MUNICIPAL MANAGEMENT SERIES

Principles and Practice
of Urban Planning

THE MUNICIPAL MANAGEMENT SERIES

William I. Goodman

EDITOR

Professor and Chairman
Department of Urban Planning
University of Illinois

Eric C. Freund

ASSOCIATE EDITOR

Associate Professor
Bureau of Community Planning
University of Illinois

Principles and Practice of Urban Planning

Published for the
Institute for Training in Municipal Administration
by the
International City Managers' Association

Copyright © 1968
by the International City
Managers' Association
1140 Connecticut Avenue, N.W.
Washington, D.C. 20036

Fourth edition, 1968

Library of Congress
Catalog Card No.: 67–30622

Printed in the
United States of America

Principles and Practice
of Urban Planning
is dedicated to
the late
DENNIS O'HARROW

Providing inspiration and guidance for all who were associated with the preparation of this book, Dennis O'Harrow served as chairman of the committee that planned its focus and content.

Since 1948 as associate director, and as executive director of the American Society of Planning Officials from 1954 until his untimely death in the fall of 1967, he worked to make urban and regional planning an integral part of democratic local government. His wisdom came from practical experience. He was the first village president of Park Forest, Illinois, and a member of the Park Forest Planning Commission and Zoning Board of Appeals. He had been a commissioner of the Northeastern Illinois Planning Commission since 1961.

His scope was world-wide, serving as the U.S. member of the Bureau of the International Federation for Housing and Planning for 14 years—as its president in 1966–67, becoming only the second American thus honored by this organization, as he was the second American named an honorary member of the Town Planning Institute of Britain.

He was a recipient of the American Institute of Planners Distinguished Service Award for "outstanding professional service to urban and regional communities through outstanding quality of practice of the art and science of planning."

Foreword

PRINCIPLES AND PRACTICE OF URBAN PLANNING provides a framework for better understanding of current urban problems as well as a guide for local government administration of planning. Concepts and emerging trends are covered as well as methods and techniques.

This is the fourth edition of a book that has been widely used by local government administrators in all parts of the United States, and in many other countries as well, as a continuing guide to the complex problems of urban development. Known as LOCAL PLANNING ADMINISTRATION in the first three editions, the new title recognizes the changing nature of the planning process.

This book has been published by the International City Managers' Association as part of its Municipal Management Series. Like others in the series, this book has drawn on the first-hand experience of governmental administrators, consultants, and teachers. Each book incorporates the latest developments in research and teaching. Each has been reviewed by administrators, consultants, staffs of appropriate professional organizations, and university teachers and students.

The 15 titles in the Municipal Management Series have been prepared especially for the Institute for Training in Municipal Administration. The Institute offers in-service training courses designed specifically for local government officials whose jobs are to plan, direct, and coordinate with the work of others. The Institute has been sponsored since 1934 by the International City Managers' Association and

is an accredited member of the National Home Study Council.

A special committee was organized to help in the initial planning and development of PRINCIPLES AND PRACTICE OF URBAN PLANNING. This committee included Dennis O'Harrow, Chairman, Executive Director, American Society of Planning Officials; Orin F. Nolting, Vice Chairman, Executive Director, International City Managers' Association; Joseph R. Coupal, Jr., former President, International City Managers' Association, now Director of Highways, Iowa State Highway Commission; William I. Goodman, Chairman, Department of Urban Planning, University of Illinois; Irving Hand, President, American Institute of Planners, and Executive Director, Pennsylvania State Planning Board; and Herbert W. Starick, former President, American Society of Planning Officials, and former City Manager, Dayton, Ohio.

Three persons served as resource specialists for this book: David S. Arnold and William E. Besuden, Assistant Directors, International City Managers' Association, and Jerome L. Kaufman, Assistant Director, American Society of Planning Officials.

The American Society of Planning Officials assisted at all stages in the preparation of this book. The ASPO staff helped in developing a basic outline for the book, in obtaining chapter authors, and in reviewing several of the manuscripts. ASPO will also play an important role in the training program based on this book by reviewing course materials and the training kit, assisting in obtaining instructors, and issuing a joint certificate with ICMA, certifying compliance with the training course requirements.

It is a particular pleasure to acknowledge the fine work of William I. Goodman and Eric C. Freund who served, respectively, as editor and associate editor for this volume. Special thanks are due to the chapter authors who through their efforts, often in after-hours time, made this book possible.

The editors were assisted by a number of people who should be recognized:

Students and faculty associates at the University of Illinois who worked on several of the chapter manuscripts included Virginia Blake, S. A. Kalgaonkar, and Scott Keyes.

Several of the chapter authors provided valuable insights and materials outside their specific chapter assignments: Lachlan F. Blair, Willard B. Hansen, Jerome L. Kaufman, and James H. Pickford.

Dennis O'Harrow participated actively in defining and organizing the project and served as liaison with the editors, the advisory committee, the authors, and the staff of the International City Managers' Association.

David S. Arnold, ICMA Assistant Director, Publications, worked closely with the editors in reviewing manuscript for the entire book to help in providing a clear and consistent text.

Mrs. Mary A. Vance reviewed and revised the chapter bibliographies and established guidelines for format and style. Mrs. Phyllis Smith typed and checked all of the manuscript.

It is especially appropriate to acknowledge the cooperation of three persons who made outstanding contributions to earlier editions. The first edition of this book was published in 1941 under the editorship of Ladislas Segoe, City Planning Consultant. The second edition was largely the work of Howard K. Menhinick, then Director of the Department of Regional Studies, Tennessee Valley Authority, and now Regents Professor of City Planning, Georgia Institute of Technology. The editor for the third edition was Mary McLean, then Director of Research, American Society of Planning Officials, and now on the staff of Tec-Search, Planning Consultants.

This volume, as with others in the Municipal Management Series, has been prepared under the general supervision of David S. Arnold, Assistant Director, Publications, ICMA.

ORIN F. NOLTING
Executive Director

The International City
Managers' Association

Chicago
June, 1967

Preface

The first edition of LOCAL PLANNING ADMINISTRATION appeared in 1941. The nation was still shaky from the effects of the Great Depression, although World War II promised a temporary industrial stimulant. There were about 132 million persons living in the United States, 57 per cent of them in cities. Ours was a mature nation; the demographers saw the population curve leveling off in a few years, after which we might even have a decrease in population. Subsistence farming seemed to be a likely way to solve many of our problems.

Admittedly, our cities were pretty messy. The art of city planning, however, was offering some solutions. Getting off to a slow start in the early part of the twentieth century, city planning had come out of its City Beautiful stage during the thirties as a result of the massive intervention of the federal government into city building and rebuilding. While planning was not truly a science, it was using a number of technical and legal tools that were more precise than the intuitive methods of its infancy.

More important, planning was beginning to be taken seriously by politicians and public administrators. No longer was it merely the play-thing of well-meaning citizens and impractical aesthetes.

Literature in planning was beginning to expand, but still in 1941 there was nothing much in the nuts-and-bolts classification. There was a growing number of persons with the civil service classification of "planner" who were doing their best, but for whom ecstatic descriptions of Central Park and Piazza Navonna were less than a satisfactory background for preparation of a zoning ordinance. The first edition, 26 years ago, of LOCAL PLANNING ADMINISTRATION was a god-send, undoubtedly the most influential planning book in the United States during the first half of the twentieth century.

World War II came to an end, as did much of our faith in economic and population predictions. Instead of returning to the prewar doldrums in a flattened population curve, the nation moved into unprecedented economic growth and a population explosion. Instead of subsistence farms, each family with its own turnip patch, farms got larger and mechanized. The farm population dropped precipitously and the urban population expanded enormously. Cities burst their boundaries and urbanization spread over the countryside.

City planning was complex enough in 1941 to make multiple authorship of LOCAL PLANNING ADMINISTRATION advisable, and the first edition was prepared under the direction of Ladislas Segoe and six collaborators. The second edition came out in 1948. Although some advances had been made, the intervening years were dominated by the war, and in 1948 it was possible for one man, Howard Menhinick, to revise the earlier edition and bring it up to date.

By 1955, however, the urban explosion was obvious, there had been ferment and change in techniques, and there were some new factors present, notably urban renewal and the technology of mass-building. It was clearly necessary, if LOCAL PLANNING ADMINISTRATION were to reflect the reality of urban problems, to completely redo the book. This time it required 12 authors instead of seven, under the editorship of Mary McLean.

At the time of publication of the first edition of LOCAL PLANNING ADMINISTRATION, five universities in the United States were offering professional degrees in planning. From these five schools there were being graduated about 35 or 40 planners each year. In 1955 there were 19 schools turning out some 200 graduates each year. In 1967 there were 50 schools of planning, graduating something over 600 planners annually. In addition, there were perhaps 50 university institutes devoted to urban research.

Research and university activity in any field means innovation, the critical examination of old habits of thought and ways of doing things. Between 1955 and 1966, when preparation of this fourth edition was started, the advances in methodology and approach were again so great that complete rewriting was necessary. The new title for the fourth edition, PRINCIPLES AND PRACTICE OF URBAN PLANNING, reflects the broader coverage of this book.

Perhaps the most important advance in technique in the 11-year interval was the introduction of systems analysis and automatic data processing. The most important expansion of objective was the increased emphasis on the social welfare implications of planning. And the most important stimulus to planning generally was the massive federal financing of urban development. Again the rewriting of the book has had to be total, using some 21 authors

under the editorial and general direction of William Goodman and Eric Freund.

I have written this preface around the history of the book because it seems to epitomize the change and, I trust, the growth of city planning over the past quarter century. If I were to be asked, I would predict that the next edition too would have to be substantially if not completely rewritten. But this is not to say that this book is out of date the moment it is printed. In fact, anyone in 1967 carefully following the techniques and theory set forth in the 1941 edition would be doing a more effective job of planning than would be found in the majority of communities in the United States.

Planning strives hard to be a science, but it will always remain fundamentally an art. Which is to say that while techniques are important and constant improvement is desirable, the personal skill of the planner—of the artist—is paramount. What he does is not nearly as crucial as how he does it. And instruction in that aspect of planning is difficult to put between the covers of a book.

DENNIS O'HARROW

Chairman
Committee on Fourth Edition,
    Local Planning Administration

Executive Director
American Society of Planning Officials

Chicago
June, 1967

Table of Contents

Figures

Tables

Principles
and Practice
of Urban Planning

Introduction

THE PURPOSES OF THIS BOOK ARE: to provide some insight into the methods which characterize local planning; to review current problems of planning, particularly with reference to information processing and other areas of recent concern; to provide a training guide for planning directors and other local government administrators and for university teachers and students; and to provide general information and understanding of the governmental and administrative framework for local planning.

The current edition of this book—previously titled LOCAL PLANNING ADMINISTRATION—is now much broader in coverage, in recognition of the expanding nature of the planning process. The present is a time of excitement for all local government administrators because of the sweeping technological, educational, cultural, and economic changes affecting life in the United States. It is a particularly exciting time for planners, city and county managers, urban development directors, welfare agency executives, and others who are on the frontiers of urban affairs. The future holds great promise, especially for the design-minded, the science-oriented, and the socially motivated. As a consequence, this edition includes three major kinds of chapters to provide an appropriate perspective of local government planning.

1. Position papers or think pieces about functions not yet clearly seen or of extremely recent prominence. Chapters 9, 10, and 11 constitute such a group; most of the other chapters also include significant points about emerging trends.

2. Surveys of ideas and actions, over time, that bring disparate kinds of information together to form a coherent picture of the institutional framework for planning. This is characteristic of Chapters 1, 2, and 12 where a review of past or recent history points to the evolution of meaningful patterns of action within the governmental structure.

3. Procedural guides and methodologies which make up the balance of the book and cover the many tasks that are the continuing responsibility of planning agencies. Most of these chapters provide basic information required for effective performance. They may be based on refinement of earlier techniques, or they may represent the distillation of long experience and careful judgment, hitherto unrecorded, as in Chapter 19.

This range of materials constitutes not only a basic guide to the administrator and technician but also a set of credos espousing certain value judgments and expressing strong convictions. The individual authors occasionally present divergent attitudes to the same problems. In a forum such as this, and in a profession whose solutions must be open-ended, this is inevitable and should be welcomed.

Sequence

The book opens with chapters on the development and interrelationships of planning—a context within which current planning programs and practices can better be understood.

Part Two deals with studies of a research and analytical nature that are basic to the work of a planning agency. Examples are provided, and certain procedures and methods are described. Part Three includes chapters on the enhanced use of systematic approaches in the aesthetic, the quantitative, and the social areas—aspects of planning where considerable rethinking is taking place on concepts and methodologies.

Parts Four and Five cover implementation. Some of the chapters deal with the culmination of the process of analysis and design, variously emphasized in maps and plans, reports, policy statements, and action-oriented recommendations and programs. Other chapters describe specific statutory tools and formalized programs that are integral to planning implementation.

The last section of the book looks directly at the planning agency—how it is organized, how it operates, and how it relates to the public. This section is most important to the professional on the job, and it seeks to draw together the effective application of techniques and programs covered in earlier sections. The last chapter is particularly relevant in describing the interactions between planners and members of society in a democratic environment.

Current Concepts and Trends

Out of the various fields of study and application which have played a dominant part in shaping the profession, planning seems to have emerged under its own identity. Yet some of the most significant "missions" now being pursued in planning are forging close working relationships with these same disciplines out of which planning grew. It is appropriate therefore to single out these missions here.

Indeed, this volume, if it is to be effective, should make it possible for the planner to take a long look at the nature of his contribution to society, in addition to briefing him on his intrinsically professional tasks. Furthermore, the related professions may find it useful to focus sharply on the special concerns of planning in their own areas.

For this reason, it is appropriate to bring together some of the relevant points made in more extended fashion in the various chapters. On the basis of the contents of the 20 chapters that seek to delineate the field today, planners seem to be making a mark in at least four

directions: quantitative techniques, aesthetic considerations, political-behavioral imperatives, and social welfare concerns.

QUANTITATIVE

Planning has become more "quantitative" because of the operational complexities brought about by an expansion of the basic responsibilities in the field: from a preoccupation with physical design at the city scale to a concern with the interrelatedness of social, economic, and physical analysis and programming at many scales and at all levels of government.

Planning has therefore launched itself fully into the use of mathematical techniques, notably the systematizing of information through high-speed electronic data processing and the construction of mathematical models. Terms like "systems analysis" and "regression curves" are in as common usage in the profession today as in the sciences and engineering from which they mainly emanated. This development has been quickened by the opportunities for federal aid on behalf of communities and by the consequent demands for more scientific underpinning to formulate public policy.

Over the next several years planning may be expected to make even greater use of quantitative techniques, due both to the demand for more and better data as a means of support for the other interests and to the continuing advances in the basic mechanics and procedures themselves.

AESTHETIC

"Design" is a wonderfully versatile word as well as an uncomfortable one in planning. It is generally taken by the public to mean either the appearance of the community and sections thereof, or the arrangement of separate buildings and projects. Neither stereotype is fully workable in a professional sense. Without documenting in detail the differences in the interpretation and usage of the term by the several "design professions"—architecture, landscape architecture, and engineering—several tenets should be stressed.

Design in urban planning is directed at the distribution, over a whole settlement, of buildings, activities, and open spaces rather than at single objects or with systems of public facilities. The client is largely impersonal, and the program is fluid. Above all, there can be no state of finality but a continuing process at work.

Our current achievements in design have been confined largely to such utilitarian areas as suburban shopping centers, campuses, and downtown office blocks.

There is a dilemma faced by the planner here. On the one hand, it is felt widely both within the profession and among members of the public that overzealous restrictions place too great a constraint on the developer. However, it is also true that citizens clamor increasingly for a higher standard of environment as expressed, for instance, through the beautification movement.

In these circumstances, planners can try a number of approaches:

1. Design by government of an entire city, e.g., Brasilia and Chandigarh.

2. Control of the key facades of the city like the boulevards laid out by Haussmann in Paris.

3. Design of publicly owned properties: public buildings, parks, and highways.

4. Rebuilding of deteriorated areas through measures like urban renewal, beautification, and acquisition of open space. These are particularly significant because they accomplish two objectives that have been the cornerstone of our political system: the avoidance of perpetual ownership of land by government, and fusion of the efforts of government with those of private enterprise.

POLITICAL-BEHAVIORAL

It was not so long ago that planners considered themselves aloof from politics. Indeed their earliest attachment to local government, through autonomous planning commissions, was intended to stress the so-called nonpartisan and independent status of the planning function.

No experienced professional maintains such a view today. He is interested in seeing his proposals implemented, and he participates in various ways in the process of implementation. In some cases, he is now directly attached to the office of the chief executive, and, in most instances, he admits unblushingly to being in the forefront of political stress. The result is that the planner has become sensitized to a number of phenomena—however shadowy and elusive—that condition the success of his program.

One of these is the "power structure" of the community, a collection of movers and shakers from public, professional, and other strata who provide a touchstone for public proposals, and who seem to provide a gauge to the rate at which change will be accepted and what the character of such change will be.

Another direction is that of citizen participation. The federal government is especially concerned with the consensus aspect of planning and has made it a constituent part of the "workable program" of the community as well as of each urban renewal project.

These are factors external to the technical program but important nonetheless. Internally, the planner is concerned with perfecting the tools of management, of being able on the one hand to keep the broad perspective with which he is charged and yet at the same time to fulfill individual assignments in relation to one another and to the big picture. So we find sophisticated devices like the Planning–Programming–Budgeting–System (PPBS) being introduced into planning offices as a means of evaluating the best "mix" of policies and actions.

Finally, and highly important for the mission of this book, planning is increasingly practiced as an integral part of the governmental process. Planners know that they must work closely with the legislative body and the chief administrator to see plans put into effect. They know that planning is done by every city and county department; that teamwork must be practiced by planners, the chief administrator, and the department heads in looking at the major resources for growth and investment. Mayors, managers, and planners must work closely together, not only in physical development planning but also in budgeting, programming, intergovernmental negotiations, and socioeconomic research.

SOCIAL WELFARE

For most of the time that city planning has been practiced in this country there was tacit acceptance of a doctrine that the physical environment was a major determinant of social behavior and of the level of individual welfare. With singular detachment, therefore, the planner could proceed to prescribe his City Beautiful therapy, assured that it would lead to the correction of social pathologies.

As the complex web of interrelationships in our society was revealed, however, the simplistic concentration on the physical gave way. For example, we find that equal emphasis in urban renewal schemes must now be given to highly personalized elements—relocation as well as reconstruction, social adjustment to a new environment in addition to adjustment of utilities.

In large measure the changes can be traced to a shift in focus on the part of the nation as well as within the profession itself. As a people we have discovered and recognized that amid affluence there exist pockets of severe economic poverty; their elimination has indeed taken on the status of a national purpose. We have likewise acknowledged that hand in hand with economic inequality usually go other ills— discrimination, lack of education, and physical deterioration.

Within city planning the urgencies presented, as well as the opportunities afforded to alleviate them, have turned the spotlight away from the urban fringe areas smack upon the inner areas and the central core. So planning finds itself enmeshed in problems of race, income, and social disorganization.

When the courts speak, they declare that schools must be planned as foci of social interaction, not simply as a neat pattern of service districts. Or they say that zoning cannot classify land so that low-income groups are in effect excluded from the community.

The area of urban social welfare is still largely uncharted, alike for city and county managers and planners—who are novices in this realm—and for social welfare workers— whose responses are geared to the individual client rather than to the broad scope of the municipality.

Conclusion

The urban environment obviously means many things to different people. It is organic, metropolitan, overcrowded, value-laden, pluralistic, and diverse. It is the center of population growth and mobility and makes possible most of the education and technology that are remaking our country. Planning and urban management, relatively young professions, have an exciting future at a time when change is a way of life. This book, hopefully, provides some of the guidelines for local government administrators who want to provide a better urban environment.

Part One

The Context
of Urban Planning

1

Antecedents of Local Planning

IN ORDER TO understand the development of urban planning in the United States, it may be instructive to consider two popular museums. One, the restoration of colonial Williamsburg, is located in tidewater Virginia. The other is the Museum of Science and Industry, which stands near Lake Michigan on the south side of Chicago.

Each museum is connected with an important aspect of the American local planning tradition. The original Williamsburg was one of the highly successful products of a self-conscious attempt to create a town culture in the colonies. Laid out in 1699 under the most detailed piece of town planning legislation adopted in the English colonies, Williamsburg reflected "a disciplined exercise in axial planning—formal, yet never pompous."[1] The Museum of Science and Industry was also planned—but not as a museum. Few of those who now descend into its simulated coal mine, wander through its submarine, and enjoy the demonstrations of the laws of probability are aware that they are in the last remaining building of a world's fair. Still fewer realize that this fair, the Columbian Exposition of 1893, is the event from which the modern phase of American city planning is usually dated.

By recalling a past, museums help to make sense of the present. In the case of Williamsburg, the visitor is invited to contemplate an urban environment that is difficult to make relevant to the contemporary situation. There appears to be little in its small scale, its careful

design, or its integration of architecture and site plan that would give perspective to the problems of planning the 20th century city. Williamsburg is undoubtedly appealing to the modern visitor, but the attraction may be grounded simply in the desire to escape. To the extent that this is so, Williamsburg stands in danger of being considered as merely "quaint." Unless one understands the social and political environment of the colonial towns, he can easily overlook the fact that the processes through which Williamsburg was originally established hold important lessons for modern urban life.

By contrast, the relevance of the Museum of Science and Industry is easily understood. From the standpoint of a history of urban planning, it is altogether appropriate (and more than slightly ironic) that a remnant of the Columbian Exposition should house a collection of technological memorabilia. Within a structure of classic proportions, the exhibits are archetypical of the forces that have created the modern industrial metropolis. It is almost as if the Louvre became the home of a permanent auto show.

Thus, modern visitors are more at home, culturally, than the crowds who were dazzled by the Exposition fairgrounds. In 1893, a galaxy of notable architects and landscape architects created a "White City" that was in striking contrast to the drab and grimy aspect of the 19th century city. The modern visitor is not so dazzled. He may be bemused, but only because the variety and complexity of the displays are a microcosm of his urban environment. He understands the Museum as intuitively as he understands his city.

[1] John W. Reps, THE MAKING OF URBAN AMERICA, A HISTORY OF CITY PLANNING IN THE UNITED STATES (Princeton: Princeton University Press, 1965), p. 114.

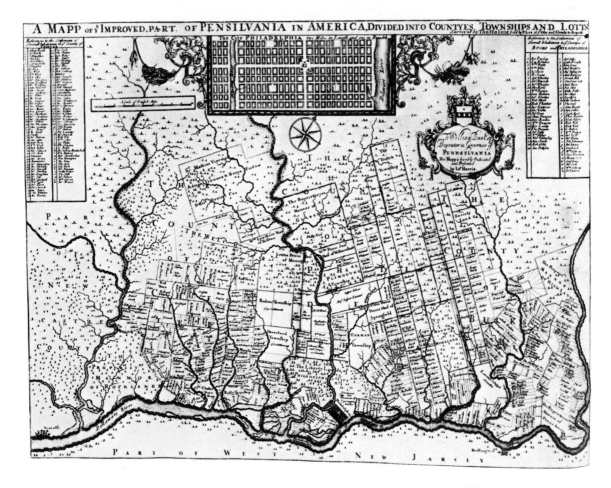

FIGURE 1–1. *Plan of Philadelphia, Pennsylvania, and vicinity: c. 1720*

The environments that produced the colonial towns and the Columbian Exposition were very dissimilar. American culture had radically changed. Yet urban planning had been only peripherally involved in the transition. Between the town planning tradition of which Williamsburg was a leading example and the rebirth of planning that began in 1893, there was a basic discontinuity. A new urban environment emerged in a society that did not admit the legitimacy of comprehensive town planning policies.

The problems of urban planning in the United States may therefore be viewed as a product of the cultural distance between Williamsburg and the Museum of Science and Industry. The 19th century hiatus helps to explain certain aspects of our two museums, such as the seeming anachronism of Williamsburg and the apparent contradictions of the Museum of Science and Industry. More important, the discontinuity is important for understanding the current status of local planning. American cities have been engaged since 1900 in the reconstruction of a planning function that is as relevant to modern conditions as colonial town planning was to a pre-industrial age.

The Colonial Town Planning Tradition: A Case of Infanticide

Williamsburg was by no means an isolated example of urban planning in the colonies. It was not even the first attempt to lay out a major city. Seventeen years prior to the time that Francis Nicholson, the governor of Virginia, undertook the planning of his new capital, William Penn had adopted a plan for a city on the lower Delaware. Philadelphia was as much of an achievement and a source of satisfaction for Penn as Williamsburg was for Nicholson.

Ample evidence exists that Penn—himself London bred and a visitor to the urban centers of Europe—was as fascinated by the prospect of founding a great city as he was concerned with establishing religious freedom for his fellow Quakers.[2]

Although Penn was unable to accompany the first settlers in 1681, he gave explicit instructions to his representatives about selecting the site and drawing the city plan. After a site between the Delaware and Schuykill rivers had been selected, the surveyor general, Thomas Holme, began to lay out the town. Penn himself arrived in October, 1682, and contributed to the final plan.

The major features of the Philadelphia plan were (1) a gridiron street system, (2) a system of open spaces, and (3) uniform spacing and setbacks for the buildings. The gridiron pattern consisted of nine streets from river to river, and 21 streets perpendicular to them. Considering European standards, the 50-foot street width was quite generous. Furthermore, the two streets intersecting at the center of the town were made 100 feet wide. A central square of 10 acres was placed at the intersection of these two major arteries. In each quarter of the town was an eight-acre square, which was available for use by all residents, not merely by those whose property fronted on the square.

The pattern created for Philadelphia in 1682 is important for its general features and for its influence on other American cities. The gridiron is a major type of street system and continues to dominate the American townscape. Perhaps because it was a principal port of entry, Philadelphia was widely copied as towns sprang up in the West. Travelers quickly saw the similarity.

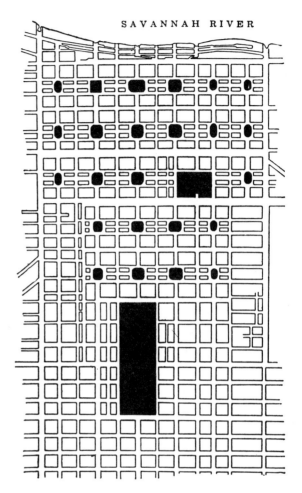

SAVANNAH RIVER

FIGURE 1–2. *Plan of Savannah, Georgia*

'Rambling through and round the city of Lexington,' William Faux recorded, 'the outline is large and resembling Philadelphia. . . .' 'The town is built on the model of Philadelphia,' Henry B. Fearon observed in Cincinnati. . . . John Cotton remarked that Pittsburgh's streets 'are mostly laid out like those of Philadelphia.' Smaller towns also followed Eastern leads, and John Palmer, visiting Zanesville, Ohio, pointed out that the plat was drawn up 'after the manner of Philadelphia.'[3]

Another gridiron-with-open-space was the plan of Savannah, Georgia. This accomplishment of James Oglethorpe could be considered the most successful example of town planning in colonial America, if only because its growth was guided until 1856 by the basic plan of 1733. Oglethorpe's unit for urban development was a ward of 40 house lots. Each ward was

---

[2] *Ibid.*, p. 158.

[3] Richard C. Wade, THE URBAN FRONTIER (Chicago: The University of Chicago Press, 1964), p. 314.

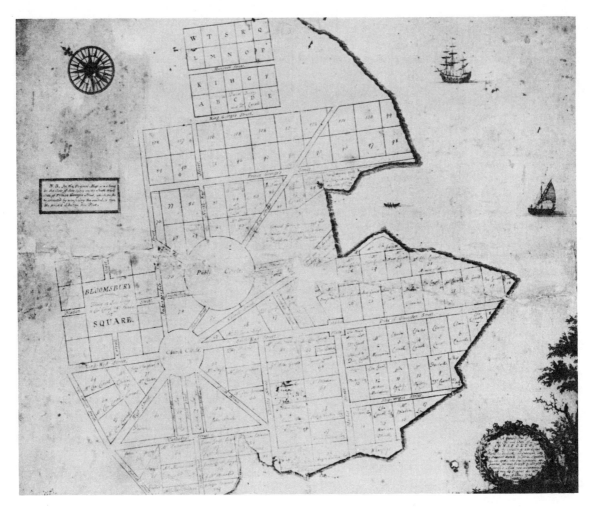

FIGURE 1–3. *Plan of Annapolis, Maryland, 1718*

bounded by major streets 75 feet wide, and contained an interior square. On two sides of the square, lots were reserved for public uses, such as churches or places of assembly. The wards were what contemporary planners would call neighborhood units. They "provided not only an unusually attractive, convenient, and intimate environment but also served as a practical device for allowing urban expansion without formless sprawl."[4]

The plantation system kept the South largely rural, and Savannah never rivaled Philadelphia or New York as a base for westward migration. This seems to be the reason why the plan had little impact elsewhere. Brunswick, laid out in 1771, is the only town that adopted Savannah's urbane neighborhood pattern.[5]

Although the gridiron seemed ubiquitous, there were other significant contributions to urban design during the colonial and early federal periods. The 1695 plan of Annapolis was an innovation in the baroque style. The major features were a square and two large circles, from which diagonal streets radiated. One circle was the statehouse site; the other contained the church. Annapolis was designed by Francis Nicholson, who was to conceive the Williamsburg plan four years later.

[4] Reps, *op. cit.*, p. 199.

[5] *Ibid.*, p. 202.

There is some evidence that Nicholson proposed elements of the Annapolis plan when he first began to consider the new Virginia capital. But diagonal streets and circles were, fortunately, rejected for Williamsburg, and the final layout used two intersecting streets as formal axes leading to the town's focal points. The major axis was the Duke of Gloucester Street, which was terminated at one end by the College of William and Mary, and at the other by the capitol. The palace green, 200 feet wide and 1,000 feet long, was the perpendicular minor axis, opening to the north about halfway between the college and the capitol. The governor's palace terminated this vista. A market square was placed on the Duke of Gloucester Street, near the green. Thus education, government, and commerce served as symbolic foci of community life.

In addition to Annapolis, baroque design concepts were evident in the planning of Washington, D.C. Major Pierre L'Enfant, an artist and engineer, was commissioned to prepare the plan for the capital city. In April, 1791, he wrote to Thomas Jefferson asking for plans of the major European cities, so that he could apply the best ideas of each in his treatment of Washington. Having spent his youth in Paris, L'Enfant already knew Versailles, the Tuileries, and the Place de la Concorde.

The plan was completed in six months. It provided for a combination of diagonal and radial streets, which were superimposed upon a traditional gridiron. This grand plan clearly showed the influence of French civil design.

In the works of Le Notre, his contemporaries, and their followers we can see the same concern with axial treatment of building masses and open spaces, the same delight in sweeping diagonal avenues, the same studied use of monuments or important buildings as terminal vistas to close street views that L'Enfant employed in his plan of Washington. This was the language of civic design that came most naturally to him, and he spoke it fluently and with conviction.[6]

The five examples of colonial town planning we have just examined by no means exhaust the catalog of early plans. They are treated

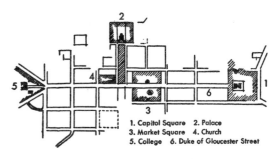

FIGURE 1–4. *Williamsburg, Virginia (An example of the American baroque city plan.)*

here because of their impact on other cities, or because their layouts constitute a typology of colonial plans. The fact is that town planning was widely practiced in the colonies from the Laws of the Indies, the Spanish city planning legislation of 1573, until the Revolution. By 1800, there was widespread interest in planning, and extensive planning experience to draw upon.

Looking back from our contemporary world, we would be tempted to consider the colonial town plans as simply a rudimentary form of subdivision control. Indeed, the towns themselves were no larger than many modern tract developments. However, we must render final judgment in light of the conditions of the era. From this perspective, the colonial plans were quite adequate. They made significant contributions to urban design, as for example, in the reservation of open spaces, the differentiation of major and minor streets, and the emphasis on foci of community life. As drab as they might be, American townscapes would be the poorer had they been denied aesthetic contributions like the circles of Annapolis and Washington, the central square of Philadelphia, and the formal axes of Williamsburg.

The colonial plans also accommodated the technology of the time. There was no factory system then, and most commercial enterprises were carried on in the home. Since agriculture was the economic base of the colonies, town plans often went beyond the built-up area. In Savannah, each holder of a town lot received a five-acre garden plot, located beyond the common that surrounded the town, and a 44-acre

6 *Ibid.*, p. 252.

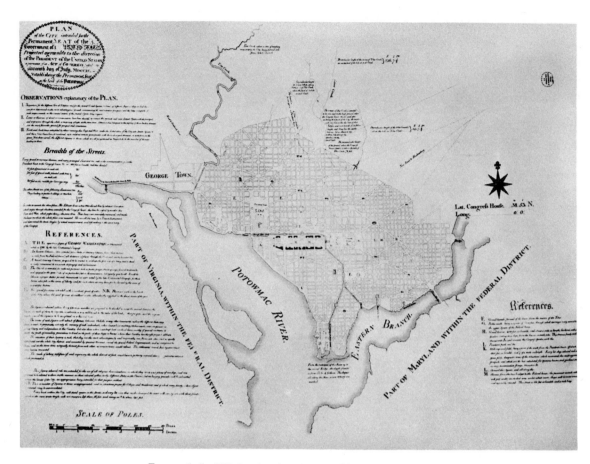

FIGURE 1–5. *L'Enfant's plan for Washington, D.C., 1791*

farm beyond the garden plots. William Penn laid out "liberty lands" and agricultural villages in the countryside around Philadelphia. Both the Spanish pueblos and the New England towns were designed to be self-contained rural-urban units, with several types of land holdings for individual and communal use. This was genuine regional planning, because both rural and urban land uses were subject to integrated control. Considering the various types of land holdings and their different uses, John Reps concludes that fairly sophisticated concepts of collective ownership and communal land management guided the early years of these relatively simple communities.[7]

In summary, the colonial town planning tradition was in step with urban development.

There is no need to romanticize the period and to deny that urban problems existed. But it does appear that, by and large, colonial planning succeeded in managing the forces by which cities were established. After the Revolution, however, new social and economic forces created a hostile environment for planning. We now turn to the four factors in the American experience that finally destroyed the vitality of this early planning tradition.

Two factors simply made it difficult to focus on urban problems. First of all, there was the anti-urban bias of American intellectuals. Thomas Jefferson's view of great cities "as pestilential to the morals, the health, and the liberties of man" was widely shared. The whole body of ideas that informed American civic virtue in the 19th century was grounded in ruralism. The doctrine of civil disobedience was

---

[7] *Ibid.*, p. 54.

formulated by the shores of Walden Pond. Even populism, the only native radicalism, was a product of the prairie. In the face of such hostility, an ideology of humane urban life could hardly be expected.

Economic competition among cities also served to deflect attention from the urban environment. From the beginning of our history, U.S. cities were commercial centers, and largely remained so until 1860. Each saw its destinies wrapped up in capturing the trade of as large a tributary area as possible. Unlike Europe, competition for vast hinterlands became a continuing aspect of American urban history. Men of affairs had every reason to look outward beyond the city limits. Their attention and their resources went outside, in the form of canals, railroads, and other weapons of the struggle for hegemony. The quality of life within the city had to take second place to concerns outside the city.

Ironically the American Revolution, a boon to so many other aspects of American life, adversely affected the continued development of urban planning. The impact was unintended, but nonetheless significant. The Revolution seriously undermined the capability of local governments to control urban growth. From medieval through colonial times, the concept of the municipal corporation had implied a melding of economic and political power. The city was a positive instrument of the public welfare, for it could not only proscribe but also promote. The Albany Charter of 1686 illustrates the wide range of accepted municipal powers. In addition to the usual public safety functions, the city of Albany had a monopoly on trade with the Indian tribes. It owned all vacant land within its boundaries, and the council alone had the power to allow an individual to practice a trade or craft.

The Revolution changed all this by substituting the state governments for the crown or the proprietor. Becoming "creatures of the state" *de jure,* city governments soon found themselves in conflict with the state over both substantive powers and adequate financing. Although the cities were successful in securing the power to provide services, effective control over the use of private property was not attained. Nor did the post-Revolutionary cities have the "private" powers granted to colonial towns.

Perhaps the most important effect of the Revolution on town planning was the encouragement it gave to land speculation. In one stroke, it both opened the west for settlement and abolished the remaining feudal aspects of land ownership, such as quitrents, entail, and primogeniture. Thus began a century of cheap land.

A veritable army of speculators arose after the Revolution. They were greatly aided by the Ordinance of 1785, which established the rectangular survey system. Since the survey accurately located every parcel, it now became as easy to trade in western land as in corn or wheat. It was not even necessary to visit the site. The Ordinance also reinforced the tendency to use a gridiron street system, which is the easiest to lay out when speed and speculative gain are of greatest importance.

Washington, D.C., provides a good example of the effect of speculation on the effectuation of a plan. In the agreement by which the Potomac site was selected, the federal government gained control of half the lots in the District. Needing money to construct the capitol and the White House, the Board of Commissioners held auctions in 1791 and 1792. Neither was successful. The Board finally accepted the proposal of a syndicate to buy 3,000 lots at a reduced price. One member of this group was Robert Morris, Philadelphia merchant and "financier of the Revolution." A successful speculator, he controlled the North American Land Company, which owned six million acres by 1795.

The syndicate extracted more concessions from the government, and finally controlled one-third of Washington's building lots. In 1797, the syndicate went bankrupt. This helped to give Washington a reputation as a bad place for real estate investment. Benjamin Latrobe, who supervised construction of the public buildings, was one of those who commented on the ruin left by speculators.[8]

[8] Charles N. Glaab, THE AMERICAN CITY, A DOCUMENTARY HISTORY (Homewood, Ill.: The Dorsey Press, Inc., 1963), p. 34.

Under the impact of these four forces—an anti-urban political theory, economic competition among cities, the decline of municipal government, and the rise of land speculation—the colonial town planning tradition died. There was no inclination in the polity to interfere with the operations of an expansive, laissez-faire economy. If the economics of urban development emasculated a plan, there were few to complain.

Both Philadelphia and Washington suffered from the changes that were made in their original plans. William Penn had hoped that the City of Brotherly Love would be dominated by open spaces and single-family dwellings. His instructions of 1681 asked that:

> every house be placed in the middle of its plat, so that there may be ground on each side for gardens or orchards or fields, that it may be a green country town, which will never be burnt, and always be wholesome.

But as early as the middle of the 18th century, houses were being built from lot line to lot line. As continuous rows of buildings shut off access, alleys were cut through the center of the blocks, and more homes built there. In 1811, James Mease noted that, of the five squares set aside for public parks, not one had been exclusively used as planned. One open space area had been rented out as a lumber yard.[9]

In 1803, Nicholas King wrote to Jefferson about the substantial departures from the L'Enfant plan for Washington. King complained, first, that more than 130 new building squares not on the published plan had been created. These were usually carved out of the open spaces at the intersections of avenues and streets. Second, King emphasized the importance of controlling river front development. The plan provided for a continuous street on the waterfront, at which the other streets terminated, and beyond which no building was to be allowed. But in 1795, the Commissioners published regulations allowing owners to build wharves, docks, and slips as they pleased beyond the street, so long as they did not inter-

fere with the channel. King observed that this was a great danger to the public health. Finally, King noted that the number and direction of streets had been changed from the original plan. Like many planners since that time, King strongly urged the authorities to establish a definitive plan from which no further departures would be allowed.[10] It was a futile request.

If any one event could be said to signal the death of the colonial tradition, it was the rejection of the Mangin Plan for New York City in 1800, and the subsequent adoption of the 1811 Commissioners' Plan. The appointment of the three-member Commission in 1807 stirred up a speculative fever. Owners platted their lands, hoping that they could force the commissioners to confirm their plans. Evidently, the commissioners were most accommodating.[11]

The 1811 plan imposed a rigid gridiron, unrelieved by open space or any other design feature, upon all but the upper end of Manhattan Island. The street system was completely unrelated to the topography, and the commissioners justified their failure to provide sufficient open space by saying that the city was destined to be such an important commercial center that all land should be put into intensive use.

The sole rationale for the plan was its suitability for the buying, selling, and improving of real estate. It certainly gave no encouragement to the creation of an attractive urban environment. Several decades later, Frederick Law Olmsted was to render an appropriate and acerbic judgment:

> Some two thousand blocks were provided, each theoretically two hundred feet wide, no more, no less; and ever since, if a building site is wanted, whether with a view to a church or a blast furnace, an open house or a toy shop, there is, of intention, no better place in one of these blocks than another. . . . Such distinctive advantage of position as Rome gives St. Peter's, London St. Paul's, New York under her system gives to nothing.[12]

---

[9] *Ibid.*, p. 37.

[10] *Ibid.*, pp. 38–42.

[11] Reps, *op. cit.*, p. 297.

[12] John Nolen, NEW IDEALS IN THE PLANNING OF CITIES, TOWNS AND VILLAGES (New York: American City Bureau, 1919), p. 41.

The legal basis for the 1811 plan was the Dongan Charter granted to the city of New York in 1696. As in the case of Albany, the provisions of this document gave the municipality ownership of land not yet allotted to individuals. Public ownership of such a vast tract offered an unparalleled opportunity to control urban expansion. But the speculative temperament prevailed, as it did in most American cities.

Savannah was a notable exception. The common land located between the town and the garden plots became the property of the municipal corporation after the Revolution. As Savannah expanded, the city authorities required additions to follow the original Oglethorpe pattern. This state of affairs lasted until 1856, when the old common was totally developed and vacant land was all in private ownership. In Savannah, at any rate, public ownership of land was a key factor in orderly city growth.

The 19th Century Precursors of Modern Urban Planning

After the death of colonial town planning, it was almost as if the word "planning" had disappeared from the American civic lexicon. City lots were now a speculative business, not a matter of community policy. Town promotion in the trans-Allegheny region demonstrates to what a low level urban planning had sunk by 1835. During the first two decades of the 19th century, the western migration was mainly composed of *bona fide* settlers. But after 1830, there were increasing numbers of speculators, who saw in the cheap government land an opportunity to make large gains. An article in the *American Review* of October, 1845, called it the era of imaginary villages. The author even claimed to have seen a party of surveyors in mid-winter laying out a town on the ice; the land was so low and wet that a boat was needed for summer transportation. He described these midwestern buccaneers as follows:

The method of operating was simple, and but little money was required to get up a respectable village on paper. About two hundred acres of land was necessary. . . . Then a surveyor would be employed to divide the land into lots of about three rods by ten, leaving streets between every second tier, and others running at right angles, and stakes were then driven into the ground making the divisions. Afterwards, came the 'map,' drawn with precision and care, and the more splendidly executed the better; next the erection of a few buildings, generally of logs or loose boards, except one which must be large and gaudily painted, as it was to be 'the Hotel.' All this required but little money, and now the operator was ready for business. He would circulate the maps over the country, and write puffs for publication in the newspapers, wherein was duly heralded 'great sales of village property'—'flourishing village in the center of a rich and growing country'—'on the great thoroughfare between the East and the West'—'emigration [sic] rapidly pouring in'—and much more, set forth with all the flourish of Western eloquence. Mock auctions were held in distant towns, at which one conspirator would buy of another and sell to a third, at rising prices of course, and this was also published. Some simple-minded men, allured by all this display, would be induced to purchase a few lots on a long credit, and build upon them; and this was sufficient to keep up the excitement, until the original proprietor, by dint of perseverance, would at least effect a sale of the whole 'village' to a speculating company from abroad, at a profit of a thousand per centum. Many villages created in this way have since been turned into very respectable farms, to the benefit of the neighborhood.[13]

From the beginning of the 19th century, towns were laid out as if the gridiron pattern had been received from on high. Little regard was given to the topography, and the reservation of open spaces was rarely considered. Apart from building regulations designed to prevent conflagrations in the densely-settled areas of the city, governments had almost no inclination or capacity to regulate the uses of land, or to take steps to correct abuses. In fact, local policy was often used to reinforce the voracious demands of the urban land market. For example, the town of Jeffersonville, Indiana, was laid out in 1802 according to a plan suggested by Thomas Jefferson. This proposal required the alteration of vacant squares and subdivided blocks, like a checkerboard. However, speculation proved stronger than plan-

[13] Glaab, *op. cit.*, pp. 148–49.

ning, and in 1816 the Indiana legislature authorized the replatting of all the land laid out according to the 1802 plan. This compulsory pooling of land for redevelopment converted Jeffersonville to a typical gridiron. The Jefferson checkerboard was followed in the original plan of Jackson, Mississippi, in 1821. This also fell before the influence of land speculation and the temptations of unearned increment.[14]

For the most part, people accepted uncritically the way in which American cities were developing. This attitude is not surprising, because an urban society hardly seemed to be in the making. The 1840 census showed only twelve cities of over 25,000 population, and only three with more than 100,000. So long as the scale of urban growth was small, the antiplanning of the 19th century was more an annoyance than a disaster.

But rapid urbanization was just ahead. Technology was forging the instruments through which an urban society would become viable. Between 1830 and 1840, railroad mileage increased from 23 to 2,818. The first telegraph message was sent in 1844. In 1852 Otis invented the passenger elevator, and the first Bessemer converter was put into operation a year before the end of the Civil War. Centralized business services became possible in 1867, when the first practical typewriter was developed. The telephone was invented in 1876, and two years later occurred the first practical application of electric arc lamps. The 1880's were boom times in building, as skyscraper frame construction was introduced.

The cumulative impact of these technological innovations was to centralize population. By 1880, there were 77 cities with populations of over 25,000, and 20 cities of over 100,000. It would have been difficult in any event to manage changes of such magnitude. The lack of urban planning policies made it impossible. Congestion was as inevitable as centralization.

A few Americans rejected the new urban, industrial life by fleeing to small utopian communities. These were primarily religious groups, some with overtones of early socialistic

doctrines.[15] Several enjoyed economic and social success, such as the Amana, Iowa, groups, the Rappites in Pennsylvania, and John Humphrey Noyes' Oneida community in New York state. The Rappites, in fact, had tamed the wilderness of New Harmony, Indiana, before selling out to Robert Owen, who was to fail as completely as the Rappites had succeeded. On the whole, the impact of the utopian communities upon the physical patterns of city building was negligible. The successful settlements did not depart from typical American planning practice. The Rappites used a simple gridiron. The Mormons, who had the most extensive experience in building cities, planned their settlements at Kirtland, Ohio, Nauvoo, Illinois, and Salt Lake City according to a strict gridiron pattern. It is interesting to note that the utopian communities that exhibited unusual schemes for physical layout were spectacularly unsuccessful.[16] Apparently visionaries like Robert Owen, Etienne Cabot, and Fourier neglected the ancient admonition to put first things first. "But seek ye first the kingdom of God, and his righteousness; and all these things shall be added unto you."

CRUSADES FOR IMPROVEMENT

Thus, uncritical acceptance and escape were major 19th century reactions to urbanization. However, two small groups made an effort to meet the city on its own terms, not to escape from its demands. The housing reformers and the park planners were the precursors; they paved the way for a rebirth of planning at the end of the century. Both groups began to raise a crucial question that had not been faced since colonial times: to what extent was community control over private actions necessary to create and preserve a satisfactory urban environment?

Urban housing first became an issue through the concern with sanitation. Serious epidemics of typhoid, cholera, and yellow fever periodically swept sections of the country, and they were most severe in the cities. New York City

---

[14] Reps, *op. cit.*, pp. 314–24.

[15] See Charles Nordhoff, THE COMMUNISTIC SOCIETIES OF THE UNITED STATES (New York: Hillary House Publishers, Ltd., 1961). This was first published in 1875.
[16] Reps, *op. cit.*, pp. 439–74.

paid attention to the problem at an early date: in 1834 and 1845, reports on sanitation blamed bad housing as a major cause of disease. A state legislative committee surveyed slum areas of New York and Brooklyn in 1857, and its report deals both with the relationship between disease and poor housing, and with the process by which urban housing became blighted. The latter was described as the familiar pattern of abandonment of houses by upper income groups, their management passing into the hands of real estate agents, who then subdivided them into many apartments. Said the report:

> . . . entire blocks of buildings, worn out in other service, were let in hundreds of sub-divided apartments, and rates of rent were established, as well as seasons and modes of payment, which, while affording the wretched tenantry some sort of shelter within their scanty means, secured at the same time prompt payment of weekly dues, and an aggregate of profit from the whole barracks (risks and losses taken into account) of twice or thrice the amount which a legitimate lease of the building to one occupant would bring, if granted for business purposes at the usual rate of real estate interest.[17]

Glaab observes about the report as a whole that it:

> reflects views often found in the writings of municipal reformers—that the city, for better or worse, was here to stay; that it historically had been a center for civilization and decent living and could be the same in America; and that its problems had to be solved through community action.[18]

After 1865, the large cities of the country became increasingly congested. New York reached a density of 326 persons per acre in 1870. At the time of the Columbian Exposition, slum sections of New York, Boston, Chicago, and Cleveland were more densely populated than almost any cities throughout the world. These conditions finally produced legislative action and attempts to improve low-cost housing design.

In New York, the usual tenement of the mid-nineteenth century was built on the "railroad" plan. Six- and seven-story buildings were placed on 25-foot lots, each structure abutting the other. The only "open space" was a 10-foot yard in the rear, where the privies were located. The practice of building exterior walls on the lot lines meant that the interior rooms had no windows.

The first New York tenement legislation was passed in 1867, the year following the establishment of the city health department. It was an ineffective law. The "dumbbell" plan dated from 1879. It merely reduced lot coverage from 90 per cent to 85 per cent by providing a small interior light shaft along the lot lines. Finally, the dumbbell was outlawed by the "New Law" of 1901. Lot coverage was now reduced to about 70 per cent, with a greater use of interior courts, rather than light wells. A 50-foot lot tended to replace the old 25-foot width.[19]

The Tenement House Act of 1901 was vigorously enforced. Its adoption was a tribute to the efforts of Lawrence Veiller, a municipal reformer who was later to become president of the National Housing Association.

Within a few years, New Jersey, Pennsylvania, and Connecticut established similar codes, and between 1905 and 1908 Chicago, Boston, Cleveland, and San Francisco adopted effective municipal ordinances.[20]

After fifty years of work, the housing reformers finally persuaded the public to assume some community responsibility for the conditions under which the other half lived.

The park planners performed a similar function. Their ability to convince a number of cities after 1860 that parks and boulevards were desirable and could not be provided without planning and land controls was important in altering the dominant *laissez-faire* attitude toward urban growth. In both parks and housing, the claims of the polity were beginning to be reasserted.

It is ironic, as well as indicative of constraints upon American civic action, that the urban parks movement succeeded because it based its arguments upon rural virtues. Its

---

[17] Glaab, *op. cit.*, p. 270.
[18] *Ibid.*, p. 267.

[19] Arthur Gallion and Simon Eisner, THE URBAN PATTERN (Princeton, N.J.: D. Van Nostrand Company, Inc., 2nd ed., 1963), pp. 67–69.
[20] Glaab, *op. cit.*, p. 266.

leaders justified the provision of open spaces as a means of counteracting the baneful influence of urban life on simple neighborliness. In an article written in 1870, Frederick Law Olmsted developed an argument that is a remarkable anticipation of Louis Writh's urban sociology. Like Wirth sixty years later, Olmsted asserts that life in cities is characterized by secondary contacts:

> Our minds are thus brought into close dealings with other minds without any friendly flowing toward them, but rather a drawing from them. Much of the intercourse between men when engaged in the pursuits of commerce has the same tendency—a tendency to regard others in a hard if not always hardening way. . . . (Thus) it happens that men who have been brought up, as the saying is, in the streets, who have been most directly and completely affected by town influences, so generally show, along with a remarkable quickness of apprehension, a peculiarly hard sort of selfishness. Every day of their lives they have seen thousands of their fellow-men, have met them face to face, have brushed against them, and yet have had no experience of anything in common with them.[21]

Therefore, the park was, to Olmsted, an opportunity for "neighborly receptive recreation," an atmosphere equivalent to an informal family gathering.

Many of the design principles of the parks movement originated in the layout of cemeteries in the 1830s. New theories of informality, romanticism, and the picturesque were applied to Mount Auburn Cemetery in Cambridge, Massachusetts (1831), Philadelphia's Laurel Hill Cemetery (1836), and New York's Greenwood (1838).[22] These attractive areas were immensely popular, and began to acquaint people with the skills of the landscape architect. The next step was to draw an analogy to municipal parks. By 1844, William Cullen Bryant was strongly campaigning for park space in New York City. Political support developed, and in 1853 the acquisition of Central Park began. This was the first large public park in America.

Frederick Law Olmsted was appointed superintendent. Associating himself with Calvert Vaux, he submitted the prize-winning plan for the development of Central Park. The whole nation was the beneficiary of the extraordinary quality of this plan, for Central Park became a great example for other cities. In their report of 1868, the Commissioners noted that park planning was proceeding in Baltimore, Philadelphia, Cincinnati, Chicago, St. Louis, and other cities. Chicago was to purchase 1,900 acres for park development in 1870. The great Minneapolis system took shape between 1872 and 1883, while the Boston Metropolitan Park Commission was established in 1892.

Olmsted himself had found his life work. He became the acknowledged leader of the parks movement. Sometimes, in cooperation with Vaux, he produced parks plans for a score of American cities. He laid out several suburban communities, such as Riverside, Illinois, and Roland Park in Baltimore. In the latter, his contribution included a set of deed restrictions for management of the common property of the community organization. He was a leading participant in the design of the 1893 Columbian Exposition. By the time of his death in 1903, he had trained a number of associates, including his son. In the history of American civic design, there were few to equal his talents.

As the 19th century drew to a close, the times seemed ripe for a rebirth of a conscious city planning movement. Sanitation was bad, and housing was worse. In 1890, the Superintendent of the Census announced that the frontier had ended; cheap Western land was no longer even in theory a "safety valve" for the urban masses. With the establishment of the AFL by Samuel Gompers in 1886, the labor movement was entering its modern phase. For the first time, many Americans were facing the fact that an urban, industrial society was forming, and that there was no reversing the trend.

Urban life even began to get some defenders, who provided partial alternatives to the anticity bias of American intellectual and popular thought. The most dramatic examples were the utopian novels. The plot of Edward Bellamy's *Looking Backward* was set in an ideal city. It has been judged the most widely read American novel, other than *Uncle Tom's Cabin*, and

---

[21] *Ibid.*, p. 248.
[22] Reps, *op. cit.*, pp. 325–26.

societies were formed to promote the realization of its projections. Less well known was Chauncey Thomas' *The Crystal Button Or, Adventures of Paul Prognosis in the Forty-Ninth Century* (1891). Thomas' city of the future featured zoning restrictions on building heights, low-income public housing, home demonstration agents, and the use of expressway median strips for rail rapid transit.[23]

This was also the period of intensive municipal reform. Almost every American city government had its boss and his machine, which thrived on corruption. Progressive reformers often attributed boss rule to the cynical manipulation of masses of uneducated immigrants. In part, this was true, but the simple exchange of votes for services is not enough to explain the persistence of the phenomenon.

The big money was not in immigrants, but in public services. After 1860, city development was a great expansive force in the American economy. The needs of dense settlements created goods and services that had not existed before, such as paved streets, sewerage and water systems, and public transportation. As evidence for the pressure to provide such services, it is worthy of note that municipal debt rose from $200 million in 1860 to $1,433 million in 1902.[24] Even if private enterprise were responsible for an activity, public officials were usually involved through such legal requirements as utility franchises. The construction contract and the franchise provided opportunities for honest and dishonest graft. In sum, the important symbiotic relationship in municipal corruption was politician-businessman, rather than politician-immigrant. As Lincoln Steffens and his fellow muckrakers demonstrated, the cesspool under city hall was usually dug by businessmen.

The Columbian Exposition of 1893 was held in this period of ferment. It was a *tour de force*. Beginning in 1890, a group of the nation's most prominent designers hammered out a unified plan. Frederick Law Olmsted was the consulting landscape architect. Daniel H. Burnham and John Root were retained as con-

sulting architects. The noted sculptor, Augustus Saint-Gaudens, advised on the execution of fountains and statues. Although Louis Sullivan condemned the classical style of the Exposition as a "virus," it was an immediate popular success.

The Chicago Fair of 1893 changed the architectural taste of the nation and led to a new direction in American city planning. The sight of the gleaming white buildings disposed symmetrically around the formal court of honor, with their domes and columns echoing the classic buildings of antiquity, impressed almost every visitor.[25]

The Fair catered to a latent interest that was ready to be aroused, and it signaled the revival of urban planning.

1900–1930: The Partial Recovery of a Planning Function

It would be pleasant to recount a simple tale in which, after the dark ages of the 19th century, urban planning emerged from bondage, gradually gathered to itself a panoply of techniques, powers, and ideals, and finally became totally equipped to grant cities a comprehensive salvation. To describe such a process of linear, cumulative development would indeed be heartwarming—but inaccurate. In fact, the American planning movement after 1900 followed a path that was to lead it into serious irrelevance thirty years later. The recovery of an adequate planning function was not to be an easy task.

In 1900, the centennial year of Washington, D.C., the annual meeting of the American Institute of Architects was held in the capital city. Several important papers dealt with the beautification of areas containing the principal government buildings. These plans came to the attention of Senator James McMillan. As chairman of the Committee on the District of Columbia, McMillan was instrumental in obtaining a Senate authorization to prepare plans for the District's park system. The subcommittee responsible for the work immediately consti-

[23] See Glaab, *op. cit.*, pp. 318–25.
[24] *Ibid.*, p. 177.

[25] Reps, *op. cit.*, p. 498.

tuted a Senate Park Commission, the members of which were Daniel Burnham, Charles McKim, Augustus Saint-Gaudens, and Frederick Law Olmsted, Jr. The old Columbian Exposition team had been reconvened.

A European trip was first on the agenda. The group visited the major cities, including Paris, where they saw the elements of civic design that had inspired L'Enfant and the improvements made by Haussmann from 1854 to 1889. These later achievements were of a monumental character, with wide, sweeping boulevards to let in light, air, and infantry.

The final plan was completed in December, 1901, and made public a month later. Primarily the work of Charles McKim, it replanned the Mall, provided for the axes that terminated on the Lincoln and Jefferson Memorials, and recommended areas for grouping public buildings. Modern Washington shows that the plan was substantially followed. The plan also had repercussions far beyond the District of Columbia. Reps observes that

By a coincidence which was to have profound influence in the subsequent course of American city planning, it was in the Washington of L'Enfant that the new doctrines of monumental planning were first carried out. Because the principles of Renaissance planning were so easily revived in this city, since its basic framework had been conceived in that spirit, the impression was soon created that these planning precepts could be successfully adopted elsewhere.[26]

The impression was shared in many American cities. The publicity given to the McMillan Commission's plan stirred widespread interest in civic beautification. Business leaders formed improvement groups devoted to applying the new gospel of planning in their own cities.

This earliest manifestation of the rebirth of planning is usually called the City Beautiful Movement. Since the only available models were the Columbian Exposition and the Washington Plan of 1902, the content of the plans was invariably restricted to three elements: civic centers, thoroughfares, and parks. Boulevards and parkways were the design elements

that tied together the schemes for impressive public buildings and open spaces. As the leading practitioner of the Movement, Daniel Burnham, asserted in his San Francisco plan report, "A city plan must ever deal mainly with the direction and width of its streets."[27]

By 1913, 43 plans were in existence, and four years later, the American Institute of Architects reported that 233 cities were engaged in some kind of civic improvement program. Frequently, these were simply monumental civic center plans, as in Cleveland, Buffalo, or Harrisburg. The roster of more comprehensive schemes included the nation's leading cities: San Francisco in 1905; St. Louis, Roanoke, and Los Angeles in 1907; Chicago and Des Moines in 1909; New Haven in 1910; Dallas and Rochester in 1911; and Portland (Oregon) in 1912.

The apogee of the City Beautiful was Daniel Burnham's *Plan of Chicago* (1909). In scope and in understanding of a city, this masterful composition in civic design went far beyond Burnham's 1905 plans for Manila and San Francisco. The report began by placing Chicago in its regional context, pointing out the need for control of development beyond the city limits. Then Burnham progressively narrowed the focus of the plan from the city as a whole through the central area to a great plaza-civic center. As in the case of Washington, Chicago was to implement many of the proposals.

The City Beautiful Movement was the beginning of comprehensive planning. Professionals like Burnham saw that there was a need to relate buildings to each other and to their sites. In emphasizing the three-dimensional quality of urban planning, they reasserted the vitality of one part of the colonial planning tradition. Hereafter, city planning would no longer be equivalent to a street map.

The Movement had inspirational value in popularizing and dramatizing the need for city planning. Furthermore, it was not completely blind to the interconnections between physical planning and the sociopolitical aspects of urban life. In the Plan of Chicago, Burnham recognized the problem of the slum neighbor-

---

26 *Ibid.*, p. 502.

27 *Ibid.*, p. 517.

hood and warned that the city might soon be forced to provide public housing as a matter of simple justice.

Despite these undeniable contributions to the revitalization of a planning function, the City Beautiful Movement quickly revealed certain deficiencies. To begin with, beautification and adornment had limited practicability for most cities. In light of other demands upon the municipal treasury, the benefits hardly seemed worth the high costs involved. A more serious defect was the lack of legitimation of any public control over the private actions that were decisive in setting the quality of the urban environment. The early planners merely avoided the issue when they made "planning" coterminous with parks, boulevards, and civic centers. This choice of a focus had two unintended consequences. It made sure that the claims of the polity did not become an issue, since the achievement of these limited goals required public investment, rather than controls. At the same time, the choice created a special upper-middle class constituency for planning. By nature suspicious of governmental controls, particularly at the local level, this group would respond enthusiastically to an all-rewarding objective like beautification through public investment.

The ironic aspects of this approach to urban planning were pointed out by Graham R. Taylor in his book, *Satellite Cities*. Written in 1915, Taylor's description of metropolitan expansion contains one of the first critiques of city planning. He discusses the rise of industrial suburbs, and asks whether the brilliant technological innovations of the new mills and factories were being matched by equivalent imagination in new town design. Gary, which U.S. Steel laid out on the dunes of northwestern Indiana in 1907, and Flint, Michigan, provided an answer:

Our general failure to bring city planning to bear where it will count for most—that is, in zones of new construction—was personified in this instance by those Middle Western officials of the Steel Corporation who, as members of the Commercial Club of Chicago, were at this time contributing from their own pockets toward the $100,000 fund raised to work out in map and design the present magnificent

city plan for Chicago, in which the genius of Daniel H. Burnham had its final expression. Yet as company officials, they had not thought to secure the services of an expert city planner to lay out a brand-new town which, including the plant, involved an investment of over seventy-five million dollars. The Chicago city plan calls for a cutting of diagonal streets through old territory at enormous expense; the Gary town plan is likely to create in a decade conditions which can only be remedied by a similar Caesarean operation.[28]

How far we have yet to go in these directions in guiding development with reference to the community as a whole is illustrated by the fact that even at Flint—where a few years ago public-spirited citizens secured a well-known city planner to lay out a scheme for parks, boulevards and other civic features—one section after another of the industrial quarter was laid out adjacent to the automobile plants 'without any special regulation except the understanding that no street was to be less than sixty feet in width.'[29]

An event in 1911 foretold the direction in which city planning would go in the next two decades. Two years before, the first national Conference on City Planning was convened at the call of the New York Committee on Congestion of Population. The Committee represented those who were primarily interested in housing and thus was anchored in one of the two groups that kept planning alive during the 19th century. The theme of the 1909 Conference was using planning to deal with social problems. The papers dealt more with economics than aesthetics. They called for an urban planning process based upon a type of research alien to the City Beautiful leaders. As explained by Benjamin Marsh, executive secretary of the New York Committee,

This means that we shall make a survey, if we may adopt this term, of the economic and industrial conditions in the city, and preeminently of housing conditions and the ownership and control of land, since the land question is fundamental to a proper solution of the housing questions.[30]

By joining in this Conference, the planners were associating themselves with the main stream of municipal reform, which at this time

[28] Glaab, *op. cit.*, pp. 441–42.
[29] *Ibid.*, p. 443.
[30] Robert A. Walker, THE PLANNING FUNCTION IN URBAN GOVERNMENT (Chicago: University of Chicago Press, 1941), p. 11.

was undertaking a number of "social surveys" patterned after Charles Booth's *Life and Labour of the People of London* (1903). But the association was brief. In 1910, the National Planning Conference was established, and was soon dominated by architects and landscape architects. The New York Committee independently organized the National Housing Association, which, beginning in 1911, held its own conferences. The two groups diverged, not to find common interests again until the 1930s. The divorce was a principal factor in keeping the planning movement out at the fringe of the major efforts to improve cities during the first three decades of this century. It also helped to stereotype planning as mere beautification of the urban facade.

Not all planners were comfortable with this reputation. As sensitive a man as John Nolen returned again and again to the problem of restricting the scope of planning to streets, civic centers and parks. In 1919, he quoted, without comment, an unnamed "English writer" on the subject, and ten years later he used the same quotation in a textbook prepared under his editorship. But in 1929, Nolen added his own observation, "This criticism is typical of many others, and in the main it is true."[31]

One English writer said, 'In America it is the fear of restricting or injuring free and open competition that has made it so difficult for cities to exercise proper and efficient control over their development. The tendency therefore has been to promote those forms of civic improvement which can be carried out without interfering with vested interests. To impose severe sanitary restrictions, to limit the height and density of dwellings, or to prevent the destruction of amenities on privately owned land, may all help to reduce the profits of the speculator—hence if he has any influence over the local governing bodies he will secure that nothing but what is absolutely necessary and legal shall be done in these directions. But to purchase large public parks and to develop civic centres adds to the value of the privately owned land and buildings in the city. . . .'[32]

The City Beautiful Movement established two aspects of local planning that remain in common use today: the professional consultant and the quasi-independent planning commission composed of leading citizens. The consultant system emerged quite naturally. There was no separate planning profession; the emphasis was upon the production of a one-shot plan; and the architects and landscape architects who became planners were accustomed to the client-consultant relationship. Given these conditions, there was really no alternative method for providing a professional staff. However, the exclusive reliance on consultants became more and more dysfunctional for effective planning. Summarizing the defects of the consultant system, Walker noted that:

it generally involves the flaring and burning-out of the enthusiasm of civic groups, the expenditure of considerable sums within a short span of time, and a subsequent complacency on the part of public officials who view the resultant neatly bound volume as a *fait accompli*.[33]

Planning as an official function of local government became established almost as quickly as the consultant system. Although the first City Beautiful plans were prepared under private auspices by civic organizations, there was early recognition of the need for placing responsibility under public authority. Cities turned to a familiar device: the appointment of prestigious citizens to an unpaid commission. The first city planning commissions were in Hartford (1907) and Milwaukee (1908). Chicago followed suit in 1909 with a rather unusual organization. The mayor and the council appointed a commission of 328 members. In reality, this was an association of influential civic leaders for promotion of the Burnham Plan, but it did receive an appropriation of public funds. The Massachusetts legislature, in 1913, made it mandatory for all cities of over 10,000 population to create official planning boards. Only 18 cities had planning boards or commissions in that year. However, the number had grown to 185 nine years later.

[31] John Nolen (ed.), CITY PLANNING (New York: D. Appleton and Company, 2nd ed., 1929), p. 22.

[32] John Nolen, NEW IDEALS IN THE PLANNING OF CITIES, TOWNS, AND VILLAGES (Boston: Marshall Jones Co., 1927), pp. 133–34.

[33] Walker, *op. cit.*, p. 210.

During the 1920s, city planning became increasingly popular. Although there were some changes in emphasis, the general trend was to move in the directions charted by the City Beautiful Movement. Cities continued to show little inclination to add planners to the full-time municipal bureaucracy; in 1929 only 46 cities had planning budgets of more than $5,000. Thus the itinerant consultants grew in numbers and prestige. Semi-independent planning commissions multiplied, as this way of organizing the local planning function became imbedded in the enabling statutes of state after state. The U.S. Department of Commerce gave additional sanction to the use of planning commissions in its 1928 model law, *A Standard City Planning Enabling Act*. Because the leadership of most local planning commissions rested in the hands of Chambers of Commerce and well-to-do citizens, their plans paid no attention to slums or poverty. Through their decisions and actions physical layout remained supreme.

The major changes in local planning during the twenties were (1) the addition of engineers and lawyers to the ranks of the planning profession, (2) the beginnings of state and metropolitan planning, and (3) the rapid rise and immense popularity of zoning. This last change was the most important of all. Zoning became to planning what the sacraments are to the Bible—a visible sign of grace.

A separate planning profession had been slowly emerging since 1909, when Harvard's School of Landscape Architecture offered the first university course in city planning. A decade later, the Harvard curriculum included principles of city planning, practice and design, principles of construction, and planting design. Eight other educational institutions were offering some instruction in city planning. The course work was, like Harvard's, usually offered by landscape architecture faculties.

When the American City Planning Institute (now the American Institute of Planners) was organized within the National Planning Conference in 1917, its membership consisted primarily of architects and landscape architects. Lawyers and engineers were attracted in increasing numbers during the 1920s. The former came in because of their role in the development of the law of zoning and subdivision control. The latter were required because of the need for competence in transportation and public works. It should be recalled that automobile registrations increased from 458,000 in 1910 to 8,132,000 in 1920, and then soared to 22,973,000 in 1930. Engineers could plan street improvements and transit facilities. The City Efficient became as admirable an objective as the City Beautiful, and the chief staff person in local planning agencies, aimed at furthering this new image, usually received the title "Planning Engineer."

Because the automobile and an expansive economy made rapid suburbanization possible after World War I, attention turned to both state and metropolitan area planning. New York State created a temporary commission on housing and regional planning in 1923. Its 1926 report is usually considered the first comprehensive state plan. New Jersey, Wisconsin, and Illinois set up planning agencies between 1929 and 1931.

At the metropolitan level, planning efforts were usually carried out by private groups; it was not until the 1950s that metropolitan planning was to become primarily a governmental function, supported by public funds. The New York Regional Plan Association, which was established in 1923 and financed by a large grant from the Russell Sage Foundation, attracted much attention. Its activities inspired similar organizations in large metropolitan areas like St. Louis, Philadelphia, Chicago, and Pittsburgh. However, some metropolitan planning was carried on under governmental auspices, even at this early date. The Los Angeles County Regional Planning Commission was created in 1922; the Boston Metropolitan District Commission set up a Division of Metropolitan Planning in 1923; and Niagara Frontier Planning Board came into existence in 1925. An analysis of the proceedings of the National Planning Conferences shows that metropolitan and county planning was a major subject of professional consideration from 1923 through 1925, and from 1929 through 1931. The Conferences gave minor attention to state planning from 1923 through 1926.

The hallmark of the 1920s was the widespread acceptance of comprehensive zoning. Building upon a limited legal base that had allowed municipalities to control "public nuisances," lawyers like Edward Bassett and Alfred Bettman began to develop zoning as a method for effectuating a community plan. In 1913, the New York Heights of Buildings Commission, chaired by Bassett, adopted a report that laid the foundation for the 1916 New York City ordinance, the first comprehensive zoning ordinance to be enacted by an American city. This new technique received a great deal of publicity. The National Planning Conferences had lengthy papers and discussions on zoning each year from 1916 through 1925, and again from 1928 through 1931, when the emphasis shifted to the administration of zoning ordinances.

Five years after New York's pioneer action, seventy-six cities had passed zoning ordinances. In 1922, the U.S. Department of Commerce published the first edition of *A Standard State Zoning Enabling Act*. By 1926, when the Supreme Court established the constitutionality of comprehensive zoning,[34] there were 564 cities with such ordinances. In 1931, there were 800.

The remarkable popularity of zoning deserves closer examination. Since, in theory, it had become the chief means of guiding urban development according to a comprehensive plan, an observer might be tempted to conclude that Americans had, at last, changed their *laissez-faire* attitudes toward the urban land market. Such a conclusion would be erroneous. Zoning became popular precisely when it became touted as a method of stabilizing and protecting property values. The practice of zoning was substantially different from the theory. Single-family residential areas were secured from the intrusions of undesirable uses, but multi-family, commercial, and industrial areas were commonly overzoned. New York's ordinance, for example, could legally provide enough business and industrial space for a city

of 340,000,000 people.[35] Walker summarized the way in which zoning had been co-opted when he wrote:

> Zoning became primarily a static process of attempting to set and preserve the character of certain neighborhoods, in order to preserve property values in those areas, while imposing only nominal restrictions on those areas holding a promise of speculative profit.[36]

In sum, local planning on the eve of the Great Depression had attained status and self-identity. American cities had recovered a planning function. Yet the relevance of most planning programs to basic urban problems seemed questionable. Organization for planning was in the hands of quasi-independent commissions composed of business executives, realtors, and the high priests of the economic order— lawyers, architects, and engineers. For the most part, these lay leaders looked upon planning as a citizens' effort, to be "sold" to recalcitrant politicians.[37] Lacking funds for a permanent staff of any size, the commissions employed consultants to prepare a "Master Plan." In due course, the Plan would be presented, and anyone at all acquainted with the field could anticipate the sections of the report: (1) streets, (2) transit and transportation, (3) parks and recreation, (4) civic appearance, and (5) zoning. These headings had almost become stereotypes. Except for zoning and transit, the scope of the plans went little beyond the framework developed by Burnham and his contemporaries. If the politicians could be induced to adopt the recommended zoning ordinance, planning was completed. The commission could think of little else to do, other than advocate the bromide that the Master Plan should be kept up-to-date.

This was the typical pattern for local planning in the late 1920s. As Alonso observes:

---

34 Village of Euclid, Ohio, v. Ambler Realty Company, 272 U.S. 363 (1926).

---

35 Walker, *op. cit.*, p. 60. See also URBAN PLANNING AND LAND POLICIES, Vol. II of the Supplementary Report of the Urbanism Committee to the National Resources Committee (Washington: U.S. Government Printing Office, 1939).

36 *Ibid.*, p. 59.

37 For an occupational analysis of commissions, see *ibid.*, pp. 143–62. For attitudes toward planning, see *ibid.*, p. 205.

The planning commission in a social sense, and the zoning ordinance in a real estate sense, represented middle and upper class values and were too often holding operations against the forces of change. Since zoning combined conservatism with the planning advocated by the progressives, it (city planning) often enjoyed considerable support together with indifferent success.[38]

Norton Long had succinctly described this pattern as the "civic New Year's resolution," with the same practical effect as such resolutions usually have. Thus, in only three decades, American cities built a new planning tradition that was in danger of becoming a ritualistic art form. It is a tribute to the regenerative capacities of the planning movement that alternative patterns were soon to be developed.

Local Planning After 1930— Evaluation and New Directions

Some foundations of regeneration were laid during the 1920's. The academic disciplines most closely allied with planning practice began to undertake research in urban structure and behavior. The University of Chicago was becoming the center for urban sociology, and, in 1924, a faculty committee on community research was created. In 1925, the first issue of *Land Economics* was published at the University of Wisconsin. The economic, sociological, and governmental research initiated in the Twenties was eventually to furnish a more rigorous empirical base for urban planners.

Three events in 1929 were harbingers of new emphases in planning. One was the completion of Radburn, New Jersey, an innovation in neighborhood design inspired by the "new town" theories of Ebenezer Howard. Published in 1898, Howard's book, *Tomorrow: A Peaceful Path to Real Reform,* had had relatively little impact on American planning, which, from 1902, stressed the re-planning of existing cities, rather than the creation of new ones. The second event was the establishment of the first school of city planning, at Harvard University. After 1929, entrance into the planning profession could be accomplished through professional education in planning itself, rather than through specialized aspects of training in architecture or engineering. The third event was the publication of the *Regional Plan of New York and Its Environs.* This remarkable document was quite unlike the stereotyped plans of the period. It relied heavily upon social science research, and it broke new ground in its treatment of the neighborhood unit, public finance, government services, and the economic base of the city. Perloff asserts that it was not until the 1940s that university planning education caught up with the Regional Plan of New York.[39]

The Depression experience provided a powerful impetus toward a redefinition of local planning. When it was seen that the Unseen Hand did not necessarily assure continued high levels of economic activity, the nation's attention became focused on creating new institutional structures and coordinating their activities with old ones. Planning could not escape these questions of administration and organization. Many of its leaders saw that if planning were to be more than the civic New Year's resolution, it had to become anchored in the ongoing political process. The establishment of the American Society of Planning Officials in 1934 was an early organizational expression of the new concern with planning policy. ASPO was to serve as the vehicle through which public officials and professionals could discuss common concerns. Robert Walker's book, *The Planning Function in Urban Government,* was both an analysis of the status of planning and a plea for an alternative model to the quasi-independent planning commission. Walker believed that effective local planning required that the planning function be organized as a staff aid to the municipal executive. In the late 1930s, under the impact of Keynesian economic theories and the

---

[38] William Alonso, "Cities and City Planners," DAEDALUS, XCII (Fall, 1963), p. 826.

[39] Harvey S. Perloff, EDUCATION FOR PLANNING: CITY, STATE, AND REGIONAL (Baltimore: The Johns Hopkins Press, 1957), p. 19.

concept of a "shelf of public works," cities developed systems of capital programming and budgeting. Planning agencies began to undertake so many administrative duties that, after World War II, many planners began to wonder whether the principal job of long-range comprehensive planning was not succumbing to the pressures of these short-term tasks.[40]

In addition to forging new relationships to municipal government, planners during the Depression were also broadening the focus of their activities. Social problems assumed equal stature with physical layout as a legitimate claim on professional attention. Federal programs were of great assistance in producing the new emphasis. By 1939, the Works Progress Administration alone had furnished staff for more than a hundred studies carried out by the planning agencies of 37 cities and 2 counties. WPA expenditures for these purposes averaged about 4.2 million dollars annually in the late 1930s. Total local appropriations for planning were about 2.1 million dollars in 1936. Thus, the federal government was spending several times as much money for local planning as the local governments themselves.[41] The WPA-supported studies dealt with social and economic conditions. Most common were analyses of residential areas and conditions, which included real property inventories and child health and juvenile delinquency studies. Some planning agencies produced reports on aspects of municipal finance, such as cost-revenue studies of public services and tax delinquency data.[42]

The awakening interest in social problems served as a basis for a rapprochement between the planning and the housing reform groups. The rediscovery of common interests, after two decades of relatively little contact, was strengthened by the passage of the Housing Act of 1937. This statute set the existing pattern of federal-local responsibilities in the field of public housing. The records of the National Planning Conferences provide the best evidence of the radical change in professional attitudes toward housing problems. Except in 1918, there were no major sessions on housing at any of the annual Conferences from 1912 until 1931. Thereafter, housing was a primary topic through 1936, and received minor Conference attention each year from 1938 through 1946. By that time, however, "housing" had been converted to the problem of urban redevelopment and renewal, which has been extensively discussed at most Conferences since 1941.

In reviewing the ferment of the 1930s, it seems clear that the Urbanism Committee of the National Resources Committee was a major force in stimulating the new outlook on local planning. Composed primarily of students of public administration, the Committee accepted two major premises for making planning effective. First, it saw that there is a direct relationship between the definiteness and continuity of governmental policy and the success of the city plan. Second, it called attention to the fact that physical planning has no meaning apart from a matrix of social and economic factors. The Committee summarized its analysis of urban planning as follows:

In fact, the entire scope and conception of local urban planning need broadening. While the influence of the physical environment upon the economic and social structure of the community is everywhere in evidence, planning agencies and planners have been slow to recognize and give proper emphasis to the social and economic objectives and aspects of planning and zoning. Studies of the economic base of the community, its soundness, deficiencies, and its prospects, and the need for a selective program of industrial development, have been almost completely overlooked. The pressing problem of housing has not received the attention from planning agencies that it deserves.

Local planning should be given or must gain for itself a place in the structure of government where it will be closer to the local legislative body, the chief executive and the administrative departments. A possible way to achieve this might be the transforming of the independent planning commission or board into a planning department as one of the staff agencies of the local government, with or without an advisory committee of citizens. However, thorough understanding and acceptance of planning by the local legislative body, the chief executive, and, most of all, by the citizenry in general, would appear to be a prerequisite for such a change.[43]

---

[40] *Ibid.,* p. 16.
[41] Walker, *op. cit.,* p. 193.
[42] *Ibid.,* pp. 357–66.

Following World War II, there was a dynamic expansion of local planning in the directions pointed out in the 1930s. Budgets grew, and so did staff resources. The rise of the resident planning staff began at the end of the Depression. Some consultants, like Nolen and Bartholomew, encouraged cities with which they had contracts to hire the consultant's professionals in residence as permanent staff after the consulting job had been completed. The growing number of planning schools increased the supply of trained professionals. While only four schools offered graduate degrees in city planning in 1940, there were 19 professional degree programs a decade later. University curricula not only made more planners available, but also expanded the expertise of those entering the field. The professional programs were rapidly to make obsolete Walker's criticism of 1936 that "persons trained for social research have, in fact, been generally overlooked in staffing planning offices."[44]

Vastly more sophisticated methods of analysis became commonplace. A comparison of Stuart Chapin's textbook *Urban Land Use Planning*[45] with, say, the 1929 edition of Nolen's book shows how strongly planning now relies upon the diciplines of economics, sociology, and geography for its analytic tools. Planning techniques have been most highly refined in the model building and computer technology applied since 1955 by the massive transportation studies in Chicago, Detroit, Philadelphia, Pittsburgh, and other large cities.

Planning is now considered a governmental function at all levels—municipal, metropolitan, and state. No doubt the federal grants first authorized under Section 701 of the Housing Act of 1954 acted as powerful leverage in stimulating small cities and metropolitan areas to organize planning agencies. However, the pressures of urban growth would probably, in time,

have been as compelling as the availability of money. In large cities, particularly, the governmental character of planning has been interpreted to mean an integration of the planning function into the administrative structure. Planning departments have replaced several quasi-independent commissions. This has made it easier for elected chief executives to adopt planning as part of their political platforms and to use the planning agency for objectives far broader than physical development.

The fan-wise expansion of planning activities since 1930, with their variety and increased scope, has led Perloff to comment on the "additive" character of urban planning in the United States:

From (1) an early stress on planning as concerned chiefly with aesthetics, planning came to be conceived also in terms of (2) the efficient functioning of the city—in both the engineering and the economic sense; then (3) as a means of controlling the uses of land as a technique for developing a sound land-use pattern; then (4) as a key element in efficient governmental procedures; later (5) as involving welfare considerations and stressing the human element; and, more recently, (6) planning has come to be viewed as encompassing many socio-economic and political, as well as physical, elements that help to guide the functioning and development of the urban community.[46]

Conclusion

The diversity of which Perloff speaks has been a remarkable achievement. By creating alternative models from which to choose methods and objectives, the American planning movement has avoided a sense of closure on the limits of professional practice. The prevention of orthodoxy may have been unintentional, but it has clearly been functional for both urban planning and the cities it serves.

Looking back over the history of city planning, it becomes clear that both the term 'planning' and city planning activities have served extremely useful social ends. Planning—as an approach, a symbol, and an activity—has helped to bring . . . into the con-

[43] U.S. National Resources Committee—Urbanism Committee. OUR CITIES: THEIR ROLE IN THE NATIONAL ECONOMY (Washington: U.S. Government Printing Office, 1937), pp. 63–64.

[44] Walker, *op. cit.*, p. 200.

[45] F. Stuart Chapin, Jr., URBAN LAND USE PLANNING (Urbana: University of Illinois Press, 2nd ed., 1964).

[46] Perloff, *op. cit.*, pp. 11–12.

sciousness of governments and of the general public, the importance and desirability of being concerned (operationally) with relationships among people, physical objects, and ecological forces; of trying to see things whole; of setting goals and of trying to figure out the best ways of achieving them; of trying to coordinate and integrate the different kinds of physical improvement and development activities carried out by the government; of aiming at and working toward a better future. Thus, at least in the United States, a dynamic relationship has developed between city planning as an idea and an activity, on the one side, and, on the other, the broadening popular view of municipal government responsibility and the more widespread acceptance of the need for consciously working toward an improved urban environment.[47]

The creative interplay between the political process and the objectives of the planning movement has indeed been a hallmark of urban planning in the United States. But the problem remains that the full range of planning objectives cannot be accommodated within most local political systems. What has happened is that the four environmental factors that killed the colonial town planning tradition are still operative in American urban policy-making. Instead of pervading the total political system, as they did early in the 19th Century, they now have differential impacts. Their influence is quite decisive in many urban political environments, moderately powerful in most, and of little effect in a few. This means that the creative interplay of planning and politics is inhibited in varying degrees because of certain stable properties of local political action.

From this perspective, it is easy to account for the popularity of local planning in the late 1920s. The end result of the line of development that began in 1900 was a type of planning that did little violence to the concepts on which 19th century city development had proceeded. The planning activity of the 1920s did not challenge the view of land as a speculative commodity, but simply imposed a few ground

rules under which speculation was to be carried on. It did not ask local government to become a positive instrument of the public welfare, but assumed that public powers would continue to be exercised as the handmaiden of private development. Finally, the planning activities of the 1920s were seen as an instrument in the economic competition among cities. To have a master plan or a zoning ordinance was a badge of modernity and "progress." Concern with the quality of urban development, apart from sheer quantity, was a retrograde notion. To be bigger meant, *ipso facto,* to be better, and planning marched forward under the watchword "Grow or Die."

Since 1930, the major trends in planning have interposed a set of ideas that challenge the older ideology. Those who are concerned with effective guidance of urban development are asking the polity to adjust to new conditions by accommodating more extensive public interest claims on private actions. Some cities are experimenting with new combinations of public and private activities through such devices as non-profit development corporations. Some are attempting to integrate social and physical planning. There is a search for satisfactory alternatives to the traditional practice of zoning and subdivision control.

Yet, anyone familiar with American local politics must recognize the power of the older ideas. Urban land is not completely recognized as a community resource; the capabilities and intentions of municipal governments are viewed with suspicion; growth is in itself admirable; and many people are, at base, anti-city. As a result, two traditions of local planning exist side-by-side in the United States. One rests upon the foundations of the 1920s, the other upon the alternatives first posed in the 1930s. The latter is the more vital and timely, for it provides the concepts through which the urban polity is overcoming the conditions that, for more than a century, vitiated attempts to create a more satisfactory urban environment.

---

[47] *Ibid.,* pp. 17–18.

2

The Intergovernmental Context
of Local Planning

THIS IS THE AGE of creative federalism. It is a time marked by constant redefinition of the working relationships between governmental jurisdictions. Gone are the classic compartments drawn on the blackboards of civic classrooms. No longer is there a domain for the national government, a sector for the states, and a place for the municipality, for the web of government has become a tangled one.

The urban planner finds himself working on new levels of involvement and activity. At one end of the planning spectrum he may be with a large regional or state planning commission, or even be a consultant working across the expanse of Appalachia; at the other end, he may find himself conferring with the indigenous leaders of community action agencies that are involved in an endeavor to cope with his city's poverty problems. Instead of a single frame of reference, there is today an entire pyramid of planning jurisdictions, surmounted by the growing influence of the national government.

Professor Coleman Woodbury of the University of Wisconsin has offered the term "urban government" as the one best suited to describe the resulting complex. This term, he asserts, is more descriptive than "local government" or some other term that utilizes a mere territorial basis for definition. Urban government:

. . . takes in all governments operating within such areas: municipal government, essentially rural government (e.g., counties and townships), state and national governments in so far as they deal,

directly or in close collaboration with local governments, with the affairs of urban or urbanizing localities. It includes, of course, not only general-purpose governments but also special districts and authorities—both single and multi-purpose. It comprehends not only governmental forms, structures, functions and processes, but also the roles and relationships of individual citizens, officials, and various groups in formulating, opposing, and administering public policies and programs.[1]

This provides an able description of the milieu of planning today. But the planner has come to experience increasing involvement in urban affairs and the impetus resulting from federal rules requiring the preparation of plans as a prerequisite for the receipt of federal funds. In the federal Highway Act 1962, Section 701 of the Housing Act, 1954, as amended (the Planning Assistance Program), or in any of a growing number of other federal programs, the planning proposals for one locale are affected by rules that require them to be coordinated with neighboring jurisdictions in order to be eligible for federal aid. Within a city, the key to funds and planning actions may be a prior approval by the local anti-poverty committee.

Similarly, the planner may sometimes feel the frustration that stems from working within

---

[1] Coleman Woodbury, "Some Notes on the Study of Urban Government," PUBLIC POLICY, A YEARBOOK OF THE GRADUATE SCHOOL OF PUBLIC ADMINISTRATION, HARVARD UNIVERSITY 1963, edited by Carl J. Friedrich and Seymour E. Harris, vol. XII (Cambridge: Graduate School of Public Administration, 1963), pp. 113–14.

a complex of governmental agencies, where masses of paperwork often become a substitute for first-hand observation and communication. The regional offices of state and federal agencies become its symbols and long delays in processing become its product. A growing reliance upon elected officials in Washington and the state houses to move and expedite a particular program or funding request, is another manifestation of this condition. The result has been to forge a closer link between planning and politics.

These examples establish the point that the planner, operating in any sector of urban government, must learn to live with and apply the promise, with all its shortcomings, of a new Federalism that is itself a product of the immense changes that have overtaken our society. These changes have been eloquently recorded by planners and other urban observers. Gutkind has written of the emergence of megalopolis, that gargantuan nonjurisdiction that spreads from Maine to Virginia displaying a common spine, yet competing limbs and organs.[2] Raymond Vernon and his colleagues probed in great detail the inner workings of the New York region and the utter dependence of that area upon the separate decisions of some 1,400 governments.[3] John Gaus, writing in *Reflections on Public Administration,* speaks of "the coercions of environment and the compulsions resulting from science"[4] that demand new governmental responses so that the community is able to deal with change while maintaining its democratic institutions.

One of the most trenchant statements was made by the poet, Archibald MacLeish, in commenting on the personal impact of mass society and governmental entanglement:

The old relationship between man and the world—a relationship once heavy with myth and imminent with meaning—has been replaced by our new, precise, objective, dispassionate observation of the world. With the result that our understanding of our experience of the world has been curiously mutilated. The world is still there—more there now than ever—bright and sharp and analyzed and explicable. But we ourselves, facing the world, are NOT there. Our knowledge, that is to say, seems to exist of itself independently of us, or indeed of any knower—scientific knowledge stated in its scientific laws, its formulae and equations true to all men everywhere and always, but not for a single man alone.[5]

The urban planner today operates in a welter of relationships that demand his attention, require his participation, and press his competence. It is therefore important that he regard this situation in systematic terms, in the same way he has come to regard highway systems and land use relationships. He must learn that local self-determination—that is, planning on a map that stops at the city limits—is as outmoded as the trolley car, that governmental interdependence is a fact of life.

The Causes of Complexity

What are some of the factors contributing to the reality of this situation?

FISCAL FACTORS

The first, of course, is to be found in the inability of both cities and states to find adequate revenue sources. In many urban areas, the inability to meet even the ongoing and accustomed services is already evident, to say nothing of accommodating increasing expectations that give rise to new and greater demands for public service. The record indicates that both states and cities have been stretching their available revenue sources to the breaking point in recent years; their actual rate of increase has been greater than that of the federal government, for all its multitude of programs. While the federal government controls both the credit and the tax base of the nation, it has not

[2] Erwin A. Gutkind, THE TWILIGHT OF CITIES (New York: Free Press of Glencoe, 1962).

[3] The New York Metropolitan Region Study (Raymond Vernon, Director) was undertaken by the Graduate School of Public Administration, Harvard University in 1956. See especially Edward M. Hoover and Raymond Vernon, ANATOMY OF A METROPOLIS (Cambridge, Mass.: Harvard University Press, 1959), and Robert C. Wood, 1400 GOVERNMENTS (Cambridge, Mass.: Harvard University Press, 1961).

[4] John M. Gaus, REFLECTIONS ON PUBLIC ADMINISTRATION (University, Ala.: University of Alabama Press, 1947).

[5] Archibald MacLeish, "Crisis and Poetry," a speech delivered to the Convocation of the Alumni Association, Yale University, October 7, 1960.

sharply increased its allocation of resources to domestic, primarily urban problems, in terms of dollars.

The results of this imbalance are recognized as having a strong outward pull on citizens and taxpaying businesses who can elect the relative convenience and the temporarily reduced costs of suburban living. In their wake comes a dependency and blight that requires still greater resources for stabilization or cure. On the political level, the product has been an increase in federal influence on programs, procedures, and available funds. While there is common agreement that the urban tax problem must be resolved, the answer is not at hand.

ARCHAIC GOVERNMENTAL STRUCTURE

A solution to many problems of urban growth is further inhibited by the archaic structure and ineffective performance of the vast majority of urban governments. While much attention is currently being given to regionalization or other shifts in certain services, too little attention is being paid to the basic structure of local government.

A common tendency is to respond to a newly identified problem or a new source of federal aid with an entirely new administrative mechanism. There is persistent use of the semi-independent authority for handling a new problem, be it transit, renewal, or parking, this procedure resulting in the power of the chief executive being splintered and reduced. The powers of many a relatively strong mayor are being eroded in this well-intended manner. In Philadelphia, for example, a model home rule charter, instituted in 1952, incorporated the best features of modern administrative structure. In the years since its adoption, some 20 new agencies and coordinative mechanisms have been added to the fringes of that structure. While the vast majority of such agencies carry out a new regional, state, or federal function that defies simple placement within old compartments, the net effect of their creation is to create a tangled set of working relationships within city government and with the state and federal agencies to which they are functionally related.

POLITICAL PROBLEMS

The absence of any real degree of regional or even city-wide consensus, is a fundamental obstacle faced constantly by the planner in coping with intergovernmental problems. Part of this arises from the obvious fact that planning decisions are political decisions and are, by nature, not susceptible to unanimous views. Another part is attributable to the relative weakness of elected political leadership. In matters concerning regional problems, this is particularly likely to be the case. Parochialism and insularity dominate both sides of the central city's boundary line. Their mark is seen in many unhappy discussions involving transportation schemes, industrial location planning, and school consolidation. How frequently the planner feels his best efforts are frustrated by lack of political leadership!

In the absence of people and machinery to achieve consensus, and amid problems that cry out for attention, there has been a major recourse to legalistic solutions that involve passing the problem upward. One result is seen in the increasing prerequisites to local and regional receipt of federal and state aids and there is every reason to expect that this form of carrot-and-stick implementation will intensify in the years immediately ahead.

ECONOMIC PROBLEMS

It is a simple fact that governmental units are geographically fixed, unlike business firms and residents who are free to move about as their situations may require. The result has been to make American cities and metropolitan areas extremely competitive creatures that increasingly rely upon careful public relations programs, tax gimmicks, and other techniques to lure and win to them vital talent, industry, and tax revenues. An effect of this competition has been, all too often, to stimulate unwise planning decisions that have resulted in a duplication of facilities and misallocation of land areas and other resources. It has caused the planner all too often to suboptimize his efforts within the confines of his own jurisdiction and to avoid the facts of economic, social, and cultural life that bind the cities of a region together.

PHYSICAL PROBLEMS

There is, finally, the constant need to insert new land uses at higher standards into the built-up fabric of existing cities and regions. Not only must more people be housed, but new uses must be accommodated, such as airports, sewers, expressways, schools, and universities. Each of these new requirements, when developed by the planner, tests the ability of existing mechanisms to achieve sensible solutions.

A few years ago the city of Milwaukee calculated the impact of receiving 100 new families. This would require the availability of 100 dwelling units, 2.2 grade schoolrooms, 1.64 high school classrooms, 4 teachers, ⅔ of a fireman, 10,000 gallons of water, and 140 new automobiles. If this is multiplied by the presumed growth of metropolitan areas across the country it will provide still another way of measuring the planner's stake in intergovernmental solutions in the years that lie ahead.

Existing Intergovernmental Relationships

Existing intergovernmental relationships may be classified into two general categories for the purposes of exposition. *Vertical relationships* refer to ties that link a jurisdiction to governments of higher and broader jurisdiction. *Horizontal relationships* describe a government's relationship to its neighbors across invisible boundary lines. Together, these relationships cut across all the functional areas of concern to the planner, such as highways, urban renewal, poverty, pollution, and even natural beauty.

HORIZONTAL RELATIONSHIPS

Governmental boundary lines may be invisible to the planner on his field trip, but they are very real in legal, political, and practical terms. The walls between jurisdictions seem to grow taller even as accelerated urbanization proves how outdated they have become.

In 1960, there were some 174 metropolitan areas whose core cities exceeded 50,000 in population. In all, multiple governments rule, 25 or more being commonplace. In Greater Philadelphia, for example, the figure is 963, comprising 7 counties, 140 municipalities, 199 townships, 286 special districts, and 331 school districts.[6]

For even the simplest planning purposes, such a number of jurisdictions involves problems of coordination, competition, and political and social distance between people. To the planner, it raises the question: what can he do with his formal charge when it encompasses so small a portion of the total area's resources and needs? A number of solutions have been suggested and are being applied across these lines.

Regional Planning Efforts. In planning, perhaps the most common device has been the regional planning commission whose directors represent the constituent political bodies. The typical charge to these regional bodies has been to advise on planning problems and to derive long-term comprehensive plans for regional growth and development. Stress should be placed on the advisory nature of the bodies. Many regional organizations have been a product of primary interest in transportation planning, and have often been spawned by planing funds made available by the United States Bureau of Public Roads. Many of these groups have subsequently broadened their concern to include all aspects of regional growth and development.

In response to recent federal rulings, many now are in the process of moving from purely advisory, consensus-seeking roles to those of responsibility for the preparation of long-range plans that are prerequisite to various forms of fiscal aid. In this activity, they begin to parallel the evolution of the independent city planning commission as described in Robert A. Walker's classic, *The Planning Function in Urban Government*.[7] The prognosis would be for improved metropolitan planning on an advisory level, but with continued increase in the degree to which professional planning criteria are used in making local decisions. As Charles Adrian has pointed out, this is one way in which

---

[6] U.S. Bureau of the Census, LOCAL GOVERNMENT IN METROPOLITAN AREAS (Vol. V, 1962 Census of Governments, p. 104).

[7] Robert A. Walker, THE PLANNING FUNCTION IN URBAN GOVERNMENT (2nd ed., Chicago: University of Chicago Press, 1950).

the heavy political costs of metropolitan planning could be paid.[8]

Outside the framework of the regional planning commission, some metropolitan areas have been experimenting with the formation of leagues or councils of elected officials that may deal with specific regional problems ranging from air pollution to transit.[9] Examples may now be found in Philadelphia (Regional Council of Elected Officials) and the San Francisco Bay area (Association of Bay Area Governments). Composed directly of elected officials, this device begins to bring together political leadership in such a way as to provide a forum for conflicting viewpoints and a chance for reaching consensus on one or more specific problems. Moreover, it uses, rather than threatens, existing political units.

Recent federal legislation has led to a rapid proliferation of the council device. In 1965 councils were made eligible for matching grants for undertaking programs of regionwide application. Their further development is enhanced by the Model Cities and Metropolitan Development Act which makes the council the prospective recipient of a number of grants to foster metropolitan development. As the executive director of the Metropolitan Washington Council of Governments has pointed out:

. . . the council device provides greater opportunity for local governments to influence and control the solutions to regional problems by placing cities and counties in the mainstream of the regional policy process; and, through Section 701 (g), it triples the value of each dollar the local government chooses to invest in regional problem-solving through the council. Experience across the country is proving that this . . . a heady combination.[10]

Extraterritorial Controls. A third technique practiced in many states is the use of extraterritorial planning and administrative controls.

Through such devices, hard-pressed cities have, for example, been able to secure water rights and reservoirs beyond their territorial limits. Similar cases include the municipal ownership of sewage treatment plants, incinerators, cemeteries and recreational areas beyond local boundary lines. In thirty or more states, central cities are given the right to review the plans of subdivisions proposed in adjacent areas in order that subdividers may be prevented from developing unplanned areas that may later require city services.

Intergovernmental Agreements. Far greater use, however, has been made of intergovernmental agreements for the joint planning and administration of services and facilities. Through legal contact, some services have been shifted from city to county levels (e.g., highway, assessing, personnel, health, and welfare). These accords become binding agreements upon participating governments and follow from legislative action.

Much more numerous than such shifts of function are the thousands of voluntary agreements entered into by localities. Such agreements may be for the provision of sewer or water services, or, in some areas, for library services. There may also be highly informal, professional arrangements for sharing police and fire communication equipment or for providing emergency assistance in any one of many service areas.

These various forms of intergovernmental agreements represent the greatest breakthrough yet achieved in solving intergovernmental problems of the horizontal type. They get things done that might not otherwise be possible, while respecting local identities and foundations. Nevertheless, they have severe shortcomings. An obvious one to the planner is the shallow basis such agreements afford for long-term planning, for frequently the agreements constitute a marriage of convenience and do not contain an opportunity for long-term examination of the problems or services in question. The arrangements are voluntary and often of minimal character.

Consolidation and Federation Efforts. In a few instances, state legislation has effected a union of services across the whole or part of a

[8] Charles R. Adrian, "State and Local Participation in the Design and Administration of Intergovernmental Programs," THE ANNALS, CCCLIX (May, 1965), pp. 35–43.

[9] Royce Hansen, METROPOLITAN COUNCILS OF GOVERNMENT (Washington: Advisory Commission on Intergovernmental Relations, 1966).

[10] Walter A. Scheiber, "Evolving a Policy Process for a Metropolitan Region," speech delivered to Philadelphia Regional Chapter, American Society for Public Administration, January 19, 1967.

metropolitan area. The classic example is Boston's Metropolitan District Comission (MDC) which, since 1919, has provided water, sewer, park, and certain police functions to more than forty cities and towns in Greater Boston. The MDC is a kind of super-government whose revenues are obtained from an assessment formula applied to each participating city and town. School consolidation represents a common instance of state initiative in the rationalization of service patterns.

Despite the considerable attention paid to the activity by political scientists and reformers, the examples of actual consolidation and federation of municipal bodies are few and far between. In 1945, Baton Rouge, Louisiana was completely consolidated with its county (parish), an action which produced one set of officials, one planning commission, and a more effective service over a large geographic area. Twenty years later, however, it remains an almost solitary textbook example of municipal-county consolidation.

Dade County, Florida, supplies one of the few examples of efforts to rationalize certain functions on a metropolitan basis. Through the use of the pre-existing county, important regional functions were developed, with the cities maintaining other services as their responsibility. Planning, police, parks, taxing, assessing, and health are among the functions today performed by Dade County's county-manager government. While there have been persistent attempts to repeal the charter that supports the system, the arrangements have withstood all pressures and now appear clearly established.

Undoubtedly the best known and most far-reaching federation of governmental functions has taken place in metropolitan Toronto, Canada, where since 1953 the city of Toronto and 12 suburbs containing 240 square miles have performed a wide set of functions on a metropolitan basis. Metropolitan planning is one notable result. Services performed by metropolitan Toronto's government include water supply, sewer disposal, street arterials, transit, police, and tax assessing. Further consolidation took place in 1966 when the 13 municipal governments were consolidated into six, the city of

Toronto and five boroughs, and metropolitan powers were expanded for welfare services, waste disposal, and equalization of school finances.

Special Purpose Districts. Another form of arrangement is the special district, authorized by the state for special purposes (e.g., water, sewer, port) and responsible, not to the general public, but to its bondholders. The Port of New York Authority is a classic case and so are the countless turnpike authorities across the country.

The advantages and disadvantages of special districts are the subject of constant debate among political scientists and public administrators. There is no question that they allow flexibility, fresh sources of financing, a business-like atmosphere, and similar advantages. On the other hand, they are challenged on the grounds that they frequently become self-perpetuating units, removed from the controls of the political process; that they thus obscure decision-making; that they compete unfairly for public finances; and finally, that they further splinter the power of an elected chief executive.

Annexation. A final mechanism for rationalizing metropolitan or regional problems is the technique of annexation which, in sections of the country at least, has done much to clarify service areas and extend planning effectiveness. Impossible in closely-built eastern states, annexation has been extensively practiced in unincorporated areas of the south, west, and southwest. Viewed collectively, all of these devices for improving horizontal intergovernmental relationships fall far short of contending successfully with the problems they seek to address. The more grandiose types of solution, federation and consolidation, have been disappointing to their advocates. The defeat of such efforts in metropolitan St. Louis, Cleveland, Knoxville, and Albuquerque in recent years has made such ideas less popular. Greater hope is now being placed in solving the same problems through the same "carrot-and-stick" method employed by federal and sometimes state aid programs. A growing theory is that local tradition and other barriers to cooperation may have to be solved through directive

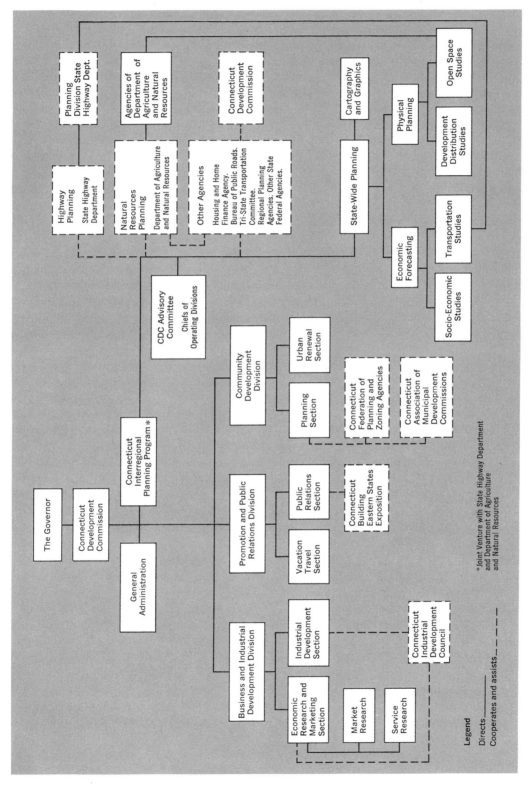

FIGURE 2–1. *Organization chart, Connecticut Development Commission*

and inducement, rather than through locally achieved consensus; through the medium of additional revenues rather than through academic arguments. Meanwhile, the problem of achieving metropolitan policy continues to engage planner and administrator alike.

VERTICAL RELATIONSHIPS

Although cooperation between local governmental units has been slow to mature, the same cannot be said of relationships between local units of government and those of higher jurisdiction, especially the national government. Here, the number of linkages has steadily been climbing, often through frustration in working out closer-to-home solutions. The results to the planner or administrator, however, may not appear dissimilar, for frustration in making these new links work is often of equal intensity. The problems are simply those of feast, rather than famine.

The State. In our federal system the state is the father of the municipality and all other jurisdictions within its boundaries. The latter derive their power from the state authorization. Thus, the range of local planning powers has been closely linked to enabling or special

legislation enacted by the state legislature. Once confined to such planning controls are zoning, official maps, and subdivisions, the list of state legislation now of interest to the urban planner extends into urban redevelopment, transportation, low income housing, and industrial development. As Professor William I. Goodman has pointed out:

> The state is no longer permissive; the municipalities are no longer insular and untouched. Indeed, the two jurisdictions seem to be moving in the direction of one another, as measured by the extent of their responsibilities and initiative, on the one hand, and their conformance to overall policies, on the other hand.[11]

Planning by the states themselves has not received the widespread attention paid to local planning efforts authorized by the states. It is only in recent years that serious attention has been paid to the state's role in solving the problems previously described. As a result, new state plans now give a more realistic context to locally developed plans. With greater planning come greater revenues usable by localities:

[11] William I. Goodman, "Urban Planning and the Role of the State," STATE GOVERNMENT, XXXV (Summer 1962), pp. 149-53.

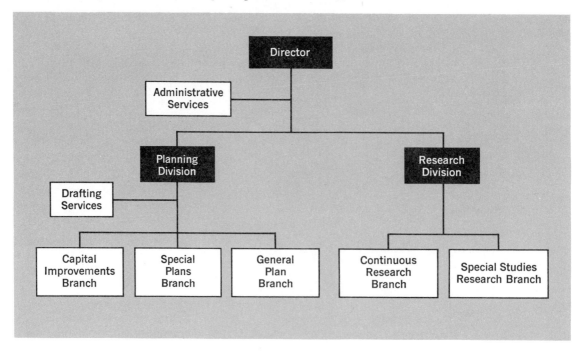

FIGURE 2–2. *Organization of the Hawaii Department of Planning and Research*

there are now funds for land acquisition, sewage systems, hospital construction, highways, and other purposes such as urban renewal.

Comprehensive planning, usually based upon regional divisions, is now under way in many states. The newest state, Hawaii, was the first to complete a statewide plan. This has been followed rapidly by significant efforts in such major states as New York, California, Michigan, and New Jersey. In Pennsylvania, these new activities have been in large measure responsible for establishment of a department of community development to coordinate all the state's planning assistance programs. In almost every case, the efforts have been stimulated by federal planning assistance programs.

In addition to the planning work they are undertaking themselves, the state planning bodies have come to play an increasing role in the supervision of local planning. This has become a precondition for acceptance of federal aid, and in small towns and cities especially, comprehensive planning has been coordinated and in some instances instituted by state personnel. In the process many states have become full-fledged partners in planning, and, as a by-product, active salesmen of planning assistance and other forms of state and federal aid. In no other field, perhaps, has the state come to exert a similar degree of partnership with national and local governments.

Summarizing all these trends, Goodman, writing in *State Government* in 1962, stressed these aspects of the state's increasing role in local planning affairs:

1. The likely emergence of a clearer hierarchy of responsibilities for planning and development made possible through the exertion of greater leadership by the states either through legislation, financing, or a combination of devices.
2. The opportunity of municipalities to receive increasing assistance from the state in conducting their local planning programs.[12]
3. The necessity for local officials to become increasingly alert to the impact of a growing array of state projects and policies on the local area so as to avoid state-local conflicts and to minimize local financial burdens.
4. A likely increase in state regulatory controls

over local growth and development for residential areas, industrial areas, and such matters as air pollution and transportation. Parallel to this will be the need for ever-increasing cooperation and communication among professionals operating at both levels.[13]

The National Government. At the national level the spate of programs produced by recent administrations has had a revolutionary effect upon the scope and context of urban planning, yet all of this has occurred without there being a single reference in the Constitution of the United States to the American city. A major share of the credit for this dramatic shift in the traditional definition of federalism is, of course, the rapid growth of urban populations and problems, and the inadequacy of state and local responses to the demands thus created. Rebuffed many times by rurally controlled legislatures, cities have set their sights directly upon their congressional representatives and the federal administration to find support for their needs. Thus, the picture today is characterized by an extensive lobby representing the nation's cities in Washington—among others, the U.S. Conference of Mayors and the National League of Cities, plus individual city representatives alert to the interests back home. At stake are an ever-increasing fund of dollars and services of incredible variety.

National Programs. A group of available services are those the national government supplies for its own purposes but which fulfill important local needs. To the planner this list is headed by the great body of research and statistical services that are vital in mounting an urban planning program. The United States Bureau of the Census produces basic planning data of great variety; these figures become the basis of countless decisions involving resource allocation, the determination of urban renewal areas, and school enrollment projections. Census information remains the spine of all urban data bank systems. There is considerable pressure now for a quinquennial census to overcome the time gap that impairs the utility of data collected only once every ten years.

---

[12] In addition to financial aid, Goodman referred to additional planning information and statistics and the sharing of high-level state-employed technicians.

[13] The author is indebted to William I. Goodman for this summary of ideas broadened in the aforementioned article in STATE GOVERNMENT.

Equally useful are data from the Bureau of Labor Statistics, the Federal Reserve Bank, the FBI, and other agencies of the national government, together with the maps and charts compiled by the Army Map Service and the United States Geological Survey that form the basis of most planning agency map files.

Other examples of federal aids of this type are: numerous White House conferences on matters of concern to the nation's states, cities, and regions; model legislation, suggested standards, and reporting systems developed by federal agencies for local use; and the well-nigh inexhaustible products of the Superintendent of Documents.

Direct Federal Services to Localities. These services have grown considerably since the time when river and harbor improvements made by the U.S. Army Corps of Engineers provided the dominant example. Now training and assistance programs are made available to urban governments in many fields. There are the airport planning and construction programs of the Federal Aviation Agency, the work of Job Corps personnel in relieving chronic unemployment problems, the practical aid programs of the Department of Health, Education and Welfare, public health grants for exploring the borders of knowledge in medical science, and the cooperative Agricultural Extension Service programs which are beginning to have urban applications in some enterprising cities. More familiar to the city planner is the public housing program which is administered through local housing authorities.

One result of the increase of direct federal services has been to relieve local revenue pressures in certain areas such as welfare. Increases in these types of programs are sometimes suggested to further relieve local fiscal pressures.

Federal Laws and Regulation. While most numerous in the field of interstate commerce, federal laws are having profound effects upon local administrative and planning efforts as seen dramatically in the problems of school and residential desegregation. The civil rights acts and related legislation are having direct bearing on the planning of public facilities and the changes induced have gone beyond the limits likely had local decision-making been the only force involved. A similar influence deriving from administrative regulation rather than legislation is found in the familiar requirements of the Department of Housing and Urban Development's Workable Program for Community Improvement (see below).

Grant-In-Aid Programs. By far the most significant form of vertical relationship for the planner in today's federal system is the grant-in-aid. Today this technique, first employed in the Morrill Act of 1864, ties all levels of government together in intricate and almost indescribable patterns.

A grant-in-aid is any federal allocation of funds to a state or local jurisdiction for specified purposes but usually with provision for at least a degree of supervision of review by the federal agency.

The Morrill Act actually made federal grants of land available to the states for educational purposes. Since then, land grants have come to be replaced by financial grants usually allocated on the basis of local matching funds according to a formula and routed, for administrative or political purposes, through state agencies acting as intermediaries. However, even this semblance of adherence to the classic lines of federalism, is being over-looked in some instances today.

The first extensive grant-in-aid affecting urban governments might be said to be the Federal Aid Highway Act of 1944. It was followed by the Hill-Burton Act for hospital and health center construction in 1948, and by the first United States Housing Act in 1949. The latter opened the door to federal funds to aid the growth and redevelopment of cities and towns.

Now the list of grant-in-aid programs is considerable, as revealed by an extensive survey made by the Office of Economic Opportunity in 1965.[14] The following are among the aids of greatest interest to urban planners:

1. *Highway Beautification* (1965). Under this program, any state highway commission may enter into an agreement with the Secretary of Commerce for a 75 per cent federal reim-

---

[14] U.S. Office of Economic Opportunity, CATALOG OF FEDERAL PROGRAMS FOR INDIVIDUAL AND COMMUNITY IMPROVEMENT (Washington: The Office, 1965).

bursement of the cost involved in landscaping and scenic enhancement of federal highways.

2. *Highway Planning and Construction* (1916 as amended). Financial assistance to state highway commissions is available under this program for constructing and planning the interstate system and all other federally-aided primary and secondary roads. State and local plans must be approved by the Bureau of Public Roads. Part of the funds are earmarked for planning studies designed to produce a well-integrated transportation and land use plan. With these funds, many starts toward region-wide planning have been initiated.

3. *Public Works and Economic Development* (1965). This program, operated by the Economic Development Administration, is designed to provide new industry and permanent jobs in areas experiencing depressed economic conditions. Long-range planning and programming of job requirements are stressed. Local initiative is called on to design successful solutions. An overall economic development program is a qualification for receiving benefits under the Act.

4. *Advance Acquisition of Land* (1965). Funds available under this program are available to stimulate localities to acquire land and land interests that may be needed in the future for public work and other municipal facilities.

5. *Code Enforcement Program* (1965). This program provides grants for planning and operating intensive code enforcement programs in eligible local areas where initial signs of blight and deterioration in housing quality are evidenced. To be eligible, a community must comply with the terms of the Workable Program for Community Development. Once a program is approved, the residents in a code enforcement area are eligible for relocation assistance and various forms of FHA mortgage aid.

6. *Community Renewal Program* (1959). This program provides a two-thirds grant to any community for preparation of a full examination of its long-term renewal requirements. Economic, physical, and social needs and resources are to be assessed in arriving at a long-range strategy for local development.

7. *Neighborhood Facilities* (1965). This new program is designed to provide federal construction funds for multi-service public facilities in local neighborhoods. Two-thirds grants are extended and priority is given to low income areas. The sponsor may be any governmental unit or non-profit corporation so long as the latter receives the approval of the chief executive of the community, and an endorsement for the local community action agency.

8. *Open Space Land Program* (1964). 50 per cent matching grants are made available to public bodies for acquiring, developing, and preserving open space for permanent public use as a park, recreation, historical, or scenic area. To be eligible for open space grants, a project application must be consistent with an officially coordinated regional plan for open space development.

9. *Urban Beautification Program* (1965). Federal matching funds are made available to beautify and improve open space and public areas in urban communities. Again, individual project requests must be consistent with an overall plan for development of such areas. Waterfronts, squares, parks, and malls of all kinds are eligible if they meet this requirement.

10. *Urban Mass Transportation* (1964). This program makes grants and loans available to local public bodies and states for developing coordinated mass transit systems. Up to two-thirds of the cost of acquisition, construction, and improvement of facilities may be received. Demonstration projects are also fundable under the program.

11. *Urban Planning Assistance Program* (1954 as amended). The "701 Program" grants funds to assist comprehensive planning in small communities, states and metropolitan areas. With the funds received, the community can prepare comprehensive plans, capital programs, and various administrative and control regulations, such as those for zoning and subdivision control.

12. *Urban Renewal Projects* (1949 as amended). Grants, planning advances, and temporary loans are made under this program which is intended to eliminate physical blight from both residential and nonresidential areas. Clearance of areas, rehabilitation, or a

combination of techniques are fundable on a two-thirds—one-third basis in most cities. Relocation assistance and eligibility for FHA and Small Business aids are made possible under this program. Compliance with the Workable Program for Community Development is a prequisite for funding.

The 12 programs referred to above are merely a selection of the available federal grants-in-aid. Omitted entirely are others that deal more directly with social and manpower problems, such as the programs of the Office of Economic Opportunity. Collectively, the federal programs play a significant role in defining the work load, the influence, and the scope of local planning operations. The planner's familiarity with the programs and their application often becomes one measure of his service to the community for which he works.

Urban Renewal—A Look at a Grant-in-Aid Program. The urban renewal grant-in-aid program is perhaps the most familiar to city planners. It provides a good example of the complexity of intergovernmental relationships, and, as such, has been examined recently in a number of books and articles.[15] These accounts point to the fact that policies underlying the programs involve Congress, the newly-created Department of Housing and Urban Development, local government, and the public itself.

Clifford Ham, writing in the *Annals*, identified the following as being illustrative of urban renewal's significance as an example of contemporary intergovernmental relations:

1. The increase of urban influence of Congress and in the administering agency, as evidenced by the widened scope of the program, the increasingly generous loan and grant programs, and the willingness of Congress to respond to urban problems;

2. The development by Congress and the administering agency of stricter standards and requirements for receipt of federal assistance;

3. The establishment of closer relationships between urban governments and the federal government, with an increasingly vestigial role for state government;

4. The development of new structures within local government for carrying out its work with the federal programs and agencies.

The urban renewal program contains within it many examples of problems that demand attention in the realm of creative federalism. There is the agonizing lead time involved in the execution process. Unable to program operations according to a fixed schedule, officials are harrassed in selling land and meeting the expectations of anxious residents within rehabilitation areas. A persistent tendency to oversell and underestimate both cost and time has hurt the program. For these reasons, there is constant talk of further refinement through changed administrative rules, and even new legislation. Open-ended budgets, reduction of review machinery, and the provision of annual grants are frequently mentioned methods. Nevertheless, urban renewal is a proper example of dynamic federal-state-local relationships. Despite the problems already referred to, it has made a significant mark on the landscape of many American cities. It has given these same cities a taste of what could happen if sufficient funds, programs, and personnel were made available to tackle the job of rebuilding urban America.

Unsolved Areas

At the present time, considerable attention is fixed upon the performance obtained under the intergovernmental arrangements previously described. The Administration, through its Budget Bureau and many departments, is probing the logic and capability of existing devices. Congress is demanding more accountability and direction of the programs it has authorized. Mayors and local legislative bodies are groping with new structural arrangements in order to be able to cope with federal and state aids with some order and initiative. All agree that satisfaction of the nation's objectives in a complex urban world requires more skills, wealth, and creativity than ever before. All agree that the machinery of government must be reshaped in the manner

15 Roscoe Martin, METROPOLIS IN TRANSITION (Washington: U.S. Housing and Finance Agency, 1963), and Clifford C. Ham, "Urban Renewal: A Case Study in Emerging Goals in an Intergovernmental Setting," THE ANNALS, CCCLIX (May, 1965), pp. 44–52.

best calculated to perform these missions well. This, in turn, means experimentation, pragmatic adjustment, and a continual shifting of the lines between the local, state, and federal government spheres. The underlying challenge is how to construct a fabric of decision-making and subsequent action that will bring better conditions and increased satisfaction to the nation's urban population.

Although his discipline calls upon him to seek a more rational plan for the future, the urban planner must learn to content himself with a pattern that continues to approach yet never achieves such goals. This is the clear consequence of a pluralistic society, a federal system, and a democratic process. In the continuing search for better instruments, however, the planner has a challenge to set targets and goals that can help to bridge the gaps between groups and governments. This is an immensely complex task in the context of the metropolis alone, much less still wider areas of concern. It requires accommodation and innovation of the highest order. It is important therefore, that the planner should know the present situation well and be aware of the new ideas that loom on the horizon of reform and improvement.

PROBLEMS OF CURRENT RELATIONSHIPS

The implications of the programs previously described are many and varied, and are being worked out daily in the governments of this country. The comments that follow relate particularly to grant-in-aid programs.

One clear effect has been to decrease the role of the state vis-à-vis the governmental creatures it has made. Despite a net gain in state participation in solving public problems, it is obvious that the states have come to play a lesser role in the wake of increasing federal participation under the grant-in-aid and direct service programs enacted in recent years. Even when political protocol has dictated that the state be involved in the allocation formula, it is very often a mere wicket through which funds are channeled with little interference or change. Only the time of processing may be affected thereby. In Mississippi, the governor's veto role in that state's anti-poverty program has been circumvented by federal administrators. In Philadelphia, state opposition to the use of federal funds to cover a suppressed highway near Independence Mall has been overcome by a union of local and congressional influence upon officials of the Bureau of Public Roads in Washington. So dominant are the lines between Washington and the big city that in some instances the state is simply ignored in the planning of key projects and programs. That kind of event may well be influenced by the political party in control of state and city. In any event, a means of circumvention exists.

A second effect of mounting federal aid is its skewing effect upon the allocation of scarce local resources. Changes in the marginal value of alternate investments may result from the availability of matching federal funds for transit, air pollution, or renewal. Their presence may alter political decisions and make local moves much easier for the local politican to swallow. This can be timed in local capital improvement programs with the advent of new federal programs. It has, for example, resulted in advancing the place of transit improvements, not otherwise affordable by many cities, to positions of top billing. The same effect is also seen in urban renewal where the search for non-cash credits as the local matching share for the federal formula has pushed streets, recreation, and school projects into priority positions that can beget federal funds.

Aid programs also have the effect of strengthening local programs and, in real measure, the efficiency of local planning efforts. Comprehensive, long-range planning has been notably extended by being made a prerequisite for participation in many aid programs. Also, urban renewal has given the locality the power of eminent domain to make a broad variety of public improvements and has greatly strengthened the power of the planner as a doer, and not simply as an idea man.

The same programs have forged a better grasp of intergovernmental political relationships and, as a result, a more complex form of communication between levels of government. This is symbolized by the regional offices of federal departments and agencies, the growth of big city lobbyists in the corridors of Congress, and the present role of the Vice President as a special emissary to the mayors and managers of the nation. The consequences of these ties may be measured by the intense competition that has existed between the nation's cities in searching for new federal installations and facilities, such as the Atomic Energy Accelerator, and the new Environmental Health Center recently awarded to North Carolina's research triangle.

Other observers would point to the impact on local initiative to get things done with local funds. The existence of a federal program may be a useful excuse for deferring or delaying involvement.

A far more profound question surrounds the impact of these new relationships upon local governmental organization. Given the growing ties between the city and the national government, what forms of local government are likely to evolve? Already, the need for a development coordinator has proved itself in countless cities involved in housing and economic growth programs. Now that need is duplicated by similar ones in the field of education and other human services.

Still another question raised is in the fact that federal programs are generally supplemental in nature, rather than contributory to basic local needs such as public education or police and fire services.

There results, at the present time, a mammoth problem of coordination across the triangle of horizontal and vertical lines of government. In a recent speech to the senate, Senator Edmund Muskie summarized the problem with great force:

During the past five sessions of Congress, we have developed the most impressive package of federal legislation since the Depression, to attack poverty, ignorance, economic distress, urban blight, discrimination, and other human problems; but the success of this legislation is only as good as the machinery which carries it to the people in the fastest, most effective way possible. During the past two Congresses, we have concentrated primarily on the substance of government; now the spotlight must be turned on the procedure. Here is where the challenge lies.[16]

---

[16] Senator Edmund Muskie, "The Challenge of Creative Federalism," CONGRESSIONAL RECORD, CCXII (March 25, 1966), p. 6500.

Finally, there is the question of manpower to run a complex and truly creative federal system. Given funds and legislative authority, there remains the scarcest resource of all to fill: talent capable of managing the resulting mechanisms with care, vigor, imagination, and clarity. This is especially required at the state and local levels if federal domination is to be avoided and a balance is to be maintained in the federal relationships. Without trained personnel to plan and administer the welter of programs successfully, little product will result. There are ample examples of this to be found today in housing, poverty, and other fields.

So unpromising is the immediate prospect for diverting the necessary talent to the public service that there are growing opinions in favor of turning to industry for greater and greater assistance. In any event, the ability to find and train talent to run complex programs becomes a severe limitation upon the success of current intergovernmental arrangements. The relative decline of state government is frequently attributed to its relative failure to cope with the talent gap and the rise of professionalism in handling governmental responsibilities.

CORRECTIVE STEPS

Paralleling the problems just recited are a growing number of steps being taken to assure a more successful response to the accelerating changes affecting urban institutions. Some of these steps are administrative, some institutional, and some involve the training and development of new skills. The following summarizes some of the more significant of these steps.

Structural Changes at the Federal Level. The establishment of a Department of Housing and Urban Development (HUD) in 1966 was a major step taken to redefine federal relationships vis-à-vis other jurisdictions within the federal system. Its new organization stresses intergovernmental relations and metropolitan affairs by assigning assistance secretaries to these aspects of urban development.

First proposed by the late President Kennedy, HUD was argued to be a proper response to obvious conditions that compel the national government to pay major attention to housing and urban development and to the major per-

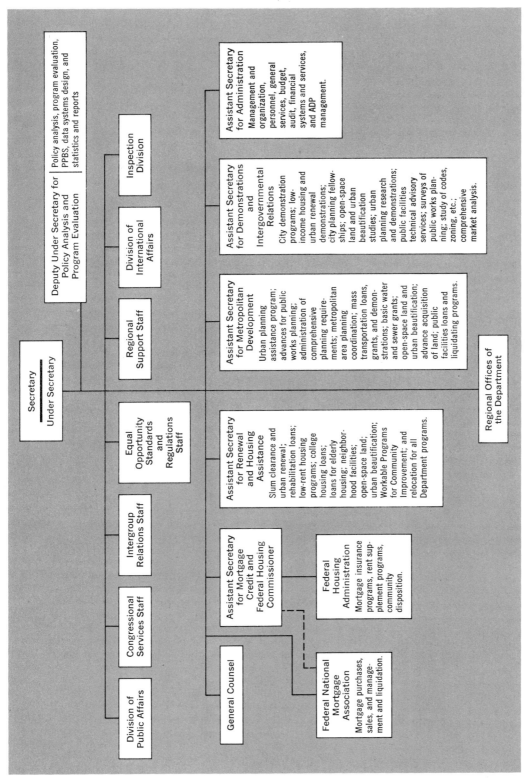

FIGURE 2–3. *Organization chart, U.S. Department of Housing and Urban Development, 1966*

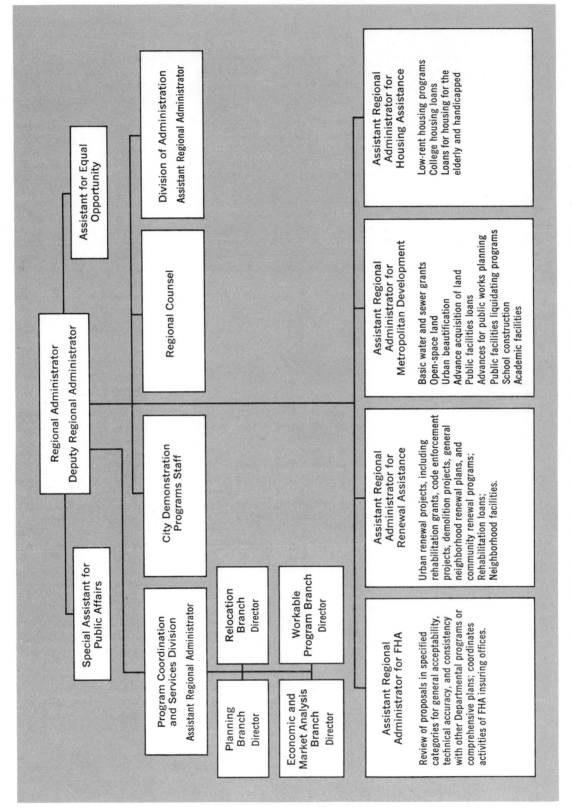

FIGURE 2–4. Organization chart for regional offices, U.S. Department of Housing and Urban Development, 1966

centage of the nation's population. It was aimed at superseding the Housing and Home Finance Agency, itself already large enough to warrant department status, but too narrow in scope to address the nation's urban problems.

The new Department was opposed by many who feared a shift in attention to urban areas and by others who feared that the growing domination of federal funds and programs would lead to the destruction of local government as presently known. To many, it was a direct threat to the familiar system. It is still too early to gauge the effectiveness of the Department. Its powers have been increased through passage of the rent supplementation and Model Cities bills, and an executive order that gives its Secretary the power to convene any and all meetings relevant to urban problems. A strong unit has been set up in the Department, under the Assistant Secretary for Demonstration and Intergovernmental Relations, to deal with intergovernmental relations.

Throughout the past seven years, an enormous impetus for reorganization has been given by the Advisory Commission on Intergovernmental Relations, a federal office that includes representatives from federal, state, and local government and provides a forum and a channel for recommendations to Congress and other bodies.

Structural Changes at the Urban Level. In addition to occasional proposals for consolidation and federation of key urban functions, there is growing interest in the long-sleeping subject of local governmental reorganization. To match the consolidation of federal services, many cities have begun to reassess and regroup their own growing functions.

Some cities have undertaken administrative studies with funds granted under the Community Renewal Program. A frequent model has been the creation of a department of development under the direct aegis of the elected or appointed chief executive. This concept has superseded prior concepts of a development coordinator, who was charged with dovetailing the actions of city departments and independent housing and redevelopment authorities. Philadelphia, for example, has proposed an Office of Development Programming that would,

close to the chief executive, be charged with maintaining a balanced assessment of all city functions dealing with development, and with corresponding regional, state, and federal authorities.

An interesting response accorded great publicity in 1966 was the series of task forces appointed by Mayor John Lindsay of New York to assess and reorganize that city's complex human service and physical development programs. The Lindsay task forces are significant not only for their proposals for sweeping changes to better accord with intergovernmental demands, but for the premium placed upon sound organization as a prerequisite for coping successfully with current programs and problems. It is a harbinger of efforts that will doubtless follow in cities across the land.[17]

Structural Changes at State Level. Although not an active partner up to this point in creative federalism, the state is beginning to adapt itself institutionally to urban needs. In the past several years, a number of states have established an office of urban affairs. The function of the office is to enable the state to give continuing attention to problems of local government, including finance, structure, organization, and planning. They encompass the function of advising the governor and the legislature, and some of the offices operate directly out of the Governor's office.

Another trend is the establishment at state level of liaison units to coordinate federal programs and determine how the state should deal with these on both a policy level and an operating context.

One of the most hopeful trends, of course, is the drive toward state constitutional reform. After many decades of dormancy, constitutional commissions are being established and conventions held. Michigan approved a new constitution in 1963 that instituted a number of state-local reforms.

Resource Allocation Mechanism. One major recommendation of the New York Task Force on Human Services was advocacy of a

17 Institute of Public Administration, LET THERE BE COMMITMENT, A HOUSING, PLANNING DEVELOPMENT PROGRAM FOR NEW YORK CITY (New York: The Institute, 1966).

new approach to resource allocation, commonly called PPBS (for planning–programming–budgeting system). Local interest is beginning to match federal commitment to this concept which features a systematic approach to decision-making and the use of cost-effectiveness and related management techniques.

Programming, the key ingredient of the approach, is a continuous process of allocating resources with respect both to the purposes they are expected to perform in the plannable future and to the results they have achieved in the past. Thus defined, programming is central to the task of getting to one's objectives and is sensitive to the changing forces that affect our communities. As a technique, it is peculiarly adaptable to intergovernmental entanglements. Application of its rational approach would do much to develop a common language among the participants in decision-making and thus lead to more readily pursuable courses across boundary lines. (See Chapters 12 and 13 for further discussion of programming within the context of comprehensive planning.)

The concept of PPBS owes it origins and present popularity to the spectacular success achieved by its use in the Defense Department. There, the system became the pivotal device in interrelating the sometimes competing and wasteful efforts of the three military systems. Agreement upon a set of defense missions, to which all resources were then directed, was the critical step from whence sprang highly involved techniques for judging alternative systems and designs. The energies of the creator of a new weapons system were not cut off; rather they were subjected to tests of relevance, capability, and performance of the established missions. The agreed upon missions, or program packages, became new compartments for looking at defense problems and for amassing a defense strategy.

As a result of Presidential orders, the basic concept is now having application in the planning of all domestic activities, but not without considerable difficulties. The job of defining missions for the urban world is far more complicated than for the kill-or-be-killed defense world. Growing experience, however, would seem to point out that missions stated in such

terms afford a sensible way of classifying, measuring, and coordinating domestic programs across jurisdictional lines.

Improved Personnel Relationships. In some fields, such as public health and natural resources, strong professional relationships already bind the personnel of federal, state, and local agencies. This itself can do much to break through the log-jam of distance and confusion that are the product of grant-in-aid and other joint programs.

There is ample evidence of the great role played by professional leadership in current solutions to metropolitan and other affairs. Police chiefs, school superintendents, and city managers, as well as planners, have found innumerable occasions on which they could share problems and deal across jurisdictional lines. They are often preliminary to the development of contractual or voluntary arrangements, for handling services. Professionals often are able to find solutions that would not be possible through official channels.

These developments are not without their shortcomings, however, for there is the danger of making decisions within the realm of closed politics and of controverting established political lines. There is the danger of functional decision-making, wherein accords are reached on transportation matters for example, without regard for other and impinging goals. Nevertheless, the reasonable work of trained men, when working in a framework that protects against parochialism is a major step on the road to sounder intergovernmental relationships. The talent shortage must, therefore be addressed in schools and colleges across the country as part of an attack on today's shortcomings and rivalries.

Federal Intergovernmental Advisory Activities. Since the 1930s, there have been administrative reviews of intergovernmental problems. In 1953, a major review was inaugurated by President Eisenhower's Kestenbaum Commission. Its works were followed in 1959 by the passage of Public Law 380 which created a permanent Advisory Commission on Intergovernmental Relations to provide a common view of problems, a forum for discussion, to consider controls in existing federal aid programs, make technical aid available to all governmental levels, and recommend, within constitutional safeguards, the best allocation of functions among governments. The presence of the Commission now gives a continuing, well-planned, and well-staffed avenue for continuing solutions to these problems.

At the present time, the Commission's recommendations include support of a general statute for automatic termination of any grant-in-aid program passed by the Congress within five years. This probationary period would force the program to be reappraised before the program had a chance to become thoroughly institutionalized. A second recommendation that is finding its way into more and more legislation is that all grants pertaining to facilities be reviewed by a planning group on a metropolitan basis before authorization to proceed is given an applicant. Further elaboration of this principle will greatly enhance the power of the planner and the importance placed upon metropolitan planning bodies.[18]

But thoughts about coordination do not end with the work of the Commission. Other recent suggestions which cover a wide range of proposals, some or all of which may find their way into practice in the years or months ahead, include:

1. A Special Assistant to the President for Program Coordination to keep abreast of current conflicts and to assist the Chief Executive in solving them.

2. Support from a special team within the Bureau of the Budget.

3. A computerized capability within the Bureau's staff that would keep abreast of the needs and current resources of all subareas within the country.

4. A Deputy Undersecretary in each federal department to coordinate intergovernmental aspects of that department's program.

5. HUD-like regional administrators that would have a purview over all aspects of that department's program.

6. Local coordinators in each metropolitan area.

7. A National Intergovernmental Affairs Council, patterned upon the National Security Council, and composed of all those in command of programs with an impact on state and local governments.

8. Reduction in the number of local governments by as much as 80 per cent.

9. County modernization.

10. Greater local home rule.

Summary

All of these proposals are attempts to strike a balance between the importance of preserving local institutions and the need to attain a high level of program performance. To some, the prospect of moving to additional echelons of federal officials is reason enough to suggest steps for greater decentralization of services.

For these, the block grant or similar proposals for redistributing federally-collected revenues to local areas without strings has increasing merits. For others, the stakes are sufficient to warrant a readjustment in favor of greater federal control and initiative. The tension between these opposing schools of thought will be affected in future years by the impact of Congressional and legislative reapportionment, to say nothing of the status of the unsolved problems that have triggered the debate in the first place. In any case, the years ahead will see a continually unfolding set of adjustments in our federal system. No one will be more concerned with them than the urban planner who, like it or not, has a daily involvement in the political and administrative arrangements that bind city to city, city to region, region to state, and all to the national government.

---

[18] William G. Colman, "The Role of the Federal Government in the Design and Administration of Intergovernmental Programs," THE ANNALS OF THE AMERICAN ACADEMY OF POLITICAL AND SOCIAL SCIENCE, CCCLIX (May, 1965), pp. 23–34.

Part Two

Basic Studies
for Urban Planning

3

Population Studies

ANALYSIS AND PROJECTION of population are at the base of almost all major planning decisions. As measures of the size and density of the various groups within the urban or regional population, they determine the level of demand for future facilities and serve as indices of most urban and regional problems. Since no other local agency normally provides projection data in a way that is useful for these purposes, the responsibility falls to the local planning office. The substantial importance of population projections to all aspects of planning programs justifies the use of adequate time and resources to produce results that are reliable, flexible enough to reflect the consequences of local change, and sufficiently detailed to serve as a basis for the design of specialized local facilities. The methods used by planners to analyze and project population are too often simple, short-cut methods which provide very shaky grounds for decisions on large investments. It is the purpose of this chapter to provide a detailed, unified strategy for population analysis and projection which, within the limitations of the usual resources of a planning office, best meets the requirements of local planning.

Although this method involves mathematical computations, it is perhaps more time-consuming than esoteric. In fact, any competent technician, even if he is untrained in demographic techniques, should be able to follow the diagrams and instructions that are incorporated in this chapter without difficulty. It is our contention that the rudiments of this method are required in order to elevate the function of population analysis and projection

above the crude level that has characterized the product of many planning offices. There is no necessity, indeed, to include a chapter on population studies at all in this volume, which seeks to reflect the most meaningful recent contributions in the field, if earlier methods are to be continued as the basis of work. Hopefully, the coming era in planning will provide for more disciplined, but manageable, research and analytical activities.

Perhaps the most serious criticism that can be made of most contemporary work by planners in the area of population studies is that little attention is given to the interrelationships between population variables and other factors. Relationships with population are relevant to almost all of the chapters of this book. These need not be recapitulated here, but they do have to be recognized in population analysis and projection. In some cases the relationship may be so strong that there is no need for population studies as such, as in the case of a region whose structure is such that the future population can best be projected as a byproduct of economic projections.

We are concerned here, however, with the more usual case in which economic and demographic factors and many others are important in determining the future of a community or region, and with providing an approach to the demographic factors themselves which permits purposeful consideration of these interrelationships. Heavy reliance is placed in our suggested approach on the *cohort survival model of population dynamics.*

The cohort survival model is not the ultimate answer, but it is the best of those operationally available to planners.

In this connection, it should be noted that as planning programs continue to shift from a long range, physical design, public works emphasis to a social welfare here-and-now concern, selective analysis of existing demographic patterns and post-censal developments will become relatively more important in relation to overall studies and projections. As the demographic base for planning shifts, we shall need to devise an appropriate data base and a set of analytic procedures to deal with this condition. The term *population* as used here refers to the number of enumerated people enumerated in households, adjusted for comparability over time to account for changes in the rules for enumeration.

Required Characteristics of Studies

Among the several special demands by local planning is the need for breakdowns of total future population into small groups which are subject to special urban policies: groups of a specific age, sex, race, and income level, or groups located in a particular planning district. For purposes of planning, the method must project each group *independently* rather than disaggregate or separate it from a general or *unitary* projection which takes no account of the special growth characteristics of each group.

A second requirement is for a projection method which allows for planned change and for other local changes not systematically included in the calculations. This is necessary because most successful elements of local planning policy have feedback effects on local population growth. A basic goal of every planner is to help make the area he serves a better environment for living. If he is successful in this undertaking there is likely to be higher net in-migration than otherwise would have occurred. The entry of new institutions into the area, the opening of land for residential development through the extension of utilities or the transportation system, annexations which change the desirability of localities because of changes in taxes and services, zoning changes,

and the provision of community facilities are all potential forces for a change in the growth and distribution of area population. While there are obvious practical problems which make analyses of these effects difficult, it is self-contradictory for a planner to propose a future environment that is designed to be attractive and yet not designed to accommodate the in-migration resulting from a measure of success in achieving the objective.

Effects of this type, and others even less tractable, are even more important for local planning jurisdictions than for larger regions, since single private decisions and incremental changes in the urban physical plant have a larger net effect. The decisions of a single-tract developer or industrial executive, construction of a freeway, and any number of other such decisions can have local effects of great magnitude.

This points up two additional criteria for estimating and projecting future local population. The method used must permit the systematic consideration of migration as an effect closely tied to the planning process. It must also meet the need for clear internal structure, displaying the key behavioral variables of change in a manner that encourages the use of judgment, apart from the computations. Population projection, like other aspects of planning, cannot be wholly scientific. While large scale aggregate projections may be able to rely on a balancing effect among small scale changes, in an urban area there is no substitute for an intimate knowledge of the area and sound judgment of the effects of various kinds of special change.

COHORT SURVIVAL METHOD

It seems clear that the varying demands on local population analysis and projection will increasingly be met by the cohort survival method, both because it is among the most accurate methods and also provides unique flexibility for the inputs and outputs of population studies. The cohort survival approach is not unknown to planners, but has been infrequently used because of its alleged complexity and demand on office time. Actually, a simplified aggregate projection by sex and by five-year age intervals can be made in a couple of days by one man using a desk calculator. The detailed series of projections by groups suggested here requires more time and would be inefficiently accomplished without the aid of a computer. Our position is that the much heralded "computer revolution" has arrived, at least to the extent that electronic digital computers of moderately high speed and moderately large capacity are within the reach of every local planning agency in North America. A recent restatement of the cohort survival approach in terms which lead to simple and direct programming for digital computers is employed in this chapter.

At the same time, the approach is not an "automated" system in which reliance on human judgment and human intervention is minimized. On the contrary, in keeping with the criteria above, the procedures we suggest are intended to focus the attention of the planner on the more critical judgments required in population studies for local planning purposes, to present him with the available data in a form which is suitable for informed decisions, and to permit the use of a computer for working out the detailed implications of the decisions which are made.

In order to develop the full strength of the special possibilities of cohort survival other methods of population projection also are described, primarily for purposes of contrast. In this context, the important distinctions between conditional and nonconditional projections are discussed, the basic causes of population change are explained, and the components of the population which can be studied separately are defined. Then attention is given to the basic assumptions for projection and the systems of local subareas for which projections are prepared. With this as background the general form of cohort survival is described. Then a simplified form of the method is presented, and separate attention is given to the special opportunities for including migration projections.

Surveys of the full range of traditional projection methods are found in several good standard sources, some of which specifically discuss operational details for the methods most

likely to be of use to planners.[1] Special problems in the data for many local areas, caused by the presence of large institutional populations, such as military installations or universities, are also treated in that literature.[2]

There are many aspects of data that will be available in the 1970 Census of the United States which have not been determined at the time of this writing. In particular, it is not known to what extent, if any, information about migration between pairs of small areas will be available. The procedures suggested here can be used with data of the kind available in the 1960 Census, but there is also some discussion of the ways in which better data could be incorporated into the analyses.

KINDS OF PROJECTIVE ANALYSES

Planners are ultimately interested in making statements about the relationships between key variables as they may or should exist at some future time. In order to make such statements, planners study the past and present conditions of the factors relevant to a given situation.

The technical vocabulary of *demography* embraces concepts and terms that are comparable. These terms are used here in their technical meanings. The most general term is "projection," used with reference to a methodology

[1] The chapter on "Population Studies" in F. Stuart Chapin, Jr., URBAN LAND USE PLANNING (Urbana: University of Illinois Press, 2nd ed., 1965), is by far the best single source for planners on the range of methods available and operational procedures for applying most of these methods. Walter Isard's chapters on "Population" and "Migration" written with G. A. P. Carrothers in METHODS OF REGIONAL ANALYSIS put these methods in both an analytical and historical perspective (Cambridge: MIT Press, 1960). Both Chapin and Isard give ample references to original sources. George W. Barclay, TECHNIQUES OF POPULATION ANALYSIS (New York: Wiley, 1958), is the standard text on demographic methodology. Any one of the many other textbooks on demography will introduce the reader to the ranges of variation and correlates of variation in births, deaths, and migration which have been observed in the United States and in other parts of the world. The best reference on the subject of the social and economic development as related to population change is still the United Nations, THE DETERMINANTS AND CONSEQUENCES OF POPULATION TRENDS (New York: United Nations, 1953).

[2] Chapin, *op. cit.*, and the introductory material in the U.S. Census volumes explain the nature of these problems, and the various definitions of "population" which are used. They suggest ways of handling problems of incompatible definitions.

or technique. A *projection technique* is one which uses facts about a population at earlier points in time to reach conclusions about that population at later points in time. If the point in time for which a projection is made is the present, or if it lies in the historical past, the result of this use of a projective technique is an *estimate.* The fact that we have hard factual knowledge of populations only for the relatively infrequent dates when census enumerations are conducted gives rise to the need for *inter-censal* and *post-censal* estimates.[3] If a projective technique is used to reach conclusions referring to a point in time which lies in the future the result is a *projection.*

In general, projections represent conditional statements: "If A, B, and C, are true in the future, then the 1980 population will be D." To put this another way, a projection is the population size implied by a given set of trends. An unconditional assertion about a future population is formally a *forecast.* But planners seldom if ever make completely unconditional assertions, so we depart here from conventional definition to use the term forecast to refer to a population projection used as an input to some nondemographic aspect of plan-making. A *forecast,* then, is a projection we put faith in for planning purposes.

The scope of population *analysis* for local planning purposes may be stated by using these terms. It begins with population data, uses these and projection techniques[4] to derive

measures of trends and population estimates, then uses projection techniques again to make alternative projections of future populations, and results in forecasts selected from the projections for use in nondemographic analyses.

Past and present population trends are analyzed in order to determine the parameters to be used in projections into the future. An *ex post facto* projection is one for which the correct answer is known, such as a projection to the date of the 1960 census. The parameters of such a projection, fitted to known data, are a form of analysis of past trends. If the projective technique used in the *ex post facto* projection is that selected for use in making projections of future populations, the analysis is in a form that is directly relevant to the primary objective. The approach presented here under the name "cohort survival" is an analytical technique as well as one for making projections into the future. In the demographic literature its application to analysis as presented here is generally referred to as "census differencing," and the term "cohort survival" is often limited to projections into the future.

COMPONENTS OF THE POPULATION

A basic distinction among projection techniques separates those which treat the population as a single aggregate from those which deal with disaggregated components of the total population. Disaggregation by age is the basic difference between the net migration and natural increase method and the cohort survival approach, for example. There are two general reasons for disaggregation: it may be necessary to have disaggregated *forecasts,* and it may be a more reliable method of projecting the *total.* In the case of population forecasts for local planning purposes, both of these reasons normally apply. Most of the uses of population forecasts in plan making imply identification of some age group. School facilities are designed to accommodate children of particular ages; the demand for some types of recreation facilities is related to people in broad age ranges; the numbers of people old enough to have drivers' licenses are useful in transportation planning; the numbers of adults of various ages are basic to estimates of the numbers of

---

[3] The distinction between this specialized definition of "estimate" and the more general use of that term to refer to any number which is approximated by some computation will always be clear from the context in which the term is used.

[4] Though any projection methodology *can* be used to prepare post-censal or inter-censal estimates, the methods which normally *are* used for these purposes cannot be used for projection into the future. Inter-censal estimates are normally based on interpolation between two census enumerations, and post-censal estimates are normally based on data, such as birth and death registrations, school enrollments, building permits, and utility connections, which are available on a more nearly current basis than are census enumerations. Post-censal estimation is discussed in considerable detail in Chapin, *op. cit.,* pp. 183–96, and in U.S. Bureau of the Census, CURRENT POPULATION REPORTS, Series P-25, No. 328, "Inventory of State and Local Agencies Preparing Population Estimates: Survey of 1965" (Washington, D.C.: U.S. Government Printing Office, 1966) .

Table 3–1

**Relationship of Future Age Groups to Population
Enumerated in 1960, Assuming No Migration**

	1960	1970	1980	1990
Survivors of Future Births				
Survivors of Past Births	0–4	0–4	0–4	0–4
	5–9	5–9	5–9	5–9
	10–14	10–14	10–14	10–14
Women's Childbearing Ages	15–19	15–19	15–19	15–19
	20–24	20–24	20–24	20–24
	25–29	25–29	25–29	25–29
	30–34	30–34	30–34	30–34
	35–39	35–39	35–39	35–39
	40–44	40–44	40–44	40–44
	45–49	45–49	45–49	45–49
	50–54	50–54	50–54	50–54
	55–59	55–59	55–59	55–59
	60–64	60–64	60–64	60–64
	65–69	65–69	65–69	65–69
	70–74	70–74	70–74	70–74
	75–74	75–79	75–79	75–79
	80–84	80–84	80–84	80–84
	85–89	85–89	85–89	85–89
	etc.	etc.	etc.	etc.

households and size of the active labor force, and so on. The best way to obtain forecasts of numbers in an age group is to project specific age groups.

The sum of separately projected components is generally more reliable as a projection of total population than a projection of the single aggregate for moderately long projection periods. In this context "moderately long" may be interpreted as meaning approximately 10 to 40 years, or from half a generation to two generations. Table 3–1 illustrates part of the reason for the general superiority of component projections. The columns in this table show ages in the four census years shown at the head of the columns. The heavy stepwise line divides each of the future populations into those born after 1960 and those alive in 1960. Even after 30 years, most of the age groups and perhaps half of the total population will be survivors of the population actually enumerated in the 1960 census. The sizes of age groups below the heavy

line will be affected by future mortality and migration, but cannot be affected by changes in fertility. The childbearing ages are within the dotted lines, which show that after 20 years most of these women are survivors of an enumerated population, and even after 30 years roughly half of the women of childbearing age will be survivors of an enumerated population. In the past few decades in the United States fertility has been much more variable than mortality, so the projections of the components below the heavy line are more reliable than those above it.

But even the size of the components above the line are more reliably projected in the cohort survival approach than in an aggregate projection. An age-specific birth rate is affected only by changes in the rate at which women of specified ages are having children, while a crude birth rate is affected by these changes and also by changes in the ratio of women of childbearing ages to the remainder of the population. For example, an increase in the proportion of the population which is over 65 will have the effect, other things being equal, of decreasing the crude birth rate. Mortality rates and migration rates do not fall to zero at any age, unlike fertility rates, but they do show very great variations with age. The use of these rates in a form applicable to the total population therefore makes them difficult to predict.

The normal practice is to disaggregate by five-year age groups. Disaggregation by sex is usual, and where there are substantial racial minorities and appreciable interracial differences in vital rates, it is standard practice also to disaggregate by two or more races. Disaggregation is desirable to the extent that there are substantial differences in specific vital rates of the subgroups, and is possible to the extent that the subgroups are separately identified in the census and vital registration data. The latter consideration rules out, as a practical matter for local planning purposes, some other promising bases for determining components of the population.[5]

CAUSES OF POPULATION CHANGE

There are three immediate precipitators of change over time in the number of residents of an area: births, deaths, and migration across the boundary of the area. Some projection techniques take into account each of these causes of change separately, others deal with a single composite as the net effect of the three, and at least one combines two of these causes and deals separately with the third. There appear to be essentially different sets of factors underlying these three causes; thus there is a theoretical basis for the empirical observation that secular changes in *fertility, mortality,* and *mobility* tend to be uncorrelated one with the other.

As a simplistic illustration of the separate

sets of underlying factors it may be asserted that fertility is primarily associated with cultural norms, socio-psychological factors, and socio-economic status; mortality is primarily associated with sanitary and medical technology, availability of preventive and curative services, and per capita income; while mobility is primarily associated with regional economic differences and the availability of housing and public services. Given that these three sets of underlying causes are really different, it is likely, *a priori,* that fairly regular trends in each of the three will result in a composite that is erratic and difficult to analyze and project. Thus there is much to gain by separating the three causes, if there are specific data available on each of the three. Data on migration comparable in quality and coverage to tabulations of birth and death registrations are not normally available except for whole nations or very large regions.

In the absence of separate series of data on migration it is always possible to estimate the total net migration during the period between two censuses by using the change in the population and the total numbers of births and deaths during the period. Estimates obtained in this manner are not fully satisfactory in that the ten year period is far too long, and such estimates are subject to large percentage errors if the net migration is a small percentage of the total population. Nevertheless, these data and others which are available in recent censuses do give some insight into past migration. Symptomatic data on the kinds commonly used for preparing post-censal estimates, such as residential utility connections, school enrollments, and building permits, also may be interpreted as information about trends and magnitudes of migration.

ALTERNATIVE PROJECTION STRATEGIES

Early projections of the national population were based on simple assumptions about a single variable, the total population. In the simplest form of such a "straight-line" projection, it is assumed that the future absolute change per unit of time will be constant. This is the result obtained by drawing a straight line on ordinary graph paper, as illustrated by the

---

[5] Other aspects of the composition of the population, particularly marital status, birth parity, and interval since last birth, which might provide a better basis for projecting fertility are discussed in John Hajnal, "The Prospects for Population Forecasts," JOURNAL OF THE AMERICAN STATISTICAL ASSOCIATION 50 (June, 1955), pp. 309–22, and N. B. Ryder, "Fertility," in THE STUDY OF POPULATION, Philip M. Hauser and O. D. Duncan (eds.) (Chicago: University of Chicago Press, 1959).

mathematical function and its graphic equivalent in Figure 3–1 (A). A slightly more sophisticated assumption is that there will in the future be a constant *rate* of change per unit time, or equal percentage increments in each successive time increment. This result can be obtained by plotting total populations against decades and describing their change by a straight line on semi-logarithmic graph paper, or by the equivalent formulas shown in Figure 3–1 (B). On regular graph paper this forms an exponential curve. It was observed in the 19th century that neither of these "straight-line" methods worked very well. The first tends to understate long-run growth, for the obvious reason that if this implies more children in one generation then there will be more parents in the next generation, provided that rates do not change. On this basis it can be expected that population will follow an exponential or compound-interest growth curve, as illustrated in Figure 3–1 (B). But it was also observed that the rate of increase had decreased during the 19th century, and that it is unreasonable to expect an exponential growth curve to continue indefinitely.[6] The formulas shown in Figure 3–1 (B) are the source of "horror projections," such as the projection that if present trends continue to the year 2811, the annual increase in the world population will be about equal to the present total world population. These simply make the point that present trends cannot continue for hundreds of years.

As demographers learned that the kinds of curves we have been discussing are inherently unsatisfactory for projection periods of more than a few years, they began to experiment with more complex mathematical functions, two of which are shown in Figure 3–1 (C). These functions were, like those shown in Figures 3–1 (A) and 3–1 (B), fitted to data on the total size of the population at discrete points in time. These and a number of similar functions not mentioned here all implicitly describe a transition between two stable situations. For all practical purposes they may be regarded as beginning at a time when there is no net change, tracing a period of net increase in the population and reaching another point beyond which there is no net change in population.[7] These methods of projection have also been abandoned because of their poor correspondence with the facts of population change.[8] One of the problems with these "S" shaped exponential formulas is that there generally is no useful meaning to the concept of an upper limit to total population. In special cases, where there is a clear and direct interpretation of an upper limit, one of these methods or the simpler exponential curve shown in Figure 3–1 (D) do give useful projections, and perhaps useful forecasts.

The population implications of effective land use control policies can be determined, for small areas and where the land use control is the effective limit on population growth, by the area capacity method. It is assumed that there is some upper limit to the population of a small area which is set by zoning, subdivision control, soil characteristics, and septic tank requirements, or by some other public policy which sets a meaningful maximum population limit. It is also assumed that the curve of actual population will tend to level off as the maximum population is approached. A mathematical function which generates a curve consistent with these assumptions is

$$P_{t+n} = K + (a)(b^n),$$

where the total population, P, at time $t+n$ approaches K, the upper limit or maximum population, as n, which may be expressed in years, increases; provided that the parameter a is negative and that the parameter b is positive and less than one, both derived by least squares method. In the application suggested here, this equation is to be solved for P, the population size, at one or more dates, $t+n$, in the future. Since n is fixed by the assumption of the dates for which the projections are desired, an alternative to the equation above is suggested. This alternative is mathematically equivalent to the exponential formulation above, more clearly

---

[6] Isard and Carrothers, *op. cit.*, pp. 8–10.

[7] In more precise terms, these curves imply upper and lower limits which are constant population sizes, and approach the upper limit asymptotically with increasing time and approach the lower limit asymptotically with decreasing time.

[8] Experience with these formulations is reviewed in Isard and Carrothers, *loc. cit.*

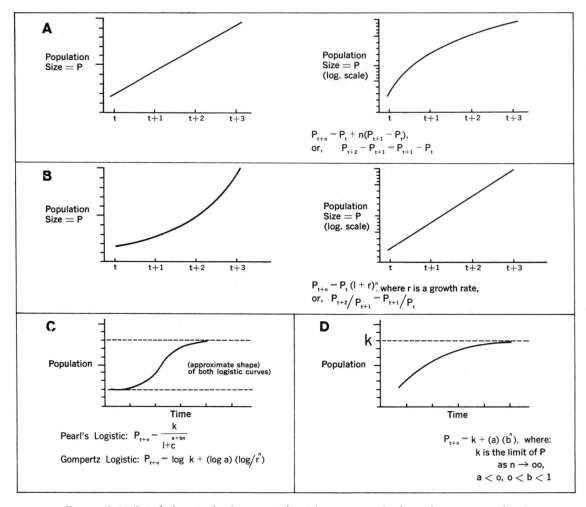

FIGURE 3–1. *Population projection strategies (A, constant absolute change per unit of time; B, constant percentage change per unit of time; C, typical logistic curves; D, constant percentage decrease in unused capacity in each time period.)*

expresses the rationale for specifying this kind of function, and is computationally simpler. The function is generated by the assumption that the unused capacity—the difference between the limiting maximum capacity and the actual population—is reduced by the same percentage during each successive increment of time. In other words, it is assumed that

$$\frac{K - P_t}{K - P_{t+10}} = \frac{K - P_{t-10}}{K - P_t}$$

where K and P have the same definitions as above. The percentage decrease may be esti-

mated from data covering at least one intercensal period in the past, and then the same relationship may be used to project the population as far into the future as is desired. This is not suggested as a method to be used for areas much larger than a census tract, and it is chiefly useful for projecting the consequences of a policy which effectively limits population growth. In order to be acceptable as a forecast there would have to be good reasons for believing that the policy would not be changed as residential preferences come into conflict with the limit that has been established.

CATEGORIES OF PROJECTION METHODS

Various forms of graphic and mathematical extrapolation have been briefly described. It is suggested that these are generally useful only for short range (up to five years) and very long range (more than fifty years) projections, the latter since they are only used for *order of magnitude* estimates anyway, and in the special case where it is desired to project the filling up of an area which is assumed to have a fixed population capacity. These methods have in common the characteristics of dealing with a single aggregate, the total population, and of treating all causes of change as a single composite. They are grouped in the upper left cell of Figure 3–2, in which general approaches to population projection are classified by the distinctions discussed in the preceding sections.

The other general projection approaches whose characteristics put them in the same cell of this table are not as simple as the projections of constant absolute change or constant percentage change, and are likely to be no more reliable. The ratio approach is based on accepting a projection for the nation, or other large area, and projecting from it the local area's share of the total population. The local proportion of the growing total may be assumed constant over time or may be projected in some other manner. This method is perhaps useful as a rough check on the reasonableness of other projections.

The analogue method assumes that all cities "of the same kind" follow the same growth curve, some starting earlier than others. The rate of growth in another city at an earlier time, when it was of the same size as the current population size of the city whose population is to be projected, is assumed to be a valid indication of the future population of the study city. This approach should be used, if at all, only with great care and in very special situations.

As explained earlier, the migration and natural increase approach is based on separate projections of the numbers of births, deaths, and in-migrants.[9] These three are combined by

---

[9] Population growth and in-migration are conveniently regarded as numbers which may be either positive or negative, and this convention is followed here. A decrease is represented by negative growth, and net out-migration is represented by negative net in-migration. Unless there is concurrent reference to gross migration, statements about "in-migration" are to be interpreted as "net in-migration" in the discussion which follows.

Treatment of Causes of Change	Disaggregation of the Population	
	Single Aggregate	Separate Components
Single composite— net change	Graphic and mathematical extrapolation	
	Ratio and analogue methods	
Separate identification of births, deaths, and migration	Natural increase and net migration	Hamilton & Perry[1] Cohort survival
		Simulation

[1] Deaths and migration treated as one composite, but births are identified separately.

FIGURE 3–2. *Classification of projection methods (Postcensal and intercensal methods estimation methods are not included.)*

using the obvious fact that population growth during a period is the sum of births and net in-migration during the period minus deaths during the period.

The usual practice is to express each of the three projections of vital statistics in the form of crude vital rates in which the numerator constitutes a number of vital events during an interval of time, usually a year, and the denominator is the total number of people in the population at the middle of the time interval. Births and deaths are almost invariably handled in this manner, but migration is sometimes projected in absolute numbers rather than as a rate. If these are annual rates they are multiplied by the base year population to give the numbers needed to project the population one year. That projection is used as the basis for a projection one more year, and so on for as many steps as are required to reach the target year. It is convenient to work with a natural increase rate which is simply the algebraic difference between the birth rate and the death rate rather than multiplying the birth and death rates by the population and then subtracting the products. Presumably this is the origin of the conventional designation "natural increase and net migration." The problems involved in projecting crude vital rates have been discussed earlier, and these problems are one of the major reasons for preferring the cohort survival approach. The disaggregation of the population which permits the use of subgroup specific rates rather than crude rates is the major conceptual difference between the two general projection approaches described above.

The Hamilton and Perry projection method is a special case of the cohort survival approach which will be described after a discussion of a more general cohort survival model. *Simulation* is an experimental approach to population projecting which has not, to our knowledge, been attempted except as an academic experiment. Because of its great potential for planning purposes it will be given some attention here, also after the cohort survival model has been discussed, even though it has not been developed to the point of operational availability for planning purposes. There are no stan-

dard population projection techniques which deal both with disaggregated subgroups of the population and also with a single composite. It is not surprising that this is the case, because a basic reason for disaggregation is to obtain better projections of the individual elements of change. An interregional econometric model, in which the sizes of the various subgroups were determined as a function of economic activity, would have these characteristics.

The "straight-line" approaches, which make a few simple assumptions and project a single aggregate, was the first stage in the evolution of a method. The second stage was the use of complex assumptions, expressed in voluminous exponential equations, to project the same single aggregate. In the contemporary standard practice, which may be called the third stage, demographers deal with many components of the population and have gone back to making simple and straightforward assumptions.

The essence of the cohort survival approach is its use of many simple assumptions, each one limited in its scope of application, and recognition of specific interrelationships among some of the components which are projected. Cohort survival is regarded by contemporary demographers as the standard projection approach. This is true with respect to populations of small areas as well as populations of whole nations.[10] Although forecasts by the cohort survival approach have not always been better than those made with other techniques, it is believed to be the most reliable of the available methodologies because it makes better use of available data and tested demographic theory.[11]

---

[10] See C. Horace Hamilton and Josef Perry, "A Short Method for Projecting Population by Age from One Decennial Census to Another," SOCIAL FORCES, XLI (December, 1962), especially page 163, pp. 163–70; and Barclay, *op. cit.*, p. 237.

[11] The cohort survival "procedure has often given rather poor estimates of future population. This has happened because the assumptions were inappropriate, not the method." Barclay, *op. cit.*, pp. 237–38. A good example of contemporary projection practice and considerable methodological discussion may be found in Jacob S. Siegel, Meyer Zitter, and Donald S. Akers, PROJECTIONS OF THE POPULATION OF THE UNITED STATES, BY AGE AND SEX: 1964 TO 1985 (Washington: Bureau of the Census, CURRENT POPULATION REPORTS, Series P-25, No. 286, 1964).

General Cohort Survival Model

A cohort survival approach adapted to the needs and data resources of local planning agencies is presented in this section. There are three major stages to be considered: analyzing past changes, determining the projection parameters, and running the projection. Since an understanding of the mechanics of the projection technique is prerequisite to discussion of the first two stages, it is convenient to describe the last stage first.

COHORT SURVIVAL PROJECTIONS

Figure 3–3 illustrates the general cohort survival model, under the simplifying assumption that migration is not a factor. There is a beginning population, here assumed to be the 1965 population, in which the numbers in each of the 36 combinations of 18 age groups and 2 sexes are known. A set of projection parameters has also been specified: 36 age and sex specific survival rates, 6 female age specific birth rates, the sex ratio at birth, and infant survival rates for both sexes. The survival rates are the probabilities of living at least five more years, so each is found by subtracting from 1.00 the probability of dying in the next five years, given the specified age and sex. Still assuming no migration, the size of any age and sex component of the 1970 population is found by multiplying the proper survival rate by the component of the 1965 population which is of the same sex and is five years younger. This process provides all but two of the components of the 1970 population—the boys and the girls who are less than five years of age in 1970. These boys and girls must be born during the five-year projection period.

The number of babies born during this period is found by multiplying the numbers of possible mothers in each of six age groups (15–19 through 40–44) by the appropriate fertility rates, and then adding the products. A female age-specific five-year fertility rate can be derived by dividing the number of babies born during a five-year period to mothers of a specified age by the number of women in the population who are of the specified age. The sum of the babies born to mothers in all six of the age groups is the total number of babies to be born.[12]

Slightly more than half of the babies will be male, so this proportion is used to separate the number of babies born into numbers of boy babies and girl babies. This is done before applying infant survival rates to determine how many of the babies will live long enough to be present in the 1970 population, because there is a substantially higher mortality among male infants. We have now estimated the size of each of the age and sex components of the age and sex components of the 1970 population. If a projection for 1975 were desired we would simply begin the process again with the 1970 population components. If there were two or more races to be considered, each race would be treated as a separate population, with its own set of projection parameters. The total population projected is simply the sum of all the separate components. While we are not yet ready to discuss migration in detail, it can be seen that the numbers of net in-migrants in each age, sex, and race component in 1970 would be added to the results of the process just described.

The substantial amount of computational effort required to do a cohort survival projection may explain, though it cannot excuse, the general neglect of this approach by urban planners. Computer programs have been written for this purpose, though considerable programming skill and effort are required to translate procedures better adapted for use with desk calculators into computer programs.[13] A recent theoretical development of the cohort survival idea, largely by Keyfitz, has the collateral virtue of leading to rather simple and direct computer programming using standard matrix

---

[12] The rare cases of babies born to mothers under 15 or over 44 are conventionally handled by arbitrarily including them in the numerator of the first or last of the fertility rates.

[13] We are specifically aware of two such programs. Jere Fidler, of the Subdivision of Transportation Planning and Programming, New York Department of Public Works, developed an IBM 1401 cohort survival program which may become available to others with access to 1401's through IBM's library of customer contributed programs. Fidler's program is described in the July, 1963 issue of Upstate New York Transportation Studies NOTES. Richard G. Ames has written a cohort survival program for use on a UNIVAC 1105 computer for the Bureau of the Census.

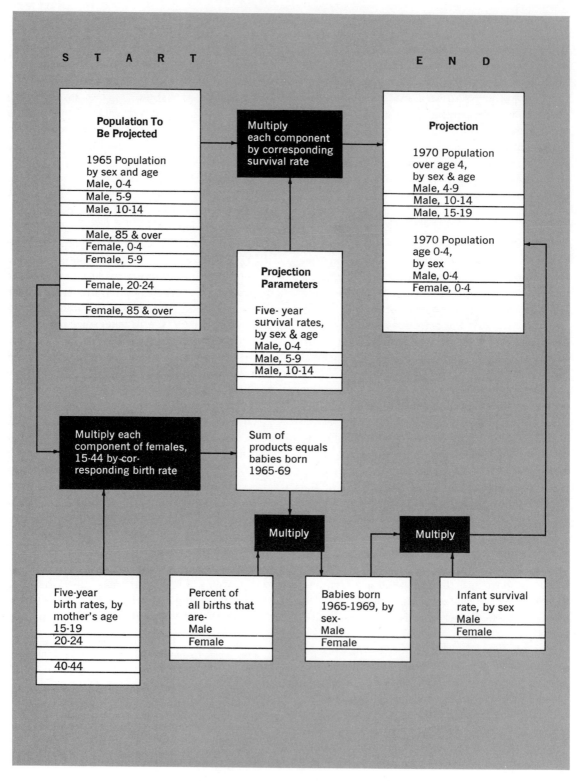

FIGURE 3–3. *Cohort survival approach*

algebra subroutines.[14] The matrix approach is the one that is developed here in operational terms.

It has been shown that a matrix, M, can be constructed which incorporates all of the projection parameters. That is, the M matrix may be used actually to carry out all of the steps illustrated generally but not specified in operational terms in the preceding discussion of Figure 3–2. In order to use this matrix to reproduce the projection illustrated in Figure 3–2 we would arrange the size of the components of the 1965 population in a vector, $_{65}P$, premultiply this vector times the matrix, and the result would be the 1970 population components arranged in a similar vector, $_{70}P$. The nature of the M matrix can best be explained by considering two matrices, F and S, the sum of which is M. The F matrix expresses fertility and the S matrix expresses survivorship.

There will be an M matrix, and hence an F and S matrix, for each combination of sex and race to be identified in the projection: four matrices of each kind if white males, white females, nonwhite males, and nonwhite females are to be separately identified. Each of the matrices will have n rows and n columns corresponding to the n age groups identified, and a P vector is a column of n age group elements, and there is one of these for each combination of sex and race groups. There are rigid specifications for the permissible age groupings. The range of ages included in each of the n groups except the last one must be exactly the same as the length of the projection to be obtained in each step. It is recommended that five-year age groups and five-year projection increments be used, because this is consistent with both the age groupings in published census tabulations and the frequency of census enumerations.

With ages defined as "age at last birthday,"

as they are in the census, the first age group would be 0–4, the second 5–9, the third 10–14, and so on. The last, n^{th}, age group may be an open-ended group, such as 85 and over. Again, this is the recommended procedure because it is consistent with the published census data.[15] For convenience of presentation, typical values rather than general symbols will be used for the range of ages and length of the projection increment, five years, and for the number of age groups identified, eighteen. And since the same methodology is to be replicated for each of the races identified it is not necessary here to specify any race.

The female sex is used as the example, and then the differences of procedure for the male sex are noted. Where it is necessary to identify one of these matrices, pre-subscripts with obvious interpretations will be used; for example, the matrix $wf70^M$ is the matrix used to project the white female population from 1970 to 1975. The element of this matrix which is in the third row and the second column is indicated by $wf70^M32$.

The eighteen columns of the M, S, and F matrices are identified as age groups one to eighteen at the start of a projection increment of five years, and the eighteen rows of these matrices are identified as the same age groups at the end of the five-year period. The elements of the M matrix are probabilities[16] linking individuals in two different age groups at the beginning and end of the five-year period. In the S matrix an individual who survives the five-year period is linked to himself as a member of the succeeding population, and in the F matrix an individual is linked to any children born to her and surviving to the end of the period.

---

[14] The leading paper on this subject is Nathan Keyfitz, "The Population Projection as a Matrix Operator," DEMOGRAPY, I (1964), pp. 56–73. The planning profession is indebted to Andrei Rogers for bringing Keyfitz's work into the planning literature and extending it to interregional analyses, in "Matrix Methods of Population Analyses," JOURNAL OF THE AMERICAN INSTITUTE OF PLANNERS, XXXII (January, 1966), pp. 40–44, and papers forthcoming in PAPERS AND PROCEEDINGS OF THE REGIONAL SCIENCE ASSOCIATION.

[15] If the last age group specified is not open-ended it must end at a sufficiently venerable age to make acceptable the approximation that nobody can live to a still older age. If it is necessary to carry the five-year age groups to this point, such as 95–99, then the final element of the S matrix should be zero.

[16] It is not appropriate here to relate these probabilities to the more familiar age-specific survival rates, if only because rigorous exposition of this relationship would require background explanation of life table rates and quantities. These relationships are discussed by Keyfitz in "The Population Projection as a Matrix Operator," op. cit., and "Finite Approximations in Demography," POPULATION STUDIES, XIX (1966), pp. 281–95.

The specification of five-year projection increments and five-year age groups means that most of the elements of these matrices are necessarily equal to zero. There are eighteen[17] nonzero elements in the S matrix; identifying rows and columns by i and j respectively, $s_{ij} = 0$ unless either $i = j + 1$ ($i = 2, 3, \ldots,$ 18) or $i = j = 18$. It should be evident that these nonzero elements correspond to the common sense observation that a person who lives through a five-year period must move from one five-year age group to the next during this period. The nonzero elements are probabilities of survival, since the only possibilities encompassed by the S matrix are survival and death. For example, the value of 0.99640 for the element s_{21}, the only nonzero element in the second row and the only nonzero element in the first column of an S matrix, indicates that all of those in age group two at the end of the period were in age group one at the beginning of the period, that 99.64 per cent of those in the first age group at the beginning of the period will be in the second age group at the end of the period, and that the other 0.36 per cent will be removed from the population by death during the five-year period.

The F matrix encompasses the introduction of new individuals into the population through births. All of those born during a five-year period will be in the first age group at the end of the period since they cannot attain their fifth birthday during the five calendar years in which they are born. Hence all of the nonzero elements in the F matrix are in the first row. The rates at which babies are born will be considered as a function of numbers of women of childbearing ages, and so all of the nonzero elements will be related to women of ages 15–44 during the five-year projection increment. Because of the nature of the data to be used in fitting parameters to this model, it is

desirable here to include all women who will be of these ages at any time during the five-year period, which includes women aged 10–44 at the beginning of the period. Thus nonzero elements of the F matrix appear only in matrices applicable to females, and only in the first row and in columns three through nine of such matrices. The values of the nonzero elements are interpreted as the numbers of children who are born to women of the specified ages and survive from birth to the end of the five calendar years during which they are born. The M matrix is simply the sum of the F and S matrices which have been described. The form of the M matrix is shown in Table 3–2, using f and s as symbols representing nonzero elements obtained from the F and S matrices respectively. The M matrix represents the demographic processes of mortality, fertility, and aging, in the sense that a vector of population by age, multiplied by M, equals another vector of population by age which is the effect of five years of deaths, births, and aging on the first. Again we are carrying out this process for the sexes individually. Yet the application of M for females to the female population will produce births, both male and female. Hence we must label the result, B, differently from P for the time being. We shall then turn to separating girls and boys in order to put them in their respective vectors, which will be called C.

$$_{t+5}B = (_tM)(_tP)$$

where:

$_tM$ = the matrix operator defined above, of order 18 by 18, for the five-year period beginning with year t.

$_tP$ = a vector of population counts by age, of 18 elements, at time t.

$_{t+5}B$ = a vector of population counts by age, of 18 elements, at time $t + 5$. Newly born children of both sexes included with the female survivors.

The limitation to populations in which the two sexes are combined will be removed first. If the computation indicated above is carried out using a female M matrix and P vector, the first age group, newly born, in the B vector will include both males and females, and the B vector computed in this manner using a male

---

[17] This assumes, of course, that there are eighteen age groups identified. It also assumes that the last (eighteenth) age group is openended (85 and over). The condition i = j = 18 is predicated on this openended group, since it is possible for an individual to survive five years and remain in this final age group. Rogers felt that it was satisfactory for his purposes to assume that there were no persons age 90 and over, and so in his S matrices the only nonzero elements are those meeting the i = j + 1 criterion.

Table 3–2

**An M Matrix, Showing Locations of Nonzero Elements
Obtained from the F and S Matrices Whose Sum is M**

j. (columns), specify numbers of population by 5-year age groups at the beginning of a projection period.
i. (rows), specify these numbers at the end of the period.

	Age at Beginning of Period																	
	j = 1	2	3	4	5	6	7	8	9	10	11	12	13	14	15	16	17	18
i = 1			f	f	f	f	f	f	f									
2	s																	
3		s																
4			s															
5				s														
6					s													
7						s												
8							s											
9								s										
10									s									
11										s								
12											s							
13												s						
14													s					
15														s				
16															s			
17																s		
18																	s	s

Age at End of Period (row axis label)

M matrix and P vector will have a zero population in the first age group. We may allocate the infants to the vectors of the appropriate sexes by using the ratios of males and females in the first age group (ages 0–4) in a recent census. Assuming for the sake of illustration that 51 per cent of the population of age 0–4 enumerated in the last census was male, we may compute corrected population vectors for the two sexes at time $t + 5$, $_{t+5}C$, as follows:

$$_{m,t+5}c_1 = (.51)\,(_{f,t+5}b_1)$$
$$_{f,t+5}c_1 = (.49)(_{f,t+5}b_1)$$

With the exception of the first age group, the elements of B and C are identical. The sex ratio in the first age group is not likely to change appreciably over time, and so it may be taken as a constant from a recent census. This is not the same as the sex ratio at birth, however, because of the higher mortality among male infants.

Formal demographic methodology is least applicable to the problems of projecting *migration,* and, conversely, this is the area in which the professional judgment and detailed knowledge of the planner is most relevant. For these reasons it is suggested that migration be introduced into the projection simply by adding a vector, $_{t+5}N$, of net in-migrants by age to the $_{t+5}C$ vector defined above. That is,

$$_{t+5}P = {}_{t+5}C + {}_{t+5}N$$

We shall return later to the problem of estimating and projecting net migration for small areas. This projection methodology is completed by noting that the $_{t+5}P$ vector which has been defined may be used as the beginning point for another five-year projection increment, which results in the computation of a $_{t+10}P$ vector, and so on for as many cycles as are required.

ANALYSIS OF PAST CHANGES IN PROJECTION PARAMETERS

There are two somewhat different reasons why planners pay attention to past changes in the population of a locality. One is the need for the best data available on birth and death rate trends in the recent past in order to project these trends into the future, which, it is assumed here, will be done in a fairly mechanical manner. The other is the planner's interest in local migration behavior, which should be of interest both for the light it sheds on the relative attractiveness of an area as a whole, and of various parts of the area, during the recent past and as a part of the information to be used in making judgments about probable or possible future patterns of migration. It is assumed here that the data available are the decennial census enumerations of population: by age, sex, and race, birth and death registrations; by place of residence for the locality; by sex and race without age; and by specific birth and death rates, by age, sex, and also race, for some larger area, such as a state of which the locality is a part. These data may be used to derive M matrices for past periods of time, and to estimate net in-migration by age, sex, and race during these same periods.

The elements of the F and S matrices which are summed to obtain an M matrix may be estimated by assuming that the five-year age specific rates for some larger area are valid in proportional distribution, though not in absolute magnitude, for the locality being analyzed. This is a reasonable assumption because it has been found that the relationships among age specific birth and death rates change much more slowly than these rates themselves, which is to say that the individual rates tend to change in the same direction and by approximately the same proportionate amount. This is generally the case for comparisons over time and for comparisons among areas which are fairly close geographically and culturally. This permits use of the cohort survival approach where age specific rates are not available.[18]

Let us assume a set of annual age specific death rates, $_td^*_j$ $(j = 1, \ldots, 18)$ believed to be valid in proportional distribution though

not necessarily in absolute magnitude for the locality being studied. The asterisk is used to express this reservation. (For convenience of exposition, the qualification "sex and race specific" has been dropped here, though both are important in this context and the computations to be described should be done separately for both sexes and all races present in substantial numbers.) If these rates were valid in absolute magnitude they could be used to compute the total number of deaths during a year, as

$$\sum_{i=1}^{18} {}_td^*_j \cdot {}_tp_j = \text{"expected" deaths } (j = 1, \ldots, 18)$$

where:

$_td^*_j$ = an age specific annual death rate
$_tp_j$ = an element of the $_tp$ vector of population at time t

But the actual number of deaths during a year in the past, though not recorded by age, is assumed to be known from registration of deaths of residents of the locality, and so the relationship between actual and "expected" deaths may be used to adjust the assumed age specific death rates which, applied to the population in the area at the appropriate time, will reproduce the correct number of deaths.

$$_tu = {}_t\text{registered deaths} \div \sum_{j=1}^{18} {}_td^*_j \cdot {}_tp_j$$
$$(j = 1, \ldots, 18)$$

$$_td_j = {}_tu({}_td^*_j)$$

These are annual rates, and so they must be multiplied by five before they are subtracted from one to obtain the five-year survival rates required in the $_tS$ matrix. Again using i and j to designate row and column positions:

If $i = j + 1$ $(j = 1, \ldots, 17)$ or if $i = j = 18$;
$$_ts_{ij} = 1 - 5_td_j$$
Otherwise;
$$_ts_{ij} = 0$$

The age, sex, and race specific survival rates are sufficiently stable over time so that they may be estimated with sufficient accuracy for planning purposes by interpolating between rates computed for census years. This avoids the errors in estimated rates that would otherwise be introduced by migration between cen-

---

[18] A similar assumption is made in a much more intensive analysis and projection of age specific fertility for the United States done for the Bureau of the Census (Siegel, *et al.*, *op. cit.*, pp. 17–18), and Hamilton and Perry's projection methodology assumes that the ratio of age specific rates for a county at two points in time is the same as the corresponding ratio for the state as a whole. See page 168 of C. Horace Hamilton and Josef Perry, *op. cit.*

suses or by errors in inter-censal and post-censal population estimates. However, it would be desirable to take as the total number of deaths the average of the figures for the three years centered on the census year to minimize the effect of shortrun variation in death rates.

The estimate of inter-censal migration derived by a *census differencing* procedure will be used in making estimates of fertility rates, so the migration procedure will be described next. If there were no migration the population aged 10 and over in year $t + 10$ could be obtained from the $_tP$ vector of population by age in year t and the appropriate S matrices. Let us denote population vectors derived this way as E to avoid confusion with the P vectors, which include the effects of migration. Where t and $t + 10$ are years for which we have census enumerations, we can estimate each element of a vector of net in-migration of age 10 and over at $t + 10$, $_{t+10}n_j$ $(j = 3, \ldots, 18)$ as follows:

$$_{t+5}E = {}_tS({}_tP)$$
$$_{t+10}E = {}_{t+5}S({}_{t+5}E)$$
$$_{t+10}N = {}_{t+10}P - {}_{t+10}E$$

There is no harm in using the entire matrices and vectors, rather than deleting the elements which involve persons not yet born at time t, so long as it is remembered that the $t + 10^n1$ and $t + 10^n2$ elements are meaningless. Lack of migration data on persons under age 10 is not important, since it can be assumed without appreciable error that children of these ages move only with their families.[19] The estimates of net migration obtained in this manner are not the best that might be obtained, since the residual term which is interpreted as net migration also includes the net effects of errors in death registrations and census enumerations. However, these are the best data generally available for localities of the kind we are concerned with. These estimates have the virtue of being age-specific, which is important because the magnitude of net migration is almost invariably different for different age groups. It is not uncommon for net in-migration at some ages to

coexist with net outmigration at other ages.

These estimates share a defect with the more familiar procedure for estimating net in-migration, which is based on inter-censal application of the natural increase and net migration approach: the defect of not providing information on changes within an inter-censal or on post-censal changes. The other approach uses the same data plus birth registration data. The recent censuses have provided data on place of residence either one year or five years prior to the date of the census. These are tabulated so as to give information on gross in-migration to small geographic areas. The other kinds of data which are useful in studying net migration or gross migration are the wide variety of time series referred to collectively as "symptomatic data," including school enrollments, building permits, utility connections, drivers' licenses, and many others. There is so much variation from one place to another in the availability and quality of the various symptomatic data that no useful generalizations can be made. This is but one of the reasons that the local planner must rely heavily on his own judgment, experience, and ingenuity in the analysis and projection of migration.

Let us return now to the problem of estimating the birth parameters which appear in an F matrix. As in the case of the survival parameters it is suggested that these be based on a correction factor applied to some set of age specific rates in a manner so as to reproduce the aggregate results observed in the locality being studied. There is a significant difference between the procedures for estimating the rates appearing in the F and S matrices, however, in that the rates in the F matrices are composites of both birth rates and survival rates over a range of ages during which there is enormous variation in mortality.[20] For these reasons the

---

[19] Obviously this assumption would be wrong where there is a large orphanage, for example, but "institutional" populations like this should be excluded from the census data used in the P vectors in any case.

[20] Mortality during the first few weeks of life is far higher per unit time than at any subsequent age, higher than even the mortality per unit time experienced at ages such as 90 or 95. Mortality decreases very sharply during the first few months of life, and then at a less rapid rate during the next few years, so that by age 4 it is approaching the minimum age specific mortality experienced somewhere between ages 5 and 15. Not only is there a great variation in mortality rates within the first five years of life but the change during this period is very markedly nonlinear.

approach which is suggested does not use vital registration data to estimate the correction factor to be applied to the assumed age specific birth rates.

It is taken as before that the assumed set of rates are valid in proportional distribution but not in absolute magnitude for the locality of the study. Before the correction factor to be applied to these rates can be determined, it is necessary to estimate the numbers of net in-migrant children in the first two age groups.

For this purpose it is suggested that an assumption be used which is quite crude but perhaps no more seriously in error than other alternatives which require more extensive data or complicated computations. Let us assume that the ratio of surviving children to women of ages which include most of the mothers is the same among the net in-migrants as the comparable ratio in the local population. Some 90 per cent of births in the United States in recent years have occurred to women between the ages of 15 and 35. When the survivors of these births are aged 0–4 the mothers of about 90 per cent of them are aged 15–39, and when the survivors are aged 5–9 about 90 per cent of their mothers are aged 20–44. From the census enumerations the ratios of these age groups can be determined, and these ratios may then be applied to the numbers of female net in-migrants estimated by the procedures which have been described above. The estimated numbers of net in-migrant children may then be divided into boys and girls by use of sex ratios for the appropriate age groups. The numbers of net in-migrants under age 10 will be subtracted from the enumerated population of these ages at the end of an inter-censal decade to obtain the estimated numbers of children in the first two age groups attributable to the population resident in the locality at the beginning of the inter-censal decade.

In the discussion of the estimation of the rates in the F matrix which follows it is assumed that annual age specific birth rates are used. Because of the very substantial variation in birth rates from one age group to another, and the extension of these rates over five years (which will be reflected in the correction factor to be determined), it is desirable to adjust the rates to a midperiod base.

The rationale of this adjustment is as follows. For half of the projection increment of five years a woman who is 22.5 years old at the beginning of the period will be in the age group 20–24, and for the other half of the period she will be in the next higher, 25–29, age group. Thus her probable childbearing is best represented by the average of the rates applicable to these two age groups. This reasoning can be extended to all those in the five-year age group in which she falls, as approximately representing their aggregate experience, on the assumption that all ages within the range 20 through 24 are equally represented. Adjustment of the rates is more convenient for this purpose than the more common practice of adjusting the ages. It is also convenient to express the adjusted rates in the form of a vector, G, which may be subscripted in the same manner as the vectors of population with which it will be multiplied. Using the symbol $ASBR_j$ to represent the annual age specific birth rate for the jth age group, G is defined as:

$$g_j = 0 \quad \text{for } j = 1,2,10,11,12, \ldots ,18$$
$$g_3 = ASBR_4/2$$
$$g_j = ASBR_j/2 + ASBR_{j+1}/2 \quad \text{for } j = 4,5,6,7,8$$
$$g_9 = ASBR_9/2$$

The variable $_tv$ may be used to adjust the assumed set of rates to rates which will reproduce the numbers of surviving children at the end of a five-year period beginning at time t. It is defined in the equations

$$_tv \cdot \sum_{j=3}^{9} (g_j)(_f,_tp_j) = {}_{t+5}e_1$$

where the t subscripts refer to years and the f subscript to females, and:

v = a correction factor

g_j = an element of the vector G of assumed birth rates, as defined above, ($i = 1, \ldots , 18$ age groups)

e_1 = the element representing the first age group in the vector E of population by age attributable to the population resident in the area five years earlier.

Having solved for $_tv$ we may write the elements of the F matrix for females as follows:

If $i = 1$ and $2 < j < 10$, $_tf_{ij} = _tv(g_j)$
otherwise

$$_tf_{ij} = 0$$

This completes the determination of the S matrix which relates a population at one point in time to its survivors five years later, the F matrix which relates the population to the survivors of births to it during a five-year projection increment, and the N vector of numbers of net in-migrants.

PROJECTION OF POPULATION PARAMETERS

The computations which have been described lead to empirical values of projection parameters, the $_tu$ and $_tv$ variables which have been described, in the context of analysis of past trends, as "correction factors" which summarize local trends of mortality and fertility. While these are not in a form which can be easily comprehended by the general public as descriptive of past trends, they are in a form which is directly relevant to planners' interests in future population. Local planners should generally be willing to make the assumption that local trends in fertility and mortality will parallel the national trends which demographers who have prepared national projections consider reasonable possibilities. The $_tu$ and $_tv$ variables which have been defined above may be directly related to summary measures of national fertility and mortality experience and demographers' extrapolations of these measures.

The life expectancy at birth is a measure derived from age specific death rates through the life table method of analysis. In the most recent national projections by the Bureau of the Census there is a discussion of some alternative projections of mortality and a tabulation of life expectancy by sex since 1940 and alternative projections to 2000.[21]

The Bureau of the Census analysts felt that a single series reflecting "slightly declining mortality" could be used in all of the principal projections presented in their report, and their justification of this and illustration of the very small differences between projections using alternative reasonable assumptions about future mortality levels is likely to persuade local planners to follow their example.

It is not necessary for the planner to compute a local life expectancy at birth in order to link assumptions about local future mortality to the assumptions stated in the Bureau of the Census report. The $_tu$ variable and the life expectancy at birth can both be interpreted as reflecting changes in overall mortality levels from one date to another. Thus percentage changes over time are comparable from one variable to the other. In most cases a planner will probably assume that the percentage change in the future in the $_tu$ projection parameter will be the same as the percentage change in life expectancy at birth in the mortality projections used by the Bureau of the Census for the same time period.

The range of reasonable extrapolations from the recent history of fertility is greater than is the case with respect to mortality. It is suggested that planners will want to make several alternative projections which differ in assumptions about fertility but assume the same trends of mortality. The Bureau of the Census projections currently available present four different series of fertility assumptions which imply a decrease from recent actual levels, plus a series which assumes continuation of recent levels of age specific birth rates.[22] The gross reproduction rate is analogous to the $_tv$ factor defined above, and thus may be used to make alternative assumptions about future values of $_tv$. For example, it might be desirable to have three sets of projections which could be labeled "moderately high fertility," "medium fertility," and "moderately low fertility," which would indicate quite different numbers in the younger age groups. Chapin has discussed the desirability of using alternative forecasts for various purposes and projection periods.[23]

The range of reasonable alternative assumptions about migration is, in most areas, sub-

[21] Siegel, *et al., op. cit.,* pp. 24–27, Table P, and Appendices A and B. This is the most recent of the national projections published occasionally by the Bureau of the Census in the P-25 series. It will no doubt be superseded in a few years, as this 1964 projection replaces a 1958 projection and two interim revisions of the 1958 projection.

[22] *Ibid.,* pp. 12–24, Appendices A, C, D, E.

[23] Chapin, *op. cit.,* pp. 196–202.

stantially wider than is the case with fertility. The extent to which a plan is implemented and is successful in attaining its objectives (these are not necessarily the same) will influence future migration. Unforeseeable changes in the economic base of an area may change migration patterns very greatly. Extreme instances of such changes, such as the location of the Cape Kennedy complex in a sparsely settled part of Florida, totally obviate previous population projections. But the possibility of such a change does not absolve the planner from responsibility for tracing through the implications of more probable changes, and in most cases there are several different sets of assumptions about factors influencing migration which should be explored. The planner using this system has maximum flexibility for incorporating alternative assumptions of many different kinds, because the migration input to the mechanical part of the population projection system is left in the form of a set of numbers of net in-migrants.

Consider as a hypothetical example an area which has experienced relative economic decline and substantial out-migration during the past two or three decades. It is reasonable to assume that many of those who left the area because of job opportunities will return, as the head of the household reaches retirement age. Many assumptions could be made about the size of this return flow, but they are relatively independent of future changes in the local economic base. This area is one of many competing for new industry. The degree of success in attracting new generators of employment to the area is a major determinant of net in-migration of younger adults and their families, but the strong competition for mobile industry makes forecasting very difficult. In this case it might be wise to have two or more alternative sets of assumptions reflecting "pessimistic" and "optimistic" expectations about future demand for labor.

Intrametropolitan migration will also be affected by variables which cannot be foreseen with any degree of assurance. Perhaps it is believed that a major cause of intrametropolitan migration has been relative changes in the quality of the various public school systems in the area. If improvement of the school system in the central city is one of the planning goals it is reasonable to assume that this will change the migration picture, but the timing and extent of the change might be so problematical that it would be wise to set up a couple of alternative assumptions.

In summary, it is suggested that a number of alternative projections be made, based on alternative assumptions about the future course of events. Mortality assumptions and alternative assumptions about fertility can be made quite simply by relating changes in the $_tu$ and $_tv$ factors to national projections of life expectancy at birth and to the gross reproduction rate, respectively. Assumptions about migration require and deserve the close attention of planners familiar with the local situation, and the projection system which has been described is intended to relieve the planner of much routine work so that he can focus his attention on the linkages within the planning and effectuation process which interact with population trends chiefly through migration.

Further attention will be given below to projection of migration in connection with areal distributions of population.

COHORT SURVIVAL ASSUMING CONSTANT RATES

The Hamilton and Perry method is useful as a very quick, simplistic way to arrive at an estimate which can be used in pressing situations, particularly when migration is minimal, or as a base projection to which more accurate projections can be compared. It can also be used to get a quick feeling for the community's natural internal demographic growth.

If the assumption is made that trends in age specific fertility, survival, and migration rates observed during the last inter-censal period continue unchanged into the future then it is not necessary to quantify these rates in order to make a cohort survival projection. In the paper in which Hamilton and Perry present such a projection method[24] an argument for using this as a forecasting method is developed. It is said that the 1950–1960 decade was a rather "normal" one for the nation as a whole and for

---

[24] C. Horace Hamilton and Josef Perry, *op. cit.*

most localities, in the sense that it is reasonable to expect in the future a fairly similar mixture of relative peace and limited war, of prosperity and mild recession, of rising fertility followed by falling fertility, and so on.

The position taken here is that this is a reasonable assumption where it is not possible to give detailed attention to the trends and prospects of a specific area, for example, when making projections for all of the counties in a state, but it is not a forecasting assumption for a local planner to seek out. Nevertheless, a projection based on these assumptions does provide a datum against which alternative projections can be compared. That is, the assumption that nothing changes leads to a useful projection but not to a forecast acceptable for local planning purposes.

The assumptions which are required if a very simple projection formula is to be used are:

1. There are no changes in the relevant definitions of the population or area involved.

2. Age specific rates of mortality, fertility, and migration do not change between the last inter-censal decade and the decades for which the projection is made.

3. The effect of errors of enumeration for the past two censuses will be the same in the future.

Given these assumptions, an exact projection of those old enough to be enumerated in the last census can be obtained from the formula below. Assuming that only decennial census data are available, this is used for 10-year periods.

$$t+10p_x = (tp_{x+10}) \frac{-tp_x}{t-10p_{x-10}}$$

where p is the population enumerated at the censuses conducted in the years t, $t + 10$, and $t - 10$ who are in the age groups x, $x + 10$, and $x - 10$ years. The reasoning behind this formula is more clearly seen by putting it in the form of a proportion and substituting years and age groups for the letter subscripts,

$$\frac{1970p_{30-34}}{1960p_{20-24}} = \frac{1960p_{30-34}}{1950p_{20-24}}$$

In other words, the assumptions above are equivalent to the statement that the ratio of a cohort's present population is to the size of that cohort ten years earlier as the size of a given cohort is to its size ten years later.[25]

Hamilton and Perry describe a procedure for estimating the numbers in cohorts which were not yet born at the date of the last census which is based on an assumed set of age specific birth rates and birth registration data. Their procedure is generally similar in concept to the methods suggested above for estimating the values of the nonzero elements in the projection operator matrix, and it should be considered by planners as an alternative to the procedure suggested above for finding the values of tf_{ij}. It is obvious that the Hamilton and Perry method can be applied to any combination of sex and race subpopulations, and can be used to project as many decades into the future as is desired.[26]

OTHER PROJECTION METHODOLOGIES

Two kinds of analytical techniques which are of potential utility in population studies for planning are described briefly in concluding this section, although neither uses the cohort survival model. The first, simulation, may be viewed as a possible alternative to cohort survival, while the second, multiple regression, is of interest chiefly as a supplement to cohort survival models.

Statistical simulation has been used in research on planning problems of other kinds,[27] but has not been used in population studies except in some experimental work at the national scale. Quite satisfactory projections of national population, labor force, and variables

---

[25] This paragraph is based directly on Hamilton and Perry, *op. cit.*, pp. 165–66.

[26] The reader is referred to the original paper for further details and discussion of the method. An IBM 650 computer program utilizing the Hamilton and Perry method was used to make projections by age, sex, and race to 1980 for each of the 100 counties in North Carolina, for the Bureau of Community Development of the North Carolina Department of Conservation and Development.

[27] Considerable discussion of simulation techniques and several examples may be found in the May, 1965 special issue of the JOURNAL OF THE AMERICAN INSTITUTE OF PLANNERS, XXXI, 2, which is devoted to "Urban Development Models: New Tools for Planning."

related to personal consumption were obtained in a simulation experiment by Orcutt and his colleagues.[28] We know that the probabilities of births, deaths, being in the labor force, household formation and dissolution, and migration, and variables such as family size derived from these, are interrelated as well as related to age, sex, race, income, occupation, and so on. In principle this complex chain of interrelations can be roughly approximated by a general cohort survival model, but the conceptual problems and others associated with the ways in which data are collected and tabulated are so formidable that this is never seriously contemplated for more than a handful of variables at a time.

In the simulation approach a sample of the households derived from a census enumeration is taken as the initial population, and all of the relevant characteristics of these households and their members are noted. Each cycle of the simulation moves this population forward through an increment of time, adding to the ages of the household members and changing characteristics of households or individuals by a random selection procedure which is consistent with the predetermined probabilities and with the characteristics of the particular households or individuals involved. This procedure generates one of the possible outcomes or projections which is not inconsistent with the specified projection model, and the most likely outcome can be estimated from the outcome of a number of separate runs of the model. We foresee far greater reliance on simulation approaches to population projection when there has been more experimentation with them, because simulation has the potential capability of integrating demographic, employment, and housing considerations in a sensitive and realistic manner. Some progress along these lines has come out of Community Renewal Program studies, notably in San Francisco and Pittsburgh.[29]

[28] Guy H. Orcutt, M. Greenberger, J. Korbel, and A. M. Rivlin, MICROANALYSIS OF SOCIOECONOMIC SYSTEMS: A SIMULATION STUDY, (New York: Harper, 1961).

[29] See W. A. Steger, "Review of Analytic Techniques for the CRP," JOURNAL OF THE AMERICAN INSTITUTE OF PLANNERS, XXXI, 2 (May, 1965), for a general review and citations of particular reports.

Multiple regression is not a technique well suited to population projection in general, but it is used in making post-censal estimates and may be useful in projecting the migration component of a cohort survival model. The reason that it is not believed to be useful as a general projection technique is that the interdependencies within the data create technical problems of multicolinearity and the identifiability of coefficients which could best be solved by reproducing the essence of the cohort survival model. However, where the problem is to estimate a variable that is dependent on the joint effects of a number of separate variables, as migration may be said to depend on employment opportunities, availability of attractive housing, quality of local public schools, numbers of out-migrants in prior decades, and so on, multiple regression is an appropriate analytical and projective technique.

The general multiple regression model may be expressed as

$$Y = a + b_1X_1 + b_2X_2 + b_3X_3 + \cdots + b_nX_n$$

where Y = the dependent variable, such as net migration during a decade, value of which is to be predicted

X_1, X_2, etc. are values of the separate independent variables

a, b_1, b_2, etc. are coefficients which may be estimated by a least-squares procedure and are related to the amount of effect the independent variable with the same subscript has on the dependent variable.

Subject to the constraint that the number of independent variables must be less than the number of independent observations (which in this example might be the number of areas for which data are available,) variables which may or may not have a significant effect on migration may be inserted in the model and then tested to see if in fact they do appear to be significant. Some of the variables will probably be matters over which there is public control, such as the quality of schools as measured by expenditure per student, and probably other significant variables will be matters such as employment and housing which are considered by planners and influenced by public decisions but not directly determined by public policy.

Thus the multiple regression model would appear to have a potential for incorporating some feedback effects within the planning process and for exploring some implications of alternative policy assumptions.

Areas and Systems of Areas

Local planning agencies can seldom limit their concern to the population within a single geographic boundary. In most instances it is important for an agency to study both a broader area which includes its own formal jurisdiction, and also smaller subdivisions of its jurisdiction. Consideration of the trends and potentials of a whole urban area is necessary if one is to make reasonable projections of the population of a political unit within the urban area,[30] so the geographical area of concern to a planner can seldom be limited to his area of planning jurisdiction. Planners must also give special consideration to spatial distributions within the geographical area which they serve.

In the context of population studies, this requires subdivision of their area of jurisdiction into planning districts or analysis zones and consideration of the present and future populations in each of these subareas. The discussion which follows can be simplified by referring to these three levels of geographic distinctions as "metro area," "city," and "district," though it should be understood that the points to be made here are fully applicable to places which are not metropolitan or even urban in character. This generalized discussion is also simplified by assuming that only three levels of areas are necessary for analytical purposes, and by assuming that the only distinction necessary at the metro area level is between the urbanized area and the rest of the world.[31]

---

[30] This point suggests an obviously desirable and mutually beneficial subject for a collaborative effort involving all of the planning agencies concerned with parts of a metropolitan area.

[31] In many cases these are not appropriate assumptions, but the extension of the ideas presented here to more complex situations will become obvious. Where the planner's area of jurisdiction is in a large metropolitan area or an emerging megalopolis or urbanized corridor a more extensive system of geographical distinctions will be required.

Analysis and projection of migration to or from the metro area will be largely related to studies of judgments about the economic base and employment of the metro area. There are two kinds of formal models which appear at first sight to be useful in projecting metro area migration but are not likely to be of much use to local planners. The data requirements of Rogers' interregional extension of the cohort survival approach[32] make it unavailable to most local planning agencies. The data required include the numbers in each sex, race, and age group of those moving from one area to another, for all pairs of areas. Such data are available only for some large regions and for the nation as a whole, generally from sample surveys. There is a strong argument for either doing sample surveys which would provide estimates of these numbers at the metro area or county scale, or for making tabulations based on change of address information obtained from routine reports such as the annual income tax returns. This type of model appears more promising for planning purposes than the various formulations of the gravity model and Stouffer's intervening opportunities model. Both of the latter fit quite well the data for the nation as a whole, but are likely to give very poor predictions for a specific locality.

It is well established that migration is invariably "selective migration," in the sense that the socio-economic characteristics found among a given stream of migrants differ on the average from those of the general population of the areas of origin and destination and from those migrating in the opposite direction. Past migration viewed in this perspective may give some clues about future migration. It may be that the reasons for the migration which can be inferred from characteristics of the migrants are changing, or that the opportunities for migration are changing. For example, there are areas in which there has been so much rural-urban migration of erstwhile farm workers that the farm labor force is sufficiently depleted to make continuation of the past level of migration quite unlikely. It appears that out-

---

[32] The relevant literature is cited in footnote 14 above.

migrants are likely to return eventually to the area from which they moved, and so an area which has experienced heavy out-migration of young adults in the past will probably have some in-migration of older persons in the future. But planners' assumptions about future metro area migration will no doubt continue to be based chiefly on judgments about the migration implications of economic projections and plans. It is at this point that the major interaction between planners' economic studies and population studies must occur.

The geographical units distinguished at the "city" level as defined above are defined by political boundaries, and these boundaries have no significance for migration unless they separate areas with quite different kinds of residential development or substantial differences in levels of residential services provided and taxes imposed on residents. In this context, school district boundaries are likely to be more significant than the boundaries between general-purpose local government units. Thus the "city" level should be ignored in migration studies in many areas, and projections for cities allowed to emerge simply as totals of the projections for the districts which constitute the city.

As economic base and labor force considerations dominate the analysis of migration at the metro area level, so housing availability and levels of residential services and amenities dominate migration studies at the district level. The factors involved here are too well known to professional planners to require repetition. Districts may be regarded as competing for population on the basis of their predominant type, density, and quality of housing, levels of residential services such as schools, social prestige, safety, and amenity, and considerations of cost and accessibility to employment and region-serving facilities. Though highly judgmental, this process is disciplined by the requirement that all of the migrants to one district must also appear as migrants from other districts, and vice versa. Areas of recent heavy migration are likely to be characterized by heavy migration in the future. A relatively small number of householders who are frequent movers account for a relatively high pro-portion of the number of moves.

The data which show that about one-fifth of the U.S. adult population can be expected to move in a given year also show that about half of the U.S. adult population will stay in the same residence for at least five years.[33] The annual school-age population censuses conducted in some areas can, where the data are of adequate quality and provide sufficient detail, be used to obtain relatively good information on migration flows among small areas.[34] The 1960 census tabulations provide some information on place of residence in 1955 and on length of residence at the April 1960 address. The 1950 census included a question on place of residence one year earlier, and it can be assumed that the 1970 census will also provide some information on residential mobility, though final decisions about the questions and tabulations of the 1970 census will not be made in time to be included in this chapter.

Conclusion

Population studies in comprehensive local planning work are often not given sufficient thought and effort. Frequently a quick and overly simplistic population projection is used as a basis for much more thorough analyses of other subjects and as a part of the design and policy recommendation process. And population projections prepared as a first step in the planning process are often left without later revision based on findings from other kinds of studies and on the policies recommended in the plan. Changes in the size, composition, and distribution of the population have effects on many of the other subjects covered in a comprehensive plan and on various governmental policies which, regardless of their relationship to the plan, certainly affect migration and thus

[33] Karl E. Taeuber, "Duration of Residence Analysis of Internal Migration in the United States," MILLBANK MEMORIAL FUND QUARTERLY, XXXIX (1961), p. 121.

[34] See Sidney Goldstein and Kurt B. Mayer, METROPOLITAN AND POPULATION CHANGE IN RHODE ISLAND (Providence: Planning Division, Rhode Island Development Council, 1961) for a good example with quite adequate methodological discussion and investigation of the extent to which total migration is reflected in the data for families with young children.

the future size, composition and distribution of the population.

It must be recognized that professional planners do not have unlimited time and resources. The population studies suggested above are designed to make efficient use of the time and knowledge of planners. This efficiency is obtained in three ways:

1. The analysis of past population changes is done in a manner which produces information in a form directly applicable to the projection of future changes and the solution of current problems.

2. The analysis and projection of changes in fertility and mortality is set up so as to require a minimum of professional planning judgment. This enables the planner to devote more time to the study of migration, which is the aspect of population change most requiring the specialized skills, judgment, and local knowledge of the planner.

3. The sequence of studies suggested here is expressed in a form which lends itself to the use of electronic computers, thus enabling the planner to obtain alternative or revised projections at less cost and far less time than would otherwise be possible.

The need for flexibility in population studies is obvious if the planning process is visualized as one in which tentative conclusions and analyses are refined and modified during the preparation of a comprehensive plan, and the recommendations and forecasts in the plan are then revised as a result of public reaction, changing opportunities, and unforeseen events. This need for flexibility is one reason for the emphasis in this chapter on alternative assumptions about future trends and alternative projections and forecasts.

Secondly, the planner has to use forecasts about future populations, and needs the best forecasts he can make, but he can never assume that his forecasts will be correct. A forecast based on a cohort survival projection is more likely to be correct, other things being equal, than one based on an unnecessarily crude projection method, but there is always some unknown probability of error. By making projections based on a number of alternative sets of assumptions about future trends the planner can see which kinds of variables are most critical in the area with which he is concerned, and he can select as forecasts the results of appropriate projections. In most cases, and at any stage in the planning process, there should be three projections considered as forecasts: one that is considered the most probable future population; a second that is higher and is used where the costs of overestimating are greater than the costs of underestimating population; and a third which is lower and is used where it is conservative to overestimate rather than underestimate. The second would generally be used in the design of capital improvements of fixed capacity, for example, and the third for estimating market demands, tax revenues, and similar variables.

Perhaps the most important of these reasons for retaining flexibility in the population studies done for local planning purposes is that of providing for feedback to the population forecasts from other kinds of planning studies and conclusions. Such feedback in the planning process is consistent with the fact that population does change in response to environmental changes. If population studies are done in this manner they will be a much more valuable aspect of planning than they generally have been in the past.

This chapter was prepared with the assistance of Ralph C. Gackenheimer, Associate Professor of City Planning, University of North Carolina.

4

Economic Studies

STUDIES of the urban economy have the underlying purpose of improving our understanding of the economy and how it works. Methods of urban economic analysis now available perform rather well in telling us what the economy of an urban area is in a structural sense. They are notably weak in explaining how this type of economy operates. The operational deficiencies are found both in theory and in analytic techniques. It may well be that the troubles we encounter with respect to the dynamics of urban economies are traceable, in part, to misconceptions concerning the method of structural description. This is uncertain. Despite these imperfections, however, there is a distinct sense of confidence among city planners that they can work in a far more enlightened way with than without economic studies.

Purposes and Objectives

City planners must keep in mind the fact that economic studies are intended to improve not only their own understanding as technicians but also the understanding of local public officials and citizens. Hence economic studies are to be prepared as a public document or series of documents. A method of analysis and presentation is therefore required that will accomplish this end.

It must be pointed out that for some planners economic studies are merely a formality, a recognized and orthodox step in the process of planning. Once the "proper" studies are completed there may be very little integration of the results with other basic studies and with the more detailed phases of planning that follow. As a consequence, although the planner's understanding may be improved by economic studies, such understanding is sterile if not applied in his work.

In a technical sense economic studies have two purposes. A principal purpose is to provide materials about the local economy that will assist the community, with the aid of the planner, in arriving at a series of goals and objectives. A second technical purpose is to provide quantitative estimates of future employment and population. Population estimates based on employment estimates are then usually cross-checked and reconciled with population forecasts that have been computed by demographic techniques. Quantitative employment and population forecasts are intended to serve as gross guides to the formulation of plans of land use, transportation, open space, and facilities.

A more refined and effective application of the results of economic study to the process of physical planning combines certain qualitative measurements with the quantitative estimates metioned above. By this is meant a breakdown of the gross employment estimate into principal economic activity lines such as food and kindred product manufacture, retailing, finance, government administration. Refinement of employment estimates into economic activity lines can be made even more effective by a further extension, resulting in the estimate of occupational classifications likely to result from growth and change within the activity lines. It is perhaps obvious that cumulative refinements, primarily by categories of occupation, income, education, and sex would have meaning for the anticipated population composition. These estimates in turn are directly related to the requirements for land use, transportation, recreation, and facilities.

Additional purposes of economic studies, at present emerging in a few planning operations, pertain to economic development and to social welfare. While these two areas are closely associated they deserve separate comment. Economic development programs of an informal type have been conducted in American cities for many years. In only rare instances has such development activity been associated with organized city planning departments. This is logical in view of the fact that the city planning profession has traditionally focused on physical planning as its field of competence and responsibility. On the other hand the development operations of *ad hoc* community groups have made the economic aspects of planning not only highly visible but also a challenge to the professionally oriented person with training pertinent to this kind of activity. In addition there is a growing appreciation on the part of city planners of the critical relationship of the urban economy to physical plans. Planners are already aware that the character and evolution of a local economy is strongly influenced by physical plans. But planners are only beginning to understand that the realization and effectiveness of physical plans is almost completely dependent on the local economy and its prospects, guided or unguided. Therefore, as a physical planner he is aware of the necessity of economic planning as a means to the principal end of his profession.

Of more recent origin and roughly coincident with the appearance of the Federal Poverty Program is the developing consideration given by the city planning profession to social welfare. With roots in the predominantly physical planning programs of public housing and urban renewal, social welfare planning is emerging as an independent concept at the city level. In common with economic development activity, urban social planning in America has passed through a long and generally short-

sighted history of organized personal and family welfare. Social welfare activity shows itself in a myriad of citizen-based community welfare programs, formal philanthropic groups such as the Volunteers of America, as well as in city and county relief and welfare departments. Recognition by city planners of the inseparability of physical planning problems and social problems suggests the imminent integration of the two. A moment's thought shows, in turn, the close relationship of urban economic planning to social welfare planning. Certainly, welfare in its broadest sense is one of the general objectives of economic planning. More specifically, economic planning is aimed at many of the key problems associated with what is ordinarily implied by social welfare at the city level. These key problems include, by way of example, employment opportunity, employment regularity, income level and distribution, property tax policy, housing finance and subsidy systems.

Speed of acceptance of these newer purposes of city planning and of economic studies will, of course, depend upon the vision, mental flexibility, and cooperativeness of the principal parties involved—not only organized city planning staffs with their controlling mayors or managers and councils, but also those individuals and official city bodies who have been on the firing line of economic development and social welfare for many years.

In summary, the purpose of urban economic studies can be expressed as a series of practical, direct, and interrelated questions. Weighting of the questions will vary by community but all will invariably be present.

1. *Why does the community exist?* The answer to this question must have historical perspective. Present economic forms, functions, and problems are partly explainable in terms of the past. From the past, through the present, and extending into the future, there is a deeper answer to the question, however. What factors explain the continuing development, or lack of development, of the community? Is it a matter of location, labor force composition, intangible leadership factors, physical community layout and facilities, or weaknesses of competitive communities and areas?

Histories of certain well-known cities provide some guidance in answering the lead question. Pittsburgh's evolution from defense point and trading post to major manufacturing stature is highly familiar. Not so familiar is its more recent emphasis on service and administrative functions concurrent with a relative decline in the importance of manufacturing. Chicago shows similar tendencies with, however, greater strength in manufacturing, traceable, in large part, to diversity as compared to Pittsburgh's greater manufacturing specialization. Washington's economy has from the start exhibited the solid undergirding of federal services. With rapid growth in size, however, its professional, service, and retail economy have burgeoned and made the city more like many other major metropolitan areas of the nation.

2. *What are the principal causes of change in the economy?* The answer to this question is partly historical: what have been the principal influences of change in the past? For the present and more remote future cause of change must be related closely to economic function. For the extractive and manufacturing economy, forces of technologic and market change and competitive strength may be the most pertinent. Professional and service economies are highly responsive to change in social custom and general income distribution. Institutional impacts of government regulation and policy decision will have differential impacts depending on their type and timing.

3. *What are the most important forms of imbalance in the community economy?* Few urban economies are perfect in terms of economic balance. It is, therefore, necessary to determine the type and degree of seriousness of these imbalances. Roughly classified, economic imbalances can be viewed as self-adjusting and non-self-adjusting.

Self-adjusting imbalances include such factors as wage levels, labor force housing supply, labor force skills supply, and competitive effectiveness of plant equipment.

Imbalances that usually require some managed adjustment involve economies where sharp cyclical and seasonal production shifts are evident. Imbalances reflecting inadequate economy size and diversification also frequently require managed adjustment.

4. *How can the imbalances of the economy be remedied?* Remedies for economic imbalance will vary widely depending on the particular structural conditions encountered. By way of example, remedies may range from the importation or local creation of new industry or product and service lines, to the abatement of the causes of labor unrest.

5. *How can economic problem remedies be expressed as community development targets?* Targets for community development must be expressed in terms that are not too technical, and yet specific and practical. These targets may take the form of "1,000 electronic industry jobs by 1970"; "development of tourist service activities in sufficient volume to counterbalance summer and fall employment slump in wood products manufacture"; "doubling of annual output of new housing units rented or sold at price levels below $12,000"; "500 acres of industrial park development by 1975."

6. *How do the facts of community economic structure, problems, problem remedies, and targets relate to other community problems and targets in which the planner is involved?* The principal elements in the answer to this question include:

(a) Consideration of priorities. Are economic issues to lead or follow other elements of the plan? If they follow, what is the order?

(b) Feasibility. To what degree is the feasibility of implementation of other parts of the planning program dependent on practical feasibility of the economic development plan?

(c) Appraisal of the consistency of economic means and goals with the means and goals of other elements of the community plan. What are the feedbacks, plus and minus, of one part to the other?

Concept of the Economic Base

Among the numerous approaches to the making of studies of the urban economy, the economic base method has, until the present, been the most frequently employed.

The term "economic base" has two general meanings in the literature of the social sciences and of city planning. In one sense it is a way of looking at or classifying the economy of the city. This is usually what is meant when reference is made to the "concept" of the base. The other meaning of "economic base" pertains to a *technique* or method of handling urban economic data, in which the "concept" plays a fundamental role. A substantial portion of this chapter is devoted to an explanation of the base technique.

There is no complete agreement among authorities on the question of what the concept of the economic base is. One group, representing the minority, maintains that the *total* of economic activities and relationships that can be identified within a city is the base which supports the city or urban area, however it may be defined.[1] A majority of writers and practitioners claim that the economic base is a portion of the total city economy. This economic portion is composed of the producers of goods, services, and capital who export all, or a predominant part, of their output from the urban area. The export function is considered of fundamental importance in the foreign trade sense that it is the "money earning" portion of the economy, it is the exchanger of goods and services with the outside world. Both the makeup of the base and the changes which occur in it are thought to have an important bearing on the total health of the city's economy, on population total and composition, and on land use distribution.

A preliminary comment on the economic base technique will assist in showing its relationship to the concept and to the planning process. The economic base technique is, essentially, a multiplier approach to urban economic-population relationships. As sketched above, the procedure is one in which the export segment of the city economy is identified and quantified according to some appropriate universal measure, such as sale dollars or employment. A similar measure is applied to the residue of the economy, which is engaged in production for the local market only. A ratio is calculated between the total of base operations and the total of local operations.

Another ratio used in working with this technique is one in which sums of the totals of the base and local activities are related to total population.

While other ratio variations are used in the base technique these two are probably the most important. The ratios are, of course, descriptive of conditions at one point in time. To be useful in a planning sense they must be made dynamic. In this technique, "movement" is introduced by study of the growth prospects of the export or base elements of the city economy, and derivation from this study of the estimated level of employment or of sales dollars at some future date. To this estimate are applied the ratios described above. By multiplication, the volume of purely local market activity can be determined and, next, the volume of population at the future date can be derived. A carry-over to land use allocations and facility needs is the next logical step.

A shortcoming of this technique for the planning process rests in its quantitative character. Internal analysis and evaluation of the export and local economic sectors is necessary in order to obtain qualitative perspective. The findings, however, are not readily convertible to ratios. This type of analysis is usually carried out in economic base studies, but is in no sense peculiar to the base technique.

The essence of the economic base *concept* is extremely old—it would be pointless to document and prove its beginnings. A simple example or two may therefore suffice. Venice or any one of the trading cities of the ancient Hanseatic League between the 6th and 12th centuries was intensely concerned with the relationship of export operations to its general welfare as an urban settlement. The policy and theory of 18th century mercantilism would be a national version of the same emphasis on exports in the economic structure. Mercantilism had an additional twist *not* found in the modern concept of the base, namely, the discouragement of imports. This variation is worth mentioning because of the fact that the economic base concept is frequently accused of being mercantilist in nature.[2] Finally, a little reflection will bring

---

[1] Ernest M. Fisher and Robert M. Fisher, URBAN REAL ESTATE (New York: Henry Holt and Co., 1954), p. 278.

[2] Avoidance of emphasis on imports will be discussed in more detail at a later point.

to mind the fact that for centuries a myriad of small urban communities the world over have depended for their very existence on the export of goods and services to their rural hinterlands. In short, the emphasis on the export sector of trade expresses a significant portion of the exchange equation, which in turn explains more current phenomena such as functional specialization, division of labor, and urbanism.

---

[3] The following references in time sequence are representative of theoretical treatments of the economic base concept and technique since its beginnings in the 1920's:

M. Aurousseau, "The Distribution of Population: A Constructive Problem," GEOGRAPHICAL REVIEW, XI (1921), p. 574.

Robert M. Haig, MAJOR ECONOMIC FACTORS IN METROPOLITAN GROWTH AND DEVELOPMENT: VOLUME I OF REGIONAL SURVEY OF NEW YORK AND ENVIRONS (New York: Regional Plan Association, 1927).

F. L. Nussbaum, A HISTORY OF THE ECONOMIC INSTITUTIONS OF MODERN EUROPE (New York: F. S. Crofts & Company, 1933), p. 36.

Richard Hartshorne, "A New Map of the Manufacturing Belt of North America," ECONOMIC GEOGRAPHY, XII (1936), pp. 45–53.

"Oskaloosa vs. The United States," FORTUNE, XVII (April, 1938), pp. 55–62.

Arthur M. Weimer and Homer Hoyt, PRINCIPLES OF URBAN REAL ESTATE (New York: The Ronald Press Company, 1939).

M. C. Daly, "An Approximation to a Geographic Multiplier," THE ECONOMIC JOURNAL, L, No. 198–99 (June–September, 1940), pp. 248–58.

Homer Hoyt, "Economic Background of Cities," JOURNAL OF LAND AND PUBLIC UTILITY ECONOMICS, XVII (May, 1941), pp. 188–95.

Victor Roterus, "The Economic Background for Local Planning," PLANNING 1946, Proceedings of the Annual Meeting of the American Society of Planning Officials in New York, May 6–8, 1946 (Chicago: 1946), p. 86.

Richard U. Ratcliff, URBAN LAND ECONOMICS (New York: McGraw-Hill Book Company, Inc., 1949).

George Hildebrand and Arthur Mace, Jr., "The Employment Multiplier in an Expanding Industrial Market: Los Angeles County, 1940–47," REVIEW OF ECONOMICS AND STATISTICS, XXXII (August, 1950).

John Alexander, "The Basic-Nonbasic Concept of Urban Economic Functions," ECONOMIC GEOGRAPHY, XXX (1954), pp. 246–61.

Charles M. Tiebout, "The Urban Economic Base Reconsidered," LAND ECONOMICS, XXXII (February, 1956), pp. 95–99.

Gerald E. Thompson, "An Investigation of the Local Employment Multiplier," REVIEW OF ECONOMICS AND STATISTICS, XLI (February, 1959), pp. 61–67.

Ralph W. Pfouts (ed.), THE TECHNIQUES OF URBAN ECONOMIC ANALYSIS (West Trenton, New Jersey: Chandler-Davis Publishing Company, 1960).

Charles M. Tiebout, THE COMMUNITY ECONOMIC BASE STUDY (New York: Committee for Economic Development, 1962).

The historical beginnings of what approximates to the economic base *technique* are of relatively recent origin. From the early twenties until the mid-sixties the concept of the base was sharpened and quantified. Significant applications of technique began about the middle thirties and multiplied enormously, despite rising challenges from other methods which appeared most conspicuously in the late fifties. Credit for the theoretical development of base technique is about equally divided among one historian and several geographers and economists.[3] Geographers were apparently the first to break ground, and economists followed up as most assiduous tillers of and tenders of the growing crop.[4] It might be said that planners may end up being the stewards of the harvest in the interesting absence of concern on the part of either geographers or economists for the broader applications and meaning of these techniques. Applications of the economic base technique are to be found in literally scores of studies, involving principally cities in the United States.[5] These studies, when sampled at

---

[4] Economists interested in base technique range from land economists and econometricians to federal reserve bank staff economists and students of economic structure.

[5] Some of the early economic base studies which are of good quality and at the same time contain a limited amount of theoretical discussion are listed here in time sequence, along with products of more recent vintage.

U.S. Federal Housing Administration, BASIC DATA ON NORTHERN NEW JERSEY HOUSING MARKET, Washington, D.C., July 1937. This was one of the first of a series of studies produced by Homer Hoyt under the direction of Ernest M. Fisher for the Federal Housing Administration. Although the objective of these studies is housing market analysis they each contain a section on economic background which introduces in precise quantitative form the ratio or multiplier characteristic of the urban economic base.

The Regional Plan Association, Inc., THE ECONOMIC STATUS OF THE NEW YORK METROPOLITAN REGION IN 1944 (New York: 1944). This study was also conducted by Hoyt and updated the survey of 1928.

Detroit City Plan Commission, ECONOMIC BASE OF DETROIT (Detroit, Michigan: 1944).

Cincinnati City Planning Commission, ECONOMY OF THE AREA (Cincinnati, Ohio: 1946).

Federal Reserve Bank, Kansas City, Missouri and the University of New Mexico, THE ECONOMY OF ALBUQUERQUE, NEW MEXICO (Albuquerque: University of New Mexico, 1949).

John W. Alexander, AN ECONOMIC BASE STUDY OF MADISON, WISCONSIN (Madison: University of Wisconsin, 1953).

time intervals, show the evolution of the technique and the problems of its application. The debate relative to the base technique follows a pattern which underscores both its immaturity and its evolutionary character. Discussion of "terminology," "classification," "measure," and "identification" are symptoms. At a fairly recent date (1955) a prominent planner pronounced a death sentence over the concept and thereby the technique.[6] His judgment was based largely on the view that the importance of export activities in the urban (metropolitan size) economy was grossly overemphasized and that local market activities represent the true base. In 1963 an equally prominent economist expressed amazement at the persistence of a technique (base) that was burdened with substantial imperfection.[7]

Economic Base Technique

It will be the purpose of this section to examine the important details relating to application of the economic base technique: as a consequence, much of the finery of theoretic discussion is cut away. Intricacies of technique design can be traced by the interested reader via footnote or from general bibliographic reference.

The bare bones of economic base technique have, over the past 20 years, become relatively standardized. After a short introductory com-

ment of terminology, the principal sections that follow outline the generally accepted lines of thought, practice, and most frequently encountered problems associated with the technique. These sections are, in part, a reflection of a procedural sequence, but also represent decisions and situations that must be considered on a simultaneous and feed-back revision basis. Specifically, the subjects treated include area delimitation, economic functional classification, base identification, unit of measure selection, economic ratios, and the projection of economic data.

TERMINOLOGY

It is important for any field of study or profession to have general agreement on the terms it uses. Despite the 40 or more years that the economic base technique has been under discussion, there is no general agreement on terms. The principal area of disagreement seems to be usage descriptive of the two principal parts of the urban economy. The urban economic base is generally accepted as the exporting portion of the local economy. It is most frequently referred to as the "base," or "basic" activities. In the past it was variously labeled as "primary," "urban growth" (activities), and "town builders." The residual portion of the urban economy, frequently many times larger by any measure than the base, is most often described as "non-basic." Terms now apparently discarded or disfavored which refer to this non-exporting portion of the economy are "auxiliary," "secondary," "urban serving" (activities), "town fillers," and "service."

If this question in terminology is looked at as a matter of efficient communication of ideas, it would seem that terms more precise and therefore more descriptive would be preferred. For example, the term "basic" means "export market activity"; "non-basic" means "local market activity." These longer positive terms give the precision which is desired but are clumsy in use. Therefore, they could be abbreviated to "export" and "local"; producing expressions such as "export-local ratio," and "local activity" analysis. The expression "base" could, of course, be retained for general discussion purposes when it is not being used in close

Denver Planning Office, WORKING DENVER (Denver, Colorado: 1953).

E. T. Halaas (consultant), ECONOMIC BASE: A PLANNING DIMENSION (Canton, Ohio: Stark County Regional Planning Commission, 1959).

Virgil C. Crisafulli, AN ECONOMIC ANALYSIS OF THE UTICA-ROME AREA (Utica, New York: Utica College Research Center, 1960).

Wisconsin Department of Resource Development, DOOR COUNTY PLANNING PROGRAM, Chapter 2, Population and Economy (Madison, Wisconsin: 1964).

Byron B. Brown, Jr., EXPORT-EMPLOYMENT MULTIPLIER ANALYSIS OF A MAJOR INDUSTRIAL COMMUNITY (Houston, Texas: University of Houston, 1964).

[6] Hans Blumenfeld, "The Economic Base of the Metropolis," JOURNAL OF THE AMERICAN INSTITUTE OF PLANNERS, XXI (Fall 1955), pp. 114–32.

[7] John R. Meyer, "Regional Economics: A Survey," AMERICAN ECONOMIC REVIEW, LIII, No. 1 (March, 1963), pp. 19–54.

association with the term "local." The terminology just suggested will be used in the balance of this chapter.[8]

SOURCES OF DATA

Primary and secondary urban economic data are available from federal, state, and local sources. While too numerous to list individually, the principal reference sources include:

Federal:

1. U.S. Bureau of the Census, *County and City Data Book* (available on an approximate biennial basis). Includes primary data from nongovernmental agencies as well.

2. U.S. Bureau of the Census, *Directory of Federal Statistics for Local Areas, A Guide to Sources, 1966,* Washington, D.C., U.S. Government Printing Office.

3. Special cross tabulations and unpublished tape data are available at a user charge from the Bureau of the Census. Analysts can then make known the nature and cost of what data are available. Published census sources that can be further refined include, by example, the Censuses of Population, Business, Agriculture, Manufactures, and Mining.

State:

1. A reference source which shows the form, location, and availability of primary urban economic data from state agencies is listed here. Although this reference is only for Wisconsin, other states will tend to parallel it rather closely: Richard B. Andrews, Lawrence Sager, and Collen L. Schuh, *General Economic, Population, and Public Finance Statistics Available from Public Agencies of the State of Wisconsin* (University of Wisconsin, Bureau of Business Research and Service, School of Business), Volume II, Number 5, Wisconsin Project Reports, 1965.

Local:

Local primary and secondary urban economic data are available from a large number of sources. Representative of these sources are:

1. Special economic studies and data collections in the city's planning department files.

2. City and county operating department annual reports and detail data, i.e., assessor, building department, comptroller.

3. Regular monthly and annual reports, and special studies of the chamber of commerce.

4. Annual review of local economy in the daily paper.

5. Special studies of economy by local colleges or universities.

AREA DELIMITATION

Delimitation of the area which is to be the subject of economic studies is of special importance when the economic base technique is used. This is true because of the necessity of distinguishing between export and local market activities. Delimitation is almost always an arbitrary matter in any field. The present case is no exception. Establishing the limits of the "economic community" is as difficult as determining the limits of urban settlement and, in some respects, more difficult. What, therefore, are some of the most pertinent questions or considerations that can lead the analyst to a semi-satisfactory answer in this matter?

The most straightforward approach to the delimitation question is a determination of the economic area of which the community under analysis is a part or the focus. An urban economic area may be measured by at least two rather similar methods.

Labor market area delineation is one of these methods. As set up by the U.S. Department of Labor, and followed by state employment and labor departments, the labor market area concept originally relied heavily upon transportation facility and commuting time limits. In miles this means an average radius from the study center of 30 to 40 miles with a *maximum* time limit of about 90 minutes. It is certain that labor market areas which are on interstate highway systems will have their limits extended considerably in the direction of these systems. While local analysts may use labor market standards for area delineation they may also apply their own standards to the commutation measure. This would mean, for

---

[8] A recent study (1964) has used the complementing expressions "export employment" and "import employment." An inaccuracy results from the use of the term "import"; *both* segments of the urban economy import, only one exports.

example, including counties or portions of counties that contribute more than a certain minimum percentage of total labor force to the city or principal county under study. While commutation origins are available on application from the Bureau of the Census for 1960 and will assumedly be available in 1970, there is no inter-censal reporting of these data. Distance from the most recent census year will therefore be one way of determining the necessity of local adjustments and survey work.[9]

The other method of delineation is a part of the technique whereby Standard Metropolitan Statistical Areas are defined. Without going into the details of the definitions (which can be found in the introduction of the census volume on metropolitan areas) it may be sufficient here to state their emphasis. Counties included in SMSA's are expected to show a strong degree of social and economic integration. Economic integration is measured by arbitrary minimum non-agricultural employment shares of peripheral counties in the combined total of the counties considered, i.e., at least 10 per cent of the number of non-agricultural workers employed in the county containing the largest city in the area. Other required minimums of the SMSA definition are (1) if 15 per cent of the workers living in the county work in the central county of the area, or (2) if 25 per cent of those working in the county live in the central county of the area. As with labor market area determination there is no federal inter-censal measure of these integration conditions. Therefore, for rapidly growing metropolitan areas and for areas of less than metropolitan status, independent local survey is required to arrive at an up-to-date delineation.

These remarks on area delimitation have pointed to certain problems which deserve additional comment. The question of economic area delimitation for the small city (less than

50,000) is particularly bothersome. County size units as representative of the "economic community" of small cities often seem unrealistic. The disproportion of the county unit is great when there are other small cities within it, when the small city is a central city suburb within a metropolitan county, or when the major portion of workers in the county outside the small city work in an adjoining non-metropolitan county. The solutions to these situations cannot be standardized. However, it may be best to apply the *standards* of labor market area or metropolitan area identification on a minor civil division basis (townships and villages) surrounding the small city. The difficulty of this approach is that not only the original identification, but also subsequent economic data must be obtained almost entirely by local effort. Economic data collected by the federal census relate for the most part to counties and large cities. Deriving the localized share from a county total base is fraught with perils. Suburbs, largely on the dormitory types, in which commutation represents an important segment—if not an exclusive representation—of the export market portion of the city economy, is yet another special case. In this situation a logical approach would be to extend the radius of economic influence of the suburb beyond its municipal limits to include contiguous or adjacent subdivisions that are within its *convenience* trade area for goods and services. The convenience emphasis suggests the daily or high frequency contact type of association that is considered so important in distinguishing integrated economic situations in metropolitan areas.

The economic area delimitation problem of the metropolitan suburb calls forth a procedural suggestion that can be applied to other community types. In the case of the commuting suburb it is quite clear that its economic welfare is entirely dependent upon the market in which its commuters sell their services, namely, the central city or other suburbs. Consequently a broader framework, that of the metropolitan area, is necessary for proper analysis of the commuter market. In the event that the metropolitan area is composed of more than one county, analysis should be sharpened by a

---

[9] When a locality is forced to perform the survey work necessary for delineation, the economic activities of the locality should be classified by economic category (standard industrial classification) and then detailed by operating plant. Operating plants will provide the necessary place of residence data. Industrial classification is discussed in an ensuing section on classification of the economy.

breakdown on an individual county basis. This line of discussion does not suggest that the suburb must take the initiative in inaugurating metropolitan economic studies. But if they have not already been conducted, the suburb may well play the role of prodder and expediter.[10]

Another problem of delimitation worthy of comment relates to the dynamics of study area boundaries. It is generally assumed that the economic limits of the community are expanding over time. However, general contractions and localized variations in an area perimeter that do occur on a secular or cyclic basis will, if unadjusted, introduce defects of description and analysis. The problem of directional shifts of economic area boundaries may not always result in quantitative change or even in qualitative change for the area economy. But the fact of directional shift is nonetheless of immediate practical significance to the physical planner. Industrial plant and interstate highway locational policies are only the more obvious examples of forces likely to cause a directional shift in the boundary of the economic area.

Much of the difficulty of area delimitation is a data problem. From the foregoing discussion one might well assume that federal and local municipal survey data are all that the analyst has available to him. However, it is encouraging to know that some states maintain sampling and estimating systems by employment

category that can be used in meeting not only delimitation problems but also other problems associated with local economic studies. All states maintain unemployment compensation records which, within the limitations of their coverage, provide additional data leverage.

CLASSIFICATION

The concept of the economic base is a classifying idea in itself. A community's economy is classified thereby into an export sector and a residual, which is here called the local market sector. In a general sense it may be said that all theories classify. One of the important scientific objectives of the classification operation is clarification of the meaning of a thing, or a situation, by breaking it into parts, or sub-classifications, that have a cause-and-effect relationship to one another, and which help to explain on-going action and anticipated change. At present classification of the two major portions of the urban economy via the base concept is in an unsettled state. Variations of classification occur with each field study. Academic writers have individual classification preferences. Reasons for this variability are not difficult to guess. Differences among the academics are often a reflection of their social science backgrounds. There is even a difference between the views of the general economists and the land economists. Differences in field study classifications are likely to represent reactions to the academic backgrounds of the study directors and specific local problems and objectives. The range of differences in economic classification can be summarily explained by variation in *function* of the classification system. If, therefore, the purpose of the classification is physical planning, the way in which the two major parts of the local economy are subclassified and related will (or should) be adapted to this end. This is not to say that other classification systems will not contain concepts of value for the planning process. However, it is usually true that their total system has other disciplines or ends in mind. Parts of classification systems that appear to have meaning for the planning process will be presented in the following paragraphs.

Almost all classification systems first divide

---

[10] In general, urban economic analysis at a less than metropolitan level is an extremely hazardous undertaking. Whereas it must be performed in order to temper other judgments concerning a single community's outlook and problems, projections based on such analysis are likely to be unreliable if there is no larger metro study to use as a benchmark. Part of the difficulty, with or without a metro study, is that of making geographical allocations of projected growth and problem impacts within the area. In the absence of a metro benchmark study there is also a bothersome question concerning the mobility of production factors, particularly labor, within the area. The effect of economic development plans of competitive communities within the metro area on single community projections provides yet another complication.

There are urban development economists who argue that even the metropolitan area is too small a unit of analysis. They maintain that the multi-county district with a full-range hinterland and complement of satellite cities is a more realistic concept of the economic community for development planning purposes.

the total urban economy into the structural parts that have long been established by economists and the Bureau of the Census. These structural parts are formalized in a standard industrial classification system, which appears in the *Standard Industrial Classification Manual* published by the U.S. Bureau of the Budget. In this manual the table of contents lists the major divisions into which an economy can be divided. These divisions include, for example, agriculture, mining, construction, manufacturing, transportation, services, and government. Divisions are essentially the same as the economist's "sectors." Each of the divisions is then broken down into major groups to which are assigned standard industrial classification (SIC) numbers. For example, Division D, Manufacturing, includes among its 21 major groups such classes as Major Group (SIC) 28, Chemical and Allied Products; Major Group (SIC) 37, Transportation Equipment; and Major Group (SIC) 26, Paper and Allied Products. Identification of economic units within each group is on the basis of the "establishment" such as a factory, a store, or a mine. Two-digit designations of the major groups are broken down step by step in the *Manual* to a four-digit level. Each successive digit added represents a description of a deeper level of specialization within the group. Most economic base studies classify only through the two-digit level. For planning purposes, the deeper the classification the better. Two digits are considered too gross at the local level, three digits represent a compromise, in view of published data difficulties, with four-digit classifications.

With the total urban economy classified along the lines described, refinements can move in a number of directions. The essential question is, however, how shall the SIC data be arranged once the export and local market division has been made.[11]

The simplified classification just described is probably the best starting point for the economic analyst. It is from this simplified version

that he will make his employment estimates and his employment-based population estimates. It is, moreover, the version which will have the most meaning to public officials, legislators, and the public at large. Finally, it can be described as the classification from which the analyst not only branches out in his studies, but also the one to which he returns in order to summarize his results. An abbreviated example of this form of classification appears in Table 4–1.

Beyond this point in the classification process how the analyst moves is determined by local objectives, problems, analyst abilities, data availability, and budget. It will, therefore, be the purpose of the following paragraphs to sketch the nature and use of a few basic classification approaches.

A classification refinement that is occasionally encountered breaks down export and local market activities by the *degree* to which a particular SIC is export and local market oriented. Thus food product manufacture (SIC 20) in Table 4–1 which shows 200 employees in the export category and 100 in the local market category may be registered as 66⅔ per cent export and 33⅓ per cent local. Usually percentage brackets are used for this purpose, i.e.,

Table 4–1

Economic Activities of City X Classified by Economic Division, Major Group, and Export and Local Market Status (employment measure)

Economic Division and Group	Market Status		
	Export	Local	Total
Total, all activities	1,635	1,265	2,900
Services (total)	885	115	1,000
Hotels	175	25	(200)
Auto repair	100	50	(150)
Legal	270	30	(300)
Medical	340	10	(350)
Manufacturing (total)	400	100	500
Food	200	100	(300)
Textiles	200	…	(200)
Construction	…	200	200
Trade (total)	350	850	1,200
Retail	200	800	(1,000)
Wholesale	150	50	(200)

[11] The techniques of dividing total urban economic activity into export, local and auxiliary elements will be discussed at a later point in connection with the process of identification.

(10%–20%) ; (21%–30%) ; (75%–100%), etc. The brackets are inserted under the table titles of "export" and "local." Thus a clearer view in proportional terms is obtained of the export local weights of each activity line. Degree of orientation of a particular economic group toward the export side or the local market side of the economic ledger has important implications for location and development policies. For public presentation purposes, this classification is more effective in chart form.

A further classification refinement which may accompany the form described above, or be applied independently to the original simplified version, is that which breaks down the major group two-digit data into three-, and, where possible, four-digit arrangements. The food product manufacturing classification of Table 4–1, which is SIC 20, might then break down as follows: SIC 201, meat products; SIC 202, dairy products; SIC 203, canning and preserving fruits, vegetables, and sea foods. Each of the three-digit classes may be subdivided again, SIC 202 can represent two or more sub-classes such as SIC 2021, creamery butter; SIC 2022, natural cheese. Whether the major two-digit groups need this much refinement in any one community study will depend on the actual distribution of local activity below the two-digit level. If the preponderance of employment, sales, and income of a major two-digit group is focused in a single three- or four-digit group, like dairy products—natural cheese, there may be no point in detailing the other thinly represented three- and four-digit activities of the broader class, except to designate them under SIC 20 as "other."

A variation of classification which can be of great significance in large urban areas involves a further breakdown of local market activity. This refinement segregates local household transactions from transactions of local business firms, government, and institutions. The degree of segregation is usually expressed by means of an employment allocation. Major groups, or portions of them, whose purchases and sales circulate within the non-household and usually non-retail portion of the economy, are sometimes described as "auxiliaries." When this identification can be made, it is then possi-

ble to gain a clearer idea of the internal business linkages of the community. The planning implications of this information are probably obvious. This method of local market activity classification is, however, quite crude. A matrix approach is far superior in that it shows the origin and destination of these local transactions, while the method under discussion describes only transaction destinations.[12] A simplified version of the classification appears below.

$$\begin{array}{ccccc} & Total & Export & Local & \begin{pmatrix} House\text{-} & Auxil\text{-} \\ holds & iaries \end{pmatrix} \\ \text{SIC 20} & 300 & 200 & 100 & \begin{matrix} 70 & 30 \end{matrix} \end{array}$$

Local market activity has been broken down further by at least one economist.[13] This method identifies the proportion of local market employment which can be attributed to investment activity. Local investment purchases by business in plant and equipment, similar purchases by government, and the housing investment of households is included. Investment classification provides at least two advantages to the urban economic analyst. On the one hand it gives a more complete conception of linkage relations within the local economy. Investment classification also assists in differentiating between rapid and slow consumption portions of the economy, which have cyclical implications for estimating. Investment observations can, with caution, be used as independent indicators of economic health and change. Finally, investment in buildings, and in buildings and equipment, provides the physical planner with an important datum in his land use work and in his capital budgeting, via tax revenue potential.

An approach which complements local activity refinement applies segregation to the export market phase of the economy. The most frequently encountered example is one which classifies the export market according to *private* purchasers, *government* purchasers, and *institutional* purchasers. Measure is, again,

[12] The matrix approach will be described at a later point in this section.

[13] Charles M. Tiebout, THE COMMUNITY ECONOMIC BASE STUDY (New York: Committee for Economic Development, 1962).

generally by an employment allocation based on sales distribution. Using the same SIC as in the preceding example the classification form would look like the line below. This type of market classification is meaningful only in those instances where export income from government and institutions is of significant size. This is *not* likely to be the case in a very large number of cities.

	Total	*Export*				*Local*
		Total	*Private*	*Govt.*	*Inst.*	
SIC 20	300	200	150	40	10	100

One classification approach which has special significance for the urban planning process is based on physical movement of goods, services, consumers, and employees. This classification can be applied to both the export and the local side of the economy by SIC group at the two- or three-digit level. Let us start this brief description with the *consumers*.

There are a great many activities or establishments within a community which transact business with customers who come to them. Such activities are a typical and familiar part of the local market portion of the economy.

This distinction is, however, more variable and has a more significant feed-back effect on the export side of the ledger. For example, the student "customers" of a large university are likely to come from outside the economic limits of the community and as a consequence bring in, and expend, disposable income that is equivalent to a community export. In the course of their stay at a university, over the period of a school year, they purchase goods and services from the community. The number of firms, or activities, that are significantly dependent on this source of trade, or are influenced by it (as government services), is usually a function of the university's size and operating policy. Medical centers, army bases, recreational centers all exercise this consumer multiplier effect on an urban economy in varying degrees. The multiplier impact on income, employment, and ultimately population, will be influenced primarily by the time duration of consumer contact and its purpose.[14]

[14] When duration of consumer stay is long, the possibility of the consumer entering the labor force on at least a part-time basis increases. Such a condition is likely to influence total employment projections and economic development policy.

Table 4–2

Consumer Movement to Major Industry Groups by Consumer Origin and Time Stay as a Per Cent of Sales, 19__

Major Industry Groups	Total* 1–2–3	Consumer Origin and Time Stay				
		Local 1–2–3	Trade Area 1–2–3	State 1–2–3	Region(s) 1–2–3	Foreign 1–2–3
Retail (SIC 52).......94– 6– 0%		70–0–0%	22–0–0%	2–5–0%	0–1–0%	0–0–0%
Recreation (SIC 79).......20–70–10%						
Medical (SIC 80).......50–30–20%						
Education (SIC 82).......70– 0–30%						
Total (weighted average)†.....40–30–30%						

* *Time-Stay Key:*
    1—Under 1 Day
    2—Under 1 Week
    3—Over 1 Month

† Note that values add across the table but not vertically. The footing total is, therefore, not a sum but a weighted average.

Income levels of consumers are an important additional variable, but are likely to vary from function to function and city to city. The shorter the time stay and, therefore, the more frequent the turnover of consumers, the more important for the planner is the mode of movement used by the consumer. In the event that the time duration of stay is very long, as with the university student, the greater the chance that the travel mode of arrival and departure will differ from that used within the community. The most pertinent data surrounding consumer origin and time stay could be organized as shown in Table 4–2, with Retail (SIC 52) as the example.[15] These data can then be extended to include the mode of consumer movement. No attempt is made to show mode in this table because of space limitations, and the fact that

there tends to be more than one consumer mode per type of origin. The data for this table are not available from published sources. Local survey sampling by means of questionnaires and interviews would be required, as in most detailed aspects of urban economic analysis.

Goods movement and, to a lesser extent, services movement, from producer to distributor and consumer, represent another highly significant part of the economic classification of urban movement patterns. Service movement is played down in this discussion, partly because of the heavy dominance of goods movement, and partly because of the fact that a great many service movements occur via communication systems such as the mails and telephone. Consequently, although major service groups are included in demonstration Table 4–3, they are not likely to show many or very significant entries. Nonetheless in some community situations they could be of greater importance and should therefore always be considered. The

---

[15] Table 4–2 by breaking down "origin" not only makes the distinction between export and local but refines the external geographic source of income represented by consumers who purchase in person.

Table 4–3

Goods and Services Movements of Major Economic Groups, 19__ by Origin of Purchases and Destination of Sales, Classified by Dominant Movement Mode*
(proportion of Total $ Transactions)†

Purchases / Sales	(A) Local 20	22	52	80	82	X	Total Sales	(B) Trade Area	(C) State	(D) Region	(E) Region Other	(F) Foreign	Total Sales
(A) Local													
(20) Food........ 5T	20T		5T			(30)		5T	40T	20R	5R	...	100
(22) Textiles...... ...													
(52) Retail....... ...													
(80) Medical...... ...													
(82) Education.... ...													
(X) Households... ...													
Total local purchases......... (5)							Total sales B – F	...	...	...	...	...	100
(B) Trade area........ 30T													
(C) State........... 40T													
(D) Region.......... 25R													
(E) Regions (other).... ...													
(F) Foreign......... ...													
Total purchases ... 100													

* Movement mode key:
   T—Truck   AR—Air   C—Private Car
   R—Rail   W —Water   P—Pipeline
† Proportions may be applied to other measures such as employment or units of input and output.

goods and service movement analysis table is designed in matrix form. The matrix can be considered two-dimensional, in that it shows purchase and sale interaction by economic activity group, including a household sample, and by geographic origin and destination. As with consumer movement analysis these movements may be further refined by movement mode. Food product processing (SIC 20) is used as an example in Table 4–3 to show the manner in which gross purchases and sales might be distributed. It should be kept in mind that in this table Households operate only as a purchasing group. Households, in fact, *sell* the labor service of their principal wage earner. Therefore, it is possible to include such sales activity in the table.

Employment movement classification is sketched in Table 4–4. A geographic interaction matrix is used. Individual matrices are set up for each major economic activity group with the exception of households which, of course, represent the labor supply source. Once again the demonstration group food products processing is used to show how a hypothetical distribution might appear. Insertion of movement mode can be made, as in Table 4–3, if this refinement is desired. It may be clear to the reader that the form of classification shown could be used at an earlier stage in order to delineate the appropriate economic community or study area. In the case of small cities, for example, the county may often be too large to present a realistic reflection of the commutation area. In

such cases a shift to the township basis is advisable. However, the analyst must keep in mind that use of the township will complicate his economic data collection procedures later on, particularly when such data are taken from census reports. This is due to the fact that census report economic data are not refined below the county level for unincorporated civil districts. Commutation classification into many separate major group patterns, while it may appear to be an overly complex process, can and should be consolidated into a master table of total commutation movements.

In concluding this general discussion of functional classification, the idea must be re-stressed that, with the exception of the broad distinction between export and local market activity, classification depends entirely upon the objectives, abilities, and budget of the analyst. Data problems, of various kinds, are so universal that they are usually taken as a "given." Inasmuch as the emphasis of this publication is city and metropolitan physical planning, a few additional classification topics should at least be mentioned.

Land Use by Area. While the major economic groups of an urban community would be designated by map and table, such results are usually too gross in any meaningful land use study. Land use classification may, too often, break manufacturing into broad classes such as "light" and "heavy." But little attempt, if any, is usually made to classify the broad groups by SIC so that the *kind* of activity and,

Table 4–4

Commutation Area Employee Movement by Origin and Destination for Industry Group SIC 20, Food Products, 19___

Employee Movement From/To	Total	Central County	Peripheral County A	Peripheral County B	Peripheral County C
Central county (or city)	60	50	5	5	. . .
Peripheral county A (or township)	17	12	5	. . .	. . .
Peripheral county B (or township)	12	10	. . .	2	. . .
Peripheral county C (or township)	11	10	1	. . .	. . .
Total	100	82	11	7	. . .

therefore, its land requirements, in a more specific sense, become evident. Moreover, it is important for the physical planner to have his economic activity area data in a form which will report floor area, loading area, parking area, exterior storage area, and the like. It is quite feasible to think in terms of obtaining such detail, since items pertaining to inventory and space data need only be added to a questionnaire or to the duties of a survey team at each establishment address.

Personal and Corporate Income. Each of the forms used here should, for best planning results, be classified by SIC. Personal income can be aggregated under SIC according to information available through annual payrolls.[16] Where either record systems or interview systems allow a broad-scale frequency distribution of wage and salary, totals can be added to the classification. Corporate income data by SIC should, for maximum utility, be subclassified by gross and net before tax. The former is usually difficult to obtain, but the latter is available on a total corporate basis[17] from public records in states with a state corporation income tax.

IDENTIFICATION

Studies of an urban economy which use the economic base technique must contend with the step of identification. Identification involves the distinction of export market from local market activity and in some cases from auxiliary activities. On first consideration this may seem to be a relatively simple procedure, which it is in principle. Difficulties arise, however, because of the fact that reliance is placed for this purpose on published records, usually those of the U.S. Census. The Census presents SIC data in employment term totals by metropolitan area and county. The question is, how shall these employees be divided among the export, local, and auxiliary classifications of the *local* economy? If the physical establishments which compose the total economy mar-

keted their goods and services exclusively to *one* of the three classifications mentioned, there would not be a very great problem in identifying the market destination pattern. For a few activities in most urban areas this is the case. The activities are, as a rule, well known and easily distinguished by the layman. However, for most activities, the majority of economic establishments will have mixed markets, usually with varying strength in the three directions. There are a few generally recognized convenient techniques for segregating aggregated SIC employment data into at least export and local form. All these techniques are very crude in their results. Unless the economic analyst is working under the most spartan of time schedules and dollar budgets he would be advised to avoid them. These identification shortcuts are briefly described here with an explicit caveat, "Use in emergency only!"[18]

Oldest, and also lowest in reliability, is the *assumption* method. A simple and deadly type of commonsense pervades the method, which operates on the assumption that broad economic sectors or divisions such as manufacturing, wholesaling, and mining are invariably export in nature; whereas retailing, government, education, and services are invariably oriented toward the local market. No attempt is made to examine major groups within the divisions; no recognition is given to the fact that any one economic division can have major groups that are *either* export or local. Auxiliary operations are given no recognition.

Location quotients have greater respectability, but very little, if any more, reliability than the assumption method. In brief, identification by location quotients works on an assumption that there is uniformity of demand patterns nationally. Specifically, it argues that if a certain industry group in a city claims a greater percentage of the local labor force than its counterpart does at the national level of the nation's labor force, the excess is assignable to the export sector. Therefore, if a city's labor force is 50,000 and its SIC 20 (food products)

---

[16] This classification is not intended to reflect all sources of personal income within a community, only locally earned wages and salaries.

[17] State income tax records show *total* corporate status or total state share status and cannot, therefore, always pinpoint the earnings of a particular plant.

[18] A concise but lengthier treatment than given here of "indirect measures" of the economic base is given by Charles M. Tiebout in his THE COMMUNITY ECONOMIC BASE STUDY, pp. 46–50.

claims 10 per cent or 5,000 of the force, and if at the national level SIC 20 claims only 5 per cent of the force, then the excess 5 per cent at the city level, or 2,500 employees, is assignable to the export sector. It is assumed that the other 2,500 employees or the other 5 per cent of sales (whichever measure is used) can be equated with local demand.[19] If the local percentage is less than the national, it is then assumed that no exporting occurs and that all activity is local. The deficiency is made up in a trade balance sense by importing. Thus, industry by industry, at three-digit levels in many cases, it is possible to compute the division of activity in the city. The divisions can then be summed to produce a total community breakdown between export and local market activity. No attempt is made here to identify auxiliary operations separately, although these may be assumed in cases of industries that show a strong export quotient, but are known to make all or a heavy proportion of their sales locally. However, this latter fact cannot be determined from the quotient alone. Weaknesses of the method include the assumption of uniform demand, disregard of variability in productivity, and the problems of product mix. Product mix difficulties arise in connection with the digit level used; two digits (SIC 20) may show no exports whereas SIC 2024 may show heavy exports in a specific community. Some of these weaknesses may be partially compensated by determination of local tastes and productivity. But if this is done the advantages of speed and convenience gained by use of the quotient are practically eliminated. In short, this method of identification has important flaws.

A third, well-recognized technique of identification, which is similar to the location quotient method, is the *minimum requirements* technique. In this procedure, the community under study is compared to a large number of other communities which are similar to it. For each community, computation is made of the percentage share which each economic activity claims of the community's total labor force. Comparisons can then be made of identical activities among the universe of communities. Inspection of such across-the-board comparisons reveals the high and low percentage shares. The technique assumes that the *lowest* percentage share of an activity type indicates the hard core of local demand for that particular good or service, in other words the minimum *local* requirement. This minimum then serves as the benchmark for determining the degree of excess which is assumed to be export oriented employment. The process is repeated for each economic activity in the spectrum of comparison communities. Summation in employment terms of the minimums and excesses, industry by industry, will produce the total export-local identification desired for the study community. The crudities of this technique are probably apparent. There are some compensating devices which can be traced in the Tiebout reference. The method is no better than the preceding ones, and should be avoided.

Reliability in export-local-auxiliary share identification for one point in time can be approached only by direct investigation of the local situation. This is best accomplished by a combination of questionnaire and personal interview. Small cities have been the typical users of the direct technique while large cities tend to use the derivative, indirect devices outlined above. Differences in approach reflect, in the main, personnel and budget constraints in relation to observations to be made. Little has been attempted, so far, in the application of structured sampling to the larger metropolitan economies. In addition to the apparent fact that greater precision of identification is possible by direct contact with a firm within an activity group, is the associated fact that additional data may also be obtained which will make possible a more elaborate and meaningful classification. Ultimate projection of total industry group activity will also gain in precision by means of the interpretation of trends and plans of the constituent parts of the econ-

---

[19] Tiebout presents a formula for the location quotient computation which is as follows:

$$\frac{X}{\text{Total Local Employment}} = \frac{\text{National Employment in Industry}}{\text{Total National Employment}}$$

X represents the major industry group that is being locally identified or split. Another way of computing the quotient is to divide the smaller area percentage (10%) by the larger area (5%) which produces a quotient of 2 or double the nationally uniform level of 1.

omy provided by executives. Direct identification is accompanied by some significant difficulties aside from expense, personnel, and time problems.

The most prominent of these difficulties is associated with the construction of questionnaires and interview techniques that can meet the highly variable situations encountered in these urban economies that are complex in their makeup. Problems resulting from uneven or inadequate questionnaire and interview response are to be expected. Because of the natural disinclination or inability of most respondents to provide absolute data on sales or income, they must render many of their answers in estimated proportions, i.e., percentage of total sales made to trade area, to local industries, to purchasers in the state and so on. These proportions applied to employment (which is much more willingly reported) [20] will give the desired identification of export, local, and auxiliary classes. However, the proportions *are* estimates more frequently arrived at after a moment's thought, and less frequently from records. Part of the difficulty is that the geographic division of sales asked for may be completely new and strange to the respondent. With knowledge that no easy cross-checks are available, willful distortion of estimates is probably high in some industry categories. The partial counter-balance of such distortions by occasional estimates in an opposite direction does not guarantee a smooth averaging-out effect.

The closely associated procedures within the economic base method of identification and classification, both suffer from common difficulties of data availability, and the cost in time and money of industry group contact. Students of the economic base, and planners, have for many years considered universal coverage of an urban economy and precise identification of the major parts of the economy an indispensable requirement of good results. There can be little doubt that these are proper objectives. However, the work that must be invested to

implement these procedural goals has all too often either completely discouraged the initiation of economic base studies, or encouraged the use of shortcuts that have seriously undermined the reliability of the results.

With these problems in mind another type of shortcut, of considerable promise, has been offered in recent years called the *dominants* method. The dominants method is, essentially, a specialized direct sampling approach to the processes of identification, industry analysis, and projection. The "sampling" method, if it can be so called technically, extracts from the context of a total urban economy those industrial groups, preferably of the three-digit and higher variety, which dominate the economy. Dominance is an individually determined concept. In general, dominant industries are those which account for the majority of employment within a community. Other measures of dominance will, however, be discussed shortly. Dominant industrial groups of the economy are then classified by their degree of class tendency. For example, if the dairy products manufacture group, SIC 202, were considered to be dominant in a particular economy, and if this group exported 80 per cent or more of its output or sales, it would, in total, be classified as an export segment of the economy. In this case it would be designated "Export: Heavy," meaning strongly oriented to the export side. If SIC 202 had exported between 55 and 75 per cent of its output, the designation would have been "Export: Light." Any dominant, with less than 55 per cent of its output exported, is considered a marginal exporter, and classifiable with the local market side of the economy. On the local market side a similar "light," "heavy" breakdown is observed. Hospitals, SIC 806, may show in a specific community sales that are 60 per cent within the local market. The group would be designated "Local: Light." Auxiliary enterprises which are dominant are broken down in two directions, toward the export side, or toward the local market side, of the economy. Industries engaged in the manufacture of paperboard containers and boxes, SIC 265, may, for example, sell well over 50 per cent of their output to the local dairy products manufacturers, SIC 202. In such a

---

[20] A very heavy proportion of urban economic activities, by firm, regularly report their employment totals and averages for unemployment compensation records or other reporting systems.

Table 4–5

Dominant Industries Classified by Export Market, Local Market, and Auxiliary Market Tendency, 19___
(absolute employment measure)

Dominant Industry Group (SIC#)	Export		Local		Auxiliary		Dominant Employment Total
	(1) Heavy (75– 100%)	(2) Light (55– 75%)	(3) Light (45– 70%)	(4) Local (70– 100%)	(5) Export (50%+)	(6) Local (50%+)	
Dairy products (202)	700	...	...	...	...	...	700
Paper boxes (265)	...	...	...	...	100	...	100
Canning and preserving (203)	...	...	...	...	...	...	...
Department stores (531)	...	...	...	600	...	...	600
Hospitals (806)	...	...	350	...	...	...	350
Accounting services (893)	...	...	...	...	...	150	150
Market class Total	700	...	350	600	100	150	1900
Total community employment (estimated or on record)							2700
Dominants proportion of total employment							70%

case SIC 265 would be classified "Auxiliary: Export." If the dominant were SIC 893, accounting, auditing, and bookkeeping services, the orientation might be well over 50 per cent toward the local market, hence, "Auxiliary: Local." The tabular appearance of these relations is shown in Table 4–5. Summation for a total community identification of dominants can be deduced from such a table. The essential difference between this method of identification and classification, and the more traditional approach, is in the use of *tendency,* compared to precise splitting or allocation of sales and employment. An assumption of the dominants method which is important in analysis and projection work involves the economy segments classified in the column heads of Table 4–5. The essence of this assumption is that the more strongly a dominant segment (i.e., export, light [2]) is oriented in the direction of export markets, the more pervasive will be the effect of changes that occur in it over the rest of the economy. Conversely, the stronger the local market orientation, the less the potential for general change in community employment and income levels resulting from a change in the category. This assumption sets up, therefore, a

priority order of impact for change in the order 1, 2, 5, 3, 4, 6, according to the column number sequence of Table 4–5.

Determination of dominance for most favorable results should extend to more than one measure: employment expresses but one aspect of dominance. Where data and budget allow, dominance should be further determined by payroll volume, sales volume, plant investment, tax revenues returned, and similar factors. The guiding principles which permit the selection of a suitable aggregate level of dominance are found in (1) a "sample" which represents well over half of community economic activity, however measured, and (2) a range of major industry groups that is sufficiently restricted to permit continuous depth study and frequent repetition of economy analysis. Studies using this method have worked well when applying a four per cent minimum total employment within a SIC, modified by other weights as described above. Auxiliaries are likely to be smaller than export and local classes and therefore can be subject to a much lower proportional level of dominance. For *preliminary* identification purposes, there is no problem in choosing the export and local dominants from published sources. There will, of course, exist problems of three-digit identification in smaller urban communities. However, the principal difficulty arises in connection with preliminary identification of auxiliaries. One logical approach of auxiliary identification is in connection with the interviewing of the preselected export and local dominants. In the course of interviews or the completion of questionnaires, the dominants identify their local purchase sources by industry type. Subsequent investigation of these purchase sources

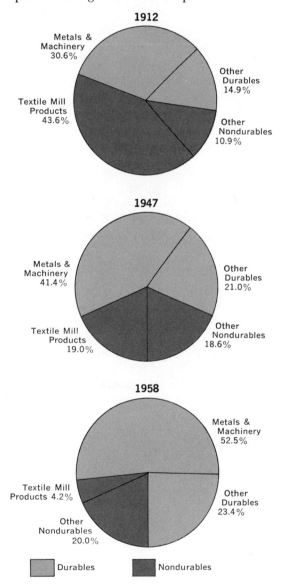

1912

Metals & Machinery 30.6%

Textile Mill Products 43.6%

Other Durables 14.9%

Other Nondurables 10.9%

1947

Metals & Machinery 41.4%

Other Durables 21.0%

Textile Mill Products 19.0%

Other Nondurables 18.6%

1958

Metals & Machinery 52.5%

Textile Mill Products 4.2%

Other Durables 23.4%

Other Nondurables 20.0%

Durables   Nondurables

FIGURE 4–1. *Distribution of manufacturing employment, Utica-Rome SMSA, 1912, 1947, 1958*

can determine whether or not they qualify for auxiliary and for dominant status (see classification matrix Table 4–3).

Analysis by the dominants method, therefore, creates certain advantages that are of great importance in effective community economy analysis. The most important of these advantages is the depth of research into the structure of industrial groups that is made possible. The principal consequences of depth research are improved understanding, and more reliable projections. The feasibility of continuing depth research and the synthesis of this research into frequent reanalysis and reprojection of the economy is also enhanced. Finally, the adaptability of most of the classification techniques, described earlier, to the dominants system, is of no small importance. Less than full coverage of an economy will quite naturally result in some shortcomings for the planning process. The most significant of these shortcomings is, probably, curtailment of an effective base for land use projection for the nondominant portions of the economy. There is also the difficulty of projecting an employment or income total from a selective base.[21]

MEASURE

The question of how the parts of an urban economy are to be measured has been discussed both directly, and by implication, in the materials covered up to this point. As a consequence the following statements will be by way of explaining the reasons for choosing the measures thus far used, and for omitting others.

Examples presented in this chapter have almost exclusively been focused on *sales* and *employment*. The justification for use of these measures is based, in part, on the tedious but real constraint of availability of data. This is not to say that dollar sales by major income group are easily come by, for they are not. But it does mean that most respondents will give an estimated geographic and functional breakdown of sales, as well as purchases. Manage-

[21] For additional comment on the dominants method see R. B. Andrews, "Urban Economics: An Appraisal of Progress," LAND ECONOMICS, XXXVII (August, 1961), pp. 219–27. Also refer to Andrews, "Economic Planning for Small Areas: An Analytical System," LAND ECONOMICS, XXXIX (May, 1963), pp. 143–55.

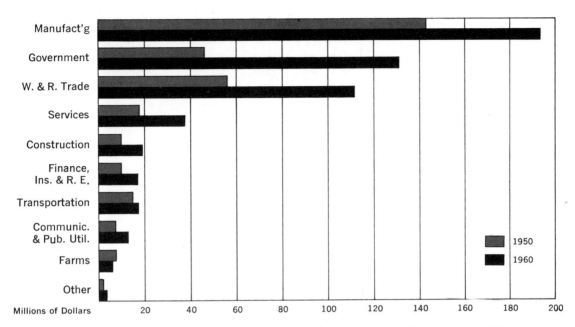

FIGURE 4–2. *Personal income from wages and salaries by major employment group, Utica-Rome SMSA, 1950 and 1960*

ment is also inclined to give out current employment information. Such information in less current form is available from public records and government publications. Another reason for using these two measures is that the sales estimates can be applied in their geographic proportional form to employment, for the purposes of quantifying these proportions, and establishing structural identification. Thus 25 per cent of sales derived from exports would be convertible for a major industry group into 25 per cent of current employment that is export-oriented. Successive industrial group conversions to employment can then be summed to arrive at a total community identification of export, local, and auxiliary. Employment has additional significance as a measure, in that it has a very direct relation to the family unit, several types of land uses, total population, marriage rates, birth rates, and certain public expenditures. Consequently its importance for the planning function is patent. Difficulties in using employment as a measure are principally associated with rendering the count on a basis which will compensate for part-time and overtime work. This can be done

by computation of full-time equivalents. Seasonal fluctuations must also be converted to a median or typical level.

Payroll income is a useful supplementary measure to employment. When converted to a per capita or employee basis by industry group, it is an indicator of general employee welfare; in gross form it will give a rough idea of the comparative multiplier effect strength of industry groups on the rest of the community economy. However, payroll data are not freely available, and must be regularly adjusted for changes in the value of the dollar. Much the same may be said for business income which, at best, may be obtained only in net taxable form from state income tax returns. Even in this form, however, a very crude impression may be gained of the degree of change in business welfare. Where sales dollar data can be found, combining these with income data furnishes a further approximation of the conditions of business growth.

Physical production measures such as *units of output* and *tons shipped* are satisfactory supplementary measures for the types of economic activity to which they apply, but they are specialized, rather than general measures like employment. *Value-added,* which, essentially, is the difference between sales and the cost of materials and power purchased, is a measure which will give a picture of business income or productivity at the community level. However, if value-added is to be locally computed from state or even corporation returns, there is the problem of separating out a single local plant contribution to value-added, from a multi-plant report. Moreover value-added cannot be meaningfully applied to some service activities such as a university, public services, and similar elements.

Earlier, reference has been made to the process of weighting, which is of particular importance when the dominants method is used, but is a desirable refinement in every case. Where, for example, employment is the measure, the weighting of the employment with payroll, will produce a far more accurate picture of the

economic significance of an industrial group that the employment measure alone. For portions of a local economy that keep and make available standard business records, the combination or weighting of sales data with reported earnings, can give an even deeper perspective on economic welfare.

RATIOS

Economic base analysis depends upon a system of ratios that expresses not only the quantitative proportional relationships between the parts of an urban economy but also the relationships between these parts and the community's population. One of the principal objectives of classification and identification is to provide the data that will permit the establishment of these ratios. With a system of ratios available, the planner is in a better position to explain and forecast economic change and, by derivation, the changes that can be anticipated in the

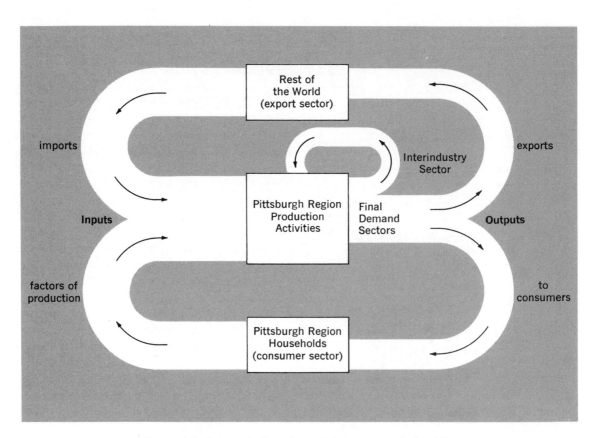

FIGURE 4–3. *Schematic flow chart of intersector relationships*

other community characteristics that are of professional interest to him. A typical set of ratios is shown below expressed in symbols and representative numbers.

$$B:LM :: 1:2$$
$$B:TE :: 1:3$$
$$LM:TE :: 2:3$$
$$TE:TP :: 1:2$$
$$B:TP :: 1:6$$
$$LM:TP :: 1:3$$

B = export market activity (base)
LM = local market activity
TE = total employment (B + LM)
TP = total community population

Auxiliary activities are not separately classified and identified in most applications of the base technique, and are, therefore, likely to be buried in the total LM factors in the ratios shown. However, when the auxiliaries are identified, their ratio positions to B, net LM,[22] and TE can be empirically computed in the same way that is used for deriving the other ratio positions. When conditions of change are injected into the ratio system via B, net LM, and the Auxiliaries, the multiplier effects can be computed in the absolute terms of such measures as employment.[23] When the dominants approach is used, the B and LM designations are modified with subscripts to show that they represent only a major portion of each element, i.e., B^D, net LM^D, $Ax^D(L)$, $Ax^D(B)$, TE^D. If in a particular community study *total* B, net LM and Ax have been identified, then the ratio system may be elaborated to include such additional ratio relations as $B^D:B$; net LM^D:net LM; $Ax^D(L):Ax(L)$; etc.

Ratios vary from community to community, and within the same community in response to variable conditions. Consequently, the analyst cannot assume constancy, which would be one of the most desirable virtues of a ratio system. This means, therefore, that the ratios must be used, particularly in relation to projection work, with this dynamism in mind. The series of simplified diagrams below is intended to

show some of the more important variables that are suspected of having an influence on the ratios. The diagrams are only partially successful in making their point and must, therefore, be tolerantly interpreted. They will be briefly described in terms of a single community although inter-city comparisons would be possible.

Diagram A (Figure 4–4) says that as a city grows the quantitative relation of B and LM reverse themselves over time.[24] Customarily the employee size of B is larger than LM in the early years, as with a trading center. As B, LM and the community grow in size, the change in local market scale alone makes possible types of retailing, service, and office operation that were not previously feasible. Diversity of population often accompanies population growth, and creates fields of taste and need that had not previously existed. Size also encourages the appearance of industries closely linked in the process of production. This latter factor biases the apparent growth rate and level of LM, which would be deflated somewhat if the third classification, auxiliary, were added to the diagram.[25] Ultimately LM size exceeds B, and then after continuing to outstrip it, is likely to stabilize in its ratio relation to the base.

In the environment of a dynamic regional or national economy, the two variables of city size and age are likely to be positively correlated. However, in order to separate out the effect of the one variable as against the other, Diagram B (Figure 4–4) assumes population as relatively constant. Relations of B and LM are likely to be much the same as in Diagram A. The principal difference between the two is that the population multiplier, employment (B in particular), is relatively constant. Although LM changes its position relative to B, it does so in far less dramatic fashion than in Diagram A, and therefore terminates at a much lower ratio. With virtually no growth in B, or in commu-

---

[22] Net LM means LM minus Auxiliaries which leaves household purchases.

[23] The use of TE in this example assumes employment as the measure. However, others may be used.

[24] Of necessity time and change in size must be considered together.

[25] Not much is known of the action pattern of auxiliaries in the context of the diagrams used here. However when *size* is the variable it is likely that the origin point of auxiliaries would be the lowest of the three, might climb as steeply as LM but terminate well below B and LM.

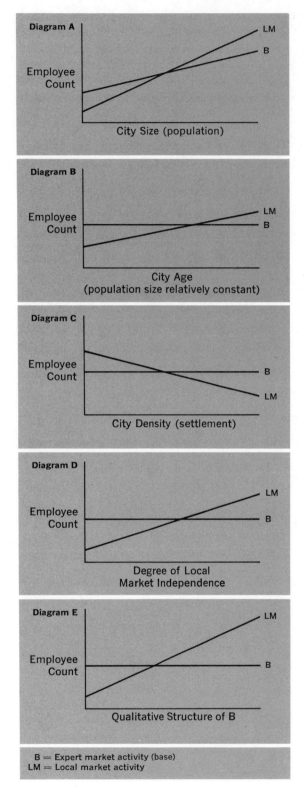

Diagram A

Employee Count

City Size (population)

LM
B

Diagram B

Employee Count

City Age
(population size relatively constant)

LM
B

Diagram C

Employee Count

City Density (settlement)

B
LM

Diagram D

Employee Count

Degree of Local
Market Independence

LM
B

Diagram E

Employee Count

Qualitative Structure of B

LM
B

B = Expert market activity (base)
LM = Local market activity

FIGURE 4–4. *Effect of specific variables on the quantitative relation of base to local market activity*

nity population, independent growth in LM is dependent on influences from outside the community. These exogenous influences include, for example, secular increases in real wages and salaries as a result of federal legislation, union action, industrial productivity, or regional competition for labor. As the community ages, savings accumulate in both local and outside investments with returns on these investments supplementing the rising wage and salary flow. To the flow, is added the actual and released cash of expanding governmental transfer payments (social security, unemployment compensation), plus private pension funds and other accumulating fringe benefits. When all these factors are joined with a proliferating taste for more and better goods and services on the part of community residents, it is little wonder that the LM portion of a local economy should show independent growth tendencies in spite of a relatively stable base and population.

Density of settlement is the variable shown in Diagram C (Figure 4–4). The general argument is that as density of settlement increases, population size remaining constant, fewer employees and fewer square feet of floor space are required for LM activities. Justification for this view rests principally on accessibility. B is generally considered to be unresponsive in size terms to changes in density, although it is, of course, responsive in an internal *locational* sense to these changes.

In Diagram D (Figure 4–4) the rough relationship of B to LM is shown when the variable factor is the degree of independence of the local market; that is the degree of freedom from direct competition with another local market. For example, a metropolitan area is considered to be semi-monopolistic in the sense that competition from other community LM's for the dollars of its residents is virtually absent.[26] At the other extreme is the case of the dormitory suburb within a metropolitan area. Here the base is likely to be largely represented by the services exported through daily commutation of the employed residents to the central core, or

[26] There exists, of course, variance in the degree of metropolitan monopoly depending on size, location, and complexity of the particular LM.

satellite communities within the metropolitan area. Local market activities, on the other hand, are certain to be thinly represented. A small LM sector is the consequence of superior competition from the central city and its major satellites, plus the built-in tendency for commuters to make many purchases near, or enroute to and from, their places of work.

In conclusion, Diagram E (Figure 4–4) pictures the influence of the B–LM ratio of qualitative differences in the structure of B. The fact of differences or changes in base structure between cities and within the same city over time are well known. The quantitative and qualitative impact of these changes on LM is not as easily distinguished. However, enough observations have been made to indicate that as the principal emphasis of structure in B moves in time or space along a continuum from primary type activities (extraction, agriculture, fisheries) to secondary (manufacturing), to tertiary (goods, sales, and services), to quartiary (research and administration) the response of LM will be strongly positive. The reasons for this tendency are to be found in the increasingly diverse social pattern that evolves over the continuum, in the greater real per capita income available, and in the wider range of tastes that require satisfaction.

The reader of the diagram descriptions must keep in mind that they are only abstractions from reality, and are not completely verified. Moreover, any one city represents a combination of all these factors in movement. This condition alone may suggest the difficulty of forecasting ratio relationships. The dominants method tends to diminish this problem appreciably.

A fundamental assumption of the system of ratios used in the economic base method is that there is a high degree of constancy in the ratios of any one community. Deviations from these ratios are short-run in duration; the ratio elements tend, in the longer run, to return to their original levels. Thus the ratio of B to LM in a particular case may be 1:2; B expands as a result of new plant construction and extensive hiring; the employment ratio of B to LM consequently shifts to 1:1 (other ratios in which B plays a part also change); multiplier effects

begin to operate which in the long-run raise the absolute level of LM to the original 1:2 ratio with B.[27] Other ratio elements, particularly population, also respond to this change. The shift can, of course, be positive or negative. Reliance on the assumption of ratio constancy is a great aid in prediction and projection. There appears to be some validity in this assumption for certain spans of a city's economic history. Review of the generalized diagrams reveals, however, some of the variables that are at work in all urban environments. Consequently, the duration of a particular "normal" ratio relation and the imminence of a relatively lasting change in it are not easily determined, except by continuous depth analysis. A similar ratio problem which, though difficult, can be solved is that of determining what the *normal* ratio relation actually is. Trend analysis provides the answer, but involves a contingent problem of several successive identifications. These back identifications of B and LM can be expensive in the absence of reliable shortcuts and available records.

PROJECTIONS

In simplest terms, the process of projection associated with the economic base technique relies on an aggregated projection of the various parts of the export economy, which is then used as a multiplier, guided by observed ratios to derive future local market activity, total employment, and total population. Auxiliary activities may, of course, also be included in this ratio and projection sequence. For example, assume the present observed ratio of the urban economy is as follows:

$$B:LM :: 1:1\frac{1}{2} \ (1,000: 1,500 \ \text{employees})$$
$$B:TE :: 1:2\frac{1}{2} \ (1,000: 2,500 \ \text{employees})$$
$$TE:TP :: 1:2 \ (2,500 \ \text{employees}: 5,000 \ \text{persons})$$
$$B:TP :: 1:5 \ (1,000 \ \text{employees}: 5,000 \ \text{persons})$$

Analysis of B indicates a decade increase to 1,500 employees. Application of the ratios shows that at the end of ten years LM will have 2,250 employees. Total employment in the community will be 3,750 and total population

[27] It is not unusual for LM on the upswing to overcompensate the "normal" ratio level but it soon adjusts back to normal.

Table 4–6

Employment Patterns, Evansville SMSA, 1950–1963
Annual Averages (in thousands)

Year	Total Employment	Total Mfg.	Manufacturing Durables	Manufacturing Non-Dur.	Non-Mfg.[1]	All Other Non-Agric.[2]	All Other Agric.[3]
1950	75.9	32.3	23.8	8.5	35.6	6.7	1.3
1951	77.6	33.3	24.4	8.9	36.4	6.7	1.3
1952	83.6	38.7	29.7	9.0	36.8	6.7	1.3
March 1953	97.5	51.4	41.7	9.7	38.1	6.7	1.3
1953	91.4	44.7	35.1	9.6	38.7	6.7	1.3
1954	80.2	33.6	24.5	9.1	38.6	6.7	1.3
1955	85.5	34.1	25.3	8.8	39.5	8.0	3.7
1956	81.7	30.1	21.2	8.9	39.9	8.0	3.7
1957	82.6	31.2	22.2	9.0	39.7	8.0	3.7
1958	74.9	26.3	15.3	9.0	38.3	7.7	2.7
1959	73.6	25.0	16.1	8.9	38.6	7.6	2.5
1960	72.4	23.8	14.6	9.2	38.9	7.3	2.4
1961	71.9	23.1	13.8	9.2	39.3	7.3	2.3
1962	73.3	24.2	14.7	9.5	40.0	7.3	1.8
July 1963	75.7	25.9	16.5	9.4	40.5	7.3	2.0

[1] Wage and salary workers employed in mining, construction, wholesale and retail trade, utilities, finance, insurance, real estate, service, government, and others.

[2] Self-employed, domestics, and unpaid family workers.

[3] The erratic movements in this column are primarily a result of changing coverage and definition.

Source: Compiled from data supplied by the Indiana Employment Security Division and the U.S. Department of Labor.

about 7,500 persons. A decline in B would bring forth a similar but reversed multiplier effect.

This simplified view of the projection process must be subjected to numerous refinements before it is put in final form. Some of the qualifications relating to the ratio system have already been discussed. The most prominent of these is the general set of variable conditions that are constantly at work altering some of the ratios; i.e., community age, size, location, density, and base composition. Trend analysis represents the best technique for detecting the nature and direction of movement of these variables.[28] If trend analysis is not possible, for data or budgetary reasons, cruder and more informal means must be used to derive the

answers, and adjust the ratios, for the projection year. Note must also be taken of conditions of semi-independent growth in local market and auxiliary activities, which will alter ratios and therefore influence projections. Inasmuch as population projections are derived, in this system, from their relation to employment, they should be refined and tested in at least two ways. Demographic analysis, described in Chapter 3, provides one of these tests. Qualitative application of the base and local market projections to the gross population figure is the other refinement. This latter procedure refers to the impact of changes in B, net LM and AUX on occupational distribution, age structure, family count, income, and similar factors. As this discussion of projection refinement may make clear, the word "projection," which often suggests mechanical extrapolation, does not quite describe what goes on. "Calculated forecasting" is a more accurate term.

---

[28] Regression analysis is not advisable in this situation because of the dearth and irregularity of observations as well as the presence of non-quantifiable variables.

Table 4–7

Estimated 1985 Population and Labor Force of Kalamazoo County

Item	Number of Persons			
	Total	Male	Female	% Female
Total population	435,000	207,600	227,400	52.3
Population 14 years old and over	274,200	126,400	147,800	53.9
Labor force	156,300	97,200	59,100	37.8
Employed	150,000	92,300	57,700	38.5
Unemployed	6,300	4,900	1,400	22.2
% of labor force	4.0	5.0	2.4	
Not in the labor force	117,900	29,200	88,700	75.2
Population under 14 years of age	160,800	81,200	79,600	49.5

Source: Estimates of the Institute of Urban Life based upon 1950–60 labor force and population trends in Kalamazoo County; 1960–1985 labor force and population trends for the East North Central Region and United States estimated by the National Planning Association.

Conversion of gross employment and population forecasts into forms necessary for land use projection work is also highly dependent on the approaches in refining details as listed above. In order to determine acreage or square foot allocations by land use category, each of the main elements of the economy (B, net LM, AUX) must be reclassified on a land use basis and then expressed in the physical measurement unit used, i.e., square feet per employee, or acres per 100 employees. Forecasts of employment change can then be converted to forecasts of space need, subject, of course, to refinement based on such factors as the changing technology of production, the effects of excess plant, and local locational selection limitations.[29]

Use of the dominants method of economic base analysis, in general, reduces the complexity of projection refinement. There are, however, a few drawbacks to use of the method at the projection stage. One of these drawbacks is the simple fact that total employment is projected from a thinner volume of observations. Therefore, error tendencies will be magnified as the projection period is extended. Such error will be magnified again when the labor force

participation rate is computed and projected, and then used for population estimating purposes. Direct projection of population from the dominant base is also risky, unless a long series of observations of this relationship is available. Finally, land use projection would be incomplete in that only use projections based on the selected dominants could be computed. The significance of incompletion would, of course, depend on the proportion of the total economy accounted for by the dominants and on the qualitative range of the economic uses omitted.

Limitations of Economic Base Technique

The economic base technique is a device which is very far from perfection, both in conception and in application. Division of a complex piece of urban economic machinery into two, and at most, three parts, for purposes of description and analysis, is rightfully considered an oversimplification likely to produce crude and inaccurate results. It is, therefore, fair to say that the main burden of criticism is on the broad-gauged crudity of the method, although results that can truly be called accurate are still the unattained goal of the other known methods as well. While sub-classification and matrix-type arrangement of data can lessen the crudity, they can by no means eliminate it. It is difficult if not impossible, in the more typical applica-

[29] The economic base technique does not provide answers on internal locational allocation although some researchers have attempted to so adapt it. See Norbert Stefaniak, "A Refinement of Haig's Theory," LAND ECONOMICS, XXXIX (November, 1963), pp. 429–33.

tions of the method, to obtain a picture of the detailed interactions of all parts of the economy with one another. The feedback effects of these interactions represent the true meaning of change for the economy when it occurs. It is, moreover, with the highly complex patterns of change and their impacts, that the urban planner should be most concerned. He will not obtain a view of these patterns in their full flower from the base technique.

In addition, economic base analysis by its fundamental theoretical stress on exports, and secondarily on internal transactions, ignores almost completely the import side of the economy. For a method which leans so heavily on an analogy to international trade, this is a strange and serious omission. Avoidance of imports in the analysis leaves the observer in the dark concerning the net economic effect of change. Therefore, what may appear in any one instance to be an economic gain to a city may actually be a loss or a stalemate. Lack of import analysis can also conceal serious diseconomics and trade inefficiencies. Matters such as these should be particularly disturbing to the planner.

The problems of the analyst in attempting to make a sharp distinction between exports and local activity have been discussed earlier. Two of these will be mentioned here. First, there are within the economy businesses that are actually indirect exporters, but which by crude classification are labeled "local." While an auxiliary classification may reduce this vagueness, it still leaves a substantial twilight zone. The second general problem involves proportional distribution (base, local) of a firm's activity. This is usually an estimated division. The chance for error here is sizeable. Moreover, the distribution in percentage terms is, in some cases, likely to be highly fluid, possibly reversing the B–LM relation.

Employment is the commonest, though not the only measure of economic activity used by the base technique. The inability of employment alone to indicate business strength · or welfare in productivity terms is self-evident. Yet productivity is one of the most important facts which both economist and planner need to know about a particular activity. It is no solace

to remember that all techniques have trouble with the question of productivity at the urban level.

One other defect which deserves special mention is the difficulty encountered in determining *normal* ratio relationships. Without a fair idea of the normal, the analyst is unable to determine where an economy stands in the short run, and where it is headed in the long run. Secular shift of the normal complicates this determination and, in the opinion of some critics, seriously calls into question the meaning and utility of the ratios for predictive purposes.

Other Theories and Techniques

Within the past fifteen years, several other theories and techniques have been introduced which have varying suitability for urban economic analysis. However, unlike the economic base technique, not one of them was originally designed for urban analysis conditions. Nonetheless some of these other approaches show great potential, if not immediate applicability, for urban planning purposes.

In the paragraphs that follow, only the briefest of descriptions and evaluations for each of the most prominent methods is presented. The reader is urged to examine the concepts in more complete form in the references provided.

INPUT-OUTPUT[30]

Designed for the analysis of national economies, the input-output technique employs an industry interaction model which appears in the form of a multi-sector or industrial matrix. Input-output theory is simple and eminently

[30] Walter Isard, METHODS OF REGIONAL ANALYSIS (New York: The Technology Press of M.I.T. and John Wiley and Sons, Inc., 1960) . See Chapter 8, Interregional and Regional Input-Output Techniques, written by John H. Cumberland.

A clearly-stated, well-written exposition of the input-output method as applied to a major metropolitan area is to be found in REGION WITH A FUTURE, Vol. 3 of Economic Study of the Pittsburgh Region by Pittsburgh Regional Planning Association (University of Pittsburgh Press, 1963) . See Chapter 6, The Future Economic Structure of the Region.

sound; it says that an understanding of the structure of a particular economy is dependent on a complete picture of the sources of purchases procured, and the destination of sales of goods and services produced, for each of the sectors or parts of an economy. This portrait of economic interdependence is of particular value in predicting the ramifications of change within an economy. When change is expected in one or many sectors, so goes the theory, the purchase-sale allocations or proportions observed at one point in time, the "bench-mark," will prevail. The impact of the expected change in the one or more sectors is traced through the entire economy by a multiplier process known as iteration. Input-output invariably uses a dollar measure of purchases and sales. It is possible to convert the dollars to employment by the establishment of ratios.

Conceptually, input-output is the most comprehensive and refined of any of the broad-scale methods that have been adapted to the analysis of urban economies. Its system of identification of interconnections of all parts of an economy is almost flawless; its mathematical procedures for tracing the impact of change through the complicated twists and turns of a large economy is impressive. The fact that input-output has not been more widely applied to urban situations is traceable to a few critical shortcomings.

Although data problems present difficulties for all techniques, they are unusually serious for input-output. Sales data, on which the technique depends, are not freely available, and when available must be precisely classified by destination. Some industrial classifications, such as education, government and research, cannot always convert their revenue positions into a realistic sales equivalent.

Another problem is encountered with the coefficient, or multiplier system, used by input-output.[31] Theory requires that the coefficients be constants in order to have predictive value. But in reality, conditions of competition, changes in taste, technology, and economic structural shifts cause the coefficients to

change. The change is slow in some sectors, rapid in others. Thus the coefficient system of input-output can be said to have no more reliability than the economic base ratio system.

There is an apparent general tendency for input-output to increase in reliability and predictive force as its economic-geographic scope expands: at the national level it is claimed to be highly effective. "Degree of openness" is another way of describing this same situation.[32] At the national level the economy is considered relatively closed; at an urban community level relatively open. Population and employment size, as well as economic structure of the urban community, will also influence the degree of openness. For urban economic analysis, therefore, input-output is not too highly reliable because of the great degree of openness at this scale of the economy.

Despite these drawbacks the input-output technique is so effective in analysing the internal workings of any economy, that it has been adapted here, with variations, to the economic base approach. Its effect on ideas presented in this chapter will, no doubt, already have been noted.

INDUSTRIAL COMPLEX ANALYSIS[33]

Another respected approach to the analysis of an economy is represented by industrial complex analysis. As its name implies, it is not a comprehensive system like input-output or economic base analysis. Instead, this system is brought to bear on selected industrial complexes which are represented within a single nation or region. The term "complex" refers to

---

[31] Coefficients are derived from the percentage distribution factors of the sales of each sector, i.e., .05; .10; .04 up to a total of 1.00.

[32] The absolutely closed economy is one in which *all* purchases and sales occur *within* the economy; conversely an urban, or open economy, is one in which a heavy proportion of purchases and sales are made outside the economy. Hence an urban input-output matrix can explain only a part of the urban economic interaction system and is, of course, highly subject to economic determinants from the massive external economy of which it is a small part.

[33] Isard, *op. cit.*, see Chapter 9, Industrial Complex Analysis, prepared by W. Isard and Eugene W. Schooler.

For a detailed case study of this method see Walter Isard, Eugene W. Schooler and Thomas Vietorisz, INDUSTRIAL COMPLEX ANALYSIS AND REGIONAL DEVELOPMENT (New York: The Technology Press of M. I. T. and John Wiley and Sons, Inc., 1959).

the network of procurement, production, and marketing contacts involved in the creation of a single product, or series of closely related products, i.e., crude oil, gasoline, plastics. Although industrial complex analysis is most frequently applied on a regional and interregional basis, it has substantial potential for small region (metropolitan) analysis.

The basic purpose of complex analysis is that of determining the locational activity patterns of an industry group, with the intent of discovering the potentials for industrial development, not only for the whole pattern, but also for specific locational points within it. Clearly such a process also contributes to an understanding of the mechanics of industry group structure. Execution of this system is highly dependent on input-output techniques that determine interindustry and interactivity patterns measured in physical production terms such as barrels, pounds, tons, and btu's. The resulting interactivity matrix reveals degrees of interdependence of product and process. In essence, therefore, industrial complex analysis produces a broader and more highly integrated perspective than would be gained from a deeper comparative cost analysis on an industry-by-industry basis.

The shortcomings of the techniques are not numerous, but some are serious. Data, particularly in physical terms, may be difficult to obtain. Many times it must be filled out by engineering estimates. There is a substantial question, moreover, concerning the effectiveness of the system when applied to service industry complexes. Critics also indicate that this system lacks the depth of comparative cost analysis. Finally, the technique requires high execution skills that are not generally available. The fairest characterization of industrial complex analysis is that it is a valuable complement to other methods but that it is not expected to stand alone. For urban study purposes it appears to have greatest potential in connection with development, rather than with analysis operations.

INCOME AND SOCIAL ACCOUNTS

In the preparation of effective economic studies the urban planner must concern himself intimately with income—its volume, source, distribution, and trend. A special methodology for this purpose is called "income and social accounting." Based on the theories, definitions, and terminology of national income accounts, income and social accounting is usually rendered in major regional terms.[34] However, some experimentation has been conducted with urban regions.[35]

It is on the most notable of these urban area experiments that the following remarks will be focused. Leven, in his Elgin-Dundee metropolitan area study, employed three basic tables or double entry account forms: (1) a rest-of-the-world account, (2) a gross regional product account, and (3) an account of regional product and income measures. The system, like the economic base technique, places fairly heavy emphasis on the export relation to its rest-of-the-world account. This would, of course, be a must with any open economy such as a metropolitan area. However, this particular account, as with the second account—gross regional product—also includes import dollar volumes. By way of example, other significant components of this set of accounts include net receipts of interest, rent, dividends, and profits from abroad; excess of out-commuter wages over in-commuter wages; purchases of goods by local consumers; total disposable personal income of residents. The accounts can tell the planner many things, such as the position of metropolitan area money claims on the outside world versus claims against the area; the net position of the area relative to payments made to, and receipts from, state and federal governments; and resident regional income (gross and disposable) .

Weaknesses of the technique, aside from data problems, and very heavy reliance on esti-

[34] Ideally the construction of regional accounts will eventually enable, by summation, a more refined national income account total.

[35] Charles L. Leven, THEORY AND METHODS OF INCOME AND PRODUCT ACCOUNTS FOR METROPOLITAN AREAS, INCLUDING THE ELGIN-DUNDEE AREA AS A CASE STUDY (Ames, Iowa: Iowa State College, 1958) , mimeographed. A short discussion and evaluation of the method appears in Isard's METHODS OF REGIONAL ANALYSIS, Chapter 4, pp. 109–15. See also Werner Z. Hirsch (ed.), ELEMENTS OF REGIONAL ACCOUNTS (Baltimore: The Johns Hopkins Press, 1964) .

mating, are principally traceable to lack of wide experience with the technique. Too few applications of the approach have been made to metropolitan situations. Consequently there are many rough spots, thin spots, and gaps, that are waiting to be treated by the professional research economist. The practicing planner is advised to await the outcome of research now in progress, rather than experiment with this method on his own.

MATHEMATICAL MODELS[36]

For the urban and regional planner the applicability to economic studies of mathematical models is still open to question. The reason for this state of indecision is the same as that for income accounts, namely the largely experimental nature of the procedures being applied. Prominent among the mathematical approaches to economic analysis are linear programming and simulation. However, their major applications to date have been to regional and interregional situations.[37] Of the two approaches, linear programming is the more prominent at present. Linear programming has a strong developmental bias in that it is usually thought of as an optimizing technique aimed at identifying the most efficient management of a given set of resources and prices subject to a given technology. It is usually considered as less than a complete system, and can be applied to only those parts of

an economy where complete linearities of production supply and marketing linkages exist.[38] These are not normally present in an urban framework. Nevertheless, as in the case of industrial complex analysis, it is likely to be highly effective in the special situations to which it naturally applies. Stated somewhat differently, *linear programming* problems in planning are usually "mixing problems" that attempt to determine how given resources can be combined or "mixed" in order to produce a particular output or employment target most efficiently. The variables are expressed in mathematical symbols presented in linear equation form, i.e., $y = a + bx$.

Simulation is the term assigned to the experimental use of mathematical models for the purpose of determining the effects of certain changes in some variables, on the values of others. The commonest variable in this system is time. The purpose of the model application is to imitate, or simulate, a real life economic system in operation under varying assumptions and inputs, thus mathematically testing various economic planning approaches.

In conclusion it is worth while observing that not one of the analytic techniques examined in this chapter possesses the whole truth: all have significant defects; all suffer from data problems; all have *some* degree of utility for urban planners. It is therefore appropriate to say that where economic analysis systems are to be used, the planner should be pragmatic and eclectic and should choose a system or combination of systems suited to his purpose and workable for him, and for his community.

[36] Walter Isard, *et al.,* METHODS OF REGIONAL ANALYSIS, Chapter 10, "Interregional Linear Programming." See also Chapter 10 of this volume for a detailed treatment of mathematical techniques in various facets of planning.

[37] Kenneth J. Schlager, "Simulation Models in Urban and Regional Planning," Southeastern Wisconsin Regional Planning Commission THE TECHNICAL RECORD (II, no. 1, 1964).

[38] Linear programming can however treat a broader interindustry framework than industrial complex analysis.

5

Land Use Studies

"HOW SHALL WE GROW?" is a recurring theme in communities throughout the nation. Growth takes many forms—more people, more homes, more schools, new job opportunities, new flows of information, higher levels of aspiration, higher levels of learning, higher standards of living, increased family wealth, increased community capital, increased gross national product, and so on. There can be growth in many directions, on different scales, and on diverse frontiers—spatial, material, institutional, cultural, and spiritual, for example. This chapter is concerned primarily with the accommodation of spatial growth; that is, the increased use of land for urban activities.[1]

Anticipating Urban Growth

For public agencies, "Plan Ahead" has become a slogan with a cutting edge matching the "Think" signs displayed by a well-known manufacturer of computer hardware. When communities do not plan ahead or think in terms of meeting future needs, mounting urban growth problems can create crises and rob urban living of its many qualities. Water pollution, air pollution, transportation bottlenecks, power failures, water shortages, overloaded septic tanks, overcrowded schools, and overtaxed central cities are some of the more prevalent problems arising from rapid growth on the urban periphery coupled with the abandonment of older areas of established municipalities. The list is longer, but need not be detailed here.

Planning and programming for optimal use of land, water, air, and human resources are thus becoming a vital instrument for guiding urban growth and providing a healthful and aesthetically pleasing community environment. The importance of long-range planning is highlighted by projections, such as those published by Resources for the Future, that urban land requirements between 1960 and 2000 are likely to grow from 21,400,000 to some 45,000,000 acres (medium projection), in effect doubling in less than forty years.[2]

---

[1] For readers concerned with a theoretical approach to urban growth, there are a number of worthwhile publications. As an introduction to recent urban theory, see the review article by F. Stuart Chapin, Jr., "Selected Theories of Urban Growth and Structure," JOURNAL OF THE AMERICAN INSTITUTE OF PLANNERS, XXX (February, 1964), pp. 51–58. The following are included, among others: Richard L. Meier, A COMMUNICATIONS THEORY OF URBAN GROWTH (Cambridge: M.I.T. Press, 1962); Melvin M. Webber, "The Urban Place and the Nonplace Urban Realm," in Webber (ed.), EXPLORATIONS INTO URBAN STRUCTURE (Philadelphia: University of Pennsylvania Press, 1963), pp. 79–153; "Introduction" and Chapter 13 in F. Stuart Chapin, Jr., and Shirley F. Weiss (eds.), URBAN GROWTH DYNAMICS IN A REGIONAL CLUSTER OF CITIES (New York: John Wiley and Sons, Inc., 1962); Lowdon Wingo, Jr., TRANSPORTATION AND URBAN LAND (Washington: Resources for the Future, Inc., 1961). See also Chapin's Chapter 2, "Toward a Theory of Urban Growth and Development," in URBAN LAND USE PLANNING (Urbana: University of Illinois Press, 2nd edition, 1965), pp. 69–99; William Alonson, LOCATION AND LAND USE: TOWARD A GENERAL THEORY OF LAND RENT (Cambridge: Harvard University Press, 1964); and Britton Harris (ed.), "Urban Development Models: New Tools for Planning," Special Issue of the JOURNAL OF THE AMERICAN INSTITUTE OF PLANNERS, XXXI (May, 1965), pp. 90–184.

[2] Hans H. Landsberg, Leonard L. Fischman, and Joseph L. Fisher, RESOURCES IN AMERICA'S FUTURE: PATTERNS OF REQUIREMENTS AND AVAILABILITIES 1960–2000 (Baltimore: Published for Resources for the Future, Inc., by The Johns Hopkins Press, 1963), Table 18–14, p. 371, adapted from Marion Clawson et al., LAND FOR THE FUTURE (Baltimore: Johns Hopkins Press and Resources for the Future, 1960).

LAND USE TRENDS

While the growing population (human and automotive) accounts for a major portion of the expected doubling in urban land use, the tendency of increased use per unit, such as larger residential lot size or reduced coverage on industrial parcels, also contributes to the urban land explosion. Counterbalancing the trend toward decreased densities are the growing acceptance of planned unit development (clusters of housing types providing for more effective use of communal space) and the continuing organization of related activities into efficient commercial, industrial, medical, cultural, and governmental complexes.

An analytical study of recent land use trends has shown that within the larger cities of the nation, net land use densities are declining for population and manufacturing employment, and that commercial employment densities appear to be holding constant. Examination of changes in the proportion of major types of land in urban use indicates that vacant land in the reporting cities is rapidly disappearing. Consequently, the conclusion is drawn that "unless large amount of vacant land exists inside the city limits, the average large city appears to have nearly reached its upper limit of population and employment in manufacturing and commerce."[3] The implications of these findings for enforcing coordinated land use planning are clear.

Looking ahead to urban land use patterns in the 21st century, a contemporary planner foresees that:

urban agglomerations will claim not only a larger percentage of the population but a larger absolute number. As they grow they will spread. However, concentration will take place at the same time. A substantial percentage of the new development will be at relatively high densities. Some of it will continue to be at very low densities also. However, the cities and urban areas will not consume a tremendously larger percentage of the total land surface. Concentration will take place among the cities themselves. The larger urban centers will become locations of larger and larger percentages of eco-

nomic activity and, therefore, attract increasing populations. . . . Rural-urban migration will continue, and it will be supplemented by a higher rate of urban-urban migration than we have experienced in the past. . . . New flows and counterflows of migration will be established throughout the country.[4]

TYPES OF STUDIES

With a broad sweep of the urban growth problems related to land use, observed land use trends, and a look at the future, the focus switches to types of land use studies which a community should consider in preparation of its preliminary land use plan. Land use studies are designed to provide basic data on land characteristics and the various activities that occupy land in the planning area. These data are used in analyzing the current pattern of urban land use and serve as the framework for formulating the long-range land use plan. The land use plan establishes the character, quality, and pattern of the physical environment for the activities of people and organizations in the planning area.

Land use planning depends on reliable population forecasts, sound economic projections, and thorough understanding of the interrelationship of all types of urban land use, that is, for living, livelihood, and leisure.

Urban Land Use Planning lists a series of basic studies that furnish information on the use, nonuse, and misuse of urban land.[5] These include: (1) compilation of data on physiographic features, mapping the urban setting; (2) the land use survey; (3) the vacant land survey; (4) hydrological and flood potential study; (5) structural and environmental quality survey; (6) cost-revenue studies of land use; (7) land value studies; (8) studies of aesthetic features of the urban area; and (9) studies of public attitudes and preferences regarding land use. The study of activity systems, defined by Chapin as "behavior patterns of in-

[3] John H. Niedercorn and Edward F. R. Hearle, RECENT LAND-USE TRENDS IN FORTY-EIGHT LARGE AMERICAN CITIES, Memorandum RM-3664-FF. (Santa Monica: The Rand Corporation, June 1963), p. v.

[4] Barclay G. Jones, "Land Uses in the United States in the Year 2000," in Charles M. Weiss (ed.), MAN'S ENVIRONMENT IN THE TWENTY-FIRST CENTURY (Chapel Hill: Department of Environmental Sciences and Engineering, School of Public Health, University of North Carolina, 1965), pp. 171–95. (Quotations on pp. 185–86.)

[5] F. Stuart Chapin, Jr., URBAN LAND USE PLANNING (Urbana: University of Illinois Press, 2nd edition, 1965), pp. 254–338.

dividuals, families, institutions, and firms which occur in spatial patterns that have meaning in planning for land use," is also recognized as a basic source of information in planning for urban growth.[6]

Closely related to the foregoing land use studies are the transportation and thoroughfare studies which provide concomitant data on the movement of people and goods.

Depending on staff, resources, and nature of land development problems, some studies may have to be postponed until the basic mapping and surveying stages are completed. Actually, to formulate a long-range plan for the year 1990 or beyond, each of the studies listed and possibly others still being field tested may prove essential. Furthermore, examination of special problems, such as flood plain characteristics, may require a high priority.

Maps for Land Use Studies

In preparation for the land use and vacant land surveys, the planner makes use of a variety of maps, depending on the resources of the city and county, including an engineering survey map, which is generally maintained by the public works department or city engineer; a topographic map showing contour lines, drainage courses, and other natural features; tax maps showing property lines; and miscellaneous reference maps, such as insurance maps showing structures, and highway maps.

Using these maps and recent aerial photographs, if available, the planner prepares a series of base maps of the planning area.[7] Depending on the size of the area, the scale of the base map will vary. For smaller urban areas a scale of 200–400 feet to the inch is practical. For larger urban areas 600–800 feet to the inch may be necessary, unless the map is prepared in atlas or book form. However, since survey data

are marked directly on the field map and land use measurements are made from that map, a larger scale is necessary for working purposes. If large-scale base maps are not available, tax maps, insurance maps, or aerial photos may be used temporarily.

The first of the base maps includes street right-of-way lines, railroads, watercourses, lakes, and civil division lines. A second map adds property and easement lines and is used in detailed studies of neighborhoods and problem areas of the city. The final base map includes structures and is used in the planning office for recording changes in land use, demolition or conversion of structures, new subdivisions, new construction authorized, and other improvements to the land.

In addition, a general-purpose planning base map is prepared, showing street names and major points of interest in the city. It is reproduced in various scales: a small handy sheet for public distribution, larger sheets for rough studies in the office, and an oversized sheet for wall display. Mosaics of aerial photos may also serve the need for a wall map, with key streets and municipal boundaries identified for reference purposes. If the planning office is tied into a data bank, or simply processes its information on punched cards, a grid-coordinate system superimposed on the general-purpose planning base map will facilitate coding of data and machine analysis of small areas for special purposes, i.e., renewal, transportation, or utility planning.[8]

Land Use Survey

Depending on the size of the area, the size of the planning staff, and the time available, the actual land use survey can be accomplished on foot or by automobile, i.e., "windshield inspec-

[6] *Ibid.*, p. 224.

[7] For further information on the use of aerial photography in the preparation of planning maps, see the following series of articles: Fred H. Bair, Jr., "Mapping Program for Planning, Tied to Aerial Photographs," FLORIDA PLANNING AND DEVELOPMENT, XII, No. 5 (May, 1961), pp. 1–5; XII, No. 6 (June, 1961), pp. 1–5, 10; XII, No. 7 (July, 1961), pp. 1–5.

[8] For a discussion focused on electronic data processing, geographic identification of data, and mapping, see Robert E. Barraclough, "Mapping and EDP," in PLANNING 1965 (Chicago: American Society of Planning Officials, 1965), pp. 313–18. Observing that large inefficiencies result from inadequate maps, Barraclough concludes that "Cost-benefit studies in the mapping field are few and far between, but it can be safely asserted that in many cases the cost of better mapping would be small compared to the benefits that would result."

tion." If an automobile is used, at least two persons are required: one to drive and one to observe and record the observations. For scattered development and residential areas, windshield inspection is quite satisfactory. In areas of mixed land use and particularly in the central business district, the survey should be done on foot.

In addition to maps for recording data, a classification system must be established in advance. Furthermore, field notations corresponding to land use classifications should be determined prior to the survey. To assure uniformity of results, it is recommended that a manual of instructions for the field survey be prepared in the planning office and that it be reviewed in detail and tested before the survey team starts out. Where a punched card file of land use is maintained and machine tabulations of the field data are made, it is essential that field notations be completely standardized.

CLASSIFICATION OF LAND USE

Since land use patterns vary from community to community, the classification system adopted by a planning agency should correspond to the types of land use existing and emerging in the planning area. There is no prescribed system suitable for all communities, even those of similar population size or stage of development. Nevertheless, there are some broad categories of land use that prevail in most classification systems. Simplified to a system of major land use categories, which in effect washes out community differences in subcategories, the "universal" categories are conveniently identified on maps in color (see Table 5–1).

For analytical purposes a much more detailed system of classification is required than shown in Table 5–1. However, it is not necessary to build up such a system from scratch. Frequently communities can adopt the system followed by planning agencies operating in adjoining metropolitan areas, particularly if there is interest in coordinating land development at the metropolitan or regional level. The *Land Use Classification Manual*, developed by the Detroit Metropolitan Area Regional Planning Commission

Table 5–1

Illustrative Major Urban Land Use Categories for Generalized Presentation, Ground Area, and Buildings

1. Residence
   Low density—yellow
   Medium density—orange
   High density—brown
2. Retail business—red
   Local business uses
   Central business uses
   Regional shopping centers
   Highway service uses
3. Transportation, utilities, communications—ultramarine
4. Industry and related uses—indigo blue
   Extensive
   Intermediate
   Intensive
5. Wholesale and related uses—purple
6. Public buildings and open spaces—green
7. Institutional buildings and areas—gray
8. Vacant or nonurban use—uncolored

Source: Based on Table 21 in F. Stuart Chapin, Jr., URBAN LAND USE PLANNING (Urbana: University of Illinois Press, 2nd ed., 1965), p. 276.

is designed to make possible a coherent description of the land use structure of a township, a village, a city, or a metropolitan region. The code may be used at the level of detail needed to serve the purposes of each survey.[9]

The manual has been recommended as practical and usable—the tool which planners needed but did not have until this publication appeared.[10]

The federal government has also recognized the need for a standard land use coding system to facilitate the interchange of statistical information and research findings between communities and public and private organizations. The lack of uniformity, it is said, has led to duplication of effort. In the past, land use data have been collected for one specific purpose and then collected again in another format for another purpose. This is particularly relevant

[9] Detroit Metropolitan Area Regional Planning Commission, Land Classification Advisory Committee, LAND USE CLASSIFICATION MANUAL (Chicago: Public Administration Service, 1962).

[10] Dennis O'Harrow, "Foreword," *ibid.*, p. iii.

PARCEL (e.g., ownership parcel)

Location	Area of parcel*	Slope*	Soil type	Ownership	Land value*	Zoning	Etc.

STRUCTURE (e.g., building)

Type of structure	Total floor area*	Ground floor area*	Height*	Number of floors*	Condition of structure	Value of improvements	Etc.

SPACE USE (e.g., residential)

Activity	Ownership (activity)	Floor area*	Nuisance characteristics	Number of household units*	Number of residents*	Number of employees*	Etc.

FIGURE 5–1. *Example of characteristics commonly used to describe a land parcel (This figure is neither definitive in the number of characteristics shown nor does the sequence indicate relative importance. The unshaded area labeled "Activity" is the characteristic being given primary consideration in this coding system. Characteristics with an asterisk (*) can be described by an actual figure or a range in figures representing magnitude. The other characteristics cannot be described numerically; therefore each will need a series of "word description" categories.)*

to the collection of land use information that is equally useful to urban development planning and transportation planning programs. Amendments to Section 701 of the Housing Act of 1954 in 1959 and in 1961, and the Federal-Aid Highway Act of 1962 have placed greater emphasis on the need to integrate urban development and transportation plans. As noted in the *Standard Land Use Coding Manual,* the land use inventory and the land use forecast are common denominators to urban development and transportation planning processes.[11] The Urban Renewal Administration and the Bureau of Public Roads have both recommended that "where appropriate the detailed system of categories presented in this publication be used for the activity collection and coding of information describing land use activity."[12] While recommending a standard system for identifying and coding land use activities, the sponsoring agencies underscore the fact that *this recommendation is not to the considered as a requirement in any programs sponsored by the two agencies.*[13]

The federal government's *Standard Land Use Coding Manual* is likely to be widely used, although because of its relative newness little can be reported on its successful adaptability to different types of communities. However, all communities, small and large, would do well to familiarize themselves with its contents and approach which are sketched very briefly in the paragraphs and figures that follow. One of the problems in the adoption of the system in the manual is the desirability of using a computer to facilitate analysis. While the smaller communities may not have ready access to computers, the idea of metropolitan data banks is spreading, and it may be feasible to tie into a metropolitanwide service.[14] In fact, it is not unlikely that some day state-operated municipal data banks may serve as depositories and processors of urban land inventories.

As an example of characteristics commonly used to describe a parcel of land, which is the building block of the *Standard Land Use Coding Manual,* Figure 5–1 illustrates some twenty-one items, many of which are quantifiable. As noted, the figure is neither definitive in the number of characteristics shown nor

[11] U.S. Urban Renewal Administration and Bureau of Public Roads, STANDARD LAND USE CODING MANUAL (Washington: 1965), p. iii.

[12] *Ibid.*

[13] *Ibid.*

[14] Tulsa Metropolitan Area Planning Commission, METROPOLITAN DATA CENTER PROJECT, Demonstration Project Number Oklahoma D-1 (Tulsa: 1966).

Table 5–2

A Standard System for Identifying and Coding Land Use Activities— One- and Two-digit Levels

Code	Category	Code	Category
1	Residential	11	Household units.
		12	Group quarters.
		13	Residential hotels.
		14	Mobile home parks or courts.
		15	Transient lodgings.
		19	Other residential, NEC.*
2	Manufacturing	21	Food and kindred products—manufacturing.
		22	Textile mill products—manufacturing.
		23	Apparel and other finished products made from fabrics, leather, and similar materials—manufacturing.
		24	Lumber and wood products (except furniture)—manufacturing.
		25	Furniture and fixtures—manufacturing.
		26	Paper and allied products—manufacturing.
		27	Printing, publishing, and allied industries.
		28	Chemicals and allied products—manufacturing.
		29	Petroleum refining and related industries.
3	Manufacturing (continued)	31	Rubber and miscellaneous plastic products—manufacturing.
		32	Stone, clay, and glass products—manufacturing.
		33	Primary metal industries.
		34	Fabricated metal products—manufacturing.
		35	Professional, scientific, and controlling instruments; photographic and optical goods; watches and clocks—manufacturing.
		39	Miscellaneous manufacturing, NEC.*
4	Transportation, communication, and utilities	41	Railroad, rapid rail transit, and street railway transportation.
		42	Motor vehicle transportation.
		43	Aircraft transportation.
		44	Marine craft transportation.
		45	Highway and street right-of-way.
		46	Automobile parking.
		47	Communication.
		48	Utilities.
		49	Other transportation, communication, and utilities, NEC.*
5	Trade	51	Wholesale trade.
		52	Retail trade—building materials, hardware, and farm equipment.
		53	Retail trade—general merchandise.
		54	Retail trade—food.
		55	Retail trade—automotive, marine craft, aircraft, and accessories.
		56	Retail trade—apparel and accessories.
		57	Retail trade—furniture, home furnishings, and equipment.
		58	Retail trade—eating and drinking.
		59	Other retail trade, NEC.*

Table 5–2

(continued)

Code	Category	Code	Category
6	Services	61	Finance, insurance, and real estate services.
		62	Personal services.
		63	Business services.
		64	Repair services.
		65	Professional services.
		66	Contract construction services.
		67	Governmental services.
		68	Educational services.
		69	Miscellaneous services.
7	Cultural, entertainment, and recreational	71	Cultural activities and nature exhibitions.
		72	Public assembly.
		73	Amusements.
		74	Recreational activities.
		75	Resorts and group camps.
		76	Parks.
		79	Other cultural, entertainment, and recreational, NEC.*
8	Resource production and extraction	81	Agriculture.
		82	Agricultural related activities.
		83	Forestry activities and related services.
		84	Fishing activities and related services.
		85	Mining activities and related services.
		89	Other resource production and extraction, NEC.*
9	Undeveloped land and water areas	91	Undeveloped and unused land area (excluding noncommercial forest development).
		92	Noncommercial forest development.
		93	Water areas.
		94	Vacant floor area.
		95	Under construction.
		99	Other undeveloped land and water areas, NEC.*

* NEC = not elsewhere coded.

Source: U.S. Urban Renewal Administration and Bureau of Public Roads, STANDARD LAND USE CODING MANUAL (Washington: The Bureau, 1965), pp. 29–31.

does the sequence indicate relative importance. It does, however, reflect the type of information considered by planning agencies when describing a parcel of land. The activity associated with space use is highlighted as the characteristic given primary consideration in the manual's coding system, which is clearly central to all land use planning analysis.

STANDARD IDENTIFICATION AND CODING SYSTEM

The classification system proposed in the manual expands from 9 one-digit categories (2 of which cover "manufacturing") to 67 two-digit categories, 294 three-digit categories, and 772 four-digit categories. The one-digit categories are the most generalized and the four-digit categories the most detailed. Planning agencies can utilize the system at whatever level of detail is required for area analysis and development programming. Table 5–2 includes the one- and two-digit categories, and Table 5–3 illustrates the development of new classifications within the standard system for central business district planning, general transportation planning, and general urban planning.

For those familiar with the Standard Industrial Classification (SIC) employed by a number of federal agencies, including the Bureau of the Census, Bureau of Employment Security, Bureau of Labor Statistics, and Social Security

Table 5–3

Developing New Classifications—Three Applications of the Standard Land Use Coding System*

Central business district planning (example classifications)	Standard code	Local code	General transportation planning (example classifications)	Standard code	Local code	General urban planning (example classifications)	Standard code	Local code
Residential:			Residential:			Residential:		
Household units.......11.			Household units......11.			Household units......11.		
Group quarters.......12.			Group quarters.......12.			Group quarters......12.		
Resdential hotels.....13.			Residential hotels.....13.			Residential hotels....13.		
Transient lodgings.....15.			Mobile home parks or courts.............14.			Mobile home parks or courts.............14.		
Manufacturing.........2 and 3.			Transient lodgings....15.			Transient lodgings....15.		
Wholesale trade:			Manufacturing, communication, and utilities:			Manufacturing and nonmanufacturing. industry:		
With storage area.....51.			Manufacturing.......2 and 3.			Light and heavy manufacturing.	2 and 3.	
Retail trade and services:			Communication......47.			Warehousing and storage..........637 plus all land use activities with an auxiliary code of 4.		
Convenience goods— retail.............52, 54, 553, 591, 592, 594, 596, 598, and 599.			Utilities............48.					
			Transportation:					
			Passenger terminals...4113, 4122, 4211, 4212, 4213, 4312, and 4411.					
Shopping goods— retail..............53, 551, 552, 559, 56, 57, 593, 595, and 597.			Freight terminals...4114, 4221, 4313, 4412, and 4414.			Contract construction...66.		
			Passenger and freight terminals. 4115, 4314, and 4413.			Transportation, communication, and utilities.	4.	
Personal services......62.								
Repair services.......64.			Right-of-way........4111, 4112, 4121, 4311, 4391, and 45.			Commercial and service:		
Banking services......6111.						Wholesale trade......51.		
Offices...............All land use activity with a 1 or 2 in the auxiliary code position plus those categories listed in table 1.			Automobile parking...46 plus all land use activities with an auxiliary code of 5.			Retail trade........52, 53, 54, 55, 56, 57, 58, and 59.		
						Finance, insurance, and real estate services.	61.	
						Personal services......62.		
			Wholesaling and warehousing:			Business services......63.		
			Wholesale with storage area..........51.			Repair services.......64.		
Warehousing and storage................637 plus all land use activities with an auxiliary code of 4.			Warehousing and storage...........637 plus all land use activities with an auxiliary code of 4.			Professional services...65 (excluding hospital service code 6513)		
						Community:		
						Hospital services......6513.		
Transportation, communication, and utilities................	4		Retail trade and services:			Executive, legislative, and judicial functions.	671.	
Public and quasipublic institutions:			Retail trade.........52, 53, 54, 55, 56, 57, 58, and 59.			Government protective functions.	672.	
Hospitals and medical clinics............6513 and 6517.			Personal services......62.			Postal services.......673.		
Government protective services.......672.			Repair services.......64.			Educational services...68.		
Postal services.......673.			Offices...............All land use activity with a 1 or 2 in the auxiliary code position plus those categories listed in table 1.			Religious activities....691.		
Educational services...68.						Welfare and charitable services.	692.	
Religious services......691.						Cultural activities and nature exhibitions.	71.	
Welfare and charitable services.............692.						Public assembly, miscellaneous purposes.	723.	
Cultural activities and nature exhibitions...71.			Public and quasipublic:			Playgrounds and athletic areas.	742.	
Entertainment and recreation:			Hospitals and medical clinics............6513 and 6517.					
Entertainment assembly............721.			Government protective services.	672.		Leisure:		
Public assembly, miscellaneous purposes....723.			Postal services.......673.			Entertainment assembly..........721.		
Eating and drinking...58.			Correctional institutions..............674.			Sports assembly and activities..........	722, 741, and 743.	
Bowling.............7417.			Educational services...68.			Amusements........73.		
Gymnasiums and athletic clubs..........7425.			Religious activities....691.			Parks and reserves....76 and 921.		
Parks (leisure and ornamental).......762.			Cultural activities.....711.			Agricultural and open areas:		
Vacant or unused:			Military bases and reservations.	675.		Agriculture..........81.		
Undeveloped and unused land area......91.						Commercial forestry production and nonreserve forests (undeveloped).	831 and 922.	
Water areas.........93.								
Vacant floor area.....94.								
Under construction....95.								

* This table is for illustration purposes only. The combination of categories under each of the three types of planning studies are not to be considered the recommended categories for these studies.

Source: U.S. Urban Renewal Administration and Bureau of Public Roads, STANDARD LAND USE CODING MANUAL (Washington: The Bureau, 1965), pp. 26–27.

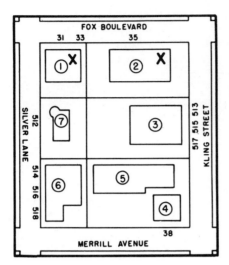
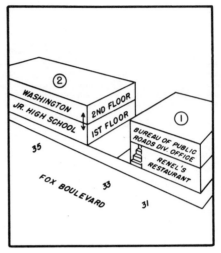

FIELD OPERATION										OFFICE OPERATION				
Street No.	Street Name	Building No.	Floor	Description of Activity	Auxiliary?	Activity Ownership	Residential Structure Type	No. of Household Units		Activity Code	Auxiliary Code	Ownership Code	Structure Code	No. of Household Units
1	2	3	4	5	6	7	8	9		5'	6'	7'	8'	9'
31	FOX BOULEVARD	1	1	RENEL'S RESTAURANT	—	PRIVATE	—	—		5810	0	20	—	—
33	FOX BOULEVARD	1	2	BUREAU OF PUBLIC ROADS, DIVISION OFFICES (ADMIN.)	X	FEDERAL	—	—		6710	1	11	—	—
35	FOX BOULEVARD	2	1+2	WASHINGTON JUNIOR HIGH SCHOOL (GRADES 7-9)	—	MUNI-CIPAL	—	—		6813	0	15	—	—

FIGURE 5–2. *Example for describing and coding land use activities (Top left, block plan; top right, parcel schematic; bottom, land use entries on field listing form.)*

Administration (OASDI), the land use activities categories may look very familiar.[15] There is indeed a close relationship between the two systems, inasmuch as the SIC category titles have been adopted, as well as the detailed identification of activities wherever feasible. However, no correspondence in the four-digit codes is maintained, and the user is forewarned that adoption of the same terminology does not necessarily make the land use data collected and coded under this system of categories compatible with the economic data collected using SIC specifications.[16]

In addition to the basic activity code, a one-digit auxiliary code has been set up for supporting land use activities that are generally found separated from, but are functionally and organizationally linked to, basic activities.

---

[15] U.S. Bureau of the Budget, STANDARD INDUSTRIAL CLASSIFICATION MANUAL (Washington: 1957); and SUPPLEMENT TO 1957 EDITION (1963).

[16] U.S. Urban Renewal Administration and Bureau of Public Roads, *op. cit.*, p. 13.

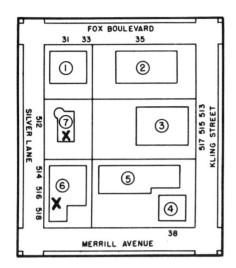

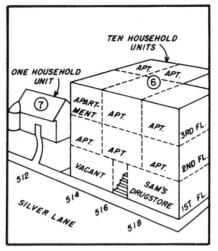

FIELD OPERATION									OFFICE OPERATION				
Street No.	Street Name	Building No.	Floor	Description of Activity	Auxiliary?	Activity Ownership	Residential Structure Type	No. of Household Units	Activity Code	Auxiliary Code	Ownership Code	Structure Code	No. of Household Units
1	2	3	4	5	6	7	8	9	5'	6'	7'	8'	9'
518	SILVER LANE	6	1	SAM'S DRUG STORE	—	PRIVATE	—	—	5910	0	20	—	—
516	SILVER LANE	6	2+3	HOUSEHOLD UNITS	—	PRIVATE	WALK-UP APART.	10	1100	0	20	31	10
514	SILVER LANE	6	1	VACANT FLOOR AREA	—	—	—	—	9400	0	—	—	—
512	SILVER LANE	7	1	HOUSEHOLD UNITS	—	PRIVATE	SINGLE UNIT— DETACHED	1	1100	0	20	11	01

FIGURE 5–3. *Example for describing and coding land use activities (Top left, block plan; top right, parcel schematic; bottom, land use entries on field listing form.)*

These include: (1) central or administrative offices; (2) sales offices, without stock; (3) research and development; (4) warehousing and storage; (5) automobile parking; (6) motor vehicle garage (maintenance and/or storage of vehicles); and (7) steam and power plant.[17] While these are all important space uses in themselves, they are basically significant in their relationship to the parent activity served. For

example: pharmaceutical preparation—manufacturing, basic activity code 2834, has an auxiliary code for its research and development activity, 3; and the combined activity code is 2834–3. Groceries—retail, basic code 5410, and an auxiliary code for its automobile parking facility, 5; and the combined activity code is 5410–5. The use of auxiliary codes is almost a necessity in large commercial or industrial areas, where conceivably research and development may be a basic activity (code 6391) or a sup-

[17] *Ibid.*, pp. 10–12; 16–17.

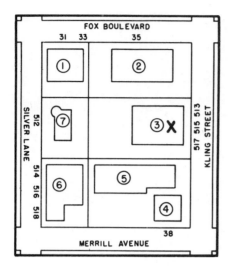
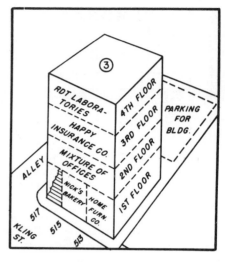

FIELD OPERATION									OFFICE OPERATION				
Street No.	Street Name	Building No.	Floor	Description of Activity	Auxiliary?	Activity Ownership	Residential Structure Type	No. of House-hold Units	Activity Code	Auxiliary Code	Ownership Code	Structure Code	No. of House-hold Units
1	2	3	4	5	6	7	8	9	5'	6'	7'	8'	9'
513	KLING ST.	3	1	HOME FURNITURE CO. (RETAIL)	—	PRIVATE	—	—	5711	0	20	—	—
515	KLING ST.	3	1	NICK'S BAKERY (WITH OVENS IN REAR)	—	PRIVATE	—	—	5461	0	20	—	—
517	KLING ST.	3	2	BIG TOWN REAL ESTATE CO. (REAL ESTATE AGENTS & BROKERS-OFFICES)	—	PRIVATE	—	—	6152	0	20	—	—
517	KLING ST.	3	2	PHYSICIAN'S OFFICE	—	PRIVATE	—	—	6511	0	20	—	—
517	KLING ST.	3	2	JONES CHEMICAL CORP. (SALES OFF. OF AGRICULTURAL FERTILIZER MFG.)	X	PRIVATE	—	—	2870	2	20	—	—
517	KLING ST.	3	2	AJAX CONSTRUCTION CO. (GENERAL OFFICES – HOME BUILDERS)	X	PRIVATE	—	—	6611	1	20	—	—
517	KLING ST.	3	2	LAW FIRM (OFFICES)	—	PRIVATE	—	—	6520	0	20	—	—
517	KLING ST.	3	3	HAPPY INSURANCE CO. (REGIONAL OFFICE OF COMPANY)	X	PRIVATE	—	—	6141	1	20	—	—
517	KLING ST.	3	4	RDT LABORATORIES (DEVELOPMENT LABORATORIES FOR RDT INDUSTRIES–RADIO TRANSMITTING EQUIPMENT MFG.)	X	PRIVATE	—	—	3436	3	20	—	—
513–517	KLING ST.	—	—	PARKING FOR VISITORS & EMPLOYEES IN THE REAR (20 SPACES)	—	PRIVATE	—	—	4600	0	20	—	—

FIGURE 5–4. *Example for describing and coding land use activities (Top left, block plan; top right, parcel schematic; bottom, land use entries on field listing form.)*

porting activity and automobile parking similarly (basic activity code 4600). Taking inventory of land use activities is facilitated through a clear recognition of differences in categories included in the two complementary codes, as are analysis of space use and projection of future land requirements for linked and independent activities.

Examples drawn from a hypothetical block,

with seven structures fronting on four streets, are illustrated in Figures 5–2, 3, 4, and 5. These examples show the type of land use activity data that should be collected to utilize fully the standard coding system. The block plan in each figure identifies the parcel and structures being inventoried. The parcel schematic focuses on the structures on each parcel and shows the types of activity by floor. All this

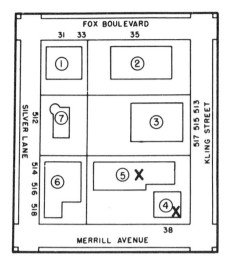
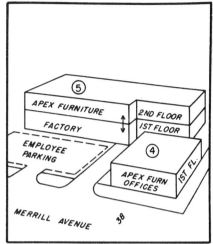

				FIELD OPERATION						OFFICE OPERATION				
Street No.	Street Name	Building No.	Floor	Description of Activity	Auxiliary?	Activity Ownership	Residential Structure Type	No. of House-hold Units	Activity Code	Auxiliary Code	Ownership Code	Structure Code	No. of House-hold Units
1	2	3	4	5	6	7	8	9	5'	6'	7'	8'	9'
38	MERRILL AVE.	4	1	APEX FURNITURE FACTORY (AD-MINISTRATIVE OFFICES OF FACTORY)	X	PRIVATE	—	—	2520	1	20	—	—
38	MERRILL AVE.	5	1+2	APEX FURNITURE FACTORY (FACTORY PRODUCING WOOD OFFICE FURNITURE	—	PRIVATE	—	—	2520	0	20	—	—
38	MERRILL AVE.	—	—	APEX FURNITURE FACTORY (EMPLOYEE PARKING-36 SPACES)	X	PRIVATE	—	—	2520	5	20	—	—

FIGURE 5–5. *Example for describing and coding land use activities (Top left, block plan; top right, parcel schematic; bottom, land use entries on field listing form.)*

observed detail is actually listed on the field sheet. While the illustrations are based on only one type of activity per establishment,[18] if more than one activity is carried on by the same firm on the same premises, such as manufacturing and retail sales, only the activity occupying the largest floor area would be identified. The *Standard Land Use Coding Manual* prescribes that the predominant floor area for activities in a structure or predominant land area for activi-

[18] Where only one type of activity is carried on by an establishment, by definition the activity and establishment become synonymous terms. See, U.S. Urban Renewal Administration and Bureau of Public Roads, STANDARD LAND USE CODING MANUAL (*op. cit.,* p. 4), for definition: "The term 'activity' for purposes used here is defined as an organizational unit for performing a special function and occupying identifiable space at a fixed location." The difference between this definition and that of others engaged in activity systems analysis should be recognized (for example, Chapin, *op. cit.,* p. 224).

ties not in a structure will determine the activity that is coded.[19] Communities may have under way or projected planning programs for which a further breakdown of floor area activities is required (for example in central business district and/or renewal planning), and significant space users, while not predominant by floor, should probably be included on the listing sheet.

The office coding operations, also illustrated in Figures 5–2 through 5, involve primarily the addition of the four-digit basic activity code and the one-digit auxiliary activity code. While smaller communities may not require the full four-digit classification system to code their relatively simple land use diversity, the *Standard Land Use Coding Manual* points to the advantages of having a common base of detailed activity data for entire metropolitan areas.[20] Classifications can be reduced from four- to three-, two-, or one-digit categories for simplicity, or can be regrouped into new categories to fit special studies. However, if the original field survey is based on less than the four-digit system, then the opportunities for coordination of data resources, analyses, and forecasts for entire metropolitan areas may have to be sacrificed.

To complete the field listing form, three other columns are filled in as part of the office operation. Two-digit codes are added for ownership (public, by type, or private),[21] and for structures with housing units (single family, two family, multifamily, converted, mobile, or primarily nonresidential).[22] The last column, number of housing units, is a transcription of the field column, standardized for number of digits, as shown in Figure 5–3. This item provides for an immediate machine count of the number of housing units in the community, planning area, or neighborhood, whenever the land use activity data are coded and key punched on data processing cards and/or stored on magnetic tape. If electronic data processing

or computer services are not available, the data can still be tabulated directly from the listing forms. All that is required for straight counts is a reliable adding machine and a willing clerical assistant.

It should be noted that the listing form illustrated does not provide column space for inserting measurements on ground coverage or floor space area occupied by basic and auxiliary activities.[23] These measurements are generally made from field maps, with a planimeter or nomograph, depending on the coverage involved and the precision desired.[24]

Other data important for land use analysis and projections not included in the field listing sheet concern the characteristics of vacant land suitable for urban use and the site and structural qualities of residential and nonresidential parcels for continuing use. Evaluation of qualitative characteristics generally requires special appraisals surveys as noted below. However, in smaller communities it may be desirable to include selected quality characteristics in the basic land use inventory in order to provide concurrent data and to economize on field survey time.[25]

APPRAISAL

While the *Standard Land Use Coding Manual* has set up a category for undeveloped land and water areas (9100–9900), it does not provide a direct means for determining the suitability of vacant land for major types of urban use. For example, slope and drainage characteristics should be recorded to indicate whether the

---

[19] U.S. Urban Renewal Administration and Bureau of Public Roads, *op. cit.,* p. 18.

[20] *Ibid.,* pp. 23–25.

[21] See Appendix 1 for ownership classification system, *ibid.,* p. 107.

[22] See Appendix 3 for classification system of structures containing household units, *ibid.,* pp. 110–11.

[23] See Chapin, *op. cit.,* Figure 26, p. 228, for another illustrative general-purpose field listing sheet which includes columns for floor area measurements. This sheet is intended for space use surveys conducted in developed areas of a city where data are to be stored on punch cards.

[24] Machine methods also make it possible to compute area coverage directly from large-scale aerial photographs. (Chapin, *ibid.,* p. 296.)

[25] For an informative critique of the classification system recommended in the STANDARD LAND USE CODING MANUAL, see: Marion Clawson and Charles L. Stewart, LAND USE INFORMATION, A CRITICAL SURVEY OF U.S. STATISTICS INCLUDING POSSIBILITIES FOR GREATER UNIFORMITY (Baltimore: The Johns Hopkins Press for Resources for the Future, Inc., 1965), pp. 137–41.

Table 5–4

Statistical Summary of Land Use, Thomasville Planning Area
(figures in acres)

	Northwest	Northeast	Southwest	Southeast	Subtotal City	Outside City	Total
Residential:							
Single family	209.69	414.78	220.16	293.21	1,137.84	1,994.55	3,132.39
Duplex	17.74	18.14	2.13	5.43	43.44	2.76	46.20
Apartment	5.14	3.30	1.47	2.09	12.00	2.76	14.76
Retail business:							
Retail regional and offices	10.40	15.98	6.24	3.53	36.15	24.39	60.54
Retail local	10.79	13.08	3.71	6.20	33.78	11.71	45.49
Retail highway	—	5.85	—	—	5.85	25.58	31.43
Wholesale	1.54	3.89	.84	.62	6.89	3.22	10.11
Manufacturing	24.28	13.92	32.43	56.48	127.11	28.93	156.04
Construction	22.44	1.18	2.31	10.17	36.10	8.95	45.05
Public:							
Schools	8.45	36.07	4.74	12.46	61.72	14.70	76.42
Recreation	13.66	22.41	11.61	11.65	59.33	8.49	67.82
Other public	1.14	15.50	147.32	2.98	166.94	7.58	174.52
Semipublic:							
Social religious cultural	6.87	5.62	1.87	9.18	23.54	18.60	42.14
Streets and railroad	90.55	108.66	72.40	153.21	424.82	529.51	954.33
Total urban land use	422.69	678.38	507.23	567.21	2,175.51	2,681.73	4,857.24
Vacant	407.41	573.10	531.92	385.37	1,897.80	6,354.13	8,251.93
Total area	830.10	1,251.48	1,039.15	952.58	4,073.31	9,035.86	13,109.17

Source: Cynthia E. Gubernick, George C. Hemmens, Richard L. Sutton, and Morris A. Trevithick, A PRELIMINARY REPORT FOR PLANNING FOR THE CITY OF THOMASVILLE, NORTH CAROLINA (Chapel Hill: Graduate students in the Department of City and Regional Planning, University of North Carolina, 1958).

land is suitable for construction. Nearly level land (5 per cent slope or less) is necessary for industrial sites. Prime sites ready for industrial development would have large acreage plus water supply, sanitary sewerage, storm drainage, highway accessibility, and railroad sidings or airfreight service. Residential sites ready for development would have a safe water supply; adequate means of sewage disposal; proximity to schools, recreation facilities, and neighborhood shopping; and access to good transportation facilities to major employment centers in the community and surrounding area.

These qualitative standards for vacant land are equally appropriate for appraising the suitability of developed land for continued use and for earmarking areas for possible reuse.

Application of these standards would be in addition to an evaluation of structural characteristics and environmental factors in housing and nonresidential building surveys—generally carried out in connection with urban renewal planning. Detailed structural and environmental standards relating to residential land use have been promulgated by the Committee on the Hygiene of Housing of the American Public Health Association.[26]

For nonresidential land use, a demonstration project of the St. Louis City Plan Commission

[26] American Public Health Association, Committee on the Hygiene of Housing. AN APPRAISAL METHOD FOR MEASURING THE QUALITY OF HOUSING, Parts I, II, and III (New York: The Association, 1950).

of St. Louis has developed three comprehensive appraisal schedules. The "structure schedule" covers 80 items in six major groups: tenure-use, structure layout, facilities, maintenance, site and land use, and codes. The "occupancy schedule" has 50 items. These are intended to appraise conditions that accrue to the occupant rather than the structure. Finally, the "block analysis score sheet" includes 22 environmental features, such as, traffic, paving, street lighting, parking, water supply, and sewerage.[27] Clearly a pioneer effort, the St. Louis appraisal method merits close attention by communities with aging commercial and industrial areas.[28]

ANALYSIS AND PRESENTATION OF DATA

Once the measurements of land use are completed, according to major categories or in greater detail as may be required, a statistical summary is made for each subunit of the planning area and then a final total is prepared for the entire area. The subunits may be census tracts, well-defined residential neighborhoods, or somewhat arbitrary areas delineated for analytical purposes. In the latter case, these areas would be identified by natural or structural barriers (e.g., streams or transportation routes), or by service area (e.g., elementary school, neighborhood shopping center, local park, and playground). An example of this type of summary, using the four quadrants of the Thomasville, North Carolina, Planning Area as statistical subunits,[29] is given in Table 5–4. The land use survey data can be consolidated in a black-and-white map as was done in Kingsport, Tennessee (Figure 5–6).

Larger planning areas generally require additional categories in both statistical summarization and mapping. Land use maps are likely to be in color, in order to provide more shades for the different uses. An example of the land use summary of a more complex metropolitan area, comprising 26 municipalities and an urban unincorporated area in Dade County, Florida, is given in Table 5–5.[30] The accompanying map of existing land use, not reproduced here, consolidates the classifications with 14 shades of color: residential (3), commercial (2), tourist (1), industrial (1), institutional (1), parks and recreation (1), transportation and utilities (2), agriculture (1), water (1), and glades or marsh (1). Drawn at a scale of 1 inch = 2 miles, the map is folded to a convenient size of $8\frac{1}{8} \times 9\frac{1}{4}$ inches and inserted in an open envelope attached to the inside back cover of the report.

Smaller planning areas are also tending to use color in their land use surveys. Although color reproductions are more costly than black-and-white plates, they are likely to be more effective in conveying information and in appealing to the public. If color is preferred to black-and-white patterns for reporting purposes, a standard color scheme should be adopted after careful consideration. One such scheme is included in Table 5–1. When the color code is adopted to illustrate existing land use, it should be maintained consistently in the mapping of proposed land development as part of the comprehensive plan. Use of identical colors to represent different residential densities, that is, existing and proposed, may be unintentionally confusing.

[27] St. Louis City Plan Commission, MEASURING DETERIORATION IN COMMERCIAL AND INDUSTRIAL AREAS (St. Louis: The Commission, 1957). For another experimental approach, see Albert Z. Guttenberg, "New, Old Criteria Explored in Search of Means of Evaluating Non-residential Property," JOURNAL OF HOUSING, XXI, No. 2 (1964), pp. 73–79.

[28] See Brian J. L. Berry, COMMERCIAL STRUCTURE AND COMMERCIAL BLIGHT (Chicago: University of Chicago, Department of Geography Research Paper No. 85, 1963), for a classification scheme of possible forms of commercial blight, Table 76, p. 181.

In a report by Arthur D. Little, Inc., to the Philadelphia City Planning Commission, THE USEFULNESS OF PHILADELPHIA'S INDUSTRIAL PLANT: AN APPROACH TO INDUSTRIAL RENEWAL (January, 1960), a method of classifying industrial sites and structures according to their current and potential usefulness is formulated and field tested.

[29] Cynthia E. Gubernick, George C. Hemmens, Richard L. Sutton, and Morris H. Trevithick, A PRELIMINARY REPORT FOR PLANNING FOR THE CITY OF THOMASVILLE, N.C. (Chapel Hill: Graduate Students in the Department of City and Regional Planning, University of North Carolina, June, 1958).

[30] Metropolitan Dade County Planning Advisory Board and the Metropolitan Dade County Planning Department, PRELIMINARY LAND USE PLAN AND POLICIES FOR DEVELOPMENT, prepared for the Board of County Commissioners, Metropolitan Dade County (Miami: 1961).

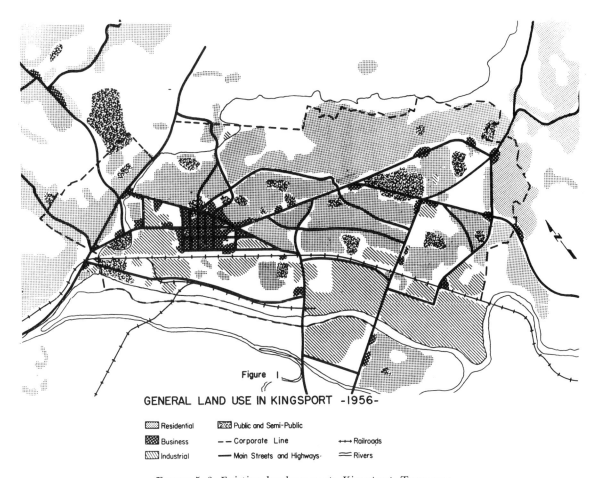

Figure I

GENERAL LAND USE IN KINGSPORT -1956-

Residential   Public and Semi-Public

Business   – – Corporate Line   +–+–+ Railroads

Industrial   —— Main Streets and Highways·   Rivers

FIGURE 5–6. *Existing land-use map, Kingsport, Tennessee*

In addition to the general inventory of land use as the basis for future land use and transportation planning, the land use survey provides information for many special needs. In his book on *Land Uses in American Cities,* Bartholomew has stated the case for land use analyses most succinctly. The statement, quoted below, serves as a capsule summary of the operations discussed in the foregoing paragraphs, as a gentle admonition to keep data collection current, and as an introduction to the problems of forecasting the community's future land requirements.

LAND USE ANALYSIS

The applications of land use data for planning purposes are manifold. For example, they can be used to determine commercial markets, to locate institutions such as churches and schools, or for zoning purposes. Therefore, the type of statistical analysis in any given situation will be determined by the problems under study. In zoning studies, with which we are concerned here, it is essential to know the amount of land used for various purposes. Computations of lot and parcel areas, arranged according to each major type of use, should be made for individual blocks, then summarized for permanent unit areas or neighborhoods, and finally for the entire community. The result of these summaries is generally expressed as an area in acres, in percentages of total areas, and as a ratio of land used to given units of population. Zoning that is based on the facts of actual use of land will have far greater validity than that based upon opinions unsupported by such facts.

The land use map represents the conditions on a given date, and its validity becomes progressively less with each change in use of property. Thus, it is important to keep this graphic and statistical infor-

Table 5–5

Existing Land Use, Metropolitan Dade County

Category	Acreage	% of Urban Area	Category	Acreage	% of Urban Area
Residential			**Parks & recreation**		
Single family	39526	31.0	Parks	2629	2.0
Two family	1800	1.4	Play Grounds	218	0.2
Multifamily	1783	1.4	Golf Courses	1604	1.3
Rooms	78	0.1	Cemeteries	344	0.3
Camps	24	0.0	Total	4796	3.8
Trailers	328	0.3	**Transportation**		
Mixed*	708	0.6	Terminals	6784	5.3
Total	44248	34.8	Railroad	830	0.6
Commercial			Utility	529	0.4
Retail	3940	3.1	Streets	22966	18.0
Mixed*	458	0.4	Parking	249	0.2
Total	4398	3.5	Mixed*	158	0.1
Tourist			Total	31516	24.6
Hotels	549	0.4	**Agriculture**		
Motels	264	0.2	Groves	687	0.5
Mixed*	57	0.0	Crops	2102	1.7
Total	870	0.6	Mixed*	48	0.0
Industry			Total	2837	2.2
Extraction	339	0.3	**Undeveloped**		
Light mfg.	639	0.5	Vacant	29815	23.4
Heavy mfg.	434	0.3	Glades	20	0.0
Light storage	569	0.4	Marsh	78	0.1
Heavy storage	250	0.2	Total	29913	23.5
Mixed*	343	0.3	**Water**		
Total	2575	2.0	Lakes	1104	0.9
Institutional			Courses	1290	1.0
Education	1909	1.5	Bay		0.0
Cultural	199	0.2	Total	2394	1.9
Medical	232	0.2	Total, all categories	127381	100.0
Religious	498	0.4			
Public admin.	641	0.5			
Penal	6	0.0			
Mixed*	351	0.3			
Total	3835	3.1			

* Indicates two or more categories of use on the same parcel of land.

Source: Metropolitan Dade County Planning Advisory Board and the Metropolitan Dade County Planning Department, PRELIMINARY LAND USE PLAN AND POLICIES FOR DEVELOPMENT (Miami, The Department, 1961), p. 18.

mation current. In the interim, changes in land use can be recorded from building permits issued or from insurance atlas records; however, these are never fully effective. Periodic revisions, yearly if possible, should be made.

In conclusion, the value of land use surveys tabulated in the manner described lies in comparative statistics. But, as with all comparisons of this nature there are definite limits of applicability. A community's future land use requirements cannot be projected with complete accuracy on a basis of current ratios. Likewise, a comparison of land uses between two or more communities will disclose differences due to character and physiography. However, in both cases such comparisons can be instructive. In combination with other basic studies, and with good judgment, current land use data offers a factual base for improved planning and zoning practices.[31]

[31] Harland Bartholomew assisted by Jack Wood, LAND USES IN AMERICAN CITIES (HARVARD CITY PLANNING STUDIES, XV) (Cambridge: Harvard University Press, 1955), pp. 18–19.

Forecasting Space Requirements

ANTICIPATION OF SPACE NEEDS

There are no universal standards or multipliers for determining the amounts of land needed in the future for each class of use or activity located within the planning area. Reasonable estimates can be made, however, of the future "space requirements" for each class of use in a community, and these estimates can be employed in the preparation of the land development plan. The measures used to estimate space requirements are frequently based on current space use, modified by anticipated impacts of new technology, and legal requirements in zoning, subdivision, and housing codes. Allowances for auxiliary space needs for off-street parking, off-street loading and landscaping are added, plus a sizeable safety factor. Space standards are based on a unit of measurement, such as a person, household, a worker, or a shopper, among others. For this reason, population forecasts and economic trend projections (discussed in earlier chapters) are fundamental in determining future space requirements.

A brief review of the estimating sources and measuring units for the major types of land use may be helpful as an introduction to the process of forecasting space requirements, some of which are based on a level of activity and others, predominantly on a community or neighborhood level. In Metropolitan Dade County, for example, the optimum size of service unit has been studied for each type of facility (police, fire, water, sewer, waste, schools, parks).[32] The three levels of service unit found to be feasible for this particular metropolitan complex are illustrated and described in Figure 5-7. While these service units are focused on land uses related primarily to government services, a parallel distinction should be made for region-serving uses, i.e., industrial, wholesale, commercial; and neighborhood uses, i.e., residential and local shopping, schools and playgrounds.

Industrial Land. Employment per net industrial acre tends to vary with the location of

the plant, the nature of the manufacturing process, and the extent of automation. In-town plants by necessity economize on land. Outlying plants allocate considerably more structural space, as well as open land for future expansion. It is noteworthy that in her detailed study of *Space for Industry,* Dorothy A. Muncy observed that employment by peak shift rather than total employment is a more realistic yardstick for determining density, that is, number of employees per acre.[33] In addition to projecting space requirements to accommodate normal expansion of existing plants as well as new industrial activities, it is advisable to set aside an "industrial reserve" for one or more industrial districts, or possibly for unforeseen very large industrial enterprises in developing areas. A helpful guide to the development of industrial districts is The Urban Land Institute Technical Bulletin No. 44, *Industrial Districts: Principles in Practice.*[34]

Wholesale Land. Employment has also been used as a measure for projecting future wholesale space needs. However, this has been done with considerably less success because of the lack of detailed information on land requirements for the various wholesaling activities as classified by the Bureau of the Census. Projections made on the basis of inlying and outlying locations in the planning area, with separate allocations for petroleum bulk stations and large-scale warehousing, offer a more realistic approach. Further study of space requirements within each of the major wholesaling functions has been a longstanding need among the techniques available for future land-use planning.[35]

Commercial Land. Space needs for commercial uses, which are composed primarily of re-

---

[32] Metropolitan Dade County Planning Advisory Board, *op. cit.,* p. 29.

[33] Dorothy A. Muncy, SPACE FOR INDUSTRY, Urban Land Institute Technical Bulletin No. 23 (Washington: Urban Land Institute, 1954), p. 9. See also Richard L. Meier, DEVELOPMENTAL PLANNING (New York: McGraw-Hill, Inc., 1965), pp. 242–43, for experience in application of new space standards in Puerto Rico.

[34] Robert E. Boley, INDUSTRIAL DISTRICTS: PRINCIPLES IN PRACTICE, Urban Land Institute Technical Bulletin No. 44 (Washington: Urban Land Institute, 1962).

[35] Wholesaling activities, particularly those involving warehousing, storage, and truck terminals, are often combined with industrial space studies. See: Arthur D. Little, Inc., *op. cit.,* pp. 48–59.

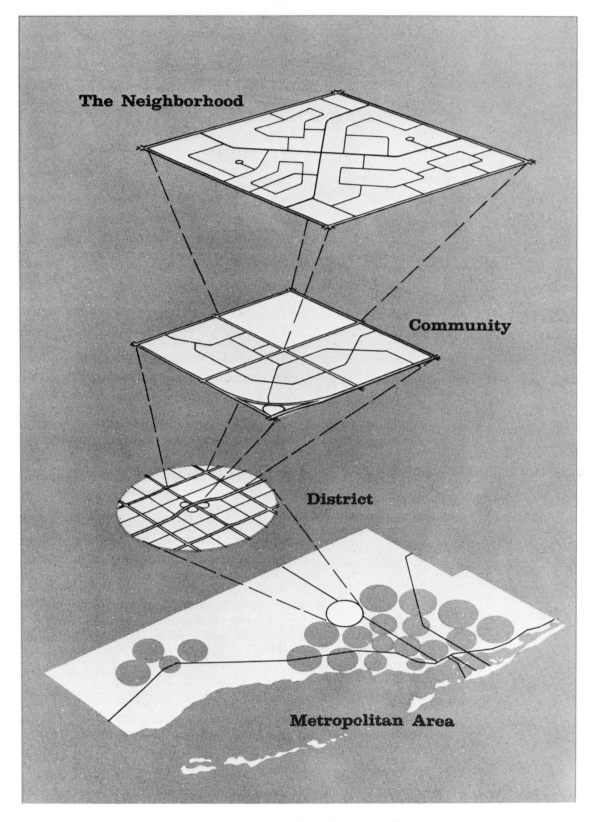

FIGURE 5–7. *Delineation of land service units, Metropolitan Dade County*

tail stores and office buildings, can be based on a number of units of measure. Future population growth is extensively used as a simple measure. However, projection of retail sales volume, based on future income estimates, has been widely applied by market analysts in determining space needs of new shopping centers. This technique has also been used in the planning of commercial areas in new towns, such as Greenbelt, Maryland, and in renewal areas.[36]

To determine the amount of land to be allocated to office buildings, employment is considered a more suitable indicator than future population growth. Because persons employed in offices are not enumerated by location, representative categories need to be chosen, such as employment in finance, insurance, and real estate and in professional and related services, as reported in the decennial census. Since these groups are major office space users, projections based on them may be interpolated to determine requirements for total office use. However, in larger cities and rapidly developing suburban areas, the possibility of office decentralization and job opportunities closer to home needs to be considered.[37] Land area requirements in commercial areas that serve regions should be distinguished from those in commercial areas that serve neighborhoods, and separate projections should be made for each category. Neighborhood requirements are related directly to the population to be served.

Daytime population is another unit of measure that offers considerable promise for estimating nonresidential space requirements. Daytime population is particularly useful in estimating future space needs of the central business district. Employees, shoppers, and persons coming to the CBD for business and social purposes interact and generate demand for businesses and services other than those associated with their immediate destinations. These activities, too, must have land space allocations. Origin-and-destination studies, which include trip purpose, continue to be the most readily available source of information on daytime population. It has been suggested that origin-and-destination data on CBD population (compiled at the peak hour) be used to estimate total floor area used by each segment of the population in determining future land space needs.[38]

Governmental and Institutional Land. The amount of land needed for public buildings differs in each planning area, particularly where a number of governmental units, such as, city, county, state, or federal, are involved. While these space needs are related most closely to population growth and the area's stage of urban development, other factors may be decisive. Legislators may procure federal or state government activities for the home town, and, on occasion, ambitious local leaders have dedicated their careers to monumental building programs. On account of these influential factors, some areas may be overbuilt with government offices while others may be sadly in need of new facilities. There are no general standards—except possibly for educational, hospital, and recreation facilities. Nevertheless, present deficiencies (or surpluses) can be de-

---

[36] See discussion in Shirley F. Weiss, THE CENTRAL BUSINESS DISTRICT IN TRANSITION: METHODOLOGICAL APPROACHES TO CBD ANALYSIS AND FORECASTING FUTURE SPACE REQUIREMENTS (Chapel Hill: Department of City and Regional Planning, University of North Carolina, reprinted 1965), pp 29–32. See also Larry Smith, "Space for CBD's Functions," JOURNAL OF THE AMERICAN INSTITUTE OF PLANNERS, XXVII (February, 1961), pp. 35–42.

[37] Refer to: Raymond Vernon, THE CHANGING ECONOMIC FUNCTION OF THE CENTRAL CITY (New York: Committee for Economic Development, 1959), particularly "Office Job Movement," pp. 55–60; and Donald L. Foley, THE SUBURBANIZATION OF ADMINISTRATIVE OFFICES IN THE SAN FRANCISCO BAY AREA (Berkeley: Real Estate Research Program, University of California, 1957). See also: Norbert J. Stefaniak, UTILIZATION OF CENTRAL OFFICE SPACE BY MILWAUKEE AREA INDUSTRIAL FIRMS, prepared for the Division of Economic Development of the Mayor's Office and the Central Industrial Office Development Committee of the Mayor's Economic Growth Council (Milwaukee: Division of Economic Development, Mayor's Office, 1964).

[38] F. Stuart Chapin, Jr., "Edited Memoranda from Persons Solicited for Comment on 1960 Census Proposal," in FINAL REPORT (draft), Committee on the 1960 Census, Population Association of America (Princeton: Work Group to Consider Proposals for Inquiries on Journey to Work, Daytime Population, Commuting, 1957), p. 37.

termined by survey and future land requirements estimated accordingly. In all of these calculations, projections of population groups to be served are the basic ingredient.[39]

Transportation, Communications, and Utilities. Pending up-to-date survey data, or specific long-range plans, space needs for this group of linked uses can be related to population growth, the status of present facilities, and expected technological advances. Particular attention should be given to probable distribution of the future population, to trends in industrial growth, to public and private policies on industrial development, and to expansion in communication channels. The importance of conducting parallel transportation studies and preparing a comprehensive thoroughfare plan cannot be overemphasized.[40]

Residential Land and Neighborhood Facilities. Finally, the amount of land to be devoted to residential use depends on the rate at which new families are formed; on in-migration; and on the effect of housing codes, slum clearance, and private demolition on the supply of dwelling units. Population forecasts can be converted to housing forecasts (that is, dwelling units) by assuming an average household size for the forecast period. The actual amount of space allocated to housing will of course depend on the densities selected and the assumptions made regarding the percentages of single-family units, duplexes, row houses, garden apartments, and high-rise apartments to be built. Neighborhood facilities are closely related to residential development, so that schools, playgrounds, and local shopping areas can be computed on a per-family basis, or according to the total population of the neighborhood.

Standards observed in planning studies of neighborhood areas tend to reflect those promulgated by the Committee on the Hygiene of Housing of the American Public Health Association, in *Planning the Neighborhood.*[41] These standards will be considered further in the section which follows. Other major reference sources are the publications of the Urban Land Institute and the National Association of Homebuilders,[42] and those of the Federal Housing Administration.[43] The *Environmental Health Planning Guide,* of the Public Health Service, provides a series of yardsticks for "evaluating health related services and facilities from a planning standpoint." Among the factors contributing to a healthful environment, the following are considered: air pollution control, housing programs, radiological health, refuse collection and disposal, sanitation programs, sewerage services, and water supply services.[44]

---

[39] See: U.S. Office of Education, PROBLEMS IN PLANNING URBAN SCHOOL FACILITIES, Bulletin No. 23 (Washington: The Office, 1964); U.S. Office of Education, SCHOOL SITES: SELECTION, DEVELOPMENT, AND UTILIZATION (Washington: The Office, 1958); American Hospital Association and Public Health Service, AREA-WIDE PLANNING FOR HOSPITALS AND RELATED HEALTH FACILITIES (Washington: The Association, 1961); American Society of Planning Officials, STANDARDS FOR OUTDOOR RECREATIONAL AREAS, ASPO Planning Advisory Service Report No. 194 (Chicago: ASPO, January, 1965); National Recreation Association, STANDARDS FOR MUNICIPAL RECREATION AREAS (New York: The Association, 1962); H. Douglas Sessoms, "New Bases for Recreation Planning," JOURNAL OF THE AMERICAN INSTITUTE OF PLANNERS, XXX (February, 1964), pp. 26–33; National Advisory Council on Regional Recreation Planning, A USER-RESOURCE RECREATION PLANNING METHOD (Loomis, California: The Council, 1959); U.S. National Outdoor Recreation Resources Review Commission, OUTDOOR RECREATION FOR AMERICA (Washington: The Commission, 1962).

[40] See: National Committee on Urban Transportation, BETTER TRANSPORTATION FOR YOUR CITY. A GUIDE TO THE FACTUAL DEVELOPMENT OF URBAN TRANSPORTATION PLANS (Chicago: Public Administration Service, 1958).

[41] American Public Health Association, PLANNING THE NEIGHBORHOOD (Chicago: Public Administration Service, 1960).

[42] Urban Land Institute, Community Builders' Council, THE COMMUNITY BUILDERS HANDBOOK (Washington: Urban Land Institute, Executive edition, 1960); Urban Land Institute, INNOVATIONS VS. TRADITIONS IN COMMUNITY DEVELOPMENT, A COMPARATIVE STUDY IN RESIDENTIAL LAND USE, Technical Bulletin No. 47 (Washington: Urban Land Institute, 1963).

[43] U.S. Federal Housing Administration, LAND PLANNING BULLETIN No. 6: PLANNED-UNIT DEVELOPMENT, WITH A HOMES ASSOCIATION (Washington: Federal Housing Administration, revised edition, 1964); LAND PLANNING BULLETIN No. 7, LAND USE INTENSITY (Washington: Federal Housing Administration, interim edition, 1965); MINIMUM PROPERTY STANDARDS FOR ONE AND TWO LIVING UNITS, FHA No. 300 (Washington: Federal Housing Administration, looseleaf, reprinted to include General Revision No. 5, 1965).

Table 5–6

Land Area of all Neighborhood Community Facilities Component Uses and Aggregate Area, by Type of Development and Population of Neighborhood*

Type of Development	Neighborhood Population				
	1,000 persons 275 families	2,000 persons 550 families	3,000 persons 825 families	4,000 persons 1,100 families	5,000 persons 1,375 families
One- or two-family development*					
Area in component uses					
1) Acres in school site................	1.20	1.20	1.50	1.80	2.20
2) Acres in playground..............	2.75	3.25	4.00	5.00	6.00
3) Acres in park....................	1.50	2.00	2.50	3.00	3.50
4) Acres in shopping center...........	.80	1.20	2.20	2.60	3.00
5) Acres in general community facilities†......................	.38	.76	1.20	1.50	1.90
Aggregate area					
6) Acres: total.....................	6.63	8.41	11.40	13.90	16.60
7) Acres per 1,000 persons...........	6.63	4.20	3.80	3.47	3.32
8) Square feet per family.............	1,050	670	600	550	530
Multifamily development‡					
Area in component uses					
1) Acres in school site................	1.20	1.20	1.50	1.80	2.20
2) Acres in playground..............	2.75	3.25	4.00	5.00	6.00
3) Acres in park....................	2.00	3.00	4.00	5.00	6.00
4) Acres in shopping center...........	.80	1.20	2.20	2.60	3.00
5) Acres in general community facilities†......................	.38	.76	1.20	1.50	1.90
Aggregate area					
6) Acres: total.....................	7.13	9.41	12.90	15.90	19.10
7) Acres per 1,000 persons...........	7.13	4.70	4.30	3.97	3.82
8) Square feet per family.............	1,130	745	680	630	610

* With private lot area of less than ¼ acre per family (for private lots of ¼ acre or more, park area may be omitted).

† Allowance for indoor social and cultural facilities discussed in Section 22 (church, assembly hall, etc.) or separate health center, nursery school, etc., unallocated above. Need will vary locally.

‡ Or other development predominantly without private yards.

Source: Committee on Hygiene of Housing, American Public Health Association, PLANNING THE NEIGHBORHOOD (Chicago: Public Administration Service, 1960), Table 11, p. 53.

STANDARDS FOR THE ENVIRONMENT OF RESIDENTIAL AREAS

In *Planning the Neighborhood* the Committee on the Hygiene of Housing points out that

The present volume should be considered not as a manual of design but rather as a formulation of those principles and standards which the technician will use in combinations to be determined by him in the course of his design solutions; and as a frame of reference against which the nontechnical policymaker can test the adequacy of solutions finally presented to him by the technicians.[45]

While there have been notable changes in design concept and technique since the first edition was issued in 1948, the standards have served planners well in allocating space for future residential areas and in testing the adequacy of existing housing stock and facilities with the Committee's guidelines for the residential environment. As a working definition,

---

[44] U.S. Public Health Service, ENVIRONMENTAL HEALTH PLANNING GUIDE, Public Health Service Publication No. 823 (Washington: Division of Environmental Engineering and Food Protection, Public Health Service, Rev. Ed., 1962).

[45] *Ibid.*, p. v.

healthful housing "includes not only sanitation and safety from physical hazards but also those qualities of comfort and convenience and aesthetic satisfaction essential for emotional and social well-being."[46]

A revision of the APHA standards is currently under way (1967), and a new edition may be expected in 1968.[47] While some of the standards are likely to be different from those published some twenty years earlier, they are also likely to be higher.[48] Consequently, the risk in publishing the existing standards is one of likely obsolescence within the biennium. Yet the 1948 standards have not been met in many parts of the country, and perhaps the chance of their acceptance or serious consideration is more likely now than ever before, with the promise of revised guidelines by 1968.

In Table 5–6, the recommended land area requirements of all neighborhood community facilities are given. Neighborhood populations, depending on density allocations, vary from 275 families (1,000 persons approximately) to 1,375 families (5,000 persons approximately). Acres in school site, playground, park, shopping center, and general community facilities are given separately for one- or two-family development and for multifamily development. Community facilities are based on access standards relating to walking distance from the farthest dwelling. As noted in Table 5–7, provision is made for school buses "in exceptional circumstances" and for public transit to indoor social, cultural, and recreation center and to health center, "where facility cannot be provided within neighborhood or walking distance." Use of the automobile is clearly not encouraged in the access standards recommended. It remains to be seen whether the 1968 revision will reinforce the neighborhood concept by maintaining walking distance standards and/or whether driving time standards will be adopted in recognition of the widening use of the automobile as a means of access to local activities. Clearly there is room for choice in this decision area, as long as the implications of the different transportation facilities vis-à-vis land development patterns are understood and evaluated in terms of the community's long-range development objectives.

ESTIMATING PROCEDURES FOR PRELIMINARY LAND USE PLAN

A comprehensive text in urban planning and/or technical reports of selected planning agencies should be consulted as guides in the

Table 5–7

Access Standards for Community Facilities Within The Neighborhood Recommended Distance, with Maximum Limit

Neighborhood Facility	Walking Distance (one way) From Farthest Dwelling
Nursery school	¼ mile*
Kindergarten	¼ to ½ mile
Elementary school	¼ to ½ mile†
Playground	¼ to ½ mile‡
Park	¼ to ½ mile
Shopping center	¼ to ½ mile
Indoor social, cultural, and recreation center	½ mile§
Health center	½ mile§

* Where nursery school cannot be provided within ¼ mile it should at least be within 15 minutes elapsed time by public or special transit.

† In exceptional circumstances, the limit may be ¾-mile walk or 20 minutes elapsed time by school bus, if children may obtain hot lunches at school at nominal cost.

‡ One-half mile permissible only in planned neighborhoods meeting all requirements for safe access, and where playground is adjacent to elementary school.

§ Where facility cannot be provided within neighborhood or walking distance it should at least be within 20 minutes elapsed time by public transit.

Source: Committee on the Hygiene of Housing, American Public Health Association, PLANNING THE NEIGHBORHOOD (Chicago: Public Administration Service, 1960), Table 5, p. 44.

---

[46] *Ibid.*

[47] ASPO NEWSLETTER, XXXII (February, 1966), p. 1. AIP NEWSLETTER (June 1966), p. 10: ". . . the American Public Health Association has decided to begin work on a new edition. . . .

"The action was taken at a meeting of the Program Area Committee on Housing and Health of APHA, held in Washington on May 10. AIP and ASPO national offices are advising on the project. Persons with suggestions for inclusion in the booklet should communicate with the chairman of the Committee, Charles L. Senn, c/o Los Angeles County Health Department, 220 North Broadway, Los Angeles, Calif. 90012."

[48] Observation by Dennis O'Harrow, ASPO NEWSLETTER, *op. cit.*, p. 1.

Table 5–8

Estimating Net Increase in Space for Retail and Office Functions in CBD by Component Analysis, 19___

Type of Space Use	Space in Thousands of Square Feet		
	Retail	Office	Combined Total
Total floor area	XXXX[a]	XXXX[b]	XXXXXX
Ground floor area	XXX[c]	XXX[d]	XXXX
Ground area for new parking[e]	XXX	XXX	XXXX
Ground area for new loading[f]	XXX	XXX	XXXX
Other ground area[g]	XXX	XXX	XXXX
First subtotal of ground area			XXXXXX
Allowance for flexibility[h]			XXXX
Second subtotal of ground area			XXXXXX
Deficiencies in parking and loading for existing uses[i]			XXXX
Total ground area required			XXXXXX

[a] Before this entry can be inserted, assumptions as to the distribution of new region-serving retail space must be made. To illustrate, it might be assumed that 50 per cent of new floor area is to be accommodated in the CBD, 30 per cent in satellite centers, and 20 per cent in all other locations. Under such assumptions, the entry would be 50 per cent of the aggregate new floor space expected to be added in the metropolitan area during the planning period.

[b] As in the case of the retail item, assumptions concerning the distribution of office space are introduced here. If, for example, 90 per cent of new office floor area is expected to develop in the CBD, then the entry here would be 90 per cent of the aggregate of all new floor area in office uses expected in the metropolitan area during the planning period.

[c] For estimating purposes, an average story height for retail uses is assumed here. If, for example, upon examining the prevailing average height to which retail uses build, it seems reasonable to expect new uses to build to an average of 1.9 stories, then to derive this entry, the total floor area in the entry immediately above would be divided by 1.9.

[d] Two assumptions are involved here. First, the per cent of floor area in offices in the CBD which can be expected to be added to floors above retail activities already provided for in the entry immediately to the left is assumed, let us say 40 per cent. Second, as in the case of retail structures, an average story height of CBD office buildings is assumed, say 5 stories. Then, under this example, the entry here would be 60 per cent of the total new office floor area expected to be added in the CBD (60 per cent of the item immediately above), divided by 5.

[e] Assumed parking ratio standards are introduced and applied to *total* new floor area figures. Differential standards may be used, or a crude general standard may be applied to the entry for combined floor area in the right-hand column. If a portion of the parking area is to go into multideck structures, a procedure similar to that followed in Note d would be followed in order to "factor out" the space in upper-deck areas and obtain a ground area total.

[f] On the basis of design standards, an estimate of space required for new loading areas is made in this entry. Crude standards for both retail and office structures are sometimes developed on the basis of a survey of areas presently judged to be well served in this or other cities. Some studies have used rough estimators such as one square foot of loading area for every 20 square feet of *total* floor space.

[g] This is to take care of waste area and private open spaces not included in estimates above. According to anticipated changes in the intensity to which ground area is to be used, an entry for these space needs is made here. On the basis of recent construction in the CBD, some studies simply follow the trend observed, adjusted or unadjusted, and increase the ground floor area by, say, 10, 20, or 25 per cent to provide for "relief space" and planted areas.

[h] The flexibility factor is an allowance for unforeseen expansion in the CBD, including at the same time latitude for choice of location among leasing users of CBD floor area. This factor is estimated locally on the basis of vacancy rates assumed reasonable for the period ahead and an adequate allowance for flexibility. It usually takes the form of a simple per cent increase of the aggregate ground area represented in the first subtotal, say a 20 per cent increase.

[i] This entry involves an analysis of the adequacy of present off-street parking provisions. It reflects the aggregate deficiency in parking and loading areas that must be treated as new space requirements under assumptions concerning the elimination of on-street parking and loading and any significant changes in driving habits anticipated.

Source: F. Stuart Chapin, Jr., URBAN LAND USE PLANNING (Urbana: University of Illinois Press, 2nd ed., 1965), p. 407.

process of preparing estimates of space requirements for the preliminary land use plan.
Considerable time can be saved in following a
logical sequence of steps in allocating vacant
and renewal land by major categories of use.
The following procedures have been selected
from *Urban Land Use Planning* as examples for
determining space requirements for manufacturing, wholesale, region-serving business, and
residential uses.[49]

Manufacturing Uses

1. Determine the salient characteristics of existing
manuracturing uses in the urban area, existing industrial densities, and the prospects for future manufacturing activity as determined in previous studies
of the urban economy.

2. On the basis of these studies and considering
modern-day industrial plant requirements, develop
local standards for future industrial densities.

3. Apply industrial densities to future manufacturing employment estimates to obtain estimated
land requirements.

4. Determine from summary of vacant and renewal land how supply matches up with estimated
need, and, referring to location requirements, make
a trial distribution into areas considered prime for
industrial use, carrying over the surplus for realloca-
tion in the vacant land tally.[50]

Wholesale and Related Uses

1. Analyze the characteristics of existing wholesale
and related activities in the urban area.

2. On the basis of anticipated growth in wholesale
activity as determined in studies of the urban economy and expected changes in the intensity of use,
estimate future ratios of land area per employee for
inlying and outlying locations.

3. Apply these ratios to future wholesale employment estiates to obtain estimated land requirements.

4. Determine from summary of vacant and renewal land how supply matches up with estimated
need, and, referring to location requirements, make
a trial distribution into areas identified as having potentialities for this use, earmarking the surplus for
use in subsequent analyses of other uses.[51]

*Central Business District and Satellite Business
Uses*

1. Delineate the CBD study area and satellite
business centers and analyze existing space usage by
floor area and ground area.

2. On the basis of this analysis and studies of
retail business trends in the primary trade area,
develop estimates of probable changes in intensity
of use, parking needs, and so on, and determine
future space needs.

3. Determine from vacant and renewal land summary the amount of land available for CBD expansion and determine what additional space is expected to become available due to decentralization
moves of wholesale and manufacturing uses presently in CBD. Establish space deficit, if any. As
necessary, earmark for CBD expansion strategically
located areas, and summarize data on areas presently
in other uses needed for CBD expansion. Repeat
these space investigations for satellite centers.[52]

Residential Uses

1. Organize data relative to the existing supply of
dwelling units and density of development and summarize by planning districts.

2. Develop working assumptions as to future residential trends, and on the basis of these assumptions, determine additions to total supply of dwelling units required and estimate how this total is to
be allocated to assumed future housing types and
residential density classes.

3. On the basis of the supply of vacant and renewal land suited to residential development and its
approximate effective net holding capacity by planning district, make tentative allocation of additions
to total dwelling unit stock for the several density
classes to the various planning districts.

4. Summarize space requirements and population
estimates by planning district.[53]

As noted in the foregoing examples, the final
step in each estimating procedure calls for a
check of vacant and renewal land to determine
how supply matches up with estimated need.
The computation of new space requirements is
facilitated by well organized tables for tallying
the estimates of the net additions and net re-
ductions in space. Tables 5–8, 9, and 10 illustrate
tabular layouts for estimating the components
of CBD space use, total CBD and satellite center requirements, and local business center
needs. Other tabular layouts are provided in
Urban Land Use Planning for major and component uses, including: industrial areas;[54]

---

[49] Chapin, *op. cit.*, Chapter 11, "Space Requirements," pp. 383–456.
[50] *Ibid.*, p. 386.
[51] *Ibid.*, p. 397.

[52] *Ibid.*, p. 403.
[53] *Ibid.*, pp. 422–23.
[54] *Ibid.*, p. 391.

wholesale and related uses;[55] current stock of dwelling units and net densities by housing type;[56] derivation of total new dwelling unit requirements;[57] new residential space requirements by density type distributed among planning districts;[58] new space requirements for schools by planning district;[59] new requirements for local recreation areas by planning district;[60] and derivation of gross space requirements for entirely new residential communities.[61]

The space for residential communities is allocated *after* region-structuring uses, which also include the open space system and public service facilities. The efficient interplay of all these uses in a regional and a local context and their arrangement in the urban landscape to provide healthful living, convenience, and aesthetic satisfaction are some of the more obvious objectives in shaping the future land use pattern.

Welding the Land Use Plan

After the mapping, surveying, classifying, tabulating, and estimating procedures, there still remains the important task of welding the land use plan. The allocation of space for future land use and reuse must be reviewed in relation to a meaningful open space system and an efficient transportation network. The basic questions to be asked, and answered, are: "Do the various elements of the plan fit together?" "Is there a logical organization of land use activities, open spaces, and transportation movements?" "In terms of the community's goals, does the plan really succeed in tackling basic problems and issues?" "Can the community afford to pay for carrying out the improvements envisioned in the plan?" "Have public and private interests been given full consideration?" "Is there a place for citizen participa-

tion and identification with the program required for carrying out the plan?"[62]

LAND DEVELOPMENT GOALS

The goals of the community are fundamental to the entire planning progress. They form the basis for making plans, considering alternatives, and evaluating results. In short, they provide the means for making choices and affirming decisions in terms of explicit community goals. A number of these goals are likely to concern the land development pattern of the community, and it is important that these goals be utilized as guidelines throughout the process of formulating the land use plan. It has become the practice of the sixties to relate goals and descriptive urban development patterns. Terms such as "radial corridor," "satellite," "strong core," "multiple centers," "spread city," and variations of these are being used increasingly in land use studies, although the patterns may be more fashionable verbally than fitted structurally. Whatever the proposed land development form may be termed, clearly it is important that it reflect the full array of goals of the community.

One of the most comprehensive attempts to enumerate a set of goals and to formulate alternative growth patterns for achieving a balance of goals is the recent work of the Joint Program, an inter-agency land use–transportation planning program for the Twin Cities Metropolitan Area.[63] As noted by the Program staff, "Goals are hard to determine because they are essentially concrete expressions of values which are highly elusive, complex, and frequently inconsistent. They are seldom stated explicitly."[64] The results of an attitude survey carried out in the winter of 1963–64 were used in determining area development goals and also in judging

---

[55] *Ibid.*, p. 400.
[56] *Ibid.*, pp. 424–25.
[57] *Ibid.*, p. 427.
[58] *Ibid.*, p. 439.
[59] *Ibid.*, p. 447.
[60] *Ibid.*, p. 450.
[61] *Ibid.*, p. 452.

[62] For an extensive checklist of questions covering physical planning and its implementation for land use and circulation, see: William I. Goodman and Jerome L. Kaufman, CITY PLANNING IN THE SIXTIES: A RESTATEMENT OF PRINCIPLES AND TECHNIQUES (Urbana: Bureau of Community Planning, University of Illinois, 1965), pp. 15–16.
[63] The Joint Program, GOALS FOR DEVELOPMENT OF THE TWIN CITIES METROPOLITAN AREA, Report No. 3 (St. Paul: The Joint Program, November, 1965).
[64] PROGRAM NOTES, Vol. 1 (December, 1965), p. 2.

Table 5–9

Total Space Requirements for CBD and Satellite Region-Serving Business Centers, 19___

		Net Acreage of Ground Area				
			Deductions from Other Uses			
Type of Center and Use*	Total Needs	Resi-dence	Whole-sale	Mfg.	Other	Total
Central business district............xx		x	x	x	x	xx
Retail uses......................xx		x	x	x	x	xx
Office uses......................xx		x	x	x	x	xx
Civic uses and parks..............xx		x	x	x	x	xx
Transportation uses................xx		x	x	x	x	xx
Other uses......................xx		x	x	x	x	xx
Satellite business centers.............xx		x	x	x	x	xx
Center A........................xx		x	x	x	x	xx
Center B........................xx		x	x	x	x	xx
Etc.............................xx		x	x	x	x	xx
Other scattered....................xx		x	x	x	x	xx
Total...........................xx		x	x	x	x	xx

* Acreage figures for each center and type of use include parking, loading, and other miscellaneous areas associated with these uses.

Source: F. Stuart Chapin, Jr., URBAN LAND USE PLANNING (Urbana: University of Illinois Press, 2nd. ed., 1965), p. 408.

Table 5–10

New Space Requirements for Local Business Centers by Planning District, 19___

		Net Additions in Space (acres)								
	Net Reduction in Space (acres)	Community Shopping Centers			Neighborhood Facilities			All Local Business Facilities		
Plan-ning District		Inva-sion	V & R*	Total	Inva-sion	V & R	Total	Inva-sion	V & R	Total
1	xx	x	x	x	x	x	x	x	x	x
2	xx	x	x	x	x	x	x	x	x	x
etc.	xx	x	x	x	x	x	x	x	x	x
Subtotal central city	xx	x	x	x	x	x	x	x	x	x
10	xx	x	x	x	x	x	x	x	x	x
11	xx	x	x	x	x	x	x	x	x	x
etc.	xx	x	x	x	x	x	x	x	x	x
Subtotal fringe area	xx	x	x	x	x	x	x	x	x	x
Planning area total	xx	x	x	x	x	x	x	x	x	x

* "V & R" is an abbreviation for "vacant and renewal land."

Source: F. Stuart Chapin, Jr., URBAN LAND USE PLANNING (Urbana: University of Illinois Press, 2nd. ed., 1965), p. 443.

alternative growth patterns proposed.[65]

Communities undertaking land development plans would do well to follow the example of the Joint Program in developing their own goal list based on a survey of community attitudes. The Twin Cities' list[66] is cited below as an example of an explicit statement of goals. Obviously, it cannot and should not be adopted in whole by other areas with different values and attitudes. Yet, only time will tell whether there are universals among the goals set for themselves by communities throughout the nation.

Housing Goals of the Twin Cities Metropolitan Area

1. Enough housing for all area residents.
2. Broad choice of housing types in the metropolitan area.
3. Housing choice within neighborhoods.
4. Identity and individuality.
5. Convenience to other activities and facilities.
6. Safe, healthful, and blight-free residences and neighborhoods.

Commercial Goals

1. An adequate supply of goods and services.
2. Varied sites suitable for a variety of outlets.
3. Functional, safe, and attractive design and display.
4. Minimum conflict with other metropolitan activities.
5. Effective use and development of old centers.

Industrial Goals

1. Enough industry to meet industrial employment needs.
2. A variety of types of industry.
3. Adequate supplies of suitable industrial land.
4. Minimization of industrial blight and the blighting effects of industries on their neighbors.

Open Space Goals

1. Satisfaction of the people's outdoor recreational needs.
2. Conservation and effective use of natural landscape qualities.

Public Facilities Goals

1. Adequate and efficient service.
2. A fair distribution of costs and benefits.

Transportation Goals

1. Ease of movement throughout the metropolitan area.
2. A variety of modes of travel to meet the needs of different people and activities.

Government Goals

1. Authority and capability to deal with metropolitan as well as local problems.
2. Effective coordination among all branches, units, and agencies of government.
3. Fair and adequate acquisition and distribution of tax revenues.

Urban Design Goal

A visually pleasing, coherent, and workable environment.

EVALUATION OF ALTERNATIVE SCHEMES

As preparation for policy review and selection of the optimal urban growth pattern, a systematic evaluation of the land use proposals must be related to the potential achievement of the community's development goals. Conversely, the impact of each scheme on the community's public revenues and expenditures should be considered, as well as social and private costs and benefits. While few communities may be in a position to make detailed analysis as part of the preliminary land use planning process, the importance of undertaking meaningful evaluations should be underscored.[67]

In the staff proposal for a general plan for the Maryland-Washington Regional District, a simple form of comparative analysis of four development patterns was introduced.[68] The analytical technique, illustrated in Table 5–11, is based on a rating system of plus, zero, and minus marks which correspond to "positive contribution toward achievement of goal,"

---

[65] PROGRAM NOTES, Nos. 2 and 3, as cited in No. 5, *ibid.*

[66] The Joint Program, *op. cit.,* p. 1.

[67] In THE CITY PLANNING PROCESS: A POLITICAL ANALYSIS (Ithaca: Cornell University Press, 1965), Alan Altshuler makes the following pertinent observation: "In the long run, I suspect, general planning and evaluation will have little effect on American cities unless their goal premises can be established in sufficiently compelling fashion (both politically and intellectually) to make politicians take notice" (p. 332).

[68] The Maryland-National Capital Park and Planning Commission, . . . ON WEDGES AND CORRIDORS: A GENERAL PLAN FOR THE MARYLAND-WASHINGTON REGIONAL DISTRICT IN MONTGOMERY AND PRINCE GEORGE'S COUNTIES (Silver Spring: The Commission, 1962), p. 148.

Table 5–11

Comparative Analysis of Development Plans
(illustrative example)

Goals	Alternatives			
	Sprawl	Av. Den.	Satellite	Corridor
1. Use land efficiently..........................	−	0	+	+
2. Encourage an orderly conversion of undeveloped land to urban use.............................	−	+	−	+
3. Protect natural resources and encourage their proper development...........................	−	+	+	+
4. Maintain large open spaces...................	−	0	+	+
5. Expand opportunities for outdoor recreation.......	−	+	+	+
6. Facilitate the orderly and efficient arrangement of public utilities and services...................	−	+	−	+
7. Provide an efficient transportation system including rapid transit.............................	−	−	+	+
8. Encourage greater variety of living environments....	−	−	+	+
9. Invite imaginative urban design.................	−	−	+	+
10. Assure implementation of the plan..............	+	+	−	+
Acceptance Factor*.............................	−8	+2	+4	+10

* Number of plus factors minus number of negative factors:
    + = positive contribution toward achievement of goal.
    0 = achievement of goal not decisively helped or hurt.
    − = works against achievement of goal.
Source: Maryland-National Capital Park and Planning Commission, . . . on WEDGES AND CORRIDORS: A GENERAL PLAN FOR THE MARYLAND-WASHINGTON REGIONAL DISTRICT IN MONTGOMERY AND PRINCE GEORGE'S COUNTIES (Silver Spring: The Commission, 1962), p. 148.

"achievement of goal not decisively helped or hurt," and "works against achievement of goal." The sum of the plus marks less the minus marks provides the evaluating measure, called the "Acceptance Factor." While the degree of precision may be questioned, the rating system apparently provides a basis for ranking alternative schemes related to explicit goals. The staff evaluation of the Maryland-Washington Regional District proposals reports as follows:

Summarizing the advantages and disadvantages of the four alternative development patterns in terms of the ten goals, the corridor pattern rates highest overall, with satellite second, average density third, and sprawl a poor fourth. The satellite pattern would have rated nearly as high as the corridor except that it was more expensive and harder to implement. The average density pattern has several advantages but they are offset by disadvantages. Sprawl's only advantage is its ease of implementation.[69]

TOWARD PLAN ADOPTION AND COORDINATION

Having evaluated the alternative land use schemes and prepared the technical findings and recommendations, the planning staff is ready to submit its report for the final policy review leading to adoption of one alternative as the community's future land use plan. From goals to plan, as illustrated in Figure 5–8, the end product is the result of a circular sequence of steps which involves successive multiple levels of analysis and policy review.

Characterized as a "progressive planning ap-

[69] *Ibid.* See also: Greater Bridgeport Regional Planning Agency, PRELIMINARY REGIONAL PLAN: RECOMMENDED DEVELOPMENT POLICIES (Trumbull, Conn.: The Agency, 1963) for evaluation of three alternatives, including projections of public expenditures and full property values, pp. 21–28. The Strong Core Plan is recommended; the Lineal Plan is considered for further study; and the Spread Plan is rejected.

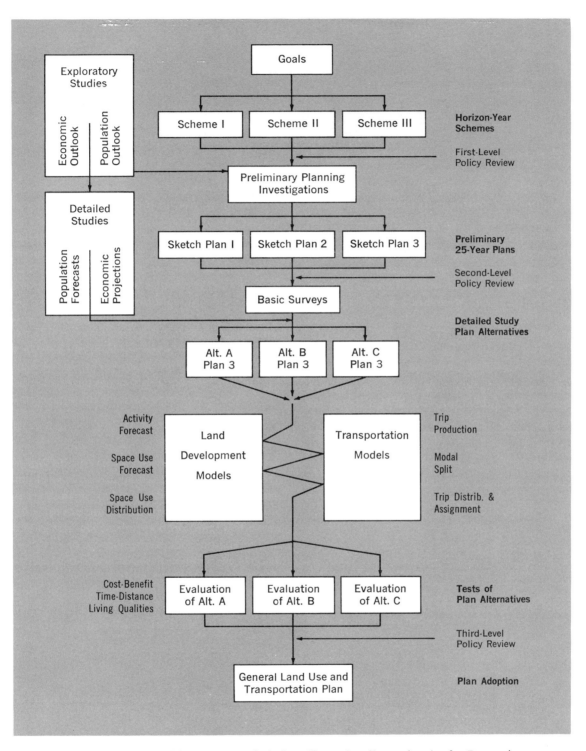

FIGURE 5–8. *Sequential aspect of technical studies and policy review in the Progressive Planning Approach (As indicated in the right-hand column, this approach involves cycles of planning, each involving more detailed and exacting forms of analysis than the preceding one. Plans are presented in the form of alternatives, with one emerging from each level of policy review and providing the basis for consideration of alternative policies at the next more detailed stage of analysis. The general land use and transportation plan is the end product of this sequence. This is not a straight-line but rather a circular sequence; with adoption of this plan a new sequence is set in motion.*

proach,"[70] this procedure of systematically working toward plan adoption has many advantages. It proceeds from planning schemes and policy decisions of a broad and general nature to refined studies and detailed proposals modified in keeping with policy reviews scheduled at each major sequence in the planning process. As delineated in Figure 5–8, the procedural example integrates forecasts of land development and transportation models and tests plan alternatives according to measures of cost-benefit, time-distance, and living qualities. Responding to public discussion and reaction, modifications are made in the land use plan which is finally adopted.

Implementation of the land use plan as adopted goes hand in hand with implementation of the comprehensive plan, of which it is a key component. Complementary plans for servicing land use, zoning and subdivision regulations, housing and renewal programs, and capital budgeting, are important implementation tools. These subjects will be discussed in later chapters. The stock of techniques for shaping and reshaping urban growth, however, is still in the early stages of trial and error. The effectiveness of some of the traditional techniques is

being questioned, as new attitudes and changed activity patterns call out for new combinations of land use and new public-private cooperation in guiding urban development. The notion of *urban development guidance systems,* as proposed by Chapin, may well fulfill the need for conscious direction through one coordinated framework:

The concept is a simple one. A guidance system draws upon the general plan [ed.: of which the land use plan is an important component] of the metropolitan area for the underlying rationale in the location and timing of urban expansion—land development, the construction of essential links in the transportation networks, and the provision of required community facilities. In serving as an organizing force, the general plan thus becomes a key technique for steering both public and private actions so that they produce the desired pattern of development in the metropolitan landscape. But at the same time an urban development policies instrument that specifies under what conditions public services will be extended to new areas of development, and a public works program that sets forth the schedule under which facilities will be built in order to supply these services, become the key techniques for formalizing actions in the public sector. By the same token, an over-all urban development code and a broad-gauge civic education program become key techniques for regulating and insuring more informed action in the private sector. . . .[71]

---

[70] Cited by Chapin, URBAN LAND USE PLANNING, *op. cit.,* p. 351: "First perfected in test demonstration studies by the National Resources Planning Board at the beginning of World War II, the 'progressive planning approach' was later set down in ACTION FOR CITIES, Chicago: Public Administration Service, 1945."

[71] F. Stuart Chapin, Jr., "Taking Stock of Techniques for Shaping Urban Growth," JOURNAL OF THE AMERICAN INSTITUTE OF PLANNERS, XXXIX (May, 1963), p. 86. Reprinted by permission of THE JOURNAL OF THE AMERICAN INSTITUTE OF PLANNERS, May, 1963, Vol. no. 39, No. 5.

6

Transportation Planning

TRANSPORTATION planning is the process by which transportation improvements or new facilities are systematically conceived, tested as to present and future adequacy, and programmed for future construction. Modern transportation planning emphasizes the total transportation system, rather than one or more isolated facilities. It considers all modes of transport which are economically feasible to a state, region, or urban area. It considers all types of improvements, including traffic engineering improvements, such as more efficient signal systems, channelization of traffic at intersections, better signs, and off-street parking facilities; major reconstruction of existing facilities, such as road widening; and the construction of new arterials, expressways, and transit facilities.

Much of this chapter is concerned with planning in urban areas for streets and mass transportation systems. The basic principles of such planning are applicable to all types and sizes of urban areas. The methodology used in the planning process varies widely depending upon the kind and magnitude of the transportation problem and the size of the urban area. The process described in this chapter has been developed and utilized in a number of areas of all sizes.

The characteristics of urban travel and the component systems providing for travel are described first, followed by a description of the planning process involved. The purpose of the chapter is to outline the methods used to obtain economic solutions to urban transportation problems. The first major section of this chapter covers Streets, Highways, and Mass Transportation; the second major section covers Intercity Transportation.

I. Streets, Highways, and Mass Transportation

Our cities are an accumulation of different urban patterns. Each of these patterns was influenced not only by the previous form of the city and by its site, but also by the contemporary economic, social, political, and technological systems of the inhabitants. Within all these patterns, travel has prevailed as a constant condition of urban life.

In pre-19th century cities, urban settlements were generally small enough to permit travel by foot, horse, cart, bearer, or other primitive means.

From the mid-1800s, mass transportation developed as a new means of carrying people in cities. Consequently the railroad, the horse car, and the cable car began to affect urban form. Extensions of urban development poked fingers into the countryside along the fastest travel routes, with suburban railroad stations giving birth to the suburbs—small nuclei then quite divorced from the central city.

Subsequent developments in mass transportation accentuated the earlier trends. The electric street cars in the 1880s and 1890s, the steam (later electric) elevated trains of the same era, and the subways—all of these provided a means for moving and concentrating people with unprecedented efficiency.

The nature of mass transportation required

high-density development, not only of work places but also of living quarters. During the late 19th and early 20th centuries, high densities were provided of necessity because the only practicable method of moving about within cities was by foot or by mass transportation facilities. The forms of our present cities still bear the imprint of this type of growth, with a spoke-like pattern focused on a center that dominates the economic, social, and political scene.

In a similar fashion, the automobile has greatly influenced the form and shape of modern cities. In effect, locational constraints which resulted in high-density cores and radial development along mass transportation lines, have been lifted; mass transportation is no longer the sole mode of transportation influencing urban development. During the past several decades, the areas which have developed most rapidly are those having few mass transportation services. With increasing automobile ownership and the resultant increase in personal mobility, vast areas around existing cities have been brought into urban use. This is most apparent when the newly developed areas are served by freeways.

From this brief review of the development of transportation in cities, certain conclusions can be drawn. There is a pattern of technological advance of which improvements in transportation technology form only a small part. The rate of technological progress is faster now than before, and seems to be accelerating. For example, individual air travel in the future city may be an element to consider. Population growth and greater per capita automobile ownership will continue to provide additional means for improving transportation.

What form the city will take, and how provisions for future changes will enter into planning equations cannot be seen clearly, but this much can be said: transportation plans must consider the activities that will continue to generate traffic, and the different modes of transportation must be planned together since they are integral parts of the total system which moves people within cities.

Throughout history, the need of the traveler for improved transportation has been much the same. Travel is not purchased as an end-product, but rather to make other products and services available.

Economical, safe, pleasant, and fast transportation are but a few of the many goals of urban life.

Travel in Urban Areas

An understanding of the nature and characteristics of travel in urban areas is desirable as a basis for the design of transportation systems. Travel is to the transportation system what current is to an electrical network or fluid to a hydraulic network. The design of the system must be based not only on the characteristics and functions of the conductor, but also on the properties of that which passes through the conductor.

Since most current knowledge about travel in urban areas has been gained from origin-destination surveys, it is desirable to learn some of the terms used in these surveys. The unit of travel is customarily the "trip"—that is, a one-way journey that proceeds from an origin to a destination by a single type of vehicular transportation. For example, a journey from home to work proceeding by bus, then by suburban railroad, and then by taxi, is normally considered to be three trips. In some surveys, these trips have been linked into a single trip, so that the overall purpose, length, and time of the journey may be better studied. The "purpose" of the trip is the reason for making the journey—that is, to go to work, to go home, to shop, to conduct personal business, and so on. The type of transportation used—for example, automobile, bus, suburban railroad, or taxi—is called the "mode" of travel.

A journey made completely by foot is not considered to be a trip in the typical origin-destination survey. The walk made from home to a mass transportation mode, however, is considered a part of the overall trip by mass transportation, as is any walking at the end of a mass transportation trip.

A rewarding or a profitable activity is the main purpose of travel and it can be said that such activity generates travel. Whatever the purpose of the trip it can be looked at in two ways: from the viewpoint of the type of activity involved, or from the viewpoint of the person making the trip. For transportation planning, the most accurate description of the acitivty is land use, and the most accurate description of the person's viewpoint is purpose. Land use is perhaps the more convenient measure of the two, because it enables travel to be related to a tangible, and relatively predictable quality. However, it must be thoroughly understood that *people* make trips, and that land use is only a convenient indirect measure of the type and geographic location of trips made.

LAND USE AS A TRIP GENERATOR

Because most travel data are obtained by means of interviews in the home—a technique employed by origin-destination surveys—trip generation is often related to the dwelling, which is the unit sampled in such surveys. The rate of trip generation per-dwelling unit varies from city to city and from place to place within a city. In the Chicago area in 1956, the average trip rate was 5.5 trips per dwelling per day, while in Detroit in 1953 it was 6.2. More recent average trip rates of 7.8 and 8.6 have been obtained in Buffalo in 1962 and Rochester in 1963.

Within a city, trip generation seems to be related to income, automobile ownership, and distance from city center. The higher the income and the greater the automobile ownership, the more travel is performed. These two factors are correlated, because automobile ownership is partially a function of income.

Tables 6–1, 2, and 3 show these relationships, as obtained from Buffalo data in 1962. Why

Table 6–2

Average Weekday Number of Person Trips per Dwelling Place by Automobile Ownership, Buffalo, 1962

Number of Automobiles Owned	Average Number of Person Trips Per Dwelling Place
0	2.28
1	8.34
2	12.78
3	16.66
4 or more	27.04
Average for study area	7.84

Source: Subdivision of Transportation Planning and Programming, New York State Department of Public Works, SUMMARY OF HOME INTERVIEW SURVEY DATA (Albany: The Subdivision, 1964).

Table 6–1

Average Weekday Number of Person Trips per Dwelling Place by Income Range, Buffalo, 1962

Family Income Range	Average Number of Person Trips Per Dwelling Place
$ 0 to $ 2,999	2.76
3,000 to 3,999	5.48
4,000 to 4,999	6.66
5,000 to 5,999	8.17
6,000 to 6,999	9.87
7,000 to 7,999	10.12
8,000 to 8,999	10.99
9,000 to 9,999	11.45
10,000 to 11,999	11.85
12,000 and up	12.89
Average for study area	7.84

Source: Unpublished data from the Niagara Frontier Transportation Study.

Table 6–3

Average Weekday Number of Person Trips per Dwelling Place by Distance from CBD, Buffalo, 1962

Ring	Average Number of Person Trips Per Dwelling Place
0	2.85
1	4.38
2	6.39
3	8.86
4	10.35
5	10.02
6	8.99
7	8.34
Average for study area	7.84

Source: Subdivision of Transportation Planning and Programming, New York State Department of Public Works, SUMMARY OF HOME INTERVIEW SURVEY DATA (Albany: The Subdivision, 1964).

travel varies with income cannot be explained with certainty, but it might be hypothesized that trip-making, relative to income, is less costly as income increases. Another explanation might be that trip-making is easier in low-density areas, and more difficult, and hence less frequent, in the high-density areas close to the center of the city. In high density areas, many trips are undoubtedly made by walking, whereas this is not feasible in low density areas. Since new subdivisions are generally occupied by middle- and upper-income families who own more cars, and since these subdivisions are farthest from the central business district, it follows that greater rates of trip generation can be expected in growing areas than for the city as a whole.

Trip generation can also be measured for nonresidential land uses with data from origin-destination surveys. The unit of measure is often in trips per net acre (streets excluded). Unfortunately, per-acre rates do not include any correction for density, and this is why working with per-dwelling unit rates is advantageous in the case of residential land.

Floor-area generation rates, a density measure, may in the future be used to study the effect of density in commercial and industrial areas.

Tables 6–4 and 6–5 give the rates of trip generation by net acres of land use for Detroit and Chicago. The declining rates of trip generation per acre are a reflection of the decreasing intensity of land use with increasing distance from the city's center.

The implication of trip generation is that if the amount of land and its type and intensity of use can be forecast, then the amount of travel can also be predicted. Further, travel to different parts of the city is not likely to grow indefinitely but will reach stability when there is no more growth in any given area.

TRIP PURPOSE

Looking at trip-making from a traveler's viewpoint, a similar picture is seen. Data obtained from home interview surveys present a cross section of trip purposes made by each dwelling unit. These trips are made for all the likely reasons: to work, to shop, to go to school, to conduct personal business, to enjoy social-recreation, etc. Figure 6–1 shows the distribution of automobile trips by purpose for two San Diego subdivisions and for the metropolitan area of San Diego.

The proportion of trips made for different purposes changes as the number of trips per household increases. Households making more

Table 6–4

Average Weekday Number of Person Trips per Acre of Land Use, by Ring, Detroit, 1953

Ring	Description	Internal Trips per Acre of Land Use					
		Residential	Commercial	Industrial	Public Open Space	Public Buildings	Average Rate for all Used Land
0	Core of CBD	733	1797	153	—	945	1522
1	Remainder of CBD	186	207	209	29	362	222
2	Remainder of 3 mi.	65	194	92	10	89	74
3	3 to 6 mi.	56	218	48	3	26	58
4	6 to 9 mi.	42	280	38	8	46	50
5	9 to 12 mi.	26	325	36	3	33	32
6	Over 12 mi.	14	182	8	2	17	15
	Average rate for study area	29	269	37	3	33	36

Source: John R. Hamburg, "Summary Comparison of Trip Generation for Chicago and Detroit," C.A.T.S. RESEARCH NEWS, Vol. 2, No. 11 (June 27, 1958).

Table 6–5

Average Weekday Number of Person Trips per Acre of Land Use, by Ring, Chicago, 1956

	Approx. Distance (miles)	Internal Trips per Acre of Land Use						
Ring		Resi-dential	Com-mercial	Manufac-turing	Transporta-tion	Public Build-ings	Public Open Space	Average Rate for all Used Land
CBD	0.0	2120	2096	3343	265	1910	121	1149
I	1.5	213	182	229	36	241	31	142
II	4.1	123	118	78	15	120	25	90
III	6.1	104	141	85	11	97	27	85
IV	8.6	66	208	50	13	76	14	65
V	11.7	42	176	26	5	56	6	36
VI	15.8	30	129	14	2	45	2	19
VII	23.4	19	122	14	6	13	1	13
Average rate for study area		47	177	47	8	51	4	37

Source: John R. Hamburg, "Summary Comparison of Trip Generation for Chicago and Detroit," C.A.T.S. RESEARCH NEWS, Vol. 2, No. 11 (June 27, 1958).

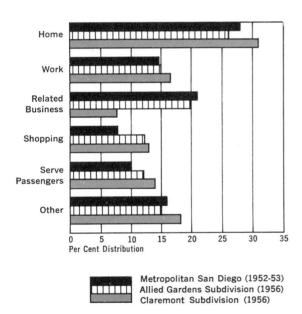

FIGURE 6–1. *Percentage distribution of weekday trip purposes for San Diego and two subdivisions*

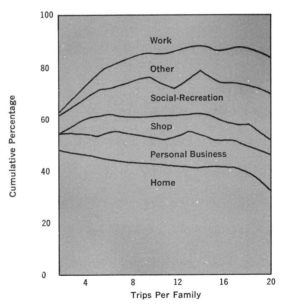

FIGURE 6–2. *Distribution of trip purposes as a function of person trips per dwelling place, Chicago, 1956*

trips have higher proportions of shopping and social-recreation trips (see Figure 6–2).

TRIP LENGTH

The distribution of trips by length follows a regular pattern. Most trips are short; as trip length increases, progressively fewer trips are made. The short trip is relatively inexpensive and may be made more often and for less important purposes. For example, a trip to the corner delicatessen for pumpernickel bread can be made without much cost or effort. A trip

Table 6–6

Percentage Distribution of Trip Purposes by Airline Trip Length, Chicago, 1956

Trip Length (in miles)	Home	Work	Shop	School	Soc. Rec.	Eat Meal	Pers. Bus.	Total
0.0 to 1.9	33.4	26.7	48.6	47.5	37.1	45.5	41.6	34.5
2.0 to 3.9	25.1	20.2	29.8	31.6	23.8	25.9	26.7	24.6
4.0 to 5.9	14.2	15.3	7.4	10.3	15.8	15.8	12.6	14.6
6.0 to 7.9	10.7	14.7	6.3	4.9	8.1	2.9	8.8	10.3
8.0 to 9.9	6.2	7.7	3.5	2.9	3.8	1.9	3.4	5.6
10.0 to 11.9	4.0	5.6	0.6	0.7	5.6	2.5	2.4	4.0
12.0 to 13.9	3.0	3.8	1.5	—	3.8	3.2	2.6	3.0
14.0 to 15.9	1.5	2.5	2.3	2.1	1.2	1.7	1.0	1.7
16.0 to 17.9	0.4	0.5	—	—	0.2	—	—	0.3
18.0 to 19.9	0.6	1.3	—	—	0.2	—	—	1.1
20.0 and longer	0.9	1.7	—	—	0.4	0.6	0.9	0.9
	100.0	100.0	100.0	100.0	100.0	100.0	100.0	100.0

Source: Howard W. Buels, "Trip Length Distributions for the Chicago Area," C.A.T.S. RESEARCH NEWS, Vol. 2, No. 8 (April 25, 1958).

across the United States, on the other hand, may be made perhaps once in five or ten years and only for an extraordinary vacation or because of a change in family location.

Trip purpose, therefore, is related to the length of the trip. Trips to work are longer trips; trips to shopping and school are shorter trips. The distribution of trip purposes by trip lengths for the Chicago area is shown in Table 6–6.

Trip length has an important bearing on the planning of transportation facilities. Since most trips are short, it seems clear that a logical street pattern is one that is laid out to permit short journeys to be made directly to the known short-trip generators: schools and shops. These short trips should not encumber the freeways, which are more efficient when they serve long-distance travel. Rapid transit lines specialize in serving long-distance travel and would be rendered inefficient if they carried an excessive number of short trip riders; buses are more suited to short trips.

MODE OF TRAVEL

Purpose affects the mode of travel chosen and hence the operations of mass transportation. Trips made to and from work use mass transportation to a greater degree than any other type of trip (except school trips). One reason is that the central business district of most cities is still the largest single employment area and is the focus of mass transportation routes. Trips made for social and recreation purposes are almost exclusively made by automobile. In between these two extremes lie the range of other trip purposes (See Table 6–7).

DESIRE LINES

Trips may be portrayed on a map as a series of straight lines connecting the origin and destination of each trip. These lines are called "desire lines" because they are the most direct paths that one would desire to use in going from origin to destination and, because they express a desire to travel between two locations. An accumulation of such lines on a map is an indication of the desire of many people to travel in a particular direction and suggests where transportation service might be provided. The lines should be regarded merely as indicators, however, and not as a precise tool for planning purposes.

The density of desire lines on any part of the map of an urban area is an indication of the traffic that would flow through the area if pavements were provided there. These desire line densities can be drawn as isopleths, producing

Table 6–7

Percentage Distribution of Trip Purposes by Mode, Chicago Area, 1956

Mode	Home	Work	Shop	School	Soc. Rec.	Eat Meal	Pers. Bus.	Serve Pass.	Total
Auto driver	47	55	55	10	42	54	52	98	49
Auto passenger	28	13	28	25	47	40	29	2	28
Suburban railroad	2	4	1	1	—	—	1	—	2
Elevated subway	2	7	3	4	1	2	2	—	3
Bus	21	21	13	60	10	4	16	—	18
Total	100	100	100	100	100	100	100	100	100

Source: C.A.T.S. RESEARCH NEWS, Vol. 2, No. 4 (February 28, 1958).

"contour" lines, a technique that is most useful for display purposes.

Figure 6–3 illustrates the travel desire pattern for Detroit. This map illustrates effectively how the total trips from all parts of the city build to peaks at and near the central business district. These peaks of travel desire completely overshadow local traffic considerations near the central area. As one moves toward the fringe of urban development, the desire line densities fall off rapidly, and patterns of local traffic focused on outlying shopping areas are visible. Still farther out, the influence of some long-distance travel shows up on a few major roads connecting Detroit with neighboring cities.

Patterns of truck desire lines are not substantially different from automobile patterns—they seem to remain at about 10 to 15 per cent of the total traffic stream throughout the urban area. Truck trip length follows a frequency distribution pattern wherein short trips constitute the bulk of the total and where there are progressively fewer trips as trip length increases. Truck trips are, however, shorter than automobile trips: they are usually made during the hours of 8:00 A.M. and 5:00 P.M. with relatively few trips occurring during the remainder of the day.

Taxi trips are a highly specialized and relatively unimportant part of the total travel picture. They seem to be concentrated at a few points such as the central business district, airports and railroad stations, and high-density housing developments.

External trips, made by nonresidents and by trucks that are not registered locally but come into the area from outside, may be quite important in the smaller cities. As city size increases, the percentage of external trips declines, unless there are peculiar geographic considerations. Given a population of 100,000 making, on the average, about two trips per capita per day for a total of 200,000 trips, it would take an entering highway with a daily traffic volume of 10,000 vehicles (heavy traffic for an intercity route) to equal 5 per cent of the total trips made in the urban area. External trips have the longest average trip length of any type of travel in an urban area, since each trip starts at the geographic limits of the area and moves toward the center or on through the area.

The distribution of travel during the day is pictured in Figure 6–4 for the average 24-hour weekday period in the Chicago area. The morning and afternoon peaks dominate the picture, and it is for these peaks that most facilities have to be designed. The travel cycle starts from the home in the morning, with the bulk of the morning peak hour traffic proceeding to a work destination. In the evening the cycle is completed as traffic returns to the home from work, shopping, and other destinations. In the evening, social and recreational trips figure prominently in travel after 6:00 P.M., completing a time distribution of travel that is remarkably consistent among cities in the United States.

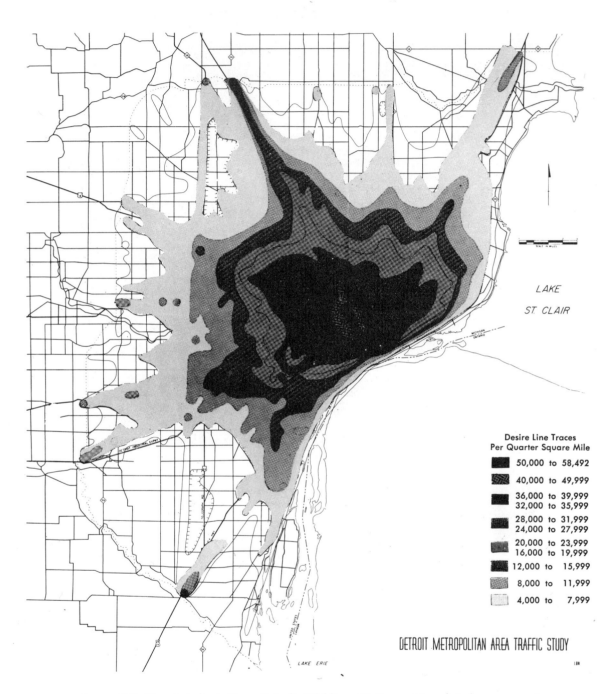

FIGURE 6–3. *Travel desire pattern, Detroit, Michigan (Pattern of travel desire movement of 2,959,348 vehicle trips inside or across the cordon line on an average weekday in the fall of 1953. All desire lines are traced through a one-half mile grid system.)*

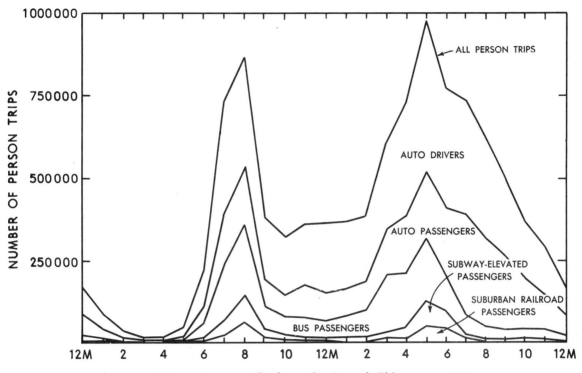

FIGURE 6–4. *Internal person trips by mode of travel, Chicago area, 1956*

The Urban Transportation System

The transportation system is the circulatory system of a city. It brings people and goods into the community and provides the means by which they can move freely from one activity to another. Since circulation involves the vehicular movement of people and goods throughout the city, the transportation system can be considered as three basic inter-related subsystems.

1. *The Travel Way.* Circulation takes place over permanent pathways, namely streets of all types and, in larger cities, separate rights-of-way for railroads and other types of mass transportation facilities. The travel way is the major structural element of the urban community, since these facilities occupy up to 30 per cent of the total land area. They influence the shapes of blocks, and thus of the lots within them, and help fix the boundaries of residential communities and other major land uses. The quality of the circulation system directly influences the volume and orientation of travel within the city and thus, indirectly, its economic well-being. The different types of facilities—local, collector, and arterial streets, freeways, and mass transit rights-of-way—are the components used in building the circulation system.

2. *The Vehicle.* Automobiles, buses, trucks, and rapid transit cars are simply different types of vehicles: each has its function and efficiency in transporting persons or cargo. In terms of use, the automobile accounts for some 85 to 90 per cent of total travel on freeways, arterials, and local streets and trucks for most of the remaining travel. The number or percentage of trips made by bus or rapid transit varies widely, depending upon the density, physical, and economic characteristics of the city, and the type, extent, and service offered by the mass transportation system. Outside the 15 largest metropolitan areas in the United States, the amount of travel by mass transportation is relatively small. For example, in a medium-sized city having only bus transportation, it is unusual to find that more than 10 per cent of

residents' personal trips are made by bus.

3. *Terminal Facilities.* A terminal is any facility providing for the delivery, receipt, and temporary storage of freight or the embarkation of passengers, and providing for temporary storage of the vehicle itself. Off-street automobile parking garages and lots are forms of terminal facilities, as are railroad yards, airports, truck terminals, and docks.

The planner must understand thoroughly all elements of the transportation system and their inter-relationships to be able to plan effectively for the present and the future. All three subsystems are equally important, even though the planner must usually accept the vehicle subsystem as it presently exists. On the other hand, he can influence directly the circulation system and the provision of off-street parking facilities.

THE CIRCULATION SUBSYSTEM

It has been said that much of the present difficulty in moving people and goods in cities results from various elements of the circulation system being called upon to fulfill functions for which they were not designed: hence the importance of understanding the appropriate functions of different elements to prevent misuse and failure of the system.

Streets, the principal component of the circutation system, can be divided into four categories: local, collector, and arterial streets, and freeways, although other ways to differentiate streets are sometimes used. Another element in the circulation system is the right-of-way used exclusively for mass transportation purposes.

Local Streets. Local streets have a variety of functions to perform that can be listed as follows:

1. The principal purpose of a local street is to provide access to property abutting the public right-of-way; this includes both vehicular and pedestrian access.

2. Moving traffic is a secondary function of the local street. This traffic is generally so light that the primary function is not impaired. Since land service is its primary purpose, the local street should not carry through traffic; buses and heavy trucks should be excluded except where the local street is in a commercial or an industrial district of the city.

3. The local street serves as an easement for all types of utilities, such as sewers, water lines, gas mains, electrical and telephone conduits, and poles.

4. The local street serves as an open space between buildings to provide light and air to adjoining properties and to serve as a fire break.

5. The local street functions as an element in urban design; it is a site for buildings, and its arrangement in curves or straight lines, together with trees, shrubbery, grass, and flowers, can form the basis for a large-scale design composition. In residential areas the street serves as temporary storage space for vehicles, and in densely populated areas it may have to be used for all-night parking.

Cross-sections of local streets vary with building practices, abutting land uses, parking, weather conditions, planting of street trees, and other considerations. For residential streets, common right-of-way widths may vary between 50 and 65 feet. Pavement widths generally vary from 26 to 48 feet. With a prohibition against all-night parking and with fairly low residential densities, a 26- to 28-foot pavement width is adequate and inexpensive to build and maintain. In multifamily areas where there is more or less continuous daytime parking, 40 to 48 feet of pavement is needed in order to leave room for two moving lanes of traffic.

Setbacks required by local ordinance are almost an integral part of street design. They vary in depth depending on local conditions such as lot depths, building types, and climate. Zoning regulations requiring off-street parking and off-street loading are also necessary to maintain the operating efficiency of a street.

In commercial developments, greater widths are necessary for local land-service streets. Right-of-way widths of 60 to 100 feet are proper, depending on the type of parking, sidewalk widths, and the volume and turning movements of vehicles. Most modern shopping centers are provided with off-street parking areas designed so that a local street is not required. Driveways perform the function of moving vehicles from nearby arteials to these parking areas or to passenger or freight loading areas. A well-designed shopping center layout illustrates how separating parking and moving vehicles prevents the conflicts that make the improvements of existing, multifunction streets so difficult.

Industrial areas usually have their own local streets. The designer of such streets must consider the predominant type of trucking and whether the maneuvering of trailers must be provided for. Parking requirements, drainage and curbing, and the setback of buildings must also be considered. Street rights-of-way from 60 to 100 feet may be desired. For the layout of industrial street systems, the planner must consider railroad sidings in addition to buildings and the probable distribution of industrial plans of various sizes. Grades and utilities are also important, but where traffic volumes are small and distances short, circulation is less important than land service.

The system design of local streets greatly affects traffic. An unduly long street builds up traffic volumes. Cross streets and intersections with acute angles are likely to cause accidents. Bringing every local street into an arterial creates unnecessary friction points, which also cause accidents and slow vehicles on the arterial. It is better to bring the local streets into a collector, which then feeds into an arterial.

Collector Streets. The collector street is primarily a residential phenomenon, which filters traffic from local streets before their capacity is exceeded and then conducts it to arterials or to local generators such as shopping centers, schools, or community centers. In commercial areas, traffic volumes build up too rapidly for the efficient use of collectors, and local or land-access streets should therefore connect directly with an arterial, but in large industrial areas, a collector street may be needed occasionally.

The main function of a collector street is to conduct traffic from local residential streets to arterials or freeways. Land access should be a secondary function of a collector, and its design and operation should reflect this fact. Parking should be discouraged, and residential buildings should not have driveways entering the collector. As in the case of the local street, a collector functions as an easement for utilities, as an open space furnishing light and air, and as a design element in the residential area.

For obvious reasons, the collector street must not have a cross-section less than the local streets entering it. Right-of-way widths will probably vary between 60 end 80 feet with pavement widths of 40 or 48 feet.

The design of collector streets is a most important factor in traffic safety. Local streets should not cross the collector directly, planting should be held back from the street, and the sidewalks should be separated from the pavement by a wide lawn or esplanade. Sight distances at intersections should be adequate, with no visual barriers adjacent to corners.

The way in which collectors are located with respect to other street types and to the total street system is influenced by their function, namely collecting traffic from residential streets and conducting it to arterials. The spacing of collectors is therefore partially controlled by the factors that affect residential trip generation such as car ownership, population density, and the use of mass transportation. An interval of one-half mile is a rule of thumb often followed. Spacing will also be influenced if the street is used to delineate neighborhood boundaries or to focus on community centers such as shops or parks. It is not desirable for collectors to form a continuous system, since there may then be a tendency for traffic to use the collector as an arterial, thus violating one of the basic principles of residential planning—to keep through traffic out.

Traffic volumes on collector streets may vary greatly, from 2,000 or 3,000 up to 8,000 or more vehicles per day. Since streets with lower volumes seem to carry higher proportions of their 24-hour volumes in the peak hour—12 to 14 per cent on streets like collectors—it is better to locate collectors at intervals sufficient to attain the lower loading. Any collector carrying more than 8,000 vehicles per day is probably taking through traffic and doing the work of an arterial. This volume is an indication of a need for increasing road capacity in the vicinity, either by construction of freeways or improvement of arterials.

Arterials. The arterial, more than any other

type of street, illustrates the conflict which may arise between traffic service and land service, two functions which are basically incompatible. When volumes of traffic are low and the abutting land is not used intensively, the conflict is not serious, but when traffic volumes are high and the adjoining land is used intensively, the conflict increases almost geometrically, and the situation quickly becomes intolerable. A highway in open country, for example, has relatively few locations for potential accidents, but an urban arterial with parking and pedestrian crossings may have thousands of potential accident or friction points per mile.

Three ways of improving arterials should be considered by a planning agency. The first is to provide additional capacity for movement (for example by building freeways near by), which will reduce or stabilize the volume carried on the arterials. The second is to ensure that the design of future arterials is improved, and the third is to alleviate conditions on existing arterials as far as possible, by eliminating on-street parking or by improving signalization.

The first and most important function of the arterial is to move large volumes of vehicles such as automobiles, trucks, and busses and includes, as the name artery implies, longer trips from one part of a city to another.

Land access should be a secondary function of arterials but owners usually have a legal right to such access. Historically, traffic brought people, people brought trade, and trade led to commercial development. Zoning has tended to perpetuate the location of commercial strips on arterials but the design of streets and the development of abutting properties has not recognized the problems created by increasing traffic volumes. Parking on arterial streets is, however, one function that is being increasingly controlled due to the pressure of increased traffic volumes.

The arterial, as in other cases discussed earlier, serves as an easement for utilities and is also an open space, providing light and air. The greater width of arterial streets, creates an opportunity for impressive design on a grand scale, but this opportunity has seldom been utilized, and arterials—with their utility poles, advertising signs, billboards, and tasteless architecture—are without doubt the ugliest streets in American cities.

Cross sections of arterial streets are extremely variable, ranging from a simple 60-foot right-of-way with a 48-foot pavement to a right-of-way 100 feet or more in width, with median strips and service drives. Arterials should be designed primarily for traffic, with such compromises as are necessary to service adjoining properties. The responsibility for design is in the hands of the traffic engineer whose experience with signalization, median strips, and lanes for turning movements is especially important for attaining the maximum capacity from a fixed right-of-way.

Often little can be done with older arterials because the street width is narrow and buildings project to the property lines. As the city grows, however, a natural adjustment sometimes occurs for the retail outlets may die out and be replaced by wholesale houses or industrial plants whose access requirements are not so demanding. It may then be possible for buildings to turn their backs on the arterial and gain principal access from side or rear yard parking lots. The planning agency would do well to encourage such developments.

The key to the design of newer arterials is greater width, preferably with rights-of-way measuring 150 to 200 feet and adjoining lots measuring 150 to 250 feet deep or more. Such right-of-way widths permit traffic to flow more freely on divided roadways, access to abutting property being provided by service roads. Such a design is, in effect, a small scale freeway, with access permitted but carefully regulated and lesser widths may be desirable if no access is permitted.

The design of a system of arterials cannot be specified precisely, but two principles are predominant. First, the spacing of arterial streets should be a function of density: in older parts of the city, they should be spaced about one-half mile apart, while at suburban densities, one mile spacings produce reasonable traffic volumes. The second principle is system continuity: roads should *flow* through an urban area, with no stubs, jogs, or T-intersections. This continuity permits an even disperson of traffic and minimizes traffic distribution problems brought about by localized overloading.

Traffic volumes on arterials have an extreme range and may go from 2,000 vehicles per day to as high as 25,000 vehicles per day. In some places, volumes may reach 50,000 vehicles per day, but this number is exceptional and requires street designs which eliminate or seriously reduce all access to adjoining land.

Arterial street capacity is generally calculated in capacities per lane: 600 vehicles per hour per lane is a rule of thumb often used. This figure may be set higher or lower, depending on such factors as turning movements, one- or two-way design, percentage of commercial vehicles, parking, and bus stops. A four-lane arterial may carry up to 2,400 vehicles per hour during the peak hour. Since peak-hour traffic is generally split directionally, with less going in one direction than in the other (60–40 is a common ratio), 2,000 vehicles per hour is the more usual peak hour load. With the peak hour carrying 8 or 10 per cent of the daily load, a four-lane arterial may then carry 20,000 to 25,000 vehicles per day.

Freeways. The term "freeway" means an access-free, high-speed road with grade-separated interchanges. It is technically more correct to use the word "freeway" than the words "expressway" or "superhighway." ("Expressway" in traffic engineering terms means a high-class arterial.) A "parkway" is a freeway restricted to pleasure vehicles and having some scenic qualities.

The freeway has only one function—to carry traffic. Because it is thus specialized, with controlled access, no parking, and no grade intersections, it is a highly efficient carrier. Freeways are not generally used as sites for public utilities or communications lines. The depressions and elevations, and especially the grade-separated interchanges, make the construction and maintenance of utilities too difficult.

The freeway is a new visual element in the city and metropolitan area. In cut, at grade, or on fill, it is a major barrier separating land uses on the one side from those on the other. To the motorist the freeway opens up vistas of the city never seen from arterials or local streets, and even at high speeds it gives a sense of the magnitude and structure of the urban commu-

nity. In coming years these design aspects will be more fully exploited.

Freeway traffic capacities are generally calculated at 1,500 vehicles per lane per hour, although volumes of 2,200 vehicles per lane have been achieved. Peak hour taffic on freeways is a lower percentage of daily volume (8 to 9 per cent) than on any other street type. Freeways have a very even, and hence efficient, use pattern. With a 60–40 directional split, a four-lane freeway can carry as many as 60,000 vehicles per day, although better performance is achieved at lower volumes.

The cost of building freeways is enormous, principally because of the cost of urban lands taken for rights-of-way. Costs may vary from $1 million per mile in rural areas to over $20 million per mile in congested parts of the city. The closer the freeway goes to the central business district, the higher the cost, not only because of land values but also because utility relocations and grade separations are generally more frequent. Obviously, freeways are designed only after the most careful planning studies have been made.

Mass Transportation. Mass transportation operates over two types of facilities: (1) that which runs within a public street right-of-way on the surface and has intersections with other streets at grade such as the streetcar, trolley coach, or bus; and (2) that which operates within a right-of-way reserved exclusively for its use such as subways, elevated lines, and suburban railroads. In the former case, the mass transportation vehicle shares the right-of-way with automobile and truck traffic. The speed of operation depends on the speed of the traffic stream within which it operates and the number of stops per mile. With more stops per mile, the speed is necessarily slower, so that while there may be a gain in convenience to the individual as a result of more stops, there is a loss in convenience to the group as a result of a longer journey time.

In contrast to surface mass transportation, rapid transit provides faster service, especially over long distances, since it operates in its own right-of-way. It is similar to the freeway, being a single-purpose, specialized type of transportation having no conflicts with abutting land uses, or (as in the case of buses) with motor vehicle traffic. Rapid transit, however, is peculiar to large cities and is restricted to the radial routes focusing on the central business district.

There are several types of rapid transit. One basic type is suburban railroad, in which heavier equipment operates at high speeds with intervals of one-half miles or more between stations. The other basic type is the subway-elevated system (generally electrified) using lighter, self-propelled cars with an ability to accelerate and decelerate quickly, permitting more frequent stops. Within these two basic types many variations are being proposed. The so-called mono-rail (invariably running on two or more surfaces) is one variation, while a computer-controlled bus system on its own right-of-way has been demonstrated in Pittsburgh. A decision on the type of rapid transit facility to be recommended in any particular case should only be made after careful, specialized study.

The Vehicle Subsystem

The history of transportation has been one of technological advancement of the vehicle subsystem, particularly during the past 50 years. There is every reason to expect that this process of development will continue in the future. However, because of the size of the total investment in present modes of transportation it may be expected that most changes will be evolutionary. There is little evidence to suggest that any radically new type of transportation system will gain widespread acceptance and use during the next several decades.

In urban transportation planning, the alternatives are usually whether to add new expressways, arterials, bus lines, rapid transit lines, or even commuter railroad service, or to improve and upgrade existing facilities. Although public investment is mainly in circulation and terminal systems, the choice is often influenced by the performance characteristics of the vehicle subsystem. The choice is almost never made to limit a system to one type of vehicle, but to provide a balanced system designed to serve varying needs in different parts of the region.

Many factors should be considered by the transportation planner in making a decision

on the type of facility to be recommended. These will include:

1. *Cost.* The cost of a vehicle system is the resultant of many different internal and external factors, most of which are highly interrelated. Components of the total cost include fixed charges and expenditures which vary with the use of the vehicle. Fixed charges include the capital recovery costs associated with the purchase of the vehicle, organizational overheads, and the various franchise, registration, and insurance fees which are independent of vehicle use. Variable costs include such items as fuel, the wages of operating personnel, vehicle maintenance, and accident costs not reimbursable by insurance.

Each individual considers costs from a different viewpoint, depending on his needs, resources, geographical location, his family size, and many other factors. Most cost comparisons are made on a basis too unrefined to have validity when extended across a metropolitan area. Figure 6–5 shows how the relative costs for an automobile and for transit may change as a function of the amount of travel a person performs per year. In this figure, capital as well as out-of-pocket costs are included.

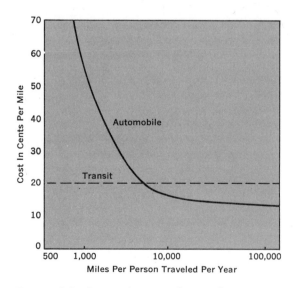

Figure 6–5. *Comparison of time and movement costs per mile, and number of miles travelled by mode of travel*

As his income rises, the ability of a person to command more and better transportation increases: hence costs become relatively less important, and other factors become more important.

2. *Speed.* Few people travel for enjoyment alone. The reasons for traveling are associated with the gain to be obtained from the activities taking place at the trip destination: hence, the time spent traveling is basically unproductive. Most people attempt to minimize the time spent traveling within the choice of modes available to them, therefore the advantage of one type of vehicle over another is often measured in terms of its relative speed, or difference in time taken from origin to destination.

The only meaningful speed or travel time is door-to-door or origin to final destination. In the case of an automobile trip, this speed includes walking to the vehicle, driving time, parking, and walking to the destination. In the case of a trip made by bus or other forms of transit, it includes time spent walking to the bus stop or station, waiting for the vehicle, riding time, and time spent walking to the final destination. It may also include waiting and riding time on other transit vehicles, should a transfer be necessary. Comparative door-to-door journey speeds as surveyed in the Chicago Study are given in Table 6–8.

Speed is relative: a small time saving on a long trip is probably of little consequence to the average traveler, whereas the same time saving on a short trip may be significant in the selection between alternate modes of travel. A large time saving will influence the choice of mode regardless of the trip length. In comparing different modes, both time ratio and time savings are subjectively used in evaluating speed and hence choice.

3. *Safety.* Safety is the condition of being able to transport passengers to their destinations without mishap resulting in personal injury or property damage. It refers to the safety of the passengers as well as to the safety of the vehicle and system and is based on an ideal, for no mode of transportation is completely safe. Personal accident costs include property damage, medical bills, insurance overhead, court and legal expenses, cost of accident prevention programs, and lost wages and nonevaluable costs brought about by socio-economic dislocations, loss of production, and death. Accident accounting systems commonly recognize as measures of performance the number of accidents resulting in property damage, personal injury, and deaths and the total number of persons injured and killed. These statistics can be readily converted to a vehicle-mile or person-mile basis.

Each automobile or truck trip is under the direction of a driver operating his vehicle independently of all other vehicles and of the support system. This reliance on human control is at the root of the accident problem in urban areas, but it is difficult to foresee how mechanical systems can replace human guidance for intraurban automobile travel. Transit systems utilizing their own rights-of-way offer a more immediately promising area for the replacement of human control with computer-mechanical control. Systems of this type have always exhibited a far better safety record than highway systems. Among the different types of highways, freeways are by far the safest in terms of accidents per vehicle mile traveled, whereas local streets have very high accident rates per vehicle mile driven (see Table 6–9).

4. *Comfort and Convenience.* Different vehicle subsystems provide varying kinds of comfort and convenience—performance characteristics which are very difficult to weigh because they are a subjective experience for each individual. Furthermore, a person may evaluate the comfort and convenience of a vehicle dif-

Table 6–8

Comparative Portal-to-Portal Journey Speeds by Mode, Chicago, 1956

Mode	Average Speed (miles per hour)
Automobile	11.1
Bus	6.2
Subway/elevated	8.9
Suburban railroad	14.4

Source: Chicago Area Transportation Study, FINAL REPORT (Chicago: The Study, 1960), Vol. II, p. 123.

Table 6–9

Number of Accidents by Type of Street Chicago, 1956

Type of Street	Number of Accidents per 100,000 Miles of Vehicle Travel			
	Fatal	Injury	Property Damage Only	Total
Local streets....	007	1.132	9.069	10.21
Arterials.......	003	0.454	1.968	2.43
Expressways....	001	0.091	0.418	0.51
All types.......	004	0.531	2.940	3.475

Source: Chicago Area Transportation Study, FINAL RE-PORT (Chicago, The Study, 1962). Vol. II, p. 11.

ferently depending on the purpose of his trip, or the time of day.

With higher standards of living becoming more universally available, it is certain that future passengers will want more comfort and convenience from their transportation than before. Adequate seating, air conditioning, cleanliness, and pleasant surroundings will have to be provided.

In planning for different modes of transportation, comfort and convenience are not recognized as factors which determine the choice of mode. Speed, safety, and cost factors are undoubtedly more influential. Nevertheless, in any system planned, attention must be paid to these higher standards.

5. *Capacity.* The carrying capacity of different types of vehicles is important in determining how the demand for movement with vehicles of different types may be met. It should be realized that the full carrying capacity of any vehicle is utilized only during certain hours or under somewhat unusual circumstances.

The average automobile can carry 5 to 6 persons, but the average loading is approximately 1.5 persons per vehicle. This may vary from about 1.2 persons for a work trip to about two persons per vehicle for social-recreation trips. This means that one expressway lane rarely carries more than 2,400 persons per hour.

Buses carry approximately 50 persons each with all seats filled, and are frequently expected to carry 50 per cent more standing during peak hours. The capacity of a bus line depends on bus size, the ratio of persons per seat, and the headways (time interval between busses on the same route). Take for example, a bus route with 50-seat busses with all seats filled. On a 60-second headway this route will carry 3,000 persons per hour one way; on a 3-minute headway this drops to 1,000 persons per hour; and on a 15-minute headway it drops to 200 persons per hour.

The capacities of rapid transit lines are extremely high. Capacity is a function of the passengers-per-seat ratio (usually 1.5), car seating (generally 50), and no standees, the number of cars per train, and the headways between trains. For example, take a rapid transit route with eight car trains, 50 seats per car, and no standees. On a two and one-half minute headway this route will carry 9,600 per hour one-way. The figure drops to one-half (4,800) on a 5-minute headway, and to one-quarter (2,400) on a 10-minute headway. For trains with fewer cars, or greater headway between trains, the figures are reduced proportionately.

THE TERMINAL SUBSYSTEM

Elements of the terminal subsystem include parking, truck terminals, railroad yards and depots, bus terminals, and airports.

Parking. Parking is an integral part of the automotive transportation system; it is the terminal storage of vehicles while drivers and passengers are occupied elsewhere. Where terminal storage capacity is inadequate, back-ups in streets and excessive hunting for parking spaces may affect the circulation system. One objective of a good transportation plan is to provide a balance between circulation of motor vehicles and terminal storage, with due regard for other types of transportation, for buildings, and land values. How to reach this balance has not been clearly determined, but there is some merit in knowing that a balance ought to be achieved and what elements should be considered.

Parking in the outskirts of the city is easy to provide. Most modern zoning ordinances insist that off-street parking be provided at the developer's expense. Where land costs are relatively low, this is a reasonable requirement because it helps insure that the heavy public expenditures in streets are used for circulation and not for storage. One hundred per cent off-street parking for residential development should be considered standard practice. This proportion should also be the target for commercial, industrial, and institutional activities.

In the older parts of the city, especially at the center, there has been a continuing effort to accommodate the automobile and truck with more and more parking spaces. How this has been done depends greatly upon city size. In smaller communities where buses are the only form of mass transportation, the end-product will probably be complete off-street parking, with curb parking only on side streets. In the largest cities, continuation of the central business district in its present concentrated form depends upon continuation of mass transportation, subsidized if necessary. Between these extremes, the problem is more difficult; a successful solution will probably depend on continuation of some mass transportation. Good design must then relate compact building areas to open parking areas, so that the end result does not resemble a war-damaged city as is now often the case.

The original form of parking was curb parking, free and unregulated. With the increasing use of automobiles and trucks (and the resulting greater demands for parking), regulation of curb use was necessary. The parking meter became the most effective means of controlling parking and increasing turnover. The meter provides a source of revenue well over the cost of installation and maintenance. Nevertheless, curb parking takes up one full lane that might be better used for moving vehicles, and it also impedes flow in the second lane when drivers maneuver to park.

Off-street parking in older commercial districts has developed with all types of financing. This may range from complete municipal construction and operation of a parking lot or garage, perhaps financed by bonds backed by the revenue from street parking meters, to complete private operation paid for by commercial establishments. In between these two extremes is a variety of financing and operating plans that involve government, public authority, or private financing. In most cases the user is required to pay part of the cost. Rates may be varied to hasten turnover, which is desired to accommodate shopping trips and to discourage all-day parking in commercial areas where facilities are limited.

Off-street parking may be provided in a variety of forms, any one of which may be selected to satisfy local conditions of appearance, cost, available area, and access. In addition to the surfaced lot, there are parking machines, parking buildings, and underground buildings. Notable examples of the latter are the lots in San Francisco, Detroit, Chicago, and Pittsburgh.

The quantity of parking required to serve an area is a function of the total number of trips generated in that area; the proportion of automobile and mass transportation use; the duration of parking and pricing; walking distances; and hourly, daily, and seasonal travel patterns. Calculating the effect of each of these variables is a complicated but not impossible task. It is more difficult to decide how much of the demand should be satisfied. This is a question of economics. Supplying enough spaces for periods of peak demand may be inefficient in terms of cost and the return that might be gained if capital and land were used for other purposes; it also may have the effect of reducing mass transportation use.

Transportation Planning Process

The basic steps in the transportation planning process are shown in Figure 6–6. The elements are: organizing, stating the objectives, obtaining the information, preparing and evaluating land use and transportation plans within the framework of the objectives, selecting the best plan, and working for adoption and implementation.

The actual planning process may vary considerably from large to small areas. An urban area of 5 million persons might require the evaluation of alternative land use patterns and several different transportation systems com-

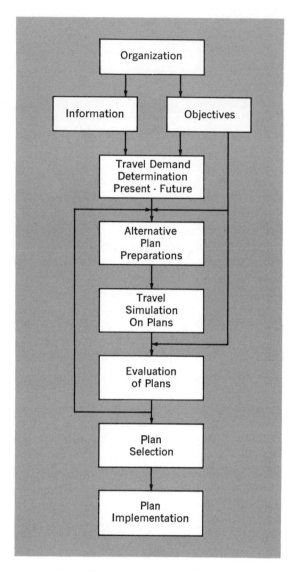

FIGURE 6–6. *The transportation planning process*

Subdivision of Transportation Planning and Programming within the New York State Department of Public Works; ad hoc groups such as the Chicago Area Transportation Study; and combined regional planning and transportation planning organizations such as the Cleveland–Seven Counties Land Use Transportation Study. Regardless of structure, the organization must achieve two objectives: it must have the support of metropolitan policy makers and must possess a competent staff large enough for the planning task.

Confidence, support and intergovernmental coordination can be achieved by including metropolitan policy makers in the organization. This may be accomplished by forming a policy committee composed of elected public officials and transportation officials. This committee should be charged with the responsibility for establishing the planning objectives, approving the final plan, helping in its implementation, and studying proposed revisions.

The policy committee should be served by a planning or technical subcommittee of chief planning advisers. The planning subcommittee might thus include the city planner, regional planner, city traffic engineer, county highway engineer, urban renewal director, and a transit organization representative.

The day-to-day tasks of preparing a transportation plan should be the responsibility of a staff reporting to the policy committee. This staff should be a team composed of urban planners, urban transportation analysts, traffic engineers, highway engineers, transit engineers, computer programmers, mathematicians, economists, and other specialists. Without an interdisciplinary staff it is nearly impossible to perform the broad range of work involved in a transportation study. To effectively carry out the planning tasks, each staff member should have a clear understanding of his work load, and the internal administrative organization.

OBJECTIVES

Defining objectives is probably the most important and difficult task in the entire planning process. Transportation plans in a democratic society are created to satisfy certain human desires. These desires must be determined and

posed of freeways, rapid transit, and surface transit for each land use pattern. However, an urban area of 25,000 persons might require a study to determine whether to widen Main Street or to make Oak Street and Elm Street a one-way couple. Regardless of size, the basic goal of the planning process does not change: to test alternative transportation plans based on public desires and relevant facts.

ORGANIZATION

There is a wide variety of organizational structures among the groups engaged in transportation planning: central agencies such as the

translated into objectives. This step determines the tone and direction of the entire planning process.

An important principle in determining planning objectives is to avoid statements that specify the means to be adopted. For example, a statement which defines a specific system such as a rapid transit system or freeway system should be avoided. Transportation facilities must be planned to serve people and to fulfill their desires. Consequently, transportation planning objectives must be stated in terms of desires to be fulfilled instead of systems to be planned.

Objectives fall into two classes: user objectives and general community objectives. User objectives include the desires of the public as individual users of the transportation system; community objectives deal with general goals such as stimulating economic growth.

Several user objectives are often stated in transportation planning—increased speed, safety, convenience, and reduced cost—but each of these objectives deals with improving transportation service. The most general user objective is the removal of existing travel congestion and the prevention of future congestion. Achieving this objective would not only reduce travel aggravation to the public but would also reduce accidents, operating costs, and travel time. Another similar user objective is the reduction of travel costs. Briefly these objectives can be summarized by the statement: "Invest public funds in transportation improvements to save travel time, lower operating costs, and reduce accidents."

Community objectives generally include promotion of economic growth and creation of a desirable environment. A frequent community objective is to create relatively traffic-free residential areas. Another common community objective is to preserve or restore older urban areas such as the central business district. A constant community objective is to minimize taxes, an objective which acts as a restraint upon all plans. Another frequently stated community objective is to stimulate economic growth by expanding existing establishments and attracting new undertakings.

Unfortunately objectives can be competitive:

the desire to increase accessibility can conflict with the desire to create traffic-free residential areas; an objective of low taxes can compete with a desire for better transportation service. Some method is needed to resolve this competition and to enable the best plan to be selected. There are many ways to resolve this competition; the best method is to establish some objectives as absolute constraints and to leave the others as ideals to be achieved to a greater or lesser degree. For example, the nonpenetration of neighborhoods can be an absolute constraint, while the removal of congestion and reduction of transportation costs are ideals to be considered in terms of volume/capacity ratios and the rate of return on transportation investment.

One common pitfall in preparing objectives is a preoccupation with the effect of accessibility on urban form. A frequently stated objective of the transportation system is to aid in the creation of certain urban forms. For example, a rapid transit system may be suggested to strengthen the central business district or a bridge crossing may be planned to spur development. The staff should make certain that the role of the transportation system in creating the desired urban form has not been overstated, otherwise the transportation plan would be prepared for an unattainable urban form—and an unattainable goal.

The key to sound planning is to measure performance of plans in relation to objectives. This measurement procedure is the time bridge between plans and the objectives they are attempting to fulfill. As objectives are established, plans are made and their performances measured, the results of each plan are being compared to see how well they are meeting the objectives. This is the only way to determine which of the plans offered is the best and thus to work toward the best possible solution.

Reduction of total transportation costs within a rigid set of land development constraints is a favored procedure. The costs to be minimized include the capital cost of the transportation facility, the operating cost, the cost of accidents, and the travel time cost. An interesting relationship between the scale of investment in facilities and the cost of travel is shown in Figure 6–7. Usually any additional capital investment will reduce the cost of travel; however, a point of decreasing return is reached where a dollar invested will not yield a dollar in reduced travel costs. In fact the total transportation costs will increase with additional investment. This relationship is helpful in establishing the economic amount of capital which should be invested in facilities.

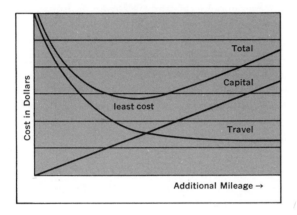

FIGURE 6–7. *Total travel cost for additional freeway mileage*

This process is also useful in determining where the investment in transportation facilities should be made. Often the facilities which give the highest travel cost reduction per dollar invested are located in highly urbanized areas and have a high capital cost. Similarly the lowest return per dollar is more often associated with low capital cost facilities located in the least urbanized areas.

This procedure is an excellent indicator of decreases in congestion since reducing congestion is one way of reducing travel costs. However the procedure is usually reinforced by an inspection of specific overcapacity transportation facilities.

Often a minimum service constraint is applied to the minimum cost procedure to insure that all persons have some form of transportation available to them. Specifically, this constraint usually dictates a minimum transit system which may or may not pay its way. Whether or not the transit system pays, it is a needed service and should be supported by diverted tax funds if necessary.

INFORMATION COLLECTION

Knowledge of the specific transportation traits of an urban area is necessary before any attempt is made to plan a transportation system. Basic data are required on the present transportation system, its performance, the present travel pattern, travel characteristics of the area, land use pattern, and urban economy. These data can be obtained through a series of inventories.

The inventory of transportation facilities has three specific objectives: to obtain a better understanding of existing routes (this is not attained until the data have been clearly presented) ; to survey the transportation system for obvious trouble spots, noting places where improvements can be made; and to gain some insight into the ability of the facilities to render service, and into their carrying capacity under varying conditions of speed, cost, and convenience.

The inventory process consists of locating and describing each link of the transportation circulation system. This description includes a measure of both the present capacity and use of the specific link and a statement of its performance characteristics.

The physical and traffic control data which should be considered a minimum for a highway inventory are the length, pavement width, right-of-way width, number of signals, signal timing, number of lanes, and parking control. The traffic engineer must have this information to determine highway capacity.

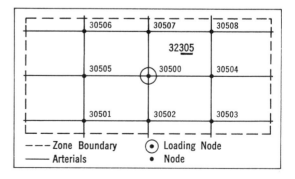

FIGURE 6–8. *Network coding*

The minimum physical data needed for the transit inventory would be location, operating schedules, average headways, number of seats per vehicle, and operating speeds.

The location description of each link should be in digital form to facilitate the data reduction and processing as shown in Figure 6–8. Electronic graphic devices are available to digitize each system and to plot any system information in map form. A specific example of the use of these devices is the electronic plotting of highway or transit volume flow maps as shown in Figure 6–9.

The existing use of the transportation system is obtained by sampling or counting the number of vehicles or passengers on each component of the system. Ideally, the inventory would count each component for an extended period of time. This type of inventory would be expensive and only slightly more reliable than a statistically structured counting program utilizing short counts from a selected sample of facilities, controlled by a still smaller sample of long counts. Highway use may be obtained, for example, through a counting program which integrates a large number of two-hour traffic counts with a few selected 24- or 72-hour counts. The longer counts are used to obtain the hourly variation by day, and the short counts are used to obtain the relative use of that highway section. A highway system volume map showing the 24-hour volume on each highway section is the end result of this phase of the transportation inventory.

The use made of the total transit system can be ascertained by reviewing company fare records, but the volume carried by sections of the route may be found only by counting the passengers on the transit vehicles. Surface transit operation usually requires that any volume counting program be conducted on board. For rapid transit systems simultaneous counts can be made of persons entering and leaving the system at each station. The final product of this phase of the inventory is an average daily volume flow map for the transit system.

The capacity of collectors, arterials, and freeways should be determined by using the 1965 Bureau of Public Roads *Capacity Manual* and the physical and traffic control characteristics

of the highways. This phase of the inventory should be assigned to a traffic engineer. This information can be used to compare existing use or future demand with the street capacity to spot deficiencies. The determination of deficiencies should also reflect the standards for service that are a part of the objectives to be attained through the plan: a minimum resultant from the entire transportation inventory should be a map of volume-capacity, pinpointing the location and magnitude of present traffic problem areas.

The capacity of a transit system is flexible. The existing system capacity is fixed by the number of operating vehicles. The capacity of the travel way can thus easily be increased by adding to the number of operating vehicles. The present number of vehicles being operated on each transit route (usually called the "level of service") is an important transit fact that must be recorded. The usual level of service index is seat-miles per square mile. This is determined by multiplying the route-miles in a specific area by the number of transit vehicles operating during the specified time period and the seating capacity of the vehicle. The index is then adjusted as required to reflect normal operating conditions in the area.

The present level of service is easily measured from transit schedule records. The conventional measure of transit service is the "seat-mile" of service. This information can be mapped in the same manner as the highway capacity and the number of seat-miles of service provided can be compared with the system use measured in passenger-miles.

Several measurements can be used to determine how well the existing transportation system performs. One performance measure is the average time required to travel over the system. For instance, the highway subsystem travel time rate can be measured easily by driving test vehicles at various time intervals over the highway system. The transit system's average travel time rate can be obtained from transit company schedules. A special study of transit and highway system terminal times should be made to determine door-to-door travel time. This travel time information can be displayed by plotting travel time contour lines based on the

FIGURE 6–9. *Electronic volume plot (Mechanically produced volume flows on street network in center of Buffalo, New York.)*

location of the metropolitan center.

Another statistical measurement which should be obtained is the frequency of accidents by location. This information can be supplied by the local or state police and/or the state motor vehicle department. The accident frequency for the transit system is best obtained from transit company records. This information can be displayed by an accident pin map which illustrates trouble spots.

Travel Inventory. Inventories provide data on the origin and destination of all trips, the purpose, travel time, and length of trip, the mode of travel, and the land use at the points of origin and destination. This information then serves as the basis for predicting future travel.

Origin-Destination Surveys. If a city has not undertaken an origin-destination (O-D) study within the past 10 years, such a study should be conducted. Historically, O-D studies are usually made by or under the auspices of the state highway department, sometimes in collaboration with local governments. A large share of the cost is borne by the United States Bureau of Public Roads. One and one-half per cent of all federal funds spent for primary and interstate highway systems is allocated for research and planning; this is the primary source of funds for origin-destination studies.

The origin-destination survey is designed to interview a representative sample of all kinds of travel that originates within or passes through an urban area. The sum total of vehicle and person trips in an area is composed of three elements: the travel of persons who live outside the area and of commercial vehicles that are registered outside the area; the travel of commercial vehicles (trucks and taxis) registered within the area; and the travel of persons who reside in the area. Each of these requires a separate type of listing, sampling, and interviewing.

1. *External Travel.* The importance of travel by persons and commercial vehicles not living or registered in an urban area depends on the size and position of the urban area. While external travel is of little importance (3 to 5 per cent of the total average daily travel) in most cities of 100,000 population or more, these data must be collected. For smaller cities,

especially those on a direct route to a large city, external traffic may be of considerable importance. In either case, the interviewing technique is to draw a cordon line around the area, to stop a sample of all vehicles (perhaps 20 to 35 per cent), and to question the driver on his origin, destination, and trip purpose, and the land use at origin and destination.

2. *Internal Commercial Travel.* Commercial vehicles generally account for 10 to 15 per cent of the total trips made in an urban area. These vehicles, whether truck or taxi, can be sampled from lists of registrations obtained from the state government or from municipal lists if such vehicles are licensed or taxed by the municipality. The sample can be drawn from the complete list, and the interview conducted by telephone, by mail, or by personal visit. Although more expensive, the personal visit is a more thorough and trustworthy technique. The sample rate may vary between 5 and 20 per cent, depending on city size, interviewing technique used, and required accuracy.

3. *Internal Residential Travel.* Travel performed by residents can be obtained by home interviews, telephone, and interviewing at a series of multiple "screen lines" cutting the travel area into segments. The best technique is undoubtedly the home interview; it insures a thorough interview and a well-controlled sample. The other techniques are harder to control, and it is difficult to add the pieces together to present a reliable picture of total travel. Lists of residents (actually dwelling places) may be obtained through field listing, from the Bureau of the Census, directories, or utility lists. Data obtained on travel of residents should include origin, destination, purpose, time, land use at origin and destination, and mode of travel.

Sample selection and sampling rates are difficult technical problems, requiring a considerable knowledge of statistics and a weighing of costs, administrative requirements, data processing problems, use of data, and required accuracy. The sample rate may vary between 1 and 10 per cent, depending on city size. Since each home interview costs from $10 to $12 (including editing, coding, and key-punching), a decision on the size of sample to be taken must be made carefully.

An origin-destination study involves a major campaign, requiring three to eight months to plan, two to six months for interviews, and one or two years for data processing, analysis, and the planning of transportation systems. Costs may range from $100,000 to $3 million, but there is a trend toward smaller sample size, hence somewhat lower costs.[1] State highway departments have had the most experience with this work. Advice and manuals are available from the Bureau of Public Roads or state highway organizations.[2,3]

The urban planner is not normally involved in the conduct of origin-destination studies, but he should be consulted. For example, the location of the cordon line, which sets the limits of the planning area, should be such that most population growth taking place within the planning period will be inside the cordon line. The urban planner will also want to check to see that travel inventories call for data on the land use at the origin and destination of each trip. This information is necessary to obtain land-use-trip generation rates for forecasting.

The designation of analysis zones (the small areas for which trip data are tabulated for analysis purposes) may require compromises. It may seem desirable to have such zones coordinated with neighborhoods, planning areas, or census tracts. However, rapid analysis and mechanical presentation may require the delineation of analysis zones in regular fashion.

Inventory of Land Use. Information on land use, when combined with population information, is a good index of the intensity and spatial distribution of development in the urban area. A land use inventory should be made to quantify the present development of the urban area and to provide needed data for transportation planning.

The essential features of a land use inventory are: (1) employment of land-use categories corresponding to those in the travel inventory; (2) measurement of all land areas; (3) use of the same analysis areas by the land-use inventory and the travel inventory; and (4) employment of some method for measuring the intensity of land use. This last feature can be accomplished by a simultaneous floor-area survey; however, in residential areas it can also be achieved by knowing the number of dwelling units per unit of land area and in nonresidential areas by knowing the number of employees per unit of land area. By these means the expensive method of measuring intensity of land use by collecting floor-area data can be restricted to small areas such as the central business district.

Economic Inventory. The economic inventory of the metropolitan area is important to the planning process—especially the predictive phase. Total population, total automobiles, total employment, total labor force, and worker productivity levels should be known. Fortunately most of this information is readily available from the state labor department and /or the United States Bureau of the Census.

The existing geographical distribution of population, income, and automobiles must be determined. This information can be obtained from the standard home interview portion of the origin-destination survey or the Bureau of the Census for the census year.

PREPARING THE TRANSPORTATION PLAN

Once an organization has been formed and staffed, the planning objectives stated, and some of the more basic information collected and processed, the actual planning of a transportation system can begin. The goal is to develop a plan for all modes of travel, both for goods and people, in coordination with land use planning. In practice this goal is generally reached by stages.

The preparation of a plan can be considered

[1] Roger L. Creighton and David I. Gooding, SAMPLE SIZE AND STUDY DESIGN (Albany: New York Department of Public Works, Subdivision of Transportation Planning and Programming, 1964, unpublished).

[2] Frederick W. Memmott and Charles R. Guinn, HOME INTERVIEW SURVEY MANUAL (Albany: New York Department of Public Works, Subdivision of Transportation Planning and Programming, 1965).

[3] Frederick W. Memmott and Charles R. Guinn, EXTERNAL SURVEY MANUAL (Albany: New York Department of Public Works, Subdivision of Transportation Planning and Programming, 1963); and, Frederick W. Memmott, TRUCK AND TAXI SURVEY MANUAL (Albany: New York Department of Public Works, Subdivision of Transportation Planning and Programming, 1964).

as a four-part process: identification of present and future problems, preparation of alternate proposals, testing these proposals by estimating use, and evaluating these proposals against previously stated objectives to see how well the objectives have been satisfied by the various alternative plans. While the methods used in this four-part process will vary with each city, primarily as a function of size, these four components are basic to all methods.

Planning, particularly in smaller communities, often starts with an identification of present problems. One simple technique is to compare volumes and capacities on all major thoroughfares and by this means identify deficiencies. The relative importance of the problems then stands out, and solutions will often suggest themselves. Similar methods can be employed for transit systems, although management generally adjusts capacities to demand. Grade crossing conflict maps, accident dot maps, and other devices can be used to identify problem areas. The main point here is that measured, objective data, whether in the form of lists or maps of one kind or another should be available to aid the planner in evaluating the location, nature, and true scale of problems. Only with this essential background material can planning be started.

In larger communities—and as the second stage in planning smaller communities—an estimation of future problems must be undertaken. This is forecasting, which in itself is a complex operation. Basic inputs are forecasts of population and economic activity for the region or area being planned. But these aggregate forecasts must then be distributed over the region. This can be done by measuring a future land plan, by making a mathematical distribution,[4] or by combining plan and forecast.

When future land use has thus been estimated, trip generation can be deduced. This calls for applying trip generation rates to population employment and/or land uses. Crude estimates can be developed quickly, but more accurate estimates require information on car ownership, land use density, and even the presence or absence of transportation facilities of various types. There are a variety of formulas, but the end product of this step is a distribution of future trips throughout the region.

Future trips must be converted into travel volumes on roads and transit lines. This is the traffic assignment process which enables future requirements to be matched by specific plan proposals for various modes of transportation.

Preparing alternative transportation plans for testing is something of an art, although a number of techniques exist which permit the planner to zero in fairly rapidly on the most suitable scale and network configuration. One technique is the use of optimum spacing formulas[5] which indicate the approximate best spacing of arterial and expressways as a function of trip density, construction cost, travel costs, and relative speeds on arterials and expressways. Variations on these formulas estimate the volumes to be expected on each type of facility.[6] Maps showing existing expressways, topography, rail lines, and barriers to transportation facilities (neighborhoods, institutions, residential neighborhoods, etc.) should be used freely to aid in laying out transportation links.

High densities of residence and employment provide clues to the possible location of rapid transit facilities. Rapid transit lines are almost exclusively radial, since the central business district is generally the largest single center of trip making in any urban area. This makes the transit planning task somewhat simpler.

The costs of each proposed link for any type of transportation facility must be carefully estimated, both in relation to construction and right-of-way costs. Relocation problems must similarly be estimated. All these costs are the price a community must pay for gaining other objectives, and the price must be realistically weighed.

[4] George T. Lathrop, John R. Hamburg, and G. Frederick Young, AN OPPORTUNITY ACCESSIBILITY MODEL FOR ALLOCATING REGIONAL GROWTH (Albany: New York Department of Public Works, Subdivision of Transportation Planning and Programming, 1965).

[5] Chicago Area Transportation Study, "Derivation of Formula for Optimum Spacing," TRANSPORTATION PLAN, FINAL REPORT, Volume III (Chicago: Chicago Area Transportation Study, 1962), pp. 121–23.

[6] New York Department of Public Works, Subdivision of Transportation Planning and Programming, DIRECT ASSIGNMENT TRIP TABLES (Albany: The Department, 1964).

Testing alternative transportation plans is the third step in the planning process. Here the modern transportation study is able to record the representation of an entire transportation network—both transit and road systems—and to estimate the choice between modes and the use of each link within the system. Volume flows are then mapped directly by a computer-directed plotter, as shown in Figure 6–9. Of equal importance is the fact that the computer prints out a record of the time, accident, and vehicle operating costs associated with each plan tested.

In cities from 25,000 to 50,000, more limited results than those described above can be obtained by manual methods. Origin-destination surveys indicate where trips begin and end, and hence the use of proposed facilities can be estimated with reasonable accuracy. In such cities substantial new construction is less frequent except where regional roads are involved, and these can generally be located in by-passes on the basis of roadside interviews.

Once the future travel pattern has been simulated, the planner must evaluate the results to determine what proposal is best. What is the rate of return to the community (in terms of reduced time, accident, and travel cost) in relation to the investment? Is adequate provision made for those who cannot use automobiles? Are land uses well served? Are neighborhoods preserved? Is the region accessible to all its residents? Are scenic values preserved?

Evaluating each proposal is a long and demanding task, and many hours in committee may be required before all present are convinced that no further improvements in the plan can reasonably be expected.

Plan Implementation

Plan selection is not the final step in the planning process. The plan must be "sold" to the public and implemented. Too often good plans have been discarded or greatly altered by a lack of effort in this phase.

Establishing public confidence in the planning organization should be the best route to establishing support for the final plan. This procedure should be started almost upon organization of the planning effort. Frequent publication of intermediate findings usually is helpful in establishing this confidence.

The final "sales campaign" should be completely organized prior to public release of the final plan. The presentation of the final plan should include a comparison between the results of implementing the final plan and making no improvements. The measures of the benefits resulting from the plan such as lives saved, accidents prevented, dollars saved in operating expenses, hours saved by the average traveler per year, and improved access should be used to support the plan. The beneficial effect of the transportation plan on regional development and economic growth should also be measured and stated. The simple message which must be conveyed to the public is: "This is the best transportation system for achieving our regional goals."

The actual implementation of the plan must be phased since it should require 20 to 25 years to complete. The usual technique is to divide the planned facilities into four or five stages of five years each.

The selection of facilities for each stage is a necessary but difficult task since many conflicting criteria must be considered in staging the plan. The facilities which provide the most immediate benefits should be included in the first or second stage; however, they are usually located in the most urbanized areas where right-of-way acquisition is both expensive and time consuming. The rights-of-way for these facilities may also be more easily acquired at a later date through urban renewal, and this fact must receive due consideration. The facilities in the least urbanized areas are usually those that are not immediately beneficial, but these facilities are also the easiest to build. At a later date the same rights-of-way may be much more difficult to acquire. Thus, the final staging must be arrived at by weighing conflicting criteria—one which should be followed is to provide a continuous system at all times, for disjointed transportation improvements usually provide limited benefits.

The staging schedule should be subject to fairly frequent review, about every two years. The actual staging must remain flexible since the relative benefits obtained by implementing a specific facility may change over time.

The final step in the planning process is to provide a continuing study to furnish a basis for refining and updating the transportation plan. The plan should be updated every 10 years.

In conclusion, it is worthwhile to think about the changes that are likely to occur in transportation planning in the coming decade. Such forward thinking is useful in preventing undue reverence for present procedures. A helpful guide in such estimation are the trends which have emerged during the past two decades.

Undoubtedly one of the strongest trends during this period—and one which will certainly continue—is the planner's increased power to calculate and deal with large volumes of data through use of the computer. This has revolutionized transportation planning. Formerly, origin-destination data could only be hand applied to one or two plans to see what loads new roads would carry. With the Chicago study's use of computer assignments, more than six plans were tested. In the Niagara Frontier in 1965 more than 20 plans were tested, and economic evaluations of each were produced. This was possible only with the tremendous power of second and third generation computers.

The computer has opened up for serious consideration certain kinds of problems which could never have been attacked before. One is the critical problem of simultaneous planning for two or more modes of transportation. The Chicago study in 1960–61 made separate assignments to transit and to highways; shortly thereafter the Washington, D.C., transportation study developed and used a two-mode model. A more complex program was made operational by the New York State Department of Public Works in 1966, featuring sensitivity to changes in interzonal accessibility by either roadway or transit line. There is little doubt that by the seventies computer models will be able to handle entire regional networks for four or more modes of travel, by persons and by goods.

Paralleling the development of modal models has been increased interest in the coordination of land use and transportation planning. Can transportation significantly affect metropolitan development patterns? The studies

made in the Puget Sound (1960), Penn-Jersey (1959), and Minneapolis-St. Paul (1958) programs were interested enough in this possibility to propose alternative land development plans to be coordinated with different transportation plans. Various computer models have been developed which estimate land development patterns as functions of different kinds of accessibility. More work will certainly be done in this area, forced by particularly strong national interest in better cities, by whatever means they can be obtained.

The trend in transportation planning is now toward longer-term planning and toward devising means to obtain a variety of end-products. A shortage of funds for road building in the 1940s inhibited long range planning. The interstate highway program of 1956 did much to improve financial capability. Now, funds for transportation construction are seen as a continuing investment, needed not only to improve intraurban area accessibility and to lower total transportation costs but to achieve greater personal safety and promote regional economic growth and development. Transportation planning can no longer be considered solely to justify isolated facilities, but rather as an integral component of the comprehensive study, planning, and staged construction of multimode regional transportation systems, in partnership with overall planning for land development.

II. Intercity Transportation

Previous sections have dealt mainly with travel within urban areas, particularly within individual cities and their immediate environs. This section refers to *intercity* transportation.

The distinction between transportation systems that circulate people and goods within cities and transportation systems that move them from one city to another is partly artificial, for each type is an extension of the other. In some cases the connection between the two is hardly discernible as, for instance, when an interstate highway proceeds from rural areas into a city with scarcely a change in cross-section or design. In other cases the transition is abrupt, involving obvious terminals and transfers, as with railroad stations, ports, and airports.

In many areas of the United States most transportation movements of any length still have an identifiable city–rural–city geographic sequence, and are easily classified as intercity. In addition there are specific rural-city and urban-city movements. The increasing urbanization of the United States however, together with its associated concentrations of economic activity, is producing increasing numbers of transportation movements wholly within urban areas and yet of sufficient length to classify them as intercity in other parts of the country. It is possible to classify movements by mileage groupings, but the relativity of distances presents a problem. Perhaps a formalization of transportation movement terms such as intraurban, interurban, intercity, intraregion, and interregion is called for.

The ultimate purpose of a transportation system, whether intraurban or interurban, is to link people and their social and economic organizations together. Goods and services must be brought from the places where they are prepared to the places where they are needed,

and people must be carried from one activity to another. These requirements emphasize the interlocking character of intercity and intracity transportation.

The means by which people and goods are moved between cities is constantly changing, and this is one of the local planning agency's basic problems. The dynamics of the situation are indicated by looking at the proportions of intercity freight traffic moved by five different types of carriers during the years 1940 to 1964 (see Table 6–10).

At the turn of the century, railroads probably carried 90 per cent of all intercity freight traffic, but by 1954 this had been reduced to 50.5 per cent. In addition, trucks carried 18.6 per cent, inland waterways 15.2 per cent, oil pipelines 15.7 per cent, and airways .04 per cent, for a total traffic volume of 1,144 billions of ton-miles.

In the 10-year period to 1964, the share hauled by train decreased by 12.9 per cent, whereas the freight transported by truck increased by 21 per cent, by inland waterways 6.6 per cent, by oil pipeline 9.6 per cent, and by airways 250 per cent. While these changes in mode of transportation were taking place, the

Table 6–10

Percentage Distribution of Domestic Intercity Freight Traffic by Type of Transportation: 1940–1964

Year	Total Traffic (billions[1] of ton miles)[2]	Railroads[3]	Motor Vehicles	Inland Waterways[4]	Oil Pipelines	Airways[5]
1940	651	63.2%	9.5%	18.1%	9.1%	. . .[6]
1945	1,072	68.6	6.2	13.3	11.8	0.01
1950	1,094	57.4	15.8	14.9	11.8	0.03
1954	1,144	50.5	18.6	15.2	15.7	0.04
1955	1,298	50.4	17.2	16.7	15.7	0.04
1960	1,330	44.7	21.5	16.6	17.2	0.06
1964	1,545	44.0	22.5	16.2	17.2	0.10

Source: STATISTICAL ABSTRACT OF THE UNITED STATES, 1965, p. 559; 1966, p. 561.

[1] Note: U.S. billion—1,000,000,000; U.K. billion—1,000,000,000,000.
[2] U.S. ton = 2000 lbs.
[3] Includes electric railways, express, and mail.
[4] Includes Great Lakes, Alaska all years, Hawaii beginning 1959.
[5] Domestic revenue service only. Includes express, mail, excess baggage.
[6] Less than 0.01%.

growth of the national economy caused more traffic to be carried than ever before, increasing 35 per cent during the period to a terminal volume of 1,545 billions of ton-miles in 1964. This increase occurred while the national population went up 18 per cent, industrial production 53 per cent, and Gross National Product 42 per cent.

Table 6–11 indicates a considerably different distribution in mode for passenger travel.

It will be noted that from 1950 to 1964 the share of passenger traffic carried by railroads dropped from 6.4 per cent to 2.1 per cent, representing a decrease of 67.2 per cent. In 1954, railroads carried 4.4 per cent of domestic intercity passenger traffic, commercial motor vehicles, 3.8 per cent; inland waterways 0.2 per cent; and airways, 2.9 per cent. Private automobiles carried the predominant share or 88.7 per cent. During the 10 years ending 1964 the share hauled by railroads and commercial carriers decreased by 52.3 per cent and 34.2 per cent respectively, while that for private autos rose by 1.3 per cent, inland waterways 28 per cent, and airways 90 per cent.

The total volume of freight carried in terms of ton-miles increased from 1,144 billions in 1954 to 1,545 billions in 1964. This increase was reflected in the various modes of freight transportation with railroads carrying an additional 17.8 per cent, trucks 63 per cent, inland waterways 44 per cent, oil pipelines 18.3 per cent, and airways 278.8 per cent.

In the realm of passenger transportation, the total number of passenger-miles traveled increased from 673 billion in 1954 to 895 billion in 1964. The effect of this total increase was to raise actual auto passenger-miles by 34.3 per cent, inland waterways by 66.8 per cent, and air by 153 per cent, while the passenger-miles run by busses declined by 11.4 per cent and the railroads suffered a decrease of 37.6 per cent.

These statistics present an overall picture of particular interest to the urban planner. They indicate heavy increases in the total amount of freight hauled and the total number of passenger miles traveled, as might be expected during a period of steady economic growth. They also indicate changes in the fortunes of the different types of carriers. Commercial motor vehicle carriers have increased their freight hauling activity considerably, while at the same time suffering a decline in passenger traffic. The railroads, while increasing the actual amount of freight hauled, have declined in the overall proportion of available freight carried, and in addition have suffered a heavy loss in passenger traffic, both in terms of volume carried and

Table 6–11

Percentage Distribution of Domestic Intercity Passenger Traffic by Type of Transportation: 1950–1964

Year	Total Traffic (billions[1] of passenger miles)	Railroads[2]	Private Autos	Com'l Motor Vehicle Carriers	Inland[3] Water-ways	Air-ways[4]
1950	508.5	6.4	86.2	5.2	0.2	2.0
1954	673.4	4.4	88.7	3.8	0.2	2.9
1955	716.1	4.0	89.0	3.6	0.2	3.2
1960	784.2	2.8	90.0	2.5	0.3	4.3
1964	895.2	2.1	89.6	2.5	0.3	5.5

Source: STATISTICAL ABSTRACT OF THE UNITED STATES, 1966, p. 561.
[1] Note: U.S. billion = 1,000,000,000; U.K. billion = 1,000,000,000,000.
[2] Includes electric railways.
[3] Includes Great Lakes.
[4] Includes domestic commercial revenue service and private pleasure and business flying.

share of available business. However, the airways have experienced a significant increase in freight and passenger traffic, both in terms of volume and share. Oil pipelines have increased both their traffic and share situations. While increasing their volume of freight business, waterways appear to be just holding their own relative to the proportion of traffic handled. However, in terms of passenger-miles run, they have improved their position both in volume and share.

At the turn of the century people traveled almost exclusively by rail, and to a minor extent by waterways. By 1964 the situation was completely changed with almost 90 per cent traveling by private automobile and the remainder selecting the other modes of transportation, with a significant number traveling by air.

These changes are largely the result of technological innovations such as the development of the motor car, the airplane, and the whole range of auxiliary inventions and developments that have made possible a full utilization of the primary inventions to solve man's varied transportation needs. Among the prime movers are the helicopter, the jet airplane, the diesel locomotive, and the many specialized adaptations of the motor car, some involving the use of diesel power, such as earth moving tractors. Among developments considered secondary to transportation, but primary in their own right, are radio; radar and electronic computers to control air, rail, and road traffic; and "piggy-back" trains which enable road and rail freight transport to be more closely integrated.

The impact of public expenditure on highway facilities should not be overlooked. Government spending on highway facilities is now over $10 billion per year, much of which is urban oriented. Waterways are, in effect, subsidized by several hundred millions of dollars each year. Trunk airlines are generally self-supporting, but subsidies of several hundreds of millions of dollars still flow into local airlines, airports, and operational facilities. The railroads are self-supporting, but federal funds are now being applied in urban areas to improve passenger traffic facilities and service. The long-range effects of this type of federal

financial investment cannot yet be determined.

All the factors which have been mentioned have a profound effect upon the economy and land-use structure of the urban area, as well as on the planning of sites for terminals and the routes for intercity transportation systems. Any system must be planned realistically on present technology, but technical advances now occur with such rapidity that changes are singularly difficult to anticipate and evaluate. However, the constraining effect of vast capital investment in existing plant and equipment should not be overlooked in dealing with the application of radical advances to any particular system.

It would be desirable to have a plan for all types of transportation on a national scale that would assign to each carrier the business that it is best suited to serve. At this time (1967) there is no national policy that embraces all types of transportation, although the different modes experience both government regulation and subsidy. Although the Federal Department of Transportation, established in 1966, will be giving more systematic attention to national transportation policy than has ever been possible before, a planning agency must act without an overall national policy framework.

In formulating a plan for its area of jurisdiction, the responsible agency must consider the economic effects of changes in intercity transportation. These effects might be evaluated as a part of the planning agency's economic base studies. Ease of transportation, plus a city's resources and geographic position, determine to a great extent the growth of the economy of any urban area. Intercity transportation permits specialization of production in various cities, just as intraurban transportation permits specialization of functions and hence greater productivity within cities.

Detroit, for example, exports automobiles and trucks and imports food and raw materials. Many cities in the South and Midwest are assembly points for the export of food and the import of farm machinery and consumer goods. A good transportation system permits profitable specialization to take place. Changes in transportation may sometimes also have adverse effects. Oil and gas pipelines have undoubtedly contributed to the decline of the coal industry and have thereby hurt cities in coal producing regions. Some small towns, previously on main routes, have been bypassed by new highways, thereby decreasing their economic bases.

Transportation changes also affect the form of cities and the ways in which cities are grouped in regions. The local planning agency will have little control over the regional influences, but it should be aware of the effects of transportation on land use and be able to anticipate some of the effects on the locality.

Generally, improvements in transportation tend to benefit the larger cities—jet aircraft, for instance, will serve only the larger metropolitan areas. However, the interstate system of highways may accelerate the growth of medium sized cities as has been the case along the New York state thruway. Whatever their overall regional effect may be, it is clear that an increase in the number of types of carriers available will reduce urban densities. The railroad system tended to concentrate cities, but roads and pipelines, which feed naturally into the internal distribution of a city without having to be transshipped, act to reduce centripetal forces. Even the airport—through its requirements for location, and present and future area—helps produce lower urban densities.

Site requirements are also affected by changes in transportation. Airports are becoming larger and noisier due to the development of larger jet aircraft. Small feeder lines may be accommodated on very small tracts of land because of the development of the helicopter. Railroads have centralized and streamlined their operations due to the transition from steam to diesel and the reduced emphasis on passenger service. Port designs may change in the future and, of course, other types of transportation may be developed.

These site changes will also affect the areas surrounding terminals of intercity transportation systems. The site planning of various transportation terminals is not generally a public responsibility, except in cases where the facilities are publicly owned, yet the planning agency must be aware of internal site requirements to plan appropriate external connec-

tions more intelligently and efficiently.

Changes in terminals and lines of intercity transportation occur infrequently and are rarely subject to public programming. When they do arise, they are apt to be brought to the planning agency as an urgent problem with pressure generated for an expression of opinion or the immediate execution of a research project. A well-functioning agency will be ready for such eventualities. It will be acquainted with technological developments and the likelihood of their application to the area of jurisdiction. Queries may then be dealt with against a background of progressive research, and intelligent decisions made.

Once a problem has been identified, specialized knowledge must be applied to carry out the analysis necessary to isolate the critical factors. The planning agency will rarely include personnel who are sufficiently skilled to discuss technical matters with experts in the various transportation fields, except in cities large enough to warrant retaining a specialist staff for this purpose. The role of the planning staff will usually involve keeping abreast of the current community situation, anticipating problems, and then cooperating with appropriate specialists for their solutions.

Technological developments have a profound effect on the means by which people and goods are moved between cities. Carriers are always striving to improve their competitive positions by making innovations in service. These changes have an influence on cities due to the nature of terminal facilities, land occupancy, and the general location and manner of bringing in people and goods.

The planning agency should keep up to date on new developments in order to anticipate effects on the community. In providing for change, the planning agency should seek to avoid controversy on detailed points and should adhere to the comprehensive view.

Having reviewed in some detail the results of the operation of various modes of transportation, both freight and passenger hauling, it is now appropriate to examine more closely the operation of each mode and its impact on immediate surroundings and the community at large.

FREIGHT TERMINALS

Freight terminals have certain common features, and it is therefore convenient to deal with them as a group, although the design and location of any individual unit will be determined by the mode of transportation involved, the goods being hauled, and the quantitative capacity considered appropriate. Clearly there will be great differences between grain, livestock, farm produce, and general merchandise terminals. Due to the variables involved, each terminal of any significance will tend to create a unique problem for the urban planner.

For most terminal situations, however, experience has produced a series of guidelines or standards relating the physical dimensions of loading platforms, freight houses, or transit sheds to the quantity of traffic and the number of trucks, railroad cars, or ships being handled. In all cases physical plant design is closely related to the overall turn-around time of the particular mode. The highway truck is turned around in one day; where ships or barges handle bulk cargoes such as iron ore or coal, special provisions are made for loading and unloading and they can have a similar turn-around time. However, the general cargo ship is commonly in port for several days.

Railroad cars have a turn-around pattern similar to cargo ships, but for different reasons. It is true that for hauling bulk materials on a regularly recurrent basis, contractual unit trains are being operated with special loading and unloading facilities. A highly sophisticated example of this may be found in Labrador, Canada, where completely automated trains haul iron ore from mines to port for transhipment. In contrast to the specialized one-cargo train, the average freight car spends only about 11 per cent of each day in actual load hauling, the remaining time is spent in loading or unloading, in terminal and classification movement, or on standby. Thus railroad freight yards require large areas of land in urban areas.

Technological and operational improvements in the railroad industry should not be overlooked. These advances tend to diminish the scattered space needs of the ton-miles per train-hour of freight, which increased from 23,877 in 1954 to 32,640 in 1964. In 1954 the average freight car moved 43.8 miles per day in line-haul service, but in 1964 it moved 50 miles. During the same period carload freight increased from 41.4 tons to 47.8 tons, and the introduction of progressively larger cars increased average capacity from 53.7 tons to 58.3 tons.

In the case of truck freight, increased tonnages demand larger terminal facilities, as with all modes of transportation. In 1954 there were 9.8 million trucks registered; this had increased to 14 million in 1964. Although the increase in size of equipment demands greater areas for maneuvering, it does bring relative improvement in terminal efficiency due to the smaller number of bays required for a given capacity. To enable a 50-foot combination unit to back up to a platform, a setback of 70 feet is required. Care should be exercised to insure that this large intercity equipment is prohibited from servicing buildings via ordinary streets, which often creates traffic jams.

Of all intercity modes of transportation, air travel is having the most noticeable impact on urban planning. The effects of rapid increase in use, introduction of jet aircraft requiring greater runway lengths, and increases in aircraft size require air terminals to become more regional in nature, while retaining efficient lines of communication between the terminals and the communities they serve.

Some factors external to the mode involved, which influence terminal location and design, are worthy of note. These may involve considerations such as whether the purpose of the terminal is to break bulk (e.g., from rail to truck) or is more truly terminal, like a produce market where market transactions take place before reshipping, perhaps requiring from 8 to 100 acres of land. Market and seasonal requirements must be considered—the degree of perishability of the goods and their sensitivity to bruising, temperature, and humidity, together with the lot-sizes demanded by the market. Also to be considered would be the requirement for adjoining business offices and the availability and cost of required movements by different modes balanced against the cost of land, traffic, and availability of markets.

The interacting effects of technological change within the various types of transportation should also be considered as well as changes within particular industries and changing patterns of world trade in both raw materials and finished products.

The development of truck-trailer "piggy-backing" is an interesting example of the first of these effects. Between 1955 and 1965, piggy-back loadings increased from 168,510 to 1,031,210. Another example: in 1940, about 41 per cent of new automobiles were shipped from factories by rail; by 1959 this method reached a low of only 8 per cent. By 1965 a level of 40 per cent had been recaptured by the railroads through aggressive pricing, the use of extra-long double and trilevel cars, and specialized terminals.

The decentralization of the meat-packing industry is an example of the second situation (changes within industries). Moving livestock traditionally was a railroad activity; it is now estimated that about 95 per cent of cattle, virtually all hogs, and 82 per cent of sheep and lambs arrive at major markets by truck. Thus, even for that proportion of livestock which continues to be carried by rail, the operational dimensions and handling facilities required differ completely from past practice.

The decline in importance of iron ore deposits in the United States is an example of changed patterns of international trade. The movement of iron ore into the U.S. from Canada and overseas has created an expansion of specialized shipping on the Great Lakes and other waterways.

In terms of both tons and ton-miles, trucks predominate in hauling meat and dairy products, candy, beverages, textile products, apparel, rubber and plastic products, furniture, fabricated metal products, machinery, and instruments. Rail carries the majority of canned and frozen food products, paper, chemicals, lumber, primary iron and steel, nonferrous products, and motor vehicles.

The urban planner should be aware of the characteristics of the various modes of transportation available for handling the same commodity. For example, grain shipment is normally by rail and is then transferred to shipping for overseas export. To unload rail freight cars a gang of men with power shovels can process some 5,000 bushels per hour, whereas an automatic dumper can handle some 15,000 bushels per hour. The grain can be moved into a million-bushel elevator at a similar rate, although in loading ships through multiple spouts significantly higher rates can be achieved.

The combined effects of changes in technology, and the more abstract factors of management and government regulatory practices, are illustrated by the reorganization of the Railway Express Agency (R.E.A.). As the number of centralized area terminals increased, the number of local offices was reduced. In shipping, the truck-air combination was developed significantly and in truck-rail movements, standardized highway and rail vehicles were produced to carry standardized containers which could be moved from truck to rail by special power equipment.

Turning to air transportation, modern jet aircraft can now carry up to 47 tons of freight, or 250 passengers, and larger and faster types of aircraft are promised. Airlines are perhaps even more interested in the development of freight containers than shipping companies. Much of the airline's freight traffic consists of less-than-carload or truckload lots. The development of aircraft that can be used for passengers or freight, by sliding out the passenger seats and fittings in blocks, is an attempt to increase the utilization of airplanes so that both markets may be tapped without the necessity for two types of specialized aircraft. The possibilities thus afforded for night freight hauling and daytime passenger hauling may be clearly appreciated.

The field of transportation is still advancing, and the innovative curiosities of today may well be the accepted modes of tomorrow. The downtown helicopter terminal is already a fact in some large cities, and may someday become commonplace in much smaller communities. The use of rivers and other waterways for hydrofoils and air-cushion vehicles is a fact in some locations and may become much more widespread in the world of tomorrow. The traditional airfield may in due course be modified under the influence of vertical take-off and landing (VTOL) aircraft now in existence.

Many of these developments are already upon us and it is not unrealistic for the planner to keep them in mind, for he is dealing not only with the present but also in many cases with plans which will culminate in the year 2000. As discussed in the last chapter of this book, developments in communications will undoubtedly have an effect on terminal facilities and upon land uses generally, perhaps to such an extent that the traditional concept of city shape and form may be altered dramatically in a future that may be remote in terms of the life of man, but close in terms of historical development.

Highway Facilities

Although urban highway transportation was discussed earlier in this chapter, the relationship of city and intercity traffic should be examined.

In 1964 a total of 842 billion vehicle-miles were traveled in the United States, of which 52 per cent were rural and 42 per cent urban. Of the rural travel, 78 per cent was by automobile, 21.4 per cent by truck, and .6 per cent by bus. For urban travel the percentages were 85.5, 14, and .5, respectively.

Although freight is moved increasingly in private trucks directly to individual local wholesale and retail distribution points, the true truck terminal, which has already been described, is a land use activity which can have a significant effect upon surrounding traffic patterns. For example, even long-distance trucks moving directly to shopping centers create a specialized land use for small-scale local truck terminals. The demands of truck terminals generally are, in some respects, becoming greater, due to the increasing size and weight of truck units. Whereas a private automobile may require a minimum turning radius of 30 feet, a truck unit requires 47 feet, and the truck may be three times as long as the auto. Due to the length of the units, loading platforms require setbacks from the road of at least 70 feet.

The horsepower of truck engines has been increased considerably over the years, but has been absorbed in net and payload weights so that performance characteristics, such as acceleration, have hardly changed. A large truck may be considered generally to be the equivalent of from two to eight automobiles in relation to traffic flow, depending upon traffic control and grade characteristics. The nature of the performance of heavy trucks should be considered in the design of intersections and the ramps and weaving sections of controlled access highways. An auto can accelerate to 30 mph in approximately 12 seconds, whereas a heavy truck requires closer to 30 seconds, distances of 400 feet and 900 feet respectively. These factors obviously have an impact on highway design.

Data collected on main intercity rural roads indicate that only 31 per cent of the vehicle-miles are covered by tractor-trailer truck combinations but that they account for some 74 per cent of the ton-miles. In 1953 most trailers built were from 32 to 34 feet long; in 1964 these lengths had increased to 38 to 40 feet.

The ultimate destination of highway traffic that approaches cities varies considerably with the size of the city involved. Traffic with destinations beyond the city will range from 42 per cent down to 8 per cent as city population increases from 5,000 to 1 million persons. Traffic to the central business district ranges from 29 to 15 per cent whereas, for the same population range, the attraction of the other parts of the city increases from 22 to 77 per cent as size increases.

The increasing significance of highways is indicated by the fact that in 1964, 72 million cars and 13 million trucks and busses were registered in the United States; projections suggest that there may be 97 million cars and 19 million trucks and busses in 1975.

Railroad Lines and Terminals

In his book *Land Uses in American Cities,* Harland Bartholomew observed that about 5 per cent of development land in the cities studied was used by railroads.[7] This is generally more than is used for all commercial purposes and about the same as is used for public open space. Most railroad land is taken up by yards

[7] Harland Bartholomew, LAND USES IN AMERICAN CITIES, (Cambridge, Massachusetts: Harvard University Press, 1955).

and terminals; very little is used for main line rights-of-way.

Apart from occupying large areas of urban land, railroads actively use their properties. The noise and vibration of passing trains makes large areas adjacent to yards and main line tracks less than desirable for residential purposes. Although almost 100 per cent of all locomotives are now diesel powered, there is still dust and oily exhaust fumes near the tracks. Consequently the presence of railroads tends to lead to the classification of adjoining properties as industrial. This is an important element to be considered in zoning, and not without reason, since railroads and industry are mutually helpful.

Railroad property as a whole generates relatively little person or vehicular traffic—about as much per acre as generated by public open space. This is because yards and tracks are extensive rather than intensive users of land. Passenger and freight terminals, however, can throw concentrated loads on nearby street systems, requiring careful traffic planning.

Railroad lines and yards frequently interrupt street systems, requiring the consideration of grade separations to eliminate delays and accidents and substantially influencing the layout of street and highway systems. At rail-highway intersections, the high speed main line will usually require the highway facility to adapt to the rail-line configuration when grade separation is being carried out. A branch line may permit on-grade crossings with appropriate automatic crossing warning protection, although some multiple intersections require careful research and track-circuit planning by railroad staff. For the industrial feeder and spur line, automatic warning may be required, but a little-used rail line can be protected manually by train crews. Particular attention should be given to problem crossings where slow-moving or standing trains are a source of traffic congestion. Improvement of rail-highway crossings normally involves joint financing by the railroad and the highway authority.

Consequently, as railroad facilities are fixed in location they are an extremely important element, affecting the planning of cities and metropolitan areas. Although alterations some-times can be made, for the most part little can be done except to recognize that the railroads are there, and to plan land uses and transportation facilities around them.

Elements of a Railroad System. The main line tracks of a railroad line generally proceed as radials toward the heart of the city. The radial pattern is due to the fact that railroads once held a near monopoly on intercity passenger and freight business, and they sought to bring their depots as close as possible to the most convenient location for the pick-up and delivery of passengers, mail, and luggage.

Many main line tracks have become a natural site for industrial location. Within the limits of the switching district, where there is no extra charge for delivery or pick-up of freight cars, it has been convenient for the railroads to construct parallel or spur switching tracks leading directly off the main line tracks to serve industries. Even if new main line tracks are proposed, these industries have a continuing need for rail connections. This is one reason why it is extremely difficult to reroute main line tracks, which are among the most permanent elements of the railroad system in cities.

Belt lines are circumferential routes permitting cars not destined to a city to be shifted from one rail line to another. In railroad parlance, a belt line is any track that extends from one railroad to another in order to exchange cars. The proportion of exchange movements is related to city size and the number of rail lines serving it. In the largest urban areas, two belt lines may be required; Chicago has three. Often thought of only as part of an ideal rail system, belt lines may become more important with consolidation of railroad companies and attempts to make the handling of freight cars more efficient.

Belt lines offer excellent sites for industrial development, especially if they are located in undeveloped parts of an urban area. Because the belt line connects two or more railroads, there is better chance for fast connections and quick receipt and delivery of freight cars. There seems to be no standard pattern of ownership of belt line railroads. The San Francisco and New Orleans belt lines are publicly owned; the outermost belt line in Chicago is owned by a subsidiary of the United States Steel Corporation; and the belt line in St. Louis is owned by an association of railroads.

Classification yards are places for the assembly and reclassification of the individual units which make up trains, principally freight trains. They also serve to store cars not in use or awaiting repair and maintenance. Classification yards are often combined with repair shops and roundhouses, where locomotives are stored and serviced. Larger yards are becoming increasingly automated with electronic controls and a number of other devices that permit the more rapid assembly and turnaround of freight trains.

The changing technology of railroad operation is bringing about a reduction in the number of classification yards through consolidation and relocation to the outer edges of urban areas. This provides an opportunity for making significant physical changes and for conversion of marginally used land to industrial sites. In some cases the ideal solution might be the provision of one very large yard, to include locomotive and car servicing facilities, together with a few localized yards. Under such an arrangement, most freight cars entering an urban region would be sorted and classified in the large yard, and the new trains would then proceed to local yards, or freight-houses, or on to other cities.

Classification yards require large land areas. Tracks are usually arranged so that as trains enter they are scanned by television or automatic car registering devices, the locomotive detached, and the train units pushed over a "hump" where they roll by gravity to their proper positions in the new train being assembled. This assembly is performed under the guidance of a completely automatic or semiautomatic system based on punched cards or lists prepared to describe the operations required for the correct placement of the cars.

In addition to the main and subsidiary yards, and the freighthouse yards for rail-truck transfer, there may be specialized terminal facilities in separate locations for bulk cargoes which are not sorted and classified, for "piggyback" operations, and for trains carrying automobiles and trucks. Such specialized terminals may be located in suburban industrial areas or close to the dense centers of urban areas.

Railroad terminals may be classified in a number of ways and include passenger terminals for commuters or long-distance travelers and freight terminals or various types. Terminals are known as "dead-end" where trains are required to back out, or "through" where trains can proceed to their next destination.

Despite the decline in numbers of passengers using railroads, the passenger terminal appears to be one of the more stable elements of railroad operation in the city—in part because such terminals are used for such purposes as administrative offices and handling of mail, baggage, and express freight.

Where terminals are located in the heart of the city, the railroad has an advantage over the airplane. For intercity journeys the time taken to travel to and from an outlying airport is of significance compared to the total time to make the basic journey. The availability of overnight sleepers for intercity journeys is also a deciding factor in the selection of a mode of travel by some passengers. In the larger cities, commuters are heavy users of the passenger terminal, and this may become an even more significant factor if new high-speed rail schemes are developed.

Railroads in the City Plan. A survey of railroad operations as they affect the public interest may be a desirable way for a planning agency to plot its course regarding railroads in the city plan. The elimination of grade crossings is an action generally initiated by public authority, but there are many instances where repeated accidents have aroused public feeling to such a degree that prompt action has been taken by the highway authority and the railroad company. There is no doubt that a planning agency should give all support necessary in cases where public safety is involved.

The consolidation of terminals, both freight and passenger, may be proposed by other than railroad interests, and possible alternative uses for marginally used railroad yards may be pointed out by the planning agency. Finally, the agency should, as a part of its industrial and residential land planning, determine the uses and control the platting of land adjacent to the railroad in the developing sections of the city so that past mistakes are not repeated.

1. *Terminal Consolidation.* The replacement of two or more passenger stations with a union terminal is a change that has been frequently suggested, and in some cases already implemented. There would not seem to be much advantage to be gained by such an expensive undertaking in a period of declining passenger traffic; however, the possibility of eliminating one or more rail routes through a city, of improving the total grade-crossing situation, and of making more land available for other urban uses may, in some cases, make terminal consolidation a feasible proposition.

The New Orleans Union Passenger Terminal, completed in 1954, was only part of a much larger project with a total cost of nearly $55 million. The Cincinnati Union Terminal, completed before World War II, cost nearly $40 million. A proposed consolidation of terminals in Chicago has been an issue for nearly 50 years.

2. *Railroad Grade Crossings.* In cities traversed by railroad lines, crossings at grade present one of the most perplexing planning problems, often difficult and expensive to correct. Crossings at grade are unwelcome legacies from a past era where highway transportation was slow and minimal. They now occasion considerable losses through road traffic delays and accidents, inefficient railroad operation, depressed real estate values, and often serious inconvenience and annoyance to the public.

In 1964 there were approximately 218,700 railroad-highway grade crossings in the United States, nearly 9,000 less than in 1950.[8] Each is a potential deathtrap. In 1965, 1,534 persons were killed and 3,801 injured in 3,820 accidents at grade crossings; over 93 per cent of the deaths and over 96 per cent of the injuries involved automobiles. It has been found that the protection of crossings by gates, signals, or watchmen, and the design of the crossing to assure adequate views of the railroad track in both directions is not sufficient.

For example, on one railroad about 40 per cent of the total grade crossing accidents occur at crossings protected by watchmen, signals, or gates. Fifty-four per cent of the accidents occur in broad daylight, most involve persons who live in the community and who are familiar with the crossing and the schedule of trains. It is therefore obvious that the only safe highway-railroad intersection is one where levels are separated. Progress in this direction is slow. In 1964 only 159 were treated on separate levels in the United States as compared with 61 in 1950.[9] The total number of grade crossings has decreased substantially since 1950, as already noted, but this has been due to abandonment of lines rather than improvement of crossings.

Grade separation is so intimately related to broader problems of the arrangement and operation of railroad facilities, the community street plan, and the general development of the city that, in order to avoid costly mistakes and insure proper coordination, the problem needs to be studied concurrently with these major elements of community development. It would be unrealistic and inexcusable, for example, to spend large sums of money for the separation of grades along a railroad line that might better be relocated or abandoned, or to construct utilities where they would have to be removed at great expense when grade separations were constructed in the future.

All grade crossings are objectionable and theoretically should be eliminated, but it is clear that this cannot be done in all cases. The practical solution is to concentrate automobile traffic on a few main thoroughfares and to separate the grades where they intersect with principal rail lines. Any large-scale grade separation program will take many years to complete. It is important therefore that a comprehensive grade-separation plan be prepared and adopted in order that future railroad, public, and private improvements may be designed in agreement with it.

To determine priorities for grade crossing separations, it is desirable to establish a comparative rating of grade crossings measured by their relative hazard and by the economic

---

[8] U.S. Bureau of the Census, STATISTICAL ABSTRACT OF THE UNITED STATES: 1966, 87th edition, No. 850 (Washington, D.C.: Government Printing Office, 1966), p. 586.

[9] *Ibid.*

losses which they engender. One method is to prepare an accident "dot map" where intensity of dots indicates maximum hazard locations. Another method is to multiply the average daily traffic volume crossing the grade intersection by the number of trains passing at that point. This calculation yields an index of probability of accident occurrence. Physical conditions such as visibility, street approach grades, and the angle at which the street intersects the track will also affect the degree of hazard. In preparing a program for eliminating grade crossings, care should be taken to include those that will be more heavily used in the future.

3. *Railroad Air Rights.* Air rights comprise ". . . the rights vested in the ownership of all the property at and above a certain horizontal plane, as well as caisson and column lots essential to contain the structural supports of the air rights improvement."[10] The utilization of such air rights consists of construction "in space" above an existing surface use, in this case the railroad.

In the largest cities, where land costs are very high, the use of air rights over downtown railroad lines, yards, or terminals, may be economical for construction of new buildings. The pressure to develop structures on air rights is strongest in the heart of the business district where railroads are usually focussed and where land values are at a peak. The use of air rights enables valuable land lost to transportation systems to be reclaimed for other urban purposes, provided that the value of sites in the location under consideration is sufficiently high to make the operation economically feasible.

Improvements over railroads are not a new idea—indeed, the first air rights construction, the New York Central Terminal development in New York City, was started in 1908 and completed in 1913. Park Avenue was built over the New York Central tracks leading into the terminal and by 1929, 18 skyscrapers had been built over the tracks, the most recent being the 59-story Pan American building.[11]

Interest in air rights developments has increased as pressures for land have built up in city centers. The most numerous examples are found in New York City and Chicago, but instances exist in Cleveland, Ohio; Kew Gardens, Long Island; El Paso, Texas; and other cities.

4. *Land Uses Abutting Railroad Tracks.* In the past, the steam locomotive produced noise, vibration, ash, and smoke which created an industrial atmosphere that was highly detrimental to adjacent land uses. The railroad facilities of today still have this effect, though on a less dramatic scale. A diesel-hauled freight train running at higher speeds than in the past, still produces severe noise levels, vibration, and some air pollution, and a rail terminal remains associated with industrial land use and depressed adjacent residential areas.

Cities continue to grow, and unless their growth occurs in a controlled manner in accordance with a rational plan, the problems now presented by the railroad will continue to multiply. Existing grade crossings in fringe areas will become more heavily used, and new housing will be built adjacent to railroad tracks and yards. Only realistic proposals formulated by the planning agency can prevent the mistakes of the past from being repeated to procreate the urban blight of the future.

Industrial land use is most frequently associated with railroads. This is certainly the most appropriate use in some cases, assuming that industrial sites can also be served by good arterial streets. Of course, if all the land adjacent to railroad lines were zoned for industry, there would obviously be an excess of industrial lands. The area to be zoned must conform to the calculated needs of the community over a realistic planning period, and other uses must be found for the remainder of the land.

Commercial uses—especially automobile sales, lumber yards, monument works, and other uses that involve storage—are not damaged by proximity to the noise and vibration of railroad trains. Recreational areas, particularly large playing fields, may also coexist with railroads. Residential areas, on the other hand, require protection from railroad rights-of-way to minimize noise, vibration, and pollution. This may be achieved, to some extent, by plat-

---

[10] American Society of Planning Officials, AIR RIGHTS, ASPO Planning Advisory Service Information Report No. 186, (Chicago: The Society, 1964) , p. 2.

[11] *Ibid.*, pp. 1–2.

ting lots that back on to railroad tracks so that they are at least 200 feet deep, or by establishing a buffer zone of public land between railroad and residential lots. In either case, land adjacent to the tracks should be planted with shrubs and trees of suitable variety to minimize the presence of the railroad.

PORTS

In the period from 1940 to 1964, waterborne imports and exports in United States trade with foreign countries increased from 111 million to 422 million short tons per year. In the same period, the freight carried on inland waterways more than doubled in volume. This increase was not concentrated in the Great Lakes, but was distributed among many river systems, as indicated in Table 6–12. Clearly the increase in waterborne cargo movement has an influence on many cities, including inland as well as coastal ports. This suggests that planners should give proportionately increased attention to the problems that may exist in ports under their jurisdiction.

Ports, like railroad terminals and airports, are transportation terminals used for the han-

dling of freight that requires transshipment in order to reach its final destination. Industries such as steel, aluminum, and power—which are located on the water and process or handle cargoes directly on the spot—do not use ports, although they generate a large proportion of the maritime traffic. Developing facilities for the economic and efficient transshipment of freight is the major port planning problem and the reason for its existence.

Planning port and harbor facilities is mainly an engineering job, just as planning the terminal arrangements of railroad terminals is a task for the railroad engineer. Port planning requires a knowledge of ship construction, cargo handling techniques, pier construction, and experience with the functional administration of a port facility. In short, it is a highly specialized undertaking which does not normally fall within the province of the municipal planning agency. This does not mean that the planners in such an agency should be disinterested in the internal operation of a port facility under their jurisdiction. On the contrary, the agency should be concerned that the port is provided with adequate transportation links, particularly highway and railroad facilities. To do this well the planner should have a workmanlike understanding of how a port operates.

Major Elements of Ports. A port consists of a harbor, which is a protected body of water sufficiently deep for the entrance of the ships to be handled, plus all the land facilities that make possible its use for shipping. The depth of water in the harbor controls the types of ships that can enter. Only a few United States ports have water depths at piers or wharves greater than 30 or 35 feet. The St. Lawrence Seaway permits ocean-going ships that draw no more than 27 feet of water to enter the Great Lakes, but on major inland waterways no more than a nine-foot channel is usually required.

Ship berths are the water areas alongside wharves or piers where the ships are moored during loading and unloading. A pier is usually placed at right angles to the shore line, and is appropriate on gently sloping shores and places where there is a premium on waterfront space. A wharf is constructed so that the ship is moored parallel to the natural shore line, al-

Table 6–12

Freight Carried on Inland Waterways, by System: 1940 to 1964 (in millions of ton[1]-miles; excludes Alaska and Hawaii except as noted)

System	1940	1964
Atlantic Coast rivers..........	1,859	27,860
Gulf Coast rivers.............	593	20,686
Pacific Coast rivers...........	1,229	6,347
Mississippi River system[2]......	13,934	89,348
Other waterways[3]...........	10	12
Canals and connecting channels[4]................	4,787	...*
Great Lakes system...........	95,645	105,912
Total.....................	118,057	250,165

Source: STATISTICAL ABSTRACT OF THE UNITED STATES, 1966, p. 603.
[1] Short ton = 2000 lbs.
[2] Includes main channels and all tributaries of the Mississippi, Illinois, Missouri, and Ohio Rivers.
[3] Beginning 1960, includes Alaskan waterways.
[4] Except Great Lakes.
* Beginning 1955 distributed by inland waterways. Volume in 1950—8,639.

though the term is often used loosely to include piers. A quay is, in effect, a masonry wharf, more common in Europe than in the United States. A levee is a paved, sloping area, extending above and below water line, suitable for handling shallow draft vessels in river systems having variable water levels. Levees were provided at many points along large navigable rivers throughout the U.S., particularly during the heyday of the passenger river boat. The amount of traffic at that time may be judged by the size of the levees—the levee at St. Louis, Missouri, is an outstanding example.

On the pier or wharf three types of areas must be provided for loading and unloading activities. Immediately adjacent to the ship is the apron—an open working space to which goods are transferred from the ship by derricks or cranes and other mechanical devices. It is comparable to the platform used for unloading freight cars at a railroad freight terminal. Behind the apron, or between two aprons in the case of a double-berth pier, is the transit shed, a covered area used for temporary storage of cargoes being loaded or unloaded. Finally, areas must be reserved for trucks and trains bringing freight and sometimes passengers to and from the port. In some cases railroad spurs may be located on the apron itself, and in others they may be located between two transit sheds on a broad pier.

Ports may include facilities for refueling and repair of ships, oil storage, storage of goods in transit, and firefighting. Where passengers and cargoes from foreign countries are handled, facilities are provided for customs officials and for holding goods in bond, pending transshipment or the payment of import duties.

Ship berths for general cargo handling should be 600 feet long, although tankers, ore boats, and passenger liners are much longer, ranging from 800 to more than 1000 feet. Piers and wharves are, therefore, usually designed in multiples of 600 feet, or other appropriate ship length. The width of piers and wharves may be from 200 to 300 feet, the trend being toward a greater width adapted to the mechanical handling of cargo. A medium-size port may have 100 cranes, so that when considered with the lighting required for night operation, the area

becomes a concentrated load-point for electric power.

Ports in the City Plan. In almost all cases, the site of a port has been determined by the physical facts of water depth, topography, and the form of a coastline or river. Since cities have grown up around the best natural ports, most port problems are not those of finding suitable sites, but rather of developing and redeveloping existing sites usually located in the oldest section of the city.

Probably the most important aspect of a port relative to the city plan is its relationship to rail and highway transportation systems. A large part of the cost of waterborne transportation lies in terminal operations. If these can be streamlined, a considerable economic advantage is gained. Some excess costs are attributable to the design of the terminals themselves, which are often outmoded, but some can be attributed to congestion in surrounding streets and to inefficient rail connections.

It was once common practice to construct a wide marginal road on the land side of all piers or wharves, often with railroad tracks let into the pavements. These marginal roads were often 150 to 200 feet wide. Due to curb parking; loading and unloading in the street; and the movement of trains, trucks, and automobiles, marginal roads are frequently congested. Under today's conditions it would seem to be more desirable to require extensive offstreet truck loading areas, and to direct long distance trucks quickly to an expressway system. Such an arrangement would leave marginal roads free for short trips.

Rail facilities must also be planned to serve the port. Piers are often more difficult to serve than wharves, because spurs must be constructed with unusually sharp curves to enter the piers if the main track parallels the waterfront. In almost all cases there is also conflict between rail and road traffic at grade in the vicinity of the transit sheds.

In the United States, both imports and exports contain a high proportion of bulk cargoes such as petroleum products, ores, wood, paper, coal, grains, flour, and scrap iron. The handling of these bulk goods is largely mechanized. Oil, for example, can be pumped directly from ships into storage tanks and then to pipelines or refineries. Only a few men are needed to tend the installations involved. Other technical innovations reduce manpower requirements and thus the cost of handling cargoes. The fork-lift truck handling freight on wooden palettes, various types of conveyors both suction and mechanical, and ships designed to carry truck-trailers are examples of the application of mechanization to loading and unloading. Improvements in handling may be expected to continue. Their possible effects on port transportation requirements should be noted and studied by the planning agency.

Under the United States Constitution, certain harbor rights are vested in the federal government. Design, construction, and maintenance are the responsibilities of the U.S. Army Corps of Engineers. In many cases cities and states pay for the cost of improvements, but work is carried out under the supervision of the federal government. The planning agency should be aware of the extent of federal regulation in this area.

Land planning near ports must be considered on the individual merits of each case. Where considerable differences in elevation exist near the port, land on higher elevations can be used most effectively for residential purposes or for public open space, since a busy port with ships moving about can be an attractive spectacle, particularly in cases where sailing events are held. Unfortunately, the presence of heavy industries on the waterfront and the required movement of trucks and trains usually makes land in the vicinity of ports industrial in character. Industrial and commercial redevelopment projects are appropriate means for clearing old buildings in waterfront areas and improving land use and circulation patterns.

Airports

The principal concerns of the planning agency relative to air transportation are the location of new airports, provision of adequate ground transportation facilities to serve these and existing air terminals, programming and financing airport improvements through the capital improvements budget, and planning and zoning adjacent land uses. The design and layout of an airfield and its terminal buildings and facilities is a highly specialized undertaking requiring not only technical competence in many areas, but also a thorough knowledge of the regulations and standards of the Federal Aviation Agency and the applicable state agency which, in Illinois, is the Department of Aeronautics. Although the planning agency is rarely involved in the actual design of an airport, its members as in the case of the port facility, should make themselves aware of the general characteristics and requirements governing its operation.

If the past record is examined it requires little imagination to forecast a great expansion for air travel in the future. In 1940, approximately 2.5 million revenue passengers were carried on domestic flights compared to just over 92 million in 1965. International air travel in the same period increased from 163,000 to almost 11 million. From 1964 to 1965, domestic passengers increased from over 79 million to over 92 million, while international passengers increased from almost 9.4 million to 10.8 million. As might be expected, the average size and speed of aircraft increased steadily, as did the amount of freight and mail carried domestically and internationally.

This remarkable growth has been reflected in an increased use and expansion of many airports, and the construction of others. Airport location and servicing will obviously become an increasingly frequent problem to planning agencies, particularly those in large cities, for it is from the larger airports in these cities that the majority of domestic passenger and air cargo traffic emanates, as well as all international flights. Agencies in such cities should seek every opportunity to realistically appraise future air traffic that their airports will have to handle. These projections should be accommodated in the overall plan with provision made for all necessary supporting services.

Airport planning is particularly difficult because of the rapidly changing technology of flight. Within the past few decades both the helicopter and jet aircraft have developed from experimental models to fully operational commercial use. It is likely that other types of aircraft now in the experimental stage will be perfected and used for specialized segments of the transportation market. These will include the more successful among the bewildering number of "vertical take-off and landing" (VTOL) machines and "short take-off and landing" (STOL) machines now being developed. There were at least 75 different types in existence throughout the world in 1963.[12]

Other types of vehicles which use the air, but are not strictly aircraft, include the air cushion vehicle, more commonly known as the Ground Effect Machine (GEM), such as the British Hovercraft, which is already in regular passenger service in a few locations. Larger models are being developed, and may be expected to play an increasing role in both passenger and freight transportation. The Hovercraft can surmount small obstacles and make a smooth and uninterrupted transition from water to land. Assuming that suitable unobstructed routes could be identified—later versions may be expected to clear obstructions up to 10 feet high—there is no reason why the craft should not make a valuable contribution to the overall transportation system, including its use for feeder services to main airports. Rockets may be used in the future for civilian purposes, perhaps at first for the delivery of freight over long distances with great speed, then later, fitted with passenger modules, for international passenger service.

At the present time it is difficult to accurately anticipate how these new types of vehicles may be used, or the range of facilities that will be needed for them. The only types of airports that can realistically be considered are those that serve existing types of aircraft, such as the standard propeller, jet planes, and helicopters. Prudent design would suggest reserving land for later expansion of an airport. Hopefully, this would provide a degree of flexibility to meet the requirements of future aircraft.

Airport Types and Functions. Airports are often classified by the types of aircraft they can accommodate, and thus by the service they render to the flying public. The Federal Aviation Agency (FAA), when recommending design criteria, has used the term "secondary airport" to apply to all airports serving small aircraft.[13] In the 1959 National Airport Plan (FAA) these general aviation airports were further classified by function, but no data were presented for the various functions. These were described as follows:

Executive, accommodates intercity flights by corporate, air taxi, or air charter aircraft.

Commercial, local flying operations including instructional and aircraft rentals in the vicinity of the airport.

Industrial, primary use by aircraft engaged in crop dusting, aerial photography, fire patrol, or utility patrol.

Airports larger than the "secondary airports" are used for air carrier service. The classification and functional descriptions used by the FAA for air carrier service are as follows:[14]

Local, airports to serve on local service routes providing service in the "short-haul" category normally not exceeding 500 miles.

Trunk, airports to serve on airline trunk routes and engage in intermediate length hauls normally not exceeding 1,000 miles.

Continental, airports serving long nonstop flights exclusive of coast to coast, normally entirely within the confines of the continental United States. These airports serve nonstop flights up to 2,000 miles.

Intercontinental, airports to serve the longest range nonstop flights in the transcontinental, transoceanic, and intercontinental categories.

The size of an airport is determined mainly by the length of its runways. These will vary in accordance with types of aircraft to be accommodated, average temperature, height of the airfield, gradient of the runways, and barometric pressure. The FAA has made suggestions for the length of runways that might be employed in the various categories of airports. These are shown in Table 6–13.

[12] F. G. Swanborough. VERTICAL FLIGHT AIRCRAFT OF THE WORLD (Temple Press, Aero Publishers, Inc., 1965).

[13] U.S. Federal Aviation Agency, SMALL AIRPORTS, (Washington, D.C.: Government Printing Office, 1959), p. iii.

[14] U.S. Civil Aeronautics Administration, RUNWAY STRENGTH AND DIMENSIONAL STANDARDS FOR AIR CARRIER OPERATION, Technical Standard Order N6b, (Washington, D.C.: Government Printing Office, looseleaf, undated).

Table 6–13

Runway Geometric Design Standards

FAA Classification	Runway Length (feet)
General aviation	
Secondary	1,600– 3,200
Air carrier	
Local	3,201– 4,200
Trunk	4,201– 6,000
Continental	6,001– 7,500
Intercontinental	7,501–10,500

Source: FAA AIRPORT DESIGN MANUAL, Technical Standard Order (TSO) Nob., which includes complete Runway Geometric Design Standards, from which the above is abstracted.

The runway lengths indicated in the table appear to have been calculated with reference to the average types of aircraft that could be expected to operate from the type of airfield specified. Each aircraft would, of course, have its own characteristics which later FAA manuals permit to be taken into consideration.

One of the most recent FAA manuals presents "those widely accepted engineering and design procedures and principles that should be followed to assure proper airport development."[15] The manual emphasizes that an airport serving a particular community or area must be economically designed to meet the present needs of the locality and be readily adaptable to future needs. Specific requirements vary with each airport location and no fixed design criteria can be applied to all circumstances. However, the manual covers design fundamentals that must be considered to insure that safety and functional use factors are incorporated in the development of any airport.

All categories of aircraft are covered. In the case of secondary airports used mainly by general aviation, tables are provided which enable runway lengths to be calculated for various types of aircraft under 12,500 pounds maximum weight under various maximum atmospheric temperature conditions. Corrections are also provided for airport altitude and runway gra-

15 U.S. Federal Aviation Agency, AIRPORT DESIGN, (Washington, D.C.: Government Printing Office, 1961), p. iii.

dient. In the case of airports for air carrier service, specific nomograms are provided for various types of aircraft which enable runway lengths to be calculated with precision, taking into account aircraft characteristics, airport elevation, atmospheric temperature, and take-off or landing weight, for both operations must be considered. Corrections can also be made for runway gradient.

Connected with the runways by a series of taxiways are the aprons where aircraft park while being loaded or serviced. Immediately adjacent to the aprons is the terminal building which houses all the necessary ground operations except the actual repair and regular maintenance of airplanes. In large airports the terminal building may consist of a complex of two or three interconnected buildings each dealing with a particular category of traffic. Using FAA nomenclature, one might be designated for the use of general aviation, another for local and trunk flights, and a third for continental and intercontinental flights. A basic range of facilities would be required for all categories, but special facilities would be provided as appropriate for each type of flight activity.

The terminal building is the focus of ground transportation, and, in a large city, a most important generator of vehicular traffic. Parking, both short-term and long-term, perhaps up to seven days in some cases, must be provided for travelers, employees, and visitors. In the future, some of the major airports will incorporate rapid transit terminals. Plans for London Airport already incorporate such a terminal, and Gatwick Airport, used as a diversionary alternative to London, is provided with a structural link to the London-Brighton electric railroad.

While the development of vertical take-off aircraft has not yet proceeded far enough to permit design of major landing facilities, the helicopter has created the need for a new small airfield called a "heliport." This specialized branch of aviation has witnessed a boom since 1945, particularly in large cities such as New York City and Chicago where traffic congestion between the airports and downtown is severe. Some authorities believe that helicopters may eventually become the principal type of aircraft used on commercial feeder lines up to 100 miles in length. At regular airports helicopters can land on allocated sections of the aprons used for taxiing and servicing conventional aircraft, but in downtown areas special heliports need to be built or accommodated on the roofs of suitable existing buildings.

The Port of New York Authority in its 1955 publication *Heliport Location and Design,* indicates that a major heliport needs a landing and take-off area of 200 by 400 feet, or about two acres. A secondary heliport would require less area or 150 by 400 feet. In addition, parking locations should be provided for four or five helicopters. An approach zone of appropriate dimensions at each end of the landing area would have to be available, and this should preferably be lined up with the prevailing wind directions.

In order to examine the progress of advancing technology in VTOL and STOL aircraft, the Federal Aviation Agency established a program designated as "Project Hummingbird" to examine the types of vehicles of this class which might be used in civil aviation. The report on this program[16] examines five main classes of aircraft: the Helicopter; the Compound Aircraft; the Tilt-rotor Aircraft; the Tilt-wing plus Deflected Slipstream Aircraft; and the Turbojet V/STOL Aircraft. It concludes that the helicopter holds the most promise in the immediate future for use by markets such as (1) utility-industrial; (2) private; (3) business; (4) air taxi; and (5) urban area airline. When certain inherent problems, such as noise, have been overcome, the FAA foresees a future for the Compound Aircraft in the short-haul and feeder line market (stages 50 to 100 miles long) and to a lesser extent the business aircraft market. The Tilt-rotor Aircraft could some day compete in a similar market.

Airport Location and Size.   The area re-

---

[16] U.S. Federal Aviation Agency, THE HELICOPTER AND OTHER V/STOL AIRCRAFT IN COMMERCIAL TRANSPORT SERVICE: PROJECT HUMMINGBIRD (Washington, D.C.: Government Printing Office, Nov., 1960) ; also U.S. Federal Aviation Agency, A TECHNICAL SUMMARY AND COMPILATION OF CHARACTERISTICS AND SPECIFICATIONS ON STEEP-GRADIENT AIRCRAFT: PROJECT HUMMINGBIRD, (Washington, D.C.: Government Printing Office, April, 1961) .

quired for an airport will depend on the class of the airport, its required runway dimensions and placement, and the particular physical characteristics of the site. It is hard to provide a rule of thumb under such circumstances. The size of the airport is not decided by the population of the community in which it is located—more significant is the number of people who are expected to use the airport and how it will be used. This use covers the type of service to be accommodated and the kinds of aircraft that will use the airport.

The FAA notes that "secondary airports" are generally designed for personal flying; for business or pleasure. The popular kinds of aircraft in use at these airports range from single-engine, low horsepower trainers to light twin-engine aircraft of medium horsepower. These vary widely in size and performance, affecting the required length of the landing strip. This length is also affected by the site elevation above sea level, the longitudinal slope of the strip, and the temperature of the air—a higher temperature requiring a longer take-off distance.

In addition to these factors, the amount of land required for an airport will also depend on the space required to accommodate buildings and hangars, and aircraft and automobile parking areas. Future development must also be considered.

The FAA notes that specific requirements for land cannot be given, due to the variable conditions involved, but it does indicate some general minimum areas, based on landing strip lengths corrected only for elevation, minimum building area, and clear-zone requirements. These requirments, to be used for secondary airports only, are shown in Table 6–14.

In addition to the actual airport site, additional land must be acquired or controlled for safety purposes, and to allow for maneuvering aircraft under all conditions. At the end of each runway is an "approach zone," defined as to shape and slope by the FAA which specifies the type and loading of commercial aircraft that may operate from any given runway. The approach zone, together with other specified "clear zones" to be free from obstructions, form part of a complicated envelope of imaginary

Table 6–14

Approximate Minimum Land Areas Required for Small Airports at Specified Elevations

Elevation of Site in feet	Landing Strip Dimensions in Feet[1]			Acreage Required[2]	
	Width	Length			
		Minimum	Maximum	Minimum	Maximum
Sea level......250	250	1,800	3,400	27	43
1,000.........250	250	1,900	3,600	28	45
2,000.........250	250	2,100	3,900	30	48
3,000.........250	250	2,200	4,100	31	51
4,000.........250	250	2,300	4,400	32	53
5,000.........250	250	2,400	4,600	33	55

Source: U.S.F.A.A. SMALL AIRPORT (Washington: Government Printing Office, 1959), p. 13.

[1] Landing strip lengths are shown to the nearest 100 feet after correcting sea level lengths for elevation.

[2] Based on minimum rectangular parcels of land for strip with rectangular parcel at side for building area. In addition adequate property interests should be acquired in the 16 acres contained in clear zones at each end of the strip.

surfaces that completely surround an airport, and into which no projections from the ground must penetrate. The dimensions of the approach zones and other imaginary surfaces will depend on the size of the airport and whether its runways are used for instrument landings. The specific details and diagrams which describe these dimensions are too numerous and detailed to be included here. Reference should be made to the various FAA Technical Standard Orders which describe them (such as TSO N-18). Figure 6–10, although taken from one of the earlier FAA manuals, illustrates the nature of the approach, and horizontal, and transitional surfaces that are involved for obstruction protection on and around a runway on which instrument landings are taking place. The dimensions shown are subject to periodic alteration by the FAA.

Any given urban area is likely to have only a few sites that are available and suitable for the development of new airports. Standards for airport location are based on general principles established by the FAA, but the choice often must be made between a relatively small number of sites, each of which has been subjected to careful study. Factors to be considered include topography, subsoil conditions and

drainage, local weather conditions, land and development costs, location, flight patterns of other airports in the vicinity, and accessibility. The site of the airport should be practically level, or one that can be made level at a reasonable cost. Sites with nearby hills, tall chimneys, or other structures that project into the required glide paths of aircraft should obviously be avoided. Assistance in planning and site selection may be obtained from the nearest FAA District Airport Engineer.

The land area required for secondary airports has already been discussed. A "community" airport with two 2,500-foot runways might require only 160 acres, while an "intercontinental" airport might occupy as much as eight square miles. Area depends largely on whether or not land is acquired to protect the approach zones from encroachment by buildings. It is particularly important that acquisition calculations allow for expansion, for once a substantial investment has been made in an airport, it is difficult to justify scrapping it and starting all over again. Location of additional airports requires consideration of airspace requirements of both existing and new fields. The FAA has suggested that the following radii be reserved around each airport in accordance

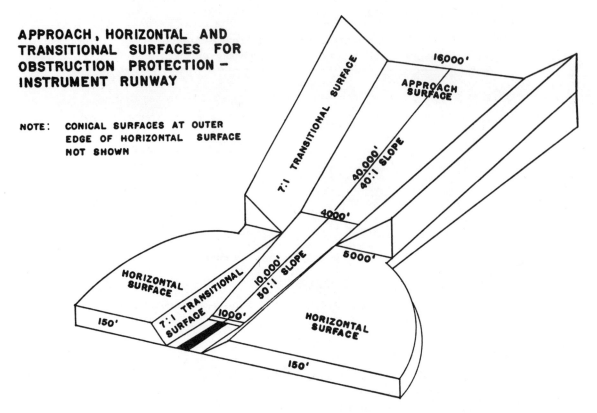

FIGURE 6–10. *Airspace standards for airport approach zones*

with the type of airport: community (small private planes), one mile; secondary, two miles; local and trunk, three miles; and continental and intercontinental, four miles.

Thus the minimum distance between a secondary and a trunk airport would be five miles. Since so much depends upon runway alignments and the locations of instrument runways, it is essential to consult state and federal authorities in the early stages of site selection.

Accessibility is of major importance in airport location. Driving times in excess of 20 or 30 minutes between the airport and the central business district seriously diminish the over-all journey time advantage that people pay for when they purchase air transportation. Distances permitting these driving times can easily be calculated: if a freeway allows 50 miles per hour speeds, an airport can be located about 20 miles from downtown within a 30-minute driving time, allowing five minutes to get to the freeway.

Present and future land uses should play an important part in determining airport location. Airports are noisy neighbors, and while they do not have the same immediate blighting influence that a railroad yard might have, they can detract from residential property values, particularly where larger aircraft and jets are involved. However, because of the fast transportation available, they may be advantageous to nearby industrial districts that rely on air transportation.

Noise and the possible danger of crashes during take-off and landing indicate that the greatest forethought should be put into placing runways and controlling land use so that the construction of a few hundred homes will not force the abandonment or curtailment of a public investment of millions of dollars. It is desirable to locate the airport near rivers or other waterways and to line up the runways with these or other natural open spaces, assuming local meteorological conditions permit this. By this means, the approach and clear zones at the end of the runways can be protected permanently, without the necessity for acquiring sites. Some airport runways at Boston, New York, and Washington, D.C., have this advantage.

The airport should be located so that hills, power lines, tall chimneys, television towers, and other vertical obstructions do not project into required air spaces. It is desirable for the airport to own all the property in the half-mile "clear zone" at the end of each runway, since this is the area in which most crashes occur. This may not be possible in all cases due to the cost of land. Then, airport zoning can be used to limit the height of structures.

Airport Zoning. Technically speaking, airport zoning regulates the height of structures in certain prescribed zones near the airport. Consequently, it is a type of control that can either be part of a standard comprehensive zoning ordinance, or, in the case of a very large airport requiring extensive controls, it can be a separate regulation enacted by a municipality empowered to do so by state government. There are, however, other types of provisions related to airports that may be part of a comprehensive zoning ordinance. One type relates to the zoning of the airfield itself, the other to the uses of lands in the vicinity of airports.

The use of airport zoning to protect airspaces in the approaches to airports is a comparatively recent zoning extension. Under such zoning an "airport" or "flight" zone is shown on the zoning map, and for this zone additional restrictions—principally height restrictions—are required by the text of the ordinance over and above those normally required for zoning districts upon which the "airport zone" is superimposed.

Court support of airport zoning depends on whether the airport zone is a reasonable application of the police power in the interests of public welfare and safety. For example, an airport zone restriction that limits the height of all buildings in the approach zone to five or ten feet would clearly be unconstitutional, because the severity of the restriction amounts to taking of property by preventing reasonable use without compensation. It is the unusual structure—the tall chimney, the television tower, and the transmission line—that is the greatest hazard to air navigation near airports. These structures can normally be located elsewhere, and the prevention of their construction will rarely constitute a taking.

The airport itself may be zoned either as a commercial or industrial use depending on the structure of the local zoning ordinance. In addition to facilities for air passengers and visitors and handling mail and express freight, airport areas often have repair shops, airplane storage, automobile parking, restaurants, shops, and, in some instances, plants for the manufacture of planes and parts. Probably the industrial classification provides the better set of restrictions, but this may not be desired if the airport is located in a predominantly residential area. Under some zoning ordinances airports are treated as exceptions or special uses that the board of appeals may authorize in residential districts subject to adequate conditions and safeguards.

Airport and related city planning must also consider the dangers to persons on the ground caused by possible aircraft crashes. Most crashes take place within a half-mile of the end of a runway. For this reason the FAA is pursuing a policy of having airports acquire property in the clear zone which is in this vicinity. It has been suggested that a comprehensive zoning ordinance may be used to prevent the location of schools, hospitals, and other places of public assembly in the approach zones, to eliminate the possibility of a catastrophic accident involving a large number of persons. The legality of this action is not clear, however, and care must be taken not to limit the use of land to such an extent that the regulation amounts to taking of property without due process of law. For example, the Brunswick, Maine, zoning ordinance prohibits the erection of churches, schools, hospitals, and other places of assembly in "flight zones." By this means, the chance of more than a relatively few persons being killed by a falling aircraft is eliminated.

Ownership, Budgeting Improvements. Except for smaller community airports, which are often owned and operated by a private corporation as a business, most airports are owned and operated by municipalities, governmental authorities, and states. Military airports imply federal ownership, although in some cases there may be arrangements for both military and civil use of a field.

The Federal Aviation Agency furnishes grants for the construction of runways, land purchase, control tower operations, and radio navigation. Acceptance of these grants may entail obligations to continue to operate an airport for a period of years. The FAA also prepares an annual National Airport Plan pursuant to the requirements of Section 3 (a) of the Federal Airport Act and Section 312 (a) of the Federal Aviation Act.[17] It identifies existing and new airports characterizing the national system of airports and recommends development to meet the needs of civil aviation. The cost of such developments is eligible for consideration for federal financial assistance under the Federal-Aid Airport Program, although it does not represent ability, intent, or commit-

ment to proceed on the part of local communities or the federal government. Privately owned airports are not eligible for this assistance.

If there is sufficient traffic, airports may operate at a profit as far as maintenance and operating expenses are concerned. Airport capital costs, however, must be considered as nonrecoverable grants whose purpose is to permit a faster form of transportation to service an urban area. Airport improvements should be included in a capital budget, like other public works.

This kind of budgeting requires coordination with FAA authorities to take advantage of state or federal grants if they are available. Unfortunately, many airports are still legacies whose responsibility falls on the central city in a metropolitan area, when, in fact, they are metropolitan services which should be financed on a metropolitan-wide basis.

---

[17] For example, see: U.S. Federal Aviation Agency, 1965 NATIONAL AIRPORT PLAN, 1966–1970 (Washington, D.C.: Government Printing Office, 1965) .

Foregoing sections of this chapter were prepared with the assistance of Roger L. Creighton, President, Creighton, Hamburg, Inc., Planning Consultants.

7

Open Space, Recreation, and Conservation

Since the mid-fifties there has been a growing interest in recreation, conservation, open space, beautification, pollution abatement, and a myriad of other ways to improve the "quality of the environment." As the exploding population presses on a limited resource base for its needs and activities, the task of providing a satisfying and stimulating living environment clearly becomes a greater and greater challenge. How can these limited resources best serve the population? What role does open space play?

The challenge is not caused solely by the sheer increase in the numbers of people, over 100 million in the last 60 years in this country alone, but also by the geometrically multiplying demands of this population. Increasing leisure, shrinking work weeks, greater mobility, higher incomes are only some of the factors creating this environmental challenge.

This challenge takes many different forms. For those who have been able to take advantage of the technological strides of the twentieth century, who have two cars in the garage, maybe a boat too, two houses, and plenty of free time, the problem is to provide facilities and opportunities so the benefits of leisure can be maximized and the physical resources effectively utilized. In contrast to this mainstream of affluence are the many areas of poverty and depression where both human and physical resources are under-utilized. Here the very basic problems are to use the resources to stimulate economic activity, restore human dignity, and truly enhance the quality of life. And between these two extremes there are many gradations of affluence. In all of these, the critical factors to be considered are the use of the open spaces, the physical resources, the air, water, and lands in planning for a satisfying environment.

And this challenge can be met. Despite recent literature and the desperate "going, going, gone" philosophy, there are unused, overlooked, and forgotten open spaces even in the most crowded of metropolitan areas. Within a 50-mile radius of New York, the Outdoor Recreation Resources Review Commission found a surprising amount of undeveloped land. Thus the problem is not the quantitative or absolute loss of land but rather a qualitative one of what land is disappearing where and what land is being left where. Are we effectively using the physical resources? Are the open spaces serving positive functions? Or are they just the spaces leftover from development?

What Is Open Space?

In this chapter, open space is defined in the broadest of terms as space which is not used for buildings or structures; in other words, it is the counterpart of development. It may be air, land, or water—located in the "big city" or in the open countryside, remote from urban development. It may be an active recreation area like Coney Island in New York, or a vista of the San Francisco Bay from Russian Hill, a

FIGURE 7-1. *Valley Stream, Long Island, 1933 (above), 1959 (below)*

large national forest like the George Washington National Forest in West Virginia, a balcony in Marina Towers in Chicago, or just a tree-lined suburban street. It may be publicly or privately owned; it may be owned in full or may be only partial rights or easements. It may be used for recreation, water supply, tourism, economic development, resource development, or amenity. How it is built into the environment and what functions are emphasized is highly relative to the needs and the opportunities presented by the location to the community.

What is done with open spaces will obviously affect the character of development and what is done with development will likewise affect open spaces. Open space must be seen not just as space remaindered from development or green splotches for parks on land use maps, but as an essential element determining the character and quality of the urban environment.

There are basically three functions which open space serves: (1) It can meet *positive human needs*—both physically and psychologically—in recreation amenities; (2) It can enhance and protect *the resource base*—the air, water, soil, plants—and, in turn, the animals; and (3) It can affect *economic development decisions* like tourism, development patterns, employment, real estate values, etc.

MEETING HUMAN NEEDS

The underlying justification for most open space has been on health grounds—for fresh air, sunlight, physical exercise, and psychological release. Physical and psychological benefits have provided the basis for action on open space from the early zoning legislation in the 1920s to the recent beautification and recreation legislation.

Although little research has been undertaken to determine the positive benefits—both physical and psychological—of open space on human beings in different situations, we do have some indications of the role that open space can play in providing a healthful environment. From a negative point of view, we know of certain noise thresholds, toxicity levels, pollution quotients, and density patterns

which can become intolerable to human beings in certain situations. We are learning more about the effect of different spatial relations on human relationships and on communication. For instance, the location and design of open space can play an important role in bringing people together as in a neighborhood park, an office or apartment courtyard, or a clustered subdivision's open area. Likewise, it can be a barrier or buffer separating different uses or neighborhoods. The more we learn of the effects of different open space locations and designs on human beings, the more thoughtfully and effectively can open space programs be planned. The social functions of open space must be studied along with its economic and physical functions.

ENHANCING THE PHYSICAL RESOURCES

The productivity and efficiency of the physical resources—the air, water, and soils—as well as their amenities are critical factors in determining open space programs. By protecting and preserving these resources, flood damage can be reduced, water supplies protected, air cleansed, soils nourished, wildlife enhanced, and many economic activities, from farming to lumbering, assisted. The misuse of these resources has presented us with dramatic but uneconomic results—polluted waters, smogged air, costly flooding, decreased animal and fish production, and millions of tons of lost soil through erosion.

Concern for thoughtful management of physical resources ranges beyond mere sentiment to maintain the purity of a pre-man ravaged world: rather, it extends to contemporary realism. With man's expanding demands on the resource base, and with the gradual recognition that resources are not inexhaustible, open space action will be increasingly concerned with the protection of the natural environment throughout this country. The dependency of urban settlements on the produce of a well-managed resource system is making the soil conservation agent, the hydrologist, the geologist, and the ecologist essential members of the planning team for the metropolitan area. These are not just rural concerns, but urban as well.

EFFECTING DEVELOPMENT DECISIONS

The size, character, location, and shape of open space can have a profound effect on current and future development, for open space is a basic of such development.

This does not mean that a superimposed, packaged design of geometrically shaped green areas, as designated on a map, is going to meet the problems and needs of developed or developing areas. But where careful research has been undertaken to determine the potentialities of the physical resources and the needs and desires of the people, open space can be located and designed to influence many other development factors. In a depressed rural area, the objective may be primarily tourism; in the fringes of a metropolitan area, open space acquisition may be a temporary holding action on development prior to final decisions. In other situations, advanced acquisition of open land may help to locate new communities. And in many built-up areas, the location of parks can influence neighborhood patterns and real estate values as well.

Open space can affect more than the ducks and the toddlers; it can help provide a more economically productive town, city, or region.

Planning the Open Spaces

Planning for parks, for watersheds, for scenic beauty, for tourism, for conservation, and for amenities cannot be undertaken as a single function. Open space planning, further, must be integrated with all the other land use, economic, social, and transportation considerations involved in community, regional, and state planning.

Such statements may seem to be truisms, but it is also true that open space planning has been limited in its focus and in the resulting programs. Open space functions have rested at the bottom of the list of land use elements, with the funds and the lands relegated from the remainders of other activities. Open space should not necessarily receive one sort of priority or another, but rather should be planned and programmed in conjunction with other functions and purposes. As the Chicago Planning Department stated, "The physical development and design of parks are also tied to policies for other community facilities."[1] Thus, the data gathered on population characteristics, economic activities, and resource capabilities are as useful in the planning of transportation systems or industrial locations as they are for open space systems.

AREAWIDE APPROACH

Not only should open space planning be based on the consideration of a wide spectrum of data, but for maximum effectiveness it should be undertaken with full knowledge of the regional context.

This means that local government, while continuing to exercise responsibility for certain functions especially related to open space, must collaborate with metropolitan and state units of government in planning and acquiring open space. Indeed, the most recent federal programs provide for extra subsidies to areas whose approach is organized in a comprehensive manner to embrace all of the logical units concerned.

To a greater degree than is perhaps characteristic of many other public programs, open space cannot be neatly confined to a single jurisdiction, but poses questions of intergovernmental relations and responsibility. It is indicative of demands which both people and governments will gladly travel long distances to satisfy, e.g., recreation, water, etc. The shortage of facilities in any given locality, due to factors like overbuilding or an under-endowed landscape, simply means that users must seek their objectives farther from home. There will consequently be some areas of "deficit" and others of "surplus," and the flux of people from one to another will have an impact that dictates a joint approach.

The physical resources are regional in nature; water and air, for instance, are not affected by jurisdictional boundaries. Similarly, human desires and needs are not jurisdictionally limited. The services that people require

[1] Chicago Department of City Planning, BASIC POLICIES FOR THE COMPREHENSIVE PLAN OF CHICAGO (Chicago: The Department, 1964), p. 36.

utilize resources found throughout a region—or even a state. While the city dwellers may want to enjoy the larger lakes, ocean, and mountain facilities in the more distant parts of a region, the exurbanites may need the zoos, museums, coliseums, and ball parks traditionally found near the centers of the regions. Consequently, what is done in one jurisdiction will affect what should be done in another jurisdiction. This interdependence on both the supply and demand side of the picture argues for an areawide approach to open space planning.

A fluid and kinetic viewpoint is needed to comprehend the interrelationships of needs and services in a given area. A standard study of geographically rooted land uses does not often reflect the dynamics of such needs. This kinetic approach can also be extremely useful in selling a regional plan to local communities.[2]

A multiplicity of organizational arrangements is available for producing a regional approach, depending on the extent of planning jurisdictions, statutory authority for open

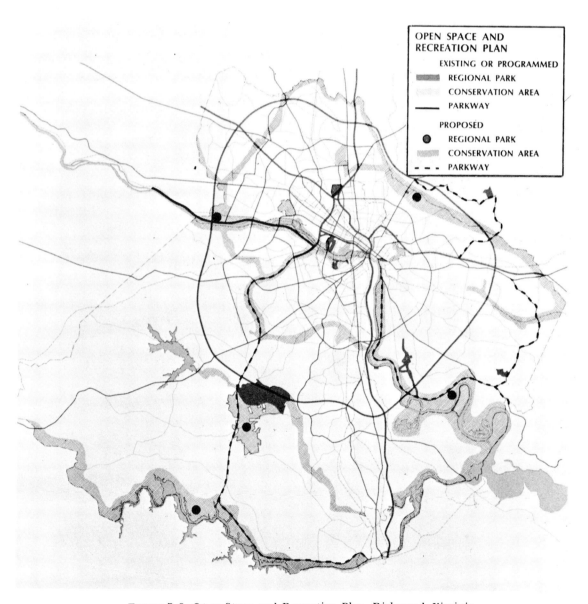

FIGURE 7–2. *Open Space and Recreation Plan, Richmond, Virginia*

space planning, availability and effectiveness of existing planning organizations, and the number of political jurisdictions in the area. Clearly, there is no pat organizational structure to follow.

In some cases a single county, like Dade County (Miami), Florida, covers an entire metropolitan region or a more rural region, such as Berkshire County in western Massachusetts. But not many regions are fortunate enough to enjoy single-jurisdictional boundaries that encompass neat geographic planning regions. In most cases, towns, cities, or counties must be merged into regional planning organizations. The guidelines of the Department of Housing and Urban Development as well as the Department of Commerce's and other federal agencies' programs and aids have been fostering the establishment and operation of regional and metropolitan planning throughout the country. Whatever the administrative and institutional arrangements, it is clear that open space planning must be done 1. in conjunction with other functional planning, and 2. on a regional basis.

WHAT IS INVOLVED?

The nature of the planning process is the critical determinant of plans and programs. The process should be flexible enough to permit new data and techniques to be fed back continuously into the process. Plans and reports should periodically present the guidelines and directions for public and private actions, but these plans must be constantly reevaluated and updated so they accurately reflect the latest needs and demands. This is well understood in most planning, but somehow parks, recreation, and open space planning has too often become a static, single-function activity.

However, several stages of the open space planning process are continuously interacting:

---

2 "The problems most amenable to regional treatment are those that are kinetic rather than static; they embody movement to, from and through a community and are therefore more demonstrably joint problems of neighboring independent governments. Movement is a prime characteristic of air and water, floods, water supply, traffic and transit," said Dennis O'Harrow in the AMERICAN SOCIETY OF PLANNING OFFICIALS NEWS-LETTER, XXXI (November, 1965), p. 113.

1. The analysis of goals and policies for the town, city, region, or state—or whatever the planning unit. This includes life styles, development patterns, etc.

2. The analysis of basic data—
   a. the physical resources,
   b. human needs, and
   c. institutional framework.

3. The synthesis of the above data with goals and policies into a plan.

4. The determination of means of implementing the plan and programming the action required.

THE ANALYSIS OF GOALS AND POLICIES

What are the long-term goals of a region? What type of life styles are desired? What do the consumers—the public—want? How can the resources be most effectively used to enhance the environment so they are positively contributing to human betterment?

This task requires a thoughtful, penetrating analysis into the dynamics of the social, economic, and physical factors affecting the urban development process. This is the first step in all planning—and as relevant to open space planning as to transportation planning. It should be a creative operation utilizing the talents of a wide range of social scientists.

In the past, the goals stage has involved a deductive reasoning process, usually beginning with attempts to adapt alternative geometric developments to a given land base. Recently there have been some interesting cases where much freer and hence more comprehensive discussions of community and regional goals have taken place. The planning for many of the new towns in this country has forced developers, as well as public agencies, into some hard thinking of these basic goals.

The work that has been done on the development of a new town in Maryland (Columbia, midway between Baltimore and Washington) has been unusually interesting. J. W. Rouse, the developer of this new community, planned for 125,000 people, assembled a team of people from fifteen fields, including sociologists, architects, planners, public administrators, lawyers, economists, transportation ex-

FIGURE 7–3. *Land capability classes determined by experience in using land in local situations plus scientific knowledge of soils, agronomy, hydrology, etc.*

perts, and anthropologists. They met as a "human planning commission" over a period of months to discuss the goals and dynamics for such a community.

This "nondirected" approach to goals planning was extremely productive in that it started from scratch and examined the needs and desires of potential occupants. There were no preconceived patterns or frameworks into which people would be fitted. Rather, this was an attempt to build the community in response to the people. Such an approach could be applied in all phases of planning, and the uses and nonuses of open spaces are just one function which could profit from such an analysis.

ANALYSIS OF THE BASIC DATA

Another stage is the more traditional analysis of the basic data on resources, people, and institutions. With the application of electronic data processing equipment, it is now possible to collect, correlate, and even map an extremely wide range of data. Much of this will be collected for general planning purposes, especially Community Renewal Programs, but the following aspects discussed below are especially applicable to planning open spaces in the community.

Analysis of the Physical Resources. An inventory and analysis of the capability of the resources—the water, land, and air—for the region to be planned is the first order of business. Such an analysis demands a multidisciplinary approach by a team of geologists, foresters, hydrologists, botanists, ecologists, geographers, agronomists, and soil scientists, among others.

This analysis would include a study of the quantity and quality, current and potential uses, economic value, recreational functions, and amenities of the resources. Not only should each resource be analyzed for its own capability but also for its ecological relationships with other resources. Maps, descriptions, and studies would cover the following:

Water resources: streams, rivers, lakes, ponds;

Land resources: topography, including steep slope, floodplain, forest, soils, including prime agricultural land, poor development soils, mineral sources, plant patterns;

Water related resources: wetlands, marshes, swamps, underground water supplies, water table;

Air: quality of, movement pattern;

Animals and wildlife: locations of, dependence on resources.

Much source material is already available in the U.S. Geological Survey maps, the U.S. Soil Conservation Service soil surveys, as well as in special studies made by federal, state, and regional agencies. For instance, the Soil Conservation Service can classify land by its capabilities. Aerial photography can be useful especially in the less urbanized areas as resource patterns can be identified and potential recreation and development discovered.[3]

In many instances the job will not involve much original mapping but rather will entail a search for work already done which can be correlated into meaningful maps. Here electronic mapping can be useful. Not only should these resources be analyzed for their physical characteristics but also for their quality and character in relation to man.

The quality and character of a given area depend on its physical determinants—the soil, slope, vegetative, and hydrologic patterns—and how these physical determinants are viewed by human beings. The same physical feature can evoke many different reactions. For instance, a clump of trees is clearly more significant in an arid stretch of the Southwest than it is in a wooded area of the Northeast. Likewise, a lake in northern Minnesota is just more of the same while in the Southwest it is a landmark. The need to infuse such viewer reactions, and hopefully subtler ones, of the land and cityscapes into the open space planning process is gradually being recognized.

This type of viewer analysis of the landscape can be made for many different types of places at different scales: from the neighborhood to the region and from center city to wilderness. Pioneering work has been done on the visual reactions of people to the "imageability" of the cityscape and roadside by Massachusetts Institute of Technology's Kevin Lynch and Donald Appleyard. Pittsburgh, aware of its striking topography, has issued an interesting report on its design image prepared by Patrick Horsbrugh.[4]

On a regional and state scale, Philip Lewis's work in Illinois and Wisconsin has been a pioneering attempt to analyze the visual impact of landscape on people. Environmental corridors, described in the 1962 Wisconsin recreation plan, *Recreation in Wisconsin,* have been identified as linear configurations of land with distinctive landscape character, as determined by patterns of significant topography, water, and wetland. These environmental amenities are seen as sources for local and state recreation, as well as for the tourist-vacation industry.[5]

In judging the resource/landscape, the following factors should be considered in the areas of states and regions, or towns and cities:

1. The ecological role—how can it best function to provide a healthful area of clear water

---

[3] The Organization of American States, located in Washington, D.C., has prepared some interesting annotated indices of aerial photography and mapping of topography and natural resources as well as some integrated resource studies. Selection of recreation sites by aerial photography is discussed in the U.S. Outdoor Recreation Resources Review Commission's study Report #8; POTENTIAL NEW SITES FOR OUTDOOR RECREATION IN THE NORTHEAST (Washington: Government Printing Office, 1962), p. 20.

[4] Patrick Horsbrugh, PITTSBURGH PERCEIVED: A CRITICAL REVIEW OF FORM, FEATURES AND FEASIBILITIES OF THE PRODIGIOUS CITY (Lincoln, Neb.: Woodruff Printing Company, 1963).

[5] See DOOR COUNTY, published by Wisconsin Department of Resource Development (Madison: 1964), pp. 12–17, for a listing of 194 types of "resources," as well as a system of symbols for identifying these in map form.

and air, healthy vegetation, and needed wild-life?

2. The economic role—how can it best provide good soils for agriculture, forests for lumber, minerals for excavation, and sources for employment?

3. The recreation role—where and how can

given resources meet the growing need for a variety of recreation needs?

4. The amenity role—how can the landscape be developed and designed to enhance the liveability of the area?

Several plans and studies done in Wisconsin, particularly the Door County and Lake Supe-

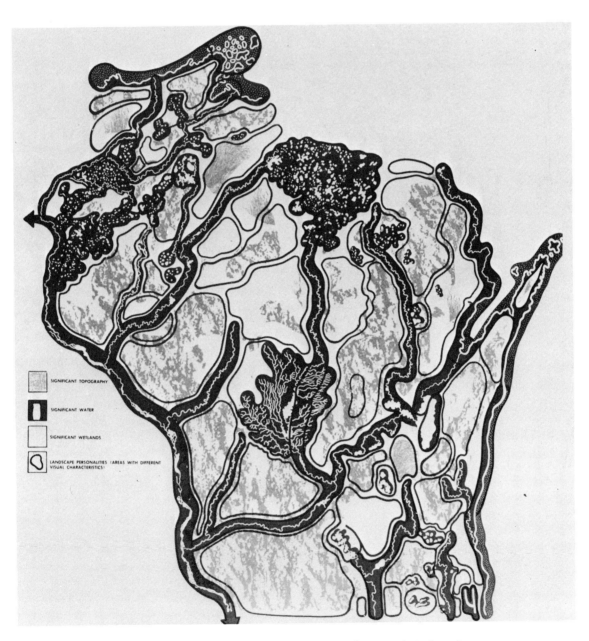

FIGURE 7–4. *Areas of distinctive landscape character in Wisconsin*

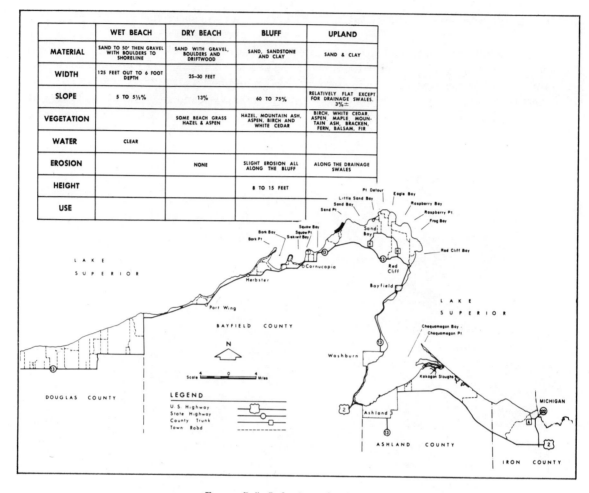

	WET BEACH	DRY BEACH	BLUFF	UPLAND
MATERIAL	SAND TO 50' THEN GRAVEL WITH BOULDERS TO SHORELINE	SAND WITH GRAVEL, BOULDERS AND DRIFTWOOD	SAND, SANDSTONE AND CLAY	SAND & CLAY
WIDTH	125 FEET OUT TO 6 FOOT DEPTH	25–30 FEET		
SLOPE	5 TO 5½%	13%	60 TO 75%	RELATIVELY FLAT EXCEPT FOR DRAINAGE SWALES. 3%±
VEGETATION		SOME BEACH GRASS HAZEL & ASPEN	HAZEL, MOUNTAIN ASH, ASPEN, BIRCH AND WHITE CEDAR	BIRCH, WHITE CEDAR, ASPEN, MAPLE, MOUNTAIN ASH, BRACKEN, FERN, BALSAM, FIR
WATER	CLEAR			
EROSION		NONE	SLIGHT EROSION ALL ALONG THE BLUFF	ALONG THE DRAINAGE SWALES
HEIGHT			8 TO 15 FEET	
USE				

FIGURE 7–5. *Lake Superior shoreline*

rior shoreline reports, have imaginatively related these factors in trying to realize the maximum economic gains and to accommodate the increasing tourists without destroying the existing resources.[6]

Analysis of Human Needs and Desires. Only after a study of the needs, motivations, desires, and habits of people is it possible to determine how best to utilize physical resources, meet recreation needs, stimulate the economic climate for the functioning of resources, and generally provide a congenial living environment.

---

[6] See comprehensive plan for Door County, Wisconsin, and WISCONSIN'S LAKE SUPERIOR SHORELINE, a special report by Zube and Dega Associates classifying shore types—all published by State of Wisconsin's Department of Resource Development.

Although the basic justification for most of the programs and legislation on recreation, beautification, and open space relates to ways to improve the lot of human beings, little has been studied with respect to the effect of these open spaces upon the lives of human beings. Planners must conscientiously pursue this problem.

The aura of sentiment and unquestioned faith on the part of open space supporters needs to be backed up with some hard-headed analysis. The assumptions underlying much of the thinking and work need to be tested—not only to produce plans and programs more realistically geared to the needs of an area but also to provide some more substantive and solid support for the legislation.

What type of an environment is wanted? What types of outlets do people desire? What kinds of recreation activities are liked? What sorts of escapes and challenges do different groups of population seek? Are distant recreational facilities needed if less crowded, more varied, and more accessible close-in facilities are available? Do people "drive for pleasure," for lack of anything better to do or because they enjoy it for its own sake? Are people afraid of exposure to wild, undeveloped, natural areas? What type of social interactions are wanted which can be fostered by manipulation of spaces and resources? These are some of the questions which need to be asked.[7]

How is this analysis of psychological, motivational, and physical needs to be undertaken?

Much of this work is covered, or should be covered, in the comprehensive planning process, in the Community Renewal Programs, in the poverty programs, and in the transportation work. For example, origin and destination studies, as well as the more sophisticated desire line networks and elements for modelmaking, can provide indications of some behavior patterns. It will be necessary to extrapolate from these studies only those factors most relevant to open space planning and then determine what further studies are needed to complete this sociobehavioral picture. In cases where this psychological and motivational work has not been undertaken in other planning work, a broad-based sociobehavioral study will have to be designed for use, not merely in open space planning, but in all phases of planning.

The most fruitful source of quantitative information on population characteristics is of course the United States Census. Many of the major elements of the census have a direct bearing on open space planning: population statistics, age, size of families, density, race, income, education, mobility, cultural characteristics, employment, car ownership, type of housing.[8]

These quantitative data could benefit from the thoughtful and creative analysis of a team of experts, like anthropologists, sociologists, planners, psychiatrists, architects, and others, depending on their availability and range of interests. As with the case of goals analysis, an independent thinking group is extremely helpful. Although such an advisory group can be especially helpful in the design and analysis of research, their contribution to periodic reviews of operations should not be overlooked.

It may be necessary to undertake questionnaires and depth interviews to explore more fully the qualitative aspects of behavior patterns. Simple preference questions as undertaken in the Outdoor Recreation Resources Review Commission's study program do not provide adequate information on which to base recreation, much less the more broadly based open space plans. The whys and wherefores are needed.

Recreation—just one aspect of open space—desperately needs the infusion of behavioral data to direct its plans and programs. One large metropolitan park system discovered that people were venturing only a few hundred feet from their parked cars in their parks. In investigating the reasons for this, it appeared that fear, not of being raped behind the laurel bushes but of being in totally strange, alien, and unknown terrain, prevented them from freely exploring untrampled nature in the inner reaches of the park. Translating such insight into park planning, in this instance, it might follow that linear park systems, rather than large aggregate chunks of parks, would be used by more people. This isolated example does not rule out the role of larger wilderness-like parks in metropolitan areas, but it does indicate the needs of one specific and large group of users. More important, perhaps, this

---

[7] A report prepared by Marcou, O'Leary and Associates in conjunction with Kevin Lynch, Marvin J. Cline and Carl Feiss, entitled OPEN SPACE FOR HUMAN NEEDS has been submitted to the Department of Housing and Urban Development. This report explores ways in which open space lands in cities can best be designed to meet human needs. It develops the elements of a new approach to open space planning to meet these needs and illustrates the application of the approach in two areas in Washington, D.C.

[8] The Census material can be presented in a workable and meaningful format so it can be easily interpreted. The National Capital Planning Commission in Washington, for instance, published a volume entitled FACTS BY TRACTS which arranged the Census data for the District of Columbia into useful categories.

experience in Cook County, Illinois, points to the importance of understanding the public and their wants and needs.

The total metropolitan area is made up of pockets of different neighborhoods and different towns and counties, each with a variety of different needs. What is done in the in-city ghettoes with dense populations of carless, low-income families who are not familiar with the city beyond their block in many cases, much less beyond the city boundaries, is quite different from what needs to be done in the affluent suburbs where leisure facilities abound.

Recently, with the development of interest in and attention to deprived and underprivileged people, there has been a welcome awareness of the special needs of the ghetto areas. Karl Linn, in his work in Philadelphia, Washington, and New York on "neighborhood commons" has been able to transform an unused lot in a slum area into a neighborhood asset by the combined efforts of local craftsmen and workers, plus some outside design help. These commons become a spark of pride in the neighborhood—a place for the toddler to play, the oldsters to enjoy watching, the teenager to have rock and roll concerts at night.

New York City has creative approach to park planning and programming. Not only is the New York City Park Department giving the Harlems-Stuyvesants-Bedfords some overdue park areas, from vest-pocket parks to simple street-play areas, but it is recognizing the changing nature of neighborhoods and thus the changing needs for recreation.

An example of this new approach to park planning in New York is the introduction of a mobile recreation program. This involves the use of portable and semiportable equipment like swimming pools and skating rinks for rooftop or small neighborhood on-the-ground parks to meet the immediate needs of a neighborhood. Public lands, awaiting the construction of schools or renewal projects, for instance, can temporarily provide recreation opportunities. When recreation planning and programming can introduce this type of flexibility, there is hope that the recreation-open space planning programs can better meet human needs.

The interrelationships of human needs and the interdependence on the same resource within a metropolitan area or region need to be studied. What is the relation of indoor facilities to outdoor facilities? Perhaps an air-conditioned movie is more attractive than an open air baseball field in mid-August to a Negro teenager. What effect would a subsidized transportation program to outlying, inaccessible recreation facilities have on metropolitan recreation programming?

To relate the needs and desires of the people to the potentialities of the available physical resources within a sound institutional framework is an extremely complicated task. No national quantitative guide or standard can uncover the formula for such planning. The traditional equation of numbers of people to numbers of areas was derived from playground equipment standards in the 1930s. No matter how it is rearranged, it is still inadequate. As the Toronto Planning Board stated, standards

are more a measure of park deficiency than park adequacy. . . . Park standards are primarily a measure of relative adequacy between different areas. By providing a rough method of determining the general areas of greatest park deficiency they act as a guide to the assignment of priorities.

—Quality is not considered nor are

differences in character of residential development which might significantly affect the need for public park facilities: or differences in the age composition of the population which would also affect the type and quantity of parkland required: or significant differences in habits and customs, which are decisive in determining the extent to which park facilities are actually utilized.[9]

Clearly, a more flexible, locally- or regionally-oriented means of relating human needs to physical resources is needed. The type of approach suggested in *Open Space for Human Needs*[10] is highly promising.

Analysis of Institutional Framework. An examination of both public and private agencies, whose programs relate to open space activ-

---

[9] Toronto Metropolitan Planning Board, THE OFFICIAL PLAN OF THE METROPOLITAN TORONTO PLANNING AREA (Toronto: The Board, 1957), p. 227.
[10] Marcou, O'Leary and Associates, *op. cit.*

ities, is needed. This takes in a broad spectrum of agencies.

Innumerable federal departments, agencies, and commissions are concerned with open space, from the Department of Housing and Urban Development to the Department of Agriculture. Each state also has several departments working on open space matters from conservation, wildlife, economic development, welfare, and recreation to transportation and highway departments. And similarly, on the local and regional level, there is a variety of public as well as private agencies involved in open space activities. Far more recreation agencies than parks departments are charged with responsibilities for functions related to open space.

The importance of private organizations, citizen action groups, and nonprofit corporations in assisting in action for open space cannot be overemphasized. Such private groups can be used by public agencies in lobbying for legislation and supporting public open space action programs. Although the role and effectiveness of these energetic private groups and citizen leaders has not been carefully analyzed, we do know from experience in urban renewal and other planning fields that these private organizations can be effectively used to back up public action. The town conservation commissions, for instance, which were authorized in Massachusetts, have undertaken constructive action in local situations.[11]

Private citizens, from individual developers to organizations such as garden clubs and conservation groups can provide invaluable direction for open space action from developing imaginative subdivisions to acquiring valuable threatened open spaces.

There are no set patterns for effective administration or institutional productivity. This is because the role of different constitutional and administrative mechanisms depends upon the legal authorities, administrative structures, financial resources, and leadership. And ultimately this variety in institutional arrangements is due to the diversity of problems and peoples in different areas to which these institutions are responding.

The production of open space plans, for instance, illustrates the range of possible institutional mechanisms for a given open space task. On the whole, most recent regional open space plans have been prepared by the regional comprehensive planning agencies rather than single-function agencies or departments. On the state level, open space, recreation, or conservation plans have been prepared generally by single-function agencies although coordinated with the plans of the state planning or development agency. However, many other kinds of arrangements are in operation, ranging from an ad hoc transportation planning agency like New York's Tri-State Transportation Commission, which is undertaking a regional plan for the New York metropolitan area, or a single-function agency like New York State's Department of Conservation, to an arrangement whereby a specialist agency collaborates with a planning agency, as in Los Angeles County, where the Regional Planning Commission and the Parks and Recreation Department have prepared the open space plan.

SYNTHESIS

The preceding sections of this chapter have defined and analyzed the information that goes into the making of an open space plan, from the analysis of goals and policies through the examination of physical resources, human needs, and institutional capabilities.

In each case, suggestions have been made on the need for taking a freer and therefore more comprehensive look into these elements of the open space planning process.

Goals and policies need to be operational, recognizing the social, economic, and physical aspects of urban life and their potential for change and evolution over the planning period.

Physical resources, both existing and potential, need to be analyzed in a free and comprehensive way, quantitatively and qualitatively.

The aspirations and behavior of population in regard to open spaces need to be surveyed, recognizing the many differentials in the population and significant trends in human needs

---

[11] A. J. W. Scheffey, CONSERVATION COMMISSIONS (New York: Conservation Foundation, 1965).

for open space in their daily living.

Suggestions were also made for identifying institutions that can play a role in open space activities in a broad and comprehensive way, from local antipoverty citizen action groups to regional and state agencies.

The open space planning process usually begins with an analysis of existing and future population—numbers and distribution—and the grouping of this population into neighborhoods divided by natural or man-made barriers or centered around nuclei of neighborhoods such as schools. To these population numbers and groups are applied "standards" relating most often to conventional facilities: a playground or a neighborhood park for "so many" units of population. And thus are derived measures of present and future deficiencies.

These demands when compared to existing facilities yield present and expected, mostly quantitative, deficiencies in open space and recreation areas. These geographically distributed deficiencies are in turn related to vacant or undeveloped land and locations for open space and recreation facilities are determined from these deficiencies.

The process of open space planning need not be solely a mechanistic matching of "supply" vs. "demand" to define present and future open space "deficiencies." The application of a free and comprehensive approach to the formulation of an open space plan can yield more than maps, tables, and charts showing sizes, locations, and stereotyped functions of proposed open space acquisitions.

The open space plan needs to concern itself with all facets of open space functions and activities. The greatest potential for introducing variety, choice, and flexibility in open space activities can best be achieved through a comprehensive system of spaces that embraces the small vacant lot in an in-town neighborhood as well as the large water conservation area. Those spaces need not be confined to only the established and accepted types: neighborhood parks, playgrounds, or playfields, but should be extended to include spaces seldom mentioned in open space planning such as important vistas, bicycle trails, or hobby yards.

The proposed open space system, because it is concerned with only one of the many facets of urban environment needs to be constantly related to all other aspects of the urban environment. Its functional relationship to the land use structure, the transportation network, the broader natural setting need to be stated in written and graphic form.

In particular, the specific relationship that the system of open spaces has to its users needs to be stated and documented. For whom is this space to be provided? What are the needs of the potential users of this space? How can the space itself be designed to meet these needs? This last question points to the need for continually taking into account and incorporating into the open space plan relevant design considerations, expressed in the form of text and graphics. Design guidelines may range from large-scale abstract statements dealing with the form and character of the region and its extensive open spaces, to specific site plans that concern themselves with the fine-grain design of an in-town park.

Of equal importance to spatial considerations in the open space plan are the activities that take place in those spaces. Here again, a freer approach to programmed activities could yield a treasury of exciting opportunities. Consider some activities that the New York City Parks Department is currently programming: miniature golf courses in Central Park, a dating computer in Manhattan's Bryant Park, free dog shows, kite-flying and tire-rolling contests, outdoor fashion and rock'n roll shows, and painting "happenings." In Washington, groups of teen-agers have been painting murals on the temporary fence around the construction site of the John F. Kennedy Center for the Performing Arts.

A program for these and more conventional open space activities needs to accompany and be a part of an open space plan.

Briefly, the conventional open space planning process can be modified and improved to reflect better the needs of our expanding population. It can benefit from a more comprehensive approach to the definition of the types of open space that it considers. It can be strengthened by a closer relationship to planning for the other components of the environment of which it is a part. It can be made to focus more clearly on the specific human needs it is intended to serve. The plan can benefit from incorporating design integrally into the formulation. And the process can also benefit from a broader and more imaginative approach to the definition of activities for which open space is the locale.

The open space planning process evolves into a system of priorities and a financial plan for acquiring, developing, and managing open space areas. Here again, priorities and financial programs cannot be developed without the context of an overall planning framework and must recognize competing needs, limitations on financial resources, comparative costs, and limits of community support, among other factors.

Fortunately, the growing interest in improving the "quality of the environment" has been paralleled by the evolution of an ever expanding kit of tools for implementing the open space plan.

Programming Open Space Action

Opportunities for building open space into the environment are so varied that they have stimulated the energy and imagination of professionals concerned. Depending on local conditions, it is possible to incorporate open space into urban areas by taking steps to reserve natural drainage channels, wet lands, and flood plains against undesirable development; encourage cluster development in residential areas; acquire scenic or other special easements; adopt special zoning districts; and acquire land outright in the traditional manner.

The recent interest in open space action has spurred an unprecedented wave of legislation, programs, new techniques, and incentives to assist in public acquisition and control of open space for specific recreation and conservation purposes as well as for more general development and amenity purposes.

The imagination of legislators, lawyers, and technicians in providing a plethora of tools and techniques unfortunately is seldom matched by imaginative open space planning or action. There is no shortage of tools; new and innovative ideas are being constantly developed. Compensatory regulations, real estate syndicates, easements, zoning for transferable density, development corporations, conservation commissions, installment purchasing, and natural resource zoning are only some of the new aids for open space acquisition and control currently available. However, there are few examples so far where these techniques have been tried.

The main categories of tools for open space acquisition and control are: 1. acquisition, 2. regulation, and 3. taxation. Each has its advantages and disadvantages, so to assure a variety of and accessibility to open spaces, an imaginative application of a mixture of the tools is necessary. Programming choices depend on priorities, goals, timing, and institutional capabilities. The following discussion of the different tools is focused primarily on the utility of these tools.

ACQUISITION

Acquisition of full or partial rights to land is the most certain means for public agencies, be they local, regional, or state, to preserve open space. This may be done through condemnation, donation, or purchase.

There are no legal deterrents to purchasing or condemning land for traditional recreation and conservation purposes. And it is also likely that "structuring urban growth" according to an approved plan is an adequate public purpose for purchase or condemnation of full or partial interests, if the case is carefully made. In general, if it can be clearly shown that a public purpose is served, there should be no constitutional barriers to public open space acquisition by either purchase or condemnation. And in recent years the courts have upheld public purchase, regulation, and condemnation as long as public benefit would result.

The bulk of open space land is acquired by purchase, condemnation, or donation of the full rights to the land. Where heavy public use is made of the open space, this is undoubtedly the best means of acquiring the space.

Installment purchasing is a way for buyers to stretch out their payments and sellers to maximize tax advantages.

Leasebacks and Salebacks. Aside from owning and directly controlling land, public agencies can use leasebacks and salebacks in which the land is acquired and controlled but not necessarily occupied by the owner.

A public agency can acquire tracts of land and then lease them to private persons for specific open space uses in accordance with the approved public plan for the area. Although the public agency's renting out of the land has the usual landlord's management problems, the land can be kept productive. The lands can produce rent for the public body as well as products and activities for the public, like farm produce and recreation opportunities.

In salebacks, land bought by public agencies can be resold with restrictions attached to insure that the open space purposes set forth in local and regional plans are being followed.

Both leasebacks and salebacks offer a way for public agencies to acquire open space and yet provide for continued use of land for farming, for instance, and also acquire some income. Cook County Forest Preserve, Illinois; Cedar Rapids, Iowa; and Bowling Green, Kentucky, among many other public agencies, have been using leaseback arrangements to expand their open space programs.

Easements. Another acquisition tool is the purchase of easements or partial rights. When a public body acquires an easement, it acquires certain specific rights. These may be affirmative rights giving the public agency, and the public, the right to use land for certain purposes such as fishing, biking, or riding; or these easements may be negative, giving no public right to use the land but rather restricting the uses to which an owner may put his land.

Conservation easements limiting land use to farming, forestry, or wetlands, or scenic easements along highways are examples of negative easements. Affirmative easements, on the other hand, have been used for riding and hiking trails, and for fishing and hunting access.

Such easements, both positive and negative, have been utilized by public agencies when full ownership has not been necessary or has been too costly to achieve some open space goals like protection of watersheds, prevention of floods, or preservation of large scenic areas. Clearly,

easements make it possible for public agencies to stretch their dollars in acquisition programs by reducing cost of acquisition as well as cost of maintenance. Easements also allow land to continue to produce tax revenue for municipalities.

Easements are primarily useful for land and water areas which do not involve heavy on-site public usage. Scenic easements will probably account for the greatest bulk of acreage to be acquired this way.

Monterey, California, was one of the first communities to become interested in scenic easements. The Washington, D.C., metropolitan area has two excellent examples of scenic easements. South of Washington in Prince George's County, Maryland, directly across from Mount Vernon, scenic easements have been granted to preserve the rural view from Mount Vernon. The land with these easements in Prince George's County has been recently allowed a reduction in property taxes.

Northwest of Washington in Fairfax County Virginia, the Department of the Interior acquired easements on the Merrywood estate to protect the Potomac shoreline and prevent an apartment development. At the same time owners of property adjacent to nearby Merrywood donated scenic easements on their riverfront properties. This was the first case to come under the Internal Revenue Service's ruling that such donations can be deducted for tax purposes.

Scenic easements can be broadly used for highway, stream, and riverbank control. Legislation in the highway field offers new opportunities for easement acquisition. The model study of the Potomac River Basin also indicates the possibilities for imaginative use of easements, both to protect the natural atmosphere of the riverbanks and to make them accessible for hiking and bicycle trails.

The use of easements for limited public use of land for activities like fishing and hiking is also promising. Although the acreage under this type of easement may not be large, accessibility to recreation areas or just the provision of recreation areas like trails, is opened up. The state of New York has traditionally acquired easements along trout streams. Pending federal legislation (1966) for trails will undoubtedly increase the usage of this type of

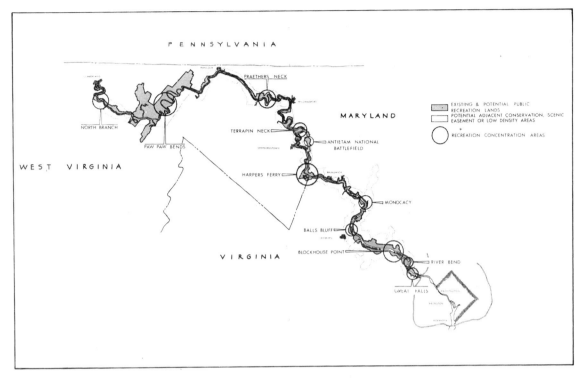

FIGURE 7–6. *General map, Potomac Valley Park*

positive easement for limited public use.

Despite the considerable publicity for ease-ment acquisitions and donations, this tool has not been widely used. For instance, the Open Space Land Program in its first five years of operation (1961–66) had no applications for funds to acquire easements. Easements can be costly in built-up areas and do not provide for mass, public-usage parks, which explains why fee simple purchases have been the main type of acquisition for parks. Nevertheless ease-ments are seldom as costly as fee simple acquisi-tion, and they can satisfy many open space purposes.

REGULATION

Open spaces can also be acquired through reg-ulatory means, which today are exercised al-most exclusively by local governments. Regula-tory tools still provide some of the most basic controls on the "quality of the environment" in terms of guiding the pattern and design of development from setbacks to densities. The main types of regulation to keep land open are (1) zoning, (2) subdivision control, and (3) the official map. As regulation does not involve compensation to the landowners, care must be taken to avoid too stringent restrictions which might be interpreted as confiscatory and hence unconstitutional.

Zoning. Of the regulatory tools, zoning of-fers most promise for preservation of open space. There are two major types of zoning: development and natural resource. Develop-ment zoning includes large lot and cluster zon-ing which are primarily applicable in urban areas. Natural resource zoning, on the other hand, includes floodplain, agricultural, and forest zoning and is more relevant in the less heavily developed areas where natural re-sources are still available.

•Development zoning by large lot zon-ing—or low residential zoning—is by far the most popular type of zoning technique. Large lot zoning can go up to five acres but is usually one or two acres. It is thought that by discouraging development and thinly spacing housing the open character of an area can be retained. Such zoning does preserve open space for back-yard recreation and does minimize housing density. When used alone, however, large-lot zoning is normally ineffective in maintaining the open space character of an area or in providing open space for active recreation or conservation.

FIGURE 7–7. *Crofton plan puts golf course in middle*

•Cluster or density zoning, on the other hand, is a means of providing for open spaces which can both serve neighborhood recreation and conservation needs and also enhance the open space character of the area.

Density zoning establishes a maximum density for an area, usually in acreage per dwelling unit, and then allows the developer to alter the lot size for each house as long as the total subdivision does not exceed the maximum for the district. Thus one section or all of the subdivision may be developed at high density, allowing the remainder to be kept in open space dedicated to the use of persons in the subdivision or in the community as a whole.

There are many advantages to density zoning: it reduces building costs as only land suited to building need be used; it reduces costs of providing services since there need be less street mileage; utilities from electric and tele-

phone lines, and even garbage pickups are easier and cheaper since routes are shorter. Moreover, if several subdivisions are planned cooperatively, it may be possible to link open spaces from one subdivision to another, forming a larger linear open space stretch, or a greenbelt to benefit more residents.

Before adopting cluster or density zoning, local governments must decide how the open space in such subdivisions will be both preserved and maintained. To have permanent preservation, there must be covenants or restrictions attached to the land to prevent any possible future changes to the zoning. Local governments must also decide whether such open space should be dedicated to the local government for public use or whether it should be privately owned and maintained. If it is privately owned and maintained, a decision must be made, whether by an individual or property owners' association.[12]

Clustering is an old principle found in developments like Radburn, New Jersey, and Sunnyside Gardens, New York, in the late 1920s. Recently it has become popular and can be found in sizes of developments from in-city projects like Morrell Park in Philadelphia or more suburban projects like Parkwood adjoining the Research Triangle in Durham, North Carolina, to large new towns as well.

•Natural resource zoning may be used to protect marshes, floodplains, agricultural land, sources of water supply, and other natural resources where they are serving urban demands. Although this zoning has not often been used, it is a means not only of conserving the resources but also of providing limited recreation opportunities. This type of zoning is not a secure method of preserving open space as it cannot resist development pressures. When there is a discrepancy between the productive value of the land for conservation purposes like farming and its realizable urban development value, or when a reasonable return cannot be made, then such zoning will be considered an unconstitutional taking of property

[12] U.S. Federal Housing Administration, PLANNED-UNIT DEVELOPMENT WITH A HOMES ASSOCIATION, Land Planning Bulletin #6 (Washington: Government Printing Office, 1963).

FIGURE 7–8. *Aerial view of Lake Anne Village in Reston, Virginia*

without just compensation. Although it cannot be counted on permanently to preserve open space, it can be effective when used in conjunction with acquisition and easement programs.

Several types of natural resource zoning have been used. They are floodplain, agricultural, and forest zoning.

•Floodplain zoning is a means of prohibiting and restricting development within floodplains to prevent property loss, to insure human safety, and to enable the safe and natural flow of streams. The floodplain is most accurately determined by mapping the actual areas which have been flooded, as well as mapping the extent of alluvial soils.

Floodplain zoning has not been widely adopted despite considerable technical assistance and information from the federal government. Nine states specifically list flooding as a purpose for zoning, although such enabling legislation is always a necessary prerequisite to floodplain zoning. Lewisburg, Tennessee, with the aid of TVA and the Tennessee State Planning Commission has a well-prepared floodplain zoning ordinance.

•Agricultural zoning has been used to pro-

tect fertile land from encroaching development but with little success. As mentioned before, agricultural zoning cannot withstand development pressures. When agricultural land is faced with the greatest development pressures, when effective measures for preserving open space may be most needed, agricultural zoning collapses. For instance, Santa Clara County has been using agricultural zoning since 1954, but the agricultural land is swiftly dwindling. Recognizing the problems, the County realizes the need for stronger and more effective measures like the acquisition of easements.

•Forest zoning has been used in rural areas to protect the forest crop but it, like agricultural zoning, cannot hold up to development pressures of urbanizing areas. In rural areas forest or agricultural zoning may serve their purpose, but they are not effective in urban or urbanizing areas.

Subdivision Controls. Subdivision control ordinances can affect open space preservation through regulating how developments are laid out and what public improvements are to be provided. Dedication of a certain percent of each subdivision for permanent open space might be required, or a payment in lieu of dedication equivalent to cost of open space, or a choice between the two. Required dedication of open space is justified on the grounds that each subdivider should provide community open space in relation to the demand generated by the development.

Aside from provision of open space areas, usually for recreation, subdivision regulations can affect the appearance and ecology of an area by requiring planting of trees, or prohibiting cutting of certain sized trees, or special grading—which can contribute considerably to the quality of an area.

Legally the required dedication of land has generally been upheld in the courts while the option of payment in lieu of dedication has not held up as the land purchased with payment may not directly benefit the subdivision.

Usually subdivision regulations require a dedication of a fixed per cent of land to be subdivided, rather than relating land needed to the size and density of the population. Baltimore County in 1963 adopted an ordinance which requires the dedication to be geared to the density of development with a maximum dedication of three acres and a minimum of 20,000 square feet.

Official Mapping. Official mapping has been used to preserve open space, but it has quite limited applications due to its questionable legality. The official map is an indication of the local government's intention to acquire specific sites for public purposes (usually for streets) but also for parks in many states. Building is usually prohibited in those areas mapped for later public acquisition.

TAXATION

Taxation is another means that has been proposed for helping to maintain low-density development and hence open-space character of land. Taxation is thought to be a factor in influencing development decisions as well as providing incentives for the retention of open land in underdeveloped uses. Since many think that high taxes force open space into development, local governments are using tax exemption, preferential assessment, deferral, and differential rates through a system of classification

of land uses to try to keep land open. A study, *The Present and Potential Role of State and Local Taxation in the Preservation and Development of Open Space in Urban Areas,* by the Urban Land Institute, discusses in detail the utility of these different methods of taxation.[13]

Tax Exemption. Public open space—parks and public conservation areas—are usually exempt from property taxation. The partial or full exemption of private open-space lands is commonly determined by their benefit or use to the public. These benefits are not just for the users of the facilities, but for adjacent areas where amenities and real estate values have been boosted.

Preferential Assessment. Preferential tax assessment for agriculture is a device for keeping agricultural land assessed at its agricultural value rather than its development value to encourage the continuation of farming. It has been thought that the high assessments of undeveloped land in the urban fringes, usually based on development values, have forced farmers to succumb to the tempting offers of speculative developers.

The preferential tax assessment in Maryland has not worked out that way, at least not in Prince George's and Montgomery counties. Farming has been carried on in many cases, but many of the farm owners are now speculators taking advantage of the tax benefits and look-

Table 7–1

Type of Dwelling Units in Subdivisions

Zone	Type of Unit	Per Cent Allocation in Subdivision
R-10	10,000 sq. ft. lots	3
R-6, Zone 1 family	6,000 sq. ft. lots	5
R-6, Zone 2 family	10,000 sq. ft. lots	6
R-6, Zone 2 family	8,000–9,200 sq. ft. lots	8
R-6, Zone group house	2,000–5,000 sq. ft. lots	12

[13] John E. Rickert, THE PRESENT AND POTENTIAL ROLE OF STATE AND LOCAL TAXATION IN THE PRESERVATION OR DEVELOPMENT OF OPEN SPACE LAND IN URBAN FRINGE AREAS (Unpublished manuscript for the Urban Land Institute, Dec., 1965).

ing forward to the day when the cornfields will be filled with split-level houses. Certainly there are instances where the "good guys," the owner-operator farmers, are benefiting from the tax relief, but on the whole the Maryland preferential tax assessment has not solved the problem it set out to tackle. Reduced tax rates by themselves have not been enought to prevent unwanted development.

Tax Deferral. Another tax scheme geared to preserving low density—open space uses like farming—and also to conquering the problems uncovered in the Maryland experiences is a tax deferral system for open space sites. The Northern Virginia Regional Planning and Economic Development Commission proposed that:

Under a tax deferral system, all taxes on land, located within *a planned or an existing open space site,* would be deferred as long as it remains in an open type land use (taxes on improvements would still be collected). However, if an owner of such a site decides to develop for a non-open space use then all deferred taxes would have to be paid before a subdivision plan or building permits would be issued. If the property is sold the tax lien goes with it and the market price should be reduced by the amount of the tax lien. If the land is subdivided and sold but not developed the tax lien is proportioned, based on the size of the subdivided parcels. . . . If the public eventually buys the land, the deferred tax would reduce the market value of the property and could be considered as installment payments on the property.[14]

The tax deferral idea has a precedent in Virginia's forest yield tax which the Department of Conservation and Economic Development administers. Taxes are suspended on all forest land suited for timber growth when it is offered as a temporary game, fish, or recreation reserve. The forest yield taxes, however, must be paid at the time of cutting when the owner can bear the burden. The major objective of this program is to prevent premature cutting. This open space deferral scheme for the sale of agricultural lands, with its penalty of the payment of back taxes, offers a better means than Maryland's preferential tax assessment method for retaining open space.

How much of a burden back taxes constitute for an investor or builder who anticipates hundreds of thousands of dollars of profit is open to question. A developer can quickly recover the payment of back taxes by raising the price of each house by $100 or by charging a few dollars more per square foot in a commercial building.

However, tax deferral is a device to be used in open space programs, as it is an inducement to owners to keep land open, especially owners of recreation facilities like golf courses, riding stables, or lakes, who are trying to hold on to their recreation areas in the face of soaring taxes. In Fairfax County, Virginia, in the metropolitan Washington area, for instance, taxes shot up from $5 per acre in 1953 to $4,500 in 1963. On the whole, this tax system will be useful only when tied to other land use controls like zoning and acquisition. By itself tax deferral will have little effect on preserving the open space as it does not impede the worst threat to open spaces: large-scale speculation and development.

NEW TOOLS

To implement the open space plan and launch an effective program to insure the maximum benefits from open space for a given locality or region, it is clearly necessary to skillfully combine the various tools and regulations previously discussed. Each of these tools and regulations has its flaws. Many of them like the regulatory techniques are extremely weak at the very time when the pressures are greatest and when they are most needed. The most effective tool is the most expensive one: namely, the acquisition of full or partial rights.

Fortunately, some imaginative new ideas are being brought forward, primarily by the legal profession, to try to correct some of the inadequacies of present tools. Although most of these new tools have not yet been experimented with, they are worthy of discussion. Their focus is usually on broader development decisions than open space, and their effectiveness is usually based on a strengthened regional governmental system.

New Towns. The growing interest in new towns or new community developments is en-

---

[14] Unpublished report of the Commission, written in 1965.

couraging; today there are many new towns that are being developed in this country. In the future there may be stronger large-scale development controls: public ownership of land, public ownership of land with leasebacks and salebacks for controlled private development, or even national ownership of development rights. Current (1966) federal legislation on new communities and advanced acquisition point to some solutions of land assembly and land development problems on a large scale.

Timed Development Zoning. By controlling the timing and location of development by zoning, it may be possible to utilize temporary open space in urbanizing areas for public use. Such zoning would allow development in specified districts and prohibit development elsewhere until all available land in the development district had been utilized. In those districts not slated for immediate development, it would be possible to preserve the open spaces temporarily. Aside from the obvious merits of timed development zoning for much broader development control, this type of zoning does offer one means of providing temporary open space, which should not be overlooked when assembling a program of techniques for enhancing open space in an urban area.

Transferable Density. This is a new approach to density zoning that allows more desirable concentration of development as well as a greater amount of open space. This proposal would average out the overall density of an entire community. The same average density as large lot zoning would exist, but large amounts of open space would be available by concentrating the densities.[15] This technique applies to residential uses only, and has a more limited objective than the next technique discussed.

Large-Scale Development Zoning. This is cluster or density zoning expanded to the scale of the neighborhood or town, including all uses normally found in a town. Such zoning permits the development of new towns which offer the promise of planning for community life with well-integrated open space among other things. This type of zoning depends of

course on long-range plans for future comprehensive development for the region. But through such zoning it is possible to plan open spaces so they will be an integral part of the community. Pending federal legislation (1966) may foster this type of development.

Compensable Regulations. This is a means of strengthening zoning and providing compensation for controlled land.[16] Compensable regulations severely restrict the uses which may be made of land yet compensate the property owner for any decrease in value of his land caused by the regulations. Under these regulations, permanent open space as well as open space reserves for future development can be provided. Land would remain in private ownership under these regulations thereby producing taxes and not introducing any new public maintenance costs.

Acquisition of Partial Rights. Interpreting open space to include all undeveloped space—not just land and water for recreation and conservation—calls for a broad acquisition of partial rights to land, water, and air. It has been proven that acquisitions of full or partial rights is the only certain means of assuring permanent open space. Tools like conservation easements make it possible to control land without the cost of full fee acquisition and problems of maintenance. Recent interest in the acquisition of air rights is another means of providing open space, vistas, and recreation opportunities, especially in the densely developed cities where such open space is most needed.

Real Estate Syndicate. Another new idea which copes with some of the most stubborn of economic issues, inequitable distribution of profits from planned land development, and also provides for planned control of open space, is the *real estate syndicate* idea proposed in *The Plan for the Valleys,* in Baltimore County. To protect the natural character of the valleys in Baltimore's Green Spring and Worthington Valleys and also accommodate the anticipated future population, it proposes

---

[15] Urban Land Institute, NEW APPROACH TO RESIDENTIAL LAND DEVELOPMENT, Technical Bulletin #40 (Washington: The Institute, 1961).

[16] Jan Krasnowiecki and Ann Louise Strong, "Compensable Regulations for Open Space: A Means of Controlling Urban Growth," JOURNAL OF THE AMERICAN INSTITUTE OF PLANNERS, XXIX (May, 1963), pp. 87–97.

to concentrate development in the plateau between the two valleys.[17]

A real estate syndicate would be formed of all the property owners in the area. Then the syndicate would purchase the land in the valleys, either in fee simple or certain rights. By buying and later selling the land on the plateau, the syndicate could acquire funds to buy the land in the valleys. The syndicate, in other words, would provide a means for all landowners in the area to equitably share in the costs as well as the benefits of the planned development program.

Such a profit-sharing device might be applicable in a situation where several public agencies or even jurisdictions share a common resource such as a body of water like the San Francisco Bay.

Summary

Open spaces are vital elements in our environment. They perform necessary and positive functions: they provide recreation opportunities for people, protect physical resources like water, air, soil, plants, and animals, and finally affect a wide range of economic development decisions from employment to tourism.

Every aspect of planning and development should be infused with a concern for imaginative and effective uses of open spaces. As in planning for any other urban functions, open space planning should interlock with other functional planning on both a substantive and geographic basis. The interdependencies of city and country, rich and poor, and work and play force a multidisciplinary regional approach into planning for open spaces.

Throughout the complex process of open space planning, there are three factors which must constantly guide policies and programs: variety, accessibility, and imagination.

A *variety* of open spaces is needed to serve diverse populations and to enhance multiple resources. Wildernesses are called for as well as rooftop parks; junk playgrounds as well as formal malls; marshes as well as beaches. To meet the different and constantly changing needs of people and resources, variety must be built into the types, designs, and programs of open space.

Both physical and psychological *accessibility* to open spaces is a basic consideration for all open space planning. The mountain park does the carless ghetto inhabitant little good if it is inaccessible by public transportation. Likewise the enjoyment of a river is not possible if its banks are lined with a barrier of freeways.

Imagination is the key to stimulating open space planning and action so open spaces can serve the positive functions they should in urban society. Never before in this country has there been such a wave of interest in the environment, nor so many grant-in-aid programs for the acquisition and development of open spaces, nor such a plethora of legal tools and techniques to help obtain and control open spaces.

The application of imagination to some of the overlooked resource problems close at hand can open up both recreation and economic opportunities. For instance, in Boston the Boston Redevelopment Authority stated that:

. . . the existing nonrecreational uses of Boston's harbor and river frontage constitute blighting influences and an unnecessary and expensive burden on public services, when if they were turned to recreational purposes, they could bring in a considerable economic return to the City.[18]

Some cities have seen the possibility of an "in-town resort area" for places like the Toronto Islands or Chicago with its projected landfill peninsulas with beaches on the north side and marinas on the south side.

Open spaces must be seen and treated as an essential part of the planning process for urban development. With the application of the growing sophistication and technology found in other functional planning today, open spaces may be able to provide a variety of accessible opportunities to people and become a means of enhancing the quality of living in our urban environment.

---

[17] Wallace-McHarg Associates, PLAN FOR THE VALLEYS (Philadelphia: The Associates, 1964).

[18] Boston Redevelopment Authority, 1965/1975 GENERAL PLAN FOR THE CITY OF BOSTON AND THE REGIONAL CORE (Boston: The Authority, 1964), pp. vii–5.

8

Governmental and Community Facilities

MUNICIPAL FACILITIES are physical manifestations—buildings, land, equipment, and whole systems of activities—of governmental services on behalf of the public and of major segments thereof. They are important components of a city and add immeasurably to the quality of urban life. Some services are necessities—the provision of pure water, for example—while others are highly desirable for cultural or educational enrichment.

Municipal facilities are often called "public facilities" to denote that they are owned by the public (or municipality) and are operated for the benefit of the community (public). The term "community facilities" is somewhat broader in scope, and includes not only those facilities owned by the public but also those owned and operated by private enterprise for the benefit of the community.

The demand for more and varied community facilities and services increases as urban areas expand, population grows, old facilities become outmoded, and living standards and public expectations rise. While the demand and need for traditional community facilities such as water or sewer lines continues, the demand for other services, such as health clinics or junior colleges, is increased by a more sophisticated and expectant public. A service or facility that a few years ago was a luxury may now be regarded as a necessity.

With the increasing demands placed upon public budgets, intelligent planning of facilities is essential. Planners and urban planning agencies will be expected to help determine needs, priorities, and standards for a wide range of public service facilities.

The purpose of this chapter is to provide a general introduction to planning facilities, such as city halls, civic centers, decentralized municipal administrative centers, libraries, fire stations, police stations, municipal garages and yards, water lines, sanitary and storm sewers. Substantive space and location standards will be noted and discussed.

The sequence of facilities considered begins with those where the planner is likely to play a contributory but not a primary role (higher education and health), then to: relatively new or significantly expanded municipal functions which are less likely to have been encountered previously by the professional in planning; one-of-a-kind facilities, such as civic centers; and finally, to the most widely distributed and common facilities.

Two key problems in planning for any facility or system of facilities are finance and intergovernmental relations. Because of space limitations and the objectives of this chapter, these two aspects will not be considered for each facility; however, these facets of planning for public facilities are of crucial importance and are discussed in general terms in Chapters 2 and 14.

Any discussion of financing techniques would soon become dated as these are evolving with the various state and federal loan and grant-in-aid programs which change each legislative year. Of necessity, the most up-to-date financing methods have to be studied for a particular project. For example, a growing range of financial assistance is becoming available through the Community Facilities Administration of the U.S. Department of Housing and Urban Development.

Various kinds of facilities will be provided in a multitude of ways by various levels of government including special benefit districts within a city, the city, the county, the metropolitan area, and the special district. This will be done through contractual service agreements and joint agreements between cities, between cities and counties, or between counties and states. For excellent studies of the problems of intergovernmental relations the reader is encouraged to consult the publications of the Advisory Commission of Intergovernmental Relations.[1]

Particular emphasis in this chapter will be placed upon the role of the planner and the planning agency. This role ranges from the purely advisory to one involving the detailed staff work necessary in preparing plans. Thus a planning agency staff member may serve as liaison with an advisory committee to a health planning agency and at the same time be responsible for preparing the detailed plans for municipal administrative facilities.

When considering the planning for particular kinds of facilities the planning agency may also find that it will either have to work with or hire professionals who are specialists. The average planner on the planning agency staff may not possess the expertise of a campus planner, hospital planner, or library building consultant. In working on community facility plans the planning agency will be working with a host of specialists, such as civil and sanitary engineers, hydrologists, architects, urban designers, librarians, educators, manage-

ment consultants, fire underwriters, building engineers, and police officials. On the professional level, planners will find that new opportunities for specialization are constantly occurring in these various related fields: for example, universities and health agencies are using planners, and some movement of personnel between fields is already apparent, both from general planning into special planning and from one special planning area to another.

In providing for community facilities the planning agency will find that the focus of its interest and work will be shifting as time goes by. Typical is a process whereby the planning agency may move into planning a new system of facilities. As an appropriate department of government assumes more responsibility for planning or operating its facility, the continuous detailed planning of the facility and system of facilities is increasingly taken over by operating departments. Thus the kind of work that was originally a pioneering effort by the planning agency might be assumed by the planning staff of the police department, for example. The agency then finds itself moving into even newer areas, such as the planning of health facilities, where there are little or, at best, only token attempts to plan and coordinate such facilities with urban development as a whole.

In summary, this chapter will introduce some planning principles for both the traditional and the evolving responsibilities of the planning agency. Space and location standards will be presented and discussed, and throughout the role of the planner and the planning agency will be emphasized.

Higher Education

Urban planners and officials are becoming aware that facilities for higher education are an important part of our urban, social, and cultural environment.

College and university expansion is taking place so rapidly that announcements by educational authorities that a new building is being built or a new campus planned are commonplace. One authority has recently estimated

[1] See the following publications by the U.S. Advisory Commission on Intergovernmental Relations: *Alternative Approaches to Governmental Reorganization in Metropolitan Areas*, June, 1962; *Intergovernmental Responsibilities for Water Supply and Sewage Disposal in Metropolitan Areas*, October, 1962; *Performance of Urban Functions: Local and Areawide*, September, 1963; *The Problem of Special Districts in American Government*, May, 1964. (Washington, D.C.: The Commission).

that about three to four million dollars a day is being spent on higher educational facilities.

Planning agencies seldom participate in framing higher educational policies and curricula; nor do many planning agencies engage in campus planning. Planning agencies can work *with* higher educational institutions, a role more appropriate for the typical agency.

In general, the planning agency should cultivate close relationships with colleges and universities within its jurisdiction. If the institution has a campus planner these relationships may be forged more easily, but if not, the planning agency may use its influence to persuade the institution to obtain professional help. The planning agency can also help alleviate "town and gown" tensions. Hopefully, such amicable relationships could permeate policy-making levels. There are many areas of mutual concern, such as taxes, services, and relationships with surrounding neighborhoods, that need careful and unemotional discussion. The planning agency's goal should be to foster a climate where both city and institution can understand each other's problems and reach mutually acceptable conclusions.

INFORMATION

The university should inform the planning agency of enrollment and development policies and supply future estimates of student and faculty population. If the institution is interested, the planning agency could supply it with population and economic data and projections. The planning agency should keep institutions alerted to proposed capital improvements and programs, such as urban renewal projects, the location of new highways and mass transit facilities, and other factors that influence campus development.

CAMPUS PLANNING

The details of campus planning may have important implications for the surrounding area. Equally important are public plans for the neighborhoods surrounding colleges and universities, particularly in larger cities where university neighborhoods may have declined. Joint urban renewal efforts are becoming much more common, particularly since Section 112 of the U.S. Housing Act of 1954, as ame permits the inclusion of an institution penditures in an urban renewal area as p the local contribution. Universities may purchase land for expansion in an urban newal area that might not otherwise be ava ble in suitable parcels at reasonable prices.

The size of enrollment and the density of development are key elements in determining campus size. While some private institutions may limit their enrollments, public institutions must often accept an increasing number of students. With both private and public institutions, city and university officials should, if possible, agree upon a maximum size for the institution. Such decisions may of course be made at a higher level, and a city may have little control except for the influence it may bring to bear on state boards of education or state legislatures.

The planning agency will also be vitally interested in the physical form of the campus, whether it be a low-rise, spread-out campus, or an intensively developed, high-rise campus. If the campus is to expand in area, the planning agency should play an important role in determining the *direction* of that growth. Future street and highway improvements, the availability of utilities, as well as urban renewal area boundaries may influence these decisions.

Planning agencies will also be interested in the number of students, faculty, and staff members that commute to the university each day. A large institution can create as much or more traffic than a major industry or a shopping center. The amount of traffic depends upon the number of students and faculty that live on the campus, the number of students and faculty that live within walking distance, the student automobile ownership policies of the university, the extent and number of cultural and sports events that attract public attendance, and other similar factors. Where possible, university expansion and related public facilities, such as mass transit lines and highway interchanges, should be coordinated. Traffic patterns in surrounding neighborhoods may also need close study because of the possibly undesirable effects heavy traffic may have on surrounding residential areas.

The planning agency will be vitally concerned with the university neighborhood. While in the past some universities and colleges have ignored their surroundings, there is a growing feeling among university administrators that the vitality of the institution depends on the quality of life in the surrounding area. Many urban universities are faced with a problem in attracting and holding faculty because of deteriorating housing in the university's immediate neighborhood. Some universities and cities are cooperating in urban renewal and rehabilitation efforts, but these have at times created other problems—relocation of low income and minority groups or upgrading of the surrounding area to such an extent that the cost of housing is prohibitive for faculty members.

A persistent headache for many city planning agencies is providing adequate student housing in surrounding neighborhoods. Although the campus may include housing, some students prefer to live off campus. The problems arise when single-family houses are converted to rooming houses. Although universities may require certain qualitative standards in off-campus student housing, both the planning agency and the city have the important obligation of carrying out a careful and intensive housing code enforcement program in these converted single-family homes.

Almost every campus will have an adjacent business area that caters to the faculty and students. These business areas may create traffic problems, and adequate off-street parking may be the only solution. At the same time the community may be concerned about the marginal appearance of many student-supported business establishments. This is largely inevitable and perhaps not too important unless actual physical deterioration is also present.

Universities are spawning both planned and unplanned industrial and research facilities. Many industries will locate in areas completely separated from a university and base their locational decisions on the fact that a particular institution is in the city. However, some research and development facilities may be located very close to the university and may present problems, unless development is carefully controlled through the use of industrial performance standards, for example.

The university may also influence the development decisions of other educational and cultural institutions. In Boston, Pittsburgh, and Cleveland, for example, universities and other institutions have begun to plan their immediate environs jointly to create an educational or cultural center. Institutions may find it advantageous to share some facilities and to have mutual relationships in terms of faculty, students, and research activities. The planning agency and the city can play important roles in helping institutions plan their environs, but the problems associated with such educational center complexes are much greater than for a single institution. The planning agency must also be aware of the problems associated with creating what some critics have called "cultural ghettos."

The benefits of educational institutions to a city in terms of their economic attractiveness are becoming increasingly recognized. An industrial establishment, when studying a city with a view to locating there, will want to know what college and university facilities are available, not only for the families of employees but for the continued education and development of its own highly skilled personnel. In summary, the city should consider institutions of higher learning as one of its most important resources.

Health Facilities

There are important elements of a city that traditionally receive much attention in city plans. One example that promises to receive a growing amount of attention in the future is the planning of health facilities. This emphasis will not only include planning specific local health facilities, such as a particular hospital, but also on planning for a *system* of health facilities.

HEALTH FACILITY PLANNING AGENCIES

A significant medical and sociological development of the sixties has been the growth in the voluntary hospital planning. In 1960 there were about 10 area-wide metropolitan health facility planning agencies. By 1964 the number had grown to 57.[2] As yet, although there are health facility planning agencies and "health planners," the health planning field is still a "movement" rather than a field with established theories and techniques.

Early health facility planning agencies emphasized the physical aspects of building hospitals where they were most needed. Recently, the focus has shifted to the interrelationships between existing facilities coupled with a growing awareness of technological advances, patterns of medical care, and organizational changes in the medical field.

Health planning agencies collect and dispense information on the construction, development, and use of hospitals and related health facilities, such as mental hospitals, TB clinics, nursing homes, rehabilitation centers, and medical education facilities, on an area-wide basis; measure the present and future needs for such facilities; and carry out research and special studies. Principles and standards of service are developed, the public and health practitioners are kept informed, and proposals for new facilities are reviewed.

In the future, these agencies will spend more time determining and projecting needs for interrelated services and facilities, providing more information for decision-makers, developing principles and standards for evaluating facilities, maintaining a central source of data on health facilities, analyzing new trends in medical and health care, and improving cooperation with governmental and private planning agencies.

The relationship between health planning agencies and city planning agencies has not been extensively developed. Nevertheless some general guidelines to the future role of the city planning agency in the health facility planning field can be made.

ROLE OF THE PLANNING AGENCY

If the planning agency is to play a role in health planning it must first familiarize itself

with the field. It is highly technical and complex, and expertise may never be achieved by a planning agency staff member. However, if a local health planning agency exists, the staff members can be valuable sources of information and can make judgments about the kinds of information the urban planner can use. The health planning field is not one in which the planning agency can be involved without prior invitation. If no health facility planning agency exists, the planning agency may use its influence to establish one, but it should not attempt to assume such a task itself.

One possible role for the planning agency, although atypical, is for the staff to act for a health planning agency. An example is the Santa Clara County (California) Planning Department which has acted as staff for the hospital commission of Santa Clara County. A more typical arrangement, however, might be for the planning staff to cooperate with a health planning agency.

As with other agencies and organizations, the planning agency can cooperate with health planners by exchanging information and data. The health agency can provide the planning agency with specific requests for the kinds of information it needs. The planning agency in turn can provide the information on population growth, characteristics, and movements; economic projections; land use; transportation and capital improvement plans; and other information that may affect the general planning of a health system and the development of particular sites. The informational requirements of the health agency may be satisfied adequately if the urban planning agency operates or helps to maintain a "data bank." When information is gathered for a data bank the health agency may request that specific types of information, such as the incidence of certain diseases by population groups and census tracts, be collected and correlated with other data.

The planning agency also can help health planning agencies draft locational and site development standards for distribution of hospitals, nursing homes, and clinics. It can review specific sites chosen by a health agency and make comments on their suitability relative to

[2] American Medical Association, *Profiles in Planning, AMA Directory of Health Facility Planning Agencies,* prepared by the Department of Hospitals and Medical Facilities (Chicago: The Association, 1965), p. 1.

soil characteristics, availability of utilities, adjacent land uses, transportation and transit, and any urban renewal or development projects planned for the area. The health agency may also ask the planning agency to make site location recommendations for a particular facility.

The planning agency is sometimes called on to study the characteristics of various health facilities and compare them with activities that may be described in the provisions of the zoning ordinance. It is well known, for example, that many zoning ordinances needlessly discriminate against some types of health facilities and force them to locate in undesirable or unsuitable parts of the community. The outright prohibition or marginal treatment that mental institutions often receive in zoning ordinances is unfortunate. Other kinds of changes in zoning ordinances that might be suggested by a planning agency relate to permitted intensity of development, required off-street parking, and the development of health facilities systems.

The planning agency and the health agency together can prepare a health facilities' plan for inclusion in the comprehensive plan. Such action would inform community decision-makers about yet another important system of facilities that might influence other development decisions.

As with educational and cultural institutions, the health facility, more particularly the hospital, can play an important role in urban renewal. Many hospitals are in deteriorating neighborhoods where it is difficult to retain medical and technical staff. Some hospitals have hired their own planning staffs and have acted as a positive force in renewing and rehabilitating their immediate environs. As in the case of educational institutions, hospital capital expenditures in an urban renewal area may be considered as part of the local financial contribution.

A hospital can serve as the focus for a section of the community. It can provide employment and may benefit the community in many indirect ways. Hospitals may also serve as a center in which related and ancillary facilities may locate, such as medical schools, nursing schools,

doctors' offices, laboratories, and nursing homes. The planning agency has an important role to play in this context. Although the primary burden is on the health agency, the planning agency can make a contribution to better planning of a system of health facilities. The future city planning document may well include chapters on health facilities which are just as fundamental as those now included on parks, recreation, and transportation.

Governmental Administrative Centers

Planning the system of administrative facilities for local government is an important function in which the planning agency should be involved, not only because capital improvements will be made but also because placement of such facilities is related to other planning and development factors. In this section planning city halls and civic centers will be discussed, followed by an examination of the problems that may be encountered if these facilities are decentralized.

PLANNING THE CITY HALL

Apart from financial considerations, four basic steps in planning a new city hall are: (1) determining the need for a new or expanded structure; (2) studying space requirements; (3) choosing a location; and (4) developing the site and building.

Determining Need. The first step in evaluating an existing city hall is to ascertain structural defects and operational inadequacies. An architect should determine the type of construction, structural condition, and state of electrical, plumbing, and heating facilities. Such a survey might indicate, for instance, that the structure was unsound or that restrooms for the public were not satisfactory. Even if the building were structurally sound it might have poor ventilation, inadequate space, and poor office layout.

Space Requirements. The second step is to undertake a study of future space requirements. Although it may be easy to see that the existing accommodation is overcrowded, it is much more difficult to anticipate space requirements for the next ten or 20 years. A new city hall may last a half century or more, and must therefore be carefully planned for future as well as present needs.

In studying space needs, future population growth and the resultant demand for municipal services and personnel must be determined. A survey of space needs can be carried out by the planning agency, but the advice of an architect is most desirable at this point. Each city or county department should list the number of existing employees and unfilled positions and the space needs for personnel, equipment, and storage. Based on the level of municipal services anticipated, projections for, say, the next 20 years should be made, divided into five-year phases.

The size of a city hall will depend both on its desired significance and on the activities it houses. In the smallest cities almost all offices, including police and fire departments, should be located in the same building. In larger cities certain activities, such as public works departments, garages, and libraries, will be located elsewhere. The key test in determining functions to be housed in the city hall is administrative efficiency; in general, all administrative offices should be located there. A particular function should be excluded when inconvenience to the public might result, when a city hall location might interfere with its operation, or when other local conditions suggest a separate location.

Another factor in determining space needs is whether provision is to be made for other agencies. For example, a number of cities have built joint city-county administrative buildings or a city hall may house a court. In the small community the city hall may also function as a community meeting place. Under these circumstances, a city council chamber might be planned to handle much larger groups of people than would normally attend council meetings.

The space study, in addition to providing information for city officials, will also provide the architect with detailed information on the departments, the number of employees, appropriate types of furnishings and equipment, and special requirements such as type and amount of storage space. As a new building may have to serve for over 50 years, space needs should not be underestimated and should be planned for expansion.

Location. Government offices must be accessible to the people who use them. For convenience the city hall is best located near the center of transportation and business activity. In older cities this is the central business district; in suburban areas such a location might be near the community shopping center. The city hall should be near other offices—government and private—with which it deals frequently. City officials may thus consult with county and state officials frequently, and attorneys may consult records in the city hall and visit other government agencies.

Sites with suitable land values should be chosen. The site should allow ample off-street parking for both employees and the public. If possible, the location should be coordinated and integrated with other development proposals; thus a new city hall might be located in a downtown urban renewal area. A city hall should not, however, be located in such a way as to interfere with the efficient functioning of a business district.

Naturally, the analysis of a potential location should include site development costs and information on availability of utilities and any drainage difficulties.

An arrangement that is sometimes adopted is a joint city-county building. At least 40 cities and counties have cooperated in this way. There are two main advantages. First, the joint location is frequently a convenience to the public and to government agencies that work with each other. Second, a single building often can be constructed and maintained for less money than two separate buildings. The majority of cities that occupy joint space feel that the arrangement is satisfactory. One disadvantage is a lack of room for expansion. Planning for expansion is more complicated when two separate governments are involved. In addition, problems connected with the equitable sharing of the expenses involved in running and maintaining the structure may arise.

Another type of location for a city hall is within a civic center complex. The advantage of so locating a city hall is that it may be combined with other administrative and governmental buildings to make it convenient for the public. Intergovernmental relations may also be strengthened if other agencies are located in the same center. For example, the San Jose, California, civic center contains the city hall, public health building, communications building, police garage, county office building, sheriff's department and jail, criminal-legal building, and juvenile center. A single site may also reduce heating and cooling costs if a single power plant is used. If other facilities such as a municipal auditorium are included, the differing hours of operation may make it possible to use the same parking facilities.

A civic center also offers an opportunity for urban design, but it can be a disadvantage if it is poorly located or if some facilities are used infrequently. In this case the city hall would not only be less accessible but also would be in a location seldom populated except during day-time hours.

Site and Building. Whether the city hall be located in a civic center or by itself, the site should have room for expansion and adequate parking. The city hall should be designed as an office building and should not attempt to be monumental. Municipal officials should not hesitate to engage outstanding architects, for a desire to save taxpayers' money should not result in mediocre design. The building should be planned internally with a stress on good functional relationships and convenience. Detailed interior design considerations are beyond the scope of this chapter, and other sources should be consulted.[3]

CIVIC CENTERS

The civic center is one of the traditional concepts in city planning; since ancient times it has received much attention from town planners and architects alike. A civic center is a distinct area, located at or near the center of a city, within which are located the city's major

administrative, and sometimes cultural, activities. During the "City Beautiful" movement[4] almost every city plan contained a proposal to group certain governmental and cultural functions at one location, typically in the central business district, but the majority of these centers were never built.

During the fifties and sixties there was a reawakening of interest in the civic center concept because of a growing need for administrative and cultural facilities in urban areas and for a variety of public buildings. Many civic center proposals are still on paper, but an increasing number are being built. A certain amount of criticism has arisen however, and the dissentient arguments deserve careful consideration by each city considering a center.

Advantages and Disadvantages. Some of the advantages of a civic center have already been mentioned in connection with city halls. In essence grouping public buildings is convenient both to governmental officials and to the public in transacting business that requires visits to various agencies. With the growing web of intergovernmental relations the advantages to public officials are growing. Analyses of the operations of governmental agencies show that certain agencies (city and county police and the courts, for example) have frequent contact, and administrative costs can be significantly lowered when offices are in proximity.

A civic center also makes it possible to use joint parking facilities and power plants. Joint use of janitorial services, research and reference library facilities, and electronic data processing equipment may also be possible. Finally, the civic center may provide an opportunity for imaginative civic design and may sometimes be located, with advantage, in an urban renewal area.

Some of the disadvantages of civic centers should also be considered. For example, planning a civic center is much more complicated than planning a single building. Coordinating various agencies and levels of government may be extremely difficult. Some agencies may prefer to act independently in choosing the loca-

[3] See Beryl Robichaud, SELECTING, PLANNING, AND MANAGING OFFICE SPACE (New York: McGraw-Hill, 1958) and Kenneth H. Ripnen, OFFICE BUILDING AND OFFICE LAYOUT PLANNING (New York: McGraw-Hill, 1960).

[4] Arthur B. Gallion and Simon Eisner, THE URBAN PATTERN (New York: D. Van Nostrand Company, 1963), p. 81.

tion, method of financing, timing of construction, and design of their buildings. Various agencies will have differing locational requirements that cannot easily be coordinated. Land acquisition costs may be higher since premium prices may have to be paid to obtain a single large site. In addition, some agencies may have no relationship whatsoever to each other and may never coordinate personnel, records, or services. This is true when governmental administrative offices are combined with art institutes, auditoriums, and museums.

The most vocal critics of civic centers[5] suggest that such centers are obsolete—that they have little validity in the modern metropolis. There is also the fear that a civic center might turn out to be of poor architectural quality, thus deteriorating rather than improving the environment. Civic centers may have an adverse influence on their environs; that they may be deserted after office hours and may, even in extreme cases, add to law enforcement problems.

Where areas have been cleared for the erection of a new civic center, some feel that existing neighborhoods and districts have been destroyed needlessly, with a consequent loss of urban functions and vitality. When community activities are centralized, there is always the danger that abandonment of older facilities may result in the needless destruction of landmarks that still have a useful life.

Planning agencies should study carefully the advantages and disadvantages of civic centers before making their recommendations on proposed projects of this type. Until more experience is available perhaps the tentative generalization might be made that in the larger city the disadvantages of civic centers may outweigh the advantages, but in the smaller city the civic center may provide an opportunity for good urban design and an intensification of uses which may well be an asset.

Planning the Civic Center. Planning a civic center is obviously more complex than planning a single building. Essentially the problem is to determine the space requirements for each use, to examine the effect of combination, and to determine functional relationships and conflicts. Because progressive errors are possible, professionals in architecture and site planning should be retained from the outset.

The location of a civic center will depend upon city size and land use intensity. Civic centers are typically located at the edge of a central business district to take advantage of lower land values and also to prevent the interruption of any possible future business expansion. The site should be served by mass-transit facilities, and the local street system should be studied since the assembly of a site suitable for a civic center might necessitate closing a number of streets. Major street improvements may have to be made in the immediate area and in the central business district as a whole to change traffic patterns.

Important design decisions will also have to be made about the size, mass, shape, and arrangement of buildings and their relationships in terms of circulation and appearance.

ADMINISTRATION DECENTRALIZATION

The "branch city hall" is not a new idea,[6] but a number of major metropolitan areas have only recently begun to consider decentralizing certain administrative functions to bring governmental services closer to the people. Recently, urban planning critics have stressed the need for government and services at the neighborhood or community level.

Some municipal services have traditionally been decentralized. Fire stations, libraries, and police precinct stations are common examples. Opportunities to serve the public more effectively as well as to gain other development objectives, such as variety in design, should be investigated by the planning agency. Various kinds of governmental services can be decentralized, depending on local circumstances. These include fire stations, libraries, police stations, health centers, receiving hospitals, and auditoriums. Also offices for utilities, building

[5] See Jane Jacobs, THE DEATH AND LIFE OF GREAT AMERICAN CITIES (New York: Random House, 1961) and Richard A. Miller, "Are Civic Centers Obsolete?" ARCHITECTURAL FORUM, CX (January, 1959), pp. 94–99.

[6] An early discussion of the concept can be found in Clarence E. Ridley and Orin F. Nolting, "Taking City Government Back to the People," PUBLIC MANAGEMENT, XXI (April, 1939).

and zoning inspections, engineering services, licenses and permits, courts, city and district attorneys, registration of voters, property taxation and assessments, and welfare. Other public uses such as state license centers, post offices, and YMCA's can also be decentralized. In larger cities other opportunities for the coordination of public services exist. For example, a number of cities' urban renewal project offices dispense information on urban renewal and on housing and building codes. The Economic Opportunity Act has enabled certain major cities to open "urban opportunity centers" where a number of services for the needy are brought together in one building.

Planning for branch city halls or sub-civic centers must begin with the decision that certain services can be decentralized. A survey of existing city agencies is necessary to determine those which already have decentralized services and those which can increase efficiency and service to the public by decentralizing certain operations. Some operations, of course, cannot easily be decentralized—a county recorder of deeds or the central laboratory of a health department are but two examples.

The planner of branch administrative facilities will immediately be faced with the problem of determining suitable district sizes for the various functions and services. For example, the service area of a fire station is carefully calculated according to fire protection standards. Police and library services are calculated on an entirely different basis and identical district boundaries may be difficult to achieve. One solution is to adjust the boundaries of the "more administrative" kinds of functions that do have exact district boundary requirements. Such a plan might result in either using an existing fire station or a police station location as the site for a branch civic center, or boundary difficulties might present such a problem that in certain centers no police or fire facilities would be included.

An entire range of services need not be duplicated at each center. Some departments have larger service districts than others and it is possible to vary the services that are included in each center. The Los Angeles system has "major" and "minor" centers that cover larger and smaller geographic areas with varying ranges of services.

The location and the services offered in a particular branch center would depend on the area to be served, and the size, density, and characteristics of its population. The site should be close to the center of population, located on a major street, and served by public transportation. The center should be near other community facilities such as shopping centers, frequently used by the public. The site should be relatively level, have stable soil conditions, be well drained, and have adequate utilities. Finally, the branch center should be used as a positive element and force in the design and development of the community and neighborhood.

Library Planning

With an expanding population, growth in leisure time, higher educational goals and attainment, and a significant increase in the proportion of young people in the population, the public library is an important community facility. Planning agencies have a role to play in helping to plan the expansion of existing libraries and the development of new branches.

Although planning agencies will not be concerned with the operation and maintenance of the library, it is important for them to know some of its essential services. Basic to determining the kind and level of services required is a knowledge and understanding of the community to be served. Information about government and tax structure, population characteristics such as age, educational level, occupations, and general social structure is needed. Since library services are not performed in a vacuum, it is also necessary to examine the resources of other educational and cultural agencies within the community, as well as service and financial relationships with neighboring municipalities, and county, state, and federal governments. Fundamental is the need to know both the short- and the long-range objectives of the library in the community: decisions relating to the public to be served and the level of service to be achieved are important items of information.

When we examine the services that modern libraries perform it is apparent that the concept of a library as a source of recreation for housewives and children, or as a facility to serve the intellectual elite, is out of date. The growth in population and in the educational level of the average American, has brought about a significant expansion in the type and level of services provided by libraries.

Children's departments have been traditional with libraries: with population growth this service will continue to expand significantly. The library serves children by introducing books and other materials to them. These materials are often used to augment the facilities available at school. In addition, the library generally cooperates with other community and social agencies that serve children.

Service to young adults is also increasing. In the past this age group was "lost" to the library shortly after leaving high school. Now, with increasing educational attainment and more leisure time available, the young adult is using the library more, particularly if he is continuing his education. Thus the public library situated near a community college often has a high proportion of students to serve.

The demand from adults is increasing rapidly with the realization that the library can play an important part in further education. Not only are services available for recreational and educational reading, but they are often performed for special interest groups such as business, industry, or labor.

This brief discussion cannot do justice to the many and varied types of services provided by the public library; however, it should alert planners to the need to investigate the kinds of services that may be provided in the library so that intelligent decisions can be made relative to the location of this important facility in the community.

PLANNING FOR LIBRARY BUILDINGS

Most cities, when approaching the planning of a library system, are usually faced with one of two problems: first, the need to build a new main library in the community that is now without one or is abandoning an older building; second, the older community that has a main library is considering the establishment of branches.

The two problems are distinctly different, and this section will deal with the two types of planning considerations that must be faced.

Planning the Main Library Building. The

Table 8–1

Experience Formulas for Library Size and Costs

Population Size	Book Stock—Volumes per Capita	No. of Seats per 1,000 Population	Circulation—Volumes per Capita	Total Sq. Ft. per Capita	Desirable, First Floor, Sq. Ft. per Capita	1961 Fair Estimated Cost per Capita[1]
Under 10,000	3½–5	10	10	.7–.8	.5–.7	15
10,000– 35,000	2¾–3	5	9.5	.6–.65	.4–.45	12
35,000– 100,000	2½–2¾	3	9	.5–.6	.25–.3	10
100,000– 200,000	1¾–2	2	8	.4–.5	.15–.2	9
200,000– 500,000	1¼–1½	1¼	7	.35–.4	.1–.125	7
500,000 and up	1 –1¼	1	6.5	.3	.06–.08	6

Source: Joseph L. Wheeler and Herbert Goldhor, PRACTICAL ADMINISTRATION OF PUBLIC LIBRARIES (New York: Harper and Row, 1962), p. 554.

[1] Without furnishings (add 15%) or air conditioning (add 10%).

planner's primary interest is in the general aspects of the library building, its location and site. However, planning for a library building begins from the inside. The planner can make important contributions to the planning of libraries and library systems, but should recognize his own limitations and realize that the planning of the services and spatial relationships within the building are not within his professional province. He should, however, understand something of the techniques of the library planner and the architect.

The first stage of library planning is the preparation of a "program statement." This is a crucial step, normally undertaken by the librarian, and outlines the basic policies of service and the implied requirements that must be met. The statement will reflect the prior study of the community (economic and social characteristics) and the kinds of services the library wants to provide. This statement is often prepared with the assistance of a library building consultant. Such a consultant is essential if the librarian has not had previous experience in planning a system.

From general policies and requirements the program statement moves into space requirements for books, readers, staff, group meeting rooms, mechanical equipment, and all other space-consuming facilities.

Table 8–1 provides general empirical guidelines for programming the floor space for the total building. Table 8–2 provides empirical guidelines for determining minimum interior space requirements in relation to population and size of the book collection. Space requirements thus derived are then discussed with an architect who prepares alternate design possibilities to accommodate the stated requirements.

One of the most important sections of the program statement, from the point of view of the planner, is the selection of an appropriate site. It is to this aspect that the remainder of the discussion will be devoted.

1. *The Need for a Central Location.* The library serves people, and should be located to be accessible to the largest number of potential users. Although this idea seems obvious to the planner, it has not been well accepted by

public officials who often seem to know little about how libraries function. The principle of maximum accessibility has been advocated by a majority of experienced library administrators for some time, but unfortunately, their judgment has often been overruled by misguided public officials who are often more interested in building monuments than in providing the best public facilities.

A central location would be in the central business district or in a major shopping center that is the main business district of a suburb. Here there is a heavy concentration of retail stores, office buildings, banks, public transportation, and parking facilities. Just as the retail store market analyst studies pedestrian traffic to assure a maximum number of customers, so a library planner should locate a library to be prominent and accessible to attract a large number of people. Maximum accessibility and use is of fundamental importance to the successful operation of a public library. Libraries are not intended to house collections that are not used; furthermore, unit costs are important, for the greater the number of users, the less the cost per user.

2. *Where Not to Locate A Library.* Even after hearing such arguments as the foregoing, some public officials still believe that libraries should be located in civic centers, parks, or where quiet surroundings or parking facilities are available. Those who suggest libraries on such sites do not understand the library or its users. Libraries are not museums—they are dynamic educational centers whose services and resources must be easily accessible.

Remote or uncongenial locations should be avoided. For instance, a civic center is often unsuitable, for with the exception of those civic centers that have auditoriums, activities usually stop at 5:00 P.M.; however, evenings and weekends are prime hours for libraries. Experience has proven that a civic center is usually a poor location for a library. In some cities attempts have been made to overcome the problem of remoteness by establishing a branch in the downtown area. Unfortunately, these endeavors are expensive as well as unsatisfactory, and would not be required if the central library were located downtown.

Table 8–2

Guidelines for Determining Minimum Space Requirements

Population Served	Shelving Space[1]			Reader Space	Staff Work Space	Estimated Additional Space Needed[3]	Total Floor Space
	Size of Book Collection	Linear Feet of Shelving[2]	Amount of Floor Space				
Under 2,499	10,000 vol.	1,300 linear ft.	1,000 sq. ft.	Min. 400 sq. ft. for 13 seats, at 30 sq. ft. per reader space	300 sq. ft.	300 sq. ft.	2,000 sq. ft.
2,500–4,999	10,000 vol. plus 3 bks. per capita for pop. over 3,500	1,300 linear ft. Add 1 ft. of shelving for every 8 bks. over 10,000	1,000 sq. ft. Add 1 sq. ft. for every 10 bks. over 10,000	Min. 500 sq. ft. for 16 seats. Add 5 seats per M. over 3,500 pop. served, at 30 sq. ft. per reader space	300 sq. ft.	700 sq. ft.	2,500 sq. ft. or 0.7 sq. ft. per capita, whichever is greater
5,000–9,999	15,000 vol. plus 2 bks. per capita for pop. over 5,000	1,875 linear ft. Add 1 ft. of shelving for every 8 bks. over 15,000	1,500 sq. ft. Add 1 sq. ft. for every 10 bks. over 15,000	Min. 700 sq. ft. for 23 seats. Add 4 seats per M. over 5,000 pop. served, at 30 sq. ft. per reader space	500 sq. ft. Add 150 sq. ft. for each full time staff member over 3	1,000 sq. ft.	3,500 sq. ft. or 0.7 sq. ft. per capita, whichever is greater
10,000–24,999	20,000 vol. plus 2 bks. per capita for pop. over 10,000	2,500 linear ft. Add 1 ft. of shelving for every 8 bks. over 20,000	2,000 sq. ft. Add 1 sq. ft. for every 10 bks. over 20,000	Min. 1,200 sq. ft. for 40 seats. Add 4 seats per M. over 10,000 pop. served, at 30 sq. ft. per reader space	1,000 sq. ft. Add 150 sq. ft. for each full time staff member over 7	1,800 sq. ft.	7,000 sq. ft. or 0.7 sq. ft. per capita, whichever is greater
25,000–49,999	50,000 vol. plus 2 bks. per capita for pop. over 25,000	6,300 linear ft. Add 1 ft. of shelving for every 8 bks. over 50,000	5,000 sq. ft. Add 1 sq. ft. for every 10 bks. over 50,000	Min. 2,250 sq. ft. for 75 seats. Add 3 seats per M. over 25,000 pop. served, at 30 sq. ft. per reader space	1,500 sq. ft. Add 150 sq. ft. for each full time staff member over 13	5,250 sq. ft.	15,000 sq. ft. or 0.6 sq. ft. per capita, whichever is greater

Source: American Library Association, Subcommittee on Standards for Small Libraries, Public Library Association, INTERIM STANDARDS FOR SMALL PUBLIC LIBRARIES: GUIDELINES TOWARD ACHIEVING THE GOALS OF PUBLIC LIBRARY SERVICE (Chicago: The Association, 1962), p. 15. This brief 16-page report is based on standards set forth in ALA's, PUBLIC LIBRARY SERVICE; A GUIDE TO EVALUATION WITH MINIMUM STANDARDS. It is intended to provide interim standards for libraries serving populations of less than 50,000 until these libraries can meet the standards of ALA's PUBLIC LIBRARY SERVICE.

[1] Libraries in systems need only to provide shelving for basic collection plus number of books on loan from resource center at *any one time.*

[2] A standard library shelf equals 3 linear feet.

[3] Space for circulation desk, heating and cooling equipment, multipurpose room, stairways, janitors' supplies, toilets, etc., as required by community needs and the program of library services.

One of the problems of a central location is that of parking. For some, the availability of parking may be the main consideration in using the library. However, many surveys have concluded that a pedestrian-oriented location is the most important factor in the use of the public library. If a community has a strong and vital central business district it no doubt has already made the policy decision that every building need not provide parking on its own site.

3. *The Site.* The library site should be prominent; the corner of a busy intersection might be suitable. It should be level and suitable for a street entrance, be large enough for expansion, service vehicles, and bookmobiles, and a small amount of landscaping. It should also be rectangular in shape, since libraries function best with rectangular interiors.

The library should be located reasonably near parking areas and sufficient space for staff parking should be reserved. If drive-in service is to be provided, the site must be large enough for the provision of service drives. Finally, under certain circumstances it may be advisable to reject a large site and instead, purchase a smaller site on which horizontal expansion may not be feasible, but on which it is possible to expand vertically to achieve the same goals for library needs.

Planning for Branch Libraries. Because the services of the public library become most effective when brought close to its members, a system of branches is often desirable. When a city reaches 100,000 population a single main building is often inadequate. In cities of 50 to 75 thousand, branches with specialized services are sometimes necessary if the community is extensive or has some remote sections.

In the vocabulary of library planners a branch is an "extension agency" of which there are five categories:

1. *The Regional Branch*—a large comprehensive service branch used in larger cities that also serves smaller branches.

2. *The Community Branch*—a major library unit serving a population of not less than 55,000 with a full professional and clerical staff. Some smaller community branches serve 25,000 to 50,000.

3. *The Bookmobile*—a library on wheels that services scattered population and districts remote from schools. Visits may be infrequent, but are on a regular and well-timed schedule. Bookmobiles are often used to determine locations for future branches.

Branch libraries provide a convenient way for services to be extended on a neighborhood or community basis with the main or regional library serving as a principal resource. The branch is the direct link between the reader and the system of library resources.

When planning a branch system the fundamentals of planning for any system of public facilities apply. Studies must be made of the existing agencies and services, the population, educational and economic characteristics, the topography of the area, any natural or industrial barriers, and the policy to be adopted relative to the level of service to be provided for various locations and population groups. A branch system must also be planned in the light of community change and shifting population, the development of new shopping centers and residential areas, and changing transportation patterns. Whereas in planning the library building interior the planning agency may play only a minor role, it should play a major role in the planning of any branch system, for this cannot be done without use of the extensive data found in basic studies for comprehensive planning.

In most large cities the problem of planning effective branch library services is complicated by existing libraries in areas undergoing population changes or changes in land use. In addition, new residential areas are located in outlying parts of the city or beyond the central city. These areas frequently contain residents with high economic levels and educational attainments, who exert effective pressures for new services. The renewal of older neighborhoods has also placed great burdens on library systems, for existing branches have either had to expand, relocate, or adapt their services. For example, the substantial increase in population density and the number of schoolchildren in public housing projects often creates great stresses in an in-city library system which the city must face.

Planning a branch system within a county or metropolitan area will necessitate making decisions concerning the establishment of new services in outlying areas as well as the expansion, relocation, and adjustment of services within the central city. A good library plan will contain priorities for service that will be related to other public improvements and new growth.

1. *Location and Distribution.* Patterns of branch location and distribution are often less than ideal. In the past, branches may have been located in neighborhoods that have changed either in their service demands or in land use. In addition, it has always been difficult to coordinate the expansion of a system with existing facilities. Although at times it is desirable to abandon a particular branch, it is often difficult to do so, due to public resistance or because traditional library buildings cannot be sold.

Libraries will never be able to react quickly to changing and expanding populations; however, the impact of change can be lessened by adopting a policy of "fewer and better" branch libraries. The branches that have failed in the past have done so mostly through the ineffective and limited amount of service provided. In many ways the branch library has gone the way of the small independent shopkeeper; larger branch units prove to be more effective in the long run.

General standards for the distribution of libraries over a large area have not been established; however, plans drawn for individual cities may prove helpful, particularly those for Dallas, Los Angeles, and certain other cities.[7]

A recent study shows that in cities over 300,000 population the range in population served is from 97,000 per branch in Dallas to 20,000 in Oakland. The median is 40,000. In Denver the main library, located in the downtown area, serves as a "branch" for nearby residents. If the main library were to be included in a calculation for other cities the population per branch would be lower still. In general, recent plans require that a branch should serve more than the stated median. In Dallas a plan to service one million people with fourteen branches, an average of 71,000 people per branch, has been adopted. In Tulsa the goal is to serve over 50,000 persons per branch.

The distance between libraries can vary considerably, depending upon population density; the range can be anywhere from one to over two miles. The service radius of a branch library will also vary, and the size of the library building can vary with the population involved and the types of services provided.

In establishing the location for a branch library, the principle of maximum accessibility applies as in the case of the main library; however, locations for a branch library differ. Some may be in a shopping center, while others are in a quiet, semi-rural center; some have their own buildings, while others occupy rented quarters. In small communities branch libraries sometime share space in public buildings planned for multiple use.

A branch library should serve a minimum of twenty-five to thirty thousand people within a radius of one to one and one-half miles, subject to topographic conditions. The branch should be located within reasonable distance of a residential area so that a considerable number of children and adults will be within walking distance. With the universality of the automobile it is also important to be near a major street or highway intersection, particularly if public transportation is also available. An excellent location is within or adjacent to a major neighborhood or regional shopping center. Here, as in all locations, the branch should be built where it can be clearly seen and it should have parking space equal to its floor area. Space should also be provided for bicycles and delivery vehicles. Finally, the branch library should have a street level entrance with as little setback as possible.

---

[7] See Los Angeles Bureau of Budget and Efficiency, ORGANIZATION, ADMINISTRATION AND MANAGEMENT OF THE LOS ANGELES PUBLIC LIBRARY (Los Angeles: The Bureau, 1948–51); Lowell A. Martin, BRANCH LIBRARY SERVICE FOR DALLAS (Dallas: The Library, 1958); and, Philadelphia Free Library, A REGIONAL LIBRARY SYSTEM FOR PHILADELPHIA (Philadelphia: The Library, 1956).

Fire Station Location

The location of fire stations should be selected with care for the best possible fire protection.

Fire stations are a "system" of facilities and are capital improvements related to land use and population density. Urban planners can therefore make important contributions in their location. However, two factors should be made clear: first, that fire protection studies should be carried out only with the active, joint participation of fire protection officials and planners; and second, that creative innovations have little applicability in this kind of planning since standards are set quite explicitly by the American Insurance Association. (The Association was formerly known as the National Board of Fire Underwriters.) The American Insurance Association has published many informational aids and the nearest office should be consulted to determine the most recent standards advocated.

Table 8–3

Required Fire Flow

Population	Required Fire Flow for Average City, gpm	mgd	Duration, Hours
1,000	1,000	1.44	4
1,500	1,250	1.80	5
2,000	1,500	2.16	6
3,000	1,750	2.52	7
4,000	2,000	2.88	8
5,000	2,250	3.24	9
6,000	2,500	3.60	10
10,000	3,000	4.32	10
13,000	3,500	5.04	10
17,000	4,000	5.76	10
22,000	4,500	6.48	10
27,000	5,000	7.20	10
33,000	5,500	7.92	10
40,000	6,000	8.64	10
55,000	7,000	10.08	10
75,000	8,000	11.52	10
95,000	9,000	12.96	10
120,000	10,000	14.40	10
150,000	11,000	15.84	10
200,000	12,000	17.28	10

Over 200,000 population, 12,000 gpm, with 2,000 to 8,000 gpm additional for a second fire, for a 10-hour duration.

Source: STANDARD SCHEDULE FOR CITIES AND TOWNS OF THE UNITED STATES WITH REFERENCE TO THEIR FIRE DEFENSES AND PHYSICAL CONDITIONS (New York: American Insurance Association (National Board of Fire Underwriters), 1956 ed.)

WATER SUPPLY FOR FIRE FIGHTING

Water supply is one of the most important factors in fire protection. This chapter will not go into the engineering details of planning water systems for fire fighting purposes; however, it is necessary to introduce the concept of "required fire flow." The American Insurance Association has set up requirements for adequacy of the water system, shown in Table 8–3, based upon average conditions found in communities of various sizes.

DISTRIBUTION OF FIRE COMPANIES

Fire officials when discussing fire station location planning often examine distribution of "equipment and personnel." In larger cities the basic organizational unit is the "fire company," the unit assigned to operate either a pumper truck or a ladder truck, two basic types of fire equipment. In larger cities a company may have two pieces of equipment; and ladder companies may have various kinds of apparatus, including a lighting or rescue vehicle. Although there are an infinite number of variations, the term "fire company" is used typically to describe the force assigned to operate one pumper or ladder truck.

The fire department in a small community is usually a single pumper company that can deal only with small fires. Over 70 per cent of the communities in the United States and Canada with fire departments have only one, or at most, two companies. When the community is able to provide three companies (two pumpers and one ladder truck) it has the capacity to fight fires in uncongested single family residence districts or other small buildings. When two simultaneous fires occur, such a department must call a neighboring fire department. In the absence of nearby communities the fire department should have at least six companies. The goal for the small community should be the ability to handle two simultaneous fires of moderate intensity such as might occur in commercial and industrial districts or institutions such as churches, schools, and hospitals.

Smaller communities usually start with a one pumper company. With 10,000 population a community should have two pumper companies and one ladder company. With about

Table 8–4

Fire Company Distribution Standards

	Optimum Service Radius in Miles	
District and Required Fire Flow	From Engine, Hose, or Engine-Ladder Company	From Ladder Company
High-Value District (commercial, industrial, institutional)		
Where required flow is 9000 gpm or more	¾	1
Where required fire flow is 4500 to 8999 gpm	1	1¼
Where required fire flow is less than 4500 gpm	1½	2
Residential District		
Where required fire flow is more than 2000 gpm or where there are buildings in the district three or more stories in height, including tenement houses, apartments or hotels	1½	2
Same as above, but where the life hazard is above normal	1	1¼
For buildings having an average separation of less than 100 feet (and a fire flow requirement of 2000 gpm or less)	2	3
For buildings having an average separation of 100 feet or more (and a fire flow requirement of 2000 gpm or less)	4	4

Source: American Insurance Association (National Board of Fire Underwriters) FIRE DEPARTMENT STANDARDS—DISTRIBUTION OF COMPANIES AND RESPONSE TO ALARMS. Special Interest Bulletin No. 315, January, 1963.

Note: The above distances shall be reduced if a severe life hazard exists; if streets are narrow or in poor condition; if traffic, one-way streets, topography, or other unusual locational conditions hinder response; or if other circumstances peculiar to the particular district or municipality indicate that such a reduction is needed.

30,000 the community should have four pumpers and two trucks. Eight pumper companies and four truck companies are needed for a population of 70,000 and double that number for a population of about 200,000.

The smallest community usually has one station near the municipal building or near the center of town. When additional stations are needed, the distribution standards recommended by the American Insurance Association are used. These standards are more stringent for business, industrial, and other high-value or high-hazard districts, than for scattered residential districts. Table 8–4 illustrates the recommended standards for the distribution of pumper and engine companies. The response distances are based on extensive studies by both the American Insurance Association and state rating bureau of engineers. The standard distances have been increased within the past few years due to overall improvements in apparatus,

streets, and other factors that influence response.

Fire officials are particularly interested in fire protection for high-value districts such as central business districts. Standards in these areas are related to multiple response of companies. Thus, a high-value district requiring a 12,000 gallon-per-minute (gpm) fire flow must have 15 companies located within five miles. The standard for ladder company concentration for this type of district requires seven ladder companies to be located within five miles. Both engine and ladder company concentration would be correspondingly less for districts requiring smaller fire flows. Consideration should also be given to the concentration of companies for first alarm response; the standard for a district requiring a 12,000 gpm fire flow being three engine companies within one and one-half miles and two ladder companies within two miles.

Experience in the amount and kinds of

equipment that must be delivered to various types of fires in different districts is important, as well as experience of the problems associated with covering all parts of the city when there are several fires at the same time.

The foregoing discussion is intended merely to introduce the reader to the publications of the American Insurance Association, which should be consulted and studied in detail.

APPLICATION OF DISTRIBUTION STANDARDS

Most planners will be working with cities that already have a number of fire stations and are anticipating construction of new ones. The existing stations should be temporarily ignored when preparation of a fire station location plan is commenced. Standards should be applied so that existing stations are ignored and the "ideal" fire protection layout is prepared in map form. The object of this procedure is to determine to what extent existing stations meet or fail to meet modern standards. In any growing city there will be areas that are not receiving adequate fire protection, and many cities have had to readjust fire station locations. Cities under 100,000 population may be deficient in the number of companies; larger cities tend to have enough companies, but not well distributed.

Readjustments in distribution often result in greater efficiency and lower operating costs. With changing national standards, the growth of population, and shifts in land use and population, the relocation of existing fire stations is inevitable. A poor distribution of fire stations is also likely to be found in the suburban communities of metropolitan areas. The built-up sections and the location of high-value districts seldom bear any relationship to the individual municipal boundaries, and each municipality often organizes its own fire department without conscious regard to the location of fire companies in adjoining communities. Much more cooperation and study of the advantages of mutual aid agreements are necessary.

Substantial fire protection and financial benefits have been realized through the wholesale reorganization of fire station locations in a number of larger cities. Such reorganizations have been undertaken in Omaha, Chicago,

Hartford, Boston, Providence, Buffalo, Rochester, and Philadelphia. The magnitude of financial saving thus possible is evident in the reorganization of the Providence, Rhode Island, system. This was financed by a $1,750,000 bond issue that reduced the number of fire companies from 37 to 30. Six existing stations in good condition were retained and nine new stations were built. The city now has 15 buildings to maintain instead of 29, with an estimated saving of $200,000 a year. Similarly, in 1964, Chicago made a 15-year plan to reduce fire stations by 27 from 132 to 105. The plan eliminates 16 pumper companies and adds three truck companies, and the resulting better distribution in manpower will be achieved with no increase in cost.

Many officials hesitate to abandon existing stations to build new ones because of the expenditure; however, if a city adheres to an inefficient distribution pattern it will not have adequate protection at an economical cost. The best long-range approach is first to locate the companies properly and then provide stations to house them. A wrong location is an expensive error; one properly located station can often replace two old ones, particularly if structures which can house several companies are built.

THE PLANNING AGENCY

Many fire station location plans have been made without the assistance of city planning agencies. However, in those situations where there are changes in land use or rapid growth, the active participation of the planning agency is essential. It can provide information on existing conditions and forecasts of development as well as plans for future improvements. Fire protection officials are often handicapped by an outlook which tends to emphasize the present with little regard for the future. There seem to be particularly detailed standards on planning which they can follow for an existing situation but few guidelines relative to anticipating the future. The planning agency can fill this vacuum and may also have the personnel needed to gather information, analyze data, and write reports. The typical agency is probably better equipped to carry out studies than the typical fire department since only the very large fire departments would have personnel with a staff planning function, in contrast to daily operating duties.

The planning agency can analyze existing and future access barriers. Barriers lengthen the time required to reach a fire and they reduce the effective service area of a fire company. The most obvious kinds of barriers are rivers, canals, and other waterways that may not have bridges at frequent points. Similarly, an expressway with a reduction in the number of cross-streets is a barrier. The planning agency can point out the barriers that will be caused by future expressways and, of course, the planner who is aware of fire protection districts will also have them in mind when determining which streets may or may not be closed by expressway construction. Other kinds of barriers are railroad grade crossings, drawbridges, large open spaces such as golf courses and parks, and topographic conditions such as steep hillsides and valleys which can slow response significantly. Another barrier is heavy traffic: a busy street will obviously be a hindrance to rapid fire company action.

The way in which a city is developing is particularly important in planning fire station locations. This aspect has been discussed in a fire station study prepared by the Phoenix Planning Department. The planning department pointed out some of the basic characteristics of growth: larger lot areas with increasing distance from the city; a pattern of urban sprawl; residential development in the midst of rural land; major decentralization of retail activity; and predominance of automobile transportation. The report goes on to point out other development factors of particular interest from a fire protection point of view: the speed of growth, the extensive use of one-story masonry construction; the regularity of the major street system at section and quarter section lines; the irregular, long block pattern of local streets inside the grid; and the unique canal and topographic situation, together with lack of railroad and bridge crossings.

The report points out some implications of this kind of growth for fire protection. Fire stations must be built in both concentrated and low density developments and wide variations in accessibility will result. Fire runs are mainly restricted to the major street grid because of the discontinuous local street pattern that eliminates bypasses and shortcuts.

THE FIRE STATION SITE

When the general location pattern of fire stations is determined, specific sites must be selected. A station should not be located in such a way that its response in a particular direction would be hindered by having to make a long run up a hill, across a railroad at grade, or over a drawbridge. Heavily traveled streets are usually bad locations since it may be difficult to enter the flow of traffic. Similarly, a site too close to an intersection may prevent fire equipment from leaving the station because of traffic that is backed up waiting for a signal to change. In general, a good location is a street that runs parallel to or across a major thoroughfare; locations on one-way streets should be avoided.

When stations are to be built in outlying areas the ultimate development pattern should be considered. The location should not be so close to the city limits that the response area is reduced, or in such a position that the station is poorly located when an adjacent area is developed.

It is difficult to set exact standards for the size of a fire station site. The size will vary considerably from the central city site which will be very small, to the outlying community site where there will be open space surrounding the station. However, the site should be large enough for the station to be set well back from the curb line for safety and to provide parking facilities and space for holding company drills.

FIRE STATION BUILDING

The prime requisite for a fire station is to provide a building for housing fire equipment and men. The general layout of the station centers around the apparatus room: the minimum floor area required for a modern pumper truck is about 16 by 32 feet, for a ladder truck 20 by 50 feet, and for an aerial ladder truck approximately 20 by 75 feet. A minimum ceiling height of 13 feet is necessary. All doors should be at least 12 feet wide and should be installed in such a way that each piece of equipment has direct access to the street wherever possible; the overhead door has become standard equipment in new stations.

The modern station should have an architectural style that will blend with the surrounding neighborhood; thus the station design may vary throughout the city. Some two-story stations are still being erected, but the one-story layout is becoming more popular. The fire station may be part of a building used for other municipal purposes, but the area should be separated from the remainder of the building.

In addition to space for equipment and men, the fire station must contain office space, racks for drying hose, equipment maintenance rooms, offices, recreation rooms, kitchenettes, training classrooms, and other facilities such as underground gasoline tanks.

Police Stations

Unfortunately, there is a dearth of literature on the subject of police station planning,[8] but some broad outlines can be discussed.

The basic kinds of information needed are statistics on crime, the nature of the police department work load, the relationship to other city departments such as the city attorney's office, and to the sheriff and the county jail. A knowledge of local development patterns with particular emphasis on the location of special problem areas such as a skid row or a street of taverns is essential.

SMALLER CITIES

In smaller cities the police department will usually occupy one section of a civic center or a single building that houses all city departments. When police facilities are located in the same building as the city hall and fire depart-

ment, particular care should be taken to see that the portion devoted to the police department is separate so that the public can enter other departments without passing through the police area. A typical layout might have all administrative entrances on one side, those to the fire department on another side, and those to the police department on yet a third side.

Planning a small city police station is more a matter of interior architectural arrangement and will not be discussed here at length. It should, however, be emphasized that the interior should be carefully planned as most small cities have a limited number of personnel and the layout should enable them to operate the station efficiently.

LARGER CITIES

In larger cities the police station may or may not be attached to a civic center. If the police department is in the city hall or civic center, problems may occur if the location is not separate from the administrative offices. The prisoner entrance should be separated from the public entrance; in addition, any possible noise from the jail must not be permitted to reach other portions of the building. If possible, it is preferable to have the police department at a separate location or so placed that the business of the police department does not interfere with other governmental operations.

The larger city is confronted with a far more complex police problem than the smaller town. The central police facility in a larger city must cater to many more functions. In a New Orleans study[9] the central police facility was required to accommodate the following functions: an administration building to house police operations, administration and service divisions; a central lock-up for the temporary detention of prisoners; a police department house of detention to house longer-term prisoners; a garage for the police, court, and employees; public parking; a maintenance garage for police vehicles; and space for traffic and municipal courts. It was decided that pounds for abandoned, stolen, and impounded cars could not be provided at the central site.

[8] The "standard" reference is: University of Washington, Bureau of Governmental Research and Services, *Police Stations—Planning and Specifications,* Report No. 128 (Seattle: The Bureau, 1954). Also see O. W. Wilson, POLICE PLANNING (Springfield, Ill.: Charles C Thomas, 1958).

[9] New Orleans City Planning Commission, *Public Buildings Report No. 1—Central Police Facilities* (New Orleans: The Commission, 1960).

The planning of district stations may provide an opportunity for the planning agency to be helpful to the police department. Studies of population growth and density, the location of major commercial centers, and major streets should be studied in conjunction with crime and accident statistics. The New Orleans study pointed out those areas of the city that were experiencing the greatest population growth with new development. In addition, residential densities and crime rates were studied. (Obviously, high crime rates are related to many other factors.) The planning department pointed out that crime rates did not necessarily increase in high rise areas but rather in areas where there was a combination of high density low buildings, with high land coverage. The high crime rate was also associated with low personal income levels and was found in commercial centers and older sections of the city, a pattern quite typical for large cities. With the exception of isolated industrial centers, housing projects, and large commercial centers, the crime rate generally decreased with distance from the core of the city, as population density decreased. The lowest crime rates were found in the newly developed outlying areas.

Crime statistics were mapped and showed two interesting features. When the address of the arrestee was checked with the location of the offense, it was found that although the greatest percentage of both offenses and residences of persons arrested were found to be in the central city, offenses were committed also in the new outlying residential areas. These were far in excess of the number of apprehended persons residing there. Thus, in planning police facilities not only must the central business district and the surrounding area be kept under close surveillance at all times, but outlying residential areas must also receive a high level of police protection.

Using the collected data and comparing it with existing precincts the New Orleans study established some rough guidelines for setting standards for the optimum operation of districts and district headquarters.

No absolute population or density figure could be used in establishing the area for a police district. However, it was determined that high density residential areas with mixed industrial and commercial uses could be policed only in small sections, while low density residential areas with neighborhood type commercial centers could be policed in larger sections. The New Orleans study recommended that, as a rough guide, a density of up to 25 persons per acre should have a police area of between 5,000 and 10,000 acres. With population densities of above 25 persons per acre the area for a police district should be between 2,000 and 5,000 acres.

A district should comprise, if possible, a homogeneous area, unbroken by impassable barriers such as expressways, railroads, or rivers that provide natural barriers. In addition, a district should have convenient major street access throughout the area.

The district headquarters should be near the geographic center of the service area; on a major street with good access to all parts of the service area; near concentrations of commercial and industrial uses and the highest crime rate; preferably not in residential areas, but adjacent to a commercial area; and district headquarters should emphasize administration and service to the public rather than the long-term incarceration of prisoners.

Municipal Garages and Yards

Planning agencies can assist municipal public works departments in planning the extent and location of municipal garages and yards[10] thereby contributing to the efficient management of maintenance and public works functions. Municipal garages and storage yards provide space for the storage and maintenance of equipment and supplies used in refuse collection and disposal, street cleaning, street maintenance and construction, sewer maintenance, street lighting, street signs and traffic devices, and other housekeeping functions. Of-

---

[10] For detailed case study examples and additional sources of information see The American Public Works Association, Committee on Equipment, PUBLIC WORKS EQUIPMENT MANAGEMENT (Chicago: Public Administration Service, 1964) .

fice space for these functions may also be provided.

Municipal garages and yards are also used for equipment maintenance and repair. The average city has police cars, trucks, jeeps, mechanical sweepers, snow blowers and plows, rollers, tractors, ambulances, and other vehicles that need maintenance and repair.

The size and kind of garage and yard facilities depend largely upon the city's size and services. No exact standards have been developed, but many cities have conducted studies that would be helpful to the planning agency.

For the smaller city a single garage and yard facility is probably the most economical. Maintenance services may be duplicated with scattered locations which may have small sites that are difficult to expand.

The larger city or county has a problem of a different dimension. With expanding services and a growing geographic area, running times for vehicles and employee travel increase and operations become uneconomical. The solution is often found in a systematic decentralization of facilities in order to create a system of garage, yard, and maintenance facilities.[11]

One example of planning a decentralized system is found in a Phoenix study.[12] The city was faced with the problem of overcoming increased service costs because of the growth in population, geographic area, and decreasing population densities that resulted in increasing operating costs. The original municipal service facility was geared to a smaller population with compact distribution. By 1963 service crews had to travel up to 15 miles from the central yard to reach job locations. The result was a substantial accumulation of nonproductive man-hours and in-transit equipment expenses. When a vehicle broke down it had to be taken back to the central yard for repair. The decision was made that garages and yards nearer to job areas would be built.

One of the first steps in planning a city-wide

system of service facilities is to study existing decentralized operations. (The issue of decentralization must of course be considered first. In Phoenix there was already a degree of decentralization, and the problem was to make adjustments in the existing situation and plan for additional service centers.) The study found 20 separate locations used by five major municipal divisions: building inspection, water production, water distribution, street maintenance and sanitation, and police. In addition, three locations of the street maintenance and sanitation division had shared facilities with the department of parks, water, and fire.

The basic purpose of the Phoenix plan was to create a few, strategically located service facilities. Each center would serve as a decentralized base for the joint use of different city agencies. Existing yard facilities would be consolidated into the new combined centers and several other municipal divisions, now located only in the downtown area, could initiate their own decentralized programs.

Each regional center would be scaled to the present and future needs of each division. Space would be included for offices, assembly areas, equipment and material storage, employee and vehicle parking, and routine mechanical service facilities. A mechanical maintenance shop could not be provided at every existing small service yard. Through the combined centers, however, a fleet of vehicles large enough to provide demand for services would justify a maintenance shop.

The Phoenix study differentiated a "public contact" from a "nonpublic contact" type of service. Public contact services are those that deal directly with the citizen, such as issuing building permits and business licenses, and other face-to-face services. The other type of service does not involve personal contact. The first type is discussed elsewhere in this chapter and the second, including services such as garbage collection, street maintenance, and water line maintenance, are functions that are carried out without public contact and are based in municipal service centers. The two kinds of municipal services have different locational requirements. While one may be located anywhere where offices are permitted, the latter

[11] See Phoenix City Planning Department, A PLAN FOR REGIONAL SERVICE FACILITIES (Phoenix: The Department, 1963) and Roanoke Department of City Planning, MUNICIPAL OFFICES AND SERVICE CENTER (Roanoke: The Department, 1964).

[12] Phoenix City Planning Department, op. cit.

often require a large fleet of trucks and other heavy vehicles and many acres of land for equipment and storage.

Through study and departmental surveys it was determined that the following activities should participate in the regional service centers: engineering, traffic engineering, building inspections, electrical maintenance, street maintenance, mechanical maintenance, sewer and water system maintenance, purchases and storage, and field operations of the police department.

Once it was determined which departments would conduct decentralized operations it was possible to develop some locational and siting criteria. It was determined that a service center should be near the center of an area producing the heaviest, most consistent service demands. Although this point would differ with each department and also change with time, it was assumed that the best location would be near the geographic center of a service district. A modification of the central location would be made in districts where large areas did not contain urban development. In these cases population density was used as a guide. The location would be in an industrial-warehousing type of district because of the need for large truck operation, storage, and repair. In any district in which there was not land already developed for industrial-warehousing types of uses, new buildings would require good architectural design, larger side yards, more landscaping and ground maintenance, and careful traffic control.

The site should be large enough for both present and future needs. The center should be near a major arterial street or the intersection of two arterial streets. With frequent and somewhat slow ingress and egress of trucks, direct access to yards should be from a service road, not from the arterial street. For internal circulation at least two entrances should be provided. The site should also have subsoil and topographic conditions that make for low development costs.

Another important step in planning a system of yards and service centers includes the determination of the sizes and layout of districts that each center would service. In Phoenix it

was determined by analyzing travel time and other similar factors, that the upper limit in district size should be between 45 and 55 square miles, and that a service district of 15 to 20 square miles would be large enough to support a center containing at least some of the basic activities, if not a full range. With a range of standards relating to district size it could be possible to vary standards as a city grows. A single existing service center might handle newly annexed areas as they grow; then when these areas become large enough they could each support a service district and center. The older district would then revert to its former size and the new district absorb subsequent growth.

In determining the boundaries of districts, expressway location was the most significant factor. Although an expressway is a barrier to vehicles that must cross it, it can also greatly increase the distance that a vehicle can travel along it in a given time, compared with a similar stretch of arterial street. Ultimately, the service center operation would gain the maximum benefit from having access to the expressways; thus each district would have an expressway through it or as near to its median as possible.

After a district plan was adopted in Phoenix, size estimates for the service centers were made. These estimates were obtained by taking a detailed survey of each department that was to be decentralized. Each department completed a questionnaire on estimates of space required by both employees and vehicles for offices, employee parking, city vehicle parking, shop facilities, open and enclosed employee assembly areas, and open and enclosed equipment and material storage areas. To ensure consistency in growth projections, the planning department provided each department with a map of the proposed district boundaries and a chart showing the area in square miles and a 20-year population projection for each district in the community.

The final step in the process of planning for a city-wide system of garages, yards and service centers is an analysis of specific sites, to determine how they meet locational and site requirements, how much they will cost to develop, and their final cost complete with buildings and facilities.

The detailed planning of a garage site and its interior is largely an architectural problem that must be worked out in close cooperation with the architect and the department heads most familiar with the function and operation of their own departments. However, the gathering of basic data on space estimates and location as well as participation in policy-making at a higher level make the contribution of the planning agency an important one.

Cemeteries and Crematories

Few people would deny that the reservation of areas for the interment of the dead is an important facility which must be provided in any community. It should be regarded as a community responsibility in the same way as provision of water and an adequate sewerage and drainage system, all of which, of course, also have a bearing on public health.

Cemeteries, or burial grounds, are provided and administered in various ways. They may be provided as an adjunct to a church, particularly in older communities; they may be provided and run by the community as a public service; or they may be provided by private enterprise and run as a business through a cemetery association. Some small private cemeteries also exist.

Similar factors are present for each type of cemetery: suitable land must be provided, the land must be developed to make it suitable for a cemetery, a staff must be available for interment and general maintenance, and an administrative organization must be set up to operate the facility.

The administrative responsibility for management of a cemetery has no defined duration, for once a cemetery is located, it is rarely moved. The problem of general perpetual care must be faced, together with the more particular responsibility of the perpetual care of specific plots. Where a burial ground is under the control of local government, it is assumed that this will be for all time, and no particular problems arise that differ appreciably from those involved in other functional responsibilities. A similar situation obtains in the case of a church cemetery administered by church officials.

In the case of cemeteries run as a private enterprise, special problems arise as far as public responsibility is concerned. The enterprise, which may be a partnership or association, has a partial, if not complete, monopoly in its operations, and in turn has an obligation to perform its services to the public in a proper manner. In the case of perpetual care, monies paid for the continuous upkeep of a grave must be properly applied, and a special responsibility is placed on the management. In many ways a cemetery association is similar to a utility company, and its special role is reflected in the regulations enforced in most states to protect the public welfare.

As far as the planner is concerned, the extent and location of land to be reserved for burial purposes will be his prime considerations. The area of land required may be calculated by the application of appropriate standards to be found in references such as those cited in the Selected Bibliography. The suitability of the terrain for interment involves considerations of an engineering character, such as the nature of the subsoil, drainage, proximity to community water sources, accessibility, and other similar practical factors. It is in the location of the area to be used as a cemetery that the main planning problems lie.

Many normal persons do not like to face the fact of death, or to be reminded of it. It follows that this feeling of repugnance will be reflected in a disinclination to live in the vicinity of a cemetery, and this may not be influenced by the particular esthetic qualities imparted by landscaping.

In planning for cemeteries it must be recognized that not only will a considerable area of land be used for the purpose, but that it will probably be so used in perpetuity, for once reserved, burial grounds are rarely moved due both to the practical and to the legal difficulties involved. It would also be reasonable to assume that residential development will not take place in the immediate vicinity.

A cemetery should thus be related to the size

of the present and future population, in terms of area, and should be placed in an accessible location, having suitable physical characteristics. It should not be placed where residential development is desired, although it can be provided in conjunction with parks, recreational facilities and airports. Room for expansion should, of course, be provided as required.

Cremation is more popular in some parts of the country than in others. Due to the relatively small number of cremations carried out as compared with normal burial, the location of the requisite facilities assumes a regional significance, and whether provided by private enterprise, or by the public, would have to be assured of adequate support to justify the expense involved in the provision of the appropriate site, buildings, and special equipment.

Crematories are often run in conjunction with a normal cemetery operation, and similar problems are encountered in their location. The area of land required is, of course, far less for cremation than for traditional burial, and the mounting pressure for the more economical use of land in some areas may influence the popularity of this operation in the future. The whole question of the disposal of the dead is, however, surrounded by religious custom and sentiment, and no provisions should be made by the planner which assume a dramatic change in community customs unless good evidence for this is available.

Water and Sewer Systems

Sewer and water system planning is an engineering problem, and most systems are designed by engineers. Planning agencies play only a small part in the detailed technical aspects, but they play an extremely important role in general policy planning—unfortunately, often neglected. The planning agency can contribute to the conduct of any sewer and water study by providing basic information to the engineer and by helping to make utility plans useful implementation devices that will guide urban growth patterns.

WATER

Water planning is a well-developed branch of the engineering sciences and the planner must rely on the professional for technical advice. However, the fundamental aspects of water supply should be understood and the engineering texts on water supply listed in the Selected Bibliography should be consulted for more detailed information.

Water Sources and Supply. The primary sources of water are rivers, lakes, springs, and subsurface supplies. Geographical and geological conditions will dictate both availability and supply. The United States Geological Survey and state water departments are often able to furnish valuable data. In rural and some suburban areas individual wells provide water for residences; however, with increased population densities supplies may become inadequate or unsafe. In many metropolitan areas underground sources of water are being contaminated by inefficient methods of sewage disposal. Water tables are falling because of the decreasing amount of water being returned to the soil through land now covered with streets, rooftops and parking lots.

Because streams and other sources of water seldom bear any relationship to municipal boundaries, water resource planning is a function best carried out at the metropolitan or regional level. Regional water studies, gross quantities available, and the location of water resources, are determined and compared with urban growth and future needs. Although some metropolitan areas located in semiarid regions have long known the importance of proper water resource planning, it is interesting to note that some older metropolitan areas along the eastern seaboard experienced water shortages during the mid 1960s.

Quantity. Demand for water is related directly to population and is typically expressed as gallons per capita per day (gpcd). Per capita consumption varies from the small predominantly residential suburb with a consumption of no more than 40 gpcd, to the large city with extensive industry that consumes up to 250 gpcd. An average for all communities is about 150 gpcd. Demand averages also include commercial and industrial uses, and fire fighting and street cleaning requirements; the latter uses are likely to create the major demand and must be studied closely. Probable peak hour demands must also be examined. This amount is generally controlled by the peak domestic demand plus "fire flow"—the water used in fighting a major fire. (See section on Fire Station Location earlier in this chapter.) Peak hourly rates may vary substantially (up to six times the average daily rate) [13] and storage and distribution systems must be designed to handle such peaks demands.

Treatment. Water should be free from bacteriological or other contamination; clear, colorless, odorless, and pleasant to the taste; and contain a moderate amount of soluble mineral substances. The amount and character of treatment will vary with the source and quality of the water. The character of the water will also dictate whether solids must be removed by filtration and whether tastes and odors must also be removed. Nearly all public water supplies are protected against bacteriological contamination by chlorination or other processes.

Planning agencies will have little if anything to do with water treatment, except insofar as they may make suggestions or studies concerning the proper location of a treatment plant.

Collection and Distribution Systems. There are three types of collection and distribution systems: the gravity system, in which the source is at an elevation above the community sufficiently high that adequate pressure is directly available; the distributing reservoir system, whereby water is pumped to a reservoir whose elevation enables the water to flow by gravity through the main; and the direct pressure system, wherein water is pumped directly into the main. Most large municipal systems are combinations of each.

Unless water is taken directly from a river or lake, major metropolitan areas usually have impounding reservoirs. The protection of these reservoirs is extremely important and scattered residential development with inefficient septic

tank disposal systems should be prevented from contaminating them. If reservoirs are planned in conjunction with park and recreation systems it is possible to have a multiple-use facility where picnicking, boating, fishing, and even bathing may be conducted under controlled circumstances.

Water from impounding reservoirs, holding several months' supply, is carried in large viaducts to distributing reservoirs close to or within the city. The distributing reservoir holds enough water to take care of daily variations and holds a reserve of water for fire fighting and other emergencies. These reservoirs may be either closed standpipes or open ponds; and if the latter, may be developed in park and recreation areas. A third type of reservoir is the elevated storage tank that assures uniform water pressure, provides for hourly variations in demand, and supplies water to tall buildings or higher portions of the city.

The distribution system, which carries the water from the reservoirs or pumping stations to users, consists of a network of underground pipes following, in general, the street network. Since water is under pressure, water lines can be laid up hill and down, following topography as desired. Water lines are laid at a depth sufficient to protect against frost damage. The minimum size of pipes is usually set by fire protection requirements.

A good distribution system should provide an adequate quantity at adequate pressure. The distribution system is a network with ample connections between mains, with duplicate mains between the source of supply and the distribution system, and duplicate units and alternate sources of water for pumping installations together with other standard precautionary measures. A well designed water system will keep to a minimum the number of dead-end pipe lines in order to assure proper circulation of water. Valves will be provided at strategic locations so that service will be interrupted in only a small area in the event of a breakdown.

Water mains that serve as trunk lines will vary in size depending upon the service area and the water demands of users (e.g., an area served by a high water-using industry versus a

[13] Kenneth J. Carl, "Fire Protection, paper presented at panel discussion on Extension of Public Services to Suburban Areas," JOURNAL AMERICAN WATER WORKS ASSOCIATION, LXVII (October, 1955), p. 965.

typical residential area); most residential areas are served by 6- or 8-inch mains.

Water for Industry. As a result of advances in technology, industry has become much more independent of specific site facilities and often enjoys a wide range of choice when seeking a location for a new plant. Very often the desirability of the community as a place to work and live becomes a most important factor, in which case the range of community facilities available comes under review, together with civic attitudes and the progressiveness of the local governing body.

Some facilities such as sanitary sewers, storm water sewers, and water supply are essential, and among these water holds a high place. An adequate supply of water, both in quantity and quality, is often a key factor in industrial location together with the cost at which such supply can be obtained.

The quantity of water required for different industrial processes varies greatly, and sometimes the availability of independent sources of supply from rivers, streams, or ground water, and the ability to discharge treated process water into public streams are significant locational considerations.

Some industries, such as steel mills, oil refineries, paper mills, and chemicals, use large quantities of water both for cooling and processing, and need to be located near a large, reliable source of supply. Frequently, accurate information on the amount of water consumed by various industries is not readily available unless it has all been supplied by a local utility company. In the absence of accurate figures a table of industrial water requirements similar to that indicated in Table 8–5 forms a useful reference.

The quality of water required for industry is, in general terms, the same as that required for domestic use, but for certain specialized industries these requirements should be ascertained by referring to an appropriate engineering source book such as *Elements of Water Supply and Waste-water Disposal* by Fair and Geyer, listed in the Selected Bibliography. The requirements for cooling water will not, of course, be so stringent as those for water used in specialized manufacturing processes.

Table 8–5

Industrial Water Requirements

Type of Establishment	Gallons of Water	Per Unit
Breweries	470	Barrel of beer
Laundries	4.3–5.7	Pound of "work"
Canneries		
Grapefruit juice	5	Case of No. 2 cans
Peas	25	Case of No. 2 cans
Spinach	160	Case of No. 2 cans
Coke	3600	Ton of coke
Gasoline	7–10	Gallon of product
Meat-packing plant	5.5	Hog killed
Meat slaughter house	5.5	Hog killed
General dairy	0.34	Pound of raw milk
Oil field	180	Barrel of crude
Oil refinery	770	Barrel of crude
Paper mill	14,000–39,000	Ton of product
Pulp mill, chemical	60,000–85,000	Ton of product
Textiles		
cotton sizing	0.8	Pound processed
bleaching	0.3	Pound processed
dyeing	4.8–19	Pound processed
woolens	70	Pound processed

Source: JOURNAL OF THE AMERICAN WATER WORKS ASSOCIATION, January, 1946.

SANITARY AND STORM SEWERS

A sewerage system is a network of drains and sewers used to collect the liquid and solid wastes of a city for subsequent treatment or disposal. Sanitary sewers collect sewage from the plumbing systems of buildings and carry it to a sewage treatment plant. Storm sewers are used to collect and carry rain or surface water to some natural water course or body of water in such a way as to prevent flooding. In a sense, storm sewers are artificial watercourses. At times, particularly in older cities, sanitary and storm sewers are combined into one system.

Sanitary Sewers. Sanitary sewage is collected from individual buildings by a network of sewers, including the building sewer (called the house connection), lateral or street sewers, branch or trunk sewers, and finally, main or interceptor sewers. The size of each type of sewer depends on the anticipated load it must carry. Ordinarily, planning agencies are concerned only with the location and capacity of main sewers and treatment plants, since these represent upper limits placed upon the density of development.

While there are no set rules on population density, it is a general practice to consider the installation of sewerage when land is subdivided into lots of less than one acre. The quantity of sewage is generally a direct function of the quantity of water consumed. Lateral sewers are designed on the assumption that the area served will be fully built-up. The design of main sewers should be related to land use and to population projections for the tributary area for 25 years or more. Per capita sewage flows per day vary widely from community to community, due to differences in population, population density, industrial development, the numbers of hotels and apartment buildings, the size of residential lots and the per capita water consumption.

Sewage is collected by a gravity flow system, in contrast to pressurized water distribution systems. Sewers must be so laid out as to flow continually down hill so that the lines will quickly concentrate the flow in the valleys and thereafter follow the trend of the valleys to the end of the system. In flat cities pumping may be necessary at some points, or when the crest of a drainage basin is crossed.

Sewerage problems vary with the size of the city, but increase in complexity much faster than the size of the city. The small town produces only a small amount of sewage, which may not have to be conveyed any great distance. Large city systems have continuous lines which may run ten or twenty miles. The sewage, if not adequately treated, might pollute watercourses. The problem is further complicated by liquid wastes from industries, discharged into the municipal sewerage system. In some cities industrial wastes can constitute over 50 per cent of the sewage treatment load.

In planning a sewerage system many technical phases of the work are pure engineering problems and can be left to an experienced sanitary engineer; however, the planner or public administrator can participate in formulating questions and issues that must be re-solved. In addition to the problem of shaping urban growth, which will be discussed later, other questions might include:

1. What is the present type of system and should it be continued or changed? What are the respective advantages of combined and separate systems? If a change is necessary, what are the long-range implications?

2. In presently developed areas of the city will population increases in number or density require additional sewer capacity?

3. How does local topography affect sanitary sewer construction?

4. How thoroughly is the present sewage treated?

5. Are there any special industrial waste problems?

6. How do sewers relate to the other utilities in the public streets? (In large cities this is a complicated, technical problem.)

7. What are the financial implications of sewage plants? What about costs of operation and maintenance of the system?

Perhaps one of the most difficult decisions that must be made is whether to combine or separate sanitary and storm sewer systems. In the 19th century most large cities provided culverts for storm drainage, but did not treat their sewage. However, as sewage treatment became necessary, cities began to use the same systems for both purposes. The result is that often treatment plants must handle storm water and thus increase costs. In addition, when heavy rainstorms occur, sanitary sewage may back up into buildings causing serious health problems as well as inconvenience. Where it is financially feasible, a city should attempt to develop separate sanitary and storm sewer systems.

Sewers must ultimately discharge at a plant, or plants, whose purpose is to render the sewage innocuous. Sewage is usually organic in nature and therefore may be processed by decomposition, utilizing the oxygen present in the carrying water. The strength of raw (untreated) sewage is indicated by its biochemical oxygen demand, this being an indirect measure of the decomposable matter to be treated.

Sewage reaching a treatment plant is most complex in its composition in a large industrial area, for instead of containing purely organic substances, it will also contain grease, oil, chemicals, including varying quantities of detergents, and other nonorganic ingredients. Treatment consists of various steps aimed at separating out the various constituents into solids and liquids, and rendering them harmless. The liquids can then be discharged into rivers or streams via outfall sewers when the required degree of purity has been attained. The solids are first obtained in the form of sludge, the disposal of which presents the most difficult problem in the complete treatment process.

Sludge has considerable bulk due to its high water volume and has a high organic content. Digestion, or decomposition by bacteria, is accompanied by the production of gases, some of which are combustible and may be used for plant lighting or treatment purposes. Digested and dried sludge may be disposed of in landfill operations, or it may be used as a fertilizer if possessing suitable qualities. Sludge can also be incinerated, before or after drying, and the residue used for landfill purposes.

Treatment plants often require the use of extensive land areas, not only for the active parts of the plant, but also for the ancillary sludge drying beds and sanitary landfill areas. If properly designed and operated, the plants need not constitute a nuisance; however, considerable prejudice exists on the part of the public toward them, and this makes the location of treatment plants of particular importance to the planner.

In addition to the reservation of an appropriate area of land for the plant or plants, the effect upon the residential development of adjacent land and the recreational potential of rivers and other bodies of water, should be considered. The fact that development is likely to be inhibited in the general area of the plant, as it is in the area of refuse disposal sites often presents a problem in location which should be considered in relation to its effect upon the complete pattern of land uses desired for the whole community.

Storm Sewers. A dilemma in planning a storm sewer system for a drainage area is that it has to be done in reverse. If main trunk lines could be installed last—after an area is fully built-up and the necessary local and collector drains installed—there would be little doubt about size, design, location, or financing. In practice, however, the trunks must be in place first, to receive the discharge from a local system; otherwise damage to downstream property will inevitably occur.

Because a storm sewer system is actually a replacement for a natural drainage system, the concept of a drainage area is used. The terms "drainage area" or "drainage basin" are used interchangeably with "watershed." The watershed of a river or stream is composed of the many smaller watersheds of its tributaries. When urban development occurs the natural drainage is disturbed. Before development, water strikes the land surface and is absorbed, and some water penetrates to underground layers (infiltration). With heavy rainfall, the absorption and infiltration process does not absorb all of the water. The remaining water runs along the surface of the ground directly into creeks and rivers and is called "surface run-off."

But with urban development, former forests and natural open areas are replaced by roofs, sidewalks, parking lots, and paved streets. The porous surfaces are sealed and the hydrological cycle as it formerly operated is changed substantially. Much of the water that would have been absorbed runs on the impervious surface of the ground; thus, curbs and gutters, storm drains, retention basins and other facilities must be built.

Hydrologists and engineers have devised various formulae for computing the amount of run-off. Table 8–6 is an example that was prepared by the San Antonio (Texas) Department of Public Works.

The results shown in Table 8–6 should not be used blindly without local study. Although a run-off characteristic can be computed for a small subdivision, the problem becomes exceedingly complex in an entire drainage basin with various kinds of conditions and various kinds of storm drainage structures to be taken into account.

Although the planning of a storm drainage system is complex, a number of suggested steps can be taken. Obviously, these do not reflect the amount of detailed engineering and statistical analysis that must be made before a plan is completed. The steps are as follows:

1. *Determine boundaries and areas of watersheds.* This information can be determined from topographic maps.

2. *Compile data on storm and flood frequency.* This information is essential to determine the "design frequency" for trunk storm drainage facilities. Thus, if a system is designed so that it handles a five-year storm interval the storm sewer will operate at capacity once every five years. The bigger storm, which may occur once every ten years, will cause flooding because the storm drainage system, designed for a five-year storm, cannot handle it. Determining the proper interval is extremely difficult and requires the advice of an expert hydrologist. Naturally, the economic implications of various designs may help to determine the proper choice.

3. *Map soil characteristics in the drainage basin.* The Soil Conservation Service of the United States Department of Agriculture, as well as state agricultural colleges have made soil surveys in nearly every state. Soils vary in their drainage characteristics and these characteristics must be known in order to calculate the rate of run-off.

4. *Estimate future growth in density of population within each drainage area.* The comprehensive plan can be useful at this point if it goes into sufficient detail.

5. *Collect and map existing facilities and determine new trunk sewer construction needed.* To adequately handle total run-off from tributary watersheds, several trunk lines may be necessary.

6. *Plan new trunk line construction needed both in built-up and new areas.* Locations, relation to existing drainage facilities, and a schedule of recommended priorities should be indicated.

With proper advance planning a considerable amount of money can be saved if natural stream channels are used to the maximum. If these channels can be preserved, the total cost of a drainage system can be decreased since large trunk sewers are the most expensive to construct. If water courses can be acquired, including the lands along the banks to a considerable width, and can be improved, then the development can become an aesthetic asset and also function as a buffer between neighborhoods and various kinds of land uses. However, the lands should be developed and maintained so they are not mistreated by the public to

Table 8–6
Per Cent of Storm Water Runoff by Types of Development*

Character of area	Average slope			
	Up to 1%	1 to 3%	3 to 5%	Over 5%
Businesses or commercial area (90% or more impervious)	95	96	97	97
Densely developed area (80 to 90% impervious)	85	88	91	95
Closely built residential area	75	77	80	84
Undeveloped area	68	70	72	75
Average residential area	65	67	69	72

Source: Prepared by the San Antonio, Texas, Department of Public Works; International City Managers' Association, PLANNING AND FINANCING STORM SEWERS, Management Information Service Report No. 171, (Chicago: The Association, April, 1958), p. 4.

* In all cases, wet antecedent conditions shall be assumed. Runoff rates shall be computed on the basis of ultimate development of the entire watershed contributing runoff water to the proposed subdivision. For determination of time of concentration, velocities shall be assumed on the basis of concrete lined channels and streets carrying storm waters in the contributing watershed area. Rainfall intensities shall be obtained from Figure X [a graph showing the value of i for various durations and frequencies].

become dumps and eventual serious threats to public health.

THE ROLE OF THE PLANNING AGENCY

Traditionally, water and sewage system planning has been treated merely as an engineering problem with only a token effort being made to shape urban growth patterns. The typical pattern has been to provide for past, unmet needs and to extrapolate present development trends; little attention has been paid to alternative policies concerning design, location, and timing of utility systems to guide new growth in a predetermined direction. What has been known intuitively for some time has been substantiated by research: that the provision of utilities often acts as a triggering device influencing the direction and rate of land development.[14]

In recent years a great deal of research and general discussion has taken place on the development patterns of metropolitan areas and on the service and financial implications of various kinds of growth. Urban areas can develop in a number of ways, compact, or in patterns that are sprawled, scattered, linear, or nucleated. There are variations of each of these patterns, and each involves different physical problems. For example, much has been written about urban sprawl and the resulting waste and duplication in the provision of highways, water systems and other community facilities.

The planning agency can analyze local development patterns and ascertain the implications for utility patterns. Other public facilities such as transportation and open space will also influence the direction that a community wishes to take, but water and sewer plans are powerful tools to implement chosen development policies.

A planning agency may or may not have staff participating in the actual conduct of the study. The most important function the agency can perform is to make recommendations at a higher *policy* level. No water or sewer study

should be carried out without the active participation of the agency. If there is an advisory committee connected with the study, the planning agency should be represented. If it has personnel working on the study, work elements should include growth and development problems as they relate to the utility systems, as well as to proposed development policies. Even if no technical personnel are involved in the study, it should be considered incomplete until the planning agency has had an opportunity to comment in detail on the urban development implications.

The agency should formulate and recommend policies that will implement particular land development decisions. For example, a recent hypothetical example considered alternative policies for the placement of treatment plants, the timing and location of distribution and collection systems, and the policies for the extension or withholding of services for a nucleated urban development pattern and for an alternative stellate development pattern. In broad outline the hypothetical policies examined for these two patterns of land development were as follows:

(A) *Nucleated.* Under this approach, it would be a firm policy that land development would be closely related to a series of 'utility cores' and their service areas at pre-determined locations and with fixed capacities. Optimal limits on the expansion of existing systems would be determined, and as capacities of these systems were reached, new cores would be established. No utility services would be provided except in the pre-determined service areas of these cores under established development-timing criteria.

(B) *Stellate.* In recognition of the propensity of land development to fan out into the countryside from central areas, this approach calls for channeling this growth into one central service area and a system of radial utility corridors at pre-determined locations and of limited capacities. After adoption of an integrated utility plan for cities of the defined region, a 'utility service line' would be established beyond which service would be provided only in pre-determined corridors and according to established timing criteria.[15]

[14] F. Stuart Chapin, Jr. and Shirley F. Weiss (eds.), URBAN GROWTH DYNAMICS IN A REGIONAL CLUSTER OF CITIES (New York: John Wiley and Sons, Inc., 1962), Chapter 13.

[15] *Ibid.*, pp. 450–54.

There are, of course, a very large number of types and variations of urban development patterns and of policies that might be adopted to implement them. In essence, each policy would be geared to the development pattern chosen and would mean that utilities would be constructed *in advance* of actual need, coupled with a refusal to extend them in directions or patterns not in accordance with the adopted overall policy.

Also, as a practical matter, utility extension policy would also be related to the operational level of municipal management. For example, the planning agency could participate in formulating decisions as to the provisions required of subdividers, the method of financing to be employed, the capacity of utilities, and other policy matters.

Location of Underground Utilities

It would seem reasonable to assume that if a system of underground utilities exists, then a plan of the system should be available; however, this is not always the case. The principal underground utilities are water, sewers, gas, telephone, and electric power.

If accurate plans of all underground utilities are available, many advantages are gained. The first, of course, is that the private or public agency responsible for a particular utility will be able to locate all sections of the supply lines at will, thus enabling repairs, extensions and renewals to be carried out expeditiously. In addition to saving time, disturbance of the road or sidewalk surface is kept to a minimum. The second advantage is that the various agencies are enabled to coordinate operations so that interruption of vehicular or pedestrian traffic may be minimized, and costs reduced through economies in excavation. The third is that utility agencies are able to coordinate their activities with the department responsible for street repair and construction, thus insuring that the street surface will be disturbed to the minimum extent necessary.

If the locations of existing utility lines are known, it becomes possible to formulate plans for their extension, alteration, and renewal in an organized manner. Plans indicating the location of underground utilities are properly the concern of the planner and should become a part of every comprehensive community plan.

Although the supply of information necessary to prepare such plans would be the responsibility of the utility agencies concerned, the initiative for such preparation might well come from the planning agency. This might be accomplished by suggesting the formation of a joint advisory committee comprised of appropriate representatives of each public or private enterprise agency responsible for a utility, and of those responsible for street improvements.

Work would commence by the assembly of existing information and by the institution of surveys required to update this to give a true record of existing conditions. The joint committee could then exchange information on proposals for future extensions, alterations, or improvements of the existing utilities, at which time the planning agency might discuss how utilities might be provided in furtherance of proposed policies relative to the community plan.

Such a joint advisory committee would be a valuable addition to local government resources and could continue on a permanent basis, meeting regularly to exchange information on street and utility programs and problems. If properly organized and administered under local government aegis such a group could be of great mutual benefit, an incentive which would rebound to community advantage.

Gas Distribution Systems

Gas is delivered to consumers mainly for heating purposes under uniform but comparatively low pressures. Gas lines can follow the topography but are usually laid with a slight gradient to allow for the drainage of water caused by condensation.

Gas may be of two main types: coal and

coke-oven gases, which are usually locally produced and stored; and natural gas, which is transported considerable distances through high pressure lines. Other types of gases, such as water gas, producer gas, and blast-furnace gas, are produced and used in industrial installations.

In most areas natural gas has superseded manufactured gas, but some plants still exist on either a full-time or emergency basis. Many industries use natural gas in manufacturing processes and constitute the largest volume consumer group.

In the past, single gas mains were often laid in the center of streets, but the modern practice is to lay two mains, one on each side of the road in the planting strip next to the curb, or under the sidewalk. Mains are also sometimes laid in rear lot easements where one pipe may serve two rows of houses.

In the case of natural gas, cross-country high pressure gas lines of 24-inch diameter or greater are tapped, and pressure reduced before distribution by the supply company. Gas regulating stations and other control devices are located by the company where required, in accordance with conditions usually specified by the local authority.

Gas manufacturing plants are regulated, together with other industrial establishments by zoning ordinance provisions, so that they are compatible with adjoining land uses. Gas regulating stations are often permitted as special uses in almost all districts. Other special regulations are aimed at appropriate design for safety.

The planner will not be concerned with the engineering aspects of gas supply. He will, however, wish to see that appropriate easements are available for such supply in newly developing areas, and that it can be made available in any area that is scheduled for industrial development to the extent called for by the type of industry that is anticipated.

When a new zoning ordinance is being drafted, or an existing ordinance reviewed, the advice of the planner will be called for in relation to gas installations and the regulations that should be applied to them.

As in the case of other utilities, problems and conflicts can be avoided, or mitigated, through the establishment of a joint advisory committee as discussed above under Location of Underground Utilities.

Steam Distribution Systems

The distribution of steam over large areas in an economical manner presents considerable problems. High pressures and temperatures must be maintained, condensation kept to a minimum, and the mains, which are often surrounded by a housing some five feet square, must be easily accessible, heavily insulated against heat loss, properly supported and well drained.

The system is most suitable where a large number of customers can be served over a concentrated area—namely in the center, or most populated areas of large cities such as New York. Some systems are found in a few small and medium-sized cities, such as Lansing, Michigan, and within building complexes, such as civic centers and university campuses.

Where a new system has to be installed in an existing downtown area, many difficulties present themselves in the form of obstruction by existing water and gas mains; sewers; electric light, power, telephone and telegraph cables; and other subterranean facilities. As the mains are so large, the problem of the relocation of other services is considerable.

In addition to the difficulty and cost of installation, the cost of operation is high and the return on the investment low during the summer months. However, in certain circumstances installations can be run economically.

A study carried out for the city of Wilkes-Barre, Pennsylvania, and published in 1963, indicated that in this city of approximately 65,500 persons (1960), central station steam heat was supplied to 500 customers in the central business district. At that time there were about four miles of underground mains, with the farthest customer about 5,400 feet from the boiler plant. The ratio of commercial to residential consumers was about 3:1 and the heating season from September 15 through May 31, with adjustments for exceptional weather conditions.

Increases in supply rates are controlled by the Pennsylvania Public Utilities Commission and an additional adjustment is permitted in respect of fluctuation in fuel costs.

New service connections are installed by the company, the customer being billed for that section between the curb line and the basement. Defective lines are replaced in the same manner. At the time the report was written no definite plans had been made to enlarge the service area, but consideration was being given to increasing the boiler plant capacity in the event of renewal in the future.

Electric Power Systems

The typical power system consists of six vital elements: a power station which changes prime energy into electrical energy; transformers to raise the generated energy to the high potential required for economical passage through primary transmission lines; the transmission lines; the substations where the power is reduced to the potential used in secondary transmission lines; the secondary transmission lines; and the transformers which again reduce the secondary potential to the voltage used by the consumer. This latter action is often performed by transformers affixed to transmission poles.

A generating station contains a prime mover, such as a water or steam turbine, diesel or other internal combustion plant; this drives an electric generator. In 1959, approximately 78 per cent of the electric power produced in the United States was generated in steam plants. Another 20 per cent was produced by hydroelectric (water turbine) plants, the balance being generated by other means. In the future, other forms of motive power will undoubtedly be employed. Some nuclear power plants already exist, wherein a nuclear reactor replaces the conventional furnace, the generated heat being used to produce steam, which then drives a conventional turbine. Due to the necessity for technical development to overcome problems of shielding and control, nuclear power plants are not yet serious competitors to other forms of power production, but the time is not far removed when they will slowly replace established conventional methods.

The planner is not, of course, primarily concerned with the engineering aspects of power production and transmission. His concern is to see that appropriate service is available to all parts of the community without conflicting with other existing or planned land uses. In regard to primary transmission, he will want to know the exact location of proposed steel lattice towers in relation to proposed airfields and other development which might be injuriously affected by their presence. He will want to see that appropriate easement reservations are made in new developments so that secondary transmission lines are made as unobtrusive as possible, with full access for servicing and repair. In other areas he will want to negotiate with the power supply company (whether public or private) to insure that new cables are laid underground, or that old overhead lines are converted to underground cables in accordance with an agreed program.

Other actions might be concerned with public safety and convenience. This would arise in connection with advising on the provisions of a new zoning ordinance, or the adequacy of an existing one. In addition to the position of the primary generating station, the location of substations and other required equipment would be considered.

The prevention of air pollution is another area in which the planner might find himself concerned with the performance of a local generating station, particularly if steam-operated and guilty of the production of an undue amount of soot, fly ash, and other air pollutants. In the future, the arrival of the near or in-town nuclear power plant will give rise to special problems of public safety, both in regard to general operation and to the periodic disposal of nuclear waste.

Many of the above problems could be reduced, or mitigated, by the existence of a joint advisory committee on utilities, to which reference is made above in the section on Location of Underground Utilities.

Overhead and Underground Utility Wires

Many utilities, such as electric power, telegraph, telephone, fire alarm, and similar systems, have traditionally been carried above ground on poles. In rapidly growing areas such an arrangement lends itself to speed of erection, and thus of supply, and speed of repair and ancillary connection.

In the past, the city planner has been concerned mainly with the location of these utility lines to insure that they are placed in an orderly and consistent manner either in street rights-of-way or in special easements provided at the rear of lots. Subdivision regulations commonly contain provisions which direct the developer to provide rights-of-way in specific locations in new subdivisions. These provisions make for some degree of order and insure that utility companies may obtain access at all times for the purposes of inspection and repair.

Even where overhead wires are placed in easements on rear lot lines it cannot be denied that they are unsightly. Their effect can be held to a minimum by placing several wires in one core, or by running several utilities on common poles, but the problem of unsightly poles, crossbars and wires still remains. When run in street rights-of-way poles and wires are not only unsightly but are hazards in fighting fires and conflict with the proper growth and formation of street trees. Wires on poles are also most susceptible to damage during storms.

The answer both to unsightliness and to vulnerability is, of course, to run utilities underground. This is being done in progressive communities, usually beginning with downtown areas and proceeding on a programmed basis along main thoroughfares and other locations where they may be offensive. Recent federal programs directed toward beautification of town and country have given an impetus to the drive to place utility lines underground. Usually utility companies are willing to cooperate, but the motive power for action must still come from the local level where government should take every reasonable opportunity to insure that the community environment is improved, not deteriorated, by actions over which it has either direct or indirect jurisdiction.

Refuse Disposal

Planning agencies have little to do with municipal refuse collection, but should take an active interest in refuse disposal. Disposal of refuse can have significant effects on the aesthetic, health, and land use characteristics of an urban area. In areas where county or metropolitan planning agencies exist, these agencies should take an active part in planning for refuse disposal needs.

Refuse is defined as the solid wastes of a city, in contrast to liquid wastes (sewage), and is a general term which includes garbage, rubbish, ashes, abandoned automobiles, and industrial refuse.

Planning for refuse disposal, in essence, is a process that begins with a calculation of the amount of refuse generated by a given population. According to the American Public Works Association, the median amount of refuse collected and disposed of in cities is approximately 1,420 pounds per capita per year. Amounts will vary widely depending upon such local conditions as the weather and the use of home incinerators and garbage disposal units; for example, a recent report for the northeastern Illinois metropolitan area estimated that the per capita refuse collected was about 1,000 pounds.[16] The second step is to translate refuse weight into cubic yards since refuse disposal is largely a matter of space allocation. Various methods of refuse disposal, such as (1) on site disposal, (2) swine feeding, (3) open dumping, (4) incineration, (5) composting, and (6) sanitary landfill, must be examined in terms of past local practices. Future estimates of the land area requirements for disposal will then have to be made and com-

---

[16] Northeastern Illinois Metropolitan Planning Commission, REFUSE DISPOSAL NEEDS AND PRACTICES IN NORTHEASTERN ILLINOIS (Chicago: The Commission, 1963), p. 1.

pared with available sites. In addition, the various policy decisions concerning methods of disposal and their desirability for the particular urban area must be made. When these steps are completed, a plan and policies statement can be made and examined in terms of capital expenditures and final execution of the plans.

Although the subject of refuse disposal is broad and somewhat technical, an attempt will be made in the remainder of this chapter to introduce the reader to refuse disposal methods and their implications for urban planning. For further details, sources cited in the Selected Bibliography should be consulted.

ON-SITE DISPOSAL

The typical method of on-site disposal in residential areas is the home incinerator. Unfortunately, most gas-fired or electrically heated refuse burners are often improperly installed and do not function at sufficiently high temperatures to ensure complete combustion; air pollution therefore results. Outdoor fires in wire baskets or drums are particularly bad offenders. Some apartments also contribute to air pollution by operating an "incinerator" as part of a central-heating furnace; as in the case of the home incinerator this method is highly inefficient.

Mechanical grinding units fitted in the kitchen sink are another type of on-site disposal. This method lessens collection, and a few communities have passed ordinances requiring the installation of these devices. If these disposal units operate properly they present no insurmountable problem in the operation of sewage treatment plants.

SWINE FEEDING

At one time swine feeding was a popular and profitable method of garbage disposal. However, various states have enacted laws requiring that garbage fed to swine must be cooked. This has meant the installation of expensive equipment, and thus swine feeding has become insignificant as a method of garbage disposal.

OPEN DUMPING

The open dump is the simplest method of disposal and also the least satisfactory. An open dump is an area where refuse is deposited and allowed to remain exposed to the atmosphere. Dumps form a breeding ground for rodents and flies, and the outbreak of fire at some creates an air pollution problem. Some are also swampy and water-filled and under these circumstances the probability of ground water contamination is high. Both burning refuse and stagnant water cause serious odor and health problems, and in every way the open dump is both undesirable and an unnecessary hazard to public health. In brief, the open dump is a relic of a past era and cannot be considered an acceptable method of refuse disposal today.

INCINERATION

A central incineration operation can reduce substantially the volume of refuse. The resulting residue is inert and can be used for landfill; however, the high initial cost of incinerators is often a deterrent to its wide-spread application. Many early incinerators did not operate efficiently through poor design, slow combustion, and unskilled operators. The economics of incineration require large plants that are efficiently operated. Economies result through a lowering of the volume of refuse that must be used as landfill, and by lower hauling and collection costs.

An incineration plant must be located with great care. It should be in an industrial district and as close as possible to the center of population to be served so that collection costs may be reduced to a minimum. Efficient and highly trained personnel are necessary to prevent odors and air pollution. The location must also have good access since the noise and congestion of collection trucks may be objectionable to adjacent land users. The size of the site needed for an incinerator is not large; for example, a plant of 400 tons per day capacity can be placed on a three acre site. However, a larger site may be necessary if screening is needed or if special provisions have to be made for access or truck storage.

COMPOSTING

Composting is a process whereby refuse is converted into humus, an organic product that is used as an agricultural fertilizer. Although quite widespread as a method of disposal in Europe, composting has not been too popular in the United States. There is a small market for compost in the United States since farming generally is much less intensive than in Europe and Asia. It is unfortunate that composting is not economically attractive, since it does not produce air or water pollution. In addition, although it is more expensive to produce, it is more naturally assimilated by the land than ordinary landfill material.

Other kinds of salvaging operations, such as the removal of rags, metals, glass, or papers can also be carried out. The market for these items is very unstable and no governmental body should rely on an income from this source.

Sanitary Landfill

The sanitary landfill is a substantial refinement of the open dump method. It does not create a nuisance as it does not produce odor, air, or water pollution. An efficient sanitary landfill operation will inhibit flies and rodents, will seal in odors, prevent water infiltration, and will minimize blowing and scattering. Perhaps most important from the urban planner's point of view, is that it is a method whereby a community disposal problem may be solved in an economical manner, and also provide opportunities to create improved sites and to shape the landscape.

In a sanitary landfill operation the site is prepared by digging trenches or cutting into slopes with earth-moving machinery. The refuse is dumped into the cavities and the refuse covered with a layer of earth taken from either the trench or the slope.

In selecting the site for a sanitary landfill, the nature of the subsoil must be considered carefully. Low areas, such as ravines, swamps, and borrow pits may be suitable; however, not all sanitary landfills need be directed to the reclamation of waste land, and fill sites should not be limited to problem areas. For example, a community on flat terrain can create a landscape with a gently rolling topography for aesthetic variety, which can be used ultimately for parks, recreation, or even construction sites.

The process of making the decision to commence a sanitary landfill program and of selecting a site may provide many headaches for planners and public officials alike. From the popular public point of view there seems to be little difference between a sanitary landfill and an open dump.

A great deal of misconception still exists, and officials who contemplate a sanitary landfill operation should be prepared to precede its inauguration by a program of public education to give assurance that serious nuisance will not result.

Conclusion

The discerning reader will have noted that although many elements falling within the broad category of "community facilities" have been dealt with in some detail, others will, inevitably, have received little or no attention. It is the purpose of this section to touch on some of these omissions, and to comment on some planning aspects of community facilities as a class.

The definitions given at the opening of the chapter may have given warning that some of the territory is not well charted. As is so often the case with familiar things, we tend to take them for granted and refer to them in terms which are not uniform or precise. In this, the planning profession is as guilty as the public at large and it is hoped that the definitions provided will enable the reader to place all the elements contained within the wide spectrum which we refer to as "community facilities" in the proper perspective.

It will be noted that specific mention has been made of such buildings as city halls, civic centers, libraries, police stations and firehouses, but that other buildings commonly provided for public use or public service are not described. These omissions are intentional and have been made either because they constitute details of the general items discussed (sewage pumping stations or telephone exchanges, for instance) or because they form an integral part of an element discussed in another chapter, as in the case of schools. In another limited category fall items which are sometimes provided for public convenience, but not found universally. Overground or underground public toilets or garages might be an example of these.

Among obvious omissions, to which reference is made in other chapters, are those connected with recreational facilities. These may be provided and run by the public or by a combination of public and private enterprise and might include: sports pavilions, skating rinks, restaurants, auditoriums, stadiums, theaters, museums, swimming pools, marinas and other waterfront or lake facilities, golf courses, zoological gardens, camping areas, and other facilities falling within this broad category. These are included by implication in the appropriate chapter. In similar manner public housing is included in Chapter 17.

Another area of omission is concerned with transportation, and would include central depots and other service facilities provided in connection with city and long distance bus lines and railroads. It would also include the many modern facilities now being provided for city airports and heliports. All these would vary in significance from the extensive big city bus depot down to the small town shelter, and from the world famous airport terminal down to the smallest local airfield control building. These are considered to be included when transportation is discussed, together with port and dock facilities.

There would seem to be no universally recognized structure to which reports should adhere when dealing with community facilities. Some planners appear to prefer dealing with all facilities under the general heading of "community facilities" while others prefer to deal with them under the separate categories of "public buildings," and "utilities," with other elements being mentioned under their specific service areas such as "transportation," "recreation," and "schools." Some reports differentiate between facilities provided by private and public enterprise, some do not, and others deal only with those provided by the public, and may include all levels of government.

Whatever method of presentation is adopted, it should obviously be appropriate to the community and to the range of facilities provided therein. All of these should be covered in a well structured manner to provide a comprehensive coverage to which quick reference may be made. Complete coverage requires that private facilities be included as well as public facilities, so that the planner may relate all these to the physical design proposals contained in the plan for the future development of the community. The traditions and values of the community, as well as its size and range of facilities will suggest the weight that should be given in dealing with each segment.

As populations grow, as technology becomes even more advanced than at present, and as higher living standards are achieved by an increasing proportion of the population, public expectation will demand more and better facilities of an increasingly wider variety. The rarity of today may well be the commonplace of tomorrow.

An increasing public concern for the proper provision and coordination of these facilities, coupled with a growing sense of governmental responsibility for the attainment of a properly coordinated range of facilities, may result in more government control, or in the assumption by government of responsibility for the provision of services that can thereby be made available more satisfactorily than under private enterprise.

Throughout this evolutionary process the planner will exercise his responsibility at various levels. These will range from suggestions related to direct control of facilities on the ground, to the financial provisions that should be made in the capital program to achieve an appropriate level of facilities in the future. In the exercise of this responsibility the planner should be conscious of the effect of the provision of facilities on development. This will insure that all proposals are made in furtherance of approved municipal policy, thus underlining the strong relationship between the provision of facilities and land use planning.

Part Three

Special Approaches
to Planning

9

City Design
and City Appearance

DESIGN IS A confused word in environmental planning. Tautologies such as "design plan," or vague phrases such as "the design element," are symptoms of an oscillation between two equally incorrect conceptions: either that design is concerned solely with apparent finish, or that it is principally a matter of planning buildings. This chapter will deal primarily with the appearance of cities, but it cannot avoid the broader issue of design.

Appearance and esthetic quality are not final touches; they are fundamental considerations that enter into the design of a thing from the beginning,[1] but they are only one consideration. Similarly, architectural design is only one kind of design—many others affect city form. For our purposes, we may usefully distinguish at least four:

Object design—of a single object, or a standardized series of them (a building, a chair, a bridge);

Project design—of a defined geographic area, however large, in which there is a definite client, a concrete program, a foreseeable time of completion, and effective control over the significant aspects of form (a housing project, a new campus, even a small new town);

System design—of a functionally connected set of objects, which may extend over large areas but do not make a complete environment (an arterial street system, a lighting system);

City or environmental design—of the general spatial arrangement of activities and objects over an extended area, where the client is multiple, the program indeterminate, control partial, and there is no state of completion.

These types of design are so diverse in their nature as to call for different techniques, attitudes, and criteria. The misapplication of project design techniques to problems of city design has resulted in such sterilities as the monumental axis of the past, or the "megaform" of today. City design is so complex and fluid, so uncertain and beset with conflicting values, as to be thought an impossibility by many thoughtful critics.[2]

Yet in fact we *do* design our cities, however imperfectly, and it is even possible to analyze, and in some measure control, their sensuous qualities, as will be described below. There are serious gaps in the continuity and coherence of the design process, and substantial ignorance as to the consequences of city form. Our esthetic achievements are small: our past efforts have most often led to isolated monuments, or to patterns appreciable only on paper, or to pathetic applications of cosmetics. Yet the city is a great (if disordered and uncomfortable) sensuous spectacle, and could be manipulated for the joy of its inhabitants.

Design is the imaginative creation of possible forms and arrangements, together with the

---

[1] Designers have a dirty word for the idea that appearances come last. They call it "cosmetics." They are unjust, of course: cosmetics is an honorable art, when you have decided you can do no more than change the visible surface of a thing.

[2] See, for example, Jane Jacobs, THE DEATH AND LIFE OF GREAT AMERICAN CITIES (New York: Random House, 1961), pp. 372–91 and Werner Hegemann and Elbert Peets, THE AMERICAN VITRUVIUS (New York: Architectural Book Publishing Co., 1922).

means of achieving them, which might be useful for human purposes: social, economic, esthetic, technical. One designs a possible piece of sculpture, but one also designs a possible gear, a possible crop layout, or a possible population distribution. City design is the technical core of the process of city planning, and its concerns are equally broad. Design does not focus solely on appearance, nor indeed on any single factor which is affected by form.

The immediate sensuous quality of an environment—the way it looks, smells, sounds, feels—is one consequence of the way it is put together, and of how and by whom it is being perceived. Occasionally, this is the most important characteristic of a form, as in an ornamental garden or a festival. Occasionally, it is of no importance, as in a sewer layout or an automated warehouse. In most cases, wherever men are acting in the environment, this quality is one of the several significant consequences of form. The city is such a case.

In the esthetic experience, the dialogue between perceiver and the sensuous environment is intense, and seemingly detached from other consequences. But environmental appearance also has other functions: comfort, orientation, or the communication of status, for example. These characteristics are not easy to disentangle from each other, nor is it always profitable to try.

Planning consists of three processes, all continuous, concurrent, and mutually linked: formulating objectives and criteria, obtaining and organizing information, and designing, or the creation of possible sets of actions. Whenever these processes come into a reasonable fit they lead to intermittent decisions to take action. Within this framework, this chapter will cover two subjects which are commonly confused with one another:

1. *Appearance:* the sensuous quality of the environment as one of the several major aspects of environmental form. It is analytically separable from these other aspects in the process of gathering information, and to some extent in formulating criteria. Except in special cases, it cannot be separated from them in the process of design.

2. *Design:* the role of design in local plan-

ning. Only passing reference can be made to the general subject of city design, which is dealt with at some length throughout this volume. Somewhat more attention can be given to project and system design, particularly as they relate to city design in general, and to sensuous quality in particular.

What Is Good Appearance?

Our first question is whether the appearance of an environment is of any importance to its inhabitants, and how we can derive criteria for judging better or worse. Sensations which crowd the limits of our biological abilities—too much heat, cold, or noise—are obvious sources of discomfort, and some of these may have long-term, cumulative effects of which we are not fully aware.[3] Through our senses, we gather information which we organize and transform as a basis for action. If this information is ambiguous or false, we are unable to carry out our purposes effectively.[4] The environment serves as a medium of social communication, by which men transmit data, values, feelings, or desired behavior to each other. As such, its look and smell and sound support the fabric of society. We have some evidence that the form of the environment can encourage or frustrate individual growth.[5] The look of our surroundings is obviously crucial to the esthetic experience, the joy of sensing the world immediately and intensely, which is an experience not confined to the gifted few.

In all these ways, the appearance of the environment affects its users, and in many cases it can be substantially improved. As more desperate questions of survival or conflict are met, and as we have the courage to go beyond criteria which are easily quantified, these psychological attributes of cities may come to be the central concern of environmental designers. For the present, they are surely significant.

[3] René Dubos, MAN ADAPTING (New Haven: Yale University Press, 1965).

[4] George Miller, Eugene Galanter, and K. H. Pribram, PLANS AND THE STRUCTURE OF BEHAVIOR (New York: Holt, 1960).

[5] Harry Fowler, CURIOSITY AND EXPLORATORY BEHAVIOR (New York: Macmillan, 1965).

There are patent difficulties in developing and applying these criteria. Perception of the environment depends not only on its visible form, and its objective nature, but also on the nature of the individual, his history, his needs and purposes, and his social environment. The same object may be seen quite differently by two people of different class, or different visual acuity, or different upbringing, or different immediate tasks. The consequences of appearance are only partially predictable—there are some pervasive effects due to the nature of men as biological organisms; others which are common to large groups, based on class, culture, environmental history, or typical tasks or character traits; and others which vary widely, according to individual idiosyncrasies. The problem of providing for common, frequent, or large group needs, while minimizing intergroup conflict and tyranny over the individual, is a familiar one in environmental design. It is not unique to questions of appearance.

The taste or need of one group may too easily be taken to be the proper esthetic standard. Current campaigns for "beautification" are a reflection of middle and upper middle class taste, with its emphasis on tidiness, appropriateness, and camouflage. The junkyard, abhorrent to the garden club, is a rich mine of form for the sculptor. A lower class citizen may be attracted by visible signs of security, durability, newness, or upward mobility, and take pleasure in forms which to an upper class observer seem coarse, hard, and vulgar. A good environment provides satisfactions for both groups, while offering new possibilities to tempt each to enlarge their desires. Since the designer is usually a person of special class, as well as special temperament and training, his intuitive judgments of appearance, while sophisticated, may not be widely held. His value to society lies in his ability to create new possibilities, rather than to set criteria or to make final judgments.

Criteria must embrace the multiplicity of need and place even as general statements. In emphasis and concrete detail, they will necessarily vary with the particular situation. This relative emphasis will lie at the heart of any decisive evaluation. Criteria must be directly related to form, so that one proposal may be evaluated in comparison to another. The best source for such a set would be an environmental psychology. Lacking that for the time being, we may use hints from art criticism, or from professional consensus, or from individual experience. We may seek indications from current political decisions, or go to community organizations as sounding boards. Unfortunately, the public expression of sensuous criteria is often inarticulate, confused, and conventional, and unrepresentative as well. Our best source for the present may be the user himself, either by watching his market choices, asking for his preferences (which is a slippery affair), or observing his behavior (whether real, as on a shopping street, or simulated, as in an orientation test or a real-estate game). Yet all these methods only test reaction to the present environment. There is little indication of how users might value a setting that they have not yet experienced.

SOME PERCEPTUAL CRITERIA

A general list of criteria can be useful as a checklist, and as a guide to applied or basic research. Some criteria are intangible and difficult to set forth in any systematic way. They cannot yet be used as a commonly-accepted basis for public decision. Other criteria can be more clearly defined and are likely to enjoy substantial acceptance. Our knowledge regarding criteria of this latter kind can be summarized as follows:

1. Sensations should be within the range of comfort, and not interfere with the activities that people wish to pursue: not too hot, noisy, bright, cold, silent, loaded or empty of information, too steep, dirty, or clean. Climate, noise, pollution, and the level of visual input are perhaps the most critical factors. The acceptable range has a partly biological, partly cultural basis, and will vary for different people engaged in different tasks. But in any one group there will be large areas of agreement as to what is unpleasant or intolerable. We have some specific information on the effect of temperature or noise on health or efficiency, and these data could be expanded. The discomfort of our cities is a common complaint.

FIGURE 9–1. *Diversity of environment offers a wide choice of activities: Golden Gate Park in San Francisco*

2. Within this range of toleration, a diversity of sensation and setting will give the inhabitant a choice of the environment he prefers, and correspond to his pleasure in variety and change. Diversity is an important support for human cognitive development, and, indeed, for the very maintenance of the perceptual and cognitive system.[6] Adequate diversity is more difficult to define, as are the critical elements that should be diversified. To some extent, we may look to market behavior, and the expression of preferences, to find the kinds of diversity people presently seek. But present choices are constrained by past experience and

perceived possibilities. The effective designer opens up new choices.

Given the low level of environmental diversity in our cities and the even lower visibility of such diversity as exists, given our evident appetite for novelty and our human ability to cope with it, we are for the present safe in striving to increase environmental diversity, to make it more visible, and to broaden its spectrum by experimenting with novel environments. Experiments which involve human beings must always be cautiously designed; novelty and diversity can sometimes be felt as a threat. The safest tactic is to increase the availability of diverse environments, without forcing them on the user, and then to monitor the way in which those users choose to operate in the new settings.

We can guess at some of the important variations which people may seek: the range from lonely to gregarious places for example; or from highly defined and structured surroundings to ones which are free and loose; from calm, simple, slow worlds to rapid, complex and stimulating ones. Diversity is not a matter of mixing together a large number of varied sensations, but rather of constructing consistent and directly accessible sub-environments of contrasting character. A secluded garden opening directly off a busy street is one example. Diversity must be not only present but accessible and be perceived as accessible. The door to the garden must open, and no one should fear to turn the handle.

3. Places in the environment should not only be diverse, but have a clear perceptual identity: recognizable, memorable, vivid. A street should not look like all other streets. Every place in a large environment cannot be radically different from all others; important centers may be unique, most places will vary only subtly. But this quality of identity, or a "sense of place," is the cornerstone of a handsome and meaningful environment.[7] Without it an observer cannot make sense of his world, since he cannot distinguish or remember its parts. Wide regions of the contemporary city

[6] Donald W. Fiske and Salvatore R. Maddi, THE FUNCTIONS OF VARIED EXPERIENCE (Homewood, Ill.: Dorsey Press, 1961).

[7] Ian Nairn, THE AMERICAN LANDSCAPE (New York: Random House, 1965).

are visibly faceless and gray, yet conceal much social differentiation. If the setting is vividly identifiable, the observer has a concrete basis for a sense of belonging. He can begin to make relations; he can savor the uniqueness of places and people; he can learn to *see* (or to listen or to smell).

Identity can be tested for, by recall or by identification in the field, and its presence can be predicted in planning proposals, if the user's viewpoint is simulated. A sense of identity also depends on the knowledge and past experience of the observer, and can be conveyed to him indirectly just by verbal symbols. But a unique set of perceptual characteristics is a powerful, concrete reinforcement of this symbolic identity. The designer will accentuate any special traits of form and activity that he can find, or invent and encourage new ones. The typical units within which people function or into which they mentally organize their environment, or the elements which can realistically be manipulated for identity of character, will set the strategic scale at which places should be given identity.

4. These identifiable parts should be so arranged that a normal observer can mentally relate them to one another, and understand their pattern in time and space. This is not a universal rule, since there are occasions when it is desirable that parts of the environment be hidden, mysterious, or ambiguous. But at least the general framework of a living space, and the linkages between its public places, must be legible—in the street and in memory. Legible structure has an obvious value in facilitating the practical tasks of way-finding and cognition, but it has other values as well. It can be a source of emotional security, and one basis for a sense of self-identity and of relation to society. It can support civic pride and social cohesion, and be a means of extending one's knowledge of the world. It confers the esthetic pleasure of sensing the relatedness of a complex thing, a pleasure vividly experienced by many people when they see a great city panorama before them. The structural chaos of our great urban regions is notorious, and lies behind some of our distaste for city life.

Legible structure will have to be simple and adaptable to maintain itself in a constantly changing city. It must also be flexible enough to facilitate different ways of organizing the environment (map organization, sequence organization, and schematic organization, in particular). It must be designed to work for the wide-eyed tourist, the old inhabitant intent on his practical task, and the relaxed and casual stroller. Different groups will search for different clues which they wish to link together: work places, historic spots, or specialty shops for example. Yet certain elements will be crucial to almost all of them: the main system of circulation, the basic functional and social areas, the principal centers of activity and of symbolic value, the historic points, the physical site, and the major open spaces.

Legibility of an existing environment can be tested by field reconnaissance and by interviews of the inhabitants.[8] We have some clues for designing for spatial legibility in large environments, particularly through shaping the circulation system as a comprehensible sequence and a comprehensible geometry, but also through the pattern of open space, centers, and important districts, and through such design techniques as form simplicity, perceptual dominance, articulation or clarity at the joints, and increasing visual range and exposure. Simply to make important elements and activities visible, for example, particularly those which carry high levels of potential information or are of common significance, may be a strategic way of increasing legibility. It can be heightened by keying other informational aids to the visible landscape: giving coded telephone exchanges a visible spatial reference, for example, or keying maps to real objects, or bestowing evocative and relatable place names.

Spatial legibility is the more obvious aspect of our subject, but temporal legibility is equally important—space and time together are the dimensions within which we live. We would like to know not only where but when we are, and how "now" relates to time past and to come. By emphasizing the clues of time and

---

[8] Kevin Lynch, THE IMAGE OF THE CITY (Cambridge: The Technology Press, 1960).

season, by exposing the scars of history and the signs of future intention, the visual environment may effectively be used to orient its observers to the past, to the present with its cyclical rhythms, and to the future with its hopes and dangers.

Historic preservation is a common way of preserving orientation to fragments of the past, but no one has yet paid much attention to clarifying cyclical time in the environment (day/night, winter/summer, holiday/workday), nor to smoothing or explaining current transitions (the visual shock of urban renewal, for example), nor to making the known future visible.

5. The environment should be perceived as meaningful—that is, not only should its visible and identifiable parts be related to each other in time and space, but they should seem to be related to other aspects of life: the natural site and its ecology, functional activity, social structure, economic and political patterns, human values and aspirations, even to individual idiosyncrasies and character. The city is an enormous communications device—people read its landscape, they seek practical information, they are curious, they are moved by what they see. Great cities are expressive environments, but in ours the information is often redundant or trivial, false, suppressed, or unintelligible. Unfortunately, the symbolic role of the urban landscape is little understood, and to deal with meaning at the community scale is most difficult, since significant meanings and values differ widely between various groups in our society. The formal legibility discussed above is at least a common visible base on which all groups can erect their own meaningful structures.

It would be desirable, however, to make this visible structure at least congruent with functional and social structure, so that visual units correspond to social units, or a visually dominant tower occurs at a focus of intense activity, or at a point of high symbolic significance. As one effective example, the visible setting may be used to convey the structure of "territories," or "behavior settings," by which much normal behavior is regulated: the public, private and semi-public areas; the places in which one should be decorous, and those in which one can be free.[9] Proper behavior is socially learned; but the visible marking of territory can reduce the distress and conflict of inappropriate action. The environment can also express the temporal organization of behavior; light, or changeable forms, will convey when as well as where an action is proper. In general, congruence of the visible and social world, to the extent that it can be managed, will facilitate action and make both worlds more comprehensible. In the same vein, city forms can accent and be congruent to the basic features of the site—hills, rivers, escarpments.

The designer can deal more directly with the explicit communications in the city landscape; the signs and symbols by which people openly speak to each other, using established formal codes. Although city signs are generally damned on esthetic grounds, they perform an important function and add to the interest and liveliness of the scene. The designer's task is not to suppress but to clarify and regulate the flow of information, so that priority signs (such as public control messages) cannot be missed, but also so that a greater flow of other kinds of information is transmitted more easily to the observer, while still giving him the possibility of ignoring it. Signs in themselves are an effective and relatively inexpensive way of enhancing identity, legibility, or congruence.

Not only can they have the graphic clarity that we find in some European cities, but policies can be set about their location, their timing, and their relevance to the place to which they are attached.[10]

They may consciously be used to expand what a man can learn about his city: store locations and goods for sale (which are important), but also history, the site and its ecology, the presence of people and what they are doing, the flow of traffic and information, the weather, time, politics, or events to come. The individual or a small group should be able to transmit messages when they so desire, and this can be kept

[9] Sidney N. Brower, "The Signs We Learn to Read," LANDSCAPE, XV (Autumn, 1965), pp. 9–12.

[10] Massachusetts Institute of Technology, Department of City and Regional Planning, SIGNS IN THE CITY (Cambridge: MIT Press, 1963).

in mind in the design and regulation of residential structures, for example.[11]

If we go beyond simple congruence and the regulation of explicit communications in an attempt to make the environment more meaningful, we strike numerous difficulties. It is sometimes desirable to increase the transparency of the urban landscape, for economic and social processes are increasingly hidden from sight. Building construction is fascinating because it is one of the few industrial processes left open to view, and city policy might well be directed to making transportation, industry, or meetings and celebrations visible.[12] Public places should be provided where people can congregate and parade—to see and be seen. On the other hand, we risk an intrusion on privacy, the exposure of persons or activities who choose to be hidden. Similarly, if we wish to make our cities symbolic of our society and its values, we are faced with such questions as the diversity of values, and the confusion and emptiness of much of our symbolic vocabulary (or even our embarrassment, should we reveal our society as it really is).

6. The environment plays a role in fostering the intellectual, emotional and physical development of the individual, particularly in childhood, but also in later years.[13] Certainly, the negative effects of highly impoverished environments can be shown. We can speculate on the sensuous characteristics of cities that might facilitate human development.

Some of the characteristics noted above are valuable: perceptual diversity, legibility and meaning, particularly if they are not immediately obvious but communicate a simple pattern which becomes more complex and subtle as the object is attended to more closely. This condition of "unfoldingness" is easy to specify

FIGURE 9–2. *Environment can stimulate discovery and learning: a detail from a home for homeless children by Aldo van Eyck, near Amsterdam*

in general, but difficult to identify or achieve at city scale. An educative city would visibly encourage attention and exploration, particularly at those times when the observer is not task-oriented, for example when he is at play, travelling, or just waiting. It would provide opportunities for children to manipulate the environment directly, whether by building, reshaping, or even destroying it. It would alternate between situations of high stimulus and times of quiet and privacy. It might even present visual shocks, puzzles, and ambiguities—challenging the observer to find a satisfactory organization for himself.

The use of the city environment as a teaching device is a fascinating topic going well beyond questions of sensuous form. We have done little careful thinking and fewer experiments on it. The subject warrants close attention, since many social problems and possibilities revolve about the subject of education.

[11] Julian Beinart, "The Pattern of the Street," ARCHITECTURAL FORUM, CXXV (September, 1966), pp. 58–62; Sidney Brower, "The Expressive Environment," ARCHITECTURAL FORUM, CXXIV (April, 1966), pp. 38–39.

[12] Stanley F. Moss, "A Policy for the Visual Form of Industrial Areas," Master's thesis in City Planning, M. I. T., 1964.

[13] Clarence J. Leuba, "The Concept of Optimal Stimulation," in Fiske and Maddi, THE FUNCTIONS OF VARIED EXPERIENCE, *op. cit.*

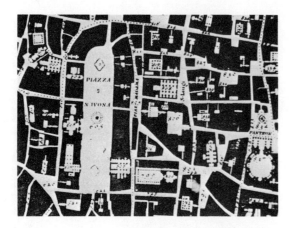

FIGURE 9–3. *The intricate web of indoor and outdoor space in 18th century Rome*

The criteria for city design which it can provide are as yet meager and uncertain.

There is more to a fine visual environment than can be compressed under the headings above, but it becomes progressively more difficult to define. Moreover, if we achieve a landscape which is comfortable, diverse, identifiable, legible, meaningful, and developmental, in the senses we have given those words, we have the basis, and indeed much of the essence, of a beautiful landscape.

In any application, these general criteria must be turned into specific statements. Where does background noise rise above a certain level more often than a given number of occasions per year, or which major routes cannot visually be differentiated one from another, or where is essential public information unreadable? The nature of these questions will vary from place to place, in relation to the environment, the needs and values of the people served, and the purposes of the planning operation. We lack the space here to discuss the difficult question of how such specific criteria (or any planning criteria) are decided upon in the course of the planning process. Sensuous criteria will interlock with other criteria at many points, and must be consistent with them. Visual legibility may be emphasized, for example, in order to increase circulation efficiency, or to develop a better sense of civic cohesion.

Gathering Information

Data on the appearance of the environment must be gathered in order to prepare designs and take action. Professional uncertainty as to what is relevant at the city scale, and how it may best be organized for analysis and manipulation, has made it difficult to include visual considerations in city designs. The nature of the data, and the language in which it is recorded, always have a profound impact on the nature of proposals. We tend to forget that many other arts (architecture, music, for example) have well-developed languages which can be used to describe, to manipulate form symbolically in design, to evaluate, and to transmit solutions and give directions for achieving them. They are economical and fluent, concentrating on essentials but allowing endless complexity and variation. Unfortunately, for us, architectural language is both too detailed and too limited to be very useful at the community scale.

Data on the sensuous characteristics of an environment may conveniently be classified into: (1) the pattern and quality of the relatively objective and separable sensuous elements; (2) syntheses of these elements into more compact and interdependent clusters of information; (3) descriptions of the system of observer and observed: the environment as perceived and remembered; (4) an appraisal of these characteristics in terms of the criteria.

SENSUOUS ELEMENTS

The sensuous elements are those particular characteristics of the city environment which seem significant to its perception, and which can be recorded with some objectivity by trained observers. The quality of the environment is founded on these raw materials. Diversity in particular can be measured from their distributions.

Spatial form: a central concern to man as a mobile animal. At the city scale, we must deal with the major publicly-accessible spaces, both external (which is a traditional subject of city design) and also internal (lobbies, halls, arcades, and concourses). We are concerned with their location, their scale, their general form and clarity of definition, and the linkages between them. We may also wish to record the *texture* of spaces throughout a city district—their typical scale and form, without reference to exact location. All these qualities may be recorded in models, in two or three dimensional diagrams, in long sections, coverage plans, or in isometric views. This is a well-developed and much-discussed subject, and we have acquired a rich variety of form possibilities.[14] We are less prepared to consider these spaces as a linked, city-wide system, although the legibility of an environment is anchored here. Modern transportation and use have made it difficult to maintain well-defined external spaces of the classic type. Will it be possible to specify the characteristics of an area-wide spatial system, without controlling building form in detail?

Visible life and activity: the sight of other people in action, a constant fascination for all observers, which conveys much of the meaning and "warmth" of the city scene. Visible evidence of plant and animal life is similarly important. Diagrams, diagrammatic models, and selected photographs or sketches can be used to convey the location, apparent intensity, rhythm, and type of life and activity open to view. This is a fluctuating condition, and its diurnal and seasonal rhythm is important. Visible activity is distinct from the usual planning concept of objective use or activity: an intensely used place may *seem* quite empty or "dead." The disposition of objective activity, its exposure to view, the nature of the actors, and the proportioning of space to activity will determine the subjective sense. Many city designs are prepared without reference to this crucial quality.

Ambience: the set of encompassing conditions—light, noise, micro-climate, smell. Light is the medium for visual perception, and the typical rhythms, intensity, and texture of both natural and artificial light will always be important. Artificial light, in particular, now offers largely unexploited resources of color, form, and sequential change. Prevailing micro-climates, by small areas, and the intensity, character, and rhythm of city sound affect all observers. Both can now be recorded accurately, and to some degree be manipulated. Smell, while a more subtle sense, and one difficult to record, can also occasionally be crucial, and not only in a negative way.

Space, visible activity, and ambience will prove to be the key factors, but there are many others that are often worth recording.

Visibility: the general visible form of major landmarks, and the locations from which they can be seen—skylines, land forms, and building masses. To this may be added the key viewing positions. Manipulation of visibility is a well-known device of the environmental designer.

Surfaces: generalized descriptions of the visual and tactile texture of walls and floor, visible evidence of the surface we inhabit, or the material of which the environment is constructed: topography, earth, rock, water, pav-

14 Hans Blumenfeld, "Scale in Civic Design," TOWN PLANNING REVIEW, XXIV (April, 1953), pp. 35–46; Gordon Cullen, TOWNSCAPE (London: The Architectural Press, 1961); Ivor DeWolfe, THE ITALIAN TOWNSCAPE (London: Architectural Press, 1963); Camillo Sitte, CITY PLANNING ACCORDING TO ARTISTIC PRINCIPLES, translated from the German by G. R. Collins and C. C. Collins (London: Phaidon Press, 1965).

FIGURE 9–4. *Visible human activity is the crucial aspect of city appearance: the Galleria in Milan*

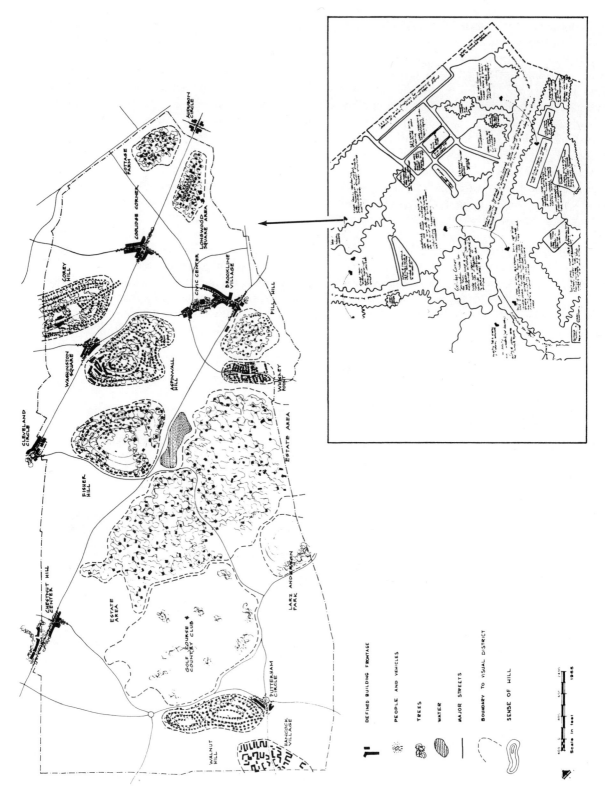

FIGURE 9–5. *A cartoon of the visible character of the principal centers and districts of Brookline, Massachusetts, with a fragment of a more detailed recording*

FIGURE 9–6. *The city seen in motion: San Francisco*

ing, facade character. Much of the city floor, in particular, is already under public control, and it usually is a salient perceptual feature.

Communications: the location, intensity, clarity, type of information, and "rootedness" (relation of a sign to its locality) of explicit signs and symbols in the environment.[15] As noted in the discussion of meaning, these explicit symbols play a very important visual role, and they are amenable to control.

SYNTHESES

These studies will produce a mass of data which is difficult to use in the initial process of design, however useful for analysis or for detailed design. It is more efficient to coordinate this material into a set of sensuous character-

istics which correspond to typical ways in which people organize their surroundings. The pattern and nature of these sets are the physical basis for the diversity, identity and legibility of the environment. Selection and judgment are required to make such descriptions, and thus they must already include some recognition of the nature of the observer.

Focal and district character: the environment as a pattern of regions and points: (1) The spatial form of the important focal points, their fill with light and activity, their climate and noise, the approaches to them and the views in and out of them, the ways in which they are linked together, and how they relate to their immediate environs. (2) The characteristic spatial and surface textures, activities, skyline, planting, detail, light, noise, and climate of the major city districts.

---

[15] SIGNS IN THE CITY, *op. cit.*

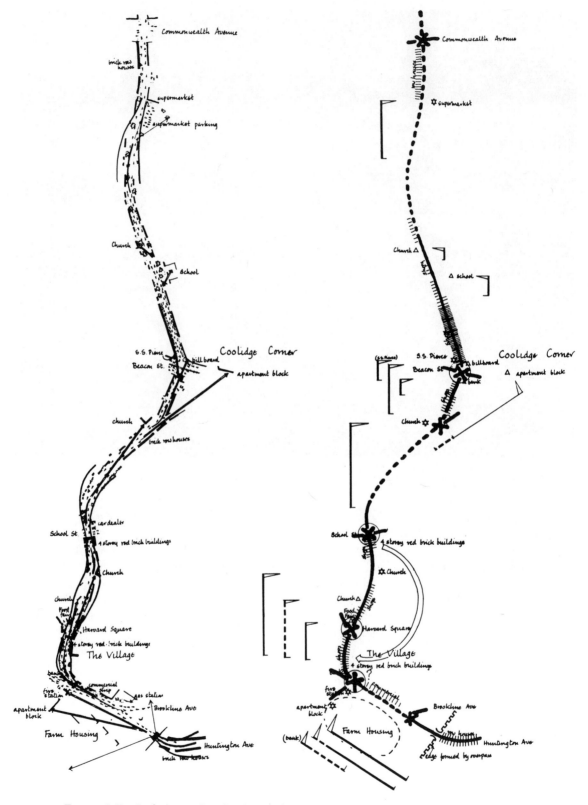

FIGURE 9–7. *Analysis of the visual experience of Harvard Street in Brookline, and a diagram of its structure*

The analyses must indicate how the characteristics fluctuate according to cyclic rhythms of light, activity, and climate, and also how they are changing over the long run.

Sequence system: the environment as a pattern of journeys: the visual continuity, the rhythm of events, and the character of goals and decision points along the important individual pathways (auto, transit, pedestrian, etc.), as well as the sequence of space, view, and motion along them. In addition, the network of paths must also be analyzed as a complete system, including its general form, coherence, and rhythm, and the nature of transitions between its parts. This is a relatively new subject of attention, for which new diagrammatic languages are being developed.[16] Information may also be recorded in special models or in compressed-time movies. Cyclical and secular changes must be noted. As population becomes more mobile, the importance of these sequence systems increases.

IMAGES

To understand the quality of the environment, we must consider the interaction between observer and observed. Here our techniques of analysis are much less secure, and more liable to revision in the near future. While such studies may begin with field surveys, which simply take observer characteristics into intuitive account, they must rely more and more on the sampling of opinion, or the observation of real or simulated behavior, to disclose how the environment is perceived and endowed with meaning. If not, the subjective bias of the typical designer will seriously distort the information. We may call this group *images,* or descriptions of the environment *as perceived.* They now bear directly on our criteria.

Significant objects: an inventory of those special objects or locales which are unique, or which are highly valued or meaningful to significant groups or people, including historic

structures, elements of special design quality, sentimental or symbolic things, etc. This type of inventory is especially useful in conservation work.[17]

Territory: division of the environment into spatial or temporal regions symbolically controlled by various individuals or groups, or within which certain types of behavior are expected: private or public territories; prohibited, decorous, or free areas; wilderness; quiet zones. This is a particular (and particularly useful) subdivision of a more general topic:

Public image: the differentiation and structure of the general (or large group) image of the environment, as organized into districts, centers, pathways, edges and landmarks, all as determined from various field and memory interviews and tests. Here the criteria of identity and legibility may be tested.[18] To this may be added information on how this image is changing.

Value and meaning: by tests and interviews, or perusal of existing descriptions, or by watching behavior, information may be gathered as to the values and meanings that observers coming from various significant groups impute to their surroundings.[19] This is an important factor, but difficult to analyze, and little studied to date in any systematic way.

APPRAISAL

All this material is only brought to the point of usefulness if it results in a set of judgments, organized in some way congenial to design and decision. Any set of data must be reduced to text and diagrams which pick out the problems, strengths, and potentialities (for better or for worse) of the existing sensuous environment as perceived by its users, in the light of the chosen criteria. The nature of the data will affect the

[16] Donald Appleyard, Kevin Lynch and John R. Myer, THE VIEW FROM THE ROAD (Cambridge: M. I. T. Press, 1964); Mahmoud Yousry Hassan, THE MOVEMENT SYSTEM AS AN ORGANIZER OF VISUAL FORM (M. I. T., Ph.D. thesis, 1965); Philip Thiel, "A Sequence-Experience Notation," TOWN PLANNING REVIEW, XXXII (April 1961), pp. 33–52.

[17] Stephen W. Jacobs and Barclay Jones, "City Design Through . . . Conservation" (unpublished); Oakland, Calif. City Planning Department, DESIGN RESOURCES IN THE OAKLAND CENTRAL DISTRICT (Oakland: 1963).

[18] Kevin Lynch, *op. cit.*

[19] Gyorgy Kepes, "Notes on Expression and Communication in the Cityscape," DAEDALUS, XL (Winter, 1961), pp. 147–65; R. Richard Wohl and Anselm L. Strauss, "Symbolic Representation and the Urban Milieu," AMERICAN JOURNAL OF SOCIOLOGY, LXIII (March, 1958), pp. 523–32.

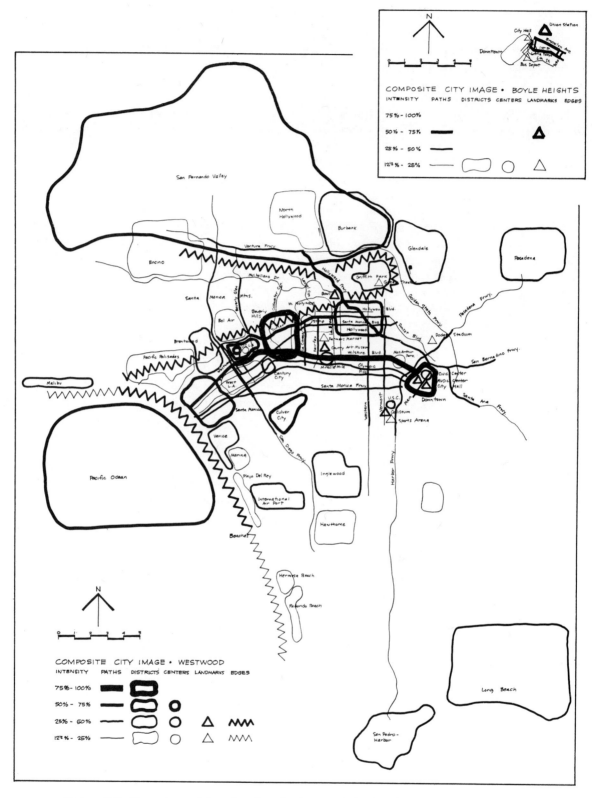

FIGURE 9–8. *Two views of Los Angeles: the image of the Mexican Americans of Boyle Heights compared to that of the upper middle class residents of Westwood*

choice of criteria and vice versa. Appraisal may reveal certain goals to be improbable or untestable, or it may uncover previously unstated goals. When working with few resources or little time, it may be most efficient to begin by identifying problems and possibilities directly in the field, shortcutting any more systematic gathering of information.[20] Data on those sensuous elements which bear most directly on critical problems can then be gathered in a selective way. Evaluative judgments should be organized into forms suitable for design, pointing out problem clusters, major opportunities, latent form, pivotal points for manipulation, and so on.

One of the difficulties in dealing with the appearance of cities has been the lack of a developed and accepted language for noting sensuous conditions at that scale. While conventional means may do in certain cases (microclimate, visibility, significant objects) in others it is necessary to use newly-evolved techniques (sequence, public image), and in still others an effective language has yet to be created (light, focal character, meaning). In most cases, we have yet to evolve a language which is useful for design as well as for description. The information itself is still typically gathered by field reconnaissance, but new techniques of interview, the observation of behavior, or the use of games in simulated situations, are all beginning to develop. In the future, we may be able to store these data, not simply in texts with illustrations, but in movies, constantly changing models or diagrams, or in visual data banks based on computer storage, which could maintain constantly updated records of sensuous conditions, including sequences or views at special or even at generally distributed points, so that it would be possible to call up a representation of any point in a city, or to simulate any trip.

What we have gone through is a content

[20] Kevin Lynch, AN ANALYSIS OF THE VISUAL FORM OF BROOKLINE (Brookline, Mass.: Brookline Planning Board, 1965).

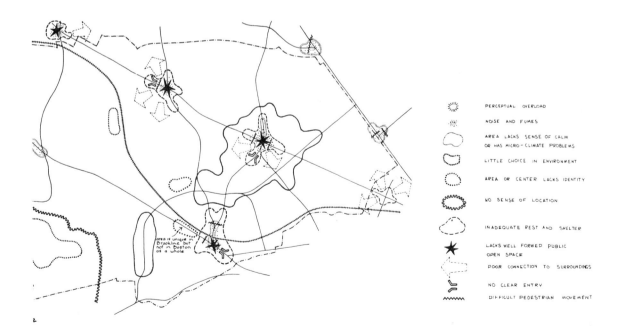

FIGURE 9–9. *Analysis of the perceptual problems of centers and districts in Brookline*

checklist. No agency in its right mind would gather all this information as a matter of routine. Although some evaluative statement is always needed, all the other items will be dealt with or neglected according to the situation. In general, surveys will focus on those items which are amenable to public policy, and which seem to be relevant to the scale, the problem, and the key criteria. (In return, designs and criteria will have to focus on items for which there is information.) The scale of the environment, as one example, will indicate whether floor texture is important. One survey may concentrate on signs, because these can realistically be controlled and are at the heart of a current controversy. A transportation study may focus on the sequence system, while a long-term analysis will be directed to the public image, and to the values people ascribe to these elements.

Sensuous intelligence will have to fit in with other data collection, so that questions must be found which can be employed in an origin and destination survey, or data compiled on an area basis compatible with other statistics. In the past, visual information has been gathered as though it were something special and remote from all other concerns, and the result is often that the information is in a form which cannot be applied in making comprehensive decisions. On the contrary, sensuous data are relevant to many other questions. The quality of visual sequences bears on traffic flow and safety; visual identity affects market value; stimulus load has a meaning for health; and so on.

There is a need for continuous intelligence about the appearance of the city, however simple or selective that intelligence may be. Since appearance depends heavily on dynamic conditions such as activity or light, and on the character and purposes of its observers, it is itself a constantly changing phenomenon, requiring constant re-analysis. The planning agency must know what perceptual changes are being introduced by other agents, and in particular it must look candidly at the results of its own efforts. If a program has put potted trees on downtown streets, then what has been the resulting change in appearance, and how do users view it? The absence of feedback in city

design is even more notorious than in building design.

Designing the Sensuous Form

Design is not normally confined to visual ends, nor indeed to any other single purpose. In two special cases, however, we may speak of "sensuous design." In the first case, the design may be dealing with a predominantly visual system, in which other factors are of lesser importance, or can easily be dealt with by solving their requirements in any reasonable manner. This will be true in a minority of cases at the city scale, but may occur in the design of a festival, or of planting, paving, or artificial lighting in an ornamental area, or in the provision of special viewing points. It can also occur even where other important interests are involved, but where the sensuous factors are felt to be the critical ones. Control of signs or of a city silhouette, the improvement of climate or pollution, the design of a recreation area, are examples. In these cases, we are sometimes justified in designing for the sensuous characteristics first, and then checking to see that other factors are within reason, just as we so often (and often wrongly) design an environment from an economic or technical point of view, and then adjust to social or sensuous factors.

In the second case, a designer making a more comprehensive plan may deal with major factors one at a time, until he has a better feel for the whole problem. He may concentrate on certain criteria (low cost, for example), or on certain elements (the transportation system), or at certain scales (the block), and develop sketch designs which deal with that element. It is a convenient way of exploring the implications of various factors, and of looking for interfits between them. In this way, the designer can develop a system of visual sequences through an area, even before he looks at circulation requirements, or may play with silhouette before he understands the requirements for enclosed space, or may work up a desirable image structure while still in a functional vacuum. Odd as this may seem, it is neither more nor less reprehensible than the other way around. The results will be revealing but exaggerated caricatures, useful as temporary steps in constructing an integrated design.

Except for these cases, design cannot deal with sensuous aspects alone. "Design plan" is an absurd tautology. "Beautification" is an ugly word, with overtones of fraud. Yet a good design deals with the sensuous qualities of its object, and only in special cases are these qualities of small importance. The best design language, therefore, is one which expresses all the relevant aspects of a thing, as an architectural drawing can simultaneously convey appearance, structure, and (to some extent) function.

Designs for large environments become too complex to be compressed into a single display, and thus diagrams of activity distribution or structural density or traffic flow may be accompanied by diagrams of spatial texture, lighting, or focal character. None of these diagrams is a separate plan. All of them are particular aspects of a single integrated design, and they will change together.

Sensuous aspects need not be communicated solely by graphic means. They may be expressed in words, where words are most appropriate, as in setting general policy or describing sequential actions with various alternatives. Unfortunately our verbal (and as often our graphic) abstractions do not refer precisely to the concrete visual characteristics intended. The language is full of ambiguous generalities: "proper," "harmonious," "balanced," "suitable," "an orderly framework."

An environmental design need not include exact specifications of material and form. It is often more efficient and flexible to prepare a sensuous *program*. That is, the design can state that there be a landmark structure at an important junction, which shall be visibly full of activity, easily identifiable as distinct from its surroundings, continuously visible from a mile away up to the junction itself, and that it have a form which can be used to distinguish the various approaches to the junction. This visual program can be satisfied by many particular forms, according to the market and the abilities of the building designer. The design for a large environment may therefore contain a spatial pattern of visual performance characteristics, or programs, covering such items as space

and form, visibility, texture, visible activity, apparent motion, signs, noise, light and climate. These characteristics would be expressed verbally and diagrammatically—best of all, perhaps, in a diagrammatic model.

The design will also specify form, but in a very general way. Thus it will locate the major paths and the rhythm of views from them, the principal visual centers, the axes of view and the barriers to view, the landmarks, the districts of consistent visual character and the major boundaries between them, the form of the dominant open spaces, and the land and building masses. It is for these major elements, arranged in space as prescribed, that the visual programs will be specified. All this is part of a comprehensive design, which also deals with objective activity location, flow, and objective physical form.

Preferred sensuous form is as dependent on goals as any other aspect of design. Alternatives should be prepared for public evaluation. Different groups will have different interests, and designers should represent them. Visual form is also a subject for political debate. It is not holy ground.

At the moment, this appears to be a likely way of dealing with large-scale sensuous form. It is applicable from the project scale even up to the metropolitan region. However, we have produced very few examples of this technique, and have little concrete experience by which we can test its effectiveness.[21] Under pressure, we are thrown back on more familiar methods: the site plan, which specifies the shape of building exteriors; the illustrative sketch, or "artist's conception," which conveys mood or character by the use of selected detail (usually fraudulent); or the verbal statement of general policy, often ambiguous. These older methods are useful under certain conditions—the site plan in particular, when working at that scale and when in realistic command of building form. They are dubious when expanded to a larger scale—one cannot lay out a city as though it were a single subdivision, or model its three-

---

[21] Donald Appleyard and Kevin Lynch, "Opportunities in Kendall Square" (unpublished); Okamoto and Liskamm, MISSION DISTRICT URBAN DESIGN STUDY (San Francisco: 1966).

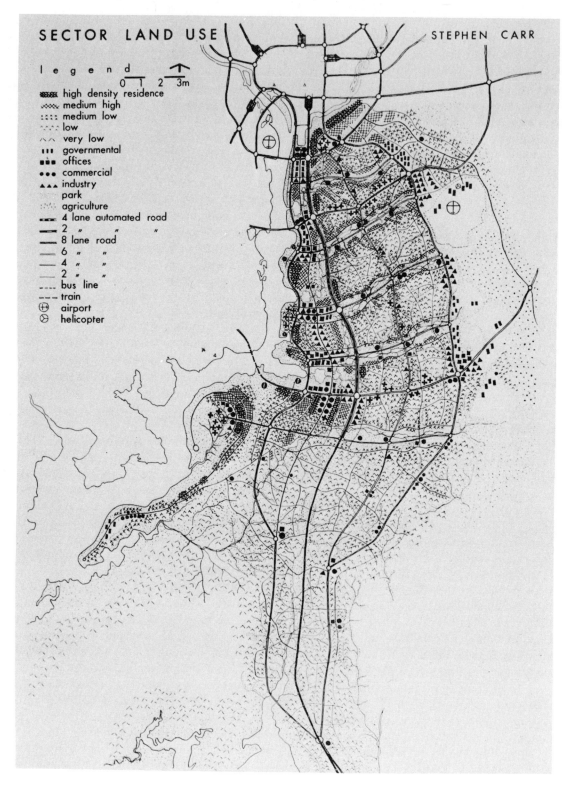

SECTOR LAND USE   STEPHEN CARR

l e g e n d   0 1 2   3m

▨▨ high density residence
⋌⋌ medium high
∷∷ medium low
⋰⋰ low
∧∧ very low
┃┃┃ governmental
▪▪▪ offices
●●● commercial
▲▲▲ industry
park
agriculture
▬▬ 4 lane automated road
▬ 2 "   "   "
▬▬ 8 lane road
6 "   "
4 "   "
2 "   "
- - - bus line
--- train
⊕ airport
⊗ helicopter

FIGURE 9–10. *Proposed visual texture for a sector of the Washington metropolitan region: a design by MIT students*

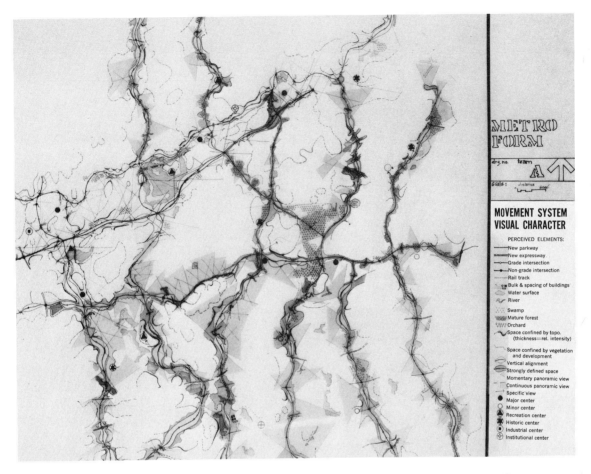

FIGURE 9–11. *Proposed system of highway sequences in a sector of the Boston metropolitan region, showing horizontal and vertical alignment, space definition, views, and relation to the landscape: a design by MIT students*

dimensional form as if it were a piece of sculpture. But one might design an urban region as a constellation of distinctive focal points connected by a cobweb of identifiable paths; or as an organized mosaic of visual districts; or as a visible spine of mass and activity along a major topographic feature; or as a coordinated grid of visual sequences. Specificity of form necessarily decreases as the scale of design increases. A proposal at metropolitan scale will consist of visual programs, illustrative designs and standards for typical situations, and the general location of the fundamental visible elements. A community design may include site plans, the exact location and expected visual performance of elements, even the detail and finish at crucial points.

CITY DESIGN

Design at the city scale, in its comprehensive sense, of which the above techniques are only aspects or partial approaches, is too large a subject to be treated here. Much of the text of this volume is concerned with just this topic. City or environmental design deals with the spatial and temporal pattern of human activity and its physical setting, and considers both its economic-social and psychological effects (of which latter the sensuous aspect is one part). The concepts and techniques for manipulating this complex pattern are as yet half-formed. The ambiguity of our graphic notation system, and its lack of inclusiveness, is one symptom of this inadequacy. The goals for which this pat-

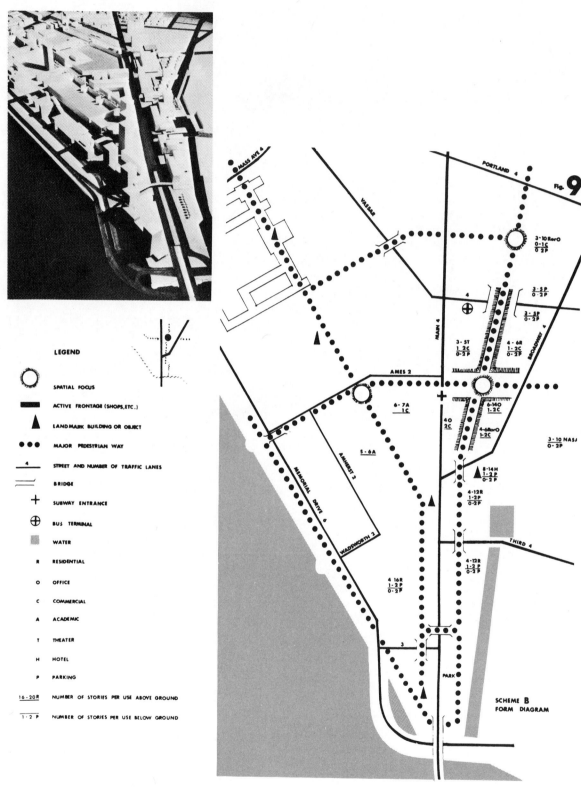

LEGEND

⊚ SPATIAL FOCUS

▬ ACTIVE FRONTAGE (SHOPS, ETC.)

▲ LANDMARK BUILDING OR OBJECT

●●● MAJOR PEDESTRIAN WAY

4 STREET AND NUMBER OF TRAFFIC LANES

═ BRIDGE

✛ SUBWAY ENTRANCE

⊕ BUS TERMINAL

▨ WATER

R RESIDENTIAL

O OFFICE

C COMMERCIAL

A ACADEMIC

T THEATER

H HOTEL

P PARKING

16-20R NUMBER OF STORIES PER USE ABOVE GROUND

1-2 P NUMBER OF STORIES PER USE BELOW GROUND

FIGURE 9–12. *Program for the visible form of a development, and an illustrative sketch model of one way of carrying out that program*

tern are manipulated are not clearly stated, and their relation to pattern is imperfectly known. Our vocabulary of city form is impoverished: the need for innovative ideas is correspondingly strong. Yet it is clear that city form is a critical aspect of the human environment, and design it we must.[22]

PROJECT AND SYSTEM DESIGN

Project design is usually what people refer to when they speak of "urban design" or of the "design input" in city plans. Project design is a better developed subject than city design. We have substantial experience with various aspects of it, a rich vocabulary of form, a history of success and failure, and a partial set of principles. We are accustomed to training professionals to deal with it.

System design is similar to project design in its concreteness of program and timing, but concerns a group of objects which may not all be in the same location, and do not make up the total environment in any area. This is a type of task to which the industrial designer is habituated. In this chapter, we can only point out typical examples of system and project design in the city environment, and briefly discuss their connection with city design.

The classic areas for project design in the city (with which chapters on design in former editions of this volume have largely been concerned) include such features as boulevards, parks, civic centers, cultural institutions, waterfronts, and garden cities. Most of these are settings for leisure, or for so-called "higher" activities: governments, museums, churches, schools.

This focus implies a hierarchical ranking of activity, a feeling that the remainder of the city must of necessity be unattractive, subject only to "practical" requirements. The garden city made an effort to include all aspects of life in a humane environment, but elsewhere the bias is obvious, and carries over today in the linkage of design with special events, or with upper middle-class taste. Some of these former design

preoccupations have lost their importance for us, such as the boulevard and the civic center. Others are still live issues—parks, new towns, large institutions—although the forms are shifting.

The design of new towns and of large institutional campuses are two examples which lie on the border between project and city design. Typically, they are marked by well-established central control of form, by a definite area (however large), and by an explicit future program (however mistaken it may often be). But the time span embraced by the design, and the complexity of its elements, make them akin to city design. Some of our best design talent is currently engaged precisely in these hybrid areas, and new ideas for city design are evolving there, including the management of future flexibility, the use of activity location for visual effect, the establishment of a formal framework for individualized building design, a creative attention to circulation, and so on.[23]

Current project design in the stricter sense is concentrated on shopping centers, suburban or in-town housing developments, plazas and other special open spaces, and sites for natural or historical preservation. The urban renewal program has opened up many opportunities for project design, particularly high or medium density housing, and partial replacement of the central business district. We are learning many new lessons about project design in the process.[24]

Inevitably, these design foci will shift, to some extent in response to shifts in design fashion, to a larger extent as social need and possibility evolves. We may guess at an increased role for system design, as in lighting or sign systems, mobile housing, open space networks, and systems of automobile, transit and pedes-

---

[22] Kevin Lynch, "The Quality of City Design," in Holland, ed., WHO DESIGNS AMERICA? (Garden City, N.Y.: Anchor Books, 1966), pp. 120–171.

[23] Oscar Newman, "The New Campus," ARCHITECTURAL FORUM, CXXIV (May 1966), pp. 30–55; Leslie Hugh Wilson, "New Town Design—Cumbernauld and After," ROYAL INSTITUTE OF BRITISH ARCHITECTS JOURNAL, LXXI (May 1964), pp. 191–201.

[24] Robert Montgomery, "Improving the Design Process in Urban Renewal," AMERICAN INSTITUTE OF PLANNERS JOURNAL, XXXI (February 1965), pp. 7–20; Jack Lynn, "Sheffield," in THE PEDESTRIAN IN THE CITY; ARCHITECT'S YEARBOOK XI, ed. David Lewis (London: Elek Books, 1965), pp. 53–97.

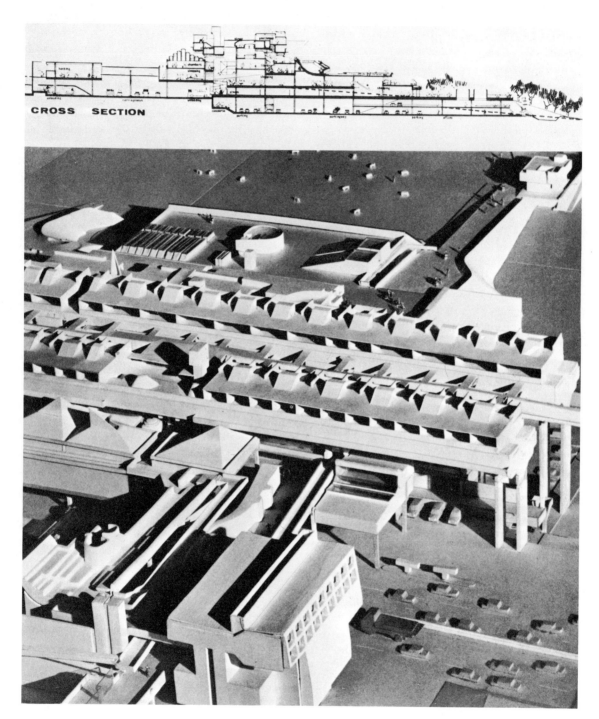

FIGURE 9–13. *Model of Phase I of the center for the new town of Cumbernauld: multiple uses occupy a complex linear structure overlying the main roadway*

FIGURE 9–14. *Living units overlap academic spaces in a single structure designed to replace an existing campus incrementally: proposal for Tougaloo College by Gunnar Birkerts and Assoc.*

trian movement. We may hope for attention to urgent environmental problems which have been considered beneath the notice of design, such as the slums and "gray areas," the strip commercial street, or the industrial complex. The concern for new towns and large suburban development may grow into the problem of designing new cities, which returns us to our original subject. We may begin to consider designs for the development of areas previously thought uninhabitable: mountains, deserts, water surfaces, wastelands, arctic tundra.

The joint between project and city design is always a crucial issue. City designers may be so remote from action that they recommend policies which cannot be carried out, or which have unanticipated or indefinable outcomes. Project designers may wreak havoc on other areas of the city. Urban renewal and campus design have by now furnished us with many bitter lessons on coordinating these two levels of attention. Until we have developed more skill, our only answer is that both concerns must overlap. That is, the city designer, in preparing his comprehensive framework, must test his ideas in the form of illustrative project designs or be to some extent involved in implementation. Vice versa (and this is rarely done), the project designer must see what consequences his particular scheme has for the general form of the city. Both professionals must therefore be at least familiar with the techniques of the other. Since city design is rarely taught, and many practicing city designers were originally project (architectural or landscape) designers, this linkage works somewhat better in the one direction than in the other. Even if mutual knowledge were improved, the institutional barriers between these two professionals, and the discrepant values they must work for, are formidable.

Public Policy and City Appearance

Many attempts have been made in history to control the look of a city. Most often they have failed. A few successful efforts have been carried out by strong central authorities, and many beautiful old cities were produced by the guidance of restricted technology or strong custom rather than by conscious design. Today those historic constraints have little controlling force. City design successes have typically been confined to the ceremonial areas: palaces, squares, religious compounds, parades. Few of these have direct relevance for us.

Our present achievements have been concentrated in planned suburban housing for the affluent, shopping centers, some campuses, and a few parks and squares. Many of our control systems have in reality gone wide of their mark, or broken down under the stress of the market and political conflict. Other attempts at control—"look-alike" ordinances, the specification of allowable style, powerful review boards—have often succeeded in stifling design innovation. "Design studies" which accompany city plans are usually done by separate specialists. They exhort, but do not often affect development decisions. Yet popular demand for a better environment is rising, and steam is collecting in the political boilers.

There are perhaps three general ways of managing city appearance: direct design, regulation, and influence. Let us take them in that order.

DIRECT DESIGN

Direct design implies that a central authority specifies the form that the environment will take. Direct design of the entire environment is possible at the project scale. At the city scale it is a dubious affair, requiring immense power and superhuman foresight. The inner city in Peking was done in this way, Fatehpur Sikri in India, central Le Havre and Brasilia in our time. Many architects dream of designing cities as they would a single building. Even aside from the political power required, the technical demands—staff, ability, and information—are staggering. Breakdowns are normal.

More frequently, even in the past, design focused on the outward form of certain key elements, a public square or the flanking facades of a major street, while leaving internal design and the bulk of the city to private developers. This was the strategy of Sitte and Haussmann, and the key idea in the City Beautiful movement. It continues today in such projects

as Pennsylvania Avenue (Washington, D.C.). Where the stakes are high, and authority is willing to exert its power, the strategy can be effective at the central focus of a city or along a major processional way. But to hope to control the entire appearance of a city by this means is unrealistic.

Design efforts may concentrate on those elements that are normally built by the public: post offices, city halls, hospitals, schools, streets and highways, transit lines, parks. They make up a large proportion of the city landscape, and must somehow be designed in any event. Unfortunately, separate government agencies may be more resistant to design improvements than are private builders (who have something to gain from cooperation), but it is true that good public design, particularly of such common elements as streets and open space, could make a strategic change in city appearance.[25]

The maintenance and constant renewal of these public elements is even more important than their original design. Money, energy, and skill must be applied regularly. The public areas of many European cities, and the current revival of the New York City park system, are striking examples of what can be done by good housekeeping, imaginative remodelling, lighting, and decorating.

It is also possible to design particular areas directly, where these have been previously delimited and programmed. Urban renewal, in particular, has offered this possibility to us, and so does institutional growth. If the current results have been sterile or chaotic, we have some grounds for hoping for better as project designers learn their trade. Too often, they are still designed as a collection of unrelated buildings. Unfortunately, even these projects are usually small, and their pattern a patchwork. Where areas are larger, as on the urban fringe, the potential is correspondingly greater.

Finally (and this is a technique as yet hardly used by public agencies) it is possible to design systems (highways, corridors, connected walkways or open spaces, night lighting), or to

---

[25] David A. Crane, "The Public Art of City Building," ANNALS OF THE AMERICAN ACADEMY OF POLITICAL AND SOCIAL SCIENCE, CCCLII (March 1964), pp. 84–94.

develop prototypes for frequently encountered problems (a local commercial intersection, a pocket park, a trailer park), or to innovate what Maki calls "group forms": elements which can be repeated, although with detailed changes, and whose flexible agglomeration can produce harmonious variations of general form.[26] The row house is an example of the latter, and the visual character (and functional adequacy) of many old towns is due to the consistent use of some such well-developed form. Standardized forms still characterize the great bulk of building today. Innovations in group form, in systems, or in prototype designs may be one of the most effective ways in which a central agency can affect city appearance, and they will be of great future importance. For reasons that go far beyond those of appearance, there must be a massive increase in public control of land and development in this country. But even under these conditions, we will find that the strategies of selective design, visual programming, systems and prototype design, and coordination and control will still be fundamental techniques for managing the resulting complexities of site, function, and agency.

PUBLIC REGULATION AND REVIEW

Visual form controls may be area-wide, similar in principle to zoning ordinances or even made part of them. The height limitations in Washington are an example, as are the specification of allowable materials in a housing development, setback lines along main ways, the regulation of signs, or the control of noise or light emission. These controls are applied to the entire city, or to large regions of it, or to all areas of a similar use.[27]

Almost all regulations of development— zoning ordinances, subdivision regulations, fire and building codes—have an impact on appearance. Density, building location, and open space requirements; rules as to street, block, and lot geometry; the regulation of parking, signs, landscaping, fences, earth removal or noise, should all be reviewed for their sensuous implications. In particular, they should not be so worded as to prevent good visual results, as they so often and unwittingly do. Regulations have typically been directed to the single object: the building or lot. They will be more effective where they refer to the group of objects as in cluster zoning or rules for integrating building forms. Just as in direct design, the move from the object to the system scale may be especially strategic.

Area-wide controls must of necessity be simple, and have often been supported by non-visual arguments, even when the motive was esthetic. They cannot produce a fine environment, but may prevent the worst or ensure consistency. Whether it is possible to control form indirectly, and thereby produce a visible harmony without interfering with the flexibility of individual design, is still a moot point. One strategy is to concentrate on specifying some salient element, such as the shape and material of the roof. Another is to develop a vocabulary of allowable forms, materials and colors, which can be combined at pleasure, but are calculated to sit well together. Both these devices are usable in strong control situations, such as renewal or a single-developer subdivision.

More recently, special controls have been used as strategic points—at landmark locations, for example, or to keep open important views. A visual easement may be purchased, or the immediate environs of a monument be protected, or unique regulations even be imposed on a single lot at a highly visible position. These entail compensation to the owners of the property affected.

Historic districts and landmark zones are by now familiar cases of special form controls, usable where a unique environment already exists, and the purpose is to preserve, rather than to create. Typically, a special commission is given veto control over all exterior changes within the district. It might indeed be desirable to vary visual regulations area by area, consistently over an entire city, to heighten

---

[26] Fumihiko Maki and Masato Ohtaka, "Some Thoughts on Collective Form," in Gyorgy Kepes, ed., STRUCTURE IN ART AND SCIENCE (New York: George Braziller, 1965), pp. 116–27.

[27] Joint Committee on Design Control, PLANNING AND COMMUNITY APPEARANCE (New York: Regional Plan Association, 1958).

area identity and make a closer fit between the form and meaning of each place. Such a sophisticated set of controls has not yet been attempted.

Controls may be applied more flexibly by the use of boards of review. These boards review development plans and make advisory suggestions, or they may have the power to prohibit undesirable form. In the latter case, the veto power may be more or less detailed. It may be guided by administrative rules or left to judgment on the spot. Discretion of the latter kind can take into account particular situations and integrated effects, playing a creative rather than a purely restrictive role. But the administrative energy consumed in each decision is large, and such a board may itself become mechanical and arbitrary.

For the former reason, it is impossible to review the detailed form of all development proposals in a city. The review process would break down under the load. Review must be confined to strategic points—historic areas, important centers, highly visible locations, or zones where strong control is easily achieved, as in public buildings and urban renewal. For the second reason, it is dangerous to give review boards powers of control which are based solely on their own judgment, except perhaps in cases of preservation, or when a board is temporarily created to pass on one unique site. Preferably, their work should be guided by a set of detailed criteria.

It is at this point that visual programming (see p. 263 and Figure 9–12) is particularly useful. If the general plan contains detailed statements of what the visual form should achieve in the various locations of the city, then the board's recommendations can be based on them. Even prior to review, they will act as persuasive guides to the developer and his designer.

Review has most often been applied at the moment of decision, when a design is complete. Changes are difficult and the confrontation may be savage. Review is much more effective if it enters into the initial stages of a design, when the program is being formulated and first sketches are being made. Changes involve fewer commitments, and new ideas may be received with interest. Frequent informal advice and persuasion, applied flexibly to design difficulties as they develop, is the correct tactic.

The review process is a useful way of controlling visual form. It should be confined to strategic locations and strategic types of development, and occur during the process of design, rather than at its terminus. It is preferably based on a well-developed visual program for the environment as a whole. It can be most effective as an advisory procedure, except in cases of preservation, or in some unique location of special public interest. The review function may be carried out by the regular staff of a planning or renewal agency, rather than by a separate board.[28]

A public agency can also affect environmental quality by influencing the selection of the designers who will plan it in detail. This influence may simply be informal, by recommendation and indirect pressure, or there may be a public list of recommended designers. Some European cities admit designers to practice in crucial areas only by special license. These are sensitive policies. An accepted means of controlling the selection of the designer is by the design competition, organized and judged by recognized procedures. This is a useful device for key landmark locations (and also a useful way of arousing public interest), but too unwieldy to be used often.

INFLUENCE

Controls and direct design are overt means of shaping sensuous form. What might be called sensuous information and design influence is an equally powerful tool. When people with visual design ability are present at a top decision level, or at key staff points where development is being planned, there will be an obvious impact on the resulting form. An alert design staff may often exercise important leverage by "brush fire" work—intervening persuasively with suggestions and criticism at the moment of public or private decisions. This requires tact, and also the ability to recognize the correct moment: when decisions will soon be made, but are not yet fixed.

---

[28] Roger Montgomery, "Improving the Design Process in Urban Renewal," *op. cit.*

Influence may be formalized by offering design services to public agencies or small developers who do not have such capabilities. In return for supplying design service at a nominal fee, and for imparting its superior knowledge of the future setting of the design, the agency gains influence over decisions, and can inform itself of the motives and capabilities of those who actually construct the environment. The resulting feedback, in its turn, will modify the proposals of the agency. This act of design liaison is as important as the services being directly rendered. By assigning staff (or even volunteer) designers as area service and liaison, the quality of the environment may be sharply improved simply because of the improved flow of information between the public and private agencies, large and small, which are shaping that environment.[29]

The flow of information may be improved in other ways. Visual surveys and analyses of the existing environment, coupled with predictions of future change and its impact, will by themselves influence the actions of builders. Communicated to the general public, they may help to generate political demands for an improved environment, increase public interest or pleasure in the cityscape, or make necessary controls more acceptable. Illustrative designs (which are despised by many designers) are another source of information. Far from being mere window-dressing, they communicate new possibilities, and transmit the intentions of the public staff in a more concrete way than abstract criteria and generalized diagrams. But these illustrations must depict real possibilities. Too often, they are drawn to show unlikely or distorted scenes—they convey false information with the intent to deceive and "sell."

ORGANIZING To DEAL WITH VISUAL FORM

Given the wide range of devices for influencing visual form, the multiplicity of situations in which this form can be a matter of concern, and the prevailing ambiguity between the concepts of design and appearance, it is difficult to generalize about best ways of organizing to manage environmental appearance. We can only note a few elements of organization which might be usable in a large public staff, concerned with continuous environmental planning for an extensive area:

1. The general "design" or "planning" section (meaning the staff which is preparing alternate possibilities for the general form of the area) should regularly include the capability to deal with visual form, along with other implications of form. It would be best, of course, if all members of the team had some such capability, however they concentrate their efforts. But since many points of view are pressing for attention in a large staff, and since city planners trained to deal with visual form are rare, it will probably be necessary to include specialists, or a special group, in the design team. However, there should not be a separate "visual design" staff, producing a "visual plan" which is disconnected from other design decisions.

2. It may be legitimate, however, to provide for a separate visual intelligence section, since factors can often be separated analytically if not in design. The function of this intelligence section would be to conduct a continuing analysis of the present and future sensuous form of the environment, by means of field surveys and studies of attitude and behavior. It could also be used to evaluate proposals, to test accomplished plans, and to communicate all this information to the public, to staff, and other designers. Members of this section might be specialists in perception, or behavioral science, or visual form.

3. There could be a liaison and review section, dealing primarily with the project and system designs made by other agencies and individuals. Again, it would necessarily deal with the designs as wholes, and not simply with their visual aspects. Its functions could include process review and "brush fire" intervention, design liaison and service, and recommendations for the maintenance and treatment of existing public areas.

4. Finally, a large staff may have one or more design task forces, which are composite

[29] Mary Hommann, WOOSTER SQUARE DESIGN (New Haven: New Haven Redevelopment Agency, 1965).

teams temporarily set up to do certain strategic project or system designs. Such task forces may also be used to develop prototype or illustrative designs, and in general to explore new possibilities. They will be composed of project or system designers, along with specialists peculiar to the particular problem.

While project design and project appearance are matters of long tradition, city design and city appearance are not. Techniques and criteria for dealing with the latter are still developing. Much of what has been said may be superseded. Certainly it will be expanded and clarified.

New powers, new public attitudes, new means of training professionals will all be required. But the key may be a better understanding of how the sensuous form of the environment affects us, a better knowledge of what we want, and a richer store of form possibilities. Given those, we can define and seek the power we need. Meanwhile, we know enough of some of the consequences and possibilities of the environment, and are backed by a sufficiently strong (if diffuse) public desire, to build, even now, a more comfortable, delightful, meaningful world.

This chapter was reviewed in draft by Stephen Carr, George Kostritsky, Roger Montgomery, Boris Pushkarev, Paul Spreiregen, and Carl Steinitz, and many useful ideas were received. The author's obstinacy is responsible for the remaining errors.

10

Quantitative Methods
in Urban Planning

FROM ITS VERY BEGINNINGS early in this century urban planning in the United States has become progressively more "quantitative" through growing use of numerical data and introduction of large-scale information-handling procedures and mathematically formulated analytical techniques. In the past few years significant new needs and capabilities have quickened that trend to the point of a methodological revolution.

On the demand side this recent development may be attributed to the greatly increased operational complexities implied by a drastic broadening in the scope of planning activity during the 1960's—from an almost exclusive emphasis on physical city planning to an inclusive concern with the whole range of physical, social and economic programming at the metropolitan, county, municipal, and submunicipal levels.

On the supply side, major contributing factors included the adaptation of mathematical techniques for use by the sciences concerned with socioeconomic, management, and policy techniques; the emergence of high-speed electronic data processing; the expansion in general-purpose data collected by public agencies; and the establishment of sizable federal aids for planning purposes.

Since quantitative methods are now an integral part of planning, they are touched on in a number of other chapters with reference to the particular subject matter at hand. (See Chapters 2, 3, and 6 for discussion of specialized activities related to quantitative methods.) The present chapter will augment those discussions by placing quantification in a broader perspective. This will be done by summarizing its general characteristics. Although some mathematical-statistical terms are used in the chapter, particularly in the subsequent section, the emphasis is not on operation of these concepts and techniques but on the overall role of quantification in current and future operations of comprehensive urban planning agencies. A number of recommendations to enable quantification to function effectively in public and civic affairs have been incorporated in the chapter.

Nature of Quantitative Methods

Quantitative methods are standardized operational sequences that involve large-scale assembly and/or processing of information by manual, mechanical, or automatic means. Such methods fall into three principal classes: (1) analytical techniques, (2) physical control mechanisms, and (3) data-handling procedures.

No inclusive integrated vocabulary exists for the use of quantitative methods in urban planning because the subject matter is in a state of rapid evolution and the methodological and substantive disciplines involved have their particular universes of discourse. We shall therefore adopt our own specific set of terms and attempt to follow it consistently in the text. "Neologisms" will be avoided in favor of words which have already gained reasonable acceptance.

Some key methodological concepts are set out below and illustrated with elementary examples.

ANALYTICAL TECHNIQUES

A *quantitative analytical technique* creates numerical solutions, through the mathematical treatment of input data, in order to perform one or more of the following basic types of analysis: empirical estimation; hypothetical estimation; structural estimation; prediction; prescription; calibration. Generally speaking, quantitative analytical techniques comprise a set of mathematical models and a series of associated computational operations. In all cases they have a conceptual as well as a procedural dimension.

Mathematical models, a central feature of quantitative analysis, may be defined as abstractions presented in the form of symbols which express an aspect of the real world in terms of a sequence of simplified processes or as a complex of relationships among numerical entities.

The basic types of quantitative analysis are perhaps most readily characterized by their objectives and some of their end-products.

Empirical estimation treats partial or "proxy" observed data to generate values describing a corresponding universe of occurred and directly observable states or events, e.g., expanded population sampling results, or income figures that derive from reported rent levels.

Hypothetical estimation treats observed or projected empirical data to generate values expressing not directly observable concepts of an interpretative and/or normative nature, e.g., cost of living indexes, service quality ratings, "access" measures, dwelling density standards.

Structural estimation yields quantified measures of general relationship among different classes of observable phenomena, e.g., correlation coefficients, beta coefficients.

Prediction produces values which forecast a set of empirically verifiable future states or events, e.g., anticipated employment levels as of specific years, or anticipated investment volumes during specified periods.

Prescription produces values which propose a set of desired future states or events, e.g., recommended land use amounts, as of specified years or recommended highway improvement outlays during specified periods.

Calibration assigns values (a) to the numerically non-specified constants of individual mathematical models, e.g., regression-based parameters, input-output production parameters; (b) indexes that assess the efficacy of those models for estimating or for predictive purposes, e.g., standard errors of estimate, coefficients of determination.

PHYSICAL CONTROL MECHANISMS

A *physical control mechanism* is a method for operating selected components of a mechanical-electronic system over time, on the basis of continuously received input data which monitor the progress and prospects of that system's performance and of its environment.

The essence of control mechanisms inheres in their self-regulating properties, their reliance on feedback information, and their consequences for immediate judgment and action. Modern manufacturing processes are, of course, totally dependent on such devices. A more pertinent example is afforded by current methods for phasing traffic signals in instantaneous response to monitored data on vehicular flows within a given highway network.[1]

Data-Handling Procedures

A data-handling procedure is a method which works with relatively large amounts of numerical, verbal, or graphic intelligence in order to perform one or more of the following basic types of information management: collection;

---

[1] Incidentally, analogous approaches are applicable to quantitative analysis with regard to the progressive updating of numerical solutions—e.g., the automatic modification of regional employment forecasts as a function of monitored intelligence on local job changes that are actually observed, new plant locations, and national business cycle developments.

recording; storage/retrieval; reduction; presentation; transmission.

The subject matter of data-handling is information and the elemental substantive unit involved here is the individual information item. The range of possible item categories is broad and varied. It includes numerical values, conceptual constructs, textual narratives, pictorial illustrations, cartographic mappings, etc.

The six basic types of information management may be briefly described as follows:

Collection embraces the systematic assembly of individual information items by means such as interviewing, visual inspection, photography, reading, etc.

Recording refers to the standardized transfer of information to and among physical media such as questionnaire forms, film, computer tapes, library accession cards, books, etc.

Storage/Retrieval entails the orderly filing and cataloguing of recorded information and its ready release upon user demand.

Reduction involves the mathematical manipulation of retrieved data with a view to increasing its general usefulness or adapting it to the input specifications of analytical techniques or control mechanisms, e.g., summarization of block population data by census tract, aggregation of detailed employment figures into a smaller number of broader categories, and computation of arithmetic means or variances.

Presentation refers to the reporting of retrieved data by such means as graphic displays, written summaries, numerical tables, etc.

Transmission entails the movement of information between facilities which are relatively distant from one another, e.g., dissemination of census data via teletype, computer operation by remote control.

The foregoing concepts are meant to provide an elementary guide to the almost boundless subject matter of quantitative tools in general, and to serve as a basis for classifying some of its more important methods. Obviously, several types of analysis, control, and information management are often carried out on an interrelated basis, due to the operating needs of applied fields such as planning. With respect to analysis, for example, structural description and calibration would probably be part and parcel of any estimating, predictive, or prescriptive effort, which would in turn depend on the whole range of data-handling activities. Similarly, physical control mechanisms would operate in a completely integrated manner with data-handling and analytical methods.

The Place of Automation

Automation should be briefly noted at this point, since it cuts across the entire spectrum of quantitative methodology. As a rule the data assembly and processing sequences under discussion here lend themselves to automated operation and in many cases actually require it for effective use.

Automated means are appropriate whenever one or more of the following circumstances obtain:

—Large amounts of data must be handled, e.g., reduction of land use survey results.

—Complicated calculations must be carried out, e.g., linear programming solutions for a prescriptive resource allocation model.

—A given task is not amenable to manual or mechanical methods because of time limitations or technical difficulties, e.g., recording of "perishable" census data, Monte Carlo solutions for a predictive model incorporating millions of individual decision processes.

The array of activities that can currently be automated includes data storage/retrieval and calculation; visual information display; quantification of graphic data; physical design; textual scanning; long distance data exchange. In all cases automation involves the use of "hardware" equipment, e.g., electronic computers, and translation into "software" operating methods, e.g., computer programs.

Quantitative Methods as "Systems"

A "system" is an autonomous administrative, physical, or analytic construct designed to perform a set of given tasks by carrying out a variety of activities subject to centralized controls. Factories, electronic computers, and mathematical models are respective examples of organizational, physical and analytic systems. Currently popular terms such as "systems engineering" and "systems analysis" have come to denote the design and use of systemic constructs for a variety of purposes and, more broadly, to signify a rational and "holistic" approach to the performance of complicated tasks.

Generally speaking, the quantitative methods discussed here are systems in this sense. It should be made clear however that these methods constitute only one of many possible application areas of the systems approach.

SOME OVERALL IMPLICATIONS

The quantitative methods described are applicable to a wide variety of disciplines. While most of them owe their inception and original use to fields like chemistry, physics, biology and engineering, they have been considerably advanced by the military, and are rapidly being adopted by the social, management and policy disciplines. Urban planning practice, by virtue of the "quantifiability" that characterizes much of its subject matter, is especially suited to such methods; in fact, the profession would be helpless without them, given the complexities and information loads which face planners today and which are bound to become even greater in the future.

Essential as they may be to successful professional practice, quantitative methods are not easy to live with. They make heavy material, intellectual and emotional demands on their users. This is particularly true in fields such as comprehensive urban planning which, unlike engineering for example, have come upon these tools only recently and with comparatively little relevant preparation. Several important facts of life must therefore be recognized.

Not a Panacea. Because of the remarkable accomplishments of natural science and engineering derived with the help of quantitative methods, the recent wholesale adoption of such methods by social, management and policy disciplines has been accompanied by hopes for comparable success in these disciplines. Consequently, resultant equations and computer data printouts sometimes assume an aura of precision and unchallengeable authority in the eyes of the urban planning practitioner (and the spectator). Moreover, they appear to confer a special kind of status on individual users and their agencies. (A countervailing tendency to engage in blanket denunciations of the quantitative approach arose within the profession some years ago, but this seems to be subsiding.) Without disparaging their many actual and potential contributions we must qualify the applicability of quantitative methods to urban planning by pointing out two ways in which the field differs from natural science and engineering. First, the urban social, economic, and spatial structure is inherently more difficult to measure, understand, and predict than are physical or biological phenomena. Second, the urban planning process is more subject to "non-quantifiable" political and bureaucratic decisions than is the typical laboratory, factory, or construction site.

Quantification Demand Rigor. All terms must be sharply defined and all procedural steps logically consistent with one another in order that processed data will yield meaningful results and computer programs will work. The use of quantitative methods thus requires a degree of exactness which is both laborious and time-consuming and which calls for a firm grounding in conceptual and mathematical logic. This is not always compatible with the planning profession's traditional reliance on intuitive approaches and with the very real pressures for quick results to which public agencies tend to be subject. Nevertheless, if quantitative methods are to be genuinely productive, they will need an administrative environment that can evoke rigorous job habits and provide enough time for sustained precision.

Quantification Depends on Specialized Skills. Consider a group of quantitative methods which includes such diverse items as statistical sampling, regression analysis, mathematical programming, stochastic process analysis, and computer program writing. Effective use of any of these procedures in a given work effort depends on the collaboration of two kinds of highly trained experts: first, a person for whom that particular method constitutes a primary professional interest and who is reasonably familiar with the subject matter to which it is being applied; second, a person who is a full-fledged practitioner in the substantive field of concern. In the case of urban planning, specialists of the former type must be recruited from such outside disciplines as data processing, operations research, and statitsics, while those of the latter must be found within the profession itself. Naturally, both types of talent tend to be in short supply. A planning agency may often need to retain them from universities and private consulting firms or from other public agencies.

Quantification Is a Mass Consumer of Data. When quantitative analysis is adopted by an applied discipline, a great deal of numerical information that meets specified standards of accuracy is usually required for its development and use. Much of this may need to be obtained from original sources, and all of it should be carefully managed—from its initial intake through every stage of the work process. Data demands tend to be particularly heavy when, as is often the case in urban planning, individual methodological applications must be calibrated or formulated by the user himself before being put into practice. Thus, calibration of traffic forecast models for Southeastern Wisconsin utilized 12 million separate data bits from a home interview survey of the 1963 travel behavior of 18,000 sampled households.

Quantification Requires Elaborate Technical Equipment. The tasks which quantitative methods can perform best tend to be analytically intricate or to entail large and varied volumes of data. As a result, automation tends to become a necessity. With regard to urban planning procedures, for example, current and prospective means for achieving automation include such complicated devices as high-speed computers and optical scanners. It would probably be fair to say that urban planners as a whole are not noted for their interest in electronic hardware or their ability to use it. The fact remains, however, that this type of equipment is associated with many quantitative methods and that its management and operations must be based on technological competence.

Quantification Implies Continuous Development of New Methods. One hundred man-

hours might have been needed in 1952 to write a typical regression program (in machine language) for an IBM 650, one of the most advanced non-military computers then in existence. It had a storage capacity of 20,000 characters and took 20 hours to solve a medium-sized multi-varied regression program. In 1967, the same program-writing (now in FORTRAN) might take 10 man-hours for a comparably-priced IBM 360 computer possessing a storage capacity of 120,000 and the ability to solve a corresponding problem in one or two hours.

Within a 15-year span, drastic improvements in data processing technology have brought about complete revision in computer programming procedures and a quantum jump in capabilities for data handling and analysis. In turn, this has increased the range of quantitative methods available to various applied disciplines, forcing the latter into a state of rapid methodological change which is bound to become even swifter in the future. For urban planners, the resulting opportunities are accompanied by a number of problems. These include the cost of adapting new techniques to agency work, the continuing need for updating obsolescent personnel skills, and the difficulty of reconciling frequent methodological innovation with stable agency practices and sound staff morale. It should also be pointed out that individual planning units will increasingly be called upon to collaborate in the development of techniques which, while intended for profession-wide use, require experimental testing in the context of a specific agency situation.

Quantification Calls for Systematic Programming and Control. Since quantitative methods tend to be associated with analytical complexity, heavy data loads, and major equipment usage, their application in a particular work effort usually generates a large number of interdependent activities involving a variety of organizations, specialists and financial arrangements. Take, for example, current agency practice with respect to the prediction of intrametropolitan locational changes. This may entail collection of large amounts of land use data[2] (planning agency field crews) ; computerized

---

[2] Items in parentheses refer to logically-related personnel and organizations.

reduction and storage of the collected data (commercial EDP facility); calibration of a computerized locational forecast model (private consulting firm No. 1), with input variables obtained from the concurrent calibration of a trip distribution model (state highway department); and, finally, use of the calibrated forecast model to predict future locational patterns (planning agency staff) as a function of separately projected metropolitan growth aggregates (private consulting firm No. 2) and as a function of travel times and land capacities deriving from a separately formulated metropolitan policies program (planning agency staff)—with the resulting model outputs serving as direct input to the trip generation phase of an intrametropolitan traffic prediction sequence (state highway department). Clearly, a plan-making effort that embraces the foregoing array of work elements should be regarded as a management problem of the highest order. Unless systematic operations programming and control are exercised, such an effort is bound to break down or at best "muddle through" unproductively. It must be said that the urban planning field does not yet appear to be truly receptive to the systems approach that is called for here. Much of this difficulty stems from the political and bureaucratic pressure within which planners operate, but the *ad hoc* mentality dominating the profession is also an important contributing factor. In addition, the model-makers themselves can be faulted for failing to make clear the nature of their assumptions and their value structure.

Quantification and Political Issues. The large volumes of data entailed in quantitative methods can provide a great deal of detailed knowledge of existing community conditions. At the same time, the application of such methods can indicate the likely consequences of contemplated public and private actions in stark and objective terms. For these reasons quantification may lead to political pressures aiming to inhibit some of its efforts and to promote others. While pressures of this type are, of course, traditional to the field they are bound to grow as the scope of planning agency information increases.

Quantification Is Expensive. Large field crews add up to sizable payrolls, since sophisticated statisticians and computer programmers command impressive salaries, and data processing services are billed at several hundred dollars per hour of machine time. In the case of urban planning practice, this means that a long-standing tradition of modest agency budgets must give way to expenditure patterns which may be illustrated by some current examples: a $300,000 outlay to develop locational forecast models for a major regional planning project; a city planning agency's $18,000 salary offer for a systems analyst; an annual item of $100,000 for computer services to aid in the preparation of metropolitan land use and transportation plan. In the long run, sufficient funds for this type of work will no doubt be made available by an affluent society such as the United States, largely through its federal government.[3]

In summary, the obvious and healthy attitude toward quantitative methods combines respect for a powerful set of working tools with a continuing awareness of their limitations.

The New Planning Agencies

During the latter 1960s and early 1970s the primary mission of urban planning agencies, regardless of organizational form, is likely to revolve around the preparation of comprehensive plans for the long-range development of given jurisdictional areas as a whole or by sub-section. The "prescriptive scope"[4] of these

---

[3] It should be noted, moreover, that a high level of agency expenditures necessitate elaborate internal fiscal procedures, particularly in view of the accountability requirements imposed by federal funding units.

[4] We define the term *prescriptive scope* to denote a range of action types which are embraced by a comprehensive area plan and with regard to which the plan-making agency chooses to make recommendations of its own. As a rule action types are included by virtue of having major area-wide implications, requiring middle- or long-range goals and falling directly subject to governmental initiative. Over the years the prescriptive scope of comprehensive area plan-making has widened progressively as a result of the growing complexity of urban society and the increasing role of government in urban affairs. This progression has in turn precipitated continuing and far-reaching changes in the technical content of planning agency work.

QUANTITATIVE METHODS IN URBAN PLANNING 283

plans may be expected to cover such functional facets of area development as transportation, recreation, health, education, welfare, housing, culture, social relations, personal and business services, trade and manufacturing.

In addition to carrying out its primary assignment of long-range plan preparation, the typical comprehensive urban planning agency of the latter 1960s and early 1970s can be expected to exercise a collaborative role in two closely-related governmental efforts, with respect to its jurisdictional area, i.e., in plan-implementation and in general-purpose information management. With regard to plan-implementation this is likely to occur through direct administrative involvement in the regulation of land use and in the realm of socio-economic measures; in the short-run operational coordination of public facilities, services and aid programs; and in the mandatory review of individual public and private development projects. With regard to general-purpose information management, the planning agency's role will derive from its assembly, maintenance, and analysis of the massive data files which are required for plan-making purposes and which are bound to make up a substantial portion of an area data repository that seeks to be substantially inclusive of vital information.

Quantitative Methods and Planning Agency Operations

Planning agency tasks call for a wholehearted systems approach centering on the use of two broad constructs, one of them organizational and the other analytic. *Organizationally,* the entire work of a particular agency should be administered as an integrated complex of activities. *Analytically,* the course of development experienced by an agency's jurisdictional area as a whole should be expressed in the form of an inclusive conceptual model of areal structure. Although they are not being applied to any appreciable degree at present, the two constructs suggested here will most likely become increasingly necessary as the scope of planning agency operations becomes greater and greater. At the same time the quantitative methods

summarized elsewhere in this chapter will make the use of such constructs increasingly more feasible. A brief review of the formal characteristics of systems should serve to introduce the construct in more detail.

By previous definition a system is an autonomous administrative, physical, or analytic construct designed to perform a set of given tasks by carrying out a variety of interdependent activities subject to centralized controls. In terms of its individual components a system may be said to comprise:

(a) an integrated complex of precisely formulated and staged operations which interact along

(b) designated time segments and from

(c) a determinate initial condition to convert specified categories of

(d) input into specified

(e) end-product categories, and

(f) by-product categories; and which are directed by

(g) a central control mechanism with reference to that mechanism's continuing perception of

(h) a delimited germane environment, with the aid of a set of

(i) fixed resources and on the basis of

(j) explicit system-wide objectives and

(k) a generalized operational configuration.

Since a system moves forward over time it may be viewed in either of two ways: as a *process* during any particular *period,* or as a *state* at any particular *time-point.* Also, it is usually possible to disaggregate or separate a given system into functionally distinct parts or to mask it into more inclusive systemic constructs.

Planning Agency Operations: An Organizational System. Most of today's comprehensive planning agencies are loosely administered, lacking a clear-cut conception of their own scope, objectives, and operating procedures, and of their place within the community decision-making process. This is a contributing factor—though not the only one—to the low achievement levels that have plagued planning to date.

A first and strategic implementing step is to

propose the systems concept as an overall organizing principle. The premise is that the operations of a typical planning unit can and should approximate the formal character of an administrative system by virtue of their task-orientation, diversity, interdependence, and amenability to centralized control.

Consider a comprehensive planning unit which operates as a governmental agency for a medium-sized American city and which has been carrying on for a number of years in the disjointed manner that is common to organizations of its kind. How could the work of this agency be cast into a systems format by a future planning executive and his technical and managerial advisors?

The activities in which a total community is engaged, in order to facilitate a community's comprehensive planning, involve many forces which are not amenable to centralized control. Hence our proposed systems orientation is advisedly restricted to the planning *agency,* as distinguished from the planning *process.* This calls for some attention to certain end-products that do not constitute "planning services" as such, e.g., the review of zoning ordinance amendments. It also means that numerous aspects of plan-making proper—political interventions, for example—will be placed in the system's "germane environment" rather than in its "integrated complex of precisely formulated and staged operations." Even with regard to the latter, the matter of "precision" is a question of degree, along a scale that descends from mathematical assignment of trips to the choice by judgment of major area development alternatives open to the community.

Reiterating the formal components enumerated previously (items [a] to [k] p. 283), the organizing team might proceed as follows:

Area Development: An Analytic System. In carrying out its primary task of comprehensive plan preparation, an urban planning agency is faced with the problem that "area development," the central substantive concern of this work, covers a virtually boundless multiplicity of phenomena. Before any meaningful plan-making can begin, these phenomena must be conceptualized into an analytically manageable abstraction. The kind of abstraction that is required should encompass and be confined to three principal features: the various action-proposal categories of the plan-maker's prescriptive scope; those aspects of area structure that are to be anticipated endogenously for evaluating action-proposal consequences; and any other aspects of area structure that are proposal designs.

Drawing on our previously enumerated components (items [a] to [k] on p. 283), one might conceptualize the course of area development as follows:

ANALYSIS, CONTROL AND DATA HANDLING

In addition to calling for a two-fold overall systems approach, the task groups that have been outlined for the planning agency will require application of a great variety of quantitative methods. Many of these methods are already available, a host of others are currently under development, and still others represent promising ideas that should—and probably will—be translated into useful operating procedures. The following methods 'represent, therefore, a combination of advocacy and anticipation.

Planning Agency Management. Predictive and prescriptive analytical techniques based on the "critical path" approach, e.g., PERT and CPM, will be used by all larger planning units to organize their internal operations. Such methods provide forecasts of the time and dollar costs of individual task items, as well as producing periodically updated work schedules which divide an agency's many activities into phases, so that available resources are used to full advantage and stipulated deadlines are met to the greatest practicable extent.

Description of Past and Current Development. Mathematical estimating techniques will be used by planning agencies to describe the past and current course of development experienced by their particular jurisdictional areas—as a basis for plan-making and as a general-purpose information service for public and private decision makers. These techniques will center on mathematical models which produce indexes that summarize, interpret and evaluate quantifiable development aspects possessing general area-wide significance or direct and

PLANNING AGENCY OPERATIONS
(Formal Components)

Basic Component	Illustrative Elements or Considerations
Formalize a central control mechanism (g).	The executive and administrative elements of the agency.
Delimit a germane environment (h).	The overall course of municipal change in relation to extramunicipal events, political and bureaucratic forces inside and outside the municipalities, as they bear on the planning agency's operations.
Specify system-wide objectives (j).	Preparation of a comprehensive municipal development scheme; participation in plan-implementing activities and in general-purpose information management; extension of miscellaneous kinds of assistance to other municipal agencies.
Specify detailed end-product categories (e).	Prepare the format of the comprehensive municipal development scheme, public project review items; zoning amendment review items; data contribution items for the metropolitan information center; special services for the mayor's office.
Formulate a generalized operational configuration (k).	Task flow charts; task precedence diagrams.
Specify detailed input categories (d).	Primary data; secondary data; staff and consultant services; computer services.
Specify detailed by-product categories (f).	Incidentally generated substantive data; internal management information.
Designate a time segment for system operation (b).	E.g., a five-year future period extending from the earliest practicable starting date.
Detail an initial system condition (e).	Task completion status and fixed resource availability as of the designated starting date.
Allocate fixed resources (i).	Personnel, equipment, office space, funds.
Formulate and schedule individual operations (a).	Planning agency work program and budget.

FIGURE 10–1. *An organizational system for planning agency operations*

PLANNING AGENCY OPERATIONS
(Area Development: An Analytical System)

Basic Component	Illustrative Elements or Considerations
Central control mechanism (g).	Technical decision criteria adopted by the planning agency's upper echelon technicians.
Germane environment (h).	The future course of development outside the jurisdictional area.
System-wide objectives (j).	To provide an indication of the area's future development; to place the planning agency's action proposals and their consequences within the context of this development.
Time segment for systems operations (b).	The planning period, e.g., 1970–1975.
Detailed end-product categories (e).	Anticipated area structure for future dates and structural change for future time intervals.
Generalized operational configuration (k).	Procedural flow chart for anticipating exogenous and endogenous development aspects.
Detailed input categories (d).	Planning agency's action proposals; anticipated characteristics of the germane environment.
Detailed by-product categories (f).	Intermediate output required solely as input for the anticipation of endogenous development aspects, e.g., highway link driving times.
Initial system condition (e).	Base date description of areal structure.
Fixed resources (i).	Raw data underlying input categories.
Individual operations schedule (a).	Complete definitions of variables and functional relationship.

FIGURE 10–2. *An analytic system for area development*

specific relevance for proposals-design. Examples of the resulting output might include periodic "empirical estimates" of population levels, investment volumes and income distribution, as well as periodic "hypothetical estimates" of community well-being, public service quality, and degree of ethnic segregation. Although this type of analysis is already fairly common, the future is likely to bring a considerable expansion in its frequency of use, its substantive range, and in the reliability of the mathematical indexes that are utilized.

Exogenous Aspects of Future Area Development. Traditionally, urban planning practice has treated many aspects of future area development as exogenous or outside factors, because it was presumed that they had no impact on the action-proposals embraced by comprehensive area plans, that they represented "non-dependent" aspects. As a result of their ready quantifiability, however, some of these exogenous aspects, e.g., aggregate metropolitan population levels, or per capita productivity ratios, did in fact occasion the initial use of mathematical techniques in planning. Now, with the growth of governmental action in urban development, and with the widening prescriptive scope of plan-making, the range of truly non-dependent aspects is bound to shrink progressively.[5] More and more, area-wide economic and demographic aggregates and quantified behavioral/technical relationships are therefore likely to be predicted by endogenous techniques which allow for the effect of specific planning agency proposals (see section below on Preparation of Comprehensive Area Plans).

Adoption of Area-Development Goals. Mathematical techniques for proposals-formulation and evaluation incorporate quantitative norms, i.e., numerically expressed objectives, standards and rating indexes. As the use of such techniques in plan-making becomes more common (see section below), planning agencies will tend increasingly to state their broad area-development goals in a manner which permits direct numerical elaboration.

Consider the general aim of furthering the economic well-being of an urban community. For operational purposes, the concept of well-being might appropriately be phrased in terms of personal income. This would provide for direct translation of the general aim into specific quantitative norms: for example, maximization of the aggregate income as the functional objective of a linear programming model that allocates public subsidies to disadvantaged population groups; specified levels of aggregate community income and individual income as, respectively, target objectives and minimum standards in the design of public assistance services; per capita community income as one rating index for evaluating the overall consequences of alternative area-development schemes.

Preparation of Comprehensive Area Plans. In preparing its comprehensive plan, the typical planning agency will follow a sequence of repetitive steps embracing the design of action-proposal sets, anticipation of consequences of proposals, and evaluation of the proposals in terms of their anticipated consequences. This sequence will lead to the formulation of an Area Development Scheme which details a preferred action-proposal set and its evaluated consequences. Throughout the process there will be considerable reliance on mathematical techniques of prescription, prediction and hypothetical estimation.[6]

With respect to *proposals design,* mathematical prescriptive methods such as linear programming will be utilized to schedule governmental projects involving facilities (e.g., highway improvement) and services (e.g., manpower retraining programs); and to arrive at fiscal and regulatory recommendations. Generally speaking, this type of method will operate to prescribe that configuration of a specified category of future governmental actions which most closely achieves quantified objectives within the limits of a quantified set of "norma-

---

[5] Consider, for instance, the substantial effect of expressway building or federal business loans on the economy of a medium-sized metropolitan region.

[6] As noted, planning agencies will also make heavy use of mathematical techniques in the three preparatory activities that are fundamental to plan formulation—describing their area's past and current development, anticipating its exogenous future aspects and adopting goals for its future growth.

tive" or "circumstantial" constraints. An illustrative list of objectives might include capital cost minimization, personal income maximization, service equalization and attainment of a "target" distribution of land use classes. A corresponding list of constraints might include mandatory site density ratios, maximum acceptable air pollution counts and minimum acceptable wage scales (normative), as well as the given total amount of available land, size of tax base and magnitude of the total labor force (circumstantial). All quantitative objectives and normative constraint values will be likely to derive from the planning agency's overall development goals (see section above) and all circumstantial constraint values will be produced as part of the agency's forecast efforts.

At present, the mathematical prescriptive techniques available to urban planning agencies are mainly limited to a few disparate, narrowly-defined proposal categories (e.g., highway improvements) that utilize extremely simple objectives and constraints (e.g., travel time minimization; total funds available for road building).[7] Continuing methodological research and the widening prescriptive scope of comprehensive area planning are bound to lead to procedures which are directed at a progressively larger range of proposals and which work with an increasingly greater number of objectives and constraints. Nevertheless, individual techniques will probably always be "sub-optimal" in the sense of covering only a segment of the total prescriptive scope that prevails during any particular plan-making period. No single technique is likely to be all-inclusive. Moreover, substantial portions of the widening prescriptive scope will probably always remain subject to non-mathematical procedures for such technical reasons as non-quantifiability and analytical complexity, and for non-technical reasons of political and bureaucratic intervention.

With respect to *anticipating proposal consequences,* mathematical predictive techniques will be applied increasingly to make *endogen-ous forecasts*[8] of the quantifiable aspects of area development. Typically, the output of current application represents a staged future distribution of phenomena, serving to convey a picture of endogenous area developments and to provide a numerical basis for evaluating alternative proposal sets. The corresponding input allows for the combined effect of initial conditions, exogenously forecast future phenomena, the specified plan proposals themselves, and certain endogenously forecast future phenomena that have been projected by other techniques.

Most current applications operate to forecast patterns of location, traffic, and fiscal activities—as a function of variables which express development proposals dealing with transportation facilities, urban renewal, open space, and land use regulation. As the role of government, and the prescriptive scope of urban plan-making, continue to expand, the substance of endogenous forecasting generally will be augmented in three important ways: (a) through the introduction of output elements which express proposal consequences that urban planning agencies have traditionally projected in an exogenous manner (e.g., aggregate metropolitan population growth) or not at all (e.g., educational attainment, incidence of disease and delinquency, atmospheric pollution levels); (b) through the introduction of input elements which reflect supplemental aspects of initial condition and exogenous future development that must be allowed for in forecasting the added output elements; (c) through the introduction of input elements which reflect additional kinds of *physical* development proposals (e.g., air pollution controls) as well as an entirely new range of recommendations dealing with socio-economic services such as vocational training, crime abatement, birth control assistance and medi-

---

[7] Occasionally, there has been other meaningful work undertaken, such as by the A. D. Little firm on the Community Renewal Program in San Francisco.

[8] We define *endogenous forecasting* as the projection, for purposes of a given plan-making effort, of area development phenomena which are presumed to depend on action-proposal types embraced by the plan-maker's prescriptive scope. Note the difference between this and *exogenous forecasting,* which projects phenomena that are presumed to be non-dependent on the plan-maker's action-proposals (see section on Anticipation of the Exogenous Aspects of Future Area Development).

cal aid. It should be clear that such a drastic increase in output and input requirements will greatly complicate the endogenous forecasting task and call for intensive studies of the physical, social and economic interrelations of urban structure in the context of public policy.

With respect to *evaluating proposals* in terms of their anticipated consequences, urban planning agencies will place growing reliance on the use of quantitatively scaled rating indexes such as per capita personal income or community "livability"—specified by themselves or relative to their respective levels at prior dates. This type of appraisal is based on the calculation of rating index values that are a function of endogenous forecasts and (where a comparison with initial conditions is desired) current estimates. Some indexes will take the form of a simple measure whose values are directly obtainable from the results of forecasting and estimating, e.g., per capita income. More and more frequently, however, indexes will be defined as composites of normatively weighted forecast and estimate values. In these latter instances it will be necessary to calculate the desired index number of means of a hypothetical estimating equation, whose parameters operate as normative weights to produce a single numerical score from a whole series of input values, e.g., a community "livability" index computed by adding differentially weighted magnitudes of per capita "consumer facilities access," personal income, tax payments and daily commuting time.[9]

In all cases, rating indexes used in evaluation of proposals should derive from the agency's overall development goals and be compati-

ble with the indexes that are employed to describe past and current area development. The problem of assigning meaningful numerical values to the normative weighting terms is of course a difficult one and must be regarded as a major unresolved issue in contemporary urban planning practice.

Generally speaking, mathematical prescriptive techniques will be applied segmentally to the design of some but not all of the items that make up a planning agency's inclusive proposal set. By contrast, endogenous forecast and evaluation techniques will be applied across-the-board to appraise the consequences of the proposal set as a whole and to do this for the agency's entire jurisdictional area. The fact that a particular proposal item may have been produced by a "sub-optimizing" technique will not of course prevent its incorporation in the appraisal sequence and would not preclude major subsequent changes in the item on the basis of the more complete picture revealed by that sequence. At the same time the prospective effect of individual proposal items may occasionally be traced out, by holding the remainder of the set constant as a complete series of endogenous forecasts and evaluations is performed—first with and then without the proposal item in question. This type of impact analysis is also applicable to the review of project recommendations that originate outside the planning agency (see section on Participation in Plan-Implementing Activities).

With respect to *development scheme formulation,* planning agencies will come to pattern their product after the analytic system of area development that was outlined above. As such, the typical scheme will comprise the following elements:

—All adopted overall development goals and operational norms.

—A description of area structure as of a base date.

—All anticipated exogenous aspects of future area development.

—A detailed scheduling of the preferred action-proposal set.

—Descriptions of anticipated changes in area structure for a number of contiguous time intervals, extending from the base to

---

[9] Note that hypothetical estimating models are also utilized to produce certain non-normative indexes which represent composites of various presumed, projected, or estimated values and which are required as input to endogenous forecasting and evaluation. "Consumer Facilities Access" is one such measure. Thus, future subregional access levels may be obtained by hypothetical estimation from the separately projected pattern of consumer service facilities and from inter-subregional highway travel times. In their turn, these access levels provide input for a prediction of subregional residential growth and (in their area-wide aggregate) for an evaluation of the overall inter-areal access characteristics implied by the planning agency's proposals.

the final date of the planning period (including endogenous forecast data).

—Descriptions of anticipated area structure as of the terminal date of each time interval (including endogenous forecast data).

—All evaluations of the anticipated proposal consequences.[10]

Most development scheme components will be quantitative, in the sense of constituting actual numerical values, e.g., population forecast results, or lending themselves to numerical identification, e.g., the map grid coordinates of an expressway link. This will enable a planning agency to record a large portion of its scheme on computer tapes, thereby greatly facilitating the job of changing the many components that are necessarily affected when the agency modifies an individual norm, an exogenous forecast value or, an action proposal, or when it traces out the impact of an independently advanced recommendation.

Participation in Plan-Implementing Activities. The typical new planning agency is likely to have direct responsibility for reviewing independently submitted public and private project proposals with respect to their conformance to agency plans. Here, the endogenous forecast and evaluation techniques discussed above in relation to plan-making will find additional use in impact analyses which indicate the prospective implications of such projects for area development as a whole.

Take a recommendation for the establishment of a nuclear processing plant that has not been included in a given comprehensive area development scheme. In reviewing this proposal, the planning agency concerned would be able to document its approval or non-approval by means of evaluated forecasts of the manner in which area growth—traffic loads, employment distributions, tax yields, etc.—might be expected to occur if the plant were built in the future setting envisaged by the development scheme.

Participation in Centralized Data Service Activities. In a rudimentary manner, and largely

by default, urban planning agencies currently tend to serve a repository function for various kinds of data that have general usefulness for their particular jurisdictional area. During the remainder of the present decade this repository function will probably be assumed by metropolitan information centers—an emerging organizational device devoted to the maintenance of general-purpose data and to the contractual performance of assignments related to data storage and processing for individual public and private users. At the same time, however, urban planning agencies operating within a metropolitan area that possesses such a center will continue to be important consumers and producers of the general-purpose information files involved. As consumers they will make use of many kinds of raw data collected by other agencies, e.g., building permit statistics. As producers they will contribute the raw data which they themselves collect, e.g., land use survey tabulations, together with the analytical results of their description of past and current area development and their forecasting of exogenous future aspects. In addition to taking part in this exchange of general-purpose data, urban planning agencies will be likely, in their internal operations to call on many of the contractual services offered by metropolitan information centers.

Creation of Planning Agency Procedures. A considerable amount of work is involved in conceptualizing the kinds of methods discussed above and in calibrating them for operational use. In situations in which a quantitative procedure required by a planning agency has not been developed or exists only in primitive form, the agency will find it necessary to undertake much of the needed development work itself. Statistical techniques for investigating the dynamics of urban structure, e.g., correlation and factor analysis, will be applied to past observations to conceptualize substantively plausible variables and equation types which can operate on potentially available data and computational facilities and yield reasonably reliable results. Statistical techniques such as regression analysis will be employed to calibrate the conceptualized models, i.e., to compute parameter and efficacy index values, for

---

[10] The first and last one excepted, these items would derive conceptually from the analytic system of area development used in this chapter.

use in the agency's particular jurisdictional area.

MATHEMATICAL MODELS OF URBAN DEVELOPMENT

Any particular effort with models applied to the subject matter of urban planning tends to be dominated by one of two overriding drives: (1) a desire to uncover the dynamics of urban development for its own sake; (2) a desire to explain, anticipate and/or influence the course of urban development for reasons of public or private interest. Social scientists are usually impelled in the former way and urban planners in the latter. Both have an important place, and their work is of reciprocal benefit. However, the distinction between them is significant and must be borne in mind. As will be readily apparent, the present discussion is guided largely by the second motive.

Essentially, a mathematical model is a device for making some part of reality analytically manageable. Relative to the infinite complexities of real-world phenomena, the number of elements and relationships that can be handled in this way is extremely limited; any model will therefore grossly oversimplify the phenomena which it is meant to encompass.

Granted this relative simplicity, mathematical models nevertheless tend in their own right to be complicated constructs whose development and use involves many different kinds of operations. Even the most "naive" attempts incorporate a sizable number of elements and relationships, and their data needs and computational loads may exceed the present capabilities of many metropolitan agencies.

A model is a system in the sense of being an autonomous and stable construct designed to perform a set of given tasks by carrying out a variety of interdependent activities subject to centralized controls. Moreover, a model is usually meant for use as an integral part of a larger complex of analytical activities, receiving information from some and furnishing it to others. This makes for the obvious and rather readily met requirement that individual model components be designed in relation to one another, e.g., a residential construction variable and a residential capacity variable must embody the same definition of dwelling. It also imposes the more difficult task of designing these components in relation to analytical activities outside the model. For example, identical criteria for delineating residential subregions should apply with regard to different models that are to be used together; a driving-time variable in a locational forecast-model may need to be formulated for double duty as input to a separate trip distribution equation.

In arriving at an overall formulation of his construct, the model-builder is faced with the choice of treating his subject phenomena either in terms of relationships among behavioral aggregates or in terms of behavioral processes involving individual actors. The former approach, which our two examples illustrate, tends to be much easier and is generally followed in fledgling fields of application such as urban planning. It leads to the specification of algebraic forms—e.g., $Y = a + b(X_1) + c(X_2)$, and parameter values—e.g., $c = 0.01$, that serve to approximate real-world relationships for purposes of analysis. Here, numerous algebraic alternatives are available to a model builder. The choice of any particular form is dictated in part by substantive considerations of theoretical and/or empirical appropriateness and in part by the need to keep all formulations as simple as possible for reasons of computational manageability and (with regard to regression-based equations) statistical reliability.

Any mathematical model is based on the very fundamental premise that real-world processes and relationships are sufficiently regular and (within given time ranges, at least) sufficiently enduring to justify abstraction by means of stable conceptual constructs. Generally speaking, algebraic forms are designed to hold for any area over a 20–30 year period (as in the case of both our examples), while parameter values are often permitted to vary by area and period.[11]

---

[11] Current methodological approaches probably still under-state the actual fluidity of urban structure, which is changing at a rapidly accelerating rate as a result of technical and social innovation. Nevertheless, "conservative" assumptions about the pace of structural transformation will continue to be made, largely because this type of change is so difficult to allow for in model-building.

The parameters that serve to quantify relationships among variables of a model are of two kinds: those which have substantive meaning, e.g., production coefficients in an input-output model, and those which simply act as algebraic proportioning or weighting factors, e.g., the regression coefficients of an econometric model. Generally speaking, the actual values assigned to these parameters represent technical or behavioral coefficients in the former case and regression coefficients in the latter. Model relationships which incorporate substantive parameters are preferable to relationships which incorporate algebraic ones, since they come much closer to capturing the true dynamics of urban development and since their parameter values can be changed with relative ease to reflect conditions in differing time periods and urban areas. Thus, a production coefficient may be assigned differing figures for the 1965–70 and 1970–75 periods on the basis of anticipated changes in industrial technology. No substantive basis exists for a corresponding adjustment of regression coefficients, and one would need to resort to the tenuous device of trend extrapolation in order to allow for their change over time. It might be added that algebraic parameters are usually employed in situations where little is known about the substantive dynamics at work, while the introduction of technical and behavioral coefficients reflects a maturing understanding of the subject matter.

When models are developed for applied fields such as urban planning the nature of the output should be defined early in the game and with special care. This is important because the categories of a model's output determine its particular contribution to the planning process and because they govern the choice of input variables and contextual units.[12] In that regard, broadly defined output variables may be too heterogeneous for a single model and may need to be broken down into more homogeneous components for separate treatment. For

example, instead of predicting subregional population changes with one general model, a metropolitan agency might achieve greater accuracy if it used a separate construct to "build up" future subregional dwelling volumes and then "occupied" the resulting housing stock by means of a relatively straightforward population-assignment equation.

The need for precision in model work can hardly be exaggerated. Pedantic as their wording may appear, the definitions found in our two examples are still much less detailed than actual operating practice would require: e.g., what exactly do terms such as "private dwelling" or "subregional dwelling capacity" mean to the agency technician who is to obtain data on these variables?

Models can relate to public policy in a variety of direct and indirect ways. To begin with, they may actually generate proposals for governmental action toward achievement of governmental goals, in the manner in which our plan-model would be used to prescribe intra-metropolitan public dwelling patterns promoting the policy objective of cost minimization. In addition, some of their input categories may constitute policy decisions, as illustrated by the minimum aggregate number of apartments stipulated for a linear programming allocation of public housing units. Finally, many of their input categories may derive from policy decisions, as in the case of a traffic forecast model's inter-subregional driving times which would be calculated from the link lengths and speeds of a specified public highway network. Today, almost any class of model input is likely to be sensitive to public policy in some respect—an incidental commentary on the key role of government in contemporary urban affairs.

Various means are available for assessing the efficacy of mathematical models. They include summarizing measures of output accuracy (e.g., the standard error of estimate S_y and the Coefficient of Determination R^2) measures of parametric reliability, etc. Moreover, in addition to being expressed in the usual way as a single determinate number, the values of individual variables and statistically obtained parameters may be described in the form of a probability distribution that yields an expected value

---

[12] Possibly as a result of the load which social scientists have been taking in models development for urban planning, output definition often seems to receive rather casual treatment in comparison with the emphasis given to structural relationships and "causative" factors.

(mean) and indicates the degree of dispersion (variance).

The question of accuracy and reliability leads directly into one of the thorniest aspects of model work in the urban planning field. Empirical estimating and predictive perform-ance tend to be poor when judged by conven-tional measures such as Sy and R^2. The problem stems from a lack of needed data, an inade-quate understanding of urban dynamics, an extremely limited ability for translating what little knowledge does exist into workable ana-lytical constructs, and a shortage of qualified operating personnel. These difficulties are com-pounded by the sometimes doubtful validity of currently used efficacy indexes and by an ab-sence of consensus as to what the acceptable performance levels might be in a given situa-tion. Future prospects in this regard are subject to some countervailing factors. On the one hand, the rapidly increasing intricacies and imponderables of urban development, together with sheer structural change itself, would ap-pear to preclude any major improvements. On the other hand, those complicating trends may come to be offset by our growing data resources and technical sophistication. It might be said in passing that the progressively greater role of public policy in urban development could af-fect model efficacy in either a positive or a negative way. If governmental projects are un-dertaken on an *ad hoc* basis this simply acts to augment the array of "lumpy" urban im-ponderables. If such projects are undertaken within the framework of an effective compre-hensive planning process, however, they can greatly expand the range of urban phenomena that a planning agency could treat with a rela-tive degree of certainty.

Clearly, model development in applied fields such as urban planning calls for a rare mix of technical competence, administrative aware-ness and artistic judgment. Many practical and conceptual considerations must be balanced in such work and agonizing compromises are the rule. The well-tempered model resulting from this is likely to combine adequate levels of efficacy, operability and substantive plausibil-ity—without necessarily starring in any single one of these respects.

While all of the basic types of model-analysis[13] have become a part of U.S. urban planning practice, their individual histories differ considerably. *Empirical* and *hypothetical estimating* techniques, being easiest to develop, came into the field at an early stage. Tech-niques of *structural estimation* and *prediction* were introduced later, starting with area-wide demographic/economic projections in the 1940s and progressing to more refined area-wide forecasts and to traffic and land use pro-jections in the 1950s. *Prescriptive* techniques were the last arrival, having been initially ap-plied in the 1960s to public improvements pro-gramming and planning agency work schedul-ing and, more recently, to the delineation of recommended locational patterns. With re-spect to all these types of analysis, methodolog-ical innovation has assumed a virtually explo-sive pace during the past decade, primarily as a result of two factors: the emergence of the dis-cipline of regional science and the rise of feder-ally-aided metropolitan transportation studies.

During the coming decade the urban plan-ning field may be expected to make increas-ingly greater use of model-techniques, in response to further rapid methodological prog-ress and to the institution of "Planning-Programming-Budgeting-System" procedures at all levels of government. Here, the single most significant development is likely to center on the introduction of prescriptive models as a basis for designing recommended comprehen-sive "end state" patterns and for staging many different categories of public facilities and serv-ices. At the same time, the scope and detail (although not necessarily efficacy) of predic-tion and structural estimation are also bound to expand. In addition, growing use will proba-bly be made of hypothetical estimating proce-dures for the evaluation of alternative proposal schemes.

Profession-Wide Logistics of Quantification

Effective use of quantitative methods by the new planning agencies will call for substantial logistical efforts in behalf of planning practice

---

[13] See discussion of Analytical Techniques above.

as a whole. As suggested in a previous section, these efforts will need to center on data service activities, research and education. Factors related to optimum operation, and recommendations to achieve these, are discussed here.

DATA SERVICE

Federal, state, and local agencies are already providing a great variety of "basic" and "framework" data[14] for planning practice and or many other public and private activities. However, the absence of central coordinating mechanisms makes for serious duplications, inconsistencies, and information gaps. The federal government should therefore proceed with establishing a national system of area-data services through the participation of federal agencies such as HUD, the Bureaus of the Budget, Census, and Labor Statistics, and the National Center for Health Statistics; and in cooperation with corresponding agencies in the individual states. These data services should include the following:

A comprehensive program for storing, processing and retrieving federal, state and local data; to comprise an integrated complex of computer facilities situated in Washington, D.C., and in the state capitals and larger metropolitan areas, linked by a data transmission network, and readily accessible via console to planning, development and research organizations throughout the country.

A comprehensive program of unified national and subnational projections for population, employment, industrial production, consumer expenditures, transportation, construction, agriculture, etc. making full use of existing efforts such as the census demographic projection series, while enlarging and standardizing their work to achieve greater coverage.

---

[14] In the present context the term *basic data* is applied to "raw" numerical information on observed employment, building activity, topographic conditions, land use, travel, social behavior, etc. The term *framework data* is applied to the results of estimates and projections having general utility, e.g., current summaries and future forecasts of national and state population, which serve as input to the demographic projections performed by individual urban planning agencies.

RESEARCH

Quantitative innovation for urban planning involves detailed analyses of the dynamics of urban structure, formulation of mathematical models which embody the resulting structural knowledge, and creation of data-handling procedures for research and for practice. Such investigations are so complex, expensive and time-consuming that any single agency can only hope to meet a small fraction of its research needs through its own efforts. This, together with the fact that the product of individual studies tends to have general applicability, suggests that concerted profession-wide action ought to supplant the piecemeal work common today. More concretely, several specific approaches are in order. First, the planning profession as a whole must organize to arrive at a consensus about the technical content of the area planning process (at least in its basic elements), thereby providing a substantive framework for setting research priorities and interrelating specific studies. Second, experienced and analytically competent planning practitioners must be encouraged to specialize in quantitative research through advanced academic training; at the same time, social scientists and systems-information engineers should be brought into the urban planning field by means such as agency internships. Third, some specialized planner-researchers should take a direct lead in the formulation of mathematical models for urban planning, while others should become active partners with social scientists in the study of urban structure and with engineers in the adaptation of relevant data-handling techniques. Fourth, academic and governmental mechanisms should be established for the express purpose of carrying out quantitative research projects and disseminating the results of this work to planning agencies and to other interested investigators. Fifth, the greatest possible number of planning agencies should be made to participate in individual research projects which require the kind of "laboratory" setting that only an operating agency can provide.

11

Social Welfare Planning

The appearance for the first time in Local Planning Administration (as this book was formerly titled) of a chapter on social planning and its relation to city planning reflects significant changes within the United States since publication of the third edition in 1959. In the interim, the nation has recognized the tremendous disparity in opportunities available to different members of society.

The United States is noted for its continuous efforts to reduce inequalities. The first drive, culminating in the Civil War, was toward freedom, an open society, and political equality. The next, embodied in the labor union movement of the late 19th and early 20th centuries, strove toward economic liberation, and held as its goal the widespread distribution of material affluence. The third drive, gaining momentum a decade after World War II, was a combination of the former strivings toward both political freedom and economic justice. "The Movement" personifies this most recent thrust toward social welfare, including, most notably, civil rights and other activities to organize and educate the poor.

It was not without embarrassment that the American people acknowledged the existence of basic problems such as poverty in their midst. Once the problem was recognized, its elimination gained the status of a "national purpose," strengthened by congressional and presidential commitments to action, notably the War on Poverty, announced in 1964. But the distance to be traveled before American society provides all its citizens with a reasonable opportunity to develop and participate in

society is great. Moreover, for good reason, many people still criticize the government's commitment as being nominal. Therefore, a major social question is *when* the conditions of a just society will be achieved. This is of particular importance to the planner, concerned as he is with the time dimension, to estimate both the costs and the benefits of measures and of different rates of movement over time toward social goals.

Other social problems also confront American society; although often closely related to poverty, these affect members of all economic and social classes. Included are racial discrimination, criminal behavior, drug addiction, alcoholism, the high divorce rate, mental illness, and indifference to environment and society.

The Planner's Approach

Physical and social problems are interrelated. Having realized this, city planners have begun to change their profession's approach to both physical and social problems. There has long been an acceptance, albeit unconscious, of the doctrine of physical environmental determinism. Professor Melvin Webber characterizes this doctrine as follows:

For generations it had been generally understood that the physical environment was a major determinant of social behavior and a direct contributor to individuals' welfare. Having accepted professional responsibility for the physical environment, the city planner was thus accorded a key role as agent of human welfare: the clearly prescribed therapy for the various social pathologies was improvement of the physical setting. If only well-designed and well-sited houses, playgrounds, and community facilities could be substituted for the crowded and dilapidated housing and neighborhoods of the city's slums, then the incidence of crime, delinquency, narcotics addiction, alcoholism, broken homes, and mental illness would tumble. Acculturation of ethnic, racial, and other minority groups to the American, middle-class, urban ways-of-life but awaited their introduction to the American, middle-class, physical environment. . . .

As the findings of systematic research into the relations between social-and-physical aspects of environments and social behavior have been accumulating, however, what were once stable pillars of understanding are melting down to folklore, heartfelt wishes, and, more typically, partial truths embedded within complex networks of causes. . . . The simple clarity of the city planning profession's role is thus being dimmed by the clouds of complexity, diversity, and the resulting uncertainty that seem to be the inevitable consequences of scientific inquiry and of the deeper understanding that inquiry brings.[1]

Social problems greatly increase the intensity of physical problems. Such problems as racial discrimination, and the concomitant fear of whites by Negroes, encourage ghetto dwellers to express their hostility in antisocial ways rather than through procedures like voting or appealing to political leaders. Thus, for example, ghetto dwellers have been known to throw empty bottles from windows and to participate in large-scale physical destruction through rioting. When a group of people is limited to occupying a neighborhood whose land and buildings are owned by absentee landlords, it is naturally less concerned with physical conservation. The result of emotional indifference, or even hostility, toward society and its physical structure is, in part, physical deterioration.[2] This, in turn, discourages those individuals who do own property (including landlords) from trying to improve the condition of their property. Physical deterioration prompts the more responsible citizens to move away if they can, or, if they cannot, to become less responsible. A vicious circle results.

Statistics show that physical problems do correlate with social problems: Robert Weaver, as Housing Administrator, estimated in 1964 that there were still nine million substandard dwelling units in the United States, of which over five million were occupied by families earning less than $3,000 a year. The income of a large portion of the remaining four million or so families who live in substandard housing is also at, or barely above, the poverty line.[3]

City planning grew from the same roots as social welfare planning: from protests by segments of the middle class over the emerging problems of the industrial city. Between 1910 and 1940 the two fields separated as a result of specialization.[4]

As a logical expression of the doctrine of physical environmental determinism, mentioned above, early city planning efforts focused attention on the architecture and pattern of cities and towns: this concern culminated in the City Beautiful movement. But concern for layout was also seen as a means for fostering better social and economic conditions, because the land use pattern of communities was considered to be a means for establishing viable local economies. These should be capable of providing employment opportunities for the residents of the communities and a local tax base sufficient to support the public services and facilities required.

Similarly, city planners were concerned with the physical conditions of slum dwellers. Planners who played an active role in planning new housing and eliminating slum and blight through urban renewal, sought physical means to improve social conditions.

Recent emphasis on the central city, rather than on peripheral growth, has brought the more acute social problems of slum dwellers to the forefront. However, the problems of peripheral growth remain crucial in the city planner's attempt to solve the problems of slums and central-city blight, for the fractionation of

---

[1] Melvin Webber, "Comprehensive Planning and Social Responsibility," JOURNAL OF THE AMERICAN INSTITUTE OF PLANNERS, XXIX (Nov., 1963), p. 233. Reprinted by permission of THE JOURNAL OF THE AMERICAN INSTITUTE OF PLANNERS, Nov., 1963, Vol. no. 29, No. 11.

[2] Charles A. Silberman, CRISIS IN BLACK AND WHITE (New York: Vintage Books, 1964), p. 47.

[3] George M. Raymond, "Prologue," in PROCEEDINGS OF THE 1964 ANNUAL CONFERENCE, Newark, American Institute of Planners (Washington: American Institute of Planners, 1964), p. 148.

[4] Robert Perlman, "Social Welfare Planning and Physical Planning," JOURNAL OF THE AMERICAN INSTITUTE OF PLANNERS, XXXII (July, 1966), p. 237.

suburban governmental jurisdictions allows those techniques at the disposal of city planners in peripheral areas—namely zoning, subdivision regulation, and building codes—to be used for exclusive and selfish purposes. Central city problems cannot be solved if poor and socially rejected people remain concentrated in the central city.

During the last few years two positions have developed within the city planning profession concerning the planner's responsibility for helping solve major social problems. The discussion revolves around whether the responsibility should be by direct confrontation with social issues or through the more traditional and indirect means of controlling the physical environment.

Proponents of the latter approach feel that planners can offer the most expert assistance to cities by dealing primarily with physical factors affecting urban conditions. They recognize social and economic means as important but consider them largely outside the competence of city planners. This position has traditionally been held by the American Institute of Planners. The AIP's Constitution presently defines the scope of the city planner's work in the following words:

(The) particular sphere of activity shall be the planning of the unified development of urban communities and their environs and of states, regions, and the nation, *as expressed through determination of the comprehensive arrangement of land uses and the land occupancy and regulation thereof.*[5]

In recent years uneasiness at this position has been growing. Some planners have believed that the social, economic, political, and physical factors affecting urban development are so interrelated that successful planning requires a more complete view of the community than is permitted under the definition of the planner's function adopted by the AIP. Proponents of this position, including an AIP committee recently appointed to study and recommend the proper scope of the professional planner's work, have suggested that the AIP amend its constitution to broaden the scope of the field

beyond the present limits. The proposed amendment would eliminate the words underlined in the section quoted above.

A number of years ago the New York Chapter of the AIP contrasted the two alternative views of the planner's role discussed here. The language in the alternative proposals is useful in understanding the choice now (1967) being considered within the profession[6] (Figure 11-1).

At this time it is not possible to state with assurance the direction the city planning profession will select. With the greatly increased allocation of public expenditures to combat poverty, however, it seems assured that the profession will find it desirable and expedient to include the planning of socially oriented programs within its domain. This should occur at least to the extent that greater attention will be given to coordination of the planning of facilities with the planning of services conducted within them.

Even if some or all members of the city planning profession limit their concern to the traditional area of physical development, all city planning will probably come to reflect increased public concern with the social issues of poverty, ill-health, and poor housing. In addressing a special meeting of the AIP a number of years ago, Webber set forth some propositions which provide a common base for all planners, no matter how widely they define the scope of their profession. He asserted that:

We are coming to comprehend the city as an extremely complex social system, only some aspects of which are expressed as physical buildings or as locational arrangements. As the parallel, we are coming to understand that each aspect lies in a reciprocal causal relation to all others, such that each is defined by, and has meaning only with respect, to its relations to all others.

As one result of this broadened conception of the city system, we can no longer speak of the physical city versus the social city or the economic city or the political city or the intellectual city. We can no longer dissociate a physical building, for example, from the social meanings that it carries for its users and viewers from the social and economic functions of the activities that are conducted within it. If distinguishable at all, the distinction is that of constituent components, as with metals comprising an

---

[5] Paul Davidoff, "Advocacy and Pluralism in Planning," JOURNAL OF THE AMERICAN INSTITUTE OF PLANNERS, XXXI (Nov., 1965), p. 336.

[6] These statements, prepared in 1954–55, by Henry Fagin are shown in Figure 11-1.

NEW YORK CHAPTER, AMERICAN INSTITUTE OF PLANNERS
Proposed Alternative Statements

A More Traditional Approach

The American Institute of Planners is the professional organization of persons engaged in planning comprehensively for the development of urban communities, regions and the nation, as expressed through the determination and regulation of the use and occupancy of land.

This activity has an important influence on economic and social conditions; and it entails many considerations, techniques, and insights taken from the related fields of economics and sociology. Nevertheless, the professional work characteristic of AIP members is distinguished from those planning activities that may directly undertake to give direction to the economy or to influence social organization by its essential orientation around physical development and its main emphasis on physical means for improving the environment.

In short, the planner is a specialist in dealing with the physical development aspects of questions, and he has a responsibility for bringing his special skills to bear wherever public decisions are being made that involve physical development or affect it. His specialized competence centers on the physical planning considerations that enter into such decisions.

A Modified Approach

The American Institute of Planners is the professional organization of persons engaged in planning, the broad purpose of which is to further the welfare of the people in the city, region, state, and nation by aiding in the creation of a more efficient, healthful, and attractive environment. The means for accomplishing this purpose are manifold, but most of them are related, directly or indirectly, to the determination and regulation of the use and occupancy of land.

This activity has an important influence on economic, social, and aesthetic conditions; it entails many considerations, techniques, and insights taken from economics, engineering, sociology, architecture and other physical and social sciences and design professions. The planning profession is essentially concerned with the coordination of the knowledge and skills of all of these groups in order to achieve long-range, comprehensive and general solutions to environmental problems related to efficiency, health, and aesthetics. Although a planner may have a detailed knowledge of one or several of the sciences and design professions, his special interest, skill, and competence as a planner is expressed in terms of his knowledge of the general and interrelated application of the knowledge and skills of all of the sciences and design professions . . .

In short, the planner is a specialist in dealing with the interrelationships of social, economic, design and other considerations related to the long-range, comprehensive, and general development of environments, and he has a responsibility for bringing his special skills to bear wherever public decisions are being made that involve these considerations.

FIGURE 11–1. *Proposed alternative policy statements, New York Chapter, American Institute of Planners*

NEW YORK CHAPTER, AMERICAN INSTITUTE OF PLANNERS
Proposed Alternative Statements

A More Traditional Approach

The planning professional must recognize, however, that physical considerations are only a portion among many factors which enter into the determination of policy. He has an obligation to clearly limit the contribution he makes in the mantle of an expert to those planning aspects and implications that actually are within his competence. He should not pretend to expertness with regard to the many other elements that enter into the choice of legislation, action programs or other public activities. He should refrain scrupulously from vesting his lay views with the prestige of the planning profession when he weighs the other aspects that enter the determination of policy against physical planning considerations . . .

The Institute, therefore, properly limits its expressions regarding public policy to physical development aspects; both the anticipated effects of policy on physical development and of proposed physical development on other things. The Institute may propose legislative enactments, action programs and other public activities, or it may review measures initiated by other bodies. At all times, however, it must recognize the presence of considerations beyond its competence that also must be weighed. The final determination of public policy involves the balancing of physical needs against political factors, operational requirements, and the other tangibles and intangibles of the social and economic scene; and it entails an ultimate choice among all the contending needs. This last step is beyond the proper scope of the Institute.

A Modified Approach

The planning professional must recognize, however, that his knowledge of the general interrelationships and application of the sciences and design professions will not be sufficient for the determination of policy. Often detailed economic, engineering or other considerations, with which only experts in the respective fields are familiar, will be essential to sound policy formulation. The planner has an obligation, therefore, to clearly limit the contribution he makes in the mantle of an expert to those planning aspects and implications that are actually within his competence. He should not pretend to expertness with regard to the many other elements that enter into the choice of legislation, action programs or other public activities. He should refrain scrupulously from vesting his lay views with the prestige of his public position when he weighs those other aspects that enter the determination of policy against his specialized knowledge . . .

The Institute, therefore, can properly concern itself with . . . questions . . . related to civil liberties and industrial location, housing, etc. (They) should be and can be discussed in an objective and constructive manner. If such discussions should yield conclusions, the public should be informed of the nature of those conclusions. In order to insure the widest possible dissemination of information, it is essential that the conclusions be embodied in programs, resolutions, etc., and be submitted to legislative bodies at all levels of government.

FIGURE 11–1. (*continued*)

alloy. . . . Planning for the locational and physical aspects of our cities must therefore be conducted in concert with planning for all programs that governmental and non-governmental agencies conduct.[7]

Webber did not say that the city planner had to coordinate the planning of all programs. His statement implied this but also the alternative, namely that city planners could work in concert with other planners. Under either of these circumstances city planners would be required to understand certain social, economic and political conditions within their communities.

It appears quite likely that a growing number of city planners will become engaged in the future in one or more aspects of social planning. The exact nature of their work cannot now be precisely defined for the field is evolving. There is a great demand for social planning, but little consensus at this time as to what it involves from the technical point of view.

Current and Emerging Role

Professional city planners presently participate in aspects of social welfare planning in a number of ways: (1) in land use planning and zoning; (2) by giving advice to those various line agencies of a city government such as recreation, public aid, and police; (3) through the focus of their data collection and research; (4) in urban renewal and public housing;[8] (5) as advocate planners for private groups that wish to change government planning proposals.

PHASES OF THE PLANNING PROCESS

Planning typically passes through several phases: (1) goal formulation, (2) data collection and research, (3) plan preparation and programming, and (4) implementation. The field of social welfare planning is fairly new, and planners have not yet articulated these four phases with respect to this field. Nevertheless, we can cite examples of professional work related to these areas and attempt to draw inferences from them.

Because American society has not yet reached complete agreement on the goals of social welfare, planners must treat the phase of goal formulation delicately. One recourse is to encourage citizen participation, in order to learn what the client desires. Thus, for example, the Social Plan of Providence, Rhode Island, provides for a phase of "neighborhood organization" to begin two years prior to urban renewal action, during which time private social work agencies, the Division of Community Services under the Department of Urban Renewal, and the Redevelopment Agency, are to assist citizens' groups to react to the government's tentative plans and to formulate counter-proposals if necessary[9] (Figure 11–2). The federal government has made the requirement of citizen participation one of the strictest parts of the Workable Program component of a Community Renewal Program.

Social welfare planning requires collection of data on both needs and resources. The first of these can be fairly straightforward—for example, data about income levels; about consequences of urban renewal on families by socio-economic characteristics; about the incidence of crime and disease correlated with socio-economic characteristics, etc. The second kind of data, on resources, is more complex, because it requires not only a listing of available resources, but an evaluation of the effectiveness of each, correlated with the various socio-economic groups and with various geographic areas.

Philadelphia's Community Renewal Program Technical Reports No. 11 and No. 16 make a start here. Report No. 11 describes a survey made of 11 kinds of areas in West Philadelphia to determine how social rank, family

---

[7] Webber, op. cit., pp. 235–36.

[8] Highway planning often has the same effect on social welfare as does urban renewal, although as yet highway planners have not formally recognized the social-welfare consequences of highway construction. For example, the highway department is not required to relocate displaced residents. Nevertheless, highway departments often contract to use the relocation services of urban renewal agencies, for since 1962 relocation advisory assistance and payment has been authorized for people displaced by federally aided highways.

[9] Rhode Island Council of Community Services, Inc., A SOCIAL PLAN FOR COMMUNITY RENEWAL OF THE CITY OF PROVIDENCE, R. I. (Providence: The Council, 1964), p. 35.

This list describes the separate but related pieces of work comprising the study of social foundations of urban renewal. Each piece of work is a limited study in itself and was designed to supplement and to complement all other pieces of work.

1. **The Social Goals of Urban Renewal Actions.**—This document briefly treats the historical background of the City and outlines and explains four social objectives for urban renewal actions: rehousing, the provision of social utilities, integrity of neighborhood units, opportunity for participation in community change.

2. **Delineation of Planning Districts for the City of Providence.**—Planning districts were formulated as the units within which inter-organizational forms of citizen participation and administration of human services could best take place.

3. **Theoretical Framework for the Effective Concentration of Human Services.**—This document presents a set of principles and hypotheses to be used in formulating the plans for services and for citizen participation.

4. **Social Pathology Index.**—This component documented the incidence of some forty-five health, standard of living, family and child rearing, educa-tional and behavior problems in the City of Providence by the residence of people facing such problems.

5. **Analysis of Program Areas for Human Services.**—Program areas are multi-ple enumeration districts which are delineated according to the degree of social problem concentrations they con-tain. Four types of areas were formu-lated and delineated.

6. **Problem Perceptions of People Liv-ing in Program Areas.**—An analysis was made of the difference between documented problems (by means of the S.P.I.) and perceived problems (by means of individual and group inter-views).

7. **Inventory of Services Rendered by Agencies.**—The purpose of this docu-ment was to examine the services of-fered by agencies in sufficient detail to match those services to documented and perceived problems.

8. **Attitudes toward Service Agencies in Program Areas.**—The purpose of this component was to point up how ac-ceptable a given agency appears to residents of program areas.

9. **Delineation of Providence Neighbor-hoods.**—In 1950 the Council and the Providence City Plan Commission jointly mapped out the boundaries of Providence's neighborhoods. These boundaries were reviewed in terms of how the residents of neighborhoods view them by means of group inter-views in neighborhoods.

10. **Description of Action Modes in Neigh-borhoods.**—In order to determine the kind, volume and intensity of commu-nity organization services needed in Providence, the ways in which neigh-borhoods solve problems were analyzed by means of group interviews.

11. **Attitudes toward Providence's Ur-ban Renewal Program.**—By means of group interviews in neighborhoods.

12. **Analysis of Social Treatment Types.**—Four types of treatment were devel-oped for tying in human services with urban renewal treatments.

13. **Board Members' Attitudes toward Participation in Urban Renewal Ac-tivities.**—An opinion questionnaire was sent to approximately 350 members of voluntary and tax-supported agency boards of directors.

14. **Analysis of Urban Renewal as a Social Process.**—The development of the ur-ban renewal program in Providence was traced as abstracted from news-paper accounts since 1947.

FIGURE 11–2. *A social plan for community renewal, Providence, Rhode Island*

rank, and race can be used to predict neighborhood sentiment (i.e., commitment and evaluation), neighborhood behavior (i.e., use of local resources like stores and doctors), and orientation toward urban renewal.[10] Thus a beginning was made in collecting data on those social factors that should be considered in the development of a long-range physical and economic urban renewal plan. The data collected were (1) social resources, (2) residents' attitudes and actions in different types of areas in reference to key items related to urban renewal decisions, and (3) social structures in differing geographic areas. Report No. 16 suggests the additional data needed before a scheduling of renewal program "mixes" can be developed for each of the significant, identifiable geographic sections of the city.[11]

Providence has tried somewhat the same kind of analysis as Philadelphia's CRP Report No. 11, but on a more restricted basis.[12] Providence chose only one area, Lippett Hill, and compared the residents' attitudes (correlated according to race and occupancy type) toward their neighborhood and its rehabilitation, rather than comparing the potential for urban renewal among various neighborhoods (correlated by demographic Census data).

Reiner, Reimer, and Reiner have also developed a method for analyzing needs and resources within a single framework.[13] They call it "client analysis." The method is to examine existing programs and to deduce the various goal positions of sectors of the community from the number and behavior of people confront-

ing these programs and participating in or rejecting them. Information on the effectiveness of agency operations as well as on the changing size of the social commitments of government are important products of the analysis. The analytic steps go from data on needs, eligibility, and services rendered to clients, to data on benefits resulting from service rendered.

To the extent that the goals and data have not yet been finalized, the programming stage is still in flux. But two other forces are also keeping it fluid: (1) the fact that older bureaucracies are reluctant to take on new responsibilities or adapt to new needs means that whole new departments or bureaus must be created to perform these functions, notably the function of overall coordination and programming, and (2) the impact of new social welfare activities which often changes the whole context of the problem as, for example, when it awakens a particular group or neighborhood from apathy and provokes counter-organization, sabotage, or, on the other hand, active cooperation, on the part of the residents.

George Schermer, studying the Penjerdel region in 1963, found that:

planning in the health and welfare field is largely a process of coordinating existing services, preventing overlapping and the like. In the larger cities there is liaison with city planning, urban renewal, and public housing. (But) woefully little social planning is done at all.[14]

Certainly in 1963, when Schermer made the statement, it was true, even in Philadelphia, where the Community Renewal Program was pioneering in this field by developing a model to describe the full range of public and voluntary actions necessary to impact the problems found in housing and the physical environment.[15]

A problem of timing remains in the pro-

[10] Donna M. McGough, SOCIAL FACTOR ANALYSIS, Philadelphia Community Renewal Program Technical Report No. 11 (Philadelphia: The Program, 1964), *passim.*

[11] Richard H. Uhlig, PLANNING IN THE URBAN ENVIRONMENT, Philadelphia Community Renewal Program Technical Report No. 16 (Philadelphia: The Program, July, 1965), *passim.*

[12] Urban League of Rhode Island, A STUDY OF THE RESOURCES, CAPABILITIES FOR REHABILITATION, AND PREFERENCES OF FAMILIES LIVING OR OWNING PROPERTY IN THE LIPPETT HILL REHABILITATION AREA AND THEIR ATTITUDES TOWARD THEIR NEIGHBORHOOD AND ITS REHABILITATION (Providence: Providence Redevelopment Agency, 1962), *passim.*

[13] Janet S. Reiner, Everett Reimer, and Thomas A. Reiner, "Client Analysis and the Planning of Public Programs," JOURNAL OF THE AMERICAN INSTITUTE OF PLANNERS, XXIX (Nov., 1963), pp. 270–82.

[14] George Schermer, MEETING SOCIAL NEEDS IN THE PENJERDEL REGION (Philadelphia: Pennsylvania-New Jersey-Delaware Metropolitan Project, 1964), p. 48.

[15] Philadelphia Community Renewal Program, COMMUNITY RENEWAL PROGRAMMING, Technical Report No. 4 (Philadelphia: The Program, 1962), *passim;* Health and Welfare Council, Inc., Research Department, A STUDY OF THE SOCIAL ASPECTS OF THE COMMUNITY RENEWAL PROGRAM, Philadelphia Community Renewal Program Technical Report No. 5 (Philadelphia: The Program, n.d.), *passim.*

gramming phase. It is difficult to get social and physical planners to coordinate their efforts, for the former usually follow one-year budget schedules, while the latter plan for at least five-year time periods.[16] However, Philadelphia has devised an "Annual Development Program" which schedules targets for accomplishment over a five-year period, but reviews and revises the schedules annually.[17]

The implementation phase is often the primary responsibilty of an agency other than the planning department, which has advisory functions in this respect. In order to develop a closer connection between planning and implementation, however, a considerable degree of administrative reorganization is occurring or being discussed in many cities. The culmination is frequently a tie or a merger between the various municipal functions that relate to land: planning, development, control, and management.

In this respect, the reader is referred to the closing section in Chapter 17 on Demonstration and Model Cities. This is a relatively recent program, still waiting to be tested, but it provides perhaps the greatest potential of any tool available to urban areas for combining physical planning with economic and social planning in an action-oriented context.

FUNCTIONS AND PHYSICAL SYSTEMS

Planners are concerned directly with housing, education, health, and recreation, because these aspects of welfare require careful location, extensive land areas, and expensive facilities, all of which are central considerations in physical planning.

Housing. This constitutes a welfare problem because it has generally been left to the free market to provide, whereas the American market fails to meet housing needs for many reasons.[18]

It is not feasible for the inflation-prone private housing industry to build single-family homes (which dominate the housing market) for families with less than $5,000 annual income. Even rehabilitation and apartment building is often too expensive to house the large number of families with incomes below $5,000.[19] Even with eminent domain and subsidy provided by government, profits from rehabilitation have often not been high enough to attract private capital into the lower-income housing market.[20] Moreover, inflation tends to steer investment away from the mortgage market in residential construction; under such conditions, interest rates remain high despite substantial government intervention.[21]

Members of minority groups, against whom discrimination is practiced, are restricted to ghettos where landlords have an incentive to raise rents to an artificially high level and to keep improvements artificially low. These incentives are enhanced by "guaranteed rents" from welfare payments, usually Aid to Families with Dependent Children and by low taxes on slum property.[22]

Present financial arrangements do not take into account the fact that families reach their greatest space needs before they reach their greatest earning power, and thus often do not satisfy their needs until after these needs have disappeared[23] (e.g., they acquire their biggest house after the children have grown and are ready to leave home). The "stickiness" of the market discourages older people from renting or selling their large houses, and discourages all homeowners from adjusting quickly to their needs. The poorest families can afford the least percentage of their budgets for housing, and yet often have the greatest space needs in terms of family size.

---

[16] Harvey S. Perloff, "Pomeroy Memorial Lecture: Common Goals and the Linking of Physical and Social Planning," PLANNING 1965 (Chicago: American Society of Planning Officials, 1965), p. 183.

[17] Philadelphia Community Renewal Program, Technical Report No. 4, *op. cit.,* second page of foreword.

[18] Raymond, *op. cit.,* p. 49, indicates that this is definitely not a problem of lack of manpower.

[19] Bernard J. Frieden, "Toward Equality of Urban Opportunity," JOURNAL OF THE AMERICAN INSTITUTE OF PLANNERS, XXXI (Nov., 1965), p. 326; and Rhode Island Council of Community Services, Inc., *op. cit.,* p. 24. Frieden quotations reprinted by permission of THE JOURNAL OF THE AMERICAN INSTITUTE OF PLANNERS, Nov., 1965, Vol. no. 31, No. 11.

[20] Rhode Island Council of Community Services, Inc., *op. cit.,* p. 27.

[21] Nelson N. Foote and others, HOUSING CHOICES AND HOUSING CONSTRAINTS (New York: McGraw-Hill Book Company, Inc., 1960), pp. 18–19.

[22] Rhode Island Council of Community Services, Inc., *op. cit.,* p. 36.

[23] Foote, *op. cit., passim.*

The government, on the one hand, has not adequately compensated for deficiencies in the private housing market. Local governments restrict housing construction often without intending to do so, by means of outmoded building codes (which discourage cost-saving innovations); "fiscal zoning"; decisions about utilities and transportation networks; and lax enforcement of building codes (permitting landlords to crowd in many more families than their buildings were intended to accommodate, and thereby making unsafe, unhealthful buildings profitable).

When the federal government has intervened, for example to clear slums, it has not always provided for replacement of an equal number of dwellings at prices that the displaced persons can afford. This is partly due to allowing neighboring cities, both of which are engaged in urban renewal, to cite each other's vacant housing as being available to their own displaced citizens. Some cities consciously try to replace their existing poor residents with those of higher income or with commerce and industry, through clearance and relocation.[24] But in determining the acceptability of dwellings for relocation, urban renewal relocation services have been known to use standards lower than those used for determining the need for clearance![25] The paradoxical result is that a family may be displaced from a building that is of better quality than the building in which it is relocated. Government programs such as highway building cause displacement of poor residents without conscious intent, but these programs often provide no relocation services at all.

Robert Weaver noted that:

urban renewal too often seemed to be an instrument for wiping out racially integrated living in one area at the same time that it failed to provide for an equal degree of racial integration on the site or in another section of the city.[26]

On the other hand, eligibility for public housing is highly restrictive, in both monetary and psychological terms, and such housing is often not suitable for accommodating large families.[27]

The deficiencies must be corrected before housing can become a beneficial aspect of social welfare. Planners play a varied role in the arsenal of governmental tools that deal with housing, in some instances making a primary contribution, in others playing secondary or no roles. Planners make their most significant contribution in the area of urban renewal. Urban renewal is used partly to reduce the price of land that is needed for new residential development.

Requirements for and inducements to metropolitan-wide planning, together with planning proposals for metropolitan-wide housing inventories, can help to reduce the double-counting of housing available to UR displacees. Attempts have been made to build public housing on vacant land prior to demolition of neighboring blighted residences. Some cities have improved their relocation services and coordinated them with case work. Attempts could be made through education to make poor people more effective housing consumers, as Alvin Schorr suggests.[28] But as Bernard Frieden correctly points out, what is needed most crucially is not counseling but rather a larger supply of low-cost housing.[29] The Social Plan of Providence, R.I., suggests that a Housing Authority could sell dwelling units to tenants, thus encouraging self-sufficiency and homeownership, and freeing public funds for more housing for still other slum residents.[30]

In their role as land use planners, urban planners can also affect the price of land and thereby its availability for housing the poor. Wise policies of utility extensions and zoning help to discourage land speculation, and thereby reduce the price of land. Passage of modern building codes should also help to-

[24] Frieden, op. cit., p. 325.

[25] U.S. General Accounting Office, INADEQUATE POLICIES AND PRACTICE RELATING TO THE RELOCATION OF FAMILIES FROM URBAN RENEWAL AREAS (Washington: Government Printing Office, 1964), passim.

[26] Robert C. Weaver, THE URBAN COMPLEX: HUMAN VALUES IN URBAN LIFE (Garden City, N.Y.: Doubleday and Co., 1964), pp. 53–54.

[27] Rhode Island Council of Community Services, Inc., op. cit., p. 24.

[28] Alvin L. Schorr, SLUMS AND SOCIAL INSECURITY (Washington: Government Printing Office, 1963), p. 59.

[29] Rhode Island Council of Community Services, Inc., op. cit., p. 27.

[30] Frieden, op. cit., p. 325.

ward this goal.

Zoning and utilities and transportation facilities are sometimes planned to encourage new residential development, and can be used to control the type of development in accordance with the needs and financial abilities of housing consumers.

To achieve social welfare through housing, planners must be supported by actions taken by other government authorities. The following measures have been implemented or suggested as being requisite to achieving housing welfare:

1. Government-insured mortgages have induced the housing industry to build for families of lower income than previously, although a $5,000 minimum is still too high to meet the housing needs of the population.

2. Open-occupancy laws and building code enforcement being initiated in several cities will discourage ghettos and thereby reduce incentives for price discrimination.

3. Tax policies can be used to discourage real estate speculation and thereby to reduce the price of land for housing the poor.

4. Government subsidy to house the poor has been used ever since public housing subsidies were introduced by the New York state legislature in 1926 and by Congress in 1933. A rent subsidy provision, finally passed in the Housing Act of 1965, is the most recent effort to help house the poor.

5. Through a direct requirement of the Federal Highway Program, through bonuses under the Open Space program, and through administrative policy under the Water and Sewer programs, the federal government has encouraged metropolitan-wide planning, which can be used to discourage "fiscal zoning." Movement toward various types of metropolitan consolidation and concomitant tax equalization will also reduce the stimulus for fiscal zoning and alleviate its consequences. Another partial solution to the problems that give rise to fiscal zoning is the growing reliance on state and federal taxes and on equalization formulas for distributing revenues; this tendency will proportionately decrease the reliance on local property taxes, although it will not eliminate the conditions conducive to fiscal zoning, since

property tax rates have been increasing in absolute amounts.

6. The management of public housing has sometimes been persuaded to make restrictions less onerous to occupants of public housing, for example, by eliminating the cyclone fences that had prohibited the enjoyment of patches of grass. However, abusive restrictions are still rampant. Some public housing planners have attempted to disperse public housing units throughout a community, but have usually met with overwhelming opposition. Financial limitations sometimes prevent the "more humanitarian" low-rise public housing from being any more attractive than the much maligned high-rises; however, public education could help to overcome those design limitations that are imposed by a public morality that insists on punishing the poor merely for being poor.

Education. In recent years, mainly due to the inception of New Frontier legislation, the traditional system of education has become a prime target of attack in an attempt to break the circle of poverty. Education of the culturally disadvantaged, job training, government anti-poverty loans to college students, and adult education are all a part of the increasing concern at the role of education in achieving social welfare.

The urban planner's responsibility toward education is becoming more complex. His role as planner of physical facilities now leads him into fundamental questions of educational policy. For instance, in regard to the grade system, should it be 6–3–3, 6–2–4, 8–4, 3–3–3–3, and with or without kindergartens? And in regard to the size of school districts should there be "neighborhood schools" or "educational parks"? Urban planners are now also being consulted about higher education, involving policy questions relating to the population to be served such as: Should colleges be for commuters who are generally poorer, or for away-from-home residents, who are generally more well-to-do? They are also being consulted about the location of junior colleges. Should they be in high schools or on separate campuses? What should be the vertical (age) and horizontal (functional) separation of higher educational institutions, and what might be the effect on neighborhoods of new campuses or campus expansions?

The planner has a responsibility for gathering relevant data, above and beyond the traditional age-relevant demographic projections. And now that the Poverty Program has begun to obtain cooperation between educational authorities on the one hand, and various government and public agencies on the other hand, the city planner will probably be given increasing opportunities to influence education, as a coordinator between agencies and budget requests.

Health. Health is a traditional field of social welfare, and is probably the least controversial. Schermer found that in the Penjerdel region 60 per cent of expenditures for "health and welfare services" was for health.[31] However, of this portion, 90 per cent was for hospitals and clinics, and only 10 per cent was for what might be considered preventive health.[32] This seems to reflect a *lack* of policy, and the human characteristic of responding to problems only after they develop, instead of anticipating them and planning for their prevention.

In the field of health, the city planner selects sites, allocates space, and advises on budgetary allocations.

Recreation and Leisure. "The value of leisure-time activities, play, and recreation is usually conceded to lie in a nervous release which the social order imposes upon us."[33] As such, the provision of recreational facilities and opportunities is clearly important to the whole society. However,

so common is the identification of leisure and recreation with 'going somewhere' and 'spending money' that the lack of money clearly excludes the family with a low income from many outside associations and activities.[34]

Recreation and leisure thus also become functions intimately connected with planning for social welfare in the narrower sense of the term.

Planning for recreation and leisure includes the provision of large land tracts, such as parks and playgrounds, and of specific facilities such as assembly rooms and lounges in a housing project for the elderly, swimming pools for ghetto children, and bicycle paths for sophisticated New Yorkers. Parks require long-range land-use planning and foresight; they are traditionally the responsibility of physical planners. Budgetary planning is necessary as well as the cooperation of social scientists to show which kinds of facilities are needed by what kinds of people.

A caveat must be introduced here. George A. Lundberg writes that:

leisure or recreation of a certain type is neither leisure nor recreation in any basic biological or psychological sense. Slavish pleasures and mechanical leisure are contradictions in terms. That the shorter working day necessarily means more leisure of a desired or desirable kind is a *non sequitur* which is almost universal but is palpably false. All it necessarily means is more time for other pursuits, or for simple boredom. Boredom is receiving increasing attention as a factor in mental disease. As Edman has said: 'Leisure is an affair of mood and atmosphere rather than simply of the clock.'[35]

Thus, the city planner should direct his efforts towards variety of, and opportunity for, recreation and leisure, while maintaining some perspective vis-à-vis the results of his efforts.

SELECTED OBJECTIVES FOR CITIZENS

The following areas in which planners play a role affect the economic, social, and psychological welfare of the community's residents in more intangible ways than by the building of facilities. These areas of public policy involve: (1) the restriction or provision of opportunities, for example, for residence and business; (2) the attainment of financial security, both collective and individual, through rational public expenditures and taxing policies, through financial aid to the unemployed, the poor, and those displaced by urban renewal and through job training; (3) the enhancement of psychological security, through well-advertised urban renewal relocation services, through policies regarding the phasing of urban renewal and the placement of public

---

[31] Schermer, *op. cit.*, p. 48.

[32] *Ibid.*

[33] George Andrew Lundberg, Mirra Komarovsky, and Mary Alice McInery, LEISURE: A SUBURBAN STUDY (New York: Columbia University Press, 1934), p. 17.

[34] *Ibid.*, p.187.

[35] *Ibid.*, p. 18.

housing, through job retraining and job placement, through psychiatric counseling, and through participation in community affairs.

INCOMES AND THE ECONOMY

According to Webber,

there are no more direct routes to human betterment than improvements in the educational systems and stimulation of the regional economies. No other public activities are likely to be more effective in equipping individuals for self-dependency and growth.[36]

The opportunities and responsibilities of regional planners are indeed numerous, and have grown immensely within the last five years, due mainly to federal legislation such as the Appalachian Program, the Area Redevelopment Act, and the War on Poverty.[37]

Through the activities of the city planner, economics has taken on a new significance. Here, the field can be divided into three interrelated categories: (1) the general economic viability of the whole community; (2) the fiscal condition of the community's government; and (3) the economic condition of the residents. Urban planners have been traditionally, though sometimes peripherally, concerned with the first and second of these, and only recently with the third.

Decision by government to accept responsibility for economic conditions came slowly, and involvement is still at quite an elementary level. However, where a *local* government does consider itself responsible for improving local economic conditions, it often takes measures that are indirectly harmful to neighboring communities:[38] for example zoning out all nuisance industries, zoning out low-income people, temporarily or drastically lowering taxes on certain "desirable" industries; providing no public housing and only minimal welfare services; or clearing slums without providing relocation for those displaced.

City planners can work in ways that have a positive, constructive influence on the local economy without harming neighboring communities, e.g., by carrying out feasibility studies that would encourage the growth of diversified industry; or by suggesting the most economical patterns for land use zoning. In advising on budget schedules and in programming capital improvements, the city planner can influence the fiscal condition of the local government without influencing neighboring governments adversely.

Only recently, with the advent of the Community Renewal Program have city planners been forced to turn their attention more directly to the question of the economic condition of the residents, because urban renewal activities were having a greater impact on those people with economic problems than zoning, subdivision regulation, and land-use planning. With the Community Renewal Program the federal government began to show what was meant by "creative federalism" by requiring, for example, metropolitan-wide planning, and relocation of urban renewal displacees. This last requirement made even more visible than before the fact that many of those displaced by urban renewal cannot afford an economic rent. However, new federal requirements have been tempered with inducements such as rent subsidies, 100 per cent federal grants for urban renewal relocation, area redevelopment funds, and War on Poverty funds.

Today the urban planner's responsibility, vis-à-vis economic problems, has widened to encompass the gathering of economic data needed to carry out economic-rehabilitation programs related to physical rehabilitation and capital improvement programs.

SOCIAL WELFARE PROGRAMS

Since many social welfare problems stem from the apathy resulting from discrimination and other forms of social injustice, from a lack of knowledge of opportunities, and from emotional problems caused by poor living conditions and poverty, the planner should be familiar with programs to alleviate these problems. He can encourage such programs through coordination, research, budget advice, provision of service facilities where available, and Community Renewal Program recommendations.

[36] Webber, *op. cit.*, p. 235.
[37] William L. Batt, Jr., "Planning for the Unemployed, the Underemployed, and the Poor," in PROCEEDINGS OF THE 1964 ANNUAL CONFERENCE, Newark, American Institute of Planners (Washington: The Institute, 1964), pp. 253–56.
[38] Frieden, *op. cit.*, p. 323.

Service facilities can involve counseling on mental health problems or can involve marriage counseling, vocational guidance, assistance on job interviews, help in filling out job applications, and group discussion sessions in preparation for job training.[39] Counseling can be undertaken at one level by doctors in mental health clinics and hospitals, at another level by case workers, and at still another level by the non-professional residents of a ghetto.[40]

The urban renewal planner can affect the social rehabilitation of families crucially, for it is precisely at the time that rehousing becomes mandatory that many needy families are first brought into contact with the community's social agencies. Urban renewal programs can be materially assisted through the Poverty Program and others such as the Ford Foundation's "grey areas program." A program of housing code enforcement provides this same opportunity to work with the residents of poor areas.

Improvement in social relations was the intention of President Kennedy's 1963 Executive Order on Equal Opportunity in Housing, which prompted the Urban Renewal Administration to require every new or amended Community Renewal Program to include studies of the extent of housing discrimination and segregation in the community. Recommendations were also to include an affirmative program of local action to end discrimination and to establish a truly free market in housing and related facilities.[41] Providence's Social Plan, for example, recommends that neighborhoods into which urban renewal displacees are to be moved should be prepared to receive the newcomers.[42]

ADVOCATE PLANNING

The ways in which city planners participate in social welfare planning, discussed earlier, involve the planner as an employee of, or consultant to, local government. The role discussed here—that of advocate planning—involves him as a citizen, often as a protagonist against the local government.

The role of advocate planning has developed only in the last few years. It is based on the thesis that not all city planning proposals must be developed by a public agency and its consultants; that citizens holding special sets of values about community development might call upon the assistance of a professional planner to prepare a plan advocating their views. The essence of advocacy planning is the encouragement of organization on the part of those people who are most often the objects of planning activities—that is, those most often "planned for."

Some planners feel modest about their ability to plan for others, in recognition of the fact that others may have goals differing from their own. Professor John Dyckman feels that the caretakers' interests and the long-run interests of the client often conflict, and that it is legitimate to ask whether expert judgments made by planners are inherently better than individual free choices made by clients.[43] It is obvious, at any rate, that some planning activities undertaken with the intention of helping the underprivileged were actually more painful than the conditions the planners were trying to alleviate; and since these planning activities were only partial solutions, the supposed beneficiaries were unable to make positive use of them. For instance, a family is moved into public housing; the father remains unemployed; and thus, to support the family, the father must leave so that his wife can collect Aid to Dependent Children payments.

Some planners have also felt that certain planning activities specifically disregarded the interests of the underprivileged.

The Canadian planner Adamson feels that J. S. Mill's statement of a hundred years ago still

---

[39] Allegheny Council to Improve Our Neighborhoods-Housing, Inc., ACTION FOR EMPLOYMENT; A DEMONSTRATION NEIGHBORHOOD MANPOWER PROJECT TO Nov. 30, 1964, Midway Report (Pittsburgh: The Council, 1965), p. 29.

[40] *Ibid.*, pp. 11–23.

[41] William L. Slayton, "Impact of the Community Renewal Program on Urban Renewal," in PROCEEDINGS OF THE 1964 ANNUAL CONFERENCE, Newark, American Institute of Planners (Washington: The Institute, 1964), p. 155.

[42] Rhode Island Council of Community Services, Inc., *op. cit.*, pp. 33–34.

[43] John W. Dyckman, "Social Planning, Social Planners, and Planned Societies," JOURNAL OF THE AMERICAN INSTITUTE OF PLANNERS, XXXII (March, 1966), pp. 70–71. Reprinted by permission of THE JOURNAL OF THE AMERICAN INSTITUTE OF PLANNERS, March, 1966, Vol. no. 32, No. 3.

holds true that "the concessions of the privileged to the underprivileged are seldom brought about by any better motivation than the power of the underprivileged to extort them."[44] As we have already seen, the underprivileged in today's society, as always, are at a disadvantage in two particular ways in attempting to obtain concessions: the first is their apathy, their sense of powerlessness,—they do not even try to exert power; the second is their lack of knowledge about what is going on and of government plans that will affect them. Frequently, the first time those in urban renewal areas become aware of the government's intention to clear sites is when they receive a notice to evacuate—sometimes within 48 hours.

Advocacy planning could provide professional services for those people who are affected by planning activities. At one time a planner would have had difficulty in giving such services for he was in the position of having to initiate and organize opposition to the plans his own agency was developing. More recently, however, the task of organizing such opposition has been assumed by minority groups themselves, so that now an "advocate planner" can recognize the legitimate claims made by these groups, and urge the agency to accede to reasonable requests on grounds of political expediency.

In addition to these practical arguments in support of advocate planning, there are more theoretical arguments. Advocate planning seems most adaptable to what John Dakin calls the "process theory" of planning, which holds that planning is "dynamic, not static, and is part of an on-going process; . . . that goals are really less important than the process of moving towards them, for in accomplishing goals, we change them . . ."[45]

Advocate planning groups, usually representing themselves as sympathetic to the needs of low income families, have been established in Boston, New York, Philadelphia, and San Francisco. A national planning organization,

Planners for Equal Opportunity, was created in 1964. At present, advocate planners working to assist low income neighborhoods frequently do so without pay or at very low salaries, often provided through foundation support. Advocate planning may become an important part of city planning in due course, but its future depends on whether resources can be found to support professionals who work for indigent clients. It is possible that in the future financial support may be forthcoming for such assistance in the way that legal aid is now provided.

Planning by Social Welfare Workers

SOCIAL WELFARE COUNCILS

The most common type of social planning in urban areas is that of social welfare planning carried out by councils of health and social work agencies. These councils act either on behalf of their constituent agencies or as consultants to planning and anti-poverty groups.

Health and welfare councils began in Pittsburgh and Milwaukee in the early 1900s.

Through exchange of information about programs and policies the early councils sought to eliminate overlapping and duplication of effort and thus to move from a collection of unrelated individual programs toward a coherent community program.[46]

The health and welfare councils also generally took on the responsibility for administration of the funds raised annually through the united charitable fund drives. In spite of drives toward development of coordinated welfare services aimed at filling the needs of the community in a systematic way, the work of health and welfare councils has tended to remain largely coordinative in nature. In effect, their role has been to coordinate the various services already being carried out by member agencies such as social work counseling, group work, soup kitchen operation, Girl Scout clubs, and homemaker services. Consequently, although such councils may have definite goal orientations, their achievements tend to be condi-

[44] Anthony Adamson, "Physical Planning and Social Planning," PLANNING 1965 (Chicago: American Society of Planning Officials, 1965), p. 192.

[45] John Dakin, "An Evaluation of the 'Choice' Theory of Planning," JOURNAL OF THE AMERICAN INSTITUTE OF PLANNERS, XXIX (Feb., 1963), p. 26.

[46] Harry L. Lurie, ed., ENCYCLOPEDIA OF SOCIAL WORK (New York: National Association of Social Workers, 1965), p. 802.

tioned by the kinds of services they can coordinate. Elizabeth Wood, in an essay for the Pratt Community Education program, noted that "The social planner is concerned with those resources and institutions which society offers to enable people to meet their personal goals."[47] It is the resources, not the goals, that are the focus of social welfare planning. Most social plans, prepared by social welfare councils are based on an assumption that the client population of various welfare programs is inadequately served. This may or may not be true as, without coordination, each agency may be ignorant of the others' methods and purposes. Some plans have moved from this assumption to the formulation of a set of recommendations for greater coordination and communication among the staffs of social work and social improvement agencies both public and private.

Although the assumptions and recommendations are to a large extent true and helpful, they may be criticized on the grounds that they fail to specify (1) the nature of the client population and its goals, together with the goals the social agencies have set for their clients and themselves; (2) the ways in which these sets of goals can be reconciled; (3) the changes in services that would implement the revised goal statement.

Thus the failings of these social plans mirror those of the physical plans prepared by city planning agencies. They lack techniques for ascertaining facts about the client population, and for determining democratic and open processes for setting goals. The possession of such techniques would make their recommendations useful for achieving personal goals.

Another example of social welfare planning by social work councils is that of the Health and Welfare Association of Pittsburgh for ACTION-Housing, Inc., through study of the social needs of a Pittsburgh neighborhood, Homewood-Brushton.[48] The Health and Welfare Association (HWA) worked with the Homewood-Brushton Citizens Renewal Council, a neighborhood association which had been at the forefront of planning for physical rehabilitation and renewal. The HWA was assisted by the community organizer that ACTION-Housing, Inc., had supplied to the Council. Using information supplied by the Community Council, by the organizer, and by other social agencies operating in the neighborhood together with census data, school board information, and other resources, the Association prepared a social plan for the neighborhood. The plan specified the levels of schooling, job training, counseling, and other social services and facilities needed over a 20-year period. The plan's assumption was that since the neighborhood's residents were at a disadvantage with respect to that of the city as a whole, extraordinary efforts by the city government were needed to reduce the levels of unemployment, family instability, and other factors that existed in the Homewood-Brushton community.

A third type of social planning carried out by social work agencies is that of social survey work in areas that have been designated for renewal, rehabilitation, or other kinds of project action by city planning agencies. The social work councils here act in their capacities as expert judges of the needs of the client population. An example of this type of planning is that carried out by the Health and Welfare Council of Philadelphia for the CRP program of the Philadelphia City Planning Commission. Here the Council carried out an extensive series of interviews—one set with a random sample of household heads,[49] and another with a number of individuals in the target communities known to be 'community leaders' by the local social work agencies.[50] The findings were incorporated in the CRP's recommendations on the types of project action such as clearance, rehabilitation, and the purchase of housing by the public housing authority, which might be appropriate in a given community.

In the Philadelphia case, the social work

[47] M. Miller, "Book Review—Social Planning: A Primer for Urbanists, by Elizabeth Wood," JOURNAL OF THE AMERICAN INSTITUTE OF PLANNERS, XXXII (July, 1966), pp. 248–49.

[48] ACTION-Housing, Inc., SOCIAL AND PHYSICAL PLANNING EXPERIENCES IN THE HOMEWOOD-BRUSHTON NEIGHBORHOOD OF PITTSBURGH 1960–63 (Pittsburgh: ACTION-Housing, Inc., May, 1964), passim.

[49] McGough, op. cit., passim.

[50] Mary W. Herman, COMPARATIVE STUDIES OF IDENTIFIABLE AREAS IN PHILADELPHIA, Philadelphia Community Renewal Program Technical Report No. 9 (Philadelphia: The Program, 1964), passim.

council was acting as aide to the staff of the planning commission in the processes of fact-finding and goal formulation. Thus the Council was not engaged in "global" social planning, but merely the partial process of adding a social dimension to physical planning.

WELFARE-RELATED FUNCTIONS OF LOCAL GOVERNMENT

Some kind of planning, even if it amounts merely to annual budgeting, is carried out by all the welfare-related units of local governments and special districts, for example the park departments, public aid departments, police departments, and school boards. However, the various line agencies and special districts have not, in the past, attempted to integrate their functions in such a way as to stimulate needy people to overcome their economic or social handicaps successfully.

The local public agency most directly responsible for helping people to overcome such handicaps is the public welfare agency, whose main activity is casework.

Eligibility for casework assistance has been, until recently, limited by arbitrary income formulas and budgets imposed on the agency. Agencies have tended to be essentially custodial, and eligibility highly restricted. Casework has also been traditionally handicapped by low salaries and inadequate staff. Finally, because of the self-imposed passiveness of welfare agencies vis-à-vis their legally eligible clients, "intake" has been limited to recipients who come on their own initiative, and who apparently appear, disappear, and reappear at unanticipated times—"testimony to the fragile nature of their situation and to the failure of our conventional public welfare programs to alter their life chances decisively."[51] It is not surprising that welfare recipients should call public aid "welfare colonialism."[52]

But new social values have been expressed in the Juvenile Delinquency Act of 1961, the Social Security Act of 1962, the Economic Oppor-

tunity Act of 1964, and the Housing and Education Act of 1965. These acts presage a redefinition of public welfare away from custody by passive welfare agencies over a limited number of eligible clients, and toward social reform. Public welfare units have not been found in the vanguard of this social reform. Very few have lobbied for higher minimum wages, have become engaged in shaping the municipality's response in those cities experiencing organized Negro protests, or have forged links with human relations groups or with urban renewal relocation services.[53] It appears that public welfare agencies had become too staid and bureaucratic in their custodial functions and were reluctant to expose the inadequacies of their former practices. Nevertheless, the new currents of social action aimed at institutional change promise to carry welfare agencies in their wake.

This is indicated by the fact that progressive welfare agencies have replaced terms of eligibility and income maintenance with theories of "case movement." They have replaced the term "assistance" with the term "investment." They now emphasize "prevention." They are more willing to admit that dealing with the individual has its limitations, and thus have turned also to group counseling. Plans are now being carried out on a neighborhood basis, which is uniquely suited to social action efforts.[54]

Under the pressure of identifying case movements, measured by objective indices such as income, occupation, education, and housing, welfare agencies are increasingly subjecting recipients to statistical classification and research, physical and mental tests, and case management by abstract principles. In Hartford, for example, persons tested and found by the Connecticut State Employment Service to be capable of further education are forced to attend classes or forfeit assistance. Day care attendance may become mandatory for children on Aid to Dependent Children, with the mother required to work or attend school, on the principle that this might be the best way to subsidize the ADC family—a good example of the application of the theory of preventive social

[51] Edward A. Lehan, "The Municipality's Response to Changing Concepts of Public Welfare," in THE REVOLUTION IN PUBLIC WELFARE: THE CONNECTICUT EXPERIENCE, ed. by R. Levenson (Storrs: Institute of Public Service, University of Connecticut, 1966), p. 47.

[52] Silberman, op. cit., p. 313.

[53] Lehan, op. cit., p. 48.
[54] Ibid., p. 49.

work. Hartford now plans to include day care centers in new schools and routinely applies housing code standards to general assistance recipients, through cooperation among welfare, housing code, and relocation personnel. In appropriate cases a homemaker-teacher is assigned, furnished through a contract with the Family Service Society.[55]

In addition to the change in outlook and values that have helped to provoke a rejuvenation of public welfare, a second factor—that of physical urban renewal—is bound to have a similar impact on the administration of public welfare, for now municipalities will no longer be able to limit their intake of welfare clients.

The relocation function of urban renewal alone brings public administrators face-to-face with 'problem people' in a context which involves every nook and cranny of the locality and focuses responsibility on a wide spectrum of public officials in a way never felt before. . . . Hartford's urban renewal plan, for example, is founded on the idea that every family to be moved will be the subject of intensive efforts to modify its status upward long before the act of relocation.[56]

Here welfare workers will play a leading role in the interagency neighborhood field organizations, working without close departmental supervision, in harness with planners, redevelopers, relocators, policemen, housing inspectors, and employment counselors assigned with them to a particular neighborhood. Each field organization will work under the direct control of the city manager's office.[57]

Yet, as a strategic matter, the municipality must limit and subdivide its intake over the short run; thus, the need for planning and coordination among agencies, to establish priorities.

THE FEDERAL ESTABLISHMENT

A third major area of social planning includes the federal agencies directly responsible for social welfare programs and the agencies and other lobbies for congressional and executive action to alter present programs or create new ones. The primary agency responsible for social programs is the Department of Health, Education, and Welfare. Its constituent parts, e.g., the Office of Education, Social Security Administration, and Public Health Service each administer major segments of social service and social change goals. Additional agencies involved in the social welfare field are the Office of Economic Opportunity, Department of Housing and Urban Development, and Department of Labor.

The planners' roles in these agencies consist of developing programs to implement federal legislation, and programs upon which new legislation may be based. Research sections of the federal agencies carry out extensive research and demonstration programs designed to test and gain acceptability for new departures in social legislation.

At the national level, goal setting for the federal social agencies is carried out by the staffs of the agencies themselves, working in conjunction with the Office of the President, and by national lobby groups representing major public and private groups with an interest in the fields of legislation under consideration. Innovations in social welfare legislation are reached through congressional compromises among the interests of the various groups opposing and favoring new legislation.

This national goal-setting and implementational process has been attacked as inadequate for the needs of new social legislation because it inadequately represents the clients of many of the social-welfare programs—the poor, the elderly, and the minority groups. These are seen as relatively helpless to express their interests through national lobbying and other influence-wielding devices available to the wealthier and more powerful groups. This criticism has led to a recent innovation in goal-formulation techniques, as exemplified by the citizen participation requirement of the Urban Renewal program and the "maximum feasible participation" provision of the poverty program. The innovation consists of the provision for goal formulation at both the federal government and the local neighborhood levels.

Once a general goal such as slum elimination or poverty elimination is established, machinery is set up for accomplishing this goal, which includes that of consultation with the popula-

[55] *Ibid.*, p. 50.
[56] *Ibid.*, pp. 52–53.
[57] *Ibid.*, p. 53.

tion most directly affected by the actions stipulated in the law.

ANTI-POVERTY PLANNING

A very specialized type of planning, the planning of programs to combat poverty, represents the final and most recent major type of social planning by people other than city planners. At the outset it should be noted that this type of planning might entail the broadest type of planning—the planning of national social policy to eliminate social and economic injustice. But the meaning given here to anti-poverty planning is a narrower one. The social planning referred to here is that planning associated with the growing number of programs arising out of the Economic Opportunity Act (EOA) as well as other federal legislation associated with what Gans called policies of "guided mobility."

The need for planning arises in the various training programs on which much of the anti-poverty fight is based. These programs include those intended to give a "headstart" in education to children from poor families and those intended to offer new vocational opportunities to teenagers and to adults. Another anti-poverty program which will increasingly call upon the help of planners is economic development. The federal Economic Development Act, successor to the Appalachia Bill, establishes federal support for local development programs, particularly those favoring communities or sectors of population in great economic need. This program will direct economic expansion away from general expansion, as is frequently the goal in commercial and industrial urban renewal, and toward more direct assistance to areas in greatest need of help.

But the major area for planning work is in the development of Community Action Programs (CAP) established under Title II of the Economic Opportunity Act. The CAPs are devices established specifically for the purposes of obtaining local support through planning for programs aimed at reducing poverty.

One of the great and unsolved problems associated with Title II of the EOA is just how much its requirement of "maximum feasible participation" by the poor will seriously handicap efforts of professionals to assist in the planning of programs. Many strong arguments both pro and con have been put forth concerning the exclusion from the CAPs of non-poor, particularly, technicians representing middle-class oriented professions. Professional planners can play a strategic role in assisting these programs, but it may be a role which will have to be played from a distance so that the wishes of the poor may be respected and their power developed.

The Community Action Programs of the anti-poverty program have adopted a variety of techniques for meeting the participation requirement. One technique is that of special elections in poverty-stricken neighborhoods, with a requirement that the income of those elected to poverty boards shall be below a certain level. Another technique is that of including on decision-making boards the board members of neighborhood social-service groups who have had long experience in working with social service staffs and upper-income board members of charitable organizations.

The anti-poverty program differs in significant ways from other social welfare programs that originated in the New Deal era. Like the public housing program, it is designed to affect only selected parts of the population—those living in slums and other urban and rural "poverty pockets." This is in marked contrast to the New Deal programs, which were designed to offer various forms of social security to the entire population of the nation, regardless of income level. The second major innovation is that it does not rely only on national decision-making processes for the formulation of social goals, but rests on an assumption that the clients of the program must be involved in second-level goal setting and in implementational decisions.

This assumption brings us back to the local action groups discussed in the section on advocacy planning. Local political action groups are not planning groups, but they are crucial ingredients in the accomplishment of planning goals. First, in pursuing goals such as decent housing and individual economic self-sufficiency, planning and welfare agencies are blocked by the pervasive apathy of their "clients." Local action groups are a means for overcoming this apathy, through education and *involvement*. Secondly, local action groups characteristically have such by-products as self-education, clean-up, fix-up, and school improvement campaigns, among others, all of which involve the mobilization of private resources towards the very goals that planners are trying to achieve.

Saul Alinsky's Industrial Areas Foundation is the best known effort to organize local action groups. The democratic basis on which Alinsky creates mass organizations allows the so-called "little man" to "gather into his hands the power he needs to make and shape his life."[58] Alinsky's stimulus wrought amazing results in private urban renewal in Back-of-the-Yards, Chicago, during the late 1930s. Since then his nonprofit IAF has organized some 44 groups across the nation, including, most notably, Mexican-Americans in California and Negro-Americans in the Woodlawn neighborhood of Chicago.

The Anti-Poverty's Community Action Programs should regard such local private initiative as a valuable tool, and should encourage the organization of local action groups.

Resources and Level of Operation

It is difficult to separate funds from personnel when speaking of social welfare resources. However, it is safe to say that government provides more financial than manpower resources. In the first place, the government contracts with private agencies and universities to carry on research and to implement social welfare projects. In the second place, many cities carrying out Community Renewal Programs prefer to rely as much as possible on existing voluntary welfare agencies.[59] Not only private agencies but also private citizens can be used on a volunteer basis in social welfare planning and programming and, of course, implementation. For example, Pittsburgh's Action for Employment (a demonstration neighborhood manpower project) used nonprofessional, "in-

digenous" ghetto residents to recruit and counsel unemployed people in relation to a job training and job placement program; the planning directors in this case felt that such tasks required native ability more than advanced skills.[60] Several of the more successful experiences in social welfare planning have shown the importance of using the energies of the "grass roots." New Haven concludes that "the people who are going to be called on to put a program over, to support it, or even to cooperate with it had better be involved from the beginning in putting it together."[61]

An important source of funds for pilot or demonstration projects has been various large private foundations, notably the Ford Foundation, which, for example, gave $3.2 million between 1960 and 1963 for a series of educational experiments focused on the needs of culturally disadvantaged children, and $12.1 million between 1961 and 1963 for Community Development Programs in the "grey areas" of four cities and one state.[62]

The Penjerdel Study reports the following financial sources of five counties in southeast Pennsylvania for health, welfare, recreation and "central services related to health and welfare":[63]

local government	15.2%
state government	21.0
federal government	9.1
fees from users	41.1
contributions	7.7
investments	2.8
all other	3.1

Schermer points out that while private contributions and investments represent less than one-seventh of the dollar volume of health, welfare, and recreation expenditures, nevertheless a very high ratio of what is invested in planning and preventive work, and those ser-

---

[58] Silberman, *op. cit.*, pp. 321–28.

[59] Rhode Island Council of Community Services, Inc., *op. cit.*, p. 26.

[60] Allegheny Council to Improve Our Neighborhoods-Housing, Inc., *op. cit.*, pp. 19–23.

[61] Gregory R. Farrell, A CLIMATE OF CHANGE: COMMUNITY ACTION IN NEW HAVEN (New Brunswick, N.J.: Rutgers University, Urban Studies Center, 1965), p. 58.

[62] National Association of Housing and Redevelopment Officials, AMERICAN COMMUNITY DEVELOPMENT, PRELIMINARY REPORTS BY DIRECTORS OF PROJECTS ASSISTED BY THE FORD FOUNDATION IN FOUR CITIES AND A STATE (New York: Ford Foundation, 1963), p. 1.

[63] Schermer, *op. cit.*, p. 32.

vices that can be individualized, comes from private sources.[64]

There is not total agreement among planners about the use of existing institutions, however. Schermer found them only partially useful, because of "institutional inertia."[65]

GEOGRAPHIC SCALE FOR SOLUTIONS

Needless to say, both private and governmental resources are available at all geographic levels. The particular geographic scale at which funds and personnel are recruited becomes a more crucial question when governmental rather than private voluntary action is sought, because government schemes are more restrictive then private resources. Even so, Schermer feels that the geographic scale of private social welfare activity can help to determine the geographic scale at which the government attempts to solve welfare problems, because private charity fosters in citizens a sense of commitment to the area served by the charitable organization.[66] Thus, if a regional (interstate or intercounty) charity can be organized, there is more likelihood that the same region will develop intergovernmental cooperation, and thus provide a presumably more logical jurisdiction for solving welfare problems.

The jurisdictional level which provides the funds and personnel for social welfare is not necessarily the same jurisdictional level at which the solutions are actually administered. This is to be expected, since solutions are naturally administered at the level which has the closest contact with "the people," whereas such local levels are unable to levy the taxes needed to cover welfare programs and other activities of local government. Moreover, taxes can be collected more efficiently (i.e., for less cost per $1 collected) at the higher levels than at the lower levels of government.[67]

There are two main reasons for the inability of local jurisdictions to cover their own costs: (1) they are in competition with other local areas to attract taxpayers and to repel welfare clients; thus, local jurisdictions have an incentive to lower taxes and to cut down on welfare programs and other governmental services; (2) welfare problems often occur at unpredictable times and in unpredictable places, but not continuously nor nationwide; thus, a locale that is suddenly hit by a welfare problem, e.g., unemployment, is unable to assume the unexpected burdens, just as individuals are unable to assume unexpected financial burdens without sharing these burdens through a collective insurance program.

For the above reasons, many leaders, notably the economist Walter Heller, have proposed plans for tax-sharing among levels of government. The grant-in-aid programs presently used, are criticized for destroying the autonomy of local governments. Automatic tax-sharing plans avoid this "strings attached" criticism. Automatic sharing plans could distribute according to any number of criteria, e.g., inversely according to income levels, which the Elementary and Secondary Education Act of 1965 includes in its formula; or directly according to population; or directly according to the amount of taxes contributed by each state, although such a formula as this would probably never gain political acceptance, since the American polity has come to favor a certain degree of income equalization.

Preference among fund distribution systems depends mainly on the accepted hierarchy of values: as between, for example, local self-determination and equality of opportunity. Those who are concerned with social welfare would tend to place equality of opportunity above local self-determination, since the latter value is of primary benefit to the local power structure and not of benefit to welfare clients who, for subjective psychological reasons or for objective economic and educational reasons, have almost no political power with which to help determine local decisions.

This is not to say that welfare recipients would not welcome the opportunity for self-determination. In fact, ghetto organizations have actually rebuffed offers of stepped-up governmental aid, precisely because the decision to extend this aid was not determined by the

---

[64] *Ibid.*, p. 36.
[65] *Ibid.*, p. 25.
[66] *Ibid.*, pp. 42–51.
[67] Sam M. Lambert, NINE QUESTIONS ON FEDERAL SUPPORT FOR PUBLIC SCHOOLS (Washington: National Education Association Legislative Commission, 1960), pp. 1–2.

ghetto residents themselves.[68] However, as long as the governmental structure remains as it now is—that is with local politicians making decisions for entire heterogeneous cities, largely unhampered by the objectives or nominal policies of other elements of the polity (e.g., federal representatives and civil servants lacking effective authority; or the "disenfranchised" poor and uneducated), an automatic tax-sharing plan would not solve the welfare recipients' desires for self-determination.

The geographic level at which physical planners attempt to deal with welfare problems may differ from the level at which social planners choose to solve these problems. One reason is that each has traditionally worked on a different geographic scale: social planners traditionally focused on neighborhoods, while physical planners focused on larger areas. However, urban renewal is now bringing the physical planner down to the neighborhood level, while the previously mentioned obstacles to social welfare planning will, hopefully, cause social welfare planners to become more cognizant of the need to work on a much larger geographic scale.

There is no one geographic scale at which it is preferable to attack all social welfare problems. In the first place, no one jurisdictional level could handle the problems alone; thus, there must be cooperation among levels. Usually it is the federal government and the states that provide a large portion of the financial resources, while the local government decides what it needs and how it will go about meeting its needs, and then actually carries out the program.

Cooperation is needed not only among governmental levels, but also among neighboring jurisdictions at the same level. Frieden makes this point very strongly:

Conflict between local governments arises from a context of intergovernmental relations in which considerations of municipal finance join with social prejudices in creating incentives for public officials to prevent the poor from living within their jurisdictions, or at least to hold their number to a minimum. A fundamental objective for all groups concerned with human welfare in urban America must be to change the intergovernmental setting in ways that will provide greater incentives for socially responsible policies. Until the legal and political context of local government is changed in this direction, city planners alone will be able to accomplish little in enlarging the choices available to the poor or opening the gates for a freer movement of all people throughout urban areas.[69]

Wherever the conflict between governmental units at a given level is insoluble, it is likely that a higher governmental jurisdiction will intervene to resolve the conflict.

NATIONAL

Regarding the level of government best suited for various social welfare functions, it must be said that not all planners are agreed on this matter. They differ, for example, on the degree to which they would expect to be able to rely on the national level of government. John Dyckman states that most social gains will be engineered from Washington, D.C.[70]

Anthony Adamson says that:

. . . planning, as the vital concept in government for the formation of social policy, for the formation of public institutions, and for the formation of good physical environment is now recognized at the top.[71]

Although he believes that it is mainly the local level that harbors the inhibitions to planning that arise from vested economic interests and beliefs, from rigid governmental institutions, from bigotry and uncharitableness, Adamson is nevertheless optimistic in thinking that these inhibitions are currently "giving way at a time when we are very prosperous indeed."[72]

Applied to the United States, Adamson's statement should be modified to state that the local governments are still poor, while the nation as a whole is wealthy, and it is the national wealth that is not only *allowing* us to overcome our inhibitions against planning, but is now *forcing* these inhibitions to give way.

However,

enlightened federal policies will not produce better results in practice if local governments continue to use programs to attract middle-income

---

[68] Silberman, *op. cit.,* pp. 313 and 344.

[69] Frieden, *op. cit.,* pp. 322–23.
[70] Dyckman, *op. cit.,* p. 75.
[71] Adamson, *op. cit.,* p. 193.
[72] *Ibid.*

families rather than to give fresh opportunities to the poor.[73]

INTERSTATE

The interstate regional scale was studied specifically by Schermer in the Penjerdel area. He found that this scale would be the best at which to approach the following aspects of social planning:

1. Expensive and specialized facilities such as hospitals, clinics, post-high school training, college and postgraduate institutions;

2. Economic development, promotion of employment opportunity, job recruitment, and on-the-job training;

3. The alleviation of inequities, racial restrictions in employment and housing, and overconcentration of low-income and nonwhite population in the central cities;

4. Major recreational and cultural facilities.

STATE

The state level is often a good scale at which to attack certain economic problems, but as can be seen from the Area Redevelopment and Appalachia programs, their solution usually requires a regional approach of interstate dimension.

For those social welfare problems that can be approached at a smaller-than-interstate scale, the role of the state government is usually one of coordinating efforts and the provision of financial aids and incentives to yet smaller "problem areas." North Carolina established the first statewide agency in the United States with the explicit purpose of making an all-out assault on the problems of poverty; but even so, it was felt that significant results were likely to come from experimental educational programs in *a number of carefully selected communities* rather than from mere per capita or "equalized" income-maintenance funds distributed throughout the state.[74]

METROPOLITAN

In general what has been said of the regional scale applies also to the metropolitan scale, but it seems that as the constituent governmental units become more local (from states to coun-

ties to incorporated suburbs), so the forces of authority seem to become more provincial and exclusive. This would seem to indicate that metropolitan areas will find it more difficult to plan for social welfare than regions. However, they do have the advantage of being specific entities, recognized both by the people (which Schermer thinks is a crucial ingredient for success) [75] and by the higher levels of government (e.g., the federal government, Bureau of the Census).

COUNTY

Health problems are currently being attacked most energetically by the county which also provides some recreational and educational facilities. The county's role varies according to whether it is near a metropolitan area or not. It is often in a strategic position to provide an opportunity for alleviating the results of the racial and ethnic discrimination that is often found in the exclusive suburbs of a metropolis, for open occupancy laws passed by county boards of supervisors might help to discourage massive invasions by minority groups into those suburbs that might pioneer in policies of non-discrimination in housing.

CITY

The level at which urban planners have traditionally worked is the city, and this is the scale at which social welfare problems are most visible. It is at the city level that most private, voluntary social welfare agencies exist, social casework is organized, the school system is directed, a park and recreational service is provided, public housing is built, and urban renewal is carried out. It is also, of course, the level at which most public facilities and services such as water, sewerage, streets, sidewalks, street lighting, and garbage collection are provided, and the level at which zoning, subdivision, and building code regulations are most common—all of which relate to the social welfare of the immediate residents and neighboring communities.

The city has been assisted by recent national legislation in many areas of its responsibility, including water and sewage treatment, high-

---

[73] Frieden, *op. cit.,* p. 326.

[74] National Association of Housing and Redevelopment Officials, *op. cit.,* p. 32.

[75] Schermer, *op. cit.,* p. 50.

ways, schools, public housing, urban renewal, and in regard to the War on Poverty. However, in metropolitan areas, federal aid is increasingly being made contingent upon intergovernmental cooperation and planning, so that while the city within a metropolitan area is perhaps the most important implementer of social welfare within its jurisdiction, and while it is being forced increasingly to engage in general planning, nevertheless its role in general and social planning tends to diminish as governmental units of wider jurisdiction assume greater responsibilities.

While much significant work could be done at the city level, the power structure tends to be conservative. It is likely to oppose ordinances that prohibit racial or ethnic discrimination. Reinforcing this situation is the fact that some "liberals" might not support very progressive legislation at the city level through fear of attracting undue numbers of persons with social problems.

NEIGHBORHOOD

Social welfare at the neighborhood level, even more than at the city level, has traditionally made use of private resources, such as settlement houses and neighborhood improvement organizations. It is at this scale, of course, that any existing social welfare problems are most patent, since residential areas tend to be grouped according to economic and racial characteristics.

There has been growing interest among planners in the neighborhood as a focus for the implementation of specific social welfare programs for it is here that the obstacle of apathy can best be attacked. Pittsburgh, Philadelphia, Providence, New Haven, and Hartford, for example, have strongly emphasized the neighborhood. Philadelphia is using this as the basic unit of research to determine what kinds of neighborhoods react best to given urban renewal activities.[76] Eventually the Community Renewal Program in Philadelphia will differentiate between neighborhoods on the basis of the readiness of the residents to work at particular programs aimed toward general goals

for the neighborhood.

Hartford has worked out a program for integrating services at the neighborhood level. Here experiments have been carried out with a field organization which at various times combined the welfare department, the Connecticut State Employment Service, housing code enforcement, the police department, and public works personnel, all working together within a limited geographic area. Based on lessons learned from this experiment, Hartford is now setting up a series of interagency field organizations, each working under the direct control of the city manager's office.[77]

Interest in the neighborhood is not, of course, new. It has been popular in regard to the design and administration of school systems ever since Clarence Perry introduced the concept of "neighborhood schools." The idea has been widely adopted, but now that desegregation has become an important factor in the eyes of those concerned with social welfare, the neighborhood school is now considered by many as an obstacle that must be eliminated. Thus, recently, the idea of the "educational park" has gained prominence, and this may inhibit the use of the grade school as a community center or neighborhood center, for stimulating self-help activity and organization among the apathetic residents of ghetto areas.

Adjustments in Dealing with Social Welfare Problems

Since physical and economic development and planning are merely means of achieving human and social objectives, it would seem fair to limit this discussion to a definition of social objectives, even though urban planners are often preoccupied by immediate physical and economic considerations.

Methodologies for the definition of objectives are undergoing change. Two opposing philosophies can be identified which, to some extent, correlate with the philosophical differences between what Dyckman calls administrative rightists and leftwing social planners,[78]

[76] See footnotes 4 and 5, under section on social welfare councils.

[77] Lehan, op. cit., p. 53.
[78] Dyckman, op. cit., pp. 73–74.

and also between traditional comprehensive planners and those who would like to be "advocate planners." These two philosophies also conform somewhat to the political philosophies of "idealism" on the one hand and "democratic pragmatism" on the other.

One approach to the definition of objectives postulates that a given community has common interests and that these can be ascertained by some knowledgeable persons (presumably planners) and action based upon them. The second approach states that "there are no neutral grounds for evaluating a plan; there are as many evaluative systems as there are value systems";[79] and because of the need for value determinations in science (in regard to criteria and measures), a scientific decision model must resemble a democratic decision model.[80]

Examined in relation to the whole society at this point in time, it is difficult to accept the first approach, namely that there are identifiable common interests. Experience seems to suggest that at this level the second approach is followed almost entirely; that is, very little directive planning is done other than that made legitimate through *political contests* among different interest groups.

In 1964 Perloff argued that in the field of social planning, it is less a matter of the "nonexistence" of community objectives than an "operational non-recognition" of them; . . . that there was agreement on the following goals:[81]

1. Maximizing the proportion of families who are self-supporting, thus reducing dependency;

2. Increasing the lifetime earning power of individuals, through such expediencies as reducing mortality and morbidity, preventing mental illness, providing useful work for the handicapped and the aged, and encouraging individual entrepreneurship;

3. Providing at least minimum support, either monetary or psychological, for those who cannot provide it for themselves;

4. Seeking to make the social services as effective and as economical as possible;

5. Enlarging the scope for individual and small-group decision and action, since individuals and local groups are in the best position to determine what contributes most to their own welfare.

Such goals are meaningless, however, unless they are implemented by a government or private voluntary program, and unless they are quantified. Most of these goals are currently being pursued by one government program or another, but with standards so low that the services either do not benefit the needy or are rejected by them. To accomplish these goals would require more money than any private voluntary agency has, and more money than the effective political forces in our society are currently willing to spend via the government.

In going from goal-formulation by a society to goal-formulation by specific agencies involved in social welfare, a concern for "coordination of efforts *toward* known objectives" becomes more justified. In 1965 Perloff argued that at the local bureaucratic level the lack of coordination resulted from the fact that physical planners and social planners each define their goals too narrowly, and that the following "integrating concepts" would help make their goals coincide:[82] (1) a decent home and suitable environment for every family; (2) jobs for all and a minimum family income; (3) adequacy and equality in public services and facilities.

These integrating concepts could easily prove to be points of political controversy. For example, what is decent, suitable, minimum, adequate, and equal? And more important, what would achievement of such standards cost? While standards remain unquantified, analysis and policy-making can only be considered as remedial; they move *away* from ills rather than toward known objectives, and it is therefore difficult to pursue comprehensiveness. Only after *political* decisions have been made—that is, how much will be spent on social welfare—is it meaningful to speak of a coordination of efforts such as might exist

---

[79] Davidoff, *op. cit.*, p. 333.

[80] Paul Davidoff and Thomas A. Reiner, "A Reply to Dakin," JOURNAL OF THE AMERICAN INSTITUTE OF PLANNERS, XXIX (Feb., 1963), p. 27.

[81] Harvey Perloff, "Social Planning in the Metropolis," in THE URBAN CONDITION, ed. Leonard J. Duhl (New York: Basic Books, 1963), p. 335.

[82] Perloff, in PLANNING 1965, *op. cit.*, pp. 171–74.

among the various departments of a city government.

Professor Dyckman has suggested three definitions of social planning which, in effect, distinguish societal goal-formulation from agency goal-pursuit. Rather than being competing ideas, these definitions might be viewed as compatible concepts appropriate to different levels of social intervention. They are:

1. At the societal planning level, social planning means the *selection of the social goals* of the nation or state, and the setting of targets for their achievement. It requires a ranking of these goals, and assessment of the cost (in terms of other objectives) of achieving them, and judgments of the feasibility of such programs.

2. Social planning, in a closely related meaning, involves the application of social values and action criteria to the assessment of programs undertaken in the pursuit of economic or political goals. Thus, it can mean the *testing of consequences*—in terms of intergroup or interpersonal relations—of everything from broad economic development programs to specific redevelopment projects.

3. Social planning can mean specifically 'social' programming arising from the broad social goals of the community. The traditional welfare activities of public and private agencies have been the principal focus of such planning in the United States. The *coordination of programming* for and by the multitude of caretaker agencies that have grown up in our free enterprise economy is a popular task for this type of social planning.[83]

Dyckman, quite properly, warns of overemphasis on the third category "without an adequately specified set of objectives at the first and second levels."

Returning to the tactical distinction between the "idealist" philosophy of "authoritarian justice" and the "democratic pragmatic" philosophy of "equalitarian justice," there are two further arguments for favoring the latter. First, a recognition of *conflicting interests*, rather than belief in a *community interest* both (1) forces the planner to relate the range of public activities to the diverse groups of the population having distinct preferences and aims,[84] and (2) makes more apparent and explicit the values underlying plans. Paul Davidoff feels that advocacy planning achieves this second purpose because its "legal brief" nature would

upset the tradition of writing plan proposals in terminology which makes them appear self-evident.[85] Dyckman feels that "client analysis" (mentioned earlier) presents this same advantage because it avoids subsuming the clients' interests in vague categories of public interest, and avoids ascribing the prejudices of the bureaucracy to the long-run best interests of the poor.[86] Dyckman believes that social scientists cannot supplant the goal-making role of ideology or the political decision-makers' responsibility for setting goals.[87]

If this second approach is accepted, then the planner's main concern in the stage of goal formulation is to stimulate meaningful citizen participation and broadened political participation.

Second, Gans suggests that perhaps "authoritarian justice" is, after all, the goal that social welfare planning is expected to pursue. In addressing himself to those programs, such as Mobilization for Youth, which preceded federally sponsored Community Action Programs under the Economic Opportunity Act, he wrote:

From a sociological perspective, such programs might best be described as schemes for *guided mobility*, since they propose to induce mobility among people whom sociologists describe as lower class . . . Social planning is a harmonious euphemism for the attempt to alter the class structure.[88]

INFORMATION AND SURVEY

In the task of information collection and analysis, planners will have to cooperate more closely with other specialists on whom they will rely for the provision of data.

Examples of new techniques for research and data collection include:

1. Providence's Social Pathology Index: a survey of residents and leaders to ascertain their concepts of the neighborhood; central records and data system.[89]

2. Philadelphia's "Model of Human and Social Needs and Resources";[90]

[83] Dyckman, *op. cit.*, pp. 67–68.
[84] Reiner, Reimer, and Reiner, *op. cit.*, p. 271.

[85] Davidoff, *op. cit.*, p. 333.
[86] Dyckman, *op. cit.*, p. 69.
[87] *Ibid.*, p. 75.
[88] Herbert Gans, "Social Planning: A New Role for Sociology," speech, 1962.
[89] Shown in Figure 11–2.
[90] Health and Welfare Council, Inc., *op. cit.*, pp. 8–11.

3. Reiner, Reimer, and Reiner's "Client Analysis Model";[91]

4. Melvin Schneidermeyer's "Metropolitan Social Inventory" which "receives informational inputs that measure the condition of human well-being or that facilitates this measurement," e.g., census data, magnetic tapes containing metropolitan origin-destination study findings, records of local utility companies, or questionnaire responses obtained for a market analysis, plus any original data gathered by the staff of the MSI.[92]

There are several advantages in processing such data automatically. Information can be updated quickly and thus retain maximum utility; it can be speedily converted to graphs, gradients, matrices, and distribution percentages. The information is cumulative; it builds on itself and increases in quantity without the attendant disadvantages of undue storage space being needed or of information retrieval being slow. Automatic data processing can change

the scale at which planning is attempted, because information can more easily be held and distributed from a central data bank. When a data center is set up, there is usually a strong accompanying motivation to centralize data, due to the technical requirements of ADP both in equipment and professional skills.

5. Perloff's "elements in direct human resources focus," i.e., family income and consumption submodel; individual submodel ("personal development" and life cycle); group and institutional support submodel; manpower submodel; regional economic submodel (e.g., economic accounts); neighborhood situation (location and ecology); and summary institutional component (agency effectiveness and institutional performance within the framework of the broader power structure).[93]

The major issues which Perloff would wish to have social planning confront are: (a) "jobs and incomes of families"; (b) "Financial support to those who cannot become economically self-supporting"; (c) "Emotional support for

[91] Reiner, Reimer, and Reiner, *op. cit., passim.*

[92] Melvin Schneidermeyer, THE METROPOLITAN SOCIAL INVENTORY: PROCEDURES FOR MEASURING HUMAN WELL-BEING IN URBAN AREAS, (thesis, University of Illinois, Urbana, Illinois, 1966), pp. 45–76.

[93] Harvey Perloff, "Social Planning in the Metropolis," in Leonard J. Duhl (ed.), THE URBAN CONDITION (New York: Basic Books, 1963), pp. 340–45.

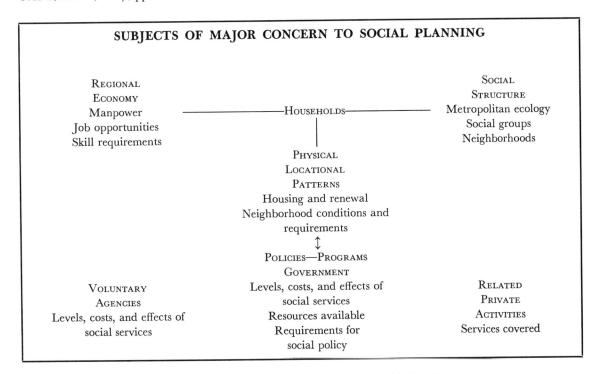

FIGURE 11–3. *Subjects of major concern to social planning*

individuals and family groups who need it"; (d) "A high level of social services, particularly education and health"; (e) "Decent housing and a satisfying physical environment for all families"; and (f) "Elimination of racial discrimination."[94]

Recognizing that "the long-term welfare of the individual and the family are the main concern of social efforts" Perloff recommends making the "household the central focus and key testing ground of social service activities."[95] But as can be seen from Figure 11–3, households are closely related measures of the regional economy and the condition of the social structure and the physical environment. In dealing with each of the major subjects of concern to social planning, Perloff has identified the types of tools required to measure social progress. The tools and their purposes are shown in Perloff's Table 11–1 reproduced below.

Perloff's "Household Welfare Indices" are measures:

aimed at evaluating the extent of realization of community objectives, such as self-support, more jobs, better income situations, and the provisions of a support floor. . . ."

For example, "The self-support index should show the number of families who are financially self-supporting, partially self-supporting and totally supported by the community.[96]

6. Schermer recommends the establishment of a Regional Data Service in the Penjerdel area.[97] This should be done for all regions.

7. In August, 1966, Senator Edward Kennedy introduced a joint resolution in Congress to authorize the Advisory Commission on Intergovernmental Relations to study the feasibility and design of a comprehensive information service system that would make use of automatic data processing equipment and other forms of advanced information technology to inform the states and localities about federal programs, aids, and projects that might be use-

[94] Harvey Perloff, "New Directions in Social Planning," JOURNAL OF THE AMERICAN INSTITUTE OF PLANNERS, XXXI (Nov., 1965), p. 297.
[95] Ibid., p. 300.

[96] Ibid.
[97] Schermer, op. cit., p. 51.

Table 11–1

Proposed Social Planning Tools

Major Purpose	Category	Tools
1. To permit a sharper focus on objectives and achievement	Households	Annual State-of-the-Region Report: showing household welfare indices
2. To permit a periodic review of changing conditions and emerging social problems and to suggest possible ways of dealing with the problems	Regional economy	Annual State-of-the-Region Report: showing (a) major changes in regional economy and in job situation (b) Regional accounts including manpower and income accounts
	Social structure	Group and neighborhood profiles
	Physical locational patterns	Neighborhood betterment programs
3. To permit improvements in social service programs and better coordination among activities	Policies and programs	Community policies plan Long-term capital and operating budget for social services

Source: Harvey Perloff, "New Directions in Social Planning," JOURNAL OF THE AMERICAN INSTITUTE OF PLANNERS, XXXI (Nov. 1965), p. 300.

ful to them. Data would include socio-economic data involving such elements as income distribution, education, law enforcement, health, and welfare; community resource data involving such items as labor force and employment, industry and trade, transportation, housing and community facilities, and finance; programs reference data, including the nature and purpose of assistance programs, conditions of eligibility, information contact, authorizing legislation, and administering agency; programs status data involving the nature and extent of usage of various aid programs, the status of obligated funds, and the names and numbers of communities involved.

8. The Advisory Commission on Intergovernmental Relations has recommended that each local governmental unit and agency within a metropolitan area, whether central city or suburban, should ascertain, analyze, and give recognition to economic and social disparities affecting its programs.[98]

9. Census data can be tied to individual parcels of land and thus worked into a comprehensive, automatically updated record system based on the revenue, planning-zoning-subdivision, and building code departments of a municipal or county government in a metropolitan area. The Census promises bright prospects for doing this, as in 1970 it plans to collect and release block statistics on developing suburban areas where data had not formerly been available on a block basis. The Census will provide this service if the suburban government undertakes to delineate the blocks. This is a challenging task inasmuch as fringe areas have not developed on the logically numbered, rectangular, small-block bases that most cities have followed.

10. The use of demonstration projects, such as those sponsored by the Ford Foundation in its "grey areas" program, and those sponsored by the President's Committee on Juvenile Delinquency.

PROGRAMMING

The Community Renewal Program has provided an excellent opportunity for integrating social, physical, and economic planning, and

has caused some propitious changes in municipal administrative and decision-making structures. For example, Providence's Social Plan proposed a change in the local administrative structure; the maintenance of a central records and data system; the phasing of the social plan to complement urban renewal activities; the use of a special "Social Treatment Model" in those areas described as most needy by the Social Pathology Index; and the establishment of various levels of citizens' organizations, to which the Redevelopment Agency and others contribute staff advice. In Providence, the Neighborhood Information Service agent, who works under the "A" Area Social Treatment Model, has a responsibility for finding gaps in services and for recommending remedial changes to appropriate bodies.[99]

Social planning is adaptable to programming techniques such as PERT (Program Evaluation and Review Technique) and Willard B. Hansen's "Two-level Task Roster for Comprehensive Metropolitan Planning."[100] However, success with such techniques will demand a great deal more basic research on social problems and their possible solutions.

On the regional scale, Schermer suggests that special purpose planning is the most likely and promising interim step toward comprehensive regional planning and thus should be pursued. He exhorts the Department of Health, Education and Welfare and the Housing and Home Finance Agency (now the Department of Housing and Urban Development) to foster region-wide integrated social planning. He also recommends that a type of "brainstorming" operation should be carried out in the form of a continuing forum at the regional level on the problems and resources of social welfare.[101]

IMPLEMENTATION

While many cities have expressed a desire for using existing social welfare agencies as far as possible, most planners *have* come to the con-

[98] Frieden, *op. cit.*, p. 330.

[99] Rhode Island Council for Community Services, Inc., *op. cit., passim.*

[100] Willard B. Hansen, PROCEDURAL FRAMEWORKS FOR COMPREHENSIVE METROPOLITAN PLANNING: AN INTRODUCTORY STATEMENT (Urbana: University of Illinois Bureau of Community Planning, 1966), mimeo.

[101] Schermer, *op. cit.*, pp. 46, 51.

clusion that social welfare planning cannot be successfully implemented by tradition-bound and stagnant agencies and thus strongly recommend the establishment of some *new* comprehensive agency.

The extent to which "city planners" take the lead in such new comprehensive planning agencies may well depend upon the direction which the American Institute of Planners chooses to follow: AIP's traditional direction of physical planning or, alternatively, the Wetmore Committee's direction of comprehensive (social-economic-physical) planning.

In some instances the local anti-poverty office might be the vehicle for comprehensive planning, since it often appears to have the closest contact with "needy" residents and a direct financial link with the federal government.

The need for a *new* comprehensive agency is also suggested by the proposal that social welfare planning subsume the other forms of planning under it, since the criteria of social planning (welfare, opportunity, security, and knowledge, for example) are more inclusive than the criteria of pure physical planning (space, location, physical condition) or of economic planning (monetary cost). However, existing social welfare agencies are not suitably equipped or authorized to undertake the responsibility for comprehensive planning.

Use of the neighborhood unit is a relatively recent innovation in implementation. Providence goes a step further: through its Neighborhood Information Service, the city attempts to integrate all the services used by a particular *family*, so that the *family* becomes the focus for implementing plans.[102] To some extent this was always done by caseworkers, but they never had

access to the authority of the several different agencies whose actions impinged on their clients' welfare. New Haven, Connecticut, focuses this kind of attention on the *individual*, through both professional and voluntary guidance and follow-up services.[103]

Part of the process of implementation should be the education of citizens to encourage them to take some initiative in distributing social welfare benefits (i.e., reducing the necessity for the agency to "reach out"). At the present time, certain welfare agencies follow the policy of waiting for the needy to come to them; however, the most needy are often not even aware of the existence of services for which they would be eligible. Other needy people reject welfare services because of the stigma of "charity" attached to them. Citizens' organizations can help to overcome the reluctance of the needy in this respect; they can also be channels for education, both by making people aware of opportunities and by making them more qualified to take advantage of given opportunities.

The city planner can encourage such organizations in four ways: (1) by recognizing organizations that have already been formed to protect the rights of "needy" people; (2) by specifying, as in Providence's Social Plan, the establishment of a neighborhood organization two years prior to urban renewal action in that neighborhood;[104] and (3) as a private citizen interested in social welfare, by helping to organize "needy" people.

---

[102] Rhode Island Council for Community Services, Inc., *op. cit.*, p. 38.

[103] Farrell, *op. cit., passim.*

[104] Rhode Island Council for Community Services, Inc., *op. cit.*, p. 34.

EDITORS' NOTE: Special contributions were made to some of the sections of this chapter by Miss Virginia Blake.

Part Four

Implementation:
Policies, Plans, Programs

12

Defining
Development Objectives

Planning for what? This is at once the most important and most vexing question to be faced by local planning agencies. To gain some sense of the importance that is attached to the task of defining development goals and objectives, it is only necessary to examine a few of many definitions of planning and descriptions of the planning process. Central to all of these is the notion of process and of goal orientation. Planning is viewed as a series of related actions and decisions that are organized around and moving toward the accomplishment of objectives. The goals and objectives themselves are viewed as the cornerstone of the planning process, for, in theory, they form the framework for public and private decision-making.

While the definitions and descriptions attest to the *theoretical* importance of defining development objectives, planning practitioners can readily attest to the difficulty, if not impossibility, of establishing a set of *operational* community goals. This skepticism is understandable, for there are many unanswered and perhaps unanswerable questions: How, for example, can one encourage citizens to be concerned with the shape of their city at a point of, say, 20 or even 10 years from now? What role does the planner play in the process of defining goals? How can conflicts between competing interest groups be resolved? Is it possible for a community to move beyond a local legislator's conception of the public interest? Can it be assumed that legislators will make decisions that contribute to the accomplishment of

long-range objectives, even when the decisions are in conflict with more immediate demands? In short, is it possible to define development objectives, and, once they have been defined, can they be applied in a meaningful way?

These are indeed complex and difficult questions to answer. Such difficulty accounts, no doubt, for the fact that many planning programs have, in the past, virtually ignored this element of planning. There is, however, evidence which indicates that many planning agencies are trying to remedy this condition.

Policies planning, or some derivation of the term, is being used with increasing frequency in the literature of planning. Certain planning reports are being called "policies plans," and "policies planning" is the subject of many articles about planning. For example, Frederick Aschman has written about "The 'Policy Plan' in the Planning Program."[1] Martin Meyerson has suggested that planning perform a "policy clarification function."[2] Stuart Chapin has advanced the concept of an "urban development policies instrument."[3] In addition, there is Chicago's recently published document entitled, *Basic Policies for the Comprehensive Plan of*

[1] Frederick T. Aschman, "The 'Policy Plan' in the Planning Program," PLANNING 1963 (Chicago: American Society of Planning Officials, 1963).

[2] Martin Meyerson, "Building the Middle Range Bridge for Comprehensive Planning," JOURNAL OF THE AMERICAN INSTITUTE OF PLANNERS, XXII, No. 2 (1956).

[3] F. Stuart Chapin, Jr., "Taking Stock of Techniques for Shaping Urban Growth," JOURNAL OF THE AMERICAN INSTITUTE OF PLANNERS, XXIX, No. 2 (1963).

Chicago,[4] and Metropolitan Washington, D.C.'s *Policies Plan for the Year 2000.*[5] The list could be expanded considerably, for there are many examples of articles and planning documents which have adopted the phrase—policies planning.

Frequency of use, however, does not mean that there is common agreement as to the nature and purpose of policies planning. Although there are planning reports which are called policies plans, and there are a few definitions of the phrase, there seems to be no general agreement as to its meaning. The differences of opinion are, in some cases, only minor. Disagreement may center around questions of terminology or emphasis. In other cases the differences appear more basic, the result of fundamentally different approaches to the subject.

One commentator, in his analysis of the relationship between planning and policy, has made the following observation concerning the different meanings ascribed to development policies.

Some view these policies plans as something akin to a statement of general principles for planning, and they are thus formulated before plans are developed. Others consider them to be embodied in the plans themselves, and when a plan is officially adopted, the proposals contained in the plan become official urban land use policies. Still a third usage considers them to be statements of the directions in which the urban area should move in order to achieve the objectives of, and implement the proposals contained in, a plan. For example, in this sense policies might take the form of general specifications for zoning, urban renewal, and such.[6]

There is no question that concern for policies is having, and will continue to have, a profound impact on the planning process: on the preparation and significance of the comprehensive plan, on the interaction of planners with government officials and private citizens, on implementation tools and techniques. This

chapter proposes to examine the major directions that can be identified in this area and to assess their meaning for professional planning.

Development Objectives—An Overview

To a considerable degree, the traditional methods of city planning have been carried over from the work done in private corporations, architect's offices, and single-function government agencies. These methods were brought to the profession by the architect, landscape architect, and civil engineer—early dominant forces in the planning movement. These methods are well suited to the unitary setting, i.e., the single client with the single site, in which they were refined, but they have not been as applicable to the complex and mercurial city. The traditional practices were noted in such factors as basic agreement concerning the goals of the organization, ability to predict the future with considerable precision, and centralized control over the resources needed to achieve the goals. Such elements are certainly more characteristic of private or voluntary organizations than of democratic local governments.[7]

The essence of our traditional approach to planning has been to view the city as a large design project. The community is thought to have a spatial, plastic form that can be grasped and reduced to manipulation and presentation by graphic means. Planning, according to this view, is the process of forming a picture of a future physical pattern and developing the control measures that are needed to move the community toward the goal. The objective is to make the community look like the map of the future, and the goals, sometimes stated but often only implicit in the map, are convenience, order, efficiency, economy, and beauty.

Typically, the city planning effort begins with an extensive survey of existing conditions and predictions of the number of people, cars, jobs, etc., that could be expected within the next 20 years. Studies are made of the existing land use, the population and economy, the

[4] Chicago Department of City Planning, BASIC POLICIES FOR THE COMPREHENSIVE PLAN OF CHICAGO (Chicago: The Department, 1964).

[5] National Capital Planning Commission and National Capital Regional Planning Council, THE NATION'S CAPITAL: POLICIES PLAN FOR THE YEAR 2000 (Washington, D.C., 1961).

[6] F. Stuart Chapin, Jr., URBAN LAND USE PLANNING (Urbana, Ill.: University of Illinois Press, 2nd ed., 1965), p. 349.

[7] Melvin Webber, "The Roles of Intelligence Systems in Urban-Systems Planning," JOURNAL OF THE AMERICAN INSTITUTE OF PLANNERS, XXXI, No. 4 (1965), p. 291.

housing stock, the circulation system, and the community utilities and facilities. The studies are for the most part quantitative descriptions and predictions, but to a lesser extent they deal with the qualitative features of the system. Once the studies and projections are completed, the estimates of people, vehicles, households, and employment are converted into the common denominator—acres of land needed to accommodate each use. The conversion from people (or jobs or whatever) to land is based upon existing ratios and modified by national averages and standards promulgated by specialists in various fields (e.g., five acres of playground space for each neighborhood of 1,000 families). The final task is to distribute these future land requirements, to establish the proper design that will accommodate the anticipated growth. The criteria used to determine appropriate locations for each category of use are based upon the existing pattern, intuition, "don't put noisy factories next to single-family homes," and the judgment of specialists "the radius of the service area for a neighborhood recreation center should be no greater than one-quarter mile."[8]

Once the picture of the future is complete, it is accepted by the planning commission as *the* city plan. The commission then uses it to advise others—the chief executive, the legislative body, and department heads—as to the action they should take. It is, of course, well known that persons who are being advised do not always agree with the advice.

Certainly it is easy to criticize the traditional planning approach, and particularly in the abreviated form presented here which serves to exaggerate the shortcomings. It suffers nevertheless from a number of oversimplifications that have severely limited its usefulness: it focuses on two-dimensional, physical plans; it is more concerned with quantitative problems (is the park large enough?) than with the performance of the system (are the public's leisure needs being satisfied?); and produces a static *end product* without determining how the city gets from "here" to "there." It must be pointed

out, however, that the traditional approach has been, and with modifications will continue to be, instrumental in improving urban communities. The pace and scale of urban development are such that it becomes essential that someone study the problem of how the disparate parts will fit together to form a functioning whole. Sooner or later someone has to make a decision concerning the size of a park or the location of a highway. Urban areas are mappable, and a picture of the future is, when used correctly, a necessary and useful planning tool. The traditional methods are particularly useful in planning for the isolated, middle-sized city, or the well-to-do suburb where there is a steady growth rate, plenty of room for expansion, adequate development resources, and widespread agreement concerning goals. The ideal setting for this approach is the new town, where land is in single ownership, resources are almost unlimited, and the planner isn't bothered with problems of existing development.

It must also be pointed out that our traditional planning practices come from, and were appropriate to, a period in which planning was a reform movement. The prevailing situation was one in which privately supported and design-oriented planners, working in a consensus environment of respected community leadership, could do little more than prepare a plan and hope that their vision of the future would stir others to take appropriate actions. These practices come from a period in which it was thought that respected members of the community could discuss a problem and arrive at a "correct" solution, or that planners could resolve value conflicts through technically rational means. They come, also, from a period in which we knew even less about the functions of a city than we do today.

NORMATIVE PLANNING

We are, of course, planning in a different context. Planners are working in a different political and social environment, facing new kinds of problems, and gaining greater knowledge of how the city "works." These changes demand new or revised planning approaches.

There are strong indications that planners are developing a new, or revised, approach in

---

[8] Henry Fagin, "Planning for Future Urban Growth," LAW AND CONTEMPORARY PROBLEMS, XXX (Winter, 1965), pp. 12–14.

their emphasis on the *normative* elements of planning—the elements that describe "where we are going" and "how we will get there." The traditional plan has been, for the planner, a technical exercise—like fitting the pieces of a jigsaw puzzle together. Effective technical planning, however, occurs only when there is a clear notion of the ends that are being pursued, and in far too many instances planning agencies have been pursuing goals that have currency within the planning profession, or they have had to assume community goals. The planning department has rarely had the guidance it needs to carry out effectively its technical responsibilities.

Normative planning is the activity of establishing rational or reasonable ends. It involves determinations concerning the objectives or ends which will guide subsequent actions. It involves decisions concerning the scope and content of action, decisions which must ultimately be based on an established value system. Normative planning develops the broad, general basis for action, whereas technical planning is concerned with specific, established purposes and the procedures to be employed in achieving these purposes. Much normative planning is done by the elected officials and their appointed administrators. They establish the goals which will either be codified as law, implemented by operating departments, or acted upon by the public. These goals are established in conjunction with the public, and are the result of a complex set of pressures, and compromises. The democratic political process establishes a series of checks and balances to keep the goals within the bounds of reality. Elections, methods of representation, public scrutiny, and the allocation of responsibilities all operate to establish an equitable short-run definition of the public interest.

The goals, once established, become the basis upon which operating departments structure their activities. These suborganizational units will be engaged, primarily, in technical planning. Their decisions need not (or should not) be concerned with the larger goals and values of the public. Their decisions will be limited to problems such as inventories, purchase of equipment, deployment of work crews, hiring, etc., all of which are subject to solution through technical planning.

The question of real importance concerns the role of the central planning office. Is it a department that is limited to technical planning, or do its functions extend to normative planning? The position to be taken in this chapter is that the planning department has a unique and dual role to play in the affairs of government. The planner exists in a middle zone between the politician (the normative planner) and the bureaucrat (the technical planner). The planner is a bureaucrat, administering the programs which have been instituted by the politicians; in addition he has a special competence and training which makes him invaluable in establishing goals.

One of the key activities of a planning department is its participation in the process of goal formulation. It has already been mentioned that the politicians, in response to public pressures, are able to establish adequate short-run goals. There are strong arguments for going beyond these minimal, short-range goals. In the first place, the public influence which helps shape goals is not evenly distributed. Certain groups will excercise greater influences on the political mechanisms than will other groups. Further, when influence tends to be equally shared by competing interests, the outcome of the conflict is likely to be a weak compromise. Finally, political decisions concerning the public interest are made only when opportunities arise. There is no systematic or comprehensive evaluation of long-term goals.

It is for these reasons that the planning department should participate in the normative element of planning. The development of general goals should result from the interaction of three groups:

(1) the public and its voluntary organizations, (2) government as expressed by the elected representatives and their appointive administrative officials, and (3) the professional and technical aids and consultants who staff urban planning offices.[9]

---

[9] Henry Fagin, "Planning Organization and Activities within the Framework of Urban Government," PLANNING AND THE URBAN COMMUNITY, edited by Harvey S. Perloff (Pittsburgh: University of Pittsburgh Press, 1961), p. 111.

Goal formulation is only one of several core activities which raise planning from the level of a technique to one that is concerned with both means *and* ends. Other activities include coordination, plan formulation, and assistance and advice to other interest groups and public agencies. Together, they exhibit a basic concern for goals, values, and the need for making basic choices.

Most of the normative work of planning agencies is being carried out under the label of "policies planning." While there is a range of opinion concerning the exact nature of policies planning, its essence is the preparation of a set of general statements that define the direction and character of future development and set forth the actions necessary to attain the desired development. The policies set the broad framework for action and form the *basis* upon which more detailed development decisions are made. They are a connective link between general goals and specific recommendations.

In comparison with the end-product plans described above, the policy statements are relatively permanent. Whereas the end-product plans set forth proposals and designate sites, the policies would only set forth the principles or precepts that would guide those who are responsible for making proposals. For example, if a plan designates a particular area in the CBD for multifamily housing, once the housing is built, or once it becomes obvious that the housing can not be built (due to changing conditions or some other unforeseen circumstance), then the plan becomes outdated and useless as a guide for community decision making. On the other hand, a clearly stated policy, like "make the CBD a dominant feature of the region by enhancing it as the center for commercial, residential, and cultural activities," remains in effect regardless of what happens to the housing proposal.

Policy at this level is properly the concern of the public and its elected representatives, although the planning agency would provide assistance in proposing and evaluating different sets of policies. To be effective, the completed statements of policy should be officially adopted by the legislative body. Although there are strong arguments against the adop-

tion of plans, these arguments would seem to apply more to the traditional master plan with its high degree of specificity. Adoption of the policies in the form of a "policies plan" does not commit the city to any particular recommendations, but it does commit it to take actions, whatever they may be, that are consistent with the policy guidelines.

Policies planning is essentially a process of establishing ends, *and* determining the means by which ends will be established. In many planning agencies, the ends are established without determining the guidelines necessary to achieve them. A *policies plan* is a statement of the general intentions of the city and thereby serves as a guide to day-to-day decision-making on the part of public officials, administrators and citizens. A policies plan contains reasonably detailed guiding principles but not specific proposals. A policies plan may state the principle that "public housing should be scattered throughout the city on sites that contain no more than 100 units," but the plan would not contain a map pinpointing a half-dozen possible public housing sites nor would it recommend that a 100-unit development be constructed next year at the corner of Fourth and Oak.

Many of the kinds of policies that would be included in a policies plan already exist in every community. They exist, however, in various places and forms. The policies exist as explicit statements in comprehensive plans, they are implied in plan maps and in the various "standards," they exist as "rules of thumb" in various public agencies, and they are embodied in the guidelines that control the decisions of various boards and commissions. Policies planning seeks to bring these policies together, resolve conflicts between them, and add new policies where appropriate. By bringing these policies together there is a greater assurance that all the individuals and agencies who make decisions affecting community development will be operating within the same framework.

THE CONTRIBUTIONS OF POLICIES PLANNING

Before describing the characteristics of policies planning in greater detail, it will be useful to set forth the benefits of policies planning *and* to describe the various pressures and changes in the planning context that have created the need for a mechanism of this kind.

Briefly, policies planning will benefit the planning program in the following ways:

1. The essential and uncluttered character of the policy statements facilitates public understanding and public participation in the planning program.

2. The policy statements permit and encourage intimate involvement in the planning process by elected officials.

3. The policies plan serves as a coordinative device, bringing together under a single framework the diverse agencies that may have an impact on development. In this respect it is particularly useful in multijurisdictional areas.

4. The policies plan provides an element of stability and consistency in the planning program in that it will not be made obsolete by changing conditions.

5. The policies plan can be useful as a guide to legislative bodies responsible for adopting land use controls, to boards and commissions authorized to administer the controls, and to the courts which must judge the reasonableness of the legislation and the fairness of its administration.

Citizen Participation. In some ways it is misleading to suggest that traditional planning practices have restricted the degree to which citizens could participate in local planning programs. It is true that the "leap" from a goal such as "a better living environment," to a precise and detailed plan makes citizen involvement more difficult. There is nothing between the general abstraction, which everybody must agree with, and the finished product. There is a void in the area where citizen debate would be most fruitful. The argument is, however, slightly misleading since it has only been during the last few years that most citizens cared about planning enough to enter into debate over a planning proposal. Planning has been an intellectual nicety, an abstraction that has rarely touched the lives of most citizens. It mattered not, therefore, whether the planning approach was conducive to public participation.

This, of course, is changing as the public increases its awareness and acceptance of the idea of planning. This is not an insignificant trend, for we have had a long history of viewing the future as a luxury. Planners have been called upon to tackle more and more public problems, and in so doing they have affected the lives of more people. Those citizens who are relocated by a renewal project or an expressway, who fight daily traffic jams, who feel they are being pushed from their neighborhoods by minority groups, increasingly turn in protest or supplication to the planning department. The large amounts of federal aid that are being poured into urban areas have been a major factor in changing planning from an academic exercise to something that may directly alter the lives of urban citizens. When a planner designates an area "deteriorating" or proposes a highway alignment, there is a good possibility that the area will be cleared or that the highway will be built. As long as plans meant nothing, or as long as the time lag between plans and projects was long, citizens had nothing to lose by supporting the *idea* of planning. But as plans rapidly become projects, citizen interest in planning is no longer casual or academic.

The increased public involvement in planning has highlighted the existence of multiple urban life styles, with distinct goals that vary widely between different social and economic groups. Most cities are witnessing a significant increase in the number and variety of voluntary organizations, all of which are demanding a voice in the affairs of government. Church congregations, slum residents, property owners associations, welfare recipients, the civil rights groups, and many others are all anxious to make their views known at city hall. Indeed, direct participation in the affairs of government by groups that have heretofore had no public voice is being institutionalized by programs such as the War on Poverty, where the poor are represented on advisory councils and where legal aid may be provided to help the poor in their struggle against, not only loan companies and landlords, but also against welfare departments and departments of urban renewal.

Policies planning is a response to the public demand to be involved in planning. Policies planning enables the public to see the relationship between the general and the specific. It encourages them to enter the process at a level between incomprehensible goals and detailed development plans. At this level it is easier to discuss and evaluate development alternatives, and it is easier for those groups opposed to the officially endorsed policies to present their own alternatives. Policies planning provides no guarantee that the public will become involved, but it greatly facilitates their involvement by shifting attention from design details and specific proposals to the essential characteristics of the future community. Debate, for example, is focused on the pros and cons of alternative principles that could be used in locating public housing units (concentrated in one area, dispersed, large developments, or small isolated projects) and not on what "that" particular development is going to do to "my" neighborhood. The latter debate will undoubtedly come later, but it will be easier to handle if some guiding policies have been publicly agreed on beforehand.

Public Officials. The public's interest in planning has, quite logically, been paralleled by an interest on the part of elected officials. Public officials, aware of the interest of their constituents and recognizing the potential impact of major development decisions, can no longer permit planning to exist outside their purview. They, like their constituents, find the traditional approach to planning largely unacceptable. They are asked to make major decisions on the basis of a recommendation that is based upon a plan they had little or nothing to do with, and made by a planning commission whose ability to interpret the public interest is at least open to question. Despite the rhetoric of planners, the traditional, detailed land use plan is not a guide for decision makers. It may guide the deliberation of the planning commission, but it is of little use to the city council. The traditional plan is a product and all the decisions are made by the planners. Public officials can either make the decisions that the plan demands or they can ignore them and be "against planning and progress." For the

public official, planning is often an "either-or" proposition. Either they accept the advice or they don't. This has forced policy makers into difficult positions where they must agree in principle with the advice and then try to develop a justification for a contrary decision. What is needed, of course, is a system which *guides* the people who will be making future decisions instead of a system that controls or forecloses all future decisions by prescribing *in detail* what the future should be.

The policies planning process enables elected officials to specify, in principle, what they as representatives of the community want. A policies plan serves as a directive to the planning department, as well as to other agents concerned with the environment. Under a directive of this kind there is greater likelihood that specific proposals will be politically realistic and thus will stand a better chance of fulfillment. A policies plan is also a reference point for a legislative body. A city council can evaluate specific proposals in light of its previously adopted statement of policy.

The policies plan is particularly suited to this function of facilitating and encouraging participation by the public and its representatives in that it is easily reviewed. The brief and essential statements of policy can be reviewed without having to grope through the maps and proposed projects of a conventional plan.

Coordination. Planners have had to question old practices and ideas as a result of their involvement in a host of new public programs. In response to the many new and complex problems that are characteristic of urban areas, local governments have been increasing the number and variety of their programs. Increasingly these programs are cutting across the traditional departmental lines as governments focus their attention on poverty, juvenile delinquency, employment, and urban renewal. These interests require an interdisciplinary approach, and frequently planners find themselves on committees designed to solve this or that problem. They find themselves working with professionals in other disciplines, which expose them to new concepts and new variables, and which force them to articulate what it is that they can do to help solve the problems being considered by the community.

The interdisciplinary approach to community problems is one of the changes that has brought planners into closer contact with social and economic issues. Regardless of the outcome of the current professional debate concerning the proper scope of planning, it is fairly clear that practicing planners have, at least, had to give greater consideration to non-physical problems. As planners become involved in the poverty program, community renewal, and, more recently, the Demonstration Cities [Model Cities] program, they show a greater appreciation for the fact that a service or program may be far more important than the building in which it is housed. It is increasingly being recognized that physical plans have relevance only to the extent they restrict or encourage the attainment of social and economic objectives. A recent and controversial example of this is the question of school location. Here the traditional standard of a quarter-mile service radius must be re-evaluated in light of the larger social issues that have been raised.

Coordination has always been listed as one of the functions of a planning agency, and the policies plan would serve as a useful device for achieving the desired levels of coordinated action. Again, the essential character of the policy statements constitutes the major advantage of the policies plan. Coordination is not a matter of solving jurisdictional disputes between different parties or coercing action toward a mutually agreed upon end. The policies plan is the statement of the desired end, and the desired coordination will be achieved if all agencies concerned with development will act in accordance with the principles set forth in a policies plan.

Traditionally, the planner's role of coordinator was thought to extend only to agencies and organizations directly involved with the physical city. However, as indicated above, the growing importance of non-physical and program planning adds a new dimension to the problems of coordination. Those commentators who consider the traditional separation of the city into social, economic, and physical packages an intellectual handicap that has ham-pered the progress of local governments argue that the policies plan will be an ideal integrative tool. The vast majority of all planning agencies do have a rather circumscribed area of concern, but there are indications that the area is being expanded. As it does expand, effective coordination and integration will, of necessity, begin at the policy level and not at the level of specific plans and programs.

The policies plan can also be used as a coordinative tool in another context. That is, it can be used to coordinate the activities of individual governments in multijurisdictional areas. Metropolitan and regional planning agencies are rarely backed by the authority that is capable of carrying out their proposed projects. They cannot dictate to the governmental units that make up the area, but they can try to get each unit to agree "in principle" to the desired character of the area. Each unit knows what the others are attempting to achieve. Naturally there is no guarantee that any given unit will abide by the agreed upon policy framework, but this approach would undoubtedly be more realistic than the "grand scheme" that appears as a threat to local autonomy.

Consistency. During the last couple of decades a great deal of planning effort has been spent in trying to estimate and predict things to the last decimal point. A comparison of actual city development with the plans or predictions of 20 or even 10 years ago reveals that many efforts to anticipate the future have been wasted time. As a result of many unsuccessful attempts at prediction, the planning profession seems to be developing a healthy respect for the unknowns of the future. Cities change often and in unpredictable ways. Large shifts in population, changes in the economy, and technological changes all make the future highly inscrutable. The fact that change is a feature of our society does not rule out the possibility of planning. In fact, it makes planning all the more necessary. It does, however, rule out the feasibility of adhering to detailed and rigid plans.

Part of our respect for the future comes from our changing perception of the city. The development of new techniques of analysis and the use of computers to handle vast amounts of data have shifted attention away from "stocks" of people, goods, buildings, and wealth to the "flows" of information, money, goods, buildings, and wealth to the "flows" of information, money, goods, and services. The interest is in how the urban system *works* rather than in *what it is*. One of the most difficult problems in the next few years will be to reconcile the theories of interaction with the traditional land use plan. Reconciliation must come, for it is impossible to think of the city in dynamic terms and plan for it with a static plan.[10]

The policies of the policies plan "may be expected to cover a greater range of future—perhaps unforeseen—specific questions."[11] The policies plan is not made obsolete by an error in a population projection, since it sets forth principles and relationships to apply when new growth occurs or to the process of renewing old development. The policies plan is a frame of reference that lends consistency to development decisions. Because the emphasis is on relationships or interaction, the policies plan has the potential for making planning more action-oriented.

Relating Plans to Land Management Controls. Concern for the relationship between plans and land use controls has served to highlight the inadequacies of the traditional unitary approach to planning. It has long been a major tenet of planning that land use controls should be "in accordance with a comprehensive plan." This was not a difficult charge to fulfill when the controls were as precise and rigid as the plans. In the case of zoning, for example, the plan was in fact little more than a preliminary zoning map. However, with the introduction of devices designed to make zoning more flexible—performance standards, floating zones, planned unit developments, density zoning, and many others—the static land use plan becomes irrelevant. The controls have responded to the need for flexibility far more quickly than have the plans.

Precisely because the controls are flexible there is an even greater need for an outside reference point. The city councils that must enact the legislation, the individuals and

boards that must administer it, and the courts who are asked to judge the legislation and its administration need some reference point to see if the results of their actions are in keeping with the desires of the community. The possibility of arbitrary or uninformed action on the part of any or all these groups is diminished if there is a clear statement of policy that outlines community objectives.

In summary, the changing character of the planning context has reinforced the need for a statement of goals and directions. Increasingly, planning agencies will find that they cannot function in ₁this new context without some method for inserting policy into their programs.

Policies in the Planning Program

A policy is a course of action adopted and pursued in attaining goals or achieving objectives. Policies are used at all levels of government. Policies are adopted by administrators responsible for carrying out a particular program. Policies are embodied in implementing ordinances and in plans, and policies are designed to guide the preparation of plans. These various policies, however, are usually formulated in response to an issue or crisis situation. They are designed individually to deal with a problem or a set of problems. Rarely do cities formulate an overall policy framework that is capable of anticipating change and guiding decisions toward community needs and wants.

The policies plan has been advanced as the mechanism to make technical planning, which is the process of translating policy into specific plans and proposals, more effective. Without such a mechanism, planners may continue to assume or prescribe what it is the public wants, and thus risk choosing objectives that never materialize as public policy.

The policies plan can best be described by placing it within a framework of more familiar elements of a planning program and in the various stages of the planning process:

First, there is the research and analysis element. This step requires an understanding of the current situation, an estimate of future pos-

[10] Webber, *op. cit.,* p. 289.
[11] Aschman, *op. cit.,* p. 110.

sibilities, and an evaluation of the constraints that will be placed on the planning efforts.

Second, there is the policies plan, the element that defines the basic policies that will guide subsequent planning efforts. The plan would contain a range of policies and would be used in the preparation of a general plan and in the preparation and administration of shorter range programs, plans, and ordinances.

Third is the general plan element. This is the element which is derived from the policies and which consist of specific long-term recommendations. It specifies general locations and suggests needed projects. It should be stressed at this point that many general plans, particularly the ones prepared during the last five or so years, contain the policies that would be a part of a policies plan. They are separated here *only* to stress the importance of the policies step in the planning program.

Next there is the element or elements that translate the plan into shorter-term programs and plans. This would include such items as zoning and subdivision ordinances, capital improvements programs, renewal projects, and the official map.

Finally, there is the action element. This is the stage in the process where funds are allocated, ordinances enforced, and programs initiated.

The Policies Plan

As indicated above, a policies plan includes, internally, a range of policies. This policy range can conveniently be compared to the elements of a trip—destination, route, and means of transportation.

The first and most general level of policy is the *destination* or objective. At this level the policies would deal with questions concerning alternative forms of development, rates of growth, character of the economy, levels of desired public services, and intensity of development. The objectives at this level may have aspatial as well as spatial dimensions. These destination points are found in one form or another in most plans. They are really statements that say "we would like . . ." or "wouldn't it be nice if . . ." However, standing alone, they are of relatively little use in guid-

ing action by the community.

The next level of policy is the *route* which specifies in general terms the way (route) the destination can be reached. They indicate the kinds of actions that will, or can, be used to achieve the objectives.

The third level is the *means of transportation*. These policies are still more detailed and can be readily translated into specific design proposals or action recommendations. They are implementing policies.

One of the values of viewing policies in this way is that it illustrates the danger of adopting policies out of sequence. If the lower levels are adopted first, and they often are in response to particular problems, there is no opportunity to consider properly all the higher levels of policy. To illustrate, if one decides to take a trip by train he immediately limits his choice of alternative routes and, as a consequence, his choice of destinations.

The following example will serve to illustrate the process a community would use in considering the policy choices for a particular area of concern:

1. *First Policy Level.* The community decides that it wants to "make the central business district a dominant feature of the region."

2. *Second Policy Level.* There are a variety of routes available to achieve this outcome. These can be determined by a citizens committee, city council, or planning commission. The planning professionals would assist in pointing out the alternatives:

A. Make the CBD more accessible.

B. Make the CBD the center for a variety of activities.

C. Improve the physical appearance of the area.

D. Make the CBD more competitive relative to other retail centers.

E. Increase the intensity of use in the area.

It is reasonable to expect that the community would pursue all these directions, but differentiate as to the emphasis placed on various of these alternatives.

3. *Third Policy Level.* At this level the policies become more detailed, and the technical judgments of the professional planners become more important.

A. Make the CBD more accessible.
   1. Support regional highway projects that will bring traffic to the CBD, and at the same time provide a by-pass route for through traffic.
   2. Provide enough parking in the area so that no major institution or enterprise will be more than five minutes walking time from a parking area.
   3. Actively support a regional organization that is now considering the feasibility of developing an areawide mass transit system.
B. Make the CBD a center for a variety of activities and uses.
   1. Top priority should be given to the central area when selecting sites for public office buildings.
   2. Provide support for the development of high-rise luxury housing in the central area.
   3. Encourage the development of a cultural center in the central area.
C. Improve the appearance of the area.
   1. The city should work with downtown merchants in preparing a sign ordinance.
   2. Eliminate the deteriorating sections of the area through urban renewal.
   3. Encourage developers to provide plazas or other forms of open space by granting them density bonuses.
D. Make the CBD more competitive relative to other retail centers.
   1. The city supports the idea of an hierarchy of commercial centers and will discourage the development of a shopping center that is large enough to be competitive with the CBD.
   2. Feasibility studies should be required for all shopping center requests.
E. Increase the intensity of use in the area.
   1. The zoning ordinance should be revised to permit higher densities in the area.

The examples of third level policy cover a range of specificity. Some are in the form of standards, others can be translated into standards, and others are simply an indication of support for a particular idea or principle.

Some can be acted upon immediately and others require further study to see if the ideas presented are feasible. Potential areas of conflict are apparent here that are not apparent at the higher levels. The policy with respect to parking areas may be in conflict with the policy of increasing the development density. The parking policy may have to be modified so as to permit or encourage all parking to be in multilevel structures. Although not indicated here, this level would also include policies relating to assesssments and taxes, levels of community services, and other items of public concern that could conceivably affect development.

An array of policies such as this illustrates what it is the community wants and how they want to achieve the "end-in-view." It begins to reveal the "price" that must be paid for achieving the end. Initiation of a federally supported urban renewal project may be too high a "price" (not necessarily in dollar terms) to pay in order to clear the deteriorating sections of the area. In that case, the community may decide to drop one of the possible policies. If this hierarchy of policies was compared with a set based on the idea of minimizing the importance of the central area (or of devoting the central area exclusively to commercial uses) there would be a greater opportunity to compare possible outcomes.

If these policies were officially approved by a governing body they would serve as a guide for preparing a central area plan, and they would be used in guiding the day-to-day decisions that boards, departments, administrators, and private citizens make that have an impact on community development.

This example relates to only one small element of the community. Other sets of policies should be adopted for all the other types of development issues that a community might face. Recently, several regional planning agencies have used this procedure for illustrating various forms of regional growth—satellite cities, dispersed development, concentrated development, and star-shaped growth. These plans are useful as informational and educational devices, and the better ones may serve to unify governments and individuals and encourage them to take action consistent with the plan's broad outlines. Often, however, several of the form alternatives merely serve as "straw men," and an intelligent public is forced into selecting the one that the planners recommend. Furthermore, many of these regional schemes do not carry the policy questions down to the level that is meaningful to most citizens. There is no indication of the routes that will have to be travelled or the means of transportation to be employed. However, the idea of presenting regional patterns of development in terms of policies (with accompanying "illustrative" maps) is sound even if the execution of the idea falls short of ideal.

In developed cities there is no opportunity to experiment with regional forms. The policies will have to be limited to more conventional areas of concern such as: density of development, distribution of commerical and employment centers, the mix of transportation, the range of housing choice, and the character of the economy. These major issues would be translated into the more detailed policies. Although there is no hard and fast rule as to the contents of a plan, it should contain "enough" policies to cover every typical or imaginable problem that occurs in land development. This means policies concerning the location of all types of uses, the relationships between uses, the nature of the communications system, and the character and density of development.

The first requirement then is that a policies plan contain a full range of policies. The second requirement is that these policies be general rather than specific. This is the most difficult aspect of developing a plan. As has been indicated, the policies can range widely in degree of abstraction and detail. If the plan contains *only* the most general policies, then it is useless as a guide to decision making; and if it contains policies that are too specific, then the guiding value of the policy statement is lost. There is a delicately-balanced mid-level policy that is essential for the plan to be effective.

This mid-level, unfortunately, creates another problem—that of conflict between policies. There is usually no conflict between the most general level of policies. A policy of "improve the residential environment" is entirely compatible with a policy of "make the central

area a dominant feature of the region." Similarly, no conflict exists between specific policies in, say, a detailed development plan. No one prepares a plan that shows a house in the middle of a street. Internally, the plan policies are not conflicting. The plan may, of course, generate controversy, and development may not occur in the manner envisioned by the plan, but the plan itself is internally consistent. At the middle levels, conflict between policies is, practically speaking, inevitable. To argue that there should be a policy to cover all situations and that all policies should be mutually exclusive so that no overlap or conflict exists between them, is to underestimate the complexity of the development process. Some conflicts can be eliminated simply by eliminating one or two policies that are contradictory. In fact, that is one of the main purposes of defining the mid-level policies, namely, to identify the conflicts. However, in many instances, overlaps will occur that cannot be resolved. Individuals make personal decisions on the basis of a number of guiding principles (policies) and when the principles are in conflict they make judgments as to which one will apply. Public, like personal, decisions are not made on the basis of strict deductive reasoning. The democratic system is set up in order to make equitable judgments, to resolve conflicts in guiding principles. The fact that conflict exists is *not* an argument against adopting policy statements. The policies help to clarify the nature of the conflict and to place it into a perspective that simplifies the problem of resolution. To be effective then, the policies must fall at the mid-level, between platitudes and specific plans and recommendations.

ADOPTING THE PLAN

Once the policies plan has been prepared, it is strongly recommended that it be adopted by the legislative body or bodies in multijurisdictional areas. The purpose of adoption is to give added status to the plan and to emphasize that it is *public* policy, agreed upon by popularly elected legislators. The legislators can, of course, ignore their previously adopted commitments or they can revise them at will. Departures from the established policies do not necessarily mean that the legislators are acting in bad faith. The departure may be a realistic and necessary action. However, the public is aware of the fact that the policies are not being followed, and they can request the legislators to offer an explanation for the departure. In this respect, it becomes a bench mark for citizens to use in evaluating the actions of their officials.

A policies statement may be of use to legislators during periods of debate on highly controversial issues. The pressures upon a law maker are many and complex, and there may be times when he needs the support of a document such as policies plan. He can use it as one more justification for the stand he takes. (Chapter 13 contains detailed discussion of the uses by the legislative body of the comprehensive plan as a policy instrument.)

It cannot be denied, of course, that political leaders are reluctant to commit themselves too far into the future. They want to be able to sense the moods of the public and synthesize a solution that satisfies the greatest number. They will attempt to make each decision consistent with previous public decisions, but they do not want to be tied down to any particular course of action.

Similarly, special interest groups may see some danger in having the governing body adhere to a set of guidelines. If the guidelines are antithetical to their interests, they may think they have a strike against them even before a particular issue arises. They may feel it advantageous to enter each situation with a clean slate. If they lost their last encounter, they may have better luck on the next; but if the community has foreclosed debate by rigidly adhering to a set of policies they are lost before they start.

Two points should be kept in mind when considering these possible limitations to the policies plan. First, the governing body does not abdicate its power to make decisions at the lowest level of administration simply because they have previously adopted a general set of policies. They can, and do, influence the most detailed level of decision making. Second, interest groups can still affect the outcome of public decisions if they can make a convincing

argument as to why a policy should be changed.

The policies plan is designed specifically to avoid the naïve practice of trying to foreclose future decisions by prescribing the future in detail. The policies say that, "when we encounter this situation we will probably react in this way for these reasons." This decision has the weight of public sanction and has been formulated in advance of heated controversy. To deviate from the decision will require an argument as convincing as the one in the plan. The policies plan informs the public—one of the important prerequisites to the democratic process.

EXAMPLES

Evanston, Illinois. In 1963, the City Council of Evanston redefined, by ordinance, the planning functions and procedures of the city.[12] The ordinance stressed that the primary responsibility of the plan commission was to develop and maintain a comprehensive plan. The plan was defined as a document consisting of a land use plan, a transportation plan, a community facilities plan, supporting studies, and "A Statement of Community Objectives and the public policies required to attain such objectives."

The statement of community objectives was, following discussion by community interest groups and public hearings, adopted by the city council as the first element of Evanston's comprehensive plan. The purpose of the statement was "to fire the imagination, serve as a general guide to planning, improve and win the support for our mutual goals."

The policies plan, or statement of community objectives, is a brief document, running only 26 pages. It contains a basic goal, 10 specific objectives necessary to attain the goal, and a series of policies designed to move the city toward the objectives. The objectives cover 10 areas of community interest, including: citizen participation, controlled growth, civic beauty, residential neighborhoods, business and industry, parks and recreation, educational and cultural facilities, transportation, special facilities,

---

[12] Evanston Plan Commission, YOUR CITY AND ITS PLANNING OBJECTIVES (Evanston, Ill.: The Commission, 1963).

and municipal facilities and services.

The objective for parks and recreation is as follows: "Provide well-designed park, playground and lakefront facilities, adequate for increased future needs, available to, and financed by all Evanston residents."

Three of the six policies include:

(1) Encourage the consolidation of Evanston's three park districts and its city parks into one agency responsible for the development, maintenance and operation of all park land and all public recreational facilities within the city.

(3) More than one-half of the total of Evanston's Lake Michigan shoreline is public property devoted to park use. Extensive beach development plans are being carried out. The city should acquire additional riparian rights and purchase additional lakefront property as it becomes available.

(5) The remaining undeveloped portions of the Sanitary District canal banks should be reserved for open park and recreational space. Expeditious action should be taken to obtain, by purchase or long term lease, (1) exclusive control over all canal banks located within Evanston and (2) either exclusive or joint control with Skokie over the Sanitary District property on the east side of the canal between Main Street and Emerson Street.

Fond du Lac, Wisconsin. In 1962, the city of Fond du Lac adopted "A Resolution Regarding Urban Development of the City of Fond du Lac."[13] The resolution was adopted by the city council following the submission of a statement by the city manager concerning growth beyond city boundaries. The statement does not cover the range of issues considered in the Evanston plan, but concentrates on one particular issue. The preamble states that:

. . . the consideration of such subjects [annexation and fringe area problems] would have more meaning in the setting of a general policy guide on urban development and would foster consistency in the City's position on points of detail with reference to such questions in the future.

Some of the policies set forth in the resolution are:

Urban services in the area should be provided by the City.

The City will press for liberal annexation laws and laws which permit extra-territorial land use control.

---

[13] RESOLUTION NO. 287, A RESOLUTION REGARDING URBAN DEVELOPMENT OF THE CITY OF FOND DU LAC.

Areas urban in character are encouraged to become annexed to the City.

The City will protest any effort to incorporate on the part of areas at its fringe.

The City will protest the creation of special service districts.

The City would generally oppose efforts by other governments to provide urban services to fringe area development.

The City will continue to seek the attachment of adjacent industrial areas.

Suggested Adaptions in the Planning Process

The above material has generally focused on policies as a sort of pre-plan, a statement of general physical development designed to work in conjunction with the traditional general plan. This need not be the case. The important point is that these policy issues are considered at some point in the planning process. In this section, we will examine three variant uses of the policies planning process described above: (1) As a replacement for the general plan, (2) As a technique for guiding urban development, and (3) As an expansion of planning scope and authority.

A REPLACEMENT FOR THE GENERAL PLAN

A review of the general plans prepared during the last decade reveals that cities increasingly are preparing plans that are simple statements of public development policy. The maps in the plans are mainly illustrative. They show in general schematic form the geographical implications of the plan, but it is recognized that these implications are only a minor aspect of the plan. The plans consist substantially of an enumeration and explanation of the policies which are to guide subsequent development.

In substance, these plans are similar to the pre-plans discussed earlier, the only difference being, perhaps, that these plans contain slightly more detail. Since the substance is similar, the functions and purposes of both types of documents are similar. However, since the general plan is defined by statute and what has been described as a pre-plan is not, there are important differences between the two. The differences involve legal issues related to the relation between the general plan and tools such as zoning and subdivision ordinances and the official map.

This distinction is critical, since adoption of the general plan by the legislative body (a practice which has been, until recently, opposed by all writers on the subject) is more than an act that simply gives added status to the plan. Adoption is meant to carry a certain legal impact, or, to use Charles Haar's term, adoption is designed to turn the plan into an "impermanent constitution."[14] Haar, who is the leading proponent of designing the general plan as a series of general policy statements and having it adopted by the legislative body argues that:

If the plan is regarded not as the vest-pocket tool of the planning commission, but as a broad statement to be adopted by the most representative municipal body—the local legislature—then the plan becomes a law through such adoption. A unique type of law, it should be noted, in that it purports to bind future legislatures when they enact implementary materials.[15]

Haar has described the general plan in the following terms:

The main task of the planner does not seem to be to develop a map or graphic description of the community as it now is or will be in its idealized form. Rather, it is suggested, it is the clarification of land-use goals of a generalized nature which, when adopted by the legislature, will become the broad framework for further implementation. This seems to be the trend of some of the recent enabling acts: the 'master plan' evolving into a series of statements —planning precepts, if you will—encompassing the greater portions of the major land functionings of the community and their critical interrelationships.[16]

Haar suggests that, "The plan should state the goals—the desirable maximum density of people per acre; the question of how to arrange them should be left to the implementing regulation."[17] The general plan should concentrate on relationships and goals. It should specify the desired relationship between an airport and residential development. It need not pinpoint the location of the airport. It should state the anticipated or desired population, the space needs for various categories of land uses, the desired type and amount of community facilities and services, and the type of transportation system that will link the various uses. To this end, Haar would amend the enabling acts "to make clear that the master plan consists of statements of objectives and illustrative materials."[18]

Boston, Massachusetts. The *1965/1975 General Plan for the City of Boston* is clearly in keeping with the kind of master plan described here.[19] Its function, according to its authors, "is to provide [a] general, ambitious, but realizable statement of policies of objectives for Boston's redevelopment." The plan provides:

1. Comprehensive, long-range standards with which land assembly and redevelopment projects must comply for state approval;

2. Guidelines for revisions of the city's zoning map and standards for passing on applications for zoning variances;

3. Guidelines for all public facilities development, particularly for the city's capital improvements program; and

4. Guidelines for the formulation of:

a. Federally-assisted urban renewal project plans, which must conform to the general plan;

b. Boston's workable program, of which the plan is an integral part;

c. A Community Renewal Program which, for federal approval, requires the substantial completion of a general plan; and

d. Other studies eligible for federal financial assistance.

The chapter on population and housing is typical. It describes the population in terms of historical trends, and in terms of age, race, and income categories. It then recommends two major policies for population. First, the city should encourage a modest six per cent increase in population. Any greater increase

---

[14] Charles M. Haar, "The Master Plan: An Impermanent Constitution," LAW AND CONTEMPORARY PROBLEMS, XX (Summer, 1955), pp. 353–76.

[15] *Ibid.*, p. 375.

[16] Charles M. Haar, "The Content of the General Plan: A Glance at History," JOURNAL OF THE AMERICAN INSTITUTE OF PLANNERS, XXI, No. 2–3 (1955), p. 70.

[17] Haar, LAW AND CONTEMPORARY PROBLEMS, *op. cit.*, p. 370.

[18] *Ibid.*

[19] Boston Redevelopment Authority, 1965/75 GENERAL PLAN FOR THE CITY OF BOSTON AND THE REGIONAL CORE (Boston: The Authority, 1964).

would require a "more substantial commit-ment to high-rise housing construction than seems appropriate for Boston." Second, the city should act to encourage the development of a diverse population that "more nearly reflects the composition of the region as a whole." This latter policy is of particular importance with respect to racial composition, and the plan rec-ommends enforcement of civil rights legisla-tion and the cooperation of all metropolitan areas as a method of making the policy a real-ity.

The number and type of housing units rec-ommended for construction or rehabilitation are a reflection of the population policies. Broad policy guidelines are set forth for new housing in three income categories. It is recom-mended that the 5,000 new public-housing units be located "in projects containing no more than 100 units on renewal sites or vacant land evenly dispersed throughout the City and well integrated with existing residential com-munities." The 15,000 moderate income units will primarily be in "row-houses and garden apartments" and be located in renewal areas outside the core of the city. The upper-income units are to be primarily "high-rise," and lo-cated "near the Public Garden, the Water-front. [and] at other points in or near the Regional Core. . . ."

King County, Washington. *The Compre-hensive Plan for King County, Washington,* published in 1964, consists of two parts: "Plan Policies" and "Plan Map."[20] The general phi-losophy of the plan is described below:

Because King County is now more than three-quarters undeveloped, and is rapidly converting its vacant land to urban uses, it is impossible to deter-mine in advance the locations of all land uses. Therefore, the conventional method of attempting to show everything in detailed map form has been replaced by a 'development policy' approach to the Comprehensive Plan. These development policies have been carefully determined and interrelated in order to translate the Regional Goals and the Urban Center Development Concept into generalized mapped proposals. They, furthermore, provide a

guide for short-range decisions, specific recommen-dations, and detailed regulations.

The use of policy statements will encourage con-sistency in administrative actions and development control. Their use will promote efficiency in han-dling frequently encountered problems in that the groundwork for making the decisions will already have been laid. Each time the same or similar situa-tion arises, the agency will not be required to start at the very beginning in its deliberations. Moreover, the policy statements provide a framework for the Comprehensive Plan [map], clarify the objectives of various implementing measures, and provide a source for public reference. The development policy statements contained in this Comprehensive Plan are not to be considered as legal controls in them-selves, but as a guide to be applied to local condi-tions.

The plan contains five general development goals and a "development concept." The devel-opment concept is presented diagrammatically as an area with a strong central core, outlying sub-centers, moderate densities, and interven-ing open spaces. The bulk of the plan is a series of literally hundreds of physical develop-ment policies which have been divided into several major categories: transportation, busi-ness, industrial, residential, open spaces, public buildings, and utilities. The policies are in-serted throughout the text of the report which provides background information and the ra-tionale behind each of the policies.

To illustrate the range and character of these policy statements, six of the 39 residential area policies are reproduced below:

Residential areas should be encouraged to develop primarily in the plateau and gentle slope areas rather than in river valleys.

Residential areas shall have varying densities dependent upon the type of development, loca-tion, and degree of improvements.

A maximum density of three housing units per gross acre shall be employed in rural tracts adjoining stream, lake, or saltwater frontage.

Areas where the allowed average residential density is three housing units per gross acre or greater should include the following minimum improvements:

    a. paved streets, curbs, and sidewalks;

    b. street lighting;

    c. underground drainage lines except where surface storm drainage facilities are deemed adequate;

[20] King County Planning Department, THE COMPREHENSIVE PLAN FOR KING COUNTY, WASHINGTON (Seattle, Wash.: The Department, 1964) , p. 32.

d. publicly approved water supply (normally publicly owned); and

e. sanitary sewers or suitable alternatives on temporary basis only.

The street system should be laid out with a minimum number of connections with major arterials. In general, intersections on the major arterials should not be closer than 1,000 feet.

Multi-family residential areas shall *always* be located functionally convenient to a major or secondary arterial highway. Adequate arterial and collector streets should exist prior to or be developed concurrently with the establishment of such uses.

Clearly, the King County plan and the Boston plan serve a number of purposes, many of them previously discussed. The key issue to be considered here, however, is the relationship between the general plan and land use controls. It is well known that the general plan and the various land use controls have developed simultaneously but largely independent from each other. For the most part, the relationship between plans and land use controls has been more theoretical than actual. The plans were either directed toward checking on the activities of other public bodies or were sketchy, first-draft zoning ordinances. When it came to drafting or administering a zoning ordinance, or when the courts reviewed the ordinance, it mattered not whether a plan existed. True, the enabling legislation specified that the ordinance was to be developed "in conformance with a comprehensive plan," but it did not take the courts long to interpret this to mean that the ordinance should be reasonable and impartial.

The lack of a meaningful connection between the plan and development controls can be traced to the fact that land use controls have been characterized by a high degree of rigidity and certainty. The landowners' rights and duties were spelled out in agonizing detail as the ordinance attempted to cover every contingency. Because of this penchant for certainty and detail, the courts were able to review the ordinance without reference to an outside source such as a general plan.

These conditions are, of course, changing. The land use controls of recent years have included many techniques designed to introduce a degree of flexibility into development ordinances. These developments are the result of a much delayed recognition that the zoning ordinance, in particular, has accounted for considerable dreary and monotonous building. In its traditional form, the zoning ordinance is well-suited to preserving existing development but particularly inappropriate for controlling the character of new growth. The new tools were developed because it was apparent that the future could not be predicted with a high degree of reliability, a point that is stressed in the King County plan.

The introduction of flexible land use controls has created a dilemma. The flexibility will certainly contribute to more imaginative development, but it also begins to conflict with American conceptions of democratic principles and our historic attachment to strict judicial review. The courts, landowners, and even the administrators of the ordinances find that there are no norms to apply to these new techniques. Many of the controls require a fairly high degree of administrative discretion, which is contrary to the American insistence on judicial control of both legislation and whatever flows from it. What was (and is) needed is some means to *effectively* relate planning and land control, a device that will facilitate: the enactment of fair and impartial laws based upon democratically derived ideals, the administration of these laws, and the judicial review of the legislation in a manner so that the court can act as arbitrator without undertaking the role of legislator.

An early response—not solution—to this need was the inclusion of policy statements, or statements of intent, within the ordinances. It was felt, and rightly so, that it would ease some of the burdens placed upon the courts and the administrators if there were some general indication of what it was the community was after. Although this is a desirable practice, it still fails to bring *all* of the community's policies into a coherent and coordinated package.

A complementary proposal is the one advanced by Haar. That is, the master plan is to be made an official statement of public policy, and be designed to provide: to the legislative body, the direction it needs in adopting the proper controls; to the individuals or commissions charged with administering the controls, a framework for guiding their judgments; and to the courts, a basis for determining the fairness of the legislation and its administration.

This proposal is not far from a similar, but more radical, idea recently proposed by John W. Reps.[21] He also envisions a system whereby the comprehensive plan, "expressed in graphic form and in statements of development objectives" would be mandatory. The plan would have to be adopted by the legislative body and reviewed and readopted periodically. However, instead of using the plan to guide the enactment and administration of development controls as they exist today he would substantially alter the nature of the controls. There would be no more zoning boundaries—no zoning map—and there would be no subdivision ordinance. The plan would be used as a guide by an "Office of Development Review" which would have broad discretionary powers to deny, grant, or modify all requests to develop or redevelop property.

These proposals are similar to the system of development control used in Britain. In this respect, it is interesting to note that a recent study prepared by an advisory group established by the Ministry of Housing and Local Government of Great Britain has concluded that most development plans prepared under the 1947 Town and Country Planning Act have been far too detailed to be of any use in making development decisions.[22] Although they should be used as guides, they have become little more than land use maps. Further, they provide no effective means for coordinating the activities of contiguous planning units. The plans have become much like our traditional master plans with their emphasis on locational detail.

One of the recommendations of the report is to change the character of the plans submitted for Ministerial approval. In place of the detailed land use allocations of the present plans, the plans submitted for approval would consist primarily of "statements of policy illustrated where necessary with sketch maps and diagrams and accompanied by a diagrammatic or 'structure' map. . . ."

Here, then, is another recognition of the inadequacy of detailed plans that are not backed by clear statements of objectives and policies. It remains to be seen whether or not general plans will ever be legally redefined and the official adoption made a precondition for the enactment of development controls. In any case, many communities are already redefining the character of the master plan, making them statements of policy rather than maps of the future. If this trend continues, it is possible that the master plan will soon be a relic.

GUIDING URBAN DEVELOPMENT

Stuart Chapin, in describing a system for shaping urban growth, views policy in the planning process from a slightly different perspective, a perspective that emphasizes the value of policy statements in achieving coordination and guiding metropolitan growth.[23] He points out that public policy must be closely keyed to the general plan (in this case a plan for a metropolitan area), and that, if the plan is to be realized, the policies of a variety of public agencies must reinforce or be consonant with the general plan. The emphasis is more on the principles and guiding policies of various governmental agencies than on the broad policy choices that are properly the domain of a governing body. In this respect, the policies are apt to be more detailed, focusing on fairly narrow areas of concern. These public policies are:

(Those) consciously derived guides that governing bodies, commissions, or administrative officials of government develop to achieve consistency of action in the pursuit of some public purpose or in the administration of particular public responsibilities.[24]

There are a great number of public policies which have a direct or indirect influence on the

[21] John W. Reps, "Requiem for Zoning," PLANNING 1964 (Chicago: American Society of Planning Officials, 1964), pp. 56–67.

[22] Great Britain, Ministry of Housing and Local Government, THE FUTURE OF DEVELOPMENT PLANS (London: Her Majesty's Stationery Office, 1965).

[23] F. Stuart Chapin, Jr., "Taking Stock of Techniques for Shaping Urban Growth," JOURNAL OF THE AMERICAN INSTITUTE OF PLANNERS, XXIX (May, 1963), pp. 76–87.

[24] Ibid., p. 80.

character, location, and timing of urban growth. For example, it has long been recognized that policies concerning the extension of public utilities can have a significant impact on determining the direction and timing of development. Decisions concerning sewer extensions are usually based upon considerations of need and the capacity of local finances, but these same decisions could also take into account the impact the extension has on future development. This is a relatively simple example, because many communities do view their utilities as a device for shaping growth and not simply a service to be extended at the request of a developer. The same reasoning which applies to utilities can also be applied to such diverse operations as schools, parks, recreation programs, police and fire protection, and transportation improvements. The distribution of these services or facilities often does affect community growth.

The policies of state and federal agencies are as important as those of local agencies. State policies concerning stream sanitation, flood plain control, air pollution, and reforestation may exert direct or indirect influences on patterns of urban expansion. At the federal level there are many programs that could affect local development. Loans for public works, defense plant locations, distressed area programs, and FHA mortgage insurance policies will all have a bearing on the character of local urban growth.

The policies relevant to these various areas of concern are almost always applied unilaterally by a single agency. Furthermore, administration of the policies is often far removed from the point of impact, and lip service is paid to the idea of coordination. Each of the agencies is likely to be so concerned with the special purpose for which it is responsible that it can give only passing consideration to the impact of its policies on urban development.

If all the federal, state, and local policies were coordinated at the local level, the impact on development would indeed be significant. Chapin advances the idea of an "urban development policies instrument" as a device for coordinating actions by all levels of government in policy decisions relating to urban de-velopment. The policies instrument,

. . . brings together relevant existing policies that impinge on urban expansion, identifies appropriate new ones, and ties the old and new into a related series of statements. Thus it considers current policies for transportation, utilities, schools, recreation, fire and police protection, and other public services to insure that such matters as levels and intensity of service, areas to be served, and method of financing are working in harmony and not at cross purposes with the general plan. In addition, tax policies, debt policies, annexation policies, and so on, would be examined as they affect land development. Similarly, policies on which regulatory measures are based would be taken into account.[25]

The policies instrument would deal with timing of development as well as with location and intensity of development. The timing problem could be handled by using "policy bundles." One bundle would, for example, contain all those policies which would tend to inhibit development. A second bundle would have policies that postponed development. A third bundle would be directed toward initiating development, and a fourth bundle would push development.

Thus, if the general plan indicated that development should be inhibited in a given sector of the region, the policies instrument would indicate that policies designed to enhance services or facilities to the area were inconsistent with the plan. In areas where development was to be initiated, the policies instrument would encourage each level of government, each board or commission, or each agency, to provide the needed services or facilities and at a level that would support the desired intensity of use.

Coordination has always been a problem in government and the problem is compounded when numerous governments are involved. A planning agency has a major responsibility in the coordinative effort and it has a choice of approaches in trying to achieve concerted action. One very effective means of coordination is to provide a common groundwork of information. By organizing and reporting factual information the planner supplies a common frame of reference for all the organizations concerned with development. Personal persuasion

[25] *Ibid.*, p. 82.

and joint meetings are also useful means for coordinating the many actions which impinge on development. The mandatory referral system provides still another means for the planner to organize activities which he cannot directly control.

Despite the number of methods of coordination available to an agency, it still finds that there are official and unofficial policies which operate at cross purposes with the objectives of the planning program. Subjecting these policies to public scrutiny via the policies instrument appears to be an effective method of achieving the consistency of purpose desired.

In some instances, inconsistent policies are the result of policy makers being unaware of the importance of their decisions relative to development. In other instances, policy makers may feel that there are overriding considerations that demand a decision that is not in conformity with the policies instrument. In this respect, the policies instrument has no more weight than the authority of its own ideas. Chapin does suggest that to be effective the policies instrument should be adopted by resolution by all the governing bodies of the region. The impact of the policies instrument could be even greater if state and federal financial aids were made available after there was joint agreement concerning the policies.

The policies instrument is neither a replacement for the general plan nor an attempt to set the goals that will be translated into a general plan. The content of the policies instrument is to be determined ". . . from the general plan, its guiding statement of goals for urban expansion, the proposals set forth for achieving these goals, and the timing of the development proposals." The center of attention is on coordination, on achieving action on the part of numerous different agents that is consistent with the aims set forth in a plan. The policies instrument becomes a tool for guiding urban expansion.

Expanding the Scope of Planning

Policies planning is being discussed among planners in still another context. It is viewed by some as being the instrument needed to move urban planning beyond its traditional physical-locational orientation.

For a variety of reasons, planning has developed with a bias toward the physical environment. Certainly one of the more important contributory factors was that reformers during the late nineteenth and early twentieth century often misread the correspondence between poor physical environment and social pathologies as being a cause and effect relationship. They felt that the introduction of a middle-class environment would lead to an immediate reduction of crime, disease, drunkenness, and delinquency. This view has led to a type of environmental determinism that to some extent still pervades planning.

Another reason for the emphasis on the physical is due to the fact that physical facilities have long-lasting consequences; they are expensive, and once decisions are made concerning them, they are not easily reversed. A highway, for example, is expensive; the consequences of its existence are far-reaching; and it cannot be easily altered once it is in place. In contrast, a decision concerning the timing of a traffic signal is inexpensive to make, easily reversible, and has fewer consequences. In other words, designing and locating physical facilities is of tremendous importance, and mistakes are costly. The need for planning the physical environment is more apparent, if not more important, than is the need for planning for programs and activities that can be easily altered.

Whatever the reasons for this emphasis on physical planning, two changes have occurred which have caused planners, and others, to question their position. The first change is the increase in the number of functions for which governments are given some responsibility. Particularly in the area of social welfare, governments have taken over functions which were formerly handled by private, voluntary organizations.

The proliferation of governmental activities has been paralleled by considerable research directed toward the urban system. Systems analysis, simulation models, cost-benefit analysis, and many other analytical techniques have been applied to the city. The result of this research is to point out that the city is an immensely complex, interwoven organization which is only partially understood. But, it is understood well enough to know that any attempt to alter the system must be comprehensive; it must not be done in isolated fragments.

As a result of the growing responsibilities of government and the increased understanding of the interrelationships between facilities and services, public officials are increasingly advocating the use of interdisciplinary approaches to problem solving. They recognize that departmental competition for limited resources is not the way to solve city problems. Social planning councils, interagency committees, and other types of interdisciplinary groups are, in some cities, taking the preliminary steps toward understanding the web of interdependencies that unite them all. They are trying to find the most effective mix of services, programs, and facilities that will contribute to the solution of shared problems.[26]

Given the changes that are taking place in our levels of understanding and in our approaches to problem solving, it is understandable that some planners argue that, "planning for the locational and physical aspects of our cities must . . . be conducted in concert with planning for all other programs that governmental and non-governmental agencies conduct."[27] Planning, therefore, is at least as broad as government itself. *Any* concern of government would be a concern of the planning office.

This is, of course, a line of reasoning which is considerably different from the views of planners who would limit the scope of planning to those things which can be expressed in terms of the arrangement of land uses. To those who opt for a broader perspective, this kind of limitation "seems an unnecessary and probably harmful effort to appropriate the common word, planning, for the exclusive use of a narrow segment of the planners in government."[28]

Henry Fagin, who has written extensively on policies planning and who thinks planning agencies must expand their area of concern, points out that planning is already diffused throughout government. Each individual and each organizational unit of government is engaged, to a greater or lesser degree, in planning. There are presently two main instruments used to coordinate these sub-units of planning. One is the physical development plan which is a means for coordinating activities of all sorts at the point where they take place. The other is the budget which controls the substance and timing of governmental activities and relates these to nongovernmental programs. These two instruments, which have developed largely in isolation from each other, can be related through a policies plan.

Fagin argues that a plan which is comprehensive with respect to time, space, and money; and which brings physical, social, and economic considerations into a common focus is a policies plan. He feels that the preparation and maintenance of a policies plan will, in the near future, be the primary responsibility of a planning office. The work would be done, however, in collaboration with the other planning centers of government, and with the agencies of metropolitan, state, and federal governments.

The wide breadth of the policies plan is indicated in the following comments.

A policies plan would be a unified document adopted in order to express the intended general goals, specific plans, and programs for urban growth and change. . . . The policies plan would express in one place the social, economic, physical, and political policies intended to guide the evolution of the particular area of governmental jurisdiction. It would contain physical plans coordinating spatial relationships; schedules coordinating time relationships; and narrative texts and tables describing and coordinating proposed activity programs. Maps, schedules, and texts also would set forth the physical, economic, and social facts, assumptions, and goals underlying the governmental policies.[29]

The plan itself would consist of these major parts:[30]

[26] Melvin Webber, "Comprehensive Planning and Social Responsibility: Toward an AIP Consensus on the Profession's Role and Purpose," JOURNAL OF THE AMERICAN INSTITUTE OF PLANNERS, XXIX, No. 4 (1963), pp. 232–41.

[27] *Ibid.*, p. 236.

[28] Fagin, PLANNING AND THE URBAN COMMUNITY, *op. cit.*, p. 111.

[29] *Ibid.*, pp. 117–18.

[30] Henry Fagin, THE POLICIES PLAN: INSTRUMENTALITY FOR A COMMUNITY DIALOGUE (Pittsburgh: Institute of Local Government, University of Pittsburgh, 1965), pp. 13–14.

- A statement on the "state of the area" which describes the current situation, trends, imminent problems, opportunities, and experience with existing plans and programs.
- A statement of goals; assumptions; constraints; and the major policies plans, projects, and proposals that express the essence of the direction in which the community wishes to move.
- The comprehensive physical development plan and a financial plan or budget.
- The instruments that will be used to implement the policies plan.
- The more detailed policies of each department or unit of government.
- Technical notes on methodology and sources of data.
- An exposition of policy alternatives that were considered but discarded.

This proposal is considerably more comprehensive in outlook than any of the schemes considered thus far. This proposal addresses itself to the problem of integrating the various disparate functions of government, whereas most of the other proposals look only to the problem of identifying and relating the policies that have a bearing on *physical development*. This does not imply that the proposals limited to the physical environment do not consider non-physical goals and objectives. Physical plans are not ends in themselves, but are means to larger social, economic, and esthetic objectives. The distinction between policies planning as described in this section and policies planning that is limited primarily to the environment is one of degree. In one case, integration of activities takes place along a full spectrum, from the most general goal statement to the more detailed level of programming and budgeting. The other is concerned with the translation of ends—ends that have non-physical as well as physical dimensions—into a plan for the environment.

The prospects for engaging in comprehensive policies planning depend in part on the development of the tools needed to understand relationships between functions and to weigh the costs and benefits of a variety of public programs. Comprehensive policies planning depends also on the attitudes of the planning profession towards defining or redefining its responsibilities. It will depend most heavily on a restructuring of local governments and the development of new sets of responsibilities. Such a restructuring will no doubt meet with some opposition from those public officials who are entrenched in the present system and who are reluctant to take a fresh look at the management of governmental responsibilities.

Conclusion

The planning profession has long recognized that "defining goals" was an essential feature of planning. For a variety of reasons, however, this theoretically important step in the planning process has often been neglected. The period of neglect is rapidly approaching an end. Significant changes in the methods and context of planning demand that planning agencies devote more of their time to charting future directions for the community. Planning is no longer a process of accommodating the inevitable. Conscious efforts are being made to change and alter the urban system. Planning is becoming more action-oriented, and the public and their elected officials want to be a part of the action.

Defining development objectives is not a process of coming out in favor of motherhood and against sin. This may be the essential grounding of a community's value system, but it need not be said. Defining community directions is a far more complex process, involving public determinations of policy that will serve to guide those responsible for shaping the city's environment.

A number of communities are trying to work out, in advance of crisis situations, the policies that will guide them. It seems clear that many others will soon follow their lead.

13

The Comprehensive Plan

T HIS CHAPTER DESCRIBES what a comprehensive plan is and how it is to be used, but it does not tell how to make a plan (i.e., what analyses and techniques to use in formulating the policies and design proposals contained in the plan). For guidance in the required planning methods, the reader should consult the other chapters of this book dealing with population, land use, transportation, etc. The preceding chapter discusses the determination of development objectives basic to the comprehensive plan; succeeding chapters explain the means for implementing the plan.

This chapter principally concerns the comprehensive plan for a municipality, rather than for a county or metropolitan government. A municipality usually has regulatory powers over the use of all private land within its territory and responsibility for most of the public activities. A county or metropolitan government often has a more limited jurisdiction because there are autonomous municipalities within its boundaries. Consequently, plans for these broader units of government tend to rely more on predictions of what will happen than decisions as to what should happen. To date there has been more experience with municipal plans, and in discussing their functions, contents, and procedures, one can cite a large body of professional materials and case examples.

What Is a Comprehensive Plan?

A comprehensive plan is an official public document adopted by a local government as a policy guide to decisions about the physical development of the community. It indicates in a general way how the leaders of the government want the community to develop in the next 20 to 30 years. Because it is general and agencies devote more of their time to charting approximate, it is not a piece of legislation. T. J. Kent, Jr., one of the leading proponents of the comprehensive plan concept, has given this definition: "The general plan is the official statement of a municipal legislative body which sets forth its major policies concerning desirable future physical development."[1]

Notice that Kent speaks of the "general plan"; this term is used interchangeably with "comprehensive plan." Another synonym, "master plan," is probably the most familiar to the ear. This phrase has fallen into disrespect among planners because of its misuse in the past to describe plans which were not general and comprehensive (such as "master street plan" or "master park plan"). The term "city plan" is also used.

It is often said that the essential characteristics of the plan are that it is comprehensive, general, and long range. "Comprehensive" means that the plan encompasses all geographical parts of the community and all functional elements which bear on physical development. "General" means that the plan summarizes policies and proposals and does not indicate specific locations or detailed regulations. "Long range" means that the plan looks beyond the foreground of pressing current issues to the perspective of problems and possibilities 20 to 30 years in the future.

---

[1] T. J. Kent, Jr., THE URBAN GENERAL PLAN (San Francisco: Chandler Publishing Co., 1964), p. 18.

Although there is some variation in the content of comprehensive plans, three technical elements are commonly included: the private uses of land, community facilities, and circulation. The first of the three is sometimes called the "land use plan," but this is a misnomer because community facilities and streets are also uses of land. Kent labels this part the "working and living areas section." Comprehensive plans may cover other subjects, such as utilities, civic design, and special uses of land unique to the locality. Usually there is background information on the population, economy, existing land use, assumptions, and community goals. Every plan includes a drawing of the community on which the major design proposals are brought together to show their interrelationships.

Among most city planners, the preparation, adoption, and use of a comprehensive plan are considered to be primary objectives of the planning program. Most of the other plans and procedures applied in the course of local planning are theoretically based upon the comprehensive plan. Many planners have chafed under the pressure of day-to-day activities which denied them the time to take a more thoughtful look at the long-range development of the community. In the past dozen years, though, the federal government has increasingly conditioned financial assistance upon conformance to a local comprehensive plan, a spur which has caused hundreds of local governments to prepare plans.

RELATIONSHIP OF THE PLAN
TO OTHER DOCUMENTS

Several other documents used in local planning are often confused with the comprehensive plan—in particular, the zoning ordinance, official map, and subdivision regulations. These are specific and detailed pieces of legislation which are intended to carry out the general proposals of the comprehensive plan. The confusion is understandable because these documents are often adopted prior to a comprehensive plan, and many communities which do not have a plan do have one or more of these. Such a sequence is contrary to good planning practice, and in some states the existence of these tools in the absence of a plan may cast doubt upon the legality of this legislation.

Particularly troublesome has been confusion between the zoning ordinance and the section of the comprehensive plan dealing with the private uses of land. Both deal with the ways in which privately-owned land will be used, but the plan indicates only broad categories for general areas of the city, whereas the zoning ordinance delineates the exact boundaries of districts and specifies the detailed regulations which shall apply within them. Furthermore, the plan has a long-range perspective, while the zoning ordinance is generally meant to provide for a time span of only five to ten years.

Other tools of the trade which are meant to effectuate the comprehensive plan include the capital improvements program and its accompanying budget and special-purpose regulations, such as a sign ordinance. A different level of plan, sometimes called a "middle-range development plan,"[2] is supposed to implement the comprehensive plan by concentrating on a particular area of the city or a particular functional element. Such plans are more specific and have a lesser time perspective, say five to ten years.

The growth of urban renewal programs since 1949 has created some confusion with the comprehensive plan, particularly when these activities are conducted by an agency distinct from the regular planning staff. More than one hundred cities have had community renewal programs prepared. To some professionals this work has seemed to overlap the preparation of a comprehensive plan. The relationships among these planning efforts have not really been clarified, but they probably will evolve gradually. Urban renewal tends to emphasize residential land and the older parts of the city; geographically and functionally, it is not truly comprehensive. Community renewal programs, while considering long-range policies, tend to recommend specific improvements to be made in the near future. It seems logical to number urban renewal and community renewal pro-

[2] See Martin Meyerson, "Building the Middle-Range Bridge for Comprehensive Planning," JOURNAL OF THE AMERICAN INSTITUTE OF PLANNERS, XXII (Spring, 1956), pp. 58–64.

grams among the activities designed to implement the comprehensive plan.

WHY IS A PLAN NEEDED?

Local government has a great deal of influence on the way in which a community develops. The buildings, facilities, and improvements provided by local government affect the daily lives of most citizens, give form to the community, and stimulate or retard the development of privately owned land. Typically about half of the land in a municipality is in public ownership. It is true that the workings of the real estate market help determine the uses of private land, but these uses are regulated by the local government. The local government is the only body with an opportunity to coordinate the overall pattern of physical development of the community. This is as it should be, since the decisions of the local government are made by a legislative body which represents the citizenry at large.

The local government is inescapably involved in questions of physical development. At every meeting of the legislative body, development decisions must be made concerning rezoning, street improvements, sites for public buildings, and so on. This has been especially true since World War II because of extensive population movements, suburban growth, and increased public expenditures on capital improvements.

The local government—and particularly the legislative body made up of lay citizens—needs some technical guidance in making these physical development decisions. This guidance can be provided by professional city planners, but the form in which they give it is important. If they give their advice on the basis of expediency of *ad hoc* "quickie" studies, then there is no guarantee that next month's decision will not negate the one made today. The local government needs an instrument which establishes long-range, general policies for the physical development of the community in a coordinated, unified manner, and which can be continually referred to in deciding upon the development issues which come up every week. The comprehensive plan is such an instrument.

It is true that it is possible to govern a municipality without a comprehensive plan; many cities have done so, and a few planners even recommend it. It has also been true, especially before World War II, that the plans of many communities have been ignored and forgotten. Probably the incentives offered by the federal government, rather than a spontaneous interest in city planning, have caused many communities to prepare comprehensive plans. Nevertheless, the fact that more and more communities are preparing plans, and are making use of them, clearly points to the success of the comprehensive plan. No one has suggested removing the federal requirements, and the federal planning assistance program (which requires matching funds from the locality) is very well subscribed. Expenditures for planning are increasing at a rapid rate, and much of this money is going toward the preparation of comprehensive plans. Public interest in planning matters has increased greatly, as a scanning of newspapers and popular magazines will show. In many cities there has been clamor for a plan and criticism over delays in preparing a plan. It appears that many painful years of experience have produced a comprehensive plan that has become a workable, useful, and accepted tool for cities.

Development of the Plan Concept

There is nothing novel or recent about city plans. The earliest known city planner was Hippodamus of Miletus who prepared plans for several Greek cities in the fifth century B.C. Throughout history, plans have been drawn for cities in Europe, Asia, and America, and many of them have been carried out. Famous early American plans include L'Enfant's for Washington, William Penn's for Philadelphia, and General Oglethorpe's for Savannah.[3] All of these plans were in the nature of architectural blueprints. They usually started with a bare site and were commissioned by a central authority which had power to execute them unilaterally.

[3] For an excellent history of these early plans, see John W. Reps, THE MAKING OF URBAN AMERICA: A HISTORY OF CITY PLANNING IN THE UNITED STATES (Princeton: Princeton University Press, 1965).

The Columbian Exposition in Chicago in 1893 initiated the "City Beautiful Movement" and brought a different type of city plan to the United States. It proposed general improvements to an existing city, emphasized aesthetics, and was sponsored by a civic organization. The best known example of this type was Daniel Burnham's plan for Chicago, published by the Commercial Club of Chicago in 1909.

The type of comprehensive plan in use today—concerned with the continuing comprehensive development of an existing city, prepared by or for the local government, and based on analyses of population, economy, and land use—came into existence about 50 years ago. Because of the incremental way in which concept of the plan evolved, one cannot point to any single plan as the first true modern comprehensive plan.[4] It was also about this time that the men engaged in city planning work became conscious enough of the special nature of their endeavors to think of themselves as forming a distinct profession: The American Institute of Planners was founded in 1917 as the American Institute of City Planning.

Olmsted

One of the early leaders of the profession was Frederick Law Olmsted, Jr., son of the famous landscape architect, who became distinguished in his own right as a city planner. At the National Conference on City Planning in 1911, he gave perhaps the first description of what a city plan is:

We must cultivate in our minds and in the mind of the people the conception of a city plan as a device or piece of . . . machinery for preparing, and keeping constantly up to date, a unified forecast and definition of all the important changes, additions, and extensions of the physical equipment and arrangement of the city which a sound judgment holds likely to become desirable and practicable in the course of time, so as to avoid so far as possible both ignorantly wasteful action and ignorantly wasteful inaction in the control of the city's physical growth. It is a means by which those who become at any time responsible for decisions affecting the city's plan may be prevented from acting in ignorance of what their predecessors and their colleagues in other departments of city life have believed to be the reasonable contingencies.[5]

Olmsted believed that the subject matter of the plan should encompass all uses of land, including private property, public sites and facilities, and transportation routes. His general conception of the plan remains remarkably valid today. While many early plans have been criticized as static pictures which soon gathered dust on city hall shelves, Olmsted emphasized the need to keep the plan up to date.

Bettman

Alfred Bettman was another of the major intellects in the formative years of the planning profession. Originally a lawyer, he was city solicitor of Cincinnati and gradually became more and more involved in city planning, until he was recognized as an expert on planning legislation. As such, he naturally formed definite ideas about the purposes, contents, and uses of the comprehensive plan. The statement he made at the National Conference on City Planning in 1928 gave a more specific picture of the plan:

A city plan is a master design for the physical development of the territory of the city. It constitutes a plan of the division of the land between public and private uses, specifying the general location and extent of new public improvements, grounds and structures, such as new, widened or extended streets, boulevards, parkways or other public utilities and the location of public buildings, such as schools, police stations, fire stations; and, in the case of private developments, the general distribution amongst various classes of uses, such as residential, business and industrial uses. The plan should be designed for a considerable period in the future, twenty-five to fifty years. It should be based, therefore, upon a comprehensive and detailed survey of things as they are at the time of the planning, such as the existing distribution of existing developments, both public and private, the trends towards redistribution and growth of population, industry and business, estimates of future trends of growth and distribution of population and industry, and the allotment of the territory of the city in accordance with all such data and estimated trends, so as to provide the necessary public facilities and the necessary area for private development correspond-

---

[4] In 1925, Cincinnati became the first large city to officially adopt a plan.

[5] Proceedings of the Third National Conference on City Planning, Philadelphia, Pennsylvania, May 15–17, 1911 (Boston: 1911), pp. 12–13.

ing to the needs of the community, present and prospective.[6]

In general, the ideas of Bettman and Olmsted constituted the accepted view of the comprehensive plan during the period from 1910 to 1930. During that time only a handful of plans was actually produced, since the planning profession was not well known.

With such a good start, one might think there would have been clear sailing for the comprehensive plan, but such was not the case. Two developments in the late 1920s combined to plunge the plan into a period of misuse and confusion which lasted until after World War II. The first development was the upholding by the U.S. Supreme Court of the power of local government to zone private property, in the famous Euclid case in 1926. This decision prompted hundreds of communities across the country to prepare zoning ordinances, and the comprehensive plan was all but forgotten. The second development was the issuance of the Standard City Planning Enabling Act.

THE 1928 ACT

Herbert Hoover, when Secretary of Commerce, appointed a nine man Advisory Committee on City Planning and Zoning which drafted the Standard City Planning Enabling Act published in 1928.[7] Olmsted and Bettman were members of this distinguished panel. Another member was Edward M. Bassett, who later wrote the first book entirely devoted to the plan.[8] The Act did a great deal to promote city planning throughout the United States, and it emphasized the importance of the comprehensive plan. However, it also contained several weaknesses and contradictions which caused much confusion and distraction in the develop-

ment of comprehensive plans during the 1930s and 1940s. This was especially true because the Act was widely accepted, and many states based their planning enabling legislation on it.

For a detailed examination of the wording of the Act, the reader should consult Kent's book.[9] Here it must suffice to summarize the four principal weaknesses of the Act. This is important, not just as an historical exercise, but because misunderstanding on these points persists today.

1. Confusion between the zoning ordinance and the private land use portion of the comprehensive plan. The distinction between the two has been explained: The plan is long-range and general, it has no legal effect on property; the ordinance is short-range and precise, it does have legal effect. Nevertheless, the two have often been confused. The zoning ordinance includes a map of zoning districts called a "zoning plan," which is often confused with the unified drawing of design proposals included in the comprehensive plan.

The Act contributed to this misunderstanding by stating that the comprehensive plan should include "a zoning plan for the control of height, area, bulk, location and use of buildings and premises"—things which do not belong in a comprehensive plan. This was a contradiction, because in footnotes the authors of the Act stressed the necessity of keeping the plan general.

As a result of this confusion and the growing interest in zoning, many communities prepared and adopted zoning ordinances without ever making the land use plans on which zoning should be based. This diverted attention from general, long-range policies to the controversial details which seem to dominate zoning questions.

2. Piecemeal adoption of the plan. The Act not only allowed but encouraged adoption of parts of the comprehensive plan separately from the complete plan. These parts could be geographical sections of the city or functional subdivisions of the subject matter. While the Act emphasized that the plan is an organic whole in which every part is interrelated with every other part, and that every part needs to

---

[6] PLANNING PROBLEMS OF TOWN, CITY, AND REGION: PAPERS AND DISCUSSIONS OF THE TWENTIETH NATIONAL CONFERENCE ON CITY PLANNING, HELD AT DALLAS AND FORT WORTH, TEXAS, MAY 7 TO 10, 1928 (Philadelphia: William F. Fill Co., 1928), p. 142.

[7] U.S. Department of Commerce, Advisory Committee on City Planning and Zoning, A STANDARD CITY PLANNING ENABLING ACT (Washington: Government Printing Office, 1928).

[8] Edward M. Bassett, THE MASTER PLAN; WITH A DISCUSSION OF THE THEORY OF COMMUNITY LAND PLANNING LEGISLATION (New York: Russell Sage Foundation, 1938).

[9] T. J. Kent, Jr., *op. cit.* See especially pp. 31–59.

be studied with these interrelationships in mind, it stated that there is no need to withhold adoption or publication of a completed part pending completion of the whole.

With this sanction, it became common practice for communities to adopt separately sections of the comprehensive plan. Often these were treated and labeled as though they were complete in themselves (e.g., "master thoroughfare plan" and "master school plan"). Of course, such plans cannot be properly evaluated without examining the land use plan, as well as the relationships between these different plans. Often communities never completed all sections of the comprehensive plan or never brought them all together in a single document.

One principal objective of a comprehensive plan is to coordinate plans for all geographical parts and functional elements of the community. Obviously this objective is defeated by piecemeal adoption. The separate preparation of sections of the plan also abets the unfortunate tendency for planners, engineers, and other government officials to develop special interests in narrow subjects and to lose the broad perspective essential to comprehensive planning.

3. Lack of a definition of the essential technical elements of the Plan. The Act did not offer a specific, clear definition of the minimum essential technical elements of physical development which should be dealt with in a comprehensive plan. Since relatively few plans had been completed up to that time, and there was no widespread concensus as to their contents, this naturally caused uncertainty among the many local government officials who were introduced to city planning through the Act. This lack contributed to the confusion with the zoning ordinance and the piecemeal adoption of the plan. It was only after many years of difficult experience that there came to be agreement that every comprehensive plan should at least cover (1) the use of privately-owned land, (2) community facilities, and (3) circulation.

In a footnote to the Act, the authors stated that "An express definition has not been thought desirable or necessary."[10] Nevertheless,

the difficulty of discussing something left vague compelled them to include in the text an illustration (which actually amounts to a definition):

. . . (the) plan . . . shall show the commission's recommendation for the development of said territory, including, among other things, the general location, character, and extent of streets, viaducts, subways, bridges, waterways, waterfronts, boulevards, parkways, playgrounds, squares, parks, aviation fields, and other public ways, grounds and open spaces, the general location of public buildings and other public property, and the general location and extent of public utilities and terminals, whether publicly or privately owned or operated, for water, light, sanitation, transportation, communication, power, and other purposes; also the removal, relocation, widening, narrowing, vacating, abandonment, change of use or extension of any of the foregoing ways, grounds, open spaces, buildings, property, utilities, or terminals, as well as a zoning plan for the control of the height, area, bulk, location, and use of buildings and premises. . . .[11]

Of course, the contradiction between the text and the footnote added to the confusion of those following the Act.

It is not known why the authors decided to exclude a specific definition; apparently they thought each community should work this out for itself. It is known that during this period Bettman opposed a standard definition, while Edward M. Bassett believed the contents of the plan should be precisely specified. Perhaps the ambiguity of the Act resulted from a compromise between the two. Incidentally, later in his life Bettman changed his mind and wrote a specific definition of the comprehensive plan.

4. Distrust of the municipal legislative body. The Act made the planning commission, rather than the legislative body, the principal client of the comprehensive plan. This idea was widely accepted and persists in current planning practice. As a result, planning was isolated from the mainstream of political decision making, and plans became very precise and technical. This was probably one reason why many plans prepared during the 1930s and 1940s had so little effect upon the actual development of cities.

The authors of the Act deliberately promoted this conception, as there was little dis-

[10] Ibid., p. 14.

[11] Ibid., pp. 14–16. Copyright © 1964, by Chandler Publishing Company. Reprinted by permission.

pute about it at the time. The Act was openly based on the belief that municipal legislators were not competent to determine and follow wise policies for the physical development of their communities. Planning was considered too complex and esoteric for them to understand, and they were believed incapable of establishing long-range policies because of their preoccupation with day-to-day affairs. The solution proposed in the Act was to set up an independent planning commission which was free of the control of the legislative body, and even restricted its legislative powers. The Act also neglected to require publication, or even public presentation, of the plan, so that it in effect became a confidential document.

The relevant provisions of the Act were:

1. The planning commission was so constituted (with six citizen members with six-year, overlapping terms) as to be independent of the mayor or legislators.

2. The planning staff was made responsible exclusively to the planning commission.

3. The plan was not to be adopted by the legislative body.

4. The legislative body was required to refer all physical development matters to the planning commission, and could override the commission's recommendations only by a two-thirds vote.

The Act thus implied distrust of the legislative body and isolated it from the preparation of the comprehensive plan, even though most specific proposals following from a plan eventually require legislative approval. The plan was to be prepared by the planning staff and planning commission, who are not accountable to the public. It was not unusual for the planners to rely on a "back-pocket plan" which was never made public. Such a plan, while it might appear to be primarily technical in content, must inevitably be based on implicit policies which are formulated by technicians and not determined through public debate.

DEVELOPMENTS SINCE WORLD WAR II

The end of World War II brought a quiet revolution in local planning and inaugurated a new era in the development of the comprehen-

sive plan concept. There was a change in attitude toward physical development and planning on the part of local government officials, caused principally by the surge of urban growth which followed the War. A backlog of needed public improvements had accumulated during the Depression and the War, general prosperity prevailed, and money was available. The population spurted upward and suburbs mushroomed, creating changes in the structure of cities.

The planning profession also expanded greatly at this time. Before the War there had been only a handful of recognized planning schools (notably Harvard and M.I.T.), but now many new ones were organized. More and more cities took on permanent planning staffs, and in many cases, the staff was given full departmental status in the local government.

Because physical development matters became so important in local government, municipal legislators became more interested in planning. Since the War, they have gradually reasserted their authority over planning decisions, and support for the independent planning commission has waned. Legislators have felt the need for a plan, emphasizing long-range policies, which would serve their needs.

The federal government also became involved in local planning, because of the high incidence of problems in the suburbs, in the older inner city, and spanning both of these areas. Starting with the redevelopment program of the Housing Act of 1949, federal legislation had a great influence on local planning. The urban renewal concept begun by the Housing Act of 1954 required each applicant to have a "workable program," one element of which was preparation of a comprehensive plan. The 1954 Act also created the "701" program, which provides matching funds to local governments for comprehensive planning.[12] Federal grant programs—for public housing and open space, for example—have increasingly required the conformance of proposed improvements to a local plan.

---

[12] Through the end of 1964, the "701" program had allocated $79 million in grants for planning in 4,462 localities. See U.S. Housing and Home Finance Agency, 18th ANNUAL REPORT, 1964 (Washington: Government Printing Office, 1965).

These forces have converged to create a tremendous growth in the number of communities which have prepared comprehensive plans. During the decade following the end of the War, several of the larger cities completed plans. During the last decade, the movement has spread to cities of all sizes, and the number of plans completed is in the hundreds. The trend shows no sign of abating.

There has been a change in the character of plans, too. As legislative bodies became more involved, the plans became more general and less specific, and more oriented to policies than planning techniques. (Of course, the technical complexity of planning has increased greatly, but has generally found its expression in other documents.) The comprehensive plan of today is quite different from the one of 30 or 40 years ago. Many members of the planning profession now think of themselves as "general planners."

Several of the conflicts of the 1930s have been largely resolved. The distinction between the zoning ordinance and the comprehensive plan is now widely understood. Piecemeal adoption of the plan is now rare. There is a consensus as to the minimum technical elements of the plan, and several credos, all essentially similar, have been promulgated.[13] However, distrust of the legislative body continues among planners. The position presented in this chapter—that the legislative body is the principal client of the comprehensive plan—should perhaps be regarded more as representing an emerging viewpoint than as reflecting prevalent current practice.

There also remain some in the profession who oppose the comprehensive plan, emphasizing that planning is a continuing process. However, now the planners who prepare comprehensive plans are also proponents of "planning is a process," with their stress on the continued review and amendment of the plan. The "one-shot plan," which is allowed to weather rather than being periodically examined and adjusted, is largely a bugaboo. The principal difference between the two schools seems to be whether the policies used to guide development decisions should ever be crystallized into a unified public document.

---

[13] See T. J. Kent, Jr., *op. cit.,* pp. 61–64.

The Setting for the Plan

THE FORM OF LOCAL GOVERNMENT

Perhaps the key principle underlying the modern conception of the comprehensive plan is that it is an instrument to be used by those leaders of the community who establish the policies and make the decisions with regard to physical development. No matter what the local situation, the persons who have the power to coordinate physical development activities will need, and probably want, some kind of plan. Here it is pertinent to refer to the different forms of local government existing in the United States, as described in Chapter 18.

IMPORTANCE OF THE LEGISLATIVE BODY

Regardless of the form of local government, it is the legislative body which ultimately makes the decisions necessary to carry out public improvements and coordinate private development. The legislative body is elected by and answerable to the citizens. The legislative body has the advantage of being a pluralistic body, encouraging the consideration of a variety of views on any issue. For these reasons, it should be the legislative body which formulates the long-range policies to guide physical development.

This poses no special questions for the weak-mayor and commission forms of government since in effect there is no chief executive. In the council-manager form, the theoretical primacy of the legislative body in policy making is clearly recognized, but because of the important role of the manager as an all-around advisor, it is only realistic to involve him significantly in planning matters.

In the case of the strong-mayor form there is a problem, since the chief executive is elected to perform the function of policy making. Under this form the comprehensive plan must be more attuned to the needs and desires of the chief executive than under other forms. Nonetheless, the mayor cannot act unilaterally to establish policies, pass laws, or approve budgets; a large amount of power still reposes in the legislative body. It is also more in the public interest for planning matters to be debated openly by the legislators, rather than decided privately by the mayor's cabinet.

Thus, even in the strong-mayor form, the legislative body has a preeminent role in planning matters. Obviously the comprehensive plan must satisfy both the legislators and the mayor, if there is to be any hope of effectuation. If a majority of the legislators generally supports the mayor, there should be no problem. If there is a political impasse between the legislative body and the mayor, it does not bode well for the plan, but such situations hopefully are only temporary in extent.

The placement of so much power over planning in the legislative body runs counter to the long-prevalent distrust of legislators. Professional administrators would prefer to keep "technical" matters away from legislators. Yet it is clearly a subversion of democratic government for bureaucrats to determine policies, and supposedly technical decisions usually depend upon value judgments which are well within the province of the legislators.

THE ROLE OF CITY PLANNING IN LOCAL GOVERNMENT

The planning function does not fall neatly into either of the traditional categories of "line" or "staff" activities in government. The proper placement of planning in the municipal organization chart has long been a matter of dispute. There are several concepts of the role of planning also described in Chapter 18, each differing in its identification of the principal client of the planner.

1. An independent activity of the planning commission to whom the technical staff is responsible. This concept predominated during the early years of city planning, and it is still held by numerous planners.[14]

2. A staff aid to the chief executive. Robert Walker advocated this concept,[15] under which the planning director is a full-fledged department head who reports directly to the chief executive and is a member of his cabinet.

3. A policy making activity of the legislative body. The third concept holds that the legisla-

tive body is the principal client of the planning agency and should make the major planning decisions.

This concept placed planning under the control of the legislators. The political content of planning is given more weight than in the other two concepts. This is a rather recent idea which has arisen from the growing concern over the policy aspects of planning. As yet, probably only a minority in the planning profession holds this view.[16]

THE PRINCIPAL CLIENT OF THE PLAN

The comprehensive plan must be useful to many clients, but since their needs will differ, it is necessary to determine the principal client of the plan, the one whose needs must be met first. Different views of the principal client follow from the different concepts of the role of planning in local government.

Those who believe in the independent planning commission think the plan should be designed primarily for the use of the commission and should be adopted only by the commission. This was the prevailing practice during the early years of city planning. Under this arrangement, the legislative body must refer all physical development matters to the commission for its recommendations, and can overrule the commission only by a greater-than-majority vote.

Those who see planning as a staff aid to the chief executive think the plan should be shaped to serve him. This idea has not developed very fully, for experience has been that the typical chief executive does not want a plan to follow; he wants recommendations from the planner on specific problems.

Some planners believe the principal client of the plan should be the planning staff. This idea does not really fit any of the concepts of the role of city planning. Those who hold this view consider planning to be too technical to be understood by laymen. Frequently these planners prepare plans for themselves to use privately as a basis for making recommendations to the planning commission or chief executive.

[14] For example, John T. Howard and Rexford Tugwell.

[15] Robert A. Walker, THE PLANNING FUNCTION IN URBAN GOVERNMENT (Chicago: University of Chicago Press, 1941).

[16] Its principal proponents have been Kent and Charles M. Haar.

Those who regard planning as primarily a policy making activity of the legislative body believe the principal client of the plan is the legislature. This concept is the one adopted by the author of this chapter, since it appears to him to offer the most promise for making city planning more effective. It is, after all, the legislative body that ultimately makes the decisions which either carry out or defeat the plan. Under this concept, the plan is primarily a legislative policy instrument, rather than a complex technical document. The planners must make their technical findings and professional judgments understandable and convincing to the legislators.

THE SCOPE OF THE PLAN

Probably the greatest controversy in the planning profession today concerns the substantive scope of city planning. Should it be broad and open-ended, encompassing anything with which local government might be concerned, or narrow and limited to subjects which directly pertain to the physical development of the community? The dispute is reflected in different views of the substantive scope of the comprehensive plan.

One faction believes that truly comprehensive planning must include the planning of social, economic, administrative, and fiscal matters, many of which are obviously interrelated with physical planning. Planning is regarded as a method or approach which can be applied to any subject matter. The city planner would become a central planner. The comprehensive plan might include plans for social and economic development and other non-physical proposals. So far there have been few examples of these types of plans. Henry Fagin has suggested that a physical plan and all the other sorts of plans should be unified in an ultra-comprehensive "policies plan."[17]

The other faction would confine the scope of city planning to physical development (i.e., matters of location, size, and spatial relationships). Planning is thought of as being con-cerned with physical things, rather than as a particular body of techniques. This has been the traditional scope of city planning, and this view is customarily held by planners with physical design backgrounds.

This group recognizes the interdependence of physical, social and economic factors in community development, and it concedes that a physical plan must take into account objectives, analyses and forecasts from the non-physical realm. The distinction is sometimes hard to pin down, but in general, a plan with a physical development scope will not emphasize economic and social development.

This faction acknowledges the need for non-physical planning, but would assign it to other than city planners. Thus, their argument depends upon who is considered to be a member of the planning profession.[18]

The trend seems to be that more non-designers are entering the planning field, and the abilities available in the profession are becoming more varied and specialized. A broader scope for planning seems inevitable, although there is a stiff rear-guard action by the limited-scope faction. In time, no doubt some type of policies plan will emerge.

For the time being, however, it seems advisable for any community undertaking a comprehensive plan to focus upon physical development. There is ample need for coordination in this area, and involvement in the polemics of the planning profession would probably be a needless distraction. There has been so little experience in social and economic planning that anyone entering this area must adopt the posture of an experimenter. There is little danger that a physical plan will ever become superfluous; it would certainly be an important element of any more extensive policies plan.

The Functions of the Plan

Describing the functions of the comprehensive plan indicates how the plan should be used by the principal persons involved in the physical

[17] Henry Fagin, "Organizing and Carrying Out Planning Activities within Urban Government," JOURNAL OF THE AMERICAN INSTITUTE OF PLANNERS, XXV (August, 1959), pp. 109–114. See Chapter 12 for an extended discussion of this approach.

[18] Hence, the membership standards of the American Institute of Planners have also been a focus for heated debate.

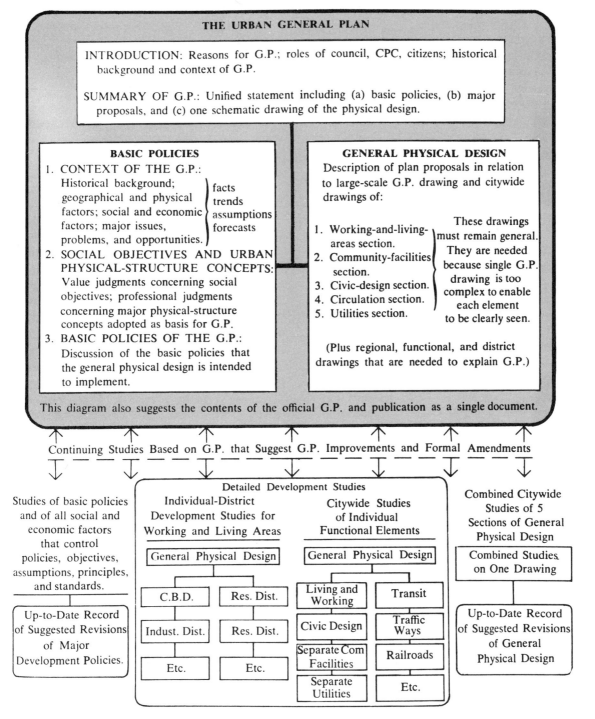

THE URBAN GENERAL PLAN

INTRODUCTION: Reasons for G.P.; roles of council, CPC, citizens; historical background and context of G.P.

SUMMARY OF G.P.: Unified statement including (a) basic policies, (b) major proposals, and (c) one schematic drawing of the physical design.

BASIC POLICIES

1. CONTEXT OF THE G.P.:
   Historical background; geographical and physical factors; social and economic factors; major issues, problems, and opportunities. } facts trends assumptions forecasts
2. SOCIAL OBJECTIVES AND URBAN PHYSICAL-STRUCTURE CONCEPTS: Value judgments concerning social objectives; professional judgments concerning major physical-structure concepts adopted as basis for G.P.
3. BASIC POLICIES OF THE G.P.: Discussion of the basic policies that the general physical design is intended to implement.

GENERAL PHYSICAL DESIGN
Description of plan proposals in relation to large-scale G.P. drawing and citywide drawings of:

1. Working-and-living-areas section.
2. Community-facilities section.
3. Civic-design section.
4. Circulation section.
5. Utilities section.
} These drawings must remain general. They are needed because single G.P. drawing is too complex to enable each element to be clearly seen.

(Plus regional, functional, and district drawings that are needed to explain G.P.)

This diagram also suggests the contents of the official G.P. and publication as a single document.

Continuing Studies Based on G.P. that Suggest G.P. Improvements and Formal Amendments

Studies of basic policies and of all social and economic factors that control policies, objectives, assumptions, principles, and standards.

Up-to-Date Record of Suggested Revisions of Major Development Policies.

Detailed Development Studies

Individual-District Development Studies for Working and Living Areas

General Physical Design

C.B.D.	Res. Dist.
Indust. Dist.	Res. Dist.
Etc.	Etc.

Citywide Studies of Individual Functional Elements

General Physical Design

Living and Working	Transit
Civic Design	Traffic Ways
Separate Com Facilities	Railroads
Separate Utilities	Etc.

Combined Citywide Studies of 5 Sections of General Physical Design

Combined Studies on One Drawing

Up-to-Date Record of Suggested Revisions of General Physical Design

FIGURE 13–1. *The urban general plan*

development of the community. It is from the use of the plan, and not the mere fact of its existence, that the benefits flow. Thus, the old distinction between "plan" and "process" is no longer relevant; the plan is meant to be part of a process. The functions are grouped here under broad categories of plan-users; because the legislative body is identified by the author as the principal client of the plan, the functions pertaining to it are discussed in more detail than for the others.

FUNCTIONS FOR THE LEGISLATIVE BODY

Policy determination. Through the comprehensive plan, the legislative body considers and agrees upon a coherent, unified set of general, long-range policies for the physical development of the community. The plan draws the legislators' attention to the community's major development problems and opportunities. It gives them a chance to back off from their preoccupation with pressing, day-to-day issues and to clarify their ideas on the kind of community they are trying to create by their many specific decisions.

Because of the unavoidable need for a "big picture" to coordinate decision making, legislators often develop tacit, unwritten policies about how the community should develop. The comprehensive plan should bring such implicit policies into the open to assure that they are determined through democratic processes. Such disclosure places these policies on record and fixes responsibility for them on the legislative body.

Policy determination covers everything from the realization that a policy is needed to the final decision on what the policy shall be. Often the early steps in the process are made by the legislative body's advisors, in this case, the planners. The final decision, though, should be made by the legislators. It would also be desirable for legislators to participate more in the early steps of formulating proposals and comparing alternatives. They should be drawn into the early stages of plan preparation and not kept in the dark until the staff has a finished package ready for them to approve or veto. Unfortunately, the latter is often the practice.

Policy determination takes place at several points in time, namely: during preparation, debate, and initial adoption of the plan; during annual review and amendment of the plan; during major reconsideration of the entire plan after five to 10 years; and during consideration of day-to-day development matters which call for review of general, long-range policies.

When the plan is adopted, it should represent the policies of the legislators; they must feel committed to it and be ready to follow its policies in their future actions. To accomplish this requires a long period of debate and education between the first presentation of the plan in tentative form and ultimate adoption in revised form. During this period, the legislators should study the proposed plan carefully, devote work sessions to it, and conduct hearings on it. This period should also be utilized to distribute the proposed plan to citizens, newspapers, and civic groups and to solicit public reactions to it.

It is a mistake for the planners to press for quick adoption of the plan. If the legislators do not feel that the plan is truly theirs, they will not feel bound by it and will readily ignore it when it suits them. This mistake will come back to haunt the planners.

Adoption of the plan by the legislative body is meant to be more than a formality. It is intended to give some assurance that the plan does represent the views of the legislative body. The crucial question is not whether the legislative body takes the formal step of adopting the plan, but whether the plan actually embodies the policies of the legislative body.

As conditions in the community change and new problems come to the forefront, the legislative body will have to modify some of its policies. Topics skimmed over in the original version of the plan will require fuller treatment. New information that becomes available, perhaps as the result of staff studies, will call for revisions in the plan. The membership of the legislative body will also change, and the plan should always reflect the policies of the legislative body currently in office.

Annual review and amendment is a formal procedure intended to encourage keeping the plan up to date. It requires the legislators to look over the plan once a year and to decide whether any of the long-range policies should be modified in the light of events that have transpired during the previous year. It also serves to refresh the legislators about the provisions of the plan and to educate any newcomers on the legislative body about the plan.

The entire plan should receive a thorough overhaul five to 10 years after initial adoption (and at similar intervals thereafter). This should be an effort comparable to that entailed in the original preparation of the plan. This is needed because some long-range trends will not be discernible in the issues which arise from week to week, or even at annual review time. Amendments to the plan will tend to reflect rather specific current issues. From time to time, the planners and policy-makers should step back and rethink fundamentals.

Besides these regularly scheduled reviews, the plan may be amended at any time. When a major issue comes before the legislators for decision, they should consult the pertinent policies of the plan and retrace the thinking that led to the policies. Normally they will reaffirm the policies, but if they should decide to change the policies, the plan should be amended. This is a kind of feedback by which plan policies are tested in the heat of battle, and are either upheld or modified.

Policy effectuation. The comprehensive plan enables the legislative body to make decisions on the specific development matters which come up every week on the basis of a clearly stated, unified set of general, long-range policies which have been previously thought out and adopted. Thus current issues are viewed against a clear picture of what has been deemed to be the desirable future development of the community. The plan serves as a practical working guide to the legislators in making everyday decisions.

It is in the exercise or lack of exercise of the policy effectuation function that most plans succeed or fail. The plan that is adopted and then put on the shelf to gather dust has become a symbol of futility to city planners. Another common failing is the discrepancy that may develop between the comprehensive plan and the zoning ordinance. These are instances in which the policy effectuation function has been neglected. To be effective, the plan must be brought to bear on the development decisions made by the legislative body at every meeting.

In performing this function, the legislative body needs the assistance of its advisors, especially the planning staff and planning commission. They should be charged with the preliminary study of current development proposals to see how these relate to the comprehensive plan. While this is sometimes accomplished on an informal, voluntary basis, it is best that it be required through a mandatory procedure of regular referral. Such a procedure requires a planning commission report on all physical development matters that come before the legislative body for action. However, this report should be purely advisory; it is not desirable to hamstring the legislative body by requiring a greater-than-majority vote to overturn a commission recommendation.

The types of specific physical development matters which require action by the legislative body can be divided into two categories: (1) those measures which are specifically designed to implement the comprehensive plan, and (2) other matters which routinely require legislative approval and should be viewed in light of the comprehensive plan.

Examples of the first category are the zoning ordinance, subdivision regulations, the official map, the capital improvements program and budget, and development plans. These instruments are drawn up by the planning staff, approved by the planning commission, and forwarded to the legislative body for its action. There is no question of regular referral for these matters, since they originate in the planning department.

Examples of the second category include rezoning cases, use permit and variance applications, subdivision plats, street closings, site acquisitions, and public works projects. These items constitute the day-to-day business of city planning. Usually they do not originate from the planning staff, but from private developers, other departments in city hall, or other public agencies. Some of these things normally pass through the planning department on their way to the legislative body, or to other boards, but some ordinarily do not and so require referral.

Clearly the comprehensive plan should be a guide to the legislative body in passing on the control instruments in the first category. For matters in the second category, the plan should at least be consulted for an understanding of the context surrounding the particular issue, but it is possible that the plan will not unequivocally indicate what action to take. Admittedly, the comprehensive plan will not answer all the small questions which come before the legislative body. It is not supposed to; it is not intended to be a zoning map or a blueprint.

The remedy to this problem is the development plan, which is based on the comprehensive plan and attempts to specify the detailed development pattern for a particular area or a particular function. If there is an adopted development plan covering the current issue, it should indicate the proper decision for the legislative body to make. In general, all of the control instruments in the first category are intended to mediate between the comprehensive plan and more detailed physical development issues.

The successful operation of the policy effectuation function will be difficult to achieve, but it is crucial that it be achieved. It will require diligence by the planning director. Legislators may tend to overlook the comprehensive plan unless they are reminded. In time, if they are induced to use the plan and find it helpful in the conduct of their week-to-week business, they will learn to rely on it.

The policy effectuation function should be the most appealing to legislators. It is the function which should be most useful to them in the regular conduct of their duties. It focuses on current tangible issues, which supposedly hold the major interest of legislators. If it is followed, the plan justifies the actions of the legislators to the public, and makes it easier for them to resist the pressures of special interest groups.

Communication. Through the comprehensive plan, the legislative body presents a unified picture of its long-range, general policies to the other persons concerned with development of the community. These include the planning commission and staff, the chief execu-

tive, other municipal departments, other public agencies, private developers, civic organizations, and the general public.

The plan enables the public and private interests engaged in development to anticipate decisions of the legislative body. They can relate specific projects to the comprehensive plan during the early study phases, before the proposals are submitted to the legislative body for approval. Government officials can use the plan as a guide to administrative decisions. The communication function cannot operate effectively unless the comprehensive plan represents the policies of the legislative body. If it represents policies from another source, then it will be little help in anticipating the actions of the legislators.

Through the communication function, the plan acts as a positive force. It persuades private developers and suggests development projects to them. Many development proposals never require legislative action—the implementation of a land use pattern which already conforms to zoning, for example. In these cases, the plan still serves an important function for the legislative body by communicating its policies, even though the legislators may not be aware of it.

Once the plan is adopted and published, the legislators themselves are not actively engaged in this function; the plan document does it for them. Nonetheless, the plan is of tremendous benefit to them. It saves them time by screening out proposals which would conflict with their stated policies. The plan is the basis for many programs and activities of the administrative staff which are aimed at effectuating the legislators' policies. The planning staff, for example, prepares a zoning ordinance based upon the land use policies expressed in the plan.

The success of the communication function requires wide distribution and understanding of the comprehensive plan. The plan should be published and made available free of charge. It should be written and designed so that it will be attractive and comprehensible to the average citizen.

The necessity for communication means that while the plan must be primarily adapted to the needs of the legislative body, it must also be suited to the needs of those to whom the legislature wishes to communicate its policies. There need not be any serious conflict here. As long as the comprehensive plan is considered to be the repository of only general, long-range policies, then the same kind of document should satisfy the needs of all users of the plan. Where the municipal staff and private developers require more detailed guides, the comprehensive plan will not prove adequate. For this, supplementary documents and implementary regulations are needed.

The communication process provides a test of public acceptance of the plan. A plan that is meaningless or displeasing to the citizens will not get much support and will not have much influence on development. Such reactions eventually will get back to the legislators. Thus, the communication function provides a stimulus for citizen participation in the planning process.

Conveyance of advice. The comprehensive plan provides an opportunity for the legislative body to receive the counsel of its advisors in a coherent, unified form which assists the legislators in determining and effectuating general, long-range development policies. The principal advisors involved are the planning staff, the planning commission, and, in the council-manager form, the chief executive.

The comprehensive plan is the major instrument by which the planning commission and staff present their findings and recommendations to the legislative body. Through the plan, they first call attention to the development problems facing the community and then propose solutions. The plan enables them to offer their advice in a studied, comprehensive form, rather than on a piecemeal, *ad hoc* basis.

It has been argued that it is really the planning staff which formulates the plan, and therefore it is really the staff's plan. It is true that planners contribute the bulk of the thought and effort which go into preparing a comprehensive plan. Professional planners have probably been involved in the preparation of every comprehensive plan; a group of laymen cannot do it unaided. But the planners should prepare the plan for the legislative body, not for themselves.

Usually the first version of the plan represents primarily the thinking of the planning staff. This is proper, although it would be better if legislators could participate more in the early stages of plan preparation. As the preliminary plan goes through the long period of study and debate leading to adoption, the plan is shaped more and more to the legislative will, and it becomes less and less the staff's plan. This process continues after adoption, as the legislators learn about the plan through using it, and modify it through amendments.

The planner may propose policies through the comprehensive plan, but he should do so consciously and openly, not through oversight or subterfuge. He should explain the plan fully to the legislators, but he should not push it as a salesman. Unfortunately, "selling" is a common approach to plan presentation. No doubt this is analogous to the accepted step by which the architect sells his design proposal to his client.

The planner-legislator relationship is not the same as the architect-client relationship. The planner is a continuing advisor and aide of the legislative body who is rewarded for his services, rather than his product. The pay-off for the planner is not adoption of the plan, but what the legislative body does with the plan over the years to improve the physical environment of the community.

The advisory function continues after adoption of the plan. It operates whenever the staff and commission recommend amendments to the plan to the legislative body. The comprehensive plan is a key instrument for advising the legislative body on specific current questions. Regular referral gives the planners an opportunity to explain to the legislators how a particular matter relates to the plan. The plan should make it easier for the planning director to put across his recommendations.

The advisory function highlights the significant role of the professional planner. Experience has shown that the proper functioning of a comprehensive plan is impossible without the constant counsel of a professional planner (either a staff member or a consultant). No legislative body is equipped or educated sufficiently to carry on effectively without assistance or with only the assistance of laymen.

The emphasis on policy is not meant to detract from the importance of technical knowledge. Every policy should have a firm basis in technical fact and professional judgment. It is the job of the professional planner to make sure that this occurs. He must attempt to convince the legislators of the applicability of his findings and the merit of his recommendations. This will require that he present his advice in a form which the legislators can readily comprehend. He must learn to express the complexities and nuances of planning in terms which laymen can grasp.

It must be acknowledged that the planning commission and staff are more than merely passive advisors to the legislative body. They offer ideas, they initiate proposals, they point out problems, they actively attempt to influence the legislators. This is one reason why there is an administrative branch of government to help the legislative branch. These activities by the planners should be conducted openly and with a sense of respect for the powers that rightfully inhere in the legislative body. In the end, it is the legislators who decide whether the ideas of the planners are to be carried out.

Education. The comprehensive plan has educational value for the legislators and for anyone who reads and uses it. It arouses interest in community affairs, offers people factual information on present conditions in the community and probable future trends, awakens them to the possibilities of the future, tells them something about the operations of their local government, and imparts some of the ideas of city planning.

While the education function is allied to the communication function, it is much broader. The plan does more than just communicate the legislature's adopted policies. In fact, it provides the context by which citizens can decide whether or not they agree with the legislature's policies. It offers a wealth of background material which can be interesting and useful. It promotes citizen participation in local government.

The plan should be inspirational as well as informative. This does not mean that it should depict a utopia, but that it should point out some of the realistic possibilities for improving the community and creating a more desirable physical environment. The plan should indicate a positive attitude towards the prospects for progress, rather than resignation to extension of current trends. This also does not mean that the plan should be presented like a Sunday supplement or a promotion brochure. It should be written and designed so as to indicate that it is a sober working document to be used by practical men.

The legislators are perhaps the major beneficiaries of the educational impact of the plan. The entire process of studying, debating, adopting, using, and revising a plan constitutes a kind of in-service training in city planning, as well as in local government in general. The planning director should continually use the plan as a basis for educating the legislators. A brief "refresher course" on the main points of the plan at annual review time can be valuable.

One important facet of this process is that the legislators learn the reactions and opinions of their constituents. Dissemination of the plan document will bring responses from civic organizations, newspapers, and individual citizens. Public hearings on the plan give the legislators an opportunity to hear from the people they represent. The comprehensive plan can improve communication between legislators and voters.

The educational value of the plan is greatest during the period of deliberation over the preliminary plan which is proposed by the planning commission. If the plan is hastily skimmed and quickly approved, the potential educational advantages will be lost. Sometimes public response to the initial presentation of a plan is disappointing. There may be apathy in the community which is difficult to overcome. Education is a continuing responsibility of the planner, and sometimes it requires years of patient effort to produce palpable results.

THE FUNCTIONS FOR OTHER USERS OF THE PLAN

The Chief Executive. The specific ways in

which the chief executive will use the comprehensive plan will depend on whether he is an elected mayor or an appointed city manager. But in either case, he will be deeply involved in planning matters, and the comprehensive plan should be a valuable instrument for him.

The policy determination and policy effectuation functions pertain to the chief executive—for the strong mayor, because he is a policy-maker, and for the city manager, because he is the principal advisor of the legislators in formulating policies. The communication and advisory functions will operate in slightly different ways under the two forms of government. The strong mayor will receive staff advice through the plan and communicate the policies agreed on by him and the legislative body through it. The city manager will use the plan in giving advice to the legislative body and will interpret their policies from it. The education function applies under either form.

In addition, the chief executive uses the comprehensive plan as a basis for implementation programs. The plan itself does not contain a detailed outline for effectuation, but its proposals imply that certain implementing steps, particularly public works, should be undertaken by the administration. Much of the responsibility for effectuating the plan falls on the shoulders of the chief executive.

The chief executive is the central coordinator of all the activities of the government, and the plan provides a framework to assist him in coordinating those activities involving physical development, especially capital improvements. Because the plan is general, however, it will not suffice to coordinate all the details of the city's physical plant. For this the chief executive will need supplementary instruments, which might take the form of administrative programs, priority lists, and budgets, or of such standard implementing devices as development plans and the capital improvements program. The preparation of such items is a logical follow-up to adoption of a plan.

The Planning Commission and Staff. The most important function of the comprehensive plan for the planners is conveying their advice to the legislative body. The plan is the key instrument by which they present their most important recommendations. This is particularly true of the initial version of the plan prepared by the staff and forwarded by the planning commission to the legislative body. It also holds for proposed amendments and for recommendations on everyday matters on which the plan has some bearing.

The communication and education functions are also of great value to the planners. It is helpful to them to be able to put a clear, printed statement of the legislative body's policies in the hands of developers, lawyers, other public officials, and ordinary citizens. It illustrates to these people what city planning is all about.

The planning commission and staff also use the plan as a basis for implementation programs. It is their job to prepare and administer many of the measures specifically designed to carry out the plan—the zoning ordinance, subdivision control, urban renewal, development plans, and so on. Since the comprehensive plan itself is not legally binding on anyone, it is essential that the necessary legislation be prepared, adopted and enforced to transform the general policies into regulations and actions which do have legal substance.

The comprehensive plan also helps the planning staff by giving some focus and purpose to its research and design activities. Instead of drifting through a series of unrelated studies, the work of the planning agency is channeled toward a definite goal. The plan is a tangible product which will give the staff the satisfaction of accomplishment. The plan also serves the staff as a vehicle for exploration, especially during the early stages of drafting the original plan, but also after adoption, when new ideas are tested by fitting them into the context of the plan.

Operating Agencies. Physical development is a prime concern of many of the line departments of the municipal government—for example, public works, urban renewal, parks and recreation, building inspection, and utilities. Occasionally other departments, such as police, fire, and library, will be concerned with sites and physical facilities. There are often other local public agencies outside of the main city government, such as the school board and special purpose districts, which are involved in physical development. The comprehensive plan can be of value to all these agencies.

The comprehensive plan gives these agencies a context into which each one can fit its own plans and programs. Coordination among the various public activities will be enhanced, so that all should be working toward the same vision of the desirable future form of the city. Of course, the plan may not be sufficient for detailed coordination, and reference to supplementary documents may be required.

Many employees of operating agencies are specialists whose training and experience predispose them to take a narrow viewpoint and to ignore the work of other agencies. The comprehensive plan should promote a broader perspective by making them aware of the interdependence of all the aspects of community development. It shows them how the operations of their agency fit into a comprehensive scheme for improving the community.

For many operating agencies, the comprehensive plan will also provide essential information and data which are needed in planning specific projects. The long-range forecasts contained in the plan may be especially helpful. While this function is important, the comprehensive plan should never be distorted into a statistical compendium.

The communication and education functions also apply to the operating agencies.

The Public. The public which uses the comprehensive plan is a heterogeneous group —realtors, builders, businessmen, industrial executives, chambers of commerce, taxpayers' groups, property owners, and ordinary citizens. The comprehensive plan serves several functions for this varied audience.

The plan represents a formal, published report to the people on the development policies adopted by the legislative body. This should be a welcome addition to the few channels of communication existing between the legislators and their constituents. The plan is unique in being a studied, comprehensive statement of policies in one entire area of local affairs.

The plan ought to have great educational value for the public. It promotes public understanding of the community, government, the

legislators, and city planning. It is important that the plan document be drafted with an eye to its educational function, so that it will be instructive and self-explanatory.

The comprehensive plan helps to stimulate citizen participation in local government. The process of preparing and using a plan offers many opportunities for citizens to express their views and to contribute to the formulation of the community's policies. This is especially important during the period when the legislative body is debating the plan prior to adoption.

The plan gives the voters a means of evaluating the legislators, since it is a clear, definite record of their development policies. It also provides a device for keeping check on the legislative body. Any citizen can consult the plan to see whether particular actions of the legislators conform to their long-range policies. Thus it deters the legislators from taking arbitrary or capricious actions. On the other hand, it makes it easier for them to resist pressures and take actions which are in line with the plan.

The comprehensive plan might also provide subject matter for the campaign platforms of local political parties. Physical development matters have sometimes been major campaign issues in local elections. It would be appropriate for a party to advocate amendments to the plan. This means the plan might be changed considerably when a new group takes control of the legislative body. The plan should be amended under such conditions, to keep it in line with the policies of the current ruling group in the legislative body.

The comprehensive plan can serve as a guide to development decisions made in the private sector of the economy. It is probably the best available forecast of the community's future. Private developers can fit their projects into a city-wide context and coordinate them with public development proposals. This kind of private effectuation of the plan is largely voluntary, but the plan is apt to have a persuasive influence. Private developments often require approval of the legislative body at some time, and a developer is better off if his project conforms to the comprehensive plan.

Other Functions. A few miscellaneous functions which do not fit under the previous headings are grouped here.

The comprehensive plan can be a guide for the courts when they are required to rule on implementary legislation or actions which were intended to carry out the plan. Legislative acts which conform to a plan are more likely to be upheld than those which vary from a plan or are not based on any plan at all. Comprehensive plans have often been used in this way, and the demands of the courts have exerted a strong pressure for communities to prepare plans.

The comprehensive plan has increasingly been a prerequisite for federal financial aid. Since the 1954 Housing Act required cities to undertake comprehensive plans before they could receive urban renewal assistance, there has been a flurry of plan-making in hundreds of cities. Now other types of federal aid are also tied to the local comprehensive plan. Occasionally this has been the primary motivation for preparing the plan. It is regrettably true that in some cases hastily-drawn plans have been adopted with scarcely a second look and then filed away. Token plans of this sort are damaging to city planning. On the other hand, the federal requirements have awakened a genuine interest in planning in many places and have resulted in some fine plans.

The comprehensive plan can be helpful in securing coordination between autonomous public agencies. It offers a medium for negotiation, a meeting ground on which compromises can be effected and recorded.

Sometimes the comprehensive plan is used for civic promotion. Legislators want something to show their constituents and colleagues from other cities. Chambers of commerce want a publication to distribute to industrial and business prospects. While promotion is a legitimate activity of city officials and civic boosters, this function should be strictly incidental.

Procedures for Preparing and Using the Plan

BASIC REQUIREMENTS AS TO PROCEDURE

The reader will by now have a general idea of how the plan is formulated and utilized. This section merely recapitulates the recommended procedures in chronological order. Local circumstances, varying state enabling acts, and the desire to experiment may justify some variation in procedures; there is no intention of being doctrinaire. Nevertheless, the conception of the comprehensive plan advocated here dictates six basic requirements as to procedure:

1. There should be only one official comprehensive plan. People other than the legislative body do have different needs for a plan, but the confusion and inefficiency that would result from multiple plans offset the possible advantages. Supplementary documents can be prepared to meet the special needs of these people, such as the chief executive, planning commission, and planning staff.

2. The plan should be formally adopted by the legislative body. This fixes responsibility for the plan's policies on the legislature and makes it clear whose plan it is. The legislators will tend to take the plan more seriously, which will enhance the prestige of the plan. It gives a desired degree of stability to the plan, so that it is not changed promiscuously. However, adoption should be more than a perfunctory gesture.

3. There should be a lengthy period of public debate prior to adoption. Considerable time will be needed for the legislators to become familiar with the plan, and for it to be modified in accordance with their views. This period provides opportunity for citizen participation. There should be a full presentation of the proposed plan, followed by wide public distribution and exposure of the legislators to citizens' reactions.

4. The plan should be available and understandable to the public. It should be published and furnished to anyone who requests it, preferably free of charge. The plan should be complete and self-explanatory, while still being as concise, interesting, and attractive as possible. It should not be abstruse, but should be comprehensible to the average citizen.

5. The plan should be formulated so as to capitalize on its educational potential. It will be an introduction to city planning for many readers. There should be an explanation of

what the plan is and how it should be used. The plan should try to correct prevalent misconceptions about the aims of planning and the roles of the planning commission and staff. The relationship of the plan to implementing legislation and detailed development studies should be clarified.

6. The plan should be amendable. It must reflect the current development policies of the legislative body at all times, and anything that tends to stagnate it will seriously diminish its utility. The procedures for keeping the plan up to date should be specified in the plan and made a formal part of government routine.

AN OUTLINE OF PROCEDURE

It is presumed that any comprehensive plan effort would start with a go-ahead from the legislative body. Since the plan is to be prepared for adoption and use by the legislature. it would be unwise for a planning director to undertake preparation of a plan without the knowledge of the legislators. Since considerable staff time and expense will be required, there may be budgetary questions. Normally staff members will have to be hired or freed from other duties to devote full time to plan preparation. Once this approval has been granted, the subsequent phases would be:

1. Preparation of the preliminary version of the plan by the planning staff and commission. Usually the initial work will be performed by the planning staff, which from time to time will present findings, proposals, and progress reports to the planning commission. It would be desirable to involve the legislators as well at an early point, at least on an informal basis. This might be accomplished by asking them to consider a statement of community goals, or by presenting some fundamental alternatives for discussion at a work session.

It would also be wise to involve citizens at an early point. Publicity should be given out from time to time. In some places an *ad hoc* citizens' committee is formed to give the planners another sounding board and to communicate their ideas better to the public. Sometimes briefing sessions are held in different parts of the community, or with organizations who are especially concerned with physical development of the community.

After the planning staff has completed its studies and settled on the preferred plan, it should present this to the planning commission. Following a period of discussion, during which adjustments would probably be made, the commission should approve the preliminary plan and recommend it to the legislative body. State law or the city charter may require the commission to hold public hearings on the plan, but the major hearings should be reserved for the legislative body.

2. Presentation of the preliminary plan to the legislative body. This constitutes an opportunity to draw public attention to the plan, perhaps by an oral presentation illustrated with slides. The legislature should take no action on the plan at the initial presentation, but might establish the period for debate.

It is customary to have copies of the preliminary plan printed at this time and ready for public distribution. However, often this turns out to be a polished, expensive publication which has a look of finality about it. When so much money is put into the preliminary plan, there is a tacit hope that the legislative body will not make many changes before adopting the plan. This is an improper approach. There must be a printed version of the preliminary plan for public distribution, but it should be a simple, unpretentious, inexpensive publication—something that has the look of being subject to revision.

3. A lengthy period of debate by the legislators and public. Probably the ideal time for this is six months to a year, but in some communities it has stretched out for two years. Formal public hearings ought to be scheduled toward the conclusion of this period.

During this time, the legislators should become familiar with the contents of the proposed plan. Work sessions might be held with the planning director or planning commission. As the legislators continue about their regular business, they will be exposed to the relevance of the plan to current issues.

Strenuous efforts should be made to attract public attention to the plan and to disseminate information on its proposals. Besides distribution of the preliminary plan document, other common means of public information should be utilized. Citizens' reactions to the plan should be solicited and noted.

The object of this period of debate is not to "sell" the plan, but to improve it and make it more responsive to the wishes of the legislative body and the community. It is to be expected that the legislators will consider changes and perhaps request the planning staff to make additional studies.

4. Adoption of the plan by the legislative

body. This step is important because it causes the legislators to take the plan seriously. They will not care to sign their names if they are not familiar with the plan and generally in agreement with it. For those who use the plan, this step helps to make clear that it is the official plan representing the policies of the legislative body (Figure 13–2).

Since the comprehensive plan is not legislation, it is normally adopted by resolution. A resolution is a good place to explain briefly

---

ADOPTING THE BERKELEY MASTER PLAN, PROVIDING FOR THE ANNUAL REVIEW THEREOF, AND PROVIDING FOR THE INTEGRATION OF THE CAPITAL IMPROVEMENT PROGRAM AND THE PHYSICAL DEVELOPMENT OF THE CITY THEREWITH.

BE IT RESOLVED by the Council of the City of Berkeley as follows:

WHEREAS, the Planning Commission of the City of Berkeley after careful study and after two public hearings has recommended to this council a master plan for the City of Berkeley; and

WHEREAS, this Council has carefully considered the master plan and has held a public hearing thereon and finds that said plan constitutes a suitable, logical, and timely plan for the future development of the City of Berkeley over the ensuing twenty-five years.

NOW, THEREFORE, Be it Resolved, that the document consisting of text, maps, and charts, entitled "Berkeley Master Plan" and dated 1955, is hereby adopted as the Master Plan of the City of Berkeley in accordance with Section 1 of Ordinance No. 3403 N.S.

RESOLVED, FURTHER, that in order that the Master Plan shall at all times be current with the needs of the City of Berkeley, and shall represent the best thinking of the Council, Planning Commission, and boards, commissions and departments of the City in the light of changing conditions, the Planning Commission shall annually review the Master Plan and recommend to the Council extensions, changes, or additions to the Plan which the Commission considers necessary. Should the Commission find that no changes are necessary, this finding shall be reported to the Council. This review procedure should be timed so that any necessary amendments to the Master Plan may be adopted by the Council prior to the commencement of the formulation of the Capital Improvement Program.

RESOLVED, FURTHER, that the Master Plan shall be the guide for the Capital Improvement Program insofar as said Capital Improvement Program affects the physical development of the City. The Planning Commission shall submit an annual report to the Council regarding the Capital Improvement Program, which shall review each project for its conformity to the Master Plan; review the program as a whole in order to suggest any improvement in economy or efficiency which might be effected through the combining of various projects; and suggest any needed improvements which do not appear in the program.

RESOLVED, FURTHER, that all matters affecting the physical development of the City shall be submitted to the Planning Commission for a report to the City Council as to conformity to the Master Plan. Such report shall be made to the Council within thirty (30) days after presentation of the matter to the Planning Commission, provided that said time may be extended by the Council. If said report is not submitted to the Council within said thirty (30) day period, or any extension thereof, the matter shall be deemed approved by said Planning Commission.

Adopted April 12, 1955

FIGURE 13–2. *Resolution of adoption, master plan, Berkeley, California*

what the plan is and how it will be used, and to make the point that it is the legislature's plan. The resolution should also spell out the formal procedures to be used in keeping the plan current.

5. Publication and distribution of the final, adopted version of the plan. Here the object is not so much to solicit public reaction as to communicate the legislative body's adopted policies to the public, and particularly to those persons involved in physical development of the community. At this point it is appropriate for the plan document to have a finished look, although of course the probability of future amendments should be indicated. As time goes by, there will be a continual stream of requests for the plan from developers, civic groups, teachers, and interested citizens.

6. Annual review of the plan. Once a year the legislators should reexamine the plan and consider possible amendments. They should reconstruct the thinking which led to the main ideas of the plan. This will not only keep the policies fresh in their minds, but will introduce the plan to new members of the legislature. Normally the planning staff would initiate proposals for amendments, which would be screened by the planning commission and then forwarded to the legislators.

There should be a regular time of year for annual review, so that it will become routine and will not be overlooked. It might best be scheduled just prior to the annual hearings on the capital improvements budget. This not only fixes a date, but means that the plan will be fresh in the legislator's minds when they are considering specific improvements.

The importance of annual review cannot be overemphasized. This is the main process which is intended to assure that the plan will be kept up to date. If it is neglected, there is danger that the plan will "ossify" and be ignored. Annual review is a fairly recent innovation; it was not practiced during the days of the much-criticized "one-shot plans." Several municipalities now have had some years of experience with annual review, and it seems to be a fairly effective procedure.

7. Major reconsideration of the entire plan after five to ten years. This should provide for an overhaul of the whole plan, including new surveys, updated forecasts, and the restudy of major alternatives. The target date for the plan, if one is specified, should be pushed further into the future. The effort expended should be similar to that put into the original plan, and the same general procedures should be followed, including a period of debate before adoption. A new plan document should be published, and the old one retired.

The rationale behind this step is that amendments made at annual review time will not suffice to keep the plan current over an extended span of years. Gradual changes may be imperceptible unless they are compared with the situation a decade before. To illustrate, during the 1950s many communities based their plans on the assumption that population would increase. The 1960 census showed, to the surprise of most planners, that in many central cities the population had begun to decline.

8. Amendment of the plan at any time. Specification of an annual review procedure is not meant to preclude amendments at other times. In the normal course of using the plan as a guide for decisions on current development issues, the legislators will become aware of provisions which seem unworkable or even undesirable. It is inevitable that they will not be fully aware of all the plan's implications when they adopt it. Possibly they may want to modify some policies in view of new developments (such as a major new industry which was not anticipated). When these things occur, the plan should be amended immediately; every effort should be made to keep it current with the legislative body's thinking.

SPECIAL TOPICS

The Interim Plan. A considerable length of time is required to prepare a comprehensive plan, especially if major surveys must be conducted. The necessary period will vary with the size of the community and the staff available, but a period of one or two years is common. In large cities, this may lengthen to five years.

Occasionally there is an urgent desire to get some kind of plan as soon as possible, so an "interim plan" is quickly prepared, pending completion of a more exhaustive plan. Usually the interim plan consists mainly of a schematic design and a written statement of very general policies.

The preparation of an interim plan seems to be an acceptable procedure, although not necessarily something to be encouraged. There is apt to be some confusion among the interim plan, the tentative final plan, and the adopted final plan. Certainly it is better to make a rough overall plan than to revert to piecemeal planning. The major danger of the interim plan is that the community will not proceed with the more complete version of the plan.

The Role of the Consultant. The discussion up to this point has been based on the implicit assumption that the plan is prepared by the community's full-time planning staff. In point of fact, private planning consultants prepare a large portion of comprehensive plans. In the past, the consultant was often depicted as a villain who blew into town with a flashy plan (not too different from the one he previously did for a neighboring city), collected his fee, and left for parts unknown. The modern consultant is more responsible and enlightened. He tries to get the community started on a continuing planning process, and sometimes provides continuing counsel for a retainer.

In principle, it is preferable to have the plan prepared by the community's own staff, if possible. Consultants are generally used in two situations: when the community cannot afford a full-time staff or when the staff is too overloaded with other work to spare time for plan preparation. Under these conditions, there is no reason not to hire a consultant to draw up the comprehensive plan. The consultant should attempt to fill the role of a local staff as much as it can, working with elements in the community, and should recognize the legislative body as its principal client.

Implementing Legislation. In theory, preparation and adoption of a comprehensive plan should be the initial step in a planning program, and should be followed by formulation of the implementary documents which are supposed to be based on the plan. In practice, such legislation as the zoning ordinance and subdivision regulations often exists before the plan is started. In this event, adoption of the plan calls for a wholesale review of these documents to make sure that they really do effectuate the comprehensive plan.

The Comprehensive Plan Document

BASIC REQUIREMENTS AS TO SUBJECT MATTER

The discussion now devolves to a concrete level, focusing on what the published plan document looks like and contains. It is not intended to prescribe exactly the composition of the plan document; the comments here should be regarded as suggestions. They do not have the cogency of the conceptual propositions advanced earlier. While there is some latitude for experimentation, there are six basic requirements which the plan document should fulfill. These have been discussed previously, and are brought together for brief mention here.

1. The plan should be comprehensive.

2. The plan should be long-range.

3. The plan should be general.

4. The plan should focus on physical development.

5. The plan should relate physical design proposals to community goals and social and economic policies.

6. The plan should be first a policy instrument, and only second a technical instrument.

OVERALL FORM

The comprehensive plan should be completely contained in a single, published document, which should include a large drawing showing the general physical design proposed for the entire community, written text, and whatever maps, illustrations, and tables are needed to support the text. Often the large drawing is folded and put in a pocket inside the back cover. The plan should be easy to read and use, and inexpensive enough so it can be widely distributed (without charge, if possible). The document should be designed so that it is attractive and written so that it is interesting. It should not look forbidding or ponderous.

It helps if the plan is of convenient size, perhaps 8½ by 11 inches. Some plans tend to be large and bulky, which makes them hard to

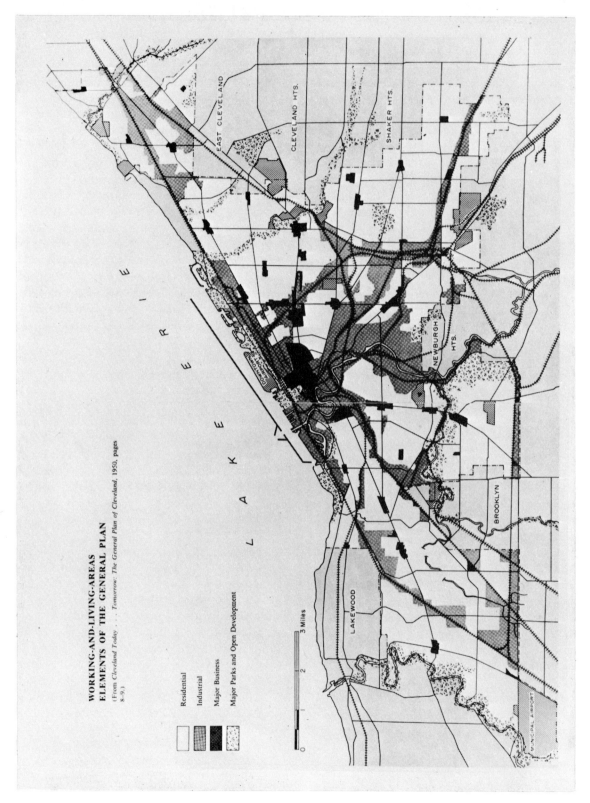

FIGURE 13–3. *Generalized land use map, Cleveland, Ohio*

carry around and use. Some provision for entering amendments should be made in the document. One solution is to use a loose-leaf binder, so that new pages can be inserted. Another is to provide a pocket where amendments may be kept.

The plan document should be self-contained, so that it will stand alone. It should not be necessary to consult other publications in order to grasp the essential ideas of the plan. Of course, some people may want greater detail, and it is appropriate to include references and a bibliography, but it should not be necessary for the average reader to undertake such research.

A final question is whether the document should be prepared as a slick or plain publication. Should the design talents of the planning staff be used to produce an eye-catcher? Often this has been done, and some very striking plan documents have resulted. However, there is an argument for conveying the image that the plan is a straightforward working document. While the legislators may be impressed with a flashy publication, they are not so likely to accept it as theirs.

CONTENTS AND ORGANIZATION

The contents of the plan document may be divided into several parts, which are discussed

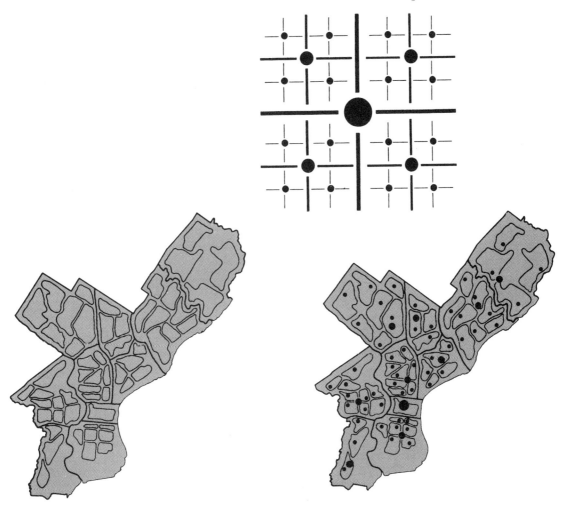

FIGURE 13–4. *Proposed service areas and neighborhood centers, comprehensive plan of Philadelphia (Above, a schematic concept for schools, hospitals, and other community facilities; bottom left, service areas for each set of facilities; bottom right, neighborhood centers for each service area.)*

in the sequence in which they would probably appear in the publication.

Introductory Material. The plan will serve as an introduction to city planning for many of its readers. Therefore, the document should open with certain material of essentially an educational character. This material should explain, in simple terms, what the comprehensive plan is, why the community needs it, and how it is to be used and implemented. It should also make clear that the legislative body bears the responsibility for the plan, and that the policies of the legislature are presented in the plan.

Such material can take a variety of forms. Often there is a letter of transmittal from the planning commission to the legislative body, or a letter to the citizens from the mayor or leader of the legislature. Another possibility is an explanatory foreword. The best technique is to reproduce the resolution of adoption, which

should explain the rationale for the plan.

There should also be a table of contents. This obvious step, often overlooked, will make the organization of the document clearer.

Background Information. Usually a sizable portion of the document is devoted to a discussion of the historical growth of the community, an assessment of current conditions, and predictions of future trends. This material helps the reader to understand the reasons for the policies and proposals presented later. This section should be not merely descriptive, but also interpretive and evaluative. The community's strong and weak points should be identified, and the emerging problems, needs, and opportunities of the future should be anticipated.

Among the topics which might be touched upon are the general history of the community, its geography, population, economy, land use pattern, and regional context. The assump-

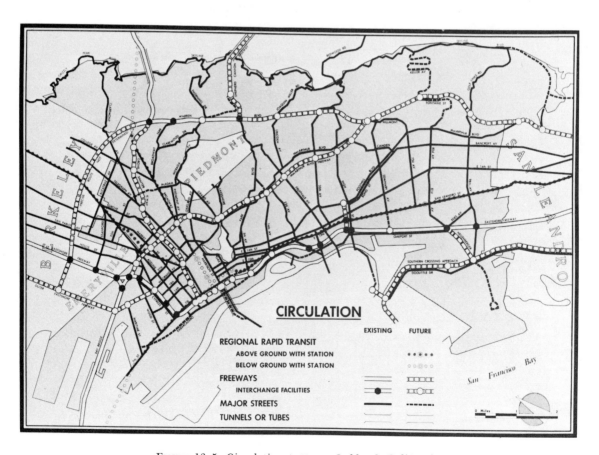

FIGURE 13–5. *Circulation pattern, Oakland, California*

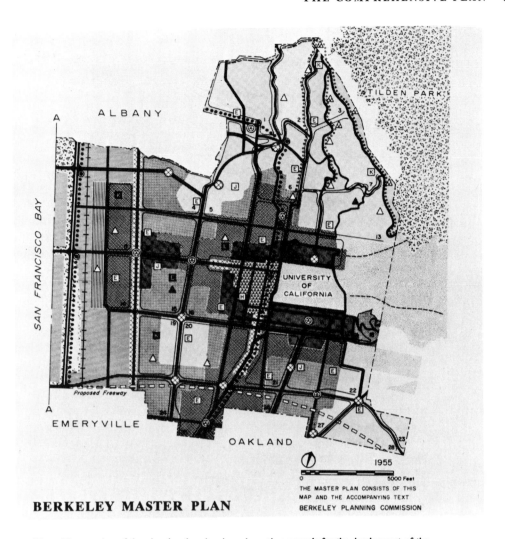

BERKELEY MASTER PLAN

(Note: That portion of the plan drawing showing schematic proposals for the development of the tidelands west of line A-A has been deleted.)

RESIDENTIAL AREAS

NET RESIDENTIAL DENSITY

0-30 Persons Per Acre
30-50 Persons Per Acre
50-80 Persons Per Acre
80-150 Persons Per Acre

6　Neighborhood Boundary and Number

COMMERCIAL AND INDUSTRIAL AREAS

Central District
Commercial Service District
Community Shopping Center
Neighborhood Shopping Center
Special Industrial District
Industrial District

PUBLIC SCHOOLS

☐ Existing
■ Proposed
K Kindergarten-Primary
E Elementary
J Junior High
H Senior High

RECREATION AREAS

△ Existing
▲ Proposed
⚠ Viewpoint
∘∘∘∘∘ Scenic Drive
--- Trail

CIRCULATION SYSTEM

Freeway
Major Thoroughfare
Secondary Thoroughfare
Feeder Street
•••• Rapid Transit Route
◉ Rapid Transit Station

FIGURE 13–6. *Generalized land use, master plan, Berkeley, California*

tions on which the plan is based should be noted. Last but not least, there should be an explicit statement of community objectives. While the planning staff is responsible for most of the background material, the legislators should be involved in formulating the objectives.

Summaries. To identify the most important ideas of the plan, it is recommended that two types of summaries be included, one written and one graphic. The written summary should be a concise list of the ten to fifteen major policies underlying the entire plan. The graphic summary should be a simple schematic diagram showing the relationships between major parts of the community and major functional elements of physical development. This should not be a precise map, but perhaps just an abstract pattern. It should be much simpler than the large general physical design drawing which also appears in the document. To date there has been little experience with such graphic summaries, although they have appeared in a few recent plans.

Instead of placing the summaries at the beginning or end, as is customary, it seems better to put them in the middle of the document, following the background material and preceding the presentation of more detailed proposals. Located here, they will make it easier to understand the proposals and view them in perspective. The location of the summaries might be indicated by printing them on a different color of paper or by a tab.

Physical Development Proposals. This is the major portion of the document; here the policies and proposals for future physical development are fully described. There may also be certain standards to guide the detailed design of specific facilities (such as the cross-section for a certain type of street) and certain principles to be followed in carrying out the broad proposals (such as elimination of industrial uses from residential areas). Reference to the unified physical design drawing should be made throughout this section, and there are usually supplementary drawings.

This section can be divided into five technical elements, the first three of which appear in virtually every plan, and the last two of which

would be desirable additions. These are: (1) a plan for the use of privately-owned land, (2) community facilities, (3) circulation, (4) civic design, and (5) utilities. Usually there is a separate chapter for each of these elements.

The first element is sometimes called a "land use plan," Kent's "working and living areas." Included are the residential, commercial, industrial, institutional, and other basic uses of land. Sometimes each of these categories is given a separate chapter. Often there is a separate drawing showing the pattern proposed for each category of uses. The residential proposals imply a plan for the distribution of the population. The commercial section usually gives special attention to the central business district.

The community facilities element concerns those structures and areas—whether public or private—which provide supporting services for the population and the basic non-residential activities. Included are schools, hospitals, libraries, police and fire stations, civic centers, parks and playgrounds, churches, cemeteries, and cultural facilities. The comprehensive plan does not identify specific sites for these facilities, but only indicates the approximate areas in which they will be needed.

The circulation element consists mostly of proposals for highway facilities and mass transit improvements (whether rail or bus). There may also be proposals for off-street parking, railroad and bus stations, airports, the port, the special needs of trucking, and pedestrian circulation.

The civic design element is intended to bring aesthetic considerations to bear on the development proposals. There should be a three-dimensional synthesis of the major proposals, and perhaps discussion of some visually important details, such as street furniture and the preservation of architecturally significant structures. Many past comprehensive plans have not included any explicit consideration of three-dimensional design.

The utilities element covers those community services which are regularly distributed to properties throughout the locality, often through pipes or wires. Among these are water, storm and sanitary sewers, gas, electricity, tele-

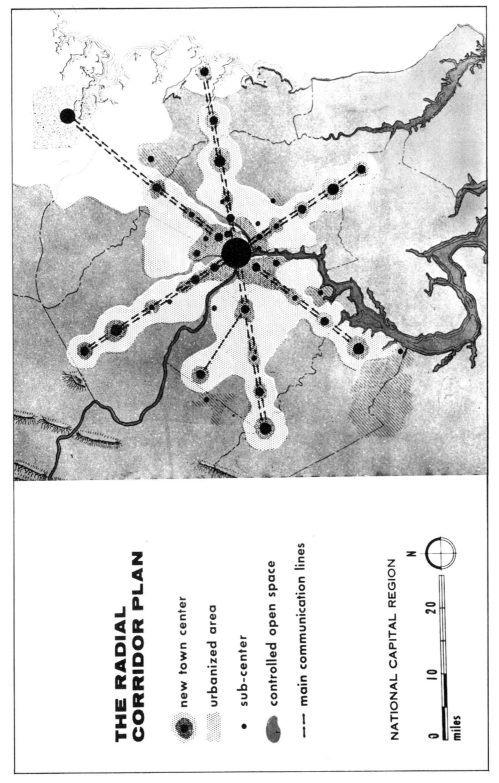

THE RADIAL CORRIDOR PLAN

- new town center
- urbanized area
- sub-center
- controlled open space
- – – main communication lines

NATIONAL CAPITAL REGION

N

miles
0   10   20

FIGURE 13–7. *The Washington Radial Corridor Plan*

phone, and refuse collection and disposal. In some cases these services require large sites (as for sewage treatment plants or dumps) which might also be covered in the community facilities element. If air and water pollution are serious problems, they might be discussed here.

Besides the five standard elements, each community may have some special feature or problem which calls for a section of its own in the plan document. This might be a major institution (a university, medical center, or state capital) or a major physical feature (tidelands, a river, or lake) which is important in the physical development of the community.

Concluding Material. There is usually a final section discussing implementation of the plan. This can be helpful to the reader who is not familiar with city planning and does not understand the relationships between the comprehensive plan, zoning ordinance, and urban renewal. There might be a restatement of the information given in the introduction on how the plan is to be used by the legislative body and citizens to guide the development of the community. This section should be purely explanatory; it should not include any detailed programs which would alter the plan's essential character of generality. Above all, the plan document should not include such implementary instruments as the zoning ordinance and capital improvements program.

To make the main text more concise and readable, it is customary to place some of the supporting data and technical analyses in appendices. Appendices might also include a bibliography, a glossary, the state's planning enabling act, and a discussion of the methods and techniques used in preparing the plan.

Large Drawing of the General Design for the Community. This is usually placed at the end of the document, although it could go elsewhere. Here all the separate proposals discussed in the various chapters are brought together in one drawing of the entire community so that their spatial relationships can be seen. While this has the appearance of a map, it is better to think of it as a diagram, since it is not intended to show precise boundaries or sites. It is important that this drawing be distinguished from the zoning map.

Problematical Materials. There is certain other material which occasionally appears in plan documents, or has been suggested as appropriate for inclusion in them.

Kent has recommended that a section be devoted to the relationship of the physical design proposals to the community's social and economic objectives. Such a section did appear in the Philadelphia plan, but it was quite theoretical and was aimed at professional colleagues rather than citizens. As yet, these relationships are poorly understood, and it is questionable whether a lucid and meaningful statement on this subject can be composed by the typical planning staff.

Some planners have suggested that cost estimates for carrying out the plan should be included in the plan document. Again, this was done in Philadelphia. It is difficult to say what is best. The comprehensive plan is meant to consist primarily of objectives and general policies; it is not a program of specific improvements. It seems wiser for cost estimates to be included in implementary documents, such as the capital improvements budget. However, it is true that decisions on general policies depend upon costs, and planners are becoming more able than heretofore to assess the cost implications of policies.

It has been argued that urban renewal should be given a special section in the plan document. The relationships between urban renewal and the comprehensive plan are still rather tenuous, since urban renewal started as a distinct program, usually outside of the planning agency. Urban renewal is a means of implementing the comprehensive plan, but in practice urban renewal agencies have had little to do with preparation of comprehensive plans. In the present situation, it does not seem necessary to devote a separate section to urban renewal. In any older city, many of the proposals for physical development will naturally be proposals for urban renewal.

14

Programming
Community Development

I T IS ASSUMED in this chapter that a local planning agency is well established as a going operation and that a comprehensive plan has been prepared. This implies that development objectives were carefully defined in accordance with the procedures spelled out in Chapter 12, and that these are now well expressed in a comprehensive plan document suitable for formal adoption by the planning agency or the governing body of the city as set forth in Chapter 13. We therefore turn our attention to the kinds of programs that can carry out proposals made in the comprehensive plan.

Many of the programming techniques described in this chapter are not dependent on the existence of a comprehensive plan. They may often be quite helpful in terms of coordination and channeling of development activities in a consistent direction, whether a plan exists or not. In many cases, a municipal government will be making use of some of the techniques described here as a part of any broad planning program.

The first section of this chapter presents an overall range of implementation measures for influencing the pattern, timing, and character of physical development. Coordination, scheduling, and financing of municipal capital improvements is then described, followed by discussion of several other types of programs relating to land development. In succeeding chapters, three significant versions for planning implementation are described in greater detail: zoning (Chapter 15), land subdivision (Chapter 16), and urban renewal (Chapter 17).

Governmental Actions
Affecting Development

The municipal government can influence the pattern, standards, and timing of development in many ways, both direct and indirect. These include construction of public facilities, regulation of private building, the use of incentives and concessions, and general information and persuasion techniques. In most communities a variety of measures needs to be applied, since each is limited in what it can do. The comprehensive plan of a typical city will ordinarily call for equally comprehensive implementation to bring about full effectiveness.

This principle is reflected in the federal government's "workable program" requirement. As a prerequisite to approval of housing or urban renewal funds, local officials must demonstrate that they are making use of the full kit of tools they have available to cope with problems of blight and to encourage sound new development. The seven elements of the program for community improvement (workable program), described more fully in Chapter 17, are examples of some of the major types of municipal actions affecting new building. These and others are discussed below.

ADVICE AND PERSUASION

The comprehensive plan itself is the number

one programming tool. It can function admirably as the major implement in a broad planning and development program to which all other implements relate. The plan document is basically a coordinated set of advisory proposals. Its effectiveness depends on the extent to which it is seen, read, understood, used, and respected. The degree of respect accorded a plan depends in turn on its soundness being evident and on its being up-to-date in relation to current problems and issues. Just as a craftsman has little patience with a tool that is dull or poorly suited for the job at hand, so a developer or a citizen can have little respect for a plan characterized in any of the following ways:

1. *Unavailable:* A plan that cannot be seen can hardly be persuasive. Enough complete copies should be published to reach every important official and to stock every library in the community; enough summary copies to satisfy everyone with an active interest.

2. *Pedestrian:* A plan that fails to capture the imagination can do little to influence the future course of development. Excitement and ingenuity in both the content and presentation of the plan can help implementation.

3. *Out-of-date:* Most people recognize that a five-year-old automobile is likely to be substandard. So it is with a comprehensive plan. Good practice calls for quinquennial review.

4. *Incomprehensible:* Far too many planning reports are obscured in technical jargon and profusion of detail. Cities are complicated enough to understand; master plans should be steps towards simplification.

5. *Unreal:* The visionary plan is, in a sense, one which by definition cannot be implemented.

6. *Neglected:* It is trite to refer to master plans gathering dust on the shelves of city hall. It is shocking that many master plans gather their dust on the shelves of planning agencies, which often overlook opportunities to relate their official actions to positions expressed in their own plans. If the planning office neglects its comprehensive plan, others will follow suit.

Why all this discussion of the comprehensive plan in a chapter on "Programming Community Development"? Because that comprehen-

sive plan, with its development objectives, policies, and patterns is the foundation on which all of the other measures of implementation can be built. In the absence of a plan, the programming measures can be only hopeful in contributing towards community objectives.

WORKING RELATIONSHIPS

The purpose of planning is to influence people. Plans are made by human beings and are expected to be carried out by people. There is room for fallibility in the processes of both plan-making and implementation. As much depends on the process of planning operations as on any other aspect of technical work, if we are to have effective carrying-out of planning proposals. The planner's relationship to citizen groups and the public is discussed in considerable detail in Chapter 20.

Perhaps the most useful rule to be observed in working relationships within municipal government is to keep people informed. The planner should not present surprises that affect people with long-term interests in a particular subject. For example, highway proposals should not be announced in planning documents before they have been discussed with highway officials. To the extent that the planner can "sell" his proposals to those expected to carry them out—making these people advocates and supporters rather than objectors and opponents—the chances of successful execution of the proposals will be increased. Methods for communicating with members of the municipal family are discussed in more detail in Chapter 19.

Coordination Measures. A fair amount of consistency in implementing community policies and goals can be achieved merely by making known the existence of the comprehensive plan and what it contains. Some degree of coordination may be expected if the plan and its proposals are widely known and kept before the public, especially those members of the public likely to carry out development activities. The planning agency should make a conscious effort to relate as many of its activities as possible to its formally adopted comprehensive plan. This carries with it, of course, the obligation to maintain that plan in an up-to-date condition, and to revise it from time to time.

The simplest means of coordination is to foster the practice, on the part of municipal agencies and private developers alike, of consulting the planning office for information and guidance in connection with any development proposals. Several planning agencies have made effective use of this technique with a series of small leaflets circulated widely as an enclosure with utility bills and bank statements. The leaflets carried a message such as "Going to Build? Check with the City Plan Office, Room 432, City Hall."

The planning agency cannot coordinate something it does not know about. If it is to function effectively as a clearinghouse and coordinator, it must encourage the habit of inquiring and checking. A useful means of doing this is to make available, to anyone who wants to see it, an atlas of information on hand in the typical planning office. Much of this material changes from time to time and is not suitable for publication without considerable expense. A prospective developer therefore must come to the planning office for information and to check particular locations which he proposes to develop.

A system of working reference atlases was effectively used by the planning division of the Rhode Island Development Council during the 1950s when one of the major objectives of state government was the stimulation of industrial growth and creation of new job opportunities to replace the employment losses in textile manufacturing. A loose-leaf atlas was set up for each of the 39 cities and towns in the state, with several dozen map sheets or colored-pencil overlays at the standard scale of a United States Geological Survey quadrangle or a state highway planning survey sheet. This meant that topography, culture, and transportation data were already shown. On separate pages for each subject and at this consistent scale, practically every bit of other information that came into the office was recorded. Among the subjects mapped were population spots, census tract data, traffic counts, soil survey information, surficial geology, bedrock geology, areas of ground water potential, locations of observation wells and test borings, land use, local zon-

ing, local master plan proposals, public properties, historic sites, potential industrial sites, flood plain and hurricane danger areas, proposals for acquisition of land by state agencies, studies and proposals by the former state planning board, locations of referral cases acted on, and subdivisions platted and recorded.

Not only were these materials useful in studies aimed at a comprehensive plan for the state, but long before such a plan existed, the atlases saved the state many times the planning division's annual budget by revealing conflicts in proposals. It was possible to leaf through a series of pages and get a relatively comprehensive picture of many factors relating to a particular location—some of which would influence development decisions. Home builders and industrial and commercial site-seekers made frequent use of the atlases.

For most communities comparable information exists, but at a variety of map scales that preclude easy correlation. The planning agency, merely by making its essential working tools available for consultation by the public, can do much to coordinate and inform, and to prove its worth and helpfulness, even if it does no planning! In recent years, planners seem to have become disenchanted with such a simple-minded atlas approach to graphic coordination of development and are devoting much attention to electronic processing of comparable ranges of data. This is certainly appropriate in our great cities, but there is a long way to go before systems are developed that can give the insights a visitor to the planning office can get from a note-laden atlas.

A more positive kind of coordination can occur when the planning office takes the initiative in contacting private developers and public agencies to determine what projects are likely to occur in the near future. The formal procedures for referring development proposals by public agencies to the planning office will be discussed later as one of the regulatory measures for implementation.

Demonstration Techniques. By setting an example, municipal government can do much to influence development. It is much easier to sell a neighborhood "clean-up, fix-up, paint-up" campaign if the city sweeps neighborhood streets, repairs street lights, and paints sign posts. Similarly, the maintenance of public buildings and their exemplary improvement can often be regarded as a prerequisite to private improvement measures. Many downtown programs are based on similar cooperative demonstrations with the city providing new public parking facilities and the merchants providing similar programs of investment in private property.

In some cases, demonstrations can be carried further. For example the urban renewal program includes provisions for a small percentage of the housing units in a rehabilitation area to be acquired and remodeled as demonstration properties in order to show private investors how the job can be done. Such demonstration buildings have become virtually a standard part of neighborhood rehabilitation programs, as described in Chapter 17.

The 1954 amendments to the National Housing Act provided for a more diverse program of demonstration projects. The federal government is authorized to make grants to assist public bodies in developing, testing, and reporting new methods and techniques for urban renewal. This activity is aimed primarily at demonstrating techniques developed in one community for application in others. Projects under the program have ranged from a publication describing record-keeping techniques for code enforcement through a series of pilot studies on varying aspects of urban renewal and relocation activities to actual physical demonstrations of self-help housing improvement.

Citizen Support Techniques. One of the more effective means of insuring follow through on comprehensive plan proposals is the use of citizen organizations. The pattern for these varies widely from city to city, both in effectiveness and in organizational structure and relationship to the official government. The range of citizen groups actively involved in support of planning activities is described in Chapter 20. A few examples from larger cities are worth mention here.

In both Chicago and Philadelphia, there are planning and housing councils independent of the city government and organized on a metropolitan basis. They operate effectively in stimulating popular interest in, and for the most part support of, the official planning programs. Such groups as these have their strongest role in stimulating planning in its earlier stages and in convincing local political and governmental leaders of the need for adequate funds and staff to cope with developmental problems. In some cases the private groups lose steam in later stages of ongoing planning programs unless there is a continuing effort to involve them in activities directly related to the work program of the planning agency.

In Boston, the Metropolitan Planning Council is in reality an agency created by the state government. The council itself is a sizable organization made up of representatives of many communities and agencies, operating under an executive committee of 15. Specialized committees, drawing from the membership of the 100-man council, are supplemented by other citizen members with particular interests in the subject area of each committee. The committees are involved in review and criticism of draft plan materials and actually function as a small support group in presentation of materials publicly and to the larger council. In effect a small advocate group is created for each of the major report products of the planning effort.

There are many citizen groups in almost every community. It is a temptation for the planner and the members of the planning board or commission to spend much time dealing with various groups in terms of generalities. This can wear dangerously thin. Such groups must be given the opportunity to take positions on real issues, but the planner and his planning board must recognize at all times that their primary responsibility is to the municipality. It is easy to have awkward situations develop where the planner is speaking more readily with a citizen's group than with the official legislative body or the city administration. Such groups, however, are useful at times in reaching around an obstinate council to achieve something in the interest of the larger community. It is a truism that politicians are responsive to numbers of voters, and a position by a sizeable group of citizens frequently will demonstrate to the legislators where the popular interest is.

The planner has a responsibility to keep these groups informed of his program and to give them the opportunity to take a position in public hearings and in formal appearances when plan proposals or independent proposals are being decided. The citizen group, however, should not be used to sidestep the need for an official planning agency position.

INCENTIVES AND INDUCEMENTS

There are many ways by which the municipal government, and in some cases higher levels of government, can provide incentives for sound development. These range from simple tax concessions or agreements to outright cash grants for developments which meet certain requirements related to the objectives of the government.

Tax Concessions. In their eagerness to attract new industries and build the tax base of the community many municipalities have granted tax concessions to builders of new factories. These vary widely in specific provisions. Some places, particularly among the depressed textile communities of New England, have granted outright freedom from local property taxes for a five- or 10-year period. Others have entered into understandings with new industries as to a fixed level of tax bill or assessed valuation for a given period of years.

In general, professionals in the industrial development field frown upon such practice, taking the view that it is in effect a kind of unfair competition. From the viewpoint of industry it is frequently misleading, because in actuality it is just a deferment or diversion of the tax impact. There is a cost of services which must be borne by the community and if some are excused from carrying their fair share of such costs the costs to others are clearly increased. It is, more directly, unfair to existing industries which may be responsible for a comparable portion of the employment in a community but which, in effect, must carry the costs of providing services to competitors excused from paying their share of costs.

For the most part such concessions do not play a strong role in the decisions of larger and better established industrial organizations seeking a new plant site. They may, however, be decisive in attracting smaller independent industrial operators. More than anything else a tax concession demonstrates the eagerness of a community to have a new industry locate there. This is particularly true if the concession is acted upon by a group such as a New England town meeting where a broadly representative body of citizens considers and votes on the matter. It is not likely to carry as much weight with industry when the decision is made by a small body of public officials.

Tax concessions for the purpose of attracting new industry have little to recommend and they should not be given lightly. The community should clearly be getting something in return for the costs which it is assuming collectively. A strong case needs to be made for serving a realistic public need, not just in terms of jobs but in terms of some positive and enduring development or investment in the community.

There is likely to be difficulty in operating any tax concession program without formal state legislative action. Most states have laws regarding assessing practices and these frequently require local assessors to value property at its full market value or a fixed ratio thereof. In order to meet the requirements of such provisions, the tax concession needs to be embodied in a formal agreement under which the community gets something in return for its action in abating or deferring taxes.

More recently a variety of tax concession has been effectively applied as a means to foster the preservation of natural areas or open space in a community. Under this arrangement tax officials agree to tax at rates suitable for agricultural or undeveloped property rather than industrial or potential commercial development use. Frequently the value of property may be effectively set by granting an easement to the community for scenic rights or otherwise limiting the use of land to specific open development uses. California's legislation in this field is a leading example. There are provisions in some laws for deferring taxes until the date when development occurs, thus, the developer of land for a more intensive use must in effect pay a substantial premium in back taxes before he can convert the land from its open use. Chapter 7 relates the use of such techniques in acquiring open space.

Bonus Provisions. Another major incentive technique for achieving higher standards of development or specific types of land use proposals is that of awarding bonus credits for good design. Such provisions are frequently worked into some of the more recent experimental zoning ordinances. There are, for example, provisions in some laws for allowing a more intensive development of the land in cases where the building design provides greater open land area at ground level than is called for in the minimum ordinance requirements. These provisions are often coupled with floor area ratio provisions in zoning. Both work toward greater flexibility and imaginativeness in building design and induce provision of better light and air at lower levels of large structures as well as increasing the amount of open space on the ground.

Bonus provisions may also be applied in subdivision design. Developers may be granted greater flexibility in the design and layout of streets and lots if they dedicate a substantial part of their tract to permanent public use or permanent open development, as would be the case in a "cluster" design with common park space.

In all of these provisions it should be quite clear that the community is not giving something away for nothing. It is granting permission to do something different than is customarily required in return for some action by the developer to assist the community in solving its problems. In effect, it works as an incentive for the developer to do things better in the community interest.

Loans and Guarantees. A third type of incentive technique is the use of loans, or loan insurance, by government to achieve certain objectives. Chiefly these apply to standards for development rather than locational requirements, although they have been most effective in influencing the broad and general metropolitan pattern of development in most communities across the nation. Almost half of the residential development in this country in the two

decades since World War II has been influenced by programs of the Federal Housing Administration and the Veterans Administration for the guarantee of mortgage financing of moderately priced privately owned housing.

During most of this time the standards for federal insurance of mortgages have paid nominal attention to zoning requirements and comprehensive plans in a community. The programs have fostered tremendous growth in suburban house building. Only since the 1959 authorization by Congress have FHA programs been developed which support rehabilitation of housing in the city center and effective means of stimulating multifamily home development.

Since almost all investment in housing and other construction depends on credit, programs which influence the pattern of credit availability have proven most effective. This is the case whether the credit financing is used by the individual home owner, the plat developer, the mass apartment builder, the public housing authority, or the municipal or other governmental agency. All of these must respond to requirements laid down by the agency that provides the financing. Although it has been the exception in the past, more and more public agencies are requiring developments for which they provide the financing credit to conform to local and metropolitan comprehensive planning programs. Most federal programs involving some form of loan or grant, whether to state or local government, private developer, or individual, set forth some forms of federal criteria for location or construction standards.

The loan technique has also been used to some extent by state and local levels of government. Several states participate in the financing of housing developments in order to reach the middle income group not served by public housing or FHA type financing. New York state's program for cooperative housing is a leading example.

As an incentive technique, the loan is widely used by higher levels of government to induce private investment to meet quality standards or to facilitate local governmental action in providing community facilities. Strings tied to the loan have been effective in setting adequate standards for construction and frequently the availability of loans to cover substantially the entire cost of development has stimulated provision of certain types of housing. Specifically, housing for relocation of displaced families and housing for certain types of nonprofit, or church related groups can be financed frequently to 90 per cent or more of the total cost involved through use of certain types of FHA loan and guarantee arrangements.

The use of loans by local governments is not nearly as common. There have been, however, some experimental programs under which municipal agencies, or local housing authorities have financed, or have assisted in the financing of veterans' housing.

Grants. Grants-in-aid for construction of specific facilities are widely used to bring about planning or development objectives. Grants generally have been made for many years by the federal, state, and local governments, and in some cases by civic or foundation groups interested in furthering community objectives.

In terms of impact on physical development, the largest single grant program has been that of the federal Bureau of Public Roads and its predecessors. This, like several other federal programs, is channeled through an appropriate state body. The Bureau of Public Roads makes its funds available primarily to the state highway agencies which follow varying patterns of distribution.

The federal government essentially follows a rule of not initiating projects, but it does set down a number of standards and criteria and has done much in researching, demonstrating, and evaluating to standardize and systematize the planning of highway facilities throughout the nation. The federal government is concerned with coordination of state highway planning at state lines and with creation of nationwide major road systems. But in general it looks to each state to carry the primary responsibility within its boundaries. The federal agency reviews and approves projects designed by the state agencies to meet minimum federal standards. In some states the federal grants, which are usually allocated on an annual formula rather than a specific project basis, are passed on to county and local highway agencies for construction of minor projects.

Federal highway grants have also been instrumental in supporting comprehensive planning for transportation and land use as required under the 1962 Highway Act. Grants to other programs for various types of public facilities are common and occur in the fields of social welfare, health, education, utilities, and other types of public facilities.

In a number of cases state agencies have contributed to the financing of local improvements, frequently to the extent of one-half of the nonfederal share required for a particular project.

Local grants-in-aid are more unusual, but not unknown. There have been, for example, a number of cases where local government has appropriated funds for capital developments to be carried out by more or less autonomous agencies such as urban renewal authorities, or industrial development groups. In some cases city owned land has been transferred to such groups, in effect constituting a grant of some importance and effectiveness in determining the location for a new facility.

Mention should also be made of grants from foundations and other civic groups. Frequently these, by their very existence, commit the community to specific sites, or specific types of improvements which might not be constructed at the time or in the location selected. In this case, they are a true incentive technique.

REGULATIONS AND CONTROLS

The municipal government can achieve many of its planning objectives through the application of regulations. These are of two main types: (1) those which apply to private development and (2) those which apply to governmental actions.

Ordinance Controls. The main type of regulation which applies primarily to private development is zoning. This is discussed in detail in the next chapter but several features of zoning regulations are described here.

The authority for zoning regulations is derived from municipal police powers and generally is based on state enabling legislation which authorizes a municipality to adopt zoning controls. Although in many cases the zoning ordinance and zoning map are prepared by the planning agency and are based upon master planning studies, the administration of the zoning ordinance involves several other agencies—customarily a building inspector, a zoning board of review or board of appeals, and in the case of changes in the ordinance or map, the legislative body of the municipality. It is good practice to have cases coming before zoning boards and city councils referred to the planning agency for comment before action is taken by these other agencies. In this way the planning office can check specific locations against current thinking and work and give up-to-date advice to guide the group which must make a firm decision.

Municipalities usually have a variety of regulations which can affect the standards of development or the location of particular types of facilities. Health regulations, building codes, and minimum standard housing codes, for example, usually apply to standards of development rather than to location. Other types of regulations, however, may involve important locational factors. Usually the city council or similar body is required to act upon applications for storage of dangerous materials including petroleum or explosives, establishment of junk yards or similar objectionable facilities, and location for licensing of liquor establishments. In some cases these matters are left to the administrative discretion of individual municipal officials. Good practice would call for referral of any important such matters to the planning agency in the same way as is done with zoning cases.

Planning Review. The planning agency cannot guide, influence, or advise on things it does not know about. For a planning program to be effective there must be a steady flow of information to and from the planning office. For this reason, many of the better planning statutes provide for a compulsory or mandatory referral of significant development matters to the planning office. Any proposal, for example, to acquire property for a municipal purpose, to dispose of city-owned land or property, or to initiate development of a public facility should be submitted to the planning agency for review and comment. The usual provision sets a time limit for the planning agency to advise

the city council or other sponsoring body in regard to the proposal. In some areas the council is obliged to follow the planning agency recommendation or can act counter to the recommendation only by vote of an enhanced majority.

In most places, mandatory referral laws apply only to municipal agencies, but there are some examples where state and county units must comply as well. This has been the case in Chicago since 1956. Although couched in somewhat involved language, the Illinois general municipal planning enabling law quoted below gives the Chicago Plan Commission the opportunity to sound off publicly in regard to the proposals of "any public body or agency."

11–12–4. Whenever a municipality of more than 500,000 population has created a plan commission pursuant to the provisions of this Division 12, every plan, design or other proposal by any public body or agency which requires the acquisition or disposition of real property within the territorial limits of the municipality by any public body or agency, or which changes the use of any real property owned or occupied by any public body or agency or the location of any improvement thereon within the territorial limits of the municipality, shall be referred to the plan commission by such public body or agency not less than 30 days prior to any election for the purpose of authorizing the borrowing of money for, or any action by such public body or agency to appropriate funds for, or to authorize such changes or the acquisition or disposition of such real property, but in no event shall such referral be less than 30 days prior to making such changes or acquiring or disposing of such real property. The plan commission shall review every such plan, design or other proposal and shall within 30 days after submission thereof report to the public body or agency having jurisdiction over such real property or improvement thereon concerning the conformity of the plan, design, or other proposal with the long range planning objectives of the municipality and with the official plan for the municipality or any part thereof if the same shall then be in effect as provided in Section 11–12–2. Such report shall be spread of record in the minutes or records of proceedings of such public body or agency. A report that any such plan, design, or other proposal is not in conformity with the long range planning objectives of the municipality, or the official plan for the municipality shall be accompanied by a written statement of the respects in which such conformity is lacking but such a report shall not bar the public body or agency having jurisdiction over such real property or improvement thereon from thereafter making such changes or acquiring or disposing of such real property. The failure of the plan commission to report on any such plan, design, or other proposal within 30 days after submission of the same to it, shall be deemed to be a report that such plan, design, or other proposal conforms in all respects with the long range planning objectives and the official plan of the municipality.

As used in this section the terms 'public body' or 'agency' shall include the State of Illinois, any county, township, district, school, authority, municipality, or any official, board, commission or other political corporation or subdivision of the State of Illinois, now or hereafter created, whether herein specifically mentioned or not.[1]

Chicago is the only Illinois city above 500,000 population at present (and the only one likely to be so in this century). It is unfortunate that comparable referral requirements for smaller communities are not yet included in the state law.

In places where a mandatory referral procedure is not spelled out in the enabling act, it is often quite helpful to informally institute the practice. In most governments the chief executive is implicitly charged with coordinating municipal departments, and he can act to implement this coordination by establishing the practice of referring development matters to the plan commission for review and comment before they are considered for final action by the city council. The planning office is the logical place to function as a clearinghouse for all development information. It can serve a significant function by indicating to other agencies whether property or development proposals are consistent with the master plan or conflict with other proposals.

It is sound practice to clearly indicate in any action taken on a referral, the specific basis for the action, and the reasoning behind it, as called for in the Illinois law cited above. In many cases city planners have made flat recommendations against a certain proposition as being inconsistent with the master plan or the city's long-range objectives without explaining why this is bad. In the planning office the referral should be regarded as an opportunity to lend status and authority to the official mas-

[1] See ILLINOIS REVISED STATUTES (1961), Chapter 24, par. 11–12–4ff.

ter plan. The planning agency's report should spell out the location involved, the master plan provisions which relate to the area in question, and the reasoning behind these provisions as well as existing conditions and ground situation which are pertinent to consideration of the case.

Far too many referral actions are taken without reference to the official master plan or to previous publications and reports of the planning agency. As has been stated earlier, this has the result of fostering neglect by outsiders of the master plan in line with the example set by the planning agency. If the city planning office does not make an obvious practice of putting its own materials and advice to use, it cannot expect others to respect them.

DIRECT ACTIONS

There are many ways by which municipal government can influence the form of community development through direct action in real estate investment or development operations. Only a few are mentioned here.

Municipal Investment. The investment of municipal funds in public facilities such as roads, schools, utilities, or public buildings clearly has an impact on the pattern of community development. Private developers consider the imminence of school facilities and community services when they decide where to open up a new plat or undertake a home building program. Planning for such public facilities and the public announcement of municipal intentions to acquire property or schedule construction of new facilities can do much to influence private decisions. Techniques for evaluating the timing of such proposals are discussed in the next section on "Capital Programs."

Land Management. The municipal government can influence the pattern of community development by the techniques it uses in managing public property. Most municipalities own more land than they realize. The amount of territory involved in street rights-of-way, for example, usually comes to between 20 and 30 per cent of developed areas. Many communities have an accumulation of tax-delinquent properties that have come into public ownership through foreclosure. A complete inventory of public land should be high on the agenda of any planning agency. Such an inventory should result in an active program of land management with clear responsibility in some agency of the municipality for the maintenance of each property. Further suggestions in this direction are made in Chapter 16.

A periodic review of property inventory should be made in order to reach conscious decisions as to the use, disposition, or retention of each parcel. A program of acquisition and reservation of land in advance of need will do much to keep down the city's ultimate cost for new facility sites. Both of these activities can be closely linked to capital improvement programming procedures discussed in the next section.

Urban Renewal. Although urban renewal is taken up in more detail in Chapter 17 it is worth mention here as the single, most important municipal program of direct action to change the face of the community. But it has larger implications in the way in which it generates or stimulates private investment. Within renewal project areas, land development and investment in most cases simply would not occur without application of the land assembly and subsidy powers. Adjacent to many renewal areas, additional opportunities are opened up by reason of the improved environment created through renewal.

Capital Programs

The typical American city carries out numerous capital improvement projects each year. They may range from extensions of utility lines to construction of major public buildings. As pointed out in the first part of this chapter, such projects can do much to influence and stimulate private development. Many projects may also have significant relationships to other projects. The construction of a school addition can be used as credit towards the local share of the cost of an urban renewal program. Savings might be possible if sewer main replacement is scheduled to coincide with reconstruction of a street. Many dissimilar projects compete for funds which are all too limited. Money needed

for construction of a water filtration plant may result in deferral of a public library branch. The wealth of federal incentives and matching grants tends to distort and confuse the efforts of city officials to set local priorities. It is far too common for projects to be selected for action solely in response to neighborhood pressures or to meet requirements for aid from the state or federal government.

With the growing complexity of both financing and development activities, even the smallest community needs to carefully analyze the way it programs funds for various improvements to be sure that it stretches its dollars as far as possible. No municipality has enough money for all the things it would like to do. This means that it must have some method for tackling first things first. The basic reason for a capital improvement program is just that: to insure that money is being spent wisely.

In municipal finance, just as in family finance, most capital investments or similar major expenditures are paid for with borrowed funds. There are usually restrictions and limitations on the amount of money which a city can borrow. If these limitations do not exist in state law or the local charter, they are effectively applied by the lending institutions which charge higher rates for the use of money if that use is not regarded as sound.

A formal method for programming capital improvements and capital expenditures is more and more being insisted upon by banks as well as federal agencies participating in many grant and loan programs. Such a method is also useful in the political realm, both in balancing competing pressures for limited funds and in demonstrating to the voters and the people that fairness and objectivity are being exercised in public spending.

An important function of capital programming lies in the area of coordination. The systematic review of proposed projects affords an opportunity to tie them together as to timing, location, and financing. A significant element of the typical capital program is the fiscal analysis usually aimed at minimizing the impact of improvement projects on the local tax rate.

A more important aspect of the capital program is that it presents the opportunity to schedule projects over time so that the various steps in the development of an area logically follow one another. It also gives an advance picture of future needs and development activities.

An often overlooked factor in the capital program involves location and distribution of projects within a city. The simple discipline of mapping all proposals often reveals interrelationships overlooked by the isolated sponsors of nearby or overlapping projects.

A final factor in favor of early introduction of capital improvement programming in a city is that it permits the programming agency to demonstrate effectively its role in serving other elements of local government. The typical capital improvement program reveals neglected needs and frequently resolves longstanding problems for which solutions had seemed futile. A capital improvement programming effort may prove to be an effective means of developing good will and understanding for the local planning agency within its governmental structure.

NOMENCLATURE

Capital improvement programming at the municipal level had its first real boost during the 1930s when local concern with public works was high and the federal government was trying to stimulate planning activity. Essentially, capital improvement programming includes scheduling of public physical improvements for a community over a certain period of time, with consideration for priorities and financial capabilities of the community. During the past several decades relatively standard procedures and terms have been developed and applied within the planning profession for the conduct of capital improvement programming. Although these terms vary, there is an increasing consensus toward the following:

Capital Improvement. Any major nonrecurring expenditure or any expenditure for physical facilities of government, such as costs for acquisition of land or interests in land; construction of buildings or other structures, including additions or major alterations; construction of highways or utility lines; fixed equipment; landscaping and similar expenditures. (Expenditures for motor vehicles or other wheeled equipment are often not treated as capital expenditures, especially in larger communities or where there is no policy question involved in the acquisition of new vehicles or wheeled equipment or the replacing of existing equipment.)

Capital Improvement Budget. The list of projects together with the amounts and sources of funds for the coming fiscal year. This is sometimes regarded as the first year of the capital improvement program. It is often treated as the capital improvement section of the annual city budget.

Capital Improvement Program. The long-range schedule of projects with their estimated costs over a period of five to 10 years. The most common period is six years. This covers a five-year period beyond the capital improvement budget for the first year. Most programs are presented in terms of specific calendar or fiscal year listings, although there are some shown in terms of several priority categories with a more flexible time schedule.

It is customary to prepare a capital improvement budget and capital improvement program annually, revising the entire program and adopting the capital improvement budget each year as part of the regular operating budget.

In 1962 an American Institute of Planners planning policy committee on "Financing the Plan" issued a report in which it said, "Comprehensive plans for the development and growth of communities should include financial plans for the realization of plan recommendations." In addition to strengthening the means for implementing the comprehensive plan, the committee introduced a new note in nomenclature for capital improvement programming, building upon the well established terms defined above. The committee proposed that for every comprehensive plan, there should be a corresponding "capital needs list," intended as a comprehensive listing of all capital improvement recommendations contained in the comprehensive plan. It should be prepared by the planning agency and be reviewed and revised each time the plan itself is reviewed.

The committee recommended that the capital needs list contain two major parts. The first would be a "capital improvement schedule" listing all improvements to be undertaken within the planning period of 20 years or more. Drawn from this schedule would be the customary five or six year capital improvement program of which the first year would be the capital improvement budget.

The second major element in the Capital Needs List would be the "planned projects reserve." This would include those improvements which suggest themselves in the plan as being desirable but unlikely to be undertaken because of present financial, legal, or other obstacles. They would presumably be catalogued as part of a planned projects reserve for completion beyond the time limit set by the comprehensive plan or earlier if new resources become available.

The committee said, "New sources of revenue, private bequests, state and federal grant programs and changes in legislation may activate such improvements and advance them to the capital improvement schedule, the capital improvement program and ultimately to the capital budget."

This is a suitable technique for insuring that all comprehensive plan proposals are presented in documents which will fit them into the capital improvement programming process. Whether they are kept in a category labeled "planned projects reserve" or maintained in the listing of deferred projects is immaterial. It is important, however, that they be carried along and considered annually as part of the capital improvements review by municipal government.

PROGRAMMING PROCEDURES

The procedures described in this chapter are fairly typical of present capital improvement programming practice. They represent a somewhat simplified and streamlined process based on experience in using materials submitted by a wide range of agencies in a number of places of varying size and scale of need. They have been effective in small towns, although the principles underlying them apply to larger units of government as well.

The process of capital improvement programming will ordinarily call for the following distinct steps:

1. An inventory of potential projects, including cost estimates and an initial evaluation of their relative priority.

2. Analysis of these project requests, usually involving discussion with the sponsor.

3. Investigation of the financing capabilities of the community and the relation of these to different project categories.

4. A schedule of project execution in a long-range program list which considers project relationships to each other and to financial requirements.

5. Selection from this schedule of a slate of projects for early action. This generally takes the form of the capital budget for the coming fiscal year.

6. Formal adoption of the capital budget against the background of the long-range recommended program, usually after some form of public review.

The specific details of this process vary with the size and structure of local government. There are also many differences in legal requirements and nomenclature among the different communities which have developed capital improvement programming procedures. One point is clear, however, in every capital program effort. This type of activity is a collaborative affair and virtually cannot be done adequately by one municipal official working alone. It matters little whether the capital improvement "ball" is carried by the local planning agency, or the city's budget officer, or some other official centrally situated within the municipal administration.

It matters very much, however, that these officials work together effectively in dealing with the various aspects of the program. Each must be involved: the planning agency, to insure coordination among the physical locations or various projects and to provide the insights needed to relate public projects to the broad goals of community development; the finance officer, to provide adequate integration of capital needs with other financial needs and operating budget implications of each project; and the city's chief executive.

It is customary to initiate the capital improvement programming procedure within a government by means of a communication from the chief executive. In a city, a letter from the mayor or city manager should inform each agency head of the purposes of the capital improvement programming operation and call for his cooperation in preparing materials to be submitted to the planning agency. It is assumed in the remainder of this section that the planning agency would be the primary unit responsible for preparation of the capital improvement program, in close participation with the finance or budget official.

The timing of the entire capital improvement program process needs to be set carefully in relation to the city's regular operating budget timetable. All of the detailed work described below should be scheduled so that conclusions regarding the initial year's capital budget are available by the time the city's operating budget is being prepared.

INVENTORY OF PROJECTS

In launching a new capital improvement programming procedure, it is important that the planning agency cast a fairly wide net to try to capture all potential projects which either will make a financial demand upon the funds available to or budgeted through the city or will have some significant relationship to offer capital improvement projects. It is recommended that a broad view be taken so that the program will be a significant device for coordinating the entire spectrum of public involvement in capital improvements. It should not be limited only to those things for which *funds* will be required within the city budget. There are, for example, significant programs carried out by other public agencies which may have great effects upon the timing as well as the financing and location of city projects. It is recommended therefore, that the planning agency poll all units of government and similar interests operating within its jurisdiction. Some of these units are described below in connection with requests which might come from them as project sponsors.

City Departments. The primary source for information on needed improvements is the operating agency of city government. These should include not only the public works department and the street, utility, and similar agencies, but virtually *every* unit of municipal government. On the theory that every unit needs some funds with which to operate, the city's operating budget can be used as a good checklist to identify potential project sponsors. Even this may be incomplete and omit some organization such as special study commissions or commissions for war memorials or civic buildings whose operating costs are minimal or nonexistent but who may be preparing plans for significant capital improvements. All of these should be provided with materials for submitting project requests.

Planning Agency. It is not unusual for a capital improvement program to be prepared without reference to a comprehensive or master plan. If such a plan exists, however, every effort should be made to have the capital improvement program represent a true means for implementation of the plan. This frequently requires that the planning agency itself develop project request forms and function in a sense as sponsor for every physical or capital improvement required to carry out the plan. This recognizes the fact that operating agencies might not be willing to give the comprehensive plan as high a status or as much respect as the planning agency might. Even though they may have participated in some of the studies leading up to the plan, it is unusual for them to become eager sponsors of plan proposals.

It is recommended therefore that project request materials be developed for *all* of the items required to wholly implement the plan, whether these items occur within the five- or six-year capital improvement period or beyond. This would ensure at least an annual review and consideration of each project needed for realization of the comprehensive plan even though many of these would repeatedly fall into the "deferred" category. This is in effect a simple administrative device to maintain plan recommendations before the public, and to stimulate definite action towards their disposition.

Other Sponsors. One way to encourage active citizen participation in municipal government would be for the mayor to invite proposals for capital improvement projects from citizens and civic groups. This tends to formalize what is generally an offhand procedure but would demonstrate the willingness of municipal officials to give careful consideration to suggestions presented by outside interests. Some of these may be significant and useful; others may be ghosts that are best laid to rest. In either case, an official statement as to the validity of the suggestion and a reasoned argument justifying its disposition will facilitate progress toward the adoption of a sound and popular capital improvement budget and program.

INFORMATION FORMS

With many diverse proposals being submitted from a wide variety of sources, it is essential that printed forms be used to obtain some consistency in presentation and to facilitate consideration of the project requests. In larger communities, capital improvement programming documents have become quite elaborate and resemble in some instances federal grant applications or income tax forms. In the typical smaller government where department heads are overburdened with operating responsibilities the distribution of another batch of complex paperwork will not be welcomed. Since the success of a capital improvement program depends on the cooperation of project sponsors and support of political leaders, materials used to solicit project requests from sponsors should be streamlined and simplified as much as possible. The basic materials needed are described below. A supply of each can be distributed to each potential sponsor with a letter of instruction.

Project Request. One of these is usually completed for each project. An example of a single form for this purpose is shown in Figure 14–1. This form has been used extensively in Massachusetts towns in connection with capital improvement studies done as part of local planning assistance programs. In the first use of this form in a community, the planner completed the forms in conference with local agency heads. In subsequent years, the agency heads themselves completed the forms. The

kinds of information asked for on the project request form were reasonably simple and largely selfexplanatory. No elaborate "capital improvement budget manual" was required; rather a two- or three-page mimeographed instruction sheet was used.

The top right corner of the form is reserved for an identification number, different for each project. Using a departmental symbol and project numbers consecutively within each department provides greater flexibility than numbering projects consecutively in each year's program. In some governmental structures it may be necessary to have a double symbol to identify the agency as a subdivision within a department.

Costs are asked for in terms of a range since it has been found that in the preliminary stages of virtually any project it is impossible to estimate accurately the ultimate costs. The breakdown of costs into several major categories is useful in identifying some elements which sponsors occasionally forget to include in the project request form.

The effect on the annual budget again is requested in terms of three categories in order to make the sponsor consider the major elements of the annual budget. Some forms call for information on new personnel not shown in this example. This information is often unreliable in the early stages of planning and frequently does not become a factor in determining project priority or scheduling. Providing a box to indicate the year in which the project is needed eliminates the need to prepare a more detailed schedule form for each department. In larger jurisdictions, however, a summary form (described below) listing all of the projects requested by each agency, is frequently helpful.

It is desirable to have the sponsor indicate his own evaluation of priority. The categories of priority indicated on the form are:

Priority A, URGENT—projects which cannot reasonably be postponed. These may be needed to complete an essential, partially finished project, to maintain a minimum, presently established departmental program, or to meet an emergency situation.

Priority B, NECESSARY—projects which should be carried out within a few years to

INDIVIDUAL PROJECT ESTIMATE

July 1, 1962–June 30, 1967

CITY OF _____

Project No. _____
Date _____ 19__

1. DEPARTMENT _____   2. DIVISION OF _____

3. DESCRIPTION OF PROJECT—
   a. Name, physical descript., location—
   b. Purpose—
   c. Shown on map attached _____
      (yes or no)
4. NEED FOR PROJECT (USE SEP. SHEET IF
      NECESSARY)
   a. Why requested—
   b. In Master Plan? _____ Page _____
5. RELATION TO OTHER PROJECTS, WHERE
      APPLICABLE
6. ESTIMATED COST—
   A. Planning (totals a,b,c)   _____
      (a) Architects
          services _____
      (b) Engineering_____
      (c) Inspection _____
   B. Land   _____
      (a) Site is secured _____
      (b) To be secured _____
   C. Construction (totals a,b) _____
      (a) Labor _____
      (b) Nonlabor _____
   D. Miscellaneous equipment
      (totals a,b)   _____
      (a) Equip. _____
      (b) Furniture _____
   E. Other   _____
      TOTAL ESTIMATED
         COST $_____
   F. Cost prior to July 1, 1962
      (included above) $_____
      ESTIMATED ADDI-
      TIONAL COST $_____
7. FUTURE BURDEN RESULTING
      FROM PROJECT— $_____
   (a) Annual cost: mainte-
       nance, repair and op-
       eration   _____
   (b) Annual estim. cost of
       new staff required   _____

   (c) Future expend. for addit.
       equip. not included
       in proj. cost   _____
8. INCOME FROM PROJECT (Estimated annual, di-
      rect and indirect)
9. ESTIMATED CONSTRUCTION PERIOD—
10. STATUS OF PLANS AND SPECIFICATIONS—
      (Place check mark opp. proper status)
      _____0 Plans not needed
      _____1 Nothing done except this report
      _____2 Preliminary estimate received
      _____3 Surveys completed
      _____4 Work on plans scheduled
      _____5 Sketch plans in preparation
      _____6 Sketch plans completed
      _____7 Detail plans in preparation
      _____8 Detail plans and specifications completed
11. PROPOSED MANNER OF CONSTRUCTION—
      (contract or day labor)
12. PROJECT EXPENDITURES BY YEARS—
      1962–63 _____ 1964–65 _____
      1963–64 _____ 1965–66 _____
            1966–67 _____
ENDORSEMENT (Questions 13, 14, 15 to be
   filled in by dept. heads)
13. PRIORITY RATING—
14. YEAR RECOMMENDED
      FOR CONSTRUCTION—
15. RECOMMENDED FINANCING:
      General Revenue   GR _____
      Service Charges   SC _____
      Utility Revenues   UR _____
      Gen. Oblig. Bonds   GOB _____
      Federal Aid   FA _____
      State Aid   SA _____
      Revenue Bonds   RB _____
      Special Reserves for Capital SR
      Expenditures   _____
      Working Capital or   WC
      Revolving Fund   _____
      Total $_____

FIGURE 14–1. *Individual project estimate for capital improvement program*

meet anticipated needs of a current departmental program or for replacement of unsatisfactory facilities.

Priority C, DESIRABLE—projects needed for a proper expansion of a departmental program. The exact timing of these can wait until funds are available.

Priority D, DEFERRABLE—projects which would be needed for ideal operation but which cannot yet be recommended for action. They can be postponed without detriment to present services.

In the space on the project request form for indicating the suggested source of funds it is anticipated that the sponsor would give his recommendations for financing. The sources might include general revenues, service charges, utility revenues, general obligation bonds, federal and state grants, revenue bonds, capital expenditure reserves, special assessments, and revolving funds.

Departmental Summary. In smaller communities where the number of project requests is small this form is not needed. In larger communities, however, it is often helpful. Ordinarily the procedure is to have each sponsoring agency list all projects in order of priority on one table. The columns on the form usually have space for the following items: project identification number, project name, priority category, target year for completion, total capital cost, federal aid, state aid, revenue bond, other, cost to the city (with subheadings for each of the six program years and a column for "beyond the capital program").

Additional Information. Each sponsor should be encouraged to submit drawings, maps, tables, and other materials that help to explain the project he is requesting from the appropriate governing body.

ANALYSIS OF REQUESTS

While a carefully prepared capital improvements program should be based on more than materials formally submitted by project sponsors, those materials can form an important base for developing the program. Tabulation of all requests to obtain total cost estimates for each program year or each priority group usually will result in figures clearly beyond the recognized financial reach of the city. However, such a tabulation is useful background in the hearings or conferences which should be held with each project sponsor. Grand total figures can often serve as something of a lever for cutting back the program to a figure that can be more readily accepted by municipal leadership.

Most project sponsors should have the opportunity to present their case in greater detail than is possible on standardized forms. In a small town, informal discussions between planning agency officials, others concerned with the capital improvement program, and the sponsoring officials would customarily be in order. In a larger community, where formal boards and relatively autonomous officials are among the sponsors, public hearings might be required.

The purpose of the hearing or conference is to gain further insight into the specifics of the requested project. Among these insights might be the personality differences among various sponsors. It is not unusual for project requests to reflect the program ambitions and strengths of different agency leaders. Public works officials are accustomed to developing specific materials for definite projects while administrators of welfare institutions—accustomed to dealing with human and social problems—may be totally inept in assemblying information for building construction. However, their needs for capital improvements may be much greater. It is incumbent upon the planning agency to help define real needs and to see beyond the submissions and their spokesmen to the things of importance to community goals.

Taking an inventory of projects in a typical city can open a Pandora's box of problems, many of which political leaders might prefer to avoid. Stirring-up of dormant issues and identification of unrecognized needs that result from a new capital programming effort makes many city administrations reluctant to get into the inventory business. In this connection the planning agency can perform its greatest service—in objective evaluation and clear recommendation for disposition of each request. Its task is to point the way towards solution of each matter that comes before it, within the fiscal and policy framework set collaboratively with other participants in the capital programming effort.

Based on the material submitted and results of discussions with sponsors of materials presented in hearings the planner should conduct his own evaluation of each project request. This will involve modifying or confirming the priority rating assigned to the project by the sponsor. Seldom would a project be raised in priority, but there are times when this might be done.

If, for example, a project has been underrated by the sponsor in its contribution toward community goals or in its relationship to other projects, there may be reason to advance it. An effort should be made to tie the arrangement of projects in priority sequence to the broad goals or objectives of the comprehensive plan. There should be, as preface to the entire capital improvement budget, a restatement of the community's basic development goals. These should be conscientiously reviewed annually and various projects tested against the contributions which they would make toward these goals.

Several rules-of-thumb would normally be developed and applied in setting up the overall capital improvement schedule. These would be used in making judgments as to the timing and scheduling of individual projects. Those projects which merit an "urgent" priority would ordinarily be tackled in the initial capital improvement budget year, unless there were financial reasons for delay. Those projects classed as "necessary" would tend to fall in the early years of the capital improvement program. Some might be undertaken in the initial year if they are funded from specialized sources. "Desirable" projects would tend to be listed in later years, and "deferrable" projects generally would only be shown beyond the six-year period.

The year-by-year tabulation of projects on worksheets will be largely a trial and error operation as various combinations are tested to determine the appropriate level of funding for the various agencies and functions of municipal government. Some factors involved in the tabulation are discussed in the next section on

fiscal programming. At this stage great care must be taken to determine the extent to which outside sources of funds might influence the scheduling of various projects. The availability of federal aid—frequently on the basis of standard formulas not directly related to project amounts needed—may influence the pace or rate at which various classes of improvements are carried out.

A significant step in project analysis, sometimes overlooked because of its simplicity, is that of mapping project requests and checking them against the kind of working atlas described in the first part of this chapter. This may reveal not only potential conflicts, but also opportunities for coordination in timing and especially for maximizing credit under federal urban renewal and model cities programs.

SCHEDULING PROJECTS

The capital improvement program cannot be completed without close collaboration with the city's finance officer. The capital improvement budget to be adopted for the coming fiscal year will be a significant part of the city's annual budget and must be closely tied to that budget. A standard capital improvement program study involves a review of the whole field of municipal finances. Schedules of the following items are customarily required for adequate study of the financing constraints on the capital program: present and projected revenues of the city, by source; present and projected expenditures, by major function category; outstanding indebtedness, present and future; and present and projected debt service.

Each of these items is readily charted when built upon the past record. Plotting data for a 10-year period in each direction is essential, and study of data over longer periods can frequently be rewarding. Bar charts and trend diagrams are useful in illustrating the relationship between future capital programs and past levels of expenditures for comparable purposes. Oversimplified comparisons, however, can be misleading because of the changing character of many financial programs, particularly the increasing ratio of federal to local funds.

The majority of capital improvements is financed by borrowing. Usually limitations are set by the state government or charter on the amount of funds cities may borrow. These are frequently stated in terms of a percentage of the total assessed valuation of the city or in a proportion of the tax revenue. These limitations should also be plotted to determine future borrowing capacity for funding capital improvements.

Many aspects of municipal finance affect capital improvements programming, but there is not space in this volume for adequate discussion. It is assumed and recommended that the planner seek the guidance and advice of a knowledgeable finance official in this stage of the capital programming effort. The bibliography to this chapter is also helpful. In addition a number of common-sense financing policies can help the planner sort out projects and determine their timing. Several which have proven helpful in many communities are listed below:

State or federal aid. The exact circumstances of availability of state or federal matching funds should be clearly understood to avoid unduly distorting project scheduling. It is too easy for the sponsor to argue that he can get three federal dollars for every local dollar only in the current fiscal year. Timing and office deadlines for such projects should be clearly understood before decisions are reached.

Non-local funds. Usually use should be made of outside funds. Even though the majority of all capital improvement monies is based fundamentally on taxes, it can be assumed that the full range of nonlocal aid money will be spent in one way or another. For the individual municipality to "get its fair share" requires that it keep up with and make full use of available grant funds from outside sources. This, of course, should apply only to those projects essential to the city's improvement. There is no need for the municipality to "cook up" projects in order to use its share of federal funds unless these projects are worthwhile.

Maximizing Credits. An eye should be kept open for maximizing the possibilities of obtaining credit for various types of projects. The best example of this is in the field of urban renewal where site or street improvements may be used as part of the local share of the net cost of an urban renewal project. Coordinating activities related to urban renewal is significant and there are many details of regulations which change from time to time. Things to watch for include deadlines relating to eligibility of a noncash credit within a future project area (construction must have been completed not more than a fixed number of months before the loan and grant application is approved under one of these rules).

Continuing Programs. Annually recurring programs, even though they are of a capital improvement nature, which are continuing at a fairly steady level should not be bonded if they are of long duration. For example, it may be perfectly satisfactory to resort to bonds for a three- or four-year street improvement program if this is the full extent of street improvement needs. If, however, the total need indicates that a 20-year program of street improvements or activities should continue over an indefinite time, the program becomes an operating budget item and it will be to the city's long-run advantage to use "pay-as-you-go" financing. Bond financing generally adds 50 to 100 per cent to the cost of a project and the city can get more for its money by paying for continuing activities from its general revenues.

As an example, assume a city projects a five-year sewer replacement program costing $100,000. It can finance this with bonds (i.e. 20 years at five per cent) with an initial debt service of $10,000 and a total cost of about $150,000. There is some advantage to this deferred payment kind of arrangement only if it is not a recurring expenditure. If at the end of five years, the city needs to go into a second program at the same level it will be paying close to the amount it would have had to pay for pay-as-you-go financing where it would be building $20,000 worth of sewer replacements annually. The great difficulty, however, in doing something about these programs is that of converting from an established bonding practice to a current revenues pattern. Some cities have done this effectively by tapering the bonding amounts down, and stepping up funding from general revenues over a period of several years time.

Bond Issue Policy. Specific policies should be set down in the capital budget document establishing the minimum level for use of bond funds. Bonds should be limited to nonrecurring expenditures of some magnitude. For example, it may be that nothing below $20,000 is worth the red tape of the additional cost of bonds.

A sound capital improvement programming procedure can benefit the city's financial rating, but public announcement of a substantial improvement program can have the opposite effect. Bond houses and rating services may interpret news stories of a capital program as indicating a "spending spree." It is essential, therefore, that the city formally inform these agencies that sound techniques have been employed in programming the city's long-range finances and insuring the soundness of the city's debt structures.

Because capital improvements programming is fundamental political policy the chief executive must participate in setting spending levels and making the basic decisions as to what types of improvements to recommend. The role of the planning agency is primarily to coordinate material submitted by others and to work with finance officials in assembling facts for decision by the executive and the council.

CURRENT TRENDS

There are several new trends in capital improvement programming and related fields worth mentioning here. One is the developing concept of the "improvements plan" as a significant element of the comprehensive plan. This is best exemplified in the December, 1966, *Comprehensive Plan of Chicago* prepared by that city's Department of Development and Planning. The comprehensive plan is presented in two major parts. The first is a "policies plan" of diagrammatic representations and statements of major policies to guide future development in seven categories of services or systems within the city. These include policies for residential areas, recreation, education, safety and health, industry, business, and transportation. The second part, the "improvement plan," sets forth specific targets for these seven

planning systems in terms of specific quantitative elements for which cost estimates have been prepared. The improvement plan is aimed at a 15-year period and is to be implemented through the annual capital budgets and capital improvement programs. In this sense, it is closely akin to the capital improvements schedule advocated by the AIP committee cited above.

Another significant development relating to capital improvement programming is the sharpening of rather sophisticated and detailed procedures best exemplified by the work being done in the Philadelphia capital program. Several references to this are listed in the bibliography to this chapter. These procedures provide for close integration of capital and operating budgets. The criteria for evaluating project requests are particularly interesting.

The whole field of governmental budgeting and decision-making has been under intensive study in recent years, arising from federal Department of Defense experience in the early 1960s. The development of a "Planning-Programming-Budgeting System" (PPBS) is being tried experimentally in a group of states, counties, and cities, with a view to improving the allocation of resources among alternative ways to attain governmental objectives. As listed in publications of the State-Local Finance Project of the George Washington University, the primary distinctive characteristics of a PPB System are these:

1. Identification of the fundamental objectives of the governmental unit, and relation of all activities to these objectives.

2. Explicit consideration of future year implications.

3. Consideration of all pertinent costs: capital and maintenance, as well as direct costs.

4. Systematic analysis of alternatives.

As in so many fields related to urban planning, the understanding of problems of municipal finance, budgeting and capital investment is changing, and the techniques for dealing with these problems are also changing. The process of capital improvement programming presented in minimal and simplistic fashion in this chapter may soon be supplanted by more effective techniques in larger communities.

Other Significant Programs

It is appropriate to include in this chapter some brief mention of other significant programs which have proven useful in relation to the control of urban growth: annexation, the selective extension of services, and official mapping. Space does not permit their full discussion here. Application of these techniques is not as widespread as the use of standard measures described in the next three chapters—largely because of the different conditions existing among the states. Nonetheless, the lessons to be learned from experience with these measures have applicability in any area where urban uses are moving into open land.

ANNEXATION

Annexation is the process by which usually contiguous fringe territory is added to an existing municipality. State laws spelling out annexation methods and procedures vary widely. In some of the New England states where the entire territory of the state is incorporated into municipal units, annexation is virtually prohibited. In the more rapidly growing sections of the country, however, annexation is a significant activity and an effective means of gaining control over developing territory.

In several states the prospect of future annexation is implicitly recognized in the grant to major communities of extraterritorial powers in regard to planning, zoning, and subdivision control. For a distance ranging from one and one-half to three miles beyond the city limits, cities are given the same controls over development as they exercise within the city limits. This insures that new subdivisions will meet existing standards within the municipality at the time the territory is annexed.

State enabling laws for annexation generally prescribe one or more of the following five procedures for determining the territory to be annexed, and may frequently include features from two or more of the methods described.

Popular Vote. Most annexation procedures require some expression from voters or property owners in the territory proposed for annexation, although some laws require a similar vote from the electorate of the enlarged municipality. In other cases, where the territory to be annexed is part of some kind of existing unit, a vote may be required from the electorate in the balance of the area not to be annexed. Such provisions are frequently troublesome although justified in terms of the principle of selfdetermination or home rule. Fear of change and the possibility of higher taxes frequently works against objective voting.

Municipal Legislative Determination. In some of the larger western states the existing city may, under certain conditions, act on its own to annex adjacent territory. Restrictions are frequently stated in terms of the character of the territory to be annexed, its size, or the class of city to which the annexing power is granted. This is an effective means of annexation but tends to give too much decision power to existing municipal authorities, who may choose to take only land which increases the tax base while avoiding settled areas needing urban services.

Judicial Finding. The laws of some states spell out a procedure under which an independent tribunal or agency, not directly involved, can take action to bring about annexation, but such procedures are often cumbersome and have been seriously questioned by students of constitutional law. In addition, the courts are not accustomed to the type of technical investigations which are appropriate for determining the desirability of expanding the boundaries of a community.

Administrative Finding. Another type of impartial determination is exercised by boards created by the enabling legislation in about eight states. These boards may take the form of a local boundary commission, as in Alaska and Minnesota, with power to regulate both annexation and incorporation proceedings.

Special Legislation. In most of the states, annexation actions can be handled by a special act of the legislature. This method is frequently used when necessary to avoid problems involved in some of the preceding methods. As with any special legislation favoring a specific municipality, the dangers of political logrolling are acute.

The planning agency should play a major

role in studying the feasibility and appropriate nature of an annexation proposal. It should pay particular attention to specific requirements of state enabling laws and limit its investigation of the proposed annexation to a careful consideration of the factors or standards specified in the law, which often differ according to the method of annexation to be used. It is customary that territory to be annexed be unincorporated, contiguous to existing city boundaries, and compact in form. Some laws may prescribe the density of development which must exist before the territory becomes eligible for annexation, while other states require some evidence of the expanding city's ability to supply services to the annexed area.

A typical annexation study will contain many of the elements of a comprehensive planning study, but will give special attention to the more limited area under consideration. Particular emphasis should be given to determining present and future population and the services needed to serve them. The annexation study will also include many aspects of a capital improvement program in relating investment and operating costs for providing services to prospective tax revenues of the area to be annexed. Close cooperation with the finance officials of the city is essential for this type of study to be realistically carried out.

A number of states have established commissions to oversee the process of annexation, so that the resulting action conforms to standards of land development and adequacy of municipal services. Chapter 2 discusses the role of the state in this area.

EXTENSION OF SERVICES

City policies regarding the extension of services can do much to determine the specific location of new development. On the outskirts of cities, whether within or beyond incorporated limits, the pattern of major roads and the time distance from centers of employment are the principal factors in discussions leading to the location of the new large-scale subdivision plats. Major developers may have greater freedom of location if their projects are large enough to absorb the costs of collector roads, but they are faced with other constraints in finding large available tracts for their projects.

In providing utilities, the muncipality's ability to control varies in accordance with investment costs and difficulty of construction involved. Telephone and electric power lines are placed with relative ease and little expense in relation to the revenues which can be derived from them. In most instances the municipality is not directly involved in the provision of these services.

However, a much greater proportion of U.S. cities—more than two thirds—supply and distribute water. A public agency usually makes the decisions for the extension of mains and the opening up of service to developing areas. It should be possible to coordinate these decisions with other factors in selecting areas for the encouragement of private development.

After road access, the most significant factor in determining the priority of development is the provision of sanitary facilities. The existence of sewer service is a primary determinant of residential density. Zoning controls for the most part recognize that urban densities are inappropriate in areas dependent on individual sanitary facilities such as septic tanks. A decision to open an area to sewer service is often the decisive factor in the timing of its development.

Through the capital improvement program, the typical planning agency—in cooperation with municipal operating agencies and, in some instances, private utility companies—can play a strong role in selecting areas for extension of services. The type of analysis needed prior to a decision by one of these agencies should be generally comparable to the annexation analysis.

OFFICIAL MAPPING

The official map is a somewhat neglected device authorized in the planning enabling legislation of many states. Basically, the official map is a document, adopted by the legislative body of the community, that pinpoints the location of future streets and other public facilities. It is based on the principle which, in early planning laws, established building set-back lines to provide for future street widening. In effect, the official map serves notice on developers that the municipality intends to acquire certain specified property. Where such mapping is carried to excess this can inhibit development. If drawn in a realistic manner, however, the official map can serve as a positive and expediting influence for sound development by reserving sites for public improvements in anticipation of actual need.

The official map should not be confused with other planning measures. It is not intended to function as a comprehensive or general plan and it is not suited to dealing with the long term periods covered in such plans. The official map should be well coordinated with the capital improvement program of a community. In general, projects which are sufficiently defined to fall within the time-period of the capital improvement program would be proper subjects to include in the official map, which places an obligation on the community to acquire the property when it is subjected to development pressures. Consequently, it is unwise to indicate items on the official map which might lead the community into premature acquisition before firm locational decisions are made.

Three principal stages in the official mapping process are established in most enabling legislation: preparation, adoption, and maintenance.

Preparation.   Customarily, the planning agency would be charged with the preparation of the official map but because its production requires some engineering precision, it is essential that it be prepared in cooperation with the city engineer or other municipal engineering official. Some legislation also requires the legal description of properties shown on the official map to be incorporated. This calls for collaboration with the city attorney.

Adoption.   The official map is usually submitted to the governing body of the municipality which customarily holds a public hearing, after which the official map is adopted in whole or in part, sometimes with modifications based on the hearing. Copies are then placed not only in the city council records, but in the appropriate office where deeds and similar public property records are maintained. The ordinance or other instrument of adoption generally prohibits any development within the areas defined in the official map until notice, within a prescribed time limit, has been served on the city. This gives the city an opportunity to acquire specific properties through normal acquisition procedures. The particular details should be consistent with state enabling laws.

Maintenance.   The official map generally is modified periodically. A well-organized planning operation calls for modification of the official map in line with specific proposals of each annual capital improvement program. Presumably, the modifications made would be consistent with the general provisions of the comprehensive plan.

The official map need not be limited to the proposals of the municipal government itself. Other agencies should be encouraged to submit proposals for consideration and adoption by the city council within the framework of the official map, but any changes proposed should of course be referred to the planning agency for review and recommendation.

The official map technique has in recent years enjoyed a wider application in relation to a number of new programs designed to deal with problems of urban growth. In a sense, many urban renewal plans are an expression consistent with the official map, and their definitions of public areas can be incorporated into the overall document. The official map can also be used in the development of expressway proposals when state highway planning agencies indicate in advance the rights-of-way which will ultimately need to be acquired. The same is true of park and school sites and some major utility proposals.

A major problem in official map programs is whether to include all existing street rights-of-way and public properties as part of the official map. In most communities, there are elaborate procedures for the dedication of rights-of-way and recording of street boundaries. It is frequently a formidable task to record all of these systematically in a single document, and to read such a document. If a choice must be made, attention should be focused on the use of the official map to protect future public land areas rather than to catalog existing rights-of-way and public properties.

Part Five

Implementation:
Regulation and Renewal

15

Zoning

It is usually accepted that the beginning of contemporary zoning was the adoption, in 1916, by the city of New York of a zoning ordinance which regulated the use and location of buildings throughout the city. Looking back on that pioneering effort, it is easy to see the great progress made since that rather cumbersome and crude document, which nonetheless represented monumental advance, since it was the first effective attempt at coordinated action to control land use by an American municipal government.

Zoning is essentially a means of insuring that the land uses of a community are properly situated in relation to one another, providing adequate space for each type of development. It allows the control of development density in each area so that property can be adequately serviced by such governmental facilities as the street, school, recreation, and utilities systems. This directs new growth into appropriate areas and protects existing property by requiring that development afford adequate light, air and privacy for persons living and working within the municipality.

Nature of Zoning

Zoning is probably the single most commonly used legal device available for implementing the land-use plan of a community. To paraphrase the U.S. Department of Commerce Department 1924 Standard Zoning Enabling Act, on which most present-day legislation is based, zoning may be defined as the division of a municipality (or other governmental unit)

into districts, and the regulation within those districts of:

1. The height and bulk of buildings and other structures;
2. The area of a lot which may be occupied and the size of required open spaces;
3. The density of population;
4. The use of buildings and land for trade, industry, residence, or other purposes.

Of major importance for the individual citizen is the part zoning plays in stabilizing and preserving property values. It affects the taxation of property as an element of value to be considered in assessment. Ordinarily, zoning is only indirectly concerned with achieving aesthetic ends, although there has been an increasing tendency to include within zoning ordinances provisions which are most solidly based on "general welfare" concepts.

An examination of cases where the courts have passed on zoning provisions which sought to impose some kind of aesthetic control reveals a very slow trend toward liberality. This is exhibited not as a specific acceptance of aesthetics as a sound basis for exercise of the police power, but rather by a liberalization of the definition of "the public welfare."

The classic case which bears on this point is that of Berman v. Parker (348 U.S. 26, 75 Sup. Ct. 98, 99 L. Ed. 27, 1954) in which Mr. Justice Douglas, in delivering the opinion of the court stated:

. . . The concept of the public welfare is broad and inclusive. . . . The values it represents are spiritual as well as physical, aesthetic as well as monetary. It is within the power of the legislature to determine that the community should be beautiful as well as healthy, spacious as well as clean, well-balanced as well as carefully patrolled. . . .

In general, it may be said that the prevailing view in the United States is still against aesthetic zoning on the face of it, but there is considerable sympathy under the surface. While no state court of appeal has upheld a provision in an ordinance directed solely at aesthetic ends, a number of decisions incorporate supporting dicta and several lower courts have taken this view.

It seems clear that aesthetics are not beyond the reach of police power protection and the degree of protection afforded may well be expected to increase in the future as the reflection of a steadily mounting concern for protection of the environment.

It is now well established through numerous court decisions, that zoning may not be used to accomplish racial segregation.

LEGAL NATURE

Zoning is an exercise of the basic power of the state, and its political subdivisions, to enact legislation protecting the public health, safety, morals and general welfare of its citizens. This means that each regulation in the zoning ordinance must bear a reasonable and substantial relationship to these ends or it will be found in violation of the "due process" clauses of state and federal constitutions. While the constitutionality of zoning has been upheld by a long series of court decisions—notably the landmark case of *Euclid v. Ambler Realty Co.* (272 US 365), decided by the United States Supreme Court in 1926—the courts will still examine the application of individual provisions to individual pieces of property to see whether the specific restrictions imposed meet constitutional requirements.

The power to zone, like other regulatory powers, is customarily derived by municipalities from the state legislature. Except for certain "home rule" cities, a municipality, therefore, must show that its zoning ordinance not only meets constitutional standards, but also meets the legislative requirements set forth in the state enabling act, relative to substantive provisions and the procedures followed in its enactment and administration. Many zoning

decisions and ordinances have been invalidated merely through defects in these two areas.

The characteristic feature of the zoning ordinance that distinguishes it from most other regulations is that it differs from district to district, rather than being uniform throughout the city. Thus, a given area might be restricted to single-family residential development with height regulations, minimum lot size requirements, and setback provisions appropriate for that kind of development. In other areas, commercial or industrial development might be permitted, and regulations for those areas would be enacted to control such development. Building code provisions or sanitary regulations, on the other hand, normally apply to all buildings in a certain category regardless of where they may be situated within a city.

This characteristic feature carries with it the special danger that local legislative bodies may be tempted to give arbitrary and discriminatory treatment to certain individual property owners. Recognizing this danger, state legislatures, in the zoning enabling acts, and the courts, through decisions involving zoning ordinances, have imposed restrictions on local legislative power.

First, the usual enabling act, while permitting regulations to differ for different districts, requires that within a district the regulations must be uniform for each class and kind of building. For instance the regulations in a certain class of residential zone must be the same for every such zone throughout the municipality.

Second, the legislatures and the courts have insisted that there be a reasonable basis for classifying particular areas differently from others.

Third, the courts have insisted that an ordinance cover the entire jurisdictional area of the city, rather than singling out a small area for regulation and leaving the remainder of the city unrestricted.

Fourth, the courts insist that the regulations be reasonable in their application to particular properties. Thus, it makes little sense to zone property for a use which it cannot physically accommodate. Residential single family zoning in areas subject to frequent flooding is an example of this restriction.

The most effective way of meeting all of these requirements is to base the ordinance on a carefully conceived land-use plan (or "comprehensive plan") for the entire city, such as described elsewhere in this book, for this tends to minimize distinctions based on the ownership of a particular piece of land and to magnify considerations of general application.

ZONING AND COMPREHENSIVE PLANNING

From the attention given the subject by legal writers and in court decisions, it is clear that confusion exists as to the distinction between "city planning" and "zoning." In reality, zoning is one of many legal and administrative devices by which city plans may be implemented. Most of the confusion has arisen out of the fact that many cities adopted zoning ordinances before embarking on full-scale planning. Consequently, persons outside the planning profession have not always understood the logical connection between the two concepts.

It has already been pointed out that a zoning ordinance is more likely to be on a sound legal basis when it is based on a carefully conceived plan. In addition, a zoning ordinance that is adopted and not based on a plan will have the following adverse effects:

1. There will be a tendency for development to be frozen in the existing pattern, if it is at all effective;

2. Wholly unexpected results may be produced, frequently of a very undesirable nature;

3. The ordinance may require amendment to such an extent, on behalf of individual property owners, that no comprehensive pattern of development in the city can result.

Many of the newer state enabling acts recognize the desirability of treating zoning as part of an overall planning program by providing that the planning commission be responsible for formulating the zoning ordinance initially, and for making recommendations to the local legislature on all proposed amendments.

ZONING AS DISTINGUISHED FROM OTHER DEVICES

It is desirable that zoning be used in a coordinated manner with other devices for carrying out plans, and that there be a clear understanding of the difference between zoning and these other devices.

Zoning has nothing to do with the materials and manner of construction of a building; these are covered by the building code. Also, the zoning ordinance may not be properly used to set minimum costs of permitted structures, and it commonly does not control their appearance. These matters are ordinarily controlled by private restrictive covenants contained in the deeds to property. There are, however, some examples, particularly in relation to historic buildings and areas, where zoning has been and is being used effectively. There appears to be a trend toward a greater acceptance of aesthetic control as a proper function of the zoning ordinance.

The zoning ordinance does not regulate the design of streets, the installation of utilities, the reservation or dedication of parks, street rights-of-way, and school sites, and related matters. These are controlled by subdivision regulations and possibly by an official map preserving the beds of proposed streets against encroachment. The zoning ordinance should, however, be carefully coordinated with these and other control devices. It is becoming more common for the provisions of many of these separate ordinances to be combined into a single comprehensive ordinance, usually called a land development control ordinance.

Zoning is primarily prospective rather than retroactive in its effect and cannot, as a result, be relied on as a major device for correcting existing conditions. These are customarily attacked through minimum housing standards, requiring rehabilitation or destruction of individual substandard structures; nuisance abatement for the correction of particularly bad conditions; and urban renewal powers for the condemnation, clearance and rebuilding of blighted areas. Finally, although in many respects it may overlap the coverage of nuisance-control ordinances, banning particular types of land use throughout specified areas or all of the city, the zoning ordinance is concerned with more than the regulation of nuisances and is not dependent upon the law of nuisance for its legal validity.

PROPERTY SUBJECT TO ZONING

The zoning ordinance is designed particularly to control private development, as distinguished from public improvements. All private property within the governmental unit's jurisdiction is usually subject to its terms. In addition, a number of state courts have held that property owned by a municipality or county for "proprietary" purposes—functions such as the water system, the electrical system or the city market—rather than for "governmental" purposes, is subject to the city's zoning ordinance. Occasionally a statute makes other types of governmental properties subject to municipal zoning; for example, a state statute in North Carolina makes property of the state, as well as the property of local units, subject to local zoning ordinances. Even if this control is not legally required, it is desirable to specify in the zoning ordinance the districts in which recreational facilities, schools, museums, libraries, city garages, land fills, incinerators, fire stations, city halls and other public buildings are permitted, and the regulations controlling them.

SPECIAL TYPES OF ZONING

Zoning has been applied to other problems besides the control of urban development. Over half of the states, notably Wisconsin, have authorized counties to zone rural areas. Under the Wisconsin act, counties may specify areas for agricultural development, forestry, and recreational use. Counties thus may prevent agricultural use of submarginal lands better suited to forestry, and they may prevent inappropriate settlement of isolated areas.

In some other states rural zoning has been used largely as a means of regulating billboards and other forms of outdoor advertising. A few states have granted their counties authority to adopt "flood plain zoning" ordinances so that citizens can receive the benefits of any federally backed flood insurance. Most states also authorize airport zoning ordinances, by means of which the height of trees and structures in the vicinity of airports may be regulated. As the national concern for the preservation and res-

toration of historic sites and buildings has mounted, more states have enacted legislation empowering municipalities to pass zoning ordinances dealing with the designation and control of historic areas. The cities of Charleston, South Carolina; Norfolk and Williamsburg, Virginia; Salem and Nantucket, Massachusetts; and Providence, Rhode Island, are among those that have well-developed proposals for action in this field.

TERRITORIAL COVERAGE

The earliest zoning enabling acts granted power only to municipalities, and restricted these powers to areas within municipal limits. It has been widely recognized for some time that this is inadequate. With an increasing proportion of new development taking place outside existing municipal limits, it is apparent that the zoning ordinance will have little effect if it cannot be applied to these areas of growth as well as to the older developed areas inside the municipal limits.

In general, three approaches have been followed in dealing with the problem of urban expansion. First, well over half of the states have authorized some or all of their counties to zone. County zoning has the advantage in most cases of affording wide geographic coverage as opposed to the control by villages, towns, townships, etc., which may cover very limited geographic areas; for instance, one township in New Jersey is totally occupied by four houses on 15,000 square foot lots. Unless the county is permitted to zone portions, as well as the whole of its area, residents of rural areas who are unable to appreciate the benefits of zoning may be able to block any effective zoning action, no matter how much it is needed in the unincorporated fringe areas around cities.

The second approach is to create a special planning region which may be composed of a portion of a single county or of parts or all of several counties. It may be established by direct action of the state legislature, by a state agency such as the state planning commission, or by mutual agreement among cities and counties involved, under appropriate enabling legislation. A planning commission for the region is customarily given the duty of preparing a zoning ordinance, which may then be adopted by the various governmental units affected, or by the planning commission itself. This approach gives coverage to the areas where growth is taking place, and provides representation for the citizens to be regulated. Legal questions may arise when the planning commission is given authority to adopt the zoning regulations, however, and practical problems of coordination may arise if this power is given instead to a number of local governmental units, but this is not to suggest that the presence of coordination difficulties should prohibit the use of this solution. Additionally, the mere meeting together of representatives of political subdivisions sometimes has a beneficial effect.

The third approach is to grant cities extraterritorial zoning powers. Although it has been common practice to give cities such powers for the control of subdivisions, there are comparatively few states which grant extraterritorial zoning powers. The constitutionality of such grants, where the distance involved is reasonable, seems to be fairly clear. The advantage of this approach is that the city ordinarily has both an administrative organization to handle the job effectively and an incentive to do so, since the areas involved are usually of primary importance to the city. The major disadvantage is a lack of representation on the municipal legislative body for citizens of the outside area affected. In some measure this disadvantage may be offset by granting representation on the planning commission and the zoning board of adjustments (or appeals).

A related problem is how to deal with the zoning of metropolitan areas cutting across the boundaries of many local government units. The solution to this problem seems to lie in a new form of governmental organization, such as metropolitan Toronto, Ontario; Metropolitan Dade County, Florida; or the Metropolitan Government of Nashville and Davidson County, Tennessee. In the absence of a metropolitan government, the courts have, in a number of cases, recognized the area-wide implications of particular zoning requirements, where the zoning actions of one municipality would have an undesirable impact upon neighboring jurisdictions or the area as a whole.

Thus it may be seen that, in general, the power to zone may be transferred by the state through enabling acts to either the local, the county, or the regional level. Some states authorize all three types of zoning, while others restrict the power to the local level, depending on the nature of development within the state and the system of land use control that would appear to be appropriate.

The principle underlying the three types of zoning is similar, as a review of various enabling acts will reveal, but the concerns of a municipal, a county, and a regional agency will usually vary considerably and will be reflected in the provisions of the zoning ordinances and in the categories of districts or "zones" shown on the accompanying maps.

The municipality will be concerned with the detailed control of development appropriate to an urban environment, and with the protection of its peripheral areas from undesirable and uncontrolled development in the surrounding county area.

The county, if it is rural in nature, may contain several municipalities, most of which will administer their own zoning, surrounded by large areas of unincorporated agricultural land, and sometimes virgin territory. The county will then be concerned with controlling development at municipal boundaries and, to the extent possible, coordinating with the municipal regulations thus preventing undesirable development and possible strain on law enforcement and health agencies.

However, it will also be concerned with the protection of the countryside, the fostering of agricultural industry and its protection from other types of incompatible industrial enterprises. It may be concerned too with the encouragement of tourism as an industry where the natural endowments of the county lend themselves to this, and with the general development of other natural resources. All these concerns will be reflected in the zoning ordinance regulations which will therefore differ in nature from the municipal counterpart, although the structure of the two documents will bear a strong resemblance. The more urban in nature a county becomes, the more it may be expected that the contents of the zoning ordinance will resemble its municipal counterpart. In some states the county may zone inside incorporated areas if such areas have not adopted a zoning ordinance.

Zoning at the regional level will differ in that it represents a coordinating function and will usually be carried out by a body with joint representation from its constituent counties. A regional planning commission constituted in this manner may have the authority to prepare various codes and ordinances for its area of jurisdiction, including a zoning ordinance, but these are advisory only and must be approved and adopted by the counties before they have force of law. However, it may be seen that complete coordination of development control may be achieved by such a regional body. It shares the same concerns as its constituent counties, but in addition, can appraise the overall situation with far greater clarity than could a single county, and can make provisions for the control of development that will be advantageous to the whole region.

Purely on the grounds of simplicity and clarity this chapter refers generally to zoning at the municipal level, but the reader should bear in mind that similar activities, problems and administrative practices may also occur at both the county and the regional level. The details will vary with the powers and obligations with which the responsible bodies are vested by the applicable state enabling acts as reflected in their zoning ordinances.

Preparing the Zoning Ordinance

The drafting of some municipal ordinances may be accomplished merely by inserting the name of the city in the appropriate places in a "model" ordinance or by substituting the name of the city in another city's ordinance. This method is not possible with the zoning ordinance, because it deals with patterns of land development (past and present) that differ from city to city. Although many provisions (especially those dealing with amendment and enforcement procedures) may be standardized, the zoning ordinance as a whole must be tailored to the needs of a specific city.

The city wishing to adopt a zoning ordinance is confronted with two sets of requirements. The first is the set of procedural requirements contained in the zoning enabling act, with which there must be rigid compliance if the ordinance is to be upheld by the courts. The second is a related set of substantive requirements, that is, there must be an adequate basis in logic for each of the zoning regulations and the regulations must produce the desired end results.

These requirements have a bearing on the legislative body's choice of personnel to assist the planning commission in preparing the zoning ordinance. In order to insure compliance with the first or procedural set of requirements, the chief legal officer of the municipality should be consulted as to the procedures required by statute, and his advice should be followed at each step. With respect to the second or substantive set of requirments, the city attorney should play a secondary role. The major part of the drafting job should be done by a trained planner, either a full-time staff member of the local government or a consultant hired for the purpose. The ordinance should be based on basic population, economic, and land-use studies and on the goals desired for the planning area, all of which have been discussed in earlier chapters. Its contents will, in general, depend more on planning considerations than on legal requirements, although it must, of course, meet both sets of criteria. The average municipal attorney cannot be expected to be an expert in planning and zoning; it is as unrealistic to ask him to undertake the functions of such an expert as it would be to ask the planner to perform as an attorney.

The exact procedure to be followed in preparing and adopting a zoning ordinance will vary somewhat from state to state, because of differences in the enabling acts. The recommended general procedure is as follows.

WHO PREPARES THE ORDINANCE?

The first step required by most enabling acts is the creation of a planning commission or a zoning commission, which is given the duties of preparing a tentative zoning ordinance, holding public hearings, and submitting the ordinance to the local legislature for adoption. Where the statute permits, the planning commission, rather than a separate zoning commission should always be given these tasks. This is because the planning commission's duties, in general, require it to make the same studies as those needed to prepare a zoning ordinance, and it would be a wasteful duplication to name another agency to act in the same area.

The zoning ordinance is one of the necessary tools for implementing the community's land use plan and, therefore, should be prepared along with this plan by the planning commission, which, as a continuing body, remains available for advice from time to time concerning amendments to the ordinance.

Where a zoning commission is appointed, the enabling act usually provides that it will go out of existence as soon as it submits an ordinance that is adopted by the governing body.

GATHERING NECESSARY INFORMATION

The group selected to prepare the ordinance begins its work by assembling information on which to base the ordinance. If the planning commission has prepared a land use plan, commonly most of this information will have been collected in the course of preparing that plan. Among the types of information that will prove useful are the following:

1. The existing use of every piece of property within the city;

2. The terms of restrictive covenants applying to large sections of the city;

3. The location and capacities of all utility lines and major streets;

4. The assessed valuation of properties in different sections of the city;

5. The location of all new buildings erected during the past five years;

6. The location and characteristics of all vacant land in the city;

7. The widths of streets;

8. The sizes of front, side, and rear yards;

9. The heights of buildings;

10. The dimensions of lots;

11. The number of families in each dwelling.

When this information has been gathered and mapped, it should be analyzed. Statistical studies of the amount of land actually used for different types of dwellings, businesses, and industries will aid in forecasting future land requirements for these uses, when coupled with other analyses. Predominant patterns of land use, yard sizes, building heights, population densities, and other data in different neighborhoods should be noted. Land valuations, restrictive covenants, and the availability of services may determine what areas are suitable for particular types of development and the direction and trends of growth may be identified. Such studies will serve as a starting point for determination of the classes of districts that should be provided and where they should be located.

PREPARING A TENTATIVE ORDINANCE

Almost all zoning ordinances consist of two parts: a map delineating the various districts or zones within the city, and written regulations controlling the manner in which property may be used in each of these districts. It is a mistake to attempt to describe district boundaries in the text of the ordinance, since they can be shown much more easily on a map which is more readily understood by the citizen. Although the preparation of both sections must proceed more or less simultaneously, in most cases it is easier to begin with the map and then prepare detailed regulations in consonance with the characteristics of the districts to which they will apply.

PREPARING THE MAP

In preparing the zoning map, it is necessary to answer a number of questions:

1. How many sets of districts shall there be?

2. How much space should be allocated to each type of district?

3. What types of land are suitable for each type of district?

4. What should be the physical relationships between various types of districts?

5. Where should the various districts be located, in general?

6. Where should the exact boundary lines of each district run?

Figure 15–1 shows a typical zoning map for a medium size city.

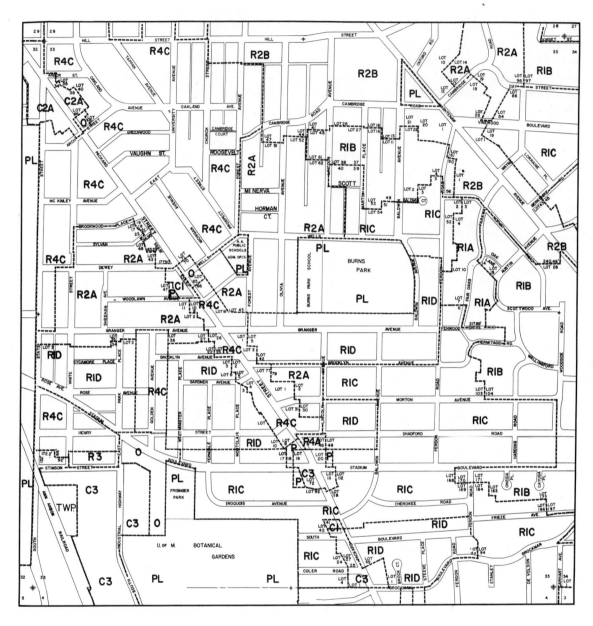

ZONING DISTRICT CLASSIFICATIONS:

AG	Agricultural District	
R1A, R1B, R1C, R1D		
	One-Family Dwelling Districts	
R2A	Two-Family Dwelling District	
R2B	" " " and Student	
	Housing District	
R3	Terrace Family Dwelling District	
R4A, R4B, R4C, R4D		
	Multi-Family Dwelling Districts	
R5	Motel-Hotel District	
R6	Mobile Home Park District	

P	Parking District
O	Office District
PL	Public Lands District
RE	Research District
C-1	Local Business District
C2A	Central Business District
C2B	Business Service District
C-3	Fringe Commercial District
M-1	Limited Industrial District
M-2	Heavy Industrial District

FIGURE 15–1. *Zoning map, Ann Arbor, Michigan*

SETS OF DISTRICTS

Although some of the early zoning ordinances had separate sets of "use districts," "area districts," and "height districts," the zoning ordinance is much easier to understand and use if a single set of districts is mapped. These districts may differ in regard to the uses permitted, the lot sizes and yards required, the permitted heights, or other criteria, but all permitted categories are shown on a single map and in a single table. The user has thus to refer only to one place in the ordinance to find the regulations applicable to his property.

TYPES OF DISTRICTTS

No standard rule can be followed for the number of district types that ought to be provided for a given jurisdiction. It is necessary to examine existing and proposed development with some care, and then to devise appropriate categories to take care of most land uses in that municipality. In general, the smaller city will have a fewer number of district types than a larger city or county, but this is not invariable. To some extent, it depends on the degree to which individual situations are to be covered specifically in the zoning ordinance.

The starting point for any categorization of uses is the "big three," namely residential, commercial, and industrial.

Residential uses may be further subdivided into two or more classes differentiated according to the types of dwellings permitted, i.e., single family, two family, multiple family; according to compatible uses in each district, for example, country clubs, hospitals, cemeteries, clinics; according to minimum lot sizes and yards required; or on some other basis.

Commercial or business uses may be subclassified according to the kinds or sizes of stores permitted; according to locations (central business district and neighborhood business districts); according to the kinds of merchandising undertaken (retail and wholesale); according to the maximum building height permitted, or on some other basis.

Industrial districts may be classified according to the type of industry permitted such as light industrial or heavy industrial, but contemporary practice favors classification by

means of performance standards which specify the degree of noise, odor, heat, vibration, smoke, dust, glare, etc. that will be tolerated.

In addition there may be special-purpose districts, such as agricultural districts, office and institution districts, estate districts, highway service districts, motor freight terminal districts, planned industrial districts, university districts and others, as may be appropriate to meet the special needs of the area concerned.

OTHER CONSIDERATIONS

A determination of the area to be allocated to each type of district, the types of land suited to particular types of development, the best physical arrangement for the various districts, and the general locations for particular districts, are all matters that should be decided in the formulation of the land use plan of the municipality. In mapping zoning districts, the planner usually is forced to compromise between the districting pattern dictated by existing development and that called for by the land use plan for the future. The land use plan then becomes a guide for this decision process, as well as for the deliberations to be followed in making later amendments to the ordinance.

A peculiarly difficult part of the districting process is the drawing of exact boundary lines between districts, since all boundary lines are somewhat arbitrary, and individual property owners are likely to raise protests that are hard to resolve. As a general rule, it is better to run the boundaries of a district along or parallel to rear lot lines, than through the center of a street. Where one side of a street is zoned for business and the other for residential use, there is a strong temptation for the legislative bodies and courts to authorize business uses on the residential side of the street. Where a district line runs parallel to side lot lines, it should avoid splitting a lot. Frequently when a block is divided in this manner, an effort is made to modify the effect of the boundary line on neighboring properties by the introduction of intermediate or "transition zone" provisions to be met by those properties.

DRAFTING THE REGULATIONS

When the city has been divided into tentative

Table 15-1

Schedule of Area, Height, Bulk, and Placement Regulations

Zoning District	Maximum Usable Floor Area in Percentage of Lot Area	Minimum Lot Area Per Dwelling Unit in sq. ft.	Minimum Usable Floor Area per Dwelling Unit in sq. ft.	Required Setback Line Minimum Dimensions in Feet				Maximum Height		Minimum Lot Size	
				Front	Side Least One	Side Total of Two	Rear	In feet	In stories	Area in sq. ft.	Width in ft.
5:25 AG	None	100,000	None	40 Min. for road-side stands only is 30.	10% of the lot width.	20% of the lot width.	50	30	2½	100,000	200
5:26 RIA	None	20,000	None	40	10% of the lot width.	20% of the lot width.	50	30	2½	20,000	90
5:27 RIB	None	10,000	None	30	10% of the lot width.	20% of the lot width.	40	30	2½	10,000	70
5:28 RIC	None	7,200	None	25	5	20% of the lot width.	30	30	2½	7,200	60
5:29 RID	None	5,000	None	25	3	15% of lot width.	20	30	2½	5,000	40
5:30 R2A	None	3,600	1 BR 600 2 BR 800 3 BR 1000	25	5	25% of the lot width.	30	30	2½	7,200	60
5:31 R2B	None	3,600 except that for dormitories, minimum lot area shall be 350 sq. ft. per occupant.	1 BR 600 2 BR 800 3 BR 1000	25	8 or 10% of the lot width, whichever is larger.	18 or 25% of the lot width, whichever is larger.	30	40	3	7,200	60

Source: City of Ann Arbor, Michigan, zoning ordinance.

zoning districts, the next step is to make detailed analyses of these districts and to draft suitable regulations. In order to pass the test of reasonableness, the regulations must bear a relationship to conditions as they exist. On the other hand, the regulations may properly be used to prod landowners toward higher standards as envisioned in the land use plan. More detailed discussion of the content of the ordinance will be found in a subsequent section of this chapter.

The form in which the ordinance is presented has an important effect on its acceptance by the city council and by the public. In general, the easier an ordinance is to use and understand, the greater will be the likelihood of public acceptance during required hearings.

Several devices have been used to simplify the presentation of a zoning ordinance. One is to include among the initial provisions a section describing in general terms the purpose of each district and the types of uses permitted therein. This provides useful background for the public and for the board of adjustment, the planning commission, city council, and the courts in interpreting the spirit and intention of the ordinance. Great care should be exercised in drafting these statements of intent, since they will be significant in guiding detailed work on the basic ordinance and will be useful in decisions on future amendments. Statements of intent are often the first item describing the regulations for each district. The philosophy underlying the detailed requirements may thus be ascertained with ease. The intellectual rigor of thinking through the purposes of a particular part of the proposed ordinance will also aid in keeping all details of the regulations in line with the stated purposes.

A second device is to present the regulations for the various districts in the form of a table rather than a text. A schedule of Area, Height and Bulk Regulations such as that shown as Table 15–1 greatly reduces the length of the ordinance and makes it easier to use. Large cities usually have complex ordinances and a tabular presentation may not be possible, although the New York City Zoning Ordinance makes good use of this technique. When it is not possible or desirable to reduce all the district regulations to tabular form, a summary table showing major regulations for each district may be employed to amplify the regular text, particularly for popularized versions. Table 15–2 illustrates such a summary.

A third method, which is becoming increasingly popular, is to include drawings in the ordinance, to simplify some of the definitions and to illustrate particular regulations. Examples of such illustrations are given in Figures 15–2 and 15–3.

A fourth device is to include a detailed set of property maps, showing the lines of each lot in the city, so as to make clear the locations of district boundary lines. These maps also prove useful to the board of adjustment, planning commission, and legislature in picturing the effects of proposed variances or amendments to the zoning ordinance.

Another helpful step is to underscore or italicize in the text of the ordinance all words defined in the Definitions section. This insures that the user will not overlook the word which may have a special meaning in that context. For example, the term "family," as used in the ordinance, may differ from popular definition.

As a general rule, it should be remembered that the zoning ordinance is normally consulted to find out how a particular piece of property is zoned and how it may be used or developed. Thus the total length of the document is not important but it is vital that the reader be able to obtain with speed and clarity information on the ordinance regulating the property in which he is interested.

HEARINGS ON THE TENTATIVE ORDINANCE

Because of its major role in shaping the future community, it is important for the zoning ordinance to reflect the citizens' views. It is also vital for the public to understand and support the ordinance, because many people who are prevented from carrying out their individual plans will undoubtedly oppose it. In order to meet these criteria, the usual enabling act provides for the holding of public hearings by the planning or zoning commission and by the local legislature prior to adoption of an ordinance.

Table 15–2

Land Use Regulations, Sacramento, California

The uses shown in this table are divided into four groups: Residential, Industrial, Commercial, and Other. To determine in which zone a specific use is allowed: (1) Find the use in one of the groups in the table. (2) Read across the chart until either a number or X appears in one of the columns. (3) If a number appears this means that the use is allowed in the zone represented by that column, but only if certain conditions are complied with. The conditions applicable to that use are those listed below the table. The number appearing in the zoning column corresponds to the number of the conditions which must be complied with. (4) If an X appears in a column the use is allowed in the zone represented by that column without being subject to any of the conditions listed.

Use	R1	R2	R2A	R3	R4	R5	O-B	S-C	C1	C2	C3	C4	M1 / M1-S	M2 / M2-S	A	F
B. Residential																
1. Apartments			X	X	X	X		1	1	1	5	13	13	13		
2. Rooming-boarding house	2	2	2	2	X	X		1	1	1	5	13	13	13		
3. Single family dwelling	X	X	X	X	X	X		1	1	1	5	13	13	13	X	
4. Two family dwelling	3	X	X	X	X	X		1	1	1	5	13	13	13		
5. Fraternity—sorority house—dormitory	5	5	5	5	15	15		5	5	15	5	13	13	13		
C. Commercial																
1. Advertising signs & structures							See Section No. 7									
2. Agricultural uses, general															X	X
3. Amusement centers, indoor only								X	X	X	X	X	X	X		
4. Auto sales, service, storage, rental									8	8	X	X	X	X		
5. Bakery or bakery goods store									9	9	X	X	X	X		
6. Bank—savings and loan								X	X	X	X	X	X	X		
7. Barber, beauty shop								X	X	X	X	X	X	X		
8. Business college, trade school								X	X	X	X	X	X	X		
9. Cabinet shop									4	4	X	X	X	X		
10. Cleaning plant, commercial									9	9	X	X	X	X		
11. Cleaning, laundry agency								X	X	X	X	X	X	X		
12. Dance, music, voice studio								X	X	X	X	X	X	X		
13. Drive-in restaurant—food stand								X		X	X	X	X	X		
14. Equipment rental & sales yard										10	10	10	10	10		
15. Florist								X	X	X	X	X	X	X		
16. Food store, delicatessen								X	X	X	X	X	X	X		
17. Furniture refinishing									4	4	X	X	X	X		
18. Furniture store								X	X	X	X	X	X	X		
19. Hotel								5		X	X	X	X	X		
20. Laboratory—medical, dental, optical							14	X	X	X	X	X	X	X		
21. Laundry, commercial plant									9	9	X	X	X	X		
22. Laundromat								X	X	X	X	X	X	X		
23. Mortuary									X	X	X	X	X	X		
24. Motel								5		X	X	X	X	X		
25. Nursery for children	6	6	6	6	6	6		X	X	X	X	X	X	X		
26. Nursery for flower and plants								X	X	X	X	X	X	X		
27. Offices							7	11	X	X	X	X	X	X		
28. Parking lot, garage or facility								X	X	X	5	X	X	X		
29. Photographic studio								X	X	X	X	X	X	X		
30. Prescription pharmacy, optician							14	X	X	X	X	X	X	X		
31. Printing & blueprinting									X	X	X	X	X	X		
32. Reducing salon—masseur								X	X	X	X	X	X	X		

Table 15–2

(continued)

Use	R1	R2	R2A	R3	R4	R5	OB	SC	C1	C2	C3	C4	M1 M1S	M2 M2S	A	F
33. Restaurant—bar								X	X	X	X	X	X	X		
34. Retail stores & services								12	12	12	12	12	12	12		
35. Service station								10		10	10	10	10	10		
36. Shop for building contractor										4	4	X	X	X		
37. Sign shop										X	X	X	X	X		
38. Tire shop, including recapping										4	4	X	X	X		
39. Trailer sales yard										10	10	10	10	10		
40. Used car lot										10	10	10	10	10		
41. Wholesale stores & distributors										9	9	9	X	X		
D. Industrial																
1. Beverage bottling plant												X	X	X		
2. Billboard manufacture												X	X	X		
3. Boat building (small)												X	X	X		
4. Concrete batch plant													X	X		
5. Cement or clay products mfg.												4	4	X		
6. Contractors' storage yard												X	X	X		
7. Dairy products processing												X	X	X		
8. Food processing plant													X	X		
9. Fuel yard												X	X	X		
10. Ice manufacture—cold storage												X	X	X		
11. Junk yard													5	5		
12. Lumber yard—retail												X	X	X		
13. Machine shop												X	X	X		
14. Monument works, stone												X	X	X		
15. Petroleum storage													5	X		
16. Planing mill													X	X		
17. Public utility yard												X	X	X		
18. Railroad yard or shops														X		
19. Terminal yard, trucking												X	X	X		
20. Truck and tractor repair												X	X	X		
21. Warehousing—wholesaling											X	X	X	X		

SPECIAL CONDITIONS: The following special conditions apply to those land uses indicated by corresponding numbers above: 1. *Residential uses* are permitted only above the ground floor of a business building. 2. *Rooming and boarding* of not more than two guests is permitted. 3. *Duplexes are permitted* on corner lots only. May be erected as one or two detached buildings if the court requirements of Section 4 are complied with. 4. *The entire business* must be conducted within a building. 5. *A Special Permit* is required to locate the use in this particular zone. 6. *A children's nursery* is permitted not to exceed four children. 7. *Offices are permitted* subject to granting of a Special Permit, but only in the area bounded by 21st–28th Streets, and alleys between H and I Streets and Capitol Avenue and N. Street. No stocking, storing, selling or processing of merchandise permitted. The maximum permissible gross floor area of a building is 6400 square feet. 8. *Auto repair* is permitted if confined to a building. 9. *The maximum gross floor area* of a building used for this purpose shall be 6400 square feet. Use may also include incidental nonnuisance producing processing, packaging, or fabricating conducted entirely within a building. 10. *Lots must be improved* to the same standards as required for a parking lot in Section 6, page 16. Repair work is permitted if confined to a building. 11. *Preliminary and final site plans* shall be submitted to the Planning Commission for review and approval. 12. *The Planning Commission* shall determine what uses may be permitted in the zone in addition to those listed. 13. *Living quarters for watchman* of commercial or industrially used property, hotels, and motels shall be the only residential uses permitted in this zone. 14. *Said use shall be incidental* to that of the office building. Principal entrance thereto shall be from inside of building only. 15. *Fraternity–Sorority House or Dormitory* is a permitted use in the R4, R5 and C2 zones inside the "Old City" only.

Source: City of Sacramento, California, zoning ordinance (minor modifications made for this book).

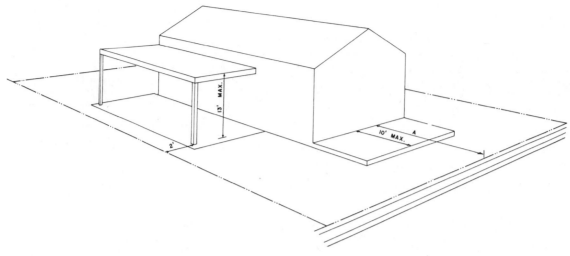

AN OPEN, UNENCLOSED, UNCOVERED PORCH OR PAVED TERRACE MAY PROJECT INTO
REQUIRED FRONT YARD "A" A MAXIMUM OF 10'

AN OPEN CARPORT MAY BE ERECTED IN A SIDE YARD IF A MINIMUM OF
2' IS LEFT OPEN AND UNCOVERED BETWEEN CARPORT AND SIDE LOT LINE.

FIGURE 15–2. *Regulation of accessory buildings*

These formal hearings are not adequate by themselves and should be preceded by activities aimed at preparing the public to play its role intelligently. When the preparation of the map and ordinance commences, the planning commission should undertake a program to build citizen understanding and support. Civic clubs, professional associations for architects, engineers, lawyers, bankers, realtors and businessmen, women's clubs, and other groups should be contacted, informed of the project, and asked for assistance. Individual citizens should also be encouraged to make suggestions and to participate actively.

After a tentative set of regulations for a district has been drafted, many commissions have found it desirable to hold neighborhood meetings, usually at a school or central meeting place. At these meetings, the tentative regulations are read and explained, and comments are invited. A secretary should be on hand to record these comments and the names of those making them. The suggestions can then be considered and the ordinance revised if this is thought desirable. A good practice is to answer in writing every suggestion made, either with news of its acceptance or detailed reasons why it was not adopted.

When the proposed ordinance is complete, most enabling acts require the planning or the zoning commission to make a preliminary report to the city council, and to hold a public hearing after due notice. It cannot be stressed too strongly that these and all other statutory requirements must be fully met or the ordinance may be held invalid. The nature of the public hearing may vary, but, in general, there should be included an explanation of the commission's work, the objectives sought, and a review of the proposed ordinance, followed by a period for questions and comments from the audience. A careful record should be kept of the proceedings and, as previously suggested, acknowledgement made of all suggestions offered by the audience.

Following the public hearing, the commission should review the suggestions, give each one careful consideration and make any further studies deemed necessary. After final revision of the ordinance, it should be submitted to the governing body with a full explanation of its provisions.

In order to insure maximum understanding of the ordinance by the legislators it is desirable that the planning or zoning commission make periodic progress reports to them while

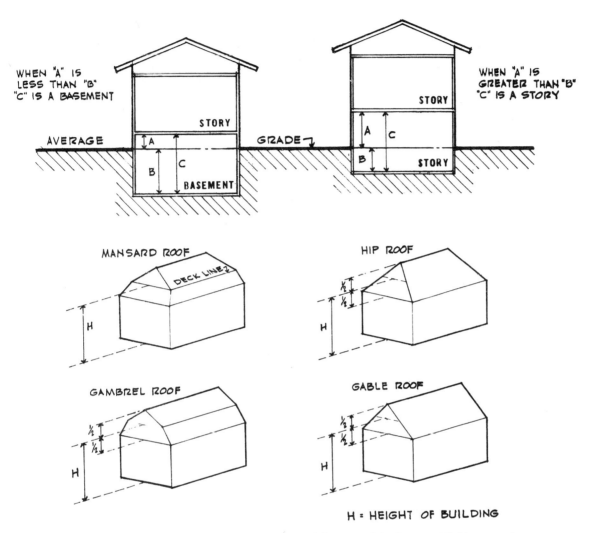

FIGURE 15–3. *Basement, story, and building heights, St. Clair County, Michigan, zoning manual.*

the ordinance is under preparation. It should also hold informal meetings from time to time with the governing body, or an appropriate committee and invite representatives to its public hearings. Without such liaison, it is likely that misunderstandings will arise.

When the governing body receives the commission's final report, it must advertise and hold a public hearing. If it requires major changes to be made in the ordinance recommended by the commission, it should request the commission's views on these changes. Before adopting any amendments that have not been considered at the public hearing, it may be necessary to advertise and hold a new hearing to comply with the enabling act.

ADOPTION AND FINAL STEPS

After all these preliminary steps have been completed, the actual adoption of the zoning ordinance is similar to that of any other ordinance. Because of its complexity and its importance to individual citizens, the zoning ordinance and map should be published and made available to the public. Real estate agents, landowners, lawyers, and architects will be particularly interested and steps should be taken to call the document to their attention. Many cities charge a small fee for copies of the ordinance, sufficient to cover the cost of printing, and a complete, up-to-date copy should always be available in the City Hall, Town Hall or Court House. Additionally, it is desirable to place copies in all public libraries.

Administrative Agencies and Procedures

Enforcement of the zoning ordinance usually involves two administrative agencies: a zoning enforcement officer and a board of adjustment (sometimes designated a board of appeals). Both the zoning enabling act and the zoning ordinance itself customarily contain provisions dealing with the creation and duties of these two agencies. Upon adoption of the ordinance, if not before, measures should be taken to put these provisions into effect. The zoning enforcement officer and members of the board of adjustment should be appointed; the board should meet, elect officers, and adopt rules of procedure.

The planning director, the municipal attorney, the governing body and other appropriate officials should have been consulted during the drafting and approval process, so that the administrative and enforcement provisions are the best that can be devised and appropriate to the community. Forms should now be prepared for building permits, occupancy permits, appeals, public notices of appeals, variations, requests for zoning amendments, and other requirements of the ordinance, and the use of these forms made clear to all concerned. In the absence of such coordination, administration of the ordinance may produce innumerable difficulties. A further discussion of this aspect will be found in a subsequent section of this chapter.

Interim Zoning Ordinances

The process outlined above seems time-consuming and cumbersome, and many a governing body faced with an immediate problem is anxious to short-circuit the required procedures. In general, two approaches have been followed in an attempt to do this. The first is to adopt a "piecemeal" ordinance covering only the district immediately involved, but as indicated earlier, courts have been quick to invalidate such ordinances as being arbitrary, capricious, and discriminatory. Even if the courts did not intervene it is not a prudent course because it initiates a continuing series of ad hoc decisions with subsequent conflict and confusion.

The second is to adopt an interim zoning ordinance designed to establish a status quo throughout the jurisdiction until a permanent ordinance can be adopted. A common type of interim ordinance specifies that when a given proportion of the existing use of a block is residential (or some other classification), the block as a whole will be restricted to that type of use. Ordinances of this type have been attacked on the basis that:

1. They must of necessity be rather crude and poorly designed, creating numerous cases of hardship;

2. They tend to debase the public's attitude toward zoning; and

3. They frequently become permanent rather than interim ordinances.

The attitude of the courts on the validity of these ordinances has varied, with most courts basing their decisions on whether there was specific authority in the zoning enabling act for adoption of an interim ordinance. An important factor, of course, is whether the ordinance is adopted truly as an interim measure, with a bona fide intent to prepare a comprehensive ordinance to replace it. In general, it is unwise to adopt an interim ordinance, except in extreme circumstances and then only when accompanied by a program of work, with firm deadlines, leading to a permanent ordinance.

Amendments

Because no area is static, it must be expected that the zoning ordinance will have to be amended from time to time. Amendments may take three general forms:

1. A revision of the entire ordinance, after re-examination of the factors on which the original ordinance was based and a review of subsequent problems;

2. Minor amendment of particular provisions or of the zoning map, in response to

situations that arise in the administration of the ordinance; and

3. Amendments, primarily to the zoning map, designed to embrace newly annexed property.

As a general rule, it is desirable to undertake complete revision of the ordinance every five years, taking into consideration operational experience, the difficulties encountered by enforcement officials and others, changing zoning principles and techniques, and unforeseen factors in the development of the community. This examination should be carried out as part of the planning commission's normal program of work and in consultation with its technical staff, the enforcement officer, the board of adjustment, and other interested parties that proved helpful during consideration of the original ordinance.

Minor amendments based on changing circumstances or new situations should be treated with caution as they may lead to an undermining of the entire fabric of the original ordinance, if the amending authority does not exercise restraint. Each proposal should be considered from the standpoint of the community as a whole, and not with the special interests of a few property owners in mind—an approach which can only lead to a weakening of the total ordinance. Amendments which give special treatment to a favored few are known as "spot zoning," and will almost certainly be invalidated by the courts if contested. Although no precise definition of spot zoning can be given, any amendment not based on community- or neighborhood-wide considerations may fall within this definition, the danger being particularly great where the amendment affects only one or two properties.

Governing bodies sometimes forget, when they extend their boundaries through annexation procedures, that this action adds a new area to their zoning jurisdiction. As a result of such an oversight, one city found to its dismay that it had no effective zoning on almost half its total area, including the residence of the mayor! There should be automatic consideration of the zoning of the acquired area when any annexation is contemplated, and zoning procedures should be initiated immediately

after annexation. Although, in one sense, the zoning of a newly annexed area amounts to an amendment of the existing ordinance, in another sense it may be regarded as the adoption of a "new" ordinance for the area. To be sure of meeting legal requirements, it is wise to comply with the statutory and ordinance provisions which specify the procedure for the adoption of a new ordinance and also with any provisions dealing with the amendment of an existing ordinance. Many zoning ordinances contain provisions on action to be taken on annexation, or provide an interim zoning category into which annexed areas automatically fall pending specific consideration.

Common Deficiencies

The following is a partial list of deficiencies frequently encountered in older zoning ordinances or their administration, and may be helpful in determining whether to undertake comprehensive revision. In general, such deficiencies fall into three classifications:

1. Defects in the ordinance as originally adopted;

2. Problems created by the administration and amendment of that ordinance; and

3. Failure of the ordinance to reflect up-to-date zoning concepts and techniques.

DEFECTS IN THE ORIGINAL ORDINANCE

The most common defects found in zoning ordinances are the following:

1. The ordinance is not based on a comprehensive plan, and its objectives have never been clearly defined; consequently individual provisions work at cross-purposes and serve primarily as an erratic brake on development.

2. The ordinance is poorly organized and difficult to use; it has separate sets of height, use, and area districts; is imprecise in dealing with specific situations, allowing undue latitude for interpretation by the enforcement officer and the board of adjustment; it is either poorly indexed, or not indexed at all.

3. Excessive areas or frontages are zoned for the more intensive uses (multifamily dwelling, business, and industry), in relation either to:

(1) the effective demand for such space, or to (2) the capacity of the streets and utility systems available to serve such districts. The result is either "spotty" development, much of it substandard, or undue congestion.

4. Extreme differences are apparent between adjoining districts, such as residential areas abutting heavy industrial areas, with no effective "buffer" to protect one from the other. A special example of this is where opposite sides of a street are zoned for conflicting purposes.

5. The ordinance provisions authorize particular uses only where the neighbors consent. This is a particularly pernicious regulation.

6. The ordinance authorizes the zoning administrator, or the board of adjustment to grant or deny permits in particular cases, with no written standards specified to guide the exercise of their discretion.

7. Nonconforming uses are regulated in a manner that tends to perpetuate them rather than lead to their eventual elimination.

8. Some uses are barred from districts where similar uses are permitted, with no logical basis for such differentiation.

9. Certain commercial uses, such as gas stations or funeral homes, are permitted in residential districts.

10. There are insufficient controls over "home occupations," doctors' offices, clinics, and boarding or rooming houses in residential districts.

11. Institutional uses such as hospitals, schools, and churches are barred from residential districts and placed in other districts which are often unsuitable.

12. Regulations for commercial districts are written loosely so as to permit the intrusion of incompatible types of industrial development.

13. Residences are permitted in business and industrial districts without being subjected to any lot area, yard, or other requirements designed to insure light, air, and privacy for the occupants.

14. Residences are permitted in industrial districts, and no vacant land is reserved for industrial development; most "industrial districts" thereby becoming substandard residential areas, furnishing neither protection for the residents nor appropriate sites for industry.

15. Neighborhood business district regulations are not designed to minimize any adverse effects of business use upon abutting residential areas.

16. Minimum lot area requirements for residences are unrealistically low or completely lacking in some or all districts.

17. Minimum lot area requirements for residences are unrealistically high in some districts, as a means of limiting development to expensive homes.

18. Height and building bulk allowances are excessive, especially in the central business district, in terms of street and utility capacities.

19. Permitted lot coverage in residential districts is too large, or yard and court requirements are too small.

Problems Created

Many of the defects listed above may be created by administrative or legislative action, particularly where this is not guided by a comprehensive plan. Maps showing zoning districts including those resulting from amendments, variances granted by the board of adjustment, and zoning violations, will sometimes highlight these and other deficiencies. Among typical kinds of problems growing out of lax administration and improper amendments are the following:

1. There are many spot zones—comprising only one or two lots whose location is not in accordance with a comprehensive plan.

2. The board of adjustment has granted too many variances, including "use variances" (even though these are illegal in many states). Use variances are essentially legislative actions taken by the board of adjustment when they permit a use not allowed in a district to be located therein. Thus the zoning map does not indicate the current use of land with accuracy.

3. The enforcement officer has issued permits for uses that do not meet ordinance requirements, or has failed to make use of occupancy permits to regulate changes in use, or has failed to carry out an active program to detect and prosecute zoning violations.

4. The enforcement officers and board of adjustment have tended to rely on complaints or

the consent of neighboring property owners as a basis for action.

FAILURE TO REFLECT NEW CONCEPTS AND TECHNIQUES

This third category of deficiencies involves developments that may have occurred in zoning theory and practice since the original ordinance was adopted. An older zoning ordinance may be lacking in several respects including the following:

1. There are no requirements for off-street parking and loading areas.

2. There is no provision for large-scale developments under single ownership, often called Planned Unit Developments, where the tract is not divided into traditional building lots.

3. The ordinance does not make use of new types of building bulk regulations that give greater architectural flexibility than is possible under traditional bulk control methods.

4. The ordinance follows the traditional districting approach rather than attempting to isolate the factors that make a particular use incompatible with its neighbors and to control those factors directly by means of performance standards.

5. The ordinance does not require the elimination of nonconforming uses.

6. The ordinance does not restrict development in flood plains and other unsuitable areas.

7. The ordinance does not limit development in the vicinity of airports or in approach lanes for aircraft.

8. The ordinance does not reflect the contemporary incidence of such developments as single-story manufacturing establishments, garden apartments, townhouses, shopping centers, and, where applicable, new towns.

PROCEDURES FOR AMENDMENT

Normally, requests for amendment of the zoning ordinance will come from individual citizens who wish the zoning of a particular property or area or the regulation relating to it to be altered. Amendments may also be initiated by the planning commission, the legislative body, and the board of adjustment or by municipal officials, such as the enforcement officer.

Although most state enabling acts do not require the council to refer proposed amendments to the planning commission for its recommendations, this is a desirable procedure. Some acts specifically provide for such reference, and require a larger than normal majority vote by the governing body before it may overrule planning commission recommendations. Occasionally, a zoning ordinance may provide for reference to the zoning commission or to the board of adjustment instead of to the planning commission, but this is not good practice.

Most enabling acts require an advertised public hearing by the legislative body prior to action on the proposed amendment and some ordinances also call for hearings by the planning commission. Where the two groups have heard widely divergent testimony at their respective public hearings, it has been found good practice for the council and the planning commission to hold a joint public hearing. On the basis of the joint hearing the planning commission will make its recommendations and the council will act.

Another procedure helpful in small communities is to limit the council meetings at which zoning amendments will be considered to one in every three months. This has the dual advantage of preventing every council meeting from being devoted to zoning matters and giving the planning commission and council a better view of the effects of the proposed amendments by permitting adequate study of a number of amendments at the same time.

A special provision in most enabling acts limits the council's freedom to adopt some amendments. This is a provision under which certain property owners can require a larger than normal majority vote of the council for the passage of an amendment to which they protest. The council should follow the statutory language precisely when this provision is invoked.

SELF-IMPOSED LIMITATIONS ON AMENDMENTS

A number of recent zoning ordinances contain two types of limitations on petitions for amendment of the ordinance and on the governing body's power to amend in particular cases. These limitations are made a part of the ordinance but are not required by state enabling legislation and can, of course, be amended. However, they are enforceable so long as they remain part of the ordinance.

The first of these is a requirement that the applicant for an amendment make a detailed showing of the justification for his proposal before it is considered. He might be required to show the effect of the amendment on adjoining properties, effect on the overall city plan, and economic and other support for his request. Even after such a showing, the council only agrees to consider his request, and may decide not to grant it.

The second limitation is a statement in the ordinance of standards to be met by any amendment. This may be expressed in terms of minimum size of the area to be rezoned, the relationship of that area to other areas, maximum permissible population densities, and other factors. Most of these standards will, of course, be derived from the studies made in preparing the land-use plan. They have the effect of reducing sharply both the number of petitions and the number of amendments allowed, while tending to focus the discussion on pertinent factors and to reduce time spent in consideration of extraneous matters.

CONTRACT ZONING

The phrase "contract zoning" is merely descriptive, not a recognized legal term. The actions within this category are of two general, but similar, types:

1. Where, subsequent to a rezoning, an owner of the rezoned property registers a covenant in favor of the governing body, placing restrictions on the property greater than those generally imposed by the zoning ordinance on the new district in which the property has been placed.

2. Where, in return for a zoning reclassification to a less restricted use, an owner enters into an agreement with the governing body, restricting the use of his land beyond the zoning requirements generally attaching to the new district in which his property has been placed.

Contract zoning seeks to limit the use of a property not only to the range permitted in the zoning ordinance for the district in which the site is located, but in other ways as well. Often the use is limited to a single purpose, and conditions may be specified as to how that purpose is to be achieved.

Many objections have been raised to contract zoning on various grounds. Some claim that such an amendment in respect of a small area of use amounts to spot zoning, and there is evidence to suggest that if the area is rezoned to a use incompatible with surrounding uses, or is rezoned for the benefit of a particular owner, that such amendments will be invalidated. A second objection underlines the fact that no contracts relating to an exercise of the policing power should be made by a legislative body. The policing power is for universal benefit and the public trust may be violated in situations where improper motives and considerations may arise in the grant of amendments by agreement.

A third point is that once a governing body has made an "agreement," then it is bound by it and cannot rezone on a subsequent occasion. This is not the case, for a governing body cannot limit the powers delegated to it by the state, either by contract or restrictive covenant. Nor can a governing body, by simple agreement, limit the statutory powers of its successor.

Among points noted is that if contract zoning is not specifically authorized by statute, the local governing body has no derived power to engage in such a practice. Again, it has been held that, as agreements involve restrictions not in the zoning ordinance and not on the zoning map, the public does not receive due notice of them. Of course, the public will be aware that an amendment of classification has been made, as this is on record, but the public has no official notice until the action is taken by the local governing body.

Contract zoning is a relatively new device and those who would use it should be wary. There are few established cases from which to seek guidance (early in 1965 eight cases were on record, in five of which the practice was upheld) and the outcome of litigation by any interested party is uncertain, particularly since the philosophy of contract zoning runs counter to that of "Euclidean Zoning" on which the legislative concept of local land use control is based. If cases on the legality of contract zoning are few, those on the enforcement of the restrictive covenants contained therein are fewer, thus presenting an additional hazard to practical implementation.

If the device is found to be universally helpful there is no doubt that legislation will be forthcoming in the future to permit local governments to enter into "zoning contracts." Until that time it might be wise for other means to be exhausted—including a careful review of zoning district uses for internal compatibility—before contract zoning is undertaken. Even then the individual case should receive the utmost care in detailed planning and execution.

Those interested in contract zoning are directed to the case of Bucholz v. City of Omaha [174 Neb. 862, 120 N.W. 2d 270 (1963)] which contains a wide variety of the elements reviewed in this general discussion.

Content of the Zoning Ordinance

Some matters relating to the content of the zoning ordinance have been discussed previously; in particular, the number of sets and types of districts for which provision should be made, and the format for the ordinance. This section will be concerned with the detailed regulations which may be included in the ordinance.

Early zoning ordinances were chiefly designed to protect the "highest class" of residential properties (single-family residences on extensive lots with large yards). They were constructed on a cumulative principle, namely that every use permitted in a "higher use" district was also permitted in all the districts "lower" on the scale. Thus, a single-family residence would be permitted not only in all categories of residential districts but also in a business district and in an industrial district. Industry was at the bottom of the scale and was restricted entirely to designated industrial areas within the community.

Under these conditions it could hardly be held that the zoning ordinance provided an effective means for carrying out the land use plan, unless it were assumed that economic forces would somehow insure that a business district would be developed only by businesses and an industrial district only by industries even though every other use was permitted there. It was not unusual to have wording in the least restrictive industrial zone to the effect that "everything is permitted except those uses in the following list." Such a technique is dangerous, since if the list is not complete the unexpected is allowed, and new uses may evolve which would be inappropriate even in this zone.

Recent ordinances have become more positive in their approach, designating the specific uses *permitted* in each district without making extensive cross-references to uses permitted in other districts. Residences have been banned from industrial districts and in some cases from business districts and businesses themselves have been divided into functional groups. Thus a given business might be permitted in one business district but not in another. This abandonment of the cumulative principle permits the planner to design a pattern of districts that is far more likely to be followed by actual land development.

Trends have developed in some recent zoning ordinances, which appear to be at cross-purposes with others. Some recent ordinances provide for many more types of districts than was formerly the practice, reflecting a desire to deal with as many specific situations as possible and to eliminate the necessity for widespread administrative discretion.

In other ordinances, the district concept is being abandoned and is being replaced by regulations aimed at permitting different classes of uses to exist side by side. For example, it is believed that if the undesirable effects of glare, smoke, dust, vibration, and noise are controlled, adequate off-street parking space is provided, plants are well landscaped with wide lawns, truck routes are controlled, and similar measures taken, then certain categories of industries might exist in the midst of residential areas without being incompatible. This proximity would permit workers to walk to work, would remove substantial traffic from the street system, and give workers more leisure time at home. Similar efforts are being made in other problem areas to identify the features that make one type of land use incompatible with another, and to control those features directly, rather than to use the more crude approach of segregating different uses completely.

A related trend is toward more consideration of particular proposals on a case-by-case basis. Instead of having specific districts in which permitted uses are listed and all others are barred, some ordinances classify a great number of uses as "special uses" permitted only after consideration by the board of adjustment then only subject to such conditions as the board may impose for the protection of the neighbors. This tendency toward the use of the "special use" technique is frowned upon by some courts and in general encourages laxity in drafting an ordinance and also indicates an unwillingness or inability to make a decision as to where a certain use should be permitted as of right.

It is not unusual now for a district to be provided in the text of the ordinance without initially being shown on the map; when a property owner can meet certain specified conditions, the ordinance declares that the city council will rezone his property to this classification. This approach, which has been termed the "floating" zone, is peculiarly applicable to neighborhood shopping districts, garden apartment developments, and similar uses that might logically be located at any one of the number of locations, among which the council does not want to make a choice until a developer is ready to move at one location. This, again, indicates lack of ability to make an initial decision on the part of the governing body, and in some cases, has been held to be of doubtful legality.

A third approach is to provide for special consideration by the planning commission and city council of large-scale housing projects, shopping centers, or where applicable, "new towns" in much the same manner as consideration of a subdivision plat and with considerable latitude for negotiation on particular features.

All three approaches are subject to serious abuse, and the ordinance should contain as many limitations as possible on the discretionary power of the agency granting this special treatment, otherwise the ordinance will be imperiled both in the courts of law and in the court of public opinion.

The following discussion of particular regulations should be read against this background of changing techniques to which the whole field of zoning is subjected. In the sections that follow, consideration will be given first to use regulations, then to dimensional regulations, and finally to certain special problems.

REGULATION OF THE USE OF LAND AND BUILDINGS

The desire to regulate uses in each area of a community is a primary reason for adopting a zoning ordinance. The underlying purpose of segregating different types of uses is two-fold:

1. To prevent the mixing of incompatible uses which may have such deleterious effects on one another as to depreciate property values and desirable environmental features; and

2. To insure that uses requiring expensive public service facilities such as major utility lines and heavily paved streets are restricted to those areas where these facilities exist or are planned to be installed.

As indicated, the basic types of districts are residential, commercial, and industrial. While some ordinances have moved in the direction of mixing uses, it is probable that there will always be the necessity for a degree of segregation of these three use classes.

RESIDENTIAL DISTRICTS

Residential properties are by far the most numerous in any city, and they occupy the most land area. Regulation of residential districts is therefore of great quantitative as well as qualitative significance.

Several theories have been followed in devising residence district regulations. In older ordinances, the practice was to divide residential districts according to dwelling types permitted. Customarily such ordinances provided for single-family districts, two-family districts, and apartment districts. Some ordinances included four-family districts, row-house districts, boarding house districts, fraternity and sorority districts, or other special residential classifications.

In general, the arguments made for this classification were that multiple family developments might damage property values in single-family districts, that they tended to cut off the light and air of single-family neighbors, that their tenants took up all the curb parking space in the neighborhood, that the increased population density overloaded the street and utility systems, and that rental tenants did not take as good care of their properties as did owner-occupants in single-family residences.

In recent ordinances some efforts have been made to eliminate particular adverse features of multi-family buildings and to permit the intermixture of dwelling classes. It is argued that neighborhoods made up of different dwelling categories are more interesting aesthetically, more socially satisfying and they have the practical advantage of enabling a family to meet its changing housing needs as it grows, without having to leave the neighborhood. Regulations embodying this theory require multi-unit residences to have increased lot areas, to hold down population density; provide larger yards, to avoid cutting off light and air from their neighbors and to afford play space for children; and install adequate off-street parking. Where differentiation among residential districts is made in ordinances of this type, it is usually based on permitted population density. Zones with higher population densities are then located in proximity to community facilities, such as roads, utilities, etc. which will provide the higher level of service necessary to service the greater number of people per acre.

If the older philosophy is followed, the city should be carefully studied in order to determine the relative demand for different types of dwellings. The single-family residence is by far the most popular. Two-family residences, or duplexes, either side-by-side or one over the other are popular in some areas, but not in others. Apartment residences tend to be more popular in large cities than in small ones, although the increasing proportion of newly

married, and older persons in the population may make this type of housing more popular everywhere in the future.

Related Uses. In the natural development of any city, certain types of nonresidential uses tend to be associated with residential neighborhoods and the zoning ordinance should make provision for such uses in residence districts. Among them are churches, day nurseries, schools, colleges, libraries, museums, art galleries, municipal buildings, cemeteries, hospitals and sanitariums, golf courses and similar recreational facilities, and semi-agricultural uses. Some related uses may be permitted only as "special uses" meeting the approval of the board of adjustment. Occasional ordinances permit certain nonresidential uses in the "lower" classes of residential districts but not in the "higher" classes. It is difficult to find a constitutional basis for discrimination of this sort. Courts have frowned on the efforts of some cities to confine such uses to business districts, where they cannot perform their functions as effectively.

Home Occupations. Most zoning ordinances permit certain "customary home occupations" to be carried on in dwellings in residential districts. Examples are physicians' and dentists' offices, professional offices, beauty salons and art studios. Many of these occupations can be carried on in the home in an unobjectionable fashion, but all pose potentially serious problems for the zoning enforcement officer.

In an actual episode in a southeastern city, a woman started making sandwiches in her home. She found a responsive market and hired a couple of assistants, after which the business continued to grow, and she expanded operations into her garage. Then she bought a fleet of trucks, and paved her backyard as a parking area. What had started out innocently enough as a home occupation had become a major business, with detrimental effects on her residential neighborhood. Almost any successful home occupation may follow this course.

To forestall these consequences, the ordinance should impose rigid controls on home occupations. It should list specifically the occupations that are permitted and severely limit the size and type of permitted signs. A flat sign with the professional practitioner's name thereon, with a maximum area of one and one-half square feet is a good standard. Employment of more than one person living outside the home should be barred. The percentage of floor area in the home that may be devoted to such an occupation must be set at a low figure, say 15 per cent, to insure that the residential use of the property predominates. Other restrictions will be suggested by experience.

COMMERCIAL DISTRICTS

The proper zoning of commercial or business districts is still a subject of considerable debate and experimentation. Perhaps the worst fault of many early zoning ordinances was the practice of overzoning for stores and other business uses. Property owners had the idea that if their lands were so zoned, they would be developed for commercial purposes and would be more valuable as a consequence. City officials thought that the best use that could be made of the frontage of all major thoroughfares and some of the minor ones was for business; civic boosters urged that plenty of space be left for business expansion. The net effect was the creation of rundown slum areas, since large land areas were zoned for business and the adjacent lands were sterilized, inhibiting productive use. No property owner would spend much to improve residential property in an area zoned for business, due to lack of protection against his neighbor. There simply was not enough demand for business property to use all the land zoned for business enterprises, so existing properties gradually deteriorated while their owners waited in vain for a commercial purchaser to appear.

Only about two to five per cent of the total developed area of an average city is devoted to commercial uses. This amount is divided among the central business district, neighborhood shopping centers and other districts scattered throughout the city. While off-street parking requirements for new commercial centers will raise the total space requirements somewhat, close examination should be given to any zoning ordinance that provides a markedly greater amount of land for commer-cial purposes than five per cent of the total.

Possibly the greatest problem in commercial zoning today is the location of neighborhood and regional shopping centers. Due to the success of some of these centers, a boom has developed, and many real estate developers are eager to follow the trend. From a planning point of view, there is frequently little basis for choice between a number of locations for a shopping center. At the same time, it is obvious that even complete service of all the natural trade area will not furnish enough business to support a center at every possible location. The planner hesitates to provide for too many shopping centers, because several partially developed centers in fierce competition with one another will not be so desirable for the community as one or two thriving centers.

At the same time, it is difficult to designate in advance any specific location as the *only* shopping center district, because this amounts to giving the lucky property owner a monopoly. A number of jurisdictions have resolved this dilemma by spelling out in their ordinances the conditions under which an area will be rezoned for shopping center purposes and by placing the burden on the applicant to demonstrate that his tract meets these conditions. The city and county of Denver is one of many jurisdictions, experiencing rapid suburban growth, which reports success with this technique.

In the older zoning ordinances it was customary to provide for a central business district, which might be subdivided into a retail business district and a wholesale business district; and for neighborhood business districts. The latter were designed for businesses such as grocery stores, drug stores, self-service laundries, and similar convenience goods establishments serving particular neighborhoods. This breakdown of business districts is still probably the most common, especially among small and middle-sized cities. The draftsman should be particularly careful, in preparing regulations for neighborhood business districts, to ban businesses of a type that will be detrimental to residential properties in the vicinity by reason of excessive noise, light, or night operation.

In cities of 100,000 and over, where the

range of commercial uses is greater, marketing experts are now called in to help develop functional groupings of businesses, and many new zoning classifications are appearing. These new districts are based on two sets of criteria: relative service areas and economic compatibility. Following the former criterion, districts are provided for convenience centers to serve the needs of their immediate neighborhoods; community shopping centers offering a wider range of goods for surrounding residential areas; major shopping centers serving large portions of the city; and the central business district. From the standpoint of economic compatibility, uses are broken down into retail uses, service uses (gas stations, theaters, and so on), and commercial uses (auto sales, small manufacturing operations, and so on).

Under this arrangement, service stations, warehouses, wholesale houses, and similar uses may be banned from retail districts, not because they are considered obnoxious in any way, but because the marketing specialists observe that they are "dead spaces" that tend to break up the pattern of pedestrian shopping from one store to another.

In smaller cities, it will also be useful to establish separate districts for professional offices and service agencies such as funeral homes. These "professional" districts might be located in the vicinity of the courthouse and hospitals and on the fringes of retail marketing areas. They serve as buffer areas between business districts and residential districts and also serve as transitional uses for old residences bordering existing business districts.

Another useful type of district is a highway service district for service stations, motels, restaurants, and similar business. Some ordinances provide for parking lot districts adjacent to the central business district, but the legal validity of this classification is questionable; it is probably better to permit parking lots as "Special Permit" uses in residence districts within a given distance of business districts and make them subject to stringent screening and construction standards.

Customarily, there have always been a certain number of mixed uses in commercial districts. Residences are ordinarily permitted, although they are required to meet the same yard, height, and use provisions as a residence in a residential district. Some ordinances prohibit residences in business districts, largely as a means of discouraging premature applications for rezoning from residential to business classification. Questions have been raised, however, as to whether it is desirable to eliminate apartments over business establishments in which owners and sales people can live. On balance, it would seem that with the provision of adequate off-street parking, this mixture would be a wise one.

Light manufacturing operations, such as bakeries, watchmakers, shoe repair shops, and oculists, are also customarily permitted in business districts, subject to restrictions on the maximum number of employees, the maximum horsepower used in machinery, and similar factors governing the size of the operation. This avoids the inadvertent creation of manufacturing zones.

INDUSTRIAL DISTRICTS

Industrial districts at one time were regarded as dumping grounds, so far as the zoning ordinance was concerned, and all land that could not otherwise be classified satisfactorily was put into an industrial classification. Today, it is recognized that prime industrial land is a relatively scarce commodity which should be identified and preserved. To compound the problem, industry now needs more space than formerly, due to a change of design from multiple story plants to single story plants and because industries are now required to provide adequate off-street parking space for workers' cars. Many firms also wish to have an appropriate setting for their plants, complete with generous setbacks and landscaping.

A major step toward the preservation of industrial areas is the banning of residences in these districts: this makes sense both for the residential property owner and for the industrialist. If it is detrimental to a residential district to introduce an industry into its midst, it is far more detrimental for isolated residences to be situated in the middle of an industrial district. Additionally, if industrial property is once divided into residential lots, the probability is that it will never again be used for industrial purposes because of the difficulty of reassembling the land. Even scattered residential owners in the area will interfere with industrial operations by demanding that the plants reduce the noise and fumes that may be incidental to their normal operations. Finally, the municipality may be forced, by reason of the residential development, to locate schools in unsuitable locations.

On the other hand, if the property owner has to wait too long before an industrial purchaser for his land appears, he may be able to persuade the courts that the ordinance has deprived him of any beneficial use of his land. This means that the amount of industrial space preserved must be based on a realistic appraisal of present and future demands.

Most zoning ordinances provide for two classes of industrial districts; light manufacturing and heavy manufacturing, although it is becoming more common to see additional special purpose industrial zones. In general, the distinction between the two is based on the degree of noxious effect usually produced by a given operation, that is, the amount of noise, smoke, odor, dust, vibration, and glare that the public has come to associate with each industry. The regulations themselves merely list permitted or prohibited industries by industry type.

Many of the newer zoning ordinances have adopted the more logical approach of prescribing "performance standards" for industry. Instead of merely listing permitted industries, these ordinances prescribe the maximum amount of noise, smoke, dust, and other external effects that an industry in a given district may produce. The worse the effects permitted, the lower the industry is on the scale of industrial districts. Theoretically, under this approach if a "heavy" industry succeeded in modifying its processes so as to minimize these external effects, it would be permitted in a "higher" district than a "light" industry which was more careless about these matters.

The permissible effects for any given industry are described in technical terms, such as for noise, decibels within a certain frequency range; for smoke and particulate matter, diam-

eter of particles, weight per unit area, and intensity as measured by the Ringelmann Chart published and used by the U.S. Bureau of Mines. The maintenance of these standards requires the perfection of measuring techniques, the use of delicate measuring instruments, and the personnel to man them.

The use of performance standards has much in its favor, but as may be seen, it does require enforcement personnel with technical ability much higher than the average—perhaps unrealistically high in terms of ordinary municipal salary scales. One solution to this problem is to require the manufacturing establishment concerned to pay the cost of technical assistance where rough tests by the enforcement officer indicate that it may be in violation of the ordinance. Other municipalities have hired specialists as part-time consultants to assist in the more delicate measurements and determinations.

Another problem of performance standards, which may be even more serious, is that some industrialists are reportedly unwilling to locate in areas where they cannot determine compliance with the law until after they have built their plants and begun operations. It is suspected, too, that city councils may not want to enforce regulations in all cases, where violations appear only at this late stage. Finally, the state of technology is not yet sufficiently advanced for the permissible levels of all types of obnoxiousness to be known. Many such ordinance requirements are still experimental at the present time.

OPEN LAND DISTRICTS

Many cities have been undecided about how to zone land that apparently is not yet ready for development. A desirable solution from many standpoints is to put this land into an "open land district" in which agricultural uses, recreational uses, such as parks and golf courses, public uses, airports, reservoirs, and similar uses, are permitted. If subdivision and development of these areas is prohibited until the land is rezoned, injurious development will probably be prevented until the land is ready for its best use. In many cases, open land uses may be the most desirable from the city's standpoint as a permanent type of development. However, the courts have been quick to strike down attempts to control the price of public acquisition of land by the device of placing unduly tight zoning regulations on it. This is an abuse of the power to zone, is not supportable at law and should be avoided.

Another type of open land district is a "flood plain district," consisting of river bottom lands and areas subject to flooding. In these areas there is a prohibition against the construction of structures that would be damaged by high waters. Regulations of this nature require extensive engineering surveys and analysis, but the value to the individual and the public can be most significant.

REGULATION OF STRUCTURES

Regulations dealing with lot sizes, yard sizes, and the height and bulk of structures are aimed directly at the qualities that collectively contribute toward "livability." They attempt to control the population density in various areas; to insure adequate light, air, and privacy; to afford safe play space for children and recreation space for older persons; to reduce fire hazards; and in general to maintain a healthful and safe environment. They have sometimes been called dimensional requirements, since they are generally shown as a series of measurements or relationships of one kind or another.

As in the case of use regulations, a pronounced trend in recent years has been toward more flexibility. At one time, dimensional regulations were almost universally expressed in terms of nonvariable requirements. Any structure erected in a given district could not exceed a specified height, and it was required to have front, side, and rear yards of certain dimensions. When all of these specifications were considered together, they constituted an invisible envelope over each lot, through which the building could not protrude, but which it might fill completely. The characteristic shape of the New York skyline is a good example of the visual effect of this kind of regulation. It

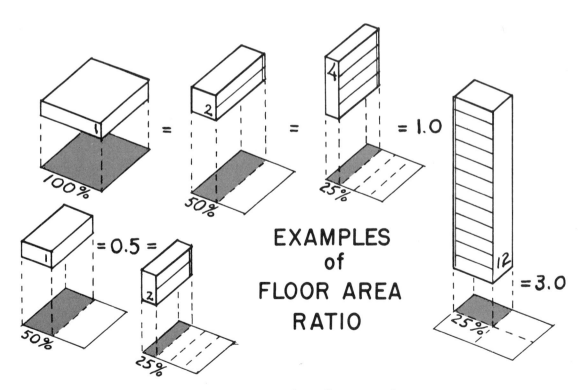

FIGURE 15–4. *Examples of floor area ratio*

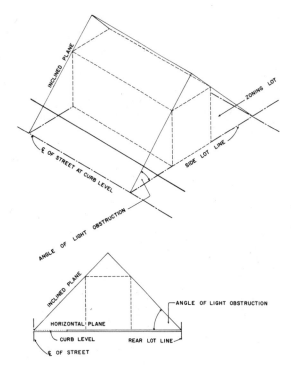

FIGURE 15–5. *"Angle of light obstruction" or "bulk control plane"*

has become evident that this approach unduly limits design possibilities, and some recent ordinance provisions have been devised to afford greater leeway to the designer without sacrificing control objectives.

An exceeding popular device is the "floor-area ratio," which is graphically illustrated in Figure 15–4. An ordinance using this control specifies the relationship between: (1) the area of permitted floor space in a structure, and (2) the area of the lot on which it is situated. The designer may then choose a variety of building forms in which this relationship is preserved. For instance, a floor-area ratio of 2.0 permits the builder to erect a two-story building covering the entire lot, a four-story building covering one-half of the lot, an eight-story building covering one-fourth of the lot, and so on.

Floor-area ratios for different classes of districts might be 0.7 for residential areas; in business districts, it might begin at 1.0 and increase to 12.0 or 16.0; and the new one-story type of manufacturing plant might be limited to a maximum ratio of 1.0 in undeveloped manu-

facturing or industrial districts. Any such regulations should, of course, reflect an analysis of existing structures to determine what is reasonable in any given district.

A second device is the "bulk control plane." Ordinances employing this device do not specify maximum heights in feet or a permitted number of stories. Instead, they recognize the purpose of height limitation, namely to assure light and air to the neighbors of the structure; and describe a plane beginning at a certain height above the ground at the lot line and sloping upward over the lot at a given angle. Thus, in effect, a pyramidal "tent" is described, and the builder may erect his building to any height and shape that does not penetrate this tent, see Figure 15–5. A variation of this device specifies an "average angle of light obstruction" and permits the builder to penetrate the "tent" with portions of the frontage of his building, if he leaves an equivalent amount of space inside the tent free of obstructions, see Figure 15–6. Another related provision specifies an area of required window exposure for each outside window, so that occupants of the building may have light and air.

A third major device appearing in recent ordinances is the replacement of nonvariable yard requirements (distributed among side, front, and rear yards) by a requirement merely that there be a certain amount of unobstructed open space on the lot for each dwelling unit, with considerable flexibility of location. Some ordinances even permit this requirement to be met by suitable space in the form of balconies or on the top of flat roofs, in high density districts. Other ordinances do not specify any amount of required yard space; instead they state the maximum percentage of the lot that may be covered by a building.

A fourth approach which is gaining popularity is to offer "premiums" to the property owner who includes certain design features in his new building. For example, a building with an arcade at street level, with a landscaped plaza, or with setbacks at particular floor levels might be permitted to exceed normal floor-area ratio or height limitations. Thus, the municipality provides an economic incentive to builders to install added community amenities. Ex-

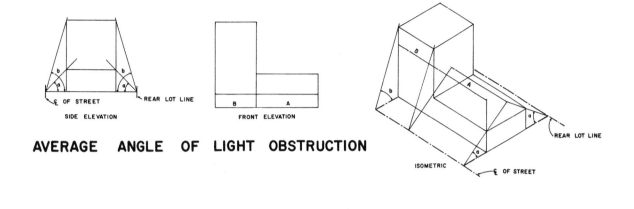

AVERAGE   ANGLE   OF   LIGHT   OBSTRUCTION

$$\frac{\text{Frontage A} \times \text{Angle a} + \text{Frontage B} \times \text{Angle b}}{\text{Frontage A} + \text{Frontage B}} \; . \; \text{(OR, is less than) Maximum angle of light obstruction specified in district regulations}$$

FIGURE 15–6. *Average angle of light obstruction*

treme care must be exercised to balance the gain to the public against encroachment due to over-liberalization of the zoning provisions.

Recently, the Federal Housing Administration has developed a new measure of land use activity, termed the Land Use Intensity (LUI) rating, which offers great promise in providing an even more sensitive control of residential development, while preserving the maximum flexibility in design solutions, mixtures of housing type and variety in dwelling size. Norfolk, Virginia and Frederick County, Maryland, have adopted ordinances incorporating this new technique and Fairfax County, Virginia, has a particularly well-designed proposal under consideration.

A technique of considerable interest, which has been successfully used throughout the country, is that of "cluster" zoning, whereby a land developer is allowed to reduce the minimum size of his lots below that specified in the zoning ordinance for the district in which his land is located, if, in return, the land thus gained is preserved as permanent open space for the benefit of the community. This procedure allows continued control of overall population density, but reduces, in many cases, the disruptive impact of development by permitting the more rugged or difficult land to be left open as cluster land.

When such devices as these are used in a coordinated fashion, they open up a whole new range of possibilities for the architect, site planner, and the landscape architect, while still advancing the objectives of zoning.

Even when such new devices are used, however, the more conventional approach is still followed in some districts, perhaps in combination with some of the newer devices. The following discussion is intended as a guide to cities concerned with older types of regulation.

HEIGHT REGULATIONS

Height regulations may be expressed in feet, stories, or with reference to the width of the street on which a building fronts, e.g. permitting a building height of "X" times the width of the street. Where limitations are given in feet, two points should be noted. First, to avoid disputes, the ordinance should specify the exact manner in which measurements are to be made. Second, there is a danger that some buildings may be built with lower ceilings than ordinarily desirable, in order to fit an extra story or two into the permitted height. When street widths vary in a district, basing height limitations on street widths may produce complicated situations. The simple measurement of a maximum number of feet is preferable.

In many cities, buildings in the central business district are permitted to exceed the maximum height, if there is a series of setbacks from lot lines corresponding to the increase in building height. This device has produced the familiar wedding-cake construction of the sky-scraper. In addition, most ordinances permit such structures as chimneys, spires, monuments, domes, cooling towers, and elevator towers to exceed the usual height limitations.

Typical height limitations in single-family and two-family residence districts are 35 feet or two and one-half stories. In apartment districts, depending on the nature of the city, permitted heights may range up to 150 feet or fifteen stories. Neighborhood business districts rarely have height limitations much in excess of adjacent residential districts, but central business districts may have permitted heights of 150 feet or more. Industrial districts frequently have height limitations of up to eight stories, but such limitations are probably excessively high for the newer districts, since modern plants are seldom more than two stories, and most often only one story high.

All of the above limitations are *maximum* building heights. A few cities have attempted to fix *minimum* building heights for their downtown business districts. Courts have characterized such requirements as being based solely on aesthetic grounds, outside the purposes for which the police power may be invoked, and have therefore invalidated them.

A special type of height limitation is that imposed on structures in the vicinity of airports. While these limitations are commonly found in airport zoning ordinances, some cities have incorporated them in their regular zoning ordinances. The latter course is preferable from the standpoint of simplifying the laws with which a citizen must comply.

Regulation of Building Bulk

Bulk regulations are closely related to height regulations. Most ordinances achieve some control over building bulk through height limitations and yard requirements, if not by the newer devices outlined at the beginning of this section. Some rely heavily on provisions specifying the maximum percentage of the lot area that may be covered by buildings. Some require increased side and rear yards when the building exceeds certain dimensions.

One type of bulk regulation deserves special mention. This is a requirement that residences must have specified minimum floor areas or minimum cubic content. The legal validity of such regulations depends largely on the city's ability to show that they represent the minimum space needed for the mental and physical health of occupants of the residence. Where the requirements are unduly high, the courts may invalidate them on the basis that they are merely attempts to preserve particular neighborhoods as sites for large and expensive homes or to upgrade the neighborhood at the expense of the newcomer. The same reasoning may be used to invalidate minimum-size requirements that differ from one type of residence district to another. If requirements are truly based on considerations of health, they should be the same in neighborhoods of modest homes as they are in wealthy neighborhoods. In most cases floor space requirements of 500 or 600 square feet per family for a dwelling, regardless of where it is situated in the city, would probably be upheld as reasonable.

Lot Area Regulations and Similar Controls

The most common method of regulating population density is through provisions prescribing the minimum lot areas that must be provided for each dwelling unit. Such requirements have additional importance as health measures in areas where sewage disposal is through septic tanks or water supply is by individual wells. In areas of this type, regulations should be based at least in part on advice of the local health authority. Minimum lot size requirements are not usually imposed on business and industrial districts, except for dwellings that might be constructed therein.

The possibility of mixing residential types in a single neighborhood has already been mentioned. Where this is done, an essential feature is a sliding scale of minimum lot sizes, based on the number of dwelling units per lot. In other words, the owner desiring to erect a multiple-unit dwelling may do so provided his lot is commensurately larger than that required for a single-family residence. Although occasionally an ordinance requires the same number of square feet of lot size for each dwelling unit, in most cases the space required for each additional unit after the first is somewhat less than that required for the first unit on the lot.

In recent years an increasing number of ordinances have provided for "agricultural," "estate," "open land," or other types of districts with very large minimum lot size requirements. Although court decisions in some states have upheld requirements of as much as five-acre lots, such requirements are extremely rare and should be imposed only where there are highly unusual circumstances. 20,000 square feet (slightly less than one-half acre) is the largest requirement to be found in ordinary circumstances, and most cities have a set of residence districts whose requirements range from 10,000 square feet down to as low as 2,500 square feet per dwelling unit.

Where very large lot sizes are required, courts are likely to insist that the municipality offer detailed factual arguments as to the necessity for such requirements. Ordinarily, requirements for the largest lot sizes are based on such factors as absence of public water or sewer facilities, efforts to encourage truck gardening, absence of adequate fire-fighting facilities, and possibly the need to protect the community's tax base through preservation of high-value neighborhoods (although some courts may reject this as a proper basis). The requirements for the smallest lots may actually be less than the desirable minima, but may be necessitated by existing patterns of land development in older neighborhoods.

To avoid evasion of the spirit of minimum lot area requirements through the use of odd-shaped lots (such as very deep, narrow lots whose rear portions are unusable because of terrain features) most ordinances couple such requirements with minimum lot width requirements. These requirements should take into consideration existing lot widths in the area regulated, but should also be large enough to provide space for construction of a ranch-style house with the required side yards in areas where that type of construction is popular. Otherwise there will be many applications to the board of adjustment for relief from side-yard requirements. A definition of how to measure lot widths in cases of irregularly-shaped lots should also be included in the ordinance.

YARD REGULATIONS

Yard regulations are usually divided into front-, rear-, and side yard requirements. Most ordinances require front and side yards in residential districts only, or for residences situated in other districts, although a growing number of ordinances require front yards in certain classes of business and industrial districts. Figure 15–7 illustrates the use of yards in an industrial park district. Occasionally the property owner is given the option of using such space for off-street parking requirements as well, although many planners regard this as bad practice because a parking space does not have the same characteristics as a yard.

Front-yard requirements are commonly expressed in four ways: (1) as a minimum number of feet between the front lot line and the front of the building; (2) as a percentage of the lot depth; (3) as a relationship to the front yards of other buildings which have already been constructed in the immediate neighborhood; (4) as a minimum number of feet between the front of the building and the center line of the street.

Most ordinances require that new buildings conform to the building lines established by certain neighboring structures (subject to maximum and minimum limits). For areas where there are no neighboring structures, a standard front-yard distance is also expressed.

Front-yard requirements are related to the

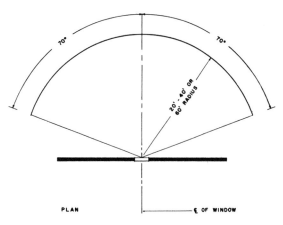

FIGURE 15–7. *Required window exposure*

setback requirements that occasionally appear in separate ordinances. Sometimes front yards are increased for lots fronting on major thoroughfares, to remove residences from the noise, smoke, dust, fumes, and traffic dangers associated with such arteries. If front yards are increased in depth along major thoroughfares, the requirement should be on this basis, rather than for the stated purpose of subsequent street widening. A number of ordinances aimed at street-widening were invalidated early in the 20th century, and those decisions may yet be used to confound the unwary.

Front-yard depths vary considerably. The usual rule of thumb for determining appropriate requirements is that the total distance between buildings facing one another (including the street right-of-way) is between two and three times the maximum height limit for the district. Common front-yard requirements in single-family districts range from 25 to 40 feet; they are usually somewhat less in older multiple-unit districts, but requirements for newer districts may be greater, in order to provide adequate play space for children.

Side-yard requirements should be based in part on fire insurance requirements, being increased in areas where fire protection is inadequate. In most cities, at least five to eight feet on either side of the building is required. Some requirements vary according to the height or length of the building or according to the number of dwelling units it contains. Although side yards are not usually required in business districts, where they are provided they should be at least three feet in width, so that they can be entered and cleaned easily.

Rear-yard requirements may be expressed either in feet or as a percentage of lot depth. Commonly, minimum depths ranging from 15 to 40 feet are required. Ordinances customarily permit the erection of accessory buildings (such as garages and woodsheds) in rear yards, provided: (1) they do not occupy more than a stated percentage of the required yard; (2) equivalent open space is left elsewhere on the lot; and (3) they are located at stated distances from all lot lines.

Corner lots present problems that should be dealt with specifically. One of these problems is to insure visibility for motorists. This is done by prohibiting any structure or planting more than a certain specified height (often two to four feet) above the curb level within a distance of 20 to 40 feet from a street intersection. Another relates to blocks where buildings face each of two intersecting streets. In this situation the "side-yard" requirement for the corner lot is usually increased to a distance more closely approximating the front-yard requirement of the neighboring lot. Any accessory buildings on the corner lot are required to remain behind front-yard lines applying to adjoining lots.

As means of affording additional outside window openings for the benefit of their tenants, many buildings contain outer courts (open on at least one side) or inner courts (completely surrounded by the building). Many zoning ordinances specify the minimum size for such courts. Required dimensions normally vary according to the number of stories above the bottom of the court, the distance from the closed end to the open end of an open court, and whether or not the structure is in residential use. The minimum widths of outer courts generally vary from four to 12 feet, and inner courts from four to 20 feet.

Most ordinances permit encroachments of various types on the required yards and courts. Such things as open fire escapes, chimneys, flues, cornices and eaves, and occasionally bay windows fall within the permitted types of encroachments. While open porches and carports are frequently added to this category, the possibility that they might be enclosed later can create enforcement problems.

OFF-STREET PARKING AND LOADING

A special type of open-space requirement is the provision for off-street parking and loading spaces. Such spaces may or may not be permitted to occupy required yard spaces (as already indicated, they probably should not); in either case, the ordinance should deal with this aspect specifically. In general, the amount of space required depends on use of the property. This is not a satisfactory solution, since the use of a building may change from time to time, when it is no longer possible to secure additional space. If a furniture store were to be sold for use as a five-and-ten cent store, for example, the need for parking space would obviously increase markedly. While the ordinance may prohibit the issuance of occupancy permits in such situations until satisfactory arrangements are made for off-street parking, a court might very well decide that such a prohibition represented an unreasonable requirement in a particular case.

Some ordinances allow the property owner to meet off-street parking space requirements by providing space on another lot within a stated distance from the lot on which the main use is located. Where this arrangement is permitted, the ordinance should specify that the parking space must be owned by the same person who owns the property under review. Unless this is required, difficult cases could arise, for instance, when a lease on a parking lot expires and the owner of the lot attempts to convert it to some other use.

OTHER ORDINANCE PROVISIONS

Nonconforming Uses. At the time a zoning ordinance is originally adopted, there are, in almost every district, some uses that existed before the ordinance was adopted, which do not conform to the use regulations or the dimensional regulations for the district. These are known as nonconforming uses. Other such uses are created from time to time by amendments to the zoning ordinance. In order to make the adoption of a zoning ordinance politically and financially feasible, and because of some doubt as to the constitutionality of doing otherwise, drafts of early ordinances allowed nonconforming uses to continue as they were at the time of adoption of the ordinance or amendment, subject only to certain provisions designed to limit the enlargement of the nonconforming use and to restrict rebuilding after damage through the effluxion of time, or by fire, weather or natural calamity. These provisions normally prohibit:

1. The enlargement or extension of a nonconforming use;

2. The resumption of a nonconforming use after discontinuance for a stated period of time;

3. The changing of a nonconforming use to any other use save one in a "higher" classification;

4. The rebuilding or reconstruction of a nonconforming use after a specified degree of damage or destruction.

Nonconforming use provisions, in practice, have not led to their general elimination.

Two new techniques for the control and elimination of nonconforming uses have appeared in some recent ordinances. One is the classification of nonconformities into:

1. Nonconforming uses of open land such as junk yards and used car lots;

2. Nonconforming uses of conforming buildings, such as a funeral home utilizing an old residence in a residential district;

3. Nonconforming uses of buildings usable only for nonconforming purposes; such as a gasoline service station in a residence district;

4. Buildings that are nonconforming only so far as they violate dimensional regulations, such as a residence in a residential district with smaller side yards than the ordinance requires.

These different types of nonconformities obviously present varying problems, and require treatment in different ways.

A second emerging technique is to provide for the elimination of nonconforming uses—immediately, after a uniform period of time, or after varying periods of time. The last approach, sometimes referred to as the "amortization of nonconforming uses," is based on the philosophy of allowing the owner to amortize over a period of time the cost of his investment. It is perhaps the most equitable, since it is obviously less difficult to eliminate a junkyard or a billboard, representing minimal capital investment, than a concrete building. The courts have given these provisions a mixed reception, depending somewhat upon the amount of the capital involved in individual cases.

There are also different methods for administrative treatment of nonconforming use Some ordinances nominate the zoning enforcement officer to inventory and control nonconforming uses. Some require the owner of a nonconforming use to secure a certificate of occupancy or use permit for that use within a stated period after adoption of the ordinance or amendment that renders it nonconforming. Failure to obtain such a certificate is prima facie evidence that the use is not entitled to nonconforming status. Some more recent ordinances require annual registration by the owners of all nonconforming uses. The pupose of all these provisions is to secure a more accurate record for use in enforcement procedures.

LARGE-SCALE BUILDING PROJECTS

The practice has already been described under which some ordinances give special treatment to the developers of large-scale projects such as "planned unit developments." Frequently these projects involve the construction of a great number of rental units on a single tract of land, and it is unreasonable to require the developer to subdivide the tract to provide lot lines from which yards and other dimensional features can be measured. Some projects involve the planning and construction of a complete community, including business districts and industrial plants. The customary procedure for such projects requires the developer to submit his plans to the planning commission for its recommendations and to the governing body for approval. He is required to meet overall density requirements and open space requirements, but often regulations may be relaxed to varying degrees consistent with the protection of the public at large, the neighboring properties and the future residents of the project. Because approval of such plans is so closely related to amendment of the zoning ordinance and to approval of a subdivision plan, this procedure is preferable to turning the matter over to the board of adjustment. Planned unit developments are dealt with at greater length in Chapter 16.

ENFORCEMENT PROVISIONS

The zoning ordinance should contain detailed provisions regulating the administration and enforcement of the zoning ordinance, as described later in this chapter. In the absence of such provisions, a court may find there has been unlawful delegation of legislative authority to the enforcement officer or to the board of adjustment, or that ordinance provisions permit arbitrary and discriminatory actions on the part of these officials.

The ordinance should provide for the appointment and specify the powers and duties of the enforcement officer and of the board of adjustment. It should provide for the issuance of building permits and of occupancy or use permits, both for ordinary cases and for nonconforming uses. It should provide penalties for violations of the ordinance. Penalty provisions usually authorize the imposition of a fine or imprisonment for each day on which a violation continues, the securing of an injunction against the violator of the ordinance, or the securing of a mandatory injunction ordering the removal of an illegal structure. Since many of these matters are covered in the normal state enabling act, that act should be studied carefully before the ordinance provisions are drafted. Here the counsel of the legal officer will be invaluable.

CONFLICT WITH OTHER ORDINANCES OR DEED RESTRICTIONS

Occasionally the requirements of other ordinances will be more severe than those of the zoning ordinance. At other times, less severe requirements of such ordinances will be cited as a reason for non-compliance with the zoning ordinance. The zoning ordinance should make clear that the most stringent provisions will prevail.

Similarly, it is well to indicate in the zoning ordinance that deed restrictions will not have the effect of overruling any provisions of the zoning ordinance and that it is not the intent of the ordinance to supersede any deed restrictions that are more stringent. In the absence of such provisions, the courts ordinarily reach the same conclusions, but many citizens are puzzled about the relationship between overlapping restrictions and a specific statement will often obviate recourse to the courts.

Administration of the Zoning Ordinance

Regardless of how much care and study goes into the preparation of the zoning ordinance and the excellence of the finished product, it will have no effect unless it is enforced. A zoning ordinance can be destroyed in three ways:

1. By laxity or indifference on the part of the zoning enforcement officer in carrying out his duties;

2. By over-liberality on the part of the board of adjustment in granting variances; and

3. By willingness on the part of the legislative body to adopt unwise amendments to the ordinance based on the applications of individual property owners.

When any of these things happen, public confidence in zoning is shaken, violators are encouraged, and judicial support for the ordinance is more difficult to obtain.

The enforcement process should not involve the legislative body: the zoning enforcement officer bears the primary responsibility for handling individual cases, subject to appeals to the board of adjustment and thence to the courts. Although some governing bodies attempt to inject themselves into the process, they are in most cases acting contrary to statutory provisions, and their actions may be challenged in the courts.

THE ZONING ENFORCEMENT OFFICER

The zoning enforcement officer is the key man in the whole administrative process, since he alone comes in contact with all the individual cases. Many property owners are completely dependent on him for their understanding of the zoning ordinance and its underlying purposes. Through his tact and persuasive abilities, widespread compliance can be brought about with the minimum of legal action. If he lacks these qualities, a continuous flow of "problem cases" can be expected.

The zoning enforcement officer may be the local building inspector or a member of the inspection department. This is because the duties of the inspector normally include issuing building permits and making inspections under the building code, and perhaps making periodic inspections for violations of that code and for fire hazards. It is a simple matter for him to check compliance with the zoning ordinance at the same time that he is carrying out these other duties.

Although making the building inspector the zoning enforcement officer is the predominant organizational arrangement, two other approaches have been followed in some cities. In some cases, it is believed that the local building inspector does not have sufficient background in the theory and practice of zoning to enforce the zoning ordinance, so this function has been placed under the jurisdiction of the planning department. Where this has been done, of course, there must be very close working relationships with the inspection department.

In other cases, separate departments of zoning administration have been created. Advocates of this arrangement point out that such a department is more apt to give attention to violations of the zoning ordinance which do not involve building construction or alteration, than is the case with the usual building inspection department. A further advantage to placing zoning administration outside the planning department is that it enables the planning staff to concentrate on studies and plans, without being diverted by day-to-day administration problems. In a few cities, the department of zoning administration has also been assigned some of the functions normally performed by the board of adjustment, including the handling of certain types of special exceptions and variances. This arrangement, too, necessitates close coordination with the inspection department.

In general, the enforcement officer (wherever located organizationally) is charged with carrying out the literal provisions of the zoning ordinance. He has no discretion to modify those provisions in individual cases. He issues zoning permits; checks to see that the work is carried out in accordance with the permit; issues a certificate of occupancy (sometimes called a use permit, which may be a more descriptive term) if the completed structure meets ordinance requirements; issues such a certificate whenever the use of the property changes; administers provisions of the ordinance dealing with nonconforming uses; makes periodic checks for violations of the ordinance; initiates court action to prevent or halt violations of the ordinance; and keeps records of individual cases. He may also serve as a secretary for the board of adjustment and see that proper legal notice is given for board of adjustment cases.

It cannot be emphasized too strongly that the zoning ordinance is not a self-enforcing piece of legislation and must, therefore, be given close attention by the members of the municipal administration. Great strides have been made in the improvement of zoning techniques, but, unfortunately, the same progress has not been made in obtaining general acceptance of the fact that a considerable amount of effort needs to be put into the enforcement of the zoning ordinance on a day-to-day basis in order to gain the benefit of these new techniques.

The Zoning Board of Adjustment

Nearly all zoning ordinances and enabling acts provide for the creation of a board of adjustment, sometimes called a board of appeals, to hear appeals on the enforcement officer's decisions and to grant relief from literal enforcement of the ordinance in certain hardship situations. This board is customarily a group of unpaid citizens working on a part-time basis. Because of the heavy workload of zoning cases in some large cities, suggestions have been made that a special zoning court, similar to traffic, housing, and domestic relations courts, might assume this function, but no such courts have yet been created.

Composition of the Board

The membership of the board of adjustment is almost always specified in the state zoning enabling act. Usually this provides for a five-member board, serving overlapping terms, although some state statutes allow up to 15 members. It has been found, however, that a five-member board is the most convenient. Because most enabling acts require the affirmative vote of four members in order to grant relief to an applicant, it is desirable that the quorum for meetings of the board be fixed at five members. With this quorum requirement in mind, some enabling acts provide for appointment of alternate members who may sit on the board when regular members are absent. Another desirable arrangement, sometimes found in enabling acts, is for one of the members of the board of

adjustment to be a member of the planning commission, to provide liaison between the two bodies. Although members of the board usually serve without compensation, where there is a great volume of work, they may often receive stated amounts per meeting attended and expenses are usually authorized.

Functions of the Board

The board of adjustment is a quasi-judicial body charged by the zoning ordinance with carrying out certain functions. It is not a legislative body with authority to substitute its judgment for that of the governing body, nor is it charged with the routine administration of the zoning ordinance, which is the responsibility of the zoning enforcement officer. The board must uphold the meaning and the spirit of the ordinance as enacted by the legislature even though it may disagree with the governing body's judgment as to the proper content of the ordinance. Where particular provisions of the ordinance seem to lead to consistent injustice, the board should recommend to the council that the ordinance be amended. The board should not attempt to "back-door" amendment through its own decisions. This would be illegal assumption of the legislative function.

The board's functions are set forth in general terms by most enabling acts and ordinances and the courts have ratified the limits of these functions rather specifically in a great many individual cases. In general, the board's functions fall under three major headings: (1) interpretation of the zoning ordinance; (2) the granting of "special use permits" or "special exceptions"; (3) the granting of "variances."

Interpretation. The board's first function in interpreting the zoning ordinance is very much like that of a court. It consists of hearing appeals from the enforcement officer's decisions, when it is alleged that he has misinterpreted the meaning of the ordinance or misapplied its provisions in a particular case. The board first determines the facts of the case and then applies what it conceives to be the proper meaning of the ordinance. For example, it might be called upon to decide whether a given type of property use in a given location would be "noxious or offensive" within the meaning of a clause forbidding "any trade, industry, or use that is noxious or offensive by reason of the emission of smoke, dust, odors, glare, vibration, or noise." Another common case under the interpretation power of the board is that of clarifying the location of a zoning boundary where the zoning map is ambiguous or unclear.

In all instances of the exercise of the power of interpretation, the board must be guided by the letter and the spirit of the ordinance and reach a judgment as a group of prudent people doing its best to uphold the cause of justice. Ordinarily, the factual findings of the board are taken as final, so long as there is some evidence to support them, but its interpretations of the meanings of the ordinance are subject to reversal on appeal to the courts.

Granting Special Permits. In the zoning of every city it will be found that there are certain uses which are necessary in some types of districts, but which may be detrimental to their neighbors if proper safeguards are not taken. A common example of this is a public utility substation which must be located in a residential district. The usual method of handling such uses is to provide that they shall be permitted in the district only when they comply with conditions that the board may impose for the protection of the neighborhood and public interest. For example, it might require that the substation be designed to look like a residence and that it be properly landscaped to fit into its surroundings. This function of the board is known as the granting of special use permits or special exceptions. Recent ordinances tend to specify the uses that may be so permitted, the standards to be applied by the board in granting them and other instructions for the guidance of the board. The number of permissible special uses should be held to a minimum in the ordinance so that the device does not become a dumping ground for undesirable uses.

The board must exercise the power of granting special use permits in the same manner as it exercises its power of interpretation: it must follow the language of the ordinance exactly and act only after all necessary findings have been made. The granting of relief is automatic when these findings appear, rather than being subject to the board's discretion. The board

has considerable latitude in the imposition of conditions, however. In general, the courts require only that these conditions be "reasonable." The board should exercise some ingenuity in devising conditions that will have the desired effect, because in doing so it will be able to insure adequate protection to the neighborhood, consistent with the intent of the zoning ordinance.

Granting Variances. Probably the major reason for the creation of the board of adjustment is to take care of the special situations that cannot be dealt with in the ordinance without making it unduly complicated. The ordinary workings of the ordinance will produce hardship cases that otherwise would have to go to court for relief. A typical example is where the topography of a particular lot makes it impossible to comply with normal front-yard or side-yard requirements.

The statutory language granting this power to the board contains only the most general standards and many boards are tempted to grant relief whenever they fancy that the ends of justice will be served. Attitudes such as this can destroy the effectiveness of the zoning ordinance and create mistrust in the minds of the citizens. In the opinion of many students of zoning, the illegal activities of boards of adjustment in the field of variances have been so flagrant as to call for the elimination of the board's power to grant them. The courts have been active, also, in defining the circumstances under which variance relief may be granted. Additionally, many of the newer ordinances spell out these court-devised rules, so that there will be no misunderstanding by the board as to its power and degree of discretion.

The enabling act usually authorizes the board to grant relief where there are "practical difficulties or unnecessary hardship" in the way of carrying out the strict letter of the ordinance. Courts have interpreted this phrase to mean that the property owner must be able to show, if he complies with the provisions of the ordinance, that he cannot make any reasonable use of his property. The fact that he might make a greater profit by using his property in a manner prohibited by the ordinance is considered irrelevant, since almost any individual applicant could make that same showing; the greater profit for that individual would be siphoned off from the value of all his neighbors' properties. At least a part of the essence of zoning is the common protection that it affords all property owners, on the theory that all will benefit if all comply, but that each individual must sacrifice some freedom of choice in order to enjoy this benefit.

A major restriction that must be observed by the board is that the hardship which serves as a basis for the granting of a variance must be unique to the property of the applicant. If the condition of which he complains is neighborhood-wide, it must be presumed that the governing body knew of this condition and deliberately chose, presumably on the basis of other considerations, to ignore it in the zoning requirements. A grant of relief by the board on the basis of a neighborhood-wide smell from a sewer line, for example, would be considered contrary to the spirit and intent of the ordinance and beyond the board's powers. Where general conditions are found to exist, the proper relief is an amendment to the ordinance, not the granting of a variance.

Other court-imposed restrictions on the granting of variances require that the hardship must result from the application of the zoning ordinance, not from the operation of a deed restriction or some other disability of the property. The hardship must be suffered specifically by the property in question, not by someone else, as would be the case where an owner seeking to erect a grocery store cites the great need of housewives in the area.

The hardship must not result from the applicant's own actions. He cannot cite expenses incurred in violating the ordinance as a reason for granting him relief from its terms. Some courts have also adopted a rule denying relief to an applicant who has bought property knowing that zoning restrictions prevent him from using it in the way he wishes.

The variance that is granted must also be in harmony with the general purpose and intent of the ordinance and preserve its spirit. In interpreting the statutory language on which this requirement is based, the courts have said that the board of adjustment may not grant a variance authorizing the applicant to enlarge a nonconforming use or in any way to make it more permanent. In most states, the courts have also held that the board may not grant a "use" variance, that is, a variance authorizing the property to be used for a purpose prohibited by the ordinance, as distinguished from a variance in the lot area, yard size, building height, or other "dimensional" requirements. This prohibition is based on the theory that a use variance amounts to an exercise of legislative authority.

Finally, in the granting of the variance, the board must take care to assure that the public safety and welfare are preserved and that substantial justice has been done. Unlike an ordinary court, the board has the function of serving as an advocate of the public interest. It should always place this consideration foremost, rather than looking upon its duties as that of a simple arbitration of disputes among private parties. The board should consider how granting a particular variance will affect neighboring properties. If more harm will be done to them by granting the variance than would be done to the applicant by denying it, the variance should be denied.

In the granting of variances as well as in the granting of special exceptions, the board has the power to place conditions on its grant. Since a variance is regarded as a special privilege rather than as a right, the property owner must, in order to enjoy it, comply with whatever reasonable conditions are imposed—even though they may go beyond the permissible range of ordinary police power regulations.

PROCEDURES OF THE BOARD

Although the board of adjustment is not a court, it should recognize that its functions are primarily judicial. Its decisions affect private property rights as surely as a court's decision, and its records are the basis for any further judicial proceedings. Under these circumstances, it is important that the board of adjustment function with the dignity and regularity that is expected of a court.

Immediately after its creation the board should establish rules of procedure for itself, and it should abide by those rules. It should, if possible, adopt standard forms for the taking of appeals, so that the parties will know what is expected of them. It should be careful to see that interested parties receive proper notice of each case, and that they have an opportunity to testify if they wish. In the conduct of its hearings it should follow orderly procedures. And finally, it should keep adequate records to show in each case that it considers: (1) the evidence received; (2) the findings of fact that it makes and upon which it bases its decision; (3) its decision. These are minimum standards that every citizen has a right to expect.

The record of the board's proceedings will normally form the basis for any court review of its actions, so that great care should be taken to insure that all pertinent information is included in this record. If, for instance, the board is required, in a certain case, to find that the permission sought will not have an adverse influence on neighboring property, it must go beyond the mere statement that no adverse influence would appear to be exerted, and record the facts, the evidence, and the reasoning on which such conclusion was based. It is wise to have this written in detail for the record so that it is always available for presentation at court should the need arise. Many boards submit a copy of their findings of fact to the governing body as a routine procedure so that the legislature remains fully informed at all times and may adopt the findings in cases where they must take final action under the provisions of an ordinance.

Where the record is not sufficient, the court will be required to remand it for amplification or will be forced to hear the matter afresh. In either case, delays will occur which could have been avoided by the presence of an adequate record made by the board of adjustment.

COURT REVIEW OF ZONING PRACTICES

In cases of local disagreement arising over the interpretation, application, or reasonableness of zoning ordinance provisions it is possible that any one, or more, of four parties might seek court review of the dispute.

1. A governing body that wishes to terminate a violation.

2. A property owner who has been denied local relief for his problem.

3. Neighboring property owners affected by, and objecting to, a grant of relief to the property owner by the board of appeals or local governing body, or

4. Any owners of property which may be affected in use or value by a violation.

The specific terms of the applicable state enabling act will determine the details of the action which may be taken in the foregoing cases. In order to give brief illustrations reference will be made to Illinois law. Under the Illinois Revised Statutes (1963) the following actions are possible:

1. Action by the governing body.

Governing body may file a complaint and bring the offending owner before the circuit court. If found guilty, a fine is usually imposed. Imprisonment is also possible but usually reserved for grave violations. Ordinances often stipulate a maximum fine of $200 per day of continued violation. A suit for injunction to restrain continuation of a violation is often more effective than a fine. The board's decision may also be reviewed by the court under the Administrative Review Act, but this is rare.

2. Action by the property owner.

When an owner has sought relief, unsuccessfully, through the board of appeals, he may apply to the circuit court to have his case considered by them. The particular type of court action initiated depends on the circumstances. The owner may also request an injunction, a declaratory judgment or a mandamus. The first restrains the governing body from interfering with the proposed use; the second declares that the zoning restrictions are invalid with reference to the subject property; and the mandamus compels the issuance of a building permit.

When the board's decision is final the owner may request a review of the denial of an application, under the Administrative Review Act. This occurs when no ratification of the board's decision by the governing body is required.

3. Actions by neighboring property owners. In order to sustain an action, neighbors must show that they suffered, or could suffer, damages in some special and different way from the public at large.

4. Actions by owners of property affected by a violation.

The Illinois Revised Statutes expressly authorize persons whose property may be affected in value or use by a violation of the zoning ordinance, to institute an action to restrain or abate this violation. This type of action is a type of "self-help" and may be resorted to if a governing body refuses to take restraining or abatement action, or maintains that no violation exists. The aggrieved owner then has a right to seek a court ruling on the alleged violation.

APPELLATE REVIEW

The decisions of the circuit court in matters relating to zoning are subject to review by either the Illinois Supreme Court, or the Appellate Court.

In general, a final judgment of a circuit court will be appealable to the Illinois Supreme Court in cases "involving a question arising under the Constitution of the United States or of the State of Illinois." In routine zoning cases the Supreme Court can be expected to transfer cases to the Appellate Court.

Conclusion

In this chapter an attempt has been made to acquaint the reader with an outline of the history and philosophy of zoning and to emphasize the fact that it cannot be separated from the planning process which culminates in a comprehensive plan of which zoning is but one of the tools of implementation.

The way in which a zoning ordinance is prepared and adopted has been explored and many comments have been made on new concepts and techniques.

When all these have been embodied into an ordinance it may be well-conceived, perfectly suited to local conditions, and technically perfect. At this stage it is still merely a document and requires the injection of two elements before it can have its intended impact on the community.

The first element is that its provisions should be understood and supported generally by the public, and the second is that the ordinance should be administered firmly and impartially. The former provision is aided by the requirement for public hearings which gives the governing body an opportunity to gauge public reaction to the proposed ordinance and to make such amendments to it as would seem to be advisable. This should be supported by a supplementary educational publicity program. The latter provision is more difficult and more lasting and involves the maintenance of a sympathetic relationship between the law and those subjected to it.

In this relationship two levels of human contact are involved. First, the zoning officer, who is usually the first point of contact between the law and the public, and second, the board of appeal (or adjustment) which must hear and decide appeals from the zoning officer's decisions and grant relief in cases where the literal enforcement of the ordinance provisions would cause undue hardship.

The zoning officer's job is very demanding and requires that he bring to it a certain degree of dedication for its proper performance. He is the first link in the chain which leads from zoning ordinance to compliance, and his influence is felt in an area where public relations and administration of the law are inextricably involved. His relationship with members of the public can make the difference between their marginal compliance and their willing cooperation, and will be reflected in the number and type of cases which come before the board of appeals for determination.

A member of the board of appeals must be no less dedicated than the zoning officer if the ideal of impartial and enlightened administration of the zoning ordinance is to be upheld. The board's function is a most important one in that the control of property values often lies in their hands. They are entrusted with the exercise of one aspect of the police power of the state and must always remain worthy of that trust.

It is incumbent upon all those involved in the process of zoning administration to strive continuously for the more perfect execution of a difficult and sensitive duty which, particularly in the smaller community, must be carried out impartially.

16

Land Subdivision

Whenever a town has been established in what is now the United States, its public or private developers have engaged in the process of subdivision of land. On the tract available to them they have mapped out the lines of streets, which both provided access and divided the land into blocks. They have further divided these blocks into lots, to facilitate distribution of the land among individual property owners. They have reserved some lands as public squares or commons or parks. They have reserved other lands as sites for schools, town offices, churches, hospitals, and other public and semi-public buildings. They have physically constructed streets and sidewalks and utilities systems in accordance with the practices of the times.

This process is still going on with little change as "new towns" are built today. But it is also continuing in older towns, as "subdivisions" are added to the original towns like new cells growing onto the chambered Nautilus.

Because this is the process by which cities are built and grow, and because initial decisions with respect to the design of the street system, lot layout, and so forth have extraordinarily enduring effects, no local planning program can be considered adequate which does not include public controls over this process.

Historical Background

Some present-day developers, impatient of any limitations on their ability to turn a profit, tend to refer to subdivision regulations as a particularly abhorrent outgrowth of 20th cen-

tury "big government." Occasionally even some city officials agree with this viewpoint.

The earliest of the new towns in this country were laid out pursuant to instructions contained in royal directives,[1] charters granted by the colonial assemblies,[2] and later charters issued by the newly-formed state legislatures.[3]

---

[1] See, for example, the "Royal Ordinances for the Laying Out of New Cities, Towns or Villages" (Archivo Nacional, Madrid, Ms. 3017 Bulas y Cedulas para el Gobierno de las Indias) promulgated by Philip II of Spain in 1573, which governed the layout of every Spanish town in North America, from St. Augustine to Los Angeles. This document prescribed the siting and orientation of the town, the layout and dimensions of the main plaza, the basic street system, the reservation of sites for churches, monastery, hospital, the Royal and Town Council House, the Custom-House and Arsenal, and the plan for distributing lots. It is translated by Mrs. Zelia Nuttall on pp. 249–254 of Volume 1922 of the HISPANIC AMERICAN HISTORICAL REVIEW.

[2] E.g., the charter for the town of Bath, N.C.: ". . . it is hereby Enacted that convenient places and proportions of Lands be laid out and preserved for a Church, a Town-House & a Market Place & that the rest of the Land which is not already laid out be forthwith laid out into lotts of halfe an Acre each with convenient streets and Passages." Laws, 1715, c. 52 (XXIII State Records of North Carolina 73). These provisions became more or less standard in colonial charters in North Carolina, with occasional modifications such as Beaufort's "Provided always, That the Principal Streets in the said Town shall be Sixty Six Feet wide, at least." Laws, 1723, c. 15 (XXV State Records of North Carolina 206).

[3] The newly independent legislators continued both prevailing types of regulation and a willingness to require dedication of privately owned land for public purposes; e.g., the requirements in the charter of Pittsborough, N.C.: ". . . That the trustees hereafter appointed, . . . shall as soon as may be after the passing of this Act, cause one hundred acres of land to be laid off in half acre lots each, with convenient streets, lanes and alleys, and an hundred acres for the public buildings." Laws, 1785, c. 60 (XXIV State Records of North Carolina 774).

Even the Continental Congress came into the process peripherally, with its regulations to guide the surveying and disposition of the western territories.[4] These legal instruments were, in a very real sense, the first subdivision regulations in America.

The first locally-enacted measures bearing on land subdivision grew out of the plans adopted or referred to in these early charters. A principal ingredient of most such plans was a map of the street system.[5] As the early towns outgrew their original bounds soon after independence, the legislatures of Pennsylvania, Virginia, Massachusetts, and New York authorized certain municipalities to map proposed extensions of their original street systems and to require property owners to observe these "official maps" as they divided up their lands.[6]

Following these early beginnings, the 19th century saw two great surges of subdivision-regulation activity. The first grew out of the excesses of the land development companies which had created many uncertainties in land titles as the continent was opened to settlement. It consisted of legislation enacted in many states, but particularly the Midwest and Far West, which required that proposed subdivisions be accurately surveyed and platted, that the survey be verified by a local governmental engineer, that the plat be approved by local officials and recorded prior to any sales of lots, and that the plat be accompanied by a certificate of a local tax official that there were no outstanding tax liens on the property.

The second reflected the same concern with the design of street systems which had appeared in the early official map legislation. This consisted of legislation adopted by many states across the country (and by Congress for the District of Columbia) which normally required that new streets tie into the town's existing street pattern, that they continue the widths and alignment of the earlier streets, and that they be dedicated to the public. Once again enforcement was to be through requiring that all additions to towns be platted and that local officials approve the street layout prior to recordation and sale of lots.

Thus, unlike zoning, the subdivision regulations which became an important tool of planning officials in the 1920s were merely a new model of a very old device, rather than a totally new type of legal control. The distinctive contribution of the 20th century legislation (which largely stemmed from the Standard City Planning Enabling Act, published by the U.S. Department of Commerce in 1928) was one of concept rather than of substance: it made subdivision regulation a part of a comprehensive and continuing program of planning and guiding the growth of cities, rather than a device used independently to achieve limited ends. As a means of effectuating this concept, major responsibility for administering subdivision regulations was transferred from such officials as the city engineer, the county surveyor, the tax supervisor, or the city treasurer to the planning commission and its staff.

Use of the new approach spread rapidly across the country, although state enabling acts frequently differed significantly from the Standard Act. A 1934 survey indicated that some 425 American cities had already empowered their planning commissions to participate in the regulation of subdivisions, either directly or in a recommendatory capacity.[7] By 1961 a survey of 1,180 cities over 10,000 population revealed that 906 had comprehensive subdivision regulations in effect as part of their planning programs.[8] Each of the 50 states has now adopted enabling legislation under which this type of regulation may be undertaken by local units of government.

The interest displayed by the federal government in its sponsorship of the Standard City

[4] An ordinance for Ascertaining the Mode of Disposing of Lands in the Western Territory, 28 J. Cont. Cong. 375 (1785), was the first of a series of such laws.

[5] The finest source book on early plans available is John W. Reps, THE MAKING OF URBAN AMERICA (Princeton, N.J.: Princeton University Press, 1965). See also illustrations of early town plans in Chapter 1 of this volume.

[6] See Russell Van Nest Black, BUILDING LINES AND RESERVATIONS FOR FUTURE STREETS (Cambridge, Mass.: Harvard University Press, 1935), p. 8, for an account of this development. He notes that the Pennsylvania law, which began with Laws, 1782, § 19441, has persisted to the present day, with some amendment.

[7] See John W. Reps, "Control of Land Subdivision by Municipal Planning Boards," CORNELL LAW QUARTERLY, XL (Winter, 1955), pp. 258–59.

[8] International City Managers' Association, THE MUNICIPAL YEAR BOOK (Chicago: 1961), p. 272.

Planning Enabling Act has continued through the years, as illustrated by the detailed subdivision standards adopted by the Federal Housing Administration for its use in administering its mortgage insurance programs, the publication by the Housing and Home Finance Agency of several editions of a set of "Suggested Land Subdivision Regulations," and similar activities. While it is occasionally charged that federal standards have delayed adoption of some particular design innovation, there can be no doubt that they have been a prime factor in raising the general level of subdivision design throughout the country far above the mechanical "gridiron" approach which once was common.

By and large the 20th century form of subdivision regulation has proved both workable and beneficial. However, recent changes in technology and in land development practices have demonstrated some shortcomings, as will be described later in this chapter, and it is likely that there will be further modifications in approach to deal with these shortcomings.

General Nature of Subdivision Regulations

As the foregoing discussion has indicated, subdivision regulations are locally-adopted laws governing the process of converting raw land into building sites. They normally accomplish this through plat approval procedures, under which a developer is not permitted to make improvements or to divide and sell his land until the planning commission has approved a plat (map) of the proposed design of his subdivision. The approval or disapproval of the commission is based upon compliance or noncompliance of the proposal with development standards set forth in the subdivision regulations. In the event that the developer attempts to record an unapproved plat in the local registry of deeds (or county recorder's office) or to sell lots by reference to such a plat, he may be subject to various civil and criminal penalties.

Objectives

Subdivision regulations may serve a wide range of purposes. To the health officer they are a means of insuring that new residential developments have a safe water supply and sewage disposal system and that they are properly drained. To the tax official they are a step toward securing adequate records of land titles. To the city engineer or public works director they are a means of assuring safe design and proper construction of new streets, utilities, and drainage systems—as well as providing a record of the location of underground utilities. To the fire chief they are a means of securing water systems of adequate size and pressure for fire-fighting and streets on which his trucks can maneuver. To the school or parks official they are a way to preserve or secure the school sites and recreation areas needed to serve the people coming into a developing neighborhood. To the lot purchaser they are an assurance that he will receive a buildable, properly oriented, well-drained lot, provided with adequate facilities to meet his day-to-day needs, in a subdivision whose value will hold up over the years. To the responsible developer they are protection against substandard competitors who might either undersell him or destroy the value of his well-planned subdivision with a shoddy one nearby.

From the specialized view of the planner, subdivision regulations are important at two distinct levels. First, they enable him to coordinate the otherwise unrelated plans of a great many individual developers, and in the process to assure that provision is made for such major elements of the land development plan as rights-of-way for major thoroughfares, parks, school sites, major water lines and sewer outfalls, and so forth. Second, they enable him to control the internal design of each new subdivision so that its pattern of streets, lots, and other facilities will be safe, pleasant, and economical to maintain.

Finally, from the standpoint of the city administrator and the local governing board, subdivision regulations may be thought of as having two major objectives. First, these officials are interested in the design aspects of new subdivisions, as are the other officials mentioned. But secondly, they are also interested in allocating the costs of certain improvements most equitably between the residents of the immediate area and the taxpayers of the city as a whole. When subdivision regulations require a developer to dedicate land to the public or to install utilities or to build streets, they represent a judgment that the particular improvements involved are (1) necessary in a contemporary environment and (2) predominantly of special benefit to the people who will buy lots from him (presumably at a price sufficient to cover the cost of these improvements) rather than of general benefit to the taxpayers of the city as a whole.

LEGAL NATURE

Subdivision regulations, like other laws governing the use of property, are an exercise of the so-called "police power" of state and local units of government. As in the case of other local regulations, their scope, geographical coverage, and procedures are largely governed by the authority under which they are enacted. Except in the case of constitutional "home rule" cities, this authority is to be found in enabling acts enacted by the state legislature. It is, of course, subject to the restrictions contained in state and federal constitutions.

Statutory Provisions. As we have noted, state subdivision-regulation enabling acts differ rather widely in their details, but they are for the most part similar to the Standard City Planning Enabling Act. This permits them to be described briefly in terms of a comparison with that act.

A critical provision of all such acts is the definition of *subdivision,* which specifies the nature of the actions subject to regulation. The Standard Act has a broad definition:

The division of a lot, tract, or parcel of land into two or more lots, plats, sites, or other divisions of land for the purpose, whether immediate or future, of sale or building development.

Most states' enabling acts exempt from this definition certain transactions such as minor subdivisions involving only two or three lots or not involving the dedication of a new street. These exemptions invariably become potential loopholes in the eyes of at least some unscrupulous developers.

The Standard Act vests municipalities with power to regulate subdivisions both inside their limits and for a distance of five miles beyond their boundaries, on the premise that much developmental activity takes place in unincorporated areas which will eventually be annexed by a growing city. All states allow at least some of their municipalities to regulate subdivisions, and about half the states give them extraterritorial powers ranging from one to six miles beyond their limits. Counties exercise similar powers in areas beyond municipal jurisdiction in about 35 states, while regional planning commissions have subdivision-regulation authority in a few states, notably Tennessee. State legislatures frequently regulate certain aspects of subdivision activity directly, through statewide acts, while in a few states a state agency such as the Highway Commission or State Board of Health plays a part in the approval process.

The Standard Act designates the planning commissions as the plat-approval agency, but only after it has adopted a major street plan to furnish a basis for its decisions. Most of the states follow the Standard Act in giving this authority to the planning commission, although some provide for approvals by the local governing board (usually with the planning commission serving in an advisory capacity). About half the states require that the planning commission adopt certain plans (usually a major street plan) before it achieves this power.

As another prerequisite to the exercise of approval authority, the Standard Act requires the planning commission to adopt written regulations stating its requirements, so as to avoid arbitrariness in dealing with individual cases. About 20 of the states give the planning commission power to enact these regulations, but a larger number treat subdivision regulations in the same manner as other local ordinances and require that they be adopted by the local governing body.

There is considerable variation in the statutory provisions which specify the permissible requirements which these regulations can make. The provisions of the Standard Act are more extensive than some, but less extensive than others:

Such regulations may provide for the proper arrangement of streets in relation to other existing or planned streets and to the master plan, for adequate and convenient open spaces for traffic, utilities, access of fire-fighting apparatus, recreation, light and air, and for the avoidance of congestion of population, including minimum width and area of lots.

Such regulations may include provisions as to the extent to which streets and other ways shall be graded and improved and to which water and sewer and other utility mains, piping, or other facilities shall be installed as a condition precedent to the approval of the plat.

Because of the many differences which exist, anyone drafting regulations in a given state should consult the statutes and court decisions of that state before deciding to include any specific requirement.

The enforcement provisions of the Standard Act have been followed fairly widely. They include provisions (1) making sale (or negotiation for sale) of land by reference to (or other use of) an unapproved plat unlawful and subject to a civil penalty, (2) authorizing the city to enjoin such a sale, (3) making it unlawful for the county recorder to file or record an unapproved plat, (4) forbidding improvements in or on new streets in unapproved subdivisions, and (5) forbidding issuance of a building permit for a structure on a lot having access only to an unapproved street.

Constitutional Basis. Court decisions have sustained the constitutionality of subdivision regulations under a variety of legal theories, as (1) an exercise of the police power designed to further the public health and safety, (2) simple conditions on the privilege of filing a plat among public records so as to simplify land title transactions, (3) a necessary adjunct of the city's power to accept or decline responsibility for maintaining particular streets, (4) a necessary aid in the maintenance of proper tax records and land titles, and (5) a protection of lot purchasers against sharp marketing practices. And it has been suggested that requirements that the developer install certain local improvements might be treated as a branch of the law relating to special assessments.

It is suggested here that subdivision regulations are all of these things and that the legal theory supporting one requirement (such as

regulation of the alignment of streets) may differ from the theory supporting another (such as a requirement that the developer install water and sewer lines). As a practical matter, much subdivision regulation is treated as a bargaining process between a developer who wishes certain city services and a city government which wishes high standards of development. Such bargaining rarely results in court actions.

Subdivision Regulations and Other Measures

To be most effective, subdivision regulations and their administration must be closely coordinated with certain other local governmental policies, ordinances, and activities. Among the more important of these are the comprehensive plan, the official map, the zoning ordinance, municipal policies for the extension of utilities or pavement of streets, and health regulations.

COMPREHENSIVE PLAN

The statutory requirement in many states that the planning commission adopt a comprehensive plan or a major street plan before it receives subdivision-regulation jurisdiction has been noted. It should be stressed that even in the absence of such a requirement a comprehensive plan is a legal and practical necessity as a basis for effective subdivision regulation. From a legal standpoint the plan is evidence that particular requirements are not arbitrary or discriminatory. From a practical standpoint, it should be evident that without a plan the subdivision approval agency is operating completely in the dark as it attempts to coordinate the layout of a particular subdivision with others in the neighborhood and to insure that appropriate provision is made for rights-of-way of major thoroughfares, park and school sites, or easements for major utility lines.

Where such a plan exists developers can design their subdivision in light of its proposals for major public facilities. In some cases they will be willing voluntarily to dedicate land for particular public uses; in others, the plan will afford a stronger legal basis for requiring such dedication. In any event the city will be in a position to acquire necessary properties before they are divided into lots and developed in such a way as to make impossible the proposed public improvement.

OFFICIAL MAP

Inasmuch as the official map designates the exact locations of proposed street rights-of-way, of street widening projects, and of open space to be reserved for parks, school sites, or playgrounds, it is of obvious importance to the agency administering subdivision regulations. What has been said of the comprehensive plan applies with increased strength to the official map, because of the latter's greater specificity.

ZONING ORDINANCE

Both the zoning ordinance and subdivision regulations usually specify minimum lot areas and frontages. Because of this overlapping coverage, the two must not conflict, so it is customary for subdivision regulations to require that lots conform to the zoning requirements of the district in which they are located. The zoning ordinance's listing of permitted uses in an area may also affect the improvements required to serve that area, and occasionally this is reflected in subdivision regulations. It is of interest that some municipalities, lacking extraterritorial zoning powers, have accomplished much the same ends outside their boundaries through astute use of subdivision regulations and through persuading developers to include appropriate deed restrictions on their plats.

From an administrative standpoint, problems arise out of the fact that a developer frequently wishes plat approval that can be given only in conjunction with a zoning amendment or the grant of a variance by the zoning board of adjustment. Where several agencies of local government are involved, or where procedural requirements for the various types of relief differ, problems of coordination and timing arise. The Standard Act recognized this potential difficulty and at least a few states have attempted to solve it statutorily, but without complete success.

MUNICIPAL POLICIES

Of considerable importance in the administration of subdivision regulations are municipal policies relating to such matters as the extension of utilities or the pavement of streets. Policy determinations, perhaps reflected in the capital improvement program, as to the areas into which major water mains and sewer outfalls will be extended and as to when the extension will take place may have considerable influence over the location and timing of subdivision activity. The availability of public water and sewerage systems within an area will affect the reasonableness of particular requirements in the subdivision regulations; required lot sizes may be made dependent upon the type of water and sewerage service available.

Policies as to the sharing of costs of particular improvements in developed areas (such as assessments for street paving, utilities, or sidewalk projects) should be coordinated with the requirements of subdivision regulations governing the same types of improvements. Differentials in policies inside and outside the city limits may influence developers to request annexation at the time of plat approval.

Other municipal policies which should be coordinated with subdivision regulations are those which specify materials and details of construction for street surfacing, utilities systems, etc., and which must be met before the city will accept maintenance responsibility for these facilities. Subdivision regulations not infrequently incorporate these standards by reference in their requirements for improvements to be constructed by developers.

HEALTH REGULATIONS

Health regulations constitute yet another area where there may be overlapping requirements. They, like subdivision regulations, may contain minimum lot size requirements for situations where individual wells and/or septic tanks are necessary, and again it is desirable that there be coordination. Since the health agency is frequently outside the city government, this coordination may not be so easy to attain as in the case of the zoning ordinance.

Experienced planners have also learned that health officials can be of considerable help in securing compliance with subdivision regulations—particularly in instances where an attempt is made to prohibit subdivisions because of health problems which will be created if any such activity takes place.

RESTRICTIVE COVENANTS

Restrictive covenants, or deed restrictions, are not properly speaking local government regulations. They are simply a special form of private contracts entered into by property owners, which may supplement public controls. They are of interest to the agency regulating subdivisions, however, because they are customarily filed with the plat of a subdivision. Knowing this, the plat approval agency may through a process of negotiation persuade a developer to include detailed regulations governing the siting of structures, landscaping, architectual design, and so forth, tailored to the particular needs of his subdivision, which it could not easily require in its general regulations. Deed restrictions cannot, of course, give a property owner immunity from governmental regulations.

Conventional Subdivision Regulation

Although there are significant differences in the state enabling acts which authorize subdivision regulation, there is a surprising degree of uniformity in the regulations actually adopted by local governments. This results in part from the issuance of "model" regulations by the federal Housing and Home Finance Agency and other organizations and in part from widespread copying of other cities' requirements. Thus there has evolved a large body of conventional or customary subdivision-regulation practices.

This section will outline the most usual procedures and requirements found in this conventional subdivision regulation. Later sections will discuss the shortcomings in this approach which have appeared with experience, partly as a result of technological innovation and changes in land development practices, and will describe some of the new directions which subdivision regulation seem to be taking in cities throughout the country.

PROCEDURES

A fairly common set of procedures involves the following five steps prior to the time that the developer is permitted to make sales of his lots. (However, it should be noted that provision is made under some enabling acts and in some regulations for a simplified set of procedures for certain minor classes of subdivisions.)

Pre-Application Procedures. Many subdivision regulations suggest (without requiring) that the developer begin by submitting a "back-of-an-envelope" sketch of his proposed subdivision to the planning staff for its recommendations, along with a map of the general location, indicating the principal features. This gives him an opportunity to secure guidance as to what will probably be required of him before he has incurred great expense in making detailed plans and provides the planner with information in undertaking a review of the plat (Figure 16–1).

In some cases this procedure has been reported unsatisfactory because the professional planning staff does not feel that it can give any commitments to the developer which will be binding upon the planning commission. However, so long as both parties are thoroughly aware that this is the case, there usually can be a helpful interchange of information at this stage.

Planning agencies in some cities have been able to prepare fairly detailed plans for undeveloped lands around their peripheries. Where this type of pre-planning has been done, the landowner or developer may find that a great deal of the expense of planning his subdivision has been eliminated.

Preliminary Plat. The first formal action normally required of the developer is submission of a "preliminary plat" for approval by the appropriate local agency. While the name suggests that the decision on this plat is rather tentative, nothing could be further from the truth. The decision made on the preliminary plat is the most important step in the entire approval process, because on the basis of this decision work will begin on opening and constructing streets, installing utilities systems,

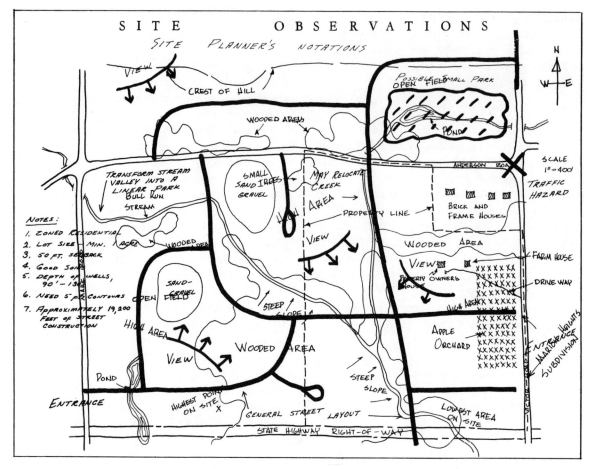

FIGURE 16–1. *Site planner's notations*

and so forth. After expenditures have been made on such permanent installations, it is extremely unlikely that any major changes will be required or made at a later stage in the approval process.

Because of this importance, regulations usually spell out in considerable detail the information to be shown on or to accompany the preliminary plat. In the absence of such information the chances of an unfortunate mistake by the approval agency are magnified, so the draftsman of the regulations must treat these provisions with some care. An illustration of such a plat is given in Figure 16–2.

The plat must be submitted in sufficient time and with enough copies to permit consideration and recommendations by various interested agencies, such as the city engineer, the department of public works, the school board,

the recreation commission, the health department, and so on. All these recommendations should be received by the approval agency prior to its hearing.

Under most ordinances the planning commission grants or denies approval of the preliminary plat. In a few instances the local governing board or an agency made up of representatives of various interested municipal departments may have this responsibility. Whatever the case, the approval agency customarily meets with the applicant after consideration of the recommendations by the interested departments and either approves, approves subject to stated conditions, or disapproves of the plat. Not infrequently there will be considerable negotiation and discussion between the developer and the approval agency, at which time agreement may be reached as to appropriate

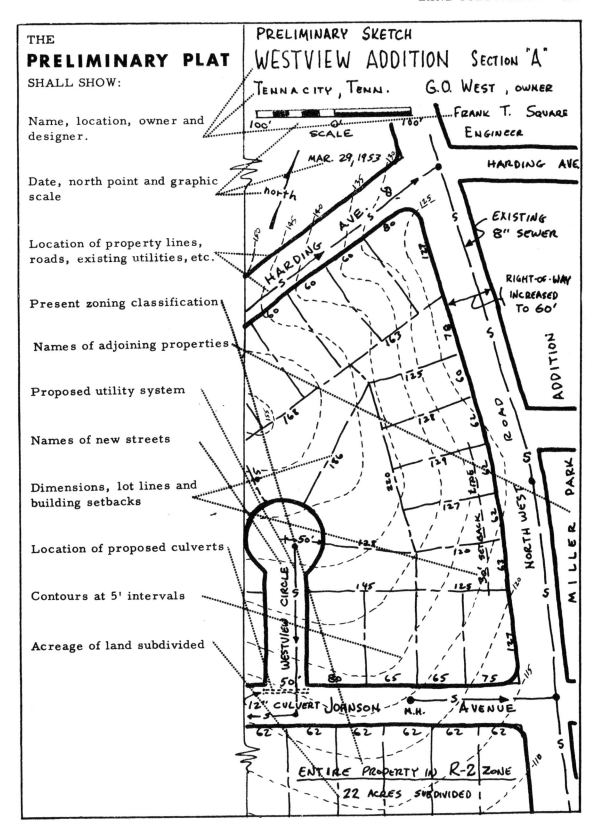

THE

PRELIMINARY PLAT

SHALL SHOW:

Name, location, owner and
designer.

Date, north point and graphic
scale

Location of property lines,
roads, existing utilities, etc.

Present zoning classification

Names of adjoining properties

Proposed utility system

Names of new streets

Dimensions, lot lines and
building setbacks

Location of proposed culverts

Contours at 5' intervals

Acreage of land subdivided

FIGURE 16–2. *Preliminary plat requirements*

modifications in the plat or conditions on the approval. Some regulations provide for an appeal to the local governing board from the decision made at this time, although this is not usual.

Construction of Improvements. Most subdivision regulations prohibit the construction of any improvements in a subdivision until the preliminary plat has been approved. Once this approval has been granted, however, the prohibition reverses and becomes an affirmative requirement that improvements be made before the final plat is submitted for approval.

Frequently the developer is given three or four options; e.g., he may (1) actually complete construction of all required improvements, (2) post a performance bond guaranteeing such construction within a given period, (3) submit a petition that the municipality construct the improvements and levy the cost against lots in the subdivision under its usual special-assessment procedures, or (4) give the municipality a mortgage on the property in the subdivision, releasable in stages as improvements are completed.

The municipality's decision as to how wide a range of options to offer developers usually turns on the extent to which it wishes to restrain the rate of subdivision activity. If it is threatened by a wave of "premature subdivision," it may put on the brakes by simply requiring that developers incur the expense of completing installation of improvements before they can make any sales of lots.

Because of the growing practice of marketing houses and lots rather than undeveloped building sites in a new subdivision, provision is made in most current subdivision regulations for issuance of building permits for construction of houses concurrently with the construction of streets, utilities, and other improvements.

From an administrative standpoint, a great deal of the responsibility for enforcement of subdivision regulations shifts during this phase from the planning staff to the city engineer and other officials concerned that proper construction standards are met. Their certificates that improvements have been completed in accordance with the city's standards are a usual pre-requisite to submission of the final plat to the municipality.

Final Plat. While subdivision regulations customarily require submission and approval of a "final plat," some cities report that it is preferable to require two rather different plats at this stage. The first is denominated an "engineering plat" which might be thought of as an "as-built" plat giving details of construction and location of the improvements which have been installed. The primary purpose of this plat is to provide the city engineer and other interested departments with a permanent record of the location, size, and design of underground utilities, for their use in the course of maintaining such installations. The second could be denominated either a "plat for record" or a "final plat," which shows primarily information relating to land titles (exact lot lines, street rights-of-way, utilities easements, deed restrictions, etc.). It is intended as the plat to be filed in the county registry of deeds (or county recorder's office). Where only a single "final plat" is required, it must show information of both types, frequently at the expense of clarity. An example of a final plat is given in Figure 16–3.

The final plat represents the final stage at which the plat approval agency can do anything about the subdivision. Usually the regulations provide for its submission in approximately the same manner as was required for the preliminary plat, with adequate time and number of copies for distribution to the interested departments who made recommendations earlier. At this time the intention is to assure that the recorded plat will be in accordance with the plans approved earlier and that construction has taken place in accordance with such plans. Under some regulations the local governing board approves the final plat, even though the planning commission was the approval agency for the preliminary plat.

Usually the final plat must be submitted within a stated period (such as a year) after the preliminary plat was approved, unless the developer wishes to start from the beginning once more. This is to prevent the developer from putting the municipal government to the trouble and expense of the approval process

THE
FINAL PLAT
SHALL SHOW:

Streets, lots, setback lines,
lot numbers, etc.

Sufficient engineering data to
reproduce any line on the
ground.

Dimensions, angles, and
bearings.

Monuments

Names of adjoining properties

Date, title, name and location
of subdivision

Graphic scale and true north
point

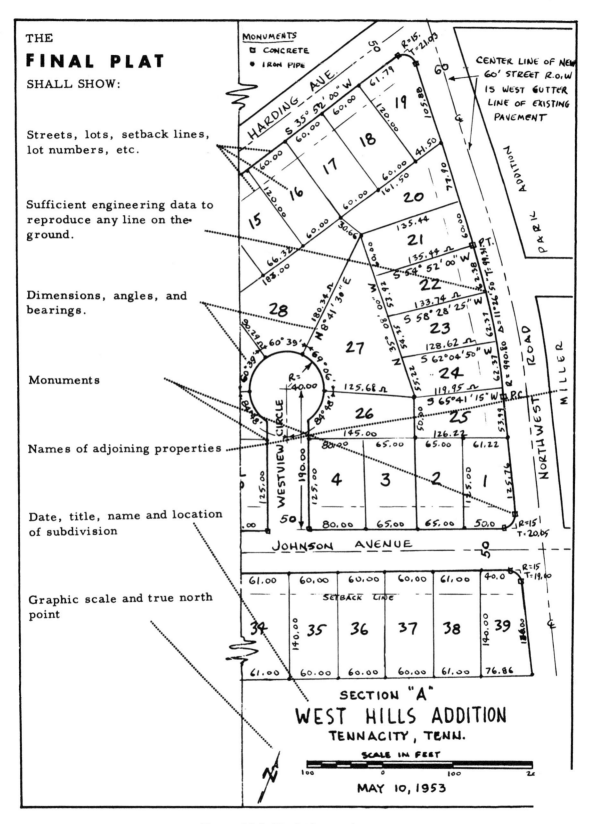

FIGURE 16-3. *Final plat requirements*

when he has no immediate intention of carrying out his plans. At the same time, the statutes of some states recognize that the developer should have some protection against a city's making major changes in its requirements between the time of preliminary plat approval and submission of the final plat. These statutes prevent changes in the zoning of the area for a reasonable period (perhaps two years) after preliminary approval.

Recording of Plat. The final step prior to sale of lots in the subdivision is the recording of the approved plat. The regulations should assure that the final plat is in a form and size which meets the requirements of the registry of deeds. It is not uncommon for other provisions of state law than the subdivision-regulation enabling act to regulate certain aspects of the recording process, such as the size of plats, required certificates of accuracy by the surveyor, certificates of ownership, or other details. In many cases it will be found wise to include such requirements in the subdivision regulations, either specifically or by reference, for the benefit of the property owner who might otherwise overlook them.

The filing of the plat serves two functions. First, it may constitute a legal dedication to the public of the streets, parks, utilities easements, and similar lands shown on the plat—particularly if a certificate of dedication is attached to the plat. Secondly, it becomes a convenient means for describing a particular lot which the developer wishes to deed to a purchaser ("Lot 9 in the Glandale Subdivision as recorded on page 19 of Plat Book 24 in the Orange County Registry of Deeds"). In the absence of such a plat, each deed would have to describe in detail, by bearings and distances ("metes and bounds"), the boundaries of the lot transferred. It is also more complicated to describe in words than on a map any rights-of-way or easements which have been dedicated over particular portions of the lot. Indeed, any developer wishing to dedicate a street right-of-way to be accepted for maintenance by a public agency is virtually required to use a plat.

Most lot purchasers are desirous of seeing a plat of the subdivision, in order to visualize the relationship of their lots to the other lots, streets, and public facilities in the subdivision and to have some assurance that a binding legal commitment has been made for provision of the promised public facilities. In addition, a great many lending agencies insist upon an approved plat as a prerequisite for any financing they make available in the subdivision. These desires serve as pressures towards compliance with subdivision regulations in general.

Fees. Because the expenses of checking both the plats submitted and the construction work which is done may be substantial, many subdivision regulations provide for payment to the city of fees to cover some of these administrative costs. The few court cases in which the legality of this requirement has been challenged have uniformly been decided in favor of the city. However, any fees imposed should bear a reasonable relationship to the actual costs incurred by the city and they should not be so great as to constitute an impediment to subdivision activity.

Fee bases vary widely. Some regulations provide for a flat fee for all subdivisions, regardless of their size. In other cases there may be a basic charge, plus an additional amount for each lot, each foot of street constructed, each foot of utilities installed, etc. Engineering inspections are particularly costly, and it would seem that a sliding scale to reflect the costs of inspecting varying amounts of improvements would be the most equitable approach.

DESIGN REQUIREMENTS

Typical subdivision regulations contain certain general provisions relating to the location and design of subdivisions, followed by more specific controls over the layout and dimensions of streets and alleys, utilities easements, blocks, and lots.

General Provisions. There are three rather distinct types of customary provisions which relate to the setting in which a subdivision is to be placed and its coordination with that setting. First, there may be a prohibition against any subdivision activity at all in areas where soil, subsoil, or flooding conditions would create dangers to health or safety if development took place. In a few states such prohibitions are supported by specific provisions of the enabling acts, but even without such support they would seem to be legally permissible. It has been proposed that such provisions might be broadened so as to attack urban sprawl, by prohibiting new subdivisions in outlying areas until there was relatively complete development closer to the center of the city, but it is not likely that this broadened approach would attract much judicial support from courts today.

Second, there may be a requirement that the proposed subdivision be in general compliance with the comprehensive plan for the area. Of particular importance is that space be reserved for major street rights-of-way, parks, schools, recreation areas, and major utilities lines which are planned. The subdivision must of course be planned to accommodate those types of land uses which the plan contemplates for the area. It should also be designed in such a manner as to avoid casting an undue burden on the street system, the drainage system, or other public facilities planned for the area, even though they may be located outside the subdivision itself.

Third, there may be a series of requirements designed to insure that the proposed subdivision will be coordinated with its immediate neighbors with respect to street connections, utilities lines, drainage facilities, and perhaps reservation of open spaces. Not only must streets connect with one another, but they must continue approximately the same right-of-way widths. Both streets and utilities systems must normally be carried to the boundaries of the subdivision to facilitate the development of adjoining properties. Although sometimes quite justified, efforts to isolate a subdivision from its neighbors as a means of "preserving the character" tend ultimately to place increased burdens on the public at large.

In order to give the plat approval agency adequate opportunity to check for compliance with these general requirements, subdivision regulations normally require the developer to submit information relating to the area surrounding his subdivision and also information as to his own long-range plans where the proposed subdivision is only a part of a larger tract in his ownership or control. For an example of such information, see Figure 16–4.

Streets. The importance of streets as an element in the design of a subdivision cannot be overstressed. They serve a major functional purpose in providing vehicular and pedestrian access to property. They serve another such purpose in providing convenient rights-of-way for the transmission and distribution lines of most utilities, such as water, sewerage, gas, electricity, and telephone systems. They physically occupy important quantities of land—up to 30 per cent of the land area of some types of subdivisions. And finally they circumscribe the land which is available for other purposes and to a large extent dictate the manner in which lots may be laid out.

The designer of the street system in a new subdivision should be required to give attention to three primary considerations: (1) the major street plan of the community as it relates to the subdivision, (2) the existing street pattern of adjoining subdivisions, and (3) the terrain.

The major street plan normally indicates at least tentative rights-of-way for streets of particular importance—those which are customarily denominated "arterial" streets and "collector" streets. It rarely prescribes the location of minor or local access streets, whose design is left to the discretion of individual developers. Obviously, if the major street plan shows a major thoroughfare cutting through the area of a proposed subdivision, the subdivision plat must reserve or dedicate a right-of-way for that thoroughfare. Even if this is not the case, the street system of the subdivision must be designed with the major street plan in mind. For example, main entrances to the subdivision should be from high-capacity streets and designed to minimize creation of traffic hazards, provision should be made for a rational and orderly flow of traffic between important traffic generators, and so forth.

Within the subdivision itself, if it is a large one, there should be a definite system of streets designed to fulfill different purposes. Even though not shown on the city's major street plan, certain streets should be deliberately de-

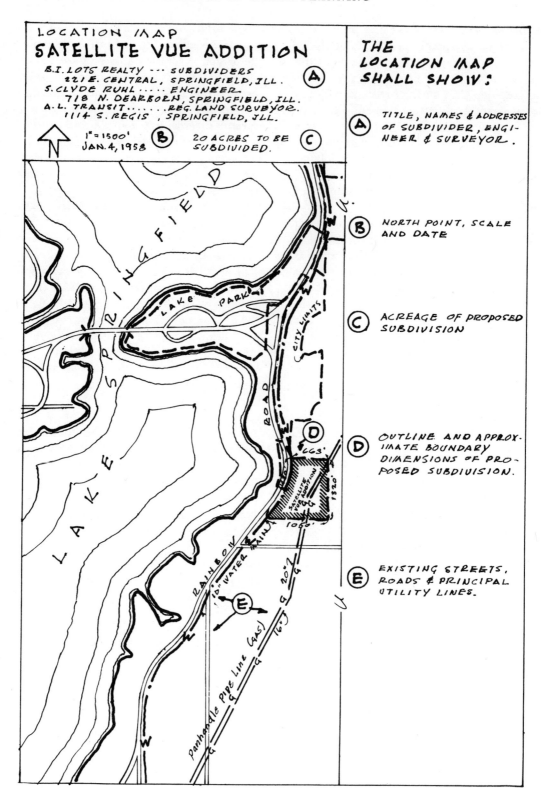

FIGURE 16–4. *Location map requirements*

signed to carry large volumes of through traffic, while minor streets should be so laid out (using devices such as cul-de-sacs and loops) as to provide access for residents but to discourage heavy traffic through quiet residential neighborhoods.

The design of areas abutting arterial streets is of particular importance, because inept design will almost certainly result in pressures to "strip zone" such areas for commercial development. Marginal access streets should be required between residential lots and the arterial highway, or else such lots should be made extra deep and faced away from the highway, with park strips, screen plantings, or other measures along the rear to protect residents from detrimental effects of the highway traffic.

The necessity of coordinating new streets with the street systems of adjoining subdivisions, both as to alignment and right-of-way width, has already been mentioned. It should be stressed again that streets normally should be carried to the boundaries of undeveloped neighboring properties, but it may be necessary to provide for temporary dead-ends with turnarounds, pending later extension of the street. At one time it was fashionable to permit the dedication of half-streets along subdivision boundaries, in the expectation that adjoining owners would subsequently dedicate the other half of the right-of-way. After unhappy experience under such provisions, most subdivision regulations today frown on this practice.

Terrain affects street design in a number of obvious ways. In the first place, the developer is interested in producing a maximum number of salable lots. In general, this is taken to mean that street alignments should be those which will permit a maximum number of lots on a level with or above the street.

Second, the developer wishes to hold his construction costs to a minimum. For this reason he is interested in street alignments which will minimize the necessity for cut and fill operations or for installation of expensive drainage systems.

Third, the designer must remember that sanitary and storm sewers, which customarily are located in streets, operate for the most part on a gravity-flow system. This means that the

streets must follow the topography in such a way as to permit such a flow, if excessive costs for excavation or pumping are to be avoided.

Finally, the streets must provide a safe means of passage. Grades must not be too steep for easy passage, and curves, both vertical and horizontal, must be gradual enough that the motorist will have adequate sight distance.

All these factors together indicate that the street system must be rather carefully fitted to the topography of the area, even with today's capability of large-scale earth movement.

It will be found difficult to state many of the above requirements explicitly in subdivision regulations, and a great deal will depend upon the negotiations between the developer's staff and the professional planners. However, there are some requirements which can be set forth precisely. The following are some of these requirements.

In general, streets should intersect as nearly as possible at right angles, both for reasons of traffic safety and to avoid difficult lotting problems (see Figure 16–5). Multi-street intersections ("Five Points") should be avoided. Intersections of minor streets with major streets should be kept to a minimum. "Jogs" resulting from failure to align streets on either side of an intersection are normally prohibited, with a minimum offset of 125–150 feet between centerlines of parallel streets being required.

Corners at intersections are rounded, with a radius of 20–25 feet, so as to facilitate turning movements. Tangents of 100–200 feet (depending upon the type of street and the consequent expected speed of travel) are provided between "reverse curves"—where the street curves first in one direction and then in the other.

To insure adequate sight distances, minimum radii of 150–400 feet may be specified for horizontal curves and 100–200 feet for vertical curves. Once again, these differ according to the nature of the street, with the greater distances being required for high-capacity collector or arterial streets where traffic tends to move more quickly.

Street right-of-way widths for various types of streets are usually specified. Requirements for arterial streets may range as high as 180 or more feet. Collector streets within a subdivision may require 60-foot rights-of-way, with pavements of 28–44 feet. Minor streets may have 40- to 50-foot rights-of-way with pavements of 18–28 feet. It is well to key these requirements to the major street plan in the case of major thoroughfares.

Maximum limits of 400–500 feet are commonly placed on the length of cul-de-sac streets, with a requirement of a turnaround at the end with a minimum 45–50 foot outside radius. Alleys are normally avoided in residential subdivisions, except in certain unusual situations, but required in commercial or industrial developments. In the latter case they must normally be at least 20 feet wide and so designed as to facilitate in-and-out movement of the rather large goods-delivery vans which may use them.

Maximum and minimum street grades tend to vary according to the nature of the terrain in the particular city. In general, a minimum of 0.5–1 per cent will be required for adequate drainage. Maximums vary according to the nature of the street, with steeper grades permissible on minor streets than on collectors or arterials. In general, 10–12 per cent is the maximum allowable on minor streets, with perhaps 5–7 per cent as a maximum for larger streets.

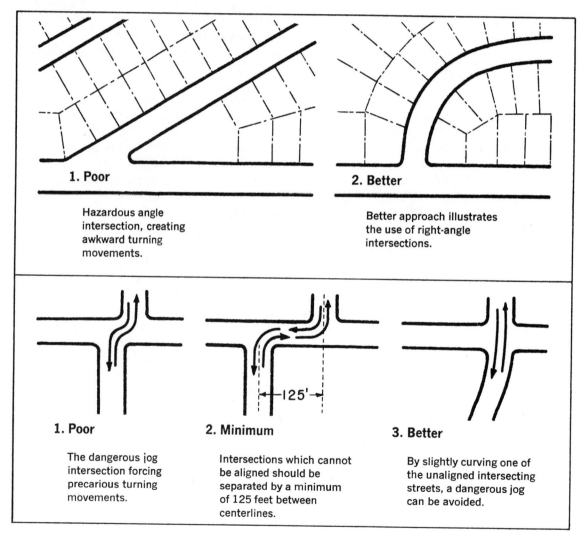

1. Poor

Hazardous angle intersection, creating awkward turning movements.

2. Better

Better approach illustrates the use of right-angle intersections.

1. Poor

The dangerous jog intersection forcing precarious turning movements.

2. Minimum

Intersections which cannot be aligned should be separated by a minimum of 125 feet between centerlines.

3. Better

By slightly curving one of the unaligned intersecting streets, a dangerous jog can be avoided.

FIGURE 16–5. *Basic intersection design*

Table 16–1

Subdivision Right-of-Way and Pavement Widths

(Width and pavement: unless otherwise shown on the master plan, the following standards shall be followed)

Type of Street	Development	R/W Width	Pavement Width (curb-back-to-back)
Residential	One-family	60′	26′
Residential	Two-family	60′	26′
Residential	Multifamily	60′	32′
Section line	. . . .	120′	
Half section line	. . . .	86′	
Quarter section	. . . .	60′	
Marginal access	. . . .	40′	20′
Alley	. . . .	20′	20′
Crosswalk	. . . .	10′	5′
Easements	. . . .	12′	None

Source: Carleton, Michigan, Ordinances, etc., VILLAGE OF CARLETON SUBDIVISION REGULATIONS (1956), p. 3.

A final aspect of street design which should be regulated, although sometimes overlooked, is assignment of names to streets. It is quite likely, if no control is exercised, that the same or similar names will be assigned to several streets in different parts of town and that different names will be assigned to continuations of the same street. Where this occurs, postal authorities encounter difficulties, and there may be crucial delays in emergency fire or police protection. It is relatively easy to control street names at the time a subdivision is being planned, but once people have become accustomed to a given address it is quite difficult to persuade them to change the name of the street. An illustration of a street naming scheme is shown in Figure 16–6.[9]

Utilities Easements. While many utilities' lines will be laid in the beds of streets, in some cases it will be necessary for them to follow other courses. Or it may be thought affirmatively desirable to run certain types of utilities,

[9] Two detailed guides to street naming and property numbering are: A GUIDE TO STREET NAMING AND PROPERTY NUMBERING (Nashville: Tennessee State Planning Commission, 1951), 47 pp.; and UNIFORM HOUSE NUMBERING, BASIC GRID SYSTEM, STREET NAMES AND SIGNS (Seattle: Association of Washington Cities, 1963), 41 pp.

such as telephone or electric power lines, down rear lot lines rather than along the street. In either event, it becomes necessary to dedicate easements for such lines, so that maintenance personnel will have a legal right to enter the property and maintain or replace them. Easements should be carefully planned in advance and located with the same care as streets. In general they should run along lot lines and not cross lots at locations which will interfere with the sitting of buildings. Minimum widths should be large enough to permit maintenance and construction machinery to operate—usually 20–30 feet.

In some cases natural watercourses are relied upon as an essential part of the storm drainage system, and in such an event a storm water or drainage easement should be designated, so that municipal personnel may enter the land and keep the channel clear of obstructions.

Blocks. In the days when most subdivision activity was done on a gridiron basis, specifications as to block lengths and widths were important. Today "block" requirements primarily have to do with the intervals at which streets must be provided in order to facilitate access from one area to another. Thus, it is common to specify that blocks may be no more

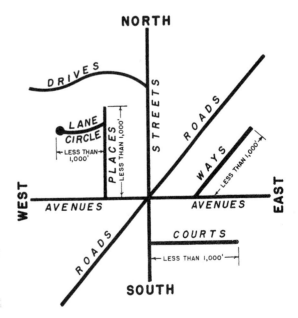

FIGURE 16–6. *Method of street naming*

than 1000 or 1200 feet long (i.e., cross streets must be provided at such intervals) and that where a block exceeds a given length, such as 800 feet, there must be a pedestrian right-of-way though the middle of the block. The latter requirement may result in a little-used seminuisance unless adequate provision is made for maintenance and lighting of any walkways thus provided.

Where there are blocks in the traditional gridiron sense, they normally are required to consist of two tiers of lots, perhaps with an alley or a utilities easement separating them. Through lots (extending from one parallel street to the next) create problems where adjoining owners cannot agree as to which direction to face their homes, and they should be discouraged.

Lots. The basic requirement of most subdivision regulations with respect to lots is that they conform to the zoning ordinance requirements as to minimum permissible area and width. It should be recognized that in some cases the zoning requirements are set lower than is desirable, because of existing patterns of development. If this is true in a given municipality, it may wish to include minimum requirements in its subdivision regulations which somewhat exceed those found in the "lower" zoning classifications. A minimum width of 60 or 70 feet and a minimum area of 6000 square feet for single-family residential lots are becoming generally accepted. Corner lots may be required to have extra width so as to have appropriate building setbacks from both streets.

Some cities vary lot requirements according to the availability of sanitary facilities, as shown on Table 16–2.

Lot lines are usually required to be substantially at right angles to straight streets or radial to curved streets. Double frontage lots (through lots) are considered undesirable, as indicated above, as are reverse frontage lots (corner lots in which houses face the side street rather than the street faced by their neighbors).

COMPULSORY DEDICATION OF LAND

From the earliest days of this country, as we have seen, it has been considered the developer's responsibility to furnish the land needed for streets and for various public areas such as the town common, squares, parks, and public building sites. This was true in the early colonial towns developed by representatives of the crown and it continued to be true right across the country as towns were developed, for example, by railroad-backed land speculators. This practice was not merely a matter of custom, for it was required by royal charters, by charters granted by colonial legislatures, and by charters granted by early state legislatures. Even the courts came into the picture, apart from

Table 16–2

Subdivision Lot Dimensions and Areas

(Size: lot dimensions and areas shall be no less than shown in the following table)

Type of Development	Sewer and Water Available	Public Water or Sewer Available	Neither Sewer nor Water Available
Single-family	60′ frontage 7,500 sq. ft.	70′ frontage 10,000 sq. ft.	100′ frontage 20,000 sq. ft.
Two-family	65′ frontage 8,000 sq. ft.	70′ frontage 10,000 sq. ft.	100′ frontage 20,000 sq. ft.
Multifamily (4 families)	75′ frontage 10,000 sq. ft.	100′ frontage 20,000 sq. ft.	150′ frontage 30,000 sq. ft.
Multifamily (in excess of 4 families)	TO BE ESTABLISHED BY PLANNING COMMISSION ON BASIS OF POPULATION DENSITY		

Source: Carleton, Michigan, Ordinances, etc., VILLAGE OF CARLETON SUBDIVISION REGULATIONS (Carleton: 1956), p. 3.

such statutory requirements, as they imposed a common-law requirement that an owner dividing his land make adequate provision for access from existing streets to any interior lots which he created.

Thus the requirements in subdivision regulations that developers dedicate street rights-of-way, utilities easements, recreation areas, and school sites are nothing new in our law, but merely a continuation of an old tradition.

It might also be noted that whenever a developer is called upon to dedicate land, the facilities thus provided become a part of the package which the lot purchaser receives, and their cost is normally reflected in the price of the lot. Without at least minimum supporting facilities such as streets there will be no market for lots at all, and many developers have found that provision of such "extras" as parks and school sites results in much larger returns on their investment.

Definitions. Subdivision regulations quite commonly require the developer to "dedicate" land for certain purposes and to "reserve" land for other purposes. There is some confusion as to the meaning of these terms, even among lawyers, and it might be well to define them briefly.

A "dedication" is nothing more nor less than a gift, by the owner, of a right to use land for stated purposes. Legally this gift is made both to members of the public in general and to certain specific members of the public, notably purchasers of lots. Since a transfer of property rights is involved, the dedication is made by a written instrument which is recorded—sometimes a deed and sometimes a plat coupled with a certificate of dedication. In order for the dedication to be complete so that it cannot be modified or withdrawn, normally there must be an "acceptance." This may consist of some action by the public generally, such as using the property for the purpose for which it was dedicated, or it may be action by representatives of the public (a city council, a county governing board, or an appropriate state agency) either of a formal nature (such as adoption of a resolution) or of an informal nature (such as assumption of maintenance responsibilities).

Most subdivision regulations making requirement of a dedication of streets or other public lands call for a "certificate of ownership and dedication" to accompany the final plat when it is submitted for approval and later recorded. They specifically provide, however, that approval of the subdivision plat does not in itself constitute an acceptance of such dedications, because that would make the local governmental unit immediately liable for maintaining the facility in a safe condition. It is generally felt that the decision to accept the dedication should be a separate one from the decision to approve the plat.

A "reservation" of land does not involve any transfer of property rights. It simply constitutes an obligation to keep the property free from development for a stated period of time. For example, the regulations might require the developer to reserve a certain tract of land for a school site. This would mean that he could not subdivide this particular tract during the period stated in the regulations, thus giving the school board the right to acquire the property in one tract and before any houses had been built on it. Unlike a dedication, in which the owner receives no payment for his land, a reservation contemplates that the governmental unit will pay the owner at the time it actually takes the property.

Problems of Dedication Requirements. In all the years in which developers have been required to dedicate street rights-of-way, few have gone to court in protest and almost none have succeeded in having such requirements set aside. To illustrate the usual run of such decisions, the Michigan Supreme Court has upheld a requirement that streets be dedicated to widths shown on the major street plan, even though they may be extensions of narrower streets;[10] the Arkansas Supreme Court has held that a developer could be required to dedicate an additional 10 feet of right-of-way for an existing street along the edge of his subdivision so as to bring the width of the street up to that shown on the major street plan;[11] and the Cali-

---

[10] *Ridgefield Land Co. v. City of Detroit,* 241 Mich. 468, 217 N.W. 58 (1928).

[11] *Newton v. American Sec. Co.,* 201 Ark. 943, 148 S.W. 2d 311 (1941).

fornia Supreme Court has held that a developer could be required to dedicate an additional 10 feet of right-of-way for an abutting highway even in the absence of such a plan.[12]

To be on the strongest legal ground, subdivision regulations should be keyed to a major street plan or to some other definite standard for determining the width of each street, so as to guard against arbitrariness in the treatment of any particular developer. In addition, it is suggested that where required rights-of-way for particular streets under the plan are so great as to bear no relation to the traffic generated by the subdivision, the public should pay for some of the extra land required. For example, it would probably be unreasonable to require the owner of a ten-acre subdivision to dedicate a 240-foot right-of-way for a limited-access throughway through the center of his land. This is not to say that he could not be required to reserve such a right-of-way for later acquisition by the highway authorities, at which time he would be paid for the land taken.

The state courts have been more divided in their holdings as to the legality of requiring dedication of park and recreation areas and school sites than they have been with reference to dedication of streets. A doctrine seems to be emerging that in order to sustain such requirements in any given case, it is necessary to demonstrate that the subdivision itself generates the need for the particular facility or area involved.

Once again, to assure the strongest legal basis, the regulations should contain definite standards as to when, where, and how much land will be required. It is legally unwise, for example, to provide merely that the plat approval agency may require dedication of such recreation areas as it deems necessary. On the other hand, a flat requirement that 5 or 10 per cent of the land area of every subdivision be dedicated for recreational purposes, while uniform and perhaps legal, might produce unnecessary land in some large-lot subdivisions and bits and pieces of poorly-sited, difficult-to-maintain recreation areas in other subdivisions. Perhaps the most reasonable solution is to require provision of certain recreational facilities scaled to the number of families to be housed in the subdivision, coupled with a requirement that land shown on the comprehensive plan as park or school sites be dedicated or reserved; a maximum limit on the percentage of land within the subdivision to be dedicated could be included.

Problems of Reservation Requirements. While the requirement of a reservation of land is not so severe a burden on the property owner as a requirement that the land be dedicated, there may nevertheless be difficulties with the courts in a particular state. The "official map" described earlier in this chapter is essentially a legal means of requiring land reservation, and the court decisions as to the constitutionality of the official map are directly relevant to the constitutionality of reservation requirements in subdivision regulations.

In general, it may be said that no serious questions are likely to arise concerning the required reservation of land for street rights-of-way unless the reservation covers so much of a particular owner's land as to prevent his making any reasonable use of it. The courts are divided on the constitutionality of reserving large areas for park or school purposes. The determining factor for some courts is the length of time for which the reservation is operative. If the owner is prevented from using his land for an unduly long time (even as little as three years according to a Pennsylvania decision[13]), with no assurance that the government will actually take his property for the purpose for which it was reserved, the courts are apt to find that the requirement is unlawful.

Payments in Lieu of Dedication. One of the aspects of dedication requirements that has disturbed many planners is the lack of equity in their application. One particular developer might be called upon to give a park or school site that was designed to meet needs generated by four or five subdivisions. Furthermore, the land which is available through dedication is not always the best located land for the particular facility.

To meet these difficulties, many cities have

---

[12] *Ayres v. City Council of City of Los Angeles*, 34 Cal. 2d 31, 207 P. 2d 1 (1949).

[13] *Miller v. Beaver Falls*, 368 Pa. 189, 82 A. 2d 34 (1951).

started permitting or requiring cash payments in lieu of donations of land. They reason that if every developer is required to pay $50 or $100 per lot, land can be purchased at the best locations for parks, playgrounds, school sites, and so forth. This requirement will apply to all developers uniformly and will therefore be as fair a system as can be devised.

The courts have again been mixed in their reaction to this approach. Several definite guidelines are becoming apparent, however, for those wishing to maximize the chances of a favorable court decision. First, there should be specific statutory authorization for such a requirement, and the requirement should be stated in the written subdivision regulations and not left to the discretion of the plat approval agency. Second, the regulations should provide that any payments received will be paid into a special park and school fund and not mixed with the general revenues of the city (otherwise the courts will probably treat them as a non-uniform tax). Third, the regulations should specify that the payments which are made are to be spent for the benefit of the specific areas from which they come. Fourth, the amount of payments required should be reasonable and bear some relation to the actual costs generated by the subdivision.

REQUIRED IMPROVEMENTS

In addition to regulating the design of a subdivision and requiring the dedication or reservation of land for certain purposes, most subdivision regulations require the developer to construct or install certain improvements. For the most part, the required improvements have to do with streets and associated facilities and with utilities systems.[14] As indicated earlier, regulations commonly give the developer the op-

tion of either constructing the improvements prior to final plat approval or of giving legal assurance that they will actually be constructed.[15]

General Considerations. In deciding whether to require a developer to install particular improvements, the unit adopting subdivision regulations should take into account a number of policy considerations. Initially, of course, it will want to know the purposes to be served by such requirements.

Perhaps the first such purpose, and most important as a legal basis, is to insure that development of an area does not create health hazards. Depending upon soil and subsoil conditions, it may be exceedingly hazardous to permit development with individual wells for water supplies and individual septic tanks for sewage disposal. Even where the conditions are such that scattered development may initially take place safely, later increase in the quantity or density of development may produce serious health problems. In such circumstances, the developer may justifiably be called upon to install adequate water and sewerage systems.

Both health and safety considerations underlie requirements that adequate provision be made for drainage of the area. Paving of streets and covering the soil with roofed structures greatly increase the rate of run-off of rain water. If inadequate provision is made for such run-off, basements may be flooded, streets undermined, house foundations weakened, soils eroded, and swampy areas interfering with sewage disposal created.

Another major reason for such requirements is the protection of unwary lot purchasers, in much the same way as food and drug laws or securities laws attempt to protect the consumer. The purchase of a house and lot is one of the most important that will ever be made by many persons. Yet all too frequently lot purchasers do not even know to ask whether their water supply is coming from a 2-inch pipe instead of the 6-inch or 8-inch main which is necessary for adequate fire protection. They see only the surface of a paved street and have no way of knowing whether the pavement is on an adequate base or whether it consists merely of a

---

[14] A 1952 survey by the American Society of Planning Officials of the subdivision regulations of cities over 10,000 showed that 85 per cent required street grading, 42 per cent street surfacing, 36 per cent street paving, 41 per cent curbs, 30 per cent gutters, 53 per cent sidewalks, 55 per cent storm sewers, 60 per cent sanitary sewers, 55 per cent water systems, 11 per cent street signs, 10 per cent gas mains, 8 per cent electrical systems, 10 per cent fire hydrants, 12 per cent street lighting fixtures, and 25 per cent planting of street trees. INSTALLATION OF PHYSICAL IMPROVEMENTS AS REQUIRED IN SUBDIVISION REGULATIONS, Planning Advisory Service Information Report No. 38 (Chicago: 1952), pp. 23–25.

[15] See page 452 above.

thin topcoat of asphalt on a bed of clay which will disintegrate at the first freeze and thaw. The city has an engineering staff capable of checking such things and insuring that the purchaser receives fair value for his money.

In addition to this essential protection of the purchaser, such requirements afford him incidental benefits. He will usually find it easier and cheaper to finance a total "package" of house, lot, and improvements at one time than to finance them separately. If he buys the house and lot without street paving, utilities systems, etc., he may very well at a future time have to finance such improvements through special assessments at a time when money is dear. Furthermore, there is likely to be considerable inconvenience if the street or his backyard has to be torn up to install a water or sewer main after he has moved into his home. In terms of expense, he will inevitably find it cheaper to pay for a sewer line at the outset rather than first paying for a septic tank and later having to pay for a sewer line.

There are countervailing cautions which should be borne in mind by the local government, however. It should carefully consider whether the improvements required are essential or merely "frills." Developers' claims that too many such requirements will price lots out of reach of lower-income groups, while frequently biased, nevertheless bear close examination. The governmental unit should recognize that in making a particular requirement it may be removing an element of choice from the purchaser—requiring him to pay for curbs, gutters, sidewalks, and street trees instead of an extra room on his house.

Even though the requirements might be appropriate for one type of subdivision, they may not necessarily be appropriate for another. The model regulations promulgated by the Housing and Home Finance Agency,[16] for example, set forth three levels of required improvements, depending upon whether the subdivision is designed for (1) apartment, row house, and similar multifamily residential types, (2)

one-family detached dwellings with typical lot widths of "X" feet, or (3) "country homes" with typical lot widths greater than "X" feet. In addition, they suggest that the planning commission itself should decide, on the advice of the city engineer, on appropriate improvements for commercial or industrial subdivisions.

This approach makes sense, because it permits the developer to decide whether to build a high-density subdivision with a full range of large-capacity and heavy-duty improvements or to build a low-density subdivision with smaller and less durable improvements—i.e., he can decide whether to spend his money on more land and less improvements or on less land and more improvements. The city's interest is preserved in either event, because the improvements required are scaled to the needs of the particular subdivision. Figure 16–7 is an illustration of one county's approach to such requirements.

Another problem which should be considered is how to provide for large-capacity streets and utilities mains, designed to serve the needs not only of a particular subdivision but also of many other yet unbuilt subdivisions. For example, an 8-inch water main might be adequate to serve the needs of the particular subdivision, but the city may consider it unwise not to run a 12-inch main so as eventually to serve projected development on the far side of the subdivision as well.

Two approaches have been followed in dealing with this problem. One is for the city itself to pay the excess costs for the extra capacity out of its general funds, on the basis that the extra-capacity facilities are for the benefit of the city as a whole. This approach is especially likely to be followed where street construction is involved. The other approach is for the city to levy acreage fees or other charges on later developers making use of the facility and to return these charges to the original developer in partial repayment of his excess costs. This approach is most often applied to cases where oversized water and sewer mains are involved.

Yet another problem to be considered is what to do about requiring water and sewerage systems in subdivisions too distant from exist-

[16] U.S. Housing and Home Finance Agency, SUGGESTED LAND SUBDIVISION REGULATIONS, rev. ed. (Washington: Government Printing Office, 1962).

ing development to permit easy connections with the town's systems. Three approaches have been followed in dealing with this problem. One is to bar any subdivision activity where there are no such connections, leaving it up to the developer to build connecting lines if he chooses and can. A second is to authorize the use of community systems for the subdivision, provided that such systems are approved by health authorities, that appropriate provision is made for their operation and maintenance, and that they are so designed that they can be tied into the town's system when that becomes feasible. A third approach is to permit use of individual septic tanks for sewage disposal but to require the developer also to install and cap a complete sewerage system which can be connected with the town system when feasible. It will be seen that any of these approaches may involve extra costs for the developer and eventually for the lot purchasers, which is probably desirable insofar as it helps to prevent "scatteration" of development.

Finally, in considering its improvement requirements, the local government should take into account future maintenance costs. The savings in street maintenance costs where curbs and gutters are installed may be very great; this factor might either serve as a basis for requiring the developer to make these improvements or it might, conversely, justify the town in making some contribution to the cost of these facilities. Similarly, the town may have a real interest, alongside the developer, in holding down the length of streets and utilities lines through careful design. An inadequately paved street may be more expensive to maintain than a gravelled street, and conversely, maintenance costs of a properly constructed street may be far less than for a gravelled street. So comparisons of original cost may present only part of the picture.

Streets. Street improvement requirements include those relating to the construction of the streets themselves and those relating to certain associated facilities. Street construction requirements begin with an almost universal requirement that the developer grade out the

IMPROVEMENTS schedule of basic facilities

PLAT PROPOSAL: Density of population — Gross desirable, people per sq. mile	Gross desirable, people per acre	Net possible, people per sq. mile	Net possible, people per acre	Lot character — Lot area in 1000 sq. ft.	Lot area, acreage	Lot width in feet	Subdivision class	Type of lots in subdivision	TYPE & CONDITION OF IMPROVEMENTS: Grading lots & roads	Storm drainage facilities	Central water supply; fire hydrants	Municipal sanitary sewerage service	Roads: type & width of surfacing — Gravel surface :16 ft.	Wet-bound macadam :18 ft.	Traffic-bound " :21 ft.	Bitum.-bound " :24 ft.	Cement-bound " :27 ft.	Sidewalk: one side	Sidewalk: both sides	Curb-gutter construction	Plant street trees	Provide street lights	Recreation facilities	Off-street parking	Landscaping	Other	
400	0.6	450	0.7	218.0	5	300	1	ACREAGE	X				X														
2000	3.7	2250	3.5	43.6	1	150	2	LARGE SUBURBAN	X	X			X														
3400	5.3	4050	6.0	20.0	1/2	100	3	SMALL SUBURBAN	X	X	X		X														
4200	–	–	–	15.0	1/3	75	4	WATERFRONT (RESORT)	X	X			X														
4900	7.7	7300	11.4	10.0	1/4	75	5	LARGE SINGLE FAMILY	X	X	X	X		X													
5700	9.0	8600	13.4	8.5	1/5	65	6	MODERATE " FAMILY	X	X	X	X			X			X									
6800	10.6	10200	16.0	7.2	1/6	60	7	SMALL SINGLE FAMILY	X	X	X	X				X			X	X							
8200	12.8	12200	19.1	6.0	1/7	55	8	MINIMUM " FAMILY	X	X	X	X					X		X	X	X	X	X	X			
							9	MULTI-FAM, ROW, APT.	X	X	X	X					X		X	X	X	X	X	X	X		

FIGURE 16–7. *Subdivision schedule showing required improvements by type of plat*

streets and make them suitable for passage. From this point there is a range of successively greater requirements as to the base which must be provided and the types of surfacing required. It is important to recognize that different types of streets are called upon to carry different loads, so that the construction requirements for one type of street may be either too little or too much for another; for example, a local access residential street need be built to only a fraction of the load-bearing capacity of a heavy-duty commercial or industrial street. Similarly, because of variations in soil conditions, construction requirements may vary widely from one area to another. Obviously the advice of professional engineers must be sought in developing appropriate standards for the various types of streets in any particular city.

Closely associated with street construction is provision of drainage facilities. These may range from culverts and ditches to "rolled" or "valley" gutters to curbs and gutters and full-scale storm sewer systems. If inadequate provision is made for drainage, streets will disintegrate more rapidly, in addition to other harmful effects which may accrue, so the engineer will be much concerned with this matter.

For some time planners and developers deluded themselves that in the age of the automobile, sidewalks as adjuncts of streets were no longer necessary. However, it is increasingly being recognized that children need hard-surfaced play areas other than the streets on which to ride their tricycles, that they need safe access to schools and playgrounds, and that many people still prefer to walk rather than drive. Although more costly, hard-surfaced sidewalks meet the requirements of users far better than dirt or gravel walkways.

More cities are also coming to recognize the necessity for adequate lighting of even their residential streets, as a means of safeguarding their citizens. Some regard this as a general municipal responsibility to be financed out of general tax receipts, some require each developer to install the lighting system for his subdivision, and some leave their responsibility to individual property owners contracting directly with local power companies—particularly in subdivisions beyond municipal limits.

Finally, some cities seeking to present a particular image to tourists and other visitors have requirements that developers provide street name signs (constructed to uniform standards), curbside mailboxes, landscaped entrance ways to their subdivisions, and street trees and shrubbery of varieties which will enhance appearance without doing damage to street and sidewalk surfacing or to utilities lines.

Utilities Systems. As the earlier discussion indicates, the most common utilities which developers are required to install are water and sewerage systems. Even though fire protection is a general municipal responsibility, it is thought not unreasonable to require the developer installing the water system to include fire hydrants. Some cities require the developer to install gas mains, electrical systems, and telephone systems. These services are commonly provided by privately-owned utilities companies, however, and where this is so the companies usually regard extension of their mains as a capital expenditure to be financed out of their general revenues and not by the developer.

Many of the more recent subdivision regulations call for electrical and telephone transmission lines to be installed underground. Where this is the case, privately-owned utilities companies may require the developer to share in the extra installation costs involved, although no uniform practice has evolved.

Monuments. One type of required improvement concerning which there is virtually no legal controversy is the installation of monuments at key points throughout a subdivision and of corner stakes on individual lots. These are intended to be permanent markers from which property lines can be accurately surveyed. In many states statutory requirements for such monuments are to be found outside the subdivision-regulation enabling act. It is generally considered desirable to make reference to such requirements in local subdivision regulations, and the city engineer commonly checks on monument location and construction as part of his duties under such regulations.

VARIANCES

Unlike the standard zoning enabling act, most

subdivision-regulation enabling acts make no provision for the granting of variances from the requirements in hardship cases. However, it is not unusual for the regulations themselves to provide for granting relief from the usual requirements in cases where they do not make sense or impose unusual burdens as applied to a particular situation. Customarily the regulations grant this variance authority to the plat approval agency, but occasionally they give it to the zoning board of adjustment. It seems greatly preferable to follow the former approach.

Because of the difficulty of writing complete specifications for many matters covered by subdivision regulations, some regulations leave considerable discretion in the hands of the plat approval agency or perhaps the city engineer. Where this has been done, there is relatively less necessity for a general provision authorizing the grant of variances.

One of the more common situations in which variances are sought is where a developer divides his land into the greatest possible number of lots barely meeting minimum standards and then seeks permission to create substandard lots out of the resulting remnants of land. The plat approval agency should remember that the subdivision regulations are intended to set forth minimum standards for development, not maximums. The intent of the regulations is clearly that these remnants of land should be used to increase the area of other lots rather than to "break" the minimum requirements. Every time that a variance is granted allowing a substandard lot, it weakens the legal position of the approval agency in the event the agency is called upon to defend its general standards.

Current and Emerging Problems

The past half-century's experience under this conventional pattern of subdivision regulation has pointed up a number of problems. Some of these are simply loopholes in the coverage of subdivision regulations—notably the "metes and bounds" loophole. Some are administrative and legal difficulties arising out of too-rigid segregation of land use controls into a series of separate legal compartments—

especially the separation between the zoning ordinance and subdivision regulations. Some are problems resulting from the failure of the draftsmen of subdivision regulations to recognize and deal with diverse types of subdivision activity. Some grow out of a simple failure to keep abreast of current technology and of changes in financing and development practices. The following sections list and describe some of the more significant of these problems and some of the techniques which have been devised or proposed for dealing with them.

Loopholes in Coverage

As every lawyer knows, it is virtually impossible to draft any legal regulation which will take care of every contingency and not inadvertently leave potential loopholes. By loopholes we mean provisions which permit an astute individual to comply with the letter of a regulation while going counter to its spirit, and thus avoid its constraints. It is not surprising that some loopholes have appeared in the coverage of subdivision regulations. Obviously, to the extent that subdivision regulations impose major financial requirements upon a developer, there will be continuing efforts by "fly-by-night" developers to identify and take advantage of these loopholes.

The major loophole which exists in many subdivision regulations today stems from the fact that enabling acts generally provide for regulating the use of plats rather than for regulating the subdivision of land. The Standard City Planning Enabling Act does not make it illegal to subdivide land without approval; instead, it makes it illegal to transfer or sell land:

> By reference to or exhibition of or by other use of a plat of a subdivision, before such plat has been approved by the planning commission and recorded or filed in the office of the appropriate county recorder.

Most current state enabling acts are similar or identical to the Standard Act in this respect. This means that in such states subdivision regulations have little direct effect upon the developer who chooses to divide up and market his land strictly by means of metes and bounds deeds. To be sure, the enabling act prevents his displaying an unapproved plat of the subdivision to a potential purchaser as part of his sales argument, and the wise purchaser of land will want to see a plat. Likewise, many lending agencies are unwilling to advance money on a subdivision in the absence of an approved plat. But a great many lots are sold to untutored purchasers at land auctions or other sales without any use of a plat; and in some cases a plat may be used surreptitiously, in a way difficult for enforcement authorities to prove in court. Unfortunately, the subdivisions thus created are apt to be the most detrimental in their effects upon their neighbors, the public health, and the general welfare.

It is curious that this loophole crept into the law in the first place, in view of the fact that most of the 19th century laws required that plats be submitted and approved in all cases when land was subdivided. It may be that the 20th century draftsmen of statutes misjudged the possibility of abuse, or they may have been motivated by legal doubts of some type.

Regardless of the source of the problem, it was soon made more difficult of solution by the courts. In a series of cases beginning with *Ridgefield Land Co. v. City of Detroit*[17] the courts based the legality of subdivision regulations squarely on the makeweight argument that they were merely conditions on the privilege of recording a plat—that no one had to transfer his property in this way and if he chose to do so, he must comply with any reasonable conditions that the government might impose on its authorization for him to make use of its recording machinery. Since most subdivision regulations can be justified on the basis of ordinary police power considerations which apply regardless of whether a plat is used or not, this was an unfortunate line of reasoning. But once it became current among the courts, cautious attorneys were reluctant to jeopardize existing regulations by seeking amendments to enabling acts which would destroy the basis for the courts' favorable holdings.

Statutory Solutions. Instead, statutory efforts have been made to block the loophole indirectly, through provisions (1) prohibiting

the issuance of a building permit for a structure on any lot which lacks access to an approved street and (2) prohibiting the public acceptance or maintenance of streets in unapproved subdivisions. Unfortunately, the impact of such prohibitions is apt to fall upon unsuspecting lot purchasers rather than upon the developer, and they are less than satisfactory for this reason. Some states have attempted to reinforce these provisions by authorizing the lot purchaser to rescind his purchase within a given period of time, but there is a feeling that this adds uncertainty to land titles.

Efforts to meet the problem head-on by amending the enabling act so as to restore the 19th century approach of requiring all subdivisions to be evidenced by plats (which would then have to be approved in the usual manner) have also encountered reluctance to act on the part of some state legislatures. Apparently this reluctance stems from a feeling that such a requirement would seriously inconvenience property owners in many situations in which the public interest is slight.

One approach toward mitigating this type of inconvenience is to identify such situations and exempt them from subdivision regulation. Thus, many enabling acts exclude from regulation any divisions of land into tracts greater than 10 acres where no street dedication is involved. This is ordinarily explained as permitting a farmer to divide his land among his children without being subjected to legal restraints. Other enabling acts exempt subdivisions involving creation of less than a stated number of lots (typically, three or four) in a given year. This approach has the serious administrative drawback of allowing transactions to take place with limited opportunity for enforcement officials to determine whether they really qualify for the exemption, and it thus creates new loopholes.

It would seem preferable to require that all subdivisions of land be platted and approved, but to classify certain types as minor subdivisions subject to much less stringent substantive requirements and more expeditious procedural requirements. A few states, notably New Jersey, have made tentative beginnings in this direction.

---

[17] 241 Mich. 468, 217 N.W. 58 (1928).

FRAGMENTATION OF LAND USE CONTROLS

Legislative bodies at every level of government normally "act" in a series of "reactions" to particular problems which have been called to their attention. A child is bitten, so the city council enacts an ordinance forbidding dogs to run at large. There is a smallpox epidemic, so the state legislature enacts a compulsory vaccination law. Seldom does a legislative body first examine existing laws to see whether a new law is needed or, if so, how best it might fit into the existing regulatory pattern. Because of this legislative *modus operandi,* it is never difficult to make an accurate demonstration that the laws in any given area are a patchwork of uncoordinated regulations.

So it is in the area of land use controls. In almost every city there is a multitude of ordinances bearing upon various facets of land use, generally from differing viewpoints. And what is worse, these ordinances spring from separate enabling acts, reflecting different concepts and objectives and calling for different organization and procedures in their administration.

As might be expected, the result of all this is confusion. The citizen being regulated, administrative officials, legislative bodies, and the courts all encounter difficulties in (1) identifying all of the regulations which apply to a given situation, (2) determining their meaning, particularly where two or more regulations seem to conflict with one another, and (3) ascertaining which administrative agencies have jurisdiction over given problems, the procedures to follow in achieving a given result, and their appropriate timing and sequence.

Some cities have alleviated a portion of these difficulties by a simple process of codification—identifying the pertinent ordinances and publishing them under a single cover as a "land development code." This approach is particularly effective where, as part of the process of codification, obvious conflicts between ordinances are noted and eliminated. But it must be noted that even where such codification clarifies the legal requirements, the situation may still be unsatisfactory because of cumbersome and time-consuming procedures which must be followed to secure desired relief in a given case. These procedures are apt to stem from the enabling acts, which means that they cannot be simplified by purely local action.

While there may be difficulties involving health regulations, urban renewal requirements, nuisance ordinances, etc., the major current difficulties in the area of land use control involve the relationships between the zoning ordinance and subdivision regulations. The difficulties in this area lie not so much in overlapping and conflicting substantive requirements as in the machinery for administering the two sets of regulations, and derive ultimately from the two separate enabling acts on which these controls are based.

As we have noted, under many subdivision-regulation enabling acts, the planning commission is the "legislative body" which adopts the regulations and any subsequent amendments; under a larger number of enabling acts it is the administrative agency which considers and approves plats; and under any local regulations it is empowered, as part of the approval process, to grant variances from the regulations in hardship cases. Under the zoning enabling act, on the other hand, the city council is the legislative body which adopts the ordinance and any amendments (usually on advice of the planning commission); a zoning enforcement officer (commonly the local building inspector) grants permits under the ordinance; and the board of adjustment grants any variances. Thus, as frequently happens, when a developer requires relief under both ordinances, it is probable that he will have to go through two distinct administrative channels involving totally different agencies and unrelated procedural provisions.

The impact of these differences can easily be demonstrated in a not altogether hypothetical situation. Let us suppose that a developer owns a tract zoned for single-family residences on 10,000 square foot lots. His designer, who is familiar with current literature on the merits of "cluster" developments, persuades him that he can produce a more attractive (and at the same time less expensive) subdivision if he divides his tract into the same number of 6,000 square foot lots and dedicates the land thus saved (amounting to 4,000 square feet per lot) to the public for a large park. He prepares a preliminary plat and submits it to the planning commission, which agrees that it is a much preferable design but informs him that it cannot approve the subdivision until there has been a zoning amendment, since the lots fail to meet the standards of the existing zoning ordinance. It then develops that the city council considers applications for zoning amendments only at quarterly intervals, and since the regular quarterly hearing has just been held, it will be almost three months before his application can be considered. Furthermore, a friendly councilman informs the developer that the council tends to pay strong attention to the view of the neighboring property owners on rezoning petitions, and he doubts very much whether the council would permit these smaller lots in that particular neighborhood; in any event, he is sure that it would not do so until the dedication of the park had actually been made and accepted. At this point the developer could hardly be blamed for shrugging his shoulders and deciding to revert to a conventional subdivision plan.

Factors Contributing to Current Importance of Problem. Such difficulties, while annoying, did not constitute a major problem in the 1920s and 1930s, because there was a fairly sharp division in the activities subject to zoning and subdivision regulation. Developers tended to limit themselves to the process of converting raw land to building lots—conduct which was indisputably within the domain of subdivision regulations. Lot purchasers then undertook the construction of houses or other structures on their lots, subject to the restrictions of the zoning ordinance. The zoning ordinance was important to the developer only insofar as it indicated how large his lots must be to be legally usable (and consequently, salable) and what types of development he could reasonably design his subdivision to serve.

But in the past 20 years there has been a revolution in development practices. The developer who sold only lots has in large measure given way to the developer-builder who constructs and sells a "package" of both house and lot. And with the introduction of mass produc-

tion techniques in house-building and the financial support of major business corporations, the scale of development has rapidly increased—from the 12-lot prewar subdivision to the "neighborhood" complete with shopping center to the "bedroom suburb" to the complete "new town." Some of these massive new developments involve traditional subdivision practices, as tracts are divided into lots which are sold with houses to individual purchasers. Some involve no division of land at all but are retained in common ownership and rented or leased to individual tenants: garden apartment developments, shopping centers, industrial parks. Some involve a division of legal title without a division of land: the condominiums, in which one may purchase an apartment (perhaps located 20 stories above the ground) and thereby secure an undivided share in the title to land and certain common facilities.

All these new approaches to land development have blurred the once-clear line between the area regulated by subdivision regulations and that regulated by zoning. It is not clear even to the draftsman just where he should place specific regulations. Consider the garden apartment development, for example, where there is to be no physical division of the land. The zoning ordinance, under the standard enabling act, could regulate the density of development; it could regulate the placement of individual structures—particularly their setbacks from streets and from each other; it could regulate maximum building heights; it could regulate the amount of off-street parking to be provided. But it could not regulate the design and widths of streets and the design and construction details of utilities systems built within the development. Furthermore, some state courts have held that the state zoning enabling act does not authorize the planning commission to issue the "special use permits" which are commonly resorted to as the device for securing detailed control over design. So there is an inclination to regulate such developments through the subdivision regulations—until it is noted that the enabling act definition of "subdivision" does not include transactions where property is merely rented or leased.

Or consider the construction of a "neighborhood" or "bedroom suburb" or "new town" where lots and structures are to be sold as well as rented. In this case there may be no hiatus in the scheme of control as there is in the case of the garden apartment development. But the physical magnitude of such developments almost insures that problems will arise under both the zoning ordinance and the subdivision regulations. It is quite probable, unless the zoning ordinance was drawn with the specific development in mind, that some rezoning will be necessary to permit development at varying densities or to permit construction of a shopping center or an industrial park at a location not shown on the existing zoning map. If the zoning ordinance contains procedures for handling these problems through issuance of a special use permit, so that an amendment is not required, these procedures also must be coordinated with the subdivision approval process. As was indicated earlier, extreme care must be taken if the developer is not to be confronted with a series of "chicken-egg" situations in which one board is unwilling to act until another has, and vice versa. And it should be remembered that in transactions of this scale, the financial cost of undue delays may be considerable.

Statutory Solutions. It is only fair to say that satisfactory answers to such problems have been long delayed. As long ago as the 1920s, the draftsmen of the Standard City Planning Enabling Act recognized that zoning requirements should be correlated with subdivision approvals. They included provisions in the Act which authorized the planning commission (1) to recommend to the city council any changes necessary to conform the zoning ordinance to the proposals involved in an approved subdivision and (2) to agree with the developer concerning detailed restrictions governing buildings within his subdivision, which restrictions should appear on the face of the plat and thereafter be enforceable as though they were part of the zoning ordinance.[18] Unfortunately,

these provisions were not widely adopted, although somewhat similar provisions appeared in the New Jersey laws from 1930 until 1953.[19]

In reality, these provisions added nothing to the powers of the planning commission where zoning changes were required, because that commission already had clear authority to make recommendations to the city council at any time as to any zoning amendments which it considered wise or necessary. The provisions thus served merely the educational purpose of highlighting the likelihood that zoning amendments might be required when subdivisions were approved, so that the planning commission would keep this possibility in mind.

A somewhat more significant solution appeared in the laws of New York in 1926 and 1927[20] and of Indiana in 1951.[21] This took the form of statutory provisions that a local governing board could, if it wished, empower its planning commission to make reasonable zoning amendments simultaneously with approval of a subdivision plat, where such amendments were necessary. Such provisions immediately raised the legal issue of whether there had been an unconstitutional delegation of legislative authority to the planning commission, due to inadequacy of the statutory standards limiting the discretion of the planning commission. The only court decision relating to these procedures sustained the standards but held that the planning commission's amendment in the particular case went beyond the intent of the statute.[22] Following this decision, the New York statute was strengthened by amendment and presumably now would not raise the constitutional issue so directly.[23]

Yet another approach has been urged recently by the Urban Land Institute, a research agency supported by private developers. A special study published by this organization suggests the adoption of a special enabling act to

[18] U.S. Department of Commerce. The Advisory Commission on City Planning and Zoning, A STANDARD CITY PLANNING ENABLING ACT (Washington: Government Printing Office, 1928), sec. 15, pp. 26–27.

[19] N.J.S.A. § 40:55–19.

[20] N.Y. Laws, 1926, c. 690 (N.Y. Gen. City Law, § 37); 1926, c. 719 (N.Y. Village Law, § 179p); 1927, c. 175 (N.Y. Town Law, § 281).

[21] Ind. Laws, 1951, c. 297, § 1 (Ind. Stat. Ann. [Burns] 534756 [7]).

[22] *Hiscox v. Levine,* 31 Misc. 2d 151, 216 N.Y.S. 2d 801 (Sup. Ct., 1961).

[23] N.Y. Laws, 1963, c. 968.

govern large-scale planned unit residential developments, which would be separate from both the zoning enabling act and the subdivision regulation enabling act and would supersede these two acts with respect to such developments.[24]

Finally, instead of making three enabling acts grow where two grew before, others are urging that the zoning and subdivision regulation acts be replaced by a single "development control" enabling act.[25] In England, they note, no distinction is drawn between subdivision regulations and zoning. All development (as broadly defined in the Town and Country Planning Act) requires permission granted through the same administrative channels. It is not inconceivable that similar legislation will soon be available in this country, although there is a natural reluctance to abandon legislation whose constitutionality has already been sustained and whose requirements have been interpreted by a multitude of court cases.

OTHER FAILURES IN COORDINATION

In addition to statutorily induced inter-agency difficulties, the agency enforcing subdivision regulations may encounter some very frustrating difficulties stemming from a simple failure of related agencies to cooperate and coordinate their programs. It is not unusual for a plat approval agency to persuade (with some difficulty) a developer to dedicate a school site, a park or playground, or a right-of-way for a major thoroughfare—only to find that the local school board, the recreation commission, or the county or state highway authority is unwilling to accept the dedication. This unwillingness may result from conviction on the part of the other agency that the proferred land is unsatisfactory from the standpoint of its needs, but quite commonly that agency has merely been unable to project its plans far

enough into the future to make a determination one way or another, and in the best bureaucratic tradition it is unwilling to commit itself until it has to.

Another type of difficulty arises when an agency in a related field of regulation proves reluctant to coordinate enforcement efforts. For example, in some localities the local health agency has been unwilling to cooperate with the planning commission staff in dealing with a recalcitrant developer who is unwilling to comply with the regulations of either.

Difficulties of both types become most acute when a subdivision lies beyond a municipality's territorial boundaries but falls within its extraterritorial subdivision control jurisdiction. In such circumstances the municipality may be regarded as only a meddlesome interloper by other governmental units, since it is not charged with providing services to the extraterritorial area but only with regulating growth. And there is no governmental agency, short of the state legislature, in a position to force cooperation among the different units operating within the area.

There is relatively little which can be done through statutory amendments to cure these difficulties, short of a reorganization of the local governmental structure. Perhaps all that can easily be done is to highlight the importance to the plat approval agency of its cultivating good relationships with other governmental agencies and attempting to aid them in their own planning efforts.

FAILURE TO CONSIDER SPECIAL SITUATIONS

Another set of problems must be blamed squarely on the limited imagination of the draftsmen of local subdivision regulations, rather than on the restrictions imposed by enabling legislation or the difficulties of coordinating activities of other governmental agencies. These are the problems resulting from subdivision regulations written as though the only types of subdivisions were those designed for single-family residences located in a more or less routine terrain setting. When enforcement officials attempt to apply such regulations to other types of situations (some exotic but many just as "normal" as the development vis-

[24] Jan Krasnowiecki, Richard F. Babcock, and David N. McBride, LEGAL ASPECTS OF PLANNED UNIT RESIDENTIAL DEVELOPMENT, Urban Land Institute Technical Bulletin No. 52 (Washington: Urban Land Institute, 1965).

[25] See, for example, John W. Reps, "Requiem for Zoning," *Zoning Digest*, XVI (February and March 1964), pp. 33–39, 57–63, and also in American Society of Planning Officials, PLANNING 1964 (Chicago: 1964), pp. 56–67.

ualized by the draftsmen), they just don't fit.

A simple illustration of this is the cemetery. The division of a cemetery into burial plots to be sold to individual owners falls directly within the definition of a subdivision under virtually all subdivision regulation enabling acts. But not one set of subdivision regulations in a thousand recognizes this fact, even to the extent of exempting cemeteries from regulation. Obviously the lot size requirements and most of the improvement requirements contained in the regulations make no sense at all when applied to cemeteries. Tacitly recognizing this fact, most plat approval agencies simply ignore the subdivision of cemeteries, rather than either attempting the Procrustean task of applying these requirements to them or following the legally-preferable course of adding specific provisions concerning them to the regulations.

The same lack of recognition occurs, in lesser degree, with respect to many other types of subdivisions more important to the planner: commercial subdivisions, industrial subdivisions, mobile home subdivisions, hillside subdivisions, and waterfront subdivisions, to name only a few of the more common ones. Also shortchanged in many regulations are possibilities of unconventional layouts which may be devised by creative designers and even desirable modifications of standard lot patterns which may be necessary to adapt them better to currently popular house designs.

Commercial and Industrial Subdivisions. Despite obvious differences in their characteristics from those of residential subdivisions, commercial and industrial subdivisions are treated skimpily if at all in most subdivision regulations. This may be due in part to the fact that probably a majority of all shopping centers and a considerable percentage of industrial parks being developed today are held in single ownership and merely leased to their tenants. These would not fit the definition of "subdivision" in most enabling acts, although they would be subject to regulations under the zoning ordinance. But there are considerable numbers of both types of developments in which there is an actual division and sale of land to particular firms, and these are deserving of coverage in the subdivision regulations.

It should be recognized that, as in the case of residential subdivisions, not all commercial and industrial subdivisions are of the same nature. The small neighborhood convenience shopping center obviously raises different problems from the regional shopping center; the industrial park designed for occupancy by research laboratories or light manufacturing operations may well have a different range of requirements from the park intended to house heavy industry. So it may be necessary to provide for a number of different contingencies. Nevertheless, it is to be hoped that as many specifications as possible can be written down, rather than leaving matters to the discretion of the plat approval agency or some other officials.

Regulations governing commercial and industrial subdivisions may differ from those governing residential subdivisions in two major respects: the design and improvement requirements which they impose and the procedures which they specify for plat approval. In the absence of any recognized models, it is advisable that the draftsman seek qualified advisers to help with the drafting of these provisions. For example, it is highly desirable to have the assistance of a professional engineer in developing appropriate standards for the design and construction of streets and utilities systems. Similarly, procedural provisions should not be drafted until one has sufficient understanding of normal business practices in developing and marketing such subdivisions to recognize when a particular requirement would cause practical difficulties.

It should be obvious that both large commercial developments and industrial parks require streets constructed to higher than usual specifications because of the characteristics of the traffic which they will carry. Unlike many residential streets, which may be deliberately designed to impede through traffic and may be fitted to the terrain in such a way as to achieve visual effects, commercial and industrial streets are strictly utilitarian. They should be designed to expedite the free movement of traffic to specific locations. Because of large numbers of vehicles entering and leaving the stream of traffic, they commonly must have additional lanes. Shopping centers may be required to furnish local access streets paralleling existing streets. Sidewalks are invariably required in commercial areas and frequently in industrial areas.

Particularly in industrial parks streets should be so designed as to facilitate movement of large and cumbersome trucks. Dead-end streets should be avoided, corners should be well-rounded, curves should not be too abrupt. Alleys are commonly required, and they too must be designed to permit easy movement of trucks. Street locations in industrial parks must be coordinated with anticipated rail spurs.

Extra-large water, sewerage, gas, and electrical systems will normally be required, scaled to the particular needs of the type of industrial or commercial development which is expected. Because of extensive areas covered by roofs or pavements, the drainage problem may be especially acute, with larger-than-usual storm drains required.

Instead of requiring dedication of school sites or recreation areas in such developments, the regulations might well require dedication of off-street parking lots in shopping centers or planting strips of various kinds around the boundaries of the development. Special attention should be paid to protecting residential neighbors against nuisance effects. In addition to provision of the planting strips as buffers, lots on boundaries with residential developments should be made extra large, with a requirement of extra set-backs. Streets should be deliberately interrupted so that they do not connect directly with quiet residential streets.

A major problem relating to appropriate procedural requirements lies in the fact that lots in industrial subdivisions (and to a lesser degree in commercial subdivisions) are usually custom-tailored to the needs of particular purchasers. Industrial plants vary far more in their dimensions than do residences, and it is extremely difficult to "pre-plan" the exact lot sizes which will appeal to particular prospects. On the other hand, industrial firms have a distaste for undue delay when they decide upon a site; they wish to have immediate assurance that the owner can deliver a particular

site, without waiting for approval by a governmental agency.

These factors suggest that the subdivision regulations for industrial (and perhaps commercial) developments might well call for approval of a plat showing the location of the streets (and hence the blocks) but not individual lot lines within the blocks. The exact location of lot lines could then be exempted from further approval requirements, possibly subject to the lots' meeting certain general standards. This approach would seem to give adequate protection to legitimate governmental interests, without unduly impairing the process of industrial development.

Mobile Home Subdivisions. One of the outstanding phenomena of the years following World War II has been the unexpected emergence of the mobile home as a major element in the nation's housing supply. And contrary to expectations, the mobile home has largely lost its mobility and become essentially a prefabricated residence. Whereas it was sited at one time in trailer camps for transients, it has progressed to more-or-less permanent mobile home parks where spaces are rented or leased on a long-term basis, and more recently to "mobile home subdivisions" where spaces are purchased outright. Mobile home parks are commonly regulated either by the zoning ordinance or by a separate ordinance or by both. Mobile home subdivisions, on the other hand, are subject to the provisions of the subdivision regulations.

It is tempting for the draftsman of regulations for mobile home subdivisions to simply copy the regulations governing mobile home parks. However, there is a basic distinction between the two situations. Title to land in a mobile home park remains in one owner, who may convert it to another use with relative ease whenever he ceases to rent spaces for mobile homes. In a mobile home subdivision land is divided and sold into multiple ownership. This impresses a legal character on the land that is apt to have remarkable permanency, for it may be extraordinarily difficult to reassemble the land thus sold. Since the characteristics of mobile homes are changing rapidly, and since all present mobile homes have relatively short lives, it is not inconceivable that the present homes will in time disappear and leave behind a land ownership pattern adapted to them but unsuitable for other types of residences which may replace them.

Thus, while mobile home parks may be thought of as horizontal apartment houses in which individual homes are crowded together in patterns designed in light of their particular characteristics, it may be extremely unwise to permit the land to be divided into those same patterns because of this longer view of the possible consequences.

With this caution in mind, a certain amount of flexibility in applying usual subdivision standards to mobile home subdivisions may be desirable. It would be well for the draftsman to begin with an analysis of generally accepted design principles for mobile home parks, as exemplified in regulations, standard texts,[26] and other sources. These principles should then be considered in relation to the ordinary subdivision regulations for single-family residences in order to determine where there are conflicts. These conflicts can then be critically analyzed to determine whether it is necessary or wise to allow departures from the usual subdivision regulations.

For example, it has been suggested that because of their general structure and floor plans, mobile homes can be better accommodated on diagonal lots than on lots whose sidelines are perpendicular to the street.[27] While this will produce the "saw-toothed" effect that some planners deplore, it is noted that this orientation will give the occupant of the mobile home a better view from his living room window than if the narrow end of the mobile home faces the street squarely. (If the regulations are altered to permit diagonal lots, they must, of course, also specify the manner in which lot width and depth are to be measured.)

On analysis of this suggestion, it would appear that the author is attempting to make the best of an arrangement wherein mobile homes are planted in parallel rows, with their narrow ends towards the street. No doubt this basic orientation was selected, in part, because the homes are 55 or 60 feet long and lot widths would have to approximate 80 feet to accommodate them broadside to the street but only 32–44 feet if they are placed this way. The planner might reasonably ask himself whether the community would not be better off with 80-foot wide (and somewhat shallower than usual) lots in the not unlikely event that the mobile homes are some day replaced with more conventional structures.

It has also been suggested that the regulations should permit the planning of mobile home subdivisions somewhat in the manner of the cluster subdivisions and other designs discussed below. In other words, the homes would be laid out in small, intimate groupings, designed to facilitate the supposed natural gregariousness of mobile home occupants. This might well necessitate allowing lots of varying sizes, shapes, and orientations. Rather than requiring dedication of a single large park in such a plan, it may be better to require numbers of small park or playground areas. It is possible that the streets necessary to serve individual groupings of homes might be narrower and constructed to lower specifications than would normally be required—particularly if parking bays are provided. Necessary modifications of subdivision regulations to permit this type of development should be carefully considered.

Because the public has not entirely accepted mobile homes yet, the draftsman might consider whether the zoning ordinance and subdivision regulations should specify only certain districts within which mobile home subdivisions will be permitted. It is also possible that he will decide to require the dedication of buffer strips between such subdivisions and their more conventional neighbors, to minimize complaints.

Hillside Subdivisions. Of all the types of unusual subdivisions described in this section, hillside subdivisions have been treated most extensively in subdivision regulations. These are commonly defined as subdivisions on land with an average drop of 15 feet or more in 100

[26] E.g., Fred H. Bair, Jr., and Ernest Bartley, MOBILE HOME PARKS AND COMPREHENSIVE COMMUNITY PLANNING (Gainesville, Fla.: University of Florida Public Administration Clearing Service, 1960) .

[27] Fred H. Bair, Jr., "Regulation of Mobile Home Subdivisions," Planning Advisory Service Report No. 145, (Chicago: American Society of Planning Officials, 1960) .

feet. While such subdivisions may present special difficulties to the developer, they can yield exceptionally dramatic settings and views. They have been particularly popular in California, which consequently is the source of most of the experience in regulating them.

Press and television coverage of particular disasters has highlighted the major problem which must be dealt with in regulations for such subdivisions—that of landslides and erosion. To meet this danger regulations commonly require that:

1. The developer present sufficient detailed information as to geologic conditions, soil types, and so forth, in order that a determination can be made as to the safety of developing at this particular location;

2. Lot sizes vary according to the slope of each, with larger lots required where the slope is greater;

3. Detailed plans be presented for any proposed cut and fill operations, which must meet detailed specifications as to the angle of slope, compaction, retaining walls, etc.;

4. Maintenance easements be provided for access to any cut and fill slopes outside street rights-of-way;

5. Sewage disposal be by means other than septic tanks, to avoid accumulations of liquid under the surface which may lead to slippage; and

6. Special attention be given to the drainage system for the same reason.

Construction of streets in such subdivisions presents a special problem, and they are usually treated specially in the regulations. Because of the generally low density of development and resultant low traffic volumes, it may be possible to authorize streets of less than normal widths. This is affirmatively desirable

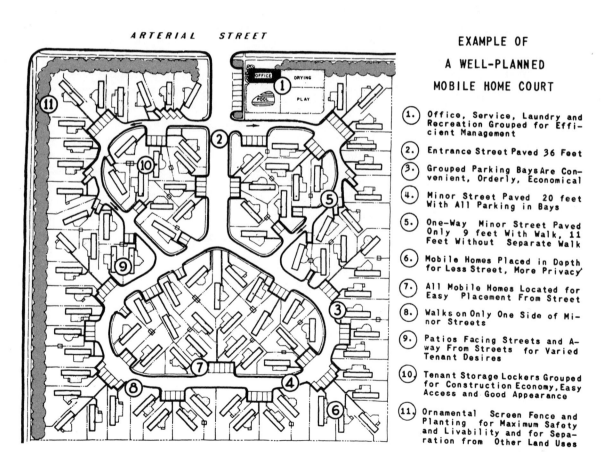

ARTERIAL STREET

EXAMPLE OF
A WELL-PLANNED
MOBILE HOME COURT

1. Office, Service, Laundry and Recreation Grouped for Efficient Management

2. Entrance Street Paved 36 Feet

3. Grouped Parking Bays Are Convenient, Orderly, Economical

4. Minor Street Paved 20 feet With All Parking in Bays

5. One-Way Minor Street Paved Only 9 feet With Walk, 11 Feet Without Separate Walk

6. Mobile Homes Placed in Depth for Less Street, More Privacy

7. All Mobile Homes Located for Easy Placement From Street

8. Walks on Only One Side of Minor Streets

9. Patios Facing Streets and Away From Streets for Varied Tenant Desires

10. Tenant Storage Lockers Grouped for Construction Economy, Easy Access and Good Appearance

11. Ornamental Screen Fence and Planting for Maximum Safety and Livability and for Separation from Other Land Uses

FIGURE 16–8. *Example of well-planned mobile home court*

insofar as it permits avoidance of excessive cut and fill and undue damage to trees and other natural features. However, provision must in this case be made for parking, either in off-street spaces on individual lots or in parking bays, and the draftsman must also consider possible interference with the movement of emergency vehicles such as fire trucks.

Because of topography, it may be necessary to allow greater than usual street grades and to reduce the required radius of horizontal and vertical curves. To avoid erosion of street surfaces, it will in almost all cases be necessary to provide curbs and gutters. Curbs serve the additional function on hills of helping to brake parked cars, and they should be constructed with this in mind.

Among the more unusual requirements of such subdivisions may be access easements for fire-fighting personnel and equipment. Obviously this will depend somewhat upon the particular situation.

Waterfront Subdivisions. Developers from coast to coast are suddenly awakening to the fact that the major single attraction they can provide for potential lot purchasers is a body of water suitable for various forms of recreation. Where lake, inlet, stream, or ocean fronts exist naturally, they are being developed; where they do not exist, they are being created artificially. Unfortunately, there are still some greedy but shortsighted developers who appear intent upon killing the ore-bearing goose by creating a maximum number of unduly small waterfront lots, providing no access to the water for interior lot owners, making inadequate provisions for sewage disposal, and allowing a honky-tonk atmosphere to develop. For this reason, there must be regulations.

In the case of waterfront subdivisions the need for special attention arises not because ordinary subdivision regulations are inapposite but because they do not cover many matters which should be regulated. Thus, unlike some of the other types we have discussed, waterfront subdivision regulations are in general supplementary rather than alternative to the ordinary regulations.

Among the matters which these additional provisions might cover are the following:

1. Filling operations in low-lying areas, including tests of underlying soils, appropriate fill materials, requirements for compaction, and provisions for drainage;

2. Provision of access to the water for members of the public or for owners of interior lots;

3. Dredging operations, with particular attention to depths, slopes of banks, and disposal of dredged material;

4. Sewage disposal facilities, which are particularly important if water quality is to be maintained;

5. Construction specifications for bulkhead, jetties, etc., designed to prevent shoreline erosion;

6. Information as to expected water levels, both normal and at high water;

7. Proposed measures for maintaining water quality, controlling insects and vegetation, controlling algae, etc.;

8. Wharf and dock lines beyond which structures may not be extended and lines marking areas within which speedboating and water skiing are prohibited or restricted;

9. Proposed covenants limiting the uses which may be made of the body of water. Other provisions might deal with such questions as how much, if any, of required lot areas may be satisfied by land lying under water.

Unusual Designs and Technological Changes. The sudden popularity of the ranch-style house following World War II served to highlight the inflexibility of many subdivision regulations. At least some developers believed that these wide but shallow buildings could best be accommodated on wide but shallow lots, but they found that local subdivision regulations required that lots be 1½ or 2 times as deep as they were wide, no matter what kind of house was to be built on them. This experience is only one example of the oft-noted phenomenon that regulations designed to prevent harmful conduct tend to sweep up the just along with the unjust.

A second circumstance in which subdivision regulations might be thought unduly restrictive is in their impact on innovative designs. A great deal of thought is currently going into development of improved designs for residential areas, but unfortunately many of the suggestions being offered run afoul of conventional subdivision regulations. It is questionable, for example, whether the world-famed "superblock" created by Clarence Stein and his associates in Radburn, New Jersey, in the 1920s would be permissible in many cities today. The same is true of the up-dated version of that concept, the "cluster subdivision." This involves groupings of lots, frequently of different shapes and sizes, surrounded by a sea of open space, with street systems and utilities systems custom-tailored to the needs of individual clusters rather than being developed to uniform specifications.

Nor does this concept stand alone. Some subdivision designers are urging the advantages of hexagonal-shaped lots, circular lots, circular blocks, and other unconventional ideas. These represent a long step away from the concept of the "gridiron with a wiggle in its streets" which underlies many regulations.

Yet a third area which may prove troublesome is the slowness of legislative reaction to technological improvements affecting the needs of particular types of development. Among the technical innovations already here or just over the horizon which may have major impacts on house, lot, and neighborhood design are (1) massive earth-moving equipment which makes possible the reshaping of almost any terrain to conform with the plans of man rather than of nature; (2) self-contained home sewage disposal plants, which may free the home from dependence upon public sewerage systems without creating sanitary problems of the types associated with septic tanks; (3) artificial lighting and air conditioning, which reduce the necessity for yards as a source of natural light and air; (4) educational television and teaching machines, which raise the possibility of education in the home rather than in schools or may have considerable impact on the size of schools (which once was thought to be a major influence on the size of planned neighborhoods); (5) nuclear power packages or fuel cells, which might free individual homes from reliance upon electrical transmission lines; (6) cost-reducing developments making underground wiring technically and financially feasible; (7) new forms of transportation which may render obsolete many of the facilities required for the motor car while possibly creating new needs. All these, with no mention of the less direct effects of new mass building techniques, prefabrication, new building materials!

The draftsman of subdivision regulations who wishes to build in sufficient flexibility to accommodate current fads in house styles, new design approaches to residential neighborhoods, and swift-moving technological changes has a formidable task. Under the current approach he must anticipate as many as possible of these needs and devise appropriate regulations to safeguard the public interest while meeting each. His only means of covering those situations which he does not anticipate is through the legally-dubious "variance" provisions.

What appears to be needed is a new approach to subdivision regulations, utilizing the "performance standards" technique which has emerged in up-to-date building codes and zoning ordinances. Instead of stating design and improvement regulations in terms of detailed specifications, the regulations would be phrased in terms of objectives, principles, and standards. These do not change so quickly as specifications, and they can accommodate considerable ingenuity displayed by able designers.

The drawbacks to this suggestion are twofold: it requires that planners and others concerned with the regulation of subdivisions think through much more explicitly exactly what it is that they wish to accomplish and why (and state these objectives precisely), and it may put a greater burden on enforcement personnel than they are prepared or trained to shoulder. However, it would not appear impossible. The recent development of the land use intensity rating technique (described below) by personnel of the Federal Housing Administration is an illustration of just such a new approach to regulation.

STATED DEVELOPMENTS

As the physical scale of new developments increases, it becomes practically necessary for the developer to work in stages, completing one

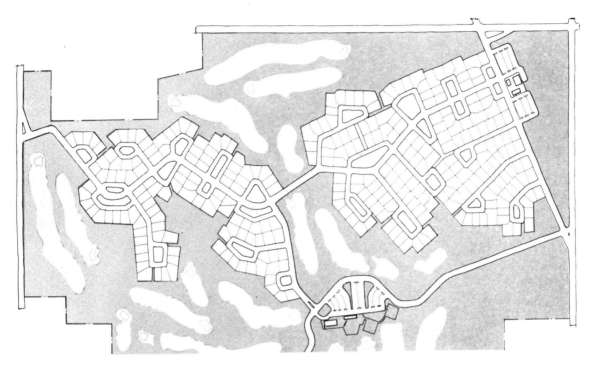

FIGURE 16–9. *Ville du Parc plan groups houses around courts*

section of his development before undertaking another. He can do this, of course, by submitting plats for each successive stage of development shortly before he is ready to undertake that stage. But frequently his financial scheme is dependent upon successful completion of the plan as a whole, and this can easily be disrupted by the city government's changing the rules when he is halfway through. It may decide to change the zoning of his as-yet undeveloped land so as to lower the permitted densities (i.e., require larger lots) or to change the permitted uses. Or it may upgrade its subdivision regulations so as to require the developer to install additional improvements or construct them to higher standards or to dedicate additional land or make increased payments in lieu of dedication.

To avert the financial hardship which such changes may impose on particular developers, the enabling acts of a few states (as has been noted earlier) provide that the zoning of an area may not be changed for a reasonable period (such as two years) following approval of the preliminary plat. This is only a partial answer and one which may have some detrimental side effects.

It may well be that a preferable solution would be to provide a system of "outline approval" for later stages in a comprehensive development, similar to that provided under British law. As described by an authority on that law:

Either before he buys his land or before he incurs the cost of preparing detailed plans, a developer may wish to know whether his proposed development will be likely to get planning permission if he applies for it. In these circumstances a developer may make an 'outline application' for planning permission which can be granted subject to a condition that there shall be subsequent approval by the local planning authority of any matters relating to siting, design and external appearance of buildings. The developer thus gets to know, before he incurs too much expense, whether in principle his proposed development is acceptable to the local planning authority. Once an outline application is granted, the local planning authority are committed to allowing the proposed development in some form or other, the only matters requiring subsequent approval by the authority being such as are specifically reserved in the permission granted on the outline application.[28]

Of course, the procedures would not be exactly the same, but the intent would be similar. The developer would submit plans showing the major physical features of his proposal, including major streets, land to be dedicated to the public, proposed land uses and densities in each area, etc. These features, as approved by the plat approval agency, would then be "frozen" for a reasonable period of time. As the subdivision plats for each stage in the development were submitted, they would be checked for compliance with this general plan, without taking into account any conflicting regulations which might have been enacted in the meantime.

Special Types of Regulation

Several areas of regulation are worthy of more extended discussion than has been given them up to this point. These are (1) the large-scale planned unit development, (2) land management measures, particularly those involving preservation of open space, and (3) measures intended to control the timing of development. In each case, subdivision regulations constitute only a part of a coordinated program of activities necessary to accomplish a given objective.

PLANNED UNIT DEVELOPMENTS

Certain aspects of planned unit developments have already been treated, notably the problem of coordinating zoning and subdivision regulations in their application to such developments. Because so large a part of recent development has been of this type, it may be worthwhile to note some additional considerations than this problem of coordination.

Historical Evolution. Planned unit developments probably had their legal genesis in the garden apartment developments which became popular just prior to and after World War II. Most zoning ordinances at that time spoke in terms of required lot areas and front, side, and rear yards, but in these developments such requirements made little sense. The owners held the entire development in single ownership, renting individual units to tenants, and it would have been foolish to require them to subdivide the tract into lots so that zoning officials would have some lines from which to measure yard sizes.

The legislative response to this problem was inclusion of provisions in the zoning ordinance which authorized the developer to submit his plans for special approval, usually by the city council on recommendation of the planning commission but occasionally by the board of adjustment.[29] Approval could normally be granted on findings that (1) the development included no uses not permitted in that particular zoning district, (2) no structure exceeded the height limits for the district, (3) the overall number of dwelling units was no greater than would have been permissible in the tract if it had been divided into lots of the appropriate size, and (4) appropriate set-backs were observed on the boundaries of the tract. Not long afterwards, similar provisions began to appear with respect to unified commercial and industrial developments.

The next step in this evolution was the appearance of "variable density" provisions in zoning ordinances. Noting the fact that the over-all density control found in the garden apartment provisions had worked well, some planners began to experiment with provisions under which developers would be given the same latitude to vary lot sizes within a subdivision as they had in garden apartment developments. So long as the total number of dwelling units in a tract remained the same, there seemed little reason to require that they have lots of uniform sizes. Where the developer chose to build on smaller lots, the space thus saved would be dedicated to the public for parks or other public purposes. In the subdivision regulations such provisions came to be known as cluster subdivision provisions, since it usually was desirable for a variety of reasons

---

[28] Desmond Heap, AN OUTLINE OF PLANNING LAW (London: Sweet & Maxwell, 4th ed., 1963), p. 56.

[29] In some states there have been court decisions that there was no statutory authority to assign this function to any agency other than the board of adjustment.

to group the smaller lots in clusters.

At the same time that this development was taking place, there were arguments that it was desirable both from a sociological standpoint and from the standpoint of architectural aesthetics to vary not only lot sizes but also dwelling types within a subdivision, ranging from single-family residences through row houses and garden apartments to high-rise apartment units.

Finally, as developments grew in scale to encompass neighborhoods and entire new towns, it became necessary to consider the possibility of authorizing commercial and industrial uses within such developments.

Throughout this evolution, roughly the same administrative organization was utilized which had been prescribed for handling the garden apartment developments. In effect, much of the burden of planning a neighborhood or new town was transferred to the developers themselves, subject to such standards as the ordinance laid down. Each development was given individual approval, based on compliance with those standards as they were interpreted by the administrative agency with approval authority. Depending upon the precision with which they were drafted and their definiteness, the standards thus became the sole safeguard of the developer against possibly arbitrary treatment at the hands of this agency.

Land-Use Intensity Standards. In this state of affairs, it was of the utmost importance that the standards for development be imaginative in their approach. Fortunately, a major breakthrough in this respect occurred in 1963, when the Federal Housing Administration announced its adoption of a new set of standards for the control of density, the land-use intensity standards (called the LUI by F.H.A. personnel). Although designed for use in its own operations of providing mortgage insurance, the F.H.A. supplied a valuable tool to planners for use in their zoning ordinances and subdivision regulations—particularly as they applied to the planned unit development.

The land-use intensity standards tie down very precisely the maximum floor area of buildings on a given area of land and the amount of various types of open spaces which must be provided on a tract for a given amount of floor area. They are presented simply, in the form of a graph, so that anyone can easily ascertain what is required of him. They are applicable, in varying degrees, to developments involving subdivision of land, to condominiums, and to garden apartment and similar developments where the property is to be kept in an undivided state. And withal, they give the designer remarkable latitude in laying out his development without sacrificing vital interests of the community.

The LUI process begins with the assignment of a land-use intensity rating to property in a given area. This is a job which would have to be done by the professional planner after careful analysis, and it would then show up in the zoning ordinance provisions relating to that area. The user of the LUI chart would then merely glance up the vertical line signifying the rating applicable to his property and note where it crosses each of six lines representing different ratios. These crossing points would then tell him which ratios apply to his property.

The first and fundamental ratio is the floor area ratio (described more fully in Chapter 15), which tells the developer how many square feet of building floor area he may put on a given number of square feet of land. He may divide this floor area among as many stories as he wishes, but there are obvious economic limits to his discretion. Having ascertained the number of square feet of floor area he can build, he then considers three other ratios. These specify how many square feet of his tract must be devoted to (1) open space, (2) "living space" (defined as open space minus off-street parking space), and (3) recreation space, which must be provided for each square foot of floor area. Finally, two ratios specify the total number of off-street parking spaces and the number of such spaces for occupants of the tract which must be provided for each dwelling unit.

This device thus permits elimination of lot size requirements, yard requirements, height requirements, and similar zoning controls throughout a planned unit development. There is no doubt that there will be many

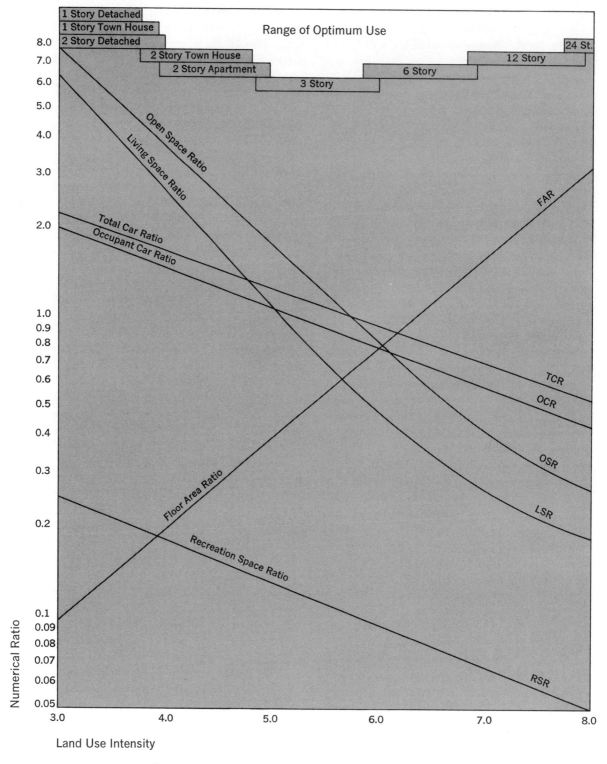

FIGURE 16–10. *Land use intensity by range of optimum use*

more ordinances making use of it as time goes by.

Maintenance of Open Space. One of the major problems encountered in planned unit developments or cluster subdivisions where the developer is permitted to reduce the lot area for certain dwelling units provided he puts the land thus saved into parks or other open areas is what legal treatment to accord to these open spaces. The first and most obvious answer is to require that the developer dedicate this space to the public. However, there are many instances (particularly where the development is located beyond a city's corporate limits) in which no governmental unit is willing to accept the expense of maintaining such areas. A second solution is to form a "homes association" of property owners in the area which is, by deed restrictions applicable to each lot, entitled to levy an annual contribution from each owner to pay for such maintenance.[30] In a sense this is more equitable, since the land was derived from reduction in their lot sizes. However, there are sometimes practical difficulties in continuing the operations of such associations over a period of time. A third solution which has been suggested is the creation of an Open Space Maintenance District, with authority to levy special assessments against benefited property owners as required for the maintenance of this land.[31] This would, of course, require specific statutory authority. A combination of the three approaches may be required to serve large planned-unit developments.

LAND MANAGEMENT MEASURES

In a civilization whose tastes and requirements are constantly changing, there is one commodity whose possession by local governments is of the utmost value in meeting unexpected needs. That commodity, of course, is land. Unfortunately, the management of this precious resource by such governments has generally been short-sighted and inefficient. One agency or

unit of local government will dispose of property at the same time another unit will be acquiring less suitable property. Whenever property is temporarily unused, and occasionally when it is very much used, a cry will go up to dispose of it and get it back on the tax books; disposition is commonly made at prices well below actual value, and shortly thereafter the same governmental unit will pay exorbitant prices for less suitable land. It is a sad feature of our economic system that slum properties must ordinarily be acquired at very high prices and then sold, after redevelopment to bring them up to appropriate standards of decency, for much lower prices—the difference being made up by all the taxpayers.

Management Agency and Program. What appears to be necessary in most local areas is an agency, perhaps similar to the federal government's General Services Administration, with general responsibility for managing the land resources of local governmental units and agencies in that area. In the absence of such an agency, a planning agency could perform at least some of the desired functions, while others might be divided among various agencies through intergovernmental agreements and intra-governmental directives.

The management activities might include the following measures:

1. Preparation and maintenance of a current inventory of all publicly held property in the area, derived from whatever source (purchase, exercise of eminent domain, gift, dedication, tax delinquency, urban renewal operations, etc.), with detailed information as to the characteristics of each piece of property;

2. Far more detailed planning than is current in most localities as to the property needs of public agencies in the area (at all levels of government) over a given period (perhaps 20 years), with liberal allowances for unexpected developments;

3. Careful screening of any land proposed for disposition to ascertain its adequacy in meeting any of the listed needs;

4. Establishment of systematic communications procedures for bringing such needs to the attention of such agencies as the subdivision plat approval agency (for its use in determin-

[30] For a compendium of such arrangements, see Byron H. Hanke and others, THE HOMES ASSOCIATION HANDBOOK. Urban Land Institute Technical Bulletin No. 50 (Washington: Urban Land Institute, 1964).

[31] Richard S. Volpert, "Creation and Maintenance of Open Spaces in Subdivisions: Another Approach," U. C. L. A. LAW REVIEW, XII (March, 1965), pp. 830–55.

ing what lands should be dedicated or reserved) and the urban renewal agency (for its use in deciding upon appropriate re-use of cleared land) ;

5. Identification, insofar as possible, of specific properties which might be available for future acquisition to meet particular needs, and communication of this information to all appropriate officials who might become aware of plans for development of such properties, so they can be acquired prior to development;

6. Establishment of revolving funds for the systematic acquisition of properties to meet future needs, at times when particular circumstances make such acquisition desirable.

In addition, the property management agency could have such responsibility as might be delegated to it for maintenance of existing property, lease or rental of temporarily surplus property, and allocation of space among various agencies in publicly-held properties.

Governmental Land Development. In recent years there have been a number of proposals, some of them in the form of bills introduced in the federal Congress, that state and local governmental units take a much more affirmative role in the development of land. These proposals call for governmental units or agencies to acquire undeveloped property, plan for the use of that property, construct the public improvements necessary, set aside lands as appropriate for public use, and then sell or lease land to private builders for construction of residences and commercial, industrial, or other structures, either for their own use or for resale. These ideas are based on (1) the very similar procedures of the urban renewal agencies in acquiring, clearing, and preparing in-town slum properties for re-use by private developers, (2) the experience of the British in building "new towns" in outlying areas, and (3) the experience of American private builders in constructing new towns (and especially the difficulties they encounter in securing adequate capital for provision of public facilities) .

There is no doubt that many legal and political problems would have to be solved before such proposals became feasible, but there is also no doubt that this could be done if attacked with determination.

TIMING OF DEVELOPMENT

One notable area in which there has been relatively little experience consists of attempts to regulate the timing of development. "Timing of development" may refer to the *tempo* of development (in which case the community may be concerned with holding development to a pace at which schools, water systems, sewerage systems, and other governmental facilities and services can be made available as the needs appear) ; the *geographical sequence* of development (in which case the community may be concerned that certain areas be more or less fully developed before development begins in other areas—an effort, in other words, to avoid urban sprawl) ; or the *balance* of development (in which case the community may wish to insure that particular types of development do not occur more rapidly than other types, to such an extent that the character of the community is sharply altered) .

In order to achieve one or more of these objectives, it is necessary that a coordinated program of "carrots and sticks" be developed and carried out. Among the legal and administrative devices which might be used in furtherance of such a program are governmental acquisition of property, governmental construction of particular facilities in particular areas, zoning restrictions, subdivision regulations imposing greater or smaller requirements on developers at particular times or in particular locations, policies for the extension of utilities (in terms of time, location, and the sharing of costs) , and various tax policies. In general it has been found easier to encourage development at particular times and locations than to discourage development, for if measures to accomplish the latter objective are too effective, they may meet with judicial rebuttal.

17

Urban Renewal

It has become commonplace when talking about middle-aged and older cities in the United States to refer to a litany of problems: the flight of middle-class white families to the suburbs, the influx of low-income Negroes, the burgeoning slums, the racial ghettos, the vast stretches of gray areas, the strain on property taxes, violence in the streets, the withering downtown, and the decentralization of industries and businesses. Some may weary of hearing these phrases bandied about over and over again in the mass media and in the professional journals, but their persistence is evidence that many observers are still unconvinced that central cities have effectively met, let alone solved, their problems.

Yet few would contend that cities are not trying. And fewer still would be remiss in acknowledging that in the past decade and a half, the principal response to the problems of older cities is the federally supported urban renewal program.[1] As Robert Weaver, Secretary of the Department of Housing and Urban Development, said in 1965: "Without urban renewal our central cities would be in a continuing cycle of disastrous decline, devoid of hope

and destined to irreversible decay."[2]

For city planning, the urban renewal program has offered and still offers great potential for accomplishing planning objectives. In its early days, urban renewal—then called urban redevelopment—was designed to clear central city slums and build new residential complexes on them in accordance with a comprehensive plan. No other planning tool offered the possibility for such radical change. As renewal evolved to encompass more and more public actions, it became in theory an even more promising tool for implementing planning. While renewal has dominated planning in some cities—rather than the other way around—in many other cities the success of comprehensive planning, more than any other factor, is attributable to the urban renewal program and the powers it enables cities to exercise.

Essentially the renewal program is important because it provides a way to loosen the Gordian knot that for years threatened to strangle the central city: the fact that run-down land which is largely or fully built-up is not easy to change in character or appearance. Because renewal enables cities to use eminent domain to assemble small and large tracts of land under separate ownership for new public and private development, it has provided opportunities to deal with a variety of problems: the slum too far gone to warrant improvement; the older single family housing area slipping badly into disrepair; the strip commercial district lined

---

[1] There are a few cities, because of strong political and ideological convictions, that have undertaken renewal-type projects without using federal money. Indianapolis, Indiana, is perhaps the most notable example. Other cities have accepted federal renewal aid, but they have not had to use federal money to renew certain areas because market conditions were so favorable and developer interest so strong that the private sector was able to do the renewal job by itself—e.g., Chicago's Wells Street, New York's Park Avenue, and Philadelphia's Penn Center. Urban renewal, as used in this chapter, however, applies only to the federally assisted program.

[2] Journal of Housing, XXII (Number 6, 1965), p. 306.

with vacant stores or clogged streets; the skid row area next to the city's central business district occupying land more suitable for expansion of the hemmed-in downtown; or the sparsely developed, flood-prone tract, on the city's outskirts, frozen into a pattern of development not adaptable to present day needs. While urban renewal has not fully lived up to the hopes of its early supporters—in part because it was impossible to achieve the many and often conflicting goals set out for it with limited funds and formidable political, administrative, and social constraints—it still has many accomplishments to its credit.

This chapter covers an important, on-going program, urban renewal, which has a sharply etched record based on techniques, many of which have been tailored from the cloth of urban planning. Since renewal is a fusion of many of the elements discussed elsewhere in this book—i.e., land use, population, and economic studies; the comprehensive plan; programming community development; and social welfare considerations—this chapter will not treat these planning tools in detail. Instead it will place major emphasis on policies and implementation. Specifically, attention is given to renewal's antecedents, its key features, its record, and the important shifts in policy, approach, organization, and implementation that have marked its growth since its formal beginning.

Accomplishments

In 16 years of existence, the urban renewal program has rebuilt or is in the final stages of rebuilding 16 square miles,[3] an area equivalent to the size of Springfield, Ohio, a city of 83,000 people. By mid-1965, 770 communities, with nearly 1,600 projects, were in the program.[4]

There is little doubt that in many cities with renewal programs a new civic pride has taken hold, resulting in a new civic image. As a direct consequence of urban renewal, cities can point

[3] William Slayton, URA Commissioner, in a speech to the American Institute of Real Estate Appraisers, October, 1965.

[4] JOURNAL OF HOUSING, XXIII (Number 1, 1966), p. 11.

FIGURE 17–1. *Downtown redevelopment, Constitution Plaza, Hartford, Connecticut*

to one or more of the following physical accomplishments:

1. Downtown areas being rebuilt with new office buildings, shopping malls, and apartment houses.

2. Areas of older housing being rehabilitated and improved with schools, parks, and other public improvements.

3. Low-rental housing projects, both public and private, being built.

4. Imposing and attractive middle-income and luxury apartment projects being developed.

5. University, hospital, and cultural complexes being refurbished with new buildings. additions to old buildings, and improvements in surrounding areas.

6. Areas of historic or architectural significance being preserved.

7. New areas being developed to quarter industrial and wholesale facilities hampered by obsolete buildings, clogged streets, and depressing surroundings.

8. Older commercial centers being rebuilt to accommodate the modern-day needs of their small business establishments.[5]

Apart from the visible improvements, cities have reaped other less tangible benefits from

[5] See the first six figures in this chapter for illustrations of a few outstanding examples of each type renewal project mentioned.

urban renewal. As a result of clearing slums and upgrading deteriorating neighborhoods, more taxes have flowed into the public coffers. The Urban Renewal Administration claims that assessed values after renewal average 4 to 5 times what they were before renewal.[6] The public dollars invested in renewal projects have triggered approximately five times as many private dollars, not only in the project areas but in the surrounding areas as well.[7] Local governments deploy talents and resources in a more purposeful manner than ever before, often reorganizing the machinery of government so that renewal will work more smoothly. Some little used but important tools like code enforcement and capital improvement programming have been dusted off, polished, and effectively employed in support of the renewal program at the local level. Renewal has also boosted our understanding of how cities function and change. In some instances, a higher level of civic design and cultural quality has been a by-product. And finally, urban renewal programs have triggered a widespread interest in city planning, lending to a greater understanding, tolerance, and acceptance.

Criticisms

In its wake, however, renewal has generated strong reactions and criticisms from divergent quarters. Some of its most ardent early supporters now have become outspoken critics. They charge that the renewal program is more concerned with bricks, mortar, and physical accomplishments than with people, hitting hardest those least able to help themselves—the Negro, the small businessman, the elderly, and the low-income large family. They claim that renewal more often intensifies than alleviates the difficulties faced by these groups. Others

bemoan the design sterility and unimaginativeness of renewal projects. Still others see the program as a harbinger of eventual control of local affairs by the federal government.

The renewal program has matured to the point where opposition, often muted in the past, is not only vocal but effective. In recent years, more and more campaigns to raise funds for local renewal programs through bond issues have failed to get public support. Referenda votes on specific renewal projects have turned out negative more often than government officials are willing to admit.[8] A growing number of books, magazine articles, newspaper editorials, and scholarly studies have been published criticizing parts of or sometimes the whole renewal program.[9] Even steadfast supporters are showing edginess. Some carp about the excessive red tape which results in slow progress and few accomplishments. Others are concerned about an overcommitment in site selection to marketable sites in order to attract developers, a condition that, if carried to excess, results in forsaking other problem areas. And still others point to the inability of the renewal program to mount a sustained attack on blight because of limited funds and other resources,[10] let alone contribute much to the

---

[6] Based on information for 518 projects in which redevelopment was started or completed as of June, 1965, assessed values jumped from $709 million before renewal to $3,238 million after renewal. (From "The Operation and Achievements of the Urban Renewal Program" by William Slayton, in URBAN RENEWAL: THE RECORD AND THE CONTROVERSY. [Cambridge, Mass.: M.I.T. Press and Harvard U. Press, 1966.])

[7] Slayton, *op. cit.*

[8] According to the JOURNAL OF HOUSING (Number 10, 1965), at least 11 cities in 1965 voted down renewal projects.

[9] Unlike the first ten years when few tangible results could be seen, since 1960 the renewal program has been subject to a rash of mild and harsh criticisms from both liberal and conservative quarters. Some of the more incisive criticisms are found in the following books and articles: Jane Jacobs, THE DEATH AND LIFE OF AMERICAN CITIES (1961); Martin Anderson, THE FEDERAL BULLDOZER: A CRITICAL ANALYSIS OF URBAN RENEWAL: *1949–1962* (1964); Herbert Gans, "The Failure of Urban Renewal: A Critique and Some Proposals," COMMENTARY (April, 1965); Scott Greer, URBAN RENEWAL AND AMERICAN CITIES (1965); Charles Abrams, THE CITY IS THE FRONTIER (1965); Chester Hartman, "Housing of Relocated Families," THE JOURNAL OF THE AMERICAN INSTITUTE OF PLANNERS (November, 1964); William Grigsby, HOUSING MARKETS AND PUBLIC POLICY (1964); James Wilson, (ed.), URBAN RENEWAL: THE RECORD AND THE CONTROVERSY (1966); Wolf Von Eckhardt, "Urban Renewal and the City," THE NEW REPUBLIC, (6 issues in September and October, 1963).

[10] Although more than 5 billion dollars of federal funds plus 2 million dollars of local funds have been committed to renewal projects from 1949 to the present, most independent studies conclude that this is far below the actual need. Dyckman and Isaacs in CAPITAL RE-

overall local housing supply.[11]

In response to the mounting opposition to urban renewal some cities have placed the program lower on their scale of priorities. A few have even changed the program's name—i.e., community improvement program—in an attempt to make it more palatable and acceptable. One student of urban renewal succinctly poses the problem and the dilemma.

Urban renewal is not the most expensive or the most far-reaching domestic governmental program of our time, yet it is one of the most widely-discussed and perhaps the most controversial. We spend far more on farm subsidies and highways, yet these programs—except for an occasional scandal—are rarely debated outside the circle of immediate participants and their scholarly observers. There are other federal housing programs—especially the FHA mortgage guarantee program—the collective impact of which has, in the past at least, been considerably greater than urban renewal, yet only rarely in recent years have they been the objects of general public discussion. The decisions of a variety of obscure regulatory commissions in Washington probably affect the lives of more people than does urban renewal, yet seldom does one encounter in print the names of these agencies, much less an argument over their policies. Urban renewal, on the other hand, has been the object of the closest scrutiny.[12]

Yet despite the fervor and emotion which the renewal program has generated, it still represents one of the few potent devices available to tackle the complex problems of older cities.

QUIREMENTS FOR URBAN DEVELOPMENT AND RENEWAL (1961) concluded that to renew all American cities within a 12-year period by the current theory of urban renewal would cost approximately one trillion dollars. The Council of Economic Development in GUIDING METROPOLITAN GROWTH (1960), estimated that the cost of replacing 7 million dwelling units most badly in disrepair and rehabilitating 2 million more would cost from 120 to 125 billion dollars. They concluded that at the present rate of federal expenditure on urban renewal, it would take 400 years to work off the current stock of slum dwellings.

[11] Philadelphia, a city with an impressive record in renewal, provides a good illustration of how much the program has actually contributed to the local housing supply. The Philadelphia Housing Association in ISSUES (December, 1965), estimated that only one-tenth of all new dwelling units brought into the Philadelphia housing inventory between 1952 and 1965—5,000 out of 65,000 new housing units—were built on renewed land.

[12] James Wilson in the introduction to a collection of articles published as a book under his editorship. Reprinted from URBAN RENEWAL: THE RECORD AND THE CONTROVERSY, quoted here by permission of The M.I.T. Press, Cambridge, Massachusetts. Copyright © 1966.

Antecedents of Urban Renewal

The seeds of the modern urban renewal program were planted many years ago. Like an embryo, it has taken different, progressively more distinguishable forms before maturing.

Concern for city slums dates back well before the 20th century. Understandably, that concern was limited because over 80 per cent of Americans lived on farms or in rural communities in the early part of the 19th century. In fact, most leading American philosophers and writers of the 19th century had a decidedly anticity bias.

Thomas Jefferson, in a letter to Benjamin Franklin after an outbreak of yellow fever in Paris in 1800, wrote: ". . . I view great cities as pestilentials to the morals, the health and the liberties of man. True, they nourish some of the elegant arts, but the useful ones can thrive elsewhere."[13]

Henry Thoreau reported that he was "ever . . . leaving the city more and more and withdrawing into the wilderness."[14]

Nathaniel Hawthorne, at one point in his novel *The Marble Faun,* advises that "all towns should be made capable of purification by fire, or of decay, within each half-century."[15]

Despite the intellectuals' disdain for the city, concern began to spread for city problems in the latter part of the 19th century. In 1894, the United States Commissioner of Labor undertook a study investigating slum conditions in four large cities—Baltimore, Chicago, New York, and Philadelphia. The concept of blight crept into some of that period's technical studies, although defined differently from today. For example, a 1907 Baltimore study used a standard of 2.5 persons per room to define one of the traditional blight factors, overcrowding. In a Baltimore study done 34 years later, the standard for overcrowding was 1.5 persons per room.[16]

---

[13] Morton and Lucia White, THE INTELLECTUAL VERSUS THE CITY (Cambridge: Harvard University Press, 1962).

[14] *Ibid.*

[15] *Ibid.*

[16] Baltimore Community Renewal Program, REVIEW OF PREVIOUS CRITERIA USED TO MEASURE THE NATURE, DEGREE AND EXTENT OF BLIGHT IN BALTIMORE CITY, Staff Monograph 3 (June, 1964).

With the development of the automobile, the influx of many foreigners to American cities, and the increasing movement of rural dwellers to urban areas in the first part of the 20th century, attention shifted more directly to the problems of cities. The settlement house movement in the 20s, which gave aid to slum residents, and the philanthropic housing ventures sponsored by Jacob Riis in New York City, the Octavia Hill Association in Philadelphia, and Julius Rosenwald in Chicago, were the first of a growing series of responses by private citizens to city problems.

On the public side, efforts were sporadic but significant. New York City adopted a model tenement building code. A spurt in playground construction in slum areas occurred after World War I. In 1926, New York state passed a limited-dividend housing law, granting tax exemptions and condemnation powers to private corporations to clear slums and build moderate income housing. And more and more zoning, building, housing, and subdivision codes were enacted by communities to deal with urban deterioration.

Not until the 30s though, was the movement for housing reform really spawned. The depression struck every sector of the economy, with the housing industry critically affected. Foreclosures skyrocketed, banks refused to lend money for new housing, and low income housing construction was at a virtual standstill.

The federal government began to stir, enacting several programs not only to help the home-building industry but also to help the homeowner and the lending institutions. The Home Owners Loan Corporation was created to give loans to prevent foreclosures. Savings and loan associations were founded to lend mortgage money insured by the federal government in the 1932 Home Loan Bank Act. Also in that year federal loans were extended to private corporations to induce them to construct low-cost housing under the Federal Relief and Reconstruction Act. The Federal Housing Administration was established in 1934 to insure mortgages for new moderately priced housing on undeveloped land. That year also saw the creation of the Federal National Mortgage Association which bought mortgages in debtor areas to save bankrupt cities and stimulate the building industry.

Paralleling the efforts to revive the home building industry in the 30s were several studies that helped etch slum conditions more sharply. The Public Works Authority pioneered by illuminating the pervasive character of slums through its real property surveys undertaken in different cities. Land use and housing surveys were conducted revealing that slums were not static, that they spread and often into healthy areas. Baltimore, Boston, Chicago, and Washington, D.C., undertook renewal prototype studies that not only sketched the qualities of blight more distinctly but also introduced terms that would later become commonplace in urban renewal such as "clearance" and "conservation."

The depression was a leveler. It exposed many people who were unaware of slum conditions in the prosperous 20s to these conditions in the difficult 30s. It also brought about the first direct federal involvement in the slum housing problem with the passage of the low-rent public housing program in 1937. Construction of public housing projects by local housing authorities, paid for entirely by the federal government, marked a radical step in the evolution toward the urban renewal program since attention was sharply riveted for the first time on the home building industry's inability to provide sufficient low-cost housing to meet the pressing needs. From 1937 to 1941, the public housing program had an unequalled period of growth—over 125,000 units were built.

While World War II diverted the nation from steady progress toward urban renewal, a lull transpired once the war ended, and pressures for housing in urban areas grew. More than any other factor, the severe housing shortage after the war accounted for the rise in attention to central city problems. The federal government met the need for a coordinated approach to housing assistance by establishing the Housing and Home Finance Agency—predecessor to the Department of Housing and Urban Development—in 1947. Several states pioneered by enacting legislation to permit localities to exercise broad public powers to redevelop blighted areas, but a lack of sufficient funds prevented cities in these states from doing much with their new powers. The financial problem was recognized in 1945 by a U.S. Senate subcommittee under the chairmanship of Senator Taft, which recommended some sort of federal subsidy to help relieve the housing problem.[17] At the same time, many began to doubt whether the public housing program would be the panacea for slums that some of its original supporters claimed. Slums began to be viewed in a larger perspective as only one of a number of problems growing out of poor city planning. Looking beyond public housing, some advocated developing land on the city outskirts with a mixture of housing types. One proposal advanced in the late 40s was to build new satellite communities, an idea that only recently became federal policy in the new towns legislation proposed in 1965.

The stage was set for the urban renewal program. After a five-year battle in Congress, the Housing Act was passed in 1949, making it possible for cities to clear slums and redevelop these lands for new housing.[18]

The program, initially called "urban redevelopment," had widespread support, partly because it meant different things to different people. Public housing and social welfare advocates saw it as a way to eliminate slums and provide the poor with decent homes through public housing in decent neighborhoods. Planners viewed it as a promising tool for implementing comprehensive planning proposals. City officials supported it for two reasons: it would (1) reduce the high cost of slum areas and (2) help correct the imbalance between cities and rural areas by giving the cities a greater share of the federal dollar. Builders

and investors thought it would be a way to secure valuable central sites otherwise impossible to acquire and deed to profitable enterprise. Downtown merchants believed the program would keep consumers from fleeing to the suburbs, thus protecting the central business district. Still others, opposed to public housing, saw it as a means of curtailing public housing by stimulating private investment in housing.

The 1949 Act coupled two key provisions: $500 million of federal capital grants for the redevelopment of slums by public or private developers and authorization to build a total of 135,000 public housing units over a six-year period. While the Act was essentially a housing measure, it still represented a remarkable accomplishment, for it gave the cities for the first time both funds and power to tackle slum conditions.

Key Elements of Renewal

The approach to city rebuilding in the Housing Act of 1949, built in considerable part around Title I of the Act, was deliberately shaped in a delicate fashion. The drafters of the legislation were well aware of several prominent constraints:

1. The political system, built upon the clear division of responsibilities between the federal, state, and local levels of government, precluded too direct an intervention into local affairs by the federal government.

2. The local revenue system, so heavily dependent on property taxes, made it virtually impossible for cities to pay themselves for what needed to be done.

3. The property rights system, built on the rights of private citizens to use their property rather freely within certain constitutionally prescribed limits, ruled out the indiscriminate taking of these rights to accomplish what some might feel was necessary to solve slum problems.

Taking into account these and other important constraints, the unique approach to urban renewal was fashioned. While there have been many modifications since then, the key features of the program remain essentially the same.

---

[17] It is interesting to note that Senator Taft rejected the notion that federal subsidies for redevelopment should be broader than just housing. Several groups testifying before Senator Taft's subcommittee on Housing and Urban Redevelopment, however, were ahead of their times when they claimed that housing was only one form of redevelopment, that redevelopment should be applied to all urban areas which needed it and should include all classes of land.

[18] For a detailed account of the struggle to enact the 1949 Housing Act, see the article by Ashley A. Foard and Hilbert Fefferman, "Federal Urban Renewal Legislation" in Law and Contemporary Problems (Raleigh, N.C.: Duke University School of Law, Autumn, 1960).

THE LEGAL MECHANISM: EMINENT DOMAIN

The use of eminent domain by government to condemn land for a public purpose, with the land to be kept in *public* ownership for highways, schools, or parks, has long been recognized as proper. The 1949 Housing Act expanded the application of eminent domain to enable cities to assemble and acquire large tracts of run-down land which could be sold later into *private* as well as into public ownership.

Eminent domain is the legal mechanism which permits cities to work on large rather than minute scales. And because most courts ruled that cities can sell condemned land to private developers—at first to build housing and later to build other nonpublic facilities—the potential for investment in renewal projects is considerably enlarged. In practice, most local renewal agencies negotiate with property owners to purchase their property directly, offering a fair market value. However, when direct purchase fails, they can initiate court condemnation using eminent domain to acquire the property.

THE FINANCIAL MECHANISM: FEDERAL SUBSIDIES

The ability to acquire several blocks of built-up city land through eminent domain must be accompanied by the ability to pay property owners for the land and structures they own. Since the cost of in-city land is high, and the city is usually strapped financially to pay for normal public facilities and services, some other means of financial assistance must be available. The principle of federal aid to help the city do the job is now well established, not only for acquisition of developed land (which is by far the most expensive item), but also for the other things that must be done to get the land ready for disposal, including demolition of structures, site improvements, property management, and payments to those displaced from the project site. With the exception of cities under 50,000 population, and cities in areas officially classified as economically depressed regions,[19] the federal government

will pay two-thirds of the net project cost.[20] The city pays the other one-third.

In addition to extending capital grants to cover two-thirds of the net project cost, the federal government also provides loans to assist in the planning and execution of renewal projects as well as insurance and purchase mortgages on property in renewal areas, and now pays part of the cost of other improvements—i.e., parks, neighborhood centers, and code enforcement programs—which support renewal projects but are not necessarily encompassed within the project area. These forms of federal aid will be discussed in later sections of this chapter.

THE INCENTIVE MECHANISM: THE WRITEDOWN

Not only did cities need a legal mechanism to acquire land tracts (eminent domain) and money to compensate property owners for their land (federal subsidies) but they also had to induce private developers to join the venture and build on the cleared land in accordance with the local renewal plan. The land writedown is the chief incentive to encourage private investment in renewal projects. By offering cleared land to private investors at less cost than they would have to pay even if they could buy the land and structures on the open market, the writedown accelerates and increases the demand for renewal project land.

The writedown is the difference between the gross cost of the project, including the land and the buildings acquired, and the lower price at which the land is sold to lure the developer to invest in the project. The actual amount varies from project to project, but the principle still holds: the writedown should be sufficient to attract the interest of the developer, particularly since he can often buy land for development cheaper in open areas of the metropolitan community.

The writedown illustrates another impor-

---

[19] The federal government pays three-fourths and the city pays one-fourth the net project cost in these communities.

[20] *Net project cost* is an administrative determination. It consists of *gross project cost*, or the total cost of carrying out all eligible operations in the urban renewal project—i.e., land donations, demolition, provision of site improvements such as streets and sidewalks—plus the value of *noncash public works* provided by the locality, less the proceeds from the *disposition of land* to private or public developers.

tant characteristic of the renewal approach—the principle of public-private partnership. Throughout its brief history, the urban renewal program has been molded by a three-sided partnership: federal aid to localities, local government responsibility for renewal planning, and private market execution of the local plan. The writedown then is the chief device to entice private capital into the partnership.

THE ADMINISTRATIVE MECHANISM:
NONCASH GRANTS

Since the federal government normally pays only two-thirds of the net project cost, the city must pay the remainder. To make it easier for the city, the federal government permits public improvements—i.e., schools, parks, and street and sidewalk improvements—provided by the city to count as part of its payment. While the city of course still pays for these improvements, they are parlayed so that its total cash obligation for the renewal project is reduced. The noncash grant-in-aid therefore allows cities to incur less new financial liability since many of the public improvements in renewal projects would normally have been built anyway.

Changing Nature of Urban Renewal

A person attending a national or regional conference on urban renewal today, who knew little about the subject, would be quite confused. If he listened carefully and had a keen sense of curiosity, he might ascertain what such terms as *workable program, conservation, rent supplements, net project cost,* or *project execution* meant. But he would probably be baffled when he heard speakers pour forth a steady stream of acronyms like CRP, GNRP, LPA, URA, or CIP, or numbers denoting sections of different federal laws like 220, 221d3, 112, 203, or 117.

To the renewal practitioner, however, these words, acronyms, and numbers have meaning and significance. They are the language of the trade, a trade becoming increasingly institutionalized as more universities offer degree programs or special courses in renewal, as the fed-

eral government continues to hold annual training sessions to fill the growing need for renewal specialists, as state associations of local renewal officials continue to be established, and as more public schools key social study classes to their local renewal programs.

Since urban renewal has altered in many ways since its inception, its language, understandably, has been modified and enlarged. And as the renewal program continues to change in the future, undoubtedly its language will too. Robert Weaver, Secretary of the U.S. Department of Housing and Urban Development, underscored the need for continuing refinement, improvement, and adjustment in the approach to urban problems when he said:

This is something we have been doing and will continue to do. Programs devised to meet the challenge of urbanism cannot be static. They must be flexible and receptive to new knowledge and techniques.[21]

The renewal program has shown considerable flexibility since 1950. Most of the changes are reflected in the federal Housing Acts, of which there have been 12 from 1949 to 1966; the extent of change in federal law can be seen in the unassuming 1950 Housing Act, which made 40 revisions from the 1949 Act. But some significant changes have also occurred at the local and state levels of government.

While new ideas, knowledge, and experience underlay many of the changes in urban renewal, others stem from controversy. The renewal program was conceived, nurtured, and has matured in controversy. The early conflicts centered around such issues as the form of subsidy, the extent of public housing, the local organization for administering the program, the provision of slum clearance versus shelter, and the balance between residential and nonresidential renewal.

In recent years, as more projects have been completed, controversy has shifted to the results of local renewal programs as reflected in relocation policy, project design, administrative delays, lack of interest by developers, lack of a comprehensive planning framework, and

---

[21] JOURNAL OF HOUSING, XXII (Number 6, 1965), p. 306.

too few low-cost housing units. The following discussion focuses on some of the more important shifts in renewal policy since its inception and the factors underlying these shifts. Table 17–1 summarizes some of the important changes in major federal renewal laws.

SLUM CLEARANCE TO BLIGHT PREVENTION

During the first few years after passage of the 1949 Housing Act, the objective of clearing slums and replacing them with better housing was foremost. This objective was reiterated in several ways. Title I of the 1949 Housing Act was titled *Slum Clearance and Urban Redevelopment*. The federal agency administering the program was called the Division of Slum Clearance and Urban Redevelopment. Federal policy emphasized the clearance of deteriorated areas and required projects to be predominantly residential in character after redevelopment. Even the sizable authorization for public housing furthered this aim. But after a few years, it became clear that the slum clearance approach was not working too well. There were several reasons:

1. Since the post-war vacancy rate of residential units was very low, clearance of slum areas tended to aggravate the already serious housing shortage and diminish the housing supply. As some pointed out, the clearance approach was really geared to the high vacancy situation that existed during the depression years.

2. Originally it was thought that the new projects would have a spreading, positive effect on the surrounding slum areas, thus helping to improve them. In reality, the opposite too often occurred, with the surrounding slums acting like barriers and slowly eroding the small pockets of redeveloped areas.

3. The rapid population movement to outlying suburbs accentuated central city problems. Slum clearance and redevelopment could not work fast enough to stem the outmigration.

4. Private developers were often unwilling to invest in slum clearance projects.

5. Because most of the limited funds were spent on clearing a few small slums, not much was done to protect other areas from deteriorating and developing into future slums.

In 1953, a close look was taken at the slum clearance program by the Advisory Committee on Government Housing Policies and Programs. The recommendations of the Advisory Committee, largely embodied in the Housing Act of 1954, set the framework for a larger and broader attack, not only on clearing existing slums but also on preventing new slums.

The term "urban renewal" came into popular usage while the objectives of the program were expanded to cover blight elimination, (which considered slums as only one of several important problems confronting the city), retention of middle class families who were tempted to move to the suburbs, improvement of the city's tax base threatened by a loss of wealthier citizens and ratables such as industries and business concerns, and creation of a better city with more diversity and quality.

The 1954 Housing Act therefore represented a major reorientation in thinking. Funds were made available to carry out improvements in two other kinds of areas: the *rehabilitation* area, predominantly built-up and threatened by incipient blight, and the *conservation* area, basically in good condition but requiring action so that it would not slip into a deteriorated state. Each participating community was required to show that it was making satisfactory progress in developing its own program to prevent blight, as well as to eliminate it, by preparing a workable program for community action. Loans were made available on favor-

FIGURE 17–2. *Morton Conservation Area, Philadelphia*

Table 17–1

Changes in Selected Provisions by Major Federal Renewal Laws

Provisions	1949 Act	1954 Act	1956 Act	1959 Act
Major themes	slum clearance; public housing	rehabilitation; conservation; workable program	relocation payments; GNRP*	liberalization of rehab, conservation, relocation; CRP†
Capital grants authorized	$500 million (1949 to 1953) with $100 million in reserve	$400 million—1955 Act (1955 to 1956)	$350 million—1957 Act	$650 million (1959 and 1960)
Cost distribution formula	⅔ federal—⅓ local			
Relocation payments			$100 family; $2,000 business	$200 family; $3,000 business
Public housing units authorized	135,000 units per year for 6 years	35,000 units per year	35,000 units per year for 2 years	37,000 units per year
Noncash credits	utility, street, school, park improvements; municipal labor and equipment to clear project areas	some credit for public buildings and improvements on projects serving areas outside the project area		credits for certain expenditures by colleges and universities; credits for public housing tax exemptions
Nonresidential renewal authorization		10% of capital grant funds		20% of capital grant funds
Comprehensive renewal planning		workable program; urban planning assistance; demonstration research grants	GNRP*	CRP†
Other federal aids		Sec. 220—aid for rehabilitation and new housing construction in renewal areas. Sec. 221—aid for relocatees to rehabilitate or build housing	aid for housing the elderly	

* GNRP = General Neighborhood Renewal Plan which is a coordinated urban renewal plan for an area too large for one project. The projects resulting from the GNRP are expected to be completed within 10 years.

† CRP = Community Renewal Program, which provides grants for information, studies, and plans of action on goals and resources for renewal, rehabilitation, code enforcement, capital improvements, social programs, etc., on a city-wide or metropolitan basis.

Table 17–1

(continued)

Provisions	1961 Act	1964 Act	1965 Act	1966 Act
Major themes	low and moderate income housing; increased nonresidential authority	code enforcement; new aid programs; training money	rent supplement; HUD; new aid programs; public housing extensions	demonstration cities; metropolitan developments; urban research
Capital grants authorized	$2,000 million (1961 to 1964)	$725 million (1964)	$2,800 million (1965 to 1968)	additional $250 million for urban renewal projects within approved city demonstration programs (1967)
Cost distribution formula	¾ federal—¼ local for cities under 50,000, in economically depressed areas, and those willing to pay overhead costs			
Relocation payments	loans to displaced small business concerns	relocation assistance program for each project; relocation adjustment payments for families, elderly, and business concerns		
Public housing units authorized		37,500 units per year	60,000 units per year for 4 years, of which 25% could be bought and rehabilitated from existing housing and 16% could be leased from private owners	
Noncash credits	credits for certain expenditures by hospitals			additional credit for city halls, public safety buildings, cultural or exhibition buildings in or near a project area
Nonresidential renewal authorization	30% of capital grant funds		35% of capital grant funds	
Comprehensive renewal planning				demonstration cities
Other federal aids	Sec. 221d3—aid for new low-interest, controlled rental housing; Sec. 221d4—aid to build housing for displacees, rent not controlled	code enforcement liberalizations; air rights; projects eligible; training and fellowship programs for community planning; open space grants	rent supplement; neighborhood facilities; urban beautification; urban parks; concentrated code enforcement	historic preservation; urban research

able terms—under section 220 of the 1954 Housing Act—to assist in financing the rehabilitation of existing housing[22] and new sales or rental housing in certified urban renewal areas. Families displaced by renewal activity were also assisted under section 221 which authorized FHA to insure mortgages for them on new or rehabilitated housing. And code enforcement activity was encouraged in rehabilitation and conservation areas to conserve the existing housing stock.

Subsequent housing acts have extended and liberalized rehabilitation and conservation incentives. In 1961, a low-interest, controlled rental housing program (section 221d3 of the 1961 Housing Act) was authorized to encourage nonprofit corporations and others who qualify to build housing for low and moderate-income families, principally in the city's gray areas. The FHA, which previously had used standards essentially tailored to new construction to gauge the feasibility of rehabilitation projects in older areas, developed a new and more realistic set of minimum property standards for rehabilitation in 1963. Also, the 1964 Housing Act created a rehabilitation program for poor-risk elderly families consisting of low interest rates and long-term payment periods.

The extent to which renewal has shifted from the clearance approach was made abundantly clear by the 1964 Housing Act which prohibits federal assistance for projects that demolish buildings unless the HHFA Administrator determines that rehabilitation of the project area cannot achieve the objectives. Still further evidence is the concentrated code enforcement program, enacted in 1965, in which the federal government pays two-thirds of the cost regardless of whether the area is certified for renewal treatment.

NONRESIDENTIAL RENEWAL

With the exception of a minor provision to allow limited industrial reuse in predominantly open area projects (usually subdivisions planted and equipped with streets and utilities but not built upon), the 1949 Housing Act did not provide for nonresidential renewal.

However, an awareness grew that cities had to revitalize the economic base, stop the rush of factories and business concerns to the suburbs, and create jobs. The housing emphasis was moderated and some renewal funds were authorized for nonresidential purposes.

The first breakthrough was embodied in the 1954 Housing Act, which authorized 10 per cent of capital grant funds to be used to convert slum housing into commercial or industrial projects. Gradually the nonresidential allotment was increased in successive housing acts to the 1966 rate of 35 per cent of the total federal grant renewal authorization. In addition, the money can be used to rebuild any area that qualifies as blighted or deteriorating, regardless of whether it has a substantial number of substandard dwellings.

By the end of 1964, roughly 2½ square miles had been designated for nonresidential reuse. Nearly 1,300 commercial and industrial buildings had been constructed with a redeveloped value of $526 million.[23] The shift away from housing is documented as well by project statistics. As of 1963, of the 600 renewal projects in the United States that were primarily residential prior to urban renewal, over 40 per cent were estimated to become primarily nonresidential after renewal.[24]

EASING THE CITY'S FINANCIAL BURDEN

In several ways, the federal government has recognized the city's increasing financial plight by easing and rendering more flexible the means of discharging the obligation of the municipality. One way has been to reduce the total amount of the city's cash obligation. The 1961 Housing Act made the first significant move in this direction when it altered the origi-

---

[22] In a speech to the American Institute of Real Estate Appraisers in October, 1965, William Slayton, then Commissioner of URA, said there were 475 urban renewal projects involving housing rehabilitation, an increase of 300 since 1960. Furthermore, he said that some 48,000 dwelling units had been completely rehabilitated with 140,000 more scheduled for rehabilitation.

[23] 18TH ANNUAL REPORT OF THE HOUSING AND HOME FINANCE AGENCY: 1964, p. 323.

[24] William G. Grigsby, "Housing and Slum Clearance: Elusive Goals," THE ANNALS OF THE AMERICAN ACADEMY OF POLITICAL AND SOCIAL SCIENCE (Philadelphia, March, 1964), p. 110.

nal two-thirds, one-third, federal-local cost sharing arrangement by upping the federal share to three-fourths for certain communities: those under 50,000, those in area redevelopment areas, and those willing to pay administrative overhead and planning costs out of their own pockets. In recent years, proposals have been made to reduce further the local share to one-fifth or even to one-tenth, but no concrete action has been taken. The principal objection to any additional cutting is that many localities would no longer feel they had a stake in renewal, thus reducing their commitment to the program.

Table 17–2

Percentages of Sources of Local Grants-In-Aid Based on 720 Projects Approved for Execution, November, 1963

Cash 35.4%
Noncash contributions 64.6
  Supporting facilities 36.4
  Site improvements 19.1
  Land donations 3.6
  Colleges and hospitals (section 112
      credits) 3.1
  Public housing (section 107 credits) 1.3
  Demolition and removal 1.1

Source: William Slayton, REPORT ON URBAN RENEWAL, U.S. House of Representatives Subcommittee on Housing, November 21, 1963, p. 401.

A more subtle, yet equally important step taken to ease the financial burden was to liberalize the definition of a local noncash contribution to the renewal project. The more noncash credits a city can claim, the less out-of-pocket money it needs to raise to cover its share of renewal project costs. Originally, street, utility, park, and school improvements in the project could be claimed as credits. In 1954, this policy was extended to allow a certain amount of credit for public buildings and improvements in the project even though they served areas outside. The 1959 and 1961 Acts permitted certain expenditures by universities, colleges, and hospitals in acquiring land in and near renewal projects, and local housing authority tax exemptions, to count towards the local

share as noncash payments.[25]

Also allowed to be counted as noncash grants were eligible public improvements started three years before federal loans and grants were committed to a project, in recognition that renewal took considerable time. The extent to which localities rely on noncash contributions to pay their share of renewal projects can be readily seen in Table 17–2.

Finally, innovative federal grant programs have been created in recent years to permit cities to undertake a new array of projects and programs. Federal grants—from 50 to 66 per cent—are now available for cities to acquire developed land for urban parks, to carry out local beautification programs, to build neighborhood centers that accommodate community service programs like tutoring and job retraining, to carry on concentrated code enforcement programs, and to demolish substandard structures in both renewal and non-renewal areas.[26]

AIDING THE RELOCATEE

One of the most sensitive, perplexing, and persistent problems associated with urban renewal is relocation. In the early 50s, when the program first got underway, families and businesses dislocated by urban renewal received the barest of assistance in the form of financial aid and services. During this period, relocation was often considered residual to the renewal process, a necessary but bothersome burden.

However, as more projects were built, more experience gained, and more criticisms expressed, the philosophy underlying relocation gradually changed. Relocation began to be viewed more positively as an opportunity to assist families compelled to move. By the end of 1964, over 185,000 families, 74,000 individuals, and 42,000 business concerns had been displaced by renewal projects.[27] Inevitably, most of the displaced were Negroes who moved into public or private rental quarters.

To a large extent, the more positive attitude of the federal and local governments towards

[25] By the end of 1964, some 154 projects were assisting 120 colleges and 75 hospitals in implementing their development plans. (1964 Annual Report of HHFA, *op. cit.*, p. 326).
[26] See especially Public Law 89, 89th Congress, 1965.
[27] 1964 HHFA Annual Report, *op. cit.*, p. 327.

relocation has come in response to a number of specific criticisms:[28]

1. Government reports claiming that most families relocated from renewal areas moved into standard housing were attacked as inaccurate. The chief complaint was that the figures were inflated.

2. Most displaced, low-income families paid higher rents when they moved—in part because there was not enough public housing for them.

3. Forced relocation caused personal disruptions, sometimes leading to intense personal suffering.

4. Many families were relocated into areas mapped for future redevelopment.

5. Negroes, in particular, had greater difficulty finding decent relocation housing.

6. Local governments took few measures to lessen the hardships and difficulties faced by families displaced by renewal.

7. Relocation tended to be severe in the business community among small business establishments, those largely dependent on a particular neighborhood market area, and proprietors too old to start over again.

For seven years after the first Housing Act was passed, Congress required only that adequate relocation facilities be made available to those displaced by renewal projects. In the 1956 Housing Act, however, a system of relocation payments was provided for the first time to cover the cost of moving and direct property losses resulting from the move. The maximum set for moving expenses at that time was $100 for families; today, displaced families can receive up to $200. Also, displaced families and elderly individuals can now receive a $500 relocation adjustment payment to help them find standard accommodations. Business firms can

now receive moving expenses and reimbursement up to $3,000 for property loss incurred in the move, an increase of $1,000 over the 1956 amount authorized. If no property loss is claimed, businesses can now be reimbursed for moving expenses up to a maximum of $25,000. Furthermore, the Small Business Administration will make loans covering a 20-year period to help a small business reestablish itself elsewhere if the firm proves it suffered substantial economic injury because of displacement.

Other steps have been taken to strengthen relocation. The section 221 program, first authorized in 1954, provided mortgage assistance for displaced families to buy new housing or rehabilitate existing housing. Localities had to develop a sound relocation program before their Workable Program was approved. Several demonstration projects, financed by the federal government, were undertaken in an attempt to improve local relocation practice. At the local level, many communities have vastly augmented their relocation services by providing such things as centralized relocation bureaus to handle persons displaced by highway as well as renewal projects, specialized services to displaced business firms, social welfare services to displaced families, and larger and more qualified relocation staffs.

INCENTIVES FOR THE DEVELOPER

Since the renewal program depends for success

---

[28] See Chester Hartman, "The Housing of Relocated Families," THE JOURNAL OF THE AMERICAN INSTITUTE OF PLANNERS (November, 1964), and Basil Zimmer, REBUILDING CITIES: THE EFFECTS OF DISPLACEMENT AND RELOCATION ON SMALL BUSINESS (Chicago: Quadrangle Books, 1964) for two of the more detailed and comprehensive critiques of the relocation program. Also pertinent is the 1965 study by the Housing and Home Finance Agency, THE HOUSING OF RELOCATED FAMILIES: SUMMARY OF A CENSUS BUREAU SURVEY, which attempts to answer some of the major criticisms lodged against the relocation program.

Table 17–3

Renewal Project Completions by Selected Periods 1958 to 1965

Date	Total Projects	Completed Projects	Per Cent of Total Projects Completed
12/31/58	648	10	1.5%
12/31/59	689	26	3.8
6/30/63	1,300	106	7.5
12/31/63	1,402	118	8.0
12/31/64	1,545	174	11.3
6/30/65	1,592	209	13.1

Source: Various HHFA annual reports and issues of the JOURNAL OF HOUSING.

on a working partnership between government and the private developer, it is important that private capital be attracted to local renewal projects. Even though the land writedown was provided as an incentive to the developers, early experience showed that developers were reluctant to invest in slum clearance projects because the risk was greater and the profit potential less than if they built housing outside the city on cheaper land, with mortgages readily insured by the Federal Housing Administration. Sometimes renewal sites would be cleared and readied for re-use, but no developers could be found. At least one out of every ten designated renewal projects in the 50s had to be dropped because cities could not get developers.[29]

Urban renewal policy has been continually revamped to reduce the developer's risk and increase his chance for profit. The section 221d3 program, mentioned above, gave developers more assurance that projects would be stable because rents were to be kept below market levels. The high mortgages which developers get under most of the FHA-assisted housing construction and rehabilitation programs also helped to reduce risk, since they meant that developers had to put down only a small amount of hard cash. Some cities make it easier for the developer by allowing him to build a single section of a project at a time; if the first part rents, he builds the balance, but if it doesn't, he can then more easily abandon or sell his interest. Risk is also minimized when developers combine forces to create development corporations so that a pool of capital can be tapped to acquire or rehabilitate property in renewal areas—i.e., ACTION Housing in Pittsburgh, the Community Improvement Corporation in New York City, and the Old Philadelphia Development Corporation in Philadelphia.

Several measures have been devised to increase the chances for developers to get more profit out of their renewal investment. A number of cities offer developers tax concessions as an incentive, among them Boston, St. Louis, and New York. A few states have passed tax relief laws in the form of assessment freezes. Section 220, authorized by the 1954 Housing Act, which provides special mortgage assistance to build new housing and rehabilitate existing housing, although riskier for the developer because it is more speculative, is potentially more profitable because there are no rent restrictions.

Liberalization of the non-residential authorization to 35 per cent also helped lure more private capital into renewal, since nonresidential projects have greater profit potential. Likewise, the tendency for many communities to select sites for middle and upper income housing re-use instead of for lower income housing also caters to the developer's demand for greater profit-potential in renewal projects.

REDUCTION OF RED TAPE

Urban renewal has been plagued constantly by delays and setbacks. In 1958, almost a decade after the first Housing Act was passed, less than two per cent of all renewal projects—10 of 650—had been completed.[30] As Table 17–3 shows, project completions have steadily risen since then—by mid-1965, 13 per cent or 209 of the 1,592 projects had been completed. Even though the pace has quickened in recent years, it still takes a long time to complete a project. Estimates vary from five to ten years, depending on several factors: when the project is started (projects started in 1950 took considerably longer to complete than projects started five years later), how large the project is, how easy or difficult it is to get a developer, and how successful the local renewal agency is in getting the several public and private groups involved to take action on schedule.

To speed up the renewal process, steps have been taken not only to make renewal more attractive to developers, but also to cut down

---

[29] For an illuminating discussion of the reasons why it was so difficult to attract developers in the early days of the renewal program, see Charles Abrams, THE CITY IS THE FRONTIER (New York: Harper and Row, 1965), Chapter 6.

[30] Projects for which federal financial participation is completed and final grant payment made, even though construction by redevelopers may not be completely finished. Some federal authorities feel that it is misleading to talk about the number of projects completed, since a number of renewal projects have been in execution for many years, and one of the reasons they are successful is that they were not prematurely completed

on the number of project reviews and to reduce the time it takes to complete each stage of the process. In the early days, the federal government, partly to be assured that its money was being spent properly, required detailed and time-consuming surveys and plans, with reviews scheduled at each step by the regional office and sometimes even the national office. When it became evident that the program was moving too slowly, several things were done to expedite matters.

By allowing cities in 1954 to pay administrative, overhead, and planning costs themselves (which reduced their share from one-third to one-fourth the project cost), the federal government in effect permitted those cities to skip directly to a later stage in the project, the loan and grant stage. In 1959, the time-consuming project eligibility stage was dropped entirely and certain of the detailed statutory requirements of the urban renewal plan were simplified. While the Workable Program added to a city's workload, partly because it had to be certified annually, some concessions were made to smaller communities—over 50 per cent of the cities with renewal programs are under 25,000 population—by requiring shorter and simpler forms for certification. Even FHA, which often slowed the pace of housing rehabilitation projects because it held conservative views on what structures qualified for rehabilitation assistance, has helped break the log-jam by revising its minimum property standards to reflect the older stock in central cities.

Some cities, accepting the fact that a renewal project requires considerable time, have taken measures to protect themselves from delays. One problem encountered is that land prices often jump sharply between the time the area is designated for renewal and the actual beginning of land acquisition. Recently, Milwaukee set up a revolving fund of $100,000 to be used to purchase certain properties as soon as they officially became part of an urban renewal area. When the local redevelopment agency was ready to acquire the property, the city would then convey the land.

ATTENTION TO AESTHETICS

While good project design was a basic, almost implicit aim of the urban renewal program, relatively little was done to assure that projects would in fact be handsomely designed. Occasionally, an excellent design plan was able to withstand pressure to cut site improvement costs in order to ease the city's financial obligation, to adhere to the often restrictive provisions of the city's zoning or building codes, or to increase the project density so as to attract developers and thus reduce the amount of open space. More often, mediocre design was the outcome, either because the pressures were too great or the site plan lacked aesthetic significance from the outset.[31]

However, as it became apparent that urban renewal was setting design standards for cities for many decades to come, concern for higher quality design increased. Key federal renewal officials began to speak out forcefully on behalf of better designed projects. Federal policy encouraged local agencies to employ the services of professional design specialists, to include design objectives among the criteria for determining the disposition of project land, and to hold design competitions to select redevelopers with the price of the cleared land fixed. The HHFA, now HUD, currently makes awards annually to the best-designed renewal projects.

Apart from the design of renewal projects, other measures followed to raise the quality of the physical environment. Cities with architectural and historic heritages launched projects, with federal assistance, to preserve these elements. Sixty-four million dollars for developing urban parks and $36 million for urban beautification—in the form of landscaping, statues, and stone work—was authorized by the 1965 Housing Act. The federal government supported civic design studies as demonstration projects or as part of Community Renewal Programs. While much can still be done to improve the quality of design in renewal projects, a new and healthier attitude toward design is clearly evident.

---

[31] An interesting case study of the problems involved in implementing the distinguished design plan for the Gratiot urban renewal project in Detroit is recounted by Roger Montgomery, "Improving the Design Process in Urban Renewal," JOURNAL OF THE AMERICAN INSTITUTE OF PLANNERS (February, 1965).

NEW INTEREST IN HOUSING LOW INCOME FAMILIES

The preamble to the 1949 Housing Act was quite specific in calling for "the realization as soon as feasible of the goal of a decent home and suitable living environment for every American family." In particular, this meant better housing for low income families. But the goal of decent low-cost housing has yet to be reached.

One renewal critic claims that the median monthly rental of all dwelling units built in urban renewal projects in 1960 came to $158, and in 1962, to $192.[32] Another contends that only one-fifth of the three billion federal dollars donated to communities through 1962 had been earmarked for projects intended to improve the living accommodations of lower income families.[33] Philadelphia provides a good example of how heavily weighted the renewal program is. Ninety per cent of the more than 18,000 dwelling units either built or scheduled to be built as of 1965 were for families in the middle or higher income brackets.[34] Even federal officials make no claim that the renewal program has provided enough low-cost housing to meet the need.

There are compelling reasons why renewal has fallen short in the low-cost housing area. Faced with declining ratables and rising costs for municipal services, many cities have used federal funds for downtown redevelopment, luxury apartments, and industrial renewal projects to shore up local finances. The avowed purpose of holding middle class families in the central city has been an important factor in funding projects in the vast stretches of gray areas to make these areas more liveable.

As already mentioned, there are difficulties in getting private developers to build low-cost housing when they can get a greater return on their investment by building more profitable developments. Even the public housing program, the traditional supplier of low-cost housing, has not been as prominent a factor as it

FIGURE 17–3. *Low-rent housing project (Mill Creek Public Housing Project, Philadelphia)*

was in the past. Not only were the annual authorizations for public housing units drastically cut in the 50s, but, because of changes in local policy, many public housing units built since the mid-50s have been for elderly people rather than for larger families in the low-income bracket.

While the record so far is not enviable, there are signs that a renewed concern for the national housing goal, reflected in several recent federal programs, and the normal activity of the building industry, will result in a larger yield of housing for low-income families in the future. Ironically, the drift to suburbia, the very trend city policy-makers are trying to halt, has indirectly led to an increased supply of housing for central city low-income residents. As middle-class families moved out, vacancy rates rose in the older neighborhoods they left. But since demand for these dwelling units from other middle-class families was not great, housing costs remained reasonably constant. Consequently, some low-income families benefited, and they were able to move into these areas without incurring appreciably higher rentals than they had in their former, more deteriorated quarters.

Recently, the federal government stepped up its efforts to improve the housing conditions of low income families. These efforts fall into two categories: to increase the supply of low-cost

---

[32] Herbert Gans, "The Failure of Urban Renewal," COMMENTARY (April, 1965), pp. 29–30.

[33] Grigsby, *op. cit.,* p. 110.

[34] Philadelphia Housing Association, ISSUES (December, 1965).

housing, either directly or indirectly; and to increase the rent-paying ability of low-income families so they can afford higher-priced housing. Since 1960, the number of new public housing units authorized has increased again after the decline in the 50s. But, in addition, local public housing authorities were given new powers to purchase, remodel, and rent existing housing in older areas as public housing units to low-income families. One optimistic estimate is that 100,000 units of existing housing will be converted to public housing in this way in the next few years.[35] It may even be possible for public housing tenants to purchase these units through long-term mortgages in the future. Providing an additional stimulus for more low-cost housing through public housing was an amendment to the 1964 Housing Act which reduced the site cost for public housing

projects in renewal areas.

The recent section 221d3 housing program, which, as previously indicated, allows non-profit corporations to obtain 100 per cent mortgages at low interest rates to build housing at below-market rentals, has already helped to increase the low-cost housing supply. As of February, 1965, some 610 of the 221d3 projects, with an average rental of $87, were in various stages of development.[36]

The other main avenue of government action to help low-income families achieve better housing is the much-discussed and recently enacted rent supplement program. Its aim is to supplement the rent-paying ability of families who live in substandard housing so that they can move into developments built anywhere in the urban area by non-profit, cooperative, or limited dividend sponsors. The rent supple-

[35] JOURNAL OF HOUSING, XXII (November, 1965), p. 596.

[36] JOURNAL OF HOUSING, XXII (June, 1965), p. 315.

FIGURE 17–4. *Middle-income housing projects (Top, River Park in Washington, D.C.'s southwest renewal area; left, Town-House-on-the-Park, Wooster Square renewal area, New Haven, Connecticut.)*

ment payment is given to the owner, amounting to the difference between the fair market rental for the dwelling unit and 25 per cent of the occupant's income. In effect, the federal government lets the owner achieve a reasonable profit on his investment and helps the tenant by partially subsidizing his rent. By May, 1966, when funds for the program were finally appropriated, applications had been received to build over 100,000 rent-supplement units.[37] Already being discussed, as a possible next step after the rent supplement program, is a program to provide annual housing subsidies to low-income families so that they can compete for better living accommodations in the *existing* stock of housing.

The new interest in low income families was further reaffirmed by the 1966 Demonstration Cities and Metropolitan Development Act. From now on redevelopment projects (predominantly clearance projects) must "provide a substantial number of units of standard housing of low and moderate cost and result in *serving the poor and disadvantaged people living in slum and blighted areas.*" (Emphasis supplied.)

COMPREHENSIVE RENEWAL PLANNING

To the city planner, one of the most significant changes in the urban renewal approach is the gradual shift toward a broader and more comprehensive basis for renewal planning. Many cities in the early days of the renewal programs picked projects on their individual merits, without much understanding of their impact on citywide problems. The natural tendency was to tackle the easiest and most attractive projects—perhaps in an area where the school board planned to build a new school so that the city could get a sizeable noncash credit, or on a site where a developer indicated strong interest in building a high-rent apartment project, or in a slum where the project would provide low-cost housing but not upset the delicate racial balance in the city. It mattered little that these projects were not coordinated in their objectives nor part of an overall renewal policy for the community. Individually, a project might have a certain merit; but collectively, they often made up a patchwork attack on the city's problems. "Projectitus" was a characteristic of early renewal efforts.

The 1954 Housing Act made a big stride toward more comprehensive renewal planning by introducing the Workable Program, extending the renewal program to cover blight prevention as well as slum clearance, authorizing $5 million in demonstration grants to develop and test techniques for blight prevention, and allocating funds for small communities to prepare comprehensive plans under section 701 as a backdrop for entrance someday into the renewal program.

The first major broadening of the renewal project concept came in 1956 when cities were given funds to prepare General Neighborhood Renewal Plans, spanning an eight to ten year period, to cover planning areas too large or complex to be executed as single projects. By the end of 1963, 166 cities had GNRPs in some stage of development.[38]

In 1959, the concept was extended further to allow cities to prepare Community Renewal Programs. Under a CRP, the blight and deterioration in the entire city could be analyzed; the city's full resources to cope with its problems identified and assessed; and an action program put forward to rid the city of blight conditions. While not required as a precedent for renewal funds, as is the Workable Program, the CRP is actually an enlargement and expansion of the elements of a Workable Program. Both the CRP and the Workable Program will be discussed in more detail in latter sections.

Carrying Out the Renewal Program

Local renewal programs take many forms, sizes, and shapes. Chicago, for example, has spent more than $200 million of its own and federal monies in the past fifteen years on 41 renewal projects, running the gamut from clearance to conservation projects for residential, commercial, industrial, and institutional purposes.[39] At

---

[37] CHICAGO DAILY NEWS, May 2, 1966.

[38] 1964 HHFA Annual Report, *op. cit.*

[39] University of Chicago Center for Urban Studies, SELECTED ASPECTS OF URBAN RENEWAL IN CHICAGO: AN ANNOTATED STATISTICAL SUMMARY (August, 1965), p. 44.

FIGURE 17–5. *Campus Green (Circle Campus, University of Illinois, Chicago.)*

the other extreme are the many small communities with renewal programs consisting of one project. Regardless of the scale of a city's renewal program, up to a point the ingredients for success are essentially the same.

Many groups must participate and synchronize their activities—the executive, the technicians, the people who determine the degree and character of market acceptance, the people who determine neighborhood support, the institutions that decide they will stay in the central city and rebuild their plants and facilities, the private developers who are willing to invest in renewal projects, the newspapers and civic leaders who determine the degree and character of public support for the program, and the

federal and state agencies who aid the program.[40]

But even when the base of support is broad, each city's renewal program must be tailored to local conditions to achieve success. If there is an abundant supply of existing vacant, low-cost housing in the city, it does not make sense for the city to duplicate this stock by investing scarce renewal dollars in low-cost housing projects. Likewise, if the city wants middle-class families to live in apartments in the center of the city, but finds that the demand for center-city apartment living is limited, it would be

---

[40] A quote from George Duggar, University of Pittsburgh (source unknown).

9 Steeple Street — Before   9 Steeple Street — After   149 Benefit Street — Before   149 Benefit Street — After

FIGURE 17–6. *Historic preservation (Before and after, College Hill, Providence, Rhode Island.)*

foolish to clear land for such purposes. The point is that careful study, taking into account the unique characteristics of the community, must be a guide in determining renewal strategy for any city.

Apart from subtle economic and market differences among communities, the steps involved in carrying out a renewal program are basically similar for most communities, including the small town serving as the center of an agricultural region, the medium-sized city with a few large industries, or the teeming metropolis. The following sections discuss the principal steps involved in making a locality's renewal program operative.

STATE ACTION

Since cities are creatures of the state, before they can undertake a federally aided renewal project they must be allowed to do so by their respective state legislatures. All but two states have passed legislation giving cities the right to contract for federal aid and exercise other powers necessary to carry out an urban renewal program.[41] However, because state laws vary, cities do not always have the same powers and authorities. For example, state laws are not always consistent with regard to the criteria used to designate renewal areas, the techniques

for disposal of property, or the controls imposed on reuse. The laws may also differ with respect to where local authority should be vested to exercise renewal powers. The earliest statutes, some of them preceding the 1949 Housing Act, authorized creation of privately financed redevelopment corporations empowering them to acquire land for redevelopment by purchase or eminent domain, subject to approval of a plan by a local public agency.

Now though, most state laws go considerably beyond this. Some designate the city government as the Local Public Agency (LPA) with responsibility exercised chiefly by a department of city government, usually called the renewal department. In other states, authority is vested in a semi-independent redevelopment agency. In still others, the powers of existing public housing authorities are extended to cover urban renewal. In most states, more than one of these options is allowed.[42] Only a few states permit a local planning agency to serve as the LPA. However, most mention the planning agency as a specific participant in the local renewal program; a few even give the agency rather than the LPA, primary responsibility for renewal planning.

The state's role in support of renewal is not

[41] South Carolina and Louisiana are the exceptions, although South Carolina communities and New Orleans, Louisiana have limited authority to undertake renewal projects providing for *public* reuse of the land.

[42] Sixteen states allow cities to select any one of the three most common LPA arrangements: the municipal renewal department, the redevelopment authority, and the housing authority. (A. Edwards, THE PLANNING AGENCY AS A PART OF THE LOCAL GOVERNMENTAL ORGANIZATION FOR URBAN RENEWAL, Master's Thesis in Planning, Georgia Institute of Technology, June, 1965.)

limited merely to enabling legislation. Beginning in 1947 in Pennsylvania,[43] state courts began to be called on to test the constitutional validity of renewal enabling acts that repeatedly came under attack. As of 1963, 34 state courts had rendered favorable decisions on their urban renewal laws.[44] By upholding these laws, the courts have clearly established the principle that slum clearance is a public purpose falling within the power of eminent domain; consequently, they have broadened the definition of what constitutes a public use. In the most famous U.S. Supreme Court Case, *Berman* v. *Parker* (1954), the court delivered an opinion that clearly extended the concept beyond slum clearance. ". . . It is within the power of the legislature to determine that the community should be beautiful as well as healthy, spacious as well as clean, well-balanced as well as carefully patrolled."

In recognition that cities are hard-pressed financially to carry out renewal programs, a few states give financial assistance. Connecticut, for example, pays one-half the local share of the renewal project cost. Pennsylvania subsidizes up to 35 per cent of the total cost for those middle income housing projects in which rents are kept significantly lower than the market normally would charge. New York, Massachusetts, and Illinois are other states that provide financial assistance. In recent years, more and more states are considering other actions to support local renewal programs by allowing cities to impose criminal penalties on owners of slum property; guarantee loans for rehabilitating properties in poor-risk blighted areas; give tax benefits to nonprofit corporations that build in renewal projects; and bill negligent landlords for repairs through court receivership programs.

THE LOCAL RENEWAL AGENCY

At different stages in any city's renewal program, different public and private groups must be involved. The planning agency may have to certify an area as eligible for renewal treatment before project planning can begin. The build-

ing department may be instructed to carry on a code enforcement program in an area as a prelude to renewal action. Residents of an area scheduled for renewal treatment may be organized into a neighborhood conservation group. Banks may be approached to lend money for housing rehabilitation to residents in certain priority areas. The school board may be asked to build a new school in a renewal area rather than in alternate designated locations, so that the city can pick up noncash credits and bolster the character of the renewed area. But one agency, above all, stands out as the chief overseer and workhorse for the city's renewal program—the local public agency (LPA).

Typically, the LPA has stronger powers for land clearance and redevelopment than it has for rehabilitation and conservation of existing neighborhoods. But no matter what type of treatment is scheduled, it is the LPA that makes the renewal program work.

Besides having power to acquire blighted or deteriorating properties through purchase or eminent domain, the LPA does many other things. It prepares applications for federal funds, undertakes studies and plans required for the project, arranges for land acquisition and site improvements, clears the sites, manages the property in the interim between clearance and sale, disposes of the land to developers, relocates displaced families and businesses, stimulates rehabilitation activity, and works with citizen groups both city-wide and in the project area.

Assuming that the state permits any of several possible LPA arrangements, what factors should be considered by a city in selecting a home for the renewal function? A first consideration is the form of local government. A city with a weak mayor or commission form of government may create a separate redevelopment authority since executive leadership is weak and power is dispersed. A strong mayor or council-manager city may create a municipal renewal department to gain the advantages of stronger executive leadership. No proof exists, however that a particular form of government warrants a particular form of renewal organization. In fact, as one expert says: "The way the form of government is utilized, buttressed, and

[43] BELOVSKY *v.* REDEVELOPMENT AUTHORITY OF THE CITY OF PHILADELPHIA, 357 Pa. 329, 54A, 2d 277 (1947).
[44] 1965 HHFA Annual Report, *op. cit.,* p. 405.

modified may offset inherent disadvantages in any one form."[45]

Another consideration is the reaction other government agencies have towards renewal, particularly since it is a new function. Some professionals contend that in the early days of a locality's renewal program, the program should be protected and insulated so that it will have time to grow and gain acceptance within the governmental family. A particular concern is to keep renewal free of overt political influence. Lodging the renewal function in the public housing authority or a quasi-independent redevelopment authority is felt by some to provide this insulation. On the other hand, a counter-pressure often exists for political integration, so that the renewal program will not have to operate in a vacuum. This often leads to the establishment of a city renewal department as the LPA.

Apart from these considerations, the principal advantages and disadvantages usually cited for the three most common LPA arrangements are as follows:

1. The *redevelopment authority* provides broader fiscal latitude since it often is given independent bonding powers and an indebtedness ceiling, and in some instances can even levy a tax. The authority arrangement further permits the city to appoint citizens with special contributions to make as members of the authority's board. The independence may also lessen the possibility that renewal projects will be delayed if there is a change in political control of the city government.

As to disadvantages, coordination of essential supporting renewal activities, such as code enforcement, capital improvement programming, and installation of site improvements, may be harder to achieve as a result of the authority's relative isolation from government. Then too, by creating a new agency, the average citizen, already beleaguered by a multiplicity of city departments and special districts, may be further confused and consequently lose interest in renewal. And finally, the redevelopment authority, because it is semi-independent, may not be responsive enough to the city administration which has had long and first-hand experience with city problems.

2. The *local housing authority* usually has a staff that is both available and experienced in handling certain phases of renewal project execution—i.e., appraisals, land acquisition, and site improvement—since it has to undertake these steps in building public housing. In particular, the troublesome function of relocation may be handled better, for the housing authority's staff has had experience in relocating families and many of those to be displaced by renewal may move into public housing. Furthermore, it may be easier to build low-cost housing in connection with renewal projects, because the housing authority is already the chief provider of this commodity.

The local housing authority arrangement has weaknesses similar to those of the redevelopment authority. In addition, the public housing stigma may work to the disadvantage of renewal. As one renewal official said bluntly, "When we pulled away from the Housing Authority, suddenly we were nice guys."[46]

3. The *city renewal department* has the advantage of being close to the chief executive and to other city agencies that play key roles in the renewal program. The feeling is that the renewal program, in the long run, will have less chance of being waylaid or stymied because it is a more integral part of local government.

The principal criticism of this arrangement is that the political integration achieved may bring the renewal program so far into the arena of politics, that the dispatch, judgment, and perspective necessary to do the right thing rather than the expedient thing may be lost.

In recent years, as the scope and complexity of urban renewal has increased, the most prominent trend in local renewal organization is towards gradually integrating the several agencies that have a role to play in the program. The trend is particularly evident in cities with considerable renewal experience since they, more than others, recognize the importance of cutting down on factionalism and overlapping programs. Chicago provides a good illustra-

---

[45] George Duggar, "Local Organization for Urban Renewal," PUBLIC MANAGEMENT, July, 1958.

[46] Scott Greer, URBAN RENEWAL AND AMERICAN CITIES, (New York: The Bobbs-Merrill Company, Inc., 1965), p. 72.

tion. In the early 50s, its renewal functions were split among a number of agencies—the Land Clearance Commission, the Community Conservation Board, and several Neighborhood Redevelopment Corporations. Today, however, only two agencies share major responsibility for renewal.

A few cities have eliminated the redevelopment authority or taken the renewal function out of the housing authority in an effort to bring renewal closer to the center of government. Others, retaining the traditional pattern, have sought greater integration by interposing a renewal or development coordinator between the LPA and the city's chief executive to oversee the renewal program. The development coordinator arrangement exists in Philadelphia, New York, San Francisco, New Haven, and Baltimore, all of which have semi-independent redevelopment authorities. The coordinator's job is not only to tune the mayor into the renwal program, but also to make sure that the different agencies involved work together more harmoniously and in sequence.

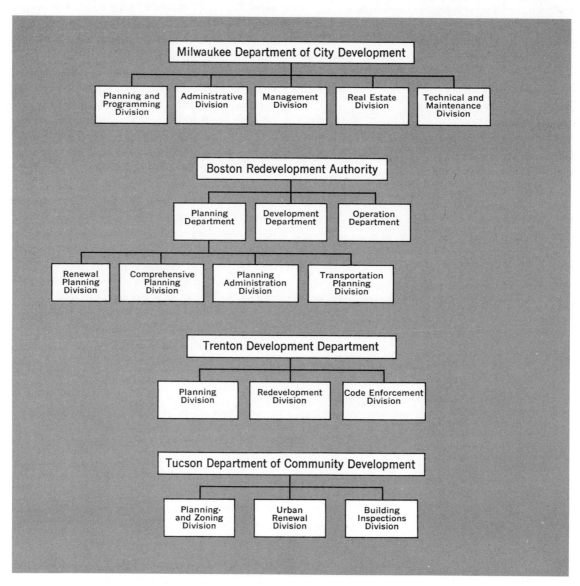

FIGURE 17–7. Organization charts for city development departments—Milwaukee, Boston, Trenton, Tuscon

Some cities have set up interagency renewal committees to achieve coordination. In Detroit, for example, a Mayor's Interdepartmental Urban Renewal Council, composed of the heads of city departments involved in renewal (including the head of the planning agency) was created to oversee the work of the city's LPA, the Housing Commission.

The most radical solution to achieving coordination at the local level is the combined department of development which brings renewal into the same agency as planning, code enforcement, and sometimes even public housing. At least 20 cities—among them Milwaukee, Boston, Tucson, and Trenton—have reorganized along this line in the past five years. Figure 17–7 shows the internal organization of the combined departments.

Proponents of the combined development department claim it achieves a closer partnership between planning and renewal, a better mesh between code enforcement and renewal priorities, a wider array of staff talents to draw upon, and a closer relationship between the agency's director and the city's chief executive (since there are fewer department heads competing for the mayor's or manager's attention). However, the size of the agency may lessen the esprit de corps among the staff and at least initially may cause some tension, since former heads of agencies would probably have to move down a notch in the hierarchy of the new agency.

Since urban renewal cuts across so many city functions—land use planning, highway planning, code enforcement, industrial development, city budgeting, public housing, capital improvement programming, community organization, and real estate management—the need for improved coordination among agencies is paramount. It is therefore likely that any city's LPA may change in character and function as its renewal program expands in scale and complexity.

The Workable Program

According to the 1954 Housing Act, no federal loan or grant can be given to a city unless it first presents an acceptable Workable Program to the HHFA Administrator (now the Secretary of the Department of Housing and Urban Development). Preparation of the Workable Program, which according to law is to be the city's "official plan of action" for dealing with its slums and blight, is therefore a first assignment for the city's LPA. Since the Workable Program must be certified each year that the city participates in renewal, it becomes a recurrent assignment for the LPA.

Seven elements constitute the Workable Program:

1. *Adequate codes and ordinances for building construction and minimum housing standards, effectively enforced.* As a general rule, a city must either adopt or make provision for early adoption of building, fire, plumbing, electrical, and housing codes before its Workable Program will be certified.

2. *A comprehensive community plan* to provide a framework for the city's future physical environment.

3. *Neighborhood analysis* to determine the location and extent of blight in the city. In addition, the analysis should include recommendations for remedial action.

4. *An administrative organization* which has the necessary authority, responsibility, and staff to attack blight on a city-wide scale.

5. *A financial plan* which shows that the city has the capacity to fund activities in support of the Workable Program.

6. *A relocation assistance program* for all families displaced as a result of renewal or other governmental activity.

7. *A citizen participation program* to obtain broad support for the renewal program, including a citizens' advisory committee and a subcommittee on minority group problems.

It is difficult to assess the importance of the Workable Program. At the very least, it has helped cities by outlining a range of activities that should be undertaken to give local renewal programs more body and endurance. It also induces—in some cases, forces—cities to adopt and amend better codes[47] and to prepare com-

---

[47] According to testimony given by William Slayton, former URA commissioner, to the House of Representatives Subcommittee on Housing on November 21, 1963, only 56 cities in the U.S. had housing codes prior to the inception of the Workable Program in 1954. As of 1963, over 700 cities had housing codes.

prehensive plans and neighborhood blight studies, all vital underpinnings of an effective renewal program. For the federal government, the Workable Program provides more assurance that its renewal dollars will be spent wisely. And, quite likely, the principle embodied in the Workable Program of committing a city to perform in a certain manner before the carrot of federal aid is extended has influenced drafters of subsequent federal-aid programs.

But the Workable Program may also cause some problems. For example, the requirement for administrative organization can result in tensions if existing agencies feel threatened by pending plans for reorganization. Or, as a result of the code enforcement requirement, enforcement activity may be initiated in areas that should not be upgraded, either because the areas require clearance or because residents would be forced to move to even poorer housing quarters.

In reality, few cities meet all the requirements of the Workable Program at the time of the first submission. This does not mean that the Program will be turned down. Usually, annual submissions are certified as long as progress is made in accomplishing the Workable Program objectives set out by the city. This view, however, has been criticized by some who feel that each requirement should be strictly enforced, particularly the codes and relocation requirements, if the goal of a better city is to be achieved. While the soft-line view still prevails, it was stiffened somewhat in 1962 when a new policy was adopted reserving capital grant funds for any additional renewal projects until the federal government carefully evaluated the city's performance on its existing projects.

ORGANIZATION OF A RENEWAL PROJECT

The planning and execution of an urban renewal project, whether it be for a one-block or fifty-block area, is a lengthy, complex undertaking, necessitating close interplay between the local renewal agency and a myriad of official and non-official interests: the local governing body, planning agency, code enforcement agency, legal department, public housing authority, area residents, and developers who play important roles in the evolution of a re-

newal project. In the final analysis, however, a good deal of the interplay is between the LPA and the Urban Renewal Administration, which sets procedure and policy for project planning and execution. Since many and often complicated steps are required from beginning to end of a renewal project, it behooves the LPA to be thoroughly familiar with the rules of the game as set up by the federal government in its Urban Renewal Manual.

Once the city has a certified Workable Program, it can, if it chooses, apply directly for federal aid to undertake a specific renewal project. But more and more cities are waiting before jumping into their first project or into new ones, until they complete either a Community Renewal Program or a General Neighborhood Renewal Plan. Both the CRP and GNRP help to create a sounder basis for local renewal decisions and therefore provide an important backdrop for renewal project planning. When the city decides it is ready to undertake a project, there are three principal stages involved: project initiation; project planning; and project execution.

Project Initiation. Over half of the state renewal laws require that before a renewal project can be planned, the city's governing body must determine by resolution that the area in which it is to be located is slum or blighted. In several of these states—California, Michigan, North Carolina, Ohio, Pennsylvania, and Wisconsin—the planning agency is specifically required to participate in the selection of prospective project areas, usually by certifying that the area is blighted and in need of renewal treatment.

The selection of a specific renewal area is of course an extremely important step in the renewal process, for it is at this point that the play of forces, issues, and values that shape the city's renewal strategy is tentatively resolved. All the more reason that the city should pause before selecting its projects, to gain the benefit of comprehensive renewal planning studies— i.e., the CRP and the GNRP—so that there will be a clearer indication of objectives and of means.

The first step in a federally-aided renewal project is usually preparation of an application for advance funds to finance the cost of surveys and plans, particularly the urban renewal plan specified in federal law. The local public agency prepares the *survey and planning application*, often with the assistance of the planning agency which provides important data. The application is a technical document consisting of statistics, financial estimates, legal papers, maps, and narrative reports. It is intended to:

1. Demonstrate that a general physical survey of the project area has been made which indicates that the area has the required minimum deterioration to qualify for federal assistance. Such conditions as structural dilapidation, over-occupancy, land overcrowding, substandard plumbing, health and safety hazards, and nuisance elements are summarized in the area survey report.

2. Demonstrate that the area is of manageable size for a project and has logical planning boundaries.

3. Determine the amount of funds that should be tentatively reserved for carrying out the project, with a breakdown of budget for estimated costs for administration, planning, real estate services to conduct marketability studies and property appraisals, land acquisition, site improvement, land disposition, and relocation.

4. Demonstrate that the community is legally empowered to undertake urban renewal.

Once the application is prepared, the local governing body must approve its submission to the federal government and also *formally* determine that the area is appropriate for an urban renewal project. When the federal government approves the survey and planning application, which may take from three to nine months, grant funds are reserved to undertake the project. In practice, the city's LPA often uses the time between submission and approval of the survey and planning application to lay the groundwork for the next phase—detailed project planning.

Project Planning. After approval of the survey and planning application and receipt of the planning advance, detailed project planning begins. In renewal parlance, the LPA prepares a *loan and grant application*, the step-

ping stone that must be crossed before any concrete action is undertaken in the project area—whether it be clearance for new uses, housing rehabilitation, spot improvement action, code enforcement, or a combination of these.

There are two parts to the loan and grant application. Part I contains the following:

1. A *project area report* with a map of structures, land use characteristics, and property lines for the project and the immediately surrounding areas. Intensive surveys are done to prepare the map, documenting in detail the area's uses and structural conditions as well as the nature of blighting influences. The survey data are essential for they help determine the kind and mix of renewal treatment. If rehabilitation is involved, the surveys must establish the structural and economic feasibility of rehabilitation.

2. An *urban renewal plan* showing the proposed land uses and a statement of project proposals, i.e., modifications to the street and utility pattern, new public improvements like schools and parks, and the proposed zoning. In many cities, the planning agency plays a key role at this critical stage, either helping to prepare or to review the plan.[48]

3. A *land acquisition and disposal report* showing which properties are tentatively to be acquired for clearance or for rehabilitation, how much these properties will cost to acquire, based on appraisals (and how much to demolish if necessary), and some indication of which properties, because of high cost or anticipated difficulty of acquisition, will require special treatment, i.e., advance acquisition or early condemnation to avoid later delays. The land disposition report, among other things, gives preliminary estimates of the marketability of parcels to be disposed of and the receipts for the sale of these parcels to developers.

4. A *relocation report* showing the number and characteristics of families and businesses to be displaced as well as the housing available to meet the relocation load. When housing is in

---

[48] The planning agency is required to review and comment upon the urban renewal plan in 32 states. (A. Edwards, *op. cit.*, p. 21.)

short supply, particularly as it often is for minority groups, then actions must be proposed to overcome these deficiencies. The report also must include a relocation plan with an estimate of relocation costs.

5. A *project improvements report* showing estimates of the cost of each improvement, local design standards for improvements, and evidence that improvements are eligible as noncash credits if claimed.

6. A *project financing report* showing the total project cost, the net project cost (all costs less the estimated resale value of the cleared land), and the proportion of the city's share that will be paid for in cash and in noncash credits.

After the LPA finishes these surveys and plans and is advised by the federal government that Part I is acceptable, a public hearing is held on the project. The local government then approves the urban renewal plan stipulating that it conform to the city's general plan and offers maximum opportunity for renewal by private enterprise. Part II of the loan and grant application consists of evidence of the public hearing and the local approvals. With approval of Part II by the federal government, the city finally can receive loan and grant funds to execute the project.

Project Execution. The planning agency, more than any other unit, plays the key role in assisting the LPA during the project planning stage. But the many talents employed in the renewal process are most evident during the lengthy project execution state. At various intervals during project execution, the LPA may have to call upon appraisers, realtors, relocation specialists, housing rehabilitation experts, community organizers, building inspectors, engineers, contractors, and architects, as well as planners, for assistance. Unless scheduling is thought out carefully and each of the inputs is made on time and in the right sequence, the already lengthy process will be drawn out even further, with project costs rising proportionately. The need for generalists at the top level in the LPA, who understand all facets of the renewal operation, is therefore particularly important.

With temporary loans now available to serve as working capital, the LPA can move into the first and by far most costly part of project execution, *land acquisition.* According to URA, nearly two-thirds of the gross project cost of urban renewal projects goes for land acquisition (see Figure 17–8). To ensure that owners of properties designated for acquisition are fairly compensated and that the public is

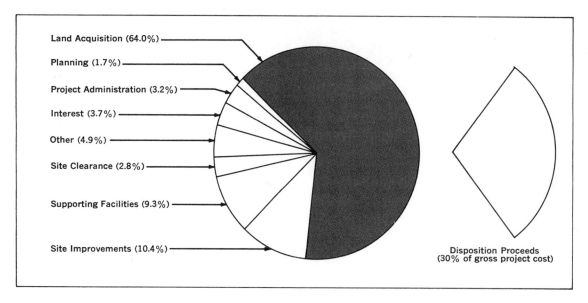

FIGURE 17–8. *Components of gross project cost (Summary of 584 projects under two-thirds capital grant formula as of June 30, 1963.)*

protected against paying excessive prices, two independent appraisals must be obtained from qualified appraisers on each property. Using the appraisals as a base, the LPA then sets a maximum price—which must be reviewed and approved by the regional URA office—for each property to be acquired. To assure flexibility in negotiating, the price offered usually falls within a range set by the appraisals of the LPA and federal review. If the owner will not accept a price within this range, condemnation proceedings are initiated through court action to acquire the property.

There is often a considerable time lapse between property acquisition, the demolition process, and disposition. During this period, the LPA must continue to *collect the rents and manage the property*, two activities sometimes farmed out to a real estate firm.

The most critical and sensitive phase of project execution is *relocation*. Early in the execution stage a family relocation service is usually established, often in or near the project site. Families to be relocated are interviewed and services available to them are explained, with referrals made to social welfare agencies when required. Information on the current availability of private rental and sales units is developed by the project staff with the help of real estate agents who have knowledge of the local market. Families interested in buying a home are given advice and guidance on how to proceed, while families interested in and eligible for public housing are advised on how to prepare admission applications as well as on how long it will take to get admitted. Although not required to do so under federal law, most LPAs also provide a relocation advisory service to displaced businesses. The system of relocation payments provided by the federal government to cover moving costs and direct property losses resulting from the move are also administered by the LPA. (See the section on Aiding Relocatees for a description of the amounts available for these purposes.)

Where *housing rehabilitation* is involved, which may go on before and after the clearance of areas, the LPA usually establishes an advisory service to help residents with the architectural, financial, and construction standards set out in the renewal plan.

After all families and businesses are relocated from the project site, the LPA proceeds to *demolish and clear the land* to be redeveloped. The removal of structures as well as the work involved in preparing the site and installing necessary street and other site improvements is normally done under contract with a private contractor. The LPA usually coordinates the installation of site improvements with the provision of supporting city facilities such as parks and schools.

When the site is cleared, the land available for new development is publicly advertised for sale. This is the stage of *land disposal*. Before advertising publicly, however, the LPA must submit to the federal government several reports relating to the methods of disposal of project land; the fair value of the lands to be sold for the proposed uses; the forms of the disposal documents. Any writedown in land cost occurs at this stage. To establish a fair value for the land to be sold to a developer, two independent appraisals must be made of the land in relationship to existing land prices in the community. In 1963, URA reported that for the program as a whole, disposition prices for cleared land averaged about $1 per square foot as compared to land acquisition and improvement costs of approximately $2.05. It is interesting also to note that the sale of land to developers amounted to roughly 30 per cent of the gross project cost. (See Figure 17–8.) Disposition methods vary, given the complexity of the marketing operation. The three most common methods are:

1. Price competition, including public auctions or the use of competitive sealed bids.

2. Nonprice competition, where a fixed price is established and announced, and developers compete on the basis of other factors, such as design criteria or moderate rentals.

3. Negotiated agreements where price and moderate rentals, design, or other criteria are negotiated, subject to public disclosure before ultimate disposal.

Unless state or local law requires a public hearing to be held on the proposed disposal by the local governing body or the LPA, the LPA can select the redeveloper under the approved disposal method, making a public disclosure.

To meet the project expenditures, the LPA periodically requisitions funds from the federal government. The local share of the cost, after noncash credits are tallied up, usually comes from borrowing in the form of general obligation bonds. California and Minnesota are two states that authorize the use of tax-appreciation bonds, payable solely out of the anticipated increase in taxes to be derived from the redeveloped area. As noted, a few states also provide direct financial aid. The LPA is subject to periodic audits and site inspections to make sure that the project is in conformance with the approved project plans. Upon completion of the project, the LPA submits a requisition for final capital grant payment.

Some New Directions

While opposition to urban renewal has mounted in recent years, there is little chance that the program will be scrapped or even cut back. Its continued expansion is assured, but the directions of growth are not entirely clear. Who could have predicted in 1949, when the renewal program was born, that in 1966 it would be faced with stiff competition for limited public dollars, as demands rose for other domestic programs like medicare, antipoverty, highways, mass transit, recreation and open space, and education? Who could have predicted in 1949 that the Housing and Home Finance Agency would be elevated in 1965 to a cabinet-level Department of Housing and Urban Development, with a concern for metropolitan development that might someday overshadow the traditional concern for central city development as reflected in the renewal program? Or who could have predicted then that in 1965, the National Association of Housing and Urban Redevelopment Officials—the principal national spokesman for urban renewal—would call for a sweeping redefinition of urban renewal to include "all community improvement activities" so that it can become "the overall urban development process"?[49] During the

[49] 1965–67 Policy Resolution of the National Association of Housing and Redevelopment Officials, adopted October 26, 1965.

17 years from 1949 to 1966 urban renewal has changed significantly in philosophy and application in response to pressures, new ideas, and criticisms. What paths might it follow in the future?

COMMUNITY RENEWAL PROGRAM

The CRP provides some answers to the future complexion of urban renewal. The 1959 Housing Act authorized federal aid to cities to cover two-thirds of the cost of preparing a Community Renewal Program. After a slow start— only 50 cities had CRP grants by 1962— interest has steadily picked up with over 150 cities participating by 1966, nearly one-fifth of them with urban renewal projects. While the CRP, like the renewal program itself, has not been the panacea its supporters hoped for, there is evidence that it is advancing both the practice and technique of urban renewal and of city planning.[50] At the very least, the CRP has helped bring into clearer focus several key issues confronting the central cities:

1. How can the city keep its industries and businesses from moving to the suburbs, yet still provide enough housing for its inhabitants?

2. How can the city keep and attract middle-income families, yet still meet lower-income family needs for housing and better living accommodations?

3. How can the city wipe out physical blight, yet still deal with the persistent social and economic problems that underlie physical blight?

4. How can the city mobilize the resources it needs to do an effective renewal job, without alienating those public and private groups, accustomed to acting independently, who must support the program if it is to work?

5. How can the city obtain greater citizen involvement and support for renewal, yet expe-

[50] For more detailed accounts of CRP experience and accomplishments, see: David A. Grossman, "The Community Renewal Program: Policy Development, Progress and Problems," THE JOURNAL OF THE AMERICAN INSTITUTE OF PLANNERS (November, 1963), pp. 258–69; American Society of Planning Officials, THE COMMUNITY RENEWAL PROGRAM: THE FIRST YEARS (1963); National Association of Housing and Redevelopment Officials, COMMUNITY RENEWAL PROGRAM EXPERIENCE IN TEN CITIES (1964); Council of Planning Librarians, COMMUNITY RENEWAL PROGRAMS: A BIBLIOGRAPHY, Exchange Bibliography 32 (May, 1965).

dite the renewal program to get concrete results in a shorter period of time?

6. How can the city create a new physical environment, yet not disrupt social life too drastically?

7. How can the city capitalize on opportunities for renewal treatment, yet still deal with the hard-core, tough areas that have little market potential?

In trying to grapple with these issues, most CRPs have devised a more comprehensive framework for programming and scheduling future renewal activities, a framework generally lacking in the 50s, when the emphasis was on individual projects, not on their relation to each other or to overall city objectives.

Piecemeal renewal planning was the principal defect CRPs were designed to correct. But there were other reasons CRP legislation was passed in 1959. Relocation problems, red tape causing delays, and a deemphasis on housing gave pause to some who felt that cities needed to rethink their renewal objectives in a larger context. Then too, there was a fear at the time that federal housing programs would be cut back and future renewal projects rationed unless there were a national estimate of urban renewal needs. A few pioneering studies done in the middle 50s also contributed by showing the value of having a more comprehensive backdrop for making renewal decisions.[51]

Federal Policy. The tone of CRP is set by federal policy. On the one hand, the city is encouraged to experiment in devising a long-term renewal program. On the other hand, it is cautioned to be realistic, with the stress on feasibility, useable results, and tangible accomplishments. Federal policy specifies that a CRP accomplish at least five technical objectives:

1. Determine the *need for renewal treatment* by identifying and measuring residential and non-residential blight throughout the city.

2. Determine the *economic basis for renewal* by conducting economic and marketability studies, as well as by forecasting changes in the residential and non-residential sectors of the economy. These studies would then be trans-

lated into anticipated demands for different types of land and structures.

3. Determine *goals for community renewal,* such as strengthening the tax base, providing adequate housing, and improving the employment structure.

4. Determine the *resources needed and available for urban renewal,* such as administrative, legal, financial, social relocation, and minority group housing resources and requirements.

5. Develop a *feasible program for renewal action* by considering the type of renewal treatment needed, priorities for renewal action, and a staged program (ranging from 3 to 20 years) to meet the most pressing current needs and to take advantage of the clearest present opportunities.

Local Variations. CRPs differ by community in terms of approach and conception. Many follow the book and adhere closely to federal policy. Others, however, have taken the federal invitation to experiment seriously, evolving novel and imaginative approaches. Among these are San Francisco, Pittsburgh, and Worcester, Masschusetts, which have developed simulation models in order to understand the city better as a system of interacting parts, where a change in one part affects all other parts. The models have also been helpful in estimating the impacts that alternative renewal programs will have on an area before a specific course of action is chosen. Philadelphia has applied U.S. Defense Department programming techniques in a highly imaginative way to test how well existing city programs achieve renewal objectives. Detroit and Washington, D.C. have pioneered in applying social analyses in their CRPs. Minneapolis has experimented in working with citizens and in tying urban design into its CRP.

The approach followed by a community in its CRP is usually based on the interaction of three factors:

1. The year that the city received its CRP grant. Since federal CRP policy was amplified in recent years to encourage more studies and programs, the earlier CRPs tend to be less comprehensive and ambitious than the later ones.

2. The local climate for renewal, as reflected in the quality of the city's executive leadership

---

[51] THE CENTRAL URBAN RENEWAL STUDY, Philadelphia Redevelopment Authority, 1954 and RE-NEW NEWARK, Central Planning Board of Newark, N.J., 1961.

and in its previous renewal history. There is a tendency for cities with more experience in urban renewal to be more cautious and less precise about what they propose in their CRPs.

3. The local agency that is accorded principal responsibility for formulating the CRP. Up to 1966 responsibility has been split evenly between the planning agency and the renewal agency, with about one of every five cities administering the CRP as a joint operation. Planning agencies tend to be more concerned with the CRP studies and analyses, while renewal agencies tend to be more concerned with the end-product, selecting projects that are feasible and marketable.

Some Contributions. While it is still too early to assess the full impact of CRPs on local renewal programs, enough have been completed to identify some of their contributions. First, the CRP has increased our *understanding of the city,* how it is structured, and how it functions and changes. We know more about the causes of residential blight and the likelihood of it spreading to different parts of the city. A greater understanding of nonresidential blight has also resulted from CRP studies.[52] The CRP has also afforded a better knowledge of the ability of government to deal with city problems because of its stress on understanding the city's resources.

Some CRPs have provided new ways of conceptualizing the city as a system of interacting parts (through systems analysis) or as a composite of different areas performing different functions, e.g., receiving ports for migrants from the rural south, terminal ports for the elderly, or way-stations for the upwardly mobile.[53] Concepts like area stability, cohesiveness, isolation from local government, investment potential, and resident skill level are used to help determine whether renewal action of a certain kind will or will not work in different areas. A greater emphasis on social analysis has led to more insights into how relocation affects the lives of displaced families, how residents of a neighborhood perceive their area, and how certain neighborhoods function in social terms.[54]

New and effective techniques of analysis have been introduced by the CRPs. The simulation models, mentioned earlier, are one kind. Because the CRP is a complex operation, some cities have experimented with more sophisticated scheduling techniques like the Critical Path Method (CPM) or the Program Evaluation and Review Technique (PERT) to achieve greater efficiency in phasing and scheduling the many studies that have to be done.[55] The application of electronic data processing techniques is common, with real property inventories being supplemented in a few CRP communities by social data banks.[56] There are even instances where computers have been used to arrange and print data on maps.[57]

In some cities, the CRP has also served a useful role as a *bridge-builder* by linking the city's planning program more closely to its renewal program. Federal policy encourages this by requiring the CRP, the eventual guide for renewal action, to be in general conformity with the city's comprehensive plan. Because of the CRP, planning and renewal—often at odds with each other in the past—have a better chance for a happier marriage. While the CRP's bridging role is important, it has also served to augment and enlarge the scope of planning. The emphasis on social planning, implicit in many CRPs, has pushed the local planning agency beyond just physical planning. And because the CRP puts such a heavy

[52] See, for example: Brian J. L. Berry, COMMERCIAL STRUCTURE AND COMMERCIAL BLIGHT: RETAIL PATTERNS AND PROCESSES IN THE CITY OF CHICAGO: A STUDY MADE UNDER CONTRACT WITH THE CHICAGO COMMUNITY RENEWAL PROGRAM, Research Paper No. 85 (Chicago: Department of Geography, U. of Chicago, 1963). Illinois Institute of Technology, Research Institute, CITY OF CHICAGO INDUSTRIAL RENEWAL STUDY: SUMMARY REPORT TO THE CHICAGO COMMUNITY RENEWAL PROGRAM (Chicago, 1963).

[53] See, for example, the Hartford, Connecticut CRP SOCIAL STUDY REPORT, 1964.

[54] Several of the Philadelphia CRP studies are illustrative of the trend towards social analysis: Technical Report No. 5, A STUDY OF THE SOCIAL ASPECTS OF THE CRP; Technical Report No. 9, COMPARATIVE STUDIES OF IDENTIFIABLE AREAS IN PHILADELPHIA; Technical Report No. 11, SOCIAL FACTOR ANALYSIS, 1964.

[55] Philadelphia, Detroit, Pittsburgh, Washington, D.C.

[56] Detroit Community Renewal Program, THE DETROIT SOCIAL DATA BANK: A REPORT ON THE DESIGN, IMPLEMENTATION, AND OPERATION. 12 pp.

[57] U.S. Urban Renewal Administration, USING COMPUTER GRAPHICS IN COMMUNITY RENEWAL, 1965.

emphasis on programming renewal action over time and in sequence, it has given support to those who feel that in order for city planning to be more effective it should move beyond the static "what" and "where" dimensions of the traditional comprehensive plan to consider "how," "when," and "in what order" planning action should be taken. The CRP has also brought more realism into planning by stressing marketability and resource capacity studies.

Then, too, the CRP has played a useful role as an *integrationist,* bringing together different groups, both public and private, to work in concert towards renewal goals. Some CRP agencies have consciously tried to involve staff from other city departments and semi-public agencies, like health and welfare councils, to get second-line support. City-wide citizen groups and technical advisory committees have been established to review the work of the CRP staff. Interagency policy committees, consisting of key local officials in those areas most closely related to urban renewal, have also been formed to guide in developing a CRP. Several cities, bypassing the planning agency and renewal agency, have placed the CRP directly under the aegis of the mayor or city manager in an attempt to integrate the program more solidly into the local government fabric. In the interest of achieving cooperation later on, some CRPs have gone out of their way initially to be of service to other departments by providing data banks, data abstracts, and advice on programming. One other reflection of the CRP's integrationist cast is the fact that interdisciplinary teams of specialists have been assembled to work on the CRP, with physical planners and renewal specialists working side-by-side with economists, community organizers, public administrators, and even operations research specialists and anthropologists. Many of the CRP reports have called for administrative reorganization to achieve a better meshing of parts, recommending development coordinators, city development departments or permanent interagency renewal policy committees.

Most of the published CRP reports do not speak out forcefully on the city's touchy issues, such as racial segregation, government agencies that are more interested in empire-building than in the city's renewal, or institutional practices that perpetuate blight, such as the reluctance of certain banks to lend money to property owners in low-income areas. In fact CRPs tend to be more cautious than bold in what they recommend. Nevertheless, the CRP has played a quiet, effective, under-the-iceberg role. Getting governmental units to talk and work together and discuss major issues and grapple with them (often for the first time), providing a reservoir of information on how the city is constrained from taking effective action, illuminating gnawing social problems, highlighting conflicts in public agency programs, and working slowly to break down public and private practices that perpetuate slum conditions, are some of the problems dealt with that are never publicized in the final report. In this sense, CRPs have played a useful role by unearthing important obstacles and working quietly towards overcoming them.

And finally, the CRP is performing a useful function by suggesting *new ways to achieve urban renewal action.* Proposals have been made to move away from the individual project approach, by focusing on programs that cut across Title I project boundaries or on specific land uses regardless of where these are located in the city, as well as by treating large areas or even the entire city as a project area, so as to get more noncash credit for public improvements. The Philadelphia CRP recommended a permanent CRP programming unit in the mayor's office to prepare annual development programs for capital as well as operating and service programs. This strikes at the heart of a long-standing criticism of renewal, that it does not take advantage of all the city's programs to support the renewal effort. Proposals have also been made to improve traditional parts of the renewal process. One city recommends that a package of services—special education, job training, and health services—be offered to displaced families when they are relocated, not just housing services. Several cities, in an attempt to reduce the disruptive effects of relocation, propose a checkerboard scheme where families are not moved from one part of a

518 PRINCIPLES AND PRACTICE OF URBAN PLANNING

project area until new quarters are built for them in another part. Others have proposed setting up risk-capital pools to help rehabilitate properties in bad-risk areas or placing greater reliance on receiverships and mandatory injunctions to supplement fines on code violators. Another proposal is to decentralize certain service and informational programs of local government into neighborhood centers, to make government more responsive to renewal area residents.

In summary, the CRP mirrors some of the directions in which the urban renewal program is moving—towards greater integration with planning, more understanding of basic city processes and constraints to action, use of more powerful analytical tools, social planning, greater coordination of the parts of government vital to effective renewal action, developing new techniques for making renewal decisions, and solving some of the problems that have perenially beset past renewal efforts.

Anti-Poverty Program

Urban renewal was an important forerunner of the Economic Opportunity Act of 1964, which launched the war on poverty. Renewal efforts not only uncovered and made social problems more visible, but they also confirmed the belief that housing and other physical improvements were insufficient measures to break the poverty cycle.

There are several signs that renewal and anti-poverty programs are converging in respect to both their purpose and their actual operation. The 1965 housing bill that was submitted to Congress contained a requirement that cities over 50,000 population must prepare CRPs, in part for coordinating renewal and anti-poverty programs. Although this requirement was subsequently eliminated from the law enacted, other provisions of the Act strengthened the link. For example, LPAs were authorized not only to build neighborhood facilities to accommodate such programs as legal aid, welfare services, and consumer information, but they also were to sell or lease these facilities to the local Community Action Program agency (the anti-poverty program's chief administrative arm at the local level). In fact,

priority is to be given to neighborhood facility applications designed to further the aims of the anti-poverty program. Some cities, like Detroit, achieved coordination at the time the anti-poverty program was started by placing the CRP and the Community Action Program agency together in the same administrative unit.

The most common link between the two programs so far is the provision of mutual services. While there are several examples of LPAs providing space to shelter CRP programs like Operation Headstart or Operation Breakthrough, more frequent are instances where anti-poverty personnel are used in various ways to assist the local renewal program. For example, nonprofessionals from the anti-poverty program have been used to:

1. Assist the LPA staff in motivating residents to undertake housing rehabilitation and in doing light rehabilitation work on housing units.

2. Assist in building code inspection programs and in improving neighborhood recreation and other facilities.

3. Assist in the relocation process by interviewing families to be displaced to see if they need personal counseling—helping them find suitable rehousing, aiding them in the move, and interviewing them in their new quarters to assess their adjustment.

4. Assist the LPA Community Organization worker by helping conduct block group meetings and aiding families with special problems.

Particularly notable are the projects funded by the Office of Economic Opportunity that relate directly to renewal objectives. In Washington, D.C., OEO funds are being used to underwrite a housing improvement school lodged in a neighborhood center. Rehabilitation of slum housing is part of one of New York City's first anti-poverty projects. A block of 37 tenements, housing 1,600 persons in 450 dwelling units, is being rehabilitated over a three-year period (1966–69) without any displacement except temporary moves to other quarters on the same block.

Demonstration Cities Program

So far, much of the renewal effort has been

directed towards keeping middle-class families, industries, hospitals, universities, and downtown business concerns in the city. The emphasis is on renewing the city to preserve its important institutions, ratables, and families. There has been a minor emphasis on promoting and developing the city's less important resources, low income families, small businesses, the elderly, to a higher level. The recently enacted Demonstration Cities [Model Cities] Program, part of the 1966 Demonstration Cities Metropolitan Development Act, indicates the renewal program may take a sharp turn in direction.

The intention of the Demonstration Cities Program is to concentrate all available resources in planning tools, housing construction, job training, health facilities, recreation, welfare, and education on slum neighborhoods. This program, when proposed by President Johnson in his 1966 housing message to Congress, was geared to a scale of $2.3 billion over six years in some 60 to 70 cities. It is significant because it will bring together the full range of improvement programs in a direct, massive attack on urban slums. After considerable debate, nearly $1 billion was appropriated for a three-year period in the 1966 Demonstration Cities Act. To qualify for what amounts to 80 per cent federal grants to undertake a Demonstration project, a city would have to meet a number of conditions, among them to show that the project will: make marked progress in reducing social and educational disadvantages, ill health, unemployment, and enforced idleness; be of sufficient magnitude to arrest blight and decay in entire sections or neighborhoods; provide a substantial increase in the supply of low and moderate cost housing; offer maximum opportunity for employing area residents in all phases of the program; develop local and private initiative and widespread citizen participation in planning and executing the project; and make major improvements in design quality.

The Demonstration Cities Program portends the day when the traditionally physical improvement-oriented urban renewal program will be merged with other equally important social and economic programs. The result may well be that urban renewal will move into a new and exciting phase of its history, a phase that will extend its recognized prominence as the most important planning tool in the hands of the medium-aged and older American cities.

Part Six

_____

The Urban Planning Agency

18

The Local Planning Agency: Organization and Structure[1]

For more than two decades a lively discussion has been waged over alternative ways to organize and locate the planning function in municipal government in the United States. Ever since publication of Robert A. Walker's book, *The Planning Function in Urban Government,* in 1941, criticizing the independent citizens' planning commission, communities have experimented with new forms of planning agencies and with reorganizing existing agencies. Experimentation still goes on and it is doubtful whether modification of the organization for planning will ever cease.

The pattern or organization of the planning agency is related to the state law authorizing community planning. In many states, communities with home rule or charter provisions are given broad authority to select an organization form most suitable to local conditions. A number of communities further supplement express statutory provisions in the state law through such informal arrangements as they feel necessary to achieve effective planning mechanisms.

Any discussion of alternative forms of organization for planning suggests that a number of different values are involved. Frederic Cleaveland has pointed out:

Some values are served by one pattern of organization, while other values are brought to the fore by a different pattern. The rational way to proceed, therefore, is to try to sift out the major values or goals to be sought, and to determine the relationship of different patterns of organization as a means to the attainment of these goals. If a relationship of means to goals can be objectively established, then the task becomes one of determining in any given local community which values are to have priority. Once this step has been accomplished, decisions as to location and organizational form of the planning function can be made.[2]

The Place of Planning

Some forms of organization serve a particular kind of local government better than others. The big task is to determine the most appropriate means of integrating the planning agency with the structure and organization of the local government. As there is no specific uniform local government organization in this country, this continues to challenge effective planning.

William I. Goodman and Jerome L. Kaufman suggest there are at least four kinds of local government situations that:

. . . call for adaptation of the planning process. These include (1) the municipality with a strong executive form of administration; (2) the municipality with a weak executive or a dispersed form of administration; (3) the area in which varying but geographically related units of government must

---

[1] Several of the charts incorporated in this chapter are based on material prepared by the author while a member of the staff of ASPO, which has published some of the material in a different form.

[2] LOCAL PLANNING ADMINISTRATION (Chicago: International City Managers' Association, 3rd ed., 1959), p. 40.

plan as a team; and (4) the area in which coordinated municipalities must plan as a team.[3]

Each locality must face one or more of these conditions and, in some cases, a community must deal with all of them to meet its planning problems.

The municipality with a strong executive includes those localities with a manager-council form of government as well as jurisdictions with the strong mayor-council arrangement. In this form of local government the executive sets the overall policy of the administration. Therefore, the planning agency must be close to the executive and must be a part of the executive staff.

The municipality with a weak or ill-defined executive includes jurisdictions governed by a weak mayor-council, a commission form of municipal government, board of trustees, board of supervisors, or a similar form of governing body in which no member has a predominant voice in making decisions. The planning agency serving this form of government usually reports to the governing body as a whole or to one of its committees, as there is no clearly designated executive head of government. In the strong executive form of government, an individual makes the final decision in virtually all the important actions of the planning program. But in the weak executive form the decisions are made by a group—there is no central point to which planning decisions can be taken.

The third condition affecting planning at the local level suggested by Goodman and Kaufman occurs in those instances where a number of units of government must plan as a team. This situation usually occurs in an area dominated by one city or several relatively large cities, all encompassed geographically within a single county. Certain governmental functions in the fringe and in the unincorporated sectors may be delegated to special districts and other autonomous units of government for provision of school, park, and sewer and water services. The development programs

of these autonomous units of government frequently are unilateral and actually or potentially conflicting, and the major problem for planning lies in developing a mechanism to assure cooperation among the units.

The fourth major type of governmental framework for local planning is exemplified by the large metropolitan area, where a number of incorporated municipalities are in close proximity. Each municipality must find ways to coordinate its planning with other neighboring communities. It is not uncommon to find in such areas several counties, cities, and special-purpose units of government where no single jurisdiction is primary. The planning agency with metropolitan or areawide jurisdiction usually does not have a parallel governmental unit to which to report. Instead, the planning unit is responsible to a commission consisting of public officials, private citizens, or a combination of both, who represent the governmental jurisdictions in the area. Thus, planning is carried on concurrently at several levels in the metropolitan area. In addition to the metropolitan planning organization, municipal as well as special-purpose bodies all function with respect to the special problems appropriate to their purview.

All these situations are important in determining the relationship of different patterns of organization for planning. There is no single structure best suited for all areas—each of the major types of planning agencies carries advantages suited to the particular governmental structure of the area.

EVOLUTION OF PLANNING ORGANIZATION

What type of organization pattern should be considered for a local planning agency? To answer this question it will be useful to review briefly the nature of the planning agency's working arrangements.

The evolution of city planning over the past half-century reveals two lines of emphasis. The first is the dominant influence and emphasis upon physical development; the second—beginning much later and growing in strength today—is the emphasis on urban planning as an aid to the chief executive of the municipality. The roots of planning may be found in the

---

[3] William I. Goodman and Jerome L. Kaufman, CITY PLANNING IN THE SIXTIES: A RESTATEMENT OF PRINCIPLES AND TECHNIQUES (Urbana: Bureau of Community Planning, University of Illinois, 1965), p. 24.

"city beautiful" movement influenced by architects, landscape architects, and engineers. The concern for planning as a staff function has grown out of interest in planning as a part of public administration and has been stimulated, particularly in recent years, by the growing size and complexity of municipal governments.

Peter Nash and Dennis Durden have suggested that the structure and organization for planning have evolved through six distinct stages.

Some communities have passed through all these stages; others are still at the initial step. However, most communities are at various stages inbetween, depending on community size, age, government, geography, and other factors.[4]

These evolutionary stages are:

1. The period when community leaders meet informally to deal with a particular problem concerning community development.

2. The period of the citizens' committee, meeting at regular intervals, to discuss common problems of the community. Technical staff assistance is absent.

3. The period when community planning is "formalized" for the first time as the citizens' group becomes a part of the local government.

4. The time when the citizens' planning board engages technical personnel on a full-time basis to cope with increasingly complex problems.

5. The later development of more centralized municipal government, especially the strong mayor or city manager forms, leading to the necessity for the chief executive to have developmental programs under direct supervision. At this point planning is recognized as a staff function and is given a departmental status. The role of the citizens' planning commission is less in the mainstream of municipal development activities, although still an important voice in the development of policy.

6. The recent organizational trend toward the development of "departments of urban development" to integrate broad general planning activities with total urban development

activities. The typical independent citizens' planning commission is further removed from points of decision.

Harvey Perloff, from another perspective, has treated the evolution of planning in terms of the emergence of the development of the planning profession.

One stream of development in the city planning field has been more or less typically professional in character; that is, the evolution of a separate skill group . . . here, a skill group concerned with shaping and guiding the physical growth and land-use arrangements of urban communities, through making and applying plans and designs covering the location and three-dimensional form of various types of public and private improvements upon the land.

. . . The other stream of development . . . has been the evolution of an administrative function of planning within municipal government. This has been essentially a staff advisory function, and increasingly a staff function which . . . is similar to other staff (or central overhead) functions such as budgeting and personnel management.

. . . these two lines of development have criss-crossed, intertwined and in some ways merged. . . . This intertwining reflects the fact that city planning in the United States, in its public form, has been developing as a rather unique governmental function which joins together general staff activities (concerned with 'integration' and balancing of municipal government operations, for example, through capital-improvement programming) and substantive activities concerned with guiding urban physical development (for example, through the preparation of master plans and the application of zoning and other controls to carry them out) .[5]

Functions of a Planning Agency

Today there is general agreement that the two lines of development—stress on physical development and growing emphasis on the general staff role for local planning agencies—are both necessary for effective operation. Urban planning may be considered, therefore, in part a line activity and in part a staff activity: that is, a mixed line-staff function.

In carrying out its activities, the planning agency is often engaged in acts that are clearly both in the nature of line and staff work.

[4] Peter H. Nash and Dennis Durden, " A Task-Force Approach to Replace the Planning Board," JOURNAL OF THE AMERICAN INSTITUTE OF PLANNERS, XXX (February, 1964) , p. 12.

[5] Harvey S. Perloff, EDUCATION FOR PLANNING: CITY, STATE, AND REGIONAL (Baltimore: The Johns Hopkins Press, 1957) , pp. 6–8. Published by Johns Hopkins Press for Resources for the Future, Inc.

Wherever the agency is integrated into local government, it must perform in this dual capacity. On the one hand, the agency's task is to provide insight into the physical, social, and economic characteristics of the community. It is involved in the work of guiding development, the performance of an operating (line) function. It must also be responsible for the execution of those policies concerning land subdivision and land use by regulating private decisions regarding urban growth. The agency is concerned, too, with numerous public actions that produce growth and development in the urban area through preparation and refinement of plans for transportation, public buildings, public utilities, and recreation areas, urban renewal, capital improvements, etc.

But the agency is also involved in assisting with coordination of the program of public improvements, and is thereby, as a staff unit, frequently drawn into the field of policy-making. The agency advises the chief executive on how public improvements conform to the land use plan or to a particular public facilities plan. It is also deeply involved in helping pinpoint and choose among alternative goals for the community, recommending one course of action as against another, and in advocating specific plans. The staff nature of planning, an indispensable element in the administration of the agency, calls for more than a skilled administrator: substantive knowledge and experience in the area of physical development is essential to the effective performance of the staff role. The major problem, however, is maintaining a requisite balance between line and staff activities.

If the planning agency is to make its whole contribution to more effective municipal government and orderly planned urban growth, it must emphasize both its substantive (line) and its administration (staff) responsibility. Preoccupation with the day-to-day pressures of zoning administration or review of proposed subdivision plats leaves little time for advance planning or for the research that must precede and support long-range planning. Furthermore, neglect of staff advisory and coordinating responsibilities can lead in time to isolation of the planning agency so that its advice is given little heed.[6]

------

[6] LOCAL PLANNING ADMINISTRATION, *op. cit.*, p. 52.

A local planning program may be classified into seven functions or categories. These are:

1. To establish community development objectives.

2. To conduct research on growth and development of the city.

3. To make development plans and programs.

4. To increase public understanding and acceptance of planning.

5. To provide technical service to other governmental agencies and private groups.

6. To coordinate development activities affecting city growth.

7. To administer land use controls (zoning and subdivision regulations).

The planning program needs a framework of overall, officially-approved development policy, to serve as both a checklist and directive for the planning agency's activities. Broad development objectives should be established, approved officially, and periodically reviewed, (1) to give the government and public a clear sense of the future city, and (2) to give the agency a clear sense of direction for its activities.

The agency must collect and analyze, on a continuing basis, all pertinent data on city growth and development in order to provide a foundation for a national planning program. The agency must be organized and staffed to analyze and use data as a matter of course in its planning programs. It should be known as the community's central intelligence headquarters on matters affecting community growth and development and should be a depository for and distributor of all relevant data and statistics needed to aid other city departments and private citizens in making informed development decisions.

The central function of a planning agency is to make development plans and programs. These should be based on careful study and analysis and geared to city development objectives, and they should provide a clear guide for governmental decisions in the construction of public facilities and in the regulation of the pace and character of private development through land use controls. Once objectives are defined, the task of the agency is to develop specific plans and programs to help achieve those objectives.

An integral activity of the planning agency is the continuing effort aimed at increasing public acceptance, understanding, and support of the program and the principles of planning. The job of informing residents of the community and public officials about the program will be handled in large part by the staff of the planning agency. This should be recognized as a part of the agency's work program and adequate time allocated to perform the continuing tasks required by public education activities. (See Chapter 19 for a detailed discussion of agency procedures.)

Furnishing of technical resources and advice is an important function of the planning agency vis-à-vis other municipal departments, governmental agencies generally, and private citizens. This is a service activity of the agency to which the staff and budget must be adjusted. At the same time, these "short-run" projects should not dominate the operation of the agency. Staff assigned to the development plans and programs functions should not be continually pulled off to work on brush-fire type projects.

Coordination is a principal objective that is related to many of the activities of the planning agency. Public and private development action must be coordinated within a framework of comprehensive development policy, if the planning program is to be effective. The agency should be given responsibility and commensurate authority to seek coherence in the development activities of the municipality and to coordinate decisions made by many private actions and other governmental levels. State legislation often requires that many proposals for public development be submitted to the planning agency for review and comment before action is taken. The agency may be required or directed by the appropriate executive to review development proposals submitted by other municipal departments, special districts, and state and county agencies that are locally based. The principal instrument for coordinating local development activity is the capital improvement program—the tentative list of public improvements to be built within a five- or six-year period. The agency may also collaborate with other governments to prepare joint plans or to develop policy on planning matters of mutual concern.

One additional function of a planning agency is the administration of land use controls, fairly and equitably enforced, and based on plans and development policies representative of the public interest.

As previously noted, the major burden of performing these seven functions falls upon the technical staff. The lay citizen commission, however, also has important tasks to perform. In addition to serving as a review and recommending body on current development proposals—zoning amendments, plat approvals, street vacations, and similar actions—the commission is also especially suited to perform four other roles. The commission may have:

1. A representation role on behalf of the public, subjecting planning decisions to citizen examination, by establishing technical advisory committees of informed citizens and officials on specific subjects.

2. A promotional role to stimulate interest in planning.

3. An advisory role to municipal officials on development policies of local government.

4. A coordinative role in working with other public and private agencies to integrate the total governmental planning effort.

Because the typical planning commission spends much of its time on development control administration and other short-run matters, the public tends to see this area as its only responsibility. However, it is important that the public also understand as clearly the total responsibilities of the lay commission. To achieve this goal may require more effort than is currently expended by many commissions. Probably the most effective method for the commission to find the time is by relinquishing to the staff as many routine duties as possible.

Major Types of Planning Agencies

There are four major patterns of organization of local planning agencies in the United States: (1) the independent planning commission with or without staff; (2) the planning department; (3) the community development department; (4) the administrative planning agency. There are, of course, variations or blends within these general categories.

INDEPENDENT PLANNING COMMISSION

The commission, stemming from voluntary activities of earlier citizens' groups, is intended to foster an objective and neutral attitude in its recommendations. Its advisory role to elected officials is determined by virtue of its independence from the local administration.

Members of the commission are usually appointed as specified by the state planning enabling legislation. Appointing authority usually lies with the mayor and city council or the county governing body. Members are selected on the basis of their demonstrated interest in the community and tend to come largely from its business and professional segments. They serve overlapping terms for a number of years that extend beyond the elected term of office of the appointing authority.

A large number of commissions serve small municipalities, and they may function without a professional staff. Such commissions operate outside the mainstream of government and are mainly concerned with the administration of zoning and subdivision ordinances. Few of these commissions attempt to coordinate development or to initiate and prepare general or functional plans, zoning ordinances, and subdivision regulations. They may rely instead on consultants for such services.

Larger communities utilizing the independent or autonomous planning commission usually have a full-time technical staff. The commission is responsible for the assignment and review of the work of its staff. Formal lines of communication between the planning staff and the chief executive of the municipality usually pass through the commission. The planning staff is theoretically outside the basic structure of the executive branch, and its relationships with personnel in the operating municipal departments may be distant, unless special attention is given to building and maintaining liaisons.

Even though many persons feel that the independent agency is limited in effectiveness, there are communities where the commission still is the most workable device for achieving an effective planning program. These include small communities, unable to hire full-time staffs because of limited financial resources, where good candidates can be persuaded to serve, and also local governments with a weak

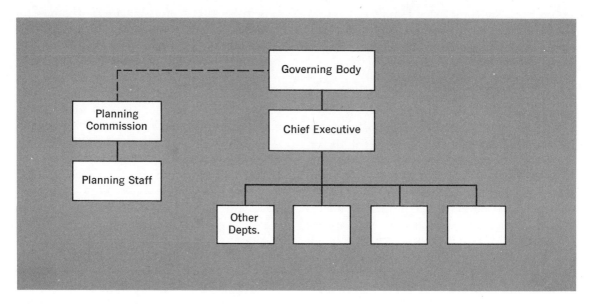

FIGURE 18–1. *Organization chart, independent planning commission*

or dispersed executive and administrative structure where the commission members themselves may be in a position to force changes on behalf of planning.

PLANNING DEPARTMENT

The major difference in organization between the independent planning commission which employs a staff and the planning department is that the technical staff of the latter is integrated within a department that is directly responsible to the chief executive of the municipality. The staff is not appointed by, nor subject to, the supervision or control of the planning commission. The commission exists but performs largely on advisory function to the department staff. In some communites, no planning commission exists. The advisory role of the commission is performed by special *ad hoc* committees appointed to review and comment on certain problems under study.

The department form of organization enables the chief executive of the municipality to assume clear authority to coordinate physical planning policy with other kinds of municipal policy covering many aspects of the administrative operations of local government. The planning staff has a direct channel to the chief executive and has a strong and influential sponsor for its recommendations. A departmental form of organization is most effective where a strong executive form of government exists—the strong mayor-council, or the council-manager form of local government.

Several cities, especially those with strong urban renewal programs, have sought better coordination between the planning agency and the executive branch by interposing a "development coordinator" between the chief executive and the planning agency. The cities of Philadelphia, Providence, New Haven, and San Francisco have established this arrangement. In a few council-manager cities, another shift has weakened the independence of the planning commission. In these cities responsibility for directing the planning operation is given to an "assistant city manager for planning." One version of this form of organization may be found in Berkeley, California. Two assistant city managers' positions were created: one in charge of plans and programs (with the planning staff reporting directly to him) ; and the other assistant in charge of administration with responsibility for seeing that approved plans and projects are completed in accordance with established schedules.

THE COMMUNITY DEVELOPMENT DEPARTMENT

A few cities have shifted the planning function toward the chief executive by combining into a single administrative unit the departments that are broadly responsible for development. A combined planning and development agency —the community development department—

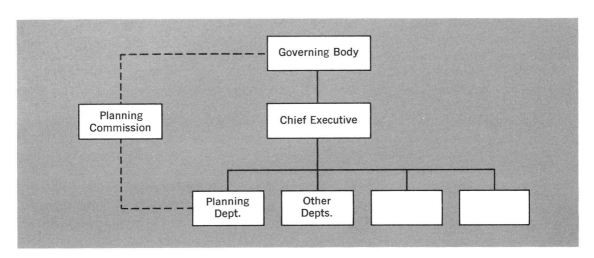

FIGURE 18–2. *Organization chart, planning department*

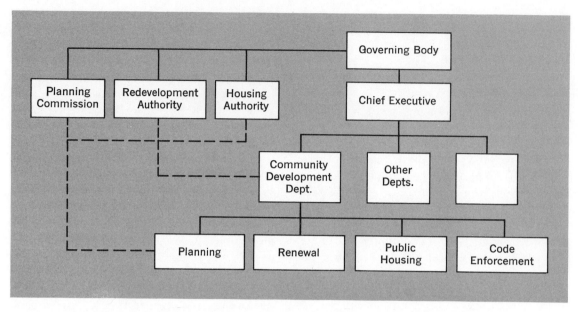

FIGURE 18-3. *Organization chart, community development department*

has been created to combine planning, urban renewal and, on occasion, code enforcement activities.

Cities have tended to assign the urban renewal function to a separate department. Coordination of the activities of the planning and urban renewal agencies often proves difficult to achieve. Since both agencies have a common objective of improving the physical fabric of the community, city officials have taken steps to merge the tasks of overall planning, rebuilding, and renewing the city within a single department. This permits renewal to be based on broad planning considerations and also enables the more specific renewal projects to be fed back to the planning staff and to test the plan. This type of consolidation has taken place in at least 15 cities, among them Milwaukee, Tucson, and Evanston, Illinois, within the past several years. In most instances the planning commission is still retained as an advisory body but with considerably reduced responsibilities.

ADMINISTRATIVE PLANNING AGENCY

Nearly 30 years ago, Rexford G. Tugwell proposed that planning be considered as a fourth branch of government because of its importance in the administrative structure of govern-ment. Planning would thus be raised to the level of the legislative, judicial, and executive arms of government.

Two major planning agencies have been organized somewhat along the pattern proposed by Tugwell: the New York City Plan Commission and the Puerto Rico Planning Board. Tugwell played a major role in both agencies, serving as the first chairman for the New York agency and later, as governor of Puerto Rico, establishing the territory's first planning board. While neither agency has assumed an importance equal to the traditional three branches of government, their organization patterns are quite different from those of planning agencies in other parts of the United States. The statutory framework in Puerto Rico, as well as the procedures followed by planning agencies, is considerably different from practices on the mainland since the Commonwealth is free from many of the specifications imposed on governmental jurisdictions here.

The administrative planning agency, as its name implies, is essentially an independent regulatory agency. The Puerto Rico planning board has most of the characteristics of an administrative agency—it makes, adopts, and enforces its plans and regulatory ordinances. It also has quasi-legislative powers. The New York City Plan Commission, however, more nearly resembles planning agencies in other cities.

One distinguishing characteristic of the administrative planning agency is that the chairman of the agency is a fulltime, salaried employee, who acts as the chief administrator of the technical staff as well as chairman of the policy-making commission. This type of planning agency offers some advantages in dealing with ordinances pertaining to regulation of land use, where the burden of administering such regulations is fast becoming too great for a nonpaid citizen group to handle.

General Background for Agency Organization[7]

An essential requirement of a successful planning agency is effective relations among staff units and staff members. The various parts of the organization must be coordinated, and each staff member must have a clear understanding of his particular contribution to the overall objectives of the organization. This is partially accomplished through simple, clear internal organization. It is also achieved through the development of personal ties among the various members of the staff and of a sense of teamwork striving toward accepted agency goals.

The work of the director of a local planning agency is complex and demanding. Not only should the director be competent in a technical sense, but also as the administrative head of an organization, responsible for execution of the many tasks assigned to his agency. As a planning agency grows, directing the organization becomes increasingly a job of administration and less one of technical planning. The director in a large agency devotes a great deal more of his time and energies to his role as an administrator, even though his training has most

[7] This discussion has been adapted from a report written by the author and published in 1961 entitled ASPO PLANNING ADVISORY SERVICE INFORMATION REPORT NO. 146: PRINCIPLES OF ORGANIZATION FOR PLANNING AGENCIES (Chicago: American Society of Planning Officials, 1961).

likely not been in this field.

In some respects, the task of the director of a small agency may be more difficult. Not only must he be the principal technician, but he must also do a great deal of administrative work that accompanies a planning agency operation. He cannot delegate these tasks as can the director of a large agency.

Twenty to thirty years ago, the tempo of the planning office was leisurely. The postwar building and development boom, however, has drastically changed the pace and scope of operations of the agency. The pressure to "produce" has forced the planning administrator to organize for the job of planning urban growth along the best lines. Whether he likes it or not, a substantial part of the planning director's time today must be concerned with administration and organization.

Organization is one of the basic aspects of administration. The planning agency, like any other administrative organization, has a structure that can be charted. The chart is a useful means to identify and depict various aspects of internal organization of planning agencies. Charting can define the chain of command or indicate the points of control or review of administrative actions.

There are only a few instances where planning agencies have planned their organization at the start of their operations. Most organizations were established structurally with little conscious design. As the planning function in local government became more widely accepted by public officials and assumed a greater role in local government, the tasks assigned to the agency became more complex to meet the increasing problems of urban development. Planning agency officials today are perhaps more concerned with matters of reorganization, rather than organization.

Nevertheless, the first step is the same. In determining the effectiveness of planning agency organization, the particular objectives of the agency must first be determined and stated. An organizational form should be developed that will best meet these objectives. In the case of reorganization, an inventory of the existing organization structure is made at the same time the ideal form is being prepared. It follows that satisfactory results cannot be expected merely through copying another agency's plan of organization.

One further point should be noted. Effective action in a planning agency is facilitated when city councils and state legislatures set down only the broad objectives of the organization of a program rather than prescribing details. The task of determining internal structure, staff relationships, and detailed work programs is better left to those responsible for seeing that legislative intent is carried out. Too often the local legislative body assuming responsibility for all administrative detail impairs the effectiveness of the planning agency through line-item appropriations or through detailed legislation that specifies a major aspect of internal organization.

Division of Responsibilities

Discussion of the organization and structure of planning agencies must take into account the size of the staff. In small agencies (up to five professional staff members), the example of leadership counts for more than the niceties of allocation of assignments or management control. For planning staffs so small, few structural organization problems exist except perhaps the

problems arising from coordination with the other departments of the local government. Staff members report directly to the planning director in these agencies. They are cellular in organization. While particular fields of investigation may be assigned to individuals because of their special training or interest, this is not rigid compartmental organization.

No positive statement can be made as to what size a staff should be before it is broken down into subunits. There is general agreement, however, that once a decision has been made to establish subunits, it should be on the basis of logically grouped functions of the organization.

The activities of a planning agency may be grouped in several different ways:

• by major technical functions, such as separate divisions devoted to land use, recreation, highways, and other significant aspects of the program;

• by the primary process or skill of the professionals involved, e.g., research design, drafting, implementation, etc.;

• by the time involved in getting out the work, which would separate current or day-to-day assignments from long-term or nonrecurring work, or service activities from policy formulation. In Figure 18–4 they are gathered together under four major functional groups:

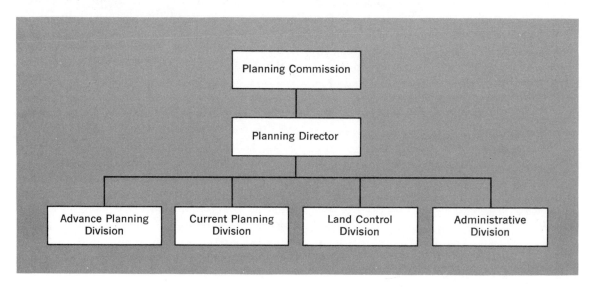

FIGURE 18–4. *Major functional breakdown of local planning agency*

(1) advance planning, (2) current planning, (3) land use controls, and (4) administration.

ADVANCE PLANNING

This group includes the preparation of all general plans, a range of activities that falls short of precise design or design review. It includes the research necessary to prepare or to support these plans and to keep them up-to-date. The preparation of statements on planning policy (rather than emphasis on a series of maps) worked out with other municipal departments, governmental units, and civic groups falls within this group. Such statements cover all the functional areas of the comprehensive plan. Probably the community renewal program, the long-range plan of renewal for the entire city, should be linked with this group. This new community renewal program, spurred by federal financial assistance, is not aimed at specific projects.

Research services may be used by other functional groups, but because they are an integral part of advance planning, a separate functional grouping may not be required. When research has been made a separate operation, independent of advance planning, the experience has occasionally developed problems of adequate communications and linkage with other work units in the agency.

CURRENT PLANNING

Current planning activities are those that are concerned with carrying out the comprehen-

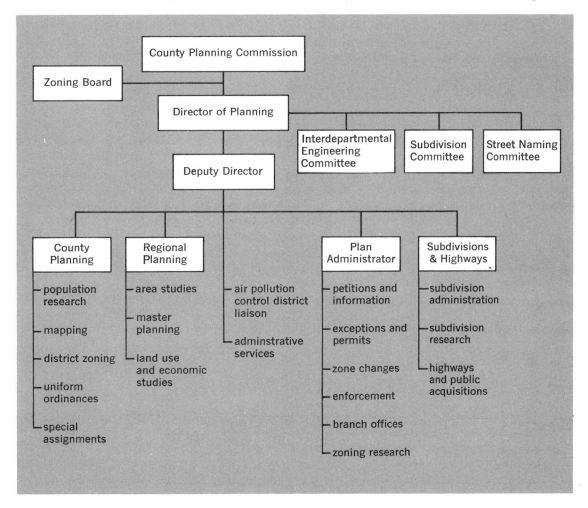

FIGURE 18-5. *Organization of large county planning agency (Office incorporates engineering functions.)*

sive plan—either reviewing proposals that affect the comprehensive plan, or initiating proposals to carry out the plan. Projects that come before the planning agency for review, such as schools, streets, parks and playgrounds, fall into this category. Preparation, certification and review studies of redevelopment projects should be considered a current planning function. The preparation or review of the capital improvement budget is also properly considered current planning. Administration of land use controls, while short-range and repetitive in nature like other current planning activities, is discussed as a separate unit because of the volume of work that is generally required in discharging that function.

In organizing and staffing a planning agency, a function frequently overlooked or underestimated is the "brushfire" operation. Because it is usually an emergency job, it can disrupt the agency's work schedule, unless such jobs are considered a normal responsibility of a particular functional area. Too often they are given to advance planning because it is felt that the schedule for advance planning can be deferred. The result frequently is that advance planning activities become stymied due to the continual barrage of requests for special jobs. The logical place for such emergency calls is in current planning.

Staff members with design skills are pulled together under current planning, both for creative work and design review.

LAND USE CONTROLS

The third functional area of planning agency operation includes the administration of the two principal regulatory tools: zoning and subdivision regulation. While these tools are necessary to carry out the comprehensive plan, they usually differ from the project and design review function assigned to current planning. The controls are, in large measure, concerned with the preservation of existing amenities and are applied to projects usually occurring through the initiative of private actions. Current planning responds to projects arising from the actions of government. Land use control administration calls for legal and engineering skills rather than for design skills.

In some cities the zoning function is considered a separate major functional area within the planning agency. However, because of the close relationship of the skills needed to service both zoning and subdivision activities, it appears wise to group them together.

Amendments either to the zoning or subdivision regulations should properly be considered a partial responsibility of advance planning, to be examined jointly with current planning. Planning policy questions are involved in such instances. The processing of exceptions, variances, and interpretations of the ordinance, however, properly fall within the functional area of land use controls.

ADMINISTRATION

The last functional area of a planning agency includes a number of services needed by all major categories. This service unit includes personnel administration, purchasing, budgeting, library activities, maintenance of files, stenography, and drafting. Experience has shown that these services are most efficiently handled if they are pooled, rather than spread throughout the planning agency.

While the senior personnel in each of the other major functional areas will be involved in public relations; the arrangement and encouragement of press, radio, and television contacts, and communication with citizen groups are basically an administrative function.

In those commissions that operate with a secretary to the planning commission, this function is also placed in the administration division if the "secretary" is someone other than the planning director. If the secretary is the director, then transcribing of minutes, arrangements for hearings, and similar routine matters are handled by personnel in the administration division.

Functional Organization

To do its job, the planning agency must parcel out specific tasks to individuals in order to carry out its work program. The planning director and his immediate subordinates cannot make decisions unless these decisions are translated into action by members of the staff at the lowest echelon. Therefore, the amount of attention devoted to directing the activities of the staff will depend a good deal on the way in which the work has been divided. Where the work of the whole organization can be divided into fairly distinct and separate subpurposes, the review process of a work project should pass through the hands of as few persons as possible.

Analysis of functional and structural organization charts of planning agencies throughout the country indicates that the major functional areas are recognized by a *division* classification in the organization hierarchy. Depending on the size of the planning agency, the division may be responsible for one or more functions. Divisions, in turn, are divided into *sections* in the larger agencies.

There appears to be no single rule to suggest the proper time for sectional breakdown of divisions, but the basis of subdivision usually occurs by fields of investigation: zoning, subdivision, urban renewal, housing, capital budget, circulation, research, advance planning, project review, and land use. In medium-sized agencies, sections set up to handle specific projects can be made up of persons who cut across division lines. As each major project comes along, a team is set up to handle it. When the project has been completed, the team is dissolved and new teams are formed. This type of organization may be satisfactory for the medium-size agency because it is flexible. But it may create difficult management problems in large agencies because of the frequent shifts in organizational relationships and because of the difficulty of timing the formation of new teams to coincide with the breaking up of teams whose projects have been completed. In this instance, a more formal sectional organization is desirable.

SMALL AGENCIES

The first consideration of more or less formal separation of functions should be made when the planning agency reaches four or five professional staff members. While no one element of the staff's work is more important than another, the preparation and periodic adjustment of a comprehensive plan is a primary function. This function should reside in a single staff division. In the smaller agency, this function should be reflected in the establishment of an advance planning division, long-range planning division, or a unit with a similar descriptive title. Thus the functional area of advance planning resides within this division.

The other subunit or division established in the smaller agency could be entitled current planning division, or planning administration division. Sometimes a separate urban renewal division is established in communities in which the planning agency is active in the urban renewal program. Division chiefs are responsible to the planning director. Two functional areas—current planning and land use controls—of a planning agency, therefore, are the responsibility of the current planning division. The urban renewal division could be considered a special projects group.

However, most smaller agencies combine the current and advance planning functions within one division. Under such an arrangement, advance planning activities are likely to take second place to the brushfire activities of the current planning function. For this reason, it is recommended that a clear and complete divisional separation be made of these two functional areas in planning agency organization, regardless of size of staff.

The fourth functional area, administration, is the major responsibility of the planning director. It is not uncommon, however, to find in many of the smaller agencies that public information and counter work is almost exclusively handled by the current planning division.

MEDIUM-SIZE AGENCIES

Agencies employing five to ten planners should usually subdivide the four functional areas into three divisions, reporting to a principal planner or to an assistant director. The divisions may be broken down into advance planning, current planning, and planning administration or into similar divisions to handle the functions. Breaking divisions down into sections may or may not be feasible, depending on the nature of the agency work program. The grouping of personnel from each of these divi-

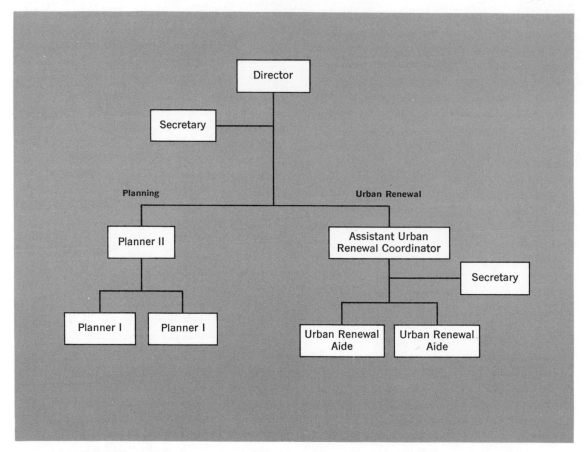

FIGURE 18–6. *Organization of small planning agency (Incorporates function of urban renewal.)*

sions into special sections to handle special projects, however, can be done with a minimum of difficulty.

It is surprising to find how many nontechnical staff members are needed to service a planning agency. These auxiliary workers in some agencies constitute half of the staff, a fact to keep in mind when determining personnel requirements. Periodic surveys of local planning agencies through the country, conducted by the American Society of Planning Officials through its Planning Advisory Service seek to establish ratios between the number of office workers and draftsmen with planners. These figures vary continually, but the proportion of non-professionals seems to be growing.

As the planning agencies grow larger, there are considerations favoring the centralization of administrative and clerical duties. For example, a drafting pool or a secretarial pool can be

established under the direction of the second-in-command or an assistant director for administration. This may go so far as to require division heads to requisition drafting and secretarial help from the executive officer as needed. If properly managed, this arrangement should provide more even workloads, and should result in increased efficiency. Private secretaries, however, are considered by some staff members as status symbols, so pooling may have to be sold with some vigor. The administration function, along with other auxiliary services, is not usually formalized by a division status in medium-size agencies, but is handled by the exective office.

LARGE AGENCIES

In agencies employing more than 10 planners, the problem is to keep the number of responsible section or division heads reporting to the next supervisor to a minimum. This should be done, to be consistent with efficient administration, through the functional allocation of parts of the work program.

The large agency should probably have a division in which each of the four functional areas described (advance planning, current planning, land use controls, and administration) is centered or substantially integrated.

Divisional nomenclature in large agencies may vary considerably, depending on local preferences, but the organization breakdown would still follow functional areas.

Large agency organization may depart from smaller agencies in two principal ways: (1) the administrative function becomes a full divisional responsibility and thus is removed from the executive office, and (2) the administration

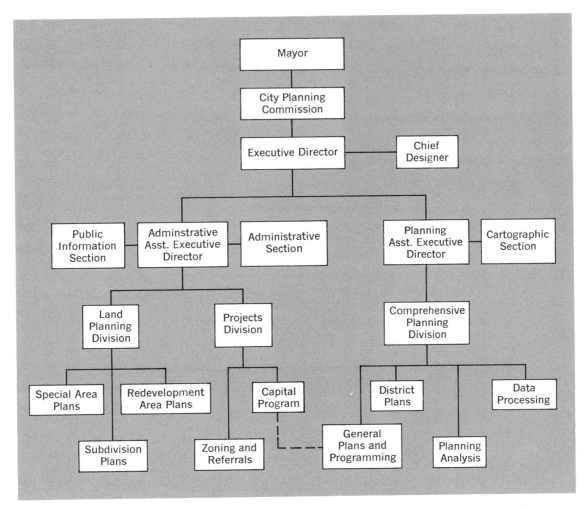

FIGURE 18–7. *Organization chart, planning agency (Shows clear distinction between advance and current planning functions. Organizational arrangement reflects strong design responsibilities of agency. Note the relationship of the Capital Program Section [in the Projects Division] with the General Plan and Programming Section [in the Comprehensive Planning Division.])*

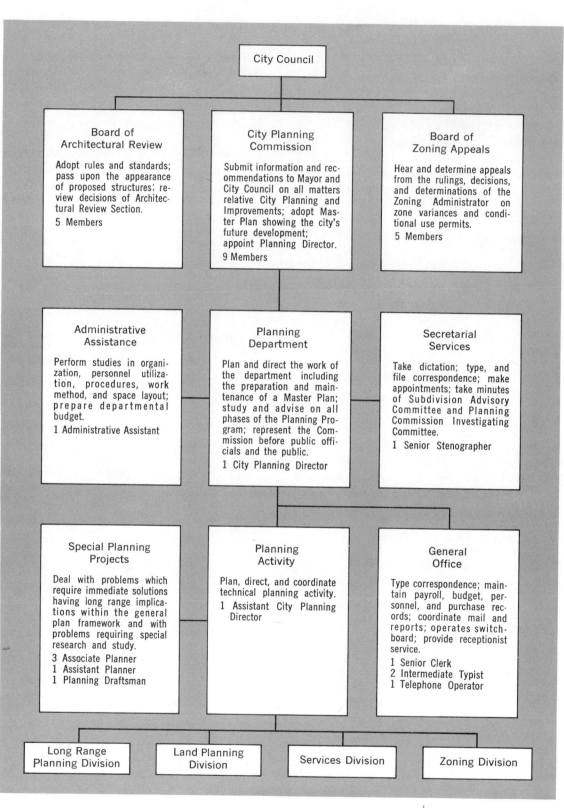

FIGURE 18–8. *General organization of planning functions (Observe method of handling brushfire operation in Special Projects Division. Other divisions are further divided into sections—annexation, transportation, research, etc.—reflecting special problems in the community.)*

of the zoning ordinance, depending on state enabling or charter provisions, may require separate divisional treatment in the functional area of land use controls. The latter departure may present some special problems. In some jurisdictions the zoning administrator is semi-autonomous or even entirely independent of the planning agency. He may have powers in making decisions not subject to control of the planning agency. And yet, in most instances, he depends on the planning agency administratively for the assignment of personnel and for recommendations on certain zoning matters.

The ideal relationship between the zoning administrator's office and the planning agency under such an arrangement will be difficult to establish. The functional independence of the administrator, if he has the power to make variance decisions, is important. To some extent his job may be considered quasi-judicial. It would seem undesirable to leave the way open for attacks on his impartiality based on his being a subordinate of the planning director. If independence is maintained, a further objection to a subordinate relationship may be that the planning director in some cases will be criticized for actions of the zoning administrator despite the director's lack of power to con-

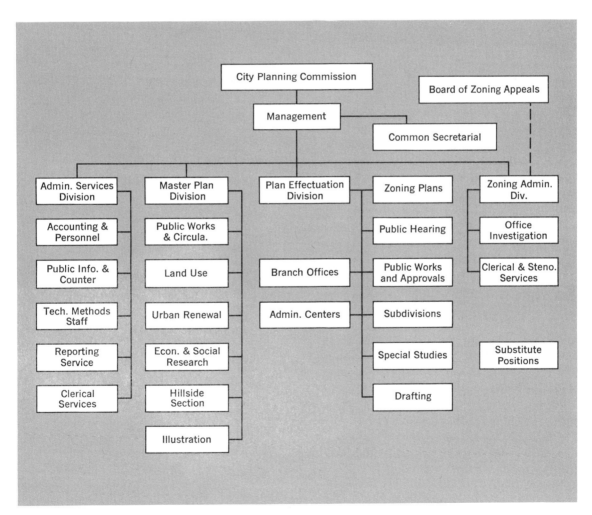

FIGURE 18–9. *Organization of planning agency (Zoning administration established as separate division. Organization reflects program geared to city areas: Branch Offices, Administrative Centers, Hillside.)*

trol or determine those actions.

In the light of these considerations, the caliber of the administrator will likely determine the quality of administration and, therefore, formal integration within the planning agency may not be important. On the other hand, administration of zoning requires a great deal of cross-checking with the planning agency, and may be carried out effectively by placing zoning administration within those functions handled under land use controls. There are close interrelations among the functions grouped here.

Several charts, taken or adapted from ASPO Information Report No. 146 (May, 1961), are shown here to indicate variations in the organization of the planning agency brought about by special local conditions.

Special Problems and Relationships[8]

The success of the planning agency in developing working realtionships with the chief executive, other departments, the governing body, other governmental jurisdictions, and the public will determine its effectiveness in guiding the development of the community. As pointed out earlier, coordination of public and private development actions is a principal objective of the planning agency. The following discussion briefly describes some of the special problems and relationships within which a planning agency works.

RELATION TO THE CHIEF EXECUTIVE

With a growing number of cities moving toward council-manager or strong-mayor-and-council government, and with counties employing a county executive officer, the chief executive is becoming the "chief planner" of municipal affairs, including physical development. The notion of a staff role for planning is built on the assumption that the executive has central responsibility for developing policy, for coordination, and for directing and supervising the local government machinery through which development plans are carried into effect.

In a very real sense the municipal executive and the planner are dependent on each other. The executive requires staff assistance and technical know-how; the planner needs support for planning and commitment to the actions necessary to carry out plans. Yet in spite of this mutual interdependence, there is also an apparent incompatibility in certain professional interests and points of view that tends at times to raise barriers to close working ties. An effective relationship between planner and city manager or mayor requires common understanding of their respective positions in the community.[9]

To the chief administrator, whether city manager, county executive, mayor, or chairman of the county board, the staff aspect of city planning is paramount. The planning process provides the rational component of city policy making and serves to coordinate consideration of each policy and decision as it relates to all other community policies. In this activity the planner with his specialized knowledge has a central position. Decisions on governmental policy almost invariably involve political choices among competing claims on limited public resources. "Each choice demands the advice of the technician who is in a position to predict probable consequences and to visualize alternative solutions." This planning and decision-making process requires "a more or less constant interchange between politician and technician up to the point where final decisions are made on matters of value and opinion."[10]

This view of planning is also fully consistent with a chief executive's understanding of his own role as policy formulator and supervising director of the local government's governmental machinery. As comprehensive planner of the entire local government program, he requires competent assistance in planning and coordinating development.

Some planners have held the view that their primary responsibility for planning is something apart from broader local government

---

[8] The material in LOCAL PLANNING ADMINISTRATION, *op. cit.*, pp. 69–74 has been edited and up-dated for inclusion in the following discussion.

[9] Robert Daland, "Organization for Urban Planning: Some Barriers to Integration," JOURNAL OF THE AMERICAN INSTITUTE OF PLANNERS, XXIII (Fall, 1957), pp. 200–206.

[10] *Ibid.*, pp. 201–202.

policy: planning is a function, largely technical in nature, to be carried out within a set of policies regarding community goals and values adopted by the city council or county supervisors and passed on to the planner. From this viewpoint the chief executive devotes most of his time to overseeing local government housekeeping and running an efficient and economical enterprise. Holding this narrow conception of the role of the chief administrator, planners are reluctant to have their offices attached to the chief executive in a staff capacity. They feel they will be "housekeepers" rather than planners.

Consequently, planners who hold this view prefer that planning be a responsibility of the independent lay commission and that the planning director report first to the planning commission and then to the governing body (city council or county board). They believe that their programs are strengthened under the auspices of an independent lay commission.

Most planners, today, however, have a different view of the planning process in relation to the chief administrators. They believe that planning ultimately is weakened when it is set apart from interrelated programs such as street improvements, parks and recreation, urban renewal, airports, and economic development. They know too that effective and comprehensive planning can be accomplished only on the basis of continuous day-to-day relationships with other operating departments and the chief administrator. Finally, they know that the governing body, regardless of the authority of the independent commission (if the local government has one), will be more receptive to planning proposals when the commission and staff are working closely with the local government administration on all planning problems.

In some local governments these relationships may involve conflicting elements: (1) the chief administrator's interest in an integrated organization with a concept of planning throughout the entire local government service and a planning agency working closely on both staff and line problems; (2) the planner's interest in maintaining the planning function somewhat apart from the local government administration and reporting to the independent lay commission and to the governing body; and (3) the planning commission's interest in keeping planning out of politics and at a level removed from the rest of the local government.

Fortunately in many local governments this conflict does not occur. In these communities the chief administrator makes every effort to instill the idea of planning in all departments and thus encourages department heads to regard planning as part of the day-to-day job. The planning director and staff have a sincere interest in developing planning as a part of every departmental program, and they view planning as an integral part of government. The planning commission, in turn, is concerned with its representative, interpretive, and advisory roles. To recapitulate, such local governments observe the guidelines suggested below:

1. The planner and the chief executive recognize that planning is both a staff activity related to policy-making and a line activity concerned with guiding development.

2. Both recognize that administrative authority and responsibility rest with the chief executive, especially in coordination of all local programs.

3. Both recognize that it is primarily the chief executive's job to be the advocate of good planning with the governing body. Thus, planning proposals are prepared under his overall direction and submitted to the governing body by him as administration proposals. The executive is the "chief advocate," not the "chief critic" of the proposals.

4. The planner and the chief executive encourage the planning commission to do the work it is best fitted for: representing the public, interpreting planning programs to interest groups and the public; and advising the planning agency, chief executive, and the governing body.

5. The chief executive recognizes, regardless of formal organization for planning, that the planning function is an integral part of government. Therefore, he gives the planning function commensurate status and prestige. Subject to his own overall responsibilities, the chief executive delegates to the planning director the authority and responsibility needed to di-

rect the planning program. This includes access to the chief executive and a salary commensurate with the duties and responsibilities of the position.

Amplifying the last point, the contribution of the planner to the work of the chief executive will depend considerably upon a close, personal relationship built upon mutual confidence and respect. Because of his line-staff responsibilities, however, the planner cannot permit his time to be fully consumed by pure staff work to the neglect of his line activities in guiding development decisions. For the executive to hinder the planner in his efforts to develop this larger network of relationships by using him as a general administrative assistant will undermine and destroy the potential contribution of an effective planning process.

The planner's close relationships with the planning commission, with operating department heads, and the people of the community, all add to his usefulness to the executive. As the chief executive fully responsible for administration of municipal affairs, the city manager, mayor, or county executive sorely needs a competent planning staff functioning at a high, professional level where its unique technical contribution both in line and in staff aspects of its responsibility can have maximum effect.

RELATION TO OPERATING DEPARTMENTS

As in the case of the relationship between the planner and the chief executive, the planning agency, operating departments, and independent boards and commissions of the city are interdependent. The planning staff looks to these agencies for supplying much of the basic data required in research and plan preparation. They in turn can profit greatly from technical assistance in making their own departmental plans. Furthermore, these agencies stand to gain in the long run from being able to fit their goals and plans into the overall framework of the community's long-range plans; as the primary staff group working on long-range urban development, the planners can provide essential guidance and advice to these agencies and departments.

On the other hand, it is important to recognize that seeds of conflict also exist in the relationships between planners and operating agencies. As a major adviser to the executive on coordination, the planner runs strong risks of appearing to line department heads as policeman and controller rather than as technical aid and guide. To be effective in a coordinating role, the planning personnel must call on professional skills, administrative skills, and, above all, skills in personal relationships.

In stimulating departmental planning, the planning agency must recognize that much substantive planning responsibility rests with the departments. Only when line departmental personnel have participated fully in actually developing plans will they support them with enthusiasm. The alternative of "package" plans prepared by the planning agency and submitted to departments for approval is totally unsatisfactory in developing planning skills and habits in operating agencies. Plans that grow out of the knowledge and experience of the department are to be preferred, despite their relative immaturity, to the fanciest plan prepared from on high.

Stated more emphatically, the planning agency should not undertake studies that can be done by other departments. Any local government has far more planning work to be done all the time than the planning agency can possibly handle anyway. The planning director should make it a point to recommend to the chief administrator those portions of the planning program that are attainable and can be carried out through existing or proposed agencies of the local government. The planning director should be particularly careful to identify those planning studies that can be done by the public works department, the parks and recreation department, the fire department, and the local board of education. In many local governments the mayor or city manager has authority to direct such departments to make special studies that are needed. Another useful device is to assign qualified employees of other city departments to the planning department on temporary duty to assist in studies of particular concern to their "home" departments. Many "community renewal program" studies have been organized in this fashion.

When viewed this way, the planning process

involves far more than just the staff and expenditures for the planning agency alone. Every department of the government, therefore, should participate in the formulation of the planning program, which is the main responsibility of the chief administrator. When plans are so developed, they will be much more acceptable because other departments have participated in the work.

Where the planning agency has responsibility for capital improvement programming, its position in coordinating departmental planning activities is strengthened. Indeed, the desire to plan for capital improvements is a strong incentive for a department to take the first steps toward systematic planning.

In many communities the coordinating role of the planning agency is further strengthened by the practice of referring capital improvement projects to the planning agency for review. Under such an arrangement, projects proposed by any department must be submitted to the planning staff for study and comment before receiving approval by the executive. In their review the planners explore such matters as conformity to general plans already adopted; potential conflict with other projects, proposed or under consideration; and the ultimate effects of the proposed project on patterns of urban growth and development.

Finally, brief mention should be made of the increasing numbers of municipal departments other than the planning agency that employ technically trained planning personnel. Housing, redevelopment, and urban renewal agencies have led the way. But boards of education, departments of health and sanitation, departments of public works, and others are also following suit. As professional expertness in planning spreads beyond the planning agency, the result should be more effective departmental planning and better coordinated overall plans for urban growth and development.

RELATION TO INDEPENDENT BOARDS AND OTHER GOVERNMENTS

Developing effective relationships with independent boards and other governmental jurisdictions is essentially similar to the job of working closely with operating departments. It may, however, prove more difficult to accomplish because of the autonomy of these bodies. School boards, recreation commissions, boards of health, and the like are inclined to be jealous of their independence from direct executive control and therefore more likely to resist efforts at coordination.

But they too have much to gain by fitting their development plans into those for the community as a whole. In part the planner's job in this instance is a selling and an educational effort. First, he has to convince the members of the board and their chief administrative officers of the value of comprehensive planning for the community. This persuasion will depend on his effectiveness in interpreting the purpose and meaning of planning as a practical administrative tool. Then, once the board members are sold on the idea, the planner may have to work closely with board personnel in training them to carry on their internal planning process and to relate this activity to the overall process of community-wide planning.

In metropolitan areas, however, much of today's planning is for individual cities rather than *effective* planning for the entire urban area. What is missing is coordination of those municipal planning and zoning actions that have an effect beyond local boundaries. One of the major challenges to effective planning today is securing metropolitan and regional coordination—in getting local governments to give heed to the regional repercussions of their acts. We have difficulty in maintaining an overview by all government agencies so that the benefits of one action are not negated by another action. This problem not only raises issues within the local government itself, but also with the actions and programs of neighboring local governments and a growing number of state and federal agencies.

RELATION TO THE GOVERNING BODY

The governing body relies on the chief executive to present the planning proposals that have been developed by the planning staff. The chief executive depends largely on the planning staff to identify alternative proposals, to evaluate their consequences for development, and to recommend action.

In the earlier stages of the planning movement there was a strong opinion that the planning agency should be attached directly to the governing body because of the latter's concern with long-range policy making. It was argued, by Alfred Bettman among others, that this arrangement would protect planners from preoccupation with detailed administrative planning, which would come inevitably with subordination to the chief executive.[11]

Prevailing contemporary opinion, however, supports location of the planning agency within the executive branch of local government so that the recommendations of the planning staff reach the governing body as recommendations of the chief executive.[12]

Aside from this formal, though indirect, relationship between the governing body and the planning agency, much can be accomplished by encouraging informal ties and communication. In some communities, for example, the governing body has a standing committee on planning with which the director of planning is invited to confer regularly. Also in some communities the governing body is represented on the planning commission by an ex officio member.[13] These arrangements help provide liaison between council and planning agency and encourage the council to make more use of the research and coordinating facilities offered by the planning agency. At least one or two legislative members are continually informed about what the planning agency is doing and what it is competent and able to undertake. Often the planning agency can assist the governing body

in its consideration of policy matters by making special reports on their implications for long-range planning. Occasionally, it is desirable for the planning commission to hold a joint meeting with the governing body for discussion of basic planning objectives.

In some local governments the planning commission and staff have been given an almost independent policy making role in an effort to protect the comprehensive plan from presumably unwarranted and ill-advised action by an unsympathetic governing body. Thus, the governing body may be required by statute to submit proposed improvements or changes in zoning to the planning commission for recommendation; if the commission recommends disapproval, the governing body is required to follow this recommendation unless it musters a two-thirds or three-fourths majority vote to override.

If city planning is conceived of as the kind of line-staff activity outlined in these pages, however, the granting of such authority to the planning commission is decidedly inappropriate. In the long run such independent decision making power will produce antagonism and conflict between the governing body and planning commission.[14] It almost certainly will discourage a close working relationship. Also it is questionable policy to impair the decision-making responsibility of the chief executive and the governing body by delegation to a body beyond popular control.

The much sounder way to protect the integrity of the comprehensive plan is to develop close working relationships among the planning agency, the chief executive, and the governing body. Mutual confidence and respect are likely to be more effective safeguards than legal formalities.

RELATION TO COMMUNITY LEADERSHIP AND THE PUBLIC

Perhaps no other activity of government is more important to the public than urban planning. In the first place, while all persons in the community have a stake in the effectiveness of

---

[11] See discussion in Arthur W. Bromage, INTRODUCTION TO MUNICIPAL GOVERNMENT AND ADMINISTRATION (New York: Appleton-Century-Crofts, 2nd ed., 1957), pp. 401–404.

[12] See Daland, op. cit., p. 204, for an interesting suggestion that perhaps the planner should have an opportunity to present his case directly to the city council on important policy proposals when the chief executive has declined to follow his recommendations.

[13] American Society of Planning Officials, PLANNING ADVISORY REPORT No. 195: THE PLANNING COMMISSION—ITS COMPOSITION AND FUNCTION (Chicago: ASPO, 1965). This survey of 443 planning agencies reported that only 9 per cent of the commissions had legislators serving as ex officio members. Chief executive officials, however, served as ex officio members 38 per cent of the time.

[14] Donald H. Webster, URBAN PLANNING AND MUNICIPAL PUBLIC POLICY (New York: Harper and Brothers, 1958), pp. 107–108.

planning, many have particular interests that are affected by planning decisions. Private organizations of many kinds, representative of different community groups and interests, seek to press their case before official bodies. As in other areas of governmental activity, the citizen is the ultimate policy-maker, setting broad community goals and directions to guide urban growth.

But in contrast to many areas of local government policy, development is actually accomplished through countless private actions—decisions, for example, on how to use certain plots of land, what kind of building to erect, when to decide traffic is so bad that commuting to work by car should be abandoned in favor of public transport or car pools. Public planning works toward its objective of planned urban growth by attempting to influence and coordinate these private decisions. How an official planning agency acts toward the community, therefore, is most important, for this relationship may have an impact on the whole process of putting plans into effect. The objectives of this relationship are to promote public understanding of the planning process, public participation in the setting and continuing review of development goals, and public insight into the consequences of specific plans and proposals for individual interests and actions. An extensive discussion of these relationships is provided in Chapter 20.

19

The Local Planning Agency: Internal Administration

Tʜᴇ ᴜʟᴛɪᴍᴀᴛᴇ ʀᴇsᴘᴏɴsɪʙɪʟɪᴛʏ of a local planning agency is to influence actions taken upon the environment. These actions are taken by others: the local legislative body, the chief executive, the operating departments; other levels of government; the private sector— investors, builders, business, industry, institutions, families. The influence is brought to bear at various time-ranges (long, middle, short) and space-scales (metropolitan, county, city, district, project). The pay-off is at the final step of project execution, whether the project is an expressway interchange, a factory or shopping center, a transit system, a school, a house, or a rehabilitated tenement. The measure of effective local planning administration is the orchestration of all of the agency's activities for maximum influence on each of the decision-making actors.

Agency Activities

The list of working activities of the normal planning agency is a recapitulation of most of the chapters of this book. Many of the activities are mandatory—that is, they are usually imposed by statute, charter, or ordinance; others, though not so formalized, are customary and necessary. It is useful to sort out a typical list of these activities by time-range, as follows:

A. *Long-range planning* (requiring a long look ahead, from 15 to 50 years) : the

decision-makers to be influenced at this range are formally only the agency itself, but informally the community at large, including other units of local government.

1. *Mandatory activities:*

a. Preparation, review and maintenance of the "comprehensive," "general," or "master" plan, including data collection, mapping, and analysis;

b. Projection and evaluation; goal formulation; design of policies and plan;

c. Devising program for carrying the general plan into effect.

2. *Optional activities:*

a. Participation in metropolitan or regional long-range studies and planning;

b. Preparation, review and maintenance of "master plans" for special areas, neighborhoods, or communities;

c. Preparation, review and maintenance of city-wide plans for special functions, in greater detail than the general plan (e.g., system of fire stations, or of off-street parking) ;

d. Servicing of civic participation in neighborhood or city-wide planning;

e. Public education on planning problems, needs, aims, and long-range proposals.

B. *Middle-range planning* (involving actions to be decided upon now, which will take effect on the ground in from 2 to 10 years) : the decision-makers to be influenced are primarily the legislative body, and also the chief executive to the extent that he influences legislative policy; but secondarily the "power structure" of the community whose concurrence or initiative is vital to major political or economic decisions.

1. *Mandatory activities* (usually, not always) :

a. Capital improvement programming—the annual preparation of a 5- or 6-year schedule for land purchase and public investment, with recommendations on financing as well as timing, location, and character.

b. Zoning studies, both initial preparation and periodic comprehensive revision of the regulations and map, also amendments to the text of the regulations.

c. Similar initial preparation and periodic revision of subdivision standards and regulations.

d. Renewal studies, specifically participating in (but not dominating) community renewal program preparation: identification of renewal areas, determination of development standards, use changes, etc.

2. *Optional activities:*

a. Initiating or participating in the framing of other programs or systems of community action, whether governmental, civic, private-sector, or hybrid; for example a comprehensive housing program, an economic development program, a "community action" program related to poverty, discrimination, or education.

b. Involvement in policy reformulation in fields which exert impact upon the physical fabric of the community but are not specifically "physical," such as real estate taxation policy, transportation, and utility rates.

c. Involvement in formulating or drafting legislation—local or state—related to the accomplishment of local planning objectives, such as revision of a state zoning enabling act or designing of a system of architectural controls.

d. Involvement in intergovernmental cooperative relationships in middle-range programming or planning, such as transportation planning.

e. Public education again.

C. *Short-range planning* (shifting further the base of operations from the general, broad-scale, or policy-and-program level to immediate action on the ground) : the decision-makers to be influenced are to a lesser degree the legislative body in its day-to-day acts, but primarily the operating arms of local (and other) government and the "families and firms" composing the private sector.

1. *Mandatory activities:*

a. Mandatory referrals: the study and report, with recommendations (which may have legal force or may be merely advisory) , covering a wide range of immediate actions by the local legislative body or by administrative agents of the local or other government, and including most importantly:

(1) Zoning map amendments (amendments to the text of zoning or of other regulatory controls are considered "middle-range") ;

(2) Urban renewal projects;

(3) Public land acquisitions or sales;

(4) Public works projects, ranging from an express highway to a playground comfort station.

b. Subdivision control, the review and (in many states) final approval of new land subdivisions, often involving substantial discretion to require plat changes, reservations or dedication of land for recreation as well as streets, preservation of trees or natural features, etc.

c. Zoning administration, which may include review of permit applications, staff services to the board of appeals, advisory reports, and, in some states, final approval on special-permit uses or site-plan review.

d. Occasionally, advisory or even regulatory controls over "civic art"—statuary, the architecture of public buildings, the design of street furniture.

2. *Optional activities:*

a. Special projects or studies for immediate action, often undertaken by the planning agency because it contains professional skills not present elsewhere in the city hall, even though the task is properly not city planning in the pure sense; e.g., site development design for public off-street parking facilities to serve a business district, or the redesign of a state highway department's express highway project to preserve "community values."

b. Advice to the chief executive, on administrative acts, such as the timing of contracts for project plan preparation or the choice of architects for a public building; or on political acts, such as vetoes, legislative messages, or even speeches.

c. Involvement with the legislative body, such as attendance at committee hearings and council meetings, both to answer official questions and defend agency recommendations, and to develop understanding and rapport.

d. Participation in current municipal administration, such as representation on a traffic control committee or an interagency recreation coordination committee.

e. Public information and education, ranging from newsletters and displays on current programs to staff participation in civic affairs.

Organization and Allocation of Work

A basic fact of planning-agency life is that there is never enough manpower or money to do all that should be done when it should be done. The problem is to devise methods and structures which will accomplish not necessarily as much work as possible but rather as effective work as possible. This has its bearing on staff organization as well as on work-program priorities.

LINES OF AUTHORITY

Regardless of how a staff is organized, it is essential that there be clear lines of authority and responsibility. Where the agency is a department (or staff) under a commission or board, their relative roles need to be sharply drawn. The board should be limited, or should limit itself, to matters of policy and to official or major decisions. Its administrative authority should be concentrated in a single agency executive, usually the planning director. It is intolerable for a board, or any member of it, to go around its executive to give orders to a member of his staff. In line with this principle is the wisdom of designating this executive as *ex officio* board secretary; otherwise confusion is inevitable. (This set of relationships between the board and its staff head, requiring for workability a state of mutual respect and

confidence, is a strong argument to exempt the planning director from civil service tenure.)

The same kind of clarity is needed within the staff. In an agency composed largely of professional-level personnel, morale requires significant delegation of initiative and sense of responsibility, but without any sacrifice of authority or evasion of final responsibility. (Extent of initiative of course varies with job level.) In brief, a staff works best when its director shoulders the blame for any staff error which he lets get past him to the board (or the outside), but acknowledges the credit for successful units of staff work.

There may be a useful distinction between lines of administrative authority and of technical responsibility. For example, a large office may have a clerical pool or a drafting pool, members of which take their orders on the task in hand from a professional to whom they are currently and temporarily assigned, but deal with an office manager or a chief draftsman on matters of vacation schedule and the like.

FLEXIBILITY OF OPERATION

The multiplicity of the usual work program requires that there will be more units of work to be carried on concurrently than there can be divisions of the staff. This in turn requires that each division be so set up that it can carry on several tasks at the same time. This suggests clear assignments of responsibility for each task to some one person, and also a sensitivity in the current scheduling of both personnel and tasks to varying pressures for priority.

Even in an agency oriented to the long, slow future, it is impossible to foresee and to schedule emergency demands upon the agency. Therefore both staff and schedule must retain a measure of adjustability. Specifically, the staff organization must be loose enough to allow reshuffling of teams without loss of either wasted work or morale.

EFFICIENCY

In a staff of any size, a division of labor is essential to efficiency. At the most obvious level, jobs must be allocated according to skills; typists type and draftsmen draft. Even at this level of demarcation, however, there is a challenge to use each person at his highest skill, and to devise ways of rematching jobs and skills. Planning offices for many years, in their striving for professionalization, have tended to use professionally qualified personnel to perform tasks which with ingenuity could be reformulated and handed down to subprofessional personnel who are less costly and less rare. (Efforts in this direction should be actively pursued, not only by individual planning agencies but also by appropriate national organizations. Such efforts should be parallel to, but certainly not in substitution of, the strenuous efforts currently being made by planners to learn to use the computer.)

STAFF STRUCTURE

Many alternatives are available for the division of staff into groups for handling separable elements of the work program. (See Chapter 18 for full discussion of this matter.) Two are presented here, as extremes to illustrate the ways in which they impinge on the allocation of assignments and the flow of work:

1. Division by the time-scale of agency functions as spelled out in "A" above: a "long-range planning" division, perhaps backed up by or including a "research" group; a "programming" division assigned to the middle-range tasks; and a "projects" division to deal with such immediates as referrals, zoning cases, and subdivisions.

2. Division by what might be called "urban function." For example: a "land-use" division, handling long-range studies and planning, comprehensive zoning work, and individual zoning and subdivision cases; a "circulation" division, and a "community facilities" division, each similarly involved with all three of the time-ranges and the space-scales of its subject matter.

The advantages and disadvantages of these two are opposite and complementary. The first permits the long-range work to proceed, with broad perspective, unhampered by the intrusion of current routines; and it also allows the short-range operations to be handled with skill and efficiency. The second maintains a constant interplay between the long, middle, and short ranges, with illumination going both ways; it

keeps the "master plan" out of the ivory tower, and keeps the project-review out of the rut.

The first is clearly more "efficient," in maximizing the units of "product" that each man can produce—numbers of words in reports, for example.

The second offers the probability of a higher quality of product, at the potential price of a disorderly office. A further advantage is a consequence of the hard fact that planners of imagination, intellectual power, and creative ability prefer to work at the long range and often at the big scale, and get bored by a routine of project review—which nevertheless requires these very qualities in order to be done well and which, as noted at the beginning of this chapter, are to a large degree the "pay-off" of the whole planning process. The second structure-type offers a way of assuring some of the attention of such planners to each of the time-ranges, concurrently.

Programming and Budgeting

PROGRAMMING

The total program of the planning agency's activities, as outlined in the first section of this chapter, must be fitted to the agency's resources of money and personnel. Since there are never enough of either, the allocations are a matter of policy—to be determined at the policy level. This level itself varies from city to city; in the usual situation it will focus on the board or commission, with varying participation of the chief administrator or the legislative body, and with varying leadership from the planning director.

At the least, the planning director will provide technical data and advice. Very often, since the multiple elements of the planning process are not well-known to his titular superiors, he will in effect make policy by formulating his proposal and securing validation for it from his board or chief executive. (This is similar, at a different scale of municipal management, to a city manager forwarding to his city council a recommendation which, upon its approval, he then administers as the council's policy.)

In any event, the policy decisions on a planning work program are political in their nature rather than technical. To the extent that the planning director participates in these decisions, he departs from the classical role of the planner as the objective technical adviser who merely carries out the will of the client. (This myth of nonresponsible objectivity crops up, of course, throughout the entire planning process.)

Translation of a work program into a work schedule, which assigns jobs to personnel and sets time deadlines is a responsibility of the planning director (not the board). Regardless of the size of the agency, some activities will be concurrent. Of these, some will be continual, on which some work must be done or will arise each week and some will be intermittent but regular, such as the capital improvements program which requires work at the same time every year.

Other activities can be classed as consecutive: mainly elements of the long-range or middle-range type which must be undertaken one after the other and repeated only every few years. This is dictated partly by limitations of funds or staff. But it is also dictated by limitations of the intellectual capacity of the agency's client (board, mayor, council, civic group, voters) to receive, understand, and digest the complex ideas and the masses of words, numbers and drawings which constitute these products. This is a major reason why a comprehensive plan should not be completely done over oftener than every five to 10 years, leaving time between for major overhaul of the zoning ordinance, for development of a community renewal program, and for presentation and debate of other large and important programs, policies, and issues.

The technical basis for choice of emphasis in the planning program is the relative urgency of planning guidance for various phases of community development, based on study and analysis of the planning problems involved. This may distort the textbook sequence of technical operations. In an oversimplified example, a small city without a master plan may need to start building a new high school within the year; the planning agency must choose between helping select a high school site and beginning on a long-range plan. The probability is that it will do the community more good, over the long pull, to bring comprehensive planning principles and skills to bear on the school site, rather than let the school board alone and get a three-month start on the master plan.

The political basis for choice of emphasis is subtly different: it consists of the relative opportunity for effective influence upon governmental decisions and for developing a recognized usefulness, and even popularity, as a basis for continued prestige and support. Using the above example, if the school board were entrenched, politically powerful, and resentful of outside meddling, while the planning agency was new and on public trial, the wiser long-run strategy might be to let the school board make a mess of this one project and proceed toward laying a foundation for better-illuminated decisions on other development issues yet to arise. It is by no means cynical to point the parallel to the dictum that the politician's first duty is to be re-elected; since the planning agency is advisory, its first duty is to get—or keep—a position from which its advice will be heeded.

In designing a work program, the base for this meld of technical and policy decisions must be the estimates of the resources needed to perform the various alternative units of work. Any experienced planner knows that this is almost impossible, but also that it must be done. The difficulty is that methods of performing various tasks are far from standardized, and planners, still dissatisfied with their techniques, are constantly experimenting with new methods.

The cost of doing anything in a way that it has never been done before is of course difficult to estimate; the usual error is to underestimate. There is another occupational hazard: planners are prone to making optimistic guesses and then getting entangled in doing a more detailed job than they intended (every consultant who has ever contracted to perform a planning job for a fixed fee is painfully aware of this).

These difficulties of estimation are in part to blame for the tendency of planning agencies to fall months or years behind in completing some of the long-range phases of their programs. When both immediate and long-range units of work prove to take longer than expected, it is naturally the long-range tasks that get set aside in order to do now what must be done now. The delay is thus compounded.

Until planning operations become more standardized, there will be no substitute in work-program estimating for experience, not only in guessing how many man-hours of what skills a certain task will take, but also in identifying the minimum degree of detail—as, for example, in a land use survey—that will generate data adequate for its purpose but not wastefully redundant.

The finally settled-upon work program must be formulated annually as a basis for budget requests. It must be designed to permit modification, not merely after the budget is adopted (too often at a lower amount than was asked) but in the course of the year when the unexpected happens.

No rule of thumb is known as to what proportions should go to what functions; obviously there will be wide variations from place to place and time to time. Perhaps, however, it is worth reporting a judgment on the average allocations for a planning agency that is established in effective contact with the community and the rest of the government and engaged in all of the activities that make up an on-going planning program.

Taking all of the resources of the agency as 100 per cent (either manhours or dollars—these figures are not sensitive enough to distinguish a difference), probably 10 to 15 per cent goes to internal administration: correspondence, board-meeting agenda and minutes, supplies and bookkeeping, personnel records and management, attendance at council committee meetings, and the like. Another 10 to 15 per cent will go to what might be called public education (though this is not merely advertising the agency's product, rather an essential ingredient to the development and maintenance of a dialogue between the community and the planners, the consequence of which is "citizen participation").

This leaves, say, 75 per cent for the technical elements of the planning program. Referring back to the time-scale sorting of activities listed in the first section of this chapter, the long-range tasks will take about 10 per cent, occasionally 15 per cent, and rarely as much as 20 per cent. Middle-range planning may range from 25 to 35 per cent, occasionally 40 per cent. Short-range activities, then, occupy the balance—a normal 35 per cent, rarely less than 30 per cent, and often 40 per cent.

This balance, with the largest share of technical effort going into short-range effort and the smallest into long-range, is not merely a reflection of the outside pressures and demands upon the agency. It is also a fair picture of the relative importance of the three time-scales, recognizing however that each must be represented and exercising its influence upon the other two.

BUDGETING

The planning agency's budget is, of course, completely interrelated with its work program, which determines the request and then is bound by the appropriation. It is a critical point of contact between the planning agency and the official decision-makers—the city's chief administration and council. It limits what the agency can accomplish. Further, it expresses what the decision-makers want and expect from the planners. Budget policies are thus significant elements of a municipality's planning policy.

Only in the smaller and more backward cities and towns is there any longer a question of whether to spend money on planning; instead the question has become how much. There still remains, however, a too-widespread misconception about what such money is for. The federal "701" program of aid to local planning has been administered, in most states and in Washington, in such a way as to foster this misconception because such funds have been available only to finance the long- and middle-range tasks, which as was indicated above amount to only about half the total needed technical planning effort.

It is of course very true that a municipality which has never had a planning program needs an extra spurt of expenditures to get started.

But the risk has been that such inexperienced communities have not recognized the nature of this initial boost and have deluded themselves that, by buying a plan (at two-thirds off), they have assured themselves of the benefits of planning.

Thus, even in those municipalities which have not previously spent money on planning, it should be made clear to those being asked to appropriate funds that this is not a lump-sum, one-shot proposition. Of course they cannot and will not commit future appropriations. But they, and the planning agency, must recognize that this initial appropriation will have been thrown away if the activities which it finances do not succeed in earning the right to continued support.

The availability to small municipalities of "701" aid does offer great hope of accomplishing exactly this. The initial quantity of planning output is much out of proportion to the city's own dollar input. It ought to be able to establish the usefulness of planning services. But there is another pitfall. Dazzled by the two-to-one matching federal dollars, the municipalities tend to put all of these first, unknowledgeable, tentative appropriations into the 701 pot, leaving nothing to get started on the short-range planning work. Experience indicates that it is far wiser to hold out some of the local funds for meeting current and continuing planning problems even though the remainder will match fewer federal dollars and command a smaller total effort on the long-range studies.

It would be hazardous to suggest a rule of thumb for what it costs to get a city well started which has had no planning before. Not only are there great differences for different sizes and kinds of city; there are also differences in the appropriate initial mix among long, middle, and short range studies, and in the most effective strategy in speeding up or stretching out the completion of major units of work in keeping with the community's capacity to absorb the planners' output and stay on top of their progress. Before World War II, the figure commonly bandied about was $1 per capita. Inflation would at least double this. Per capita costs go down with population and up with complexity and with extended time (that

is, it costs more to spread a master plan over three years than to make the same plan in one, even though it may be much wiser to take the longer time). Thus we might risk a guess that the cost of the initial getting-started push, over and above the annual planning expenditures from the beginning henceforward, might range between $1 and $5 dollars per capita.

Rules of thumb for the annual costs of continuing planning operations are a trifle less hazardous. The American Society of Planning Officials annually reports the planning expenditures of U.S. and Canadian cities by size range. To translate these current averages into norms would require determining which of these cities is spending enough! To appraise the quality, and hence adequacy, of a local planning program requires achieving real acquaintance with the city and many interviews; this has not been systematically performed. Furthermore, some of these cities are also served by county or metropolitan planning programs, or other associated activities, while others spend all their money on planning through the reporting agency.

The reported expenditures are primarily salaries plus consultant fees; they rarely include costs of office space, employee benefits, or other overhead costs. With these cautions, Table 19–1 lists the ranges in per capita expenditures for 1964 (the most recently published tabulation), and in the last column this author's judgment of the range of median expenditures that might be "adequate" (influenced by the 10 to 15 per cent increase in planners' salary rates from 1964 to 1966).

Such figures as the above may help in defending a budget request; they are clearly not presented as a point of beginning in preparing it. By the same token the work program, which is the starting point for the budget, should itself serve as a defense. "These are things that need doing, and they will cost this much."

Almost every municipality has its own form for its budget, determined by the agency in charge of such matters, which the planning agency must follow. A typical "line-item" budget will include amounts for the following items:

1. Salaries (preferably a lump sum, some-

Table 19-1

Per Capita Expenditure Comparisons

Cities (ASPO survey): Population Class	1964 Per Capita Expenditures		"Adequate" Central Range
	Range	Median	
Over 1,000,000	.10 — .54	.26	.40 — .60
500,000 — 999,999	.19 — 1.30	.42	.50 — .75
250,000 — 499,999	.27 — 1.84	.55	.60 — .90
100,000 — 249,999	.17 — 1.80	.55	.70 — 1.10
50,000 — 99,999	.23 — 3.88	.60	.80 — 1.40
25,000 — 49,999	.06 — 2.82	.72	1.00 — 1.80
10,000 — 24,999	.06 — 2.89	1.01	1.20 — 2.30

times a list of positions and salaries).

2. Contractual services (including consultants, ASPO Planning Advisory Service, etc.).

3. Materials and supplies (paper and pencils, blueprinting, typewriter repair, perhaps also telephone and postage).

4. Publication expenses (ranging from the cost of a "public notice" in the newspaper to printing of major report).

5. Transportation (local costs such as mileage for field trips, also expenses for staff and board members to attend planning conferences).

6. Agency memberships (as in a state federation of planning agencies).

Traditionally, budget estimates, justifications, and correlative accounting controls have provided the framework for common understanding of the budgetary process. Thus in most cities and counties the budget has been considered primarily as a financial control. Departments submit expenditure estimates stated in monetary terms and documented by materials, supplies, equipment, and personnel (positions and salaries). In recent years, however, more progressive jurisdictions have begun to tie costs more specifically to work performed through the "performance budget."

In broad terms performance budgeting is a program planning process which stresses functions, activities, and projects that focus upon end results. It supplements traditional budgeting by placing more emphasis on program analysis. To do so more effort must be devoted to cost accounting and manhour records upon which more sophisticated budget estimates and justifications can be built.

For the planning agency the performance budget can be built on clearly defined categories of agency operations stated in terms of projects, programs, and end results. Staff time, both professional and nonprofessional, well may be the major cost element since materials, supplies, postage, etc., make up only a small portion of the typical planning agency budget.

Since personnel services make up most of what a planning agency can offer, time sheets will be needed for allocation of work to projects and programs. Some professionals may consider time sheets beneath their dignity, but they are essential both for internal review and for effective budget estimates and justifications.

Unfortunately the need for agency programs is usually not as clear to the appropriators as it is to the agency. A number of arguments may need to be marshaled, in explanation of these needs. The most expedient, and the most foolish even when true, is that such and such a document is required for city eligibility for such-and-such state or federal aid. Yet a number of planning programs initiated under just this cynical aegis have succeeded in earning continued support in later years.

The standard set of arguments for the long-range benefits of planning is a weary litany, yet substantially true and often effective. Though it may be regrettable to the planner as an idealist, the case for the economic benefits from planning is especially relevant when it is money that is being asked for. For example:

●Conservation or enhancement of the tax base

Protection of residential areas

Stabilization of business and industry

- Assurance of maximum return for capital expenditures
  Advance land acquisition
  Proper geographical interrelation of public works
  Sound priority schedule
  Improved quality of public services—education, etc.
- Elimination of excessive tax burdens
  Slum elimination
  Efficiency of operation of systems of public services
  Orderly development of new areas for minimum public maintenance
- Contributions to the economic base
  Encouragement of industrial development
  Prosperity of business areas
- Improvements of the safety and convenience of transportation
  Highways, transit, parking, and their interrelation
- Improvement of living conditions
  Residential neighborhood improvement
  Recreation areas
  Convenience of shopping and employment
  Amenity

In addition to these long-range generalities, shorter-range benefits can be claimed. There are aids to the efficiency or effectiveness of governmental operations, such as capital improvement programming, continuing advice on legislative and administrative referrals, and special studies and services. And there are usually specific short-range problems to be attacked in the proposed work program, such as traffic or parking bottlenecks, zoning sore spots, school location, and urban renewal.

Effective tactics for presenting and defending budget requests must differ. Most effective are proofs of genuine benefits realized from work in previous years; for example (from a real case), through its advice on the disposition of tax delinquent lots, the planning agency had saved the city more than the entire planning budget in acquiring title to needed playground sites at less than market prices. If the agency is promising future benefits to be delivered, it must have a record of fulfilling such promises in the past. If it claims citizen support for the work it proposes to do, declarations by citizen groups at budget hearings will be helpful—and it is not beneath the dignity of a planning director or board chairman to solicit such declarations.

Finally and most clearly, the advance acceptance by executive and legislative leadership of the need for the planning program, and therefore for its budget, is likely to be essential. Securing this acceptance is a political operation. This fact underlines the further fact that planning is neither above nor apart from politics. Not only in winning support for its planning proposals, but even in acquiring the resources to enable it to develop proposals, the planning agency works through political processes.

Staff Management

The previous sections have stressed the importance of continuousness of planning operations. The corollary importance of continuity of planning personnel should be obvious. In principle then, if a municipality can afford even one full-time professional employee, a permanent staff is the preferable way of procuring planning services.

Use of Consultants

Many municipalities, however, cannot, or will not, spend that much every year. A general consultant is an alternative. It is a poor alternative on a one-shot basis, but there are many consultants who offer continuing services in the full range of planning activities. For a small town, a few visits a month plus some work in the consultant's home office may meet the ongoing staff needs of the planning agency.

For the next larger class of municipality, a mix of permanent staff plus a consultant on a continuing basis may prove most efficient. A one- or two-man staff is inevitably limited; it contains no specialist. Furthermore, due to the acute shortage of planners, such a staff is often quite young and of limited experience. But if these resources are backstopped by as little as one day a month of visits by an experienced consultant, the quality of planning performance can be very high indeed.

As the city and its planning staff get larger, its composition can be enriched to include specialists and will be strengthened by including older and more experienced planners. Even in very big cities, however, there may still be a use for the consultant—if only once a year with his visit serving as the occasion for the staff to think over what it is doing and take stock of its processes and progress. An isolated group of professionals, often with no one in the city outside the planning staff who speaks their technical language, needs the intellectual stimulus of occasional informed outside attention to their activity.

Two other valid roles remain for consultants. One is to provide specialized advisory services on tasks not continuous enough to warrant a staff specialist. A familiar example is the market analyst for a particular renewal project, or the demographer for population forecasts, or the economist for economic base projections; these are advisers from related professions. Examples from within the city planning field might be the adviser on contemporary zoning techniques working with the permanent staff on a major zoning overhaul, or a specialist on planning-agency structure, procedure, and work program.

The other valid role is that of the consultant as contractor rather than purely adviser, brought in to provide supplementary staff servines for a short period to complete some big unit of work—a land use survey, for instance, or some other crash program. Consultant firms have staff resources that can be efficiently deployed in one city or another, but the permanent staff cannot be temporarily doubled and a year later cut in two. Indeed, with professional shortages what they have been and will be in the foreseeable future, even modest increases in staff take a long time for the municipality to implement.

Thus the basic principle that a locality's continuing planning services can best be provided by its own permanent salaried staff does not exclude the use of consultants, so long as the spirit of the principle is honored. The key to this spirit is that, if there is any staff at all, the technical responsibility for the planning program rests in its head—the planning director.

Consultants cannot be built into local government; their work is inevitably advisory. It follows that they should operate as advisers to the planning director and should deal with the agency through him, not directly with the board or commission. (The sole exception would be the administrative study where the director's job is one of the things being examined.)

Procedures for selecting and engaging a consultant have been well spelled out by the American Institute of Planners (reprinted in the annual membership roster of the AIP). In summary, planning consultants are professionals for whom it is unethical to bid on a job. The client should select the consultant first and then negotiate both the precise scope of the work to be done and the method and amount of payment. In view of the extreme difficulty of knowing in advance exactly how much work of what kind will prove necessary, the most flexible arrangement is the most satisfactory for both consultant and client.

PERSONNEL SELECTION

For the permanent salaried staff, most cities have standard practices for job classifications, salary rates, etc., which are uniform throughout that city's services. But they are so different from city to city that any description must be general.

Subprofessional categories are relatively uniform: secretary, stenographer, typist; senior and junior clerk; senior and junior draftsman. Professional categories are not at all uniform: Planner I, II, and III may start numbering at the top in one place and at the bottom in another. Both categories are now generally under civil service, but the methods of selection vary widely.

Methods of measuring qualifications for professional titles, however, are developing strong similarities. For the lowest professional level a college degree is normally required, and probably specified to be in a relevant field (traditionally architecture, landscape architecture, and civil engineering; now also often economics, sociology, and government). Often, and properly, relevant experience may be substituted for the college degree. An undergraduate degree, however, is clearly not a *professional* qualification. More and more jurisdictions add the requirement of a master's degree in planning, for which two or three years' planning experience may be substituted.

Fully professional status would seem to require not only advanced training but also supervised experience; this is the standard which has developed in other professions and is reflected in the membership rules of the American Institute of Planners. Appropriate terminology might call a position requiring only a bachelor's degree *pre*professional; one requiring a graduate planning degree *junior* professional; and only with the addition of two years of further planning experience would the professional steps begin.

The number of steps of course varies with the size of the staff and the complexity of its organization. No staff should have less than one professional, as just defined (when a one-man-staff agency employs a planning-school graduate with no experience, both the agency and the graduate are taking grave risks). As more people are added, more levels are reasonable, both above and below that threshold. ASPO reports as many as seven professional levels in the largest agencies. Usually the levels are differentiated by two- or three-year increments of successively more responsible planning experience; the upper-level jobs in a big agency might thus require 15 to 20 years of experience.

In an old and slowly-growing profession such prolonged experience requirements might be reasonable. In city planning, they are not. It is not only that there are too few planners to fill the job openings. It is also that there have been too many instances of relatively young planners performing competently and even brilliantly in top positions, from which such rules would have excluded them. Professional techniques and planning-school curricula are developing so rapidly that younger men are not infrequently more competent than older ones.

Such an observation makes it clear that selection criteria based solely on objectively measurable and generalized qualifications are not likely to be adequate. (It is the tragedy of the civil service movement that, for administrative and professional positions, they never have

been adequate.) In a large staff with many purely technical tasks to perform, such measures may be more valid. But in a small staff, and in those positions in a large staff involving supervision or contacts outside the agency, there are equally important qualities of personality and character that are independent of age, of training, and even of experience. It is a very rare civil service operation that is capable of identifying and weighing all these factors.

These are among the reasons why the planning director should not be under civil service (others were cited earlier in this chapter). He may nevertheless be required to have certain professional qualifications; in some cities these are specified in the city charter.

In line with the principles of staff organizations set forth previously, the planning director should be the "appointing authority" for the agency's staff, rather than the board or commission. His latitude of choice may be broad or narrow, depending on local civil service procedures. It usually consists at least of selecting any one of the top three qualified candidates. The table of organization he will be seeking to fill will in large measure be of his own making, the product of the work program translated into personnel requirements.

Salary levels are normally specified outside the agency, by the legislative body or some special board. For planners these levels result from the interaction of local practices, and rates set for other professional personnel, the national supply, and the highly competitive market. The base rate is perhaps the salary offered a freshly graduated master's degree recipient with no experience save of a summer internship; this rate has risen about $300 per year for the past decade, and in 1966 hovered around $8,000 (with regional variations up and down).

In the light of this inflationary spiral, the serious problem has been to increase the rates of more senior professionals to keep ahead of the newcomers. No valid rules of thumb can prescribe increases due both to merit and seniority. The ceiling of course is probably the salary of the planning director which in turn depends on his status in the municipal hierarchy. ASPO reports for 1964 a range of medians for planning directors of about $9,500 for the smallest size-class of cities up to $20,000 for the largest.

PERSONNEL PRACTICES

Regulations dealing with vacations, sick leave, and holidays are normally set by civil service or administrative order for the entire governmental work-force; the planning agency must conform. Daily working hours are similarly uniform, but may present morale problems between the planning office and others in the municipal building if the planning professionals—who often must attend several evening meetings every week—come late in the morning or take long lunch hours in informal compensation. This can create morale problems with clerical and drafting personnel also.

One way of handling this problem is to formalize such "compensatory time off" (since the payment of overtime is usually not the practice). If someone, probably a clerk, keeps track of these occasions, they will be understood and not abused.

The other way is for professional personnel to accept the fact that theirs is not a 35- or 40-hour week, and that their salary rates already reflect the probability of overtime. Indeed, clock-watching is not characteristic of responsible professionals in any field. Although a fair-minded planning director may set up a compensatory-time-off system, he will probably find that none of his better staff take advantage of it.

Concern with matters such as these is not merely a matter of office and interoffice morale, even though this is important to the working capacity of a planning agency. In calculating how long a major task will take, it is necessary to realize that between 10 and 15 per cent of each staff-member's "work year" is legitimately spent in vacation, holiday, or sick-time. A "manyear" available to produce work is much less than 7 or 8 hours times 5 days times 52 weeks.

A further inroad upon "productive" time which is not merely legitimate but highly desirable is time devoted to staff activities and in-service training. One productive practice is the staff meeting. For a staff of any size—say,

larger than three or four—regular meetings of the entire staff may be effective, perhaps one hour each week or two hours every other week. Routine matters of office operation may benefit from these opportunities for democratic discussion.

Even more important, especially for the morale of the nonprofessional staff, is the inclusion of substantive discussion of work in progress, as a builder of job understanding. In a staff with several divisions, devoting each meeting to the work of one division or subdivision fosters an awareness of the interactions of all the elements of the planning process that is not likely to be accomplished otherwise. This contributes to the technical efficiency of each subgroup and also puts all of the staff in a position to talk intelligently to outsiders (in the city hall or elsewhere) about an operation not too widely understood.

Another kind of staff-meeting, essential in the larger offices, is the weekly conference of supervisory staff which is similarly necessary for substantive technical collaboration and also essential for job scheduling, office operation, and handling personnel problems. As little as a half-hour every week on the same day at the same time works far better than longer sessions spread further apart.

Staff meetings are a form of in-service training, providing not only gains in knowledge, skill, and morale but also experience in speaking and in leading group discussions. For individual staff members there are many other opportunities which an unimaginative planning director may not grasp. His assignment of jobs to people is one of these. It is wise to assign responsibilities which stretch competence; the gains in development of new skills and of loyalties to the work overbalance the costs in increased supervisory vigilance and in occasional failures. Job rotation from one staff division to another is another practice where the loss in short-term efficiency is exceeded by the gains in skill, worth, and morale.

There is also training through attendance and participation in nonstaff meetings, which give a chance to observe the impact of staff work upon outside people. This may need to be selective; if an entire staff comes to sit in the back row during every planning-commission meeting, the commission will consider this a waste of the budget (if the meeting is during working hours). But there is every reason for the staff group that has worked for weeks on a given project to assist in its presentation to the commission, an official public hearing, or a city council meeting. Here again, this is not merely a morale-builder. It is an invaluable opportunity for the technical crew to learn how the consumers of their product react.

Finally there is the training opportunity of attending and participating in professional groups and meetings, whether in the locality, or at regional or national conferences. These are the occasions for updating professional knowledge and techniques, whether through such annual programs as ASPO and AIP, or through the all-too-rare special course (as, for example, in electronic data processing). Increasingly public agencies are recognizing the value of these kinds of activities, to the extent of paying tuition for special courses or transportation to national conferences. At the least, it is recognized that attendance at such conferences is job-related and should not be taken out of a staff member's vacation.

PERSONNEL RESPONSIBILITIES

In return for fair and enlightened treatment by the agency and its executive head, the staff member owes certain responsibilities to the office (which are not at all unique to planning agencies). These include, of course, reasonable levels of courtesy, toward supervisors, fellow-workers, and outsiders, which are necessary to the smooth running of any group. (Even more necessary is courtesy of supervisors toward subordinates; you thank a stenographer when she puts on your desk the typing she is paid to do for you.) Promptness, diligence, consistency on the job, ample warning of necessary absences from work—these are all routine principles.

The handling of complaints is also a problem in any office with more than a few people. Complaints should come privately, directly, and freely to an immediate supervisor, or if the complaint is about him, to his supervisor. The staff should be aware of the right to complain, and do it responsibly. The need is to minimize griping without loss of constructive criticism.

The temptation for municipal professional employees to take on "outside" work is perhaps greater in planning offices than in others because of the shortage of planning professionals. In view, however, of the essentially fulltime commitment of a planning agency's professional personnel, a regular and steady outside job is clearly unfair. Occasional weekend or evening work may be acceptable; the first requirement is that it be undertaken only with the advance knowledge and consent of the planning director (or, in his own case, of the commission and perhaps also the chief administrator).

Certain types of outside jobs are nevertheless beyond the pale. These are the ones where conflict of interest appears, either in fact or (and this is just as important) where anyone from a disgruntled citizen to an opposition newspaper reporter might even *suspect* a conflict. An extreme and obviously intolerable case would be a staff planner designing a subdivision which would later be officially reviewed by his planning agency. Almost equally obnoxious would be to design a subdivision in an adjoining municipality for a developer who also operates in one's own municipality.

A safe approach might be that a planner employed by a public agency would only do professional work for some parallel public agency, and then only when there is no possible connection or conflict of the interests of the two agencies. Serving as an expert witness in a court case in behalf of the zoning ordinance of a nearby town would probably be "safe." Advising that town on a zoning-map amendment of land that adjoins your own town might not.

Beyond these potential conflicts is a professional responsibility not to compete unfairly with fellow professionals in private practice. A planner with a fulltime salary and civil-service status is in a position to charge less for his marginal time than a consultant, who has office overhead to cover, must charge for his prime time. The ethical requirements are clear; professionals do not compete with each other on the basis of price.

A further responsibility that besets the professional planning staff member, especially in periods of personnel shortages, relates to changing jobs from one agency or one city to another. There is some minimum time that a planner should stay in one job, both so that he may get the greatest personal advantage of added experience and skill, and so that he may treat fairly his employer—in view of the salary spent during his initial training period when he is probably not worth it. Planning agency work requires this period of acculturation and breaking in, probably more than most other professions, since acquaintance with a unique community must be acquired as well as familiarization with local technical procedures. This minimum time on the job increases with the responsibility level. For the master's degree holder with no experience, it is at least one year. For the planning director, it is perhaps at least six years (maybe four for very small cities and eight for very large ones). The intervening levels can be interpolated.

When the time to change jobs does arrive, either to seek a different type of experience or because the way up the ladder is blocked, the first responsibility is to advise the planning director of the intention. (It is his professional responsibility, in turn, to take the news gracefully and even to help locate the right next job). Adequate notice of departure, once the new commitment has been made, is essential and also varies with job level. At the lower professional levels, a month is the minimum. For top positions, it is not unreasonable to expect two or three months' notice.

For most professional employments, references are necessary. It is courteous to get advance permission from anyone whose name is to be submitted as a reference. One's immediate past supervisor is the reference most valued by a prospective employer; this is reason enough to seek his advance sympathy for the intent to change jobs.

There are of course circumstances in which personality conflicts or local crises cancel all rules about minimum time in one job and consent of the boss. These may range from the sheer incompatibility of two otherwise splendid people, to ethical conflicts in which resigning, perhaps noisily, is the only honorable course. Future employers may regard such an event in one's experience record as an asset rather than a liability. But a record which lists a series of job stands of a year or less immediately arouses suspicion of personal or professional responsibility.

Office Procedures

It would not be appropriate to try to compress into this part of the chapter a manual of office procedures common to all kinds of offices; what follows is an attempt to deal with matters somewhat special to planning agency offices throughout the country.

CORRESPONDENCE

Since a planning agency achieves its effectiveness largely through persuasion, it is dependent to an unusual degree on all its points of contact with the community and the rest of municipal government. But a planning staff is also likely to have a large proportion of professional personnel, each in a special position of expertise on some class of planning matters. Thus the urgency of prompt (and courteous) response to correspondence is in conflict with the probability of a scatter of sources of informed response. This suggests the desirability of a clearly-understood routine of sorting and routing for attention, performed by someone with some knowledge of the substance of the agency's work; along with a clearly agreed-upon pattern of who is to answer what kinds of inquiry, with what discretion to use initiative or seek higher approval. It also suggests the need to route inquiries (and their answers) to several other staff groups for information prior to filing.

The further problem is that, with several responsible professionals on hand, they tend for personal convenience to build up separate files on matters they have dealt with. There is, however, a strong case for having only one central file for all correspondence, because of the interrelatedness of subject-matters of the various staff sections. The need for individual files can be met through extra carbons of replies, plus photocopies of original letters where needed.

INFORMATIONAL MATERIAL

Every planning agency receives much printed material—reports, pamphlets, periodicals—of varying value and interest. Here again, some knowledgeable person must act as "librarian," with a routine for initial sorting and selective routing to staff members. The need to be on the list (say, for ASPO Planning Advisory Service reports) must be balanced by the responsibility to scan material promptly and to pass it on. The waste of staff time in plowing through stacks of material must be balanced against the "need to know." The librarian may have to be authorized to periodically scavenge through desk-piles to speed items to a central library.

Perhaps the most important quality to cultivate is that of selective disposal. Much of what comes in should be thrown away before reading; much of the rest should be discarded after staff scanning. Of the material of permanent value, perhaps the appropriate destination of a further large proportion is the public library (municipal reference branch, if any). The planning agency should retain in its own office only essential reference material that will be used. Again, the only workable system is a central reference collection, in charge of one person who can find items on request.

RECORDS

A municipal planning agency is a part of government. Many of its records are of legal significance, and their form and preciseness are of potential importance; zoning cases, for example, have been won or lost in court actions as a result of careless official record-keeping.

The most important class of records is probably the official minutes of planning commission meetings. They should be faithfully prepared by the secretary of the commission—normally the planning director acting ex officio—from the meeting agenda and his notes, supplemented by a stenographic transcript only when essential. It is the practice of some agencies to record a verbatim transcript of the entire proceedings, but this is rarely desirable. Such a substantial cost could better be spent in other ways.

Minutes should be as brief as is consistent with an adequate record of official action, including:

Call to order, roll call, and legitimization (regularly scheduled, or if special, record of due notice);

Roll call votes on each motion, unless unanimous;

Approval of prior minutes (perhaps after correction);

Identification of motions for all official acts by serial number (e.g., 1963–26), except for procedural motions (e.g., approval of minutes, adjournment);

Inclusion of summary of discussion only where necessary for explanation of action;

Inclusion of official reports by reference (e.g., "attached hereto as Exhibit B").

The officially recorded minutes, after review, correction, and formal approval, should be checked and attested by the secretary, signed by the presiding officer, and preserved in an official file-book.

Another form of record is an official plan as required by statute, charter, or ordinance. In earlier days this may have been one or more map-drawings; currently it may include substantial text in the form of statements of policy, descriptions of proposals, and verbal and numerical statements of standards. In U.S. planning practice there is colossal confusion in most published "master-plan" reports as to what is the "plan" and what is the supporting documentation and propaganda.

It is urgently recommended that the "plan" which is formally adopted, in whatever combination of maps, words, and numbers, be clearly separated from the other materials, be stated in brief and formal language similar to that of statutes and ordinances, and be acted upon independently of the published report, with all the appropriate dates, signatures, and incorporation into official minutes.

Further actions required by statute, charter, or ordinance include official agency reports to legislative or executive agencies—as on mandatory referrals or on an urban renewal project. These reports again will at some stage be incorporated in the minutes of a meeting. They should be in a relatively standard form, stating the date and nature of the action and the reasons for the action, worded as briefly as possible. The objectives of the form and content are two: first, to persuade the recipient of the report to follow its advice; second, to satisfy the judge (who may review less than 1 per cent of all such reports, but one never knows which 1 per cent) that the action recommended is legal and reasonable.

Other official acts and records include, for example, plat endorsements, endorsements on pending legislation, and endorsements on plans by other agencies requiring planning agency approval. Here, too, scrupulous adherence to legal forms is essential. Missing a date of action by one day may deprive the planning agency of its influence.

PUBLICATIONS AND MAPS

Communication is the essence of the planning agency's exercise of its function of influencing the actions and decisions of others. It must communicate effectively with a variety of receivers to accomplish its purposes. The previous section dealt with formal official communications. Whether in words or maps and drawings, the emphasis is necessarily upon precision, at a possible sacrifice of ease of reading.

At the other end of the scale are internal references—messages either to the present or to future staff. Here the material, verbal or graphic, is designed for easy technical use, without polish. Much of a planning agency's files are filled with this sort of material: memos, tables, data maps, plan studies.

Intermediate are display materials, whether reports or graphic displays. These fall into two rough groups: "official" display, for use at agency meetings and public hearings, designed to tell a clear story, but semi-technical; and "popular" display, for purely educational use, designed for attractiveness and attention, and non-technical. These are essential elements of Chapter 20.

Agency Meetings

The meetings of the planning board or commission are the ceremonial culmination of the work of the agency. They may also constitute a substantive part of the total process of influencing the community, by performing an educational as well as a legal function. The latter, however, must govern much of the superficially meaningless ritual discussed below. The requirements of legal procedure are by no means meaningless; they are a part of the cumbersome but necessary apparatus by which we protect ourselves from arbitrary, corrupt, or tyrannical treatment by our government.

SCHEDULE OF MEETINGS

Official actions may be taken only at formal meetings, either regular or special. The time and place must be made public in advance to assure minority members of the board of their right to be present as well as to permit citizen surveillance. Regular meetings under a published schedule may not call for separate public notice; their frequency will be determined by the workload. Few active agencies can get along with less than semimonthly meetings. The time of day and week will be set by the convenience of members and other officials (central-city boards usually meet during working hours, suburban boards in the evening). The place should be a public building.

Special meetings may be necessary for the conduct of emergency official business, but should be kept to a minimum. An elaborate system of notice to individual members and to the public is normally required. In addition to meeting the legal forms, informal telephoned checks and reminders may be necessary to assure a quorum.

Unofficial meetings for informal and off-the-record discussions may be essential to the education of the board and also to the morale of the staff, much of whose intellectual activity receives scant attention in the press of official business meetings. There is nothing clandestine or unethical about such private sessions, so long as no formal actions are taken. They are approximately equivalent to the caucuses which are essential to the operation of a legislative body.

PREPARATION FOR MEETINGS

The order of business at formal meetings is usually set by adopted rules of procedure or by-laws;[1] it is helpful to have such rules established in advance of the specific problem-situation which occasionally crops up. The substance of the meetings, however, is set by the agenda,[2] prepared by the planning director in his role as ex officio secretary (this function, indeed, is the main reason for combining the two roles).

It is important for efficient conduct of meetings that the agenda reach the members in advance, accompanied by such staff reports and draft resolutions that each member can be familiar with the matters to be acted upon. It is a poorly-run staff which cannot provide its board with the technical background necessary for action a few days ahead of every meeting. It is also inevitable, however, that late items will come in requiring emergency action; rules and schedules should anticipate and provide for this.

The extent of advance distribution of agenda will vary with local custom and government structure. If, for example, the city manager always attends planning agency meetings, he should know what is coming up. The press should also be informed, but should not receive advance copies of staff recommendations; the staff reports to its commission, which is entitled to receive its reports before anyone else. This is not merely mannerly, but practical; it is awkward for a board member to be telephoned by a reporter for an opinion on a staff report he has not seen.

Conduct of Meetings

The main problem on *official* meetings is whether they should be open to the public or in executive session. In many states the law requires public meetings. Even where it does not, it is sound practice, both for the educational value of public attendance and for the development of public confidence. These factors override the alternative advantages of free discussion which can be accomplished at informal meetings or in the rare executive session allowed for settlement of personnel or budget matters.

If the public is present, however, it is there to listen. It is not to take part unless the board considers it desirable (as it often will) to convert a part of its meeting formally or informally into a public hearing. In most sizes of cities, agency meetings will benefit by a large measure of informality, including a readiness to juggle the order of agenda items in order to deal first with matters of special interest to citizens or officials in attendance, and to encourage them to ask questions or make statements.

This informality, however, must not and need not interfere with meticulous adherence to the rules on any matter of official action, such as the presence of a quorum and the expression of the required majority on any substantive or procedural motion.

Public Hearings

On many matters of official action, holding a public hearing by the agency is a legal requirement. The letter as well as the spirit of applicable rules must be adhered to: public notice, a fair hearing of all sides, and a proper record of the hearing. Rules differ on whether the whole board must hold the hearing, or whether a committee may conduct it. When possible, the time and place of hearings should be set for the convenience of that part of the public most interested in the topic.

A purely pro forma hearing may meet the rules, but it may seriously damage the agency's reputation and thus its effectiveness. On a matter of any complexity, merely inviting statements from those for and against is not enough. A recommended procedure is to begin with a staff presentation of the matter to be heard, with such displays as may be helpful, followed by a question period to be sure those present understand the issue. This preliminary may well satisfy some of those who come to protest only because they misunderstand. Only after this should arguments be invited, usually first those in favor, then those opposed, then opportunities for rebuttal and counter-rebuttal.

There will be obvious differences between hearings on matters initiated by the agency—a comprehensive plan, a zoning revision—and

---

[1] For a sample set of by-laws, see Appendix.

[2] For a sample order of business at meetings, see Section 6 of the by-laws in the Appendix.

those on matters brought forth by others—a subdivision plat, a zoning map change. The difference in the agency's role should be made clear to the public.

A strong and tactful chairman is a necessity for a successful hearing in order to preserve a sense (as well as a reality) of impartiality in fair allotments of time to both sides, and to convey an attitude of receptivity to comment and encouragement of public participation. Well handled by the chairman and the staff, a potentially controversial hearing may be exploited to accomplish a major measure of public education and to build not only understanding but also good will.

This of course is equally true of unofficial public hearings, not legally required but held specifically to educate both the public and the planning agency. This kind of meeting is more appropriately a topic for Chapter 20 and is covered there.

COMMITTEES OF THE BOARD

The usefulness of committees varies with the size of the planning board; a five-man commission is probably too small for effective subdivision. Even with a large board, committees should be used sparingly in matters of technical substance. The essence of a collegial body is that it acts as a whole; delegation of authority or attention to different parts of the board on different elements of planning may lead to a lack of regard for the integrity of the agency.

A few standing committees on procedural matters may prove useful, meeting perhaps only a few times a year for special attention to such topics as personnel practices or budget and finance. Where the law allows public hearings to be held by a committee, this may be a way to relieve time-pressures on the entire board, for example when there are many zoning map amendments resulting from property-owner initiatives.

Occasionally an ad hoc committee may be useful when a particular matter is of special interest to a few of the board; an example might be a civic-center study which could benefit from the attention of architect board-members. In general, however, a board substructure which results in a few board members working with a small group within the staff tends to weaken the concentration of technical responsibility in the planning director and fragments his supervisory authority.

Conclusion

This chapter has sought to present the various processes and practices within the planning agency which contribute to the effective impact of its technical work. Smooth internal operation and know-how in intracity-hall political behavior are not substitutes for sound technical practices, creativity in design or in policy formulation, or skill in devising workable control devices and developmental programs. But the latter may turn out to be futile academic exercises or disastrous disappointments unless there is equal skill in the administration of that complex governmental function, the planning process.

20

Planning and
the Public

LOCAL PLANNING, although basically a technical process, depends in large part for its effectiveness on the attention paid to its relations with the public. To some, the work of planning at times seems to be nine-tenths public relations and "Madison Avenue stuff." This is not so, as the earlier chapters prove, but it is true that many valid and sound plans have died at birth only because of the way in which they were delivered. The presentation of plans, the communication of planning ideas, the education of people concerned with specific problems—all these are aspects of the relations of both the local planning agency and the planner with the public. The public itself is varied and includes the legislative body, the press, citizen groups, and the individuals and families affected by planning proposals.

Public relations for planning cannot afford to be the kind of one-way street literally exemplified by Madison Avenue in New York, where a heavy volume of loaded vehicles engulfs the passing citizen. Neither can it be a divided highway, with the two sides separated by an open space void. Rather it usually is a less direct route, with more than its share of obstacles, where the traffic of planners and the public frequently mixes, mingles, and turns. On such a route, speed can only be attained if there is clear sight distance ahead.

This chapter has dual functions, and the presentation reflects the dichotomy. The early sections look at some of the ways in which

planning affects people, both within the context of government and as occupants of residential areas. The attempt here is to review and clarify basic principles for dealing with citizens of the community in situations where they make contact with professional planning agencies and individuals.

Subsequent sections then relate how people learn about plans and development proposals and discuss sources and techniques for improved communications between planner and public. These sections are cast in the format of a practical guide to the participants. Caveats, rules, and aids are specified that are of direct interest to the process of interaction.

How Planning Affects People

The majority of people in a typical American community pay little attention to what their local planning agencies are doing—until they are affected personally. Publication of a comprehensive plan or an extensive renewal proposal might give rise to feelings of civic pride in some cases or concern over cost and taxes in others, but only on the part of people already aware and intellectually primed to think in such terms of the overall community interest. Publication of a detailed project plan or a plat for the condemnation of properties, however, customarily brings out surprisingly articulate "ordinary people" to defend their own homes and businesses. This is of course an oversimplification, but suggests the range of feelings and outward interests displayed when planning meets the public.

To begin to understand the ever-expanding role of planning in relation to the public we need to look in some detail at the impact of plans upon people, the constraints which our constitutional and political systems place upon public planning and citizen action, and the way in which groups work in a small area unit, such as the neighborhood, where the dimensions of physical change and human relocation can be seen and felt.

THE IMPACT OF PLANS ON PEOPLE

Some educators feel that it is essential for anyone intending to become an architect to spend a period of time as an apprentice on actual building construction work, so that he will acquire a "feel" and appreciation for the bricks and wood and metal used in creating structures of the sort he will later design. Those architects who have had such an internship period are said to be more sympathetic to design potentials of materials and more realistic in working out details of building design. There should be some comparable internship in the education of a city planner, some means of giving him an intimate understanding of the materials *he* has to work with. These materials are not just streets and buildings and systems of services, but they are people as well—people who live under a wide variety of conditions. A planner's education ought to include exposure to the ways of life and attitudes of mind of the whole range of peoples he is to serve in his future plan-making. Empathy for those affected by planning proposals can contribute greatly to the success of planning.

It will be helpful in the next few paragraphs to look at the city planning process, master plans, and project proposals from the point of view of the clientele—the individuals, families, or groups on whom such plans might have an impact. For the sake of posing issues sharply, it is assumed that the drastic steps of clearing buildings and relocating the occupants may be anticipated in a given situation.

The Individual or Family. The 1960 census showed that almost one-fifth of the people in the United States had changed homes within the 12-month period before the census date. This implies that the average family moves once in five years and suggests that periodic relocation might be taken in stride. But such is not the case; few families are average, and fewer still are receptive to involuntary removal. Planners and municipal officials customarily find problems of relocation compounded by the coincidence of disadvantaged and undereducated residents in areas of blight which call for planning attention. Their patience and skills are then put to a real test in presenting ideas and explaining the planning proposals. It is frequently not as important to be *understood* as it is *not* to be *misunderstood*.

It is difficult for the individual faced with the shock of news that his home is to be taken from him to be objective, and it matters little that the proposal is long-range if the news of it is immediate. Efforts are needed therefore to develop among those likely to be affected by planning proposals, a sense of participation in development of the plans, as well as a sense of confidence in the planners who are attempting to solve the problems of the area and its people.

In the drafting room of one of the larger city planning agencies there is a printed motto posted conspicuously on the wall, reading "If you don't understand it, OPPOSE IT!" Consciously or not, most individual citizens follow such advice. The best way of avoiding opposition is through the fostering of understanding, using all the techniques described later in this chapter.

The Businessman. The merchant or small businessman involved in relocation can usually be relied on for a reaction similar to that of an individual homeowner, but with greater intensity of feeling. He has worked for and invested in the business he operates, and not only has more at stake in terms of dollars and people, but is also accustomed to action in the hard world of reality. He may therefore act more aggressively and with somewhat greater know-how than a working class homeowner in response to planning proposals. Whether the enforced change which faces him will be regarded as disaster or as opportunity depends on the individual circumstances of his business at the time. Many retail and service activities located in areas of transition or blight are fragile and marginal ones with limited resources but with varying potentials. Careful planning would call for detailed working-out of problems on a case-by-case basis, with interviews to determine the circumstances and plans of each business operation. But this is frequently not practical and is time-consuming. Recognition that "time is money" in the business realm is prerequisite to effective planning for commercial relocation. The success of most business operations depends on the continuity of their growth. The timing of any disruption of that continuity is critical.

The Social Group. A wide range of social organizations can be found in almost every community. These form an important vehicle not only for informing people, but also in shaping opinion and in taking action. Church clubs, school associations, lodges, service clubs, political groups, and other organizations are likely to "get into the act" in varied ways during the planning and public consideration of a particular project. For the most part, their group views should be broader than those of the individual. Groups operate through their leadership, however, and it is wise to have some grasp of the extent to which democracy prevails within a particular group.

Because it takes time to gather and to agree, the group response to a planning proposal is often slower than that of individuals. For the planner, the social group structure of a community represents a very effective channel for getting information to (and also from) the people, through the leadership in whom they have demonstrated confidence. Special efforts to reach and hear from heads of local groups are warranted throughout the process of planning and execution of projects.[1]

The Community at Large. It almost goes without saying that our planning proposal or project is for the long-range good of the entire community. This broad view is often not stated clearly enough to reach the people directly affected. The upgrading of facilities and the improved economic or social opportunities which are the aims of the plan, must be brought out in down-to-earth terms and supported by respected spokesmen for the entire community. In these efforts it is especially useful to understand the nature of public opinion and how it interacts through community groups—both unstructured and institutionalized.

PLANNING IN THE POLITICAL SYSTEM

The function of city planning as we know it today is of relatively recent origin. It has evolved essentially within the past fifty years. However, its character can be traced to the basic tenets established by the "founding fathers" of this nation. Basic to this concept is the vital role of the individual in relation to state power. The "channel" for the individual remains carefully preserved and protected within the constitutional framework. Use of this channel is not automatic, however, but dependent upon the individual's willingness to utilize it through various forms of participation in the process of government.

In view of the fact that societal needs and conditions are constantly changing, and that planning is in fact a "continuing process," the planner must be able to evaluate and judge certain long-range needs and objectives in relation to the total community background. Part of this strategy includes periodic review and evaluation of priorities, including immediate and intermediate objectives, against this complex and changing pattern of interests and events.

Americans are proud of their democratic heritage, stemming from the "Town Hall" meetings which brought citizens directly face to face with their elected officials and provided opportunities for direct discussion of many of the problems of the day. Today, by contrast, the lethargy and apathy of the American people with respect to their own participation in government is the despair of many, including the politician himself.

During presidential election years, it is difficult to arouse more than half of the potential

---

[1] For further background on community groups, see Chapter 8, "Community Group Relationships," in MUNICIPAL PUBLIC RELATIONS (Chicago: International City Managers Association, 1966).

voters to go to the polls. In off-year elections, and in many local elections, it is difficult to get more than one-fourth of the potential voters to the polls. In the latter instance, it means that one-eighth of the voters decide the destiny of all. How many of these voters are adequately informed of the issues is another question of serious concern.

Former Commissioner Studebaker, of the United States Office of Education, expressed the primary purpose and concern of his office as striving to achieve "an informed citizenry." Doubtless, this has been the ideal of every city planner with respect to achieving adequate understanding, support, and active citizen involvement within the broad planning process.

Whether, or by what means, the planner can achieve the goal of an informed citizenry should be a secondary issue, as compared to the primary objective of first stating and seeking that goal. The mechanics and complexities of achieving such a goal are discussed later.

Part of our dilemma lies in the fact that the small New England town is no longer representative of the American urban settlement, as most Americans now live in megalopolitan centers characterized by sprawl and anomie. Previously, each citizen could be represented by a significant fraction, or ratio, of one elected representative to a few hundred or a thousand persons. Today, his fractional representation is in the order of one to several hundred thousand. Therefore, he feels lost, helpless, and insignificant from the standpoint of numerical strength, as well as overwhelmed by many complex problems of which he has no technical knowledge or time and special interest to investigate for himself. His isolated or insignificant protest against, or support for, an issue is of little avail, as compared to that of a large delegation.

On the other hand, the fact that planning is firmly established as an integral part of the local governmental structure, and that planning issues have become a part of the political arena in its highest sense, means that the *planner* must become involved in advocating matters of civic improvement and reform, which places him squarely in the political mainstream.

Today we find that the federal government, through the enactment of the Congress, charges each community seeking federal financial assistance under programs of the Department of Housing and Urban Development to meet certain eligibility requirements. These include filing an annual report of progress on a Workable Program of Community Improvement, incorporating an element of citizen participation. This is a must, insofar as federal requirements are concerned. However, to what degree this element is effectively carried out at the local level varies considerably. The federal government at least keeps prodding along important lines which affect the democratic health of each community involved.

It is likewise interesting to note that the National Municipal League makes an annual All-America award to a group of cities which have demonstrated outstanding achievement on civic improvements or reform that involve citizen participation.

Thus, while increasing urbanization and technical complexity are working toward making true citizen-involvement in government more difficult to achieve, many other factors are reaffirming the need for increasing participation of the public in planning.

PLANNING AT THE NEIGHBORHOOD LEVEL

Planning theory has always advocated active citizen participation. No city has yet measured up to its responsibilities in achieving overall citizen participation. Nevertheless, planning theory remains sound from the standpoint of requiring that the large communities be broken down into manageable planning areas, hitherto referred to principally as "neighborhood units." This is an important part of planning theory which has found almost universal acceptance as the service district for neighborhood facilities such as the elementary school, the park and playground, and the neighborhood shopping center, all within convenient and safe walking distance of residential areas. However, of equal importance, but subdued in recent years, was part of the original concept for providing a basis for *citizen participation* which would be meaningful to individuals at the neighborhood level. Therefore, for this purpose, we should like to review the original concept of the neighborhood, with particular reference to its potentiality for fostering genuine citizen participation.

The so-called Neighborhood Theory in city planning is generally credited to Clarence A. Perry whose hypothesis was outlined in detail in the New York Regional Plan series, *Neighborhood and Community Planning*,[2] in 1929. The essence of this concept was also included in his book *Housing for the Machine Age*,[3] in 1939.

The value of the neighborhood concept was not primarily in meeting the professional planner's need for smaller statistical areas, or in having a more functional and efficient service area for the physical arrangement of streets, utilities, and building layout, but in providing a focal point for a feasible program for bringing people together to discuss local problems of mutual concern. The underlying presumption was that citizen action and involvement could only be generated on the basis of enlightened self-interest and a mutuality of concern at the level of the small community (neighborhood).

It is interesting to note that Perry's original concept, based upon the need for "neighboring," only later became a lever for systematizing public works within defined service areas. Space standards and the basic units needed to provide various types of public works will continue to change, with changes in technology and in patterns of living, but the fundamental need for neighboring (community and communicating) endures. This has become one of the vital elements in the rebuilding process which characterizes urban renewal in residential areas.

The neighborhood concept was described as an ideal-sized elementary school district area, bounded by major thoroughfares, rather than intersected by them, and within a convenient walking distance of the elementary school building situated upon a common green (neighborhood park and playground) which

would become the community center and focal point of neighborhood activity. It was not designed to reproduce the New England town concept, but to recognize a fundamental limitation concerning the size of an area and the number of people who could effectively get together and actively participate in matters that affected them individually and as neighbors. The mere fact of recognition of the public school as the "meeting house" transcended the divisions and limitations posed by possible alternatives such as churches, lodges, and other organizations of limited membership. Simply stated, if citizens were to get together to discuss problems of common concern, they must have a convenient and acceptable meeting place. If through their discussions they could arrive at a consensus of opinion, or a course of action on a particular problem, they would have communicated, a degree of community spirit would have been generated, and an *esprit de corps* would bind them together for group action.

Prior to the 1920s the possibility of public controls and restraints, as well as long-range planning concepts, was virtually unheard of. (Today, of course, many cities are trying to put on the "harness" of controls and planning for the first time, to cope with the welter of ungoverned private decisions that have created problems of sprawl, congestion, and deterioration. This can be done effectively through adequate communication and education by the planner with the public.)

It was within the general context of this early situation that Clarence Perry spelled out the need for citizen participation at the local neighborhood level. He was also concerned about the anonymity which many people preferred, as well as with the growing laxity and apathy which were manifest, in regard to matters of civic interest and responsibility, particularly toward achieving and maintaining sound dwelling units and a wholesome neighborhood environment. The absence of such interest was reflected in the lack of adequate building maintenance and the gradual but inevitable deterioration of neighborhood facilities, which in turn led to the deterioration of property values and the eventual necessity for the public

[2] Clarence Arthur Perry, NEIGHBORHOOD AND COMMUNITY PLANNING, Vol. VII of Regional Survey of New York and Its Environs (New York: Regional Plan of New York and Its Environs, 1929).

[3] Clarence Arthur Perry, HOUSING FOR THE MACHINE AGE (New York: Russell Sage Foundation, 1939).

to undertake expensive slum clearance and blight elimination projects.

He reasoned that the school could function as the neighborhood center for a local civic improvement association to study its special neighborhood problems and to determine a course of action based upon a consensus of opinion. In other words, was it not possible to re-instill a neighborhood spirit whereby local interests could become genuinely concerned about the needs of their own particular area? In fact, could not various types of competitive improvements between neighborhoods foster goodwill and interest on a city-wide basis for *community* betterment, based upon factual information and understanding, and upon enlightened self-interest?

The introduction to *Neighborhood and Community Planning* makes reference to Emerson's *Essay on History,* wherein Emerson comments on the differences between men being essentially in their patterns of association. Perry notes as a corollary to this idea that perhaps the difference between neighborhoods and communities is based primarily upon the kind of association, or lack thereof, which occurs between residents of a particular area, namely upon citizen participation.

John Dewey wrote that there is more than a mere verbal connection between the words "community," "common," and "communication." He has expressed the thought that people come to have things in common, or a common understanding, as a result of communication.

In the same vein, Dr. Louis Wirth, noted sociologist and planner, stated:

I understand 'community' not as an arbitrary political unit like a city, county or state; I mean rather a concert of people, of interests, and functions that cannot be thought of separately. A community is any group whose problems, if they can be solved at all, can best be solved by the participation of all who have common objectives and have agreed to pursue them in common.[4]

In essence, if there is no communication or a limited degree of neighborhood organization,

there is no consensus of agreement or unified effort, or basis by which local problems can be solved through citizen participation. The degree to which this is absent in communities is an indicator of civic apathy and a type of social disorganization. Clarence Perry was well aware of this problem when he wrote:

. . . A young New York business woman was seeking a home for herself and mother. Upon being told about the attractiveness of the social life in a certain suburban development, she exclaimed, 'Oh, but I don't want to go where I have to know people!' What she really objected to was living in the kind of community where her daily comings and goings would be subject to the scrutiny and comment of neighbors. She recoiled from the tyranny of small-town gossip. Thousands of like-minded young people have sought with eagerness the freedom and anonymity of rooming-house life in a large city. Observation shows, however, that these same bachelor men and women experience a change of heart when they marry. Especially after the children have begun to come, do they again long for the detached house and yard, and the social benefits of a congenial neighborhood.[5]

A similar observation was voiced by Dr. Robert S. Lynd, co-author of *Middletown* and *Middletown in Transition:*

Many of those who migrate to our larger cities pride themselves on the fact that 'Now, thank God, I don't have to know my neighbors, go to Rotary, belong to a church, or participate in an annual Community Chest drive!' And the big city does little to disabuse them of this attitude.[6]

Lewis Mumford, with his planning insights and historical perspective, has long been cognizant of this problem, as for example in the following reference from "The Insensate Industrial Town":

As for an expression of the permanent social functions of the city in the new type of plan (the rectangular gridiron plan of our American cities) , it was utterly lacking. . . . There were no real centers in this urban massing: no institutions capable of uniting its members into an active city life. Only the sects, the fragments, the social debris of old institutions remained . . . a no-man's land of social life.[7]

[4] Louis Wirth, COMMUNITY PLANNING FOR PEACETIME LIVING (Palo Alto, Calif.: Stanford University Press, 1946) , p. 9. See also, Arthur E. Morgan, THE SMALL COMMUNITY (New York: Harper & Bros., 1942) .

[5] Clarence Arthur Perry, NEIGHBORHOOD AND COMMUNITY PLANNING, *op. cit.,* p. 25.

[6] Robert S. Lynd, KNOWLEDGE FOR WHAT? THE PLACE OF SOCIAL SCIENCE IN AMERICAN CULTURE (Princeton, N.J.: Princeton University Press, 1945) , p. 83.

[7] Lewis Mumford, THE CULTURE OF CITIES (New York: Harcourt, Brace, 1938) .

The foregoing references illustrate the scope and extent of the problem and the need to establish some sound and reasonable basis for community planning at the grass-roots level, notwithstanding the specialized function of city-wide or metropolitan planning organizations.

The widespread apathy which is prevalent today is merely indicative of the fact that certain social activity patterns which were acceptable to previous generations are no longer acceptable, and that a certain amount of social disorganization has been inevitable and will continue unless other suitable institutions and channels of communication and participation are activated.

Notwithstanding the general acceptance of the neighborhood concept in planning theory, the fact remains that it has yet to receive any broad practical application and demonstration. Most examples are limited to relatively small and piecemeal projects which are ACTION[8] oriented, but the value and need for these examples should encourage, rather than discourage, a broad approach.

The question for the planner should not be *whether* he should undertake neighborhood planning activities with local citizen participation, but *when* would local initiative, official policy, and budgetary means permit such a program to be implemented throughout the community.

Spokesmen for Planning

The typical comprehensive plan or other planning project ends up in the form of a report, usually illustrated with maps, charts, and photographs. Most members of the public never see the report, but hear of it on radio or television or read about it in newspapers. Those particularly interested may come to a meeting or look at an exhibit where details of the plan are presented, but most planning reaches people second- or third-hand, generally through a small number of spokesmen. The way these

[8] ACTION (American Communities To Improve Our Neighborhoods, Box 462, Radio City Station, New York City).

spokesmen conduct themselves and explain the plans will condition much of the response from officials, from the communications media, and from the public.

Principal spokesmen for local planning include the planning director, the political leaders he may serve, the planning board or planning commission, and a wide range of citizen groups.

THE PLANNING DIRECTOR

The technical spokesman for local planning may be the planning director, a member of the professional staff, or a consultant. The term "planning director" is used here, but what is said applies equally to any professional planner. To carry out his job he must engage not in a monologue but in a dialogue of interaction with the public, and he must perform in a variety of roles.

As a guest lecturer and public speaker before many groups varying from the sophisticated, influential, and articulate, with a wide range of interests and concerns, to local neighborhood groups with special interests and problems of immediate concern, although more loosely defined.

The planner is always challenged to communicate his message of what planning is, what values it seeks to enhance in the community as a whole, and to consider the relationship of various community groups to the planning process. In this phase of activity, by means of many direct contacts with the public, the planner is able to keep his finger on the pulse of local opinion and to evaluate the response to his programs, as well as to consider the ideas and views of his audience.

As the author or editor responsible for many technical reports and planning publications, including regular or special newsletters, and technical or general interest pamphlets aimed at informing the public generally and key officials and community leaders in particular.

This function of informing the public on broad community values and objectives is basically educational, rather than being an exercise in salesmanship, although the latter is an important by-product. The basic presumption is that if people have the essential information relative to a particular situation or problem, and a knowledge of possible alternative solutions, they will most probably arrive at a consensus of agreement on such solution through the democratic process. On the other hand, it must be acknowledged that the power of salesmanship alone, whether it be by the "hard" or the "soft" sell method, may be successful in achieving a desired result on a local issue.

As a leader and instigator of ideas, and as the city's chief technical advisor on the total community welfare, the planner is in a key position to influence, and to be influenced by, the opinions and attitudes of many individuals and groups. In many respects this is the role of the politician who, without reference to partisan politics, is rightfully concerned about the needs and welfare of all the people and their community problems.

This phase of activity is perhaps the most important factor which makes the difference between a moderately successful and a highly successful planner in achieving various programs of community improvement. The difference lies in certain personality characteristics and qualities involving both native intelligence and a degree of sophistication or *savoir faire* in getting things done.

Through direct and indirect contacts with various individuals and groups, involving both formal and informal channels of communication, the planner is in a key position both to implant ideas and to foster or encourage the ideas of others relating to local improvement programs, pertinent legislative changes, necessary appropriations, and desirable reforms. These activities may be undertaken by the planner alone, or jointly with the public, or in other ways, as appropriate to the individual circumstances.

In many respects, this phase of activity involves a high degree of coordination and strategy in both routine and extracurricular activities.

As an advisor and arbiter at public hearings, his public relations ability must be at its best. Objectivity and impartiality, supplemented by tact, are essential ingredients.

There are many planning and zoning activities which call for a public hearing which is duly advertised. In the case of zoning, hearings also require the individual notification of adjoining property owners. These situations may frequently involve a "confrontation" between opposing forces which feel strongly about the issues under discussion and feelings may run high. In such instances the planner must be able to discern impartially and advise diplomatically. There are times when the factual situation stated objectively and tactfully provides the most fruitful basis for an equitable determination. Obviously, the planner cannot be all things to all people. The facts carefully analyzed and explained, along with possible alternatives, should characterize the planner's presentation. Overtones of political expediency, or compromise, remain rightfully in the province and prerogative of the Planning Commission or the City Council.

On major problems of community-wide concern, the entire power structure of the community may be directly involved. On other matters, such as neighborhood zoning cases, only very local issues and personalities may be involved. In both cases the planner is required to make his presentation clearly, and in a way that appeals to the level of interest and understanding of his audience, if there is to be effective communication.

As an instigator and designer of surveys, the planner may frequently need the assistance of citizen volunteers from various community groups.

Whether or not a particular situation requires volunteer citizen help, it is certain that the greater the citizen participation, the better the situation from the standpoint of community understanding, support, and acceptance.

Seldom are planning budgets adequate for all anticipated needs. However, even if adequate budgets are available, there are frequently desirable benefits in utilizing the assistance of such groups as the Jaycees or the League of Women Voters for certain types of interviews, or youth groups such as the Boy Scouts on traffic counts and limited questionnaires. Furthermore, if groups are directly involved, the public relations value of utilizing these may enhance the interest in and support for particular programs.

THE PLANNING COMMISSION

The role of the professional planner in dealing with the public has been discussed so far primarily in relation to the traditional planning commission, as authorized and established through state enabling legislation. The planner's role will vary somewhat with the particular type of local governmental structure involved. Under the weak mayor-council form of government, he will be responsible primarily to the planning commission. With a strong mayor-council form of government, he will generally have a dual role involving the receipt of policy and directives from both the mayor and the planning commission. Under the council-manager form of government, the planning director also has a dual role, receiving policy and directives from the city manager and the planning commission.

The basic role of the planning commission is as advisor to the local governing body. Certain matters, such as zoning and subdivision reviews, require referral to the planning commission for recommendation to the governing body. In some instances, the council must cast a two-thirds or three-fourths majority vote to overrule the recommendations of the planning commission, so that in these cases the role of the commission is more than purely advisory.

Inasmuch as the planning commission is composed of a group of appointed citizens, notably business and professional men, the time it can devote is limited and the scope of its activities is "controlled" to some degree by the initiative, interests, and capabilities of the planning director. However, as a group of civic-minded citizens and community leaders, the commission as a whole, and the commissioners individually, will be called upon by various community groups and interests to present and discuss the planning program generally, and to receive comments and suggestions.

As the formulators of planning policy and program, notwithstanding their advisory role, the planning commission is the group entrusted to make certain decisions at the commission level. In this role the planning commissioners perform the basic function of articulating the city's views concerning the broad "civic" aspects of planning, including land use, transportation, community facilities and services, capital improvement programming, zoning, and subdivision regulations. They are not the technical experts, but they are often the virtual decision-making body in these matters, with advisory assistance from the planning director.

After planning policies have been adopted and a planning program prepared for specific undertakings, the planning commission, as well as the director, has a direct responsibility and obligation to mobilize citizen interest and support for such a program. Presumably the formulation of policies, and the preparation and adoption of a specific program, would have been guided, or tempered, through direct contacts with many citizens and groups. This procedure might be considered one of the informal "checks and balances" involved in the planning process, paralleling the role of the planning director and the technical staff.

As part of the planning process, the planning commission would exercise a continuing function and develop a working relationship directly with the public in discussing the community's needs and interests and in formulating goals and objectives which would be mutually consistent within the broad framework of policies established by the commission.

Obviously, this direct working relationship of the commission with the public is not completely separate and apart from contact and liaison with the planning director, but rather these are two activities which must be carefully coordinated.

CITIZEN GROUPS

For a variety of reasons, advisory groups of citizens, active in planning but mainly outside the realm of government, have burgeoned in recent years. There is a wide variety of such advisory groups, ranging from semi-official bodies appointed on a city-wide basis, to single-purpose self-organized groups at the neighborhood level. Each type attempts to fulfill a special need for its particular group, some selfish, some altruistic. Such groups include:

Citizen Advisory Committees. Within the past decade or two, there has been a growing trend toward the establishment of additional citizen advisory committees. This trend was given additional impetus in those communities engaged in urban renewal activities, which were required under federal procedures to establish special citizen advisory groups, which in turn would encourage citizen participation activities in relation to the seven points of the Workable Program for Community Improvement (codes, comprehensive planning, neighborhood analyses, administration, financing, relocation, citizen participation).

The fate of the Workable Program committees has been reviewed recently by Dr. Edmund M. Burke.[9] The results have been generally ineffective, although it should be recognized that any efforts in this direction are to be encouraged and facilitated. The objective is worthy, although the methods, means, and techniques have not been perfected or developed to the point of becoming genuinely meaningful. However, in isolated instances, special efforts in relation to particular urban renewal projects have proved to be quite effective.

Many of these citizen group activities have been focussed on urban renewal problems. Sometimes this has been done consciously, at other times unconsciously, depending on local comprehension of the scope of the desired Workable Program objectives.

One respondent in Dr. Burke's survey said, "In my opinion people cannot be organized into urban renewal in any way, shape or form and nothing but bitter feelings will develop from that type of approach."[10] Another response indicated that:

The critical question may be whether [citizen participation] should be viewed as a public relations policy or genuine community participation and democracy at the grassroots level, designed to give the citizens the maximum role possible in the administration and planning of public improvements.[11]

The survey further indicated that citizen participation activities were most effective in rehabilitation, rather than in clearance projects. Also, the assignment of a qualified community organization worker, or a rehabilitation specialist to the project was a crucial factor in the effectiveness of certain programs.

Citizen Planning Committees. The use of relatively large citizen planning committees appears sound from the standpoint of reviewing major elements of a local planning program. Inasmuch as the official planning commission is generally quite restricted in numbers, it is frequently desirable and important to appoint a larger review group to study and comment on various official proposals, ranging from comprehensive planning documents, to specific capital improvement projects. Such large committees must frequently delegate their assignments to a number of subcommittees in order to be able to study the problems and arrive at their findings and recommendations. From the official city point of view, such committees can be helpful as a device for obtaining opinions from a wider cross-section of community interests. In the case of capital improvement programs, approval, advice, or recommendations for modification, can frequently be helpful as a path to wider community endorsement and acceptance.

The functioning of these committees is, in a sense, a duplication of the effort and activities of the official planning commission. Therefore, on the one hand, there is the hazard that citizen advisory planning committees may upset the work and recommendations of the official commission. On the other hand, if the work has been done thoroughly, the chances are that the advisory committee will arrive at similar general conclusions and recommendations. In any event, there is need for close coordination and a direct working relationship with the planning staff and adequate technical resources. The presumption is that with adequate facts and information, reasonable persons will arrive at some general agreement.

Whether or not such committees include elected or departmental officials should be considered according to the nature of the task assigned. Generally, it would be desirable to have elected or department officials available for advice and counsel when citizen committees are functioning. On the other hand, the presence of such officials should not be construed as a method of promoting a particular viewpoint. Citizen groups should be free to function in

[9] Edmund M. Burke, "Citizen Participation in Renewal," THE JOURNAL OF HOUSING, XXIII, No. 1 (January, 1966), pp. 18–21.

[10] *Ibid.*, p. 18.

[11] *Ibid.*, p. 19.

accordance with their best judgment. Furthermore, it would hardly be consistent for a sizeable bloc of elected officials to appear with a recommending group and pass on their own recommendations.

Community-wide Housing and Planning Councils. The history of community-wide housing and planning councils indicates that they have been few and far between, but have played a most effective role in their particular communities. Generally this type of council has occurred in the larger metropolitan areas, such as New York City, Philadelphia, Chicago, and San Francisco. In part, they have been "watchdogs" in the public interest. They have spearheaded many civic improvement programs, and they have prevented some serious mistakes by well-intentioned city officials and others. Usually such councils have included important civic leaders, as well as a variety of professional people who could assist in the technical evaluation of various programs under consideration. As such, they could speak authoritatively, and they usually enjoy wide press coverage that communicates their findings to the city officials and the public-at-large.

Another important role, or function, which these councils have performed is in the general area of public information and education. Some of these groups have existed for several decades. Through their annual meetings, by means of noted guest speakers, educational forums, and special committee activities, they have helped to publicize the benefits of housing and planning. Over the years they have been primarily responsible for creating the political or civic climate for the eventual acceptance of housing and planning programs which probably could have been achieved in no other way.

Although the number of these organizations has been relatively few, their records of accomplishment have been very impressive. In general, they have served as a catalyst in pushing for legislative reform measures, and for city council support for specific projects and programs, varying from public housing to public utilities, and from school district boundaries to metropolitan and regional cooperation agreements.

New programs are generally suspect—not so much because officials are necessarily against them, but because they do not understand them. This type of citizen group can assist and support the elected officials in their deliberations on such matters. The city council does not necessarily want to function as instigator of certain reforms, but rather to be responsive to the wishes and desires of the individuals and groups who are sponsoring them.

Such groups may be particularly valuable to the planning director and the planning commission during budget hearings, when some expression of public opinion is vital to particular programs.

This group will also be largely dependent upon data and information which is available only from the city's planning department. Therefore, a close working relationship and liaison will be of paramount importance. Furthermore, the planning commission may frequently rely upon this type of group to assist in sponsoring, or co-sponsoring, public forums, exhibits, and educational institutes of various types.

Special Purpose Planning Groups. There is an ever-increasing proliferation of planning groups in this classification. Special purpose planning groups, by definition, intent, and purpose, have limited their particular interests and concerns to localized areas. Generally, such groups operate on the basis of enlightened self-interest. They are interested in areas of civic improvement, but primarily in those areas where they have a particular stake or interest. Such groups may be comprised principally of business men seeking certain improvements in the central business district, industrialists seeking improvements in a particular industrial area, or citizens seeking certain improvements in their particular neighborhood area. These groups have been the most numerous of all: they have been important and effective, but they have had certain inherent limitations.

On the whole, special purpose groups have played an important role in getting certain projects started. These might not be the most important projects at the time, nor in the proper sequence of priority. However, these groups were ready to move forward on some project which was at least important to them, and apparently was not objectionable to the officials concerned, but this is not necessarily bad.

The obvious limitation of these groups stems from the very nature of their special purpose interest, as compared to the comprehensive planning interest of the total community. Consequently, they must be viewed as a part of the whole.

When such special purpose groups can be aided by, and work cooperatively with the planners, many of the inherent conflicting interests may be resolved.

Chief among these groups are the following:

1. Neighborhood groups in conservation and rehabilitation areas. These bodies are essential for resolving many of the local neighborhood problems of mutual concern with respect to environmental deficiencies. Individual property owners can improve their own buildings and lots in conservation and rehabilitation areas, but there must be a mutuality of concern and interest in cooperating on a neighborhood basis to solve related problems such as deficiencies in streets and utilities, community services and facilities.

2. Central Business District (CBD) groups. Such prevalent groups are frequently offshoots of, or related to, organizations such as a Chamber of Commerce. Usually the business leadership of the community is articulate in voicing its needs. It has considerable amounts of money invested, and is seriously concerned about deterioration of property and about environmental deficiencies. This type of area gets prior consideration because of the mutuality of public and private interests in revitalizing the CBD through the process of urban renewal. CBD groups have frequently taken the initiative in raising thousands of dollars and in undertaking extensive technical studies in order to assist the advice of their causes. Public buildings, including state, county and city facilities, are usually a part of the CBD complex, and therefore benefit from a general environmental improvement. Notable instances of such benefit include Baltimore, Philadelphia, Detroit, St. Louis, Kansas City, Los Angeles,

San Francisco, and many others. The evidence suggests that CBD groups, on the whole, have been the most successful to date.

3. Industrial development organizations. These organizations are related to Chamber of Commerce interests and activities. Usually they are concerned with advancing the industrial development of the community, with their primary interest focussed on an increased tax base, increased employment, and greater purchasing power. Practically every community, large and small, has a committee of some kind functioning along these lines. This is a highly competitive type of activity, and therefore only the more astute and aggressive communities are successful. Urban renewal has been of some assistance, but the variety of locations suitable for industrial development makes it more difficult to focus on a particular area.

Emerging groups are currently being fostered by a number of new federally-aided programs:

4. Anti-poverty groups are being formed to assist the lower income stratum in a variety of programs ranging from education and welfare to neighborhood planning activities. These groups are less articulate than those previously mentioned, although some significant efforts are being made in several major communities to assist in their organization until they are capable of attracting the attention and support of public officials in remedying basic problems in their substandard and deteriorating areas.

5. Urban design, beautification, and open-space programs represent another category which is gaining momentum throughout the nation. Special citizen groups are being appointed to study and evaluate the need for these programs and the ways and means of implementing them. No general pattern for these groups has yet emerged but it is anticipated that they will be somewhat comparable to other planning advisory committees.

This vast array of programs underlines the hazards of piecemeal, uncoordinated planning. The need for the planner and the planning commission to assist in guiding and coordinating the activities of these various groups is evident. To a degree, the federal government attempts to assure at least minimal coordination by requiring documentation to indicate the relationship of various projects to the Comprehensive Plan. However, this technique alone is inadequate, and the basic job of coordination remains the responsibility of the local community. Local administration requirements should anticipate the needs of these newly developing programs, and make adjustments within the governmental structure to accommodate them.

Intercommunity, Regional, and National Organizations. Congressional requirements are steadily bringing about intercommunity and metropolitan cooperation for comprehensive planning purposes. This represents a culmination and a next stage for groups once confined to the individual community. This development will have an impact upon national policies affecting the various community facilities and programs. Study commissions and advisory committees as well as metropolitan and regional planning commissions and councils of government, will inevitably be established to assist in the formulation of basic policies and procedures to assure optimum services in the most economical and desirable manner.

On the national scene a number of groups have been active in the pursuit of general planning aims or of specialized objectives such as adequate recreational facilities, conservation measures, and general welfare. Each has had a significant role in the achievement of a well-balanced environment for urban living. Many local citizens and group organizations have been active participants and supporters of these important intercommunity, regional, and national associations.

The most notable of these over the past decade has been ACTION (American Council to Improve Our Neighborhoods), a national, nonprofit public service organization dedicated to the elimination of slum conditions and the improvement of America's homes and neighborhoods. It has worked with other national organizations, as well as hundreds of local citizen groups and public officials in developing effctive local leadership and action programs. The ACTION staff engages in programs of research, education, public information, and

discussion activities, with the aid of a monthly newsletter, especially illustrated publications on various problems, and a full-color animated film designed to stimulate citizen interest. During 1966 this organization merged with Urban America, Inc.

Urban America, Inc. is the rising star on the horizon, being a relatively new nonprofit educational organization which is combining the programs and resources of two national groups with the common goal of improving the urban environment—Urban America (formerly the American Planning and Civic Association) and the ACTION Council for Better Cities. ACTION's 70 "Local Group Associates" have also been invited to affiliate with Urban America. The basic objective is to assist American communities to become "more livable, more workable, and more beautiful." Their chief instrument of communication is the revitalized *Architectural Forum*, which ceased publication in 1964, after 72 years of service in the area of architectural design. Today, the *Forum* is addressed not only to architects, but to the related design professions, in whose hands will rest the task of designing and redesigning "urban America" for twice its present population by the turn of the century. The expressed purpose of this magazine is to deal in ideas, whether they be visually expressed, spoken, or written, in the general fields of architecture, technology or any related area bearing on cities and the enhancement of the urban scene throughout the nation.

Techniques for Communicating Planning

Planning reaches the public through a variety of media. A complete inventory would include not only the press, radio, and television, but also the public hearing and the informal meeting, as well as a range of specialized tools and techniques such as reports, maps, charts, photographs, models, and exhibits. All of these are useful in informing the public about a particular project, or in developing an understanding of general concepts. Some comments about the major types of media suitable for communicating planning are presented below.

REPORTS

Most of the work product of the planning agency takes the form of a report. It may be a simple letter giving a recommendation on a matter referred to the agency, or a major illustrated and bound volume presenting the comprehensive plan or a complex technical study. It may even be a simple oral report. In any case, as much care should be given to the form and method of its presentation as to the detail of its content. If that content is worth presenting at all, it is worth presenting well.

There can be many varieties of reports, and we shall not pretend here to be comprehensive by taking up the whole range from master plan elements through technical background documents, staff working papers, information bulletins, and news releases, to correspondence. It is enough to make some points about two broad categories—major reports and minor reports. Almost every planning agency needs to have a series of each. Major reports would ordinarily be printed outside the planning agency; minor ones would be run off on the office mimeograph or multilith machine.

Major Reports. The production of a major illustrated planning report is a task requiring a great deal of time and attention, not only from the technical staff but also from the leadership of the planning agency. The number of such products must therefore be limited to those subjects of top significance and enduring value. One or two a year can be expected from the average agency. The time used in preparing final materials for publication and in having them printed frequently creates problems. Several months may go by after a planning board has acted on a draft report before printed copies can be made available to the public. Some of these months can be saved if arrangements are made in advance for purchase of the printing services. If competitive bidding is needed, it may sometimes be based on outline specifications before the final copy is ready.[12]

The key to effective presentation is simplicity. Clarity of meaning should be an objective in writing a report. The illustrations should be treated as an integral part of the total presentation. A simple sketch or diagram may save many words. Photographs should be used as symbols or examples of the types of things discussed.

A common mistake of many planning agencies is to exceed their competence with tricky or elaborate reports crudely done. If capable graphic design or illustration talents are not available on the agency staff, they should be purchased from professionals, or the presentation style should be modified to fit that which the staff can do well. A clear photograph or a Leroy-lettered mechanical drawing will carry your message better than an ineptly-executed piece of freehand "art."

Minor Reports. One of the objectives of the publications of a planning agency should be to convey a sense of continuity in the planning program. A similarity in format and consistent use of the several design elements in a report will help to do this. So also will restatement in each report product of the major goals of the planning program, along with a few words relating the subject of the report to those goals.

Every planning office has its bottleneck to which the flow of material for publication is funneled. At this point may be the director, his deputy, the commission chairman or another member of staff or board. His function should be that of a sieve, improving the quality of material, rejecting some items, but not obstructing the main flow. Some planners in this critical spot act instead as a cork or stopper, holding back material for fear of public criticism. They fail to realize that some of the purposes of a publications program are the fostering of citizen response and the provision of information to guide private decisions. It is far better to maintain a steady production of modest but useful report materials than to strive for excellence on a "few-and-far-between" basis.

To facilitate the flow of production, the planning office should work towards some standardization of its minor publications. The format, size, style, organization, and procedures for review of difficult classes of reports should be clearly understood by all the staff, so that they can concentrate their brainpower on

---

[12] For further suggestions see Chapter 14, "Printing Arts and Publications Distribution" in MUNICIPAL PUBLIC RELATIONS, *op. cit.*

the content of the product.

Some Simple Rules. Regardless of the form or scale of report there are several simple rules which should be applied in any publication effort in a planning office:

1. Know your audience, and direct your report to them. In most cases this audience is, or at least includes, the city council, which ought to be able to understand what you tell them.

2. Use simple and plain English. Even the most sophisticated minds can understand it. This does not mean that you must avoid all planning jargon, but that you must make a conscious effort to be clear. Each planning office should have and use one of the books on writing, such as Nicholson's *American-English Usage* or Fowler's *Modern English Usage.*

3. Do not attempt to do what you cannot do well. If you cannot write well yourself, hire a reporter or an editor for your staff.

4. Tell your audience what is to be done with the report. The letter of transmittal should spell out the action to be taken by the recipient toward carrying out the recommendations made in the report.

5. Make it easy to follow up, by listing and numbering the findings and recommendations.

6. Let the structure of your presentation show through, not only in the table of contents, but in the visual organization of the material. Don't be afraid to let white paper show, when you want the reader to pause or to shift to a new section.

MEETINGS

Planners are perhaps the "meetingest" people in city hall. They must participate in many meetings just to comply with public hearing provisions in the laws they operate under. Further, a large part of the planning business involves coordination of diverse interests, and this can best be done by bringing people together.

A meeting is not a simple thing. It is the essence of public relations and more than any other activity of the planning agency, conditions the reception given to proposals. Arranging a meeting calls for careful attention to detail. Whether it be an informal get-together or a nationally-televised public hearing, every meeting has at least eight important elements:

    purpose
    notice
    preparations
    agenda
    participants
    place
    results
    records

Depending on the scale of the get-together, each of these elements may be simple or elaborate, informal or laden with protocol. But regardless of the scale, each element on the checklist above involves responsibility, customarily placed on the chairman or the one who calls the meeting. A few comments on each of the elements are in order, with a view to improving the effectiveness of the city planning process which operates to a large degree through the meeting channel.

Purpose. It may be belaboring the obvious, but there should be a good reason for calling any meeting. The chairman should have a clear idea as to what he wants to get out of a meeting, and should make this purpose known to the participants. The purpose of a hearing may be just to receive the views of interested parties; the purpose of a commission meeting may be to consider reports and read decisions on certain matters; the purpose of a staff conference may be simply to pass on information.

Notice. Don't expect people to show up if you haven't invited them and given them some clue as to why they should come. Whether this is by word of mouth, office memo, engraved invitation, or legal advertisement depends of course on the nature of the affair. Those who will have important roles to play should get special attention and reminders. This would apply particularly to prospective supporters who seldom appear at public hearings without prompting.

Preparations. These have to do not only with arrangements for the meeting place, food, supplies, comforts, visual aids, transportation and such mechanical things, but also with the agenda, content, reports, rehearsals, and arrangements for people to do certain things either for or at the meeting. The important feature of all preparations is that they must be done *in advance.* The time of the meeting should be set to allow for adequate preparations.

Agenda. Without an agenda or order of business, a meeting is not a meeting, it is a "happening" with no guarantee that it will come off well. Even a public hearing needs clear and fair rules as to the sequence and procedure to be followed. The participants need to know that there is a place when they will "get their chance." If copies of the agenda are not available for everyone, then it is important for the chairman to describe it at the start of the meeting and to justify any variation from it.

Participants. The most important participant is the man up front—the chairman—to whom the others are looking for direction in the progress of the meeting. His bearing and attitude can influence more than any other single factor the outcome of a meeting or hearing. His patience may be taxed, but his application of the principles of fairness in the conduct of the meeting should not waiver.

Other participants will at times include both leaders and followers, friends and foes, helpmates and agitators, table-thumpers and sitters-on-hands. Their diversity is too great to treat here, other than to note that most successful meetings are not monologues. *Participants* is a plural word.

Place. The meeting place selected should be a comfortable, convenient one appropriate to the size and nature of the meeting to be held. There may be times when nothing can be done about a dimly-lighted or poorly-ventilated hall, but there is no valid excuse for not checking facilities beforehand and making the best use of them. Few things are more disruptive of a meeting than the microphone that doesn't work or the visual aid that can't be seen.

Results. Something comes of every meeting, although it may not always be readily evident. Even fruitless sessions create impressions and contribute to the development of attitudes over time. But the kinds of meetings we want are the productive ones, which can be summarized at their close with findings, agreements, decisions. Most meetings are not ends in themselves, but steps or means. The results of these

frequently are work assignments, tasks to be done and reported on at the next meeting. No meeting is really finished until its results are stated and the next steps made clear.

Records. Seldom does everyone who should come to a meeting show up. For this reason if no other, some record should be made in order that the missing participants may be informed. More importantly, most planning work is public, and the public interest calls for certain types of records. These range from the verbatim transcript or tape recording of public hearing statements, through official published minutes of commission sessions, to much less formal types of records. If a meeting was worth having, it should have produced a result worth recording. Some planning offices find useful a simple form for listing the time, place, participants, and results of any meeting held. This is intended to be filled out at the end of the meeting, before leaving the meeting room. It can then be reproduced and sent to the participants and to all others who should be informed. Such a minimal record is nice to have as the basis for impressive statistics for annual reports. But it is far more useful as a reminder to follow up on the decisions and assignments made in the meeting.

THE PRESS

Perhaps the most important single element or channel of communication is the press, where the written word is recorded and communicated individually to many citizens concurrently. The fundamental concept of "freedom of the press" implies certain obligations toward the public in reporting the news objectively and informing the people on matters of general concern. Most newspapers today recognize that urban development is one of the more popular local issues, especially well suited to newspaper presentation. The planning office should be a regular stop on the beat of the city hall reporter, and a productive one not only for reporting on the current zoning or subdivision case, but also for longer-range and more significant stories. The larger newspapers may furnish special reporters to develop a feature series on planning with graphic and other treatment. Smaller newspapers will be more limited in their services, and therefore require additional assistance from the planner. In any case, much of the planner's work reaches the public through the further work of reporters.

Reporters are human beings. This means that they are of course in varying degrees fallible, jealous of their prerogatives, suspicious, and subject to normal human frailties. But it also means that most of them are sincere, hardworking, capable and know their job. That job has at least a couple of distinctive characteristics. One is the rather acute competition in newsgathering, not only between newspapers but among the other media as well. As in other competitive sports, winning the game is not as important as playing it fairly. Giving even breaks to the different papers in a community, including daily, weekly, metropolitan and suburban, and treating the other media with the same respect as is given to the one with a full-time city hall reporter—these are cardinal principles of fairness for getting along well with the press.

Another characteristic of newspapermen is that they live by deadlines. The good reporter is most efficient in not wasting his own time. He devotes most of that time to finding words to put into print. He knows how to cover meetings, but will appreciate technical background on complex issues. He knows how to write his own stories, but can save time by making use of simple clear news releases that tell facts. He is able to read planning reports, but will welcome (and frequently print) a list of numbered points that summarize or emphasize things in the report. He is good at arithmetic, and properly feels an obligation to report to his readers the magnitude of things, usually in the dollar terms most people understand. The good reporter is compulsive about this, and will often go to considerable effort to develop sometimes frightening grand total dollar sums unless the planners provide him with other simple and clear measures of magnitude for their proposals.

For major projects or complex reports, the newspapers need time to develop complete interpretive coverage. A downtown plan released to the press Tuesday morning may get only a half-column in Tuesday afternoon's edition

and be crowded out by national news on Wednesday. But the same plan made available to the press a few weeks before its public release date can be given several pages of coverage, including supplementary feature stories, careful layout, and special art work. Most papers, because of fluctuations in advertising volume, have certain days on which space for such coverage can be more readily provided, but this takes some planning. Planners should not be unwilling to indulge in that practice with their local editors.

For a number of years the American Society of Planning Officials has presented a series of Journalism Awards—citations for excellence in public service for outstanding news articles and presentations in advancing the cause of better understanding and appreciation of the needs and values of various types of planning problems and objectives. Such awards have included newspapers, large and small, and ranging in location from coast to coast, and border to border. Some newspapers have arranged for special reprints to assist civic leaders and citizen associates in a broader understanding of community problems in particular, and in relation to the total spectrum of comprehensive planning on the metropolitan and regional level.

The most effective use of the news media in any community will in large measure depend upon the planner and his staff providing essential facts for interpretation and presentation by the press.

BROADCASTING

Almost anything written about the radio and television broadcasting fields will probably be out of date in a few years. Despite this danger, there are some insights into these changing media that warrant consideration by planners interested in effective communication with the people they serve.

News. The broadcasting media are an important element in the field of news. A large proportion of the public learns of events only through radio or TV. Although much of the broadcast news material is drawn from the newswires or newspapers, many stations edit their own presentations. It is to the interest of the planning agency to include these local stations in its press conferences and news release lists.

Public Service. Federal regulations require broadcasting stations to devote a portion of their air time to public service programs. City planning matters make ideal copy for these programs. Whenever a planning agency issues a report, some effort should be made to tie this in with a radio discussion, or television presentation.

Radio. Today's radio operation is much different from that of twenty or even ten years ago. Many radio stations are specialized, dealing with only one type of music or with programming over the day aimed at particular age or interest groups. The multi-purpose or general interest radio station is becoming the exception. Some stations deal only in news, sports, and weather; some concentrate on classical music, others on rock and roll. There has been considerable experimentation in so-called "talk" shows: panel discussions, interviews, monologues, telephone questions, and conversations. Some of these hold considerable promise for dealing with planning topics of current interest.

Television. This is so much a part of American life today that it may be pointless to remind the reader of the pervasiveness of its influence. Planning materials, with their visual presentation of the physical aspects of cities, are particularly well-suited as television copy, provided there is some movement involved. Television costs are still high, and local station investment in programs on planning comes more easily if public-spirited sponsors can be found. The educational TV stations do well in national distribution of locally-produced features on planning, but these stations largely reach a different segment of the public than do the local affiliates of the big commercial networks.

EDUCATIONAL MATERIALS

This chapter would be incomplete without a brief discussion of notable publications aimed at increasing citizen understanding about planning. Some historic examples which indicate significant merit in the broad educational approach include the following.

Wacker's Manual of the Plan of Chicago.[13] Shortly after publication of the voluminous report, the *Plan of Chicago,*[14] prepared by Daniel Burnham for the Commercial Club of Chicago, there was prepared a school textbook, *Wacker's Manual of the Plan of Chicago,* especially written for use in the school system. It was prepared under the auspices of the Chicago Plan Commission, by Walter D. Moody, Managing Director of the Chicago Plan Commission. The first edition appeared in 1912. The effectiveness of this book in the civic courses of the schools in Chicago is credited in large measure for providing the genuine educational background for important improvements advocated in the plan, such as the reclamation of Chicago's lakeshore into the formed park development.

A sequel to the foregoing was published in 1953, *Tomorrow's Chicago,*[15] under sponsorship of the Chicago Metropolitan Housing and Planning Council. Atlanta, Boston, and a few other cities have prepared similar books.

You and Your Neighborhood. This booklet was prepared as a planning primer by Oscar Stonorov and Louis I. Kahn for Revere Copper and Brass, Inc., in 1944. It described the planning process for Mr. John Q. Public, and was graphically attractive, making use of sketches and diagrams. It merits reprinting. The Revere Company also published a series of leaflets on specialized subjects, including *Why City Planning is Your Responsibility,* and *Making Better Health Available to All.* Each was prepared by an eminent planner, architect, or related specialist.

Planning With You. This was a small booklet by the editors of *The Architectural Forum,* and copyrighted by Time Inc., in 1943, explaining the planning process in laymen's lan-

---

[13] Walter D. Moody, WACKER'S MANUAL OF THE PLAN OF CHICAGO (Chicago: Chicago Plan Commission, 2nd ed., 1916).

[14] Daniel Burnham, PLAN OF CHICAGO (Chicago: The Commercial Club, 1908).

[15] Arthur Hillman and Robert J. Casey, TOMORROW'S CHICAGO (Chicago: University of Chicago Press, 1953).

guage. It also includes an advertisement notice from the New York Times, May 19, 1943, titled "Planning, like Democracy, needs more than the experts," which states,

There are two kinds of postwar planning. One kind could only result if the citizenry shrugs its shoulders and leaves the job to the experts. Not many people, certainly not the planners, want that. The other kind of planning will result if an informed group of active citizens in every community arouses public opinion and guides the planners in gradually making each community into a better place for your wife, your children, your neighbors and you.

ACTION Publications. During the 1950s and 1960s ACTION (referred to earlier in this chapter) published a variety of citizen participation materials, including *You and Your Neighbor,* a scriptographic booklet copyrighted by the Channing L. Bete Co., Inc., Greenfield, Massachusetts, 1956, and currently distributed by ACTION. Another one is *Our Living Future—Citizen Action for Urban Renewal,* a booklet contributed as a public service by *Life* Magazine, and distributed through ACTION, New York City.

Sears Roebuck booklets. Sears, Roebuck and Co., as part of a broad community relations program directed both to its own personnel and to the public generally, published a first-rate booklet, the *ABC's of Urban Renewal* in 1957. This civic-minded company has recognized its parallel growth with that of the metropolitan area and the transition of a nation from predominantly rural to predominantly urban in character. Two other excellent booklets, *The ABC's of Community Planning* (1962) and *ABCitizens in Urban Renewal* (1959) have also been issued by Sears Roebuck, and have proven effective in aiding public understanding of these technical fields.

State and Federal Materials. Most of the state planning agencies publish and distribute educational and promotional material for use with public groups interested in planning. Many states have extension programs allied with their state universities which can be called on to assist in support of local planning.

The federal Department of Housing and Urban Development, through its regional offices and field representatives, also provides educational material and personnel to explain federal programs related to planning.

Citizens' Guides. Two small books, *The Citizen's Guide to Planning* (1961) and the *Citizen's Guide to Urban Renewal* (1962) aimed at the layman, have been published by the Chandler-Davis Publishing Company. These are among the better popular presentations, useful in working with the public.

Films, Filmstrips, and Slides. The Department of Housing and Urban Development has recently published a selected bibliography of Films, Filmstrips, and Slides on the broad subject of Housing and Community Development. Their listing includes over one hundred selections. Many of these are excellent, and available free, or at a nominal fee.

Summary

To those that seek government in the true American tradition, there is great satisfaction in knowing that elected and appointed officials, together with civic organizations, have reviewed prospective plans, and that the citizenry has also been involved through the machinery of public hearings. Involvement of the citizen is essential to the planning process under our democratic system. It is also consistent with specific programs emerging from Washington, and with local efforts that are bringing an ever-increasing sector of the community into the process.

As experience in the field has been gained, it has become evident that only genuine citizen participation can solve many of the problems associated with urban renewal. As other programs are organized within a pattern of detailed and highly localized attacks on community problems, this fact will become increasingly true for them as well.

In the future, we may well wonder at the naïveté of the planning profession in isolating itself from the people for so long through a "technical" approach to problems which can only be solved through the involvement of the majority of citizens in the community.

Appendix

Sample By-Laws
for a Planning Commission

(City Planning Commission of a suburban city of 15,000 population; council-manager form; planning commission of five members appointed by the mayor and council.)

Meetings

SECTION 1. ANNUAL MEETING:

The annual meeting of the Planning Commission shall be the first regular meeting in the month of January of each year. Such meeting shall be devoted to the election of officers for the ensuing year and such other business as shall be scheduled by the Planning Commission.

SECTION 2. REGULAR MEETINGS:

Regular meetings of the Planning Commission shall be held in the City Hall at 8:00 P.M. on the second and fourth Tuesday of each month, except in the month of August. At such meetings the Commission shall consider all matters properly brought before the Commission without the necessity of prior notice thereof given to any members. A regular meeting may be cancelled or rescheduled by the Commission at a prior meeting.

SECTION 3. SPECIAL MEETINGS:

Special meetings of the Planning Commission shall be held at a time and place designated by the officer calling the same and shall be called by the Chairman or Vice Chairman. Written notice thereof shall be given to all the members not less than twenty-four hours in advance thereof.

SECTION 4. QUORUM:

At any meeting of the Planning Commission, a quorum shall consist of three members of the Commission. No action shall be taken in the absence of a quorum, except to adjourn the meeting to a subsequent date.

SECTION 5. VOTING:

At all meetings of the Planning Commission, each member attending shall be entitled to cast one vote. Voting shall be by voice. In the event that any member shall have a personal interest of any kind in a matter then before the Commission, he shall disclose his interest and be disqualified from voting upon the matter, and the Secretary shall so record in the minutes that no vote was cast by such member. The affirmative vote of at least three members shall be necessary for the adoption of any resolution or other voting matter.

SECTION 6. PROCEEDINGS:

a. At any regular meeting of the Planning Commission, the following shall be the regular order of business:
   (1) Roll call
   (2) Minutes of the preceding meeting
   (3) Public hearings
   (4) Old and new business
   (5) Communications
   (6) Report of the Chairman
   (7) Report of the City Planner
   (8) Adjournment
b. Each formal action of the Planning Commission required by law, city charter, rule or regulation shall be embodied in a formal resolution duly entered in full upon the Minute Book after an affirmative vote as provided in Section 5 hereof.

SECTION 7. RULES OF PROCEDURE:

All meetings of the Planning Commission shall be conducted in accordance with *Robert's Rules of Order*.

Officers

SECTION 8. OFFICERS:

The officers of the Planning Commission shall consist of a Chairman, appointed by the Mayor, and a Vice Chairman, elected by the Commission at the annual meeting for a term of one year. The City Planner appointed by the City Manager under the City Charter shall be the Secretary of the Commission. In the event the Secretary shall be absent from any meeting, the officer presiding shall designate an acting Secretary.

SECTION 9. DUTIES OF OFFICERS:

The duties and powers of the officers of the Planning Commission shall be as follows:
   a. *Chairman:*
   (1) To preside at all meetings of the Commission.
   (2) To call special meetings of the Commission in accordance with these By-Laws.
   (3) To sign documents of the Commission.

(4) To see that all actions of the Commission are properly taken.

b. *Vice Chairman:*

During the absence, disability or disqualification of the Chairman, the Vice Chairman shall exercise or perform all the duties and be subject to all the responsibilities of the Chairman.

c. *Secretary:*

(1) To keep the minutes of all meetings of the Commission in an appropriate Minute Book.

(2) To give or serve all notices required by law or by these By-Laws.

(3) To prepare the agenda for all meetings of the Commission.

(4) To be custodian of Commission records.

(5) To inform the Commission of correspondence relating to business of the Commission and to attend to such correspondence.

(6) To handle funds allocated to the Commission in accordance with its directives, the law, and City regulations.

(7) To sign official documents of the Commission.

SECTION 10. VACANCIES:

Should any vacancy occur among the members of this Planning Commission by reason of death, resignation, disability or otherwise, immediate notice thereof shall be given to the City Clerk by the Secretary. Should any vacancy occur among the officers of the Planning Commission, the vacant office shall be filled in accordance with Section 8 of these By-Laws, such officer to serve the unexpired term of the office in which such vacancy shall occur.

Amendments

SECTION 11. AMENDING BY-LAWS:

These By-Laws may be amended at any meeting of the Planning Commission provided that notice of said proposed amendment is given to each member in writing at least five days prior to said meeting.

Selected Bibliography

1. Antecedents of Local Planning

ADAMS, THOMAS. *Outline of Town and City Planning.* (New York: Russell Sage Foundation, 1935.) Despite its age, this book is still an excellent overview of the historical roots of urban planning.

ALONSO, WILLIAM. "Cities and City Planners," *Daedalus,* XCII (Fall, 1963). This article is useful for its treatment of the development of the planning profession.

GALLION, ARTHUR B., and SIMON EISNER. *The Urban Pattern.* (Princeton, N.J.: D. Van Nostrand Company, Inc., 2nd ed., 1963.) Written primarily from a design standpoint, this book provides many historical materials on planning and city growth.

GLAAB, CHARLES N. *The American City: A Documentary History.* (Homewood, Ill.: The Dorsey Press, Inc., 1963.) In this set of documents, a leading urban historian has chosen to emphasize materials from the 18th and 19th centuries. The documents are well selected to illuminate both American attitudes toward the city and the capacity of local political institutions to manage urban development.

HIRSCHL, JESSE HECKMAN. "The Great White City," *American Heritage,* XI, No. 6 (October, 1960), p. 8. A detailed account of the Columbian Exposition of 1893.

HUBBARD, THEODORA KIMBALL. *Manual of Information on City Planning and Zoning, Including References on Regional, Rural, and National Planning.* (Cambridge: Harvard University Press, 1923.) This report summarizes a number of city plans of the City Beautiful period. It allows the reader to get a sense of the scope of early professional practice.

MARTIN, JOHN STUART. " 'He paints with lakes and wooden slopes . . . '," *American Heritage,* XV, No. 6 (October, 1964), p. 15. A biography of Frederick Law Olmsted.

PERLOFF, HARVEY S. *Education for Planning: City, State, and Regional.* (Baltimore: The Johns Hopkins Press, 1957.) Perloff places his recommendations for the content of professional education in the context of the history of planning. The book contains a detailed summary of important events in the development of the planning movement from 1893 to 1955.

REPS, JOHN W. *The Making of Urban America: A History of City Planning in the United States.* (Princeton, N.J.: Princeton University Press, 1965.) This is the definitive work on the history of planning from the beginning of European settlement until the first World War. Reps deals with plans and the planning process, not architecture or civic design principles.

TUNNARD, CHRISTOPHER, and HENRY HOPE REED. *American Skyline: The Growth and Form of Our Cities and Towns.* (Boston: Houghton Mifflin, 1955.) Architectural styles and civic design are the foci of this historical account.

U.S. NATIONAL RESOURCES COMMITTEE. Urbanism Committee. *Our Cities: Their Role in the National Economy.* (Washington: Government Printing Office, 1937.) A landmark in the efforts to make cities respectable and city governments effective.

———. *Urban Planning and Land Policies, Volume II of the Supplementary Report.* (Washington: Government Printing Office, 1939.) This report contains three sections of interest to the student of planning history: "Planned Communities," by Arthur S. Comey and Max S. Wehrly, "Urban Living Conditions," by Louis Wirth and Edward Shils, and "Urban Land Policies," by Harold S. Buttenheim.

WADE, RICHARD C. *The Urban Frontier: The Rise of Western Cities, 1790–1830.* (Cambridge: Harvard University Press, 1959.) Wade includes a valuable discussion of the efforts of early city governments to cope with urban expansion through regulation of private activity and the provision of public services. The cities are Pittsburgh, Louisville, Lexington, Cincinnati, and St. Louis. The book was published in paperback by the University of Chicago Press in 1964.

WALKER, ROBERT A. *The Planning Function in Urban Government.* (Chicago: University of Chicago Press, 1941.) This book propounds the thesis that the local planning function should be organized as a staff aid to the municipal executive. It was the first empirical analysis of planning agencies. Thus, it is the best summary of the status of planning in the 1930's. Walker also covers the history of planning since 1900, and a more detailed history of land use controls, especially zoning.

WILSON, WILLIAM E. "Utopia, Unlimited," *American Heritage,* XV, No. 6 (October, 1964), p. 64. Wherein Father Rapp succeeds and Robert Owen fails at New Harmony, Indiana.

2. The Intergovernmental Context of Local Planning

ADRIAN, CHARLES R. *State and Local Governments, A Study in the Political Process.* (New York: McGraw-Hill, 1960.)

COMMITTEE FOR ECONOMIC DEVELOPMENT. *Modernizing Local Government.* (New York: The Committee, 1966.)

CONNERY, ROBERT HUGH and RICHARD H. LEACH. *The Federal Government and Metropolitan Areas.* (Cambridge: Harvard University Press, 1960.)

ELAZAR, DANIEL J. *The American Partnership.*

(Chicago: University of Chicago Press, 1962.)

GAUS, JOHN M. *Reflections of Public Administration.* (University, Ala.: University of Alabama Press, 1947.)

GOODMAN, WILLIAM I. "Urban Planning and the Role of the State," *State Government*, XXXV (Summer, 1962), pp. 149–54.

HOOVER, EDGAR M. and RAYMOND VERNON. *Anatomy of a Metropolis.* (Cambridge: Harvard University Press, 1959.)

"Intergovernmental Relations in the United States," *The Annals of the American Academy of Political and Social Science*, CCCLIX (May, 1965), pp. 1–257.

INSTITUTE OF PUBLIC ADMINISTRATION, Study Group on Housing and Neighborhood Improvement. *Let There Be Commitment: A Housing, Planning, Development Program for New York City.* (New York: The Institute, 1966.)

JOINT CENTER FOR URBAN STUDIES OF MASSACHUSETTS AND HARVARD UNIVERSITY. *The Effectiveness of Metropolitan Planning*, prepared in cooperation with the Subcommitee on Intergovernmental Relations of the Commitee on Government Operations, United States Senate, Commitee Print, 88th Congress, 2nd Session. (Washington: Government Printing Office, 1964.)

KEYES, SCOTT, WILLIAM T. GELMAN, MICHAEL A. CARROLL, and CHARLES E. WHALEN, *A Guide to Federal Programs for Illinois Communities.* (Urbana: University of Illinois Bureau of Community Planning, 1966.)

MARTIN, ROSCOE COLEMAN. *The Cities and The Federal System.* (New York: Atherton Press, 1965.)

U.S. ADVISORY COMMISSION ON INTERGOVERNMENTAL RELATIONS. *Impact of Federal Urban Development Programs on Local Government Organization and Planning.* (Washington: Government Printing Office, 1964.)

U.S. AREA REDEVELOPMENT ADMINISTRATION. *Handbook of Federal Aids to Communities.* (Washington: Government Printing Office, 1966.)

U.S. OFFICE OF ECONOMIC OPPORTUNITY. *Catalog of Federal Programs for Individual and Community Improvement.* (Washington: Office of Economic Opportunity, 1965.)

WISE, HAROLD F. "Current Developments in Regional Planning in the United States," American Society of Planing Officials *Planning 1965*, pp. 47–57.

WOOD, ROBERT C. *1400 Governments.* (Cambridge: Harvard University Press, 1961.)

3. Population Studies

BARCLAY, GEORGE W. *Techniques of Population Analysis.* (New York: Wiley, 1958.)

CHAPIN, F. STUART, JR. *Urban Land Use Planning.* (Urbana: University of Illinois Press, 2nd ed., 1965), pp. 181–220.

GOLDSTEIN, SIDNEY and KURT B. MAYER. "Metropolitanization and Population Change in Rhode Island," *Rhode Island Development Council, Planning Division Publication No. 3* (1961).

HAJNAL, JOHN. "The Prospects of Population Forecasts," *Journal of the American Statistical Association*, L (June, 1955), pp. 309–22.

HAMILTON, C. HORACE and JOSEF PERRY. "A Short Method for Projecting Population by Age from One Decennial Census to Another," *Social Forces*, XLI (December, 1962), pp. 163–70.

ISARD, WALTER. *Methods of Regional Analysis.* (Cambridge: M.I.T. Press, 1960), pp. 5–79.

KEYFITZ, NATHAN. "The Population Projection as a Matrix Operator," *Demography*, I (1964), pp. 56–73.

KRISTOF, FRANK S. "The Increased Utility of the 1960 Housing Census for Planning," *Journal of the American Institute of Planners*, XXIX (February, 1963), pp. 40–48.

ROGERS, ANDREI. "Matrix Analysis of Interregional Population Growth and Distribution," *Papers and Proceedings* of the Sixth European Regional Science Congress, Vienna, September, 1966, forthcoming.

————. "Matrix Methods of Population Analyses," *Journal of the American Institute of Planners*, XXXII (January, 1966), pp. 40–44.

RYDER, N. B. "Fertility," *The Study of Population.* Ed. by Philip M. Hauser and O. D. Duncan. (Chicago: University of Chicago Press, 1959), pp. 400–436.

SCHNORE, LEO F. "A Planner's Guide to the 1960 Census of Population," *Journal of the American Institute of Planners*, XXIX (February, 1963), pp. 29–39.

SIEGEL, JACOB S., MEYER ZITTER, and DONALD S. AKERS. *Projections of the Population of the United States, by Age, Sex, 1964–1965, with Extensions to 2010*, U.S. Bureau of the Census *Current Population Reports, Series P-25 No. 286.* (Washington: Government Printing Office, 1964.)

TAEUBER, KARL E. "Duration of Residence Analysis of Internal Migration In the United States," *Millbank Memorial Fund Quarterly*, XXXIX (1961), p. 121.

UNITED NATIONS. Department of Social Affairs, Population Division. *Determinants and Consequences of Population Trends.* Population Studies No. 17. (New York: 1954.)

U.S. BUREAU OF THE CENSUS. *Current Population Reports, Series P-25 No. 328: Inventory of State and Local Agencies Preparing Population Estimates: Survey of 1965.* (Washington: Government Printing Office, 1966.)

————. *U.S. Census of Housing: 1960, Availability of Published and Unpublished Data.* (Washington: Government Printing Office, 1961.)

————. *U.S. Census of Population: 1960, Availability of Published and Unpublished Data.* (Washington: Government Printing Office, Revised October, 1964.)

4. Economic Studies

CHAPIN, F. STUART, JR. *Urban Land Use Planning.* (Urbana: University of Illinois Press, 2nd ed., 1965.) This is a text of high quality which provides the student and practitioner with excellent discussions of economic analysis concepts and methodologies. For economic study purposes the following chapters are recommended: 1, Land Use Perspectives; 3, The Urban Economy; 4, Employment Studies.

FLORENCE, P. SARGANT. *The Logic of British and American Industry.* (London: Routledge and Kegan Paul, Ltd., rev. ed., 1961.) Although the organization of materials makes for rather difficult reading, the first two chapters on industrial structure contain many ideas necessary to an understanding of the inner workings and forces of the urban economy.

HOOVER, EDGAR and RAYMOND VERNON. *Anatomy of a Metropolis.* (Cambridge, Mass.: Harvard University Press, 1959.) One of a series of studies of the New York Metropolitan Region sponsored by the Regional Plan Association, Inc. Of particular value to the urban economic analyst are Part II, The Jobs; and Part IV, The Jobs, The People, and The Future.

ISARD, WALTER, *et al. Methods of Regional Analysis: An Introduction to Regional Science.* (New York: The Technology Press of the Massachusetts Institute of Technology and John Wiley & Sons, Inc., 1960.) The principle value of this work for the urban economic analyst is found in the extensive and impartial treatment of several alternative and supplementary analysis forms such as input-output and industrial complex analysis. Chapter 6 provides a competent but unsympathetic treatment of the economic base technique.

MEYER, JOHN. "Regional Economics: A Survey," *The American Economic Review* (March, 1963), pp. 19–54. Meyer provides a thorough evaluation of the base technique and other techniques which have an essentially regional orientation. His bibliography is excellent.

PFOUTS, RALPH W. (ed.) *The Techniques of Urban Economic Analysis.* (West Trenton, N.J.: Chandler-Davis Publishing Co., 1960.) A collection of technical journal papers which reveals in depth the character, strengths, and weaknesses of the economic base technique. Considerable attention is paid to alternative approaches.

SOLOMON, EZRA and ZARKO G. BILBIJA. *Metropolitan Chicago.* (Glencoe, Ill.: The Free Press, 1959.) This economic analysis of a great city is useful to the technician in that it not only outlines the procedures employed but also evaluates them.

THOMPSON, WILBUR R. *A Preface to Urban Economics.* (Baltimore: The Johns Hopkins Press for Resources for the Future, Inc., 1965.) This book is of peculiar value in that it can stimulate the think-of the urban analyst by suggesting goals, and approaches to problems that will often seem new and provocative. Part I, Principles: Goals and Processes in the Urban Economy, is recommended for the beginner.

5. Land Use Studies

Land Use Theories, Models, and Trends

ALONSO, WILLIAM. *Location and Land Use: Toward a General Theory of Land Rent.* (Cambridge: Harvard University Press, 1964.)

CHAPIN, F. STUART, JR. "Selected Theories of Urban Growth and Structure," *Journal of the American Institute of Planners,* XXX (February, 1964), pp. 51–58.

————. "Toward a Theory of Urban Growth and Development," Chapter 2 in *Urban Land Use Planning.* (Urbana: University of Illinois Press, 2nd ed., 1965), pp. 69–99.

CHAPIN, F. STUART, JR. and SHIRLEY F. WEISS, "Introduction" and Land Development Patterns and Growth Alternatives," Chapter 13 in Chapin and Weiss (eds.) *Urban Growth Dynamics in a Regional Cluster of Cities.* (New York: John Wiley and Sons, Inc., 1962.)

CLAWSON, MARION, R. BURNELL HELD, and CHARLES H. STODDARD. *Land for the Future.* (Baltimore: Johns Hopkins Press for Resources for the Future, Inc., 1960.)

HARRIS, BRITTON, (ed.) "Urban Development Models: New Tools for Planning," Special Issue of the *Journal of the American Institute of Planners,* XXXI (May, 1965), pp. 90–184.

JONES, BARCLAY G., "Land Uses in the United States in the Year 2000," in Charles M. Weiss (ed.) *Man's Environment in the Twenty-First Century.* (Chapel Hill: Department of Environmental Sciences and Engineering, School of Public Health, University of North Carolina, 1965), pp. 171–195.

LANDSBERG, HANS H., LEONARD L. FISCHMAN and JOSEPH L. FISHER. *Resources in America's Future: Patterns of Requirements and Availabilities 1960–2000.* (Baltimore: Johns Hopkins Press for Resources for the Future, Inc., 1963.)

MEIER, RICHARD L. *A Communications Theory of Urban Growth.* (Cambridge: M. I. T. Press, 1962.)

NIEDERCORN, JOHN H. and EDWARD F. R. HEARLE. *Recent Land-Use Trends in Forty-Eight Large American Cities.* Memorandum RM-3664-FF. (Santa Monica: The Rand Corporation, 1963.)

WEBBER, MELVIN M. "The Urban Place and the Nonplace Urban Realm," in Webber (ed.) *Explorations into Urban Structure.* (Philadelphia: University of Pennsylvania Press, 1963), pp. 79–153.

WINGO, LOWDON, JR. *Transportation and Urban Land.* (Washington: Resources for the Future, Inc., 1961.)

Land Use Studies—Bibliographies

AMERICAN SOCIETY OF PLANNING OFFICIALS. *ASPO Planning Advisory Service Information Report 203: Selected References for the Planning Agency.* (Chicago: ASPO, 1965.)

CHAPIN, F. STUART, JR. *Selected References on Urban Planning Methods and Techniques.* (Chapel Hill: Department of City and Regional Planning, University of North Carolina, 1966.)

COUNCIL OF PLANNING LIBRARIANS. *Exchange Bibliographies.* (Eugene, Ore.: The Council, 1958–1966.) A series of individual planning topics, issued and updated from time to time.

Mapping

BAIR, FRED H., JR. "Mapping Program for Planning, Tied to Aerial Photographs," *Florida Planning and Development,* XII, No. 5 (May, 1961), pp. 1–5; No. 6 (June, 1961), pp. 1–5, 10; No. 7 (July, 1961), pp. 1–5.

BARRACLOUGH, ROBERT E. "Mapping and EDP," *Planning 1965.* (Chicago: American Society of Planning Officials, 1965), pp. 313–18.

CHAPIN, F. STUART, JR. *Urban Land Use Planning.* (Urbana: University of Illinois Press, 2nd ed., 1965), pp. 256–264.

Land Use Survey—Classification, Recording, and Analysis

AMERICAN INSTITUTE OF PLANNERS, SOUTHEAST CHAPTER, NORTH CAROLINA SECTION. *A Proposal for a Standardized Land-Use Classification System.* Prepared by Land Use Classification Committee. (Raleigh: Division of Community Planning, Department of Conservation and Development, periodically revised.)

AMERICAN PUBLIC HEALTH ASSOCIATION, COMMITTEE ON THE HYGIENE OF HOUSING, *An Appraisal Method for Measuring the Quality of Housing,* Parts I, II, and III. (New York: The Association, 1950.)

BARTHOLOMEW, HARLAND, assisted by JACK WOOD. *Land Uses in American Cities.* Harvard City Planning Studies, XV. (Cambridge: Harvard University Press, 1955.)

BERRY, BRIAN J. L. *Commercial Structure and Commercial Blight.* (Chicago: University of Chicago, Department of Geography Research Paper No. 85, 1963.)

CHAPIN, F. STUART, JR. *Urban Land Use Planning.* (Urbana: University of Illinois Press, 2nd ed., 1965), pp. 264–291.

CLAWSON, MARION, with CHARLES L. STEWART. *Land Use Information, A Critical Survey of U.S. Statistics Including Possibilities for Greater Uniformity.* (Baltimore: The Johns Hopkins Press, 1965.) Text prepared under the direction of a special committee organized by Resources for the Future, Inc.

DETROIT METROPOLITAN AREA REGIONAL PLANNING

COMMISSION, LAND CLASSIFICATION ADVISORY COMMITTEE. *Land Use Classification Manual.* (Chicago: Public Administration Service, 1962.)

EL PASO, TEXAS, DEPARTMENT OF PLANNING. *A Data Storage System for Land Use Analysis—A Description.* Technical Report 62–1. (El Paso: The Department, 1962.)

GUTTENBERG, ALBERT Z. "New, Old Criteria Explored in Search of Means of Evaluating Non-residential Property," *Journal of Housing,* XXI, No. 2 (1964), pp. 73–79.

LITTLE, ARTHUR D. INC. *The Usefulness of Philadelphia's Industrial Plant: An Approach to Industrial Renewal.* (Philadelphia: City Planning Commission, 1960.)

METROPOLITAN DADE COUNTY: PLANNING ADVISORY BOARD AND PLANNING DEPARTMENT. *Preliminary Land Use Plan and Policies for Development,* prepared for the Board of County Commissioners, Metropolitan Dade County (Miami: The Department, 1961.)

METROPOLITAN DATA CENTER PROJECT. *The Metropolitan Data Center Project,* Demonstration Project Number D–1. (Tulsa: The Project, 1966.)

NORTHWESTERN ILLINOIS METROPOLITAN AREA PLANNING COMMISSION. *Land Use Handbook: A Guide to Undertaking Land Use Surveys.* (Chicago: The Commission, 1961.)

TULSA METROPOLITAN AREA PLANNING COMMISSION. *Land Use: A Procedural Manual for Collection, Storage, and Retrieval of Data.* (Tulsa: The Commission, 1965.)

U.S. BUREAU OF THE BUDGET. *Standard Industrial Classification Manual.* (Washington: Bureau of the Budget, 1957; and *Supplement to 1957 Edition,* 1963.)

U.S. URBAN RENEWAL ADMINISTRATION AND BUREAU OF PUBLIC ROADS. *Standard Land Use Coding Manual: A Standard System for Identifying and Coding Land Use Activities.* (Washington: Urban Renewal Administration and the Bureau, 1965.)

Forecasting Space Requirements

CHAPIN, F. STUART, JR. "Location Requirements," Chapter 10 in *Urban Land Use Planning.* (Urbana: University of Illinois Press, 2nd ed., 1965), pp. 370–456.

Industrial and Wholesale

BOLEY, ROBERT E. *Industrial Districts: Principles in Practice.* Urban Land Institute Technical Bulletin No. 44. (Washington: Urban Land Institute, 1962.)

CHAPIN, F. STUART, JR. *Urban Land Use Planning.* (Urbana: University of Illinois Press, 2nd ed., 1965), pp. 386–400.

LITTLE, ARTHUR D., INC. *The Usefulness of Philadelphia's Industrial Plant: An Approach to In-*

dustrial Renewal. (Philadelphia: City Planning Commission, 1960.)

MUNCY, DOROTHY A. *Space for Industry: An Analysis of Site and Location Requirements.* Urban Land Institute Technical Bulletin No. 23. (Washington: Urban Land Institute, 1954.)

Central Business District and Commercial

CHAPIN, F. STUART, JR. *Urban Land Use Planning.* (Urbana: University of Illinois Press, 2nd ed., 1965), pp. 401–12.

FOLEY, DONALD L. *The Suburbanization of Administrative Offices in the San Francisco Bay Area.* (Berkeley: Real Estate Research Program, University of California, 1957.)

HORWOOD, EDGAR M., and RONALD R. BOYCE. *Studies of the Central Business District and Urban Freeway Development.* (Seattle: University of Washington Press, 1959.)

MURPHY, RAYMOND E., J. E. VANCE, JR., and BART J. EPSTEIN. *Central Business District Studies,* reprinted from *Economic Geography.* (Worcester: Clark University, January 1955.)

NELSON, RICHARD L. *The Selection of Retail Locations.* (New York: F. W. Dodge Corporation, 1958.)

SMITH, LARRY. "Space for the CBD's Functions," *Journal of the American Institute of Planners,* XXVII (February, 1961), pp. 35–42.

STEFANIAK, NORBERT J. *Utilization of Central Office Space by Milwaukee Area Industrial Firms,* prepared for the Division of Economic Development of the Mayor's Office and the Central Industrial Office Development Committee of the Mayor's Economic Growth Council. (Milwaukee: Division of Economic Development, Mayor's Office, 1964.)

VERNON, RAYMOND. *The Changing Economic Function of the Central City,* supplementary paper of the CED No. 6. (New York: Committee for Economic Development, 1959.)

WEISS, SHIRLEY F. *The Central Business District in Transition: Methodological Approaches to CBD Analysis and Forecasting Future Space Requirements.* (Chapel Hill: Department of City and Regional Planning, University of North Carolina, 1957, reprinted 1965.)

Civic, Institutional, Recreational, and Open Space

AMERICAN SOCIETY OF PLANNING OFFICIALS. *ASPO Planning Advisory Service Information Report No. 83: Civic Center Planning.* (Chicago: ASPO, February, 1956.)

———. *ASPO Planning Advisory Service Information Report No. 90: Fire House Location Planning.* (Chicago: ASPO, May, 1957.)

———. *ASPO Planning Advisory Service Information Report No. 194: Standards for Outdoor Recreational Areas.* (Chicago: ASPO, January, 1965.)

———. *ASPO Planning Advisory Service Information Report No. 173: Usable Open Space.* (Chicago: ASPO, July, 1963.)

AMERICAN HOSPITAL ASSOCIATION and PUBLIC HEALTH SERVICE. *Areawide Planning for Hospitals and Related Health Facilities.* (Washington: The Association, 1961.)

AMERICAN PUBLIC WORKS ASSOCIATION. *Municipal Refuse Disposal.* (Chicago: Public Administration Service, 1961.)

ARCHITECTURAL RECORD. *Hospitals, Clinics, and Health Centers.* (New York: F. W. Dodge Corporation, 1960.)

BUTLER, GEORGE D. *Standards for Municipal Recreation Areas.* (New York: National Recreation Association, rev. ed., 1962.)

DEERING, FRANCIS R., DON JEWELL, and LINDSLEY C. LUEDDEKE. *Auditoriums and Arenas: Facts from a Survey by the International Association of Auditorium Managers.* (Chicago: Public Administration Service, 1961.)

INTERNATIONAL ASSOCIATION OF AUDITORIUM MANAGERS. *Auditoriums and Arenas: Supplement.* (Chicago: Public Administration Service, 1964.)

NATIONAL ADVISORY COUNCIL ON REGIONAL RECREATION PLANNING. *A User-Resource Recreation Planning Method.* (Loomis, Calif.: The Council, 1959.)

SESSOMS, H. DOUGLAS. "New Bases for Recreation Planning," *Journal of the American Institute of Planners,* XXX (February, 1964), pp. 26–33.

U.S. NATIONAL OUTDOOR RECREATION RESOURCES REVIEW COMMISSION. *Outdoor Recreation for America.* (Washington: The Commission, 1962.)

U.S. PUBLIC HEALTH SERVICE. *Procedures for Areawide Health Facility Planning.* PHS Publication No. 930–B–3. (Washington: The Service, 1963.)

WHEELER, JOSEPH L. *The Effective Location of Public Library Buildings.* University of Illinois Library School Occasional Papers No. 52. (Urbana: University of Illinois Library School, July, 1958.)

Transportation

AMERICAN SOCIETY OF PLANNING OFFICIALS. *ASPO Planning Advisory Service Information Report No. 198: Helicopters.* (Chicago: ASPO, 1965.)

BOLT, BERANEK, AND NEWMAN, INC. *Land Use Planning Relating to Aircraft Noise.* (Washington: Federal Aviation Agency, October, 1964.)

FITCH, LYLE C., AND ASSOCIATES. *Urban Transportation and Public Policy.* (San Francisco: Chandler Publishing Company, 1964.)

MEYER, J. R., J. F. KAIN, and M. WOHL. *The Urban Transportation Problem.* (Cambridge: Harvard University Press, 1965.)

NATIONAL COMMITTEE ON URBAN TRANSPORTATION. *Better Transportation for Your City: A Guide to the Factual Development of Urban Trans-*

portation Plans. (Chicago: Public Administration Service, 1958.)

U.S. FEDERAL AVIATION AGENCY. *Heliport Design Guide.* (Washington: The Agency, 1964.)

————. *National Airport Plan—Fiscal Years 1965–1969.* (Washington: The Agency, 1964.)

Residential and Neighborhood Facilities

AMERICAN PUBLIC HEALTH ASSOCIATION, COMMITTEE ON THE HYGIENE OF HOUSING. *Planning the Neighborhood.* (Chicago: Public Administration Service, 1960.)

BARTLEY, ERNEST R. and FREDERICK H. BAIR, JR. *Mobile Home Parks and Comprehensive Community Planning.* (Gainesville: Public Administration Clearing House of the University of Florida, 1960.)

CHAPIN, F. STUART, JR. *Urban Land Use Planning.* (Urbana: University of Illinois Press, 2nd ed., 1965), pp. 374–78, 422–56.

CHASE, WILLIAM W. *Problems in Planning Urban School Facilities,* Bulletin No. 23. (Washington: Office of Education, 1964.)

HARMAN, O'DONNELL, AND HENNINGER ASSOCIATES. *New Approaches to Residential Land Development: A Study of Concepts and Innovations,* Urban Land Institute Technical Bulletin No. 41. (Washington: Urban Land Institute, 1961.)

KOSTKA, JOSEPH V. *Neighborhood Planning.* (Winnipeg: Appraisal Institute of Canada, 1957.)

U.S. FEDERAL HOUSING ADMINISTRATION. *Land-Use Intensity,* Land Planning Bulletin No. 7. (Washington: FHA, interim ed., 1965.)

————. *Minimum Property Standards for One and Two Living Units,* FHA No. 300. (Washington: FHA, 1965.)

————. *Planned-Unit Development, with a Homes Association,* Land Planning Bulletin No. 6. (Washington: FHA, rev. ed., 1964.)

U.S. PUBLIC HEALTH SERVICE. *Environmental Health Planning Guide,* Public Health Service Publication No. 823. (Washington: U.S. Department of Health, Education, and Welfare, rev. ed., 1962.)

URBAN LAND INSTITUTE. *Innovations vs. Traditions in Community Development, a Comparative Study in Residential Land Use,* Technical Bulletin No. 47, prepared under the auspices of the National Association of Home Builders and Urban Land Institute. (Washington: The Institute, 1963.)

Welding the Land Use Plan

ALTSHULER, ALAN. *The City Planning Process: A Political Analysis.* (Ithaca: Cornell University Press, 1965.)

AMERICAN SOCIETY OF PLANNING OFFICIALS. *ASPO Planning Advisory Service Information Report No. 160: New Techniques for Shaping Urban Growth.* (Chicago: ASPO, 1962.)

CHAPIN, F. STUART, JR. "Taking Stock of Techniques for Shaping Urban Growth," *Journal of the American Institute of Planners,* XXIX (May, 1963), pp. 76–87.

CHAPIN, F. STUART, JR. *Urban Land Use Planning.* (Urbana: University of Illinois Press, 2nd ed., 1965), pp. 457–73.

GOODMAN, WILLIAM I. and JEROME L. KAUFMAN. *City Planning in the Sixties: A Restatement of Principles and Techniques.* (Urbana: Bureau of Community Planning, University of Illinois, 1965.)

GREATER BRIDGEPORT REGIONAL PLANNING AGENCY. *Preliminary Regional Plan: Recommended Development Policies.* (Trumbull, Conn.: The Agency, 1963.)

THE JOINT PROGRAM. *Goals for Development of the Twin Cities Metropolitian Area,* Report No. 3. (St. Paul: The Program, 1965.)

LESSINGER, JACK. "The Case for Scatteration: Some Reflections on the National Capital Region Plan for the Year 2000," *Journal of the American Institute of Planners,* XXVIII (August, 1962), pp. 159–169.

MARYLAND-NATIONAL CAPITAL PARK AND PLANNING COMMISSION. . . . *on Wedges and Corridors: A General Plan for the Maryland-Washington Regional District in Montgomery and Prince George's Counties.* (Silver Spring, Maryland: The Commission, 1962.)

PUBLIC ADMINISTRATION SERVICE. *Action for Cities.* (Chicago: The Service, 1945.)

U.S. NATIONAL CAPITAL PLANNING COMMISSION and NATIONAL CAPITAL REGIONAL PLANNING COUNCIL. *A Policies Plan for the Year 2000: The Nation's Capital.* (Washington: The Commission, 1961.)

6. Transportation Planning

General

AUTOMOBILE MANUFACTURERS ASSOCIATION, *The Dynamics of Urban Transportation.* (Detroit: The Association, 1962.)

BERRY, DONALD S. and OTHERS. *The Technology of Urban Transportation.* (Evanston, Illinois: Northwestern University Press, 1963.)

BRANCH, MELVILLE C. *Transportation Developments, Cities, and Planning.* (Chicago: American Society of Planning Officials, 1965.)

INSTITUTE OF TRAFFIC ENGINEERS. *Traffic Engineering Handbook.* (Washington, D.C.: The Institute, 3rd ed., 1965.)

LABATUT, JEAN, and WHEATON J. LANE. *Highways in Our National Life, A Symposium.* (Princeton: Princeton University Press, 1950.)

MARTIN, BRIAN V., and OTHERS. *Principles and Techniques of Predicting Future Demand for Urban Area Transportation.* (Cambridge: MIT Press, 4th ed., 1965.)

MEYER, J. R., and OTHERS. *The Urban Transportation Problem.* (Cambridge: Harvard University Press, 1965.)

MITCHELL, ROBERT BUCHANAN. *Metropolitan Planning for Land Use and Transportation; A Study.* (Washington, D.C.: U.S. Office of Public Works, 1961.)

MITCHELL, ROBERT BUCHANAN, and CHESTER RAPKIN. *Urban Traffic, A Function of Land Use.* (New York: Columbia University Press, 1954.)

NATIONAL ACADEMY OF SCIENCES, NATIONAL RESEARCH COUNCIL. *A Conference on Transportation Research. Volume I: Transportation Research Conference, Woods Hole, Massachusetts.* (Washington, D.C.: The Academy, 1961.)

————. *Transportation Design Considerations. Volume II: Transportation Research Conference, Woods Hole, Massachusetts.* (Washington, D.C.: The Academy, 1961.)

————. *U.S. Transportation: Resources, Performance and Problems: Supplement to Volume II: Transportation Research Conference, Woods Hole, Massachusetts.* (Washington, D.C.: The Academy, 1961.)

NATIONAL COMMITTEE ON URBAN TRANSPORTATION. *Better Transportation for Your City: A Guide to the Factual Development of Urban Transportation Plans.* (Washington, D.C.: The Committee, 1958.)

NATIONAL RESEARCH COUNCIL, HIGHWAY RESEARCH BOARD. *Highway Capacity Manual.* (Washington, D.C.: The Council, 2nd ed., 1965.)

OI, WALTER and PAUL W. SHULDINER. *An Analysis of Urban Travel Demands.* (Evanston, Illinois: Northwestern University Press, 1962.)

OWEN, WILFRED. *The Metropolitan Transportation Problem.* (Washington, D.C.: Brookings Institution, rev. ed., 1966.)

SMITH (WILBUR) AND ASSOCIATES. *Future Highways and Urban Growth.* (New Haven, Connecticut: Smith and Associates, 1961.)

U.S. BUREAU OF PUBLIC ROADS. *Traffic Assignment and Distribution for Small Urban Areas.* (Washington, D.C.: The Bureau, 1965.)

U.S. BUREAU OF PUBLIC ROADS. *Traffic Assignment Manual.* (Washington, D.C.: The Bureau, 1964.)

WINGO, LOWDON. *Transportation and Urban Land.* (Washington, D.C.: Resources for the Future, 1961.)

ZETTEL, RICHARD M. and RICHARD R. CARLL. *Summary Review of Major Metropolitan Area Transportation Studies in the United States.* (Berkeley: University of California Institute of Transportation and Traffic Engineering, 1962.)

Highway Transportation Studies

CHICAGO AREA TRANSPORTATION STUDY. *Final Report.* 3 vol. (Chicago: 1959–1962.)

DETROIT METROPOLITAN AREA REGIONAL PLANNING COMMISSION. *Study Design for a Comprehensive Land Use Program for the Detroit Region.* (Detroit: The Commission, 1965.)

DETROIT METROPOLITAN AREA TRAFFIC STUDY. *Report.* 2 vol. (Lansing, Michigan: Michigan State Highway Department, 1965.)

JOINT PROGRAM, ST. PAUL. *The Joint Program; an Inter-Agency Land Use-Transportation Planning Program for the Twin Cities Metropolitan Area. Reports No. 1–3.* (St. Paul: The Program, 1963–65.)

PENN-JERSEY TRANSPORTATION STUDY. *Penn-Jersey Reports.* 3 vol. (Philadelphia: 1963–65.)

PITTSBURGH AREA TRANSPORTATION STUDY. *Final Report.* 2 vol. (Pittsburgh: 1961–63.)

TWIN CITIES AREA TRANSPORTATION STUDY. *The Twin Cities Area Transportation Study, v. 1: Study Findings.* (Minneapolis: Minnesota Department of Highways, 1962.)

Trucking

AMERICAN SOCIETY OF PLANNING OFFICIALS. *Motor Truck Terminals.* Planning Advisory Service Information Report No. 21. (Chicago: The Society, 1950.)

————. *Truck Terminals.* Planning Advisory Service Report No. 206. (Chicago: The Society, 1966.)

HUDSON, WILLIAM J. and JAMES A. CONSTANTINE. *Motor Transportation.* (New York: Ronald Press Co., 1958.)

McCORMICK, WILLIAM R. "Trucks, Traffic and Terminals," *Traffic Quarterly,* IV (October, 1949), pp. 329–33.

NATIONAL COMMITTEE ON URBAN TRANSPORTATION. *Better Transportation for Your City Procedural Manuals.* 15 vols. (Chicago: Public Administration Service, 1958.)

RAMSEY, GEORGE C. and HAROLD REEVE SLEEPER. "Trucks and Trucking Docks," *Architectural Graphic Standards.* (New York: John Wiley & Sons, Inc., 5th ed., 1956.)

TAFF, CHARLES A. *Commercial Motor Transportation.* (Homewood, Illinois: Richard D. Irwin Inc., 1955.)

Railroads

AMERICAN SOCIETY OF PLANNING OFFICIALS. *Rail Lines and Terminals in Urban Planning.* Planning Advisory Service Information Report No. 82. (Chicago: The Society, 1956.)

HAY, WILLIAM W. *An Introduction to Transportation Engineering.* (New York: John Wiley & Sons, Inc., 1961.)

WELLINGTON, G. M. *The Economic Theory of Railway Location.* (New York: John Wiley & Sons, Inc., 1914.)

Ports

HUGHES, QUENTIN. *Seaport—Architecture and Townscape in Liverpool.* (London: Percy Lund, Humphries & Co., Ltd., 1964.)

LITTLE, ARTHUR D. INC. *Port Development Requirements—Report to Delaware River Port Authority.* (Cambridge, Massachusetts: Arthur D. Little, Inc., 1965.)

MACELWEE, ROY S. *Port Development.* (New York: McGraw-Hill Book Company, Inc., 1925.)

NEW YORK CITY PLANNING COMMISSION. *The Port of New York—Proposals for Development.* (New York: The Commission, 1964.)

RHODE ISLAND DEVELOPMENT COUNCIL. *Port of Providence—An Economic Survey.* (Providence: The Council, 1955.)

RHODE ISLAND DEVELOPMENT COUNCIL. *Appendices to an Economic Survey of The Port of Providence.* (Providence: The Council, 1955.)

SINARD, H. F., DANIEL VANGINKEL and BLANCHE VANGINKEL. *Preliminary Port Study for the Montreal Port Council.* (Montreal: Port Council, 1960.)

Airports

BOLT, BERANEK & NEWMAN, INC. *Land Use Planning Relating to Aircraft Noise.* (Washington, D.C.: Government Printing Office, 1964.)

HORONJEFF, ROBERT. *The Planning and Design of Airports.* (New York: McGraw-Hill Book Company, Inc., 1962.)

ILLINOIS, UNIVERSITY OF, DEPARTMENT OF URBAN PLANNING. *O'Hare Airport—A Design Potential Study.* (Urbana: College of Fine and Applied Arts, 1965.)

PETERSON, JOHN E. *Airports for Jets.* (Chicago: American Society of Planning Officials, 1959.)

THE PORT OF NEW YORK AUTHORITY. *A Report on Airport Requirements and Sites in the Metropolitan New Jersey–New York Region.* (New York: The Authority, 1961.)

SACRAMENTO COUNTY, CALIFORNIA PLANNING COMMISSION. *Metropolitan Airport—Natomas Area Plan.* (Sacramento: The Commission, 1961.)

SWANBOROUGH, F. G. *Vertical Flight Aircraft of the World.* (n.p.: Temple Press, Aero Publishers, Inc., 1965.)

TULSA METROPOLITAN AREA PLANNING COMMISSION. *Metropolitan Tulsa Airports and Their Relationship with Surrounding Land Use.* (Tulsa: The Commision, 1960.)

U.S. FEDERAL AVIATION AGENCY. *Airport Design.* (Washington, D.C.: Government Printing Office, 1961.)

―――. *Airport Design Supplement No. 1.* (Washington, D.C.: Government Printing Office, 1962.)

―――. *National Airport Plan. Fiscal Years 1966–1970.* (Washington, D.C.: Government Printing Office, 1965.)

―――. *Small Airports.* (Washington, D.C.: Government Printing Office, 1959.)

U.S. OFFICE OF SCIENCE AND TECHNOLOGY, JET AIRCRAFT NOISE PANEL. *Alleviation of Jet Aircraft Noise Near Airports.* (Washington, D.C.: Government Printing Office, 1966.)

U.S. PRESIDENT'S AIRPORT COMMISSION. *The Airport and Its Neighbors.* (Washington, D.C.: Government Printing Office, 1952.)

7. Open Space, Recreation, and Conservation

AMERICAN SOCIETY OF PLANNING OFFICIALS. *Public Open Space in Subdivisions.* Planning Advisory Service Information Report No. 46. (Chicago: ASPO, 1953.)

―――. *Special Zoning Districts for Open Space.* Planning Advisory Service Information Report No. 176. (Chicago: ASPO, 1963.)

―――. *Standards for Outdoor Recreation Areas,* by John Moeller. Planning Advisory Service Information Report No. 194. (Chicago: ASPO, 1965.)

ANDERSON, KENNETH. *A User-Resource Recreation Planning Method.* (Hidden Valley, Loomis, Calif.: National Advisory Council on Regional Recreation Planning, 1959.)

ATLANTA REGIONAL METROPOLITAN PLANNING COMMISSION. *Atlanta Region Comprehensive Plan: Open Land—Regional Problems and Opportunities.* (Atlanta: The Commission, 1964.)

BALTIMORE REGIONAL PLANNING COUNCIL. *Standards for Parks, Recreation Areas and Open Spaces.* Technical Bulletin No. 2. (Baltimore: Maryland State Planning Commission, 1958.)

CALIFORNIA PUBLIC OUTDOOR RECREATION PLAN COMMITTEE. *California Public Outdoor Recreation Plan: Part I and Part II.* (Sacramento: State Printing Office, 1960.)

CARROLL, MICHAEL A. *Open Space Planning: A Selected Bibliography.* (Urbana, Ill.: Bureau of Community Planning and Department of Urban Planning, 1965.)

CLAWSON, MARION, R. BURNELL HELD and CHARLES H. STODDARD. *Land for the Future.* (Baltimore, Md.: Johns Hopkins Press, 1960.)

CLEVELAND DEVELOPMENT FOUNDATION. *Open Space in Urban Design.* (Cleveland: The Foundation, 1964.)

DOOR COUNTY BOARD OF SUPERVISORS AND WISCONSIN DEPARTMENT OF RESOURCE DEVELOPMENT. *Door County Comprehensive Planning Program.* (Madison: Wisconsin Department of Resource Development, 1964.)

GRAHAM, EDWARD H. *Natural Principles of Land Use.* (New York: Oxford Press, 1944.)

GREATER BALTIMORE COMMITTEE, THE PLANNING COUNCIL. *Jones Falls Valley Plan.* (Baltimore: The Committee, 1961.)

HAWAII STATE PLANNING OFFICE WITH THE DE-

PARTMENT OF TRANSPORTATION. *The General Plan of the State of Hawaii.* (Honolulu: The Office, 1961.)

INTERCOUNTY REGIONAL PLANNING COMMISSION. *Open Space Development Plan for the Denver Region: Final Report. A Plan for Open Space.* Master Plan Report No. 19c. (Denver: The Commission, 1963.)

KRASNOWIECKI, JAN Z. and ANN LOUISE STRONG. "Compensable Regulations for Open Space: A Means of Controlling Urban Growth," *Journal of the American Institute of Planners,* XXIX (May, 1963), pp. 87–97.

KRASNOWIECKI, JAN Z. and JAMES C. N. PAUL. "The Preservation of Open Space in Metropolitan Areas," *University of Pennsylvania Law Review,* CX (December, 1961), pp. 179–239.

LEWIS, PHILIP H., JR. *Recreation and Open Space in Illinois.* (Urbana: Bureau of Community Planning, University of Illinois, 1961.)

MANDELKER, DANIEL R. *Greenbelts and Urban Growth.* (Madison: The University of Wisconsin Press, 1962.)

MARCOU, O'LEARY AND ASSOCIATES in cooperation with Marvin J. Cline, Carl Feiss and Kevin Lynch. *Open Space for Human Needs.* An unpublished report to the Urban Renewal Administration, 1964. (To be published in 1967.)

MARYLAND-NATIONAL CAPITAL PARK AND PLANNING COMMISSION. *On Wedges and Corridors: A General Plan for the Maryland-Washington Regional District.* (Silver Spring: The Commission, 1962.)

NAIRN, IAN. *The American Landscape.* (New York: Random House, 1965.)

NORTHEASTERN ILLINOIS METROPOLITAN AREA PLANNING COMMISSION. *Open Space in Northeastern Illinois.* Technical Report No. 2. (Chicago: The Commission, 1962.)

ODUM, EUGENE P. *Fundamentals of Ecology.* (Philadelphia: Saunders, 1957.)

OPEN SPACE ACTION COMMITTEE. *Stewardship: The Land, the Landowner and Metropolis,* text by Charles E. Little and Robert L. Burnap. (New York: The Committee, 1965.)

REGIONAL PLAN ASSOCIATION and THE METROPOLITAN REGIONAL COUNCIL. *The Race for Open Space.* Regional Plan Association Bulletin No. 96. (New York: The Association, 1960.)

SANTA CLARA CO., CALIF. PLANNING COMMISSION. *Parks, Recreation and Open Space.* General Plan Series No. 3. (San Jose: The Commission, 1959.)

SCHORR, ALVIN. *Slums and Social Insecurity.* United States Department of Health, Education, and Welfare, Social Security Administration, Division of Research and Statistics, Research Report No. 1. (Washington: Government Printing Office, 1963.)

SIEGEL, SHIRLEY ADELSON. *The Law of Open Space.* (New York: Regional Plan Association, 1960.)

SKIDMORE, OWINGS & MERRILL. *Monterey Coast Master Plan—County of Monterey—Section I.* (San Francisco: Skidmore, Owings & Merrill, 1960.)

STRONG, ANN LOUISE. *Open Space for Urban America.* (Washington: Government Printing Office, 1965.)

"Techniques for Preserving Open Space," *Harvard Law Review,* LXXV No. 8, 1962), pp. 1622–44.

TORONTO METROPOLITAN PLANNING BOARD. *The Official Plan of the Metropolitan Toronto Planning Area.* (Toronto: The Board, 1959.)

U.S. FEDERAL HOUSING ADMINISTRATION. *Planned-Unit Development with a Homes Association.* Land Planning Bulletin No. 6. (Washington: Government Printing Office, 1964.)

U.S. OUTDOOR RECREATION RESOURCES REVIEW COMMISSION. Study Report No. 15, *Open Space Action* by William H. Whyte. (Washington: Government Printing Office, 1962.)

———. Study Report No. 16, *Land Acquisition for Outdoor Recreation—Analysis of Selected Legal Problems* by Norman Williams, Jr. (Washington: Government Printing Office, 1962.)

———. Study Report No. 19, *National Recreation Survey.* (Washington: Government Printing Office, 1962.)

———. Study Report No. 20, *Participation in Outdoor Recreation: Factors Affecting Demand Among American Adults* by Eva Mueller and Gerald Gurir. (Washington: Government Printing Office, 1962.)

———. Study Report No. 21, *The Future of Outdoor Recreation in Metropolitan Regions of the United States, Studies of New York, Atlanta, St. Louis, Chicago, and Los Angeles Metropolitan Regions.* (Washington: Government Printing Office, 1962.)

———. Study Report No. 22, *Trends in American Living and Outdoor Recreation.* (Washington: Government Printing Office, 1962.)

———. *Outdoor Recreation for America.* (Washington: Government Printing Office, 1962.)

U.S. URBAN RENEWAL ADMINISTRATION. *Preserving Urban Open Space.* (Washington: Government Printing Office, 1963.)

WALLACE-MCHARG ASSOCIATES. *A Plan for the Valleys,* published for the Green Spring and Worthington Valley Planning Council, Inc. (Philadelphia: The Associates, 1964.)

WHYTE, WILLIAM H. *Cluster Development.* (New York: American Conservation Association, 1964.)

WISCONSIN DEPARTMENT OF RESOURCE DEVELOPMENT. *Landscape Analysis: Lake Superior South Shore Area.* (Madison: The Department, 1963.)

———. *Recreation in Wisconsin.* (Madison: The Department, 1962.)

8. Governmental and Community Facilities

General References

HOPPENFELD, MORTON. *Planning Community Facilities for Growing Cities: A Compilation of Ideas and Information for Use by Community Planners, with Particular Emphasis for Small and Medium Sized Cities.* (Berkeley, Calif.: Mitchell Van Bourg and Associates, 1956.)

INTERCOUNTY REGIONAL PLANNING COMMISSION. *Standards for New Urban Development.* Master Plan Report No. 3. (Denver: The Commission, 1960.

NATIONAL HOUSING CENTER LIBRARY. *Community Facilities: A List of Selected References.* Bibliography Series No. 4. (Washington: National Association of Home Builders, 1959.)

URBAN LAND INSTITUTE. *News and Trends in City Development.* "Standards for New Urban Development—The Denver Background." (New York: Urban Land Institute, 1961.)

U.S. ADVISORY COMMISSION ON INTERGOVERNMENTAL RELATIONS. *Alternative Approaches to Governmental Reorganization in Metropolitan Areas.* (Washington: Government Printing Office, 1962.)

————. *Intergovernmental Responsibilities for Water Supply and Sewage Disposal in Metropolitan Areas.* (Washington: Government Printing Office, 1962.)

————. *Performance of Urban Functions: Local and Areawide.* (Washington: Government Printing Office, 1963.)

————. *The Problem of Special Districts in American Government.* (Washington: Government Printing Office, 1964.)

Higher Education

ADAMS, HOWARD AND GREELY, CONSULTANTS. *University Circle: Technical Report on a General Plan for the Future Development of the Area.* (Cambridge, Mass.: The Consultants, 1957.)

AMERICAN SOCIETY OF PLANNING OFFICIALS. "Campus Planning," *Planning 1958.* (Chicago: ASPO, 1958), pp. 142–52.

————. "Town and Gown," *Planning 1961.* (Chicago: ASPO, 1961,) pp. 109–18.

CANTY, DONALD. "New Frontier of Higher Education," *Architectual Forum,* CXVIII (March, 1963), pp. 96–103.

CARLSON, DAVID B. "Town and Gown," *Architectural Forum,* CXVIII (March, 1963), pp. 92–95.

DOBER, RICHARD. *Campus Planning.* (New York: Reinhold, 1964.)

EDUCATIONAL FACILITIES LABORATORIES, INC. *Bricks and Mortarboards, A Report on College Planning and Building.* (New York: The Laboratories, 1964.)

PERLOFF, HARVEY S. *The University of Chicago and the Surrounding Community.* (Chicago: The University, 1953.)

SAN DIEGO CITY PLANNING DEPARTMENT. *University Community Study.* (San Diego: The Department, 1959.)

WILLIAMS AND MOCINE, CONSULTANTS. *General Plan for the University Environs, Santa Cruz, California.* (San Francisco: The Consultants, 1963.)

Health Facilities

AMERICAN SOCIETY OF PLANNING OFFICIALS. "Planning for Medical Facilities," *Planning 1964.* (Chicago: ASPO, 1964), pp. 190–206.

DENVER PLANNING OFFICE. *Responsibilities of the City and County of Denver for Providing Hospital Treatment.* (Denver: The Office, September, 1962.)

OAKLAND CITY PLANNING DEPARTMENT. *Medical Center Hill.* (Oakland: The Department, 1959.)

PUBLIC HEALTH SERVICE. *Areawide Planning for Hospitals and Related Health Facilities.* Report of the Joint Committee of the American Hospital Association and the Public Health Service. Publication No. 855. (Washington: Public Health Service, July, 1961.)

————. *Procedures for Areawide Health Facility Planning—A Guide for Planning Agencies.* Publication No. 930-B-3. (Washington: Public Health Service, September, 1963.)

WISOWATY, KENNETH W., *et al.* "Health Facility Planning—A Review of the Movement," *Journal of the American Medical Association,* XC (November 23, 1964), pp. 752–56.

Government Administrative Centers

AMERICAN SOCIETY OF PLANNING OFFICIALS. *Civic Center Planning.* Planning Advisory Service Information Report No. 83. (Chicago: ASPO, 1956.)

BECKET (WELTON) AND ASSOCIATES. *Pomona Civic Center Master Plan.* (Los Angeles: Becket Associates, 1960.)

BIGGER, RICHARD, EUGENE P. DVORIN, and JUDITH NORVELL JAMISON. "Branch Civic Centers," *National Municipal Review,* XLVI (November, 1957), pp. 511–16.

FAIRFAX COMPREHENSIVE PLANNING OFFICE. *Governmental Substation Study, Fairfax County, Virginia.* (Fairfax: The Office, 1966.)

INTERNATIONAL CITY MANAGER'S ASSOCIATION. *Planning the New City Hall.* Management Information Service Report No. 212. (Chicago: The Association, September, 1961.)

LOS ANGELES CITY PLANNING COMMISSION. *Branch Administrative Centers.* (Los Angeles: The Commission, 1950.)

SAN DIEGO OFFICE OF THE CITY MANAGER AND CITY PLANNING DEPARTMENT. *A Program for the Development of Public Office Buildings.* (San Diego: The Department, 1959.)

TULSA CITY HALL-POLICE BUILDINGS ADVISORY COMMITTEE. *New City Hall and Police Buildings.*

(Tulsa: Tulsa Metropolitan Area Planning Commission, 1964.)

Libraries

AMERICAN LIBRARY ASSOCIATION. *Public Library Service: A Guide to Evaluation with Minimum Standards.* (Chicago: The Association, 1956.)

BOWLER, ROBERTA (ed.) . *Local Public Library Administration.* (Chicago: International City Managers' Association, 1964.)

DOMS, KEITH, and HOWARD ROVELSTAD (eds.). *Guidelines for Library Planners.* (Chicago: American Library Association, 1960.)

JOINT CENTER FOR URBAN STUDIES. *The Public Library and the City.* (Cambridge: The M.I.T. Press, 1965.)

NASHVILLE-DAVIDSON COUNTY PLANNING COMMISSION. *Books for Metropolitan Nashville; A Plan of Branch Libraries for Nashville and Davidson County, Tennessee.* (Nashville: The Commission, 1961.)

WHEELER, JOSEPH L., and HERBERT GOLDHOR. *Practical Administration of Public Libraries.* (New York: Harper and Row, 1962.)

Fire Stations

INTERNATIONAL CITY MANAGERS' ASSOCIATION. *Municipal Fire Administration.* (Chicago: The Association, 7th ed., 1966.)

PHOENIX PLANNING DEPARTMENT. *Fire Station Plan for the City of Phoenix.* (Phoenix: The Department, 1961.)

SEATTLE PLANNING COMMISSION AND FIRE DEPARTMENT. *Planning for Fire Station Locations.* (Seattle: The Commission, 1962.)

SPOKANE CITY PLAN COMMISSION AND FIRE DEPARTMENT. *Public Service Facilities, Part I—Fire Station Plan.* (Spokane: The Commission, 1962.)

TULSA METROPOLITAN AREA PLANNING COMMISSION. *1975 Metropolitan Tulsa Fire Station Needs.* (Tulsa: The Commission, 1959.)

Cemeteries and Crematoria

AMERICAN SOCIETY OF PLANNING OFFICIALS. *Cemeteries in the City Plan.* Planning Advisory Service Information Report No. 16. (Chicago: ASPO, 1950.)

———. *Location, Regulation and Removal of Cemeteries in the City and County of San Francisco,* by William A. Proctor. Special publication reprint. (Chicago: ASPO, 1951.)

JACKSON, PERCIVAL E. *The Law of Cadavers and of Burial and Burial Places.* (New York: Prentice-Hall, 1950.)

PARK AND CEMETERY PUBLISHING CO. *The Cemetery Handbook: A Manual of Information on Cemetery Development and Management.* (Madison: Park and Cemetery Publishing Co., 1947.)

Water and Sewers

AMERICAN SOCIETY OF PLANNING OFFICIALS. *Planning and Financing Storm Sewers.* Planning Advisory Service Information Report No. 109. (Chicago: ASPO, April, 1958.)

BABBITT, HAROLD E. and E. ROBERT BAUMANN. *Sewerage and Sewage Treatment.* (New York: John Wiley and Sons, 1958.)

FAIR, GORDON M. and JOHN C. GEYER. *Elements of Water Supply and Waste-water Disposal.* (New York: John Wiley and Sons, 1958.)

INTERNATIONAL CITY MANAGERS' ASSOCIATION. *Municipal Public Works Administration.* (Chicago: The Association, 5th ed., 1957.)

THIELE, HEINRICH J. *Present and Future Water Use and its Effect on Planning in Maricopa County, Arizona.* (Phoenix: Maricopa County Planning and Zoning Department, 1965.)

TWIN CITIES METROPOLITAN PLANNING COMMISSION. *Metropolitan Sewerage Study.* (St. Paul: The Commission, 1960.)

———. *Metropolitan Water Study.* Two parts. (St. Paul: The Commission, 1960.)

Water for Industry

See under *Water and Sewers* section, and also:

ACKERMAN, EDWARD A. and GEORGE O. G. LÖF. *Technology in American Water Development.* (Baltimore: The Johns Hopkins Press for Resources for the Future, Inc., 1959.)

GRAHAM, JACK B. and MEREDITH F. BURRILL. *Water for Industry.* (Washington: American Association for the Advancement of Science, 1956.)

HIRSHLEIFER, JACK, JAMES C. DeHAVEN and JEROME W. MILLIMAN. *Water Supply: Economics, Technology and Policy.* (Chicago: University of Chicago Press, 1960.)

NATIONAL ASSOCIATION OF MANUFACTURERS OF THE UNITED STATES OF AMERICA. *Water in Industry; a survey of water use in industry by the National Association of Manufacturers and the Conservation Foundation.* (New York: The Association, 1950.)

OAKLAND COUNTY PLANNING COMMISSION. *Industrial Water Needs.* (Pontiac, Michigan: The Commission, 1957.)

WOLMAN, ABEL. "Characteristics and Problems of Industrial Water Supply," *Journal of the American Waterworks Association* (April, 1952) , pp. 279–286.

Electric Power Systems

CHURCH, MARTHA. *The Spatial Organization of Electrical Power Territories in Massachusetts.* University of Chicago Department of Geography Research Paper No. 69. (Chicago: University of Chicago Press, 1960.)

CROWE, SYLVIA. *The Landscape of Power.* (London: The Architectural Press, 1958.)

Overhead and Underground Utility Wires

FIRST STREET TREE AND UTILITY CONFERENCE. *Our Streets Can Be Beautiful and Useful.* Conference sponsors: Edison Electric Institute; Illuminating Engineering Society; National Shade Tree Conference. (Cleveland, Ohio: National Shade Tree Conference, 1955.)

TACOMA CITY PLANNING COMMISSION. *Residential Utility Wire Distribution*. With bibliography. (Tacoma, Wash.: The Commission, 1964.)

THOMPSON, WAYNE E. *Moving Ahead from Obsolete Overhead Wiring to Modern Undergrounding*. (Oakland, California: The City Council, 1961.)

URBAN LAND INSTITUTE. *Buried Cables: A Survey of Buried Electric Distribution for Residential Land Development*. Technical Bulletin No. 48. (Washington: Urban Land Institute, 1964.)

———. *Innovations vs. Traditions in Community Development*. Technical Bulletin No. 47. (Washington: Urban Land Institute, 1963.)

Refuse and Maintenance Facilities

AMERICAN PUBLIC WORKS ASSOCIATION, Committee on Equipment. *Public Works Equipment Management*. (Chicago: Public Administration Service, 1964.)

———, Committee on Refuse Disposal. *Municipal Refuse Disposal*. (Chicago: Public Administration Service, 1961.)

NORTHWESTERN ILLINOIS METROPOLITAN AREA PLANNING COMMISSION. *Refuse Disposal Needs and Practices in Northeastern Illinois*. (Chicago: The Commission, 1963.)

PHOENIX PLANNING DEPARTMENT. *A Plan for Regional Service Facilities*. (Phoenix: The Department, 1963.)

9. City Design and City Appearance

General References

CARR, STEPHEN. "The City of the Mind," in Ewald, W. R., ed., *Environment for Man: The Next Fifty Years*. (Bloomington: Indiana University Press, 1967.)

CULLEN, GORDON. *Townscape*. (London: Architectural Press, 1962.)

GREAT BRITAIN MINISTRY OF HOUSING AND LOCAL GOVERNMENT. *Design in Town and Village*. (London: H. M. Stationery Office, 1953.)

HEGEMANN, WERNER and ELBERT PEETS. *The American Vitruvius: An Architect's Handbook of Civic Art*. (New York: The Architectural Book Publishing Co., 1922.)

JACOBS, JANE. *The Death and Life of Great American Cities*. (New York: Random House, 1961), pp. 372–391.

JOINT COMMITTEE ON DESIGN CONTROL. *Planning and Community Appearance*. (New York: Regional Plan Association, 1958.)

LYNCH, KEVIN. *The Image of the City*. (Cambridge: Technology Press, 1960.)

NAIRN, IAN. *The American Landscape, A Critical View*. (New York: Random House, 1965.)

SPREIREGEN, PAUL D. *Urban Design: The Architecture of Towns and Cities*. (New York: McGraw-Hill, 1965.)

Periodicals

Architectural Forum.
Architectural Review.

10. Quantitative Methods in Urban Planning

The literature on quantitative methods and their applications to urban planning practice is growing by leaps and bounds—as evidenced by many of the source notes accompanying other chapters in the present volume. Overall coverage of progress in this area is provided by the publications of the REGIONAL SCIENCE ASSOCIATION, the HIGHWAY RESEARCH BOARD (Department of Urban Transportation Planning) and the recently founded URBAN AND REGIONAL INFORMATION SYSTEMS ASSOCIATION. More specifically, the following current references are recommended for their treatment of major aspects of the subject matter.

HARRIS, BRITTON, ed. "Urban Development Models: New Tools for Planning," *Journal of the American Institute of Planners*, XXXI (May, 1965), pp. 90–172.

PERLOFF, HARVEY S. and CHARLES L. LEVEN. "Toward an Integrated System of Regional Accounts: Stocks, Flows, and the Analysis of the Public Sector," in *Elements of Regional Accounts*. (Baltimore: Published for Resources for the Future, Inc., by the Johns Hopkins Press, 1964), pp. 175–214. Papers presented at the Conference on Regional Accounts, 1962, sponsored by the Committee on Regional Accounts, edited by Werner Z. Hirsch.

QUADE, E. S. *Systems Analysis Techniques for Planning-Programming-Budgeting*. RAND Corporation Paper No. P-3322. (Santa Monica, Calif.: Rand Corporation, 1966.)

Scientific American (Special issue on "Information"), CCXIV (September 1966), entire issue.

11. Social Welfare Planning

ACTION-HOUSING, INC. *Action for Employment*. (Pittsburgh: ACTION-Housing, Inc., 1965.)

———. *Social and Physical Planning Experiences in the Homewood-Brushton Neighborhood of Pittsburgh 1960–63*. (Pittsburgh: ACTION-Housing, Inc., 1964.)

ADAMSON, ANTHONY. "Physical Planning and Social Planning," in *Planning 1965*. (Chicago: American Society of Planning Officials, 1965), pp. 185–93.

BATT, WILLIAM L., JR. "Planning for the Unemployed, the Underemployed, and the Poor," in *Proceedings of the 1964 Annual Conference*, Newark, American Institute of Planners. (Washington: The

Institute, 1964), pp. 253–56.

DAKIN, JOHN. "An Evaluation of the 'Choice' Theory of Planning," *Journal of the American Institute of Planners,* XXIX (February, 1963), pp. 19–26.

DAVIDOFF, PAUL. "Advocacy and Pluralism in Planning," *Journal of the American Institute of Planners,* XXXI (November, 1965), pp. 331–37.

DAVIDOFF, PAUL and THOMAS A. REINER. "A Reply to Dakin," *Journal of the American Institute of Planners,* XXIX (February, 1963), pp. 27–28.

DUCEY, JOHN M. "Citizen Participation in the Planning Process," in *Proceedings of the 1964 Annual Conference,* Newark, American Institute of Planners. (Washington: The Institute, 1964), pp. 228–33.

DYCKMAN, JOHN W. "Social Planning, Social Planners, and Planned Societies," *Journal of the American Institute of Planners,* XXXII (March, 1966), pp. 66–76.

FARRELL, GREGORY. *A Climate of Change: Community Action in New Haven.* (New Brunswick, N.J.: Urban Studies Center, Rutgers University, 1965.)

FRIEDEN, BERNARD J. "Toward Equality of Urban Opportunity," *Journal of the American Institute of Planners,* XXXI (November, 1965), pp. 320–29.

HEALTH AND WELFARE COUNCIL, INC. *A Study of the Social Aspects of the CRP.* Philadelphia Community Renewal Program Technical Report No. 5. (Philadelphia: The Program, n.d.)

HERMAN, MARY W. *Comparative Studies of Identifiable Areas In Philadelphia.* Philadelphia Community Renewal Program Technical Report No. 9. (Philadelphia: The Program, 1964.)

HOLLANDER, EDWARD D. "Arming for the Battle: Approaches and Techniques To Eradicate Poverty," in *Proceedings of the 1964 Annual Conference,* Newark, American Institute of Planners. (Washington: The Institute, 1964), pp. 262–71.

LEHAN, EDWARD A. "The Municipality's Response to Changing Concepts of Public Welfare," in *The Revolution in Public Welfare: The Connecticut Experience,* ed. R. Levenson. (Storrs: Institute of Public Service, University of Connecticut, 1966), pp. 44–54.

LUNDBERG, GEORGE ANDREW, MIRRA KOMAROVSKY, and MARY ALICE MCINERY. *Leisure: A Suburban Study.* (New York: Columbia University Press, 1934.)

MCGOUGH, DONNA M. *Social Factor Analysis.* Philadelphia Community Renewal Program Technical Report No. 11. (Philadelphia: The Program, 1964.)

MILLER, S. M. "Book Review—Social Planning: A Primer for Urbanists," *Journal of the American Institute of Planners,* XXXII (July, 1966), pp. 248–49.

NATIONAL ASSOCIATION OF HOUSING AND REDEVELOPMENT OFFICIALS. *American Community Development.* (New York: Ford Foundation, 1964.)

PERLMAN, ROBERT. "Social Welfare Planning and Physical Planning," *Journal of the American Institute of Planners,* XXXII (July, 1966), pp. 237–41.

PERLOFF, HARVEY S. "New Directions in Social Planning," *Journal of the American Institute of Planners,* XXXI (November, 1965), pp. 297–304.

———. "Pomeroy Memorial Lecture: Common Goals and the Linking of Physical and Social Planning," *Planning 1965.* (Chicago: American Society of Planning Officials, 1965), pp. 170–84.

———. "Social Planning in the Metropolis," in *The Urban Condition,* ed. Leonard J. Duhl. (New York: Basic Books, 1963), pp. 331–47.

PHILADELPHIA COMMUNITY RENEWAL PROGRAM. *Community Renewal Programming.* Technical Report No. 4. (Philadelphia: The Program, 1962.)

POPENOE, DAVID. "Prologue" in *Proceedings of the 1964 Annual Conference,* Newark, American Institute of Planners. (Washington: The Institute, 1964), pp. 122–24.

RAYMOND, GEORGE M. "Prologue" in *Proceedings of the 1964 Annual Conference,* Newark, American Institute of Planners. (Washington: The Institute, 1964), pp. 148–50.

REINER, JANET S., EVERETT REIMER, and THOMAS A. REINER. "Client Analysis and the Planning of Public Programs," *Journal of the American Institute of Planners,* XXIX (November, 1963), pp. 270–82.

RHODE ISLAND COUNCIL OF COMMUNITY SERVICES, INC., *A Social Plan for Community Renewal of the City of Providence, R. I.* (Providence: The Council, 1964.)

ROSSI, PETER H. and R. A. DENTLER. *The Politics of Urban Renewal.* (New York: Free Press of Glencoe, 1961.)

SCHERMER, GEORGE. *Meeting Social Needs in the Penjerdel Region.* (Philadelphia: Pennsylvania–New Jersey–Delaware Metropolitan Project, 1964.)

———. "Planning for Social Needs," in *Proceedings of the 1964 Annual Conference,* Newark, American Institute of Planners. (Washington: The Institute, 1964), pp. 132–40.

SCHNEIDERMEYER, MELVIN. *The Metropolitan Social Inventory: Procedures for Measuring Human Well-Being in Urban Areas.* (Thesis, University of Illinois, Urbana, Illinois, 1966.)

SCHORR, ALVIN L. *Slums and Social Insecurity.* (Washington: Government Printing Office, 1963.)

———. "The Physical Environment and Social Problems," in *Proceedings of the 1964 Annual Conference,* Newark, American Institute of Planners. (Washington: American Institute of Planners, 1964), pp. 141–45.

SILBERMAN, CHARLES A. *Crisis in Black and White.* (New York: Random House, Inc., 1964.)

SLAYTON, WILLIAM L. "Impact of the Community Renewal Program on Urban Renewal," in *Proceedings of the 1964 Annual Conference,* Newark, American Institute of Planners. (Washington: The Institute, 1964) , pp. 151–57.

UHLIG, RICHARD H. *Planning in the Urban Environment.* Philadelphia Community Renewal Program Technical Report No. 16. (Philadelphia: The Program, 1965.)

U.S. GENERAL ACCOUNTING OFFICE. *Inadequate Policies and Practice Relating to the Relocation of Families from Urban Renewal Areas.* (Washington: Government Printing Office, 1964.)

URBAN LEAGUE OF RHODE ISLAND. *A Study of the Resources, Capabilities for Rehabilitation, and Preferences of Families Living or Owning Property in the Lippett Hill Rehabilitation Area and Their Attitudes Toward Their Neighborhood and Its Rehabilitation.* (Providence: Providence Redevelopment Agency, 1962.)

WEBBER, MELVIN. "Comprehensive Planning and Social Responsibility," *Journal of the American Institute of Planners,* XXIX (November, 1963), pp. 232–41.

12. Defining Development Objectives

Books and Articles

ALTSHULER, ALAN. *The City Planning Process: A Political Analysis.* (Ithaca, N.Y.: Cornell University Press, 1965.)

ALLAIRE, JERROLD R. *Policy Statements: Guides to Decision-Making.* Information Report No. 152. (Chicago: American Society of Planning Officials, 1961.)

ASCHMAN, FREDERICK T. "The 'Policy Plan' in the Planning Process," *Planning 1963.* (Chicago: American Society of Planning Officials, 1963), pp. 105–11.

CHAPIN, F. STUART, JR. "Taking Stock of Techniques for Shaping Urban Growth," *Journal of the American Institute of Planners,* XXIX (May, 1963), pp. 76–87.

———. *Urban Land Use Planning.* (Urbana, Ill.: University of Illinois Press, 2nd ed., 1965.)

FAGIN, HENRY. "Planning for Future Urban Growth," *Law and Contemporary Problems,* XXX (No. 1, 1965), pp. 9–25.

———. "Planning Organization and Activities within the Framework of Urban Government," *Planning and the Urban Community.* Edited by Harvey S. Perloff. (Pittsburgh: University of Pittsburgh Press, 1961.)

———. *The Policies Plan: Instrumentality for a Community Dialogue.* (Pittsburgh: Institute of Local Government, University of Pittsburgh, 1965), pp. 105–20.

GREAT BRITAIN, MINISTRY OF HOUSING AND LOCAL GOVERNMENT. *The Future of Development Plans.* (London: Her Majesty's Stationery Office, 1965.)

HAAR, CHARLES M. "The Content of the General Plan: A Glance at History," *Journal of the American Institute of Planners,* XXI (Nos. 2–3, 1955), pp. 66–70.

———. "The Master Plan: An Impermanent Constitution," *Law and Contemporary Problems,* XX (No. 3, 1955), pp. 353–76.

HOOVER, ROBERT C. "On Master Plans and Constitutions," *Journal of the American Institute of Planners,* XXVI (No. 1, 1960), pp. 5–24.

MITCHELL, ROBERT B. "The New Frontier in Metropolitan Planning," *Journal of the American Institute of Planners,* XXVII (No. 3, 1961), pp. 169–175.

REPS, JOHN W. "Requiem for Zoning," *Planning 1964.* (Chicago: American Society of Planning Officials, 1964), pp. 56–67.

WEBBER, MELVIN M. "Comprehensive Planning and Social Responsibility: Toward an AIP Consensus on the Profession's Role and Purpose," *Journal of the American Institute of Planners,* XXIX (No. 4, 1963), pp. 232–41.

WEBBER, MELVIN M., *et al. Explorations into Urban Structure.* (Philadelphia: University of Pennsylvania Press, 1964.)

WINGO, LOWDEN, JR. (ed.) . *Cities and Space: The Future Use of Urban Land.* (Baltimore: Johns Hopkins Press, 1963.)

Policy Reports

BELOIT CITY PLANNING COMMISSION. *Planning Goals, Principles and Projections,* Memorandum Report No. 4. (Beloit, Wis.: The Commission, 1962.)

BOSTON REDEVELOPMENT AUTHORITY. *1965/1975 General Plan for the City of Boston and the Regional Core.* (Boston: The Authority, 1964.)

CHICAGO DEPARTMENT OF CITY PLANNING. *Basic Policies for the Comprehensive Plan of Chicago.* (Chicago: The Department, 1964.)

THE EVANSTON PLAN COMMISSION. *Your City and Its Planning Objectives.* (Evanston, Ill.: The Commission, 1963.)

HOWARD COUNTY PLANNING COMMISSION. *A Planning Policy and Design Concept for Howard County.* (Ellicott City, Md.: The Commission, 1960.)

KING COUNTY PLANNING DEPARTMENT. *The Comprehensive Plan for King County, Washington.* (Seattle, Wash.: The Department, 1964.)

LIVONIA CITY PLANNING COMMISSION. *Proposed Development Policies for 1965–1970 Growth.* (Livonia, Mich.: The Commission, 1965.)

MINNEAPOLIS PLANNING COMMISSION. *Goals for Central Minneapolis.* (Minneapolis: The Commission, 1959.)

OAHU DEVELOPMENT CONFERENCE. *Proposed Goals and Objectives of Comprehensive Planning for Oahu.* (Honolulu: The Conference, 1964.)

RICHMOND PLANNING COMMISSION. *How Should Richmond Develop in the Next Generation? A Proposed Statement of Goals.* (Richmond, Calif.: The Commission, 1962.)

RICHMOND REGIONAL PLANNING COMMISSION. *Policies for Planning.* (Richmond, Va.: The Commission, 1964.)

SOUTHWESTERN PENNSYLVANIA REGIONAL PLANNING

COMMISSION. *Alternative Regional Development Patterns.* (Pittsburgh: The Commission, 1965.)

TULSA METROPOLITAN AREA PLANNING COMMISSION. *Comprehensive Plan.* Tulsa, Okla.: The Commission, 1960.)

VILLAGE OF SCARSDALE. *Master Policies Plan Report.* (Scarsdale, N.Y.: The Village, 1962.)

U.S. NATIONAL CAPITAL PLANNING COMMISSION. *1965/1985 Proposed Physical Development Policies for Washington, D.C.* (Washington, D.C.: The Commission, 1965.)

U.S. NATIONAL CAPITAL PLANNING COMMISSION and NATIONAL CAPITAL REGIONAL PLANNING COUNCIL. *The Nation's Capital: Policies Plan for the Year 2000.* (Washington, D.C.: The Commission, 1961.)

13. The Comprehensive Plan

Conceptual Material

BASSETT, EDWARD M., FRANK B. WILLIAMS, ALFRED BETTMAN, and ROBERT WHITTEN. *Model Laws for Planning Cities, Counties, and States Including Zoning, Subdivision Regulation, and Protection of Official Map.* (Cambridge, Mass.: Harvard University Press, 1935.)

BASSETT, EDWARD M. *The Master Plan* (New York: Russell Sage Foundation, 1938.)

BETTMAN, ALFRED. "The Relationship of the Functions and Powers of the City Planning Commission to the Legislative, Executive, and Administrative Departments of City Government," *Planning Problems of Town, City, and Region: Papers and Discussions at the Twentieth National Conference on City Planning, Held at Dallas and Fort Worth, Texas, May 7–10, 1928.* (Philadelphia: William F. Fill Co., 1928), pp. 142–159.

———. "City Planning Legislation," in *City Planning: A Series of Papers Presenting the Essential Elements of a City Plan,* ed. by John Nolen. (New York: D. Appleton & Co., 2nd ed., 1929), pp. 431–71.

FAGIN, HENRY. "Organizing and Carrying Out Planning Activities Within Urban Government," *Journal of the American Institute of Planners,* XXV (August 1959), pp. 109–114.

FOLEY, DONALD L. "How Many Berkeley Residents Know about Their City's Master Plan?" *Journal of the American Institute of Planners,* XXI (Fall 1955), pp. 138–44.

GOODMAN, WILLIAM I. and JEROME L. KAUFMAN. *City Planning in the Sixties: A Restatement of Principles and Techniques.* (Urbana, Ill.: Bureau of Community Planning, University of Illinois, 1965.)

HAAR, CHARLES M. "The Content of the General Plan: A Glance at History," *Journal of the American Institute of Planners,* XXI (Spring-Summer 1955), pp. 66–70.

———. "The Master Plan: An Impermanent Constitution," *Law and Contemporary Problems,* XX (Summer 1955), pp. 353–418.

———. Land-Use Planning: *A Casebook on the Use, Misuse, and Re-Use of Urban Land.* (Boston and Toronto: Little, Brown & Co., 1959.)

HOOVER, ROBERT C. "On Master Plans and Constitutions," *Journal of the American Institute of Planners,* XXVI (February 1960), pp. 5–24.

HOWARD, JOHN R. "In Defense of Planning Commissions," *Journal of the American Institute of Planners,* XVII (Spring 1951), pp. 89–94.

KENT, T. J., JR. "Comments by a Councilman," *Journal of the American Institute of Planners,* XXVI (May 1960), pp. 131–2.

———. *The Urban General Plan.* (San Francisco: Chandler Publishing Co., 1964.)

LOVELACE, ELDRIDGE. "Three Short Articles Designed to Provoke Discussion and Re-Examination of Basic Principles: 1. You Can't Have Planning Without a Plan. 2. Needed: One-Dimensional City Plans. 3. The Flexible City Plan Is No City Plan at All," *Journal of the American Institute of Planners,* XXIV (1958), pp. 7–10.

MEYERSON, MARTIN. "Building the Middle-Range Bridge for Comprehensive Planning," *Journal of the American Institute of Planners,* XXII (Spring 1956), pp. 58–64.

NASH, PETER H. and J. F. SHURTLEFF. "Planning as a Staff Function in Urban Management," *Journal of the American Institute of Planners,* XX (Summer, 1954), pp. 136–47.

OLMSTED, FREDERICK LAW, JR. "Reply in Behalf of the City Planning Conference." In *Proceedings of the Third National Conference on City Planning, Philadelphia, May 15–17, 1911.* (Boston, 1911), pp. 3–13.

———. "Introduction," in *City Planning: A Series of Papers Presenting the Essential Elements of a City Plan,* ed. by John Nolen. (New York: D. Appleton & Co., 2nd ed., 1929), pp. 1–18.

ROW, ARTHUR. "The Physical Development Plan," *Journal of the American Institute of Planners,* XXVI (August 1960), pp. 177–85.

TUGWELL, REXFORD G. *The Place of Planning in Society.* Puerto Rico Planning Board Technical Paper VII. (San Juan, Puerto Rico: Puerto Rico Planning Board, 1954.)

U.S. DEPARTMENT OF COMMERCE, ADVISORY COMMITTEE ON CITY PLANNING AND ZONING. *A Standard City Planning Enabling Act.* (Washington: Government Printing Office, 1928.)

WALKER, ROBERT A. *The Planning Function in Urban Government.* (Chicago: University of Chicago Press, 2nd ed., 1950.)

WRIGLEY, ROBERT L., JR. "The Plan of Chicago: Its Fiftieth Anniversary," *Journal of the American Institute of Planners,* XXVI (February 1960), pp. 31–38.

Examples of Plans

BERKELEY CITY PLANNING COMMISSION. *Berkeley*

Master Plan. (Berkeley, Calif.: The Commission, 1955.)

BOSTON REDEVELOPMENT AUTHORITY. *1965–1975 General Plan for the City of Boston and the Regional Core.* (Boston: The Authority, 1964.)

BROOKLINE, MASS. PLANNING BOARD. *Comprehensive Plan, Town of Brookline, Massachusetts.* (Brookline: The Board, 1960.)

CHICAGO DEPARTMENT OF CITY PLANNING. *Basic Policies for the Comprehensive Plan of Chicago.* (Chicago: The Department, 1964.)

CLEVELAND CITY PLANNING COMMISSION. *Cleveland Today . . . Tomorrow: The General Plan of Cleveland.* (Cleveland: The Commission, 1950.)

DETROIT CITY PLAN COMMISSION. *Detroit Master Plan; the Official Comprehensive Plan for the Development and Improvement of Detroit.* (Detroit: The Commission, 1951.)

OAKLAND CITY PLANNING COMMISSION. *Oakland General Plan.* (Oakland, Calif.: The Commission, 1959.)

PHILADELPHIA CITY PLANNING COMMISSION. *Comprehensive Plan: The Physical Development Plan for the City of Philadelphia.* (Philadelphia: The Commission, 1960.)

U.S. NATIONAL CAPITAL PLANNING COMMISSION and U.S. NATIONAL CAPITAL REGIONAL PLANNING COUNCIL. *The Nation's Capital: Policies Plan for the Year 2000.* (Washington: 1961.)

14. Programming Community Development

Capital Improvement Programming

AMERICAN INSTITUTE OF PLANNERS. *Report of the Planning-Policy Committee on Financing The Plan.* (Washington: The Institute, February 1963.) A brief statement calling for a "capital needs list" as an integral part of every comprehensive plan.

AMERICAN SOCIETY OF PLANNING OFFICIALS. *Planning Advisory Service Information Report No. 151: Capital Improvement Programming.* (Chicago: The Society, October 1961.) Discussion of several of the more troublesome aspects of capital improvement programming.

————. *Planning Advisory Service Information Report No. 160: New Techniques for Shaping Urban Expansion.* (Chicago: The Society, July 1962.) A provocative review of some of the more significant trends in planning implementation measures.

BACON, EDMUND N. "Capital Programming and Public Policy," *Journal of the American Institute of Planners,* XXII (Winter, 1956), pp. 35–38. Lessons learned from the Philadelphia experience with its required program, clear policies, and fine citizen support.

BLAIR ASSOCIATES, INC. *Capital Budgeting Procedures, Supplement to Cape Cod 1980: A Sector of the Massachusetts State Plan.* (Providence: College Hill Press, 1963.) A simplified guide for small Massachusetts towns.

COUGHLIN, ROBERT E. "The Capital Programming Problem," *Journal of the American Institute of Planners,* XXVI (February, 1960), pp. 39–48. An analytic framework for selection of projects in a large-city program, dealing with objectives, comprehensive plan relationships, sequence, and importance of individual projects.

COUGHLIN, ROBERT E., and CHARLES A. PITTS. "The Capital Programming Process," *Journal of the American Institute of Planners,* XXVI (August, 1960), pp. 236–241. Detailed description of the Philadelphia process.

LOMBARDI, FRANK. "The Planning Agency and Capital Improvement Programs," *Journal of the American Institute of Planners,* XX (Spring, 1954), pp. 95–101. Description of the San Francisco programming procedure, discussion of planning department role, and plea for greater use of capital programs.

MAXWELL, WILFRED J. *A Guide to Capital Improvement Programming in Connecticut.* (Hartford: Connecticut Development Commission, 1960.) A fill-in-the-blank manual specifically tailored to Connecticut legal and fiscal requirements for smaller towns.

MOAK, LENNOX L., and KATHRYN W. KILLIAN. *A Manual of Suggested Practice for the Preparation and Adoption of Capital Programs and Capital Budgets by Local Governments.* (Chicago: Municipal Finance Officers Association of the United States and Canada, 1964.) A review of current practice in 17 larger cities, with suggested desirable practice for each step of the process.

NEW JERSEY DEPARTMENT OF CONSERVATION AND ECONOMIC DEVELOPMENT. *Capital Improvements Programming: A Guide for New Jersey Local Governments.* (Trenton: The Department, 1965.) A simple and clear manual suitable for the smaller community. Many other states have similar guides.

PARKER, WILLIAM STANLEY. "Capital Improvement Programs," *Journal of the American Institute of Planners,* XX (Fall, 1954), pp. 192–95. A strong argument by the dean of capital improvement programmers to treat the capital improvement program as an integral part of a long-range municipal financial program, prepared by the planning agency in collaboration with other groups.

Extension of Services

LAKEWOOD, CALIFORNIA. City Government. *The Lakewood Plan.* (Lakewood, Calif.: The City, 2nd rev. ed., 1960.)

METROPOLITAN GOVERNMENT OF NASHVILLE AND DAVIDSON COUNTY. Planning Commission. *Urban Services District Expansion Study.* (Nashville, Tenn.: 1967.)

SENGSTOCK, FRANK S. *Extraterritorial Powers in the Metropolitan Area!* (Ann Arbor: University of Michigan Law School, 1962.)

U.S. ADVISORY COMMISSION ON INTERGOVERNMEN-

TAL RELATIONS. *Intergovernmental Responsibilities for Water Supply and Sewage Disposal in Metropolitan Areas; a Commission Report.* (Washington: The Commission, 1962.)

———. *Performance of Urban Functions: Local and Areawide; an Information Report.* (Washington: The Commission, rev. ed., 1963.)

Annexation

AMERICAN MUNICIPAL ASSOCIATION. *Basic Principles for a Good Annexation Law.* (Washington: The Association, 1960.)

AMERICAN SOCIETY OF PLANNING OFFICIALS. *Information Report No. 114: Annexation Studies.* (Chicago: The Society, September, 1958.)

OBERLANDER, H. PETER. *Should Kelowna Extend Its Boundaries? A Study for the Planned Expansion of the City of Kelowna.* 1957.

SENGSTOCK, FRANK S. *Annexation: A Solution to the Metropolitan Area Problem.* (Ann Arbor: University of Michigan Law School, 1960.)

Official Mapping

AMERICAN SOCIETY OF PLANNING OFFICIALS. *Information Report No. 119: Protecting Future Streets: Official Maps, Setbacks, and Such.* (Chicago: The Society, February, 1959.)

GOODMAN, WILLIAM I. and JEROME L. KAUFMAN. *City Planning in the Sixties: A Restatement of Principles and Techniques.* (Urbana: University of Illinois, Bureau of Community Planning, 1965.), pp. 68–74.

15. Zoning

AMERICAN SOCIETY OF PLANNING OFFICIALS. *Planning Advisory Service Report No. 33: Forms for Zoning Administration.* (Chicago: ASPO, 1951.)

———. *Planning Advisory Service Report No. 115: Amending the Zoning Ordinance.* (Chicago: ASPO, 1958.)

BAIR, FREDERICK H., JR. "How to Regulate Planned Unit Development for Housing—Summary of a Regulatory Approach," *Zoning Digest,* XXVII (June and July, 1965), pp. 185–95, 221–30.

BAIR, FREDERICK H., JR. and ERNEST R. BARTLEY. *Text of a Model Zoning Ordinance, with Commentary.* (Chicago: American Society of Planning Officials, 3rd ed., 1966.)

BASSETT, EDWARD M. *Zoning: The Laws, Administration, and Court Decisions during the First Twenty Years.* (New York: The Russell Sage Foundation, 1936.)

BEUSCHER, J. H., ed. *Land Use Controls—Cases and Materials.* (Madison, Wis.: The College Printing and Typing Company, 3rd ed., 1964.)

BLAIR ASSOCIATES. *Salem, Massachusetts: Historic Area Study.* (Salem: Salem Planning Board, 1963.)

CHICAGO, THE UNIVERSITY OF, DEPARTMENT OF GEOGRAPHY. *Research Paper No. 56: Regulating Flood-Plain Development.* (Chicago: The Depart-

ment, 1958.)

CRAWFORD, WILLIAM H. *A Primer for Connecticut Zoning Boards of Appeals.* (Hartford: Connecticut Federation of Planning and Zoning Agencies, 1958.)

DELAFONS, JOHN. *Land Use Controls in the United States.* (Cambridge: Harvard University Press, 1962.)

FAIRFAX CO., VA. *Administration of the Zoning Process.* (Fairfax: County of Fairfax, 1965.)

GREEN, PHILIP P., JR. *Zoning in North Carolina.* (Chapel Hill: Institute of Government, University of North Carolina, 1952.)

HAAR, CHARLES M. *Land-Use Planning.* (Boston: Little, Brown and Company, 1959.)

HANKE, BYRON R. *Land-Use Intensity Standards, the LUI Scale and Zoning.* (Washington: U.S. Department of Housing and Urban Development, 1965.)

HYDE, VICTOR A., et al. *A Guide for County Zoning Administration.* (Urbana: Bureau of Community Planning, University of Illinois, 1965.)

"Land Planning and the Law: Emerging Policies and Techniques," *UCLA Law Review,* XII (March, 1965), pp. 707–1009.

"Land-Use Symposium," *Iowa Law Review,* L (Winter, 1965), pp. 243–524.

LEARY, ROBERT M. *A Model Procedure for the Administration of Zoning Regulations.* (Washington: Urban Land Institute, 1958.)

MANDELKER, DANIEL R. *Controlling Planned Residential Developments.* (Chicago: American Society of Planning Officials, 1966.)

MONTAGUE, ROBERT L. and TONY P. WREN. *Planning for Preservation.* (Chicago: American Society of Planning Officials, 1964.)

NEW YORK (STATE), DEPARTMENT OF COMMERCE. *Zoning in New York State: A Guide to the Preparation of Zoning Ordinances.* (Albany: The Department, rev. ed., 1958.)

NORFOLK, VA., DEPARTMENT OF CITY PLANNING. *Preserving Norfolk's Heritage.* (Norfolk: The City, 1965.)

O'HARROW, DENNIS. *Performance Standards in Industrial Zoning.* (Columbus, Ohio: National Industrial Zoning Committee, 1954.)

RODY, MARTIN J. and HERBERT H. SMITH. *Zoning Primer.* (West Trenton, N.J.: Chandler-Davis Pub. Co., 1960.)

SMITH, HERBERT H. *The Citizen's Guide to Zoning.* (West Trenton, N.J.: Chandler-Davis Pub. Co., 1965.)

SOLBERG, E. D. *The How and Why of Rural Zoning.* (Washington: Government Printing Office, 1958.)

"Symposium: Planned Unit Development," *University of Pennsylvania Law Review,* CIV (No. 1, 1965), pp. 1–182.

U.S. FEDERAL HOUSING ADMINISTRATION. *Land Planning Bulletin No. 6: Planned Unit Develop-

ment with a Homes Association. (Washington: Government Printing Office, 1964.)

―――. *Land Planning Bulletin No. 7: Land-Use Intensity.* (Washington: Government Printing Office, 1965.)

URBAN LAND INSTITUTE. *Technical Bulletin No. 50: The Homes Association Handbook.* (Washington: The Institute, 1964.)

―――. *Technical Bulletin No. 52: Legal Aspects of Planned Unit Residential Development,* by Richard F. Babcock and Jan Krasnowiecki. (Washington: The Institute, 1965.)

VIRGINIA GOVERNOR'S OFFICE. *Zoning in Virginia.* (Richmond: The State, 1965.)

YOKLEY, E. C. *Zoning Law and Practice.* (Charlottesville: Michie Company, 2nd ed., 2 vols, 1953.)

Zoning Digest (monthly). (Chicago: American Society of Planning Officials, 1949 to date.)

16. Land Subdivision

Manuals on Subdivision Regulation

NEW YORK (STATE), DEPARTMENT OF COMMERCE. *Control of Land Subdivision: A Manual of Subdivision Regulation for Municipal Officers, Subdivision Developers, Builders and Planning Boards.* (Albany: The Department, rev. ed., 1963.)

The above is only one of a number of excellent manuals published in various states by different agencies. It is suggested that the reader consult his state league of municipalities as to the source of any such publication in his particular state.

Written Provisions

AMERICAN SOCIETY OF PLANNING OFFICIALS, PLANNING ADVISORY SERVICE. *Organization of the Subdivision Ordinance.* Information Report No. 116. (Chicago: ASPO, 1958.)

LAUTNER, HAROLD W. *Subdivision Regulations: An Analysis of Land Subdivision Control Practices.* (Chicago: Public Administration Service, 1941.)

U.S. HOUSING AND HOME FINANCE AGENCY. *Suggested Land Subdivision Regulations.* (Washington: Government Printing Office, rev. ed., 1962.)

Subdivision Design—General

KOSTKA, V. JOSEPH. *Planning Residential Subdivisions.* (Winnipeg, Can.: Appraisal Institute of Canada, 1954.)

LYNCH, KEVIN. *Site Planning.* (Cambridge, Mass.: M. I. T. Press, 1962.)

NATIONAL ASSOCIATION OF HOME BUILDERS. *Home Builders Manual for Land Development.* (Washington, D.C.: The Association, rev. ed., 1958.)

URBAN LAND INSTITUTE. *The Community Builders Handbook.* (Washington, D.C.: The Institute, 5th ed., 1960.)

VOGEL, JOSHUA H. *Design of Subdivisions.* (Seattle: University of Washington Press, 1965.)

The Law of Subdivision Regulation

"An Analysis of Subdivision Control Legislation," *Indiana Law Journal* XXVII (Summer, 1953), pp. 544–586.

CUNNINGHAM, ROGER A. "Land-Use Control—The State and Local Programs," *Iowa Law Review,* L (Winter, 1965), pp. 415–37.

HEYMAN, IRA MICHAEL and THOMAS K. GILHOOL. "The Constitutionality of Imposing Increased Community Costs on New Suburban Residents through Subdivision Exactions," *Yale Law Journal,* LXXIII (June, 1964), pp. 1119–57.

REPS, JOHN W. and JERRY L. SMITH. "Control of Urban Land Subdivision," *Syracuse Law Review,* XIV (Spring, 1963), pp. 405–25.

YOKLEY, E. C. *The Law of Subdivisions.* (Charlottesville, Va.: Michie Company, 1963.)

Requirements for Improvements

AMERICAN SOCIETY OF PLANNING OFFICIALS, PLANNING ADVISORY SERVICE. *Forms for Performance Bonds.* Information Report No. 58. (Chicago: The Society, 1954.)

―――. *Installation of Physical Improvements as Required in Subdivision Regulations.* Information Report No. 38. (Chicago: The Society, 1952.)

―――. *Performance Bonds for the Installation of Subdivision Improvements.* Information Report No. 48. (Chicago: The Society, 1953.)

―――. *Varying Improvement Requirements in Subdivision Ordinances.* Information Report No. 174. (Chicago: The Society, 1963.)

Innovations in Design

AMERICAN SOCIETY OF PLANNING OFFICIALS, PLANNING ADVISORY SERVICE. *Cluster Subdivisions.* Information Report No. 135. (Chicago: The Society, 1960.)

―――. *Subdivision Design—Some New Developments.* Information Report No. 102. (Chicago: The Society, 1957.)

KRASNOWIECKI, JAN, RICHARD F. BABCOCK, and DAVID N. McBRIDE. *Legal Aspects of Planned Unit Residential Development.* Urban Land Institute Technical Report No. 52. (Washington, D.C.: Urban Land Institute, 1965.)

URBAN LAND INSTITUTE. *Innovations vs. Traditions in Community Development: A Comparative Study in Residential Land Use.* Technical Bulletin No. 47. (Washington, D.C.: The Institute, 1963.)

URBAN LAND INSTITUTE. *New Approaches to Residential Land Development: A Study of Concepts and Innovations.* Technical Bulletin No. 40. (Washington, D.C.: The Institute, 1961.)

Subdivisions Posing Special Problems

AMERICAN SOCIETY OF PLANNING OFFICIALS, PLANNING ADVISORY SERVICE. *Hillside Development.*

Information Report No. 126. (Chicago: The Society, 1959.)

———. *Municipal Waterfronts: Planning for Industrial and Commercial Uses.* Information Report No. 45. (Chicago: The Society, 1952.)

———. *Regulation of Mobile Home Subdivisions.* Information Report No. 145. (Chicago: The Society, 1961.)

———. *Subdivision Regulations for Industry.* Information Report No. 162. (Chicago: The Society, 1962.)

———. *Waterfronts: Planning for Resort and Residential Uses.* Information Report No. 118. (Chicago: The Society, 1959.)

BAIR, FREDERICK H., JR. *Local Regulation of Mobile Home Parks, Travel Trailer Parks, and Related Facilities.* (Chicago: Mobile Homes Research Foundation, 1965.)

RICK, WILLIAM B. *Planning and Developing Waterfront Property.* Urban Land Institute Technical Bulletin No. 49. (Washington, D.C.: Urban Land Institute, 1964.)

17. Urban Renewal

ABRAMS, CHARLES. *The City Is the Frontier.* (New York: Harper and Row, 1965.)

AMERICAN SOCIETY OF PLANNING OFFICIALS. *The Community Renewal Program: The First Years.* (Chicago: ASPO, 1963.)

ANDERSON, MARTIN. *The Federal Bulldozer: A Critical Analysis of Urban Renewal, 1949–1962.* (Cambridge: The M. I. T. Press, 1964.)

DYCKMAN, JOHN W. and REGINALD R. ISAACS. *Capital Requirements for Urban Development and Renewal.* (New York: McGraw-Hill Book Co., Inc., 1961.)

EVERETT, ROBINSON O. "Urban Renewal," *Law and Contemporary Problems,* XXVI No. 1 and XXV No. 4 (Duke University School of Law, 1960, 1961.)

FRIEDEN, BERNARD J. *The Future of Old Neighborhoods.* (Cambridge, Mass.: The M. I. T. Press, 1964.)

GANS, HERBERT B. "The Failure of Urban Renewal: A Critique and Some Proposals," *Commentary,* XXXIX No. 4 (April, 1965), pp. 29–37.

———. *The Urban Villagers: The Community Life of Italian-Americans.* (Glencoe: The Free Press, 1962.)

GREER, SCOTT. *Urban Renewal and American Cities.* (New York: Bobbs-Merrill Company, 1965.)

GRIGSBY, WILLIAM. *Housing Markets and Public Policy.* (Philadelphia: University of Pennsylvania Press, 1964.)

GROSSMAN, DAVID A. "The Community Renewal Program: Policy Development, Progress and Problems," *The Journal of the American Institute of Planners,* XXIX (November, 1963), pp. 259–69.

HARTMAN, CHESTER. "Housing of Relocated Families," *The Journal of the American Institute of Planners,* XXX (November, 1964), pp. 266–86.

HEMDAHL, REUEL. *Urban Renewal.* (New York: The Scarecrow Press, 1959.)

JACOBS, JANE. *The Death and Life of Great American Cities.* (New York: Random House, 1961.)

NASH, WILLIAM W. *Residential Rehabilitation: Private Profits and Public Purposes.* (New York: McGraw-Hill Book Company, 1959.)

PHILADELPHIA HOUSING ASSOCIATION. *Ends and Means of Urban Renewal.* (Philadelphia: Philadelphia Housing Association, 1961.)

SCHORR, ALVIN L. *Slums and Social Insecurity.* (Washington, D.C.: Social Security Administration, 1963.)

U.S. HOUSE OF REPRESENTATIVES COMMITTEE ON BANKING AND CURRENCY. *Basic Laws and Authorities on Housing and Urban Development: 1965.* (Washington: Government Printing Office, 1965.)

U.S. HOUSING AND HOME FINANCE AGENCY. *18th Annual Report: 1964.* (Washington: Government Printing Office, 1965.)

VAN HUYCK, ALFRED P. and JACK HORNUNG. *The Citizen's Guide to Urban Renewal.* (West Trenton, N.J.: Chandler-Davis Publishing Company, 1962.)

WEAVER, ROBERT C. *Dilemmas of Urban America.* (Cambridge: Harvard University Press, 1965.)

———. *The Urban Complex.* (New York: Doubleday, 1964.)

WILSON, JAMES Q. "Planning and Politics: Citizen Participation in Urban Renewal," *Journal of the American Institute of Planners,* XXIX (November, 1964), pp. 242–49.

WILSON, JAMES Q. (ed.) *Urban Renewal: The Record and the Controversy.* (Cambridge: The M. I. T. Press, 1966.)

WOODBURY, COLEMAN, (ed.) *The Future of Cities and Urban Redevelopment.* (Chicago: The University of Chicago Press, 1953.)

———. *Urban Redevelopment: Problems and Practices.* (Chicago: The University of Chicago Press, 1953.)

ZIMMER, BASIL G. *Rebuilding Cities: The Effects of Displacement and Relocation on Small Business.* (Chicago: Quadrangle Books, 1964.)

18. The Local Planning Agency: Organization and Structure

19. The Local Planning Agency: Internal Administration

AMERICAN SOCIETY OF PLANNING OFFICIALS. *ASPO Planning Advisory Service Information Report No. 1 to date.* (Chicago: ASPO, 1949–.) (Available on loan from ASPO or through subscription to the service.) See especially Report No. 208: "Expenditures, Staff, and Salaries of Local Planning Agencies," March, 1966; Report No. 146: "Principles of Organization for Planning Agencies," May 1961; and Report No. 195: "The Planning Commission

—Its Composition and Function," 1965.

————. *Administrative Study Reports* for San Jose, Syracuse, Phoenix, Pittsburgh and other cities.

GOODMAN, WILLIAM I. and JEROME L. KAUFMAN. *City Planning in the Sixties: A Restatement of Principles and Techniques.* (Urbana: Bureau of Community Planning, University of Illinois, 1965.)

Local Planning Administration. (Chicago: The Institute for Training in Municipal Administration, 1941.)

————. (Chicago: International City Managers' Assn., 2nd ed., 1948.)

————. (Chicago: International City Managers' Assn., 3rd ed., 1959.)

NASH, PETER H. and DENNIS DURDEN. "A Task-Force Approach to Replace the Planning Board," *Journal of the American Institute of Planners,* XXX (February, 1964), pp. 10–22.

PERLOFF, HARVEY S. *Education for Planning: City, State and Regional.* (Baltimore: Published for Resources for the Future by Johns Hopkins Press, 1957.)

The Technique of Municipal Administration. (Chicago: International City Managers' Assn., 1958.)

WEBSTER, DONALD. *Urban Planning and Municipal Public Policy.* (New York: Harper and Brothers, 1958.)

20. Planning and the Public

ACTION. *You and Your Neighborhood.* (New York: ACTION, 1956.)

ACTION. *Our Living Future.* (New York: ACTION, 1956.)

ALTSHULER, ALAN A. *The City Planning Process.* (Ithaca: Cornell University Press, 1965.)

ARCHITECTURAL FORUM. *Planning With You.* (New York: The Architectural Forum, 1944.) (Reprinted from Aug. 1943, Dec. 1943, and Feb. 1944 issues.)

BURKE, EDMUND M. "Citizen Participation in Renewal," *Journal of Housing,* XXIII, No. 1, (January, 1966), pp. 18–21.

BURNHAM, DANIEL. *Plan of Chicago.* (Chicago: The Commercial Club, 1908.)

CHAMBER OF COMMERCE OF U.S. *Basic Decisions in Community Development.* (Washington, D.C.: Chamber of Commerce, 1963.)

GREER, SCOTT. *Urban Renewal and American Cities.* (Indianapolis: Bobbs-Merrill, 1966.)

HILLMAN, ARTHUR, and ROBERT J. CASEY. *Tomorrow's Chicago.* (Chicago: University of Chicago Press, 1953.)

HUDNUT, JOSEPH. "What a Planner Has To Know," *Planning 1946.* (Chicago: American Society of Planning Officials, 1946), pp. 157–163.

KENT, T. K., JR. *The Urban General Plan.* (San Francisco: Chandler Publishing Co., 1964.)

LYND, ROBERT S. *Knowledge For What?* (Princeton, N.J.: Princeton University Press, 1945.)

MOODY, WALTER D. *Wacker's Manual of the Plan of Chicago.* (Chicago: Chicago Plan Commission, 1912.)

MORGAN, ARTHUR E. *The Small Community.* (New York: Harper & Bros., 1942.)

————. *The Community of the Future.* (Ann Arbor: Braun-Brumfield, 1957.)

MUMFORD, LEWIS. *The Culture of Cities.* (New York: Harcourt, Brace, 1938.)

MEYERSON, MARTIN and EDWARD C. BANFIELD. *Politics, Planning and the Public Interest.* (Glencoe, Ill.: The Free Press, 1955.)

NIXON, WILLIAM BISHOP. *Citizen Participation in Urban Renewal.* (Nashville, Tenn.: Tennessee State Planning Commission, 1957.)

PERRY, CLARENCE ARTHUR. *Neighborhood and Community Planning,* Vol. VII of Regional Survey of New York and Its Environs. (New York: Regional Plan of New York, 1929.)

————. *Housing for the Machine Age.* (New York: Russell Sage Foundation, 1939.)

SEARS, ROEBUCK AND CO. *ABC's of Community Planning.* (Chicago: Sears, 1962.)

SMITH, HERBERT H. *The Citizen's Guide to Planning.* (West Trenton, N.J.: Chandler-Davis, 1961.)

STONOROV, OSCAR and LOUIS I. KAHN. *You and Your Neighborhood.* (New York: Revere Copper and Brass, Inc., n.d.)

VAN HUYCK, ALFRED P. *The Citizen's Guide to Urban Renewal.* (West Trenton, N.J.: Chandler-Davis, 1962.)

WALKER, ROBERT A. *The Planning Function in Urban Government.* (Chicago: University of Chicago Press, 1941; 2nd ed., 1950.)

WEBSTER, DONALD H. *Urban Planning and Municipal Public Policy.* (New York: Harper & Bros., 1958.)

WIRTH, LOUIS. *Community Planning for Peacetime Living.* (Palo Alto: Stanford University Press, 1946.)

List of Contributors

The persons who have contributed to this book are listed below with the Editor and Associate Editor first followed by others in alphabetical order with a brief review of experience, training, and major points of interest in each person's background. Most of these persons have written books, monographs, reports, and articles; information of this kind has not been included.

WILLIAM I. GOODMAN, Editor (Introduction, Chapter 6, Chapter 11) is Professor and Chairman, Department of Urban Planning, University of Illinois. He has had extensive experience with city planning agencies in Detroit, Hartford, and Boston; has been on the faculty of the Department of City and Regional Planning at Harvard University; and has served as a consultant to many states, cities, counties, and federal government agencies. He was a member of the Board of Governors of the American Institute of Planners, 1962–65. His educational background includes a bachelor's from Wayne University, a master's in public administration from Wayne University, and a master's in city planning from the Massachusetts Institute of Technology.

ERIC C. FREUND, Associate Editor (Introduction, Chapter 6, Chapter 11) is Associate Professor of Community and Urban Planning, Bureau of Community Planning, University of Illinois. He has been with the Bureau of Community Planning since 1959. Prior experience includes three years in architecture and community planning in New Jersey; three years in planning and appraisal work with the Central Mortgage and Housing Corporation, Ontario, Canada; and 17 years in England where he was engaged in the general professional practice of town planning, engineering, and architecture. He has been awarded a Guggenheim Fellowship for 1967–68 and will be in England to study management of the British New Towns. He holds the Associate Degree, Royal Institution of Chartered Surveyors (England); the Associate Degree, Chartered Estate Agents' Institute (England); and the master's in city planning, University of Illinois.

RICHARD B. ANDREWS (Chapter 4) is Professor of Business, Graduate School of Business, University of Wisconsin. He has his Ph.D. in economics from the University of Wisconsin. In addition to his academic duties, he serves as Chairman of the Editorial Board for *Land Economics* and has been Study Director and later Economist and Consultant to the state of Wisconsin in the preparation of the state plan.

FRANKLYN H. BEAL (Chapter 12) is a Principal Planner with the American Society of Planning Officials. His experience includes service as a Research Assistant on the Dayton, Ohio, Regional Transportation Study and a variety of short-term engineering, teaching, and research assignments. He holds a bachelor's degree in engineering from Antioch College and has taken graduate work in city planning at the University of Illinois.

ALAN BLACK (Chapter 13) is a senior planner with the Tri-State Transportation Commission in New York. Following graduation from Harvard in 1953 he worked for six years as a newspaper reporter. He then enrolled in the graduate program in city planning and received his master's degree from the University of California, Berkeley, in 1960. He has been with the Chicago Area Transportation Study and, during the 1963–64 academic year, had a Fulbright to study planning at the Technological University, Delft, Holland.

LACHLAN F. BLAIR (Chapter 14) is Associate Professor of Urban Planning, Department of Urban Planning, University of Illinois. He has had extensive experience, including service as Chief of State Planning for the Rhode Island Development Council, 1952–56, and head of the consulting firm of Blair Associates, 1957–1964. He has been a member of the Board of Governors of the American Institute of Planners and in 1965–66 was Chairman of the AIP Division of Professional Standards. He holds the bachelor's degree in city planning from the Massachusetts Institute of Technology.

JAMES G. COKE (Chapter 1) is Director, Center for Urban Regionalism, Kent State University. He has held various teaching and research assignments with Centre College; the Fels Institute of Local and State Government, University of Pennsylvania; the Office of Community Development, University of Illinois; and the League of Minnesota Municipalities. He has been a consultant to the Southeastern Pennsylvania Regional Planning Commission and Executive Director of the Study Commission of the Philadelphia Metropolitan Area. He holds a bachelor's from Harvard and master's and doctor's degrees in political science from the University of Minnesota.

PAUL DAVIDOFF (Chapter 11) is Professor of Urban Planning, Director of the Urban Planning Program, and Director of the Urban Research Center, Hunter College of the City University of New York. He has been on the faculty of the Department of City Planning, University of Pennsylvania and a consultant to the U.S. Civil Rights Commission. He is Book Review Editor for the *Journal of the American Institute of Planners*. He holds a bachelor's from Allegheny College and a law degree and a master's in city planning from the University of Pennsylvania.

GRAHAM S. FINNEY (Chapter 2) is Director of Development, the School District of Philadelphia. He has been Planning Director for the city of Portland, Maine; Assistant Executive Director, Philadelphia City Planning Commission; Executive Director, Philadelphia Council for Community Advancement; and a lecturer in political science and planning at Tufts, Haverford, Bryn Mawr, and Yale. He holds a bachelor's degree from Yale University and a master's in public administration from Harvard.

PHILIP P. GREEN, JR. (Chapter 16) is Professor of Public Law and Government and Assistant Director, Institute of Government, University of North Carolina. He has been at the University of North Carolina since 1949 and has participated in many state and local government research and consulting activities, including membership on the Governor's Technical Advisory Committee on Area Development and the Governor's Advisory Committee on Low Cost Housing. He has served on the Editorial Board of *Zoning Digest* and in 1963–64 was a Senior Fulbright Scholar at the London School of Economics and Political Science. He received the A.B. Degree from Princeton in 1943 and the LL.B. from Harvard in 1949.

CHARLES R. GUINN (Chapter 6) is Associate Transportation Analyst with the Subdivision of Planning and Programming, New York State Department of Public Works. He has been a Transportation Planning Engineer with the New Haven Redevelopment Agency and a Transportation Analyst with the Upstate New York Transportation Studies. He holds a bachelor's degree in civil engineering from Pennsylvania State University and a master's in urban transportation planning from Northwestern University.

WILLARD B. HANSEN (Chapter 10) is Associate Professor of Regional Planning, Bureau of Community Planning, University of Illinois. He has been a Program Planning Analyst with the Boston Regional Planning Project and a Planning Analyst with the Philadelphia City Planning Commission. He currently is Chairman of the Division of Planning Research, American Institute of Planners. His educational background includes a bachelor's in sociology from Haverford College, a master's in sociology from the University of Michigan, and master's and doctor's degrees in city planning from the University of Pennsylvania.

HENRY C. HIGHTOWER (Chapter 3) is Assistant Professor of Planning, Department of City and Regional Planning, University of North Carolina. His background includes staff work with the Pittsburgh Regional Planning Association and consulting work for a number of planning agencies in North Carolina, Virginia, and Washington, D.C. He holds a bachelor's degree in sociology from the London

School of Economics and Political Science and the doctor's degree in planning from the University of North Carolina.

JOHN T. HOWARD (Chapter 19) is Professor and Head, Department of City and Regional Planning, Massachusetts Institute of Technology. His extensive background includes service with several city and regional planning commissions; he was Planning Director for the Cleveland City Planning Commission, 1942–49. He has been active in planning consulting work for many governmental jurisdictions and currently is a partner in Adams, Howard, and Oppermann, Planning Consultants. He was President of the American Institute of Planners, 1954–56. His educational background includes a bachelor's in fine arts from Yale and bachelor's and master's degrees in City Planning from MIT.

JEROME L. KAUFMAN (Chapter 17) is Assistant Director, American Society of Planning Officials. He has been with ASPO since 1961. Prior to that he was Assistant Professor of Community Planning, Bureau of Community Planning, University of Illinois, and has also been employed by the Philadelphia Redevelopment Authority and the Institute of Urban Studies, University of Pennsylvania. He has served as a consultant to the Department of Urban Planning, University of Illinois, and to the Illinois Board of Economic Development. He holds a bachelor's degree in sociology from Queen's College and the master's in city planning from the University of Pennsylvania.

ROBERT M. LEARY (Chapter 15) is Assistant General Manager, National Capital Commission, Ottawa, Canada. His planning experience has been with the Port of New York Authority; the cities of Rome, New York, and Ann Arbor, Michigan; and Fairfax County, Virginia. He also has been a visiting lecturer at the University of North Carolina. His bachelor's degree is from St. Bonaventure University, and he has master's degrees in public administration and regional planning from Cornell.

KEVIN LYNCH (Chapter 9) is Professor of City Planning at the Massachusetts Institute of Technology. He holds the bachelor's degree in city planning from Massachusetts Institute of Technology and has been at that institution since 1948. During this time he has been a consultant for several state and local governments in New England, the New England Medical Center, the Puerto Rico Industrial Development Corporation, the city of Los Angeles, and several other public and private agencies. He was co-director of a five year Rockefeller research project on the perceptual form of the city and is presently engaged in studies of visual form at the metropolitan scale.

GEORGE T. MARCOU (Chapter 7) is President, Marcou, O'Leary and Associates, Planning and Urban Development Consultants. Prior to establishment, in 1963, of the firm he presently heads, Mr. Marcou was with the Nashville–Davidson County Planning Commission (Nashville, Tennessee), was Associate Professor of Community Planning at the University of Illinois, and was with Blair and Stein Associates. He has been a visiting lecturer at several universities. He holds the degrees of Bachelor of Architecture and Master in City Planning from the Massachusetts Institute of Technology.

FREDERICK W. MEMMOTT (Chapter 6) is a Principal Research Analyst (Transportation) with the New York State Department of Public Works. He has been with the Department since 1962. From 1959 to 1961 he was a teaching assistant at the Massachusetts Institute of Technology. He holds bachelor's and master's degrees in civil engineering from MIT.

JAMES H. PICKFORD (Chapter 18) is a Senior Analyst with the Advisory Commission on Intergovernmental Relations. He has had experience with the Montgomery County Planning Commission, Dayton, Ohio; the Division of Planning, Kentucky Agriculture and Industrial Development Board; and the Pennsylvania Department of Commerce. From 1959 to 1964 he served as Assistant Director of the American Society of Planning Officials. He holds a bachelor's degree in industrial economics from Iowa State University and a master's in political science from the University of Wisconsin.

ANN SATTERTHWAITE (Chapter 7) is associated with the Conservation Foundation. She is head of the Recreation Planning Committee for the American Institute of Planners and has had experience with the Outdoor Recreation Resources Review Commission and the Open Space Land Program of the Urban Renewal Administration, Housing and Home Finance Agency. She holds a bachelor's degree from Radcliffe and a master's in city planning from Yale.

FRANK S. SO (Chapter 8) is Projects Director, American Society of Planning Officials. After previous service on the ASPO staff, he was Director of Planning for the city of Harvey, Illinois, 1964–67. He holds a bachelor's degree in sociology from Youngstown University and a master's in city planning from Ohio State University.

SHIRLEY F. WEISS (Chapter 5) is Associate Research Director and Associate Professor of Planning with the Center for Urban and Regional Studies, University of North Carolina. She has had experience in economics and planning research with the Maryland State Planning Commission and with Harrison, Ballard and Allen, Planning and Housing Consultants. She holds the degree of Master of Regional Planning from the University of North Carolina.

WILFORD G. WINHOLTZ (Chapter 20) is a partner in the firm of Runnels and Winholtz and Associates—Architects, City Planners, and Urban Design Consultants. He has had extensive experience in planning and urban renewal with Community Studies, Inc., Kansas City, Missouri; the Urban Renewal Administration of the Housing and Home Finance Agency; the South Side Planning Board, Chicago; the Detroit City Planning Commission; and other public and private agencies. He holds a bachelor's degree from the University of Utah in civil and sanitary engineering and a master's from the Massachusetts Institute of Technology in city planning and industrial relations.

Illustration Credits

Figure 1–1: John W. Reps, *The Making of Urban America: A History of City Planning in the United States.* (Princeton: Princeton University Press, 1965), p. 166. Figure 1–2: Harold M. Lewis, *Planning the Modern City* (New York: John Wiley & Sons, Inc., 1949), vol. 1, p. 120. Figure 1–3: John W. Reps, *The Making of Urban America*, p. 107. Figure 1–4: Christopher Tunnard and Henry Hope Reed, *American Skyline: The Growth and Form of our Cities and Towns* (New York: New American Library, Inc., 1953), p. 47. Figure 1–5: John W. Reps, *The Making of Urban America*, p. 251.

Figure 2–1: Connecticut Development Commission, office document, Hartford, 1965. Figure 2–2: Mildred Terauchi, *Organizing for State Planning and Economic Development* (Honolulu: Legislative Reference Bureau, University of Hawaii, 1963), p. 26. Figure 2–3: U.S. Department of Housing and Urban Development, *Department of Housing and Urban Development Organization Charts* (Washington: The Department, 1966), Chart 1. Figure 2–4. U.S. Department of Housing and Urban Development, *Department of Housing and Urban Development Organization Charts,* Chart 8.

Figure 4–1: Committee for Economic Development, *Community Economic Development Efforts: Five Case Studies* (New York: The Committee, 1964), p. 112. Figure 4–2: Committee for Economic Development, *Community Economic Development Efforts: Five Case Studies,* p. 116. Figure 4–3: Pittsburgh Regional Planning Association, *Region with a Future* (Pittsburgh: The Association, 1963), p. 199 (vol. 3 of *Economic Study of the Pittsburgh Region*).

Figures 5–1, 5–2, 5–3, 5–4, 5–5: U.S. Urban Renewal Administration and Bureau of Public Roads, *Standard Land Use Coding Manual* (Washington: The Bureau, 1965), pp. 5, 19, 20, 21, 22. Figure 5–6: Tennessee State Planning Commission, *The Use of Land in Kingsport* (Nashville: The Commission, 1957), p. 5. Figure 5–7: Metropolitan Dade County Planning Department, *Preliminary Land Use Plan and Policies for Development* (Miami: The County, 1961), p. 29. Figure 5–8: F. Stuart Chapin Jr., *Urban Land Use Planning* (Urbana: University of Illinois Press, 2nd ed., 1965), p. 458.

Figure 6–1: Highway Research Board, *Travel Characteristics in Urban Areas* (Washington: The Board, 1958), p. 11. Figure 6–2: Chicago Area Transportation Study, *Final Report* (Chicago: State of Illinois, vol. 1, 1959), p. 69. Figure 6–4: Preliminary data from Chicago Area Transportation Study. Figure 6–5: Roger L. Creighton, David D. Gooding, George C. Hemmins, and Jere E. Fidler, *Optimum Investment in Two-Mode Transportation Systems* (Albany: New York State Department of Public Works, 1961). Figure 6–9: Roger L. Creighton and John Hamburg, *State of the Art in the Urban Transportation Planning Process* (Albany: New York Department of Public Works, Subdivision of Planning and Programming, 1966), p. 5.

Figure 7–1: A. L. Strong, *Open Space for Urban America* (Washington: U.S. Department of Housing and Urban Development, 1965), p. vii. Figure 7–2: Marcou, O'Leary and Associates, *The Richmond Regional Development Plan* (Richmond, Virginia: Regional Planning Commission, 1967), p. 95. Figure 7–3: Outdoor Recreation Resources Review Commission, *Potential New Sites for Outdoor Recreation in the Northeast,* Report Number 8 (Washington: Economic Research Service, U.S. Department of Agriculture), p. 19. Figure 7–4: *Recreation in Wisconsin* (Madison: State of Wisconsin Department of Resource Development, 1962), p. 78. Figure 7–5: Zube and Dega Associates, *Wisconsin's Lake Superior Shoreline* (Madison, Wis.: 1964), pp. 12 and 13. Figure 7–6: Federal Interdepartmental Task Force, *Potomac Valley* (Washington: The Task Force, 1966), p. 45. Figure 7–7: William H. Whyte, *Cluster Development* (New York: American Conservation Association, 1964), p. 65. Figure 7–8: Reston photo by Blue Ridge Aerial Surveys.

Figure 9–1: Lawrence Halprin, *Cities* (New York: Reinhold Publishing Corp., 1963), p. 33, photo by Sunderland Aerial Photographs. Figure 9–2: *Progressive Architecture,* vol. XLIII, September, 1962, p. 160. Figure 9–3: Reprinted from *Site Planning* by Kevin Lynch by permission of the MIT Press, Cambridge, Massachusetts. Copyright © 1962 by the MIT Press. Figure 9–4: Reprinted from *Cities* by Lawrence Halprin, Reinhold Publishing Corp., 1963, New York. Photo by Donald Ray Carter. Figure 9–5: Kevin Lynch, *An Analysis of the Visual Form of Brookline,* Figs. 2, 11. Figure 9–6: Lawrence Halprin, *Freeways,* p. 15. Figure 9–7: Kevin Lynch, *An Analysis of the Visual Form of Brookline,* Fig. 10. Figure 9–8: Unpublished material prepared by Robert Dannenbrink of the Los Angeles City Planning Commission. Figure 9–9: Kevin Lynch, *An Analysis of the Visual Form of Brookline,* Fig. 6. Figure 9–10: Department of City and Regional Planning, Massachusetts Institute of Technology,

The Form of a Metropolitan Sector, p. 35. Figure 9–11: Department of City and Regional Planning, Massachusetts Institute of Technology, "Boston West," unpublished study. Figure 9–12: Donald Appleyard and Kevin Lynch, *Opportunities in Kendell Square,* Figs. 9 and 11. Figure 9–13: *Casabella,* No. 280, October, 1963, p. 16. Figure 9–14: *Architectural Forum,* vol. CXXIV, April, 1966, p. 59.

Figure 11–1: Prepared by Henry Fagin in 1954–55. Figure 11–2: Rhode Island Council of Community Services, Inc., *A Social Plan for Community Renewal of the City of Providence, R.I.* (Providence: The Council, 1964), p. 54. Figure 11–3: Harvey Perloff, "New Directions in Social Planning," Reprinted by permission of the *Journal of the American Institute of Planners,* November, 1965, Vol. 31, No. 11, p. 303.

Figure 13–1: From *The Urban General Plan* by T. J. Kent, Jr., published by Chandler Publishing Company, San Francisco. Copyright © 1964 by Chandler Publishing Company. Reprinted by permission. Figure 13–2: Berkeley (California) Planning Commission, *Berkeley Master Plan—1955,* p. 3. Figure 13–3: Cleveland City Planning Commission, *The General Plan of Cleveland; Cleveland Today and Tomorrow* (Cleveland: The Commission, 1950), p. 8–9, as reproduced in T. J. Kent, Jr., *The Urban General Plan.* Figure 13–4: Philadelphia City Planning Commission, *Comprehensive Plan* (Philadelphia: The Commission, 1960), p. C-6. Figure 13–5: Oakland City Planning Commission, *Oakland General Plan* (Oakland: The Commission, 1959). Figure 13–6: Berkeley (California) Planning Commission, *Berkeley Master Plan—1955,* p. 112, as reproduced in T. J. Kent, Jr., *The Urban General Plan.* Figure 13–7: National Capital Planning Commission and National Capital Regional Planning Council, *A Policies Plan for the Year 2000; The Nation's Capital* (Washington: The Commission, 1961), p. 47.

Figure 15–1: City of Ann Arbor, Michigan, zoning ordinance. Figure 15–3: St. Clair County, Michigan, zoning manual. Figure 15–4: Boston City Planning Board, *Zoning Policies for Boston,* 1953. Figure 15–6: Harrison, Ballard, and Allen, *Plan for Rezoning the City of New York,* 1950. Figure 15–7: Harrison, Ballard, and Allen, *Plan for Rezoning the City of New York,* 1950.

Figure 16–1: Washtenaw County, Michigan, Metropolitan Planning Commission, *A Subdivision Guide for Preparing Plats in Township Areas* (Ann Arbor: The Commission, 1963), pp. 21–22. Figure 16–2: *Subdivision Standards for the Athens Planning Region,* Tennessee State Planning Commission, 1956. Figure 16–3: *Subdivision Standards for the Athens Planning Region,* Figure 16–4: *Land Subdivision Ordinance,* Springfield, Illinois, Plan Commission, 1957. Figure 16–5: Wastenaw County, Michigan, Metropolitan Planning Commission, *A Subdivision Guide for Preparing Plats in Township Areas,* 1963, p. 38. Figure 16–6: Montgomery County, Ohio, Planning Commission, *Subdivision Regulations for Montgomery County, Ohio.* Figure 16–7: Adapted from Washtenaw County, Michigan, Planning Commission, *A Guide for Subdivision of Land* (Ann Arbor: The Commission, 1953), pp. 20–21. Figure 16–8: American Society of Planning Officials, Planning Advisory Service. Frederick H. Bair, Jr., Information Report No. 145: *Regulation of Mobile Home Subdivisions* (Chicago: ASPO, 1961), p. 24. Figure 16–9: William H. Whyte, *Cluster Development* (New York: American Conservation Association, 1964), p. 71. Figure 16–10: U.S. Federal Housing Administration, *Minimum Property Standards for Multifamily Housing* (Washington: The Administration, 1963), p. 38.

Figure 17–1: *Journal of Housing,* No. 1, 1965, p. 17. Figure 17–2: *Journal of Housing,* No. 5, 1964, p. 231. Figure 17–3: *Architectural Record,* July, 1965, p. 125. Figure 17–4: Top, *Journal of Housing,* No. 5, 1963, p. 270; bottom, *Journal of Housing,* No. 10, 1964, p. 525. Figure 17–5: Top, *Architectural Record,* July, 1965, p. 130; bottom, University of Illinois, Chicago. Figure 17–6: Providence, Rhode Island, Plan Commission, *College Hill—A Demonstration Study of Historic Area Renewal* (Providence: The Commission, 2nd ed., 1967). Figure 17–8: U.S. Congress House Committee on Banking and Currency, *Urban Renewal;* hearings before subcommittee on housing of the . . . , November 19–21, 1963: Part 2, 88th Congress, 1st session (Washington: Government Printing Office, 1963), p. 400.

Figures 18–7, 18–8, 18–9: Adapted from American Society of Planning Officials, Planning Advisory Service, James H. Pickford, Information Report No. 146, *Principles of Organization for Planning Agencies* (Chicago: ASPO, 1961).

Index

MUNICIPAL MANAGEMENT SERIES
Principles and Practice of Urban Planning

TEXT TYPE:
Linotype Baskerville

COMPOSITION, PRINTING, AND BINDING:
Kingsport Press, Inc., Kingsport, Tennessee

PAPER:
Glatfelter Offset

PRODUCTION:
David S. Arnold and Marion C. Tureck

DESIGN:
Herbert Slobin